Enigma Books

Also published by Engima Books

Hitler's Table Talk: 1941–1944
In Stalin's Secret Service
Hitler and Mussolini: The Secret Meetings
The Jews in Fascist Italy: A History
The Man Behind the Rosenbergs
Roosevelt and Hopkins: An Intimate History
Diary 1937–1943 (Galeazzo Ciano)
Secret Affairs: FDR, Cordell Hull, and Sumner Welles
Hitler and His Generals: Military Conferences 1942–1945
Stalin and the Jews: The Red Book
The Secret Front: Nazi Political Espionage
Fighting the Nazis: French Intelligence and Counterintelligence
A Death in Washington: Walter G. Krivitsky and the Stalin Terror
The Battle of the Casbah: Terrorism and Counterterrorism in Algeria 1955–1957
Hitler's Second Book: The Unpublished Sequel to *Mein Kampf*
At Napoleon's Side in Russia: The Classic Eyewitness Account
The Atlantic Wall: Hitler's Defenses for D-Day
Double Lives: Stalin, Willi Münzenberg and the Seduction of the Intellectuals
France and the Nazi Threat: The Collapse of French Diplomacy 1932–1939
Mussolini: The Secrets of His Death
Mortal Crimes: Soviet Penetration of the Manhattan Project
Top Nazi: Karl Wolff—The Man Between Hitler and Himmler
Empire on the Adriatic: Mussolini's Conquest of Yugoslavia
The Origins of the War of 1914 (3-volume set)
Hitler's Foreign Policy, 1933–1939—The Road to World War II
The Origins of Fascist Ideology 1918–1925
Max Corvo: OSS Italy 1942–1945
Hitler's Contract: The Secret History of the Italian Edition of *Mein Kampf*
Secret Intelligence and the Holocaust
Israel at High Noon
Balkan Inferno: Betrayal, War, and Intervention, 1990–2005
Calculated Risk: World War II Memoirs of General Mark Clark
The Murder of Maxim Gorky
The Kravchenko Case: One Man's War On Stalin
Operation Neptune
Paris Weekend
Shattered Sky
Hitler's Gift to France
The Mafia and the Allies
The Nazi Party, 1919–1945: A Complete History
Encyclopedia of Cold War Espionage, Spies, and Secret Operations
The Cicero Spy Affair
A Crate of Vodka
NOC
The First Iraq War: Britain's Mesopotamian Campaign, 1914-1918
Becoming Winston Churchill
Hitler's Intelligence Chief: Walter Schellenberg
Salazar: A Political Biography
The Italian Brothers

Nazi Palestine
Code Name: Kalistrat
Pax Romana
The De Valera Deception
Lenin and His Comrades
The Decision to Drop the Atomic Bomb
Target Hitler
Truman, MacArthur and the Korean War
The Eichmann Trial Diary

Working with Napoleon

The Memoirs of Napoleon Bonaparte
1802–1815

The Court of the First Empire

by
Baron Claude-François de Méneval
His Private Secretary

Original Translation by R. W. Sherrard
New Edition by Robert L. Miller

Complete and unabridged

Enigma Books

Published by Enigma Books
New York.

New Centennial Edition.
Robert L. Miller, Editor.

COMPLETE AND UNABRIDGED.

ISBN: 978-1-936274-19-2
eISBN: 978-1-936274-20-8

Publisher's Cataloging-In-Publication Data

Méneval, Claude-François, baron de, 1778-1850.
Working with Napoleon : the memoirs of Napoleon Bonaparte, 1802-1815, the court of the First Empire / by Baron Claude-François de Méneval ; original translation by R. W. Sherrard. -- [New centennial ed. / edited by] Robert L. Miller.

p. ; cm.

Translated into English from the original French.
"Complete and unabridged."--T.p. verso.
Originally published in English as "Memoirs to Serve for the History of Napoleon I, from 1802 to 1815."
Issued also as an ebook.
Includes index.
ISBN: 978-1-936274-19-2

1. Napoleon I, Emperor of the French, 1769-1821. 2. France—History--Consulate and First Empire, 1799-1815. 3. Napoleon I, Emperor of the French, 1769-1821--Contemporaries. 4. Napoleon I, Emperor of the French, 1769-1821--Relations with courts and courtiers. 5. Napoleon I, Emperor of the French, 1769-1821--Relations with private secretaries. 6. Méneval, Claude-François, baron de, 1778-1850. I. Sherrard, R. W. II. Miller, Robert L. (Robert Lawrence), 1945- III. Title. IV. Title: Memoirs to serve for the history of Napoleon I.

DC203 .M5413 2011
944.05/092

Contents

Foreword

Baron Claude-François de Méneval

A Portrait

by Robert L. Miller

To be employed by a towering military and political figure such as Napoleon Bonaparte at the height of his power offers a privileged position to an astute and highly literate observer. These exceptionally important memoirs were first published in Paris in the 1850s then translated and published in London and New York in 1894 immediately becoming one of the most authoritative documents about the French Emperor ever written. This book instantly became a required source for all historians of the Napoleonic era. Besides being a scrupulous and efficient secretary and notetaker, Baron de Méneval was a man of letters in his own right and his writing style, clear and unadorned but refined and highly cultured, offers a precise and illuminating account of history in the making during a most fascinating period.

Baron Claude-François de Méneval, served as Napoleon's private secretary from 1802 to 1813 and was attached to the Empress Marie-Louise until 1815. Secretaries, especially during those times when everything was handwritten, are by their very nature close to the person for whom they work, and Méneval was no exception. Moreover, unlike numerous other similar works, there is no doubt that Méneval was the actual author of his memoirs. He worked on them diligently over time and in 1843, a mere seven years before his own death, he also published *Napoleon and Marie-Louise, Historical Memories.*

Méneval was born in Paris on April 8, 1778, on the left bank of the Seine near the church of Saint-Germain-des-Près in what is now the rue Visconti, in the heart of the Latin Quarter. His father was a wealthy merchant who could afford to have his son brought up by an English nanny giving the young lad a solid knowledge of the language, good enough in fact for him to act later on as interpreter and translator at major conferences.

Méneval attended the prestigious Collège Mazarin where he was an excellent student and a gifted writer. He tried his hand at novels and became friendly with other men of letters in various salons among them Louis Bonaparte, Napoleon's brother. Another of the First Consul's brothers, Joseph Bonaparte also employed him as a secretary on various diplomatic missions such as the Treaty of Mortefontaine between France and the United States (1800); the Treaty of Lunéville with Austria (1801); and the Treaty of Amiens with Great Britain (1802).

With the disgrace of Louis Antoine de Bourrienne over certain financial irregularities and his ultimate dismissal in 1802, Joseph introduced the 24-year-old Méneval to his powerful brother the First Consul, who was in search of a private secretary. The job had no hours and required that he live in the palace of Tuileries, close to Napoleon's apartment, where he was constantly on call, day and night. He worked in the "interior cabinet," seated at a small table with his back to the Emperor. Napoleon sat on sofa or paced up and down dictating very quickly and refusing to repeat any sentences or words so the secretary could only move ahead leaving blanks wherever he was unable to catch single words to fill them in later. Two hours of dictation provided enough material for Méneval to stop and draft letters and reports for the Emperor's signature.

Since he had to follow the Emperor wherever he went, the secretary traveled constantly for months at a time until he fell ill and had to be replaced, much to Napoleon's disappointment since other secretaries were unable to keep up with the pace of his dictation. Upon his return, Méneval was the only one allowed to present letters and reports to the Emperor and had access to the secret papers, having the key to the cabinets where they were held.

As was his custom, Napoleon tried to control the private lives of his close associates (as well as those of his relatives). Therefore he strongly encouraged Méneval to marry, and in 1807 the secretary married sixteen-year-old Aimée Virginie Joséphine des Comtes de Montvernot. In October 1807 he was given a four-room apartment in the Tuileries and in 1810 the title of Baron de l'Empire.

From May to December 1812 Méneval took part in the Russian campaign and had to return to Paris because of frostbite and very much weakened by the brutal weather. He had to resign and was placed at the service of Empress Marie Louise in 1813 following her to Vienna. During the One Hundred Days he again joined Napoleon, who named him Duke, Councilor of State, and Minister for the Post. He was unable to follow the Emperor in exile at Saint-Helena but in 1840 he was present for the return to Paris of the remains of the man whom he had served so well.

In 1816 he was held under house arrest by the Restoration. Napoleon remembered him on Saint-Helena: "He was gentle, reserved, zealous, very private, able to work at any time whatsoever. He never gave me anything less than satisfaction and pleasantness. And I loved him dearly."

Méneval built a castle on a large estate at Gif-sur-Yvette where he lived after 1827 until his death in Paris in 1850 at the age of 72.

The family line is represented currently by Claude Napoleon, fifth Baron de Méneval.

These remarkable memoirs offer an excellent insight into Napoleon the man and the leader almost on a daily basis. While Méneval is certainly favorable and loyal to the leader he worked for, he also provides the most open and truthful image of Napoleon the man.

Preface

Méneval's Memoirs

By J. David Markham,
President
International Napoleonic Society

Memoirs—purported and legitimate—regarding Napoleon Bonaparte abound. It seems that everyone who had any connection at all to the one-time general, First Consul and Emperor wanted to tell his or her side of the story. But one must be careful, for even those whose closeness to Napoleon can't be denied often we can't trust to give us a truthful rendition of history and their role in it. Louis-Antoine Fauvelet de Bourrienne, for example, was undeniably close to Napoleon and able to witness much of his fabled career. But he fell out of favor with Napoleon and ultimately died in a lunatic asylum. His memoirs (*Private Memoirs of Napoleon Bonaparte, During the Periods of The Directory, The Consulate, and the Empire*) were mostly ghost written and designed to be read by Frenchmen under Louis XVIII. They are full of factual errors and must be handled with great care. Facts should be checked against other sources and expressed opinions should be carefully considered by the reader.

The same can be said about the memoirs of Charles-Maurice de Talleyrand. At times seemingly indispensible to Napoleon, Talleyrand served in a variety of capacities, most notably as Foreign Secretary. But Talleyrand ultimately worked for the restoration of the Bourbons and his memoirs (*Memoirs of the Prince de Talleyrand*) are often self-serving and inaccurate, to say the least. Worse, they were actually produced for publication under the direction of his niece, who had them rewritten to place her uncle in an even more favorable light than his own writing sought.

And so it goes, memoir after memoir. Fortunately, there are some memoirs that stand out as excellent resources that give invaluable insight into various aspects of Napoleon the soldier, the leader, the man. Napoleon's step-daughter, Queen Hortense

(*The Memoirs of Queen Hortense*) give an excellent and fair accounting of their long relationship. Baron Antoine-Clair Thibaudeau (*Memoires of the Consulate and the Empire from 1799 to 1815*), Antoine Marie de Lavalette (*Memoirs of Count Lavallette, Written by Himself*) and Baron John Fain (*The Manuscript of 1814. A History of Events which led to the Abdication of Napoleon. Written at the Command of the Emperor* and *Napoleon: How He Did It. The Memoirs of Baron Fain, First Secretary of the Emperor's Cabinet*) are very useful.

One cannot leave out the memoirs produced on St. Helena. Count Marie Joseph Emmanuel Auguste Dieudonné Las Cases wrote three works on Napoleon, most notably *Mémorial De Sainte Hélène. Journal of the Private Life and Conversations of The Emperor Napoleon at Saint Helena* (1823). For many years it served as the primary source of information on Napoleon. Baron General Gaspard Gourgaud also wrote several important works, of which the most important was his *Journal inédit de Ste-Hélène* (2 vols., Paris: 1899). This work gives great insight into Napoleon's mind as well as important details on some of his campaigns, especially those in Italy. Finally, there is Charles Jean Tristan, Marquis de Montholon, who wrote two books involving his conversations with Napoleon on St. Helena, *Memoirs of the History of France During the Reign of Napoleon, Dictated by the Emperor at Saint Helena to the Generals Who Shared His Captivity*; and *Published from the Original Manuscripts Corrected by Himself, and History of the Captivity of Napoleon at St. Helena*. While there is much good information contained in these books, one must be careful not to place too much faith in them. Not so Count Henri Gratien Bertrand, whose book, *Napoleon at St. Helena: Memoirs of General Bertrand, Grand Marshal of the Palace, January to May 1821, Deciphered and Annotated by Paul Fleuriot de Langle*, was only published in English in 1952 and not only gives extraordinary insight into Napoleon's last years but also serves as one of the strongest pieces of evidence that Napoleon was quite likely poisoned.

The writing of Armand de Caulaincourt, who worked closely with Napoleon and accompanied him on the fateful 1812 campaign in Russia, is also exceptional. Caulaincourt took detailed notes every day he was with Napoleon, and he was with Napoleon a great deal. They did not always agree on matters of policy, but they shared a strong mutual respect, and Caulaincourt's memoirs are essential to understanding Napoleon the man and leader. Those memoirs were recently re-published as *At Napoleon's Side in Russia: The Classic Eyewitness Account* by Enigma Books, and remain one of the most important Napoleonic memoirs in existence.

One of the people closest to Napoleon was his valet, Louis Constant Wairy (generally referred to as simply Constant). His work, *Memoirs of Constant, First Valet de Chambre of the Emperor, on the Private Life of Napoleon, His Family and His Court*, without doubt reflects the close proximity that Constant had to Napoleon. While they were largely written by another hand and must sometimes be handled with care (some of the details and stories may not be completely truthful), they nonetheless provide a great opportunity for learning about Napoleon the man.

So too do the memoirs of Baron Claude-François Méneval, who served as Napoleon's private secretary from 1802 to 1813. Secretaries are by their very nature close to the person for whom they work, and Méneval was no exception. Moreover, unlike the case of numerous other similar works, there is no question that Méneval actually wrote his memoirs. He worked on them diligently and in 1843, a mere seven years before his own death, he published Napoleon and Marie-Louise, Historical Memories.

Méneval was almost uniquely qualified to play the important role he played during–

and after–his time with Napoleon. He was very well educated in literature and wrote a number of works, including a play that was actually produced. He was fluent in English, having been raised by a British nanny. His fluency made him an important player in a number of important negotiations, most especially maritime relations with the United States of America and the Treaty of Amiens with the British. In 1802, Méneval became first secretary to Napoleon and then later, in 1813, to the Empress Marie-Louise. This promotion was based at least in part on the close associations he had developed with Napoleon's brothers, Lucien and Joseph. While with Napoleon, he essentially ran Napoleon's office, including all financial and communications arrangements. It was Méneval to whom Napoleon dictated virtually all of his correspondence.

As was his custom, Napoleon tried to control the private lives of his close associates (and, of course, his relatives). So he strongly encouraged Méneval to marry, and in 1807 he married the sixteen-year-old Aimée Virginie Joséphine Comte de Montvernot. Napoleon may have been controlling, but he could also be generous, giving the couple a very substantial financial gift and four rooms to live in the Tuileries. Some years later, he was made a Baron of the Empire and a Knight of the Legion of Honor.

Méneval was not just Napoleon's secretary. He was Napoleon's constant companion, both at home and on campaign. Napoleon not only dictated letters to him, but also involved him in various conferences, especially with the Russians. Like Caulaincourt, Méneval went with Napoleon to Russia in 1812 and upon their return, due to Méneval's health problems he was assigned to Marie-Louise.

Méneval's memoirs are as good an insight into what Napoleon was like and what it was like to be around him as one can find. While he is certainly favorable to the man who was his long-time employer and companion for such an incredible period of history, he does not hesitate to provide an open and honest image of Napoleon. Numerous pages are devoted, for example, to the controversial arrest of the Duke d'Enghein, pages that give far more insight into all that happened in that matter than is usually found in memoirs or history books.

Méneval was very explicit as to exactly why he wrote his 'historical remembrances:'

> However much my pen may be lacking in skill, I shall essay to give a sketch–pale no doubt, but true to nature–of this great man. As his former secretary, I have tried to show Napoleon just as he was, and as he will inevitably be judged when he is better known, without preoccupying myself about the reproaches of blind partiality which still-prejudiced minds will be tempted to address to me. I have wished to be just–not exclusive. I do not pretend to reveal nothing but secrets; Napoleon's government had fewer secrets than is generally supposed. Some of the things, however, which I relate, are little known, or not known at all. There are questions on which controversy has gone astray. I have sought to explain them. Amongst the facts which I have related, and the resolutions which were their consequence, are some of superior interest. Some of the stories are of value only because they speak of Napoleon's person. The principal object which I had in view in collecting my souvenirs was, I repeat, to furnish some materials likely to be useful to the future historian of Napoleon.

In this, he achieved complete success.

Introduction

Of the numberless books about Napoleon, this is one of the most interesting and authoritative, because it is both intimate and sincere.

The author, Claude François, Baron de Méneval, was in the closest relations with that historic figure, as private secretary and confidential agent, familiar with his daily thoughts and acts, during his most active years of achievement—from April, 1802, until St. Helena in 1815.

Born in Paris in 1778, de Méneval died there in 1850, and these *Memoirs* were written toward the end of his life, being finished shortly before his death. His grandson, Baron Napoleon Joseph de Méneval, edited and published them in Paris in 1894, and during the same year they were translated into English and issued in London and Paris, as an important contribution to history. A reviewer in the London *Academy* wrote: "A continual eyewitness gives a view of Napoleon in his camp, his closet, his court, and his home; no doubt favorable, but essentially correct"; adding that it "should be in the hands of all who wish to study and understand Napoleon."

Intimacy between a normal mind with so gigantic a spirit as that of Napoleon might be thought to warp anyone's judgment and lead to more favorable views of him than would be accepted by outsiders. But de Méneval was no mere amiable attendant. Without keen perceptions, broad grasp of principles, scrupulous attention to details, and swift executive ability, he would never have kept his position as Napoleon's chief and most confidential secretary throughout the tremendous activities of those years. That he did, and how he did, is told with a simplicity, a modesty, and a satisfying array of detail and documentary evidence as to facts—important and trivial alike—that lay hold on the reader's confidence. He gives intimate pictures of Napoleon's personality, moods, ways of working, and habits of living in palace and in tent, particulars of important transactions, and relations with the able men about him and with the various monarchs who came under his influence. Thus many wonders are simplified, and the human elements of that vast brain and irresistible will are made to appear. The man who could secure and keep the confidence of so exacting a master, who outworked all his ministers in council and his generals and soldiers in the field, was evidently noteworthy.

To account for his knowledge of the facts he relates—offering, he says, "nothing of which I was not an eyewitness or the direct depositary"—de Méneval begins with his own personal story. Released from the College de Mazarin, which had been broken up in the revolutionary disorder, he sought employment for his pen at the house of a literary friend in Paris. Here he met one of Napoleon's brothers, Colonel Louis Bonaparte, who in turn introduced him to Joseph Bonaparte. The latter, already in diplomatic service for the Republic, invited the youth to be his secretary. This post de Méneval retained for two years, while his superior was chief negotiator successively in the treaty with the United States of America (September 30, 1800), the Congress of Lunéville (Continental peace, especially with Austria, February 9, 1801), the reconciliation with Rome and the Concordat (July 15, 1801), and the Peace of Amiens (maritime treaty with England, March 27, 1802). During these important negotiations de Méneval met many distinguished men, of whom one gets revealing glimpses, and he details many interesting facts about the conferences, with interior views of motives and acts, showing appreciation of all and of the mastermind that controlled them. He must have acquired familiarity with governmental and diplomatic affairs, as well as shown special aptness in their treatment, for on April 2, 1802, Joseph Bonaparte introduced him to his brother, the First Consul.

After a pleasant, friendly dinner with Madame Bonaparte (Josephine) and her husband, and a few kindly questions from Napoleon, young de Méneval found himself, at the age of twenty-four, appointed as private secretary to the ruler of France. He soon lost his fear of the great man, but gave him an affection, an admiration, and a service of the most intimate and familiar kind (changing sometimes in form, but never in confidential relation) until, first, Elba and then St. Helena barred him out. Even then he was steadily faithful, attempting offices of friendship in Napoleon's interest unto the end. And after that he wrote several books in defense of the departed master: *Letters to M. Thiers* (1839), *Napoleon and Marie Louise* (1843-45), and others. While, finally, dying at the age of seventy-two, he left behind this narrative of private and public matters—"souvenirs collected," as he modestly writes, "to furnish some material likely to be useful to the historian of Napoleon."

The memory that could recall so many events, great and small, after such a lapse of time and a long life of toil and excitement, and the care with which so many memoranda, notes, letters, and varied documents had been preserved and presented in orderly disposition, suggest the qualities of the man who could endure the mental and physical strain of the office he had held. Moreover, writing of his care not to abuse Napoleon's confidence, he says: "Moderation always kept me aloof from the encroachments which a more enterprising mind than mine might have been tempted to essay." This marks his wisdom.

An affecting portion of the narrative relates his fidelity to the Empress Marie Louise during Napoleon's exile in Elba, when in Vienna she was being undermined in her loyalty to her husband, and de Méneval was vainly trying to countervail the subtle workings of her relatives and the other royalties of Europe to that end. He nowhere blames the Empress, but the facts show her shallow nature—evidenced by her later relations with Count Neipperg, whom she finally married, and then with a third husband.

De Méneval does not hide Napoleon's greatest errors—the execution of the Duke d'Enghien, the disastrous Spanish seizure and war, and the Russian campaign—but, on the whole, the reader gets new views of perplexing problems and of noble traits in the colossus of intellect and ambition. Napoleon's services in restoring a central power amidst revolution and anarchy, in establishing laws and institutions that have survived dynasties, and in the military glory making his name an emblem of splendid French achievement, enshrine him forever in France; while the rest of the world will never cease to wonder at his genius, and to study the puzzling contradictions of his nature.

Working with Napoleon

Chapter I

I had not quite completed my education at the Collège Mazarin, where I was a boarder, when the events of the Revolution, becoming every day more stormy, and threatening to destroy all ancient establishments, finally also affected the public schools. I left Mazarin, just like the monks, once the doors of their monasteries were violently thrown open. I had no precise plans. I was moved by a vague desire to benefit by my college reminiscences, to exercise myself in different kinds of literature simultaneously, without vocation, *invitâ Minervâ,* I felt, as is trivially though appropriately said about young people who have just left school, a desire to sow my wild oats. Some boyish attempts at writing drew me to a man who was at that time, it may be said, the *doyen* of litterateurs. I was received by the respectable Palissot with the kindness which he showed to young people whom the pureness of his style had led to seek his advice.

Palissot, who was naturally good and obliging, about whom a witty woman could say with truth that he had a keen wit and a dull heart, had been drawn to embrace the most thorny kind of literature, namely satire. The comedy entitled *Les Philosophes,* written at the instigation of the Duke of Choiseul, had made him a few mortal enemies. The minister, alarmed by the progress of the philosophical sect which numbered Voltaire (a secret enemy), and Diderot and d'Alembert (openly declared adversaries), amongst its leaders, desired to add to his means of repression the powerful arm of ridicule. The mordant hyperboles of Palissot of necessity attracted upon him the enmity of the philosophers, who inveighed against him in the most furious manner. A desire for vengeance inspired the author of *Les Philosophes* with an imitation of Pope's *Dunciad.* The stinging darts with which he transfixed his enemies and kindled in their hearts an inextinguishable hatred. Their rancor, which they bequeathed to their heirs, had pursued him far into his extreme old age. Palissot has frequently told me that the only reward he ever obtained, in compensation for the bitter hours with which these quarrels had filled his life, was a smile with which Madame de Pompadour felt him amply repaid. Meeting the favorite one day, accompanied by the Duke of Choiseul, who was driving her carriage, the author of *Les Philosophes* was presented to her by the minister. Madame de Pompadour deigned to stop for a moment, and, without speaking to him, thanked him with a nod of her head, and her most graceful smile, before which the good Palissot lost himself in endless bows.

On three occasions Palissot had stepped forward for a seat in the Academy. The cabal, which was assembled against him by Naigeon, testamentary executor of Diderot, and by Lalande, the Diogenes of philosophy, succeeded in defeating him all three times. At the last election, General Bonaparte, at the request of Chénier, went to the Institut to cast his vote in his favor. Intrigue turned against Palissot a step which should have been decisive in his favor. A rumor was spread that General Bonaparte had come to vote in favor of Abbé Leblanc, Palissot's competitor, the now forgotten author of a translation in verse of *Lucrèce*, and of a tragedy called *Manco-Capac*, the failure of which was determined by the following line, which has since become proverbial:

"*Crois-tu d'un tel forfait Manco-Capac capable?*"*

Abbé Leblanc, an innocuous poet who had wounded no man's vanity, was elected. Chénier, referring to this, told General Bonaparte, who was surprised at the result of the election, "General, you had to come here to be defeated."

Discouraged by the failure of his attempts, Palissot renounced the honors of the Institut. He consoled himself for his misadventures at the Academy in the bosom of his family, and by adding some lines to the *Dunciad*. The post of perpetual administrator of the Mazarin library, which he owed to the friendship of François de Neuf-Château, and the pensions which were granted to him under the Consulate and the Empire, enabled him to close with honor a career made illustrious by intrigues, which should have opened to him the doors of the Institut had it been possible to extinguish the old rancor of the philosophers.

I used to meet many more or less distinguished men of letters at Palissot's house. There was Marie-Joseph Chénier, whom Palissot had encouraged as a young writer, and whose talent reached the highest peaks, when death took him still in the full strength of his age; there was Le Brun, the lyrical poet, and Saint-Ange, the author of a translation in verse of Ovid's *Metamorphoses*, who had changed, for names which they considered more poetical, their patronymics of Ecouchard and Fariau; there was Felix Nogaret, the French Aristenetes, who affected cynicism, but who professed a veritable friendship for Palissot. Legouvé, Talma, and Mademoiselle Contat sometimes used to come and call upon the *doyen* of the authors of the Théâtre Français. The calls of his friends and a modest rubber of whist used to occupy his evenings. He rarely went to the theatre, and deplored its decadence, like all old men in whose eyes the imperfections of the present only increase the illusions and the regrets of the past. Talma and Mademoiselle Contat alone had the privilege of inducing him to return to the theatre. To these exceptional talents was to be added a growing talent which Palissot, who loved to exercise a kind of patronage, protected with the ardor which he placed at the service of his new acquaintances.

Mademoiselle Bourgoin, destined herself to play the part of the young leading actress at the Théâtre Français, had been introduced to him by M. Antoine, architect of the Mint, from whom she had received instruction. She was at that time sixteen years of age, and was very pretty, piquant, and giddy, with ingenuous manners. She had no difficulty in winning over an old man, who was only too prone to let himself be seduced by

---

* "Can you believe Manco-Capac capable of such a crime?"

her affectionate and caressing ways. M. Antoine, her master, had at one time mistaken for a decided vocation an irresistible passion which he had had for the stage. His friend Lekain had fought against the mania of his stagestruck friend with all his powers, and had prevented him from abandoning a useful and honorable profession for an uncertain and precarious career, from which he had little to hope for but mediocrity. M. Antoine was grateful for this to his friend, but could not help regretting not to have made his début in the rôle of Don Sanche of Aragon, by Corneille. The début of Mademoiselle Bourgoin was the unique object of his solicitude, and he had come to find in his neighbor Palissot one 'whose influence in the theatrical world might be useful to his favorite pupil.' Mademoiselle Bourgoin used to come almost every evening with her professor, and rehearse before Palissot different passages from the parts which she had chosen for her first appearance on the stage, receiving advice and encouragement from the poet.

Amongst other men of letters whom I had occasion to meet at Palissot's house was Urbain Domergue, a member of the Institut, and an eminent grammarian, known for his charming simplicity and kindheartedness. He had only one passion, and that was grammar, for which he had a true worship. His profound studies and his zeal to spread this art had induced him to introduce into the grammatical system certain new terms and innovations which were not received with favor. A quarrel which he had with Le Brun the most irascible of poets, and his mania for writing in verse, drew down upon him the most biting of epigrams. His happy carelessness was not disturbed by them. Enemy of everything which might disturb his idleness, he had abandoned the entire management of his affairs to a young servant, who displayed but little order and economy at his house, a circumstance which never disturbed him. In that house I made the acquaintance of one of the brothers of General Bonaparte, recently arrived from Egypt, where he had been sent on a mission by the Directoire.

Louis Bonaparte employed his leisure during his stay in Paris in attending lectures. He associated himself with the friends of literature, artists, and professors. He was preparing himself for the culture of literature, for which he had an innate taste, and which proved to be by far his best consolation in the highest rank and in his subsequent retirement. He was good, and of a straightforwardness which made him adopt as his motto: "Do what thou shouldst do, let happen what may," to which he has constantly been true. He treated me with kindness. Although it was at that time impossible to foresee the high estate to which he has since risen to, his personal merits, and his near kinship to the illustrious General Bonaparte, already gave him a superiority behind which my youth, and the first steps I was taking in the political world of that strange era, were sheltered.

It was only a few months after the return of Louis Bonaparte from Egypt that General Bonaparte unexpectedly landed at Fréjus.

Corsica had seen her illustrious child again during his crossing from Egypt to France. Forced by terrible weather to take refuge at Ajaccio, it was important for him to avoid the delays imposed by quarantine. As soon as the presence of General Bonaparte before Ajaccio became known, the Treasury paymaster, a M. Barberi, who was a friend of his family, hastened to take a boat and row to the frigate where the General was on board, to congratulate him on his return. Bonaparte asked for some fruit, and for the newspapers, of which he had been deprived for a long time. He also expressed the pleasure he would experience in landing in the midst of his fellow townsmen. While M.

Barberi was busy in sending on board what had been asked for, his father, who was President of the Sanitary Commission, explained to his colleagues the plausible reasons for which the General should be permitted to land, so as to satisfy the desire of the population, in whose hearts the news of his presence was exciting the warmest enthusiasm. The Commissioners brought up the rigors of the regulations and the responsibility under which they were held. This refusal might compromise Napoleon's plans. The President, convinced that there were no sick men on board—drawn on the other hand, by his zeal and his devotion—proposed to the members of the Commission of Health that they should go in a body alongside the frigate, so as, at least, to offer their congratulations to the General. This suggestion was adopted without difficulty. The members of the Commission embarked on the health boat under the guidance of a man who had secretly been ordered to run into the frigate, under pretext of an accident, so that the members of the Commission would be forced into contact with the ship's crew. The interdiction would then have to be raised, M. Barberi being convinced that they would not want to undergo quarantine themselves. This plan, forcefully carried out was fully successful. Napoleon, surrounded by Generals Berthier, Murat, Andréossy and others, made haste to reassure the Commissioners. They all immediately returned to land, where the General and his suite were received with enthusiasm by the entire population.

Detained by unfavorable winds, General Bonaparte tried to make the most of his enforced stay in Corsica. His first care was to remedy the pitiful state in which he found the troops drawn up to receive him. Learning that for nineteen months past these soldiers had received neither pay nor allowances of any kind, and that the paymaster, to keep them alive, had exhausted every resource, including his private means, he immediately put at his disposal, towards meeting their most pressing needs, all the money in his possession (about forty thousand francs) reserving for himself only just enough to pay his posting expenses to Paris.

While congratulating the paymaster on the disinterestedness which had been shown by his family, he expressed his indignation at the carelessness of the government, which seemed to attach so little importance to the welfare of its soldiers. These details were communicated to me by M. Barberi himself, who was at that time treasury paymaster at Ajaccio.

I may add those that follow, given to me by an eyewitness, M. Amédée Jaubert, secretary to General Bonaparte. Napoleon, impatient to continue his voyage, waited until favorable winds would allow him to sail out of the Bay of Ajaccio. On three different occasions it was thought that the wind had changed. At last, an officer sent by Rear Admiral Ganteaume, came to announce to the General, during a ball given in his honor by the municipality, that the wind had veered to the south, and that not a moment was to be lost in taking advantage of it. Everybody embarked without delay, each in the costume which he had worn at the ball. Sail was set, and the ship headed towards Toulon, where an English squadron was stationed close by. Fortunately the frigate was not sighted.

Towards the evening of the 16th Vendémiaire (corresponding to October 7, 1799) the ship was allowed to drift in the direction of the mountains that rise above Nice, and it was only at a very early hour on the following morning that it was found to be in the neighborhood of Fréjus. The Commanding General, in spite of the observations which had been made to him in the course of the night by the rear-admiral, had decided to embark in a longboat and to reach the coast, when the commander of Saint Rapheau, a small military post, situated about one league's distance from Fréjus, came in a boat to the frigate. He took Napoleon and his suite on board, and landed them at Saint Rapheau, and from there they walked to Fréjus. The frigate lay to in the offing. The foot squadron of guides, who had accompanied the Commanding General, went to finish their quarantine at Toulon and Napoleon set out without delay for Paris.

I will not undertake to describe the enthusiasm that the news of the landing of General Bonaparte spread throughout France; everywhere it was received with the prescience that the liberator expected by the nation had at last arrived. I will explain a fact on which sufficient light has not been thrown; some correspondence that remained unpublished until the day I printed it in the issue of the *Spectateur Militaire* dated May 15, 1850, will determine the opinion of the reader on the value of the generally-accredited assertion that General Bonaparte returned from Egypt against the wishes of the Directoire. When I published this correspondence I expressed the hope that its publication might entail some revelations, which would leave no doubt on the question whether the letters under consideration had been received by General Bonaparte while he was still in Egypt, and whether consequently they had authorized his return to France. I have to say how this problem of history, which today only possesses an interest of curiosity, has been solved. The letters of which this correspondence is composed are seven in number. The first was already known; it has been quoted in numerous publications. It is dated the 7th Prairial, of the year VII (May 26, 1799) and is signed by three directors, a condition exacted by the constitution of the year III for the validation of all acts emanating from the Directoire. This decision was transmitted the same day by President Merlin de Douai to Admiral Bruix. Published by itself, and unsupported by any testimony, it has been regarded up to our time as fraudulently given for authentic. In his unpublished memoirs Laréveillère-Lepeaux, a former member of the Directoire, one of the three signers of whom I have spoken, declares, it is assured, that he does not remember having signed any letter which had for its purpose the recall of General Bonaparte. M. Laréveillère-Lepeaux is betrayed by his memory in this case. The existence of this letter and the signature affixed to it by himself, cannot be doubted any more than the authenticity of the letters that accompanied it, and which still exist in their original form.

The assertion contained in the memoirs published under the name of M. de Bourrienne, which disposes of this question by declaring it absurd, has not appeared sufficiently convincing. Very much confidence cannot be accorded to the allegations contained in memoirs published under the name of a man who never wrote them. I will show later the reasoning this last assertion is based upon.

The testimony of M. Amédée Jaubert and that of General Eugène Merlin, the former being the secretary-interpreter, and the latter aide-de-camp to the commander-in-chief of the army of Egypt, merit a more serious examination. These two witnesses, each in his respective capacity, never left the person of the commander-in-chief during the course of the expedition, and were with him on board during his return to France. They were, all things considered, in quite as favorable a position as Bourrienne to know what orders were given by the commander-in-chief, and what was going on in his case both before his departure and at the moment the ship sailed. They heard nothing during the voyage home which could lead them to suspect that orders from the Directoire were recalling General Bonaparte back to France. They agree in saying that his departure seemed to have been decided by the reception of English newspapers containing detailed news about the reverses suffered by our armies in Italy and in Germany, papers that had been sent to the headquarters of the French army by the English admirals. This testimony, without being decisive, was a great argument in favor of the opinion that General Bonaparte's letters of recall were not received by him while he was in Egypt. Since these letters have been published the words of Napoleon himself help throw fresh light on this question.

In the notes he dictated at St. Helena it is said that during the siege of Acre, on the 27th of Floréal year VII—(May 13, 1799) he received letters from France informing him of the bad state of our affairs, and that this news was what chiefly compelled him to raise the siege and to retreat to Alexandria. These letters could not be those which contained the orders of the Directoire, inasmuch as they are dated the 7th Prairial—(May 26)—of the same year, and were not dispatched until the 23rd of the same month, that is to say, on the 11th of June. It is more than probable that the letters which were received before Acre were the letters sent by Joseph Bonaparte, and carried by the Greek Bourbaki; but what finally dissipates all doubt is the following fact which was communicated to me by General Bertrand, to whom the Emperor related it at St. Helena. General Bertrand is a man worthy of all confidence, from the nobility of his character, and the just esteem to which his constant fidelity in misfortune so fully entitled him.

General Bonaparte, who was believed by the Directoire to still be in Egypt, had landed at Fréjus on the 17 Vendémiaire of the year VIII—(October 9, 1799).—He was on his way to Paris when, between Fréjus and Lyon, where he met a courier bearing dispatches addressed to the commander-in-chief of the army in Egypt. These letters contained a revocation of the order which recalled him from Egypt, and enjoined upon him to remain there. It was through the perusal of these letters that General Bonaparte learned simultaneously of the order which had recalled him, and the counter-order by which he was to remain in Egypt. The Directoire also informed him of the government's intention to place General Lecourbe at the head of the main army. When we had nearly lost Italy, and the theater of war had been brought to the Var, the Directoire had felt the pressing need to have recourse to the talents of General Bonaparte and ardently desired his presence. But when the victory of Zurich and the results obtained in Holland had reassured them, like the sailor, who forgets his vow after the storm has past, they made haste to revoke the order which had been so quickly dispatched three months previously, an order which had been torn from them by the imminence of the peril which then threatened the Republic. It was accordingly only in Paris that General Bonaparte received the letters from the Directoire which Admiral Bruix had been commissioned to hand to him if he succeeded in landing in Egypt, together with the copy of the letter which the Admiral had sent to him from Cartagena, and the letters of Barras and Talleyrand.

As to the choice of General Lecourbe, on whom the Directoire had decided, Napoleon did not altogether disapprove of it. He had a high opinion of the general, and acknowledged him to possess the qualities of a soldier. He had formed a favorable opinion of him, in finding among the papers seized at the house of General Moreau, who was arrested in 1804, several letters which Lecourbe wrote to that general during the Hohenlinden campaign to urge him on to conquer his scruples, or his want of resolution, and to inspire him with courage.

The Emperor regretted losing the services of General Lecourbe, having noticed in him so much ill feeling at the time of Moreau's trial that he did not think it possible to employ him. One day, while Lecourbe was crossing the Tuileries Gardens he noticed the Emperor at the window of the palace, and cast upon him a look so full of hatred that Napoleon could never forget it. When, during the hundred days, Lecourbe came back to him, the Emperor received him cordially, and entrusted him with an important command.

Letters relating to the Recall of GENERAL BONAPARTE *to France.*

I.

To GENERAL BONAPARTE, Commander-in-Chief of the Army in the East.
Paris, 7th Prairial, An VII.

The extraordinary efforts, Citizen General, which Austria and Russia have just been displaying, and the serious and almost alarming turn which the war has taken, demand that the Republic should concentrate her forces. The Directoire has, in consequence, just given orders to Admiral Bruix to use every means in his power to become master of the Mediterranean, and to betake himself to Egypt, in order to bring back the army under your command. He has received instructions to concert with you as to the measures to be taken for the embarking and the transport of the troops.

You will judge, Citizen General, whether you can leave a part of your troops behind with safety, and the Directoire authorizes you in this case to entrust the command of them to the man whom you shall deem best suited for this post.

The Directoire will, with pleasure, see you at the head of the Republican armies, which till now you have so gloriously commanded.

(Signed) THEILHARD.
Laréveillère-Lepeaux.
Barras.

II.

Letter from THE DIRECTOIRE *to* ADMIRAL BRUIX *(written by the hand of* SECRETARY GENERAL LAGARDE, *and signed by* MERLIN DE DOUAI.)
Paris, 7th Prairial, An VII.

The Executive Directoire, Citizen General, after due reflection on the present state of affairs, has felt the necessity of uniting and concentrating as much as possible the forces of the Republic. In consequence, you are ordered to take the promptest measures to effect a junction with the Spanish fleet. As soon as this has been done you will search for the English fleet, and if, as is probable, you are then superior in force to the enemy, you will attack it. As soon as you have put the English out of the possibility of opposing your operations with success, you will make sail to Egypt with the object of embarking the army there. You will concert with General Bonaparte on the measures to be taken, and, should he deem it necessary, you may leave a portion of his forces behind you in Egypt.

You will hand the annexed letter to General Bonaparte. It communicates the plans of the Directoire to him.

(Signed) MERLIN, President of Executive Directoire.
LAGARDE, Secretary General of the Executive Directoire.

By a decree of the Directoire, dated 14th Germinal, An VII (April 3, 1799) Bruix, Minister of Marine, had been appointed Admiral in command of the naval army at Brest, a rank equivalent to that of Captain-General in Spain, so that Admiral Massaredo should have no objection to serving under him.

III.

Autograph Letter of the CITIZEN TALLEYRAND, Interim Minister of Marine, to ADMIRAL BRUIX.

Paris, 7th Prairial, An VII.

So, now, my dear Bruix, your mission has taken the form that you first desired. I am delighted at this. You are no longer in doubt; you have an object, a prescribed object, an object of the highest importance. The Directoire writes only one word to Bonaparte. I am sending him a letter from Barras to which I have added a few lines. The Directoire relies on you to inform him of our situation at home and abroad. Bring him back. You are asked to keep the strictest silence on your mission. Good-bye, I embrace and give you my best. Believe me your friend forever.

(Signed) CH. MAUR. TALLEYRAND.

P.S.—My opinion is that Belleville, our Consul at Genoa, will be your successor; that is not yet decided, but the Directoire will not make its definite selection until the first days of next decade. Sieyès will arrive here between the 20th and the 24th.

IV.

ADMIRAL BRUIX to the CITIZEN BONAPARTE, Commander-in-chief of the Army in the East.

Cartagena, 29th Prairial, An VII.

CITIZEN GENERAL,

The Executive Directoire has ordered me to effect a junction with the Spanish Fleet, then to attack the enemy, and, having defeated it, to go to Egypt to take and to transport to France the troops under your command.

My junction has already taken place, and the combined army has a strength of forty-two line vessels, but this force does not give us superiority over the English; they have sixty vessels in the Mediterranean. Nevertheless, by well concerted maneuvers, it will be possible to defeat them before they have been able to concentrate their forces. This is what I hope to do, if my constant and pressing applications to the Spanish General, and to the Court of Madrid, are successful.

Once this success obtained, I assure you, Citizen General, that I shall not lose a moment in betaking myself to Alexandria, directly after the engagement. Make your arrangements accordingly, that the fleet be detained the least time possible on the coast of Egypt. You must count, General, on all the efforts of which I am capable, to overthrow every obstacle and to join you as promptly as possible. Nevertheless, it is impossible to exactly fix the date of my arrival, and. as nothing is less certain than the result of a naval engagement, nor even that I may be able to succeed in attacking the enemy before they have united their forces, I must ask you, General, not to take final measures for embarking your army until the early arrival of the naval force be announced to you by some frigates which I shall send off immediately after the encounter.

Believe me, Citizen General that it will be for me the best day of my life, and, for the brave army which I command, a day of glory and of happiness, the day on which we shall be able to give back to the fatherland the heroes who have done so much for its glory. Receive my fraternal and respectful salutations,

(Signed) E. BRUIX.

P.S.—I promised the Greek who will hand you this letter that you would make him a present of five hundred louis. I do not think, General, that in spite of the enormity of this sum, you will hesitate in doing so.

Letters V and VI were addressed by the Interim Minister of Marine, Talleyrand, to Admiral Bruix, under dates of 13th and 27th Prairial. Amongst other instructions they repeat the orders of the Directoire on the 7th of Prairial, and insist on their execution.

VII.

Rough Draft of a Letter written by ADMIRAL BRUIX, to the CITIZEN JOSEPH BONAPARTE.

Paris, the 22nd Vendémiaire, An VII.

Receive, Citizen, the heartfelt compliment which I address to you on the happy return of your brother. The happiness of your family is everyone's happiness. I hear that you leave this night or tomorrow for Fréjus. I send you some papers which may interest you and your brother.

(1) Copy of a letter which I received in the roads of Vado. It was in accordance with this letter that I wrote him the one that I showed to you in Paris. You know how, once my junction with the Spanish effected, the superior forces of the enemy prevented the realization of my further projects.

(2) Two letters from the Directoire to your brother, which I was commissioned to hand him myself.

(3) A letter from the Citizen Talleyrand, which had the same destination and which contained a letter from Director Barras.

(4) Copy of a letter in which Talleyrand forwarded me these dispatches.

I share your joy and I salute you cordially.

(Signed) E. BRUIX

Shortly after the 18th Brumaire, as the Consuls were still occupying the Luxembourg Palace, I was at the house of Colonel Louis Bonaparte, who had been appointed to the command of the 5th regiment of dragoons. He was living at the Hotel La Trémoille, in the Rue de Vaugirard. He showed me a manuscript of about fifteen folio pages, entirely written by Napoleon. It was the draft of a speech composed by him while he was still only an artillery lieutenant, on the subject proposed for a prize essay by the Academy of Lyons: "What are the Truths and the Sentiments which it is Most Important to Inculcate to Men for their Happiness?" had tried to decipher this manuscript, but, discouraged by its difficulties, had given up the task. That was the first time that I saw Napoleon's handwriting. I seemed to have hieroglyphics before my eyes. At the same time I was impelled by strong curiosity and interest to ask Louis Bonaparte to entrust me with the manuscript. I wanted to see whether I should be more skilful or more fortunate than he had been. I spent eight days studying the words, and after infinite trouble succeeded in deciphering them, with the exception of five or six words, which I left blank. I carried the manuscript, with the translation, back to Colonel Louis Bonaparte, who, contenting himself with the copy which I had made of it, seized roughly upon the original, and before it was possible for me to interfere, had thrown it into the grate. A bright fire was burning, and this precious relic was destroyed in a moment, nor was I able to save any portion of it. The speech remained unfinished, if I may judge by the draft I read. The last part was missing. This makes me doubt that he could have received the prize, as was at first announced, and that he even took part in the competition. The impression that remained after reading this essay of his, as far as I can remember, was that he had a great deal of imagination, but little art or sequence of ideas in his composition. It contained some pleasant thoughts, a somewhat pompous approach to humanity, and a dreamy sentimentality, expressed with the exaltation and candor of youth.

A picturesque definition of feeling and melancholy, an enthusiasm for the music of *Le Devin du Village,* to whose author Napoleon would have had a statue raised for that single composition, and the sentence with which his speech ended, were the passages which most struck me. To give a definition of feelings the author took his reader to the places most favorable to meditation which he boldly described in some detail. He transported him from the shepherd's hut to the Church of St. Peter's at Rome, and gave the impressions felt by the traveler when first entering into this immense construction, under the mysterious light of a single lamp. Such is the impression I can recall of my perusal of that precious manuscript, an impression which would perhaps be modified if I were to read it over today.

The taste which Napoleon had at that time for the music of *Le Devin du Village* will seem strange to those who know that he preferred Italian music to French, and that he did not like the writing of Jean-Jacques.*

He remembered all the arias of that charming pastoral, and loved to sing them. Not altogether, as Rousseau said of Louis XV, with the most discordant voice in his kingdom, but with a voice that could not be said to always be strictly in tune. To these impressions of youth, which he retained into maturity, had come a passionate attachment to Italian music, which he listened to with delight, and which was the most effective form of recreation he could enjoy during his great and arduous labors.

* Rousseau.

But the passage in the speech which left upon me the most profound impression, and which constantly returns to my memory, is the sentence with which it ends. It is a kind of prophecy, such a prophecy as was attributed by popular belief to superior genius and to those who were dying. "Heaven lends prophetic actions to the dying." It was a kind of prescient vision of his future destiny that the great, august, and unhappy man had that day. This is the sentence, quoted literally: "Great men are meteors, destined to burn, to light their age."

M. de Las Cases relates in the *Memorial of St. Helena* that Prince de Talleyrand, either to pay court to the Emperor, or perhaps by his express command, had had the speech sought for in Lyons, and had it presented to him. Napoleon read a few pages of it and then threw it into the fire. I have since learned that, as a matter of fact, the essay had been handed in for competition. What I saw of it, then, must have been a rough draft, a composition written in the first flood of thought, the color and originality of which were weakened and destroyed by a certain number of corrections. This rough draft of the speech remaining among Napoleon's papers would later have come into the possession of his brother. I did not recognize in the speech which was printed in 1826, and which forms a part of a collection published under the name of General Gourgaud, the same one that I had read in 1800.

There remained the hope that the Count du Saint-Leu might have preserved the copy which I gave him; but a letter, written by that prince from Florence on the 31st of March, 1840, showed me that I was wrong. It is not on account of its literary merit that we may regret the loss of the original document. Its interest would be very small today, it didn't show by which serious course of study nature had endowed the man called to such great deeds. The author himself attached but little importance to it. Finding the rough draft ten years later, he wanted to throw it into the fire. He only gave it to his brother on his pressing request, and on condition that he should burn it, a condition which Louis Bonaparte, to my regret, only too loyally fulfilled.

I was part of the conscription of the year VII. I felt no vocation for a military life. My constitution was far from robust, and a state of health which, without being feeble rendered me unfit for the fatigues of war, didn't encourage me toward a military career. However, every citizen had to pay his tribute to the fatherland. None was exempt from this duty. The various applications which I made to obtain an exemption had the effect of delaying a decision on my case for a whole year. My application put me in communication with various kinds of people, and brought me at last into the presence of the First Consul. So it is that Providence guides man toward the goal it has marked out for him by ways which he cannot suspect. My efforts to escape the law on conscription were the obscure ways that placed me under the protection of a man who was reputed to be inflexible in its execution, and who would have carried its rigor to the extreme limit.

Louis Bonaparte had been appointed Colonel of the 5th regiment of dragoons. His regiment was sent to the Vendée. He invited me to meet him in Verneuil, in the Perch district, where he was quartered. I went there in the last days of June. The pacification of the Vendée was almost complete. As soon as had he took charge of the government, the First Consul turned his attention to that unhappy region, and took measures to end the discord that had torn it apart. All efforts made by the preceding governments to that effect had been completely fruitless. It was for the First Consul to put an end to this cruel war, where the victor had always reason to deplore his victory. He succeeded by the use and skilful mixture of rigor and magnanimity, and by the firmness of his will. The leaders of the Chouans, divided amongst themselves, discouraged by their reverses, and incapable of resisting the forces directed against them, were finally obliged to submit. Only, Frotté, still resisted. Taken by surprise he wished to parley, at the same time encouraging his lieutenants to wait for better days. The letters which he wrote to them were intercepted, and served as proof of his bad faith. He was brought before a court martial, and shot, together with some of his comrades.

The death of Frotté was the final scene in that bloody war. The public feeling was still such at that time that on the day Frotté and his accomplices were executed the inhabitants shut themselves up in their houses, and the streets of the town were entirely deserted. Frotté was seized at the house of the General in command at Alençon with whom he had taken refuge, and who gave him up. It was that same Guidal who was afterwards implicated in a revolutionary plot in the south, and who ended up miserably in the Mallet affair.

After having passed six months in the 5th dragoons, where my name only figured on the list as a matter of form, I was able to leave this mockery of military service without attracting any attention. Colonel Louis Bonaparte, who knew how little I was anxious to serve my apprenticeship for the *bâton* of a marshal of France, introduced me to his brother, Joseph Bonaparte, who had recently arrived from the embassy at Rome, after the outrage which had forced him to leave that city in the month of December, 1797. His rank as ambassador had not protected him from the outrage to public liberty which was committed on his person. Some partisans of the revolution had claimed the protection of the French embassy. They had been pursued by the Papal troops, who massacred a number of these refugees. In this attack the life of the French ambassador had been threatened, and he had seen General Duphot killed by his side, who was engaged to marry the sister of his wife, who afterwards became Madame Bernadotte, and who is today Queen of Sweden. Victim of his generous devotion, this general was mortally wounded while he was helping Joseph Bonaparte to induce the malcontents to withdraw, and the Papal troops to cease firing. The ambassador only owed his life to the fearlessness and calm he displayed during that terrible moment. More fortunate than the French officer Basseville, who was cruelly murdered by the Roman mob four years previously, he was allowed to escape the dangers to which he was exposed, and found a refuge in the house of the Spanish ambassador, Chevalier d'Azzara.

Joseph Bonaparte was at that time writing his story "Moïna," a work of little importance; but which can be commended for the simplicity of the subject, the gentleness of the feelings it expressed, and its pleasant style. These various circumstances put me in contact with this worthy Moecenas, who received me with the greatest kindness, and showed an interest in me from which he never departed, and for which, all my life long, I shall be profoundly grateful to him.

When he was commissioned to negotiate for peace with the American envoys he was good enough to appoint me his secretary. These peace negotiations were happily ended by a treaty which was signed on the 30th of September, 1800, by the councilors of state, Joseph Bonaparte, Roederer, and Fleurieu, on behalf of France, and by Messrs. Ellsworth, Davy, and Murray, for the United States. By this agreement, which was to last over a period of eight years, the rights of the neutrals were solemnly established. It was a victory over England. The great principle that a ship is under the protection of the nation whose flag it flies, a principle which has since been maintained and defined with such rigor, was expressly recognized. Munitions of war alone were to be considered contraband. The right of passage of neutral ships was regulated, and the right of blockade was restricted to places actually blockaded. The secretary of the Commission who was to deal with the ambassador was M. Pichon, a young man full of ardor, whose special knowledge was very useful in the various stages of these negotiations. M. Pichon, as a reward for the services which he then rendered, was appointed Consul General and Chargé d'Affaires to the United States. At the time of the expedition to Santo Domingo he was commissioned to provide for the resupply of the military and naval forces, and was unfortunate enough to sign a number of contracts exceedingly unprofitable to the state. A commission of the state Council was appointed to examine the management and the books of the Consul General. The result of this commission was that he was absolved as a bookkeeper, but condemned for his negligence. Because of this report M. Pichon was dismissed, and the various sums of which he had unduly ordered payment were put to his charge. M. Pichon, in his misfortune, deserved public sympathy. This just, but harsh sentence, filled him with a resentment which prompted him to publish, in 1814, a very bitter pamphlet full of unjust attacks against the fallen government. The government of the king was grateful to him for having placed his personal resentment at the service of the restored dynasty, and rewarded him for it by appointing him councilor of state.

The treaty with the United States was celebrated by a reception at Mortfontaine two days later. The First Consul was present with his family. The Second and Third Consuls, with the ministers, the presidents and various members of the Council of State, the senate, the legislative body, and the tribunate, were also present. The diplomatic corps was invited as well. Various persons who had formerly served in America in various capacities met together on that occasion. M. de LaFayette, and M. de la Rochefoucauld-Liancourt were present at the reception, and were good enough to undertake to invite the Americans who happened to be in Paris, and also to act as interpreters between Joseph Bonaparte and those who did not speak French. It was these two gentlemen who suggested the subjects of the emblematic devices and inscriptions which served to recall the most glorious feats in the American War of Independence. There were a number of pretty women present, at the head of which figured the two youngest sisters of the First Consul, Mesdames Leclerc and Murat.

The reception at Mortfontaine was enchanting. The beauty of the site lent itself to the taste and the magnificence that were displayed there. Mortfontaine was already at that time one of the most beautiful places in France. Today it is almost without a rival, thanks to the improvements and the embellishments that the taste of its illustrious proprietor have added to it. There is nothing particularly remarkable either about the park or the *château,* but the lakes spotted with wooded isles, and animated with the movement of boats and skiffs of elegant shapes, surrounded with shrubberies and shady avenues, offer a delightful view. These lakes are immense sheets of water separated by roadways, and communicating with one another by locks, over a distance of nearly two leagues. The hillsides are covered with many green trees and are crowned with fine timber. On their slopes are to be seen sandstone rocks, some of colossal height. One of them fully warrants the inscription which may be read:

Sa masse indestructible a fatigué le temps.—[*]
DELILLE.

Every kind of landscape may be found in this little valley of lakes, where living nature contrasts with dead nature. Hamlets and mills, grouped picturesquely, fill it with movement and life, while at the other end is a long strip of arid sand worthy of the desert, the illusion of which is completed by some ruins in the Moorish style.

A concert was given on the first day, at which Garat and the most distinguished artists in Paris were heard. On the following day a great hunt was given. In the evening there was a display of fireworks on the first lake, in front of the *château.* A flaming obelisk—on the pedestal of which were seen allegories consecrating the union of the French and American Republics—illuminated its approaches. Once the bouquet exploded a small flotilla appeared on the water, illuminated with colored globes, carrying the flags of the United States and of France interlaced.

The fireworks were followed by theatricals. Two little comedies were performed by Fleury, Dazincourt, Mlles. Contat, Devienne and Mézeray, on a stage, the back of which opened out on to the park. Through this opening could be seen a little wood, lighted by fires, producing a fairylike effect, thanks to a skilful juxtaposition of light and shade. The actors of the Théâtre Français played with their usual skill. Fleury and Mlle. Contat, invited to the fête, distinguished themselves by their good manners and their amiability. The owners of Mortfontaine greatly appreciated these two artists, so signally worthy of that name. They invited them sometimes to dinner during the following winter, at their fine house in the Rue du Rocher.

Between the two pieces, *couplets* alluding to the reestablishment of cordial relations between the two States, were sung by Garat and by Mlles. Contat and Devienne.

The festivities ended with a magnificent ball, to which more than twelve hundred persons had been invited. The First Consul and Madame Bonaparte withdrew at one o'clock, having to return to Paris.

It was at Mortfontaine that I saw Napoleon for the first time. No occasion presented itself by which his attention could have been drawn to me. Seeing him surrounded with that prestige of grandeur, which imposed respect on all those who approached him, I did not suspect that one day I should be his familiar. He was very affable to everybody. He neglected his affairs to give himself up to the pleasures of the fête. The library of the *château* in which he worked was almost entirely deserted during those days. He conversed with each on his specialty; he even spoke of music with Garat.

During the short stay which the First Consul made at Mortfontaine some gold medals, dating from the days of the Roman Empire, had been presented to him by M. Cambry, Prefect of the Oise department. These medals had been found on the borders of the department, in a little plain surrounded by hills, where the remains of an encampment could be traced. The First Consul presented these to the American Envoys, asking them to carry them back to America.

The First Consul conversed at length with M. de LaFayette, a general for whom he had a particular esteem. If his conduct during the terrible crises of the Revolution, where so many men lost their lives or their honor, did not seem to the First Consul to have always been worthy of the occasion, he considered, nevertheless, that he had always

[*] Its indestructible mass has defeated time.

acted in an honorable manner, and gave him full credit for his good intentions.

The fame of M. de LaFayette rested entirely on his unyielding perseverance in one order of ideas. He had not changed since the fall of the Bastille. He had not taken one step forward since 1789, nor alighted from the white horse on which he rode at the head of the national guards. He had dreamed for France of an American form of government, and, full of this Utopian idea, would never admit the difference between the two countries, the needs of the times, nor the mindset of the men involved. The events of the 18th of Brumaire upset everything in his past. Immovable—when all around him was changing, either by conviction or by policy—he remained faithful to his maxims at a time when anyone was ready to switch his personal convictions, and when oaths were current coin, and constantly changing. The situation of M. de LaFayette was a novelty which, in the eyes of some was original and piquant, and which inspired others with a feeling of respect.

Whatever may have been Napoleon's private opinion about him, such a man was, in his eyes, a man of real value. He must have hoped to make use of him, for he was an instrument that he could not neglect. He accordingly expressed his desire to appoint him to the senate. M. de LaFayette thanked the First Consul for his kind intentions, and begged him to transfer them to his son, alleging his desire for retirement and his disinclination to return to public life. Napoleon understood him. He had need of the father, not of the son; therefore he did not press him. Nevertheless he continued to receive him, and remained on friendly terms. Till then M. de LaFayette had been consistent, and his scruples, whatever may have been their motive, were worthy of respect. Afterwards, either because he was dissatisfied with the indifference with which his resistance had been received, or because he grew tired of the obscurity into which he had entered, or perhaps because of the strength of his convictions that drew him on, the voting on the issue of a Life-Consulate appeared as a favorable opportunity for once again drawing public attention to himself. He could have abstained from voting, but not only did he vote, he also sent his vote to the First Consul, with a letter which is too well known to need reproduction here. This act did not produce the effect that its author had expected. Its natural result was to estrange the First Consul from M. de LaFayette and cease to take any further interest in him.

Less than a month after the events which I have related above, the brother of the First Consul was appointed plenipotentiary minister to the Congress at Lunéville. The Austrian plenipotentiary was Count Louis de Cobenzl, formerly ambassador at St. Petersburg, the same who signed the Treaty of Campo-Formio with General Bonaparte. The arrival of this minister at Strasburg having been announced by telegraph, Joseph Bonaparte left Paris without delay, leaving his wife behind him, and arranging for her to join him later on. But Count Cobenzl had only stayed a short time in Strasburg, and hearing at Lunéville that the French minister had not yet arrived, continued his route to Paris. The French and Austrian plenipotentiaries met halfway. The latter wished to continue on to Paris. I accordingly gave him my place in Joseph Bonaparte's carriage, and took his place in his carriage, with M. Hoppe, his secretary, for the return to Paris.

M. de Talleyrand lent his house in the Rue d'Anjou to the Austrian minister, with whom he was already acquainted. On the following day M. de Cobenzl was presented to the First Consul. They had several conversations together.

After spending a week in Paris the two negotiators started off for Lunéville, which they reached in the first days of November. The Austrian minister declared at the very outset that he could not negotiate without the presence and cooperation of an English minister, his Court being bound by a treaty to England. The First Consul had done everything in his power to effect a reconciliation with this state. Negotiations had been opened in London through M. Otto, a French agent, for the exchange of prisoners, with the object of bringing about the signature of a naval armistice, on the same basis as the one which had been concluded with Austria.

England had asked to be admitted to the Congress as a contracting party; this demand had appeared suspicious. If this power was sincere in her desire for peace it was open to her to negotiate separately without combining with Austria. The relative positions of France and England were very different from those of France and Austria. Everything was subject for discussion with England; for twenty years no treaty had been signed between the two powers. Since then the revolution of 1789 and the wars of the Republic had entirely changed the face of Europe. England had considerably increased her possessions beyond the seas at the expense of France and of her allies, and had extended her power in India beyond all measure. All matters of negotiation had to be dealt with for the first time. With Austria the basis of the negotiations already existed; only a renewal of treaties was in question. The negotiations could with difficulty be simultaneous; obstacles were certain to arise at each step; and for this reason the French government was inclined to suspect the English cabinet of a lack of sincerity. To assure itself of this fact, and to expose the secret designs of England, it made the following proposals:—

(1) To admit an English representative to the Lunéville Congress, with the understanding that hostilities should be suspended at sea as they were on land, so that the contracting powers should, as far as possible, be in the same situation. [This demand was justified. France could not be at war with one of the powers and in suspension of hostilities with the other. If the naval armistice gave France the advantage of being able to reestablish commercial relations between her ports and her colonies, and of allowing her to resupply and to recruit her army in Egypt, the continental armistice gave Austria the means to reorganize her armies, to fortify her strong places with English money, and to prepare to resume the contest with an advantage to herself. In reply the English cabinet refused to allow munitions of war of any kind to enter any of the blockaded ports and towns, but only provisions for a fortnight, at a time when, with the exception of Malta, almost all the blockaded places were well supplied with food. This proposal tended to render the armistice illusory.]

(2) The First Consul then offered to negotiate while continuing hostilities on sea and on land, as had been the case in many previous negotiations. It was a means to accelerate the conclusion of peace, because the two allied powers, pressed by the probable successes of the French forces, would be interested in the termination of the negotiations, to avoid making the conditions of peace more onerous every day. [The proposal was not considered acceptable by the English cabinet.]

(3) A further proposal was made. France offered to accept the armistice proposed by the British cabinet, in spite of its great disadvantages, if England would agree to separate negotiations. [In this expectation the renewal of hostilities against Austria was delayed for eight days. The English cabinet refused.]

(4) As a final proposal the French government asked to be allowed to send six

frigates under a flag of truce into Alexandria, it being specially stipulated that these frigates should not carry more arms than form the usual equipment of storeships. [This was a practical acceptance of the principle of the armistice proposed by the English government. The reinforcements—of about four thousand men—which this expedition could have conveyed to the army in Egypt was by no means an equivalent to the advantages which Austria would derive from English subsidies during the prolongation of the continental armistice, which would enable her to increase her military resources. It was, moreover, a means of forcing the English to complete the negotiations rapidly, so as to prevent the arrival of the frigates in Egypt; for more than a month would have had to elapse before they could be ready to sail. These different proposals were rejected. They could only be acceptable in the eyes of a ministry really anxious to conclude peace, for where a real desire to agree exists, an arrangement is soon achieved.]

These repeated refusals clearly showed how little disposed England was for peace. In presenting herself at the Lunéville Congress as having a common interest with Austria, England, no doubt, had no intention of sacrificing herself to her ally, nor of winning for her at the price of her own conquests any restitutions of territory. All that she then desired was to gain time, and to intervene in the Lunéville negotiations for the purpose of delaying their progress and of provoking some reason to break them up. "To admit an English representative to Lunéville," said Napoleon, "would be to put into his hands the spindle and the thread with which to weave some new coalition." As a matter of fact these ruses on the part of the English government had no other result than to delay for the space of one year the peace which England so contemptuously refused in January, 1800, after the 18th Brumaire, and which she solicited on March 21, 1801.

At the end of the third note, referring to General Mathieu Dumas's work, entitled *Précis des événements militaires* which the Emperor dictated while at St. Helena, are to be found the following reflections:—

"The spectacle of the changes which were brought about in so short a time was sufficiently gratifying to a true Frenchman. In January, 1800, France solicited peace. Lord Grenville replied with a torrent of abuse, allowing himself to make the strangest insinuations. He desired that a prince of that race of kings who, during so many centuries had known how to maintain the prosperity of the nation at home and to ensure consideration and respect abroad, should remount the throne of France. He exhorted the First Consul to establish with proof the legitimacy of his government ; and today it was this same Lord Grenville who begged as a favor to be allowed to treat with the Republic, offering even to pay for this grace with new concessions.

"The negotiations for a naval armistice were broken off. The towns of Ingolstadt, Ulm, and Philipsburg were ceded by the Emperor to France, as the price of a six weeks' promulgation of the armistice. A few months later the Peace of Lunéville saved the house of Austria, and reestablished peace on the continent. And finally, shortly afterwards, the cabinet of St. James's signed the Preliminaries of London, by which the humiliated English oligarchy recognized the French Republic, aggrandized, not only by the Belgian provinces, but by Piedmont, by Genoa, and by the whole of Italy. In the meanwhile how many millions had been added to the English national debt? Such was the result of Pitt's passionate policy."

What follows was also dictated by the Emperor, but was not printed in the memoirs published under his name:

"Pitt, who did not desire peace until Belgium should have been ceded to Austria, was not sincere in asking to be admitted to the Lunéville Congress. If during the discussions between M. Otto and Lord Grenville on the question of a naval armistice, which lasted six weeks, the latter had really been anxious for the conclusion of peace he would have made his desire clear, and would have proved it in his confidential conversations. He said nothing which could remove an impression to the contrary. Lord Hawkesbury's very first words, at the time of the negotiation of the Preliminaries of London, showed the sincerity of the English cabinet. M. Mathieu Dumas shows little experience in imagining that the rupture of negotiations between the two countries depended on the admission, or the refusal of admission, of six frigates into the port of Alexandria. It would have been as mad on the part of England as on the part of France. It sometimes happens in war that an army of one hundred thousand men retreats after losing thirty or forty hussars in a reconnoitering expedition under the command of the commander-in-chief. Is so slight a loss the cause of the retreat? No, the retreat is the result of the reconnoitering expedition."

England refused all proposals, and Count Cobenzl, on his end, persisted in his refusal to negotiate without the assistance of an English *envoyé*, hostilities started up once again, in spite of the presence of the French and Austrian plenipotentiaries at Lunéville. General Moreau, who was in Paris, where he had gone after the extension of the armistice, left on the 19th of November to be at the head of the army of the Rhine. He had been received with great cordiality and marked favor by the First Consul, who presented him with a pair of beautifully worked pistols, embellished with diamonds. As he handed him these pistols he remarked that if he had not had the names of the General's victories engraved on them it was because these were so numerous that there was no room for such an inscription. Moreau received these advances and this present with an indifference which was noticed by all.

The resumption of hostilities having been declared, the First Consul drew up his plan of campaign for the ensuing winter. He was forced to abstain from taking personal command of the troops, since the state of affairs at home rendered it impossible for him to be absent from the seat of government. The army of the Rhine was destined to play the most important part in this campaign. The First Consul remembering no doubt the coldness Moreau with which had received his suggestion of a bold plan at the opening of the previous campaign, ordered him simply to take the offensive, leaving to him the responsibility of directing his operations as circumstances might dictate. The army of the Rhine was the finest of our armies; it was composed of more than one hundred thousand men, all veteran soldiers, under the command of experienced officers. To provide such an army to General Moreau, giving him at the same time a free hand, was to refute in advance the frivolous assertion that Bonaparte was jealous of Moreau's glory.

General Lahorie, General Moreau's chief staff officer, who had preceded him, had arrived in Lunéville two days before him. Instead of putting up at the house of the French minister, he went directly to that of the Austrian minister. When Moreau arrived in Lunéville the French minister, without awaiting his visit, called on him at the inn at which he was staying. I accompanied Joseph Bonaparte to see Moreau, who received us in a low room, lighted by a lamp. He was dressed in a blue frock-coat, which bore no distinctive marks of his rank, and he was smoking a pipe. Our call was short and without importance. The want of attention on the part of Moreau, and the prank played by

Lahorie, showed us fairly clearly that the relations between the commanding general and his *entourage* were not of the friendliest. Before continuing his journey, General Moreau returned Joseph Bonaparte's call, meeting Count Cobenzl at his house. After some general conversation, which did not last more than half-an-hour, he returned to his traveling carriage, which was waiting for him outside.

The preliminaries of a peace advantageous to Austria had been signed in Paris on the 28th of July, 1800, but had not been ratified by the Emperor of Germany.

Six weeks later the Austrian government asked for a resumption of the negotiations, at the cost of conceding Ingolstadt, Ulm, and Philipsburg. If Austria, abandoning her dilatory policy, had frankly entered upon the negotiations without again risking the dangers of war, she would have saved Mantua and Tuscany, and could have reestablished the King of Sardinia in Piedmont. Such an offer was made to the Austrian plenipotentiary. France's moderation encouraged Austria to increase her demands, and to insist on the admission of an English plenipotentiary. Meanwhile the armistice was coming to a close. Austria preferred to run the risk of war, but the return of General Bonaparte had brought victory back to our flag. The hopes of the cabinet of Vienna were thwarted; our victories at Hohenlinden and elsewhere in bringing our troops closer to the gates of Vienna put an end to Austria's hesitation. A new armistice—to last thirty days—had been agreed upon at Steyer, between Moreau and Archduke Charles, one month after the renewal of hostilities. Count Cobenzl then resigned himself to come to terms without the cooperation of England, but the favorable opportunity had been lost. The conditions of peace could no longer be the same after the victory of Hohenlinden. Thus did the enemies of France conspire together for her greatness and lead Napoleon by the hand to the pinnacle of power. Three times already they had they refused peace under unusually favorable conditions. The more moderate the French government showed itself, the more their demands increased; experience seemed to teach them nothing.

The point of the negotiation which the Austrian minister defended with the most obstinacy was the preservation of the German ecclesiastical States. It was his wish that the ecclesiastical electors and princes should obtain on the right bank the equivalent of what they had to abandon on the left. Austria felt that their suppression was a death-blow to her influence, and, later on, to her domination over Germany. But the compensation which Austria asked in their favor would have absorbed the greater part of the lands available on the right bank, and certain princes whose inheritance belonged to their families would have been deprived of compensation, which the losses they had suffered gave them the right to claim. Besides, the abuse of preserving to the ecclesiastical authority temporalities to defend, and the inconvenience of leaving Germany split up into thousands of little princedoms or lordships, exercising sovereign rights, had long stood in need of reform. One, only, of the four ecclesiastical electors was maintained; his seat was transferred from Mayence (Meinz) to Ratisbon.

Austria also ardently desired the preservation of the Grand Duke of Tuscany in Italy. At the opening of the Congress this prince would have been able to retain his states. Austria later on limited her demands on his behalf to the three legations which at first she had desired for herself; but she was to lose Italy as she had lost Germany. The Duchy of Salzburg was the indemnity awarded to the Grand Duke. The maritime interests of France, the safety of the new Italian States, and the necessity of removing the inimical influence of Austria from this country, decided the First Consul to take advantage of his victories. Personal overtures made by M. de Cobenzl to Joseph Bonaparte were, for the French plenipotentiary, only one more reason to insist on the cession of Tuscany, which was granted. An ultimatum was notified to the Austrian minister. In spite of all its efforts, and the threat of desperate measures, the Vienna cabinet was forced to yield, regretting bitterly not having listened to the first proposals made by France. Peace was signed on the 9th of February, 1801. The Treaty of Lunéville assured the possession of Belgium and Mantua to France, and gave her as frontiers the Rhine, and the line of the Adige in Italy. It overthrew the gothic edifice of the German Empire by suppressing the ecclesiastical sovereignties; in reducing to a small number of real sovereignties the crowd of helpless and defenseless little feudal principalities, it finally established the basis of the confederation of the Rhine.

The course of the Lunéville negotiations was marked by a notable occurrence. A suspension of arms had been concluded on the 16th of January, between Generals Brune and Bellegarde, in command of the opposing armies in Italy. By this convention the important fortified town of Mantua remained under Austrian control, blockaded only at a distance of eight hundred *toises* by French troops. By a convention signed at Lunéville, eight days later, Mantua, together with the forts of Peschiera, Sermione, Ferrara, Ancona, and the castles of Verona and Legnano, were handed over to us. Our diplomacy might well be proud of having succeeded better than our armies.

The skilful, firm, and unselfish conduct of Joseph Bonaparte seconded the genius and the power of the First Consul. The tribunate accordingly expressed the wish that a testimonial of the nation's satisfaction should be offered to the French plenipotentiary.

During the momentary interruption of the negotiations there arrived at Lunéville the courier Moustache, bringing the news of the explosion of the infernal machine of the Rue St. Nicaise. The shock into which the whole town was thrown by the news of this abominable outrage can easily be imagined. Count Cobenzl made haste to come and express his horror to the French minister, and to congratulate him on the good fortune with which his brother had escaped so great a danger. The same sentiments were expressed by the civil and military authorities.

The sons of councilors of state Portalis, Siméon, and Roederer were part of the French legation. The first two, after the fall of the Imperial government, went over to the service of the government which succeeded it. The third, faithful to the cause which he had embraced, after having honorably served the state in prefectorial offices, voluntarily retired. He applied part of his activity and of his talents to directing the glassworks, which were the foundation of the fortune of his family, and occupied his leisure hours with the study of literature.

M. de Laforêt, Secretary to the Legation, brought M. de Moustier, son of the former minister of Louis XVI—under whom he had been consul in the United States—to Lunéville. He treated this young man, who afterwards married his daughter, as a son. Moustier was appointed Secretary of Legation in Saxony, at the end of the Congress. He then and afterwards served in the embassies with the greatest zeal. His father, one of the most devoted agents of the Count de Lille, sought in vain to draw him over into the enemy's camp. The Restoration came, but then Moustier, whose fidelity had resisted a threat of disinheritance, did not resist his father, who returned high in credit with the new sovereign. It must be added, however, that he made use of his favor only in the service of old friends. He ended his career as a diplomat with a mission to the Court of Spain, which he carried out in 1827.

General Clarke was sent to Lunéville as governor of the town and commander of the department. He celebrated the anniversary of the 18th Brumaire, the day on which the conference opened, with a splendid dinner, which was followed by a ball. During the course of the Congress, there was a dance at his house almost every week. The plenipotentiaries dined alternately at each other's houses. The local authorities and leading citizens were usually invited. Mild gambling was indulged in, or an hour was spent at the theatre, where a group of actors was performing. In between the negotiations we made several excursions in the neighborhood of Lunéville, visiting the glassworks, the paper mills, and the various factories of the Vosges, the Rosières studfarms and the salt-pits of Dieuze and Moyenvic.

The former castle of King Stanislas had been selected for the habitation of the plenipotentiaries, but as it was recognized that it would be some time before it could be put into a proper state of repair, and that this would also cost a considerable sum of money, two private houses were rented for them instead. The minister of France lived at the house of a M. de Fresnel, whose son, like most of the Lorraine officers, was in the service of Austria.

There were a number of retired generals at Lunéville, who were frequently invited to the houses of the plenipotentiaries. During our stay, there arrived in Lunéville a general who seemed to have been prompted to come by the desire to show off his gold embroideries. It was apparently by the mistake of one of the representatives of the people that he had been promoted to such high rank. The naïveté of his *fanfaronades* was for a time the delight of the town. People used to get him to tell how, in a battle, his bravery and excellent appearance had attracted the attention of Suvorov, who cried out: "Who is this young Frenchman, who brings terror and death into our ranks?" "Marshal, it is General Liébaut!" "I thought so!"

M. Hugo, major of the 20th demi-brigade, a young officer full of fire and activity, who had served during the previous campaign on the staff of General Moreau, was in command of the garrison of Lunéville under the orders of General Clarke. When Joseph Bonaparte became King of Naples he summoned this officer, whom he had learned to know and to appreciate during the Congress, to his army. General Hugo followed the king to Spain, where he rendered important services, and returned to France with him in 1813. He has published some memoirs, preceded by a very interesting preface written by his eldest son, Abel Hugo, author of several highly valued works, on his campaigns, and chiefly about the military events in Spain. The youngest son of the general, Victor Hugo, has won a European reputation, and is the author of a large number of prose and poetry works, in which the beauties and the defects of a brilliant imagination, who had amply studied good models, but had freed itself from the old paths to open up a new path, may be noticed.

Brought up by a mother who was hostile to the principles of the Revolution, Victor and his two brothers acquired, from the education she gave them, prejudices which soon yielded to their more mature judgment. Since the death of his mother, Victor Hugo has returned to a more just appreciation of the genius of Napoleon. He is today one of the greatest admirers of the benefits of his rule, and of the military glory of France, in which General Hugo participated.

I must not omit to mention the arrival of young Anatole de Lawoestyne in Lunéville, who was brought there by his father to be introduced to his uncle, Count de Cobenzl. Anatole was twelve or thirteen years of age at the time of his visit to Lunéville, and was a charming child.

The events of the Revolution of 1789, which brought about the suppression of feudal rights, and caused losses of every kind to the Lawoestyne family, were the main causes which destroyed the fortune Anatole could claim. He could have still been rich. The Sillery estate had been intended for him by the first husband of his grandmother, Madame de Genlis, M. Brulart de Sillery, who became a victim during the Revolution. Count Louis de Cobenzl had appeared to have some affection for his young nephew. He had proposed to his father to take the lad with him to Austria to finish his education, and that he should enter the military service. But the French instincts of the child, and the preference which he showed for the French uniform, so glorious by victory, discouraged the Austrian diplomat in his good intentions, and easily absolved him from any further responsibility in his nephew's future.

On leaving Paris to return to Vienna, Count Cobenzl made the most splendid promises to Anatole's father; the interest he professed remained, however, without fruit. Knowing my friendship both for the father and the son, he particularly recommended his young nephew to me, thinking that my position with the brother of the Head of the government would give me opportunities of being useful to him. Lawoestyne did not follow M. de Cobenzl, and remained with us. This child, to whom I attached myself, became dearer and dearer to me, a real brother. He entered the military school at Fontainebleau at an early age. On leaving the school he entered a cavalry regiment where his bravery and brilliant qualities secured him rapid promotion. He was colonel at the age of twenty-six, and commanded the 3rd regiment of chasseurs at the disastrous battle of Waterloo. The fall of the Empire interrupted the career which he was following with such success.

Many great and heroic ideas marked this ever-memorable era. What impression must the overthrow of so many hopes have produced on the ardent and generous mind of Lawoestyne. To an era of grandeur and glory succeeded a return to gothic ideas and the reign of a prince strengthened by the misfortunes of his family in the hatred of our institutions. The indignation and contempt of Lawoestyne burst out in a scene concerted with his friends Jacqueminot and Durand, who both had a happy and original turn of mind. They went one after the other to the Café Tortoni and met together there, dressed up in the grotesque costumes of those old caricatures of the ancien régime which they humorously styled as voltigeurs of Louis XIV, obtuse minds which the great events which had occurred had been unable to lighten, and which, like Epimenides, seemed to have fallen asleep in 1788 only to awaken in 1814. Anatole and his friends played so true a scene in this café that the effect it had was immense. The sensation produced in Paris was such that the authorities thought to proceed against the main culprit. Anatole took flight to Belgium, from which his family had sprung. He settled down in the country near Brussels and lived there faithful to his memories until the revolution of July 1830. He then returned to France, and once more entered the army. He commanded for some years the department of Seine-et-Oise, with the rank of major general and has since been promoted to lieutenant-general.

Once the peace treaty was signed the plenipotentiaries left Lunéville to return to

Paris. I remember that Siméon and myself wished to celebrate this great event by some scenes to be performed by the troupe of actors at Lunéville. With this plan we stayed inside for the best part of the night which followed the signing of the treaty, but Thalia was rebellious to our wooings. We only managed a few couplets, most of which my brother in Apollo was responsible for.

Count Cobenzl and Joseph Bonaparte returned to Paris together. Conferences took place on the execution of the article of the treaty relating to the distribution of indemnities to the princes who had been expelled from their possessions on the left bank of the Rhine by the cession of these territories to France. Article 7 of the Treaty of Lunéville had stipulated that the German Empire should compensate the hereditary princes who had been dispossessed on the left bank of the Rhine with grants of land in the center of its territories, according to arrangements to be ulteriorly determined. The First Consul, satisfied with having secured to those of the secular princes who were in this situation compensation and the hope of an increase of territory, which would attach those interested to him, did not hurry on the settlement of the indemnities. This was delayed for more than a year by German procrastination and the pretensions of Austria. The French government decided not to give way, and, determined to profit from all the advantages secured by the Treaty of Lunéville, took measures to baffle the intrigues and underhanded practices meant to keep France aloof from any participation in the distribution of the indemnities. The Russian cabinet was pressed to join France in urging the settlement of this business. In consequence M. de Buhler, Russian ambassador to Munich, and M. de Laforêt, who had been appointed French ambassador to the same city, after the signature of the Treaty of Lunéville, were sent to Ratisbon to present to the Diet a general scheme of indemnification.

After seven months' discussion the allotment and the final distribution of the indemnities was effected. The control which France exercised in the new arrangements began establishing her influence in Germany. This affair was conducted by the First Consul with a skill which the school of M. de Talleyrand attributes largely to that minister, who without any doubt was a valuable agent in the execution of this great political idea. The cooperation of Russia in the operations at Ratisbon, conferred upon this power only the role of witness, France having full influence in the matter. Her dominance and the exaggerated nature of the claims of the interested parties served her purpose marvelously. The distribution of the indemnities gave rise to a number of abuses. The claims of justice were barely heeded, and it is no exaggeration to say that the territories which were to be allotted were placed at auction. But the timid complaints which arose were soon silenced and hushed up. The princes who had profited from the abuses committed made no boast of the fact, while those who had been wronged did not dare to raise their voices to reach the ear of the First Consul. He was, however, suspicious as to the real state of affairs, and this was not confirmed until many years later. The French ambassador at one of the smaller German courts, was at last able to gather a list of the extortions committed, with the names of their authors. Napoleon sent this list to Count Mollien, Minister of the Public Treasury, with orders to have all amounts unduly received paid into the sinking fund. The cares of war and various other considerations prevented him from rigorously pursuing the execution of this order. The Restoration saved the purses of the guilty, which had the double advantage of remaining unpunished and of securing the favor of the new government by claiming to be the enemies and the victims of the government which had just fallen.

Joseph Bonaparte spent most of the summer of 1801 on his fine estate of Mortfontaine. All those who, in more than one way, were most distinguished in Paris, were assembled there. Mesdames Bacciochi, Leclerc and Murat, sisters of the First Consul; Lucien Bonaparte, Count Cobenzl, who was living there for the best part of the summer; the poet Casti, author of the poem *Les Animaux Parlants* and of so many clever productions, naïf and witty, and the most independent of men; Madame de Staël, who was then protecting Chateaubriand, and who charmed the evenings with reading *Atala* and *Réné* aloud; Stanislas Girardin, proprietor of the estate of Ermenonville, whose death in 1827 was mourned by all men of heart, and by the enlightened friends of liberty; M. Miot, distinguished by the variety of his accomplishments and by his administrative talents; Roederer, journalist, writer, and witty conversationalist—these last three the constant and devoted friends of Joseph Bonaparte—Regnauld de Saint-Jean-d'Angély, whose wonderful ability and clear-headedness made capable of anything; M. de Jaucourt, a model of urbanity, who, had raised the affections of his heart to heroism, and whose attachment to the Bourbon family was awakened in 1814, but who seemed attached to his hosts by a sincere devotion; the poets Arnault, Andrieux, Boufflers, Fontanes; Madame de Boufflers, *ci-devant* Madame de Sabran, amiable and witty; Marmont, Chauvelin, Mathieu de Montmorency, who on account of a former liaison with Madame de Staël frequently came to Mortfontaine; and finally many other French and foreign politicians and literary figures found a delightful escape in this beautiful place.

The days were spent shooting, fishing, walking, and playing games; in the evenings there was music or reading aloud; sometimes a proverb or charade was acted. M. de Cobenzl knew our poets and chiefly our dramatists by heart, and would repeat comic scenes with a verve that was close to buffoonery; he used to organize little games, charades, or *tableaux vivants,* in which he always had a part, and where the sisters of the First Consul always played the principal roles. Count Cobenzl spoke French without any accent and had nothing German about him but his name. Although clumsy, big, fat, and short, his manners were easy and graceful. His conversation, as a general rule, was superficial, and abounded in witticisms; his wit was ingenious rather than profound. He affected a vivacity and an evenness of temper which was sometimes changed by some sudden preoccupation. Sometimes in the midst of a happy anecdote, such as he delighted in telling, his features would become set, a grave expression would take the place of a smile, and his wandering eyes became fixed like a machine whose movements cease suddenly without apparent cause. His affectation in appearing delighted with everything, and of finding that everything that was proposed to him was just what he had been wishing for, bothered the soul of the excellent Madame Bonaparte, who was never able to detect in him a preference for anything whatsoever.

M. Hoppé, his only secretary, was typical of a German embassy employee. He was a little man already past the middle age, with large wrinkled eyes, fatigued by the time he spent deciphering old charts and diplomatic notes. He was so short-sighted that his nose played as great a part in his work as his eyes. A minute observer of forms, he delighted in parading his knowledge of the small particularities of his profession, the high importance of which he never tired of proclaiming; insisting at the same time on his long experience. He had lived for many years in Paris, as attaché to the embassy of Count de Mercy d'Argenteau. He was a very good man, devoted to Count Cobenzl, who in return treated him with great affection. Madame de Staël, twirling a flower in her fingers, or a spray of heather, would carry on with our wits a conversation which was at times humorous, or serious, but always lightened by flashes of wit.

Joseph Bonaparte was kind enough to ask my old friend Palissot to Mortfontaine. I brought him there for a few days. This veteran of the great wits of the age of Louis XV, whose life had been spent in drawing-rooms, that had been the witnesses of his triumphs, found himself out of his sphere at Mortfontaine. Each epoch has its ideas, its tastes, and its particular character. Palissot was received with distinction and was treated with the deference due to his age. But though aware of the regard that was shown him, and though he made an effort to fit into a society which was new to him, it was clear that he felt entirely out of his element. He then returned with pleasure to the solitude which he had left for a world which was not in accordance to his habits, and which paid no attention to his memories.

The poet Casti used to recite at night what he had composed during the day. He wrote part of his poem, *Les Animaux Parlants,* at Mortfontaine. He was frequently seen sitting at the foot of one of the century-old trees, which shaded the rocks scattered here and there on the slopes of the lakes, seeking inspiration that never failed to come to his effortless talent. Casti was the "poet laureate" of Vienna. He succeeded Metastasio in this post of poet to the imperial court, which died with him. He had been presented at Mortfontaine by M. de Cobenzl. At that time he was nearly eighty years old, but had preserved all the verve and vivacity of his younger days. Endowed with an iron constitution, he had victoriously triumphed over a disease which can be cured only by the most violent remedies, and the only remaining trace was a kind of sniffling, which interfered to some extent with his pronunciation. He was in continual warfare with Mesdames Leclerc and Murat, who had selected him as their victim. Now they would snatch off his wig while he was sitting in grave meditation in his armchair, now they would come and mix up the figures on the chessboard just as he was absorbed over some difficult move. And he therefore bore them a grudge, and refused to address any of the verses which cost him so little trouble to either of them. He was better disposed towards Madame Bacciochi, and made a madrigal on her name, which was found one morning fastened to the mirror on the mantelpiece of the drawing room. This madrigal played on the words "baccio" and "occhi" and was in honor of Madame Elisa's eyes, which were very beautiful.

The good and witty Andrieux, author of charming comedies, and poems which Voltaire would not have disavowed, was one of the habitués of Mortfontaine. He had abandoned literature for parliament, but had returned to it after the suppression of the tribunate. He was anxious to translate Casti's *Animaux Parlants* into verse, but never carried out his plan. He satisfied himself with translating one of that poet's stories, called *La Bulle d'Alexandre VI.*

Frequent parties of coursing and shooting were given at Mortfontaine under the direction of General Berthier and M. d'Haneucourt, who were rehearsing—the former for the post of Master of the Hounds, and the other for that of Captain of the Hunts.

The hospitality of the proprietors of Mortfontaine was noble and honorable. They charmed their guests by a natural politeness and by their simple and affectionate manners.

The vicinity of the estate of Plessis-Charmant, which belonged to Lucien Bonaparte, made for frequent communications with Mortfontaine, and did much to enhance the charm of the two residences. There was nothing pompous about either place, but they were the rendezvous of men of different merits. In this respect Plessis was the rival of Mortfontaine. The preferred taste at Plessis was for performing tragedies; these performances were given under the direction of the actor Lafond.

Lucien had lost his first wife, Christine Boyer, who had left him two daughters. One of them has married the Roman Prince Gabrielli, the other, after the death of her first husband, married Lord Dudley Stuart. Madame Bacciochi, who was tenderly attached to her brother, spent the summer at Plessis, warmly protecting the poet Fontanes. The Marquise de Santa-Cruz, a Spanish lady whose acquaintance Lucien had made as ambassador to Madrid, helped Madame Bacciochi do the honors of the house, and was supposed to have a very great influence over him.

Joseph Bonaparte used to go on frequent excursions from Mortfontaine to La Malmaison, where I had the honor of accompanying him. We used to spend part of the day there, coming back to Mortfontaine after dinner. Dinner at La Malmaison was served at one table only, where often a family reunion might take place. The First Consul sat on one side, having Madame Louis Bonaparte next to him, and Madame Bonaparte opposite. The aides-de-camp of the First Consul were admitted to his table, and generally one of the Consuls, a minister, and one or two ladies were among the guests. Strangers were rarely to be seen.

I will mention, in a summary manner, the events that took place in the time elapsed between the signing of the Treaty of Lunéville and the conclusion of the Concordat—events which were brought about by the rise to power of the great genius who already exercised such a great influence on the destinies of Europe.

The abuse which England made of her naval supremacy, the tyranny which she exercised over the shipping of other maritime powers, our victories, the treaties come as a consequence, the wisdom and the skill of the government of the First Consul, had produced a revolution in the minds of men throughout Europe. The influence which England had enjoyed was rapidly declining. Her despotism had revolted the powers of the north, which had formed a convention to directly enforce the respect of neutrals. The Emperor Paul I was at the head of the league with his customary ardor. The general embargo under which England kept the ships of the countries which had signed this convention and her treacherous attack upon Copenhagen only tightened the bonds of the coalition against her. The First Consul had spared no effort to bring about an understanding with the Emperor Paul. There were seven thousand Russian prisoners in France, whom the First Consul fitted with clothes and sent back home ransom-free. This action finally won the heart of Paul I. He had entered into a close alliance with France and was vigorously pursuing the execution of the plans agreed upon with her, when he was ruthlessly assassinated. The particulars of the murder of this prince are well-known today, and there is no need for me to repeat them. The *Moniteur* announced this event in the following terms: "Paul I died in the night of the 24th–25th of March. The English fleet passed the Sound on the 31st." History will teach us what connection may exist between these two occurrences.

The effect of this catastrophe was the dissolution of the league of which Paul I had been the most ardent promoter. Before long a total change in Russia's policy was to take place. General Duroc had been sent to St. Petersburg to compliment the new emperor on his accession, and to pursue the relations that existed between his father and the First Consul. Duroc had been received with kindness and with protestations of a desire to continue on friendly terms with France. But, about six weeks later, the Emperor Alexander signed a treaty with England, by which he abandoned all his father's projects and submitted to the abuses of that power.

The death of General Kléber had let the command of the French army fall into the hands of General Menou, following right of seniority. He was a brave officer and a good administrator, but lacked military qualities. He was devoted to French political interests in Egypt; in pursuit of this interest he had become a Mussulman and had married a Turkish girl. The generals of the army of the east, either lacking confidence in their commander-in-chief, or from a spirit of rivalry with him, only gave him a constrained obedience, and the dissentions among them contributed to the ruin of the expedition. The English took advantage of this situation and sent an army to Egypt which combined its operations with an Ottoman army. The First Consul had made useless efforts to dispatch reinforcements of troops and supplies to Egypt. Menou made the mistake of not marching with his army to oppose the landing of the English troops and drive them back into the sea. He divided his troops, and was outnumbered everywhere. It was thus that he lost the important battle of Nicopolis, where he succumbed to greatly superior numbers. General Abercromby lost his life there. General Belliard, in Cairo, and General Menou, in Alexandria, were forced to capitulate and to accept the conditions imposed by the enemy, who agreed to allow the transport of the French army with its weapons and supplies back to France.

It was about this time that the Infante of Parma, in whose favor the Treaty of Lunéville had created the kingdom of Etruria, came to Paris with the Queen, under the names of Count and Countess of Leghorn. They spent a month there in a series of fêtes. It had seemed to the First Consul that it would be a good stroke of policy to have a Bourbon come to Paris—a Bourbon, created king by his power, by the omnipotence of a man who made men kings without wishing to be a king himself—and to admit to the Tuileries a prince who sprang from the blood which had reigned over France, at a time when his presence did not create the least sensation in Paris but when on the contrary his complete worthlessness was patently clear to all who saw him.

The conferences on the Concordat followed the negotiations for the Treaty of Lunéville. It was a firm idea of the First Consul that religion should be reestablished in France. He was absolutely convinced of the importance of religion to a nation. Catholicism seemed at its last gasp. Most of the men who had any influence in public affairs seemed ready to embrace the Protestant faith, but on the other hand the large majority of Frenchmen favored the Roman Catholic faith. This attachment is indestructible in most of the departments. In spite of the immense confidence which the First Consul inspired, his influence did not extend to the point of being able to make a selection between the two forms of religion.

From an adoption of Protestantism much dissension was to be expected, all the more violent because the memory of the religious wars had not yet been forgotten. Could a schism then be created at a time when the progress of civilization and the personal inclinations of the Head of the state prescribed the union and conciliation of all parties? But apart from the motive that, born a Roman Catholic, it was distasteful to him to abandon this religion for any other, other motives also drove him to give his preference to Roman Catholicism. France being surrounded by Roman Catholic States needed all her advantages. A repudiation of her ancient faith would have weakened her prestige, and at the same time would have aroused in Europe the anxieties which the errors of the Revolution had justified.

In maintaining the Roman Catholic religion the First Consul secured the pope to his interests and benefited from an influence which at that time could not fail to help his government. Italy remained attached to France. Napoleon's mental reservation was to bring the Catholic faith back to Evangelical purity and to effect the separation of the spiritual and temporal power, a separation which in his eyes seemed destined to assure religious peace.

This immense result, which later on was very nearly secured, would perhaps have exercised a great influence on the tranquility of Europe, and have set to rest much religious discord. In this, as in many other things, the First Consul was before his time. Someday, no doubt, the future will realize his plans. In matters of religion, however, progress must come slowly and gradually. Reforms of this nature cannot be thought up in ministries. They are the work of circumstances and of time; they must appear at the right moment; nor does it belong to any human power to hurry their development. It was a matter of primary importance to reunite people divided by religious discord, and in so doing to satisfy the almost general wish of the French people. Some of these considerations were developed by the councilors of state, who exposed the motives of the Concordat negotiations to the tribunate and the legislative body.

Full of these lofty plans the First Consul resolved to attempt a reconciliation with the Holy See. He had much resistance to overcome on the part of his ministers. Monseigneur Spina, Archbishop of Corinth, was sent to Paris to open negotiations. The preliminary articles proposed by the French government having been agreed to, with some modifications, by the Council of Cardinals, the Holy Father, to invest this act with more solemnity, and to assure its prompt accomplishment, sent his secretary of state, Cardinal Consalvi, who arrived in Paris at the beginning of June. He had several conferences with the First Consul, and the consequence was that negotiations were opened between the Papal envoys, Cardinal Consalvi, the Archbishop of Corinth, and Father Caselli, His Holiness's consulting theologian, and the French plenipotentiary, Joseph Bonaparte, to whom the First Consul adjoined the councilor of state, Cretet, and the Abbé Bernier, a former curate at Saint-Laud d'Angers. This priest, after having been the soul of the insurrectional government in La Vendée, had seconded General Hédouville's work of conciliation in that district to the complete satisfaction of the First Consul.

A national council was convened eight days after Cardinal Consalvi's arrival in Paris. Forty-five archbishops and bishops and eighty ecclesiastical deputies of the clergy met at Notre-Dame. In a new declaration of the principles of the Gallican Church, this assembly declared that the Church of France recognized the pope as its head, but denied him any right in the temporal affairs of the state. This declaration seemed destined to lay the basis of the projected convention and to support the impending negotiations. These were long drawn out, and it was only the fear lest the First Consul might yield to the persuasion of the councillors of state, the majority of whom were in favor of Protestantism, and the threatened establishment of a Gallican Church, that decided Cardinal Consalvi to come to terms.

The preliminary articles, which had been agreed upon with Monseigneur Spina,

Archbishop of Corinth, were converted into a final treaty, which was signed on the 15th of July, and was ratified by a Papal Bull dated the 15th of August. The Abbé Bernier was rewarded for his participation in these negotiations with the seat of archbishop of Orléans.

When the Concordat agreement was made public the republican party and the ideologues, as Napoleon used to call them, severely blamed this arrangement with the Court of Rome, asserting that it was a return to gothic ideas, to introduce a foreign power into the state, and to give a privilege to the Roman Catholic clergy in a country where the equality of all religious creeds had been proclaimed. Others, less passionate, while admitting that this arrangement had some advantages, expressed the wish that the marriage of priests should have been permitted by the new law. But the most regrettable omission was that of a clause setting the time in which the pope should canonically institute the bishops. This matter had been discussed in the conferences at the time of the Concordat negotiations. It was thought, however, that sufficiently large concessions had already been obtained from the pope, and that it was not proper to insist on that one. This omission has become a terrible weapon in the hands of the Head of the Church. Those who blamed the French government for not having secured freedom for priests to marry, and having omitted to establish a Gallican Church, forgot that such reforms cannot be improvised, that for the time being considerable advantages had been obtained, and that improvements which time alone can bring to fruition must be come from the march of events.

However this may be, the Concordat produced great positive results. It was a pledge of reconciliation to the large majority of Frenchmen. While abolishing the distinctions that existed between unsworn and sworn priests, it at the same time mollified the scruples felt by those who had acquired national property. Morality found once more the powerful sanction of religion, for it is the respect for religious opinions which ensures the rule of law. On the other hand the Concordat was a step in the direction of the reforms made necessary by the progress of human enlightenment, which Napoleon had in preparation. The clergy ceased to be a body in the state, it was given a salary and subjected to discipline, a discipline to which for many years it submitted in conformity with the law, restricting itself to the limits of its attributions. Restrained by the strong hand of the chief of the state, it would never have attempted to emancipate itself had not the difficulties which were later on thrown in the path of the government encouraged its pretensions, and given rise to encroachments which grew as the times worsened. It cannot be denied that the encroachments of the Court of Rome sorely tested the Emperor's patience, and often diluted the precautions which at the dictates of his foresight he had taken to protect the rights of the state against the enterprise of the priests. The troubles caused by the influential party of the clergy, encouraged in their hostilities by the reverses which our armies have suffered have gained the cause of those misrepresenting the Concordat and justified, in appearance at least, the censures passed upon this great act. The French government, without doubt, has reaped a bitter harvest from a treaty which was inspired by the desire to return peace to the Church, according to the desires of the representative of a God of peace and charity on earth; but Napoleon would have triumphed over all the embarrassments which it caused him, if the pacification of Europe had allowed him to do so.

A pastoral letter, which was issued from Rome simultaneously with the ratification of the Concordat, exhorted the French bishops to resign their sees, a delay of three months being granted them in which to pronounce themselves. Almost all the old incumbents made haste to accede to the wishes of the pope, and sent in their agreement. A very small number of former prelates, who had retired to England, remained recalcitrant, and formed a center of opposition which received the name of Little Church. Their resistance passed unnoticed. The bull, which suppressed the archbishoprics and bishoprics which had existed at the time of the Revolution, was none the less put into execution. In the place of the twenty-three archbishoprics, and the hundred and thirty-four bishoprics which were abolished, only ten archbishoprics and fifty bishoprics were created.

The articles of the Concordat were not published. No communication of this act was made to the tribunate, nor to the legislative body, after its conclusion. The apparent reason for this delay was the need for the resignation of the incumbents of the old sees, amongst whom were a certain number of *emigrés* who might be expected to refuse to resign. But the principal reason was the fear of brusquely making matters which concerned the peace of men's consciences the subject of contentious debate by the speculative minds that dominated the national tribune. The publication of the Concordat was postponed until the opening of the second session of the legislative body. This interval was used to prepare, in the council of state, various regulations required for the coordination of the religious system of the state with the needs of the nation and the progress of enlightenment.

I must speak, in connection with the Concordat, of a measure which to a great extent decided the early communication of this convention to the legislature and the tribunate. The sessions of these two assemblies, and notably that of the tribunate, had been marked by violent opposition. The majority of the laws presented to them had been unfavorably received; two even had been rejected. Hostile words had been pronounced in the tribune. This convinced the First Consul that he could not count on any sincere cooperation over there, and that the presence of these orators, whom he considered ill-disposed or led astray by an untimely zeal for public liberty, would be fatal to the improvements he had conceived. The renewal of the fifths both of the tribunate and of the legislative body, which by the terms of the constitution had to take place every year, seemed to him a favorable opportunity for ridding himself of the members who had steadfastly opposed the laws proposed by the government. The method to renew these fifths of the members both of the tribunate and of the legislative body, had never been defined by a constitutional act, the senate was free to proceed either by election or by drawing lots. The first method was adopted. At the reelection of four-fifths of the two bodies the twenty most recalcitrant tribunes were eliminated. The influence of the government was clear in this act of the senate, where, it must be said, the law had not been broken. This cleansing, which is what it should be called, brought about to this day the condemnation of honorable and independent men, who are more familiar with theory than enlightened by practice, and who for the most part profess the motto: "Let the state perish rather than principles." The measure was, however, urgently needed. The firm desire to obtain good laws had to be pursued or abandoned under pressure of men who, for the most part, thought the young government weak, and who wanted to make themselves indispensable through systematic opposition. There could be no doubt as to which of these two alternatives the First Consul would choose.

The Concordat was the first law presented at the extraordinary session called on the

5th of April. It was adopted by a very large majority. On the 18th of April, Easter Sunday, a *Te Deum* was sung in the church of Notre Dame to celebrate the reestablishment of religious worship, and the peace of Amiens. The First Consul, on this occasion, wore a green court-dress with gold embroideries; he wore the Regent, a diamond of great beauty, in the guard of his sword. This diamond was called the Regent, after, the Duke of Orléans, who had bought it during the minority of Louis XV to adorn the royal crown. Stolen from the *garde-meuble* during the Revolution, and afterwards discovered, this diamond had been pledged by the government. It was for sale at much less than its value when the First Consul bought it.

Mass was said by Cardinal Caprara, in the presence of the diplomatic corps. The bishops who had been nominated took the oath. In the evening the city was illuminated throughout. The opposition of the free-thinking party by some of the generals, was expressed in quibbles that only elicited smiles of contempt. Their first reactions had suggested the very worst designs against the person of the First Consul, who was by no means ignorant of the fact; but reflection brought wiser counsels. Many leading generals met together to discuss the matter. Some wildly excited men carried their madness to the point of suggesting that the First Consul should share the fate of Romulus. Bernadotte was amongst their number. Napoleon, who was always indifferent to his personal safety, refused to act on the reports which he received concerning this matter. His stoicism remained unshaken. He limited himself to roughly scolding the main leaders. Some he sent away. Bernadotte was packed off to the army in the west, which he had left to come to Paris. His attitude towards the head of the state became, from that time, so odd and strange that his chief staff officer, Brigadier General Simon, was dismissed from the army. I have seen Napoleon, at the time that I am speaking of, so incensed against Bernadotte, that he spoke of having him court-martialed. It was only thanks to the intervention of Joseph Bonaparte, Bernadotte's brother-in-law, that the general escaped this jurisdiction.

Of the three prelates sent from Rome to negotiate the Concordat, Cardinal Consalvi and Monseigneur Spina were very enlightened men. Father Caselli, who acted with them in the capacity of adviser on all matters of form, conscience, and pontifical protocol, was a simple and loyal man, wrapped up in the theological questions that he had studied throughout his life. Cardinal Consalvi, without openly blaming the decree of the Council of Trent, which enforces celibacy on the priests, did not in conversation reject the idea of allowing them to marry. He did not proscribe theatrical performances and, as he himself said, would have had no objection to be present at the staging of a moral play. These remarks of his, which in no way were binding, were a trifling concession to the free-thinking spirit that surrounded him in Paris. While speaking as a man free from prejudices, he could only act in accordance with the spirit of the Church. He only spoke so freely of the marriage of priests because the question had been eliminated, either in deference to the views of the First Consul, or because the latter did not wish to complicate negotiations which were sufficiently thorny without it.

The Concordat is perhaps the most important act of Napoleon's government. After having considered it with respect to politics, and in its general effect, there would be something wanting in the appreciation of this great work if the part played in it by the personal feeling of the head of the state were to remain unmentioned. Some people have thought that, in the eyes of Napoleon, religious belief was just a form of superstition consecrated by time, and that reestablishing the Catholic religion he only used it as the tool of his ambition, without considering the social influence of religion. Those who held that view were ignorant of the fact that Bonaparte was sincerely religious—I may add, he was a true Catholic. His detestation of free-thinking cynicism that preaches contempt for religion—that he considered, on the contrary, as the basis of morality and decency—was as great as his horror for the bigotry that impairs human intelligence. If, in the course of private conversation, or in the discussions into which he was drawn by his active mind, and in considering the history of the Catholic Church in its various vicissitudes he has expressed certain opinions blaming the excesses committed in the name of religion by its ministers, what a mistake it is to conclude that he was blind to the civilizing influence of Christianity, or that he was an unbelieving and skeptical philosopher. His respect for the doctrines of the gospel came from his convictions and his early training; witness the religious thoughts that the bell of Rueil, that rang as far as the garden of La Malmaison, awoke within him; and his recourse, during his final moments at St. Helena, to the consolations and comfort of religion. In reestablishing the Roman Catholic religion in France he filled the void which its absence left in the state, but at the same time he obeyed the dictates of his religious instincts.

The first measure was the creation of a Ministry of Public Worship. The direction of this ministry was entrusted to Portalis, who at first assumed the title of councilor of state charged with matters concerning public worship, and shortly afterwards that of minister. Portalis was a learned lawyer and a flowery orator, gentle and conciliatory in character. He has been accused, and perhaps with reason, of too great flexibility. But in the appointed task he was to perform this quality was an advantage rather than a drawback; he was a good man of the kind defined by Cicero as: "*Vir bonus et dicendi peritus.*"* His good deeds were as great as his knowledge and his eloquence.

Monseigneur Spina, who had been elevated to cardinal after the signing of the Concordat, remained in Paris as Chargé d'Affaires. He was replaced by Cardinal Caprara, who had been appointed legate *a Latere.* The cardinal, who arrived in Paris in September, was not presented to the First Consul until the 9th of April.

The archbishop of Lyon was sent to Rome with the title of ambassador. He was the uncle of the First Consul, the maternal grandmother of Napoleon having married M. Fesch, on her second marriage. M. Fesch was captain of one of the Swiss regiments which the Republic of Genoa maintained in Corsica at the time of her domination. Cardinal Caprara was the issue of this second marriage. The Abbé Fesch had left the holy orders at the start of the Revolution and had worked as a layman in Italy. He returned to the clergy after the 18th Brumaire. Patronized by his nephew he rapidly rose to the highest dignities in the church. He was appointed archbishop of Lyon in 1801, and promoted to cardinal two years later. He went to Rome to replace M. Cacault, French Chargé d'Affaires, when the Concordat was signed. M. de Chateaubriand, author of *The Genius of Christianity*, who had returned from emigration before the amnesty, had been presented by M. de Fontanes, his intimate friend, to Madame Bacciochi, sister of the First Consul, and to his brother Lucien Bonaparte. Brother and sister declared that M. de Chateaubriand was under their protection. The publication of *The Genius of Christianity* at the moment when Catholicism had been reestablished in France, produced a great

---

* "A good man, skilled in speaking."

sensation. Religious ideas were spreading all the more rapidly that they had been repressed for so long. No more favorable opportunity could have been found for the publication of this work, and it was received with favor by the First Consul. The protection of Madame Bacciochi, but more especially the satisfaction felt by the First Consul at the publication of a work supportive of his opinions, and giving assistance to the Concordat, prompted him to give the author a mark of his favor, in appointing him Secretary of Legation at the Holy See.

The evacuation of Egypt was keenly felt by the First Consul. The tragic death of Kléber was a disaster, for had he lived France might have retained that important conquest. The signature of the Preliminaries of London was a powerful diversion from the unfortunate conclusion of the Egyptian campaign. The object pursued by the First Consul since his rise to power was realized. His first step had been an appeal to the King of England to assist in a pacification which should be satisfactory to the interests of the two countries; this appeal had no effect. A second negotiation had been attempted, but the British Ministry did not think the new government sufficiently well-established, and these negotiations had come to nothing.

While the continental peace was being signed at Lunéville Messrs. Pitt, Dundas, and Grenville, the fiery partisans of war, believing that peace with France was inevitable, had retired to make way for a new ministry. They did not wish to incur the responsibility, in the eyes of the aristocracy and commerce of England, of an experiment which would show how peace was more advantageous to these two important classes than war.

The ministers, who were succeeded by Addington and Hawkesbury, had ordered that French fishing boats should be pursued and captured like ships of war. In answer to the communication made to M. Otto, discharging the functions of French commissioner in London, for the exchange of prisoners, communication of an order which violated every usage and every rule of war, M. Otto declared that he had received instructions to leave England, where his stay had become useless, but that his government would not take reprisals, and that French cruisers would abstain from any interference with fishing-boats. In answer to the French commissioner's note the new ministry repealed the order concerning the French fishermen. This cancellation of a measure which had given the war a character of savagery, quite unworthy of a civilized nation, made clear their less hostile dispositions. In the discussions which this matter brought about the English ministry held out the prospect of a reconciliation. As a matter of fact, one month later M. Otto received a note which contained an offer to send a plenipotentiary to Paris with authority to negotiate for peace. This overture was cordially responded to by the First Consul, who accredited M. Otto to receive the proposals of the English ministers and to begin preliminary discussions. M. Otto was instructed that no ostentatious negotiations were desired, but that the initial articles of a treaty of pacification should be secured. Lord Hawkesbury then handed to M. Otto a synopsis, written by his own hand, of the terms on which England would sign the peace. These terms demanded that France and her allies should cede to England her most important colonies, Egypt and Malta. The First Consul having refused these proposals, which already had not been considered acceptable previously, Lord Hawkesbury asked the French government on what basis it was disposed to negotiate. M. Otto made the following proposals:—

Egypt to be restored to the Porte.
Malta to be dismantled and restored to the Order.

The island of Ceylon to be ceded to England.

The Cape of Good Hope and all other establishments to be restored to France and her allies.

Portugal to be maintained in her integrity.

The English government haggled over these conditions, though, at the same time, it declared itself ready to agree with regard to Malta. It renounced its claim to Martinique, but desired to retain possession of Trinidad, which was a Spanish possession, and of Tobago, a French possession, and in this case proposed that the Dutch possessions of Demerara, Essequibo, and Berbice should be declared free ports; or as an alternative it offered to abandon Trinidad, but to retain the French islands of Tobago, Sainte-Lucie, together with Demerara, Essequibo, and Berbice.

These alternatives were embarrassing to the French government, for either Spain or Holland had to be sacrificed. To save these powers from the loss of the important colonies which England was demanding, the First Consul consented to give up Tobago, but the English government refused to be satisfied with this concession, even though M. Otto offered to add Curaçao.

At last, after six months of negotiations, the preliminaries of peace were signed. The main conditions were that all possessions which had belonged to France and her allies should be restored to them, with the exception of Ceylon and Trinidad; that the Cape of Good Hope should be opened to the trade of both nations; that Egypt should be handed over to the Porte; that the Republic of the Ionian Islands should be recognized; that Portugal should be maintained in her integrity; and, finally, that Malta should be evacuated by the English and restored to the Order; and that the power guaranteeing the independence of this island should be designated later. It was agreed upon that a congress would be held at Amiens for the settlement of a final treaty, in which certain points that had not been settled should be decided upon.

The following reflections by Napoleon on the refusal of England to accept the peace which he had offered her in 1800 will be considered of great interest:

"(1) Could the English cabinet refuse the overtures attempted by the First Consul without rendering itself responsible for the miseries of war?

"(2) Was this refusal good policy, and was it in conformity with the interests of England?

"(3) Was war then to be desired for France?

"(4) What were Napoleon's interests under these circumstances?

"(1) Pitt refused to enter upon negotiations in the hope that by continuing the war he would force France to recall the House of Bourbon and to return Belgium to Austria. If these two demands were legitimate and just, he could with justice refuse peace; but if the one as well as the other were illegitimate and unjust, he made his country responsible for the horrors of war. Now, the Republic had been recognized by all the states of Europe; England herself had recognized it when in 1796 she invested Lord Malmesbury with full powers to treat with the Directoire. This plenipotentiary had visited Paris and Lille in turn, and had negotiated with Charles Lacroix, Letourneur, and Maret, ministers of the Directoire. Besides, the war did not have the return of the Bourbons as its object. The Belgian provinces had been ceded by the Emperor of Austria at the Treaty of Campo-Formio, in 1797, and England had recognized their union to France by the negotiations of Lord Malmesbury at Lille. They formed a legitimate part of the territory of the Republic. To wish to separate them from her was to usurp, to rend, to dismember a recognized state.

"(2) Was Pitt's policy in this matter in conformity with the interests of England? Could he reasonably hope to obtain Belgium by continuing the war? Would it not have been wiser to restore peace to the world in securing real and lasting advantages? The Kings of Sardinia and of Naples, the Grand Duke of Tuscany, and the pope, would have been reestablished and consolidated on their thrones; Milan would have been assured to Austria; Holland, together with Switzerland and Genoa, would have been evacuated by the French. English influence might have extended in these countries. Egypt would have been restored to the Porte, and Malta to the Order. Ceylon, the Cape of Good Hope, and Trinidad would have assured the power of England in the two Indies. What a magnificent result for the campaign of 1799! These advantages were certain; the hopes to which they were sacrificed were of less likely realization. The coalition had been victorious in 1799, in Italy, but had been defeated in Switzerland, Holland, and the East. France had just changed governments. A man whose military talents and knowledge had been tested had succeeded five persons who were feuding among themselves, and who were less than skilful. This man had been raised to power by the wish of the nation. At the mere sound of his name the Vendée submitted and the Russians marched back across the Vistula. Lord Grenville himself admitted that even if the First Consul wished to give up Belgium, the French people would oppose any such cession. The object of the war was, then, popular in France. Berlin, Vienna, and London might deceive themselves in 1799, the circumstances were then so new. Could English statesmen be excused for falling into the same error in 1800? It was probable that the campaign of 1800 would be favorable to France, that she would reconquer Italy and, that even if her success were problematic, England would none the less be obliged to pay immense subsidies for many years; for, in order to tear Belgium from France, the combination of Austria, Russia, and Prussia would be required, or at least the joining of one of these powers to the coalition. Now no such result could be obtained by the campaign of 1800. The risks of that campaign were not to be incurred.

"(3) The interest of the Republic was opposed to the interest of England. Had she signed the peace at that time, she would have done so after losing Italy. She would have fallen back as the result of one doubtful campaign. That would have been dishonorable, and would have prompted all the kings to league themselves against her. All the chances of the campaign of 1800 were in her favor. The Russians were gone, the Vendée was pacified, the interior factions were restrained, and there was absolute confidence in the head of the government. The Republic could only, and should only, make peace after having reestablished the equilibrium in Italy. She could only harm herself and compromise her future by signing a peace on any terms less advantageous than those secured at Campo-Formio. War was at that time necessary to her to keep the energy and the unity of the state that was then badly organized. The nation would have insisted upon a great reduction of taxation and the disbandment of a large portion of the army, so that, two years after the war, France would have come on to the battlefield with great disadvantages.

"(4) Napoleon needed war. The campaigns of Italy, the peace of Campo-Formio, the Egyptian expedition, the 18th Brumaire, the unanimous desire of the people to raise him to the highest post in the state had no doubt elevated him. A treaty of peace inferior in advantages to France to the one secured at Campo-Formio—which would have ruined all his creations in Italy—would have revolted the imagination of the French nation, and would have deprived him of the force necessary to end the Revolution, and the possibility of establishing a definitive and permanent system of government. He saw this, and awaited the answer from London with impatience. The answer filled him with secret joy. The more the English oligarchy insulted the Republic, the more it was serving Napoleon's private interests, and he said to his minister: "We could not have had a more favorable answer." From that moment he saw that, having to deal with politicians so swayed by passion, there would be but few obstacles in the path towards the fulfillment of his destinies. Pitt, so distinguished by his parliamentary talents, and his knowledge of affairs at home, was completely ignorant of what is called politics. As a general rule England knows nothing about continental affairs, and especially about French affairs. The glory of France was carried to the highest point, all Europe was subjected to her, and Lord Grenville was obliged, within a few months after his insulting declamations against the nation, to sign a treaty of peace which was more advantageous to us than the peace of Campo-Formio, inasmuch as it gave us Piedmont and Tuscany.

"But for the assassin's dagger which threw the command of the army of the East into the hands of a man who, no doubt distinguished in many ways, was without military genius, Egypt would have been united to France for ever; for both the English and the French agree that Abercromby would have been defeated if Kléber had lived. The Porte had already shown herself favorably disposed towards France in abandoning Egypt to her. How heavily a fanatic of twenty years of age weighed in the balance of the world!"

It is impossible not to linger for a moment over this brilliant time. Napoleon had been at the head of the government for barely two years, and already the wounds of the Republic were healing everywhere. Finance was reestablished, public instruction had been reorganized, the civil code had been drafted, the Vendée pacified, unity restored to the Church, immense projects for the improvement and embellishment of Paris and the provinces by the construction of roads and canals were already under way, peace had been reestablished with the United States, with Austria, with Prussia, with Russia, Bavaria, the Porte, and with the Barbary Regencies, with Naples, Spain and Portugal, and all these treaties were crowned by the preliminaries signed with England. In consequence a solemn celebration throughout the territory of the Republic was ordered, to be celebrated on the 18th Brumaire following, the anniversary of the happy day from which so many beneficial actions dated.

During the first eight days following the signature of the preliminary clauses of peace with England, the respective plenipotentiaries were named: Joseph Bonaparte, negotiator of the Treaty of Lunéville, and of the Concordat, for France, and Lord Cornwallis for England.

The English plenipotentiary arrived in Paris a month later. Some preliminary conferences took place. It could be seen from these discussions that the question which would give the most trouble, and that, as a matter of fact, was to cause a break one year later, was that of Malta. The only point which seemed to be a matter for discussion was the designation of the third power which should guarantee the independence of the island; this question was frequently addressed during the discussions of the Amiens Congress.

The first conferences opened at the beginning of December, 1801. Spain and the Batavian Republic intervened in the negotiations. Spain was represented by Chevalier d'Azzara, Spanish ambassador, and the Batavian Republic by M. Schimmelpenninck, plenipotentiary minister, both accredited to Paris. These two ministers were witnesses rather than principals. Chevalier d'Azzara did not come to Amiens nor took any part in the discussions until the end of January 1802. The English cabinet, which had wanted to force the admission of an English plenipotentiary on the Congress at Lunéville, protested against the intervention of the Dutch and Spanish representatives in the Amiens negotiations, alleging the influence exercised by the French cabinet over Holland and Spain. This demand, which appears to have been put forward only for what it was worth, was not retained by Lord Cornwallis. The protocol of the conferences was held alternately at the houses of the French and the English minister, and in the French language. The first discussions turned on the question of Malta, and it seemed as if the English ministry regretted having simplified it. The British plenipotentiary appeared to be strongly interested in the future fate of that island. He desired that its protection should be assured by a large foreign garrison. He asked that if the French language were maintained in Malta, English should also be spoken. The French plenipotentiary asked that the Order of Malta should be converted into a hospitable Order, instead of being reestablished as a religious and military Order, that the fortifications of the island should be leveled, and that it should become a great quarantine station, open to all nations trading in the East and on the Mediterranean. The English plenipotentiary refused to consent to the destruction of the fortifications, because one clause of the preliminaries stipulated that the island should be restored in its existing state.

Since the discussion was not limited to the one point in the preliminary articles which remained to be settled, that is to say the designation of the power to which the protection of Malta should be assigned, the scruples which the English cabinet affected, and its respect for the letter of the preliminaries, in so far as this island was concerned, were in contradiction with the tricks of every kind which it imagined for the purpose of misrepresenting its spirit. But the English government had secret motives, later unmasked by the breaking of the Peace of Amiens, for refusing to allow the dismantling of Malta. This question was examined in every direction and discussed with a care and a minuteness which ought to have brought about an immediate understanding. But instead of that, difficulties kept cropping up, not only on this particular article but on some other points in the treaty under consideration.

At last, after long and laborious negotiations, in the course of which the shrewdness and the moderation of the French plenipotentiary were more than once put to the test, the treaty was signed. The same hand which had so judiciously directed the conferences of the peace of Lunéville, signed the maritime pacification at Amiens.

The definitive treaty confirmed the stipulations of which the preliminaries had laid down the basis. There was a derogation in favor of Holland, that obtained the restitution of the Cape of Good Hope.

The Maltese question, so obstinately discussed, was evaded rather than resolved. Malta was to be handed over to the order of St. John of Jerusalem. Neither French nor English was to be the insular language; there was to be a Maltese tongue. British troops were to evacuate the island in three months. Half the garrison was to be composed of Maltese. The King of Naples was to be invited to furnish two thousand men to complete it. Malta was to be placed under the protection and under the warranty of France, England, Austria, Spain, Russia, and Prussia. Its neutrality was to be proclaimed.

M. Dupuy, former intendant of the Isle of France, who had governed this colony during nine years, in troubled times, and had succeeded in preserving it to France, was the secretary of the French legation. His cooperation on the treaty was rewarded with a place as councilor of state, and afterwards by his appointment to the senate. His wife was one of the ladies of the Queen of Naples, and his eldest daughter was afterwards married by the Emperor to M. d'Audenarde, one of the Empress's equerries.

The son of Minister Portalis was attached to the legation at Amiens, as he had been to that of Lunéville. In the interval between the two treaties he had married a young lady of Holstein, in whose house his father had found refuge during the proscription under which he fell on the 18th Fructidor.

Lord Cornwallis, minister of England at the Congress, was a fine old man of about sixty-eight, tall, with a noble face, and with open and kindly manners. He fully justified his reputation for fair-dealing at Amiens. His first secretary of legation was a Mr. Merry, who appears to have been attached to him by the office in Downing Street to mitigate the effects of his very military frankness. This secretary was a man difficult to deal with, full of English reserve. His troublesome disposition contrasted with the frank and conciliatory ways of the English plenipotentiary. In spite of quibbles over words, the old routine of English diplomacy, the length and obscurity of the notes, and the multiplicity of the incidents created, the two ministers worked very well together. That was not always Mr. Merry's fault, and Lord Cornwallis had more than once to impose his authority.

The following act of fair play was the worthy termination of this estimable minister's mission. The protocol of the last sitting had been closed, the definitive treaty had been agreed upon, and parole had been exchanged for the signature, a ceremony which was to be solemnly carried out at the town hall on the following day. In the night which proceeded the day of signing, a courier from London brought Lord Cornwallis orders to modify in favor of England certain provisions of the treaty relating to the balance of sums due for the subsistence and maintenance of the prisoners. Lord Cornwallis had declared to Joseph Bonaparte that nothing that might happen should interfere with the signing of the peace. And though at the moment of signing he received from his government orders to claim a balance in favor of England, he considered his honor pledged, and declared that he would not go back on what he had promised.

At eleven o'clock on the morning of the 15th of March, detachments of infantry and cavalry marched to the houses of the plenipotentiaries and escorted their carriages to the town hall, to the sound of military music, and amid the cheering of a large crowd. The plenipotentiaries were received by the mayor and his deputies, and were congratulated by the prefect and the authorities. At last, when, on the order of the French minister, it was announced that peace was about to be signed, the doors were thrown open, and an orderly crowd streamed in. The plenipotentiaries then signed with due solemnity and embraced each other with such an effusion of cordiality that the rooms of the town hall reechoed with applause, and more than one onlooker was moved with emotion. In the evening the town was illuminated, and a theatrical performance was given to aid the poor.

It fell to M. Dupuy to carry the treaty to Paris. A half-hour after his arrival the cannon of the Invalides announced the news. Peace was proclaimed on the squares and *places* with the customary solemnities.

It was during the negotiations of Amiens that, at one of the conferences, the English minister hinted at a proposal to recognize the First Consul as King of France. This was no longer what Lord Grenville had said in 1800. The new English minister had understood that the recall of the princes of the ancient dynasty was an easy matter, but that, as to restoring them to their thrones, that would have been fraught with as much difficulty to their auxiliaries as to the man who would recall them, and that by its very nature such a service would have rendered them suspicious of him. The prejudices as well as the pretensions of those around them, the new interests which had arisen, the revolution that had taken place in men's minds, the new forms of government, the military system, did not all these things conspire against a durable reestablishment of the House of Bourbon on the throne of France?

Napoleon, however, paid no attention to this hint. He did not wish to reign by the grace of a foreign nation and by no means stood in need of such permission. When, two years later, the throne was once more raised in France, he was made emperor, and not king; this reign could not be a continuation of the reign of the Bourbons. A new era had dawned, the face of Europe was changed. It was not a royal monarchy that Napoleon proposed to restore, it was a constitutional monarchy that he desired to found.

General peace, that peace which the coalition had steadily refused to grant to his desire, could only bring with it the completion of institutions which had only been temporary. The times made a dictatorship necessary, and allowed only for temporary measures destined to make way for a system of government adapted to the requirements of the times, and which no man better than Napoleon could define and establish. I take a real pleasure in mentioning, in this connection, that in a sitting of the chamber of deputies, on the 3rd of March, 1827, General Sebastiani, speaking on a petition relating to the reestablishment of the jury-system in Corsica, gave the Imperial government credit for having suspended, not destroyed, the institution of trial by jury in this department, and added that in general it had only taken temporary measures which it was one day to abolish.

The English and French ministers kept house splendidly. We were invited to the houses of both in turns. M. Schimmelpenninck gave tea parties, at which his wife and eldest daughter did the honors. Madame Schimmelpenninck had left a certain reputation for beauty in Paris. She knew how to unite the domestic virtues and the duties of a good mother with her worldly successes. Her daughter was then sixteen years old. She had a charming face, and attracted all the young men of the legation by her candor and her modesty. Everyone in this family breathed the spirit of patriarchal simplicity.

It was sometimes necessary to send couriers to Paris and to London to procure additional information on important points in the negotiations. During the short intervals between their departure and return we took several excursions in the Somme department. We visited the sea at Saint Valéry, and inspected the cloth and carpet factories at Abbeville.

Lord Cornwallis used to ride his horse as exercise every day on the Paris road. He was usually accompanied by his natural son, Captain Nightingale, whom he had introduced by this name. His son, Lord Brome, and his son-in-law, Colonel Singleton, came to stay with him for some time. After dinner Lord Cornwallis and Captain Nightingale used to retire to his lordship's chamber, and spend the rest of the evening in drinking, according to the English custom.

Lord Cornwallis returned to London two days after the treaty had been signed. Before leaving Amiens he paid a compliment to the industries of this town, purchasing some pieces of velveteen at different factories there, to take back to England as proof of our superiority. He left behind him the reputation of a man worthy of all respect by the probity and elevation of his character. He looked on his participation in the treaty as the last act of a long and honorable career, and congratulated himself on having closed his public life with a mission of peace. Nevertheless, some time later, he accepted the government of India, where he died shortly after his arrival.

The French minister had taken up his abode in the house of M. de Folleville, formerly a member of the constituent assembly, where he had drawn attention to himself, amongst the members of the right, by his extreme views. Madame de Folleville, who was then middle aged, had been remarkably beautiful. Having lost a son whom she idolized, she placed his embalmed body under her bed, in the extremity of her sorrow. Her daughter married General Musnier, who commanded the Somme department. Madame de Folleville had received a man's education. She rode, fenced, and swam with the greatest courage. This masculine education had not, however, made her lose the distinctive qualities of her sex, gentleness and modesty.

M. Quinette, the prefect of the department, used to give evening parties, at which a large and brilliant company assembled. The mayor, M. Debray, would also do the honors of his house with considerable, good grace. We were invited one day to hear the reading of an unpublished song, called "L'Ouvroir" taken from the poem, "Vert-Vert." This song, which had been found amongst the author's papers, was recited by one of his relations, whose snuffling voice by no means enhanced its beauties. It seemed inferior to other songs in Gresset's poem, though it also had his flow of language and facility of style. No doubt this song had been suppressed by its author, who was the best judge and the one least open to suspicion. I believe that since then it has been published. This episode reminded us that we were in the land of a man to whom Amiens is justly proud to have given birth.

It was during the course of the Congress, in the month of January, 1802, that we heard of the marriage of Mademoiselle Hortense de Beauharnais, daughter of Madame Bonaparte, to Louis Bonaparte, later to become King of Holland. This marriage was against the wishes of both parties, whose affections were placed elsewhere. Shortly before the expedition to Egypt, Louis Bonaparte at that time aide-de-camp to his brother, being on a visit to his sister Caroline, at Madame Campan's *pension,* at St. Germain, frequently met there one of his sister's friends Mlle. E. de Beauharnais, and fell deeply in love with her. When he received orders to leave for Toulon, there to await the departure of the expedition, he was filled with deep regret at being torn from the person he loved. Bernadotte's prank, in hoisting the tricolor flag over the house which he occupied as French ambassador, which aroused the whole population of Vienna, delayed the departure of General Bonaparte, the Directoire fearing that this incident might rekindle war on the Continent. It was in the meanwhile that Mademoiselle E. de Beauharnais allowed herself to be married to Lavalette, aide-de-camp to the commander-in-chief, on the eve of Napoleon's departure to Egypt.

On his return from the Marengo campaign, Mademoiselle Hortense de Beauharnais was proposed to Louis Bonaparte, who, filled with his first love, at first refused this union. To avoid it, he asked to go to Prussia, with the intention of following the maneuvers at Potsdam. He afterwards followed at the head of the 5th regiment of dragoons, to which he had been appointed colonel, the army corps which General Beauclerc, his brother-in-law, had been ordered to lead into Portugal. An affliction, which afterwards degenerated into an incurable disease, obliged him to take the waters at Barèges. On his return he gave his consent to his marriage with Hortense de Beauharnais, who on her side only entered in upon it with reluctance.

Malevolence found in this union the pretext for a black calumny. Madame Louis Bonaparte gave birth to a son ten months after her marriage. The partiality of the First Consul for this child strengthened the lying rumor, which in spite of their proved absurdity, may have contributed to trouble the union of the two spouses, as much, perhaps, as their want of sympathy and the divergence of their tastes.

Madame Bonaparte had anxiously desired this marriage. She hoped by increasing the number of bonds which attached her to Napoleon to render more difficult a divorce which her sterility constantly prompted her to fear. The churches not yet having been reopened, the nuptial ceremony was celebrated in the drawing room of the house in the rue de la Victoire, Cardinal Caprara giving the religious benediction to the two spouses. The marriage of the Murats, which had not been consecrated by the church, was blessed at the same time. It is said that the First Consul would not take advantage of this opportunity to sanctify his union with Josephine, to whom he had only been civilly married. His subsequent divorce drew attention to an incident which passed unnoticed at the time of its occurrence.

Chapter II

The reader will pardon me for having spoken at such length on my first initiation to a period of history which occupied my full attention, and the magnificent beginning of which, marked by the most important transactions of this new era—the continental peace, the Concordat, and the naval peace—was among my most interesting recollections, for the special reason that I had been directly involved in it. The proclamation of the general peace coincided with the date of my admission into the confidence of Napoleon, and the day from which my lot was tied to his fate. Like so many others during the same period I experienced the magnetic influence which this powerful genius exercised over all those who approached him. As the collaborator I was, I responded to the prompting, and the sun in whose sphere of attraction I have never ceased to revolve had as its motto *Nec pluribus impar,* which, in this case, was the strictest expression of the truth.

I returned to Paris with Joseph Bonaparte towards the end of March, 1802. He took me aside one day, and told me that the First Consul wished to see me, and would receive me at the Tuileries the following day. He confided to me that the head of the state had decided to appoint me to his cabinet; that he was dissatisfied with Bourrienne, that as soon as I had familiarized myself with his work he would dismiss him, and that I should occupy his place.

I saw in this proposal fresh proof of the assiduous kindness of Joseph Bonaparte, and his desire to promote my welfare, but at the same time I was perplexed. I begged him to dissuade the First Consul from this project, alleging that I did not feel myself at all capable of filling the post for which he intended me, and confessed that I feared the loss of my independence.

Joseph Bonaparte said everything that the affection with which he honored me could suggest to him, persuading me not to throw away the opportunity of advancement and fortune which his friendship had given me. I remember that General Bernadotte, who was present, added his persuasive words to those of Joseph Bonaparte, to make me change my mind, pointing out the happiness of a life with such a great man, where I should be the constant witness of the inspiration of his genius. He seemed to lack words to express the admiration and devotion which he appeared to feel for the First Consul.

On the morning of April 2 Joseph Bonaparte gave me a letter from General Duroc, who was writing to tell me that the First Consul could receive me at five o'clock in the afternoon of that day. I was obliged to accept an invitation which was really a command. General Duroc took me to Madame Bonaparte, who received me with exquisite grace and politeness. She was kind enough to talk to me of the business which had brought me to the Tuileries. I was encouraged by her kindness to tell her the objections I felt to a gilded chain. She succeeded in making me agree to remain three years only with the First Consul. I should be free to retire at the end of that time, and she assured me that the First Consul would reward me with an honorable post, and further undertook to gain his consent to this arrangement.

I mention this circumstance to show with what cleverness she could enter into the feelings of others, and appear to share their illusions. On reflection I had no reason to hope that the First Consul would agree to a transaction of this kind, or would, indeed, approve of my dictating terms. Madame Bonaparte did me the honor to say that I must be her guest at dinner that night. A moment after, Madame Louis Bonaparte entered the drawing room, and the conversation became general. In the meanwhile time was passing. At last, at about seven o'clock, the sound of hurried steps on the staircase, which led to the room in which we were sitting, announced the arrival of the First Consul. Madame Bonaparte introduced me to him. He condescended to receive me with a kindness which at once dissipated the respectful awe in which I stood. He walked rapidly into the dining room, whither I followed Madame Bonaparte and her daughter. Madame Bonaparte made me sit next her. The First Consul spoke to me several times during dinner, which only lasted twenty minutes. He spoke of my studies, and of Palissot, with a kindness and a simplicity which put me entirely at my ease, and showed me how gentle and simple this man, who bore on his forehead and in his eyes the mark of such imposing superiority, was in his private life.

When I returned to the drawing room we found General Davout. The First Consul walked up and down the room with him, conversing, and a quarter of an hour later disappeared in the staircase from which he had come, without having spoken to me on the matter for which he had ordered my attendance.

I remained with Madame Bonaparte until eleven o'clock. I had asked her to be so good as to tell me whether I should go away, thinking that I had been forgotten. She told me to remain, and assured me that the First Consul would send for me. True enough, a footman came to fetch me. I followed him down a long passage to a staircase by which we reached a little door, at which he knocked. There was a wicket in this door which I examined with curiosity. My state of mind was such that I felt I was at the place of eternal imprisonment, and involuntarily I raised my eyes, to see whether I could not read over the door that inscription by Dante, *Lasciate ogni speranza voi che entrate* . . .

An usher, who had looked through the wicket, opened the door after some words with the footman, and I was shown into a small drawing room, that was poorly lighted. While I was being announced I cast a quick glance around the room, anxious to acquaint myself with what was to be my prison. The furniture consisted of some chairs covered with green morocco, and a very luxurious roll-top writing table, which was loaded with gilt bronze ornaments, and inlaid with rosewood mosaics representing various musical instruments. Afterwards I learned that these pieces of furniture had belonged to Louis XVI and subsequently sent to the *garde-meuble* as useless. A low bookcase ran round one side of the room. Some papers were scattered on the top.

I was announced, and immediately afterwards was ushered into a room, where I saw the First Consul, seated behind a writing table. A three-branched candelabra, covered with a shade, cast a strong light on the table. The rest of the room was in the semi-darkness broken only by the light from the fire on the hearth.

The First Consul's back was toward me, and he was occupied in reading a paper, and finished reading it without taking notice of my entrance. He then turned around on his chair toward me. I had remained standing at the door of his cabinet, and on seeing him turn round I approached him. After having examined me for a moment with a piercing glance, which would have greatly intimidated me had I seen it for the first time, he told me that he wished to attach me to his service, and asked me if I felt strong enough to undertake the task which he wished to give me.

I answered him with some embarrassment, with the commonplace remark that I was not very sure of myself, but that I would do everything in my power to justify his confidence. I kept my objections to myself, because I knew that he would not like them, and, besides, the way in which he had received me at dinner had weakened them considerably.

He did not seem dissatisfied with my answer, for he rose from his seat and came up to me smiling, rather sardonically, it is true, and pulled my ear, which I knew was a sign of favor. He then said, "Very well, come back tomorrow morning at seven, and come straight here."

That was all the conversation which preceded my admission into this sanctuary, which I imagined as a sort of place from which nothing but invisible oracles proceeded, accompanied by thunder and lightning.

Such was the very simple investiture which I received for a post, the responsibility of which seemed so terrible that, when it was offered to me, I could only think of it with terror. After this short audience, and this laconic dialogue, the First Consul made a sign with his hand which I took for an order to withdraw, and left me, to go into an adjoining drawing room, where, no doubt, some business awaited him. Slightly reassured by the simplicity of this beginning I went back the way I had come, preceded by my guide, who had waited for me outside the door. Nothing but solitude and silence reigned in the dimly-lit corridors through which I passed. I met nobody on my way out, except a sentry placed at the gate of the inner court.

I returned to the Hôtel Marbeuf, where Joseph Bonaparte was then living. He had gone to bed, but I sent my card up to him, and told him what had happened. He gave me fresh encouragement, and I went back to the apartment which I occupied in the house. I was in a very anxious state of mind, and felt little inclination for sleep. I needed the quiet of the night to reflect on what had happened to me that day, that proved to be so fruitful in unexpected events. I went over in my mind my introduction to Madame Bonaparte and to the First Consul, the simplicity of their home life, that simple and familiar dinner, and my reception in the evening. My ideas were confused in my head. I could not accustom myself to the thought that I was irresistibly pursuing the goal which I had desired, and that I found myself destined for a future the perspective of which was so different from the one I had imagined.

I was then twenty-four years of age. What did fortune want with me, who asked nothing of her? No doubt this change of condition was advantageous, but would I be suited to my new position? Was I not putting my neck into an iron yoke, which I should not be able to bear? I was in that state of perplexity which always besets a man in his passage from the known to the unknown. Those reflections kept me awake.

I got up before daybreak, and made my way to the Tuileries, arriving there before the appointed hour. I rather feared that I should not be able to find my way in the intricacies of the palace, and that I should have difficulty in explaining to the sentries who I was, and was very much surprised at the ease with which I reached the door through which I had passed the previous evening, and which I recognized by the wicket in it. As soon as he saw me the usher showed me into the cabinet room, which was empty.

The First Consul was in his drawing room with the Minister of Finance, M. Gaudin, who afterwards became Duke of Gaëta. I sat down at a table which stood in the recess of a window, and waited for nearly two hours for the First Consul to return. He arrived at last, holding a paper in his hand. Without appearing to pay any attention to my presence in his study, just as if I had always been there, and had always occupied the same place, he dictated a note for the Minister of Finance, with such volubility that I could hardly understand or take down half of what he was dictating. Without asking me whether I had heard him or whether I had finished writing, he took the paper away from me, and would not let me read it over, and, on my remarking it was an unintelligible scribble, he said it was on a matter well known to the minister, who would easily be able to make it out, and, so saying, he went back to the drawing room.

I never knew if M. Gaudin was able to decipher my writing. I feared that the paper might be sent back to me, and that I might be asked to explain what I had written, which would have been quite impossible. I never heard anything more about it.

The First Consul returned almost immediately. He sent for General Duroc, and ordered him to have rooms prepared for me in the palace, and to invite me to the table of the ladies and aides-de-camp in service, over which the General presided.

Just then Bourrienne entered the room, and seemed surprised to find me there. It was the first time that I had seen him in the First Consul's study. The First Consul told him to have a table arranged for himself in the outside room, and to give the table in the window, where I had written the note from dictation, up to me. Bourrienne had been in ignorance of my introduction into the First Consul's cabinet. At first he examined me with curiosity, giving me a cold salute, but his manner soon became more friendly. General Duroc took me away to lunch, and we left Bourrienne. I afterwards learned that he was accustomed to take his meals in his private rooms. I returned to the study after lunch.

The First Consul came back late, and spent almost the whole day receiving people in his drawing room, so that I had plenty of time to think over my new position, and to occupy myself with Bourrienne's arrangements and my own.

Before continuing my story, I will trace the portrait of Napoleon as I saw him at this time.

He was then in the most vigorous good health. He had recently been cured of an internal disease, from which he had begun to suffer greatly during the second year of the Consulate. This suffering was caused by a chronic skin affection, which had been driven into the system by the remedies he had taken, and of which the skilful doctor, Corvisart, had just relieved him. I have heard it said that during the siege of Toulon one of the gunners of a battery where Napoleon was, was killed. It was important that the firing should not slacken. Napoleon took the rammer and loaded the cannon several times. Some days later he was covered with a very malignant itching skin disease. He tried to remember when and where he could have caught this disease. It was then discovered that the artilleryman, from whose burning hand Napoleon had taken the rammer, was infected. In the carelessness of youth, and being entirely absorbed in his work, he had neglected to undergo any treatment. He contented himself with some remedies which only caused the outward signs of the disease to disappear, but the poison had been driven into his system, and caused great damage. This was the reason, it was added, of the extreme thinness and poor, weak appearance of Napoleon during the campaigns in Italy and Egypt.

In the second year of the Consulate, as his health began to worsen each day, he thought it necessary to undergo serious treatment. General Lannes urged him to consult Doctor Corvisart. The general's father-in-law brought Corvisart, who was his doctor and friend, to La Malmaison. Napoleon entrusted his case to the doctor. Corvisart treated him with blisters, and prescribed a regimen which, in conjunction with the treatment, produced the best results. The more Napoleon got to know Corvisart the more he held him in high esteem, and when he became Emperor he attached him to his person, as his first and only medical adviser.

Napoleon was at that time moderately stout. His stoutness was increased later on by the frequent use of baths, which he took to refresh himself after his exertions. It should be mentioned that he had taken the habit of bathing himself every day at irregular hours, a practice which he considerably modified when it was pointed out by his doctor that the frequent use of hot baths, and the time he spent in them, were weakening him and would predispose him to obesity.

Napoleon was of small stature (about five feet two inches), and well built, though his bust was rather long. His head was big and the skull largely developed. His neck was short and his shoulders broad. The size of his chest bespoke a robust constitution, less robust, however, than his mind. His legs were well shaped, his feet were small and well formed. His hands, and he was rather proud of it, were delicate, and plump, with tapered fingers. His forehead was high and broad, his eyes were gray, penetrating and wonderfully mobile; his nose was straight and well shaped. His teeth were fairly good, the mouth perfectly modeled, the upper lip slightly drawn down toward the corner of the mouth, and the chin slightly prominent. His skin was smooth and his complexion pale, but of a pallor which denoted a good circulation of the blood. His very fine chestnut hair, which, until the time of the expedition to Egypt, he had worn long, cut square and covering his ears, was clipped short. The hair was thin on the upper part of the head, and left bare his forehead, the seat of such lofty thoughts. The shape of his face and all his features were remarkably regular. In one word, his head and his bust were in no way inferior in nobility and dignity to the most beautiful bust which antiquity has bequeathed to us.

Of this portrait, which in its main features underwent little alteration in the last years of his reign, I will add some particulars furnished by my long intimacy with him. When excited by any violent passion his face assumed a terrible expression. A sort of rotary movement was very visible and would appear on his forehead and between his eyebrows; his eyes flashed fire; his nostrils dilated, swollen with the inner storm. But these passing movements, whatever their cause may have been, in no way caused disorder to his mind. He seemed to be able to control these explosions at will, which, by the way, as time went on, became less and less frequent. His head remained cool. The blood never went to it, flowing back to the heart. In ordinary life his expression was calm, meditative, and gently serious. When in a good mood, or anxious to please, his expression was sweet and caressing, and his face was lighted up by a most beautiful smile. Amongst his closest entourage his laugh was loud and mocking.

The stoutness, which grew upon him in the last years of his reign, developed his trunk more than the lower part of his body, a circumstance which made people say after his fall that his bust gave the idea of an imposing and majestic monument, the pedestal of which was not at all proportioned to its greatness.

My portrait of Napoleon would be incomplete did I not mention the hat, without trimming or lace, which was ornamented by a little tricolor cockade, fastened with a black silk cord, and the gray overcoat which covered the simple uniform of colonel of his guard. This hat and this coat, which became a trademark with him, shone in the midst of the coats covered with gold and silver embroidery that were worn by his generals, and the civil and military officers of his household.

The contradictory opinions pronounced by Napoleon's schoolmasters, or school inspectors, go to prove that as a boy he gave no signs of what he was to be one day. As a matter of fact, it was not until he left the military school that he engaged with ardor to study. He has often told me that since that date he has constantly worked sixteen hours a day. Nevertheless he already had within him the germs of the qualities which were enhanced by education, and that, under the influence of events, developed to the highest degree. These dominating qualities were pride, and the feeling of his dignity, a warlike instinct, and a genius for form, the love of order and of discipline. As a child an unjust and humiliating punishment distressed him to the point of injuring his health. A gratuitous insult to his father's name provoked him to demand reparation by force of arms, even at the cost of the loss of his career. He was then about fourteen years old. At the same age, during the winter of 1783–1784, at the head of his comrades, he collected the snow which had fallen abundantly in the court of the school at Brienne, and used it to construct forts and redoubts, which were then besieged under his orders—snowballs and cannon-balls of ice being used as projectiles—he was at one and the same time engineer and general.

Arriving at the Paris Military School at the age of sixteen he found this school used to a system of prodigality and laxity that shocked his precocious mind. On this occasion he addressed a memorandum to the deputy principal, with a plan of reform, the principal points of which he afterwards applied to the schools of Fontainebleau, Saint-Cyr, and Saint-Germain. One holiday at Brienne, having to direct a performance of the tragedy of Caesar's death, he endeavored to keep order in the theatre. The wife of the college porter, who had no ticket of admission, thinking herself authorized by her position as servant of the house, made a disturbance at the door, trying to push in in spite of the order given. She drew down on her head a sharp rebuke from the officer Bonaparte, which at once reestablished order: "Remove this woman, who brings into our midst the license of the camp."

Those who knew Napoleon in his youth agree in saying that his nature was gentle, reserved, and pensive; that he had little taste for noisy pleasures, and more inclination for the sciences than for accomplishments. He did, however, it is said, sacrifice to the muses. There are, we are assured, some pieces of poetry of his in existence, but these are only short attempts. I have never heard him admitting that he had written them.

On this point, I may add that I have more than once had the opportunity of hearing him express himself on the art of poetry in general. With the exception of true poetry, in which he recognized the elevation of ideas tied to a brilliant style, he looked upon verse as a frivolous occupation, that caused a great and useless waste of time. The mechanism of poetry, the restraint of the hemistich and the rhyme, were not at all suited to the *abandon* and vivacity of his ideas. Napoleon was a born poet. His vast thoughts, the originality of his speech and his style, his proclamations, testify to a strong and fruitful imagination. As with Plato, there was more poetry in his prose than in the verses of many poets, and just like Plato also, he would have been ready to conduct every poet, crowned with flowers, over the frontier of the Republic.

I have had in my hands a little pocketbook, which he had entrusted to me. This pocketbook contained his principal papers. His certificate of baptism, his contract of marriage, some letters, and a few sheets of paper, on which thoughts and short compositions, all in prose, were written. No traces of any attempt at poetry existed. This, however, is no proof that he never wrote poetry. It leads me to speak of an article which appeared some years ago in the *Revue des Deux-Mondes,* announcing the discovery of papers containing the youthful productions of Napoleon, partly in his handwriting.

The story of this discovery reminds me of the trick of the novelist who tries to excite public curiosity by stating that his manuscript was found in some old ruin, or in some vault, which had not been entered for centuries. I may recall that according to this story the papers had been given to Cardinal Fesch (who was certainly not the confidant that Napoleon would have chosen), that the cardinal handed them over to a priest of his diocese when he left Lyon, that this priest abandoned the box in which they were locked, that a grocer bought this box, and so on. It is a highly improbable tale.

Having thus digressed on the childhood and early youth of Napoleon, I must not let the occasion pass to mention one of the leading traits of his moral character. I mean the respect which he always showed for his parents and for his great-uncle, the archdeacon Lucien, who became, after the death of his nephew, Charles Bonaparte, the head of the family. Napoleon was fifteen years old when his father, who had brought him to France at the age of ten, died at Montpellier. The letters which he wrote to his mother and to his great-uncle on that occasion show the sorrow which he felt at this loss.

Napoleon had almost always been separated from his father, and knew him but little. Charles Bonaparte had not been able to look after the education of his children. He had entrusted that duty to Madame Bonaparte, a woman of strong character, who had fulfilled her maternal duties with a tender and severe solicitude. She had inspired her children only with sentiments that were elevated and generous, and while developing their good natural characters had been careful to remove from them all examples which might have tainted their innocence.

It was in 1787, while at the Paris Military School, that Napoleon lost his father, who died in the arms of his son Joseph. The Abbé Fesch, who afterwards became a cardinal, and Madame de Permon, mother of the Duchesse d'Abrantès, were present. Charles Bonaparte told his son that he wished him to give up the military career which kept him separated from his family, and would be pleased to see him return to Corsica to take his place. He recommended his six other sons to his care, mentioning each one by name, and made him promise that he would be a father to them as far as his age would allow. Joseph was then seventeen years old.

In 1802 the municipal councilors of Montpellier voted to erect a monument to the memory of Charles Bonaparte. Napoleon thanked the councilors for their good intentions, but, considering that his father's death had taken place eighteen years before, replied to their proposal with the words, "If I had lost my father yesterday it would be proper and natural that I should accompany my regrets with some high mark of respect, but this occurrence took place nearly twenty years ago, and is therefore not one of public interest." If he refused this homage it was chiefly because he saw it was intended rather for his personal glory than in honor of the memory of his father. Louis Bonaparte has since had the body of his father exhumed and transported to his Saint-Leu estate, where a monument has been erected.

Napoleon went to see his family in Corsica when he was an artillery lieutenant at Valence. It was then long since his uncle, the archdeacon Lucien, crippled with gout, had been forced to take to his bed. Touched by the sight of his suffering, young Bonaparte, who was then barely eighteen years old, wrote to Doctor Tissot in secret, carefully describing in his letter the state of the invalid, and imploring him, with touching solicitude, appealing to his science and humanity for advice as to the cure, or at least, as to the relief of his uncle. This letter was never answered. It was no doubt lost amongst the number of letters asking for consultations and signed by strangers which the great doctor received.

Five years later Napoleon obtained a new leave of absence, and without delay took advantage of it to return to Corsica, where he found his great-uncle on his deathbed. This sad sight recalled to him vividly the kindness with which this worthy man had always treated his nephews, and himself, Napoleon, in particular. The version of the words which archdeacon Lucien addressed to them, which is generally accredited to him, was incorrect. He was bitterly regretted by his nephews, to whom he had been a second father, and his family lost in him a guide and a protector. Napoleon united in the same gratitude the memories of this good kinsman and of his father.

I could never weary of examining the room in which I found myself since my admission to the Tuileries, and I kept looking at the papers that covered Napoleon's bureau, but had scruples about touching them as I could not imagine that from the first day he had given me a confidence I knew him to be cautious of, and of which I did not fancy myself worthy.

The room that he had made his study was moderately large, and was lighted by a single window, built at an angle, looking out on the garden. The main piece of furniture was a magnificent writing table, placed in the middle of the room, and covered with gilt bronze, the legs being in the form of griffins. The table was a sort of square box, and the lid was a sliding one, so that it could be closed without disturbing the papers. The chair was antique in form, the back being covered with a drapery of green kerseymere, pleated and fitted with silk cords. The arms also ended in griffin heads.

The First Consul, as a rule, never sat down at his writing table except to sign. His usual place was on a settee covered with green taffeta, beside which stood a small table where the day's post was gathered. Every morning the letters of the previous day were removed from this little table and put on the writing table, to make room for the day's letters. A screen with many folds shielded him from the heat of the fire. My writing table was placed within reach of his. This arrangement inside his workroom was followed in all the palaces and residences that Napoleon occupied. There was never any back cabinet.

But when space allowed it the maps which he was constantly using were placed in an adjoining room, to which the head of the topographical bureau came only when he was summoned. When it was necessary for Napoleon to follow the subject with which he was dealing, on the map, I used to go into this room to take his dictation. At the far end of the study were two large bookcases placed in the corners, and between them was one of those large clocks that are called regulators. A long glazed cupboard was placed against one of the walls. It was of breast height, with a marble top, and contained some cardboard cases. There were also a few chairs in the room, and a bronze equestrian statuette of Frederick the Great of Prussia. Such was the simple furniture of the Consul's workroom. The only luxurious object was the writing table, which had been bought at the Industrial Exhibition as a masterpiece of the skilful manufacturer Biennais. The simplicity of Napoleon's tastes was evidenced here as clearly as in everything touching his person. The only dependency of the Consul's cabinet was a topographical bureau or map room, which was the responsibility of an officer who had been formerly attached to the staff of General Clarke, and whose son, M. Cuvillier-Fleury, a distinguished man of letters, after studying brilliantly and carrying off the prize of honor at Louis-le-Grand, directed the education of his Royal Highness the Duc d'Aumale, and became his secretary of commands.

The librarian was M. Ripault, who had followed General Bonaparte in the Egyptian campaigns. He was an erudite litterateur, a learned bookman, and had been a member of the Commission of Science and Arts at Cairo, and secretary to General Kléber. In 1807 he suddenly became disgusted with his post, without giving any reason for the change. It was suspected that he was offended by his subordination to the Abbé Denina. This *savant,* author of *Revolutions in Italy* and many other valuable works, and formerly librarian to Frederick the Great, had been presented to the Emperor at Mayence. Napoleon wished to express proof of his admiration, and show him how highly he held his talents, and nominated him his first librarian, a title which was, however, purely honorary. The Emperor ordered me to invite M. Ripault to return to his post which he had abandoned, retiring to live in the country near Orléans. I wrote him several urgent letters, which he did not answer. The Emperor was then obliged to arrange for a substitute. I drew his attention to M. Barbier, who in the literary world was known for his expertise in bibliography. I had had occasion to appreciate the extent of his knowledge of that science, for I had been under his orders for a short time after I left school, when he had been commissioned to set up the libraries of the Directoire and of the Legislative Council. Since everyone spoke in his favor, the learned bibliographer was appointed the Emperor's librarian. M. Barbier is the author of the *Dictionnaire des Anonymes* and of many bibliographical and philological works, distinguished by scientific research and a judicious critical spirit.

M. Amédée Jaubert, who has since become peer of France, and a member of the Academy of Inscriptions and Belles-Lettres, was secretary-interpreter of oriental languages to the government. In this capacity he undertook a great number of translations for the cabinet. He enjoyed the complete confidence of the First Consul as a translator, many of the translations with which he was entrusted being of the highest importance. M. Lelorgne d'Ideville, who has since become *Maître des Requêtes* to the council of state, and a member of the chamber of deputies, was some years later attached to the cabinet as secretary-interpreter of northern languages. M. d'Ideville had lived many years in Germany, Poland, Russia, Sweden, and Denmark, as attaché to different French legations in those countries. He was charged in the cabinet with an important work, which consisted of extracting from the dispatches of our diplomatic agents and from foreign publications information as to the composition and movements of the enemy's armies; and to give a summary of this information in a detailed report. M. d'Ideville's reports were drawn up with such clarity and precision that the Emperor knew the condition of foreign armies as well as he knew that of the French armies. During his campaigns in Russia and Germany M. d'Ideville constantly followed the Emperor on horseback. It was his duty to question prisoners and the inhabitants of the country through which they were passing, and to translate the contents of letters or reports which might come into his hands. The Emperor, thanks to the zeal and penetration of M. d'Ideville, thus obtained information which was often of the highest interest to him.

Napoleon was surrounded by living reminders of his youth. He had with him, besides Bourrienne, Colonel Lauriston, who had also been at school with him at Brienne. Father Dupuis, formerly schoolmaster in his town, was living in peaceful and honorable retirement at La Malmaison. Although there were very few books there, and these were in Napoleon's study, which M. Dupuis never entered, he enjoyed the title of librarian. He was an excellent man, and literally worshipped his former pupil. From his management of the Brienne school he retained the practice of domestic economy rather than a taste for books and study. His principal occupation had been the cultivation of vineyards. At Malmaison there were no longer the precious vines of Champagne to be inspected, but M. Dupuis bought plots of standing vines at Garches, and at Suresnes, and through a certain process removed the greenness and acidity of the grapes for which Suresnes wine has been proverbially notorious, and managed to produce sweet and sparkling Champagne wine. The house-porter at La Malmaison was a man called Haute, who had formerly been porter at the Brienne school. This excellent man and his wife had found pleasant quarters here also. The two brothers Desmazis, who had been with Napoleon at the Military School were not forgotten. The elder was appointed director of the state lottery in 1806, and the younger, who had been Napoleon's personal friend, was given the post of director of the crown furniture. During the Hundred Days he filled the office of chamberlain.

On my arrival at the Tuileries in 1802 I found the following arrangements in force: the First Consul no longer kept common table. He dined with Madame Bonaparte and with some persons of his family. On Wednesdays, which were the days of the council, he invited the consuls and the ministers to dinner. He lunched alone, the simplest dishes being served, while for drink he was satisfied with Chambertin wine diluted with water, and a single cup of coffee. As all his time was taken he used the lunch hour to receive the people with whom he liked to converse. These were generally men of letters, or artists. General Duroc was governor of the palace. The general's tasks included regulating expenditures, and the order and supervision of the palace. He presided at the table at which the ladies and officers in waiting and the aides-de-camp dined. The military household at that time was composed of four generals commanding the consular guard, Generals Lannes, Bessières, Davout, and Soult; of eight aides-de-camp, Colonels Lemarrois, Caffarelli, Lauriston, Caulaincourt, Savary, Rapp, Fontanelli (the latter an Italian officer) and Captain Lebrun, son of the Third Consul. There were four prefects of the palace: Messieurs de Luçay, Rémusat, Didelot, and Cramayel; and four ladies, Mesdames de

Luçay, Talhouet, Rémusat, and Lauriston. One of the generals of the guard was on duty with the First Consul each week, as was also an aide-de-camp and a prefect of the palace.

The prefects of the palace were responsible for the service inside the palace, the respect of the etiquette, and the inspection of the theatres. The task of the ladies was to accompany Madame Bonaparte, and it was through them that the wives of foreign ambassadors and others were introduced. One lady was on duty with Madame Bonaparte each week. At ceremonies, or on extraordinary occasions, all the ladies and the prefects of the palace were present. A general of the guard, who was on duty, presided at the table of the officers of the guard. Already at that time the household of the First Consul resembled a court.

With the exception of these changes in the household of the head of the government, changes made necessary because of the increased power and honor given to his position, by the growth in personnel that surrounded him, the extent and the importance of the transactions in which he was engaged, by his multifarious relations with the high civil servants of the state, and the representatives of foreign powers, the private life of Napoleon had remained the same. During the first year of the consulate several plots were made against the life of the First Consul, all inspired by men belonging to the party which was vanquished on the 18th Brumaire. Some of these plots had been stopped before they could be carried out, others had failed. The one which attracted the most attention was the plot to stab the First Consul at the Opéra.

Napoleon's conviction of the impotence of the conspirators, a belief due either to his confidence in his destiny, or his contempt for danger, and his indifference to attacks against his person, had until then prevented the prosecution of the conspirators. The criminal attack of the 3rd Nivôse interrupted this feeling of security, and made him see the need to repress, by a sharp example, the audacity of the turbulent Jacobins, to whom this bloody catastrophe was attributed. The consequence was an extraordinary measure which has been severely condemned by some of Napoleon's historians. Without entering into the details of the conception of this infernal machine, let me say that the result of the explosion which took place only a few seconds after the carriage of the First Consul had passed was such that nearly eighty people were wounded, and an entire neighborhood of Paris was shaken, with several houses severely damaged. This unjustifiable crime caused general indignation, and irritated the First Consul to the highest degree. This new attack upon his life, and upon the lives of some of the population of Paris, brought about the indictment of the Opera conspirators, and led to the arrest of one hundred and thirty persons who had stained themselves with crimes under The Terror, or who were considered dangerous because of their fanaticism. The list of their names was drawn up by Fouché. Police investigations led, more than a month later, to the discovery of the real authors of the infernal machine. They were royalists under the direction of Georges, an ardent and indefatigable enemy of the First Consul. Without a doubt proscription without trial is an arbitrary act. But if one remembers the times, it would be easily understood how inconvenient and how difficult it would be to proceed against these men in a legally required way. One must admit that these blood-thirsty men, who are justly abhorred, were marked for punishment by the public's wish, which is also a court; that it was necessary to put a stop to the agitation which was caused by the impunity of these odious and dreaded men; that their expulsion beyond the frontier of the fatherland which they had covered with blood and ruins, satisfied public opinion and was a pledge to public peace; that the First Consul, dominated no doubt by sentiments of generosity, had to defend himself against the reactionary spirit of the majority of his advisers; that he restored their liberty to many Jacobins who had been arrested, and reduced the sentences passed upon those least implicated. Some, as a matter of fact, were detained in France, and later on subjected to simple police supervision. Those whose ferocity and callousness made dangerous to the public peace suffered the penalty of deportation. One of those who was affected by the senatus consultum, and whose acquaintance I made, admitted that this measure had been more of a threat, rather than rigorously carried out. This man was Félix Lepelletier, who was on the list of persons to be deported, but was pardoned by the First Consul, *proprio motu.* He was a man of extreme ideas, but of honorable sentiments. As mayor of his village, the only post which he would accept under the Empire, he distinguished himself by his skillful and good management of affairs. He had refused the decoration of the legion of honor out of a desire to be consistent with his principles. A member of the chamber of deputies during the Hundred Days, he understood that the time had come to rally around Napoleon as the only man capable of saving France from the foreign yoke. His patriotic conduct marked him as an adversary of the government of the Second Restoration, and this time he was sentenced to banishment.

Following this event Napoleon had fallen back into his usual feeling of security, and stopped worrying about the dangers that might threaten him personally. He listened with impatience to the reports on this subject that were transmitted to him by the police or by the persons around him; he needed all his calm; he made no change in his habits, and continued his work without allowing himself to be diverted from his path. When I entered the consular palace I saw none of those precautions which denote suspicion or fear. He lived in a very homey manner, especially at La Malmaison. He used to spend the hours which were not taken up by work, exercise, or shooting, with Josephine. He used to lunch alone, and during the meal, which was a relaxation for him, he received the persons with whom he liked to converse on science, art, and literature. He dined with his family, and after dinner would look in at his cabinet, and then, unless kept there by some work, would return to the drawing room and play chess. In general as a rule he liked to talk in a familiar way. He was fond of discussions, but did not impose his opinions, and made no pretension of superiority, either of intelligence or of rank. When only ladies were present he liked to criticize their dresses, or tell them tragic or satirical stories—ghost stories for the most part. When bedtime came, Madame Bonaparte followed him to his room. Napoleon wasted very little time in preparing for the night, and used to say that he got back to bed with pleasure. He said that statues ought to be erected to the men who invented beds and carriages. However, this bed into which he threw himself with delight, when he was often crushed with fatigue, was abandoned more than once during the course of the night. He used to get up, after an hour's sleep, as wide awake and as clear in his head as if he had slept quietly the whole night. As soon as he lay down his wife would place herself at the foot of the bed, and begin reading aloud. Since she read very well he took pleasure in listening to her. At La Malmaison Napoleon used to spend the time that was not taken up in his workroom in the park, and there again his time was not wasted.

Josephine spent her time as she chose. She received numerous callers during the day. She used to lunch with some friends, and with new and old acquaintances. She had no accomplishments, did not draw, and was not a musician. There was a harp in her apartment on which she used to play for want of anything better to do, and she always played the same tune. She used to work at tapestry, and would get her ladies or her visitors to help her. She had made the covering for the furniture in the drawing room at La Malmaison in this way. Napoleon approved of this busy life. The reestablishment of peace with England had allowed Josephine to correspond with some English botanists and the principal London nursery men, from whom she received rare and new plants and shrubs to add to her collections. She used to give me the letters from England, written in connection with this business, to translate into French. At La Malmaison Josephine used to visit her fine hothouses regularly, and took great interest in them. In the evening she would take the backgammon board, a game she was very fond of, and which she played well and quickly. Family theatricals were also played at La Malmaison, in a little theatre which accommodated about two hundred spectators. Eugène Beauharnais, who excelled in footmen's parts, and his sister Hortense were the principal actors, not only by rank but by talent. Next to them came Bourrienne, Lauriston, Denon and some ladies and officers of the First Consul's household. Michot, an excellent comedian, and shareholder in the Théâtre-Français, was stage manager, and directed the rehearsals. Napoleon was regularly present at the performances, which consisted of little comedies, and thoroughly amused himself. He took pleasure in praising or criticizing the actors' performances. His remarks, which were often words of praise, and that were always interesting, showed what an interest he took in these spectacles. On Sundays there were little balls given, at which Napoleon used to dance. He found a charm in this patriarchal life.

In his retreat at La Malmaison Napoleon appeared like a father in the midst of his family. This setting aside of his grandeur, his simple and dignified manners, the pleasing ways and gracious familiarity of Madame Bonaparte was very charming to me. In our leisure moments the First Consul used to go over his bookcases with me, telling me what books I ought to read. He spoke of poetry as a frivolous occupation, and advised me not to waste any time over it. He had heard that, like all young men fresh from school, I had made my attempt at verse—some attempts at tragedy. When he saw me unoccupied, he thought I was dreaming of poetry, and when I told him that I had found that I had no vocation for this art, he said: "You are right. It's a hollow science."

Napoleon had not always had this opinion of poetry; or rather, I should say, he looked upon the well-known poets of the time I am speaking, as the buglers of his fame. On his accession to the consulate he had made frequent advances not only to the scientists but also to the poets and litterateurs. He had treated Lemercier with respect and affability. Ducis, and Bernardin de St. Pierre had had no reason to complain of his treatment. He attached particular importance to the talents which both Ducis and Lemercier possessed in tragedy. He had, it is said, offered the former an honorable retreat in the senate, and later on the decoration of the Legion of Honor. This offer was, it appears, brutally refused. However this may be, Ducis accepted in 1814, from the hands of Louis XVIII, the same decoration which he is said to have considered as a badge of slavery in 1800, and with it a pension of six thousand francs.

The boldness of thought and expression which characterized Lemercier's talent, the variety of his ideas, and his creativity had attracted the attention of the First Consul, although by no means was he fascinated by him. He was ready to give him a mark of his goodwill and of the esteem which he had for his talent. The distinctions and the favors offered by the First Consul were equally rejected. After the second year of the Consulate, when, by the way, Napoleon's glory, to use the expression of those who after the fall of the Empire sought an excuse for their defection, was still "innocent," Lemercier, wounded no doubt in his republican sentiments by the show of power, suddenly withdrew from La Malmaison. No steps were taken to call him back. This indifference pushed him into systematic opposition. From that day forth he professed hatred for Napoleon, and declared this openly in his *Cours de Littérature,* published in 1817. Poets, however, must not be too severely judged. Their nervous disposition, produced by the perpetual state of excitement in which they live, their indifference to the material interests of life, that was clearly marked both in Ducis and in Lemercier, plead in their favor and prevented too severe a judgment. The experience which Napoleon had made of their susceptibility, of the mobility of their imagination, of their exclusiveness, had shown him how unfit they were for matters of any kind. He seemed to have learned at his expense what the illustrious Béranger thought about them. I have often heard Béranger say, with his usual modesty and unselfishness, that poets were really good for nothing but writing poetry.

I could not master my surprise at discovering such simplicity of habits in a man like Napoleon, who from afar seemed so imposing. I had expected him to be brusque, and of uncertain temper, and instead I found him patient, indulgent, easy to please, by no means exacting, merry with a merriness which was often noisy and mocking, and sometimes of a charming *bonhomie.* This familiarity on his part did not, however, elicit any ideas of reciprocity. Napoleon played with people without mixing with them. He desired to put me entirely at ease with him, from the very first days of my service, and, consequently, from the start I felt no embarrassment in his presence. Doubtless he impressed me to some extent, but I was no longer afraid of him. I kept these thoughts by all that I saw of his pleasant and affectionate ways with Josephine, the assiduous devotion of his officers, the kindliness of his relations with the consuls and the ministers, and his familiarity with the soldiers.

The Egyptian campaign was still recent at that time, and the memory was fresh in the minds of men. I heard it related, among other examples of his solicitude for the needs of his army, that at the raising of the siege of Acre, having given orders that all horses, without distinction, should be used to remove the wounded, he flew into violent anger with his equerry Vigogne, who had thought that the horses of the commander-in-chief were to be exempted from this general order. M. Amédée Jaubert, who had been General Bonaparte's interpreter, said that one day seeing the general returning from the trenches, harassed with fatigue and dying with thirst, he had told him that a Christian had just brought a skin of wine as a present, and that Bonaparte ordered it to be immediately carried to the ambulance.

In this vein I wish to offer here a curious document, which seems to have been overlooked by Napoleon's historians. I owe my knowledge of it to the kindness of a man, remarkable for his aptitude for the arts, which he has cultivated with great success, adopted by the fashionable world as the type of elegance and *bon ton,* and who to these brilliant advantages has added a philanthropy which will always earn him the gratitude of his fellow citizens. He is the founder of the *Société de Bienfaisance* of London, an institution destined for the relief of indigent Frenchmen. Numerous subscribers, among them kings, have endowed the asylum, thrown open by his care to all the unfortunate of his nation.

M. d'Orsay copied the document to which I am referring from the order book of the 2nd company of the 3rd battalion of the 2nd brigade of light French Infantry. This book of orders, found at Cairo, after the departure of the French army, was given to the Rev. Mr. Moore—who lent it to the Duke of Wellington—by the son of General Moncrieff.

REPUBLIQUE FRANÇAISE,
Liberté—Egalité.

AT HEADQUARTERS AT CAIRO,
1st Nivôse, Year VII.

"Every day at noon, on the squares opposite the hospitals, will be played by the regimental bands, various national airs, which inspire the sick with gaiety, and recall to their memory the most beautiful moments of their past campaigns.

"The commanding officers will in consequence give orders that the bands of the various corps shall perform in turn of service.

"For the Commander-in-Chief,
"ALEXANDER BERTHIER."

This mark of interest given to poor sick men, to unhappy wounded soldiers, sad and discouraged at the thought of their distant homes, reveals a delicate attention, a maternal solicitude, as Count d'Orsay expressed it, and that provident solicitousness which was the basis of Napoleon's character.

The partiality which the First Consul retained for his memorable Egyptian campaign was shown even in the taste which he had retained for the produce of that country. For a long time his favorite dishes were pillau and dates. He had in his private gardens both at La Malmaison and at St. Cloud, gazelles which he had brought back from Egypt, and which he loved to feed with his own hands. Sometimes he would offer them his snuff-box. They were very fond of tobacco, and would empty the snuff-box in a minute, without appearing any the worse for it. There were also for some time, in the little park at St. Cloud, some mufflons which had been sent from Corsica. Their natural wildness was, however, such that it was impossible to keep them.

M. de Bourrienne, whom as a matter of fact I had succeeded, though not titularly so, had been Napoleon's schoolmate at the military school. They had started their military careers together, and Bourrienne had followed Napoleon to Italy and to Egypt, These associations, these habits and the perfect tact of his conduct towards the First Consul had created him a position of confidence and intimacy which seemed destined to last forever. The First Consul had appointed Bourrienne councilor of state on special duty, giving him rights and prerogatives making him an important person in the state. He corresponded directly with the ministers on certain details of their service. Napoleon treated Bourrienne with familiarity, and often went out with him into the park of St. Cloud, either on foot or in a buggy. Mme. Bourrienne was almost independent, and neither ate nor slept in the palace. He had just bought a charming house at St. Cloud, had furnished it richly, and used to give dinners there to which the ministers, and particularly Fouché, the senators, councilors of state, and so on, were invited. His expenses and his purchases were out of proportion with the private fortune which the First Consul knew him to possess. Although their mutual relations did not appear changed, the First

Consul's annoyance, which he still concealed from Bourrienne, sometimes surfaced in things which he said in my presence. He seemed to me to have some private grievance against him, which he had not sufficiently investigated. The unfortunate affair of the brothers Coulon put a stop to his hesitation, and was the last straw. One Wednesday, being the day of the cabinet council, I was busy in the First Consul's study, when I saw him enter hurriedly. He asked me if Bourrienne was in his office, and on my affirmative answer he called him to the threshold of the door. Bourrienne came, somewhat troubled by the Consul's excited appearance. The Consul said to him in a severe tone of voice: "Give any papers and keys which you have of mine to Méneval, and withdraw. And never let me see you again." With these few words he returned to the council, slamming the door violently behind him.

M. de Bourrienne, at first dumbfounded by this violent tirade, gave way to extreme despair. I did all I could to calm him. I tried to comfort him with hopes which I knew to be useless, for what hope could there be after a decision so laconically and so severely formulated? During the first two or three days which followed this painful scene, we exchanged some letters, but after that all relations between us ceased on the express command of the First Consul. This is what had caused this explosion. About the same time as I was called to Napoleon's cabinet Bourrienne, thanks to his standing with the Ministry of War, had obtained a contract for the supply of military equipment and harness. Since his name could not appear in this transaction, it was with the Brothers Coulon that the contract was made. Bourrienne supplied the funds necessary to the enterprise. A banking firm advanced a sum of 800,000 francs on a mortgage furnished by the Coulons but exacted that M. de Bourrienne should guarantee the loan. The Brothers Coulon having failed shortly after, the bank proceeded against Bourrienne as bondsman. Bourrienne denied all responsibility for the Coulons' debts, but since the guarantee consisted of private deeds, defeasances, memoranda, and other papers, all in Bourrienne's writing, a lawsuit ensued, which he lost before the lower court, won before the court of appeals, and finally lost when his adversaries carried it up to the court of cassation.

This speculation, in which Bourrienne had participated as described, strongly disgusted Napoleon, who had an invincible repulsion for what is called "doing business." The object of the lawsuit and the resulting scandal revolted him. He never forgave his old schoolfellow and secretary. He spoke to me of him for a long time, and often in real pain which used always to end in bitter complaint against him.

It would be distasteful to me to enumerate the various grievances which Napoleon had against Bourrienne, and to repeat the reproaches which he used to make against the man whom I had replaced. The revelations which invariably pour in torrents on a sinking man, many of them of a very serious nature, increased the displeasure of the First Consul. He gave orders to General Duroc to ask Bourrienne for the keys of the apartment which he had placed at his disposal in the Tuileries, and which he had kept, hoping by a moment's conversation to win back the friendship which he had lost. The First Consul refused to see him. He sent word to return to the national *garde-meuble* the furniture of his apartment, as well as that of his house at Rueil. Before purchasing the house at St. Cloud, which he occupied at the moment of his disgrace, Bourrienne had acquired another house at Rueil, where he had established himself with his family. He objected that he had thought himself authorized to consider this furniture as a gift, and to keep it as his property. General Duroc took back this answer to the First Consul, who replied that his command must be obeyed without any delay, adding irritably that he gave money and not chairs.

However, as a token of their old friendship, and of services rendered, Napoleon gave Bourrienne the mission to be present each day in criminal court during the trial of the individuals implicated in the Georges and Moreau plot, and to send him a report of each of the proceedings. After the First Consul had finished reading these reports, which I handed to him, they were deposited at the archives. If they still be there, they might be compared with the accounts of the court and of the circumstances of the trial given in the memoirs published under M. de Bourrienne's name. The difference between the thoughts and the language of these two versions could be established. As I have said before, I do not think that Bourrienne was the author of the memoirs published under his name. I met him, in 1825, in Paris, and he told me that he had been asked to write against the Emperor: "In spite of all the wrong he did me," he added, "I could never make up my mind to do so. My hand would rather wither."

The ever-growing enfeeblement of his faculties, the state of financial embarrassment to which he found himself reduced, added to the deep resentment with which he remembered his disgrace, making him open to the monetary offers which he received afterwards. It is stated that the publisher of Bourrienne's Memoirs offered him, when he fled to Holstein to escape his creditors, a sum, rumored to be of thirty thousand francs, for his signature to the work. M. de Bourrienne, already seized with the disease of which he died a few years later in the hospital at Caen, agreed to allow these memoirs to be published under his name. His entire cooperation in this book consisted in some stray incomplete notes which were worked out by a few professional writers. These writers, whose names are mentioned, had to make up for the insufficiency of these notes with their own research, and with the help of materials supplied by the publisher. If M. de Bourrienne had written these memoirs himself, he would not have stated that, when he was minister for the Emperor to Hamburg, he assisted the agents of the Count de Lille in drawing up a proclamation in favor of this prince, nor that in 1814 he received the thanks of Louis XVIII. He would not have said that Napoleon had confided to him, in 1805, that he had never had any serious intentions of an expedition against England, and that the project of a landing, and its noisy preparations, was only a trick to amuse some fools. M. de Bourrienne would not have mentioned his private conversations with Napoleon nor the alleged confidences which had been made to him, since Napoleon never saw him again after the 20th of October, 1802. When, in 1805, the Emperor, forgetting his offenses, appointed him plenipotentiary minister to Hamburg, he granted him the usual audience, but did not add to this favor any return of his old friendship. He constantly refused, both before and afterwards, either to receive him or to correspond with him. I have had occasion to say elsewhere that during his mission to Hamburg, when special information beyond ministerial correspondence was required by the Emperor, it was I who had to ask it of M. de Bourrienne, just as I was to get similar information from the worthy M. Otto, French ambassador to Munich, the Emperor wishing to neglect no means of being informed about what was going on in front of and behind the great army.

I wanted to say here all that I have to say about M. de Bourrienne so as not to have to return to this subject.

The First Consul ended by resigning himself to his grievances against his old schoolfellow, and even congratulated himself on having shaken off this yoke. He did—without wishing to make any comparison—what Louis XIV had done on the death of Mazarin. In this connection he said to me one day: "I have abolished the title of confidential secretary. It has too many disadvantages, and I am forced to admit the fact. I do not wish you to call yourself anything but attaché to the First Consul. You are young, you have a long career before you; later on we will see." This title of attaché, which was imposed on me by no regulation, was the sum of the reasons which prevented the First Consul from giving me the privileges and personal preferences which Bourrienne owed to the length of their relations and the kind of familiarity which had existed between them. As a matter of fact routine prevailed. I was constantly being styled secretary to the First Consul or Emperor, sometimes even, confidential secretary. In the course of business I was constantly writing to the ministers on behalf of the Emperor and receiving their replies. It sometimes even happened that he did not sign his letters, because just at that moment he might be setting out on horseback, or was prevented by some reason, and he would then authorize me to send the letters on accompanied by a letter signed by me. Moderation has always kept me away from the encroachments which a more enterprising mind than mine might have been tempted to try. When, after his work was done, the First Consul went to spend an hour in Madame Bonaparte's drawing room, he would bid me take my hat and follow him. I went sometimes. Often I preferred to employ my rare hours of leisure on my own behalf. Later on it often happened that I had to remain in his study to expedite some urgent piece of business, and that I had only a few brief moments left to devote to my family and to my friends. I ended by contenting myself with the almost obscure position which I occupied in the confidence and familiarity of the Consul and Emperor without boasting about it or drawing attention to myself. This reserve, by the way, did not at all displease him; not indeed that he was suspicious, for I never saw any traces of this in his character. He liked to tease me about my reserve. He used to say, which was quite true, that I was totally unknown to several persons among his ladies and gentlemen in attendance. As a matter of fact there were several chamberlains who had heard my name mentioned, but who did not know me by sight. In the notes written in his writing on Fleury de Chaboulon's *Mémoires du règne de Napoléon* in 1815, at St. Helena, the Emperor says, "Méneval and Fain lived in such a withdrawn way that there were chamberlains who, after four years' service in the palace, had never seen them." However, he gave me his full confidence, and made no change in the custom that his secretary should open all his letters.

Before speaking of the work that the First Consul was occupied with at the time of my entry into his service, I should say a word about the men whom he had called to help him in the government of the state.

His two colleagues were, as everybody knows, Cambacérès and Le Brun. The former, a learned lawyer, had passed unscathed through the stormiest periods of the Revolution, thanks to his prudence and his skill. The Revolution of the 18th Brumaire found him Minister of Justice under the Directorial government. His reputation for learning and tact had attracted the attention of General Bonaparte. Cambacérès showed himself a skilful politician in all circumstances. He was the faithful counselor of Napoleon, who had entire confidence in his judgment, and who used to consult him on every point. His little eccentricities that somewhat lent themselves to jesting, by no means diminished the respect in which he was held.

The Third Consul was Le Brun. Formerly attached to Chancellor Maupeou he wrote the speeches and the writings of that magistrate, which, at the time of the reform of the parliamentary system in France, had rendered their author famous for his nobility of thought and brilliant style. A pure and elegant writer, he devoted the leisure time that business had left him to his taste for literature. Financial matters and social economy had equally been the subject of his studies. He had drawn attention to himself in the various assemblies of which he was part, from the States-General to the Council of the Ancients, by his particular knowledge of finance, and by his zeal for wise reforms. His knowledge, and his fine literary talent, made him a useful collaborator to Bonaparte, while the sweetness of his character dispelled any fear lest he might prove an unmanageable censor.

The choice of these two men proved Bonaparte's tact, and this triumvirate united the best conditions of association that could be desired.

The ministry was composed of eight members. I put at the head Talleyrand, who was Minister of Foreign Affairs. He is too well known to need speaking about at any length. His relations with General Bonaparte dated from the Treaty of Campo-Formio. His intelligence led him to see that sooner or later the general's superiority would place him at the head of the government, and, provident man that he was, he attached himself to his fortunes. Familiar with the course of business, he brought real talent, a spirit of intrigue, and a high competence to his work. He was at one and the same time a man of the court, and a man of the revolution, and it was to this dual capacity that he owed the favor of Napoleon. Endowed with a shrewd and conciliatory spirit, he had made himself agreeable to foreign diplomacy. These qualities made him better equipped than anybody else to direct foreign affairs, and designated him as the choice of the First Consul.

The Minister of Police was Fouché. The colleagues of the First Consul had rejected him, and justly so, because of his immorality, and the bloody part which he had played during the revolutionary period. His knowledge of the plans and the secrets of all the parties involved, a highly resourceful mind, a false air of frankness and independence, the art with which he knew how to persuade that he was the indispensable man, had prevailed over this repugnance, and he was maintained in the post which he had already filled under the Directoire. In appearance he reminded me of Marat, whom I had frequently seen in my early youth. Fouché was taller, very thin; his hair and eyebrows were pale, his eyes were bloodshot, and his complexion was livid. He spoke with a volubility which made one think that he was unburdening all of his thoughts. He affected a limitless devotion to the First Consul. It would sometimes happen that he would come to La Malmaison when Napoleon was away. He would then come to me, and take me out with him into the park, and speak to me at length about the vigilance with which he performed his duties, of how he intimidated the malcontents of every class, of the zeal that consumed him, and the help he was always ready to give the First Consul in whatever he might wish to undertake, invariably finishing with the words: "Be sure to tell the First Consul all I have said."

One of the most important ministries, that of Finance, was occupied by M. Gaudin. Formerly first clerk of Finances, specially charged with the management of taxation, then commissioner of the Treasury, and director-general of the post, M. Gaudin had twice refused the Ministry of Finance which was offered him by the Directoire. He accepted it from the First Consul after the 18th Brumaire. When he took possession of his portfolio, credit was destroyed; tax collection was irregular, and hampered on every side; the treasury was empty; in one word national bankruptcy was imminent. At the time of which we are speaking the vigilance and the probity of the new minister had restored confidence, the public services were reorganized, the financial administrations had been reestablished, and new ones were created; chaos had been replaced by order, and treasury bonds were negotiated with as much favor as the paper of the best banking and commercial firms. Napoleon used to say that everything that was possible to erase the evil results of a bad and abusive system, and to restore the good principles of credit and moderation, had been done by M. Gaudin in a few months; that he considered this minister an honorable and talented administrator, who advanced slowly but surely. He used to add, later, that what M. Gaudin had done initially, had been maintained and perfected during the fifteen years of his wise management, and that he had had no need to reverse any one of the measures taken, because his knowledge was certain and the result of long experience.

General Berthier was Minister of War at that time. Napoleon, accustomed to the regularity and precision with which he had always executed his orders when he was his chief of his staff, both in Italy and in Egypt, had confided this department to him. As minister Berthier always remained General Bonaparte's chief staff officer. Nature had intended him to play this part; he never raised himself above it. He was considered to be weak of mind and wavering in character. The First Consul had entrusted him with various missions in which he had acquitted himself well under his direction. Napoleon, who held him in true affection, showered him with gifts and honors to the end of his reign.

The portfolio of the admiralty was in the hands of Admiral Decrés. He owed his advance to his hardy bravery, and to the skill which he had displayed in the various commands that had been entrusted to him. He had plenty of wit and knowledge, and his conversation was brilliant. He was industrious, and an upright administrator, but he did not quite suit Napoleon, who blamed him for lack of initiative, and for being opposed to all active operations. Decrés did not like to travel. It was said that he feared that he might be replaced in his absence. Nevertheless, in a moment of ill-temper and of discouragement, he sent in his resignation. Napoleon wished to keep him, wrote to him, and sent Cambacérès, his usual confidant, to invite him to withdraw his resignation.

Decrés is said to have protected men who did not deserve his choices, and to have neglected a number of good sailors whom he did not like, a line of conduct that made him many enemies. Napoleon saw France's need for a strong and powerful navy, but his plans of maritime expeditions, on which he exhausted the resources of his genius, were not crowned with the success that he had hoped for. He saw himself forced to postpone to a more favorable opportunity his projects to develop this important branch of our national defense, an instrument indispensable to fight against the supremacy of England, and to dictate peace to a government that fomented and financed all the coalitions against France. Decrés, it may be added, was devoted to the head of the government.

The Minister of the Interior was at that time M. Chaptal. He was not only a very distinguished *scientist*. His varied knowledge of agricultural and commercial matters, his application of chemistry to the industries and the arts, his talents as administrator, and his studies of public education, had pointed him out as the right man to direct a ministry that was so wide and varied in its duties.

M. Abrial, formerly a lawyer, who had honorably fulfilled various missions during the Revolution, of which he had been a temperate partisan, and not long before had occupied the post of public prosecutor at the Court of Cassation (supreme court), conducted with zeal and probity the reorganization of the magistrates, in the important post of Minister of Justice. He was replaced, only a few months later, by Régnier, the councilor of state, who afterwards became Duke of Massa, when, after the suppression of the Ministry of Police the duties of that department were united to those of the grand-judge, Minister of Justice.

The public treasury was administered by M. Barbé-Marbois. At one time governor of San Domingo, he had rendered important services in the administration of this colony, effecting useful reforms, repressing abuses, and improving its financial position. Appointed member of the *Conseil des Anciens,* he had been proscribed as a royalist on 18th Fructidor, condemned to deportation, and shipped out to Guyana. Accustomed to the climate of San Domingo, he remained unscathed by the diseases that proved fatal to most of his companions in misfortune. At the time of the Revolution of the 18th Brumaire he was on the island of Oléron, where he had obtained permission to move. The First Consul had recalled him from exile. He had appointed him councilor of state, and then, after the death of M. Dufresne, director of the public treasury, a post which had just been raised to cabinet rank. M. de Marbois's reputation as a strict and upright administrator, and the spirit of order with which he was endowed, guaranteed a reliable and vigilant guardian to the public purse.

M. Portalis, one of the chief writers of the civil code, a man endowed with irresistible eloquence and vast erudition, at this time, was responsible for the management of ecclesiastical affairs. He was promoted later on to the rank of Minister of Religious Worship. His conciliating spirit, his great knowledge of the law, and his rare qualities as a convincing and florid orator, were very useful in his relations with the clergy.

There was a secretary of state whose duty it was to hold the pen at the council of ministers, presided over by the consuls, to communicate the decisions and decrees to the heads of the various departments, to countersign them, and to hold for safe keeping all private papers and secrets of state. Although at that time he did not enjoy the title of minister, the secretary of state filled an analogous post, his functions consisting in completing the work of the other departments and even supplementing them in some of their duties. This post had been confided to M. Maret, later to become Duke of Bassano. The scrupulous diligence with which he had followed the great discussions of the national assembly had initiated him into the business of home government. He had been the first author of the reports of the sittings of that assembly, reports which were the foundation of the *Moniteur,* over whose creation he had presided. He had acquired his knowledge of foreign affairs in the diplomatic negotiations he had been frequently led in London, and at Lille, with Lord Malmesbury and as head of a political division at the ministry for foreign affairs. M. Maret was a man of a conciliating character, and possessed a cultured mind, a trustworthy memory, and unshaken probity and delicacy. Napoleon found him one of the most pleasant of his fellow-workers, and most frequently employed him.

The council of state, divided into five sections: legislation, home affairs, finance, war, and naval affairs, drafted the laws, which members of the same council were charged to support in their discussion before the legislative body. Regulations of public administration, public affairs in litigation, the conflicts between the law courts and the administration, the inner conflicts between different public bodies, all questions of government, and sometimes of foreign politics were discussed and decided.

The council of state was the main hinge of the new government and the workshop where all the important acts emanating from it were elaborated. The various sections were presided over by councilors of state and had special duties, according to their department. The sections were presided over several times a week by the First Consul, and in his absence by Cambacérès, rarely by the Third Consul. Discussion was completely free; each councilor of state had the right to express his opinion, whatever it might be. The First Consul even solicited contradiction, protesting that all he desired was to be enlightened. It sometimes occurred that he yielded to the opinion of the majority, while declaring himself, however, unconvinced. He had summoned to the council of state all kinds of capable men, revolutionaries and royalists, without differences of opinion, demanding only good faith and a desire to assist him in the task which he had assumed. The council was therefore a rare composition of eminent and varied talents, all working with equal zeal towards a common goal.

There was no limit to the number of councilors of state. At that time there were about twenty-five exclusively employed at the council of state. There were about twelve employed on extraordinary services, fulfilling various functions with the title of councilor of state. Amongst the councilors on ordinary services MM. Boulay de la Meurthe, Regnauld de Saint-Jean-d'Angély, Defermon, and Berlier were perhaps the only ones who remained in this capacity, and who were exclusively attached to the council of state until the end of the Empire. The others were detached either for temporary missions, or for permanent employment, or else were promoted to posts that were incompatible with those of councilor of state. The extraordinary councilors of state were called upon, as required, to give their opinions and to deliberate on issues related to the functions they were in charge of. Other men of proven talent, but especially those who were distinguished by their knowledge of special subjects, would come and assist the councilors of state with their opinions, called by a department head who located competent men wherever he could find them.

The most important projects with which the First Consul was occupied at the time when I entered his service were the amnesty of the exiles, the creation of public schools—a prelude to the vast university organization—a modification of the clause of the constitution limiting the First Consul's term of office to ten years, and finally the institution of the Legion of Honor.

As a matter of fact, before a fortnight had elapsed the decree which recalled those in exile was promulgated. They were given amnesty by a senatus consultum. Exception was only made in the case of exiles who had commanded troops against the Republic, those who had served in foreign armies, those who had remained in the employment of the princes of the family of Bourbon, of the generals and representatives of the people who had conspired with the enemy, and finally of the clergy who had refused to resign their sees. The number excluded from the amnesty was ordered not to exceed one thousand, and should be reduced to five hundred in the course of the year. Nine-tenths of the one hundred and fifty thousand Frenchmen who had emigrated and who formed an anti-national population abroad, had left under fear, compulsion, or with unrealistic hopes which were soon dispelled. Little danger was to be feared from their return home. More important was the issue of giving back estates that had not been sold, because this question, above all, interested the most important and the most hostile families. To withhold their estates was to force them into violent opposition to the government. To give them back in totality was to destroy all feeling of gratitude. Forest lands constituted an immense wealth in the hands of the main exiles. A middle course was adopted by which estates of forest land exceeding three hundred arpents were not restored to their former owners. By this decision the government alienated families whose possessions consisted mainly of forest lands. But the individual restitution which the Emperor made won him back these families. It was thanks to this Restoration of their estates, and in particular to that of the forest lands, although it was a limited one, that the aristocracy, under the Restoration, was able to constitute those large landed estates which have become the appendage of what is usually called the Faubourg Saint-Germain, and the very large fortunes that they represented.

This policy, both bold and generous, was made possible by the First Consul, who could take on any potentially evil consequences and showed the strength of the new government. It generally won broad approval, and was only opposed by a small number of republicans, and by some of the generals. It pained them to see the vanquished, whom they could not help consider as their enemies, sharing the spoils with the victors.

That law was promulgated as a senatus consultum. Napoleon upon rising to power, felt it necessary to surround the necessary reforms which he was meditating, with enough formality so as to disguise their arbitrary nature, and provide them with greater guarantees of stability. He had therefore resolved to associate the first body of the state with the most important operations of the government in certain very rare cases. As time went on he extended this participation in the sovereign authority. The interference of the senate in the main political acts might be objected to. It was, however, thought that the main danger arising from the new powers of this body, could be avoided by granting it the privilege of pronouncing senatus consulta only upon the request of the head of the government. The senate respected this initiative during the prosperous days of the Empire, but seized upon it as soon as it could do so with impunity, and turned against the man who had created, honored, and enlarged it, the weapon which he himself had placed in its hands.

Due to the amnesty two men—who had enjoyed the full confidence of the princes of the former House of France—asked for and obtained authorization to re-enter French territory. One of them, the Baron de Breteuil, was introduced to the First Consul, who was very please to speak with him, hearing from this important witness curious details on his diplomatic mission, and obtaining particular information on the councils held by the princes. M. de Breteuil had asked permission to present his nephew to the First Consul, whom he begged to employ him in his administration. Young Breteuil was favorably received, appointed auditor at the council of state, and later appointed to the stewardship of the Austrian provinces ceded by the Peace of Presburg, and later on to various prefectures of the Empire, and beyond the Rhine. He served with zeal till 1814, when old remembrances returned to claim his loyalty. I must add, to be just, that the nephew of Baron de Breteuil was always grateful for the way in which Napoleon received him during his youth.

The other exile who had returned home was M. de Calonne. He did not long enjoy the benefits of the amnesty, for he died one month after his return to France. His struggles against the nobility and the parliaments, a series of difficult intrigues, his unfulfilled ambition, and his lost illusions, all contributed to shorten his days. He had not, however, given up hope of being able to impose his financial schemes. He relied upon his brilliant intelligence and his facility of argument to win over the First Consul. One of his friends, with whom I had some relations, pressed me to obtain an audience for him, convinced that if M. de Calonne could once be heard by the First Consul his cause would be won. The First Consul, however, refused to see him, his mind being fully made up on the value of the financial resources of this minister, and on the lack of stability of his principles. He was not, moreover, in the least inclined to change his Minister of Finance for anyone else. One of his brothers having asked him to put M. Roederer—a councilor of state and a man of great talent and intelligence—at the head of the Ministry of Finance, Napoleon had answered him: "I fully acknowledge all that your protégé is worth, but it might very easily happen that, with all his intelligence, he would give me nothing but fresh water, while with my good Gaudin I can always rely on having good crown pieces."

While the First Consul was preparing to reopen the doors of France to the exiles, he was closing them to those whose enmity was not diminished by the government's leniency. Mesdames de Damas and de Champcenetz were in correspondence with the enemies of the state. Madame de Damas, who had drawn attention on herself by her extreme opinions, and by her incessant attacks on the government, had sheltered Hyde and Limoëlan, who had taken part in the conspiracy of the infernal machine of the 3rd Nivôse. She was escorted to the frontier by the police, and sent to join her husband in exile abroad. Madame de Champcenetz, who was the daughter of a Dutchman named Poter, received orders to return to her own country. She corresponded regularly with M. de Vaudreuil, who was one of the members of the Count d'Artois' council to which the Bishop of Arras, Dutheil, Willot, the Swiss Colonel Baron de Roll and others also belonged.

La Harpe, who was under supervision in Paris, where he made a show of almost fanatical devoutness, after having professed atheism, was removed to a distance of twenty leagues from the capital. The reason of his expulsion was the scandal caused by his furious pronouncements against philosophy and the new institutions. His intolerance and his extreme conceit were excited by the coteries that viewed him as an oracle. Towards the end of 1802 he obtained permission to return to Paris, and died there some months later.

The law that followed right after the amnesty of the exiles was about the organization of public instruction, and was the draft of the creation of the university. Lycées were created in each district of the jurisdiction of a court of appeals. These public schools were directed by professors appointed by the state, and paid from the public treasury. To ensure the success of these establishments, six thousand four hundred scholarships were created, of which two thousand four hundred were reserved for the sons of soldiers, or of judicial, administrative and municipal functionaries. The other four thousand were distributed by competitive examination to pupils of the secondary schools. Special schools for the study of law, natural science, physics, mathematics and drawing, and a military school were instituted under the same law.

It was thanks to this law that a man whose natural gifts, rare talents, and wide range of knowledge lifted to the first rank of literature and politics was educated at the lycée of Marseille. M. Thiers comes from a family of merchants who were engaged in trade in the Levant. Since childhood he remained in the care of his mother (who was a first cousin of Marie Joseph Chénier) and of his grandmother, who had both been reduced to a state bordering on poverty. These two ladies, who belonged to royalist families of the south of France, had conceived for the First Consul an admiration which the news of the execution of the unhappy Duke d'Enghien transformed into hatred. Their feeling was so strong on this subject that although their poverty was such that they could by no means be indifferent to the advantages offered them by the law, they at first refused the offer made them by the municipal authorities of Marseille to recommend their child, who showed the greatest promise, for a scholarship at the lycée of that town. It was not until some friends had added their persuasive arguments that they agreed to benefit from the benevolence of the government. Young Thiers was placed on the list of recommended candidates, and obtained one of the scholarships which the First Consul had reserved for distribution by himself, and to which a sum of twelve hundred francs was added for the young scholar's outfit. It would seem as if a sort of prescience had revealed to Napoleon what marvelous fruits this boy's education would produce. M. Thiers, in relating this anecdote with his witty good nature, added, "Napoleon no doubt did not foresee when he granted me this favor, that he was working at the education of his future historian."

While securing the benefits of education to the sons of soldiers, civil functionaries and others, Napoleon had to provide later for the education of their daughters, in whose future he was no less interested. Houses of education were therefore created. I anticipate the time when these establishments were founded because I shall not have occasion to speak of them in their proper place. In 1806 three houses were constructed for the reception of three hundred pupils. In 1809 six hundred pupils were received into schools established in the castle of Écouen, and in the ancient abbey of St. Denis. Some of these pupils were admitted free of charge, while others only paid half fees. These schools were intended to form women for a position in life equivalent to that which had been occupied by their fathers. The terms were forty pounds per annum. The revenues of these establishments were applied to defraying, in part, their expenses. And finally, in 1810, six new schools were opened for the reception of six hundred pupils, orphans of members of the Legion of Honor. The course of education there was less ambitious. The fees were four hundred francs a year. These establishments were managed on the same principles as the schools at Écouen and St. Denis. The rules there was much stricter, indeed almost claustral. Pupils were admitted from the age of four to the age of twelve, and could remain until their twenty-first year.

The Emperor placed these establishments under the patronage of Queen Hortense. He drafted their regulations, occupied himself with the choice of the lady superiors, selected the places where the schools should be built, entered into all details of order and economy connected with them, and supervised the execution of the instructions which he had given with paternal solicitude.

The Order of the Legion of Honor was instituted at the same time. When the law creating it was introduced before the council of state it was violently opposed. The First Consul defended it successfully, by the force of reason alone, since he allowed it to be discussed quite freely. The tribunate and the legislative body finally voted the law, but with a very much smaller majority than the government had expected. The eloquence of the First Consul, the lofty range of his views, the arguments employed by the expounder and the promoter of the law before the legislative body and the tribunate could not convince some men, still imbued with the leveling ideas of the Revolution, who persisted in considering the creation of a distinction of this kind, albeit without privileges, a blow struck at the spirit and the principles of the Revolution. The great idea of a unique decoration which awarded no prerogative, itself a form of equality—to the soldier as equally as the field-marshal, the simple citizen like the prince or the highest dignitary, were eligible for it—and which has done wonders, needs no justification from me. It speaks for itself.

The project of a modification of the article of the constitution, which limited to ten years the First Consul's tenure of office, gave rise to numerous discussions between him, his two colleagues, and some of the principal senators and members of parliament. Cambacérès was his principal spokesman in this delicate negotiation. A deliberation of the senate had extended to a period of ten years the authority of the chief of the state. This addition only remedied the precariousness of the post rather weakly. On a notification from the council of state, to which the senatus consultum was submitted, this temporary prolongation was converted into a nomination for life. The First Consul wanted that this wish should be submitted to the approval of the people. Therefore a decree of the Consuls ordained that the French nation should be consulted on this question: "Shall Napoleon Bonaparte be Consul for life?" Three million, five hundred and sixty-eight thousand, five hundred and eighty-five votes out of three million, five hundred and seventy thousand, two hundred and fifty-nine citizens who took part in the election replied in the affirmative. I was charged to carry the draft of the message to the senate, to Le Brun, the Third Consul, to receive from him any observations that a fresh reading might suggest.

What things have not been said against the almost complete unanimity of votes in favor of the life consulate and the empire! Some have alleged that the public functionaries who held the registers of votes, had influenced the voters. Others have called the veracity of the lists into question; others, finally pointed out that since constitutions existed, none have ever been presented for acceptance to the people and have been rejected by it, implying thereby that governments trying this experiment know which measures to take to obtain the necessary majority. Those who were living at the time know very well that the consular government had no need use seduction, threats, or fraud. The nation's good sense, the instinct which never deceived it, showed in Napoleon the protector of its cherished interests, the man who truly loved it, and who was working to bring back to France the justice, order, and equality. Its gratitude for the great services which General Bonaparte had rendered was inseparable from the hope of a happy future which it expected from the First Consul. Napoleon could demand a national vote with confidence. Nations never refuse it to governments which feel themselves sufficiently popular to ask it.

About six weeks before my entry into the First Consul's cabinet, there was a performance of two plays. I only speak of this incident because the kind of disgrace which befell the authors caused some sensation at La Malmaison, and was still being talked about when I arrived there. The first play, *Edward in Scotland,* was by Alexander Duval. The author had been very well received by Madame Bonaparte, and by the First Consul. His play had succeeded at its public reading and had also been received with great favor at the first performance; but it was noticed that persons who were known for their ardent royalism had applauded to excess certain passages in which they wanted the public to find allusions.

The First Consul, hearing of this matter, and not knowing the play, went to see it. He found it interesting, but his attention having been attracted by a volley of significant applause, at the passages indicated, which burst from the neighboring boxes, and recognizing that these boxes were occupied by recently amnestied exiles, he was naturally irritated, and considered it his duty to forbid the performance of the play. Amongst the exiles who on this occasion made themselves conspicuous by their applause, was the Duke of Richelieu, who later became a minister under the Restoration. Although he had remained in the service of Russia, he had, by special favor, obtained the authorization to come to Paris. He received orders to leave Paris and French territory without delay. M. Duval, fearing to be compromised by this imprudence on the part of the exiles, had taken refuge with his family at Rennes. The First Consul, however, sent him word that he could come back to Paris, and added that he had no reason to be displeased with him.

The title of the second play was *L'Antichambre.* It had been written without negative intentions, but it contained situations and phrases that could be applied to the political situation and were used with such transparent malevolence by the enemies of the government that its performance could not be tolerated. The author, M. Dupaty, fell into disgrace with the First Consul, who had already been offended by the spitefulness of the imaginary allusions in *Edward in Scotland.*

M. Dupaty, was at that time and officer in the engineers, located in Paris without a regular leave of absence. He received orders to leave for Brest, and to embark with the expedition to San Domingo, but he only remained at Brest a very short time. He obtained permission to return to Paris before the expedition started, and continued his literary work. Amongst a number of very witty comedies which he wrote were several which were dedicated to Napoleon's glory. It was he who arranged the allegorical ballet, "The Hours," which was performed at the Tuileries on the occasion of the Emperor's marriage with Archduchess Marie Louise. He is the author of a rondo written in 1814 for the band of the National Guard, which was composed on the occasion of the farewell taken by the Emperor from the chiefs of this Guard, when he entrusted the Empress and his son to their care before he left to lead the army.

Since I have spoken of plays, this may be the place to relate a service which I had occasion to render to one of the most agreeable of the Opéra ballerinas at the time. This theatre was under the direction of M. de Luçay, as prefect of the Palace. He governed this republic of song and dance with severity. Mademoiselle Chevigny, who was not one of the youngest performers, injured her knee during the performance of a ballet, and remained away from the theatre for a considerable time. M. de Luçay, was getting tired of her prolonged absence, and ordered that a medical inquiry to be made. The doctors reported that the *danseuse* had a stiffened knee, and that it was impossible to say when she would be able to reappear on the stage. Because of this report, she was at once placed on the retired list. Mademoiselle Chevigny, who knew that she would be perfectly able to continue her work if she were granted two or three weeks' rest, was in despair at an exclusion which she considered most unjust. Accompanied by her husband, M. Cellerier, a celebrated architect, she applied to everybody of any influence who could help her have this decision changed. Among others she also applied to me, and I was able to get her three months' holiday, which was very much more than she wanted. Her reappearance on the stage showed that doctors' opinions are not always infallible. She had lost none of her powers, and for many years, both as a light-footed dancer and a consummate actress, she contributed to the enjoyment of the Opera public.

About this time the First Consul was exceedingly irritated against General Reynier, who had just killed General Destaing in a duel. These two generals, who had recently returned from Egypt, had quarreled violently at the time when General Menou took over the command of the army, after the death of General Kléber. Napoleon, greatly affected by the unhappy termination of a campaign which should have been so profitable to France, and so useful to his personal glory, had ordered that all mistakes made under those circumstances should be forgotten, as well as everything that would recall attention to an evil for which there was no remedy. He was very much incensed, and rightly so, at this duel. He exiled General Reynier to his estate in the Nièvre department, strongly defended the memory of General Destaing, and awarded a pension to his widow. This disgrace of one of our most distinguished generals, was also prompted by the opposition which General Reynier had manifested to General Menou, who was far from being his equal in military capacity, but who, thanks to his seniority, had been appointed commander-in-chief of the army in Egypt. This unhappy rivalry had contributed to the ruin of our affairs in that country.

The favor which the First Consul showed to General Menou, whose administrative talents, by the way, he esteemed, was prompted by his desire to protect the General against the excitement caused by the recent events in Egypt, to check its development, and make sure it disappeared.

Doctor Corvisart, being present one morning with me, at the levée of the First Consul, told him of the death of Bichat (who had died the night before) not then thirty years old. This young doctor, a savant of the greatest promise, had enriched science with works of physiology, full of new and fruitful ideas, which have largely extended its domain. This death recalled the remembrance of Desault, his master, who had been the glory of surgery. The First Consul ordered the Minister of the Interior to report on the best means of honoring the memory of these two *savants*. With the minister's report he ordered that a marble tablet perpetuating their memory and recording the services which they had rendered to humanity, should be placed in one of the wards of the Hôtel-Dieu.

The cessation of hostilities between England and France having reopened the French territory to the English, a large number came to Paris. Among persons distinguished by their rank or their birth, who came in the train of Lord Cornwallis, was the son of a Minister of State, famous for his patriotism and his energy, and a friend of Pitt, whose principles he shared. This was young Lord Henry Petty, son of the Marquis of Lansdowne, heir to the titles and to the political opinions and qualities of his father, who himself succeeded Pitt, in 1806, as Chancellor of the Exchequer. Lord H. Petty was accompanied by his tutor, the celebrated writer Dumont from Geneva, the former friend and collaborator of Mirabeau, and author of an interesting book on that celebrated and learned man. Both these gentlemen were presented to the First Consul, who received them with marked favor. |

It was especially after the Peace of Amiens that the English came in numbers to Paris. A great number of English members of parliament, lawyers, officers, and other persons of position, attracted to Paris by the fame of the First Consul, were presented by

Mr. Merry, the English ambassador, who, as I have already said, was formerly secretary to the English Legation at the Amiens Congress. Mr. Fox should be mentioned first of all. This illustrious foreigner came to Paris, less for the purpose of searching among our archives for documents concerning the history of the last two Stuart kings, which he was writing, than to make the acquaintance of the extraordinary man who enjoyed his entire sympathy. Napoleon, on his side, was drawn to Fox by a natural inclination. He received him with marked preference and, admitting him from the first to his intimacy, enjoyed numerous private conversations with him. The two did not always, it is said, agree on matters of politics, but the result of their conversations was that they left each other with mutual esteem. The First Consul ordered all the archives and public establishments to be thrown open to Mr. Fox. He used to accompany him sometimes, notably to the second exhibitions of industrial productions, which took place towards the end of the English statesman's stay in Paris.

During the year which preceded the discovery of the Georges plot, I had not seen General Moreau at the Tuileries. I have accordingly nothing to say about this general, whose peculiarities are, however, well-known. I learned that he had rejected all the First Consul's advances, and refused his numerous invitations. From the time of his marriage with Madame Hulot, to which Madame Bonaparte had contributed, his mother-in-law, a jealous and troublesome woman, did all she could to foment discord between these two rivals in military glory. Madame Hulot had complained of having to wait to be received by Madame Bonaparte, when she called upon her, and said that she had no inclination at all for the antechamber of an equal. General Moreau used to speak with affected frivolity of the hostile attempts against the person of the First Consul, or against the acts of his government. This coolness, in short, degenerated into an enmity which led Moreau to enter into an alliance unworthy of his glory, with the enemies of the state, an alliance in which he found his death—wounded, in the midst of the adversaries of France, by a French cannonball.

An interview, which attracted but little attention at the time, took place in the middle of 1802, between the Emperor of Russia and the King of Prussia, at Memel, the eastern port of the Prussian States. The latter sovereign had been reigning for five years. The Emperor Alexander had just succeeded his father, the unfortunate Paul I, who had been assassinated three months previously in his St. Petersburg palace. These princes, both young men, desired to make the acquaintance of each other. The Emperor of Russia proposed a friendly meeting, which the King readily accepted. The Queen of Prussia, in all the splendor of her youth and beauty, accompanied the King, and contributed greatly to the close friendship which bound the two sovereigns together. The result of this friendship was that from that point on Prussia was attracted into Russia's sphere of influence.

The First Consul, anxious not to appear hostile to this meeting although absent from it, and curious to know what would happen there, sent an officer of the palace, a shrewd observer, to attend. Major Dumoustier, who afterwards became general, an officer of great distinction and of really antique virtue, was charged to convey the Consul's compliments to the two kings. He carried a letter from the First Consul to the King of Prussia, which expressed Napoleon's satisfaction at the arrangement which had been concluded for the settlement of the indemnity to Prussia by the provisions of the Treaty of Lunéville, which had largely increased the territories of the King of Prussia.

The indemnity of the Prince of Nassau-Orange, the king's father-in-law, had been settled at the same time in accordance with his wishes. Large indemnities had been stipulated in favor of the houses of Bavaria, Würtemberg, and Baden, linked to the Russian imperial house by family ties. This news, coming at so favorable a moment, was received with great pleasure by the two princes, and disposed the Emperor of Russia to join with the First Consul in the apportionment of the lands for the indemnification of the small kings who had been dispossessed on the left bank of the Rhine.

This journey of the Emperor of Russia and of the King of Prussia, far from their capitals, was the prelude to those meetings of the monarchs of Germany and of the North, and of those nomadic congresses which became so frequent twelve years later.

Another officer of the palace was sent at about the same time to Algiers on another kind of mission. In spite of the peace concluded with the Barbary States, the corsairs of the regency, yielding to their habits of piracy, were recommencing their raids on our coasts, and had even dared to attack our flag. The First Consul sent a naval division before Algiers, under the command of Admiral Leissègues. He was accompanied on board by Adjutant Hulin, who was commissioned to demand reparation for these insults, and for the injuries caused to our trade by the Dey. The impression which Hulin's lofty stature, his martial attitude, and the richness of his embroideries made upon these savages, completed what had begun with the First Consul's letter, and the appearance of the French fleet. The Dey submitted on every point, released all prisoners of French or allied nationality, and sent an ambassador loaded with presents to Paris.

I witnessed the last republican celebration of the anniversary of July 14 at the Tuileries Palace. A grand parade took place that day in the Carrousel court, at which the First Consul presented flags to the light infantry regiments, represented for the occasion by the colonel and three officers of each regiment.

Just before the parade, the Prefect of the Seine department, accompanied by two of the mayors of Paris, presented the First Consul with a richly caparisoned horse of the French breed.

The diplomatic body was received in solemn audience. Foreigners of distinction were presented by the ambassadors or plenipotentiary ministers of their courts. Marriages were celebrated at the cost of the government in each of the twelve arrondissements of Paris. Banquets, illuminations, and fireworks crowned this fête.

There was no ceremony at the Tuileries on the July 14 of the following year. The First Consul and Madame Bonaparte were away, on a three weeks' journey in the Seine-Inférieure and Oise departments.

On the same day in the year 1804, Napoleon, then Emperor, rode to the Invalides, through a line formed by the troops of the garrison, preceded by the marshals and the great officers of the Empire, by the colonels of the guard, and by his aides-de-camp. The Empress, accompanied by the sisters and sisters-in-law of the Emperor, her ladies, her chamberlains, and her equerries, had preceded him at noon to the Invalides. A mass was celebrated by the Cardinal Legate. After the religious ceremony a distribution of decorations took place, handed by Napoleon in person to each legionary, as he took them from the hands of the Grand Chancellor of the Order. A *Te Deum* terminated the ceremony. In the evening all public buildings were illuminated, a concert was given on the terrace of the Tuileries Palace, and fireworks were displayed on the Pont-Neuf.

Chapter III

One night, during one of the First Consul's stays at La Malmaison, in 1802, he was awaked by a courier from Spain, who brought some very urgent dispatches from General Lannes, the French ambassador at Lisbon. As soon as Napoleon had read these dispatches he gave orders that the courier should be ready to start on the return-journey at a moment's notice. I must go back in my story to explain the preceding events.

In the course of November 1801 General Lannes, who was sole commander of the consular guard, had been forced to resign in consequence of some irregularities which had occurred in the regimental treasury. This was the truth of the matter. The First Consul had promised to pay the General's house-furnishing expenses. When the bills were submitted to him he refused to pay them, as they far exceeded what he had expected. General Lannes—who was accustomed to give and spend without counting, and had no idea at all as to how to conduct business, and had never applied to Bonaparte in vain, when in want of money—since the First Consul was so bound by the promise he had made, Lannes could think of no better plan to pay his furniture bills than to have the treasurer of the regiment of guards simply hand him the amount. Such conduct could not be tolerated, and General Lannes lost his command. The consular guard was reorganized more in accordance with its requirements, and the sole command which had till then existed was broken up into four, each vested in a colonel-general. To punish General Lannes for his unbusiness-like proceedings, and anxious to put a stop to the familiarity which had in some way prompted him to act as he had done, the First Consul sent him away for a time, ordering him on a mission to Lisbon. I remember dining with him about this time, at Joseph Bonaparte's table, and hearing with what sarcasm he betrayed his displeasure at the way in which he had been treated. M. de Champigny, who had just been appointed ambassador to Vienna, was present at the dinner.

General Lannes, little acquainted as he was with diplomatic forms, did not at first succeed in his new post. The Portuguese Ministry, and more especially the Minister of Foreign Affairs, Don Joaô d'Almeida, was devoted to England. All diplomatic documents handed in by the French ambassador were passed on to Lord Fitzgerald, the English ambassador, and the answers were concocted with him. The Prince Regent of Portugal, either deceived or dominated by his minister, was also not favorably disposed towards the French representative. General Lannes soon felt that his military pride, his self esteem, and his patience had been flouted beyond endurance. Without warning either the Portuguese or his own government, he left Lisbon suddenly, giving orders to his household to follow him. He presented himself at the first posting-establishment and demanded horses. The postmaster informed him that an order was necessary, and that without it he must refuse to accommodate him. General Lannes imperiously orders him to have horses made ready, and laying his hand on his sword threatens to strike him, unless his order is immediately obeyed. The postmaster is forced to submit. General Lannes crossed Portugal and Spain in haste, and, just before arriving at Bayonne, sends his valet de chambre on ahead with a letter to the First Consul, announcing his arrival. The valet, returning with an answer to his letter, finds his master at Orléans. The First Consul's orders were that the General should remain where the courier found him. He had calculated that General Lannes would not have passed Bayonne. Lannes, however, receiving this order at Orléans, thought himself justified from his proximity to Paris in pushing on to the capital. The First Consul refused to receive him.

In the meanwhile the greatest anxiety was felt by the Portuguese government. It was a matter of importance that General Lannes's conduct should be disapproved of, and that Portugal should not incur the resentment of France. The general had Talleyrand against him, and Talleyrand, insisting on the violation of diplomatic forms which had been committed, demanded the revocation of our ambassador to Lisbon. The First Consul would not have tolerated such conduct from anybody else, but he knew that though General Lannes was no diplomat, he was an honest man, who had too much judgment to allow himself to be made a dupe of. He finally agreed to see him, and was satisfied with his explanations, although he blamed his conduct.

Don Joaô scattered gold by handfuls in Paris to prevent the return of General Lannes to Lisbon. The Prince Regent, acting on information which had reached him, sent two men in whom he had confidence to Paris; and this without the knowledge of his minister. One of them was a Frenchman, whom I was acquainted with, and who had been living in Portugal for many years. While Almeida was assuring the Prince Regent that General Lannes had fallen into complete disgrace, the prince's agents reported that a reconciliation had taken place, and that the ambassador had altogether been restored to the First Consul's good graces. The Prince Regent then thought it right—for something decisive had to be done—to ask for his return. While the Portuguese ministers were flattering themselves that they would make good their escape from the scrape in which they had been involved, the First Consul notified the Prince Regent that he would consent to the return of his ambassador to Lisbon, and that he would forget the reasons for displeasure which the Portuguese government had given him; but that, in return for this concession, he expected a concession on the prince's part, namely the dismissal of the Minister of Foreign Affairs, whose partiality for the English, and whose bad faith, had been the causes of what had happened. The Prince Regent was only too glad to accept this settlement of the affair. Don Joaô d'Almeida was dismissed, and General Lannes returned to Lisbon. His triumph was complete. The Prince Regent received him at first with a cordiality which was more affected than real, but growing to like him eventually became on terms of great intimacy with him. General Lannes, who had plenty of natural shrewdness, understood his position. The Portuguese nobility of that time, proud and poor, held aloof, and hesitated to make the first advances. General Lannes gave a sumptuous ball, and invited everybody whose names had been inscribed on the embassy register. He did the honors of this ball with all possible refinements, and nothing else was talked about in Lisbon. Those of the aristocracy who were not present, complained at not having been invited. They were informed, in answer, that if the ambassador had thought that an invitation would have been agreeable to them, he would have sent it, and that he should be delighted and honored if they would call upon him. The hidalgos crowded to leave their names at his house. General Lannes gave another ball to which they were all invited. The invitations were eagerly accepted and from that time forward the aristocracy frequented the French embassy. Thanks to his intimacy with the Prince Regent the French *envoyé* was able to assist some of these needy noblemen. His credit at court was great, and his recommendations were always favorably listened to. The jurisdiction of his embassy, accordingly, was unlimited, nor did the Portuguese government in any way try to restrict it. No such tolerance was shown to the ambassadors of other powers. Our ambassador's influence in Lisbon was so well established, that when he returned to France he was in a position to dispose of Portugal as Napoleon might desire.

It is calculated that the sum spent in Paris to prevent the return of General Lannes amounted to four millions of francs. Where the greater part of this money went to can easily be guessed. When the General heard of this he remarked jocularly: "What clumsy fellows! If they had only offered me half that amount I wouldn't have gone back to Lisbon."

And so it happened that the cause of France was better served by our ambassador's impetuous susceptibility than it would have been by the skill of the most consummate diplomat. The First Consul understood, better than his Minister of Foreign Affairs, to what advantage he could turn it. It is true that Napoleon, at least, saw everything in the light of national interest, and in that light alone.

It is so ordained here below that, side by side with any success there is always a jealous desire to diminish its merit. And so it was that when the money-sacrifices made by the Portuguese ministers to prevent the return of General Lannes to Lisbon were heard of, it was stated, in face of the General's spontaneous exclamation, that M. de Binau, ambassador from Saxony to France, had been commissioned by him to carry a proposal to M. de Souza, Portuguese ambassador to Paris. This proposal, it was said, was to the effect that if a million francs were given to the general he would undertake to refuse to return to Lisbon, in spite of any pressure from the First Consul.

This is what Madame de Souza, the wife of the Portuguese ambassador told me on this subject. Madame de Souza being at La Malmaison one day, met the First Consul as he was going to Madame Bonaparte. He led her aside by the arm: "What does M. de Souza mean," he asked irritably, "by offering money to my ambassador to prevent his returning to Lisbon?"

Madame de Souza protested that, on the contrary, it was to M. de Souza that the proposal was made.

"And what is there to prove that?" said the First Consul.

"The treasury of the Consular Guard!" cried Madame de Souza, her excitement getting the better of her reflection, in allusion to the deficit in the accounts of this regiment when it was under General Lannes's command.

The First Consul, knowing the general's honesty, never said a word, but turned his back on Madame de Souza.

Slightly disturbed by this silence, and the tacit disapproval which the Consul's manner implied, Madame de Souza went to Josephine and told her what had just passed between the First Consul and herself.

Josephine advised her to return to Paris at once, to shut herself up and not to see anybody for eight days, so that the First Consul might see that she had not communicated with anyone.

Madame de Souza followed this advice, pretended to be ill, and took to her bed, refusing to receive anybody.

It is rather difficult to understand what the object of all these maneuvers was since they were so much trouble for nothing. The First Consul very soon forgot his quarrel with Madame de Souza, and never alluded to it again in her presence.

During the first six months that followed the Peace of Amiens, the first Consul led an almost idle life at La Malmaison, dreaming of the improvements which he could introduce into the various departments of his government; of the encouragements which might be given to agriculture and industry; of the various works which might be carried out for the improvement and embellishment of Paris and the departments, which he proposed to visit in turn; and finally of the arts of peace.

During this pause in the midst of a life so busy and so fully occupied, he had projected a league of the maritime powers for driving the Barbary people from the coast of Africa, their lands to be afterwards used for planting sugar, coffee, cotton, and produce which had to be drawn from remote colonies. If the plan of this league could have been carried through, it would have diverted him from the expedition intended for the reconquest of the island of San Domingo. The idea had been proposed by Joseph Bonaparte, and was highly approved of by the First Consul. Joseph Bonaparte was anxious that the four powers who had signed the Amiens treaty should take part in this league. It was indeed shameful that Europe should tolerate, opposite to her, a nest of pirates, who levied blackmail on her with insolence, and who each year carried off into the cruelest slavery the prisoners they had captured on sea or on land—pirates to whom nothing was sacred, and who rejected our arts and our civilization. It was useless to hope to bring them to accept the relations and the conventions by which international rights are established between civilized States.

The loss of Egypt enhanced the value of the resources which a colonization of the Barbary States, so conveniently close at hand, with a cultivation of the produce of the islands of America, would have placed in the hands of the various powers. The plan of a conquest of this vast region was carefully examined in the cabinet of the Minister of Marine. A first step towards carrying it into effect was indeed made, by a mission with which the Spanish government entrusted Badia, a clever and adventurous traveler. The *Moniteur* of 14th Thermidor, Year X, reported that two Spanish *savants,* charged with exploration of these countries, had passed through Paris. This plan of an expedition was perhaps one of the reasons for the break of the Peace of Amiens, and the renewal of hostilities which ensued that prevented the First Consul from carrying it out. The great events which were played out on the stage of Europe forced him to renounce his scheme for the time being, but he did not lose sight of a plan which, from the time of the renewal of hostilities with England, was one of the chief subjects of his thoughts.

On April 18, 1808, Napoleon, at the Château de Marrac, near Bayonne, where he had been summoned because of the affairs in Spain, wrote the following letter to the

Minister of Marine:

"MONSIEUR DECRÉS.—Think over the Algiers expedition both as a military and a naval campaign. If France could get a foot down on this part of the coast of Africa, England would have cause to reflect.

"Is there any port on this coast where a squadron of ships would be under cover from a superior force?

"What are the ports by which the army, once landed, could be resupplied?

"How many ports could the enemy blockade simultaneously?

"In Egypt there was, after all, only the port of Alexandria. Rosetta was a very dangerous harbor; still it was counted. I think that there are a dozen here.

"How many frigates, brigs, and storeships could they hold?

"Could Admiral Ganteaume's squadron enter the port of Algiers, and be sheltered against a superior force?

"At what time of the year is the air good, and the plague no longer to be feared? I imagine that it is in October.

"After having studied the Algiers expedition give your careful attention to the Tunis campaign. Write a confidential letter about it to Ganteaume, who, before coming to Paris, could get the necessary information. His inquiries should extend as far as Oran and should bear on the land, as well as the maritime, aspects of the proposed expedition. What we must find out about the inland and whether there are roads and water. I calculate that twenty thousand men will be necessary for this expedition. You will understand that the enemy is to be led to believe that Sicily is the object of this expedition, and that they will be nicely surprised when, instead, it proves to be Algiers. You need not answer me before a month. In the meanwhile get your information so that when you do answer me there shall be no 'buts,' no 'ifs,' and no 'becauses.'

"Send one of your engineers, a man who knows how to hold his tongue, out on a brig. Let him talk with M. Thainville, but be sure to select a man of tact and of talent. This engineer should have some military as well as some naval knowledge. He must walk about both on the inside and on the outside of the fortifications, and as soon as he returns home write down what he has noticed, so that he can bring us back plain facts and not merely his own dreams. Consult with Sanson as to the best man to choose. You will be able to find exact information in the archives of the Foreign Office and of the Ministry of War. Have these archives, as well as your own, looked through. Information about these countries has always been asked for in France."

Several Frenchmen who had exercised civil or diplomatic functions in the Algiers Regency, heads of French establishments in that country, engineers and naval officers who had discharged special duties there, were all consulted. M. Jean Bon-Saint-André, who had been commissioner of the government at Algiers, under the Directoire, handed a detailed memorandum, in which all the questions put to him were answered, to the Minister of Marine.

Napoleon's attention was also taken up with the scheme for reorganizing the Academies. The term "Academy" was suppressed. The Institut was divided into four sections. The first was termed "Class of Physical and Mathematical Sciences." The second, styled "Class of the French Language and Literature," answered to the formerly known French Academy. The third was the "Class of Ancient History and Literature," and the fourth that of "The Fine Arts." The "Class of Moral and Political Sciences," created by the law of Year IV, was suppressed and merged with that of *belles-lettres.* It seemed superfluous to the First Consul. He supported his opinion on this matter with reasons which I do not think it necessary to examine. His principal motive was not, as has been said, his dislike for philosophy. He often had expressed himself on this matter, but he was then convinced that the discussion of political matters had still, at that time, its disadvantages.

The eight or nine months which followed the Peace of Amiens were divided between La Malmaison and St. Cloud, which the First Consul went to live in during the spring of that year. This palace, although not vast, afforded a beautiful and comfortable residence, well suited to Napoleon's habits and requirements, and provided with magnificent gardens. His workroom was very large, and its walls were literally covered with books, from the floor to the ceiling. He had himself designed his writing-table, which was in the shape of a bass. Numerous papers were spread out on its wings. His usual place was on a settee covered with green taffeta, which stood near the mantlepiece, on which were two fine bronze busts of Scipio and of Hannibal. Behind the settee, in a corner, was my writing-table. His study was accessed through a bedroom, which he did not occupy. His apartment was on the floor above, and communicated with this room through a private staircase. It consisted of three plainly furnished rooms. The only ornament of the bedroom on the ground floor, which looked out on the garden, was an antique bust of Caesar, which stood on the mantlepiece. Beyond the First Consul's workroom was a small drawing room, where he used to receive the Minister of Foreign Affairs, who, by reason of the nature of the business of his department, had no reports to address to the council of state. This drawing room was also used for private audiences; it was decorated with a fine portrait of Charles XII. The First Consul was dissatisfied that this portrait has been selected, and had it replaced by a portrait of Gustavus Adolphus, for whom he had a particular esteem.

Paisiello came to Paris in the spring of that year, summoned by the First Consul, whose intention it was to entrust him with the direction of the Opéra and of the Conservatory of Music. Napoleon admired this celebrated composer's talents. He used to be so delighted with Nina's pastorale, *Gia il sol si ciela dietro alla montagna,* that he said he could listen to it with pleasure every evening. Paisiello was then over sixty. He had hesitated about coming to Paris, fearing to expose his gray hairs to the criticisms of his rivals, and dreading to compromise his great musical reputation. He was received with great honor by Napoleon, and with deference by the artists. He refused to accept any other post than that of chapel master, and restricted himself to the composition of masses and motets. The only opera which he composed in Paris was *Proserpine.* It was only moderately successful; a slight reversal which somewhat grieved him.

After residing in France for three years his desire to see his country again, and to take his wife home to a milder climate, induced him to return to Italy. He went home with a pension from the Emperor, and loaded with presents. M. Lesueur, whose talents he admired, succeeded him as chapel-master. Paisiello used to send Napoleon a sacred composition each year, for the anniversary of the Emperor's celebration. He also paraphrased the *Stabat Mater* of Pergolesi, which was performed in the Imperial Chapel. I have preserved many letters from this excellent man, which he wrote when sending his compositions, and in which he expressed his gratitude to and admiration for the

Emperor. I am convinced that these professions, allowance being made for their Italian emphasis, were quite sincere.

Canova was sent for at about the same time. He came to St. Cloud to execute the bust of Napoleon, and devoted himself to this piece of work for several days with a veritable predilection. The First Consul used to lunch in the large drawing room, which led into his apartments, so that the celebrated sculptor might work more at his ease during the meal. The drawing room was afterwards ornamented with portraits of the Bonaparte family. When Napoleon became Emperor he used to receive all the members of his family who happened to be in Paris at dinner every Sunday, and spent the evening with them in his drawing room. A large balcony, on to which this drawing room opened, communicated between the private apartment of Napoleon and that of Josephine, afterwards occupied by Marie Louise.

I used sometimes to remain with Canova after the sittings, and to accompany him into the gardens. He spoke bitterly of the statues he saw there, and pointed out to me the decadence of good taste which they proved. He regretted that the artists of the time of Louis XV, and especially Boucher, should have applied their great talents to works which he considered pitiful. A reproach of another kind might be leveled against Canova himself. He carried off the model of Napoleon's bust, a model true to nature, and most noble in likeness, and which, on this account, had been generally admired. I do not know why, renouncing the likeness, which ought to be the first merit of a bust or a portrait, he made an idealized head. However grand a character he may have wished to bestow on his work, he could not hope to make a more heroic face than the original.

It was after this bust that Canova executed the colossal statue of Napoleon which he sent to Paris in 1811. The statue may be admired as a work of art, but the want of resemblance in the head, and its nudity, displeased the Emperor. It was placed at the Louvre without having been previously exhibited. It was this same statue which either was bought by the Duke of Wellington, or was given to him by the government, in 1815. It was carried off to England as a trophy, and placed in a spot very unworthy of it, and in a way which does little honor to the delicacy of feeling of the victor. One of our sculptors, as remarkable for his great talents as for his national feeling, as he was returning from a walk in London, saw a number of people stopping before a partly-opened door of a mansion—the mansion of the Duke of Wellington. Prompted by curiosity to approach, his astonishment can be imagined in recognizing, in the object which was attracting the eyes of the curious, Canova's beautiful statue of Napoleon, placed at the foot of a staircase, and being used to hang cloaks and hats on.

I remember that one day the First Consul brought back a quatrain, on his return from Josephine's apartment, where he had been spending an hour. He threw the poem on his writing-table, and said that it had been composed by Madame Fanny de Beauharnais. It was a play of words on the word Bonaparte, and the last line, which is all that I remember, ran as follows: "*La bonne part sera la nôtre.*"*

The First Consul, while doing justice to the author's intentions, which he considered better than their execution, took pleasure in speaking of the good qualities of Madame de Beauharnais, Josephine's aunt. He praised the gentleness and the goodness of her character. Even if he was then under the first impression of this lady's innocent flatteries, the

* "The good part shall belong to us."

impression was a lasting one, as he never ceased his protection of Nelson and the granddaughter. The son was appointed senator in 1804, the senatorship of Amiens having been granted to him. When the Emperor married the Archduchess Marie Louise, he placed him in her service as gentleman-in-waiting. In 1806, he married Stéphanie de Beauharnais, the senator's daughter, born of a first marriage, to Prince Charles, the grandson of the Duke of Baden, whom he succeeded in 1811.

Some days later, Madame Bonaparte came and knocked at the door of the cabinet. She immediately entered, followed by the usher, who without a word placed a basket covered over with a cloth in the center of the room and withdrew. While Napoleon was waiting for the explanation of this enigma Madame Bonaparte took off the cloth which covered the basket. A little man, not more than eighteen inches high, who was lying down in the basket, raised himself with difficulty and, leaning with his two hands on the handle of the basket, turned a pair of dark and shining, but lusterless, eyes upon us. The dwarf was dressed in complete hussar uniform, with the red shako, vest, and dolman, regulation boots, and was girt with a saber which kept entangling itself in his little legs. There was nothing monstrous about him except his extreme smallness. His limbs were well-made, his features, if inert, were regular. Nevertheless the evident insensibility of this misconception, whose life seemed merely mechanical, and whose intelligence seemed destined never to develop—for he was said to be then seventeen years old—his debility, the pale and bilious color of his skin, and his wizened and sickly appearance, were thought to be disgusting.

The sight of this poor disinherited creature, nature's cruel sport, placed face to face with a full-grown being in whom the same nature had been pleased to unite a majesty of features to a superiority of genius, would have offered a singular contrast to the eyes of an observer. The fine and impressionable organism of Napoleon evidently suffered from so painful a sight, and without one word of comment, he prayed his wife to remove the dwarf from his eyes.

The union of Piedmont to France took place in the month of September, 1802. This occurrence gave rise to no recriminations; it had been expected for a long time. Piedmont, the throne of which remained untenanted after the retirement of the king to the island of Sardinia, was in pawn in the hands of France either to serve as an indemnity, or to be used in other diplomatic combinations. The fate of this country having been passed over in silence in the Treaties of Amiens and Lunéville, and Russia not having asked for its restitution to the House of Savoy, its incorporation into French territory was consummated by a senatus consultum. General Jourdan, who combined the functions of military governor of these provinces with those of general administrator, was replaced by General Menou. The First Consul had certain prejudices against Jourdan, which he afterwards discarded. Later at St. Helena he expressed his regret for having misunderstood him, and spoke of him in terms which do honor to them both.

Another event, which occurred about a month later, and which caused no more sensation, was the union with France of the Duchies of Parma and Piacenza, brought about by the death of the sovereign of those states. By the Treaty of Lunéville, Austria had lost Tuscany, which was given to the Infante of Parma, who was married to a daughter of Charles IV, King of Spain. The French government had immediately put the Infante in possession of his kingdom, and he had assumed the title of King of Etruria. In exchange for the life-crown, with which the preponderating influence of the First Consul had endowed this prince, the Duchies of Parma and Piacenza had been ceded to France, but Napoleon had desired that the old Duke should finish his days there in peace.

The latter, encouraged by the King of Spain in the hope that after his death his states would be added to the Kingdom of Etruria, had appointed the dowager-duchess Queen Regent in the name of his son, by his last will and testament. This testament, which was without value, was set aside. French officials came to take possession of the country, and M. Moreau de Saint-Méry, who was protected by Madame Bonaparte, was sent there as general administrator.

The island of Elba, which had been retroceded to France by the King of Etruria, was united to France at the same time as Piedmont.

The power of Napoleon bestowed on France two states, reserved to strange destinies. The sovereignty of the one was to devolve on a daughter of Austria, illusory pledge of an ephemeral alliance; the other was to provide the founder of the most powerful empire in the world with a modest refuge, a harbor to find shelter between two shipwrecks.

The monotony of Napoleon's sedentary life in his study was interrupted about this time by a fortnight's journey, which he undertook towards the end of October, going to visit the manufactories of the Seine-Inferieure and Oise departments. Napoleon was accompanied on this short journey by Madame Bonaparte. He left after having given General Andréossy—appointed ambassador to London—his farewell audience.

The First Consul visited the St. Cyr Military School and examined every detail. At Ivry he visited the battlefield made famous by Henry IV's victory, and, accompanied by the mayor and numerous citizens of the town, examined the positions that had been occupied by the two armies, rectifying with his martial instinct the information given to him, and judging with his eagle eye the faults or the skill of the tactics both of vanquished and victors.

Twenty young girls presented Josephine with flowers and verses at Evreux. The cloth-manufacturers of Louviers and Elbeuf, and the copper foundries of Romilly, attracted the attention of the Consul, and won his praise. Two days after leaving Paris, the First Consul arrived at Rouen, followed by the entire population. The three days which he spent there were devoted to reconnoitering the heights with which the town is surrounded—which was always the first thing he did when visiting any large town—and afterwards to visiting the factories. In his careful examination of these establishments he displayed the same spirit of investigation which always characterized him, and which was inspired by his desire to increase the nation's prosperity. He received the archbishop, the prefect, the mayors, the courts of justice and commerce, the military and civil authorities, the scientific societies, and the principal functionaries, conversing at length with each on his specialty, and with all on the questions of general interest to the welfare of the department. He appeared at the theatre, where he was received with acclamation, and afterwards at some receptions given in his honor. All the corporations were presented to Josephine, who received them with her usual good grace and tact.

From Rouen, the First Consul went to Le Havre. He stopped at Caudebec, at Bolbec, and at Yvetot. He embarked on a lugger at five in the morning to visit Honfleur, accompanied by M. de Montcabrié, who was in command of the boat. On his return, he visited Dieppe, Tréport, Forges, and Beauvais. Exhibitions of the local industries were prepared for his inspection in the various manufacturing towns through which he passed.

It is superfluous to add that this excursion, undertaken for the purpose of benefiting the various regions visited, was not a mere fruitless pleasure-trip. This journey had a political objective as well, namely, to show our eternal rivals what perfect harmony existed between the nation and its chief, and to what advantage the latter could turn the resources of the country. The First Consul and Madame Bonaparte were received with genuine enthusiasm everywhere. Companies of mounted men acted as their escort and guard of honor in each town through which they passed.

Shortly afterwards Napoleon went to visit the works of the Ourcq Canal, which had recently started. He therefore left Paris at six o'clock on a fine morning towards the end of January, accompanied by several generals and three aides-de-camp. He rode over the eighteen leagues which form the extent of the canal in five hours. He slept at Lisy, at the house of General d'Harville, uncle of Colonel Caulaincourt, his aide-de-camp, Madame Bonaparte having gone to Lisy the previous day. On the morrow, at daybreak, the First Consul rode to Marueil, where the water for the canal is taken. He found the Prefect of Paris there, and with him the chief engineer, Gérard, who directed the works. On his way back he stayed at Meaux for two hours. He received the subprefect there, the mayor, and the principal authorities, in the big room of the town hall. He returned to Paris the same evening. I accompanied him on his journey on horseback, and it was a pleasant change from the stay-at-home life, which I only grew to like once I was no longer compelled to live it.

The year 1802 brought with it the retirement of Fouché, and the suppression of the Ministry of Police. M. Régnier, who afterwards became Duke of Massa, the Grand Judge, was put at the head of the Ministries of Police and of Justice, merged into one single department. A justifiable dislike for Fouché prompted Napoleon to remove him. The way in which this turbulent man managed his ministry was a cause of anxiety to the First Consul. It offended him to see Fouché, in spite of his express commands, interfering in his home, in his private domestic affairs, under the pretence of exercising a necessary supervision. He was delighted to escape from the guardianship of such a man. Fouché was always a suspicious person in his eyes, on account of his crooked ways and his meddlesome mind; nevertheless he again returned to the ministry within two years of his dismissal. Napoleon dismissed him again in 1810, acting upon the same instinct, but once more took him on in 1815. Clear reason rejects any belief in fate, and yet who will not be struck by the sight of this evil genius, the object of Napoleon's just dislike and repugnance, twice removed from his post with an advancement in honors, and twice returning to boldly take his place at the council, dominating the destinies of the Emperor by his cunning and his spirit of intrigue, and finally taking part in his overthrow.

Napoleon used to compare the reports of the Minister of Police with those of the prefects, concerning provincial matters; and with the reports of the prefect of police, who was never in accordance with the minister, in matters concerning Paris.

His other police services, which might be called official, to distinguish them from the private police, were the service under the command of the first inspector of the gendarmerie, and that of the commander of the Paris garrison. There were one or two other police services of little importance, the reports of which he frequently neglected to read. A retired major, who was as honest as a man can be in such a profession, and who was not intriguing, was in charge of the subaltern military police of Paris.

Count de Survillers—Joseph Bonaparte—has set forth in the following brief remarks, the motives which prompted the First Consul first to abolish the Ministry of Police and afterwards to reestablish it:

"The Ministry of Police was an institution founded by the Directoire, and not by the Convention. It dates from 1796. The Revolution had the Committee of Public Safety. Napoleon found the Ministry of Police established. He preserved it until he thought that he could do without it. He united it, in 1802, after the signing of general peace, to the Ministry of Justice, so as to replace the ardent, rapid, and arbitrary action of a special administration, by the slow and methodical procedure of the magistrates and the *procureurs-généraux*. But conspiracies arose. The slow steps of justice no longer sufficed under the circumstances. A return to police measures became necessary. Réal was charged with their execution, under the orders of the grand judge. That was insufficient to reach the objective, and the Ministry of Police was reestablished. It was suppressed, as a matter of principle, in Napoleon's mind. Those were the obvious causes of the reestablishment of that ministry."

One of Napoleon's methods of government, a method in favor in almost every country, was to open letters in the post. If this method can be tolerated at all, it is only in the hands of the head of a government whose morality and prudence can eliminate the inherent danger. But this guarantee does not always exist in the man at the head of affairs, and when such a man does exist he is not immortal.

Upon his rise to power, the First Consul had found, at the general post office, a department which was known by the name of the Black Cabinet. Several clerks who had grown gray in this work, were appointed to open such letters as were indicated to them by the postmaster-general, at that time M. Laforêt, who afterwards became ambassador, senator, and peer of France. This department was used by nearly everybody at that time. The civil and military authorities in the provinces had the right to intercept letters, to open them, to make use of their contents, to send copies or even the originals to Paris, where they were read by the members of the Directoire, the ministers, and their friends. The First Consul, in appointing his former aide-de-camp Lavalette as postmaster-general, forbade that any letters should be intercepted or communicated to any authorities whatsoever, and he made the various postmasters responsible for the commission of any such offense. These precautions prove that Napoleon had it at heart to mitigate what was arbitrary in this system. The majority of the numerous agents kept in Paris by foreign ministries, a few people mixed up in political intrigues, some officials in various branches of the public service, who did not enjoy the complete confidence of the new government, or who, for one reason or another, were objects of suspicion, were named to the department, with the object of having their correspondence subjected to particular scrutiny. Some important information was obtained in this manner, but no letter, whether written by a person or addressed to him, no matter how grave its contents might be, was considered sufficient by Napoleon for his definite conviction. Until his suspicions had been confirmed, the letter was held in reserve.

Sometimes use was made of this means in support of private interests, of some denunciation, or to assist friends. The sagacity and moderation of Napoleon, and the numberless sources of information which he possessed, foiled all these maneuvers. This violation of postal secrecy, which I shall not attempt to defend from a moral point of view, because of the grave disadvantages which such a system might have presented in the hands of Napoleon's successors who possessed neither his discretion nor his perspicacity, was an instrument without danger, and often very useful in his hands. On an indication furnished by a letter, the Emperor got at the truth, by investigation, research, and contradictory reports, which never failed to enlighten him. He was often able, like a tutelary Providence, thanks to this system, to set straight an injustice that had been committed, to redress grievances, and to dispense benefits and assistance at the time when those who were the objects of his justice or of his benevolence expected it the least.

Although it was well-known that those who did not want their letters to be read, did not send them in the mail, it rarely happened that some valuable information was not gathered in this way. I remember that one day the Emperor, forgetting that since the reorganization of the post office the Minister of Finance had no connection with the Black Cabinet, said to this minister, pointing through the half-opened door to Fouché, who was in the adjoining room: "See that that fellow's letters are looked into." It is probable that Fouché would not have let himself fall into this trap, and that if he had sent any letter by the post, it would have been written to mislead the government, to which he then no longer belonged. The most absolute secrecy, moreover, involved the small number of letters which the postmaster-general communicated to the sovereign. None but he himself was allowed to read them. The copies, which were handed to the Emperor under seals, were burned as soon as they had been read, no trace of them ever remaining. If the Black Cabinet had sent any letters containing family matters, or had exhumed any scandalous anecdote of the kind which so deeply interested Louis XV, it would at once have been ordered to remain within its prescribed limits. I must make haste to add that the postmaster-general never exposed himself to reprimands of this kind.

In the first days of the month of January 1803 it was learned that General Leclerc, Captain-General of the Colony of San Domingo, after the unfortunate issue of the expedition which had been sent there to end the revolt on that island, had died of yellow fever at the Cape. The First Consul was deeply grieved by this loss. On the following day letters from Toulouse announced the arrival of the *Swiftsure* in that port, the remains of the general being on board this ship. Madame Leclerc, sister of the First Consul, and her young son accompanied the body.

Madame Leclerc, then in all the splendor of her youth and beauty, had torn herself away from the seductions of a world in which she held the first rank, to accompany her husband, and to accomplish her duties as mother and as wife. Pauline, although surrounded with adulation and homage, to which she was not altogether insensible, felt that the blood of Bonaparte was in her veins. She had resisted the order sent by the commander-in-chief, at the time of the insurrection of the Cape, to take ship home with her son. She wished to share his dangers. During the short sickness which preceded his death she had not left his bedside, and had cared for him with tender solicitude. She returned to France in broken health and never entirely recovered. She lost her son, still a child, a year later. This child's name was Dermide, a name given him by his godfather, Napoleon, who at the time had been greatly impressed with the original poetic genius of Ossian.

Bernadotte's son, who was of about the same age as General Leclerc's son, received the name Oscar. Napoleon was his godfather, and the christening was delayed until he returned from Egypt. Bernadotte, who was so obsequious towards Napoleon, did not cease conspiring against him, afterwards having recourse to everything and everybody to get his offenses pardoned. Joseph Bonaparte and his wife were as persevering in their efforts to obtain his pardon, as Bernadotte was in alternating offenses and submissions.

The First Consul wore mourning for General Leclerc for ten days. He was much affected by this loss, not only of a brother-in-law, on whose devotion he could count, but of an officer of the highest merit, who was as useful in the study as he was on the battlefield. A cultured education and brilliant services had procured him advancement which would have seemed very rapid in ordinary times. He was a general at the age of twenty-one, having risen step by step in Italy, at Toulon—where he was on active service with Bonaparte—at Fleurus, and with the army of the Alps. Appointed commander of Marseille by the Directoire, he made the acquaintance of the young sister of the Toulon artillery commander, the Bonapartes having then moved to Marseilles. General Bonaparte, on his promotion to the supreme command of the army in Italy, called him to his side at Milan. Leclerc was at that time a brigadier general. Bonaparte gave him his sister in marriage. This charming lady, one of the most beautiful women of her time, had been ardently courted by Fréron. Fréron, who after the 9th Thermidor became the leader of the *jeunesse dorée,* had not at that time yet distinguished himself by the sanguinary acts which won for him the name of Savior of the South from the society of Jacobins.

General Leclerc had not taken part in Napoleon's expedition to Egypt. During this time he served in Italy and in the west of France. He was afterwards sent to Lyon with extraordinary powers. He reestablished discipline in the army, which had been disorganized by the evacuation of Italy and dispersed over Lyon and the neighboring districts. On the 18th Brumaire General Leclerc vigorously supported General Bonaparte. After having fulfilled to the First Consul's satisfaction the mission of leading an army of twenty thousand French soldiers into Spain, for action against Portugal, he was appointed to command the San Domingo expedition.

The First Consul, upon coming to power, had invested Toussaint-L'Ouverture with the government of the island, in the name of France. Toussaint, a general division commander, was a former slave, who was a clever politician and a skillful administrator. His absolute influence over the blacks had commended him to the French government. The ambitious Toussaint, fostering at heart a secret plan to become himself the only master of the island, and to expel French troops, recognized the authority of the home country for one year. When it seemed to him that the right time had come, he threw off the mask, raised the flag of insurrection and proclaimed the independence of San Domingo. The honor and the interests of France made it necessary that he should be forced to return to the path of duty. An expedition to San Domingo was therefore decided upon. The Creoles who had taken refuge in France urged such an outcome. The fatal issue of this expedition is well-known. The failure to take prudent measures; keeping black generals and officers in their posts; the outbreak of yellow fever, which decimated the best of the French army; the cunning and the activity of Toussaint; all these factors contributed to the failure of the expedition. The seizure of some private letters from Toussaint was followed by his arrest and his extradition to France. He was imprisoned at the fortress of Joux, and died there two years later.

The First Consul, who was fully aware of the ambitious object pursued by Toussaint, and who could not believe in any kind of sincerity on his side, would have preferred his removal at the very beginning from the island. He would have preferred to receive him in France as an exile, rather than as a captive, but he could in no case allow him to be free once his treachery had been discovered.

The unhealthiness of the climate of San Domingo, and the fatigue and problems of General Leclerc, had rapidly led him to his grave. He was replaced as chief commander by General Rochambeau, who caused the final loss of the island because of his severity, just as his predecessor had weakened its loyalty through excessive indulgence. It was in accordance with the wishes of the First Consul that his sister had accompanied her husband to San Domingo together with her son. When he heard of her arrival at Toulon he immediately sent off his aide-de-camp Lauriston to bring the widow and her child back to Paris.

One of the principal grievances alleged against us by the English ministry was the mission of Colonel Sebastiani to Egypt. The splendor with which the French envoy had surrounded his mission, the assurance given to the sheiks and the chiefs of the Mamelukes that General Bonaparte, as head of the French government, had not forgotten them, and that his protection should not be wanting, and the marks of interest lavished in his name, excited the suspicions of England.

In his report to the First Consul, Colonel Sebastiani accused the London cabinet, and with reason, of working in an underhand way to turn away the chiefs of the country from their fidelity to the Porte, but he omitted to mention the friendly reception by the English commander. Napoleon, irritated at the want of good faith shown by the British cabinet in the relations which, since the signing of the Peace of Amiens, had been established between the two, powers, published the report of Colonel Sebastiani, although this had been intended as a strictly confidential document. At the same time, just before it was printed in the *Moniteur,* the idea came to him to show it to M. Amédée Jaubert, who had accompanied the colonel during his trip, and who was perfectly acquainted with Oriental countries. M. Jaubert was called in the night to the house of M. Maret, secretary of state, who showed him a proof of the report. Jaubert advised the minister to suppress several passages, which in his opinion could only produce a regrettable impression, and provoke great irritation. But as this report had to appear in the *Moniteur* of the following morning, these modifications could not be submitted to Napoleon's approval. M. Maret declined to assume the responsibility of these deletions, or of postponing the publication of the document. The report accordingly appeared in the *Moniteur,* with some slight modifications, which did not in any way affect its essential points, and thus became the starting point of the series of mutual antagonisms, which finally resulted, at no distant date, in a break of the peace between England and France.

Towards the end of 1802 some deputies of various Swiss cantons arrived in Paris, summoned by the First Consul, to discuss their respective interests with him, and to bring about a reconciliation of the different factions which for five years had divided the Helvetic Confederation. Several attempts in this direction had been made by Napoleon since his coming to power. He had imposed the recognition of the independence of that Republic at Lunéville, but the revolutions caused by the struggle between the various parties for power, the appeals to arms, and the intervention of the European cabinets called for by the aristocracy, had kept this unhappy country in a series of internecine wars and in a state of anarchy which it behooved the French government to end. The withdrawal of the French troops, which had been effected in accordance with the wishes of the Helvetic government, had only unleashed the passions of the opposing factions.

Before taking this decision, which was meant to ascertain how Switzerland would use her restored independence, it had been proposed to vest the supreme authority in this country in a hereditary chief, or *Landamman.* Negotiations then began with the Margrave of Baden. Baron Dalberg, at that time minister of this little state, who afterwards became Duc Dalberg, and a naturalized Frenchman, was the intermediary in these negotiations, which were carried so far, indeed, that the court of Baden thought to indemnify the minister for his trouble in directing foreign affairs in France. The troubles which broke out after the withdrawal of the French troops contributed to the failure of this arrangement.

The federalist faction, led by Aloys Reding, was winning, when the defeated party decided to appeal to the French government, and to request its mediation. The First Consul had several conferences, one of which lasted more than six hours, with ten deputies, selected amongst the Federalists and the *Unitaires.* He listened to the arguments of the rival factions with attention, and discussed them with the greatest impartiality. He spoke to them like a Swiss citizen, and, as the head of two great countries such as France and Italy, gave them wise advice, and constantly manifested a moderation and a logic that convinced the Swiss deputies. He commissioned four French senators, MM. Barthélemy, Roederer, Fouché, and Desmeuniers to come to an understanding with the Swiss deputies, and to draw up the draft of an act of conciliation, the basis of which should be complete equality between all the cantons, a voluntary renunciation by the aristocracy of their privileges, the division of the national debt in just proportions, and the federative organization of the eighteen cantons by which their religious creeds, habits, languages, and their interests were to be reconciled.

This wise and disinterested policy calmed all the divisive spirit, and, thanks to our mediation, Switzerland was promptly pacified. The various parties agreed to it, and Aloys Reding himself, who had declared himself one of the most ardent champions of the oligarchy, was present at the first Diet, and admitted how beneficial the intervention of the powerful peacemaker had been. All the cantons expressed their gratitude to the First Consul in numerous addresses.

The auditors were instituted by a decree of April 9, 1803. At first they were only sixteen in number, and were charged with the functions of reporters to the various sections of the council of state. They were for the most part young men of talent, with a good education, and who belonged for the most part to old families. Almost all the reporters of that first nomination reached high positions in the state. Their number was, later on, considerably increased, experience having proved the advantages of this institution. The auditors, it may be said, formed a kind of hot house of administrators trained in the school of the Empire, and intended, once familiar with the affairs of state, to occupy the highest posts in the government. With this purpose in mind they were distributed over the various ministries, in the prefectures and subprefectures, in the offices of the public prosecutors at the various courts, and in the financial administrations. They were later on commissioned to carry the portfolio containing the results of the labors of the ministers during the preceding week to the Emperor, either to headquarters, or during his journeys within France. In time of war the auditors remained at the disposal of the secretary of state, but most often were employed by the quartermaster general of the army, who used them for extraordinary missions. The majority were employed at the headquarters of those who were in charge of the occupied countries. As a reward for services rendered in the course of these missions they often received, on their return to France, advancement which had not always been won through long experience. Nevertheless, and with very few exceptions, they justified the Emperor's confidence. No complaint was ever made against their management of affairs, especially with regard to their honesty and loyalty. Almost all the families who had formerly had representatives in the departments of justice, of finance, and in the management of the principal affairs of state, were drawn upon for auditors who rendered useful services. Napoleon often congratulated himself on the advantages he derived from that institution.

I think it necessary to speak of a proposal which was made in the month of February, 1803, by the King of Prussia, to the chief of the House of Bourbon, who was at the time in retirement at Warsaw, that he should renounce his rights to the French crown in exchange for territorial and monetary advantages. The friendly relations that existed between the First Consul and the Prussian monarch, the answer made by Napoleon to the Count de Lille, on the 20th Fructidor, Year VIII—7th September, 1800—and the terms of the instructions given by the King to the President of the Regency of Warsaw, have led to the belief that this proposal was inspired by the head of the French government.

The instructions of the King of Prussia to M. Meyer are known through the copy which Louis XVIII made of them, in his own writing, that was witnessed by the Archbishop of Rheims, M. de Talleyrand's uncle, and by the Abbé Edgeworth. If such an insinuation was made to the King of Prussia, I have never heard of it. Whatever interest Napoleon might have had in the misfortunes of the fallen house, he did not think that the initiative ought to come from him. It is more than probable that the first idea of such a proposal was rooted in Prussia, because it was felt that the prolonged stay of the Pretender in the Prussian States might one day lead to difficulties, and the feelings of the First Consul toward the Bourbons were known.

Napoleon did not oppose the proposal by the King of Prussia, but declared that he would in no way participate in it. The future Emperor was particularly interested in this idea that one had very good reasons to think that he was not foreign to it. Napoleon, however, remained very circumspect, and much too shrewd not to understand that with very little common sense one could see that to ask the Bourbons to relinquish their rights, was a practical acknowledgment that the rights conferred by the vote of the nation had to be confirmed by the sanction of the family which had reigned before him.

It is natural to think that Louis XVIII thought it useful to his interests to attribute the proposal to his adversary, to draw attention to it as an indirect acknowledgment of his rights, and to take advantage of the opportunity to place himself once more before the eyes of Europe by a declaration, coming at the right time, which people found heroic. Without being unjust to this prince, it may be said that he lacked all the qualities that make a hero. Heroism above all implies the idea of danger, while Louis XVIII ran no risk whatsoever. He was a shrewd and crafty man, very selfish, and penetrated with an instinctive sentiment of his legitimacy, which always prevented him from despairing of his cause. His only arms were intrigue so carefully planned that their source could never be attributed to him, and certain proclamations, where he also sought literary renown. As to these crooked maneuvers, and the proclamations which he hurled forth from the depths of his retreat when it was impossible for him to be silent, it may be said that the former were not worthy of his cause, and that the latter, on the other hand, were more in accordance with the duties which his position gave him.

I am not in a position to contest the authenticity of the documents published by the Restoration. I will not base such a denial on the instance when the government of the Restoration published a letter written by the Emperor Napoleon to King Joachim Murat, having previously altered it. M. de Blacas, having found the draft of this letter in the archives of the Emperor's cabinet, deemed it right to publish it in the *Moniteur,* after having arranged it to suit the object which he desired to obtain by its publication. During the Hundred Days, I saw the copy of this letter written by the hand of Abbé Fleuriot, one of M. de Blacas' secretaries, with the alterations noted on the margin in red ink.

But without seeking to base any denial on the want of good faith, which certain governments do not hesitate to use when it is in their interest, it is simpler to say that these negotiations with the Bourbons, were transacted between them and the agents of Prussia. Napoleon expressed no desire to be informed as to their progress, so the zeal of these agents, and the plans of the Berlin ministry, gave the form that suited them to their proposals. This is Napoleon's own remark on the subject.

I have omitted to say why the Pretender happened to be at Warsaw. When the Emperor Paul I had reconciled himself with the Consular government towards the end of 1800, his attitude towards the Count de Lille, to whom two years previously he had showed hospitality at Mittau, suddenly changed. He ordered him to leave Russian territory, although it was the middle of a very severe winter. In his distress the Count de Lille asked shelter of the King of Prussia, who allowed him to establish himself at Warsaw. The King of Prussia, however, not wishing to displease the French government, notified the First Consul, who made no objection to the Pretender's presence in a city within the Prussian States, and tolerated it with good grace.

In support of my statement that King Louis XVIII was not a man of heroic character, I may mention the following fact: when, in the month of April, 1796, the Count de Lille left Verona, at the request of the Venetian government, he asked, with the pride and the dignity befitting his rank, that his name should be erased from the Golden Book, and that the coat of arms of Henri IV should be restored to him. But, fearing to be given up by the Venetians, or to be captured by French troops while traveling, he got the Duc de la Vauguyon to drive in his carriage pretending to be the king, while he, disguised in humble attire, made good his escape out of the district occupied by French troops. This fact is mentioned in a report from the podesta of Verona to the senate of Venice. The report in question was among the archives that were taken to France, following the French conquest of Venice.

The instinctive feeling of his legitimacy never left that prince. M. Beugnot, who in 1814 received the portfolio of the Ministry of the Interior from the provisional government, was commissioned, in this capacity, to establish Louis XVIII in the apartments of the Tuileries palace, upon his return from England. The minister has since told me that the King walked through the various rooms displaying the most profound indifference, without paying the least attention to M. Beugnot's explanation of the use to which each of the rooms was to be put. After reaching the room which used to serve as Napoleon's study, and where the writing table on which the prince used to write at Hartwell had been placed, Louis XVIII refused to go any further. He ordered that an armchair be brought up, and sat down at his writing-table as quietly as if he had only left the palace an hour before to take a walk.

Louisiana, which had formerly belonged to France, had been ceded to Spain in virtue of a secret clause of the Treaty of 1763, to the great discontentment of the inhabitants, and also to the regret of the Versailles cabinet, which for a long time continued to be in communication with that country, but finally forgot about it. England had never ceased to covet this province, which adjoined her American possessions. Our maritime and commercial cities, in the interests of our shipping to the Antilles, hoped that an opportunity to re-gain that colony might present itself. The First Consul, having been made aware of this wish, and with the future in view, began negotiations with the Court of Madrid to achieve its retrocession. By a treaty between France and Spain, towards the end of 1800, we were once again in possession of Louisiana. When the breaking of the Peace of Amiens became imminent, Napoleon considered, and rightly so, that our naval forces would not be able to protect all our colonies against the superior English fleet, and that the conquest of Louisiana, especially, would be a matter of little difficulty for England. Foreseeing even that the first operation of the campaign would be an attack on this colony, he wished to put it beyond England's reach, and at the same time to destroy all England's hopes of ever gaining possession of it, by ceding it in its integrity to the United States. Therefore he proposed to the Americans that Louisiana should be handed over to them, in return for a money indemnity. These funds, he considered, would help to pay for the cost of the war which he was about to wage with England.

An American ambassador was sent to Paris to demand indemnities for seizures which had been made on American ships during peace. The United States government did not expect to acquire the entire colony, limiting their hopes to the possession of New Orleans, and the American ambassador listened to these proposals with a certain amount of distrust, suspecting that they might hide some desire to deny him the satisfaction he was claiming. In the meantime a new envoy, a Mr. Monroe, arrived in Paris, vested with full powers. M. Barbé-Marbois, the French negotiator, immediately approached him. Mr. Livingstone, the first envoy, had offered thirty million as the price of Louisiana, while M. de Marbois was asking for eighty million. In the end the American envoys agreed to the price of eighty million, but stipulated that of this sum twenty millions should be applied to indemnifying the American citizens for their losses, so that the purchase-money would be reduced to sixty million.

Napoleon, who at first would have been satisfied with fifty millions, now wanted that the twenty million reserved for the settlement of indemnities, should also be paid into the treasury. But the news he received concerning English armaments, and the impossible claims which the English government kept putting forward, made him less exacting, and induced him to hurry with the conclusion of the agreement. He feared lest the break might take place before the cession was effected, in which case he would only have had an empty title-deed to offer the Americans. Two conventions were signed on April 13, 1803, the first relating to the payment of the price of the cession, so as not to mix up the abandonment of France's sovereignty with a monetary question of a sale. Another deed stipulated the conditions of the cession. Napoleon expressly requested that a clause be inserted in the deed, specifying that the inhabitants of Louisiana should be maintained and protected in the enjoyment of their liberties and of their properties, and in the exercise of the religion which they professed.

The English government was profoundly irritated at the fact that the Americans had become masters of Louisiana. Because of this our adversaries lost all hope of ever regaining their dominance in America. Napoleon's foresight was thus entirely justified. Only a few days had elapsed since the signing of the convention when war was declared. But Louisiana had become American property, and England could undertake nothing against that colony.

England hastened on the break. Ten thousand fresh sailors were enrolled. The militia was called out, under the lying pretext that formidable armaments were being prepared against England in the ports of France and Holland. The most convincing explanations given to the English ambassador were all in vain; the minds of the English ministers had been made up. It was obvious that in signing the Peace of Amiens the English government had only wished for an armistice with the mental reservation of breaking the peace as soon as it suited its interests to do so.

The unexpected retirement of Mr. Pitt had raised the hope that England wished for a reconciliation with France. As a matter of fact Pitt had recognized that the man who had declared eternal war with France could not sign a treaty of peace with her. His self esteem would have suffered too greatly at being forced to accept conditions so different from those for which he had once hoped. He had accordingly thought it his duty to retire, his successor being one of his supporters, Mr. Addington, son of the doctor of Lord Chatham (Pitt's father). Mr. Addington had been Pitt's schoolmate, and had remained his friend. Pitt, although absent, continued to direct the English ministry. The experiment which he had tried had succeeded. Shortly after the Treaty of Amiens, England, which at first had accepted peace favorably, found it onerous. She had enjoyed the sole monopoly of commerce; she alone during the war profited from the sea and the colonies, and peace gave her competitors and reduced her profits. The First Consul had sent his aide-de-camp, Lauriston, to London, as the bearer of the ratification of the treaty. He had been received in London with enthusiasm. The horses in his carriage had been unyoked, and he had been drawn in triumph to the house in Downing Street; but neither the government nor the big traders shared these sentiments with the people.

France had scrupulously fulfilled all the commitments made on signing the peace. The kingdom of Naples, and the Roman States, had been evacuated in less than three months, while in England no arrangements whatever had been made for the evacuation of the island of Malta; the intention to prolong the occupation was even hinted at. The English newspapers insulted the Head of the French government with the most spiteful articles, and were spreading the most lying reports. The hatred of France burst out even in the Houses of Parliament. Articles in the *Moniteur,* almost all dictated by the First Consul, replied with dignity and indignation to these venomous attacks. Napoleon was too susceptible to the libels of the journalists. Insults from a hostile country and government could have been explained. But the tolerance, the protection even, which the English pamphleteers found in a country which had recently been reconciled to France, showed him how little anxious the English government was to maintain friendly relations with him. They showed some very hostile feelings towards France. Napoleon has been blamed for his words as addressed to Lord Whitworth during the audience when he received the diplomatic corps. It had not indeed been customary till then, that the Head of the government should deal with foreign ambassadors, other than in private audiences. Sovereigns indeed only dealt with the governments of other countries through their ambassadors. This violation of a constant practice could not but profoundly offend a government whose conscience could not bear the public exposure of its politics. The bitter indignation which the unprovoked actions of the English government brought to Napoleon's mind in a sense justified such an attack. It is nonetheless true that this scene produced, and could only produce, a deplorable effect, and that it would have been much better for a man of Napoleon's greatness to have abstained from it.

The French government complained bitterly of the tolerance accorded to these indecent attacks and vile calumnies. The London cabinet replied that owing to the freedom of the press in England it was impossible to do justice to these well-founded grievances. A French newspaper written by Peltier, and the mouthpiece of the riff-raff among the exiles, gained notoriety by the violence and the atrocity of its provocations. At the request of the French ambassador, Peltier was prosecuted for inciting to murder. The pamphleteer was defended by Mr. Mackintosh, M.P., and was only condemned to a small fine, which was never paid. This celebrated barrister was, the same year, appointed to one of the most important posts in the law-courts in British India.

Among the pamphlets which Peltier's sheet—*L'Ambigu*—published, the one which provoked the most serious objection on the part of the French government, was an ode entitled "La Napoléone," written in his youth by Charles Nodier. This circumstance prompts me to point out how exaggerated the persecution that this writer was subjected to by Napoleon, has been. I even believe that he greatly exaggerated its importance himself, and that he sought to create emotions in the imaginary persecutions, and that in good faith, he imagined himself as the hero. I know of no measure taken against him emanating from the First Consul's cabinet. Nodier was a man of imagination, full of chivalrous ideas that prompted him to take sides against the victor, no matter who the vanquished might be—republicans, exiles, Chouans, or friends of the fallen government. His youthful attachments and affections mixed him up in Royalist intrigues. The thwarting of his hopes inspired him with hatred of the First Consul, when Napoleon took power, which the establishment of the imperial government by no means helped to dampen. His antipathy was expressed in *La Napoléone,* a virulent philippic, which was reproduced by the newspapers of all hostile governments, and which naturally attracted the attention of the police to its author. But it would be attaching too much importance to the attacks of a man, who had talent no doubt, but who was certainly obscure, to admit any possibility of a personal and continued struggle between so feeble an adversary and the head of a powerful state. Napoleon had something else to do besides wasting his time over the impotent hatreds which his person inspired. He could only relegate them to the vigilance of the authorities, which is what he did in this case.

The persecution Nodier complained about, was not, moreover, a very violent one, seeing that after a detention of a few months at Sainte-Pelagie he was sent back home to Besançon. His exalted state of mind led him to commit fresh acts of provocation, which exposed him to further disgrace. His unabated hostility, his relations with angry men, his love of independence, and a poetic imagination, made him leave his retreat to indulge his vague reveries in the mountains of the Jura and of Switzerland. After leading this wandering life for some time, he was allowed to return freely to Besançon, where he was even taken under the protection of the Prefect, Jean de Bry. He obtained an authorization to teach a class of literature, and thanks to the benevolence of the authorities, was allowed to live without being called to order. He later went to Illyria, where he became the secretary of his former persecutor, Fouché, formerly Minister of Police, who was at that time governor of those provinces. He occupied various lucrative posts, at that time, in the imperial government, and even edited a paper under the protection of the various governors who succeeded each other in the Illyrian provinces. The events of 1814 brought him back to France. I have perhaps spoken at too great length about M. Nodier, but, through all these particulars, I wanted to show, how in reality the rigors, of which he pretended himself to be the victim, will not stand up to investigation.

I take this opportunity to state that the existence of alleged secret societies in the army, which this same Nodier published in 1815, is entirely imaginary, and may simply be attributed to his love of romance and to his craze for conspiracies. The Emperor, in spite of all his sources of information, was never ignorant of anything that went on in the army, was never able to find any traces of mysterious associations, of hidden compacts, of sects of Philadelphians, or others, led by a single chief or a secret council. Napoleon's powerful hand, which energetically restrained all those inclinations for trouble and disorder that are hidden under the words liberty, or independence, and his vigilant eye prevented the formation of secret associations. If some secret attempts of this kind did have a semblance of execution, it was only after he had left power, or towards the end of his reign, when his power and influence were dissolving following his reverses, and when he was no longer served with the same zeal. It is only, therefore, because of the natural tendency of romantic minds, that the attempt to connect—from a common starting-point—rare and isolated facts, or solitary attempts, which bore absolutely no relation to one another was made.

This digression on Charles Nodier must not lead me to forget an event which occurred in the midst of the serious preoccupations of the time; an event which might have had fatal consequences. At the beginning of 1803, the First Consul, who was then at St. Cloud, wanted to drive a carriage with four young horses. Madame Bonaparte and her daughter Hortense were in the carriage. Napoleon mounted the box, in front of the steps of the St. Cloud parterre. On arriving at the railings which separate this parterre from the private park he lost control of the young and fiery horses. They dashed up against the railings with such violence that Napoleon was thrown from his seat and hurled ten paces away, on the gravel. I had watched his departure with some slight anxiety, but had been reassured as I saw him driving quietly away. A sudden cry and seeing the carriage stop made me fear that some accident had happened. I ran up, and arrived in time to see the First Consul seated on the ground trying to collect his thoughts. Fortunately this fall had no bad consequences; no bones were broken, or sprained; and there was no reason to fear any internal injury. Napoleon came off with a sprain and a few scratches, and was obliged to carry his right arm in a sling, which prevented him from signing any papers for a few days afterwards.

Lord Whitworth, who was appointed English ambassador to France in the month of June, did not arrive in Paris until the middle of November. General Andréossy, was only awaiting the departure of the English ambassador from London, and set out as soon as he heard that Lord Whitworth had had left. The latter's mission, was apparently to bring about a break of the peace. After the hostile proceedings and the entirely unwarranted recriminations, particulars of which are known, the English government crowned the series of its aggressions with a very clumsy manifesto, based on transparently false pretexts. This declaration of war had, according to the British custom, been preceded by an order that not only French warships, but the French merchant service and ports were to be treated as hostile.

Open hostilities had thus preceded the breaking of the peace. French vessels had been captured in ports and on the ocean, and a general embargo had been set on all ships belonging to France and to Holland, as well as on their crews and cargoes, even before the declaration of war was made public. It was to respond to these illegal and unjust seizures of men and ships, carried out in violation of all international law by the British government, that the First Consul ordered the arrest of all Englishmen, both civilian and military, located on French territory at the time of the declaration of war.

Parleys, however, continued with the English ambassador, who remained in Paris. The First Consul made every effort to maintain peace, and declared that while he could not consent to any suspension of the Treaty of Amiens, he would give England any guarantees of safety which might be considered necessary. The English ministry only replied with proposals which were contrary to the formal text of the treaty. The First Consul, taking his stand on the terms of the treaty alone, had appealed to the arbitration of the powers that had signed it. He had specifically insisted that the island of Malta should be handed over to the keeping of the Emperor of Russia. The Emperor had answered the proposal of arbitration with an offer to act as mediator. He agreed to accept the charge of the island for a period of ten years, and asked that its government, which was to have been vested in the Grand Master of the Order, should be placed under the control of the commander of the Russian garrison.

On the 25th of April, Lord Whitworth presented as the ultimatum of his government—this ultimatum being communicated not in writing but verbally—that England should continue to occupy Malta for ten years, and further that Lampedusa, a small island in the Mediterranean, which belonged to the kingdom of Naples, should be handed over. The ambassador declared at the same time, that, unless this ultimatum were accepted in seven days, he was ordered to demand his passports. The First Consul, opposing these high-handed manners in his constant desire to maintain peace, proposed to entrust the care of Malta to Russia, until the final settlement of the various differences between France and England. Lord Whitworth replied that the refusal of Russia to accept the charge of the island rendered any such step impossible; which was false, seeing that the Emperor had consented to take charge of it. The English ministry, thinking no doubt that Napoleon only demanded the evacuation of Malta to save his dignity, then proposed that he should consent, by a secret clause to be added to the treaty, to allow English troops to remain in Malta. This subterfuge was rejected by the First Consul as impracticable, and as unworthy of France.

Finally, wishing to try every possible means of conciliation, he devised a last expedient which consisted in allowing the English to retain Malta for an indefinite period, on condition that the French troops should occupy the Gulf of Taranto. Napoleon considered Taranto, due to its position in the Mediterranean, as the equivalent of Malta. It seemed to him that a French occupation of Taranto, awarded by treaty, would prompt the powers to interfere and force the English to evacuate Egypt, so that the French might leave the kingdom of Naples. But England would make no concessions on this point, and refused at any price to have her soldiers leave the island of Malta. France, on the other hand, was determined to go to war rather than abandon to the English such an important position in the very heart of the Mediterranean. Lord Whitworth refused to even listen to the statement of the arrangement proposed by the First Consul, and said that, since the *sine quâ non* conditions of his government were refused, he must imperatively demand the return of his passports. And, he left Paris forthwith and went to Calais, to await the arrival of General Andréossy at Dover.

The Russian government, by accepting the care of Malta, had asked, in its plan of conciliation, that Lampedusa should be ceded to England. To have agreed to this would have been to have given this power, if by any means Malta again was to fall under her domination, two impregnable positions in the Mediterranean; for Lampedusa would have become, in a very short time, impregnable in England's hands. Now Napoleon had always declared that France would not accept that England have the mastery of the Mediterranean. Russia demanded—besides the evacuation of Switzerland and Italy by the French, conditions which had not been stipulated in the Treaty of Amiens—an establishment in Italy which should compensate the King of Sardinia for the loss of Piedmont, etc., etc. Russia's partiality for England was made clear by these proposals. As a matter of fact the Chancellor Woronzov was a declared partisan of England, as was Count Marcov, the Russian ambassador to France, who professed the most anti-French sentiments. He used to pay professional libelers to cover the government and the person of the First Consul with insults and calumnies. He was moreover the censor of his own master, and used to say: "The Emperor has his will, but the Russian nation has her will also." The First Consul, who had suffered the antagonistic attitude of the Russian envoy during the peace, considered that his presence in Paris after war had been declared, the end of which could not be foreseen, was not only disagreeable but dangerous. The recall of this agent was therefore demanded, and he was replaced in Paris by a chargé d'affaires. At the same time the French government recalled General Hédouville, who left behind him at St. Petersburg, M. de Rayneval, also a chargé d'affaires.

The First Consul, who was on the best terms with Prussia, thought to strengthen the bonds which united the two countries. He felt that, with a bitter an enemy such as England, he needed a close and stable alliance, which could be both offensive and defensive. To use his own words, what was desired was "an evident, powerful, and complete association, the mere announcement of which should be to Europe a pledge of the stability of peace, and of the permanence of the status quo of the contracting parties, and which should warn England again to look beyond the present war." Napoleon had to choose between Austria and Prussia, but his preference was for the latter. It was therefore to the Prussian government that he proposed an offensive and defensive alliance.

The end of the Peace of Amiens disturbed Napoleon in the midst of the calm of a quiet life, that unfortunately fate hadn't in store for him. Had his indefatigable activity not been channeled to other endeavors, what prodigies might not have been created during peacetime, by the creative power of his genius, and the ascendancy he owed to the splendor of an incomparable fame. He had bound together the olive branch of peace and the laurels of war. The whole of Europe had been pacified.

What glory remained for his hands to gather? To encourage agriculture, the industries, the sciences and the arts, and to make France as happy by her peaceful development as he had made her powerful and feared by his victories. But these dreams of peace and prosperity, in which he loved to indulge, were destined to fade away before the vast and stormy career that he was called upon to follow. If any illusion about his future had ever entered his strong and penetrating mind, it was banished forever from that day on. The treacherous conduct of England made a profound impression on this susceptible mind, so sensitive to reciprocal straightforwardness of conduct, and filled with the feelings of national pride and honor. The odious machination directed by the English ministry, or paid for with its gold, against the power and the life of the First Consul; the irruption of sixty assassins, vomited out on to our shores—foul remnants of our civil wars—to consummate a cowardly and criminal attempt; the hidden intrigues carried on with a view to suborning French generals who had distinguished themselves by their victories; falsehood and corruption entering at every door, filled him with the loftiest indignation. He was forced to acknowledge that there was neither armistice nor peace to be hoped for from this irreconcilable enemy, and he had nothing further to rely on than the superiority of his power and unusual means, for it was war to the death.

From that moment forward, his sole occupation became to throw back on England all the harm that she tried to inflict upon us. His habits changed; his genius, which had appeared to slumber, awoke, full of courage and daring. He raised himself to the measure of the formidable challenges which our eternal enemies had created, and indeed rose above them. His activity became incredibly intense. From then on a new life began for him, a life of action, of combat; a life made of the hardest labors, of dangers of every kind, of the most fruitful and the most daring and bold ideas; a life from which no diversions of any kind were even allowed for a moment to turn him aside. Like an intrepid athlete, he entered upon this gigantic struggle, which was to produce such marvels—to elevate him so high, and then to cast him down so low.

The arrest of Englishmen traveling in France at the time of the declaration of war, was an energetic measure which can only be justified by the need for reprisals on a power that had perpetrated a monstrous and intolerable violation of international law. This first act was speedily followed by the conquest of the Electorate of Hanover.

Orders were given to a French army assembled in Holland to enter Germany. It marched on the double, under the command of Marshal Mortier, against the Electorate of Hanover. Leaving Nimeguen on May 26, the army entered the capital of the Electorate on June 5. A convention was signed at Subligen according to which French troops would occupy Hanover as far as the Elbe. The Hanoverian army withdrew to Lauenburg, agreeing not to fight against France during the war. All forts, artillery, munitions of all kinds, treasure-chests, and other property belonging to the King of England, were handed over to the French army. The King having refused to ratify the convention, our army pursued the Hanoverian troops into their retreat in Lauenburg, and disarmed them. The English government had sent transport ships to embark these troops, which formed an army of sixteen thousand men, but the transport ships arrived too late.

The University of Göttingen, alarmed by the approaching threat of war, had applied for protection to the First Consul through the celebrated Heine, begging that measures might be taken for the safety of the people, and the property of the University, and that orders might be given to prevent any occurrences which could trouble the calm and quiet so necessary to study. The First Consul ordered the Minister of War to reply favorably, and to instruct Marshal Mortier to protect the universities in general, and the University of Göttingen in particular.

Napoleon had made up his mind to attempt a descent upon England, so as to dictate terms of peace in London itself. He applied himself to combine the best means whereby an army of one hundred and fifty thousand men could be shipped across the channel, that being the number of men which he considered necessary for such an expedition. He decided upon the use of small ships suitable for navigation, fitted as was requisite, and adapted to the ports at which they were to land. These ships were divided into gunboats, sloops carrying guns, and barges. Some larger vessels were added to transport horses, artillery, and provisions. A certain number of large fishing-smacks scattered along the coast were purchased. All the ports, and even the river-basins, were used as docks, for the construction of the necessary boats. In a spontaneous show of enthusiasm, the departments, the townships, and the guilds offered the government gunboats, flat-bottomed boats, sloops, and frigates. The merchants of Paris set the example by voting funds for the construction of a vessel of one hundred and twenty guns, which bore the name of *Commerce de Paris*. The larger guilds, and even private individuals, paid for the construction of vessels of all sizes, destined to make up the national flotilla.

The First Consul made the necessary arrangements for the organization of six camps, to be formed on the sea coast. These camps were intended to supply the troops to be embarked on board the flotilla, whose mission it was to carry over into English territory the implacable war which the English government was waging against us.

Wishing to attack England from various points at one and the same time, Napoleon gave orders for an expedition into Ireland. He appointed for this purpose eighteen thousand men, who formed the camp at Brest. General Marmont, who was in command of an army of from twenty-two to twenty-five thousand men in Holland, was to embark his troops with the same destination in view. The First Consul had decided to place these two armies under the command of Marshal Augereau. An understanding had been reached with Irish refugees in France, and also with Irishmen in Ireland. Augereau was to march straight on Dublin. In case there was any delay on the part of the Irish insurrectionists, he was to take his stand, and, after having rallied General Marmont, to wait for the landing of the main army. After having ordered the necessary arrangements for the defense and safety of France both within and without, in the new situation in which we were placed by the unjust aggression by England, the First Consul, accompanied by Madame Bonaparte, left for the northern departments, one month after the proclamation of hostilities.

He visited all the ports on our shore of the English Channel and of the German Ocean, the manufacturing towns of Picardy, Belgium, and the Liége district, stayed several days at Brussels and at Antwerp, and returned home to St. Cloud, on August 10, by way of Rheims and Soissons. This six weeks' journey was employed in preparations for the organization of the flotilla, and in assembling the invading army at Boulogne. The men and the materials of this expedition were the objects of Napoleon's greatest care. Everywhere in the course of his journey he found an exasperation against the English, which made the war a national war, and he urged on the populations of the various districts to assist the government in the construction and the equipment of the fleet. This glow of patriotic enthusiasm had spread over the whole of France. Apart from the vessels for which funds had been voted, and had they all been built, would have exceeded the requirements of the expedition, patriotic gifts and voluntary subscriptions supplied a great part of the funds necessary for the arming and maintenance of the flotilla. More than two thousand vessels of every kind were collected together in the harbor of Boulogne and in the auxiliary ports or basins. The beds of neighboring rivers were dug out and enlarged, establishments were formed, along with the necessary work carried out to adapt them to the purpose for which they were intended. Considerable works of every kind were executed to protect the divisions of the flotilla scattered along the coast. In one word, no precaution was neglected for the execution of this memorable enterprise, in which the genius of Napoleon reached its full development, worthy of its conception.

The assembling at one and the same place, of so large a number of ships armed for war, gave rise to the belief that it was with the flotilla alone that the invasion of England was to be attempted. In order to put the enemy on a wrong path, Napoleon conceived the idea of assembling in distant waters, by combined operations, the French and Spanish squadrons of Toulon, Rochefort, Cadiz, Ferrol and Brest—some sixty line vessels—and have them return suddenly to Boulogne at the right moment, and to remain at sea during for fourteen days. Thanks to the presence in the waters of the Channel, of these squadrons that would be masters of the sea by their numerical superiority, the flotilla would be able to cross and effect the landing in England of the army of one hundred and sixty thousand men that had been collected in our ports, and notably at Boulogne. The First Consul had decided upon this plan, after having discussed various alternatives with his Minister of Marine.

Napoleon found Admiral Latouche-Tréville, to be the right man to carry out an enterprise which demanded, of the man appointed to lead it, great resolution and skill. In the letters which he wrote to him on the subject, he asked him to think over the great enterprise that he was to carry out, and to let him hear his opinion, before signing final orders on the operation, as to what would be the best way to carry it out. He informed him that he had appointed him inspector-general of the Mediterranean littoral, and added that he ardently hoped that the success of the great expedition against England would put him in a position to raise the admiral to such a degree of honor and title, that the admiral could have nothing further to wish for.

Napoleon at the same time let him know the number and the positions of the vessels which the commander-in-chief of the naval forces would have under his command, and informed him of the position of the English cruisers and squadrons. The First Consul drew this information from the reports of his bureau of foreign statistics, an office which was so well organized that he knew the exact state of the English navy, as well as it was known at the Admiralty in London. "We possess, at this moment," he added, "between Etaples, Boulogne, Wimereux and Ambleteuse, two thousand gunboats, sloops, barges, etc., able to transport one hundred and forty thousand men and ten thousand horses. Let us be masters of the Channel for six hours, and we shall be the masters of the world."

Napoleon wanted the entire operation be carried out before the winter. "Assuming that the Admiral can start before July 30, it is probable that he would not reach Boulogne before the middle of September, at a period when the night is sufficiently long, and when the weather is rarely bad for any length of time."

While planning this great expedition, the First Consul arranged with the Minister of Marine for a series of other maritime expeditions to engage the attention of the enemy, to reinforce and resupply our colonies, to seize upon insular positions that could serve as safe haven ports for our ships, and to do all the harm possible to English commerce. The organization of these different naval campaigns was the subject of almost daily correspondence between Napoleon and the Minister of Marine.

These expeditions were carried out with varying results; but, to tell the truth, they did not realize the objectives that Napoleon had in view.

I shall speak only briefly of the homage that was paid to Napoleon during his journey in the northern departments of France; of the flattering and magnificent receptions given for him, and his wife, who accompanied him; of the triumphal arches under which they passed; of the guards of honor, selected from among the most notable families in the towns through which they traveled; of the richness of their uniforms; of the young girls, dressed in white, who presented flowers; of the speeches made by the civil, military, and ecclesiastical authorities; of the *Te Deums* that were sung; of the illuminations, balls, and concerts; of the triumphal procession, so dear to the people of Antwerp, where historical, mystical, profane, or fantastic characters, were shown in a series of strange tableaux; in one word, of the extraordinary enthusiasm of the town and country people, crowding together to hail with their cries and their wishes for success, the energetic adversary of England. The newspapers of the time have reported these occurrences, and in no way did they exaggerate the truth.

Napoleon's principal object was to see for himself the naval resources offered by the departments on the coast, and to stimulate with renewed vigor the armaments against England. With this objective in view, he visited, as was his custom, the ports, dockyards, arsenals, and batteries, giving long audiences to the civil, maritime, and military authorities, occupying himself with improvements, and correcting any abuses, sparing neither encouragements nor rewards. This part of the First Consul's journey was described by the *Moniteur,* and this description is, in every sense of the word, historically trustworthy.

M. de Roquelaure, who was at that time Archbishop of Mechlin, came to Antwerp to present his respects to the First Consul and Madame Bonaparte. I often saw this prelate again in 1813, in Archchancellor Cambacérès's drawing room. He was a straight and sturdy old man, who bore with the vigor of middle age the weight of his eighty-two years and was received and treated with particular distinction. M. de Roquelaure owed this flattering reception to the wise way in which he administered his diocese, and to the spirit of concord and union which he fostered there. He was a man of great intelligence, and had been a member of the French Academy. He resigned four or five years after Napoleon's visit to Antwerp, and was appointed Canon of the Chapter of St. Denis. The Abbé de Pradt, at that time Bishop of Poitiers, succeeded him at Mechlin. When I saw M. de Roquelaure again at the Archchancellor's he was over ninety-two years old. Age had but little changed him. His sight had weakened, but his legs were as strong as ever. He was always seen standing. His memory had become curiously impaired. It broke off at the time when he was Bishop of Senlis, and first almoner to King Louis XV, high in favor with the sovereign, and honored by the patronage of the king's sisters. He had no recollection whatever of the events of the Revolution. Count Siméon was an even more remarkable man, for at a greater age than M. de Roquelaure he remained in the enjoyment of all his faculties.

It was at Brussels, on the eve of his departure from that city, that the First Consul received M. Lombard, privy councilor to the King of Prussia, who brought him a letter from his sovereign. The purpose of this letter was to compliment the head of the consular government on the occasion of his arrival in Brussels, and to express the wish that steps might be taken to relieve the townships in Lower Saxony of the charges caused by the presence of the French troops there. Nor was M. Lombard's mission confined to furthering Prussian interest alone. He was to endeavour to find out what were Napoleon's intentions as to the limits which he proposed to give to his occupation of Hanover and some other portions of the German States. These matters had been suggested to the Prussian government by Russia. Napoleon, who had at that time one only interest, namely an alliance with Prussia, received M. Lombard in the friendliest fashion, conversed with him at great length, and showed him real confidence. He spoke of the value which he attached to the friendship of the King of Prussia; he expressed his sincere desire to ally himself closely with this monarch, and to advance the interests of Prussia; and, with this in view, to do whatever might please the king. His interest, equally with that of the powers of the north, was to put an end to the maritime tyranny of England, and the only means of accomplishing this object was to close all the ports of Germany against her. He asked that Prussia should definitely agree with France, so that their mutual alliance might be genuine and effective. These explanations, made with that winning charm which was so irresistible in Napoleon, produced a great impression on the mind of the Prussian envoy. His report of their conversation delighted the King of Prussia, but, with his usual want of decision, and yielding disposition, the king feared to engage himself too far with France. He replied by making insufficient offers, and proposals of neutrality, and in the end declined the alliance, while proposing to postpone its completion.

M. Lombard was a French refugee of the French colony in Berlin. A distinguished litterateur and statesman, he had been brought up in the doctrine of neutrality. Faithful to this doctrine he made use of the credit in which he stood with his sovereign to preach neutrality in the king's council; his political sentiments and his inclination for France, from which he had sprung, have very unjustly caused him to be accused of having sold himself to the French government. His retirement, in 1806, on the eve of Prussia's call to arms, was a disaster for his country.

Whenever the First Consul wrote to the king he used to say to me, laughing: "We must be careful about the style of our letters. The King of Prussia has men in his cabinet who know how to speak and to write French very well." He referred to M. Lombard.

Cardinal Caprara, Legate *a Latere* from the Papal See, accompanied the First Consul on this journey. The presence of this prelate, distinguished as he was for his piety, his spirit of toleration, and his lofty character, had been deemed necessary in a country troubled with religious quarrels, which his conciliatory spirit was eminently qualified to appease. At Namur the Cardinal should have been lodged at the house of the bishop of the diocese, and, as a matter of fact, the episcopal palace had been got ready for his reception. But from reports received on the irregular life led by the bishop, and on his gallant adventures, it was feared lest the legate should find himself, in such an abode, in strange company. This occurrence brought forth a number of satirical verses, and allusions which, till then, had only been whispered in Namur. In consequence of the discredit which was thus thrown on the bishop, he was asked to resign his see. This he did, but only after expressly stipulating that his episcopal revenues should be paid to him during his lifetime.

On his return from this journey Napoleon spent the months of September and

October at St. Cloud, occupying himself with his accustomed ardor on the details of the Boulogne expedition, on internal affairs, and on the solution of the various negotiations which had been commenced with the different European ministries, in consequence of the renewal of hostilities with England.

In the first days of the month of November of this same year, 1803, the First Consul made a second journey, which lasted a fortnight, to Boulogne. The object of this journey was to visit the ports of Boulogne and of Wimereux, and to inspect the works which he had ordered to facilitate the assembling of the various divisions of the flotilla. He spent a day and a night in the Roads on board a gunboat, and was present, always in the front line, at an engagement between the frigates of the English cruisers, under the command of Admiral Keith, and a division of the French flotilla. The fire from our sloops, and that of the mortars on our coast batteries, forced the enemy to retire. Six weeks later Napoleon left Paris suddenly, to undertake a new journey along the French coast, which lasted ten days. Only two hours notice was given of this journey, the horses being ordered in the name of General Bessières. The preceding journey had been as secretly prepared, that time under the name of General Duroc. These precautions were taken in consequence of a suspected plot to kidnap the person of Napoleon.

While Napoleon was occupied with these preparations, while all the efforts of France were employed on the naval war, and her frontiers on the Adige and the Rhine were defenseless, Austria was marching her troops, under false pretences, towards Bavaria, Swabia, and Switzerland, reinforcing her army in Italy at the same time. The Russians, on their side, were assembling armies in Podolia, behind the Vistula, and in Lithuania; camps were being formed in Livonia, ready to descend on Pomerania, to act in concert with the Swedes and the English. Four men out of every five hundred in Russia were called to arms. And, finally, in England bodies of troops were being formed on the downs, to be shipped to Cuxhaven to join the Russian and Swedish troops. The Court of Naples was also preparing to assemble its army. Napoleon had his eye on all these movements. He took his precautions for the defense of Italy, and spared no pains to enlighten Austria on the pacific nature of his intentions towards her, and to point out to her where her real interest lay.

Marshal Mortier, having assured the submission of Hanover, returned to Paris, where he was appointed one of the four generals of the guards. He was replaced in the command of the army in Hanover by General Bernadotte.

During the First Consul's absence, his sister Pauline, widow of General Leclerc, who had died at San Domingo in 1802, married Prince Camille Borghèse, a member of one of the most illustrious and richest families in Rome. This prince, who at a very early age had embraced the principles of the French Revolution, had served in the ranks of our army in Italy during the memorable campaigns of General Bonaparte. He had attached himself to the commander-in-chief, who in his turn had taken him into his affections. The union of his sister with Prince Borghèse was accordingly entirely to Napoleon's taste. He received the overtures made to him on this subject with the greatest satisfaction. The marriage was celebrated at Mortfontaine, at the house of Joseph Bonaparte. Pauline followed her new husband to Rome, where, a few months later, she lost her son Dermide, who was General Bonaparte's godson. On Napoleon's accession to the Empire, a senatus consultum conferred on Prince Borghèse the rights of a French citizen and prince.

On the same day on which the First Consul returned from his ten days' journey to

Boulogne, the legislative body was convoked. The session had been opened, according to the usual custom, by the Minister of the Interior. Apart from the new laws which had to be submitted to the sanction of Parliament, it was necessary that the two chambers should be ready for any emergency. A vast conspiracy, of which the threads had not yet been gathered together, was suspected. It was vaguely known that Georges and his gang had entered, or were about to enter France, and that some of the conspirators had slipped into Paris, where they were lying in hiding. The investigations of the police to discover their hiding-places had so far remained unsuccessful, and general anxiety prevailed.

It would be difficult to imagine the anxieties, resulting in sleepless nights, which assailed the First Consul, as I myself can testify, during the month of January, 1804, when plots, of which he knew nothing definite, were being woven around him, and against which he fought in the dark; when he felt the earth trembling beneath his feet, and each breath of air seemed to bring with it the menace of some hidden danger. His courage was not abashed thereby. More fruitful in resource than his own police, who wasted their time in routine and impotent formalities, his clear-sightedness led him on to important discoveries, and guided his hand to seize the hidden threads of the conspiracy.

Profound was his indignation caused by the odious intrigues to which he was exposed, and by Pitt's answer to those who reproached him with wishing for perpetual war: "We do not want it eternal, but only for a lifetime." A perpetual mental strain seemed from that time forward to disturb the calm and serenity of Napoleon's mind, without, however, changing the kindliness of his nature, if such an expression may be made use of without exaggeration. It was not that he feared for his personal safety. In this respect he possessed an optimism which nothing could shake, and every open or secret precaution was repugnant to him, for he believed in his star, and abandoned himself to his fate with entire confidence. But I had opportunities for noticing that the vexation which he felt used to manifest itself in outbursts of anger, not indeed when in his family, but before witnesses, where such outbursts were not wasted. It was always in public that his displeasure burst out, usually in the form of reprimands, which were often severe, but which were always limited to words. He thought that these scenes were necessary to keep vigilance awake, and to stimulate a zeal which had to increase with the difficulties of the circumstances.

The plots which were brewed in the interior of France were favored on our frontiers by the machinations concerted between the English ministers and the French princes who were in refuge in London. The instigators of these conspiracies were the English ambassadors to the smaller Courts, Sir Francis Drake at Munich, and Spencer Smith, brother to the admiral of that name, at Stuttgart. Wickham, the English agent, had returned to Berne where he was playing anew the part of corrupter which, in 1795, 1796, and 1797, he had played towards Pichegru. Taylor was playing the same part at Cassel.

A man whose extreme opinions under the Reign of Terror had brought him into suspicion with the government—Mehée de Latouche was his name—made good his escape from Oléron, to which he had been banished, to England, passing by Guernsey. He passed himself off on Lord Hawkesbury, the minister, and the exiles who formed the council of the Count d'Artois, as the envoy of Republican malcontents in Paris, and professed to be anxious to atone for former errors by serving the Bourbons and working towards the overthrow of the First Consul. He won the confidence both of Lord

Hawkesbury and the exiles, and was sent on to Sir Francis Drake in Munich, as charged with the execution of a great conspiracy against France. This agent gave him instructions and, supplying him with money, sent him on to Paris to the imaginary Jacobin committee, the existence of which Mehée had asserted, there to contrive the best means of getting rid of Bonaparte. Mehée, on his arrival at Strasburg, being anxious, as he declared, to secure permission to return to France, revealed his business to the Prefect, who listened to his revelations and sent him on to Paris. Here Mehée communicated to the government the instructions and powers he had received from Sir Francis Drake, and gave the information which he had obtained. He was authorized to continue his correspondence, which was favored by the means in the power of the police. He pretended to have won over the usher of the First Consul's cabinet, and to be able, thanks to the offices of this man, to obtain documents from the Emperor's private cabinet at St. Cloud, which he described himself as having communicated to the secretary of the Jacobin committee to be copied. As a matter of fact these documents were manufactured by Mehée himself, and it is needless to say that he had no understanding whatever with the usher of the Consul's cabinet, and that the secretary of the committee, like the committee itself, had never existed. My name had to be mentioned to give an air of truth to M. Mehée's reports. But, as the First Consul did not wish those in whom he confided to be the objects of suspicion, Sir Francis Drake's correspondent was ordered to add that the secretary of the committee was not to be confounded with me, who was the First Consul's secretary, that this secretary was the intimate friend of General Duroc, and that on this account the First Consul gave him the work that I had no time to do. This was the only part which Napoleon would allow his cabinet to play in a hoax which covered the English agents with confusion. Mehée and Captain de Rosey, who was sent in his place to Sir Francis Drake and to Spencer Smith, as the aide-de-camp of a general who was none other than Mehée himself, and who described himself as in a position to raise several departments of France in revolt, obtained from the English agents close upon eight thousand pounds, placed at their disposal by the liberality of the English Ministry. The French government communicated to the members of the diplomatic corps in residence in Paris the various documents forming the correspondence between Mehée and de Rosey, and the agents in this work of corruption. Their comments were the condemnation of the shameful policy of the British cabinet. The agents whom he had compromised in this affair were dismissed from the courts to which they were accredited and nothing more was heard of them afterwards.

Two months later another English agent at Hamburg, Rumbold, continued the maneuvers of his colleagues, but, taking a lesson from their disgrace, acted with greater circumspection. During one night in the month of October, 1804, he was seized and removed, together with all his papers, by a detachment of French soldiers. Brought on to Paris, his papers were examined, but this examination led to no discovery. The intervention of the King of Prussia, as director of the Lower Saxony circle, restored him to liberty. A confidential and friendly exchange of letters passed, on this occasion, between the First Consul and the King of Prussia, and it is to be regretted that the letters of the King of Prussia were lost, with the original letters of various sovereigns, which have disappeared from the imperial archives.

A publication which appeared at this time showed the attempts which had been previously made by the princes of the House of Bourbon to establish communications with certain members of the French army, and with residents in the interior of France. An exile—M. de Montgaillard—who had been in the confidence of the French princes, and had been charged by them to negotiate with Pichegru and Moreau, came to offer the Consular government some very curious revelations on this subject. He was commissioned to write a book showing all the circumstances of Pichegru's treachery, and revealing all the plots which had been set on foot—either with or without the cooperation of the French princes—by the English government. M. de Montgaillard sent in to the First Consul a series of manuscripts, one of which was a memorandum on Pichegru's treachery in the Years III, IV, and V, with the text of the secret correspondence, the explanation of the ciphers used, and the key to the names. Another of his manuscripts was entitled: *Secret Memoirs of M. J. G. de Montgaillard During the Years of His Exile.* These two manuscripts, in which the author confessed that he had played a double part, contained some curious revelations on the intrigues of the exiled princes and of the English agents, and on the illusions of their nomad little court. The First Consul, whose duty it was as the head of a government, to lend his ear to traitors, and to turn the scandal of their revelations to profit, ordered that these manuscripts should be printed and published. The peculiar details which they contained, some well-drawn portraits—amongst others the portrait of the Pretender—helped to enlighten the public mind, and if they did little credit to the author's sense of honor, at least testified to his intelligence.

I was commissioned to correspond with M. de Montgaillard, and to pay over to him the sums which Napoleon allotted to him. During the time that I was in relations with this person, I received from him numerous manuscripts, of which some were printed—such as those which related to the foundation of a fourth dynasty, to the reestablishment of the Kingdom of Italy under the Emperor Napoleon, to the rights of the French Crown over the Duchy of Rome, and so on.

In 1814, Count de Montgaillard, as was to be expected of him, sang his recantation, and insulted the idol which he had worshipped. I am not aware whether this appeal to the favor of Louis XVIII stood him in good stead with a prince whose faithless confidant he had been, and whom he had afterwards branded by his revelations under the imperial government.

Since I am speaking of M. de Montgaillard I must say a few words about his brother's work. M. de Montgaillard had a brother, an abbé, who is the author of a chronological abridgement of the history of France from 1787 to 1818. This book, every page of which is disfigured by injustice and errors, was no doubt written in one of those fits of depression to which its author was subject. It seems to have served him alone as a means to pour out the most vehement invectives on Napoleon and on the most honored names of the Empire. The chronological abridgement does not justify its title. The author, instead of giving a concise statement of the principal occurrences, is careful to omit all events which do not afford him the opportunity of venting his spleen in sour and interminable diatribes on Napoleon and his acts. Although very incomplete, this book won for its author a letter of congratulation from General Foy, who was pleased with the facilities which books of this kind afford to the student of history, rather than disgusted at the spirit in which it was written.

A voluminous history of France was published after the abbé's death, under his name. This history, which is a prolix amplification of the chronological review of the history of France by the same author, is the work of his brother. The abbé would not have accepted the Count de Montgaillard as his collaborator, for it was his habit to answer anybody who asked him for news of his brother: "That is a question which I have refused to answer for the last thirty years."

Another publication which I may mention here, although it only appeared two years later, that is to say in 1806, contained certain revelations on the part which the princes, and notably the Count d'Artois, had played in our civil wars. It is entitled: *Historical Memoirs to Serve for the History of the Vendée War*. The author, Count de Vauban, great-grandnephew of the Marshal de Vauban, had followed the Count d'Artois to St. Petersburg as his aide-de-camp, when this prince went to solicit the help of the Empress Catherine in favor of the Bourbons. M. de Vauban, on his return from this journey, after having taken part in the expedition to Quiberon, went to rejoin his prince at the Ile Dieu. Then, discouraged at last by the sight of the futilities and the meannesses of which he had been the witness, he took advantage of the amnesty to return to France. Falling under suspicion of the police he was imprisoned in the Temple, and it was in this prison that he wrote his memoirs. He filled them with all the bitterest recollections, and with revelations which were in no way favorable to the party which he had served. The government, having seized these memoirs, thought it advisable to profit by this discovery, and had them published with the author's name.

Chapter IV

The discovery of the existence of the Royalist conspiracy and the confessions of some of the assassins arrested in Paris, acquainted the First Consul with the fact that the Duke d'Enghien was living at Ettenheim, that Dumouriez had been seen there, and was probably there still. He came to the conclusion that this place was the center of the various ramifications of the conspiracy. Before relating the circumstances of the forcible seizure and trial of the unfortunate Duke d'Enghien I must go further back in history. I had no desire to recall these sad memories, which have given rise to so many erroneous judgments; but it seems to me to be my duty to render strict justice to the memory of Napoleon, and I believe myself to be acting in obedience to one of his most pressing recommendations, in relating what is my personal knowledge of an affair which party spirit has so strangely transformed.

The occurrence itself is today appreciated at its just value. Provoked by the English government, the death of the last of the Condés has brought forth deplorable fruit. The principal interest attaching to this occurrence is due to the influence which it had on Napoleon's political career, and it is on this account that it occupies so important a place in the history of our times. I propose therefore to give the principal outlines of this story so that the impartial reader, from a consideration of them as a whole, may form an opinion on an act of severity to which Napoleon was impelled by a combination of fatal circumstances and an inflexible interpretation of his duties as the Head of the government, an act of which this great man accepted the responsibility with the lofty frankness and the pride of his character, and which, as he himself has confessed, was prejudicial rather than useful to his glory.

The English government, which had at first affected to consider the plan of an invasion of England with contempt, rightly alarmed by the formidable armament which was being prepared in sight of the shores of England, had ended by attaching such great importance to this expedition, that on its side it made the most extraordinary preparations against it. Redoubts and entrenchments were multiplied on the southern coast of England, works for inundating the surrounding country were carried out, the ministers themselves and the principal members of the aristocracy had assumed military uniform and figured in the ranks of the volunteers, and every man able to carry arms had been called out, and was being drilled. The general anxiety was excited and kept alive by a succession of alerts and panics, which carried dismay into the heart of London itself. A large number of families removed from the neighborhood of the seaboard and took refuge in the interior of the country.

And while the government was doing all in its power to avert the storm, it strove to prevent its bursting on British territory. All the resources of the most cunning diplomacy were called into play, and gold was scattered broadcast to induce the powers to declare themselves, and to engage on the continent the enemy which threatened England.

Not considering these means sufficient it had recourse to conspiracies. At the commencement of 1804 the French princes who had retired to London planned a serious attack on the person of the Head of the Consular government, and were favored in this by the English ministers. An order of the King's Privy Council enjoined on the French exiles to betake themselves to the banks of the Rhine, and this under penalty of forfeiting their pensions; and a regulation fixed the amount of pay to be allotted to each officer, and to each soldier. The Duke d'Enghien had previously obtained permission from the Elector of Baden to establish himself at Ettenheim, a small town situated on the right bank of the Rhine, and at a distance of two leagues from this river. At the very time when the exiles, acting under the order of the Privy Council, were assembling on the frontiers of Alsace, some determined royalists, who had fled to London after the pacification of the Vendée, and who were commanded by former Chouan chiefs, secretly landed on the Dieppe coast, and made their way to Paris by roundabout routes, finding shelter on their way in isolated farms and cottages, where they were received by peasants who had been won over to their cause. Georges Cadoudal, Rivière, aide-de-camp to the Count d'Artois, the brothers Polignac, Pichegru, and fifty other conspirators, had in this way secretly arrived in Paris, where they were hiding in places unknown to the police.

The agents of the French police in London reported that some great conspiracy against France was being prepared. The report that the Consular government was drawing to a close, that the days of its Head were numbered, and that the former reigning family were about to reascend the throne, was generally spread over England and Europe; and, indeed, had even reached our colonies. A pamphlet, entitled "To Kill is Not to Murder," which had originally been written against Cromwell, was reprinted in London, in allusion to the First Consul. A newspaper—*L'Ambigu*—written by French exiles, appeared, with a portrait of Bonaparte (with a black mark round his neck) at the head of its columns. Advices received from various sides announced that bodies of exiles would shortly land in the Vendée. The news which the First Consul received from this district induced him to send one of his aides-de-camp, Colonel Savary, to the Vendée. His report confirmed the Consul's suspicions as to the masked agitation which existed there.

The First Consul remembered that there were, in the prisons in Paris, a number of persons who had been arrested on the charge of having been sent from London for the purpose of attempting his life. Their arrest, on the seaboard, in the very act of espionage and corruption, would have sufficiently justified their being tried by court-martial, but as they had been accused of contriving to murder the Head of the state, they had been detained in prison pending the establishment of this charge. The First Consul ordered that some of these persons should be brought before a court-martial, hoping to obtain some revelations as to the object of their journey from some of them. Two were tried and sentenced. The fear of death did not cause them to waver, and they died threatening the government with an approaching catastrophe.

The reports of M. Mehée de Latouche, and of Captain de Rosey—whose mission I have related—had revealed the plots which were being hatched on the right bank of the Rhine by the English ambassadors accredited to the Courts of Munich, Stuttgart, and Cassel. The First Consul, whose mind was made up as to the imminence of the danger which threatened the state and his own person, but still to some extent in the dark, had the list of arrested Chouans once more laid before him. The entry in the jail-book concerning one of these Chouans, who was known to have acted either as servant or as confidant to Georges, during the last insurrection in the West, gave rise to the suspicion that he might know something of the matter. Querel was tried and sentenced without making any confession, but on the night preceding his execution the fear of death prompted him to speak. He related that he had been in Paris six months; that he had come there with Georges and six other conspirators, whom he named; that they had been joined shortly after their arrival by fifteen others; that more were expected to land, and that Paris was the meeting place generally agreed upon. Querel's declarations, which were rewarded with a pardon, put the authorities on the trace of some important discoveries, leading up to a former emissary of the party, a man called Troché, who was a clockmaker at Eu. The First Consul sent his aide-de-camp, Savary, accompanied by the clockmaker's son, who took the place of his father, who was a very old man, to Dieppe, where a fresh landing of exiles was expected. Colonel Savary, in company with young Troché, on arriving at Dieppe, set out at once for Béville, where the landing was to take place. Owing, however, to bad weather, which lasted several days, and to the fact that in the meanwhile, on information transmitted from Paris, signals had been made to the brig, which cruised for several days in front of the cliffs of Béville, the expected landing, which it is said would have included the Duke of Berri, did not take place.

In the meanwhile the police, under the direction of the councilor of state, Réal, taking advantage of Querel's revelations, had made active investigations, which had put them on the trace of persons in hiding in Paris. The arrest of Georges and of his accomplices, which rapidly followed, led to the knowledge of the different parts played in the conspiracy by Pichegru and Moreau. Georges had declared, in one of his examinations, that he awaited the arrival of a French prince in Paris, before acting. As new revelations arose, the importance of the conspiracy and its various ramifications were brought to light. From the extent of these ramifications, the magnitude of the danger which menaced the state and the person of the First Consul can be judged. The intrigues of the English diplomatic agents, which were plotted on our frontiers and which extended even to Paris, proved the active cooperation of England, whose government was the soul of the coalitions. The presence of Georges proved that murder was intended; the name of Moreau was a call to insurrection in the army; and a prince of the House of Bourbon was to put himself at the head of the conspiracy, and give the signal for its outbreak.

Amongst other information which was obtained was a detail which attracted attention in the highest degree. A person who was unknown to Georges' gang had had interviews with the latter. He had been received not only by Georges, but by MM. Polignac and de Rivière, with particular marks of deference. This naturally gave rise to the thought—and this would have been the case even if Georges had not declared the fact—that so important a conspiracy must necessarily be under the command of a superior chief, either present or not far distant, invested with extraordinary powers, who could make himself known as soon as the enemy had been struck down. It was concluded from this that the person received by Georges must be this head, and that he was one of the princes of the former royal family. The various members of the royal family were passed in muster. It was known where the Count de Lille—Louis XVIII—the Count d'Artois, the Dukes of Angoulême and Berri, the Prince de Condé, the Duke of Bourbon, and the Princes of Orléans—the latter living peacefully away from all centers of intrigue—were to be found. There remained only the Duke d'Enghien, of whose very existence Napoleon was almost ignorant. The belief was entertained that this prince might well be the mysterious person of whom we have already spoken. Although the description which had been made of him only tallied in a very imperfect way with that of the duke, the most striking differences in the description of a man who was totally unknown in Paris could not put a stop to the conjectures of which he was the object. The presence of the Duke d'Enghien on the banks of the Rhine, his communications with the exiles who were assembling there, the participation of the English government in the conspiracy (the fact of which was established by all the information collected by the police) the absences of the prince on alleged hunting-expeditions, his excursions on the Rhine, the suspicion that he was in the habit of going to Strasburg, gave new strength to the presumptions, already existing, that he was the chief whose name and rank placed him at the head of the conspiracy. Suppositions excited by suspicion are of rapid growth. It was consequently assumed without hesitation that the Duke d'Enghien might have come to Paris and have stayed there, and have returned to Ettenheim, within the space of eight days. So vivid was this conjecture that the principal houses in the Faubourg St. Germain were searched to see whether the prince was not in hiding there and whether no secret preparations were being made to receive him. It was even supposed that he might have found shelter in the house of the Austrian ambassador. The report to the effect that Dumouriez, the maker of civil wars, and the most active and experienced agent of conspiracies, was at Ettenheim, as the prince's adviser, changed suspicion into practical assurance.

Instructions were sent to M. Shée, at that time Prefect of the Lower-Rhine department. The report which he sent back changed suspicion into certainty. The First Consul had more confidence in his own presentiments and foresight than in the judgment of the police, which, since its suppression as a special department, was lacking in the cohesion and impetus so necessary under the extraordinary circumstances which had arisen. On rising one day, he ordered General Moncey, first officer of gendarmerie, in a confidential way, to send an intelligent officer, under disguise, to Ettenheim, with orders to find out all that was going on there, and to make a list of the people of every rank who were in relations with the Duke d'Enghien. General Moncey handed the report of the officer whom he had entrusted with this mission, direct to the First Consul, without showing it to the police. Amongst the names of the Duke's friends mentioned in this report, were those of Dumouriez and of an English colonel named Smith. It was only later that it was known that the general whom the author of the report had taken for Dumouriez was General Thumery, whose name was mispronounced in German, and that the English colonel Smith was a simple German captain, named Schmidt, who belonged to the prince's staff. This report confirmed the First Consul in the opinion that the Duke d'Enghien presided over the conspiracy of which Paris was the headquarters. The presence of Dumouriez seemed especially a decisive proof. This general, in his opinion, must be the pivot of the whole conspiracy. Napoleon was at that time in ignorance on what terms Dumouriez might be with the various princes of the former dynasty; his presence at Ettenheim was considered sufficient. He was persuaded that the arrest of this person, and the seizure of his papers, would supply exact information on the organization and the means at the disposal of the conspiracy.

To avoid acting with precipitation, he determined to consult with his wisest advisers. A kind of privy council was called together with this object in view, as soon as he had read General Moncey's report. The two consuls, the Grand Judge, the Minister of Foreign Affairs, the councilor of state, Réal, and Fouché, although the latter was not a minister, composed this council. Fouché had succeeded in making himself necessary by his extreme activity. He used often to come and tell the First Consul news which he had obtained, thanks to the influence which he had retained over the police-agents, and the confidences which he extracted from them, beating the Grand Judge in his own department.

As no official report was made of the deliberations of this council, the opinions of the various persons who took part in it have been made the subject of conjecture. It appears, however, certain—and this fact will be established or otherwise in the memoirs, which sooner or later, cannot fail to be published—that the two consuls showed themselves little disposed towards immediate severe measures, and that Fouché, on the other hand, did not hide his opinion that it was necessary to make a prompt example, so as to finish with the conspirators.

I will mention later on what influence M. de Talleyrand exercised on the determination of the First Consul. Napoleon hesitated a long time as to how to act in so serious a matter. His first idea had been to have the Duke d'Enghien tried at the same time, and on the same indictment, as Georges. He was loth, however, to couple a prince with a man whom he considered a common murderer. He next thought of giving great importance to the prince's trial, by bringing him before a High Court. Various considerations, and notably the fear of provoking party manifestations, induced him to abandon this plan, which would, perhaps, have been the best. He at last made up his mind to replace the slow and solemn forms of civil proceedings, by the rapid and secret action of a court-martial, a formidable weapon, which would strike terror into the hearts of his enemies. He had always in reserve the right of clemency.

Such was the state of affairs when on the 19th Ventôse, of the Year XII—March 10, 1804—a day on which I had not dined at the Tuileries, I was sent for at ten o'clock at night by order of the First Consul. I found him, on my arrival, in a room adjoining his study. A number of maps which he had thrown down on the floor—in looking for one of the river Rhine—were at his feet. After helping him to spread this map out on a large mahogany table, which was in the middle of the room, I wrote from his dictation a letter to the Minister of War, Berthier, giving him orders to send off, that night, his aide-de-camp, General Caulaincourt, to Strasburg, and General Ordener, commander of the mounted grenadiers of his guard, to Schelestadt to proceed to the arrest of the Duke d'Enghien. While the First Consul was dictating this letter, General Berthier was announced, and, shortly afterwards, General Caulaincourt. The First Consul dictated the rest of the instructions concerning this expedition to General Berthier, tracing on the map the route to be followed by General Ordener. He then dictated a letter to Minister Talleyrand, prescribing the diplomatic measures to be taken. By the terms of this order the Minister of Foreign Affairs was to hand General Caulaincourt a letter addressed to Baron d'Edelsheim, Minister of the Elector of Baden, which was to be delivered at its address by this officer as soon as he had heard of the arrest of the Duke d'Enghien. It was stated in this letter that "the Minister of Foreign Affairs had previously addressed to the Electoral government, a note tending to a demand for the arrest of the committee of French exiles, in session at Offenburg, when the First Consul, by the successive arrival of brigands sent into France by the English government, as well as by the developments and results of the prosecutions instituted in France, had received definite assurance of the part played by the English agents in the terrible conspiracies against his person and the safety of France; that he had moreover learned that the Duke d'Enghien and General Dumouriez were at Ettenheim; and that, as it was impossible that they could be in that town without the permission of His Electoral Highness, the First Consul had not been able to contemplate, without the greatest grief, the sight of a prince—to whom he had been pleased to give the clearest proofs of his sincere friendship—harboring his most bitter enemies, and allowing the most evident conspiracies to be quietly plotted against him; that under these most unusual circumstances, the First Consul had thought it his duty to give orders to two small detachments to make their way to Offenburg and to Ettenheim, and to seize the persons of the instigators of a crime which, by its very nature, placed those who had palpably taken part in it, outside all human law; that General Caulaincourt was charged with the orders of the First Consul; and that there could be no doubt that in his execution of them he would in no way be wanting in the respect which His Highness might consider due to himself."

The instructions contained in the letter addressed by the First Consul to the Minister of War provided that General Caulaincourt should betake himself to Strasburg, and from there to Offenburg, with two hundred dragoons, to arrest the exiles and the agents of the English government; that General Ordener should proceed to Schelestadt, where he would take three hundred dragoons, and pass over the Rhine with them to Rheinau, secretly surrounding the castle of Ettenheim and arresting the Duke d'Enghien, and especially Dumouriez, together with all persons found with them. General Caulaincourt was to put himself in communication with General Ordener and, as soon as he had heard of his arrival at Ettenheim, to send Minister Talleyrand's letter to the Minister of the Elector of Baden with apologies for the violation of his territory, which was necessitated by the urgency of the matter and the need of absolute secrecy.

Here is the scene, if I may so express myself, of this memorable evening:—The First Consul, Berthier, the Minister of War, General Caulaincourt, and myself were assembled in the large room in the Tuileries palace, which had been used as a bedroom by Louis XVI, and which afterwards was used for a similar purpose by the Emperor. This room was lighted only by two three-branched candelabra, covered with shades, so that the light of the candles illuminated a circumference of a few feet only. The minister and I wrote by the light of one of these candelabra, on a corner of the large mahogany table. The First Consul, lighted by the other flambeau, bending over the map, called General Caulaincourt up to his side and, compass in hand, showed him the route from Strasburg to Rheinau, pointing out the exact position of the ferry which joins the two banks of the Rhine, that of the village of Ettenheim and the road which leads to it.

When, on the evening of the day on which the First Consul had sent for me, I arrived at the Tuileries, I did not know what people he had seen in the afternoon. I learned that he had conversed with the consuls, with the Ministers of Justice and of Foreign Affairs, and with Fouché. Two days later, Fouché, as he was coming from the levee, said to me: "General Bonaparte is very indiscreet, he will end by letting the cat out of the bag." He was alluding to the order for the Duke d'Enghien's arrest. The First Consul had spoken at his levee of the matter which exclusively engrossed his thoughts, of the machinations of the exiles, whose proximity he tolerated with too great patience, and had mentioned the names of the Duke d'Enghien and of Dumouriez. Nobody in the Consular household, however, not excepting Madame Bonaparte, knew of the orders that had been given. The First Consul remained some days in Paris, and then left the Tuileries for La Malmaison. Although my carriage followed his he gave me an escort of some soldiers, for the greater safety of his papers.

The entire population of Paris showed an interest in the various incidents of this drama, which can hardly be conceived today. The arrest of Georges, which had taken place almost simultaneously with the order for the seizure of the Duke d'Enghien, had dispelled all uncertainty as to the existence of a conspiracy, and raised to the highest degree the general solicitude for and sympathy with the Head of the state. It was earnestly prayed that the instigators of the conspiracy might be taken and severely punished.

During his stay at La Malmaison, the First Consul appeared careworn, and indisposed for any occupation. He only received MM. Maret, Talleyrand, Fouché, Réal, the Grand Judge—Régnier—and Cambacérès. On the 25th Ventôse—March 16—the message announced that the Duke d'Enghien had been arrested in the night at the castle of Ettenheim. Orders were immediately given that he should be brought to Paris, where he arrived on the 29th Ventôse.

The First Consul was fully informed as to the details of the conspiracy. He was aware of the order of the King of England's privy council convoking the exiles of the Condé army to the right bank of the Rhine, under penalty of forfeiting the allowances attached to their rank, an edict which coincided with the presence of the Duke d'Enghien in the same place, and that of Georges and his assassins in Paris. The revelations which were contained in the letters seized on the exiles at Ettenheim, Offenburg, and other points on the right bank of the Rhine, letters which had been sent on to him by special couriers; the reports which he had caused to be drawn up and the information which he had collected on all sides, had dispelled his last doubts. Amongst the papers seized were a note from the Duke d'Enghien in answer to a letter from a certain general, called Vauborel, from which it was gathered that the prince had refused to follow the advice, given him by this general, to absent himself in consequence of the dangers to which under the existing circumstances he was exposed; and a letter from a colonel, named de Lanen, which contained similar advice. "If, as I think," this officer added, "the energetic views of the governments which protect us so particularly, are recognized by the great powers as the only means of restoring tranquility to Europe by means of peace on equitable conditions, these conditions will naturally be the Restoration of the monarchy." These papers proved the plan of hostility which had been conceived against the French government, the part taken by the Duke d'Enghien in this plan, and his relations with the exiles who were stationed on the right bank of the Rhine. Fouché had declared that a portmanteau full of papers, which would reveal all the ramifications of the conspiracy, would be found at the prince's house, but no such portmanteau was discovered at Ettenheim. Fouché's assertion was only a conjecture, though it may be that the Duke d'Enghien had been persuaded by the advice of his faithful officers, expressing their fears lest a descent might be made on Ettenheim, to remove to a place of safety all papers which might compromise his companions, while remaining himself at the post of danger.

The following note which the First Consul sent to the *Moniteur* on the day of the Princes' arrival in Paris, and which appeared in the following day's paper, gives a recapitulation of what he had learned:—

"Paris, "28th Ventôse, Year XII—March 19, 1804

"While England was sending Pichegru, Georges, and the gang of murderers, to Paris, she was assembling and hiring the services of all the exiles, who were to be found in Germany. A circular from the Prince de Condé summoned them, about three months ago. It is a fact, known to the whole town of Hamburg, that a man named Millard was entrusted with funds in this town to recruit these wretches, and to send them on to the Rhine. The right bank of the Rhine is filling daily with these new legionaries, whom England summons to be at once the toys and victims of her cruel Machiavellisms.

"A Bourbon prince, with his staff and certain officers, is fixed at this point and thence directs the movement. The Prince de Guéméné and several officers are expected to arrive on March 25 to complete the organization of the bands.

"The Continental powers make haste to disavow such elements of disorder, and the new attempt of the British government will not be any more successful than the crime, which it prepared at such great expense, against the First Consul."

The Duke d'Enghien arrived at the Vilette barrier of Paris towards three o'clock on the afternoon of March 20. He was detained there until the order arrived directing his removal to the fort of Vincennes. He entered the Vincennes prison at five o'clock in the evening.

On the same day a decree was issued ordering that the *ci-devant* Duke d'Enghien, accused of having taken up arms against the Republic, of having been and being still in the pay of England, of forming part of the conspiracies fomented by this power against the safety of the Republic at home and abroad, should be brought before a court-martial composed of seven members, nominated by the military governor of Paris, the said court-martial to meet at Vincennes. By the terms of this decree, the five colonels of the infantry and cavalry regiments in the garrison of Paris; the major of the regiment of *gendarmerie d'élite,* acting as reporter, and General Hulin, the city marshal of Paris, were designed by the governor of Paris to form the court-martial. These officers betook themselves separately to Vincennes. Silence having been observed as to the name of the prisoner whom they were to try, it was only there that they learned that it was the Duke d'Enghien. They were all in ignorance of the various circumstances of the conspiracy, but all alike were under the impression of the general indignation which had been excited by the plan of an attack on the person of the First Consul, as well as by the prospect of the chaotic disorder which would have followed on his death. They did not imagine that these plots had been under the direction of a prince of the former dynasty.

The captain reporter, Dautancourt, proceeded to a first examination of the Prince. The duke, deploring the cruel extremity to which he was reduced, expressed the desire to be heard by the First Consul. Dautancourt advised him to write a request for an audience at the foot of the report of his examination. The Prince's note was in the following words:

"Before signing this official report of my examination, I earnestly request a private interview with the First Consul. My name, my rank, my way of thinking, and the horror of my situation, lead me to hope that he will not refuse my request.

(Signed) L. A. H. DE BOURBON."

This touching appeal to the clemency of a generous enemy was never to reach the man to whom it was addressed.

The document in question was placed before the members of the military commission. Only one of the judges, namely, General Barrois, expressed the opinion that the request for an audience should be transmitted to the First Consul, but the answers of the Duke d'Enghien, the circumstances with which his arrest was surrounded, the conviction of the members of the court that the Prince was the accomplice and even the leader of the plot that was being hatched in Paris, seemed to officers judging with the rigor of the military penal code, sufficient reasons for applying the law to the Prince, his right of appeal to the First Consul after sentence being reserved. Honorable men, such as the members of the court-martial were, would not have stopped to allow their consciences to waver in the face of a sanguinary order. The First Consul, whose mind was made up, had no doubt that the Prince would be condemned; but there was no doubt that he expected that, should an incident arise, he would be referred to before the execution of the sentence was carried out. The proof of this is that at the same time he ordered his Secretary of state, Maret, who was then staying at La Malmaison, and who returned for this purpose to Paris, to write a letter to the councilor of state, Réal, ordering him to proceed to Vincennes, and to personally examine the Duke d'Enghien, and then to come and report the result of this examination to him, Napoleon. M. Maret, if I remember rightly, left La Malmaison for Paris towards seven in the evening, and it must have been about ten o'clock when his letter was handed in at M. Réal's house. By the same fatality which seems to have presided over the whole course of events in this affair, Réal, who for the last eight days had not had a moment's rest, and who had passed several nights without going to bed, had that day come in broken down with fatigue. He had forbidden his valet to wake him before five o'clock in the morning, no matter what message might be sent him. A letter coming from the state Secretary's office did not seem of sufficient importance to warrant a disobedience of M. Réal's formal order that he was not to be waked. Amongst the letters which were handed him at his awakening, was that of the Secretary of state. He dressed with all speed, and set out for Vincennes, but on his way there he met Colonel Savary, who informed him that the Duke d'Enghien's execution had taken place. Savary who was on horseback, continued on his way to La Malmaison, arriving there at eight in the morning. He was at once ushered into the First Consul's study, where I was present. Savary related the sentence and its execution in a few words. On hearing that the Duke d'Enghien had asked to see him, the

First Consul, without asking for any of those details of which he was usually so greedy, interrupted Savary to ask what had become of Réal, and to know if he had not gone to Vincennes. Hearing that he had not gone there, Napoleon remained silent, walking up and down his library, with his hands crossed behind his back, until the moment when M. Réal was announced. After listening to the latter's explanation, and having exchanged a few words with him, he fell back into his reverie, and then, without expressing a word either of approval or of blame, he took his hat and said: "It is well," leaving M. Réal surprised, and to some extent disturbed, by his manner. We heard the First Consul slowly ascending the staircase which led to the little apartment which he occupied over his library. He shut himself up here, and did not appear again for a long time.

The official report of the judgment was presented to him during the same day. The perusal of this document was a subject of fresh grief for him. Legal forms had not been respected. The irregularities and the omissions which he noticed in it caused him to order it to be rewritten. Although the First Consul had never doubted that the Duke d'Enghien would be condemned, he must have left the sentence to the discretion of the court-martial. If, as had been said, he had ordered a condemnation, the court-martial would, without fail, have been instructed in advance of the formalities prescribed by the law, formalities which the president, the judges, and even the captain reporter himself, appeared to ignore. It may be said that this judgment was that of a drumhead court-martial. This is another reason for regretting that the president of the commission did not think himself authorized to forward the request for an audience which the Duke d'Enghien had written at the foot of his examination. If General Hulin had had sufficient strength of character to resist the remarks which he alleges were made to him, and had followed the inspirations of his conscience, he would have done himself the greatest possible honor and he would have preserved the First Consul from the redoubling of hostilities of which this act became the pretext; for it can easily be guessed what Napoleon would have done under the circumstances.

These are the only facts which I witnessed. I relate only what I saw or heard. I may add that no verbal or written communication took place between the First Consul and the military commission during the time which elapsed between the examination of the Duke d'Enghien, which preceded his sentence, and the moment of execution. The means which I had of being informed on this point, and the investigations of those who had an interest in discovering any communication of this kind, totally failed to establish its existence.

If I may speak of my private impressions, I do not hesitate to say that the First Consul, justly incensed by the odious plots which were hatched against his person, wished to hurl back on his enemies the thunderbolts which they had launched at his head, and to answer war with war. Was he to allow himself to be quietly murdered, without defending himself? He appeared to me never to have doubted for a single moment that the assembly of exiles on the Rhine had a prince of the House of Bourbon for chief; that this chief was the Duke d'Enghien; that the Duke d'Enghien's mission was to enter France, after the blow had been struck by Georges and his accomplices; and that this mission had developed upon the Duke d'Enghien, after the Duke of Berri had been prevented from landing in Normandy by the presence at Dieppe of an active and determined officer, who was entirely devoted to the First Consul. Under a deep and just sense of resentment, and clearly foreseeing the sinister future reserved to France, and the bloody revolution which would have been the consequence of his death, he ordered the kidnapping and the trial of the Duke d'Enghien, convinced as he was that sufficient charges to justify a condemnation existed against this prince. What struggles took place in Napoleon's mind are shown by the order given to M. Réal to proceed to Vincennes, and to interrogate the Duke d'Enghien, and by the solitude which he went to seek at La Malmaison, less for the purpose of strengthening his resolution, than with the view of protecting himself against all outside influence, and of calmly reflecting upon his decisions, avoiding Josephine's drawing room, locking himself up for hours together in his private apartments, and refusing to answer his wife, who frequently came and knocked in vain at his door.

Although the reports received at La Malmaison, together with the letters seized on the exiles, left him no doubt whatever of the Duke d'Enghien's knowledge of the conspiracy, it is my conviction that, satisfied with the humiliation to which he had reduced his enemies, he would have leaned towards clemency if he had been informed in time of the request made by this prince to be brought before him. The evil having become one for which there was no remedy, Napoleon boldly accepted the entire responsibility of this act. He could not disavow the brave and: faithful officers who had judged as their consciences had directed them to do. He refused even to enter into an explanation of the causes which had prevented Réal from reaching Vincennes in time; and these would have convinced nobody. His dignity refused to allow him to justify himself from the accusation of seeking to protect himself by false excuses, which would certainly have been brought against him. He therefore resolved to assume the entire responsibility of the affair. He prescribed the strictest secrecy on what had happened, and allowed nobody to be compromised. He imposed silence on himself also—a silence which not even the most violent and the most persistent attacks could induce him to break.

When one looks back to these critical times and reflects on the dangers with which the state was threatened, one is forced to admit that Napoleon fulfilled a painful duty, as Head of the government, and that instead of charging him with a crime, one should rather pity him for having been placed in the necessity of accepting all the odium of an act, the deplorable consequences of which, in the future, his foresight only too clearly pointed out to him. The position of the sentenced man, and the interested feeling of pity with which the hatred of the enemies of France suddenly covered the Duke d'Enghien, have transformed an act of rigor, which the most imperious circumstances imposed on the head of a government, into a crime of savage ferocity.

Napoleon found compensation for the embarrassments in which his enemies involved him in connection with this matter in the enthusiastic attachment of the people, excited to the highest degree by the imminence of a common danger, and the vigorous measures by which it had been averted. But it is true that the first impression produced by this event on the upper classes was a very strong one, the principal and perhaps the only cause of this impression being the mystery and the precipitation with which the Duke d'Enghien had been seized, sentenced, and executed. It was only by reading the *Moniteur* that the ministers, functionaries, and persons attached to the First Consul's household, learned what had happened. La Malmaison presented a sad spectacle that day. I can still remember the silence which reigned that evening in Madame Bonaparte's drawing room. The First Consul stood with his back against the mantelpiece while Madame de Fontanes read him some book, of which I have forgotten the name.

Josephine, with a melancholy look and moist eyes, was seated at the far end of a couch; the persons in attendance, very few in number at that time, had withdrawn into the neighboring gallery where they conversed in whispers on the topic which absorbed all others. Some people came from Paris, but, struck by the doleful appearance of the room, remained standing at the door. The First Consul, anxious or preoccupied, or listening attentively to what Madame de Fontanes was reading, did not appear to notice their presence. The Minister of Finance remained standing in the same place for a quarter of an hour without being spoken to by anybody. Not wishing to go away as he had come, he approached the First Consul and asked him if he had any orders to give him; the Consul made a negative gesture in reply.

I think it useful and necessary to reproduce in this place the notes written in pencil by Napoleon on the margins of the work entitled *History of Napoleon in 1815*, by M. Fleury de Chaboulon. This book contains a long passage referring to the arrest and trial of the Duke d'Enghien. I have copied these notes from the original without changing a word, and they are as follows:

"Napoleon did not trouble himself about the Duke d'Enghien, who had been justly tried and punished by a court-martial. Already, in 1797, General Moreau—in his report to the executive Directoire, at the time of the 18th Fructidor—had complained of the intrigues in which this prince was engaged with Pichegru and his agents in the army, from his residence in Offenburg. This prince had a part in Pichegru and Georges's conspiracy. He was in consequence arrested and condemned to death by the competent tribunal. There was only one irregularity, and that was his arrest in the country of Baden, three leagues from the French frontier. But Napoleon was the protector of the House of Baden, and he had ordered Colonel Caulaincourt, his aide-de-camp, to demand the Duke's extradition, while Ordener was crossing the Rhine with three hundred dragoons and arresting the prince and his agents in his house at Ettenheim."

To the remark that the death of the Duke d'Enghien settled the question which was agitating France, etc., etc., the Emperor answers:

"The Duke d'Enghien's well-merited death injured Napoleon in public opinion and was of no political use whatever to him."

Answering the statement that Josephine, Queen Hortense, Cambacérès, and Berthier had implored him to save the prince's life, the Emperor adds:

"That is false. The Duke d'Enghien, transferred to the castle of Vincennes, was tried and shot before anybody knew that he had been arrested. Besides, everybody at that time was so indignant at the well-known conduct of the Count d'Artois, who was plotting murders in Paris, that there was a general expression of satisfaction at the news at the Tuileries, and amongst the friends and relations of the ministers and of people interested in the state."

It was asserted that the execution had been urged by Murat, who, prompted by a certain number of regicides, at the head of whom was Fouché, thought that he would be serving Napoleon, his family, and France, by the death of a Bourbon. A note in Napoleon's writing denies this assertion:

"That is false. Napoleon knew that if the court-martial found him guilty, his execution would be proceeded to within twenty-four hours."

I will add that the man who replied to the offer of the smugglers who undertook to hand over to him the princes of the former dynasty, who were retired in England, with the threat that he would have them hanged if a single hair fell from the heads of these princes, was not a man to consider the death of the Bourbons necessary to his fortune. In answer to the reproaches made against M. de Talleyrand on this occasion, Napoleon writes:

"Prince Talleyrand behaved, in these circumstances, like a faithful minister, and the Emperor never had to reproach him on the subject. If the affair of the Duke d'Enghien had to occur over again, the Emperor would act in exactly the same way. The interests of France, the dignity of the crown, and the law of just reprisals, forced him to act as he did."

It is said, in the passage in the book which was annotated as above by the Emperor, that the arrest of the Duke d'Enghien had been for a long time imputed, and was still imputed by persons who did not know the exact facts, to General Caulaincourt. On the margin is written in the Emperor's writing:

"All this is absurd. Caulaincourt, Napoleon's aide-de-camp, obeyed, and had to obey Talleyrand's order to proceed to Baden, and, at the same time that Ordener arrested the prince, to demand his extradition, accompanying his demand with an apology for the violation of territory. Ordener was forced to obey the order to cross the Rhine with three hundred dragoons and to arrest the prince. The court-martial was forced to condemn him to death, if he was found guilty. Thus, whether innocent or guilty, Caulaincourt and Ordener had to obey. If he was guilty, the court-martial had to condemn him to death, if he had been innocent, it would have been the duty of his judges to acquit him, for no order may sway a judge's conscience. There is no doubt that had Caulaincourt been appointed to try the Duke d'Enghien, he would have declined the nomination; but that, charged with a diplomatic mission, he was forced to carry it out. All that is so simple that it is nonsense to find any fault. It is true also that the Bourbon party, having persisted in calumniating Caulaincourt for the small part he took in this affair, this circumstance was the origin of the favor into which he was taken by the Emperor. The death of the Duke d'Enghien must be attributed to the Count d'Artois, who directed and commanded, from London, the murder of Napoleon by Pichegru and by Georges, and who had appointed the Duke of Berri to enter France by Béville, and the Duke d'Enghien by Strasburg, after Napoleon's death."

I have spoken of the part played by Talleyrand in the tragical end of the Duke d'Enghien. This is proved by a letter which he wrote to the First Consul under date of Ventôse 17th, Year XII—corresponding to March 8, 1804. I shall in its place relate that this former minister, after having removed all personal papers, referring either to the death of the Duke d'Enghien or to the occurrences in Spain, from the imperial archives, in 1814, consigned them to the flames. The letter in question here escaped this fate. Placed for a moment in a writing-table, together with all the documents which had been brought from the imperial archives, this letter had slipped behind the drawer of the writing table, and had remained there in oblivion. It was not till long afterwards that it was found. I have read and re-read the letter, which, on a double sheet of foolscap paper, is written throughout in M. de Talleyrand's hand, and signed by him. It will certainly be published one day. MM. Molé and Thiers have read it. The person who owns it refused to allow any copy to be taken. I recognized it as soon as it was put into my hands, for I saw it at the time it was addressed to the First Consul. Its contents, in substance, were to the effect that its author—Talleyrand—had reflected on the subject of the conversation which he had the honor of having with the General—which was the title given at that time to the First Consul—that Frenchmen loved his rule, that they placed all their hopes in him, that if anything could disturb their confidence it would be the fear lest he might play the part of a Monk, that the leaders of the conspiracy which had just been found out were men of Fructidor, that a Bourbon was at their head, and that the safety of the state demanded that all the conspirators without exception should be seized. In a final paragraph M. de Talleyrand added that the First Consul's aide-de-camp, Caulaincourt, was prudent and devoted, and that he would carry out whatever orders might be given him in a proper manner, and in accordance with the Consul's wishes.

This accusing letter appears to have been preserved for the express purpose of giving a striking denial to the assertions of Prince Talleyrand, who has frequently repeated, since the Emperor's fall, that the condemnation of the Duke d'Enghien had been entirely disapproved of by him; while, on the contrary, he did all in his power to bring it about.

This deplorable affair had a fatal influence on Napoleon's destiny. It became in the hands of his enemies, who as a matter of fact never on any occasion took any interest in the Bourbons, a weapon with which they served themselves with so much success against him, that those who had taken any part in the affair, being frightened of its consequences, did all in their power to throw off all responsibility in this compromising matter from their shoulders. Amongst these was the Duke of Vicence. The reproach of having been mixed up in this catastrophe filled his life with bitterness. He could not foresee that the execution of the Duke d'Enghien would so speedily follow on his arrest. How many times has he not spoken to me of the disagreeable things which he had to suffer on account of this affair in his family relations, and of the difficulties he had to overcome for the very same reason, after his arrival in St. Petersburg. His first care, on taking possession of the French embassy in Russia, had been to convince the Emperor Alexander his ministers, and the Russian nobility, that he had had no part in this tragic occurrence. This was the subject of the two following letters, which were written without the Emperor Napoleon's knowledge, and which were published in the *Journal des Débats* in 1814

Copy of a letter from M. DE CAULAINCOURT, French ambassador to H. I. M. THE EMPEROR OF ALL THE RUSSIAS:

"St. Petersburg, 2 April, 1808

"SIRE,

"The information which Your Majesty has received from the Rhine has cleared me of the odious calumny which has been weighing on me for the last three years. There are particulars which Your Majesty cannot know. I owe it to the confidence with which Your Majesty honors me to lay them before you. They will convince Your Majesty to what a degree I am innocent of the arrest of M. le Duke d'Enghien.

"Sent by the First Consul to Strasburg, at almost the same time as General Ordener, a confusion between these two missions has established itself in the mind of the public. General Ordener was ordered to proceed to Ettenheim, there to seize upon the person of the Duke d'Enghien. The order and the documents which I place before Your

Majesty will prove how different was my mission to his, and that, in consequence, I had nothing to do, and could have nothing to do, with this unhappy affair.

"I remain, Your Majesty's etc., etc.

"(Signed) CAULAINCOURT."

Copy of the answer of H. I. M. THE EMPEROR ALEXANDER *to* GENERAL CAULAINCOURT, *French ambassador.*

"I knew, General, through my ambassadors in Germany, how innocent you were of the horrible affair of which you speak. The documents which you communicate to me can only add to my conviction. I am pleased to tell you this, and to again assure you of the sincere esteem in which I hold you.

"ALEXANDER."

"St. Petersburg, April 4, 1808."

These two letters were preceded by an article, communicated to the newspaper, in which it was stated that it was General Ordener who effected the arrest of the Duke d'Enghien, and who conducted him to the Strasburg citadel; that the General started the day before M. de Caulaincourt, and that he had received his orders before he started; that his mission was not one of the kind entrusted to several persons; that even supposing it had been thought necessary to put him under anybody's orders, it would not have been under those of an officer younger both in years and in service, that at this the general was so grieved by what happened that he died of a broken heart at Compiègne; that Caulaincourt could so little foresee the results of this expedition that it was by the telegraph that the order to conduct the prince from Strasburg to Vincennes was transmitted; that when M. de Caulaincourt returned to Paris the death of the Duke d'Enghien had already been deplored for several days; that, like Duroc, Caulaincourt had already filled the posts to which they were definitely nominated when the Consulate was transformed into the Empire; and that, finally, General Caulaincourt's mission had two objects, as is shown by the following copy of the Minister of War's letter:—

"PARIS, Ventôse, 21st, Year XII (March 12, 1804.) "THE MINISTER of WAR to CITIZEN CAULAINCOURT.

"The First Consul commands the Citizen Caulaincourt, his aide-de-camp, to proceed by post to Strasburg. He will accelerate the construction and the launching of the light boats which are being built there for the navy. He will inform himself from the Prefect and Citizen Mehée, of the best steps to be taken to effect the arrest of the agents of the English government, who are at Offenburg and at Freiburg, and notably that of the Baroness de Reich—unless she has already been arrested.

"Captain Rosey, who is on a mission to the English ambassadors, and who enjoys their entire confidence, will give him the necessary information about the plots which are in progress against the peace of the state and the safety of the First Consul.

"Citizen Caulaincourt will inform the bailiffs of the cities on the right bank that, in giving shelter to people who seek to disturb the peace of France, they are exposing themselves to great dangers; and he will arrange with the general in command of the 5th military division for the services, in case of need, of a sufficient force for carrying out these orders.

"He will make a particular report to the First Consul of Captain Rosey's mission."

[Two paragraphs referring to Captain Rosey are omitted in the copy.]

"The Minister of War,

"ALEX. BERTHIER."

The author of the article added that the falseness of the accusations made against Caulaincourt was known to people at that time near the First Consul, as well as to the residents in the castle of Ettenheim, and to all persons with whom this general officer had to arrange the details of his mission; that his connection with the arrest of the Duke d'Enghien was limited to the grief which he shared with the whole of France and the cruel sorrows which it occasioned him to bear, so that during ten years he could only oppose to this accusation a blameless life; that he was forced on one single occasion to explain the circumstances to a great sovereign, for the purpose rather of returning his confidence than to dissipate doubts which did not exist in that sovereign's mind, as is proved by the two letters mentioned above.

We do not wish to comment in any way on this article. It will suffice us to add that the disadvantageous position in which M. Caulaincourt's susceptibility, which as a matter of principle cannot be blamed, placed him at the court of Alexander, prevented him from serving Napoleon in Russia with the energy and independence which was necessary. His object was to win back public opinion, which was unfavorable to him in St. Petersburg, and to remove the difficulties which this disfavor might throw in the way of the success of his mission. But at the same time he had contracted a tacit obligation towards the Emperor of Russia which had harmful consequences. He had given him an advantage over himself by which this prince knew how to profit. The influence exercised on the mind of our ambassador by the winning and fascinating manners of the Czar, threw the former off his guard, and prevented him from judging rightly the clear-sighted policy of the French Ministry, and from assisting to carry it out. That is the impression which the weak and partial conduct of his ambassador in Russia produced on the mind of Napoleon, who gave him full credit for his devotion and the purity of his intentions. It was owing to this impression that the Emperor consented to Caulaincourt's wish to return to France. The Duke of Vicence was recalled in May, 1811, and replaced by General Lauriston.

The truth is that General Caulaincourt did not know what fate was in store for the Duke d'Enghien. The execution took place while the aide-de-camp was still in Strasburg, or while he was occupied in the dispersion of the exiles assembled at Offenburg. It was not his mission to arrest the prince, but he could not have been in ignorance that this arrest had been decided upon, seeing that he was present when the orders concerning it were dictated by the First Consul to General Berthier and to myself, and that, together with the First Consul, he looked up on the map the positions of Rheinau and of Ettenheim on the left and right banks of the Rhine, and that he received orders to arrange with General Ordener, and to betake himself to Strasburg with a letter from Talleyrand, which he was to hand to the ambassador of the Elector of Baden, as soon as he had heard the result of General Ordener's mission; and seeing, finally, that he was entrusted with the use of a sum of twelve thousand francs for paying the expenses of the expedition.

The Emperor, at St. Helena, moved by a feeling of equity and of kindness, such as was the leading trait of his character, wrote most favorably of the Duke of Vicence in the notes in his own hand, which I quoted literally in the first editions of my Memoirs.

In relating the preceding details, I have had no other object in view than to establish the facts as they were, and to define the eagerly discussed part played by the Duke of Vicence in this occurrence, and this in the interests of truth. Far from being animated by any personal feeling, I have always felt as much esteem as respect for the character of this minister.

The sensation produced on the Continent by the arrest and trial of the Duke d'Enghien was great. Two courts, Russia and Sweden, allowed their hostility to break out on this occasion. The one was under the influence of England; the other, whose sovereign carried his hatred for the First Consul to the point of madness, had broken off all relations with the French government. The Russian Court went into mourning for the Duke d'Enghien, to whom it was in no way related. Protestations were addressed by the Cabinets of St. Petersburg and Stockholm to the Diet of Ratisbon. The Russian ambassador to Paris received orders to make the violation of the Baden territory the subject of an official complaint. Talleyrand answered haughtily to this pretension, on the part of Russia, to interfere in the relations between France and a state to which she was allied. The notes addressed by Russia and Sweden to the Ratisbon Diet were left without answer. The Elector of Baden declined the intervention of these two powers. Austria, Prussia, and the other continental States took no part in the recriminations which Russia and Sweden were endeavoring to provoke. After replying vigorously to the notes from Russia, the First Consul once more retired into the silence which, during the whole course of this affair, he had imposed upon himself.

Whatever the facts may be, this fatal occurrence has always served Napoleon's enemies as a pretext for attacking him. They have not lost one opportunity of reproaching him with it, seeming to think that all the plots directed against his life, the infernal machine, the conspiracy of Georges, and the isolated attempts to murder him, were perfectly legitimate proceedings, and that he had no right to defend himself against them. These same adversaries, on the other hand, fully absolved the Emperor Alexander for the part he played in the conspiracy which resulted in the dethronement and death of his father.

It was on this occasion that M. de Chateaubriand began his first attacks upon Napoleon. After the publication of the Concordat, this author had been appointed secretary to the French legation at Rome. His author's pride had been wounded by the indifference with which his "Genius of Christianity" had been received in the capital of the Christian world. There was, moreover, little sympathy between the ambassador—Cardinal Fesch—and the secretary, M. de Chateaubriand, who, unable to content himself with a secondary rank, claimed the right to direct the business of the embassy, and tried on every possible occasion to take the ambassador's place. It was impossible for the Cardinal to allow such an encroachment on his authority. In order to put a stop to this quarrel, which he could no longer appear to tolerate by his silence, the First Consul, yielding to the pressing solicitations of Madame Bacciochi, his sister, recalled M. de Chateaubriand, and appointed him Chargé d'Affaires to the Republic of the Valais. This post appeared a shabby one in the eyes of the person appointed. His ambition was for a post of plenipotentiary minister, and he thought that hierarchical rules might have been dispensed with in his case. The little Republic of the Valais did not play a sufficiently important part in foreign politics to warrant the presence of a plenipotentiary minister there. There was no secretary attached to this post of Chargé d'Affaires, and the salary was only twelve thousand francs. The only consideration which made the prospect of his appointment to the post in the Valais bearable, was that he would not be under the orders of any superior. His friends made him hope that he would soon be called to more important functions, and it was owing to this prospect that he neglected proceeding to his post for some time. He had already received his instructions, when the catastrophe of Vincennes occurred. This occurrence appeared to him to afford an appropriate excuse for refusing a post which he considered beneath him. The letter in which he sent in his resignation to Talleyrand, the Minister of Foreign Affairs, was not, as has been said, offensively brief; nor was it filled with generous anger. M. de Chateaubriand simply said that his wife's health was so bad that the doctors had declared that a change to so pernicious a climate as that of the Valais would be in her case, might prove fatal to her; and that under these circumstances he was forced to resign the post which he owed to the confidence of the government, and that he begged the minister to persuade the First Consul to accept his resignation, to which he added the homage of his respect. If these were not the exact expressions used in the letter, they at least convey its spirit and its substance. The letter, besides, is to be found in the archives of the Foreign Office. If the motive, namely, the mortal malady with which Madame de Chateaubriand was threatened, which was alleged by its author, was a fallacious pretext, may not this letter be described as a falsehood. If, on the other hand, it was a virtuous indignation which prompted the sick lady's husband, he should, in my opinion, have had the noble frankness to declare it. From whatever point of view one may consider the conduct of the author of "The Genius of Christianity," in this circumstance, it seems to me that it is not too severe to say that he displayed neither delicacy nor true courage.

Napoleon attached but little importance to a step, the motives of which were open to misunderstanding. He treated it with indifference, and ceased to interest himself in M. de Chateaubriand. Later on, in pursuance of his desire of drawing men of talent, with a useful purpose in view, to his side, he thought of employing him on such services as the state was warranted to expect from his talents. M. de Chateaubriand, however, persevering in a weak resistance, he decided to ignore him. This distinguished writer was drawn into this resistance by his own conceit, and by his extreme opinions, which we will at least consider sincere. But it is worthy of notice that a curious eccentricity of mind, or an excessive vanity prompted Viscount de Chateaubriand to imagine himself Napoleon's rival in superiority, establishing constant comparisons between Napoleon and himself, and setting forth their respective characters as the two principles of good and of evil, Oromaze (Chateaubriand), and Ariman (Napoleon), predestined to eternal antagonism.

I may be allowed to interrupt the chronological order of my narrative to finish what I have to say about M. de Chateaubriand. On his return from his voyage to the Holy Land, he sought on the literary staff of *Le Mercure,* the resources of which he stood in need. The spur of pride which prompted him to revolt against the immense superiority of Napoleon, excited him, while forced to admit his own impotence, to commence hostilities against the Head of the government in the articles which he supplied to *Le Mercure,* a circumstance which brought about the suppression of this paper. M. de Chateaubriand took another opportunity, later on, of defying the Emperor, by putting on mourning, an insulting affectation, for one of his cousins. Charged with a secret mission by the princes of the House of Bourbon, this cousin had been taken in the act and condemned to death. M. de Chateaubriand's publication, in 1811, of the narrative of his journey from Paris to Jerusalem, a work in which, better inspired, he nobly praised the Emperor, won back Napoleon's favor to a writer, whose talents he esteemed. The preceding year Napoleon had given him a proof of his forbearance, by repairing the omission of "The Genius of Christianity" in the report on the award of the decennial prizes. He further brought the candidature of its author before the Institut. But the obstinacy with which the candidate refused to make any alterations in his reception speech prevented its acceptance. M. de Chateaubriand had been pleased to revive in this speech his hateful memories of the Revolution, and to bring back upon a stage consecrated to literary discussions, *conventionnels* and regicides. A committee of the Institut, to whom this speech was submitted for inspection, decided that it could not be allowed to pass.

The restless and vain mind of M. de Chateaubriand, and his mobile imagination, rendered unbearable the oblivion into which he had fallen, but his pride kept him back. He decided, however, to have the Minister of Police sounded by one of his friends. The Minister of Police had been commissioned by the Emperor to form a kind of literary committee, including such men as Esmenard, Etienne, Jay, Tissot, Michaud, the author of *The History of the Crusades*, and others. A chance meeting with the Duke of Rovigo was arranged. The interview passed off to mutual satisfaction. This reestablishment of peace should have been durable if anything could have been lasting with a man like Chateaubriand, for in putting his hand into that of the minister he had expressed the hope that their reconciliation would not merely be an armistice. An article in *Le Constitutionnel,* which appeared on August 1, 1848, and which was written by the clever woman who acted as intermediary in this reconciliation, has revealed details concerning it which were only known to a few people. M. de Chateaubriand, desiring that this reconciliation should be justified in the eyes of the world by a special favor, caused a memorandum to be handed to the Emperor on the subject of the creation of a Ministry of Public Libraries, and asked to be appointed its director. Napoleon did not reject this proposal, but, as by its nature it seemed likely to create difficulties both in men and matters, and because it did not seem very opportune, it was neglected during the time which preceded the rupture of the peace with Russia. The events which followed on this rupture caused both the proposal and its author to be forgotten. M. de Chateaubriand, seeing his powerful adversary abandoned by fortune, had no other thought than to crush him. His instinct of opposition, of resistance and hostility, overflowed in furious attacks against the great and unhappy man. The high opinion which he had of his intellectual value, of the pre-eminence of the race of Chateaubriands, and of the great good fortune which a resuscitation of the ancient monarchy could not fail to bring him, made him lose all self-control and moderation.

The attempts made to effect a revolution in the state by means of the death of the First Consul had given rise to reflections on the inefficacy of a life-long tenure of the supreme post. For many months people had been struck with the necessity of creating a hereditary title, to which the Life Consulate appeared to be a preliminary. The First Consul's household and family took great interest in this important event. In the drawing room of the ladies and gentlemen in attendance this question had been the subject first of aside and then of general conversations, and the almost general wish expressed was that a hereditary title might be created. Josephine desired this also, although she sometimes expressed to people who were in her confidence that the prospect of the elevation of her husband to a hereditary dignity inspired her with some anxiety for her future. The senate had given the hint, two months previously, in an address presented to the First Consul; and this example had been followed by the other bodies in the state. The conspiracies and the machinations of the princes, and of the exiles on our frontiers, dispelled many hesitations on this point.

The tribunate took the initiative in this matter and the Council of State was consulted. Four-fifths of the votes were in favor of heredity. The First Consul was not present at the sitting at which this proposal was discussed. Hearing that the debate had been an animated one, he desired to have the signed opinion of each councilor of state. He showed no more disfavor to those who had opposed the proposal than to those who had approved it. As a matter of fact he felt respect for those who did not blindly subject their opinions to his own. They had no reason to repent having freely and in good faith expressed their way of thinking. His confidence even was forfeited by those who abdicated their independence before him. Although the vote of the council of state was not requisite, the First Consul attached importance to the opinion of a body which was justly reputed for its intelligence, and which, though apparently in his hands, was known for its independence.

The wish expressed by the tribunate, and joined in by such members of the Legislature as were present at the time in Paris, during the vacation of this assembly, was carried to the senate. On May 18 a senatus consultum was promulgated by which the hereditary imperial dignity was conferred upon Napoleon Bonaparte. The popular vote confirmed that of the great bodies of the state. Out of three millions, five hundred and twenty-four thousand, two hundred and fifty-four electors who registered their votes in the books prepared for this purpose, three millions, five hundred and twenty-one thousand, six hundred and seventy-five voted in favor of the proposal which called Napoleon to the imperial throne. There were only two thousand five hundred and seventy-nine opponents.

At the end of the sitting—during which the First Consul was proclaimed Emperor—the senate proceeded in a body to St. Cloud to present him with the senatus consultum which they had just passed. The senate next went to present its congratulations to Josephine. The palace presented that day an aspect of bewilderment and surprise which contrasted with the serenity of the man round whom all this movement centered. An immense crowd covered the steps and approaches to the palace of St. Cloud. I happened to be, after the ceremony was over, in one of the drawing rooms, conversing with a number of officers and aides-de-camp on the subject which was the one topic of the day. One of the footmen, in full livery, with gold lace on all the seams of his clothes, and dressed in white silk stockings, came to look for me in the midst of a group, and summoned me with the words, spoken in a loud voice: "Sir, the Emperor wishes to see you." These words produced the effect of an electric shock on everybody present. All looked at each other, at first with glances of surprise, but then with smiles, as if to say that it was no dream, but that all were well awake.

There are people who will not hesitate to relate, as though they themselves had been witnesses thereof, the secret communications which, according to them, took place between the First Consul, his colleagues, and their confidants, the good offices performed by these in acting as intermediaries with the influential members of the great bodies in the state, the true or false reasons alleged for necessitating or for justifying this great change, the distribution of offices, and so on. The greatest ingenuity has been displayed in forming more or less erroneous conjectures as to the reasons of Napoleon's elevation. The examples of Caesar, Augustus, and Cromwell have not been forgotten. According to these Napoleon was only a servile copy of the illustrious men of ambition of antiquity and modern times. It has pleased people to attribute to crooked and crafty ways a solution which the general tendency of public opinion rendered simple and natural. They have tried to spread the belief that he cunningly brought about an event, which pleased him, no doubt, but for the realization of which he had but let himself drift with the tide of public opinion. It has been said that he prepared this transition from the Consulate to the Empire by underhand maneuvers; that he had enshrouded himself in dissimulation and in reticence; that he had feigned astonishment at the first overtures which were made to him on the subject; that on the reception of the senate's address he had hidden his joy under the mask of indifference; that he had refused to express any opinion; that in the end he had answered with mock modesty that he desired nothing for himself; while as a matter of fact he had forced the army to offer him the Empire; and that, at the same time, he had acted upon the senate, making it fear lest the initiative should be taken in this matter by the army. The generally accepted opinion that Napoleon was the soul of all these resolutions, and that he was the mainspring of it all, has given credit to these assertions. The character of the Danish monarch, Frederick III, has prompted no historian to look for the determining motive of the resolution taken in 1660 by the States of Denmark, to ascribe absolute power to this prince, in his secret and private promptings. Neither had Napoleon any need to have recourse to subterfuges and to deceit. His glory and the influence which he had acquired by his victories and his conduct in Italy and in Egypt; success, that magical word which has such an empire over men, had won over almost the entire French nation to his side; while at the same time there had sprung up in his mind the conviction that he possessed the strength and the power necessary to raise France to the front rank amongst nations. The efforts and the recent undertakings directed against his power had confirmed him in the opinion that the counter-revolution could only be prevented by a stable form of government. He had studied the inclinations of the nation. When he was nominated Consul for life, this vote was received with general approbation. He had next been desired to appoint his successor, and this was another step in the same direction. If in the person of this successor there had been recognized a man formed by himself, this successor would scarcely perhaps have been sufficiently strong and sufficiently respected to continue his work without finding obstacles in his path. Had he been a general, rendered famous by his victories, as Moreau for instance, or any other, the first care of the newcomer would probably have been to destroy his predecessor's work. When the fermentation which the questions of lifelong tenure of the supreme post, of the appointment of a successor, had provoked had awakened the idea of a hereditary title, it was found natural that the great bodies of the state should seek out the solution of this question without being driven to do so. France was profoundly impressed with the dreadful excesses of the Reign of Terror and with the flabby regime of the Directoire. As the dangers which Napoleon had incurred were remembered, and the apprehension arose as to what fresh dangers might be menacing him, anxiety was felt as to what would become of France after he had gone. A violent reaction was feared. People were tired of changes, and determined to undergo no fresh vicissitudes. And finally it was the general aspiration to be at last able to rest under the protection of a lasting government.

The opinions on the question of a hereditary title which Napoleon emitted on the day after the 18th Brumaire, have been quoted against his conduct on this occasion. The march of events, and the constantly increasing inclination of the masses for a hereditary monarchy, had no doubt modified his ideas, and his language, on this subject. At the time when Napoleon pronounced himself opposed to the hereditary idea he declared that Europe must be brought to recognize that a state could exist with the Republican form, that a few years trial would decide this, that the Republic could only be consolidated in France by the perfect harmony of the public powers. Experience had demonstrated the want of such harmony. The opposition which Napoleon had met with in the Assemblies, against his plans of reform, gave him cause to fear a resistance which, as time went on, might become systematic. The tribunate's opposition was not popular. The nation sympathized with its chief, and applauded the acts of his government. It desired to preserve this government by placing the power of its chief magistrate beyond the uncertainties of hazard, and its government system beyond the reach of the assassin's dagger. To this feeling were due the addresses made by the army and the principal civil functionaries; also the address of the senate, asking Napoleon to complete his work. This almost unanimous state of public feeling legitimized Napoleon's secret ambition, but he had reason to be surprised at the facility with which people hailed a change towards which he was driven faster than he cared to go. It was therefore unnecessary for him either to abuse or to force public opinion. He guided it in the way in which it was flowing, and occupied himself with regulating its current; proceeding with circumspection, and conciliating the new order of things with the advantages acquired by the Revolution. The difficulties which were overlooked by the masses did not escape Napoleon's farseeing eye. He had but to moderate the impatience of the people, and of the army, and to protect himself against all precipitation. He had declared that he would only accept the imperial dignity with the assent of the French nation, an assent which he was certain of obtaining, but with which he could have dispensed. The almost unanimous answer of the votes was in accordance with his expectations and justified his appeal to the suffrages of the French people.

He was not obliged, like Caesar, to fight with a menacing opposition. The opposition which he met with in his councils limited itself to the wishes expressed by certain Republicans of perfect good faith, who were persuaded that with Napoleon France would be sufficiently strong to force Europe to live in peace with her. Napoleon, well aware of the hatred with which the monarchs regarded the French Revolution, had, as I have just said, more foresight, and consequently less confidence in the future of the French Republic. Had he only considered his personal ambitions he might, time helping, have come to an understanding with the foreign Ministries, and have ended by making common cause with them. His object was a loftier one, his ambition was more patriotic. Representing the interests which had sprung from the Revolution, he wished to definitely assure their victory by making some concessions to the old monarchies, which, as long as France isolated herself from them, feared for their future existence; a difficult enterprise, which, without being beyond the power of the genius who had undertaken to carry it out, demanded as much prudence and dexterity as resolution. Napoleon would have succeeded, in spite of the faults which were less of his doing than the result of circumstances, which he had the strength to master, had time not failed him. The proof that foreigners never ceased to consider him as the champion of liberal ideas and the enemy of privileges, in spite of the purple with which at times he had to cover himself, is that they never compounded with him, convinced as they were that he would never sacrifice the principles of the Revolution to them, and that they, could know no rest until they had struck him down. It is, moreover, evident that their suspicion and their ill will against France have survived the fall of the Empire.

It may be asked today what force gave Napoleon the high ambition to assume the crown, and to found a dynasty. The profoundness of the designs of Providence must be recognized here, when one remembers how the haughty Restoration, thinking itself firmly reestablished on the ruins of the imperial throne, fell of its own accord, and without glory, by the efforts of some men, prompted by public opinion. The nation took revenge for the way in which its rights had been ignored by this ancient race, and by the kings who rejected as illegitimate the great man to whom the national gratitude had awarded a crown, because this man was not protected by the prestige of royal birth. In one word, the inauguration of the Empire, in which the privilege of blood was subordinated to the rights and the interests of the nation, weakening as it did the prestige of ancient royalty, founded a new era and made way for the triumph of constitutional ideas in Europe.

The creation of the Empire was a revolution which the senate wanted to turn to its own advantage, and by which it tried to profit by stipulating for advantages in its favor; amongst others, for the privileges of heredity, and for extraordinary powers. The tribunate and the Legislative body demanded an increase of pay. A vulgar ambition would not have thought such concessions too high a price to pay for a crown. Napoleon was not dazzled, and saw from a higher eminence. He was not willing, by rendering hereditary the senatorial dignity, to hand over the future of the country to the mercies of an authority which, should it happen to come into conflict with the crown, would impede the onward march of the government, and which, in a time of danger, might render itself independent, and even treat with the enemy if opportunity offered itself. This event, in spite of his foresight, was destined to realization ten years later.

The following extract from a letter by the Count de Survilliers—Joseph Bonaparte—summarizes, better than I could do, the advantages of the creation of a hereditary title, and answers the reproach addressed to Napoleon of having made himself the heir to the French monarchy:

"The proclamations of the general of the army of Italy, made it sufficiently clear that if Napoleon came to power, he would establish a government other than the Republic. On the 18th Brumaire, this event was consummated. The Napoleonic monarchy dates from that day. First of all, elective and temporary; next, lifelong; and finally, hereditary; it had to undergo these modifications. The conspiracy of Georges and Moreau decided the declaration of a hereditary title. With Napoleon as Consul for a period, a *coup de main* might overthrow him; as Consul for life, the blow of a murderer would have been required. He assumed hereditary rank as a shield. It would then no longer suffice to kill him; the whole state would have had to be overthrown. The truth is that the nature of things tended towards the hereditary principle: it was a matter of necessity.

"The French monarchy had feudal rights, an exclusive and privileged nobility, a venality in public departments, entail, parliaments, convents, a landowning clergy, and a confusion of the public treasure with that of the monarch. Did Napoleon reestablish all these things? He consecrated the liberty of the individual and the liberty of property; he rendered public employment accessible to all; he established civil and political liberty in rights and taxation, the liberty of religious beliefs, the jury system, the system of public registration, the payment of clergymen, distinctions without privileges, and the separation of the public purse from the monarch's privy purse; and enforced the publication of the manner in which the public money was spent. The institution of the Legion of Honor preceded the proclamation of the Empire, but the decoration, instead of being awarded only to special and exclusive classes, was bestowed in return for services of every kind, and was the reward of all kinds of talent. There was a monarch, but he was an emperor, and not a king. It was neither hazard nor caprice, nor a puerile vanity which induced him to take one of these titles in preference to others. The constitutional imperial monarchy was a monarchy, since monarch there was; but it was something very different to the French royal monarchy."

The trial of the Duke d'Enghien was the first act of the great drama which ended in the condemnation of Georges and his accomplices. Hatched by the exiles, at the head of whom the French princes figured, and whose agents were two famous generals—Pichegru and Moreau—the plot was, as I have already said, financed by England, who placed the resources of the state, and the culpable connivance of her diplomatic agents, at the service of the conspirators.

I will not dwell upon the clemency which Napoleon wished to show towards several of the condemned men, who had not blushed to associate with murderers to conspire for his destruction and for the ruin of the state; nor on the assiduity with which his family and his household interceded on their behalf. The execution of Georges caused little regret. Murder, no matter what its object may be, is always odious. Still there was found someone to ask for his pardon. I saw a lady, accompanied by two big daughters, come to La Malmaison one day with this object. They were not received. This lady was not the most respectable agent of the royalist party, which indeed held her in very low esteem. She belonged to a Brittany family, and was the sister of a *conventionnel.* She used to say to her husband's nephew, who was auditor to the Council of State, that, if he accepted the cross of the Legion of Honor, she would never receive him again at her house.

The prosecution of the accused, and the investigation of the charges against them, was proceeded with by the French government in the full light of day. Not one circumstance, not one detail of the various phases of the conspiracy, not one loophole opened to Moreau and Pichegru, in remembrance of services which they had formerly rendered, was passed over in silence. Nothing was left for the secret historian to glean. Everything bearing upon this vast conspiracy has been published in the *Moniteur,* and a hundred other publications. The murders of Pichegru, and of the English Captain, Wright, said to have been strangled in prison, are calumnies which are refuted by their very absurdity. It seems to me unnecessary to add a single word to the denials with which this wretched and odious imputation has been met.

Moreau, after his condemnation, asked and obtained permission to retire to the United States. Napoleon cancelled the sentence of two years' imprisonment to which the general had been condemned, and made no objection to his departure for the United States. It was rumored that the judges had been secretly pressed to pronounce sentence of death on Moreau, so that Napoleon might have the opportunity of crushing his rival under the weight of his clemency. Napoleon was much too clever to take a false step with people whom he knew to be opposed to him. What has not been said besides? Certain historians have reproduced all these romances with the remarks that there was nothing improbable about these stories. If suppositions were admitted as facts, because they appear probable, might it not be said that Moreau's judges were influenced by his fame, or by the large number of his partisans? For, after all, his guilt was proved, and his name had an immense weight in the conspiracy. Napoleon must have been dissatisfied with the judgment pronounced, because he believed, and probably wrongly, that considerations unfavorable to himself had influenced the members of the tribunal and distorted justice; the resentment was not, however, of long duration. Napoleon had had an idea which was worthy of him; he had had it suggested to Moreau that he should ask him for a private interview. Had the person who was charged with this mission acted with more skill, it is probable that Moreau, in the state of mind in which he was, would have received these overtures favorably. Such a scene would probably have produced the most favorable impression about the new Augustus in the public mind.

Napoleon purchased with the police funds, the estate of Grosbois, and the house in the Rue d'Anjou, which had formerly belonged to Moreau. He gave Grosbois to Marshal Berthier, and the house in Paris to Marshal Bernadotte, whose gratitude for this new favor was as scanty as it had been for previous favors.

It was while the Georges trial was in progress before the Seine Court of Assizes that Napoleon remembered Bourrienne. "Do you know," he asked me, "whether Bourrienne is in Paris? You must find out, and write to him to go to the trial. Every evening he must send you a report of what he has heard; he is a very good man for that sort of thing." Bourrienne's reports were regularly sent in to me and transmitted by me to Napoleon. This led to Bourrienne's appointment as plenipotentiary minister to Hamburg, about a year later. Napoleon's return to him is a fresh proof of his remembrance of the services which he had rendered, and of the generosity with which Napoleon forgot the wrong done him. "Although the conduct of his old schoolfellow was far from being irreproachable at Hamburg, he tolerated him there. During one of our campaigns in Germany the necessity of being informed of what was going on before and behind our armies made Napoleon desire to receive weekly reports from his ambassadors at Hamburg and Munich. The cross of the Legion of Honor was frequently asked for by M. de Bourrienne in the letters which accompanied his reports. I was ordered not to answer these requests. As they were frequently repeated, I obtained this answer from the Emperor: "Write to him, that, as he worships the golden calf, he shall have money; but that—as to the Legion of Honor—I only give it to those who ..."

The Empire had emerged from these storms. All the combinations of corruption, conspiracy and murder had ended only in the elevation of the man whose destruction had been compassed by these infamous means. Like Hercules he strangled the serpents in his cradle. It was the presage of a greatness which will be the subject of the eternal conversation of the world.

The forms of the new court were copied from those of the ancient French monarchy, and the imperial monarchy of Germany, purged of what was servile and gothic. There were grand charges of the Empire and grand charges of the Court. Napoleon wished to associate his colleagues with his elevation, and one was promoted to the dignity of Archchancellor and the other to that of Archtreasurer of the Empire. The two brothers of the Emperor, Joseph and Louis, were created, the first Grand Elector, and the second Constable. Napoleon created twenty posts of marshal for his comrades at arms, of which four were bestowed, in reward for former services, on Generals Kellermann, Lefebvre, Perignon and Serrurier. Fourteen places were given to generals on active service, distinguished by the occupation of important commands and likely to be called to render fresh services. These were Generals Berthier, Murat, Moncey, Jourdan, Masséna, Augereau, Bernadotte, Soult, Brune, Lannes, Mortier, Ney, Davout, and Bessières. The other two places were held in reserve.

The Emperor had his chamberlains, equerries, etc. The Empress, on her side, had her ladies in waiting. The prefects of the palace were retained. The chamberlains and the ladies in waiting belonged in part to old families, who desired places at the imperial court, with the exception of some, who remained faithful to their Royalist opinions, or who made it a point of honor to figure in the opposition.

A new ceremonial was established in the services of the court, and was laid down in a code. The Sovereign's person was no longer accessible to the same persons as before. Officers who, till then, had enjoyed the privilege of approaching the Head of the state, and of presenting themselves whenever they pleased, had to yield up this privilege to the chamberlains and to new-comers, who formerly had been obliged to have recourse to the military element. The introduction of this etiquette offended the greater number of these officers. They submitted to it with disgust and grumbling.

Little by little the custom of these changes established itself. Nevertheless, although the army's zeal did not diminish, there remained in the hearts of the soldiers a keen regret for having been deprived of a right by usurpers whom they had never regarded with favor. The object in bringing to the imperial court persons belonging to families which had formerly been attached to the court, was to approach these families to the Sovereign's eyes, to interest them in the new order of things, to remove them from the intrigues of the malcontents, to withdraw them from all harmful influences, and to bring about a fusion of the various classes of society. At the same time, these new servants, more familiar with the usages of polite society, were better fitted for being placed in contact with strangers.

However much Napoleon may have been perplexed by the redoubtable crises through which he had just passed, and in spite of the diversion brought about by his accession to the imperial throne, and by the organization of his court and the imperial state, his attention had never been turned away from the serious war which he was forced to carry on against England. He pushed forward, with the same activity, administrative measures, diplomatic negotiations, and military preparations. He had ordered that several camps should be formed, amongst others one at Compiègne. This camp being nearer to Paris, and within easy reach, the First Consul, who had become Emperor, went to spend some days at the castle of Compiègne, to inspect the camp, which was chiefly composed of dragoon regiments. It was under the command of General Baraguay d'Hilliers, in his capacity of inspector general of troops of this class. At his orders the dragoons went through various exercises before the Emperor's eyes, both on foot and on horse, to show their qualities both as horse and as foot soldiers. The result of these maneuvers was not satisfactory, and the plan was abandoned.

Amongst the authorities of the department who came to Compiègne to present their respects to the new sovereign, was M. Octave de Ségur, subprefect of Soissons. He was the eldest son of Count de Ségur, who had been appointed councilor of state by Napoleon, and who was afterwards made grand master of ceremonies. This young man, who gave the highest promise, and in whose family Napoleon took a special interest, disappeared without leaving any clue that could lead to his discovery, after his return to Soissons, when the camp had been broken up. It was not known for many years what had become of him. Domestic worries, exaggerated by a morbid imagination, had disgusted him both with his home and with society. It was only after the war, in 1809, that Octave de Ségur was heard of. He had enlisted under an assumed name in the 6th regiment of chasseurs, commanded by Colonel Valin and had carefully kept his secret for six years. Taken prisoner, and being invalided, he had been sent to Hungary, where he was living on the estate of the exiled Count Baschi du Cayla, father-in-law of the Countess du Cayla. The worries of his life as an outlaw, and the privations which he had to undergo, induced him to write to his brother to inform his family of his whereabouts, and to obtain his return to France by means of an exchange. Napoleon had sincerely sympathized with the Count de Ségur's troubles, and had written him a touching letter at the time of his son's disappearance. He had never ceased to be interested in the mystery which had enveloped his flight. At last, one day, when at Pont-de-Brique, a country house near Boulogne, where his headquarters were established, he heard that Octave de Ségur was on board one of the ships of the Texel fleet under disguise. Napoleon immediately sent for his brother Philip, who was in service in the palace as captain deputy to the grand marshal of the palace, informed him of what he had learned, and gave him a plausible mission by the help of which he would be able to discover his brother. Philip de Ségur returned from his mission without being able to find any traces of the fugitive, who had either been clever enough to avoid discovery, or who possibly, contrary to what had been reported to Napoleon, had never been on the ship at all.

When Octave returned to France, he had lost precious years for his advancement in the service. The Emperor having asked him if he had the intention of pursuing his career, he answered that he preferred to remain a soldier. Touched by these chivalrous sentiments, but regretting the choice he had made of a career which should only be entered upon by a young man, Napoleon appointed him officer, on the ground of his having been a scholar at the Polytechnic School. His second début in war was unfortunate. Made prisoner near Vilna, at the beginning of the 1812 campaign, he did not return to France until after the fall of the Empire. He then entered the King's military household. A victim to extreme melancholy, he was not able to drive away the sombre fancies which pursued him, and which finally drove him to suicide.

This unhappy man had turned over his fatal design in his mind, long before his death. He used to live in the same rooms as his brother Philip. His son Raymond, who slept in a closet next to his bedroom, heard his father repeatedly getting up in the night and walking about the room, wrapped in thought which was expressed by vague exclamations, the sense of which Raymond was unable to understand. At last, one evening, Octave went to the house of a friend who owed him some money. Finding him out, he tore up the promissory note which this friend had signed in his favor, and threw the scraps of paper before the door. He then went to the St. Michael bridge, carefully filled his pockets with stones, and lying down in the bed of the river, then at low water, crossed his arms with an inflexible resolution, and awaited death. At daybreak on the morrow, he was found in this attitude, and nothing that was done could call him back to life.

Since I have the occasion to speak of this member of the de Ségur family, I will add some details about them. I spent two years as a child at Châtenay, a pretty village in the neighborhood of Paris. The Count de Ségur was living there—with his wife, his children, and his aged father, Marshal de Ségur—in a state bordering on destitution. Count and Countess de Ségur's fortune had been exhausted in costly embassies, and the loss of the colony of San Domingo, where they had important properties, had consummated their ruin. M. de Ségur, whose philosophy sustained him against adversity, was living by his pen. He used to write serious books, light comedies, and songs. He composed speeches for the deputies of the *Conseil des Anciens* and the *Conseil des Cinq-Cents*—amongst others for Baudin des Ardennes. I was present at the marriage of his eldest son, Octave, with his cousin-germane, Mademoiselle d'Aguesseau. This union, formed under favorable auspices, was not to be a happy one. The castle of Fresnes, which belonged to the d'Aguesseau family, was close to Châtenay. I can still remember a strange rumor which greatly exercised the peasants in the neighborhood. It was said that a bull from the Fresnes farm, each time that it was driven out, used to run away from the herd, and force its way to the cemetery where it would dash upon the tomb of an ardent revolutionary who was buried there, and rip up the sods on his grave with its horns, a proceeding which was generally considered a token of divine vengeance.

Napoleon, on his accession to power, called to his side all men of capacity, irrespective of their origin, and of their previous performances and opinions. M. de Ségur's merits could not escape his attention. After the 18th Brumaire, the former ambassador of France to St. Petersburg and Berlin became a member of the Legislative body. He was placed, a year later, in the Council of State, where he rendered useful services. At the time of the foundation of the Empire he was appointed to one of the great charges of the crown, namely that of grand master of ceremonies. Napoleon took this family under his protection and lavished his inexhaustible kindness upon them. The Count de Ségur's father, former Minister of War and Marshal of France, had lost his pension. Napoleon restored it to him, and when the old mutilated officer came to the Tuileries to thank him, he had the honors paid to him which were formerly attached to his rank. The Count de Ségur's eldest son, who was thought to have a vocation for the civil service, was appointed, as the readers will remember, subprefect at Soissons; the second son was destined to a military career. He was placed first of all with the so-called Bonaparte hussars, a troop which had been formed as part of the reserve army, which was then being assembled at Dijon. In order to have him near his person, Napoleon afterwards appointed him adjutant of the palace, then quartermaster, and then master of the pages. He married him to Mlle. de Luçay, daughter of one of the prefects of the palace, and endowed him with an income of ten thousand francs charged on the state, and with valuable estates abroad. In 1813 he entrusted him with the command of one of the six regiments of his guard of honor.

Countess de Ségur, grand-daughter of the celebrated Chancellor d'Aguesseau, who was distinguished by the loftiness of her character and by most amiable qualities, was nominated vice-president of the Maternity Society, of which, later on, the Empress Marie Louise became president.

The fall of the Empire did not deprive the Count de Ségur of all the advantages which he owed to the Emperor's generous patronage. He found himself, at the time, it is true, at Blois, in the suite of the Empress Marie Louise, with three hundred louis as the whole of his possessions, but some time later, he reentered the chamber of Peers as a former senator, and recovered the pension which had been allotted to him in this capacity.

In 1815 he once more fulfilled the functions of Grand Master of Ceremonies during the Hundred Days. It must be said, to Count de Ségur's honor, that he often used to express his gratitude for the acts of kindness with which the Emperor had loaded his family, and that he religiously respected his memory until the end of his life.

After his stay at Fontainebleau, the Emperor went, by way of Melun, to the castle de la Houssaie, which belonged to Marshal Augereau, who had earnestly begged for the honor of receiving him there. He spent the day there, a splendid fête having been prepared in his honor. Augereau was at that time under the influence of the genius whom fortune abetted. The Emperor expressed the wish that the park should be thrown open to the crowds of people who had come from the surrounding districts to see him.

The events by which Paris and France had been recently disturbed had shown how necessary it was to reappoint the Ministry of Police, which, before the discovery of the conspiracy, had been annexed to the Ministry of Justice. The inevitable Fouché once more got the portfolio into his hands. In order to minimize the influence of this fatally necessary person, Napoleon associated with the new minister, four councilors of state, who were charged with the correspondence, and with the carrying out of all instructions in, four districts placed under their supervision. The departments of the Empire were divided, with this purpose in view, into three circuits, or zones. The fourth was the prefecture of police of Paris.

The Emperor was always present in spirit at the Boulogne camp. He used to write several letters every day to the ministers of marine, war, and the public treasury; to Admiral Bruix, commanding the flotilla, and to the generals in command of the troops, to inform them of the plans which he had laid down. He repeated the same order several times, thinking by these repetitions to keep their vigilance awake. In spite of the short distance from Paris to Boulogne, a distance which had been still further reduced by the creation of a service of couriers, Napoleon felt that his presence on the spot was indispensable to securing a more rapid and more general execution of his orders, the time approaching when there would be a favorable opportunity for setting sail. In consequence he had a house hired in the little village of Pont-de-Brique, situated at about half-a-league from Boulogne, and established his headquarters there. It was a small country house of but poor appearance, composed of one main building with two wings, and some outhouses. The Emperor took up his abode there with a part of his military and civil households. Almost all his equerries were colonels or generals. Some of the chamberlains also had rank in the army. Napoleon used to leave Pont-de-Brique every day for Boulogne, at irregular hours, unless detained by some urgent business. He used to return to dinner, inviting two or three generals or superior officers, either military or naval, artillery or engineering, to his table. The ministers were summoned from Paris when they had some important communication to make. An auditor of the council of state used to bring him every week the portfolio containing the affairs on which the Council of Ministers had deliberated. Mass was performed every Sunday in a drawing room, which was fitted for the purpose with a portable altar. Both the military and civil officers of the household were expected to be present.

The position of Pont-de-Brique enabled the Emperor to come to Boulogne in an unexpected manner, to see all with his own eyes, and to provide for unforeseen emergencies. Not considering himself sufficiently near to the scene of his operations, he chose a site on an eminence, which overlooked the sea, and which was called "Tour d'Ordre," from which he could see the English fleet and the various divisions of his flotilla. It is said that Caesar embarked at this point for the conquest of the British Isles, a favorable omen. Napoleon had a wooden house, composed of several rooms, constructed on this spot and spent several days there. In one of the rooms was a large telescope focused on the sea, with which one could see distinctly what was going on on the water, and as far as the coast of England. Other huts, for the use of the Admiral and the Minister of Marine, were built not far from his. A battery of mortars of unusual caliber had been placed, by his orders, on the Tour d'Ordre. Enormous shells could be fired with these cannons, which had a range of six thousand yards. Ships of the English fleet, which sailed too close to the flotilla, were often struck by these bombs. The detonation of these new mortars was so loud that blood came to the ears of the gunners, and the soil of the Tour d'Ordre trembled beneath their feet. During his stays in his wooden house, Napoleon used to explore the camps and the coast, or, embarked on a flat-bottomed boat, would engage his flotilla in small combats with the English fleet, often pointing a cannon with his own hands.

He superintended the fitting out of the boats, and tested different systems of stowage, being anxious to ship munitions and provisions for twenty days. He considered the stowage of munitions of war and provisions for horses and baggage, and their disposal in the best order, and the least possible space, as a very important part of the campaign. He had the soldiers and sailors drilled, ordered sham embarkations and landings both at day and night, and spent the best part of his time with the sailors or the soldiers, sharing their labors, urging them on to renewed effort, and inspiring them with the confidence that he felt. He scoured the beach on foot and on horseback, followed by the admiral and the principal naval and military officers. Thanks to this vigilant activity, fresh improvements were every day produced in the details of the armament, while the training of both soldiers and sailors gave the best results.

The land forces were encamped in huts, constructed of mud and branches, and were divided into streets. Each regiment, each brigade, and each division had its quarters, separated from the others by broad avenues. Inscriptions expressing patriotic sentiments or testimonials of devotion to the Emperor, some heroic, some comic, could be read on the fronts of these huts.

The gunboats used to leave the various points of assembly in detachments, coming to the general meeting-place under command of naval officers, replying to the fire of the English cruisers, which were frequently driven back, doubling promontories under the protection of coast batteries, and with the escort of trains of artillery which accompanied them along the coast.

When one thinks of these Homeric times, when the genius of Napoleon was multiplying his gigantic preparations for the invasion of the British Isles, with the determination of striking our eternal enemy to the heart, there comes to one's mind a regret, which is often renewed. This regret is caused by the fact that the Emperor, who had a prescience in things really great, should have thought it necessary to submit the

American Fulton's invention, that is to say the application of steam-power to navigation, to the examination of the savants of the Institut. The members of the Institut, after two months deliberation and experiments, declared that this invention was chimerical and impracticable. Experience has since shown on whose side was the error.

Holland had not made less efforts than France to take part in the expedition against England. Nearly four hundred and fifty vessels were assembled in the ports of the Escaut and the Meuse. It was a dangerous enterprise to bring them up to the French fleet. Napoleon wished that the honor of this undertaking should fall to a Dutch sailor, and Captain Verhuell was chosen by the Dutch government to be vested with this command. On his refusal, his brother, a simple lieutenant who asked for the post, was appointed. Lieutenant Verhuell had been retired from service for some years, but, encouraged by the choice and the instructions of his brother, he accepted this perilous mission. The junction of the two fleets was effected with full success at Ostend, and in spite of the efforts of the English fleet under the command of Sir Sidney Smith. The brilliant way in which Verhuell directed this expedition, bravely attacking the English frigates, won the rank of rear-admiral and the post of aide-de-camp to Napoleon for this able and intrepid officer. Admiral Verhuell, entering the French service was later on rewarded for his talents, with the post of General-Inspector of the Northern coasts of France, by his admission to the senate, and by his naturalization. He was for a long time one of the most distinguished members of the chamber of Peers.

It was at Boulogne that the Emperor received the news of the death of Admiral Latouche-Tréville, which had occurred on August 19, 1804, on board the admiral's ship, the Bucentaur, in the roads of Toulon. The Emperor was exceedingly grieved by his loss; he had placed great hopes on the talents and the energy of this general officer, both as regards the Boulogne expedition, and the reorganization of our navy.

To replace Admiral Latouche-Tréville, Napoleon had to choose amongst Admirals Bruix, Villeneuve, and Rosily. Admiral Bruix could not be removed from the command of the Boulogne flotilla, for which he was eminently suited. The Emperor admitted the zeal and ardor of Admiral Rosily, but feared his long absence at sea. Decrés, Minister of Marine, guided his choice to Admiral Villeneuve, who was in command of the Rochefort squadron. Later on Napoleon had reason to bitterly regret his choice of this officer, who though brave and experienced, was a man of irresolute character.

During the Emperor's stay at the Boulogne camp, Joseph Bonaparte was nominated colonel of the 4th infantry regiment, and at the same time was appointed Grand Elector. Joseph, after having served under the command of his brother, General Bonaparte, at the commencement of the Italian war, had retired from military service with the rank of major, and, as has been seen at the commencement of this narrative, had taken up a civil career. The Emperor, who reserved for his brother an exalted position, in which military character had to be united to civil character, considered it indispensable that he should resume rank in the army. At the time of the breaking up of the Boulogne camp, the colonel of the 4th infantry regiment became general of brigade. He was therefore already vested with this rank, when the Emperor appointed him his lieutenant, and entrusted him with the command of the army which was destined to conquer the kingdom of Naples, after the signing of the Peace at Presburg.

The Emperor's fête was celebrated at Boulogne with unusual pomp and ceremony, and afforded those who were present a really magnificent spectacle. Napoleon—raised aloft on a throne, which was canopied by the flags and colors taken from the enemy, surrounded by his ministers, marshals, chief officers, senators, deputies, and others present with the army—towered over the camps and the sea. One hundred thousand armed men, grouped around his throne, were, at once the spectators of and the actors in this triumphal feast. The Grand Chancellor of the Legion of Honor presided over the ceremony of the distribution of decorations, which had been placed in the helmets, or on the shields, of Bayard and Duguesclin, which had been brought for the purpose from the museums in which they had been resting. The Emperor handed each man his decoration. The chair which had been prepared for him had not been chosen with the same happy inspiration as the magnificent pieces of armor which served as receptacles for the crosses of the Legion of Honor. It was a chair which was held in some ridicule by the popular mind, it was, namely, the chair of King Dagobert.

During a space of three hours the various regiments marched before the imperial throne to the sound of a hundred thousand cries of "Long Live the Emperor!" to the noise of a thousand drums, and the salutes of three thousand pieces of artillery. In the meanwhile attention was attracted to the sea by the bustle caused by the arrival of a fleet of fifty ships from Havre, in stormy weather, and under the eyes of the English cruisers.

Tables laid for four hundred covers each, had been set up in front of the camps and along the quays. All the members of the Legion of Honor, numbering two thousand, took their places at these tables. A display of fireworks was postponed till the morrow, owing to the violence of the wind.

The preparation of this solemnity, which was remembered for years, had been made during Napoleon's absence on a visit of ten days to the ports of Calais, Dunkirk, Furnes and Ostend. The Emperor had written to Princess Hortense complaining of having received no news of her. This princess, accompanied by the Prince and Princess Murat, came with her son Napoleon, to spend a few days at Boulogne after the Emperor's fête. They lived in a small country house on the banks of the river Liane, quite close to headquarters. Princess Louis often took her son to see the Emperor, who was very fond of his little nephew.

It was during one of his stays at Calais that Napoleon deprived M. Chaptal of his portfolio as Minister of the Interior. This department was entrusted to M. Portalis, Minister of Public Worship, pending the appointment of a successor to M. Chaptal, an event which took place two days later, M. de Champigny being nominated Minister of the Interior. M. Chaptal entered the senate. I have heard Napoleon complaining about this minister on the ground that he did not take any opportunities of speaking to him, that their personal relations were too few and far between, and that he too rarely informed him of the various affairs which were being dealt with in his department. It may be that the Emperor yielded to certain prejudices, which were inspired by his recollections of the failure of the experiment he had tried, in entrusting the same ministry to Laplace, who had had to be replaced by Lucien Bonaparte. He may have thought that savants lost by being diverted from their studies, and were incapable of devoting themselves entirely to the numerous details of a great administration. This was, however, not the case with M. Chaptal, who was a practical savant. As a matter of fact, however, he continued to enjoy Napoleon's favor and esteem. The Emperor took constant opportunities of showing this distinguished savant the high esteem in which he held his talents, and gave him many proofs of his favorable disposition towards him.

M. Chaptal had succeeded Lucien Bonaparte, in November 1800, first of all as charged with the portfolio during his absence, and afterwards as his definitive successor. It is known that Lucien's removal was occasioned by the publication of a pamphlet entitled *Parallèle de César, Cromwell, et Bonaparte* which, it was thought, was intended to prepare the public mind for the foundation of a new dynasty. On the publication of this book, Fouché, who was Lucien's enemy, came and pointed out that it was producing a bad effect, and offended those who, in the various bodies of the state, in the army, or in different ranks in society, had not abandoned their republican sentiments. It is not probable, as has been reported, that this book was planned out by the two brothers together. Napoleon had no need to sound the hearts of the people, or to prepare the nation for the hereditary idea, since he was very well aware of the existence of a general tendency of the public mind towards these ideas. Fontanes, who lives in the confidence of Lucien and of Madame Bacciochi, was the author of the *Parallèle.* He had just returned from exile, and was receiving an allowance from the Ministry, and, being an ambitious man, took this opportunity of showing his zeal to his patrons, and of getting himself known. Lucien adopted Fontanes's work and accepted all responsibility for it, allowing it to be sent out under the stamp of his Ministry, thus giving it official publication in the departments. Excited by the exaggerated reports of the Minister of Police, Napoleon blamed his brother. This circumstance, together with their disagreements on matters of politics and of government, and with Lucien's pretension to be his powerful brother's sole confidant, brought about a coolness between them. Lucien received orders to go to Spain, and to induce the government of that country to unite with France in forcing Portugal to break off her relations with England.

Whether, then, this publication was made by the Minister of the Interior with or without Napoleon's consent, the part which Lucien took in it proves the error of those who have been pleased to attribute to him a spirit of opposition to his brother's plans for the future, or who have considered his alleged resistance to these plans as the reason of their disagreement.

Lucien Bonaparte filled his mission in Spain with brilliant success. He snatched this country away from English influence, and concluded at Madrid numerous diplomatic conventions, which were very favorable to France. On his return to Paris he became first deputy, and then senator, and was endowed with a senatorship on the left bank of the Rhine. He supported the laws presented by the government, before the tribunate, with remarkable talent. The Institut admitted him to its membership.

Lucien enjoyed in peace the goods and honors which the First Consul bestowed on his family, and all the respect which his name and talents had won for him. He was called to share the lofty destinies which awaited his brother, when a marriage, which could not meet with Napoleon's approval, once more disturbed the good understanding which seemed to reign between them. It was in vain that Napoleon pointed out to his brother what objections there were to his entering upon this marriage. He went so far as to I forbid the mayor of the 10th circumscription of Paris to perform the ceremony of the marriage. Lucien left Paris suddenly, went to Plessis-Charmant, a country house which he possessed in the neighborhood of Senlis, and had the civil and religious ceremony of marriage performed by the village priest, who was at the same time mayor of the commune, before the First Consul could interfere. This open rebellion against the Head of the government and his family, rendered it necessary for Lucien to leave France. He asked for permission to retire to Italy, and ended by settling down in the Papal States, where he was received with deference by the pope who, some time afterwards, conferred on him the title of Prince de Canino. Lucien ceased to wear the insignia of the Legion of Honor. Showing a French general one day, at Rome, the cross of his order, which he had put away in a drawer, and being advised by the general to wear it, he answered: "No, one must not humiliate oneself too much." He took no steps to reconcile himself with his brother, being firmly decided not to submit to the *sine qua non* of such a reconciliation, namely a separation from his wife. A last attempt was made by the Emperor at the interview which Joseph, King of Naples, had arranged between the two brothers, at Mantua, in 1807, at the end of which they separated not to see each other again till 1815.

Napoleon's great displeasure at his brother Lucien's marriage was shortly afterwards provoked afresh by the union which Jérôme Bonaparte, the youngest of his brothers, contracted in the United States. Jérôme, who was at that time serving in the navy as lieutenant, had, towards the end of 1803, married a Miss Eliza Patterson, daughter of a Baltimore merchant. He was nineteen years old at the time. Napoleon, in his double capacity as sovereign and head of the family forbade the transcription of the marriage deed on to the civil registries. Without having recourse to the law-courts, he declared the marriage void, on the grounds that it had been carried out without his consent, without publication of the banns, and while the two parties were minors. He asked the ecclesiastical authorities to annul the marriage, but the pope, who was already for certain reasons antagonistic to the Emperor, taking the interests of a Protestant woman, refused to sever the religious bond which united her to a Roman Catholic.

Recalled to France by the Emperor, Jérôme Bonaparte only returned towards the end of April, 1805. He had arrived at Lisbon on an American vessel, accompanied by his father-in-law and his wife, avoiding the vigilance of the English fleet. There he was forced to separate from them and, after a sad leave-taking, departed for Madrid. Mr. Patterson and his daughter immediately returned to America.

Jérôme executed to the satisfaction of Napoleon a number of missions with which, as commander and rear-admiral, he was entrusted. He then left the navy for the army, a service for which he had long had an inclination. In 1807, having a body of Bavarians and Würtembergers under his orders, he went through a brilliant campaign in Silesia. One after the other he reduced all the fortresses in a province which had been fortified by Frederick the Great. After the Peace of Tilsit, which by one of the clauses of the treaty raised him to the dignity of King of Westphalia, he married in August, 1807, Catherine, daughter of the King of Würtemberg, a princess whose noble character and admirable conduct under adversity, entitle her to a place in history, and to the praises of all. This marriage having destroyed Madame Eliza Patterson's last hopes, she resigned herself to the annulment of the union which she had contracted in 1803. She addressed herself, in 1808, to General Turreau, who was French ambassador to the United States, and declared to him that she yielded to circumstances which imposed a painful and humiliating sacrifice upon her, and that she placed her own lot and that of her son in the Emperor's hands. Napoleon, who was at that time in Spain, replied that he would see Madame Patterson's son with pleasure, that he would take him under his protection if she would send him to France, that she could rely on his esteem and his desire to be friendly with her, that in refusing to acknowledge the marriage he had had to yield to political considerations, that he was moreover determined to assure her son's future in a way which would meet her wishes, but that the matter must be treated with prudence and without publicity.

Lucien and Jérôme Bonaparte had not been included in the terms of the senatus consultum, referring to the hereditary dignity of the imperial family, because of the marriages which they contracted without the assent, or contrary to the wishes, of the Head of the state. The reasons of this exclusion were well-founded, because it was not possible to separate Napoleon's authority as sovereign from his authority as head of his family. Numerous examples can be cited, if need be, to justify his claim to a right which he believed to be his. In our own days, the Duke of Sussex, son of King George III of England, having married Lady Murray at Rome, had his marriage annulled, although he had taken the precaution of having it celebrated for a second time after his return to England. His efforts remained without result, and the marriage was declared void because it had been effected without the consent of the English sovereign.

The Emperor went to visit Aix-la-Chapelle, and stayed there eight days. The day after his arrival he received the ambassadors and plenipotentiary ministers who handed him their new letters of credence, and letters of congratulation from their Courts on his accession to the Empire. They were presented at his audience by Minister Talleyrand.

Napoleon went to visit the manufactories of the town and of the little suburb called Borcette, a small manufacturing settlement, about three quarters of a mile from Aix-la-Chapelle, examining all the manufactures exhibited there, and accepting invitations to all fêtes given in his honor. He received in turn the departmental and municipal authorities, the judges, the military, and the clergy, and was present at the singing of a *Te Deum* which was given in Aix cathedral. The clergy showed him the relics of Charlemagne, who founded this church, and other relics, which formerly had attracted pilgrims to Aix. These relics had been dispersed during the revolutionary period but had been recovered by the Church.

On the eve of August 15, his fête, the Emperor had taken advantage of his presence at Aix-la-Chapelle with the Empress Josephine, who had preceded him there, to celebrate Charlemagne's fête with all the pomp of military, civil, and religious ceremonies. A pontifical mass was held in the cathedral, in the presence of the Empress, with all her court. It was not to the saint of the legend that this homage was rendered but to the founder of the Western Empire, of which Napoleon considered himself the restorer.

Certain events, more private than public in character, took place during the new Emperor's stay at Aix-la-Chapelle, about which I should like to say a few words.

The indirect part played in the affair of the Duke d'Enghien by General Caulaincourt had been the origin of the favor into which he had been taken. General Lauriston, on his side, had been Napoleon's schoolfellow at the military school, and had become one of his most distinguished, as he was one of his oldest, aides-de-camp. Various positions in the household of the First Consul had been conferred upon him, notably the important post of Master of the Horse. General Lauriston, accordingly, thought that he had a claim to the post of Grand Equerry when the Empire was founded, and was accordingly hurt when this post was given to General Caulaincourt, his junior in service, and his inferior in rank. He complained about the matter to the Emperor, and no doubt made use of expressions which offended Napoleon, for after a most stormy interview with the Emperor at Aix-la-Chapelle, he received orders to start for Toulon to embark on the fleet under the command of Admiral Villeneuve, and to take over the command of an army of seven or eight thousand men in transport. In the course of this expedition, General Lauriston, by a bold stroke, captured a fort in Dominica, the Diamond, which was a source of trouble to the trade and shipping of the island of Martinique. In the end he was present at the fatal battle of Trafalgar, after which he returned to Paris. All remembrance of the unpleasant scene which he had had with Napoleon at Aix-la-Chapelle seemed to have been effaced. The Emperor appeared to have forgotten it, but General Lauriston's attitude in 1814, and since, has shown that he at least remembered it. After his return from his maritime expedition, Lauriston resumed his service, and was employed in the *grande armée* in important commands, which won for him, later on, under the Restoration, his nomination as Marshal of France.

It was also, I think, at Aix-la-Chapelle, unless it were at Boulogne, that the Emperor caused Colonel Mouton, afterwards Count de Lobau, to be presented to him. This officer was then commanding the 3rd line regiment. He had opposed Napoleon's elevation to the imperial dignity, and had voted against this proposal. The Emperor, satisfied with the discipline which Colonel Mouton maintained in his regiment, and with his knowledge of tactics, was anxious to attach an officer of such merits to his person. He forgot his opposition, and sent for him. The military tribune was converted after a short conversation. Napoleon made him his aide-de-camp, and from thenceforward showed him a confidence which this officer justified by the services he rendered.

While the Emperor was at Aix-la-Chapelle, a fact came to his knowledge which disposed him very unfavorably towards M. de Talleyrand. The matter was in connection with certain territorial advantages which Napoleon wished to bestow on the House of Nassau, in which he was interested. He had reserved to himself to settle this matter with the King of Prussia, with whom he was at that time on the best terms, when he learned that a negotiation, followed up by the French ambassador at The Hague, had been entered upon with a view to obtaining an indemnity of twelve millions from the Dutch government for the same consideration. The Emperor wrote officially to the Minister of Foreign Affairs to complain that the Dutch government, already greatly in arrears in carrying out its commitments for the equipment and armament of the flotilla, and whose finances were involved, should be thinking of presenting the Prince of Orange with a sum of money, which was much too great for its resources. Napoleon then spoke in a confidential manner to the minister about the part which it was alleged had been played in this matter by his ambassador. M. de Talleyrand, however, pretended to be ignorant of it. M. de Sémonville was accordingly ordered to Aix-la-Chapelle to meet the Emperor, and commanded to explain. Our agent at The Hague, thereupon, produced the instructions which he had received from the Minister of Foreign Affairs himself in this matter. The Emperor was most indignant and spoke of nothing less than M. de Talleyrand's dismissal. Armed with the documents which had been handed over to him, he awaited this minister, who was to come and work with him. He had placed them in the drawer of a little table, and gave me orders not to produce them until I was told to do so. I do not know what happened in the course of this interview, which had threatened to be a stormy one, but M. de Talleyrand went away without the papers being asked for. I heard nothing more about the matter and noticed no apparent difference in the mutual relations of the sovereign and his minister. Doubtless, to make use of Napoleon's own expression, Talleyrand had been so adroitly evasive, that after a long conversation, he had been able to make good his escape, and avoid giving the explanations which the

Emperor had promised himself to hear from his lips. Such incidents, however, were so many blows struck at Napoleon's confidence in his minister.

The Emperor continued his journey by way of Cologne, Mayence, and Coblentz, and returned to St. Cloud in the middle of October, after an absence of three months.

Numerous decrees were promulgated on his own initiative, during his visit to the towns of Aix-la-Chapelle, Cologne, Bonn, Coblentz, Mayence, and other places on his route. Others were prompted by reports which he had asked of his various ministers, and which these presented him on his return. These decrees are a proof of the attention with which Napoleon examined all petitions addressed to him, and of the vivacity of conception with which at first sight he saw what improvements were to be made in the towns as well as in the rural districts, and the works of embellishment which might with advantage be carried out in these places. The institution of decennial prizes dates from Aix-la-Chapelle. These prizes were to be distributed every ten years, on the proposal of a committee of the four classes of the Institut, and were to be awarded to the authors of the best works in science, literature, painting, sculpture, and music; to the inventors of the most useful machines for the arts and manufactures; and to the founders of the most advantageous establishments for the furtherance of national agriculture and industries. The disastrous events which occurred in 1814, at the time of the expiration of the first term of ten years, prevented this noble plan, which would have given a salutary impulse to arts and letters, from being carried into execution.

Chapter V

The question of heredity had been settled by the creation of the Empire. Napoleon's nature was all that was great. The title of Emperor, being the highest title in modern Europe, was the right appellation of the head of a nation which was high above all other nations. This title being admitted, the forms of the courts of neighboring monarchies, freed from privileges and purged of servility, became a necessity in a new Empire surrounded by ancient European States. If the new Emperor of the French, the chief of a new race, the restorer of religion in France, the most powerful of Catholic sovereigns, stood in need of a religious consecration, he could only receive it at the hands of the Head of the Church and in the metropolis of the Empire. The question of the intervention of the Holy Father in the consecration and coronation of the Emperor, became the subject of the deliberations of the Council of State. Objections were raised in this assembly, where the greatest liberty of discussion was allowed, against a project which seemed likely to prompt the Court of Rome to fresh pretensions. Napoleon's pressing arguments won the day, and Cardinal Fesch, French ambassador at Rome, was charged with the negotiation. After long tergiversations on the part of the pope and consultations with the most influential cardinals—whose opinions were now favorable, now hostile to the project—the proposals of the ambassador were accepted on conditions which were considered acceptable in Paris. Napoleon, hearing of the pope's consent, at Mayence, wrote him a dignified and measured letter, *begging him to come and give a religious character to the consecration and coronation of the first Emperor of the French.* This letter was carried by General Caffarelli, one of the Emperor's aides-de-camp, with an invitation to the pope to come to Paris in the first days of November. Napoleon's letter, which made no allusion to settlement of religious questions which were pending, threw the pope into a fresh state of perplexity. At last, however, he made up his mind to leave Rome on November 2, the day after All Saints Day.

On the 25th the Emperor left the palace of Fontainebleau on the pretext of a hunt in the forest. Informed of the exact time at which the pope would reach the cross of St. H——, on the Paris road, the Emperor arrived there at the same time. He alighted from his horse and the pope descended from his carriage. The two embraced, and then entered the Emperor's carriage, Napoleon going first, and placing the pope on his right.

The cardinals, and the Holy Father's suite, entered the other carriages of the court. The procession made its way to the palace, where the two sovereigns were received by Cardinal Caprara, the ministers, and the chief officers of the crown. After resting in his apartment, the pope paid a visit to the Emperor, and afterwards to the Empress. At four o'clock, Napoleon returned his visit, and remained closeted with His Holiness for half-an-hour. Meanwhile the ministers and other dignitaries had been presented to the Holy Father. On the morrow, and on the following day the pope dined with the Emperor. Napoleon kept constantly giving him his hand. I heard Napoleon relate, that in the course of one of their conversations, the Holy Father had pressed him to sign his name at the bottom of a document in which Louis XIV, towards the end of his life, pressed by his confessors, had disavowed the articles of the declaration of the clergy in 1682, which was drawn up by Bossuet as the foundation of the liberties of the Gallican Church. The pope promised to keep this act of complaisance secret.

On the 28th the pope went to Paris, accompanied by the Emperor in the same carriage. He was lodged in the Pavilion de Flore where, during his stay in the French capital, he received the bodies of the state, the clergy, the religious corporations, all of whom addressed him, and amongst these addresses the speech of the President of the legislative body may be noted. A large number of people belonging to all classes of society solicited the privilege of seeing the pope, and came to ask him for his blessing. Each day a crowd could be seen under his windows, begging and receiving his blessing on their knees. The pope would frequently appear on the balcony of the Tuileries, sometimes accompanied by Napoleon, and their appearance was always greeted with the loudest cheers.

The ceremony of the coronation took place at Notre Dame on December 2. The pope went to the cathedral from the Pavilion de Flore, accompanied by a large retinue of priests and prelates, in magnificent robes, preceded by his cross-bearer, who was mounted on a richly caparisoned donkey. This monk, who wore on his head a broad-brimmed hat of a rounded form, carried a large gilt cross in his hands. Public curiosity was greatly excited by the novelty of a spectacle hitherto unknown to the population of Paris.

It was three hours later that the Emperor followed the pope from the Tuileries, driving in a state carriage glittering with plate glass and gilding, and laden with pages, who hung on the doors, in front and behind. The pomp of the procession was in harmony with the grandeur of the occasion. I omit the details of the ceremonies, which are to be found everywhere, and content myself with describing the most striking incident in Napoleon's coronation. The pope, after the usual anointings and blessings, was preparing to take the crown, which was placed on the altar, when suddenly the Emperor seized hold of it, placed it on his head with his own hands, and afterwards crowned Josephine himself. The pope was reduced to the role of a mere spectator. This act, which was a reply to the objections that had been raised through the pretensions of the Court of Rome, provoked a spontaneous movement of surprise amongst all present.

On the eve of the coronation, the senate had been received in solemn audience by the Emperor, and the result of the voting on the establishment of the Empire was presented to him. Out of a number almost equivalent to that of the citizens who had voted for the Life Consulate, there were only two thousand, or thereabouts, who refused to ratify by their suffrages the elevation of Napoleon to imperial rank. The days which followed on the imperial coronation were taken up with the reception of the bishops, the presidents of the electoral committees, the scientific bodies, and the military deputations. A distribution of the new standards, surmounted by eagles, was made on the Champ de Mars to the regiments of all the forces, and to the national guards of the hundred and eighteen departments of the Empire. On the same day the Emperor and the pope were present together, at the same table, at a banquet given at the Tuileries. They were attired in their ceremonial robes, and were served by the chief officers of the crown. The event which had just been accomplished was celebrated with fêtes, displays of fireworks, and illuminations.

And as apposite to the Emperor's coronation I will here relate, in its simple truth, an anecdote which Napoleon's biographers have embellished in the most piquant manner. Napoleon lends himself so well to the imagination that it often goes astray when on this subject. But by investigating with an air of improbability stories which have no need of any such adornment, the great man is robbed of his originality, and is reduced to a commonplace person. In this way a dénouement has been added to the anecdote to which I am alluding, a dénouement alleged to have taken place at the time of his coronation, but which is a pure invention. Some days before her marriage with General Bonaparte Madame de Beauharnais sent for her notary to talk certain matters of business over with him. When M. Raguideau called he was immediately taken up to Madame de Beauharnais, who was still in bed. The persons who were present in the room withdrew on his entry, with the exception of a young man, who escaped the notary's attention, and who placed himself in the embrasure of the window. After having spoken about certain arrangements in connection with her approaching marriage, Madame de Beauharnais asked to be told what was being said about it. M. de Raguideau did not conceal the fact that her friends regretted to see her marry a penniless soldier younger than herself, whom she would be obliged to support while in the army, and who might be killed in war and leave her unprovided for, and with children. Madame de Beauharnais asked him if that was his opinion also. He had no hesitation in answering in the affirmative, adding that with her fortune—she had an income of about 25,000 francs—she could make a very much better match, and that he thought it his duty, both as a matter of conscience and on account of the interest that he took in her, to make these remarks. He concluded by saying, carried away as he was by his zeal, that no doubt this officer was a very respectable man, but that, after all, his sword and his cape were his entire possessions. Madame de Beauharnais thanked him for his advice, and then with a laugh called to the young man who had remained standing before the window, drumming the panes with his fingers and apparently paying no attention to the conversation which had been going on. It is needless to add that this young man was General Bonaparte. "General," said Madame de Beauharnais, "have you heard what M. Raguideau has just been saying?" "Yes," he answered, "he has spoken like an honest man, and what he said makes me respect him. I hope that he will continue to take charge of our affairs, for he has disposed me to give him my confidence." M. Raguideau, learning by what he had heard who this young man (whom he did not know) was, was rather disconcerted. He had, however, no reason to regret his frankness. Napoleon kept General Bonaparte's promises. He appointed him notary of the civil list, always treated him with kindness, and never again alluded to the circumstance by which he had made his acquaintance. This is the little story in all its simplicity; the rest does credit to the imagination of those who invented it. These relate that the Emperor on the day of his coronation, clad in the imperial insignia, and wearing at his side the sword in which the Regent diamond was set, gave himself the pleasure of sending for M. Raguideau to show himself in all the splendor of his rank, and said to him, in a pointed way: "Raguideau, here is the cape, and here is the sword." I regret to be forced to say that this little stroke of revenge, so wittily conceived, never entered the Emperor's mind, occupied as it was with more serious thoughts. The only thing that showed that his thoughts went back to obscurer days was an exclamation which he made to the dearest and most familiar of his brothers: "Joseph," he cried, as he looked at his brother and himself clad in the attributes of power, "if father could see us!" This reflection was inspired less by pride than by a family feeling which in Napoleon's heart towered above the intoxication of glory and the splendors of supreme rank.

The reestablishment of the monarchy rendered the adoption of a protocol or formula of the letters of the cabinet necessary. The Emperor ordered me to look up, at the Foreign Office and at the National Library, documents and traditions by the help of which a protocol was drawn up and adopted by him.

Formerly letters in the Sovereign's handwriting were tied up crossed with two silk ribbons, on the ends of which the royal seal was placed. The color of the silk was red, or blue, according to the contents of the letter. The Emperor gave up this practice of autograph letters, and the letters were simply placed in sealed envelopes. The height at which the first line might be commenced, the number of times that the words "Your Majesty" might be used, and other minute details were formerly matters of rigorous etiquette. This etiquette was abandoned. Sovereigns of the highest rank used to write to each other as "Sir, my brother"; those of lesser rank were addressed as "My brother," or as "My brother and cousin," the addition of the word "cousin" being a sign of inferiority. The Tuileries cabinet adopted the use of the formula, "Sir, my Brother," for sovereigns of every degree. The pope, as in the past, was addressed as "Very Holy Father," or as "Your Holiness," the letters addressed to him ending, as in the past, with the formula: "May God preserve you for long years to come in the government of our Mother the Holy Church." Princes and Princesses, the high dignitaries, the Marshals and their wives, and the cardinals, were addressed as in the past, as "cousins." Letters used to end with the words: "And hereupon, I pray God that He may have you in His holy and worthy keeping," when addressed to the "cousins," and "in His holy keep" only, when addressed to others; and this formula was retained. Letters addressed by the King, to persons who were not included in these various categories, used formerly to begin on the first line with "Mons. So-and-So." The word "Monsieur," followed by the name and title, was now attributed to everybody without distinction. These modifications, and those which I have mentioned, were the only concessions made to the spirit of the times.

The constitution of the new Empire received its first application on the occasion of the birth of the second son of Prince Louis Bonaparte. A message from the Emperor invited the senate to register the birth of the eldest son, born under the Consulate, and of his younger brother, and to deposit the deeds of registration in the archives. The senate, in solemn audience, delivered an official certificate as to the deposit of these deeds of registration, to the Archchancellor, and replied to the Emperor's message with its congratulations.

Napoleon had profited by the circumstance of his accession to the Empire to renew his proposals of peace to the King of England. He never hoped that this proposal would be crowned with entire success, but he was anxious to neglect nothing which might expose the disinclination of the British government for peace. The letter was addressed to the King, and was answered by Minister Mulgrave in a letter addressed to M. de Talleyrand. Its contents were to the effect that the English sovereign could not reply to the overture which had been made to him in any particular way, without having communicated it to the powers with which he was allied in general, and to Russia in particular; thus refusing to express himself in any way on the Emperor's proposal, and arousing the suspicion that nothing less than a new coalition might be presaged from this new understanding amongst the powers. More formal respect was shown than in preceding communications, but there was not any more sincerity than before in the desire to effect a pacification.

The sessions of the Legislative Corps, which till then had been opened by the Minister of the Interior, were invested with a much more imposing character by the presence of the Emperor, who came to preside over the year XIII—1805—sitting, in person, and with all the pomp of sovereign power.

On this occasion, and in order to perpetuate the memory of the benefits of the Civil Code, a statue of Napoleon was placed in the assembly room of the Legislative Corps. A special sitting, at which the Empress, the princes and princesses of the imperial family, the ladies and gentlemen of their households, the Archchancellor and the Archtreasurer were present, was devoted to the unveiling of this statue. Marshals Murat and Masséna were invited by the President to draw the veil with which it was covered. Immediately after the sitting, which was held at seven o'clock in the evening, a brilliant fête, which the Emperor honored with his presence, was given in the apartments of the President.

About this time an old Corsican peasant woman, accompanied by a young woman whom she presented as her niece, was admitted to the Emperor's presence. This woman was Camilla Hari, Napoleon's nurse, who wanted to see him again. He received her with the greatest kindness, and embraced her most affectionately. The poor woman wept tears of joy on seeing her glorious nursling again. I was charged by the Emperor to provide for her wants and her pleasures. She did not speak a word of French. She spent three months in Paris in perpetual enchantment. She was presented to the pope, who took pleasure in hearing her speak, and was touched by the simplicity of her devotion. The whole Court wished to see her, and she played her part very well indeed. While speaking with tenderness of her foster-child, she did not neglect her interests. She did not seem sorry to return to Corsica, to talk about her journey there, and to show off the presents and the money with which the Emperor and Josephine had loaded her. Napoleon gave her the best part of his paternal inheritance on her return to Corsica. He gave the husband of her niece, whose name was Carboni, a position as tax collector at Beaucaire.

While the Emperor was occupying himself, not, very long after his coronation, with the reform of the religious congregations, only maintaining those which were really useful, he received a letter from the General Superior of the Jesuits, which contained an offer of the services of his Order. The Jesuits were beginning to penetrate into Paris. They had already enlisted a number of young men from the schools, whom they were transforming into emissaries of the opposition against the Imperial government. The Emperor esteemed this religious Order for the services which it rendered to education, but detested their intrigues. As they were, moreover, the satellites of a foreign government, whose strong pretensions he had reason to fear, Napoleon forbade them to remain in France. They entered the country under different names: Fathers of the Faith, Paccarists, Ligorists, Adorers of Jesus, and so on; but his vigilance continued to keep a strict watch on their underhand practices. When, either from reports addressed to him, or from the newspapers, he heard that some new society was establishing itself at any point in the Empire, his instinct did not deceive him. The Emperor then used to make haste to write to the Minister of Police, or to the Minister of the Interior, and blame them for their want of attention, urging them to redouble their vigilance in this matter.

The care bestowed on home and foreign affairs, on fêtes, and solemnities, were only by the way; the great object of Napoleon's solicitude remained his plan of an invasion of England. Some false maneuvers by Admiral Villeneuve, commanding the combined French, Dutch, and Spanish squadrons, made the Emperor dubious of the success of his clever plan, which was to use these fleets to protect the passage of the flotilla. He also conceived the idea of a great expedition to India, and occupied himself, for more than a month, on the means of resolving the difficulties of this great enterprise.

He did not on that account sacrifice the Boulogne expedition; but it seemed to him that an attack directed against England's distant and richest possessions might favor this expedition, by drawing the entire English forces in the wake of our fleets. These, taking advantage of the vastness of the ocean to escape any encounter with the English squadrons, and having landed the troops which they were to transport, were to return to our shores and help to cover with their protection the passage across the Channel. However, after having weighed the advantages and the disadvantages of an expedition to India, and taking into consideration the advanced state of the preparations for the Boulogne expedition, Napoleon made up his mind to leave matters as they were, and in no way to complicate his original idea. Judging that it would be asking too much of fortune to attempt such a thing, he decided to postpone the expedition to India to some more favorable time, and impatiently awaited the arrival of the fleets commanded by Admiral Villeneuve. He was much embarrassed as to the choice of a general to direct the invasion of British India. Without doubt he had a high appreciation of the talents of the marshals, and the chief generals who had been formed in his school; but he did not consider them all to possess that combination of good qualities which were necessary for commanding a distant expedition, in which they would have been left to themselves. On this occasion, I heard him regretting General Desaix, whose high capacity both as a soldier and as a politician he fully appreciated. If General Desaix had still been alive at the time, it is to him that he would have entrusted the execution of his plan of campaign in 1801, which Moreau had not the courage to undertake. The remembrance of Desaix frequently came to Napoleon's mind when he was meditating some great independent military expedition. Perhaps the fact of his being deprived of the assistance of this distinguished commanding officer contributed more than once to a relinquishment of his plans. Combined with the Emperor's high esteem for the talents of the regretted general was the superstition of friendship. Desaix's soul responded to his; he would have been the Hephaestion of this second Alexander.

There was another matter in which the Emperor was strongly interested; he was anxious to definitely settle the fate of Italy. In accordance with the wishes of the Italians, he offered the crown of Lombardy to his brother Joseph. Joseph refused it, alleging his desire to preserve his quality as a French prince, and his right of succession to the throne of France; and fearing, so it is said, to alienate his new subjects by paying tribute to France, knowing how much the Italians dislike their money to be carried out of their country. His dominating motive was that he was entirely free from ambition. Napoleon, crossed in his plans, and unwilling to hand over his creation to strange, and possibly hostile hands, decided to join the title of King of Italy to that of Emperor of the French.

During the last days of his stay in Paris Napoleon received, in solemn audience, Vice President Melzi, accompanied by the members composing the state consultum, and a deputation from the various Italian colleges, who presented him with the address by which the crown of Italy was offered to him.

The next day, so as to dispose of the various matters relating to Italy, and to prepare the future of his further plans concerning this peninsula, at the same time, Napoleon went to the senate to procure a recognition of Princess Eliza, his sister, as hereditary Princess of Piombino. The title of Prince of Piombino was conferred on her husband, together with the command of the troops charged with the defense of the coasts, and of the communications between the islands, of Elba and Corsica.

At the same sitting of the senate, the Emperor caused the constitution of the Kingdom of Italy to be laid clown in a senatus consultum.

On the same day on which the Emperor was proclaimed King of Italy, Admiral Bruix—who, notwithstanding his shattered health, was struggling, with the energy born of devotion and ambition, with the heavy duties of commander of the Boulogne flotilla—died of consumption in Paris in the prime of life. This admiral had a vigorous mind in the weakliest of bodies. Napoleon, who had watched the struggle of his weakly nature, had had him sounded on the question whether he felt sufficiently strong to resist the fatigues which his command laid upon him. Bruix, either out of devotion to the expedition, or because he was unwilling to appear inferior in capacity to Admiral Latouche-Tréville redoubled his zeal and activity. But soon, his strength spent, he had to be transported to Paris, clinging to his post of commander-in-chief with the tenacity of a drowning man, till the hour when death came to put an end to this painful struggle. He was succeeded by Admiral Lacrosse.

The Emperor having provided for the dispatch of business, and having commissioned his brother Joseph to preside over the senate and the other administrative councils during his absence, which was to last three months, received a farewell visit from the pope at St. Cloud, and left on the following day, April 1, for Italy. Four days later His Holiness also left, loaded with costly presents, as were also the members of his suite. Having arrived in Paris in the winter the Holy Father had awaited the spring before returning to Rome. During his stay in the capital of the empire he had been treated with special distinction and honors. He had visited all the public establishments without exception, and a large number of industrial establishments. During his visit to the National Printing Office, Marcel, the director, presented him with a magnificent typographical work: *L'Oraison Dominicale,* translated into one hundred and fifty languages, and printed in the characters proper to each language. The pope had performed mass several times at Notre Dame, and at all the parish churches of Paris in turn. Everywhere the greatest respect and deference had been shown him. He left Paris in the first week of April, very much pleased with the religious revival which had been brought about in France by the Concordat, but disappointed in his principal hopes. He had been unable to obtain from the Emperor the concessions which he expected from his gratitude for the step he had taken, and from the influence which he hoped the now firmly established Catholicism of the French nation would have upon Napoleon's purposes. He had failed in various approaches which he had made to the new Emperor on the instigation of his secret council, which was composed of cardinals and bishops imbued with the old notions of the omnipotence of the Holy See, and who only saw in the religious revolution which had taken place in France an opportunity for enforcing their ultramontane ideas. Amongst other concessions, the pope had demanded the repeal of Bossuet's four propositions, guardians of the liberties of the Gallican Church, and the repeal of the declaration of the French clergy in 1682. He had also asked that the clergy might have the supervision of the schools, and that a public declaration should be made by the government that the Catholic religion was the dominating religion in France. These pretensions, which were put forward by the Holy Father as points of ecclesiastical discipline, were repelled by Napoleon, with all the respect Duke to the Head of the Church, but with invincible firmness. Another question, which more closely concerned the Holy See, was the restitution of the legations to the Pontifical States. Napoleon had to show himself inflexible on this point, as on the others. The pope accordingly quitted Paris regretting to have shown a condescension for which he considered himself very poorly rewarded. His Holiness joined the Emperor at Piedmont, and renewed his leavetaking at the royal castle of Stupinis. Thence he continued his journey to Rome, where he arrived eight months after his departure from the eternal city to crown the new Charlemagne in his capital. It has been noticed that the few sovereigns who were crowned by the pope went to Rome to receive their consecration at the hands of St. Peter's successor. Pope Leo III crowned, in Rome—as Emperor of the Western Empire—Charlemagne, the benefactor of the Holy See, and the first author of its power.

Napoleon was accompanied, in his journey to Italy, by the Empress Josephine. Cardinal Caprara, Archbishop of Milan, who was to crown the King of Italy, had preceded him. The Emperor had sent the grand master of ceremonies, and part of his court, on in front; the rest escorted him on his journey and Abbés Pradt and de Broglie accompanied him as almoners. These two prelates, restored to reason, appeared to be fully reconciled to the new regime which was established in our country. These two abbés vied with each other in admiration of and devotion to the genius who raised France so high amongst the nations. Their conversations with the Emperor's aides-de-camp during the journey were most secular and gay in tone, and both showed themselves very gallant with the ladies of the palace. They were both men of wit, but Abbé Pradt excelled by his unceasing flow of conversation. Woe to anyone who, in conversation with him, should chance to pause to use his handkerchief, or to take breath; the word was taken from his mouth, and there was no hope of his ever getting a chance to put in another. M. de Pradt was loaded with gifts and honors by Napoleon; but when he saw that the Empire was on its decline, the almoner of the god Mars found out that he had only been serving at the altars of "Jupiter Scapin." He made amends for this aberration in certain writings, which do more credit to his intelligence than to his heart. In one word, his disloyalty can only be described as most scandalous.

M. de Broglie did not act like M. de Pradt, who only insulted the idol when it had been overthrown. Having become first Bishop of Acqui, and then Bishop of Ghent, his attitude and his language changed as soon as the difficulties between the Emperor and the pope arose. His estrangement from the Imperial government was as sudden as it was striking. God's elect became, in this prelate's eyes, the enemy of religion and the Antichrist. He took part, resolutely, against the Emperor; and rejecting with an ardent and obstinate passion, all attempts made by Napoleon to conciliate him, refused even to accept the decoration of the Legion of Honor, wishing to take nothing from the Emperor's hands. His fanaticism reached such a pitch, that his ambition was not for the martyr's palm—the days of martyrdom having passed by—but for that of confessor of the faith. He was confined in Vincennes, and forced to resign his see to gain his liberty. He did not, however, consider himself deprived of his episcopal authority, and continued in secret communication with his clergy, bringing fresh disgrace thereby upon himself. After the fall of the Empire, he was reinstated in his episcopal functions, but lived on no better terms with the Dutch government. Three years later he was sentenced, *per contumaciam,* to transportation, by the Brussels Court of Assizes, for the crime of disobedience to the laws of the state. At the same time, he was a man of good faith, who was respected for his learning and his irreproachable morals.

The Emperor halted for several days at Lyons and at Turin. Mont Cenis was crossed in the way which was customary at that time. The carriages had to be taken to pieces, and the travelers had to make their way by steep paths, interrupted at each step. Trusty and surefooted men carried the travelers and their luggage on their backs, or in sedan chairs; other mountaineers, placed in the front of a kind of sledge, and armed with ferruled sticks, guided their rapid course with marvelous dexterity. When we again crossed this mountain, in 1807, a broad and fine road, with a gentle and easy slope, had taken the place of all this chaos. The road was so easy that it was not necessary to put the drag on the post-chaises. On his arrival at Alessandria, Napoleon visited the immense fortifications which he had ordered, and held a grand review on the battlefield of Marengo. The maneuvers, commanded by Marshal Lannes, were executed on the same plains which, five years previously, had been the scene of the battle. Napoleon had had the coat and the hat which he had worn on that memorable day brought from Paris, and put them on on the day of the review. The sight of this old uniform excited the enthusiasm of the soldiers, most of whom had seen its glitter in the thick of the fire of the great battle, and its dingy embroideries recalled more vividly a memory eminently glorious to French arms, the memory of a victory which had produced such great results.

The Emperor found his brother Jérôme at Alessandria, who had hastened thither, on his return from America, to have an interview with him. He came from Genoa, where he had left the brig *L'Epervier,* which he was commanding. The interview was a stormy one, for the Emperor refused to acknowledge his brother's marriage with Miss Patterson, contracted at a time when the young spouses were under age. The birth of a son, issue of this marriage, had prompted Jérôme to oppose a violent resistance to Napoleon's will. He was forced, however, to yield to the irresistible superiority of his brother's will and returned, immediately after this interview, to Genoa, where he awaited the Emperor's arrival on board his ship.

From Alessandria, Napoleon proceeded to Pavia, where he spent two days. He received there a large deputation, which had come from Milan to congratulate him, and which helped to swell his procession at the imposing entry which, on May 13, he made into this capital. The Emperor was received in Milan with enthusiastic demonstrations, rendered more emphatic by the Italian character. The fifteen days which preceded his coronation were employed in completing the preparations for this ceremony. He went to visit the Duomo, the cathedral of Milan, the pride of Lombardy, an immense church, ornamented with a prodigious number of marble statues. He gave orders for the completion of this fine building, which had so long been neglected, a constant subject of regret to the Milanese. It was in this cathedral that, on May 26, 1805, the coronation of the King of Italy took place with the greatest pomp. The iron crown which had been used for the enthronement of the Lombard Kings had been brought from Monza, where it was preserved as a historical relic. Napoleon placed it on his head with his own hands, as he had done with the imperial crown at Notre Dame, repeating in a loud voice, the words inscribed on the circle of the iron crown: *"Dio mi la diede, guai à chi la tocca."*

The Empress was not crowned Queen, and watched the ceremony from a gallery on the right of the altar. The coronation was followed by fêtes and popular amusements, amongst others being sports in a circus, constructed after the Roman model, a poor imitation of the antique sports. The Theatre of La Scala displayed all its talent. At the head of the leading singers of Italy figured the celebrated Marchesi, one of the most astonishing eunuchs which the musical conservatories of the country have ever produced. Marchesi's voice, which had been the object of universal admiration, was heard there for the last time. Enthusiastic about his art he had had himself operated upon, although already in the prime of life. At the time of coronation he was sixty-three years old. His voice, perfected by the excellence of his method, had remained mellow, pure, and of charming sweetness. He was, moreover, an excellent actor.

The audience granted to the Doge, and to the deputations of the senate and people of Genoa, afforded an imposing spectacle. The Order of the Crown of Iron was created, and a constitutional statute, settling the organization of the Kingdom of Italy, was presented to the Legislative Corps. Prince Eugène took the oath as viceroy. The constitution provided that the crown of Italy should be hereditary, to the exclusion of women; that adoption could only extend to a Frenchman or an Italian; that as soon as the foreign armies should have evacuated the state of Naples, the Ionian Islands, and the island of Malta, Napoleon would transmit his crown to one of his male children, legitimate, natural, or adopted: and that from that time forward the crown of Italy could no longer be united to the crown of France on the same head, and that Napoleon's successors should constantly reside on the territory of Italy.

After having provided for the general scheme and the most minute details of the constitution of his new kingdom, Napoleon left Milan to visit the different provinces. A large camp had been formed in the plain of Montechiaro, the scene of the battle of Castiglione, and a review was held here before the Emperor; when, as at Marengo, he distributed rewards and decorations. He next visited the fortified towns of Mantua, Peschiera, Verona, and Legnano. The object of these demonstrations was to teach the enemies of France, who were then agitating Germany, to appreciate our military resources, the fine deportment of our troops, their familiarity with war, and the fine spirit with which they were animated.

The union of Genoa to the Empire was accomplished at Milan. The precarious condition of this Republic, a desire to acquire its harbor, and especially the harbor of Spezia, which was large and safe enough to form the site of a large maritime establishment, and it may also be said the favorable tendencies of the people, decided Napoleon. The Genoese expected a safer future, and the efficacious protection of their commerce, from their incorporation with France. It was this that decided the senate of Genoa and the

Doge himself to go to Milan, and to express their wishes on this subject to the Emperor.

During his stay at Bologna, a deputation from the principality of Lucca, prompted by the same motives, came to ask him to take their country under his protection. There was no need of intimidation on his part to extort the expression of these wishes from these two small states. It was so much to their interest to form integral parts of the great Empire, that they were quite naturally brought to express their desire so to become. Napoleon refused the offer of the Luccans, but he gave them a constitution, and handed over the sovereignty of Lucca to his sister Eliza, who added it to the duchy of Piombino, with which a senatus consultum had three months previously invested her.

The Emperor only stayed twenty-four hours at Parma. He met there with M. Moreau de Saint-Méry, who, owing to the influence of the Empress Josephine, whose compatriot and relation he was, had been appointed councilor of state and Director-General of the States of Parma, Piacenza, and Guastalla. This director, a man of merit and probity, who, at the beginning of the troubles of the Revolution, had showed firmness as well as moderation, governed these states in a feeble manner, being almost entirely taken up with arts and literature. His way of governing was not in harmony with Napoleon's active and positive processes of administration. He had had a "Treatise on Dancing" printed in a luxurious manner, by Bodoni, and this displeased the Emperor. A mutiny of the militia of the state of Parma severely repressed by Junot—who was sent there with extraordinary powers—was imputed to Moreau de Saint-Méry's weakness. He was recalled, and the States of Parma—divided into departments, and placed under the French administration—became part of the general organization of the Empire. On his return to France Moreau de Saint-Méry was coldly received by the Emperor. Consigned to oblivion, he received as the reward of his services only a moderate pension, which was increased by the Empress Josephine's liberalities.

Napoleon kept the promises which he had made to the Genoese deputation. He went to Genoa to receive the homage of the new subjects of the Empire, and devoted his attention to the organization of the various departments of the government. The Minister of the Interior had preceded the Emperor to Genoa, and the Archtreasurer, who was commissioned to establish the French regime in this country, was there also. Napoleon was received like a liberator, with effusive demonstrations of gratitude and admiration. Splendid fêtes were given in his honor. The fête in the Roads of Genoa, at which he was present, was fairy-like in splendor. The Emperor, accompanied by the Empress Josephine, and the whole court, crossed the terrace of the Doria palace, which he occupied, and came down the great marble staircase, which goes out into the sea, and from the steps of which Andrea Doria used to embark on board his admiral's galley. Here he got on board an immense rotunda, with columns painted in white and gold, rowed by a hundred oarsmen in rich attire. This rotunda was immediately rowed off towards the harbor, where a regatta was in progress. At the close of the day, numerous floating islands, joined on to this temple as if by enchantment, formed, in the middle of the waves, a garden filled with trees and flowers, and ornamented with statues and springing fountains. As the night grew dark a display of fireworks took place, which lighted up the whole of the Roads, and the numerous buildings built in an amphitheatre around them.

The Emperor met his brother Jérôme again at Genoa. After the reconciliation of the two brothers at Alessandria, Jérôme had been promoted to the rank of commander. He was entrusted with the mission to go with a squadron of vessels to Algiers, and there to summon the Dey to hand over to him the Genoese who had been kidnapped by the Barbary pirates, and who had remained their prisoners. Having become our fellow-citizens the Genoese had a right to the immediate protection of France. The name of Bonaparte, and the commander's firmness, triumphed over the Dey, who had at first refused obedience. Jérôme, within a month after leaving Genoa, brought back to that port all the Genoese and Italians whom he had just rescued from the hardest slavery. This fortunate expedition endeared him to the people of Genoa, who hailed his return with transports of gratitude.

The Emperor, in spite of the eight days spent in Genoa in the midst of rejoicings, did not lose sight of business. Above all, he was constantly preoccupied concerning the war against England, which had been the principal motive of his accepting Genoa. He left this city with the Empress for Turin, where he stayed one day. The extraordinary powers of the Arch-treasurer having lapsed after the union of the Genoese Republic to the Empire, this high dignitary was maintained there in the capacity of governor-general. The Emperor, on his journey back to Paris, visited the convent of Mont Cenis, where the monks had prepared luncheon for him. This was his only halt till he reached Fontainebleau, towards which he pressed forward with full speed, always accompanied by Josephine, who bore the fatigues and the privations, inseparable from such rapid traveling, with remarkable endurance. It would have been useless for the Emperor to try and spare her; she was indifferent to the length of the journey and the absence of all the comforts to which she was accustomed, so long as she was not separated from Napoleon. In this hurried journey, escorts of under-officers, grenadiers, and chasseurs of the guard, had been formed to accompany the Emperor's carriage, but so fast was the pace that none of them were able to keep up with the carriages to the end. The Emperor thanked them for their zeal, and after that time the experiment was not renewed.

I think it my duty, as a truthful historian, to relate the one occasion, during the many years which I passed near his person, on which he was rather seriously vexed with me. It will also serve to throw a new light on Napoleon's character.

I had been attached to his cabinet for close upon three years. During that time I had received proof of his kindness and his satisfaction with me. No cloud had come to overshadow my relations with him, when their serenity was suddenly troubled by a particular circumstance. Since the rupture of the Peace of Amiens, the work in the cabinet had greatly increased. The hard work to which I was constantly subjected woke in me an irresistible desire for some amusement. Too young, as I was—I was then twenty-seven years old—I was wanting in maturity. I had too little ambition and care for the future not to take advantage of the few hours of leisure which were left me, and which I was able to snatch from the sedentary and monotonous life which I was leading. The Opera masked ball was then at the height of fashion. Napoleon himself used frequently to visit it. I often went there and found some people of my acquaintance, with whom I got accustomed to foregather. That led to our arranging dinner and theatre parties. Once or twice a week we used to dine at the Robert restaurant, there never being more than eight or ten people at the table. The honors were done by one or two ladies of the class it is usual to call "amiable ladies." As fate would have it, most of the men I used to meet at these parties were not in the Emperor's good graces. Amongst them was a former moderate *conventionnel,* his compatriot, and the friend of all his family, whom I had known for a long time—a keen and clever man, dissatisfied, but incapable of doing any harm. I obtained for him later on a place in the civil service, and he was appointed to a subprefecture in Piedmont. He conducted himself with so much skill and loyalty that the Emperor, considering the place he occupied was beneath his merits, put him down for a prefecture. The others were bankers, of whom some had been crossed in their speculations by the general measures of the government, but who, in spite of that, were not hostilely disposed towards it. Although they thought that they had a right to complain, they had sufficient tact not to speak to me of their grievances, to which, in no case, could I have listened. I gave myself up to these innocent pleasures without dreaming of the storm which was gathering over my head. One day when I had been to see the Empress Josephine, she happened to speak to me of the Opera ball, of certain meetings which the Emperor had made there, and which rather excited her jealousy. She added, jestingly, that she knew I was in the habit of seeing a very amiable person there, she complimented me upon my taste, said that she knew her name, and that she was sure that it was because her Christian name was Josephine also that I had chosen her. I denied that I had any such influence with this lady, as she described, and begged her to tell me how she had got to know about these matters. She was good enough to tell me, without a moment's hesitation, that it was Bonaparte who had told her. That gave me cause for reflection. The Emperor's silence towards me, considering how fond he was of joking, surprised me. Then, on thinking the matter over, I felt hurt by this mysterious conduct, and determined to wait until he spoke of the matter to me. Two days later I met him walking with Doctor Corvisart, in a covered alley which led out from the family drawing-room at St. Cloud.

As I passed before them, the Emperor barred the way, and catching me by the arm, looked at me with mocking eyes, and said to Corvisart: "Here, after all, is a man whose usual company is that of my enemies." I was prepared for this sally by what I had heard from Josephine. I was reassured by the rough frankness which the Emperor had used in speaking to me. I ought not to have taken the matter in earnest, but, dissatisfied in my mind with Napoleon's silence towards me, which implied a sort of suspicion, I answered him very seriously that I had had no occasion to see that his accusation was a well-founded one; that if the persons whom I associated with were really his secret enemies, they would find themselves in the wrong box with me; that he could not doubt my loyalty; and that I was not the man to allow anything concerning him to be even hinted at in my presence. He allowed me to speak without interruption, and I withdrew, seeing that he had nothing to add to what he had said. Corvisart, who at first had been surprised at the way in which the Emperor had spoken to me, took my part, and said, with a laugh, that he would willingly go bail for me. The day passed without any allusion being made to what had happened in the morning. Till then my absences had been tolerated, and it sometimes happened that I did not return to the cabinet until the following day. I always managed to get there before the levee, which took place at nine o'clock. When the Emperor crossed his cabinet to go to his levee, I had always taken care, that his papers should be in order, and the letters which had arrived in the morning opened and arranged on the little table which stood by the settee where he usually sat. He used to give a glance at them as he passed, but never stopped unless I told him that there was something important and urgent in the day's letters.

I do not know whether some police reports had put the friendly meetings about which I have spoken, in a false light, but from the moment when I knew that the Emperor had been informed of these meetings, I found that he got to the cabinet before me. I also learned that he had frequently asked for me after dinner, when I was away. It looked as if he was trying to get together as many causes for complaint as possible so as to have all the more right to burst out. The explosion, which took place in the nick of time, was brought about by a parcel which I had sent off by a courier, and which for some reason or other was not punctually delivered at its address. One day, on my arrival at the cabinet, a *huissier* told me that the Emperor had asked for me in an excited tone of voice. Just as the *huissier* was going away, the Emperor made his appearance. He addressed me in a very animated way, and, with an anger which seemed feigned rather than real, reproached me for my neglect of his cabinet, adding that I paid no attention at all, that I was constantly absent, that I absolutely neglected his affairs, and that an important dispatch had been lost by my fault. Then, without waiting to hear any explanation from me, he went out to call the courier, and shouted out to him all that his anger could suggest on the subject. Then returning he brusquely opened all the packets which were on his writing-table. He told me that he did not wish me to open his letters in future, and that, without having any doubts of my loyalty, he should not be able in future to trust himself to my vigilance. All this was said and done with so much volubility and precipitation that I was unable to get in a single word. I had never before seen him in such a state of excitement. After this scene he went off to his levee, and thence to breakfast, and did not show himself again. A few minutes before dinnertime I was summoned into the little drawing room which adjoined his cabinet, where I found him working with the Secretary of state. Napoleon rose on my entrance and approached me with a calm and composed air. In the presence of the minister he gave me a really paternal lecture, speaking to me of the confidence which he had placed in me, of my duties, of the honor attaching to their right fulfillment, of my future, of all the good he wished me, and so on, speaking to me with so much kindness that, although I had made up my mind to listen to him coldly, I could not help feeling very much touched. He told me that it was necessary that I should cease my absences, because he would have to work all the week. As a matter of fact he came to his cabinet in the evening remaining there a quarter of an hour before calling me, When I came in to his summons, he received me in the most cordial manner possible, calling me his "Dear Ménevalot"—dear little Méneval—a term of friendship which he often used towards me, made no further allusion to the grievances of the day, and tried to make me forget them. There ended this quarrel, which was never renewed during the long years which Providence destined me still to pass with him, I never ceased to find him good, patient, and indulgent in his treatment of me. I had occasion afterwards, I do not remember in what connection, to allude to this scene. "My dear Méneval," he said, "there are circumstances in which it is necessary for me to put my confidence in quarantine."

The Emperor's attack upon me was without doubt of a nature to hurt my feelings, but to a certain extent it was justifiable. On reflection, I was forced to acknowledge that if sometimes storms arise in the most peaceful minds, and those least exposed to the tempests of life, one cannot be astonished that a keen and ready spirit so susceptible to impressions, so agitated by so many and such various thoughts, should, in circumstances of little importance, have paid its tribute to the imperfections of human nature. The business, the papers which Napoleon entrusted me with, were sufficiently important for him to feel anxiety as to their safety. Besides, although this superior man was not insensible to pinpricks of everyday life, under great reverses, he always remained self-controlled, always calm, always serene, and armed with all his presence of mind. So, I bore him no ill will for what had happened, and neither did he towards me. I may remark, however, that the subjection to which I was constrained seemed to me harder to bear than ever.

On the morrow the Emperor's letters were left unopened on his writing-table. On his entering the cabinet he opened one or two, and handed me the rest, saying, in a tone of some impatience: "Méneval, open these letters!" I touched none of the letters which arrived subsequently. I had often thought that my work was already very heavy, and I did not want to see it increased. I made up my mind to take advantage of the scene which had occurred to get rid of a supervision and a task which, in proportion as business increased, became more and more fatiguing. The duty of opening the sovereign's letters involved their classification according to the ministers concerned, and the drawing up of a summary on the margin of each communication. Now, very often there was no time for this work. I was constantly being interrupted in it to write at the Emperor's dictation. I will not speak of the responsibility which would have rested on me, to a certain extent, supposing some dispatch had been removed or diverted from its destination, or even had simply got lost. Already, in 1803 and 1804, when the English ambassadors, in the residences the least distant from our frontiers, were acting as the agents of disorder and intrigue, and even of corruption, I had suggested to Napoleon how necessary it was that the safety of his dispatches should be provided for. He contented himself with giving me a mounted escort, on his journeys between La Malmaison and Paris, which were always made very late in the evening, and this was only done to prevent the carrying off of his portfolio.

In drawing these reflections to a close, I will add that the Emperor gradually accustomed himself to open his letters himself. I helped him in this task, when I had nothing more urgent to do. His devouring cerebral activity, which never could find enough food, and which grew as the demands upon it increased, was all-sufficient. As soon as a letter had been opened he read it, and often answered it at once, putting the others aside to be answered later, and throwing all those which did not need any answer on the floor. Sometimes the ministers sent to ask me what the Emperor had done with such or such a report. When they heard that he had thrown it aside without an answer they knew what that meant. Napoleon used to call not answering the best part of his work. When he was away, I was charged with opening the letters which might come during his absence, and in case they contained anything urgent to take them to him, wherever he might be, or to hand them to him immediately on his return, even in his private apartments. This custom was established in this way, and was afterwards observed. The little festivities and amusements of which I have spoken to the reader, and which had given offense to Napoleon, were broken off by a series of incidents, and by the absence of the Emperor on a journey in which I had to accompany him.

This episode, which I could not pass over in silence, has interrupted the course of my narrative; may I be allowed to resume it? The Boulogne expedition was ready, and all the vessels were prepared to set sail. Repeated exercises in embarking and landing had trained the troops to precision and speed without confusion, so necessary in this kind of expedition. Each regiment, each brigade, each army corps had its appointed post, and knew on what ships to embark. The most minute instructions had been given to the land forces as well as to the sailors. The winds—which were wanted to blockade the English ships in their ports, and clear the seas—were favorable. Terror reigned in the councils of the cabinet of London. England, trembling on her island, scattered gold broadcast, and used all the resources of her diplomacy to divert to Austria, or to Russia, the most imminent danger to which she had ever been exposed. The maneuver, the success of which was to bring together, at the mouth of the Channel, sufficient naval forces to ensure a free passage to the Boulogne flotilla, had succeeded. By skillfully combined maneuvers, Napoleon had succeeded in assembling, in distant waters, the largest part of the fleets of France and of her allies. I must add, in passing, that he did not always find, in his Minister of Marine, the assistance which his ignorance of the element which was the scene of his plans rendered necessary. The responsibility which rested on this minister on the eve of undertaking so colossal a maritime expedition, rendered him almost constantly negative. This officer, who was so brave at sea, was timid and hesitating in the council. This circumspection might have reacted on the admiral who was charged with the chief command, had not his irresolution and absolute want of strength of character, although he was a brave man, sufficed to paralyze the efficaciousness of the resources at his disposal. The minister's hesitation and the Admiral's tergiversation provoked the Emperor's impatience in the highest degree. Now discouraged, now regaining confidence, as news came in from the sea, he ended by doubting as to the success of the expedition; and yet, all the preparations had been completed. The Emperor, a prey to all the torments of incertitude, was still clinging to the hope that at any moment he might hear of the appearance of the fleet which he was expecting with such impatience, when he heard that his hopes were shattered by the news of Admiral Villeneuve's entry into Cadiz, where he was blockaded by superior forces. All illusion had then to be abandoned, and Napoleon had nothing else to think of than to prepare for the imminent continental war with which he was threatened by Austria. He determined, in consequence, to break up the camp at Boulogne. Faithful to his custom, to use his own expression, of always doing his work in two ways, he had given secret orders with the object indicated, without, however, making it apparent that he despaired of the success of the expedition, and finally had dictated to M. de Talleyrand directions for the drawing-up of his manifesto.

Some of Napoleon's historians have said that when Admiral Villeneuve's blunders had demonstrated the impossibility of carrying out the plan of an invasion, he sent for M. Daru, general intendant of the army, and dictated to him, in one breath, his plan of campaign against Austria from the different points from which the various regiments should start, up to their arrival at Vienna. That is not like Napoleon. I do not doubt that he would have been able to dictate such an improvised plan, and this was not the first time that he had studied the question of war with Germany. Nor could the plan of campaign have been entrusted to more loyal hands. But it was not his habit to make his secrets known, except where such confidence appeared to him necessary for the success of his plans. Now, in this circumstance, nothing obliged him to take M. Daru into his confidence. The truth is that Napoleon sent for this gentleman and sent him, four days before he himself started for Paris, to General Dejean, Minister of War, with a letter which will be found below, charging him to assist the minister in carrying out the orders contained therein in the promptest manner possible, so as avoid letting the office into the secret.

Letter from the EMPEROR to the MINISTER OF WAR:

"MONSIEUR DEJEAN—The Minister of War has no doubt given you various orders to get in readiness for war, armies for Italy and the Rhine. You may consider this war as certain. I have orders for the provision of hoods and boots necessary for the army. Let me know if you have anything at your disposal in Paris. It is necessary that you should give orders to all the cavalry regiments to provide themselves with fresh horses at any price. I see no objection to your supplying them with a million francs for this purpose. I have placed at your disposal an extraordinary sum of two million, two hundred thousand francs, of which one million is for the purchase of horses for the train of artillery, and twelve hundred thousand francs are for the hoods and boots. Look after the carts; have them made at Sampigny. There is a market for transports here; give it greater extension. I presume that you have provided that I be supplied with biscuit at Mayence and Strasburg; I have plenty here. The stock of biscuit made twenty months ago should be used now; there will remain here more than twenty thousand mouths; the biscuit made twelve months ago can be kept. It is possible that matters will be settled after a few battles, and that I shall return to the coast. Hurry on the supply of cloth for Year XIV; it is wanted as soon as possible. You will have in the whole fifth military division, nine thousand dragoon horses, eight or nine thousand horses of light infantry or hussars, four or five thousand of heavy cavalry, and fifteen hundred of the guards, apart from those of the staff. I wish the service to be carried out by the same administration as far as Boulogne, especially as regards meat and bread. Do not lose a moment in getting supplies of wine and brandy at Landau, Strasburg, and Spires. Landau will be one of the chief points of assembly. I imagine that Vanderberghe is sending the same people to Strasburg as to Boulogne. The first divisions have already started; see him about it. I have asked you for five hundred thousand rations of biscuit at Strasburg, but I have no objection to their being divided thus: two hundred thousand rations at Landau; two hundred thousand at Strasburg, and one hundred thousand at Spires. I expect you to send me two reports, in the first of which you will inform me of the number of horses in each cavalry regiment, fit for service; what funds remain in the treasuries of each regiment; and what horses they are able to provide themselves with. In the second report you will inform me of the state of the clothing of all the regiments of the main army, and at what time they will be in receipt of the clothing for Year XIV. The Minister of War will have sent you the organization of the main army into seven corps. Do not forget the ambulances, and occupy yourself without delay with the details of the organization of this immense army. I may tell you, and you alone, that I expect to cross the Rhine on the 5th Vendémiaire; prepare everything accordingly. I have to add that this letter is intended for your eyes alone, and must not be read by anybody else. Dissemble; say that I am only putting thirty thousand men on the march, to protect our frontiers on the Rhine. Make the various heads of departments, from whom you will not be able to hide the truth, feel the importance of saying the same thing. And, hereupon, I pray God to have you in His holy keeping.

NAPOLEON

"From my Imperial Camp, at Boulogne,
"The 18th Fructidor, Year XIII."

I transcribe this dispatch as a specimen of thousands of other letters which

Napoleon used to write to his ministers, letters in which, entering into the most minute particulars, he provided for everything. He deemed this necessary for the strict execution of his orders. Often he used to repeat them, to stimulate their zeal.

It has been said that the plan of an invasion of England was only a feint. The reason alleged is that the imminence of a continental war must have made him give up all idea of absenting himself from the Continent with his best army. As a matter of fact, never was there more earnest nor sincerer planning. Napoleon had at first thought of securing the alliance of Prussia, by important concessions, to protect himself against Austria. The conquest of England, with such means as he had prepared, was an expedition which had every chance of success, and which was not to last more than three months. The first victory would have opened the road to London. Communications established in Ireland and Scotland, and a general uprising against the privileged classes of the English lords, would have done the rest. The unfortunate blunder of Admiral Villeneuve, in putting into Cadiz, instead of coming to join the Brest fleet, which was expecting him, and Austria's declaration of war, were the only reasons, first, of the postponement, and then of the abandonment, of this great enterprise.

The necessity of giving up an enterprise which had cost so many efforts, which had given him so much pains, which had involved such enormous expenditure, and which would certainly have succeeded but for the cowardice and incredible irresolution which caused it to fail, filled Napoleon with sorrow and indignation. Bracing himself, however, to bear up against such a crushing blow, he armed himself with all his resignation under an evil for which there was no remedy. He cast over in his mind the best use that could be made of the flotilla, which could not be maintained in its actual state, but which would always be, in his hands, a powerful weapon for threatening England.

The Emperor's first idea was to form a camp of from sixty to eighty thousand men, and, later on, of one hundred thousand men, on the heights of Boulogne; to reduce the armament of the flotilla to five hundred boats, capable of transporting fifty thousand men and several thousand horses; to embark artillery and material; to form a line of broadsides with these boats, brought up in turn for the purpose of exercise; and to constantly menace the British territory with an imminent descent, which could be carried out immediately after the arrival of the fleet expected at Boulogne.

The advantage of this plan was that it provided for a large camp, placed in a healthy position, and easy to victual, which could be transported to Germany without difficulty, and which compelled England to keep troops on her coasts for her protection, as well as to reserve vessels in the Downs, or on the Thames.

Events and coalitions prevented the execution of this project. In 1811 the Emperor, before starting on his journey to Holland, thought to carry it out. He ordered information on the state of the flotilla at that time to be supplied to him. He desired to spend two millions of francs on the necessary repairs, and to put in order a part of the gun-boats, sloops, and barges, which could be made use of, breaking up such boats as were useless, to use the material for building fresh boats—his object being to form a war flotilla able to embark forty thousand men and two thousand horses. The Emperor had even informed the Minister of Marine of his intention of going to Boulogne to have sail put to the flotilla in his presence, and thus to stimulate the zeal of the crews.

This Boulogne expedition was combined with other armaments which he was preparing at Cherbourg and Antwerp. He considered these the three best points from which to menace the coasts of England and Ireland, and which, according to his plans, were to operate at the same time. The total force of these expeditions would have provided for the transport of one hundred thousand men, and of from six to seven thousand horses.

The English government, alarmed at the dangers with which the active and resourceful genius of their powerful adversary threatened them, strained every nerve to avert these armaments, by provoking troubles to occupy Napoleon elsewhere. The war with Russia, and the disasters which ensued, caused these enterprises once more to be neglected—enterprises which sooner or later would certainly have eventually succeeded.

The hatred which animated England against France, her perseverance in raising up enemies and difficulties against her everywhere; that policy of hers, which, as the great Frederick used to say, consists in knocking at every door with a purse in one hand, left the Emperor without a moment's peace. But his activity grew in proportion to the obstacles put in his way, and he sorely taxed my strength, which was by no means equal to my zeal. To give an idea of how the gravity of the situation had developed his faculties, and of the increase in work which had resulted therefrom, and that one may judge how his prodigious activity was equal to everything, it is necessary to acquaint the reader with the new order which Napoleon had established in the dispatch of his numerous affairs. The Emperor used to have me waked in the night, when—owing either to some plan which he considered ripe for execution, and which had to be carried out, or to the necessity of maturing the preliminaries of some new project, or to having to send off some courier without loss of time—he was obliged to rise himself. It sometimes happened that I would hand him some document to sign in the evening. "I will not sign it now," he would say. "Be here tonight, at one o'clock, or at four in the morning; we will work together." On these occasions I used to have myself waked some minutes before the appointed hour. As, in coming downstairs, I used to pass in front of the door of his small apartment, I used to enter to ask if he had been waked. The invariable answer was: "He just rung for," and at the same moment, he used to make his appearance, dressed in his white dressing-gown, with a Madras handkerchief round his head. When, by chance, he had got to the study before me, I used to find him walking up and down with his hands behind his back, or helping himself from his snuffbox, less from taste than from preoccupation, for he only used to smell at his pinches, and his handkerchiefs were never soiled with the snuff. His ideas developed as he dictated, with an abundance and a clearness which showed that his attention was firmly riveted to the subject with which he was dealing; they sprang from his head even as Minerva sprang, fully armed, from the head of Jupiter. When the work was finished, and sometimes in the midst of it, he would send for sherbet and ices. He used to ask me which I preferred, and went so far in his solicitude as to advise me which would be better for my health. Thereupon he would return to bed, if only to sleep an hour, and could resume his slumber, as though it had not been interrupted. The solid *en cas* of food, which used to be brought in at night at the Court, before the Revolution, were not supplied at Napoleon's Court, for the Emperor had not inherited the enormous appetites of the princes of the ancient dynasty. But one of the imperial cooks used to sleep near the larder to serve such refreshments as might be asked for in the night, and which were prepared in advance.

When the Emperor rose in the night, without any special object except to occupy his sleepless moments, he used to forbid my being waked before seven in the morning. On those occasions I used to find my writing-table, in the morning, covered with reports and papers annotated in his writing. On his return from his levee, which was held at nine o'clock, he used to find, on his return to his cabinet, the answers and decisions which he had indicated drawn up and ready to be sent off.

There were on his writing-table reports of the exact state of the land and sea forces. These reports, which were supplied by the ministers of war and of marine, were bound in red morocco. They were drawn up on lines which he had laid down, and were renewed on the first of each month. They were divided into columns indicating the number of the infantry and cavalry regiments, the names of the colonels, the number of men composing each battalion, squadron, and company, the departments where they were recruited, and the number of men drafted from the conscriptions, the places where the regiments were garrisoned, the position and the strength of the depots, and the state of their troops and material. If marching regiments had been formed particulars as to their composition, destination, and the dates of their departure and arrival were mentioned in these reports. The marching regiments were composed of conscripts, who were drafted from the depots to the battalions, or squadrons proceeding to the field of battle, when their numbers sufficed to make up a company, a battalion, or a squadron. On arriving at the frontier these various detachments were united into brigades or divisions, commanded by generals, and provided with officers on the way, to take the place of other officers. On their arrival at their destination, these temporary corps were broken up. The officers and the soldiers were distributed amongst the regiments, according to the number that each bore. The corps of engineers, and of artillerymen, and the batteries of artillery, were also described in these reports, which were kept with all the more care that the Emperor had frequent opportunities of testing their correctness. If, during his campaigns, he fell in with isolated soldiers, or small bodies of men, he could tell them at once, from a glance at their regimental number, where to go to, and what stages to pass under way.

The columns of the report referring to the state of the navy contained the names of warships of every class, the names of the officers commanding them, the composition and strength of the crews, the names of the departments where sailors and marines were levied, the names of ships which were in docks, and particulars as to what progress had been made in their construction. These latter particulars were ciphered in twenty-fourths.

The Emperor always had a strange pleasure in receiving these reports. He used to read them through with delight, and would say that no work of science or literature ever gave him so much pleasure. His marvelous memory grasped all their details, and retained them so well that, better than the ministers of war and marine, he knew what was the composition and the materials of each corps. The spelling and pronunciation of names were less familiar to him, and he never remembered them rightly. But if he forgot proper names, it needed but the mention of them to bring a man or a place most vividly before his eyes. When he had once seen a man, or visited a place, he forgot neither the one nor the other; and anything connected either with the individual or the locality was never effaced from his memory. He knew Gassendi's *Aid to Memory* by heart, and was perfectly acquainted with the use and application of the innumerable details of artillery weapons.

When some lengthy answer was rendered necessary by the reading of a report or dispatch; when some spontaneous idea was suggested to him by his observations or comparisons; or when this idea, having sprung up in his mind, elaborated by his meditations, had reached its maturity, and the moment to set it in motion had arrived,

Napoleon could not keep still. He could not, like the pythoness, remain attached to his tripod. He collected his thoughts, and concentrated his attention on the subject which was occupying him, taking a strong hold on his mind. He would rise slowly, and begin to walk slowly up and down the whole length of the room in which he found himself. This walk lasted through the whole of his dictation. His tone of voice was grave and accentuated, but was not broken in upon by any time of rest. As he entered upon his subject, the inspiration betrayed itself. It showed itself by a more animated tone of voice, and by a kind of nervous trick which he had of twisting his right arm while pulling at the trimmings of his sleeve with his hand. At such times, he did not speak any faster than before, and his walk remained slow and measured.

He had no difficulty in finding words to express his thoughts. Sometimes incorrect, these very errors added to the energy of his language, and always wonderfully expressed what he wished to say. These mistakes were not, moreover, inherent to his composition, but were created rather by the heat of his improvisation. Nor were they frequent, and were only left uncorrected when, the dispatch having to be sent off at once, time was short. In his speeches to the senate and to the Legislative corps; in his proclamations; in his letters to sovereigns; and in the diplomatic notes which he made his ministers write, his style was polished, and suited to its subject.

Napoleon rarely wrote himself. Writing tired him; his hand could not follow the rapidity of his conceptions, he only took up the pen when by chance he happened to be alone and had to put the first rush of an idea on to paper; but after writing some lines he used to stop and throw away his pen. He would then go out to call his secretary, or, in his absence, either the second secretary or the secretary of state or General Duroc, or sometimes the aide-de-camp on duty, according to the kind of work in which he was engaged. He made use of the first who answered his call, without irritation, but rather with a visible satisfaction as being relieved from his trouble.

His writing was a collection of letters unconnected with each other, and unreadable. Half the letters to each word were wanting, he could not read his own writing again, or would not take the trouble to do so. If he was asked for some explanation he would take his draft and tear it up, or throw it into the fire, and dictate it over again—the same ideas, it is true, but couched in different language and a different style.

Although he could detect faults in the spelling of others his own orthography left much to be desired. It was negligence which had become a habit, he did not want to break or tangle the thread of his thoughts by paying attention to the details of spelling. Napoleon also used to make mistakes in figures, absolute and positive as arithmetic has to be. He could have worked out the most complicated mathematical problems and yet he could rarely total up a sum correctly. It is fair to add that these errors were not always made without intention. For example, in calculating the number of men who were to make up his battalions, regiments, or divisions, he always used to increase the sum total. One can hardly believe that in doing so he wanted to deceive himself, but he often thought it useful to exaggerate the strength of his armies. It was no use pointing out any mistake of this kind; he refused to admit it, and obstinately maintained his voluntary arithmetical error. His writing was illegible, and he hated difficult writing. The notes or the few lines that he used to write, and which did not demand any fixed attention, were as a rule free from mistakes of orthography, excepting certain words, over which he invariably blundered. He used to write, for instance, the words "cabinet," "Caffarelli," *"gabinet," "Gaffarelli;"* "afin que," *"enfin que,"* "infanterie," *"enfanterie."* The first two words are evidently reminiscences of his maternal language, the only ones which remained over from his earliest youth. The others, *"enfin que"* and *"enfanterie"* have no analogy with the Italian language. He had a poor knowledge of this language, and avoided speaking it. He could only be brought to speak it with Italians who did not know French, or who had difficulty in expressing themselves in our language. I have sometimes heard him conversing with Italians, and what he said was expressed in Italianized French, with words terminating in *i, o,* and *a.*

It is said that Voltaire used to have a number of desks in his room, on one of which was a poem which he had begun, on another a tragedy, on others, a piece of historical writing, and a pamphlet. The author used to pass from one kind of composition to another according as the spirit moved him. Napoleon would deal with in turn, at one sitting, matters relating to war, to diplomacy, to finance, to commerce, to public works, and so on; and rested from one kind of work by engaging in another. Every branch of the government was with him the object of a special, complete and sustained attention; no confusion of ideas, no fatigue, and no desire to shorten the hours of labor, ever making themselves felt.

Napoleon used to explain the clearness of his mind, and his faculty of being able at will to prolong his work to extreme limits, by saying that the various subjects were arranged in his head, as though in a cupboard. "When I want to interrupt one piece of work," he used to say, "I close the drawer in which it is, and I open another. The two pieces of business never get mixed up together, and never trouble or tire me. When I want to go to sleep, I close up all the drawers, and then I am ready to go off to sleep."

The initiative in the drafting of all laws and regulations almost always came from Napoleon. His ideas of amelioration, improvement, and construction kept his ministers sufficiently occupied to need all their time in prescribing and supervising the numerous details of execution. If any regret can be expressed on this subject, it is that the unceasing activity of the highest intellect, which has ever been granted to a human being, should have accustomed his agents to await his inspiration and to distrust themselves; and that in consequence, so many men of talent should have found themselves paralyzed and taken by surprise in moments of danger.

Napoleon knew that I did not possess, as he did, the precious gift of being able to go to sleep at will, and that I could not sleep in the daytime. After a piece of work which had occupied a part of the night he would tell me to go and take a bath, and often gave orders himself that it should be got ready for me.

He used sometimes to spend whole days without doing any work, yet without leaving the palace, or even his work-room. In these days of leisure, which was but apparent, for it usually concealed an increase of cerebral activity, Napoleon appeared embarrassed how to spend his time. He would go and spend an hour with the Empress, then he would return and, sitting down on a settee, would sleep, or appear to sleep for a few minutes. He would then come and seat himself on the corner of my writing-table, or on one of the arms of my chair, or sometimes even on my knees. He would then put his arm round my neck, and amuse himself by gently pulling my ear, or by patting me on the shoulder, or on the cheek. He would speak to me of all sorts of disconnected subjects, of himself, of his manias, of his constitution, of me, or of some plan that he had in his head. He was fond of teasing, never bitterly or nastily, but on the contrary with a certain amount of kindness, and accompanied with loud laughter. He would glance through the titles of his books, saying a word of praise or of blame on the authors, and would linger with preference over the tragedies of Corneille, *Zaïre* or Voltaire's *The Death of Caesar*, or *Brutus*. He would read tirades from these tragedies, aloud, then would shut up the book and walk up and down reciting verses from *The Death of Caesar*. The passages which he recited with the greatest pleasure, were the following:

> J'ai servi, commandé, vaincu quarante années;
> Du monde, entre mes mains, j'ai vu les destinées;
> Et j'ai toujours connu qu'en chaque événement,
> Le destin des États dependait d'un moment!*

Or again:

> *Caesar:* Qu'oses-tu demander, Cimber?
> *Cimber:* La liberté!
> *Cassius:* Tu nous l'avais promise, et tu juras toi-même
> D'abolir pour jamais l'autorité suprême . . . .†

When he was tired of reading or reciting he would begin to sing in a strong, but false voice. When he had nothing to trouble him, or he was pleased with what he was thinking about, it was shown in the choice of his songs. These would be airs from *Le Devin du Village,* or other old operas. One of his favorite songs was about a girl who was cured by her lover of a sting from a winged insect. It was a kind of anacreontic ode, and consisted of one verse only. It ended with this line:

"A kiss from his lips was the doctor in this case."

When he was in a more serious frame of mind, he used to sing verses from the Revolutionary hymns and chants, such as the *Chant du Départ—Veillons au salut de L'Empire,* or he would hum these two lines:

> The man who wishes to bring the world under his sway
> Must begin with his own country.

Was this a piece of self-advice? I believe that he understood his country's happiness otherwise. All the powers of his ambition were strained to render the French nation great and prosperous. He never spoke of France but in terms of affection. France had no rival in his heart, nor in his mind; her greatness was the object of all his thoughts, the opinion that she had of him was his constant preoccupation, although outwardly he seemed to be indifferent to popularity.

I must also speak of that tendency to superstition which has been attributed to Napoleon; for it is a generally accepted idea that he was under the spell of superstitious

---

* I served and gave orders and won for forty years;
In my hands I held the fate of the world;
And I always knew that in each event,
The fate of nations was the matter of an instant!

† *Caesar:* What do you dare ask, Cimber?
Cimber: Freedom!
Cassius: You promised it to us and swore yourself
That supreme authority would forever be abolished....

beliefs. It has even been said that he once consulted the famous Madame Lenormand. Endowed with a vast genius and a vivid imagination, Napoleon may have, at times, taken pleasure in straying into the regions of the world of speculation as a diversion from the realities of life. But so lofty an intellect, so positive a mind, could not admit the prescience of the future, the inversion of the laws of nature, nor let himself be carried away by a sterile love of the marvelous. Like all superior geniuses he had faith in his destiny. His successes, from the very outset of his career, followed by still greater and even unexpected successes, had inspired him with the idea that he was no ordinary man, and that he was called to play a part on the world's stage. "Neither Vendémiaire nor Montenotte," he used to say, "led me to believe that I was a superior man. It was not until after Lodi that I began to think that I might become a decisive actor on our political stage. Then awoke in me the first spark of a high ambition." His march upwards afterwards confirmed him in this thought. This conviction was a surer oracle to him than the vain predictions of a witch. He drew his confidence from loftier sources. His maxim was: "The future is in the hand of God." He used to say that after he had made the best arrangements, on a day of battle, there came a moment when success no longer depended on him, and that he had to look for it from above.

He could count on his good fortune in the execution of his most daring enterprises. This confidence, inspired by the constancy of his success, was warranted. But he was always prepared in advance for every reverse which he might meet. Luck had no place in the conception of any of his plans. Before finally deciding upon them he would subject them to the minutest scrutiny; every hazard, even the most improbable, being discussed and provided for. I saw Napoleon enjoying prosperity with the keenest pleasure, but I never once saw him betray any surprise. His measures were so well taken, and adverse chances so minimized by his calculations and arrangements that if anything could have surprised him it would have been the failure of plans which he had prepared with so much skill and so much care.

It is difficult to believe that even at a time when no revelation of his future destiny had been made to Bonaparte (still in obscurity) his strong and luminous mind can ever have yielded to the temptation to address himself to the puerile practices of necromancy. It is possible that in the extreme fervor of his love for Josephine, he may have allowed himself to be drawn into being present at a consultation with a witch, and that he made this sacrifice to the waywardness of the impressionable woman whom he so tenderly loved. However it may be, he did not approve of this weakness of Josephine, and often turned it into ridicule. I was present when he forbade her to go and see Madame Lenormand. He even had this famous juggler arrested. Josephine used to shroud her relations with this woman in the profoundest mystery, and never did the keeper of her privy purse know what sums the Empress had paid for the witch's predictions.

It is a generally accepted belief that great men have been, or must be, superstitious. The vulgar mob, which in that respect is really possessed by the superstitious feeling which it attributes to others, fancies that it is impossible to accomplish great things without supernatural means unknown to the rest of humanity. Others, in short, can only forgive such men their superiority by connecting them in some way with human weaknesses. But, what is the superstition which is attributed to great men? Is it a belief in occult and undefined powers? Is it, on the contrary, the faith which they have in themselves, or in an intuitive perception of their own value? It is clear that it is in the former of these definitions that superstition lies. This aberration of the human mind cannot be applied to that inner feeling, which led Napoleon, for example, to consider himself a divine instrument charged with a mission on earth, and fated to march onward without fear, and with the certainty of success, under its powerful protection. When Napoleon used to say that the cannon ball that was to kill him had not yet been cast, he did not yield to a feeling of fatalism; he considered that his providential mission had not yet been fulfilled. When he wrote to the Directoire that having seen at the moment of landing in Egypt a sail which he believed to belong to one of the enemy's ships, he had implored Fortune not to desert him, but to grant him five days more, he mentally translated the word "Fortune" by "The Almighty God."

His exceptional situation, the consciousness of the mission which he had to fulfill, suggested to him the best means to secure its success. Thus, when in Egypt he instructed his soldiers to show respect for the religion of Mahomet, for the ministers of this religion, and for its devotees; when he himself attended the religious ceremonies of the Mahomedans, his faith had not changed in the slightest degree. He was acting in the interests of a clever and well-matured policy. His condescension towards the outward signs of Mahomedanism was limited to what was necessary to the success of his plans. His alleged meeting with adepts in the Pyramids, the oath which they exacted from him, and the instructions which they gave him, are so many clumsy inventions, and are not worthy of refutation.

In all the circumstances of his life Napoleon showed that, far from being superstitious, he was penetrated with a profound and mysterious sentiment of the divine omnipotence. His habit of involuntarily signing himself with the cross, on hearing of some great danger; or on the discovery of some important fact, where the interests of France or the success of his plans were concerned, at the news of some great and unexpected good fortune, or of some great disaster, was not only a reminiscence of his early religious education, but also another manifestation of the feeling which led him to attribute these favors or these warnings to the Author of all things. His expectation of help from above at a decisive moment in his battles, his frequent allusions in his conversations, proclamations, and reports to the "only Arbitrator Who holds in His hands all plans and all events"; the religious ideas which the sight of a church, or the sound of church bells awoke in his mind; the reestablishment of the Catholic religion in France; his taking refuge in the consolations of religion during his last moments at St. Helena; do not all these things testify to his faith in Providence?

The storm which had been gathering in the North of Europe, burst forth two months after Napoleon's return from Italy. The Emperor had been watching, for six months previously, the conduct of the Austrian government, which was trying to deceive him with pretended assurances of friendship, and by the offer of an illusory mediation between France and England, and which replied to all questions as to their armaments either with specious explanations or with formal denials. The friendly demonstrations of this power helped to mask her hostile intentions, and to gain time; she took advantage of this to enter into secret negotiations with Russia and England. The Emperor of Russia had sent one of his chamberlains, Count Novosiltzev, to Berlin, and the Prussian cabinet had asked for his passports in Paris, announcing that this extraordinary envoy was charged with a mission the object of which had not been officially notified. Napoleon, in spite of this reticence, anxious to neglect no means of conciliation, ordered the passports which had been asked for to be sent on at once. The object of this mission, which could not be carried out, was a new proposal of intervention, in conjunction with Austria, between France and England, of which the Russian sovereign took the initiative, and of which he was prepared to assume the responsibility. A mediation of this kind, this understanding between our enemies, the fatal result of which would have been to dictate the law to France, could not be accepted by us. This coalition of three great powers, one of which was making extraordinary preparations for a new war with the French Empire, while the others had never ceased to insult our government, was very naturally an object of suspicion in France. Napoleon was waiting to be informed of what was the proposed basis of the negotiation, when the news of the crossing of the Inn by a part of the Austrian army was suddenly received in Paris.

The mission of the Russian chamberlain Novosiltzev to Paris was drawing to a close at about the same time, in consequence of the union of the Republic of Genoa with the French Empire. It is well known that peace was not the real object of this mission. The Emperor Alexander, who had just formed the new coalition with Mr. Pitt, had not the least desire to prevent a war in which, with chivalrous ardor, he was only too willing to engage, with the prospect before him of the satisfaction of limiting the power of France. The mission given to his envoy had no other object than to assist the dilatory policy of the Austrian government, and to help Austria to gain the time which she deemed necessary for the completion of her preparations. When Austria had thought herself ready, and believed that the right time had come, she had thrown off the mask. In the expectation of taking the Emperor by surprise in the midst of his preparations for his expedition against England, she had marched her troops suddenly into the Bavarian territory. On September 23, 1805, the *Moniteur* announced that on the 21st of the same month "the Emperor of Germany, without preliminary negotiations or explanations, and without any declaration of war, had invaded Bavaria."

At the end of the month's journey, which Napoleon had just made on the coast, he had been obliged to renounce, in the presence of the events which we have related, both the plan of an invasion of England and that of breaking up the camp at Boulogne, casting a glance of regret on the prey which had been torn from his grasp. He marched the army which had been collected on the seacoast to the Rhine, and an official order announced the new destination of the army which from that moment was called "The Great Army." The Emperor's plan was to march his various corps at full speed into the center of Germany so as to prevent the junction of the Russians and Austrians, and in the hope of giving battle to the allies separately. The expedition to Ireland became out of the question, and Marshal Augereau, who was commanding the corps destined for this expedition, received orders to proceed to the Rhine. This corps, which was only to arrive a fortnight after the others, formed the rear-guard. The Emperor wrote to M. Otto, his representative in Bavaria, that the Bavarian troops would have to join the troops commanded by Bernadotte, and to follow his movements. These troops, together with those of Würtemberg, Baden, and several other German principalities who declared in favor of France, added about forty thousand men to the French effective forces. Augereau's army covered the distance which separated it from the scene of war with a rapidity and a precision worthy of the Roman armies.

On the 23rd of September the Emperor proceeded to the Military School, where the Prefect of Paris, with the municipal corporations, handed the keys of the city over to him, which he returned, as though to entrust them to their keeping. He then went to the senate, there to denounce the triple coalition of Austria, Russia, and England, and announced his departure for the army. As a matter of prudence he had reorganized the national guard, which he charged with the maintenance of order in the interior, and with the defense of our frontiers and coasts, under the command of four senators, former generals. He had moreover summoned to active service a certain class of retired soldiers, who were still fit to carry arms, granting them various advantages.

Prince Joseph was to preside over the senate, and the other councils of the government, during the absence of Napoleon.

On September 24 the Emperor left Paris, accompanied by the Empress Josephine, whom he left behind at Strasburg, with her court and M. de Talleyrand. He arrived at Ettlingen, a castle belonging to the Elector of Baden, on October 1. The old Elector, accompanied by his sons and grandsons, had gone there to receive the Emperor, and to seal their alliance with him.

Napoleon was at Louisburg next day. The Elector of Würtemberg, who was awaiting him there, gave him a brilliant reception. This prince, surrounded by the whole of his court, had at his side his second son, and the Electress, the eldest daughter of George III. He offered his own apartment to the Emperor, and though he was not generally considered a very affectionate father, everything in this home wore a most patriarchal aspect, the stuffs which covered the furniture being in part the work of his children. The Emperor's arrival had put a stop to the Elector's hesitations. He signed a treaty with the French sovereign by which Würtemberg undertook to supply the French army with a corps of troops, with horses, wagons, and artillery. Napoleon spent a week at Louisburg, the object of constant attention and respect. He even accepted an invitation to dine in public with the whole electoral family, to please the Elector. The second son of this prince, Prince Paul, showed himself most attentive to the Emperor, being always at his side, and accompanying him on horseback on all his excursions. Prince Paul had recently married a princess of Saxe-Hildburghausen. This same prince, whose sentiments afterwards changed greatly, for what reason I do not know, at the time of the war with Prussia, in 1806, suddenly left Stuttgart without his father's knowledge, and went to offer his services to the King of Prussia, who gave him a command in his army. He was amongst the number of Prussian officers who were made prisoners at the battle of Jena. The Emperor took no revenge on him for his disloyalty, beyond refusing to see him, and sent him back, out of regard to the King, his father, who had him imprisoned in a fortress. The Elector of Bavaria, who had in vain asked Austria to be allowed to remain neutral, had fled from his capital on the approach of the Austrian army, and took refuge at Würtzburg. Napoleon only saw him at Linz, where the prince came to see him. The Elector returned to Munich, after Bernadotte's army had driven the Austrians out, which took place about a fortnight after the opening of the campaign. The Emperor received the Austrian general Giulay at Linz. He was one of the Austrian generals who had been made prisoner at Ulm, but whom Napoleon had restored to liberty. He came with a request for a suspension of hostilities with a view to opening negotiations for peace. Napoleon asked him if he was vested with sufficient powers to treat for peace then and there. The Austrian general answered that his master could agree to nothing without having first consulted his ally the Emperor of Russia. Such a step could have no other object than to delay the onward march of the French army.

Napoleon, in his answer to a letter from the Emperor of Austria—brought by M. de Giulay—said that he was wrong to refer to the Emperor of Russia, who had not the same interest as they had in the war; that this war was only a caprice on the part of the Russian sovereign, while for France and Austria it was a struggle which absorbed all their means and all their faculties; that he, Napoleon, was disposed to settle the dispute with the greatest promptitude, but that he could not hide from the Emperor Francis the fear which had risen from the delays and the intrigues the bitterness of which, considering the past, was still fresh in his memory.

After some hesitation, before the crossing of the Inn by the Austrians, the Elector of Bavaria had accepted the French alliance, and had added his troops to our army. There remained Prussia which, owing to the personal feeling of the King, was observing neutrality. The passing of Bernadotte's corps through the principality of Anspach gave the war-party in Berlin the desired pretext for persuading the King to assume a menacing attitude. In consequence of this Minister Hardenberg listened with a very bad grace to the explanations which were given him about the march of this corps of the French army. The sudden appearance of the Emperor Alexander in Berlin finally triumphed over the irresolution of the King, and a treaty of alliance was signed between the two monarchs at Potsdam, on November 3. It was sealed by oaths taken on the tomb of the great Frederick, a scene which had been prepared by the Queen. The king, however, caused certain reservations which he considered prudent—on account of the success of the French army, and notably by the capitulation of Ulm, a triumph which till then had been unparalleled in the history of our armies—to be inserted in this treaty.

I will mention the fight at Güntzburg, where the Emperor lost a very distinguished officer, who had been his aide-de-camp. This officer, nephew of General Lacuée, had incurred Napoleon's displeasure by his caustic tongue, and by the utterance of certain sarcasms against influential persons who had disposed the Emperor against him. Colonel Lacuée was killed during the attack on the bridge at Güntzburg, fighting bravely at the head of the 59th infantry regiment. Napoleon mourned the loss of this officer and ordered all the troops assembled at Güntzburg to be present at his funeral. The Emperor removed his headquarters to Augsburg, the center of his operations, and stopped three days in this city, to await the effect of the movement of the different corps, and to occupy himself with important details in the administration of the army. He had the town protected against any attempt at a surprise, and established a general depot of arms, magazines, and ambulances. He ordered all the Austrian artillery which had been captured at Ulm to be transported there.

The Emperor stayed in the palace of the former Elector of Treves, who did the honors of his episcopal palace, with the princess Cunégonde, his sister. He was a prince of the House of Saxony, who, after the loss of his electorate, which had been suppressed by the Treaty of Lunéville, had retired to the bishopric of Augsburg, amalgamating the title of this see with that of Elector of Treves. The income from this see and various pensions, including one of a hundred thousand florins, enabled him to live at Augsburg in a very honorable manner. He was anxious to show, by the cordial hospitality with which he received the Emperor, how grateful he was to him for the comforts which he enjoyed in his old age—comforts which he owed to the influence which Napoleon had formerly exercised on the secularizations.

The battles which preceded and followed upon the taking of Ulm brought after them results of the highest importance. On October 11 General Dupont, having arrived at the village of Haslach with two regiments of infantry and a brigade of cavalry, attacked one of the corps which were leaving Ulm, and which General Mack was endeavoring to rescue from this place to march them on to the Tyrol and Bohemia. General Dupont sustained, during the whole day of the 11th, an unequal fight of seven thousand men against twenty-five thousand, dispersed the enemy, captured two thousand prisoners, and by audacious tactics prevented the march of the enemy to Bohemia. Who could then have thought that the career of this general, called to so high a military destiny, would have ended three years later in so deplorable a manner? The other columns which had escaped from Ulm met with a similar fate at Albeck, Neusheim, Nordlingen, and before Ulm itself. The investment of this place began by the seizure of the bridge, and of the abbey of Elchingen. All these feats of arms were carried out in the worst weather imaginable. The soldiers, up to their knees in mud, a prey to privations of all kinds, were reanimated by the sight of the Emperor, himself drenched, harassed and covered with mud. I can remember my stupefaction on looking at the sinuous ramparts of the village of Elchingen, rising in an amphitheatre above the Danube, surrounded by walled gardens and houses rising one above the other. These gardens and houses—filled with troops, and from which constant firing proceeded—were topped by the vast buildings of the fortified abbey which was vigorously defended by formidable artillery. Marshal Ney won his title of Duke of Elchingen there, and fully deserved it.

We spent five days at the abbey of Elchingen in almost absolute starvation. The Emperor used to leave it every morning to go to the camp before Ulm, where he used to spend the day, and sometimes the night. The French army had become master of the heights which commanded Ulm. The Emperor had some shells fired into the town, and sent a summons to General Mack, commander-in-chief of the Austrian army, who had allowed himself to be shut up in the town with the larger part of his army. This unhappy general found himself reduced to the last extremities. He at first affected great courage and declared that he would eat his last horse before he would surrender. He had so entirely lost his head that he did not notice that in saying this he was confessing that the town was without provisions. He parleyed for several days unsuccessfully, thinking to save his honor and military reputation by proposals which could not stand a moment's examination. He was at last forced to sign a capitulation by the terms of which he agreed to surrender, unless relieved within six days. The Emperor being certain that Munich was in the hands of his troops, that the columns which had come out of Ulm were being pursued and beaten in every direction, that the Russians had not crossed the Inn, and that Mack had no chance of being rescued, consented to give him this satisfaction. Mack, however, shortened the term which he himself had asked for. On the 20th of October, from noon till six in the evening, the Austrian army shut up in Ulm, numbering thirty-three thousand men, and under the commander-in-chief, eight field-marshals, and seven lieutenant-generals, marched past the Emperor. Arms were laid down, and the army was transported to France. The officers were allowed to remain in Austria on parole not to serve against France until they had been exchanged. The first column of prisoners left the next day for France. The Emperor treated the general officers well, and deported himself towards the commander-in-chief with the respect Duke to misfortune. He severely repressed certain humiliating remarks of which the vanquished had been the subject.

On the 21st a proclamation to the soldiers of the Great Army, congratulating them, and announcing the immense successes of this fortnight's campaign was followed by a decree which ordered that the month which had just elapsed—from September 22 to October 24—would count as a campaign for the whole of the army.

On the morrow of the day on which this glorious feat of arms was accomplished at Ulm, our navy met with a great disaster. While our Great Army, led by the Emperor, routing his enemies on the continent, was forcing its triumphal way on to Vienna, the splendid combined fleet, which, in protecting the passage of the flotilla across the Channel at Boulogne, was to realize such lofty hopes, met its doom at Trafalgar. It needed the glorious victory of Ulm, and the prospect of the successful issue of the further operations which Napoleon had prepared, to console him for a catastrophe which postponed, indefinitely, all hope of ruining the English fleet. The Emperor felt that the only resource left to him was the execution of a vast continental blockade, and the extraordinary measures which would complete its effectiveness.

The unhappy Villeneuve, the responsible author of the ruin of the expedition, and author of the disaster of Trafalgar, having fallen into the hands of the English, and having been released by them, put an end to his life in a moment of despair.

Of all the battles which preceded the entry of the French into Vienna, the one which took place at Dirnstein was the most remarkable, because of the critical situation in which Marshal Mortier found himself, and from which he was fortunate enough to escape. The Marshal, who was skirting the left bank of the Danube, engaged in the pursuit of the enemy in the narrow defile which, at this place, is formed by the river and the mountains had only half his *corps d'armée* with him, the rest of his troops being disposed in echelons at one or two marches distance. Mortier easily drove the enemy before him, but these were soon reinforced by superior troops. In the meanwhile a Russian division had come down from the mountains behind him, and had placed itself between his feeble corps and the Dupont division, which was following him. Mortier, thus shut in between two hostile forces, had no other alternative than to cut his way through them or to perish. In this extremity he turned against the weaker enemy, and charged the Russian division, which was pressing on in his rear, and was followed by the enemy which he had previously attacked from the front. But at this moment the scene changed. The Dupont division which at the sound of the cannon had hurried up, came behind the Russian division, which was now caught between two fires from the French troops. This hostile division had only just time to make good its escape by the ravine which they had followed in coming down the mountain—a retreat which would have been closed to them if the Dupont division had been able to reach this ravine before they did. Marshal Mortier, having rallied this division, was now in a position to drive back the other Russian corps which he previously had to resist in front. This corps of the French army owed its safety to the Marshal's coolness and to the promptness of Dupont, and the intrepidity of the officers and men. The Emperor had halted at St. Polten, a village situated almost opposite Dirnstein, alarmed by the loud cannonade which echoed through the rocks. He did not leave St. Polten until he had received reassuring news of Marshal Mortier and of the corps under his command.

The castle of Dirnstein, which overlooked this scene, and which recalls the memory of the captivity of Richard Coeur de Lion, added to the moral effect produced by the combat which had just ended in so happy a way. The sight of these old towers inspired

Napoleon with reflections which are thus reported by General Pelet in his *History of the Campaign of 1809*:

"The Emperor was riding between Berthier and Lannes, when a guide pointed out to him, between Moelk and St. Polten, the towers of the castle of Dirnstein, which could be seen far off. The Emperor halted and spent some time in looking at these ruins. Continuing his ride he said to Berthier and Lannes: 'He also had been to fight in Palestine. He had been more fortunate than we were at Acre, but not braver than you, my good Lannes. He had defeated the great Saladin. And in spite of that hardly had he returned to the shores of Europe than he fell into the hands of people who were certainly not his equals. He was sold by an Austrian Duke to an Emperor of Germany, who shut him up, and who is only remembered by this act of felony . . . The last of all his court, Blondel alone, remained faithful to him, but his people made great sacrifices for his deliverance...' Napoleon seemed unable to turn his eyes away from these towers. He added: "Such, indeed, were those barbaric times which people are foolish enough to depict as so grand, when the father sacrificed his children, the wife her husband, the subject his sovereign, the soldier his general; when everything was done without shame, and even without disguise, for the lust for gold or power. . . How times are changed since then! What progress our civilization has made! You have seen emperors and kings in my power, besides their capitals and their States, and I have exacted from them neither ransom nor any sacrifice of honor. And this successor of Leopold and of Henry, who is already more than half in our power, no more harm will be done to him than last time, in spite of his somewhat treacherous attack...." Abandoning himself gradually to profound reflections the Emperor fell into a sad melancholy, to which we all remained foreign; for who could follow the master of Europe, the giver of crowns, in his mighty thoughts. What things must have risen before his eyes. He alone knew the fury of his enemies, and all that they would dare, if ever they had the power over him which he so often might have used against them. Who could foresee, at that time, that this new Coeur de Lion would have to envy the fate of him of the eleventh century?"

While the Emperor was at St. Polten, he received a second visit from General Giulay, coming on behalf of the Emperor of Austria to renew his proposals of an armistice. This application was as unsuccessful as the first. Its result was rather to accelerate than to retard the onward march of the French army.

The Grand Army entered Vienna the next day, the Austrians having decided not to defend their capital. They had thought of disputing the crossing of the Danube, in spite of the fact that the bridges had not been broken down, and inflammable material had been prepared to blow them up on the approach of the French. The taking of these bridges, and of the big Tabor bridge by surprise, carried out by an audacious ruse by Marshals Ney and Murat, rendered the French masters of these most valuable approaches.

The Emperor went and established himself in the castle of Schönbrunn, where he spent two days, using this short time to advantage in organizing the Vienna police. Napoleon appointed General Clarke governor of the city, and ordered him to maintain the most rigid discipline, and to protect the citizens. At the same time he prescribed military arrangements for protecting his rear. He thereupon left Schönbrunn to pursue the Russian army, which, after having joined in with the remnants of the Austrian army, was retreating upon Moravia.

Before leaving Schönbrunn the Emperor received the news of the submission of the Tyrol, which Marshal Ney had been ordered to occupy. A touching scene took place at Innsbruck, after the Marshal's entry into this town. An officer of the 76th infantry regiment discovered in the arsenal two flags which had fallen into the hands of the enemy during the preceding war, and whose loss had been deplored by the whole regiment. The sight of these glorious insignia, riddled with bullets, and so gloriously recovered, brought tears to the eyes of the old soldiers. It was a real family feast when Marshal Ney handed these flags back to the regiment. The Emperor ordered the memory of this scene to be perpetuated by a picture and a medal.

Crossing through Vienna only, the French army, accordingly, continued its march in pursuit of the Russian army. The rearguard of the army was caught up at Hollabrunn, a village situated halfway between Vienna and Brünn. The meeting gave rise to a sanguinary battle, from which the baggage corps was only able to make good its escape through the darkness of the night, leaving behind them a goodly number of prisoners in our hands and a battlefield covered with their dead. The Russians set fire to all that they passed, and destroyed the most beautiful villages in Moravia. The Emperor, on his way to Hollabrunn, was delayed on his journey by the burning of one of these villages. He spent more than an hour in the midst of the frantic inhabitants, using his escort to help them save their house and to arrest the progress of the flames.

The French army was so fatigued that, in spite of Napoleon's wish not to grant the Russian army a moment's respite, he thought it necessary to give his soldiers a day's rest. His first columns entered into Brünn the next day, where they found abundant provisions of all kinds. During Napoleon's stay at Brünn, before the battle of Austerlitz, he had received M. d'Haugwitz, the Prussian envoy, who had come to his audience-chamber by means of a secret staircase. The persons in attendance were sent out and it was I who was charged to introduce him. This was on the eve of the Emperor's departure, Napoleon wishing to make all speed to join his bivouac between Brünn and Austerlitz, where he spent the week which preceded the great battle. He refused to listen to any communication from the King of Prussia's envoy, postponing all explanations until after the battle which, according to all appearances, was about to be fought. When he returned victorious to Vienna, he gave audience to M. d'Haugwitz, on the very evening of his arrival in Schönbrunn. The minister took good care not to show the Potsdam treaty which he had brought with him. He complimented the Emperor on his victory, and Napoleon replied, "That is a compliment whose destination has been changed by fortune." Indeed, the past ten days had totally changed the situation for everybody, and the Prussian envoy was inspired with very different sentiments from those with which he had come. He decided, and rightly so, that the time for threats had passed by, that he had to get himself out of a scrape, and thought of nothing but how to get Napoleon to forget the hostile attitude which the government of his King had taken up.

The Emperor received M. d'Haugwitz with kindness, the envoy's attitude not being hostile to France; but he was not chary in blaming the Prussian cabinet for the perfidy of its conduct. He dictated the terms of a treaty to M. d'Haugwitz, which the latter accepted, and by which Napoleon offered Prussia, in the form of an alliance which it was his desire to make lasting, a chance of safety of which Prussia was foolish enough not to take advantage.

The Austrian general, Giulay, presented himself for the third time to the Emperor at Brünn, accompanied by M. de Stadion. These two envoys came to renew the offer which the first of them had already made twice—at Linz and at St. Polten—to come to an understanding as to the conditions of peace. Napoleon consented to treat then and there, and to decide upon the preliminaries of peace. But he could not commit the mistake of accepting a simple armistice, without taking advantage of his position. The Austrian envoys did not think fit to accept the conditions which he imposed. The Russians, before the battle of Austerlitz, had asked for nothing less than the return of the French army to the Rhine, and had proposed several other unacceptable conditions, which were in harmony with those which later on they tried to impose on the Emperor at Prague.

The Emperor had sent General Savary from his bivouac to present his compliments to the Emperor Alexander, and at the same time to take notice of what was going on around him. Savary brought back with him Prince Dolgorouki, one of the most influential of the Emperor's young counselors. This officer considered the French army in jeopardy, and did not doubt that Napoleon would be glad to escape an imminent disaster. The retreat which the Emperor had ordered for the purpose of choosing his battlefield and the position of his camp had confirmed Prince Dolgorouki in this opinion. He addressed the Emperor with assurance, and argued on political questions with a presumption which revealed his inexperience in these matters. He undertook to demonstrate to his master's redoubtable adversary, the necessity of abandoning his conquests, and of giving up possession of Italy, and even of Belgium, in the interests of a durable peace. Napoleon listened to this strange talk, and these unseasonable insinuations, which were simple braggadocio, with great patience and coolness. The only answer he gave was by making his final arrangements for the battles which he was going to fight.

In the night which preceded this memorable day, the Emperor visited the bivouacs of his troops on foot. He was soon recognized, in spite of his incognito, and was received with an enthusiasm difficult to describe. By a concerted movement the camp was suddenly illuminated by thousands of straw torches, which each bivouac raised aloft to salute the Emperor, and to celebrate the anniversary of his coronation. Napoleon, deeply touched by this improvised act of homage, expressed his regret, on returning to his bivouac, at having on the morrow to fight a battle which would rob him of a large number of these good fellows, and added that he considered this the best evening of his life. The sun shone the next morning on the battle of Austerlitz. The Emperor, on horseback from the break of day, surrounded by his marshals kept them by his side, until the mist, which in that season betokens a fine morning, had been entirely dispelled. Then, on a signal which he gave, each galloped off to his corps. I saw General Junot, who was rather late, rush up and throw himself into the saddle with an air of resolution which showed that he had no intention of sparing himself. It was not long before the sound of the cannon was heard. The Emperors of Austria and Russia witnessed, from the heights on which they were placed, the complete routing of their armies. This battle—which was one of the greatest that Napoleon ever won, and the issue of which, thanks to his skilful tactics and the madness of the adversaries, was never in doubt for an instant—ended this campaign, which had lasted two months.

Prince John of Lichtenstein presented himself in the morning of the next day at our outposts. He came to ask the Emperor Napoleon to grant an interview to the Emperor of Austria. Napoleon consented, after some hesitation, and could not help saying, after he had taken leave of the prince: "This man makes me commit a great mistake. It is not after battles that conferences can be held. I ought today to be nothing but a soldier. As such I ought to follow up my victory, and not listen to words of peace." The interview was fixed for the morrow at a bivouac near the Sar-Uschitz Mill, about three leagues from Austerlitz.

On December 4 the Emperor Napoleon set out on horseback, at nine o'clock in the morning, accompanied by Marshal Berthier, the chief officers of his military household, and a part of his guard, for the meeting which had been agreed upon. He arrived there before the Emperor of Austria, who drove up shortly after his arrival in an open carriage, accompanied by Prince John of Lichtenstein, several field marshals and generals of his army, and escorted by a squadron of Hungarian cavalry. The Emperor went to meet the Emperor of Austria, and embraced him. They drew up to the fire, while their suites withdrew to fires which had been lighted within view, but sufficiently far off to prevent what the two sovereigns were saying from being heard. The conference lasted about two hours, and the two monarchs agreed upon an armistice and the principal conditions of peace. The Emperor Francis asked that a truce might be granted to the Russian army. Napoleon consented on condition that the Russians should evacuate Germany, and Prussian and Austrian Poland, and return to Russia. In the movement caused by the separation of the two Emperors their officers approached them, and overheard the Austrian monarch saying to Napoleon, apparently in answer to some remark of his: "I promise not to fight you anymore."

The Russian army was surrounded on all sides, and had no chance of escape. The Russian troops were fleeing in such disorder that the Emperor Alexander, separated from his followers, was in danger of falling into the enemy's hands. He sent flag of truce after flag of truce to Marshal Davout, to obtain a suspension of arms; but the Marshal pursued his onward march.

General Meerfeld, whose vanguard had been routed by Marshal Davout's soldiers, sent the Marshal the following note, written in pencil:

"Colonel Count Walmoden will go with a bugler to the French general in command of the third division of the corps d'armée and will inform him that there is an armistice lasting from six o'clock this morning till six o'clock tomorrow morning, H. M. the Emperor of Germany being in conference with the Emperor of the French at Uschitz. By order of H.M. the Emperor of Russia,

"(Signed) MEERFELD, Lieutenant General"

Marshal Davout, having answered M. de Meerfeld that his note did not seem to him a sufficient guarantee, he having very naturally to be on his guard against these little ruses, and quoting to him, amongst examples, that of Steyer, declared that he required a written assurance from the Emperor Alexander. M. de Meerfeld assured the Marshal that he should shortly receive satisfaction in this respect, and that all his doubts would be dispelled. Colonel Walmoden immediately set out to search for the Emperor of Russia, but did not know, in the extreme confusion which reigned in the Russian army, where to look for him. At last, after numerous comings and goings, he saw afar off some mounted guards, whom he recognized by the height and the shape of their helmets. He rode in this direction and found the Emperor Alexander with Prince Czartoryski, his Minister of Foreign Affairs. The Russian sovereign, on hearing what was demanded of him by Marshal Davout, declared that he could not write this note, and ordered Prince Czartoryski to write it in his name. Colonel Walmoden having pointed out to him that Marshal Davout would not stop his movement unless an assurance was given him in the Emperor's own writing, Alexander, in order to avoid being taken prisoner by the French troops, who were approaching, consented to write the letter. It was written in the following words, and in pencil, pen and ink not being procurable:

"General Meerfeld is authorized to tell Marshal Davout from me that a truce of twenty-four hours has been agreed upon for the interview which the two supreme chiefs of their nations will hold together today at Uschitz.

"(Signed) ALEXANDER"

One of the Russian Emperor's aides-de-camp, accompanying Colonel Walmoden, carried this note to Marshal Davout. The Marshal was forced to believe this formal assurance of the suspension of hostilities, and the meeting of the two Emperors. He accordingly halted and took up his position at Josephsdorf, where he happened to be, sending word to the Russian commander-in-chief Kutosov, who had also written to him, that hostilities would be suspended until six o'clock on the following morning, and that in order to avoid all error or surprise notice of the end of the truce would be given one hour previously. The Emperor Alexander, delivered from the extreme perplexity and the great anxieties which had beset him, took refuge at Holitch, on the left bank of the March. The confusion of the various scattered corps of the Russian army was so complete, that the Emperor Alexander remained separated from his servants for nearly a week, and that Prince Czartoryski, his minister, had, so to speak, to act as his valet.

It should be added, in the interests of truth, that the assurances given by the Russian monarch to were not strictly true. An armistice between the Austrian and French armies had certainly been agreed upon by the Emperor Napoleon and the Emperor of Austria, but the truce, as far as the Russian army was concerned, though consented to in principle, had not yet been notified. Another hour's march and Davout would have made the Czar his prisoner. The marshal, to clear himself, sent the note on to the Emperor, who ordered me to preserve it in his portfolio as one of the most important documents of the history of this war.

The Emperor showed himself generous towards the Emperor Alexander. He ordered his aide-de-camp Savary to go and tell him that if he would consent to return with his army, he would suspend the onward march of the French troops and leave the Russians a free retreat. He sent also back, without any ransom, Colonel Repnin, and all the prisoners of the Russian Imperial guard, with a flattering message about their bravery.

The French army in Italy, commanded by Marshal Masséna, had rivaled the *Grande Armée* in ardor and devotion. Opposed to the French army was an Austrian army, of almost equal strength, under the command of Archduke Charles. After a series of bloody fights, and a great battle, in which the Archduke had heavy losses, and on receipt of the news of the capitulation of Ulm, and the march of the French on Vienna, the Austrian commander-in-chief ordered a retreat. Closely pursued by the French army, and driven from all the strongholds in which he halted to protect his retreat, in turn, he arrived at Laybach to hear that his brother, the Archduke John, had had no better fortune than himself, and had evacuated the Tyrol, seeking to make his way to Hungary with the remnants of his troops.

On his return to Schönbrunn, the Emperor granted an audience to the deputation of mayors which had been sent him from Paris, and commissioned them to carry back to Notre Dame the enemy's flags taken at Austerlitz, and which he intended for this cathedral. He had published a series of decrees in which he awarded pensions to the widows and children of soldiers of all ranks, generals, officers, or privates, who had perished at Austerlitz, granting them further the permission to add Napoleon to their names. He further ordered that a triumphal column should be erected on the Place Vendôme, the metal to be taken from the Russian and Austrian cannon captured at Austerlitz.

The peace conference was opened at Brünn, but the negotiators removed shortly afterwards to Presburg, where the treaty of peace was signed on December 26, 1805. This celebrated treaty confirmed all our conquests, and put us in possession of the whole of Italy. Bavaria received the Tyrol. The electorates of Bavaria and Würtemberg, enlarged with territories ceded by Austria, were elevated to the rank of monarchies. The electorate of Baden, which in spite of its increase of territory, was not of sufficient importance to be made a monarchy, was raised to a Grand-duchy. Austria received Salzburg, and Archduke Ferdinand, former Grand-Duke of Tuscany, to whom Salzburg had been attached by the Treaty of Lunéville, was transferred to Würzburg, this principality being raised, in his favor, to a grand-duchy. The war indemnity, which Napoleon had at first fixed at one hundred millions, was reduced, by his consent, to forty millions of francs.

The day on which peace was signed at Presburg, the Emperor met Archduke Charles at the castle of Stammersdorf. This interview was brought about by a mutual feeling of esteem. On taking leave of the Archduke, Napoleon presented him with a sword.

After the great disaster inflicted on the Russian and Austrian armies at Austerlitz, the Emperor regretted the necessity which he could not avoid, of having to sign a separate peace with Austria without forcing Russia to join in the treaty, thus depriving himself of the fruits of his victory; but a whole Russian army remained intact in the hands of his enemies. The Austrian army from Italy, which was in Hungary, united with the debris of the armies which had escaped Austerlitz, and strongly reinforced, could have been formed into a formidable army, and have prolonged the war. The enmity of Prussia, the vacillating and timid character of the King, who might easily be led away to make common cause with our enemies, aggravated the danger to which Napoleon would have been exposed, and made him fear lest his rear might be seriously menaced. He accordingly contented himself with exacting that the Russian troops should evacuate Germany and Poland, and should withdraw to Russia. In the bottom of his heart he had a strong feeling of resentment for the perfidious conduct of the Prussian Ministry which, after avoiding any alliance whatever with the French Empire had, by its equivocal attitude, foiled all Napoleon's good intentions for increasing the strength and power of Prussia. This government, without directly encouraging Austria to attack us, had allowed this power to hope that, in case of a war with France, she would easily be able to draw over to her side an irresolute prince under the influence of a hostile cabinet. Exposed by this dangerous uncertainty to a menacing peril, forced to postpone the accomplishment of his designs, and his dream of general pacification, to an indefinite epoch, Napoleon had already had occasion to witness the full ingratitude and hostility of the Berlin cabinet, on the specious pretext of a violation of territory, on the occasion, namely, of the marching of French troops through Anspach, which before then had been crossed by the Austrians and the Bavarians. He had, from that time on, no feeling for the pusillanimous character of the King of Prussia but one of contempt and disdain. His irritation against this monarch was constantly manifesting itself, and this irritation only increased after he had made his personal acquaintance. Napoleon considered the King to be fated, from the circumstances of his unfortunate birth, to moral and physical clumsiness. He gave up his plan of making him his ally. In the place of his favorable feelings toward Prussia, and his ardent desire to unite himself to her by strong ties, there arose in the Emperor's mind the determination to regard as an enemy the power whose alliance he had not been able to win.

While the French army was following up its successes in Austria, the Court of Naples, struck with blindness, was violating its promises of neutrality, and opening its ports to the naval and military forces of our enemies.

Napoleon, hearing of this imprudent act of disloyalty after the victory of Austerlitz sent orders to his brother Joseph, who was then at the head of affairs in Paris, to proceed to the army in Italy, which was under the command of Marshal Masséna, to take over the command of it, with the grade of general of division, and the title of lieutenant to the Emperor, and to march on Naples, where a crown awaited him.

It was reported to the Emperor that extortions and abuses had been committed in this army, which his brother Joseph was leading to Naples. He gave orders for their repression. A fund of eight hundred thousand francs, produced by illegal requisitions, had been fraudulently appropriated and deposited in a Milan banking-house. The heads of this house, having denied that any such deposit had taken place, and evaded the restitution of the amount, the Emperor had the bank's paper seized and boycotted in every market. This interdiction was only raised after the entire sum had been restored.

Immediately after the ratification of the treaty of peace, the Emperor left for Munich. He wrote a long letter from this town to the major general, containing a general order for the execution of the provisions of the treaty. This order summarized with the foresight and precision which characterized all Napoleon's purposes, all arrangements concerning the army, 'the successive evacuations of the various parts of the enemy's territory, the occupation of the provinces which had been ceded, the cantonment of the troops, the transport of the wounded, the putting the sovereigns of Bavaria and Würtemberg in possession of the territories to which they were entitled by the treaty, the payment of the war indemnities, what the engineer and artillery regiments had to do, the return of the armies of General Marmont and Marshal Masséna into Italy, and so on.

The Empress Josephine had preceded the Emperor to Munich. The marriage of Prince Eugène with Princess Augusta, eldest daughter of the King of Bavaria, was celebrated there, and formed, as one of Napoleon's best historians—Thibaudeau—has said, the first link in the chain which was to unite forever the new Napoleonic dynasty to the ancient dynasties of Europe. This Bavarian princess had previously been betrothed to the hereditary prince of Baden. Politics decided it otherwise. In this case interests of state did not disturb the reciprocity of sentiments which this union awoke in the two spouses.

The Emperor informed the senate of this marriage by a message in which he associated this body with his family joys with a paternal feeling. He informed them, at the same time, that he had adopted Prince Eugène as his son, and that he had appointed him his successor, in default of direct successors, to the hereditary throne of Italy.

The 10th Nivôse of year XIV of the Republic—corresponding to December 31, 1805—was the last day of the Republican calendar. The Gregorian calendar had the advantage of being used by almost all the peoples of Europe and America, while the Republican calendar, apart from its inconvenience for our relations with foreigners and the isolation which resulted therefrom, had the further disadvantage of deriving its origin from a period which was remembered with as great disfavor in France as in the rest of Europe.

The great corporations of the state and the people of Paris prepared to receive the victor of Austerlitz with solemnity. The senate on the initiative of the tribunate, which went in a body to the Luxembourg Palace, to carry the flags which the Emperor destined for it there, decreed, in the name of the French people, that a triumphal monument should be erected to Napoleon the Great, that the senate should go to meet him in a body, and that the letter by which the Sovereign entrusted the care of the flags captured from the enemy to the high assembly, should be engraved on a marble tablet and placed in the sessions-chamber.

The Paris municipality handed over to the metropolitan clergy with great pomp and ceremony the flags which the Emperor had destined to be hung up in Notre Dame.

Napoleon and Josephine, received with general enthusiasm, reentered Paris on January 26, 1806.

The Emperor's return was hastened on by a very grave crisis which affected the Bank of France. The intensity of this crisis was attributed to various causes which are mentioned in detail further on. The depreciation of public paper occasioned thereby was aggravated by a maneuver arranged in London, and about which the English newspapers of the time boasted. This maneuver consisted in producing by concerted means a bad rate on the Paris market, in order to spread doubts as to the Bank's solvency, and to excite a public panic, which would send all the holders of Bank of France notes rushing to the Bank to get cash in exchange.

The primary cause of the fall in public securities was the emission of a very large number of receiver-general debentures which were negotiated for the realization of funds necessary for an operation made in the name of the contractors to the French provision company. This company had been previously charged with the supply of all the provisions for the Spanish fleet at Brest. This colossal operation proceeded from an agreement which M. Ouvrard, the representative of the company, had induced the King of Spain, who was to share in the profits, to conclude. The company undertook to supply the Spanish-American colonies with everything they required in the way of provisions, and to export all the productions, and all gold and silver which these countries produced. This double commercial and banking operation, almost unexampled, and beyond the forces of the richest banks of the present day, would have secured prodigious profits to the company, had it been able to carry it out. While awaiting the realization of the funds which were to be drawn from the Spanish colonies, immense capital was necessary. The funds at the disposal of the provision society were far from being adequate. The Bank, thanks to the influence of one of its governors, who was one of the directors of the company, readily accepted all the company's paper. The Public Treasury, on its side, gave the company receiver-general debentures in exchange for their promissory notes, so that the Bank was in the position of having issued more notes than it had cash to meet them with, and the Treasury had nothing but the company's paper in its chests, instead of bills of real value. The company succeeded in drawing from the Treasury bonds to the extent of more than one hundred million francs in the financial year of 1806. The negotiation of these bonds having become known, and malevolent maneuvers having intensified the evil, the public took alarm, and stormed the bank to get its notes converted into cash.

The Emperor heard of this financial crisis with great anxiety. Immediately after his return to Paris he called together a council, in which he caused himself to be informed on all the operations of the provision company, the embarrassed state of which was in consequence exposed. The Minister of the Treasury could with difficulty defend and justify such financial transactions. The Emperor could only accuse him of a want of prudence—for his honesty was above doubt—and blame him severely. The Emperor made M. Ouvrard come to the council as the principal author of operations which he was bound to consider as fatal to the Public Treasury. Still under the impression of the critical situation to which the want of resources would have reduced him, and of the incalculable disasters which would have come upon France if he had lost the battle of Austerlitz, Napoleon addressed the severest reproaches to M. Ouvrard. He said, amongst other things, in a violent fit of indignation, that he wished he could raise a gallows sufficiently lofty to hang him on, as a lesson to the whole of France. M. Ouvrard, who was standing behind the Grand Judge's chair, bore this attack without appearing in the least affected by it, and without saying a single word in his defense. He withdrew without any confusion, although the Emperor had very roughly ordered him to go away. Whenever bankers were in question, Napoleon always remembered with bitterness how he had been forced, on the 18th Brumaire—all the public chests being empty—to address himself to the bankers to procure the means for governmental necessities, and how he had to make arrangements with them of the kind which young gentlemen of family make with usurers. This resentment, which was perhaps too exclusive, will not surprise those who know how much he detested speculative financial operations and usurious profits, and to what a degree he esteemed regularity, order, and economy.

Napoleon pursued the job-mongers without respite, and when he was unable to bring them into the clutches of the law, he would disgrace them forever by means of the printing press. The *Moniteur* is full of articles holding them up to public contempt. The examination which he had made of the accounts of people who had the audacity to represent themselves as creditors of the state had proved, on the contrary, to his satisfaction, that the claims were unsound, and that they were debtors to the Public Treasury. The experience which, in this respect, he had acquired in Italy, and in the command of the armies, had inspired him with a prejudice against the jobbers, which was often only too well justified. As Napoleon had found amongst the contractors more; robbers of the public purse, and more corrupters of morals, than anywhere else, this class more particularly excited his detestation. As much as he hated the publicans, who had grown rich by immoral means, so much did he respect those whose fortunes had an untarnished source, and who had acquired them by their honesty, their industry, and their intelligence.

On the morrow of the painful scene which M. Ouvrard had had to endure, one of his friends, a M. Haller, came to dine with the Minister of Finance. He spoke to the minister of the bankers' affair, which at that time was occupying everybody's mind, and told him that he had heard with pleasure that this matter, which at first had appeared so menacing for its authors, was under way of settlement, that the Emperor had not wished to appear satisfied with M. Ouvrard's explanations, but that in his heart he readily admitted his genius for finance. M. Haller went so far as to add that M. Ouvrard expected to receive later on the decoration of the Legion of Honor, as a mark of the Emperor's appreciation of his talents. The minister was stupefied at the effrontery of those who gave such a complexion to the issue of an operation of which the promoters had so little reason to be proud. If the man who had been the soul of this enterprise entertained such a hope, there is less reason for surprise. His confidence in his own genius was unshakable, and he yielded blindly to his vocation for enormous financial enterprises. During the Hundred Days, the Emperor addressed himself to M. Ouvrard, who was to be commissioned with the supplies for the army. The loss of the battle of Waterloo put an end to their relations.

Napoleon obliged the bankers to return all the bonds they held to the Treasury, and sequestrated their property as security for what they still had to restore.

Authentic documents give a total of one hundred and forty millions as the amount owing to the Treasury by M. Ouvrard and his partners. Sixty millions were paid by Spain, by means of a loan which the Spanish government contracted in Holland, and thanks to the cooperation which M. Mollien obtained from Messrs. Hope and Baring for the recovery of Spanish piastres in Mexico. The balance of eighty-two millions was covered in part by fourteen millions produced by the seizure of real estate belonging to the bankers; by large returns to the Treasury, which were recovered as the result of a lawsuit between the various partners, in their fight for the spoils; by what was found due to them by the army and navy departments, when their claims against these two services were gone into; by the value of the stores which were seized in their depots for the army and navy; and, finally, because they only received the third, or the half of the price of their supplies during the years 1806 and 1807, until their liabilities toward the government were fully discharged. Thanks to these palliatives, the Emperor, continuing the company's commission to supply the army and navy departments, controlled his resentment, and did not put into execution the severe measures which he had ordered against Ouvrard and his partners.

The general secretary of the Ministry of the Public Treasury who was guilty of having allowed himself to be bribed by the bankers, was dismissed from the service and forced to restore to the sinking fund a large sum which he was alleged to have received from them. His wife frequently came to the palace bringing petitions and letters of justification, which the Emperor always refused to receive.

M. Barbé-Marbois lost his portfolio. Everybody was surprised at the reason of his disgrace. He was considered the Cerberus of the Treasury, and showed, in the exercise of his functions, a severity which had made him enemies. A caricature represented him standing on the balcony of the Ministry building, noting down the clerks who came late, in a little book; while his secretary who was standing behind him was drawing millions out of the minister's pockets. There are circumstances in life when the mind slumbers, and allows itself to be led away, during this suspension of its free will, to commit unexplainable acts. The Emperor no doubt thought so; for two years later he gave his former minister a proof of the trust he had in his honesty in appointing him first president of the Audit Office. Later on he gave him a place in the senate. Nevertheless—it must be because wounds inflicted on vanity are incurable—M. Barbé-Marbois, who had been recalled from exile by Napoleon, and who owed all to him, assisted in Napoleon's overthrow, in 1814, with an ardor which the Emperor might well describe as ungrateful.

M. Barbé-Marbois had succeeded to M. Bertrand-Dufresne in the general direction of the Public Treasury, which, six months later, was raised to a Ministry. M. Dufresne had been proposed by Consul Le Brun, who respected him for his honesty and his talents. He had justified the First Consul's choice by introducing a system of order and clearness into the bookkeeping, which enabled one, at a glance, at any time, to see the exact state of the Public Treasury. This was an invaluable quality in Napoleon's eyes and he showed the greatest regret at the loss of M. Dufresne. He went to see him some days before his death, and ordered a bust of him to be placed in one of the rooms of the Treasury. He had given a fresh proof of his political tolerance in occupying M. Dufresne, whose attachment to the Bourbons was well known to him. It was learned after the Restoration that, in accepting the direction of the Treasury, M. Dufresne had had his acceptance ratified by the Count de Lille. He had written to this prince on the subject and had received from him an answer which was printed in 1814. He was, moreover, not the only one who looked on the Count de Lille as the lawful master of France. MM. Royer-Collard, Becquey-Beaupré, Cuvier, Boscheron-Desportes, and others, used to correspond with the brother of Louis XVI.

M. Mollien, who combined the strictest integrity with the widest experience of financial matters, and considerable wit, which is never in the way, owed his acquaintance with Napoleon to Joseph Bonaparte. He had submitted to the government a plan of organization of the sinking fund, and had been placed at the head of this department. The Emperor called him to the Ministry of the Treasury after M. Barbé-Marbois's disgrace, and replaced him at the sinking fund by Bérenger, the councilor of state. M. Mollien rendered eminent services in his management of the Public Treasury, both by the creation of a service fund, and by other important improvements.

The blow struck by the financial crisis at public credit was promptly effaced by the vigorous action of the government. But, in investigating the various causes which had contributed to produce this crisis, the police had discovered that the royalist opposition, in duping the public by means of false alarms, had created a panic amongst the holders of public bonds, and was undermining the credit of the state.

Twelve or fifteen individuals were condemned by the police as incorrigible, and their removal from Paris was proposed. Mesdames d'Avaux, de Chevreuse, and Récamier, and MM. de Duras, Lassalle, Montrond, and others were of the number. With the exception of Madame de Chevreuse, the order for the banishment of all was sent on from Munich to the Ministry of Police. Fouché did not omit to tell them that he was only obeying a direct order from the Emperor, whereas, as a matter of fact, it was he who had brought it about. M. de Talleyrand, who was with the Emperor, was in communication with the Duchesse de Luynes, Madame de Chevreuse's mother-in-law. He averted the blow which was about to fall on the latter, undertook to be surety for her, and advised the Emperor to appoint her lady-in-attendance in the Empress's palace; although, as a matter of fact, Madame de Chevreuse was the leader of the royalist intrigues of which the Luynes mansion was the theatre. The disgrace into which this lady afterwards fell was caused by the unceasing sarcasms and bitter railleries which she allowed herself to indulge in at Josephine's court, and which were patiently endured by the kindhearted Empress. Napoleon, however, was deeply hurt by this inconsiderate conduct, and his patience, under this persevering and malevolent opposition, broke down one day, when Madame de Chevreuse replied to a lady-in-attendance, who had told her that she had been selected to attend Marie Louise, Queen of Spain, with the words: "I was not made to be a female warder." He was disgusted with Madame de Chevreuse for renewing her offenses, after she had accepted her pardon and a place in the Empress's household at his hands. He exiled her to forty leagues from Paris, and would not allow her to return, in spite of all the applications and petitions which were made to him to grant her her pardon.

Madame de Récamier had been drawn over to the opposition by Madame de Staël, and by her own animosity against the Emperor. This was the reason of, her enmity: M. Bernard, Madame de Récamier's father, being director of the post office, had lent his name and patronage to a periodical edited by one of his friends, the Abbé Guyot, which attacked the government, the First Consul, and his family. He was arrested. His daughter in vain protested his innocence. M. Bernard having been found guilty of abuse of confidence might have been sent to trial; he was only dismissed. The Récamier firm having failed during the financial crisis of 1806, Madame de Récamier was forced to leave Paris, which she visited from time to time, spending her time partly there and partly in Coppet, from which place she brought with her the quarrelsome spirit of Madame de Staël and her coterie. She found herself in consequence involved in Madame de Staël's disgrace. Madame de Staël was flattered at being able to hold in bondage a woman celebrated for her beauty, who was the object of the admiration of all the fashionable world.

It delighted her to hear people say that the connection of two women famous the one for her graces and the other for her wit, was the alliance of genius and of beauty. During Madame de Récamier's stay at Coppet, Prince Augustus of Prussia, son of Prince Ferdinand, and nephew of the great Frederick, fell violently in love with her, and went so far, it is said, as to sign a promise of marriage with his blood. This promise was returned to him some time later, and was only accepted with reluctance, for he remained constantly attached to her. It was for her that he ordered from the painter Gerard the fine picture of Corinna's improvisation at Cape Misene. Madame de Récamier was not banished. She had condemned herself to voluntary exile in the provinces. It was only when she began to take an active part in Madame de Staël's opposition that she was forbidden to return to Paris. After three years spent at Châlons, Lyons, and Geneva, she made a journey in Italy, and did not return to France till 1814.

As to Madame de Staël, the merited literary reputation which she enjoyed, her virile talents, her passion for fame, her irresistible mania for meddling with the affairs of the government, her quarrelsome nature, the charm of her conversation—which always sparkled with flashes of wit—had given her an influence over the political men of the period which she abused. Madame de Staël had been an ardent admirer of General Bonaparte. Although her overdone flattery had inspired him with an aversion towards her, he still received her while he was First Consul, but he answered her importunities with coldness. This contempt for her advances was sufficient—although it has been said that some financial interest was mixed up in it—to change Madame de Staël's devotion into an antipathy which soon revealed itself in open opposition. The interest which is naturally inspired by a weak woman, who cries out against the tyranny of an all-powerful man, gave her the popularity of persecution. But it has not been said that the Head of the state put up with her continual hostilities during three years; that during this period she had treated his warnings and notices with contempt; that this tolerance had encouraged her to stir up opposition against him on every side, with a view to punishing him for not calling her to his council; that her drawing room was a political club where the acts of the government were bitterly censured, and where, without any concealment, people were urged on to open revolt against the authority of the Head of the state; that this woman was a power who crossed Napoleon in the work of conciliation which he had undertaken; and lastly, that it was only after three years of long-suffering that she was finally removed from Paris. But this woman, who could not endure an existence far from the theatre on which her active mind wished to bestir itself, took recourse to the most urgent solicitation to be allowed to return to Paris. She knocked at every door, she even managed to creep up close to the beloved Paris, to which she always hoped to be able to return. I had spent several months of the summer of 1801 with her and her two children at Mortfon-taine, where she was putting forth all the seductions of her wit to captivate the proprietor of this charming retreat. She took advantage of this circumstance to write me, from Blois, some twenty most eloquent letters to which, however, I was unable to answer in conformity with her wishes. I had no consolation to give this woman, who was as much to be pitied as to be blamed, victim as she was of her nature, and whose judgment, as Napoleon used to say, was not on a level with her brilliant imagination and rare faculties. Madame de Staël was forced to return to Coppet. Her resentment then knew no limits and she went to seek the echoes of her hatred amongst our enemies. She has filled a book—which in the interest of her reputation had better not have been published—with all the bitterness of her feelings, expressing the hope that France should suffer reverses which would open her eyes to the fact that Napoleon was the author of all her troubles, and stir her up to shake off this yoke.

This book, entitled *Ten Years of Exile*, was printed after her death. I have seen a copy which had belonged to Commissary-General Boisnod. After the title was written: "A work written to justify Napoleon's persecution of the authoress."

The virulence of this famous woman's temper, and her mental excitability, could not go without food. Several liaisons were made and broken off at the retreat in Coppet, to while away her leisure hours. M. Barante, a retired magistrate, who was at that time Prefect of Geneva, patronized Madame de Staël, and treated her with more tolerance than was approved of by Napoleon. In the course of this magistrate's frequent visits to the Château of Coppet his son made Madame de Staël's acquaintance, and captivated her with his remarkable intelligence. To such a degree indeed, that when the younger M. de Barante left Coppet to go to Paris to enter upon a career in which, owing to his talents, he could look for a high position, Madame de Staël was so affected by his loss that she tried to commit suicide.

It has been thought that Napoleon was fascinated by the old nobility of the Court. The object which he had in view in drawing to the imperial court representatives of the old families was part of his system of fusion, and proceeded from the determination he had taken to render himself responsible for whatever was distinguished in France. It is certain that he always had a preference for the classes who by the length of their services, as well as by a good education, more particularly attracted his attention. He used to consider them more interested in the stability of the things he had founded than the Republicans, who were always hostile to the principles of his administration, and who dreamed of an ideal government. This is the reason why he has always been considered to have taken the inheritance, not the maxims, of the monarchies which had preceded his. That was one of the reasons of his partiality for M. de Talleyrand, who was one of his principal agents in this work of amalgamation and conciliation. Napoleon had already begun it, from the time of his accession to power, by appointing the Dukes de Choiseul-Praslin and de Luynes, Senators. He had continued it with success, and there can be no doubt that if his reign had lasted longer all trace of division amongst the classes would have disappeared. He had recognized the fact that, especially in his relations with the governments of Europe, his ambassadors, if chosen from old families, would be better able to assume a part in the courts to which they were delegated, and that their affiliation to the freemasonry of aristocracy would be of real service to him.

At the time of the Emperor's return to Paris, Mr. Pitt closed, on January 23, his short, laborious career. This minister, who had entered Parliament at the age of twenty-two, and had become Chancellor of the Exchequer at twenty-three, died at the age of forty-seven after having, by the ascendency of his genius, exercised for many years an almost absolute empire over the destinies of England and Europe, worn-out with work and the cares of office, his constitution undermined by an inherited disease, and mortally wounded by the victory of Austerlitz which overthrew all his plans. He bequeathed to his country the legacy of war to the death against the French Revolution and its representative, as well as a national debt beyond counting. Events unconnected with any plans, and catastrophes which it was impossible to foresee, have given the victory to a policy of constant and irreconcilable hatred towards France. Its fruits were not harvested by England until many years after Pitt's death, whose last moments were troubled by the doubts—with which he descended into the grave—of the success of his plans.

This implacable adversary of Napoleon was succeeded by an illustrious rival, a partisan of peace, who was all the more disposed towards a reconciliation with France, because of his recent relations with the Head of the French government: we mean Mr. Fox.

The same policy which had united a princess of Bavaria to Prince Eugène, determined the marriage of the hereditary prince of Baden to one of the Empress Josephine's nieces. This prince of Baden succeeded his grandfather in 1811, his father having died, in 1801, from the effects of a fall which he met with as he was returning from St. Petersburg, where he had been to visit his daughter, the wife of the Grand-duke Alexander, who afterwards became Emperor of Russia. The Prince of Baden, had, in 1806, two other sisters, married to the Kings of Sweden and Bavaria. This house, which owes its elevation to Napoleon, only possessed a simple margravate in 1803, and, in spite of this, three of its daughters had already then been placed on thrones.

The reigning Grand-duke felt sincere gratitude towards the Emperor, but his heart was animated with anti-French feelings. The union of the young heir-apparent with Napoleon's adopted daughter was disturbed, at first, by abominable intrigues. I can remember the minute detail contained in M. de Thiars's letters on the insulting expressions which the young prince's mother, the Margravine, and the Margrave Louis, his brother-in-law, used in reference to Napoleon's brothers and sisters-in-law, and on the efforts which were made in this hostile camp to sow discord between the two spouses. M. de Thiars, one of the Emperor's chamberlains, who during the emigration had established certain relations in some minor German courts, had been sent to Carlsruhe, without any official character, to prepare alliances with the houses of Bavaria and Baden.

The Princess Stéphanie's virtue and the Emperor's solicitude preserved Josephine's niece from the pitfalls which had been prepared for her. The couple were reconciled by Napoleon's attentions, and the peace, once reestablished, was not again disturbed. The Grand Duke, having had the misfortune to lose his son at an early age, was succeeded—at his death in 1818—by his uncle the Margrave Louis Augustus William. The most sinister rumors were set afloat on the premature death of the Grand Duke's son and a disappearance rather than a death, is still believed in in Germany. If public rumor is to be believed this child was the Jasper Hauser, whose appearance in 1826 gave rise to so many conjectures. The mystery which still envelops this new Man with the Iron Mask has given the reins to the dreamy imagination of the Germans. Jasper Hauser had been brought up in such a state of sequestration that this wretched child had never seen a human being during the earliest years of his childhood; his intelligence, deprived of all food, had not been able to develop. When he made his appearance, in 1828, in Nuremberg, he could hardly make himself understood, his language being almost unintelligible. This wretched child was suddenly kidnapped from the hands of those to whom he had been entrusted and, some days later, was found bathed in his blood. Having barely recovered from this attempted murder Jasper Hauser was murdered, and the authors of this double crime were never discovered. It was supposed from the fatal issue of his cruel destiny that his persecutors, fearing the effects of public interest in the wretched youth, and the discovery of his origin, had sacrificed him for their safety. The well-known feelings of the Margrave Louis, the interest which he had in removing the obstacle which stood between him and the throne, the tendency of human imagination to assign tragic and extraordinary causes to mysterious occurrences in which lofty personages are involved, having given rise in this matter to the strangest suppositions.

The grand duke Charles Louis Frédéric, Princess Stéphanie Napoleon's husband, had declared, before dying, that the Counts of Hochberg, his half-brothers, the issue of a morganatic marriage contracted by his grandfather the Margrave Charles Frederick, in 1777, with the Countess of Hochberg, were eligible for the succession to the throne. The grand duke, in calling the Counts of Hochberg to the throne, had thus realized the wishes of Napoleon, who was greatly interested in them. The two elder brothers had served in the French army, under his eyes, with distinction. Prince Leopold Charles Frederic became reigning Grand Duke in virtue of this decision.

The marriage of Stéphanie Beauharnais with the hereditary Prince of Baden took place on March 4, 1806. Prince Eugène and Queen Hortense, adopted by the Emperor, had added the name of Napoleon to theirs. The same took place with Princess Stéphanie:

"Paris, March 3, 1806

"It being our desire that the Princess Stéphanie Napoleon, our daughter, should enjoy all the prerogatives Duke to her rank—she will place herself at our side in all Court drawing rooms, fêtes, and at table, and in the case of our absence she will place herself to the right of the Empress

"(Signed) NAPOLEON"

The result of the latest victories had been the establishment of new kingdoms and grand duchies in Germany. What Napoleon had done for foreign princes, who might one day forget what they owed to France, he considered his power sufficiently well established to repeat in the heart of his vast empire. It was naturally in his own family that he had to look for support. Prince Joseph, his elder brother, was placed on the throne of Naples; and Prince Louis, his other brother, received the crown of Holland. Prince Murat, his brother-in-law, received the grand duchy of Berg, composed of provinces which had been ceded by Prussia; Prince Eugène had the viceroyalty of Italy. These princes retained their dignities as Grand-Elector, Constable, Grand Admiral and Archchancellor of state. In conferring these independent sovereignties on the members of his family, Napoleon wished to retain them at the same time in the interests of their mother country by bonds destined to remind them at all times of their origin, and their duties towards France. The establishment of the principalities and duchies in Italy was an outcome of the same system. A new dynasty needed to be supported by an intermediate and powerful class, more particularly interested in the stability of institutions, and in the solidity and splendor of the throne; and which might give, as Napoleon expressed it, points of correspondence and support to the Great Empire. These high dignities were in no sense a danger to public liberty, and did not violate the principles of equality which had been consecrated by the French Revolution. They conferred neither rights nor particular privileges on their titularies; they were purely honorary, and were open to all citizens of every class, in proportion to their services and their capacities. They were the means of bestowing rewards which had been deserved and had been promised. They had also the advantage of stimulating a salutary emulation by holding out to all kinds of merit the prospect of these splendid proofs of public gratitude.

The Emperor bestowed the Duchy of Guastalla on his sister Princess Pauline Borghèse. The province of Neufchâtel was raised to a principality, and the sovereignty given to Marshal Berthier, Napoleon's oldest comrade-in-arms. The Archchancellor Cambacérès was created Prince of Parma; the Archtreasurer Le Brun, Prince of Placenza; Talleyrand, Prince de Bénévent; and Bernadotte, Prince de Ponte-Corvo.

Twelve Duchies were created in Italy. These Duchies conferred no authority, but each carried with it an income of sixty thousand francs, taken from the revenues reserved to the Emperor. These were the Duchies of Dalmatia, Istria, Frioul, Cadora, Belluna, Conegliano, Treviso, Feltre, Bassano, Vicence, Padua, and Rovigo.

The kingdom of Naples supplied four more, namely the duchies of Gaeta Otranto, Tarentum, and Reggio, without counting the principalities of Bénévent and Ponte-Corvo. These two small territories, wedged into the territory of the kingdom of Naples, had been incorporated into this state to the great displeasure of the Papal government, which alleged a claim to their possession.

Duchies situated in the kingdoms of Italy and of Naples were held in reserve, to be distributed as rewards for new services. The principal city of Lucca had to its charge the duchy of Massa, which was not filled till 1809, in the person of M. Régnier, the former Grand Judge. In the month of April, 1806, a deputation composed of high Dutch functionaries came to Paris to agree with the Emperor on the basis of a treaty by which a monarchy, based on constitutional laws, should be founded in Holland. After negotiations which lasted several months this monarchy was proclaimed on June 15, and conferred on Louis Bonaparte, whose personal inclinations had not been consulted, and who would have preferred the government of Genoa or of Piedmont. Napoleon, however, declared to him that he had no right to refuse a throne which he (Napoleon) had erected for him in the interests of the Empire. The death of the last Stadhouder, and his heir's renunciation of his rights, smoothed over the difficulties and calmed the new king's scruples.

King Louis of Holland left, accordingly, a week later to take possession of his States, accompanied by Queen Hortense and their children. During the week which preceded their departure, he occupied himself with the Dutch deputation in acquiring a general knowledge of the affairs of their country, and had daily conferences with the Emperor. He proceeded at first to the Castle du Bois, near the Hague, and some days later made his formal entry into the capital of the Netherlands, where he received the fealty of the former masters of the country, his new subjects. Royal honors had been paid him during the whole of his journey across French territory. On his entry into Holland the people, and all classes of society, received him with great enthusiasm and manifestations of joy. The new sovereign applied himself from the moment of his arrival, with the assiduity and conscientiousness which characterized him, in providing for the principal needs of the government. He afterwards went to Wiesbaden, near Mayence, to take the waters, hoping by these means to check the progress of a disease which had been torturing him for several years past. The first steps which King Louis took in the government of his kingdom, without any thought of opposition, crossed the views which the Emperor had had in sending him to Holland. Animated by the most straightforward intentions, Napoleon's brother was only acting in obedience to the impulse of his nature, and he always had the courage of his faults. Married against his will, created a king in spite of himself, he revolted at the thought that he was the victim of the arbitrary will of his powerful brother. He wished to be independent on a throne which he thought purchased by the sacrifice of his will and his tastes, as if he had acquired the crown by the right of birth. Jealous of his liberty of rule, encouraged in his resistance by the interested approval of our enemies, we shall soon see him taking pleasure in defying the consequences of his opposition.

The changes inaugurated in Germany by the Treaty of Lunéville, and consummated by the Treaty of Presburg, had disorganized the ancient German empire, whose edifice was falling into ruins. Austria and the German princes fought for the fragments; the diet was by this fact dissolved. Napoleon was asked by the Prince Elector, the Chancellor Dalberg, and by various other people, to take Germany under his protection. He decided in consequence to form a new confederation which should include the Southern German States. The Elector Archchancellor became the principal agent in these negotiations. The King of Bavaria and Würtemberg, the grand dukes of Baden and of Berg, and the Landgrave of Hesse-Darmstadt subscribed to this reorganization. Austria professed indifference to what was happening. Prussia, who would have been glad to take over some part of the inheritance of Austria, was more active, but was not consulted in the matter, and was excluded from all the arrangements made. At last the negotiations, which had been carried on in secret for three months, having been concluded, a treaty establishing the new confederation was signed on the 12th of July, and published some days later. The confederation was placed under the protectorate of the Emperor of the French, and took the title of the Confederation of the Rhine, a title which determined the limits of its sphere of action. The principal negotiator was rewarded with the dignity of Prince-Primate, and with the gift of the Grand duchy of Frankfort which was created in his favor. The Landgrave of Hesse-Darmstadt became Grand Duke.

To the notification of the treaty, which was made to him, the Emperor of Germany replied by resigning this title and assuming that of Francis I, Emperor of Austria. Prussia was invited to form a confederation of the North which would have been composed of the Electorate of Hesse-Cassel, the ducal Saxonies, the two States of Mecklenburg and the secondary principalities of Germany. This overture was received with favor by the Berlin cabinet, but soon suspicion as to the sincerity of the French government was aroused. The Berlin ministers gave credence to certain false allegations, which were supported by the reports of the Prussian agents, accredited to countries which were hostile to France. The adversaries of the French alliance persuaded the King of Prussia that the Emperor Napoleon was secretly offering provinces belonging to Prussia to the princes of states which were to form part of the confederation of the North, so as to draw them into the Confederation of the Rhine. The truth is that on the contrary Prussia wanted to subjugate the Kingdom of Saxony, and to dominate the Hanseatic towns by drawing them into the confederation of the North. Napoleon, for political reasons which it is easy to understand, approved of Saxony's refusal to subscribe to this scheme, and declared that the Hanseatic towns were to remain separate from any confederation. The Court of Berlin submitted and raised no further objections. It had already acknowledged the Confederation of the Rhine, and appeared to have no other object in view than to form a confederation of the States which were the neighbors of Prussia. Thus brooded and grew the rancor of Prussia against France, in spite of Napoleon's very sincere desire to make an ally of this rival of his ambition.

While occupying himself with these lofty political speculations the Emperor's attention was equally bestowed on the details of the government of the interior of his Empire. He had heard that the prisons of Brussels were crowded with people who had been arrested on the denunciation, too carelessly listened to, of old brigands, who had tried to gain their freedom by denouncing to justice alleged criminals who had escaped punishment. Napoleon wrote the following letter on this subject to Berlier, a privy councilor:

"MONS. BERLIER—I hear that there are a large number of arrested persons in the prisons of Brussels, and that they are deprived of the necessaries of life. My desire is that you proceed without any delay to this city, there to confer with my imperial procurer, the president of the criminal court, and with the prefect, that you interrogate each of the prisoners in turn, and that you report to me what is the reason that such a number of persons are under arrest, and why they are not brought to trial. You know how anxious I am that criminals should be severely punished, but also that no innocent man should suffer. You will base your line of action on these principles. And hereupon I pray God to have you in His holy keeping,

"(Signed) NAPOLEON"

"Paris, March 17, 1806"

The result of M. Berber's mission was that five hundred prisoners were set at liberty, their innocence having been proved. The Emperor ordered the Grand Judge to assure M. Berber of his satisfaction.

Napoleon had ordered the erection of the triumphal arch on the Place du Carrousel, dedicated to the glory of the French armies during the campaign of 1805. He had the intention of having others erected. The following is a letter on the subject which he dictated on May 14, 1806.

"Triumphal arches would be futile works, and productive of no effect whatever, and I should not have ordered them had I not thought that this was a means of encouraging architecture. I wish to stimulate sculpture in France, by means of these triumphal arches, for ten years. M. Denon will lay a plan before me. The Minister of the Interior is to erect another triumphal arch at the Etoile. A clear understanding must be come to with regard to the description of all the designs. One must be the arch of Marengo, and the other the Arch of Austerlitz. I shall have another built in some other part of Paris which will be the Arch of Peace, and another, the Arch of Religion. By means of these four arches I expect to advance sculpture in France for twenty years. It is well, however, that M. Denon should know that there are to be four arches, so as not to put on one subjects which are better suited for another. I beg M. Daru to let me know how far the statue of Charlemagne has progressed, and to come to an understanding with M. Cretet on the subject of the two fountains which are to be erected, one on the Place de la Revolution, and the other on the site of the Bastille; they are monumental. There must be statues and bas-reliefs. These subjects may be taken, to begin with, from the Emperor's history; next from the history of the French Revolution; and next from the history of France. No opportunity for humiliating the Russians and the English must, generally, be neglected. William the Conqueror and Duguesclin might be honored on these monuments."

It does not come within the scope of this book to enumerate the various works of improvement and embellishment carried out in Paris, and in the departments of the Empire, or the encouragements which were given to agriculture, the arts, commerce, and industry. In the midst of mighty wars the conduct and details of which absorbed the whole of his attention, Napoleon, in the few moments of leisure at his headquarters, went over in his mind the condition of the public works, as laid down in the reports of his ministers, or as the result of the observations he had made himself during the passage through the various old and new departments. He went over in his mind such works as had been begun, those which had been put under examination, and those which would really benefit the localities which had asked for them. When the temporary submission of his enemies gave Napoleon a short respite, he used it in making himself acquainted with the state of progress of these public works, in urging on their completion, and in awarding the necessary funds for this purpose; all this was done without the state being burdened with any debt. The Emperor often presided over commissions of men competent in these matters. At these meetings plans studied in advance were minutely discussed; adopted, if after a careful examination they had been declared satisfactory; or adjourned for ampler information. It was owing to this intelligent system of public works that Napoleon covered old and new France with monuments of all kinds, of which some were worthy of ancient Rome: roads, canals, bridges, fountains, and harbors fitted to shelter numerous fleets. It was thus that he was able to reestablish, or to create innumerable manufactures and factories of all kinds, giving considerable development to our national industries, naturalizing in France productions for which we had formerly to go abroad; improving our breeds of horses, etc., etc., creations realized in a period of less than fifteen years, and for which many long and prosperous reigns of former days, even in the midst of complete peace, would have been insufficient.

Napoleon—satisfied with the march of events, proud of the patriotism with which the glory and the prosperity of the Empire inspired the nation—was in the full enjoyment of his high destiny and public happiness. He accepted a fête at the Château de Grignon, which he had presented to Marshal Berthier, and spent two days there, in the course of which, laying aside all cares of politics and of government, he showed himself animated by the best of humors. He took part without any reserve in the amusements which were provided for him. Hearing at dinner that the Château de Grignon had belonged to that famous speculator Law, author of the financial system which bears his name, Napoleon was just about to say something unfavorable to this speculator, when he noticed the presence of General Lauriston, who was one of the financier's descendants. So he checked himself, and changed the conversation to avoid hurting the feelings of his aide-de-camp. In the evening, little parlor games were played, and the Emperor behaved very gallantly towards the ladies; he was one of those perhaps who took most pleasure in so-called innocent games, because they helped him to forget the gravity of his rank. The importance of political affairs left the chief of so great an Empire very little time for such amusements.

Before entering on a description of the events which were being prepared in Prussia, I will say a few words about Napoleon's private life so as to make known his method of work, his habits, and the order established in the management of the imperial household.

As a general rule I used to take the morning papers to the Emperor, while he was finishing dressing. I read him such articles as he pointed out to me, or which I thought likely to interest him. This reading almost always provoked some remark from him, sometimes a notice or an order to one of his ministers.

His first doctor, Corvisart, or his surgeon-in-ordinary, Yvan, were often present at his toilet. The Emperor liked Corvisart's conversation. When he received him it was rather for the sake of a chat, than to talk about his health, which he heeded little. He loved to tease the doctor on the impotency of the medical science, and on this subject he would pour out a rolling fire of quips and sallies against the medical profession. Corvisart defended himself under these attacks with rare presence of mind; his readiness of repartee was always quick and ingenious. While admitting the uncertainties of the medical science, he defended the utility and the services which it rendered with such a strength of argument that the sarcasms were often stayed on Napoleon's lips.

Since I am speaking about doctors I may take this opportunity of speaking of Napoleon's physical constitution. This constitution was naturally robust, and the care which he had taken from his youth to break off all bad habits had fortified it. He had all the advantages of the bilio-sanguine temperament. This kind of temperament, in spite of certain disadvantages, is considered the best. I never saw Napoleon ill; he was only occasionally subject to vomiting bile, which never left any after-effects, and which were a natural and healthy purge for him. He had feared, for some time, that he was affected with a disease of the bladder, because the keen air of the mountains caused him a kind of dysuria; but this fear was found to be without foundation. It has been noticed that men are rarely really suffering from the disease with which they imagine themselves to be afflicted. The existence of the kind of disease which killed the Emperor was not suspected at that time, and I never heard him complain of pains in the stomach. I have heard a skilful doctor maintain that affections of the kind—of which Corvisart undertook to cure the First Consul, at the beginning of the Consulate—are incurable when they are not seriously treated from the very outset. He asserted that remedies administered too late, and general care, can retard the progress of the virus, but not entirely destroy it; that its presence causes temporary perturbations in the part to which it is attached, and that sooner or later it ends by mastering it and creating mortal ravages. This doctor was persuaded that this virus was the germ of the disease to which Napoleon succumbed at St. Helena. So susceptible were Napoleon's organs that the slightest evil smell was sufficient to upset him greatly. He had so keen a sense of smell that he could detect the vicinity of a subterranean passage, a cellar, or a sewer, a long way off; or smells proceeding from places far away, which were not noticeable to any of the persons in his company. I have heard him say, on this topic, that he would have been very unhappy in the days when four or even six people used to sleep together in the same bed. He had been anxious to gain some acquaintance with anatomy, and for this purpose Doctor Corvisart had brought him some anatomical models in wax, representing parts of the heart and the stomach. The Emperor had set aside the hour which followed his luncheon for this study, but the illusion produced by the attention given to these parts of our animal organization filled him with such disgust that it used to make him sick. He tried in vain to resist this revolt of his senses, but he was forced to give up his lessons. Nevertheless the same man, riding over a field of battle after a bloody fight, was not disgusted by the contact of wounds of disgusting appearance and odor. He often used to get off his horse, and place his hand on the chest of the wounded man to see whether he still breathed; he would raise him up, with the help of his officers, and put to his lips a bottle of brandy, which his servant Roustan always carried with him.

One would be tempted to believe, if such a supposition could be admitted, that his body participated to some extent in his marvelous intellectual organization. When his coffin was opened at St. Helena, twenty years after it was closed down, Napoleon appeared to be sleeping. His teeth had preserved their whiteness, his beard and nails seemed to have grown since his death. His hands had the color of life, they were supple and resisted pressure. It is not impossible that some centuries hence some biographer of this great man should apply to his body the property which Plutarch attributed to that of Alexander the Great. The soul alone is immortal, and reason rejects the belief in such phenomena; but sentiment may admit them. It is a touching superstition which attributes privileges to the mortal remains of men of genius; for it is only another tribute paid to their memory.

Napoleon was careful in the matter of personal cleanliness. He took frequent baths. He used to brush his arms and his broad chest himself and loved to joke about the fatness of his breasts. His valet finished by rubbing him very vigorously on the back and shoulders; but he often used to make Roustan, who was much stronger, do this for him. He formerly used to be shaved, but for a long time, that is to say, since about 1803, he had shaved himself—after he had changed his valet. A small mirror was held before him, and turned as required, in the process of shaving. He then used to wash himself with a great quantity of water in a silver basin which from its size might have been taken for a vat. A sponge dipped in eau de cologne was passed over his hair, and the rest of the bottle was poured over his shoulders. His flannel singlets, his vests and pants of kerseymere were changed every day. He never gave up wearing his green or blue uniform coats—the only coats he ever wore—until he was told that they were beginning to show signs of wear. His allowance for dress had at first been fixed at sixty thousand francs; he had reduced this amount to twenty thousand francs, all included. He was fond of saying that with an income of twelve hundred francs, and a horse, he should have all he wanted. He often referred to the times when he was an artillery lieutenant, and delighted in speaking of the order he put in his expenditure, and the economies which he attempted to avoid getting into debt, especially when the triumph of the English party in Corsica had cut off all supplies from home, and he had charge of his brother Louis, whom he was bringing up and maintaining on his pay. At such times he would censure the example of luxury which his aides-de-camp, and the principal officers of his household, gave to the officers of lower rank, who were attached to his person. Nevertheless he liked to be surrounded with splendor and a kind of pomp. He often used to say to those on whom he lavished his money: "Be economical and even parsimonious at home; be magnificent in public." He followed this maxim himself. Nobody was more modest in his dress, or less particular about his food, and all that concerned him personally. He told me one day that when he was quite a young officer, he had sometimes traveled from Paris to Versailles in what used to be called the Court carriages, which were a kind of cheap coach; very comfortable, he used to add, and where he met very nice people. Only it was not a very expeditious way of traveling, for these carriages took five hours to do the journey.

Although the interior and exterior affairs of the Empire had taken a great development since the rupture of the peace of Amiens, the Emperor's usual way of living had changed very little. He had fixed hours neither for his work, nor his meals, nor for sleep. He used to come to his work-room at seven in the morning, dressed for the whole day in his invariable costume, vest and pants of white kerseymere, the green coat of the *chasseurs de la garde* during the days of the week, and the blue coat with white lappets on Sundays and reception days. He wore a colonel's epaulettes, the decorations of the Legion of Honor and of the Crown of Iron in his button-hole; the plate of the Legion of Honor and the grand cordon under his coat; and he was always dressed in white silk stockings. When he had to ride out, to save time, he did not change his stockings, and contented himself with changing his shoes with oval gold buckles for riding-boots lined with silk.

The levee took place at nine in the morning. The officers were expected to be present to receive their orders, officers not in attendance had permission to be present. After the levee certain persons who by reason of their rank or of their employments were in immediate contact with the Emperor, took advantage of the hour of the levee to pay him their respects, or to obtain a few words with him.

Napoleon used to lunch alone in a little drawing-room which was close to his work-room. During this repast—which rarely lasted more than ten minutes, but which he prolonged when he had leisure—he used to receive some savants, men of letters and artists with whom he liked to talk. After luncheon he returned to his work-room, attended to some business, and then went to work with one of his ministers, or with some official for whom he had sent, or presided over the Council of State. There were days when the work in his cabinet took up the whole of his time. The Council of Ministers, at which the

Archchancellor and Chief Treasurer were present, took place every Wednesday at noon, and lasted till the dinner hour.

This meal was served at six o'clock, but when the Emperor was busy he let the hour go by. He used to dine alone with the Empress, except on Wednesdays—when the ministers were invited, and Sundays—which were devoted to a family feast. Napoleon preferred the simplest dishes. He drank nothing but Chambertin mixed with water, hardly ever without water, and never touched liqueurs. A cup of coffee was served to him in the drawing room, and he used also to take one at luncheon, but never more. He would remain about an hour in the drawing room, at the end of which the Empress used to go down to her apartment. It was usually after this meal, and once a week, that M. Barbier, his librarian, used to present him with the new books, or books sent by authors in token of homage. The Emperor glanced over them all, throwing down on the ground or pitching into the fire those which did not interest him, or which displeased him, and putting one or two—rarely three—aside to read with greater attention.

Chapter VI

I used to take an hour's horse exercise every day, as much for amusement as for the sake of exercise. I felt more than ever the need of some assistance, and I asked the Emperor to give me a companion. The idea then came to him to create two posts of Secretary to the cabinet, and he appointed General Clarke—who, now that the death of the King of Etruria had closed his mission to this prince, was without employment—to one of these places. The Emperor appearing to neglect him, Clarke followed him step by step during his journey in Alsatia, placing himself before him each time that he had the opportunity of recalling himself to his memory. On his return from this short journey, the Emperor told me that, not wishing to interrupt the unity of the work of his private workroom, he had made up his mind to charge the general with the title of secretary to the cabinet, with a special class of work, viz., his correspondence with the ministers of war and marine; and that this would be a notable reduction of my day's work. General Clarke was accordingly established in a private office. But the necessity of sending for him to write to his ministers often kept the Emperor back from making use of his services; in one word, the post degenerated into a sinecure. The second post of Secretary to the cabinet was also vacant when the 1805 campaign took place. General Clarke, who followed the Emperor in this campaign with me, was appointed governor of Vienna. He was entrusted with several missions abroad after this campaign, and his post as Secretary to the cabinet remained as unoccupied as the second post.

The assistance which it had been the Emperor's intention to give me was accordingly only an illusory one. Another year passed without any change being made in the work in the cabinet. I repeated my application to Napoleon to obtain an assistant. What I needed above all was to be relieved of the care of the papers which had to be classified after having been answered. The multiplicity of my occupations prevented me from keeping these papers in sufficiently good order to be able to find any draft of a letter or a dispatch which the Emperor might want to see at a moment's notice. Napoleon avoided satisfying my request for some time longer, either by making promises which he did not keep, or on various pretexts. He used to urge me to get married, assuring me that he would arrange my work in such a manner that I should get some rest. Various matches were proposed to me by him and the Empress Josephine, including a lady who was one of her relations, and whom she obliged me to call upon at her house. But at that time I did not feel any vocation for marriage. Besides, I was determined that if I ever did make up my mind to get married I would choose my own wife. As a matter of fact, more than two years passed before I contracted the irrevocable bonds, the solemnity of which so impressed me. Seeing that the Emperor put off keeping his promise every day, I became discouraged and fell ill, as much from worry as from overwork. On hearing this news the Emperor showed his solicitude and sent me Doctor Corvisart, who was charged with a kind message. Pending my recovery he sent for the Empress's private secretary. M. Deschamps was one of our most agreeable vaudeville writers; he was still capable of more serious work, and lively and brisk, though past middle life. Napoleon despaired from the very first of being able to accustom him to his way of working, and especially to writing from his dictation. He employed General Duroc, the aide-de-camp on service, and the Secretary of state in turn. During my short illness I was to some extent in the position of the man who while yet alive reads an obituary notice of himself, written by some friendly pen at the news of his death. I heard that when the person to whom the Emperor was dictating did not take down his words sufficiently quickly the Emperor would cry out: "I cannot repeat. You make me lose the thread of my thought. Where is Méneval?" Pointing to the disorder on his writing-table he would cry out: "If I had Méneval here, I should soon have cleared all that away. He also used to say that he was postponing all work of importance until after my recovery. As a matter of fact my entire merit consisted in the acquaintance I had with the connection and direction of Napoleon's affairs, in the way that thanks to this knowledge I was able to foresee their development and issue, and in my familiarity with the connection of his ideas, with the precision of his style, and with the originality of his expressions. I did not know any kind of shorthand, and so would have been unable to take down the Emperor's words literally; but I used to note down the principal points which served as memoranda and also the characteristic expressions. I used to rewrite the letters in almost the same terms as he had used, and when he read it over before signing it, which only happened when it was a delicate matter, or one which preoccupied him, he used to find his own style in my writing—if I may use that expression. Those who have followed the details of the work done in the imperial cabinet for sufficient time, or who made themselves acquainted with Napoleon's method of work, have been in a position to verify the truth of what I have related.

I confess that my vanity was flattered by the reports which I heard, and the idea that the Emperor attached importance to my assistance and my work soon restored me to strength and courage. When I reappeared in his cabinet after four days, I may say without boasting that I was received with pleasure. I found Napoleon kinder to me than ever. He authorized me to mention somebody to him as assistant, adding that he left this choice entirely to my personal responsibility. M. Maret—the Duke of Bassano—who used to accompany the Emperor on his journeys as Secretary of state, was succeeded by one of his heads of departments with whom I was in relations by reason of my service. I knew him as a man trained to business by the knowledge which his duties at the state-secretaryship had given him of the various acts of the government. I further knew him to be a very industrious man and honest to a degree. Before approaching him on this subject I wished to have the opinion of M. Maret, who strongly encouraged me in the idea which I had had of suggesting the name of M. Fain to the Emperor, offering himself as bondsman. I accordingly asked the minister to back up my suggestion in favor of his subordinate. M. Fain was accepted. As far as I was concerned, I was delighted with this arrangement and as to M. Fain, I never saw a happier man. He embraced me with tears of joy and gratitude. The Emperor promulgated a decree under date of February 3, 1806, on the new organization of his cabinet. By the terms of this decree the service of the imperial cabinet was entrusted to a Secretary of the Portfolio, assisted by a reporter on petitions and a keeper of archives. I was appointed Secretary of the Portfolio, and I alone had to present for signature all the notes or letters which the Emperor had dictated. I alone had the right to enter into the Sovereign's cabinet. I was entrusted with the keeping of the keys of the Emperor's writing-table and portfolios. If in my absence the Emperor dictated any note or letter, or had any piece of work done, a copy, or at least a draft, of this work had to be handed to me immediately on my return. The reporter on petitions was M. Deschamps, already secretary to the Empress Josephine, and M. Fain was the keeper of archives. He became later titular secretary to the Emperor. Napoleon had wished to do something pleasant for the Empress Josephine and to improve the position of her secretary. The kindheartedness of this princess, and her goodwill towards her people, are well-known. The Emperor, who always loved her tenderly, never refused her anything that he thought it possible to grant.

During the first years the papers connected with affairs which the Emperor thought it advisable to withhold from sending to the archives were put into a small mahogany box, which was placed in the cabinet. The key of this box remained in the hands of the Secretary of the Portfolio. This precaution was only observed for two or three years, at the end of which all papers, with very few exceptions, were immediately sent off to the archives.

The same decree instituted two guardians of the portfolio who were in attendance a fortnight in turn. They had to wear a uniform and a sword, with a shoulder-belt of a peculiar design.

I had to wait some time still for the assistance which the Emperor had intended to grant me in appointing M. Fain. The force of habit, Napoleon's dislike to increase the number of people who shared his confidence, his habit of acting on experience, fortified by a prudence which was increased by the importance and the gravity of the constant struggle in which he was engaged, prevented him at first from entrusting M. Fain's talents and zeal with the employment on which we had counted. It was only gradually, and when the work became too heavy, that he used to call M. Fain into his workroom to dictate to him, after which the secretary used to return to his office of the archives to write out his fair copy. The Emperor accustomed himself to him gradually. He first of all employed him for dictations on questions of administration, until the time when the breaking-down of my health gave him freer access to the cabinet, which after my retirement was organized on a larger basis.

The introduction of M. Deschamps into the cabinet (reorganized by the decree of February, 1806) led us to make the acquaintance of a number of his colleagues of the Vaudeville: MM. Barré, Radet, Desfontaines, Despré, Picard and de Vigny, an actor of the Odeon, all people of approved wit and talents. These gentlemen frequently came to luncheon with us.

MM. Barré, Radet and Desfontaines were the first to think of the collaboration of several authors in the writing of a theatrical piece in which a unity of plan, idea, and action should be preserved. M. Deschamps obtained for this inseparable trio—who together had founded the Vaudeville, a theatre on which the glory of France was frequently celebrated in patriotic plays—a pension of four thousand francs apiece from the funds reserved for the press fund. I am not aware whether the authors continued to enjoy this favor under the government of the Restoration.

In the burst of his gratitude one of the new pensioners cried out: "O Vaudeville, heureuz d'avoir dans tes domaines, Des champs!"

To which Deschamps, in his modesty, suggested that he should add: "Des prés et des fontaines!"

This anecdote reminds me that a man of letters who had been received at La Malmaison, and who had had one of his tragedies played on the Court stage, obtained a pension of six thousand francs from the Emperor. At the time of the Restoration this braggart of a poet said, speaking of Napoleon: "The devil of a fellow! As soon as he saw somebody in a crowd whose head topped those of the others—bang! he disgraced him with a pension."

Now it happened that the minister who at that time disposed of pensions and pardons, reduced the pension of our man of letters to three thousand francs. In consequence of this his friends made haste to congratulate him on the fact that the Restoration had effaced half of his stain.

The interest which the Emperor took in the prosperity of commerce and industry induced him to visit an establishment which at that time was at its highest prosperity. This was the calico-factory which M. Oberkampf had established at Jouy in the Biévre valley. Napoleon went there one day in the summer of 1806, accompanied by Josephine, and followed by a part of the court. He invested this visit with a certain amount of importance. He went through the various work-rooms, and examined the various processes of manufacture with attention, desired to be informed of all its details, and even went into the meadow where the calicoes were spread out. The Emperor expressed his satisfaction to the modest author of this fine establishment. Then, looking at him with greater attention, he showed his surprise at the fact that M. Oberkampf had not yet been decorated with the Legion of Honor. Then unfastening the cross which he wore in his button-hole, Napoleon handed it to the manufacturer, saying: "Here is my cross. I am pleased with what I have seen. I like to reward services of all kinds to the motherland. Peaceful war made against the enemy in your workshop is no less efficacious than the war waged on battlefields."

During the month of March, 1806, orders had been given to the ministers of war and of the war administration to assign the places to be occupied in France by the corps of the *Grande Armée*. The garrisons which they were to hold were in the 2nd, 3rd, 4th, 5th, 6th, 18th, 24th, 25th, and 26th military divisions. The news that the Austrians had handed over to the Russians the mouths of the Cattaro, which by the terms of the Treaty of Presburg they had promised to surrender to France, suspended the surrender of the fort of Braunau to the Austrian troops, and the movement of the French army back to the Rhine. This incident, which lasted some time, having been terminated, the Emperor confirmed his previous orders for the return home of our army. On the 22nd of June he sent an order to the Minister of War, fixing the positions which the various corps were to occupy, modifying the first arrangement, although very few of the military divisions which had been named were altered. The major-general, who had remained in Germany, was commissioned with the execution of these orders. The refusal of a ratification of the treaty concluded in Paris with the Russian plenipotentiary d'Oubril; the rupture of the negotiations begun in Paris with England; and finally the armaments of Prussia caused all these orders for the return of the troops to be countermanded.

The long stay of the French troops in Germany necessarily formed the pretext for accusations of all kinds against the head of the French government. Libelous pamphlets, which so greatly contributed towards the perversion of public opinion and towards exasperating Europe against France, began to spread, and provoked the peoples of Germany to revolt. Booksellers in the principal towns occupied by the French troops printed, published, and hawked these libelous calumnies against us. One of them, Palm, a bookseller at Nuremberg, was arrested, tried by court-martial, and shot. The inflexibility of martial law and the safety of the army rendered this act of rigor imperative. Nevertheless the effect produced in Germany was terrible, and this occurrence brought down on the Emperor fresh accusations and a fresh explosion of public indignation. Palm was honored as the martyr of the German national spirit. The major-general had respited certain other prisoners who had been sentenced to death for the same crime. He asked the Emperor to pardon them and Napoleon wrote at the bottom of his letter:

"Saint-Cloud, September 4, 1806—I leave. Marshal Berthier free to act as he chooses. I find that the pardons which he asks for may well be granted."

The exasperation, however, which regained in Berlin, and the hostile preparations ordered by Prussia, increased the anti-French agitation. Prussia, who had learned no lesson from the defeat of Austria and of Russia, nor from the want of success of her bellicose intentions in 1805, entered the arena in her turn. This power, whose constant irresolutions worried Napoleon during five years, tempted by the French alliance, without definite political system of any kind, but secretly inclining towards the coalition, finished by throwing in her lot against France.

The treaty of an offensive and defensive alliance which had been signed at Vienna, by Count d'Haugwitz, after the victory of Austerlitz, ceded Hanover with other important possessions to Prussia in exchange for the margraviate of Anspach, the principality of Neufchatel, and the duchy of Cleves. Napoleon disposed of the margraviate of Anspach in favor of Bavaria. It will be remembered that the marching through this territory by Bernadotte's army had furnished Prussia with a pretext to manifest her animosity towards France. The principality of Neufchatel was given to Marshal Berthier; the duchy of Cleves was intended to form part of the grand-duchy of Berg to the sovereignty of which Murat was appointed. The balance of these exchanges was immensely in favor of Prussia, whom the Emperor, despite his well-founded grievances, wished to bind to him in a close alliance. Count d'Haugwitz, on his return to Berlin, found the Anglo-Russian spirit predominant in the King's councils, and the King himself engaged to the coalition. The negotiator of the Treaty of Vienna was accordingly blamed, and the King refused his ratification, pure and simple, demanding that the alliance with the French Empire should be neither offensive nor defensive, and consenting only to occupy Hanover temporarily, until the conclusion of peace between England and France; an event which alone in his eyes could justify Prussia's acquisition of this Electorate. Eminently pacific, this monarch wished to combine an apparent friendship for France with the maintenance of close relations with her enemies, a line of conduct which could not possibly satisfy anybody, and which could not fail to make Napoleon lose all confidence in the good faith of Prussia. The Emperor having been apprised of the hostility towards France which reigned in Prussia, sentiments which the King was powerless to restrain, refused to consider the Prussian Ministry as other than a hidden foe. This government, not daring to break off with ours, although it had torn up the Treaty of Vienna, which was so favorable to Prussia, had to accept another treaty the clauses of which were very much less in her favor. By the terms of the new stipulations Prussia was forced to accept the fee simple of Hanover (which for fear of offending England she had refused); and to close her harbors against the English ships—a clause which involved Prussia in the loss of four hundred vessels, seized upon by England. The exasperation of France increased after the conclusion of this new treaty, but was not yet sufficiently strong to break out. The establishment of the confederation of the Rhine, from which Napoleon looked for the support in Germany which he did not find in Prussia brought these hostile feelings, which did not dare to manifest themselves openly, to the highest degree of irritation. As a matter of fact the Prussian government held France responsible for the loss of the advantages of which it had deprived itself by its continual tergiversations.

While France and Prussia were in this equivocal situation the death of Mr. Pitt made way in the British Ministry for Mr. Fox. The new minister took advantage of a peculiar occurrence to approach the French government, and to address pacific overtures to France. An exile had proposed the murder of Napoleon to Mr. Fox. Mr. Fox, indignant at such a proposal, had brought it to the Emperor's knowledge. A correspondence ensued. Lord Yarmouth, who happened to be in France, where he was detained with the rest of the English travelers who were arrested on French territory at the time of the rupture of the peace of Amiens, and whose release was obtained by Mr. Fox, acted as intermediary between the two governments. The English cabinet having expressed the wish to negotiate in agreement with Russia, this proposal was evaded, and it was agreed upon that a Russian agent should be sent direct to Paris. This agent, M. d'Oubril, concluded a separate agreement with France. The negotiation with England was taking a favorable turn; it had been stipulated that she should retain possession of Malta and of the Cape of Good Hope, and should surrender all the other colonies. One of the principal difficulties, the maintenance of King Ferdinand of Sicily, would have been smoothed over, although the union of Malta and Sicily in the hands, or under the influence, of England had grave disadvantages, because the negotiations were inspired with good faith on both sides. In the course of these negotiations the French government had even undertaken, apart from the relinquishing of Malta, to consent to restore Hanover to England, without consulting Prussia, this power having shown that she attached but little value to this possession. An equivalent, and even larger indemnity of the kind likely to be agreeable to Prussia, had been stipulated for, it being proposed to give Prussia Fulda, Hoya, and some other principalities in exchange. Napoleon had undertaken to secure Prussia's consent to these arrangements. Peace was just going to be signed when Fox fell dangerously ill, and died a short time after. Lord Yarmouth was at once replaced by Lord Lauderdale, who was sent by the war party in London—who had conceived the hope of forming another coalition against us—with the mission to break off negotiations. Lord Lauderdale, in consequence, imperiously demanded, in place of the terms agreed upon with Lord Yarmouth, that each country should retain its respective possessions, with the exception of Hanover, which was occupied by Prussia, a proposal which amounted to this, that England would have kept all her conquests, and that neither Prussia nor France would have obtained any compensation from the British Ministry, since the only English possession on the continent which these powers had in their hands was Hanover. It was evident that peace was not desired in London, that all that was wanted was to obtain a declaration from France that Hanover should be restored to England, a declaration which would have rendered all reconciliation with Prussia out of the question. At the same time the Emperor of Russia refused to ratify the treaty concluded in Paris by M. d'Oubril. Lord Lauderdale demanded the return of his letters of credence.

Prussia, led astray by lying reports and perfidious maneuvers, such as are lavished by the English government, was daily assuming a more menacing attitude. The young Court of Berlin, the Queen and Prince Louis Ferdinand of Prussia breathed fire into the councils of the King, and set every head in Germany aglow. The beautiful Queen of Prussia, dressed in the uniform of the regiment which bore her name, used often to parade on horseback at its head, stimulating the enthusiasm of the troops. Prince Louis of Prussia, young, ardent but inexperienced, was the leader of a large number of young officers, who intoxicated with the remembrance of the great Frederick, and burning to measure themselves with the French, clamored aloud for war. They used to go and sharpen their swords on the steps of the French embassy, and broke the windows of the Prussian ministers whom they thought favorably disposed towards our country. Berlin was in a real state of delirium. The King was persuaded that in declaring war with France he would be carrying out the unanimous wishes of the nation. In the first days of the month of September, the Emperor, rendered anxious by Prussia's arming, and the order given to the Prussian royal guards to leave Berlin and to proceed to the frontier, desired M. de Knobelsdorf, the Prussian envoy to Paris, to furnish him with explanations on these matters. M. de Knobelsdorf, faithful to the system which had been adopted by the coalition, denied the arming, and stated that this piece of news was only the result of the action of the enemies of France and Prussia, who were jealous of the cordial understanding which existed between the two countries. Napoleon might have been lulled by so positive a denial, which of course had no other object in view. But on the first of the following October a note from M. de Knobelsdorf destroyed all illusions he may have entertained. This note contained three injunctions, the first and most important of which was formulated as follows: "The King expects that the French troops, whose presence in Germany is totally unjustifiable, shall immediately and without any exception, recross the Rhine, beginning their march back on the day on which the King expects the Emperor's reply, and continuing it without interruption, etc., etc." The Prussian ambassador added that he had to insist with earnestness—such were his literal words—on a prompt reply, so that in any case it might reach the King's headquarters on the 8th of October. An ultimatum formulated in such arrogant terms was nothing less than a declaration of war. Napoleon, forced to take up the gauntlet, was anxious not to annihilate Prussia. He earnestly wished for peace, and peace would have been secured, and Prussia would have been saved, if Fox had lived.

The Prussian Ministry was so anxious to commence hostilities that without awaiting the arrival of the Russian troops it suddenly opened the campaign. The Prussian armies were in front of the French cantonments provoking our soldiers with insults of every kind, before our army corps had received any orders to march.

The Emperor left St. Cloud for Mayence on September 25. He had sent his guard on in front. It had left Paris some days previously, driving in relays of carriages. The major-general had been ordered a fortnight previously to procure horses, and to ask the King of Bavaria for some, Napoleon fearing that his own, which had only been sent off on September the 11, might not arrive in time. Napoleon entered Germany on October 1, and went to lunch with the Prince-Primate at Aschaffenburg. He spent two days at Würtzburg in the palace of the Grand-Duke Ferdinand. The King of Würtemberg paid the Emperor a visit there to confer with him, and to make certain statements which were of common interest. During his stay in Würtzburg, Napoleon gave the necessary orders for establishing a great depot in this city. He repeated the orders he had already given and made fresh commands. Volumes would not suffice to describe the multitude of military and administrative measures which in his foresight he provided for every section of his army, and the precautions which he took against even the most improbable hazards of war. Suffice it to say that not even the minutest detail was overlooked.

Important successes were achieved in the first engagements, notably at the combat of Saalfeld, where the young Prince Louis of Prussia was the first victim of the war which he had helped to kindle. The Emperor ordered the major-general to write in his name to the King of Prussia "to express the sympathy which he felt for the sorrow which the news of the premature but glorious death of Prince Louis must have caused him." The rapidity of the march of our soldiers brought the Emperor to Jena on October the 13th. These dates should be remembered. He mounted on horseback forthwith, wishing to make use of the rest of the day to examine the locality, and, having concluded this investigation, he made arrangements for a battle which could be fought on the morrow. Part of the night was spent in widening a steep defile by which to convey pieces of artillery on to one of the heights which commanded the town of Jena and which he had chosen as his point of attack. The Emperor was present in person at this operation, and sometimes in his impatience would snatch up a torch to light the engineers.

Napoleon was on horseback giving his last orders before the break of day. Victory crowned his efforts, and before the end of the day the Prussian army was completely routed. It was only in the night and on the following days, that the immense results of this memorable encounter became known. When the Emperor reentered Jena in the evening, after having visited the field of battle with his accustomed solicitude—a pious duty in the fulfillment of which nothing was allowed to stand in his way—the whole extent of this great victory was not yet known. But in the night General Romeuf, Marshal Davout's aide-de-camp, arrived with the news of the victory won the same day, a few leagues off, by the Marshal, a victory which completed that of Jena, and which won for this intrepid warrior the warmest congratulations of the Emperor, and the title of Duke of Auerstadt. Abandoned by Bernadotte, who, yielding to a deplorable feeling of rivalry, not only refused his urgent appeals for assistance, but left the battlefield on some pretext, Davout remained alone with the three divisions of his army corps, in presence of the second Prussian army, which exceeded the number of his soldiers by more than half. The King of Prussia and the two first generals of the great Prussian army, the Duke of Brunswick, commander in chief, and Field-marshal Mollendorf, one of the comrades-in-arms of the great Frederick, were at the head of this army. Marshal Davout, in spite of his numerical inferiority, did not hesitate to oppose the enemy's passing. The Marshal's tenacity, backed by the coolness and intrepidity of the Gudin, Friant, and Morand divisions, won him a complete victory. These splendid successes, achieved before the arrival of the Russian troops, had destroyed the Prussian military forces and thrown open the gates of Berlin to the French army.

The Emperor, master of all the enemy's communications, and assured of victory, had written from Gera to the King of Prussia to declare that in spite of all his advantages, he was disposed to restore peace to the nations; that he had given the Prussian monarch no real cause for war; and that he asked him to remove from his councils the crackpots who, fourteen years previously, had wanted to take Paris, and who had provoked the present war. M. de Montesquiou, Napoleon's officer of ordinance and chamberlain, who had been commissioned to carry this letter, was detained at the enemy's outposts. The Emperor's letter was sent on to the King, who according to what he said, did not receive it till the following day when the fighting had already begun. But even if the King had received it on the previous evening its perusal would have done no good, so great was the excitement of our adversaries.

The remnants of the Prussian army, which had showed itself inferior to its great reputation, dispersed, and, flying in every direction, fell one after the other under the ardent pursuit of the French army. One month after entering the field the enemy's army no longer existed.

On the morrow of the battle of Jena, the Emperor called together the officers of the Saxon troops which had been taken prisoners, and, through my old comrade Moustier, who acted as interpreter, informed them that he would send them back home, if they would promise not to serve against France again. The Saxon prisoners numbered six thousand men and three hundred officers. This act of generosity won for Napoleon the sympathy of a prince worthy of esteem and respect, the King of Saxony, whose friendly feelings and loyalty towards him never failed, even in the midst of the cruelest adversity. At the same time it was one ally the less for Prussia.

Napoleon thereupon left for Berlin, halting at Weimar. The Grand duchess, sister of the Emperor Alexander, came to meet him with all her court, and asked for his protection for her States. The Emperor received her with courtesy, although her husband was commanding one of the Russian army corps, and gave orders that this new Athens, the home of the first litterateurs of Germany, should be respected. As he passed through Rosbach Napoleon gave orders for the removal of the monument which the Prussians had erected on this spot in remembrance of the battle of that name. This monument, which consisted of a small pillar, was transported to France. The scattered remnants of the vanquished army were pursued without respite in all directions. The troop amongst which the King of Prussia found himself tried to rally at Magdeburg. In his flight the King ran the risk of being taken prisoner at Weissensee, where he was cut off by a division of dragoons belonging to the French general Klein. The Prussian general Blücher saved his king by a trick, assuring General Klein that an armistice had been concluded. As a matter of fact the King had asked for an armistice but Napoleon had refused it. The general was blamed in an order of the day for having given credence to the mere word of the enemy in so serious and important a matter.

While the Emperor was at Wittemberg he received a letter from the Duke of Brunswick, which was brought by an officer of his household. The Duke wrote as a suppliant to commend his country to Napoleon's generosity, and to place it under

French protection. The Emperor took the opportunity to express himself very severely on the Duke of Brunswick's conduct in 1792, and in the present war, on the violent proclamation with which he had threatened the French nation with sword and fire, and the insolence with which he had summoned our brave army to evacuate Germany by gradual stages, and to flee without fighting before the Prussian eagles; and on his present abasement in coming today in person to implore the generosity of a people which he had dared to threaten with shameful chastisement. Napoleon declared that he would not take reprisals, that "General" Brunswick would be treated with all the respect Duke to a Prussian officer, but that he would only be treated as a Prussian general, and consequently not as a sovereign; but that the inhabitants of the Duchy of Brunswick would find generous enemies in the French soldiers. He repeated several times that to destroy the dwellings of peaceful citizens was a crime which could be repaired with time and money, but that to dishonor an army by requesting it to flee before the Prussian eagles was a baseness which only the man who advised it was capable of committing.

The same Duke of Brunswick who had excited this legitimate indignation was mortally wounded at Auerstadt by a cannon-shot in the head, and was conveyed to Brunswick. He did not await the French there, and was conveyed on to Altona where he breathed his last.

The Emperor, as a proof of the satisfaction which he had felt at Marshal Davout's splendid conduct and at the bravery of his army corps at Auerstadt, reserved for them the honor of being the first to enter Berlin. He betook himself there in person towards the end of October. He spent two days at Potsdam, where he visited the castle of Sans-Souci, which he explored with great interest. He made his guides explain to him with all sorts of particulars the sort of life that the great Frederick had led in this residence of his. Writing tables stained with ink were to be found in most of the rooms. There was an immense alcove in the King's bedroom in which Frederick the Great used to sleep on a small bed, which had been removed since then. In the same room were to be found a number of music-desks which had been used at the concerts, at which Frederick played the flute himself and performed pieces of music which he himself had composed with the members of his private orchestra. Everything in these rooms showed this great prince's contempt for luxury and pomp. Nothing had been changed since his death. The Emperor found the King's sword, his sash as general, and his cordon of the Order of the Black Eagle, at Potsdam. He seized upon these trophies with eagerness, considering them as priceless, and presented them to the Hotel des Invalides in Paris. We saw the apartment which Voltaire had occupied. The drawing room, or cabinet of this apartment was hung with a painted and varnished tapestry which represented apes and parrots perched on trellis-work. The governor of the castle told us that this was the same tapestry which had been there in Voltaire's time, and that the King had placed it in the French philosopher's rooms with a malicious intention.

M. Chastenet de Puységur's work *On the Art of War*, which we found in the library of Potsdam Castle, was opened at the very page where the King had finished reading it. A small volume, in bastard 18mo, bound in red morocco, printed in Holland, and marked with a "P" on the cover, as were all the other books in this library, was found lying on a small table. It was Montesquieu's work "On the Greatness and Decline of the Romans," and each page of this book was covered with marginal notes in the writing of the great Frederick. I carried this book to the Emperor, and he kept it in his library. M. de

Talleyrand, who heard me speak of it, asked me for it. I gave it to him, but was never able to get it back, though I frequently asked him for it.

The Emperor went from Potsdam to Charlottenburg, where he slept. This was one of the King's pleasances, at about one league's distance from Berlin. He was received on his entry into this beautiful residence with music, which was such that one might have supposed that it was performed by the buglers of numerous regiments of cavalry. As a matter of fact this music was performed by one of those mechanical musical instruments which are so common in Germany. This mechanism was in this case placed in a gallery, and was of extraordinary dimensions.

The harbingers in attendance found, in a drawer in the Queen's toilet table, a voluminous memorandum from Dumouriez on the best ways of injuring France.

The Emperor made a triumphal entry into Berlin, passing under the triumphal arch which adorns the Brandenburg gate, accompanied by his marshals, aides-de-camp, and the imperial foot-guards. He spent the best part of the month of November in the Prussian Capital. He occupied the King's palace or Schloss, which seemed an unfavorable omen for the future of Prussia, for Berlin was the only capital which Napoleon had conquered in which he stayed in the sovereign's residence. Napoleon's stay in Berlin was marked by respect towards the members of the royal family, by the act of clemency with which he dealt with Prince Hatzfeldt, and by the famous decree on the continental blockade.

England, abusing her maritime supremacy to the last degree, had forbidden all trade by sea between France and the neutral powers; and to carry out this measure the British Ministry had declared the coasts of France, and of the countries occupied by the French troops, to be in a state of blockade, although as a matter of fact this blockade only existed on paper.

This unexampled attempt to violate international law—which only acknowledges as blockaded a harbor that is literally blockaded by the presence of a naval force—drove Napoleon to take just reprisals by forbidding trade of any kind with England. The approach of any coast belonging to countries subjected to French arms was forbidden to the English. Any Englishman so found was declared prisoner by this mere fact; any ship having communicated with the coast of England, or with any of the English colonies, was declared to be a lawful prize; all goods of English manufacture were confiscated; all English letters, no matter what they were, were seized in the post and destroyed. The Emperor was not blind to the rigor of these measures; to the English maritime blockade he opposed the continental blockade. England forbade him the sea; he forbade her the continent. Such is the origin of the decree of Berlin, which declared the British Isles in a state of blockade. This decree was immediately notified to the maritime powers who were allied with France, and its execution strictly enforced.

The result of the battles of Jena and Auerstadt had been the total annihilation of the fine Prussian army which had stepped on to the field of battle with as much foolhardiness as courage. It vanished, to make use of Napoleon's expression, like an autumn mist before the rising sun. Generals in chief, generals in command of army corps, princes, infantry, cavalry, artillery—all was gone. The pursuit of the disbanded and scattered remnants of this army in every direction resembled a hunt. All the fortified places without exception, some of which were the strongest in Europe, fell one after another into the hands of the French, who had but to present themselves at the gates to have these opened to them. All that remained to the King of Prussia was twenty thousand men fleeing, dispersed, beyond the Oder, and the only refuge that this unfortunate monarch could find was at Koenigsberg.

The surrender of Magdeburg reminded one of the taking of Ulm: twenty generals, eight hundred officers, and twenty-two thousand soldiers marched out past Marshal Ney. There were taken fifty-four flags, five standards, eight hundred pieces of cannon, a million of powder, a large pontoon train and an immense amount of artillery materials.

Prince Jérôme, commanding an army composed of the French allies, was commissioned to reduce Silesia. He besieged and carried, one after the other, the seven great fortified places which protect this province. He was summoned from Silesia to join the *Grande Armée,* and to take part in the combats which followed upon the entry of the French into Warsaw. The reports mentioned the distinguished services which he rendered there, and the courage which often drove him right up to the enemy's outposts. He afterwards returned to Silesia and had the glory of achieving the conquest of this province. The Emperor, desiring to stimulate the spirit of emulation among the troops of the confederation of the Rhine, sent to the King of Würtemberg a part of the flags which had been captured at Glogau by the Würtembergers.

Napoleon had entered Berlin with a soul ulcerated and filled with bitterness against those who had provoked the war which had just brought him to this capital. This unexpected triumph, these decisive and immense results, however flattering they might be for his pride, would gladly have been bartered by him for an alliance which was now out of the question. They were the outward and visible signs of the disappearance of this favorite political dream. So also his words towards those who had lighted or fanned the flames which had just devoured their country, were incisive, severe, and humiliating. Fidelity to the King of Prussia no longer seemed a virtue to him. He transformed all excesses of zeal for the interests of this King into the crime of high treason. His resentment manifested itself in bitter complaints—which, however, were fully justified—against the Queen, who had allowed herself to be carried by unreasoning hatred far beyond the limits to which her sex and her rank should have restrained her; and he compared her to Armida, in her madness, setting fire to her own palace. The immoderate exaltation of this princess had been as fatal to the Prussian monarchy as the excessive prudence of her husband.

On the other hand the Emperor treated the members of the royal family, who had remained in Berlin, with respect. He paid a visit to the King's uncle, Prince Ferdinand, whose son had been killed at Saalfeld, and tried to speak some words of consolation. He also visited the widow of Prince Henry, and the King's two sisters, one of whom was in child-bed, and the other ill. He treated these princesses with delicate attentions, and provided for the wants of the second, who, in the confusion of the times, had been left deprived of all the comforts of life.

Napoleon gave orders that the pensions of Princess Henry, and of Prince and Princess Ferdinand, should be paid to them regularly, and replaced in possession of their revenues and pensions two sisters of the Duke of Brunswick, who had been mortally wounded at one of the last two great battles.

Several small principalities, independent of, though allied to, Prussia, were exempted from contributing to the war levies. The city of Leipzig was relieved of the extraordinary levy which had been laid upon her. The English goods which had been seized there were left to the merchants, who bought them in for ten million francs. The levy imposed on the Electorate of Hesse-Cassel was put to the charge of the Elector's private debtors, and these were forced to pay into the army treasury the sums which this prince had lent them. In one word the Emperor did his best to diminish, as far as possible, the burden of the war which weighed on the towns and minor states which had been drawn, against their will, into the struggle between Prussia and France. A suspension of hostilities had been signed at Charlottenburg, during the Emperor's stay in Berlin, where he was endeavoring to negotiate for peace. The King of Prussia having refused to ratify it, on the ground that a part of the Prussian States, which the French troops were to occupy, was in the possession of the Russians, the Emperor left Berlin for Posen.

If Prussia and her army were annihilated by our great victories, the Russian armies remained intact. Although the season was advanced the Emperor could not hesitate to march against them. The campaign in Poland was announced in a proclamation to the army, which was dated December 2, the second anniversary of the proclamation of the Empire. The approach of the French army had revived the undying hopes of the Poles. The people were arming in every direction, and in addresses and by deputations prayed for the reestablishment of their nationality. Napoleon would, however, make no promises. He awaited that the issue of this campaign, as he himself said, should permit him to solve "this great political problem, of which God alone, Who holds in His hands the combination of all events, was the arbitrator." Before leaving Posen, the Emperor concluded a treaty of peace with the Elector of Saxony, whose virtues and fidelity he held in high esteem. By the terms of this treaty the title of King was given to this prince, who after the Peace of Tilsitt, added to it that of Grand Duke of Warsaw.

A decree ordered the erection of the Temple of Glory in Paris. This monument was to bear on its front the words: "The Emperor Napoleon to the Soldiers of the Great Army," and orders were given that a plan of this building, which was to occupy the site of the Madeleine church, should be laid before the Emperor with the least possible delay.

The Emperor went from Posen towards Warsaw. The roads were in a fearful state. Duroc, the Grand Marshal of the Palace, whose carriage was upset under way, broke his shoulder-bone. It was only on the morrow that he could be transported to Warsaw.

The Emperor's entry into this ancient capital of Poland excited a state of universal delirium. He only spent three days there. Hearing that the Russian generals had stopped their retrograde movement and were marching to the front, Napoleon left Warsaw at one o'clock in the morning of December 23 to go and encounter them. Several fights took place, notably at Nasielk, where Colonel Philippe Ségur was taken prisoner, after bravely defending himself. When Napoleon arrived at Nasielk the Russians were evacuating this town. He followed so close upon them that he entered the town before his servants had finished cleaning out the hut where he was to pass the night. A corpse was hidden under some straw in this hut, and the servants had barely the time to remove it, almost under his eyes.

The encounters at Pultusk and Golymin ended this short campaign. The Russians had heavy losses at these places, but were preserved from certain annihilation by the heaviness of the mud, which was so thick that the cannon got stuck. Even soldiers perished in this slough, without being able to extricate themselves. It may be added that in the course of these trying marches, the indomitable courage and patient valor of the soldiers did not for an instant abandon them. The sight of the Emperor marching in the midst of the ranks on roads soaked with rain consoled them for all their sufferings, and their natural gaiety helped them to bear up against all their troubles. Sometimes a joke passed from mouth to mouth and excited general laughter. A soldier, seeing the Emperor struggling painfully against the mud and swaying on his horse which slipped at every step, began to hum this refrain of a song that was fashionable at the time:

On ne saurait trop embellir
Le court escape de la vie.*

This parody on Cynéas's advice to Pyrrhus brought a smile to the lips of Napoleon, who was not vexed at the sally. Their privations, however, and the bad weather irritated the soldiers against Poland. There was always some epigram suggested to them by their privations. They had remembered four Polish words amongst others, and used to make up dialogues with them. These were *kleba* (bread), *voda* (water), *niema* (no), *zara* (at once). The soldiers used to say: "When you ask the Poles for bread, they never fail to answer '*Niema kleba*'; but if you ask them for water *(voda),* oh, then it's '*zara zara zara!*'"

The alternations of snow, frost, and thaw rendered marching impossible, and the Emperor returned to Warsaw. He spent the whole month of January, 1807, there. During this halt, which gave the army a rest, Napoleon gave fêtes and concerts to the Polish ladies. He did not remain insensible to the charms of one of them, whose tenderness and devotion did not fail him in the days of misfortune.

Prince de Bénévent presented General Baron de Vincent to the Emperor at Warsaw. The Baron was the bearer of a letter from the Emperor of Austria, whose protestations and offers did not entirely reassure Napoleon on the equivocal attitude of this power. General Andréossy, French ambassador to Vienna, had described the tendencies of the court of Austria as being very suspicious, repeating this first warning, which he had given in the month of September, towards the end of October of the same year, 1806. He sent word that this court was certainly mixed up in the political conspiracy; that Austria, with respect to the rest of the Continent, was in the same position as Prussia had been before the battle of Austerlitz; that Count Stadion was still at the head of affairs, and that everything was directed by him; that, under pretext of cantoning the Austrian army, the troops of the Emperor Francis were being assembled on the Polish frontier; that, instead of disarming, Austria maintained the same attitude, and that her standing army might be estimated at one hundred and thirty thousand men; that, besides, the position and successes of the Great Army was the one object of Austria's politics and those of the Continent.

Marshal Ney wrote to the major-general that the examination of prisoners had informed him, apart from particulars concerning the movements and operations of the Russian and Prussian troops, "that it was generally believed that on the first successes obtained by the Russians—successes which they thought certain by reason of their numerical superiority—the Austrian army would give a diversion in Moravia and march into Silesia."

An old Polish soldier, born in 1690, was presented to the Emperor during his stay in Warsaw. This old man of one hundred and seventeen was without any infirmity, and in

---

* You can't embellish enough
The short moment of life.

the full enjoyment of his memory. He had known King Sobieski, and remembered the stories which his father had told him of the battle at which he was present when the King of Poland defeated the Turks and forced them to raise the siege of Vienna in 1683. In answer to a petition, written in Polish and in a still firm handwriting, which was handed to him by this patriarch of days gone by, Napoleon ordered that a pension of one hundred napoleons should be paid to him, and one year's pension in advance.

A serious attack upon our cantonments, made by the Russian army, forced Napoleon to take the field again, in spite of the extreme cold. He left Warsaw to fight with the Russians the battle of Preussisch-Eylau, which was bloody and hardly contested. A horrible spectacle was the sight of this battlefield, covered with corpses, and furrowed with blood, which lay in long lines mapped out on the snow. We had slept the evening before at the little village of Eylau, and returned there on the evening after the battle. The Emperor deeply regretted the loss of one of his aides-de-camp, General Corbineau the elder, who was killed while carrying an order in the course of the engagement. We had passed the night sleeping on the same straw with this officer, and he had expressed a vague presentiment that the morrow would be fatal to him.

One of the most daring cavalry actions known in the history of war must not be passed over in silence here. A body of twenty-four squadrons—composed for the most part of the division of General d'Hautpoul's cuirassiers and mounted grenadiers of the imperial guard, commanded by General Lepic—charged the Russian squares, These intrepid cavalrymen broke into the center of the Russian army, wheeled round, charged again, and forced their way right up to the third line of the enemy's infantry, which they annihilated. General d'Hautpoul was mortally wounded during this magnificent charge. Before dying he had strength enough left him to write to the Emperor to express his devotion to him. Napoleon consoled the last moments of this brave soldier with the following letter:

"Preuss. Eylau, Feb. 9, 1807

"M. LE GENERAL D'HAUTPOUL—I was extremely touched by the letter which you have written to me. Your wound is not such as to deprive your son of his father. You will live to lead other charges at the head of your brave division, and to cover yourself with fresh glory. You and your children may rely upon the interest I take in you.

"(Signed) NAPOLEON"

The Emperor, by a decree dated from Osterode on March 6, 1807, ordered that an equestrian statue representing General d'Hautpoul in his cuirassier uniform, should be made from the metal of twenty-four cannon which had been captured at Eylau.

Marshal Augereau, also, was wounded in this disastrous battle. This wound and acute rheumatic pains, with which he was tormented, temporarily affected his mind. I saw him, by chance, riding up to the Emperor, with his hat in his hand. The perspiration was pouring from his head, though it was bitterly cold at the time. This Marshal, usually so brilliant on the field of battle, came to say that he no longer understood anything about the maneuvers, and asked to be replaced. Napoleon listened to him with kindness, and said a few words of consolation, and then commissioned General Compans to take over the temporary command of his army corps. On the morrow permission was granted to the Marshal to return to France to attend to his health.

The Russians claimed the victory for themselves and, according to their custom, had a *Te Deum* chanted at St. Petersburg. But during the night which followed this bloody day, they decamped, leaving us masters of the field of battle, with many thousands of prisoners, forty cannon, and sixteen flags. One of the Russian army corps which had fought at Eylau, fell in, on its retreat, with the fifth corps which General Savary was commanding in the absence of Marshal Lannes, who was lying sick at Warsaw. From this encounter came the battle of Ostrolenka, which is mentioned in the reports as a combat, but at which, as a matter of fact, three divisions of the French army were engaged. The Russians were completely routed. Napoleon expressed his satisfaction at the way General Savary had acted, and awarded him the grand decoration of the Legion of Honor. General Savary returned to his service as aide-de-camp to the Emperor.

Napoleon spent three days at Eylau occupied in arranging for the removal of the wounded, and in hurrying on the arrival of provisions required for the army. Some days after the battle he replied to the proposals which the King of Prussia had made to him. He expressed himself anxious to put an end to Prussia's misfortunes. He offered to conclude a separate peace with him, and to reorganize the Prussian monarchy, which, as an intermediary power and as a barrier against Russia, was necessary for the tranquility of the whole of Europe. General Bertrand was charged with this letter. The King's answer was brought to Osterode by the Prussian general Kleist, who had orders to add some verbal explanations. The King of Prussia could not resign himself to sign a treaty for which his ally was to be excluded. He proposed the assembly of a congress at which Prussia, Russia, England, and Sweden should be represented. Prussia had just bound herself to England by a convention, and had already received the first installments of an English subsidy. She hoped to find a powerful ally in this state, and thought that a treaty made in conjunction with England and Russia would be less disadvantageous to her than a separate peace. The Emperor, in his turn, answered that the inevitable delay of a congress was not in accordance with the present situation in Prussia, although he also desired to come to an understanding with Russia and England. This correspondence resulted in nothing, though the communications between the headquarters of the belligerent parties were not interrupted during the time which Napoleon spent at Osterode and Finckenstein.

From Eylau the Emperor went to take up his winter quarters, at first at Osterode, so as to be near his cantonments, and spent the end of February and the whole month of March here. He issued numerous orders from Osterode to provide for means of subsistence, flour, wines, brandies, rum, and beer for the soldiers and the invalids, and forage for the horses. He ordered at the same time that detailed reports on the state of the storehouses which had been concentrated at Pultusk, Warsaw, and other places, should be laid before him. He asked the heads of the various corps for information as to how their soldiers were living. Provisions for the soldiers were the first object of his care, and he also paid great attention to the state of the hospitals. Then followed orders to provide for the salubrity and safety of the cantonments, for remounting the cavalry, to bring up distant corps, and thus to reinforce the army; to form provisional regiments at Mayence, and to march them to Potsdam and other places; to recall French divisions, the Polish legion, and the Polish lancers from Italy; and to form with the latter an observation corps, the command of which was given to the Polish general Zayonchek. Other orders provided for the distribution of the funds allotted to the artillery, to the engineers, to the commissariat, accoutrement and transport services, for the awarding of recompenses, and for watching the movements of the enemy.

On April 1 Napoleon went to live in the Castle of Finckenstein, where he spent the months of April and May. During his stay here the same labors were the object of his constant activity. He used to make short excursions from Finckenstein to visit the army corps, and to see the bridge which he had had built over the Vistula. In the prolonged inactivity of his residence in winter quarters Napoleon showed that he knew how to ally patience and tact with the impetuous outbursts of his genius. Work was his element and beguiled his impatience. The necessity of preparing decisive triumphs to master the enemies, who allowed him no hope of safety but in victory; to keep his allies to their duty, and to reassure France, all these duties made his time of waiting, so advantageously used by him, appear very short.

As a matter of fact he had barely the time necessary for the operations of the war on the one hand, and the care of the government of his vast empire on the other.

Chapter VII

It was during his stay at the Castle of Finckenstein that the Emperor heard of the results of General Sebastiani's brilliant embassy to Constantinople. I will not enter into the particulars of the important services which this ambassador rendered to the Porte on this occasion in the interests of France. Napoleon highly praised the energy and skill with which General Sebastiani had raised the courage of the Turks, and had stimulated them to put their capital and the Bosphorus into a state of defense, as well as the activity and the vigor which he had shown in directing the works himself, and in triumphing over the Ottoman apathy. The complete success obtained by our ambassador made French influence predominant in the Divan. The Emperor himself had taken care to keep up the Sultan's favorable feelings towards France. He kept writing him pressing letters, urging him to place himself at the head of his troops, reminding him of the glory of the Selims and the Amuraths—in one word he had aroused in this weak, but really gifted prince a feeling of generous indignation against the oppression of England. Selim, in his enthusiasm for Napoleon, and disobeying the law of the Koran, which forbids all representations of the human face, had desired to have a portrait of the Emperor, following the example of Sultan Mustapha, who, in his admiration for the great Frederick, had placed a portrait of this king in his seraglio—the only portrait that had ever entered its doors. Selim, in exchange sent the Emperor his portrait, which was placed in the Emperor's cabinet. It was the chevalier Amédée Jaubert who, passing through Constantinople on his way back from a diplomatic mission to Persia, brought this portrait, together with the portrait of Feth-Aly-Shah, back to Finckenstein.

It was at Finckenstein also that the Emperor decided on the plan of the monument which he wished to dedicate to the Great Army, and the erection of which he had ordered on December 2, 1806. The buildings of the Madeleine church, which had been abandoned in an advanced state of construction in 1790, and as to the occupation of which Napoleon had frequently hesitated, were definitely appropriated to this monument. The committee of the Institut, charged with the inspection of the plans submitted for the competition, had forwarded various plans, and had indicated which amongst them they had considered the most suitable. Napoleon had charged M. Fontaine, his architect, to be present at the inspection of the plans, which was to take place at the

Ministry of the Interior, and to report to him on the subject. This report not having reached the Emperor in time, he decided to accept M. Vignon's plan, which had only obtained the second place, but which pleased the Emperor by the grandeur of its dimensions and form. What the Emperor wanted was a building, not of the style of modern churches, but which would recall antique monuments, and be superior both in majesty and magnificence to the finest buildings which antiquity had bequeathed to us. No wood, and nothing but iron, marble, and gold were to be used in the construction of this building. M. Vignon's plan fulfilled some of the necessary conditions, but was wanting in general arrangement and in points of detail. M. Fontaine's remarks made Napoleon regret not to have awaited his architect's report before coming to a decision.

As the author of the successful plan had no practical experience of building, M. Rondelet, an architect, was associated with M. Vignon, to superintend the carrying out of the construction, M. Fontaine having refused the post. M. Rondelet was the most celebrated pupil of the great Soufflot, who, on his deathbed, had mentioned him as the man most capable of finishing the great cathedral of St. Geneviève, which has since become the Panthéon.

The Madeleine, a grandiose specimen of architecture under the Empire, and constructed on the model of the temples of ancient Greece, is not adapted to the requirements of a church. It was proposed to place Napoleon's tomb in this building, and this plan had the advantage of giving the founder of the imperial edifice a last home in a monument, at once religious and national, which had been erected under his reign. But the Restoration decided otherwise, and the Madeleine was purely and simply restored to divine worship.

The Emperor received the Turkish and Persian ambassadors at Finckenstein. Mirza-Rizza, a great Persian nobleman, arrived in Warsaw early in March, at the same time as a Turkish ambassador. The Persian envoy was summoned, towards the end of April, to Finckenstein where he was treated with great respect, and put into relations with the Secretary of state—Maret, Duke of Bassano. The negotiations only lasted a few days, and the treaty was signed on May 8. The learned orientalist Jaubert, dragoman secretary to the imperial cabinet, acted as intermediary between the two negotiators. The Persian ambassador offered the Emperor some pearls and shawls on this occasion, representing them as coming from himself, because he feared that they might give a lower idea than he wished of his sovereign, as a good courtier, or from a feeling of national pride. He pretended that his master's presents had not yet arrived, and presented his own, saying that he prayed the lion to receive the gifts of the ant. He accompanied Napoleon to a great review following the Emperor step by step amidst the ranks of the soldiers, walking on the ploughed fields with his beautiful slippers and trailing robe. It was very hot weather, and he returned to Finckenstein quite worn out. Throwing himself on his couch, he kept exclaiming, exhausting the whole vocabulary of admiration, "How great! How fine! How magnificent!" Below his breath he muttered: "I am dying of fatigue." The Emperor used to walk out with him in the gardens of Finckenstein every day. One day the poor ambassador found himself in a very awkward position. His supply of henna had run out, a red substance which he used for dyeing his nails and the palms of his hands, and he was as much ashamed to appear before the Emperor with white hands as the habitué of our drawing rooms in Paris would have been to present himself without gloves. One day the conversation turned on the history of Alexander, and the ambassador said that the true history of this conqueror was to be found in Persia. Mirza-Rizza departed on his way back home immediately after the signing of the treaty. He was followed shortly afterwards by General Gardanne, the Emperor's aide-de-camp, who was accredited as ambassador to the court of Teheran. Napoleon at the same time sent some distinguished officers to be attached to his legation. They were intended to act as instructors and auxiliaries to the Persian army. As to General Gardanne, who went to Teheran in the hopes of finding a treasure which had formerly been buried in this capital by his grandfather, his searches were in vain.

The Turkish ambassador, Seïb-Wahid-Emin-Effendi, arrived in Finckenstein a month later. He was as much lacking in wit and intelligence as Mirza-Rizza had been distinguished for these qualities, and was essentially a formal and fastidious person. Commissioned to tighten the bonds of friendship which united us to Turkey, he did not consider himself vested with sufficient powers to conclude a real alliance. During a conference which took place between him and the Emperor in the garden of the castle of Finckenstein, Napoleon urged him to conclude, making signs with his hand to try and make the Turkish ambassador understand that the Russians had made us proposals of peace. At last, to compel him to come to a decision, the Emperor declared to him that if no arrangement was come to between France and Turkey, peace would inevitably be made with Russia to the exclusion of the Porte. Wahid contented himself with answering that he needed fresh instructions, that the answer to his letter would not occasion a delay of more than forty days, and that he begged the Emperor to wait. Napoleon, who could not submit to delay, was made very impatient by this obstinacy.

In the meanwhile events were progressing, and in the interests of the campaign Napoleon left for Danzig. He summoned the Turkish ambassador to join him there, and to continue the negotiations with the Duke of Vicence, who was not a whit more successful. All these conferences came to nothing, and hostilities with the Russians recommenced. Wahid-Effendi proceeded to Paris, where he soon heard of Sultan Selim's decision, which deprived him of his powers.

The Treaty of Tilsitt was signed, and Turkey had missed her opportunity of uniting herself in a close alliance with France, which would have been advantageous to both states. The failure of Napoleon's efforts to bring the Porte to this line of action was of a nature to cool his feelings towards this state; however, in spite of the obstinacy which had been shown in these delays, either owing to the incapacity of the representative to Finckenstein, or to the influence of Russia on the Divan, the good understanding between Turkey and France did not appear to be in the least diminished; but M. de Talleyrand showed himself very offended that anybody but himself should have been chosen to treat either with Turkey or with Persia.

The war with Sweden continued. Marshal Mortier received orders to occupy Pomerania and to besiege Stralsund, the garrison of which was a menace to our lines of communication. The Emperor considered the war with Sweden bad policy. He bitterly regretted that the Swedes had set fire to the fine faubourg of Stralsund and that two thousand of the inhabitants were in consequence homeless.

He deplored the sufferings caused to a nation which was our natural ally. He had in consequence expressed a wish to Marshal Mortier that a suspension of hostilities might be concluded, thanks to which friendly relations might once more be established between the Swedes and ourselves. This wish for a truce was realized, although no definite treaty of peace was concluded. An armistice which had been granted for a period of ten days only, and which the Emperor had had prolonged, lasted until about the middle of July. Peace had just been signed at Tilsitt, when the armistice was broken by the King of Sweden. It looked as if he had awaited the very moment when Napoleon could dispose of all his forces to commit this imprudent act. The Swedes were thereupon expelled from Pomerania, which was occupied by the French troops, as also from Stralsund and the island of Rugen. The King, having in this way lost his possessions in Germany, returned to Sweden.

During his stay at Osterode, the Emperor had undertaken the siege of Danzig, which, for the success of his military operations, it was highly important for him to occupy. He had intended to appoint Marshal Victor to the command of the besieging army, but this soldier was taken prisoner on his way to his post by the Prussian Schill, whom we shall see playing a more important part in the war of 1809 against Austria. Marshal Lefebvre was then commissioned to conduct the siege, Marshal Kalkreuth, on his side, defending Danzig with stubborn courage. The Emperor Alexander and the King of Prussia, feeling how necessary it was to save this fortified place, sent reinforcements, but all their attempts to raise the siege were in vain. An English corvette, the Sans Peur—carrying twenty-four cannons, and freighted with powder and cannon balls—was boarded and captured by a picket of the regiment of Paris. Lacking it is true in deep science, Marshal Lefebvre displayed all his bravery and all his activity in the task which had been entrusted to him, and General Chasseloup directed the operations of the siege with skill. At last, after a resistance of two months, which did great credit to the Prussian general, at the very moment when the town was going to be taken by storm, Kalkreuth asked to capitulate. In recognition of his brave defense Napoleon granted him honorable terms. The same day, Marshal Lefebvre made his entry into the town.

It was at Finckenstein, on May 29, that the Emperor heard the news of the surrender of Danzig. He at once sent General Rapp to take over the command of this place. Napoleon went himself to spend two days there, and to visit his new conquest, He approved of the works which had been executed by the engineers, and complimented Marshal Lefebvre on his splendid conduct. He created him Duke of Danzig, and handsomely endowed the new title. He authorized him to accept a considerable sum of money, the exact amount of which I forget, which the states had offered of their own accord to the Marshal, but which he had refused to accept without the Emperor's permission. On leaving the Sovereign, the new Duke slipped. He was not superstitious, and so, picking himself up, he said good-naturedly: "Egad, my good town of Danzig is badly paved." Napoleon having distributed numerous rewards amongst the soldiers who had taken part in the siege, returned to Finckenstein by way of Marienburg, to prepare to resume the offensive.

In spite of his success and of the satisfactory state of his army, which had recruited itself in the cantonments, the Emperor was anxious on account of his difficult situation between obstinate enemies and doubtful allies, and on account also of his prolonged absence from France. He was not in ignorance of the fact that it was the victory of Jena alone which had prevented the Austrian Ministry from declaring itself against him, and the Spanish cabinet from attacking him. He strongly inclined to prefer an advantageous peace to continuing the war, although he considered himself very well able to stand against his enemies. Napoleon had showed the most conciliatory disposition. He had offered to conclude a treaty with the Russians on the same conditions as those which were signed in the preceding month of July by M. d'Oubril, at Paris. He was not indisposed to restore his provinces and capital to the King of Prussia. The Prussian cabinet had declared that it could not separate its cause from that of its ally, and, as a matter of fact, it was in the hands of Russia. The Austrian cabinet, which had sent M. Vincent to Warsaw, where the Emperor had left him with M. de Talleyrand, wanted nothing better than to intervene in the negotiation. Forced to declare itself, Austria had offered her mediation with the mental reservation of swaying the negotiations, or of crushing us in case reserves came upon us. The Emperor had accepted the mediation of this power so as to be consistent with the pacific sentiments which he had expressed. England approved, Prussia seemed inclined to accept, but the Emperor of Russia dissuaded the King of Prussia. The Czar's armies had been strongly reinforced, and the half-success of the battle of Eylau, which his generals represented to him as a victory, had given Alexander confidence. He had made tempting promises to the King of Prussia, and had induced this prince to conclude, at Bartenstein, a convention which was a trial of the agreements which were negotiated and concluded in 1813, with greater success. The object of this convention was the reestablishment of the Prussian monarchy, the Restoration of their independence to the German States, and the realization of important projects against France in the event of the war having a favorable termination. England and Sweden agreed to the Bartenstein convention, but Austria refused to take part in it. In the meanwhile the reunion of a general congress in which all the belligerent powers in Europe were to be represented had been proposed to the Emperor and agreed to by him under certain reservations. The allies expressed a wish to hear on what basis Napoleon proposed to treat, while they themselves suggested none. Napoleon had answered without hesitation that his bases would be equality, reciprocity and a system of equitable compensations. Our enemies no doubt considered this moderation as a proof of weakness on his part, and all the more in consequence staked their hopes on the hazards of war, for, at the very moment when it was thought that the last obstacle to the congress had been removed, the Russian army marched out of its encampment and attacked the French army.

The consequence of this attack was to force the Emperor to leave Finckenstein hastily. I followed him as far as Danzig. I was detained by sickness for a fortnight in this town, at the end of which time I rejoined Napoleon. Marshal Ney, attacked by a large portion of the Russian army, made a firm resistance. He retreated in good order and held his own until the French army had been assembled. It was then Napoleon who took the offensive. The victories of Heilsberg and Friedland followed. This last battle was decisive, for the Russian army was crushed and forced to take refuge beyond the Niemen. The defeat of her allies deprived Prussia of her last resources and did away with all hope of reestablishing her affairs. The Emperor of Russia was reduced to ask for an armistice, during which negotiations for peace might be entered upon. Napoleon made no difficulty in accepting this proposal and dispatched General Duroc to arrange the conditions of the truce.

My health having been restored by rest, and our great victories having also contributed to my cure, I was impatient to rejoin the Emperor. On my way through Koenigsberg, where General Savary, whose services and unfailing fidelity were recompensed six months later with the title of Duke of Rovigo, had been left as governor of the city, I saw Prince de Bénévent who was awaiting the Emperor's orders there. I preceded him by some days and proceeded in company with the Count de Turenne, chamberlain and orderly officer, to headquarters. We passed through the forest of Wehlau, which was said to be full of peasants who had taken refuge there, and who used to sally out on expeditions against the rear of the army. Although we were without escort we were lucky enough not to make any bad encounters.

The Emperor had been in Tilsitt three days when I arrived there. Almost simultaneously, General Duroc arrived from carrying the ratification of the armistice, concluded between the two armies, to the Emperor Alexander's headquarters. I heard that this was his second journey and that an interview between the two Emperors had been agreed upon. It duly took place, two days later, in a tent which had been erected on a raft moored in the middle of the Niemen. Napoleon who had arrived first crossed through the tent and went to meet the Emperor Alexander. The two sovereigns, with a spontaneous movement fell into each other's arms and embraced. It was a beautiful sight and its impressiveness was increased by the cheers of the two armies drawn up on either side of the river, cheers which starting from the right shore and echoed back from the left, mingled in one loud shout. A second interview to which the Emperor Alexander brought the King of Prussia took place on the same raft, on the morrow. The two foreign sovereigns afterwards established themselves in the town of Tilsitt, which had been rendered neutral for the time being. The two armies kept their respective positions on the two banks of the Niemen and a perfectly friendly understanding grew up between them.

On the day on which the two Emperors returned into the town, a dinner was given at Napoleon's quarters. On the morrow and following days they rode out together, accompanied by the King of Prussia. The object of their rides was to visit the various encampments of their armies. They held reviews, they ate of the soldiers' soup, and paid each other all the usual compliments. The Emperor Alexander took pleasure in exhibiting his picked men, the Russian guards and the Cossack regulars. Napoleon admired them, and even distributed some decorations of the Legion of Honor amongst them. So intimate did the two Emperors become, that, when on returning from their excursions the Czar was to dine with Napoleon, the latter would not allow him to go home to change his dress. He used to send somebody to the house where Alexander lived to fetch the things he needed. He used to send him his own cravats and handkerchiefs through his valet. He placed his big gold traveling bag at his disposal, and as Alexander had praised the carvings of the various fittings, and the way in which the bag was arranged, Napoleon made him a present of it before they separated. When they returned before the dinner-hour it was for the sake of a free *tête-à-tête*. On such occasions they used to leave the King of Prussia, and go into a little gallery which adjoined the Emperor's work-room. Sometimes Napoleon would bring the Czar into his study and ask for his maps, which included one of Turkey in Europe. I have seen them bending over this map and then continuing their conversation as they walked up and down. Schemes of partition were occupying them. Constantinople was the only point on which they were not visibly agreed.

It was easy to see that Napoleon did not wish these questions to give rise to any discussions likely to trouble the harmony which had been reestablished between them, and that a tacit agreement had been come to, to maintain, provisionally at least, the *status quo*. It would, moreover, be difficult to assign any results to the conversations which I overheard in the study, which for the most part began but did not end; or having begun outside, ended there. Nothing besides was written on this subject. In their familiar conversations the two Emperors often spoke of home politics and forms of government. Alexander used to describe a hereditary crown as a source of abuses, while Napoleon could not find arguments enough to prove that it was precisely a hereditary monarchy which assured the peace and the happiness of the people. The Emperor Napoleon in relating these conversations used to say that if the opinions expressed by Alexander were not the outcome of what he had been taught by his tutor, the Swiss colonel Laharpe, they were the effect of his tendencies to mysticism. It may be supposed, seeing that Alexander's conduct was not entirely straightforward, that his arguments, though seriously expressed, were only spoken with a purpose, and were far from being his real opinions.

The Emperor Alexander was tall, well-built, and elegant. He spoke French without any accent, and always expressed himself with grace and dignity. His way of receiving people was familiar rather than imposing, and his manners were open, though his look was not always a frank one. He used to listen to Napoleon with extreme interest, and behaved with filial deference towards him. He used to walk with his head slightly bent on one side, from the habit of bending down to listen through deafness in one ear. Possibly he wanted to resemble Alexander the Great in this respect.

The Queen of Prussia came to Tilsitt, ten or twelve days after the Niemen interview, accompanied by her mistress of the robes, Countess de Voss. The Queen was a woman of middle height but very imposing, and her profile was an admirable one. Her beauty was splendid although she was at that time no longer in the freshness of youth, being thirty-two years old. I saw her when she came to dine with the Emperor. She had relied on the resources of her wit and her charms to obtain better terms for Prussia. But though Napoleon affected a gallant and respectful bearing towards her, all the complaints, prayers, and importunities of this deeply humiliated queen, all the feminine wiles to which she had recourse were bound to fail, and as a matter of fact did fail before the stern exigencies of politics. Besides, the Queen had come after all had been settled. She effected nothing but to hasten on the conclusion of the two treaties with Russia and Prussia.

On the morrow of the Queen's arrival, three treaties were signed. One of these was between France and Russia, another was between France and Prussia. The third was a separate treaty which the two emperors mutually engaged to keep a profound secret. The two first treaties are known. The secret treaty itself has become public property since the circumstances have ceased to exist under the influence of which it was concluded. The two allied powers engaged in this treaty to make common cause in any and every eventuality, to force England to peace, to take away all the Porte's European provinces, with the exception of Constantinople, to force Portugal and the Northern powers to close their ports against English trade, and to use their influence to induce Austria to declare war on her side against England.

An article of the treaty with Russia, mentioned that it was out of consideration for the Emperor Alexander that the Emperor Napoleon consented to restore to the King of Prussia the provinces which were left to him. This loss amounted to about half of the whole territory which had belonged to the King of Prussia before the war. The principal conditions of the public treaties were the creation of a new kingdom in favor of Jérôme

Bonaparte, Napoleon's youngest brother, and the establishment of a Grand-Duchy of Warsaw out of the Polish provinces which Prussia had lost. This new state was given to the King of Saxony, with the exception of the district of Białystock, which was detached from these provinces and ceded to Russia.

The constitution which Napoleon gave to the Grand duchy of Warsaw was conceived in a manner to assure to the inhabitants of this state institutions for the protection of their liberties conciliating these with the tranquility of the Polish provinces incorporated with Russia and Austria. This constitution abolished serfdom, and made all citizens equal before the law, declared that the Napoleonic code should be the civil law of the state, and prescribed that all trials, whether civil or criminal, should be held in public. It suppressed the diets, the *pospolita,* the *liberum veto* and all the other privileges of the Polish nobility, which had been the causes of troubles and anarchy in the kingdom. The executive power was vested in the Grand Duke, the legislative power was attributed to a senate composed of a minimum of eighteen and a maximum of thirty members, and to a house of nuncios, composed of one hundred deputies from the districts and communes. These chambers had the power of passing or of rejecting the laws which in every case had to be presented to them on the initiative of the Grand Duke.

The creation of the Grand Duchy of Warsaw in favor of the King of Saxony, whose predecessors had reigned in Poland, had so great an influence on the subsequent relations between the Russian and the French empires that the mere mention of so important an event will not suffice. The Grand duchy was formed of provinces which had belonged to the old Polish monarchy, which Prussia had obtained at the various divisions, and which she had just lost by the fate of war. Russia had no scruples about profiting by a small part of her ally's losses. The importance of the creation of the Grand duchy of Warsaw cannot have been misunderstood by the Emperor Alexander and if he assisted in this matter it was because he did not feel himself sufficiently strong at the time to oppose it. We shall see him later on, when Russia had repaired her losses, had realized the most solid advantages of the Treaty of Tilsitt, and had finished the conquest of Finland, expressing his displeasure at the enlargement of the Duchy of Warsaw, which, however, could with difficulty be considered as anything else than a steppingstone. The creation of this state, as a matter of fact, seemed a kind of forerunner to the reestablishment of the Polish monarchy, and this capital question was the rock on which the Franco-Russian alliance was to break. The Treaty of Tilsitt might have become the instrument of the reconstitution of the Kingdom of Poland, and it is perhaps a matter of regret that the iniquitous parceling out of this brave nation was not repaired by its means. The Emperor, encouraged by the prodigious success of the campaign which had rendered him master of the whole Kingdom of Prussia, was for a moment tempted to dispose of Silesia in exchange for Galicia with Austria. Napoleon would in this way have been able to reconstitute the Kingdom of Poland, less the missing Russian provinces, on the most solid basis; but this Restoration could not be but the work of time. At the time of the peace of Tilsitt numerous obstacles stood in the way of the realization of Napoleon's good intentions. The Emperor Alexander could not with decency give countenance to the infliction of fresh sacrifices on his ally. By acting in spite of him Napoleon would have dissatisfied Russia without conciliating Austria, whose tendencies were the constant object of his suspicion. And moreover he was anxious for a settlement; his absence, which had already been too greatly prolonged, the distance he was from France, and other considerations—the influence of which he no doubt had appreciated, and of which he had measured all the importance—induced him to abandon a plan which, no doubt, afterwards he regretted not to have carried out to the end.

The Russian alliance sealed at Tilsitt, as well as the triumphs of the two immortal campaigns which had preceded it, lifted the power and the glory of the Emperor Napoleon to their highest summits. The consequences to France were, of necessity, immense. It was only after the disaster at Moscow that cause for blame was found. Adversity undertook, as a matter of fact, to prove that this treaty contained in germ the ruin of the Empire. Adversity discovered that the Emperor could have crossed the Niemen after the victory of Friedland, and could have followed up his successes with a powerful army at a time when the Russian and Prussian forces were almost entirely destroyed. Napoleon had good reasons for acting thus, but no doubt he had better reasons for stopping at the time we are speaking of, and for concluding the important Treaty of Friedland, although politicians have blamed him, perhaps not without reason, for placing too much trust in the Emperor Alexander, and for leaving Prussia either too strong or too weak.

The decree issued at Berlin, by which the British Isles were declared in a state of blockade, in creating the continental system, rendered it necessary to take extraordinary measures for carrying it out, so that no loophole might be left open to English commerce. The uneasiness caused by the interruption of maritime trade, tended, as can be easily understood, to tire out the perseverance of the states involved in the continental system; but the power which first violated it, although suffering less thereby than other powers, was Russia—restored to confidence and strength by her alliance with France. The Treaty of Tilsitt, which inaugurated this alliance, brought with it a system of concessions the entire advantage of which was in favor of the Russian Empire. Disadvantages and dangers were all that France ever derived from this treaty. The principal results of this agreement were to place Russia at once, and on easy terms, in possession of Finland, to involve us in the unfortunate Spanish campaign, and to prevent the Restoration of Poland. The French alliance stimulated anew the insatiable greed of Russia. This favorable circumstance, arousing the Czar's claims on the Ottoman Empire, encouraged him to ask for its division and the occupation of Constantinople. Napoleon's just refusal awoke a feeling of discontented coolness in Alexander's bosom, which he did his best to disguise under the appearance of the most captivating friendship, and which, after our troubles with Spain, and the inevitable consequences of the continental blockade transformed itself into open enmity. The difficulties created by these various causes were great, but not insurmountable. It needed the disasters of Moscow and of Leipzig to overthrow the beautiful monument of Napoleon's glory.

One of the most iniquitous and most barbarous acts of English politics, committed shortly after the Treaty of Tilsitt, excited general indignation in Europe. An English fleet, freighted with an army of thirty-five thousand men, under the command of General Cathcart, suddenly appeared off the coasts of Denmark, although the Danish government had done nothing whatever to furnish England with a pretext for an attack. The only excuse which the British government dared to make for this atrocious violation of international laws was, that to all appearances, it was the intention of the Danish government to ally its naval forces with those of France. Denmark was reposing in the security of peace; no means of defense had been prepared either at Copenhagen or on the island of Zeeland, and as the whole Danish army was on the continent it was impossible to foresee any attack on this island. An English agent presents himself and without opening any negotiation, without taking the trouble to justify his mission, without giving any alternative, signifies to the Danish government an order to hand over the Danish fleet to the admiral in command of the English expedition, and on these demands being refused, threatens to burn down Copenhagen. So insolent an ultimatum could not be accepted. Accordingly, on September 2, 1807, a day of sinister memory, there begins, without any other formality, the bombardment of the Danish capital, which lasted with horrible intensity for three days. A great part of the city was reduced to ashes, and on the 7th the governor capitulated to avoid its entire destruction. The Crown Prince, who was away from his capital, had sent orders that the fleet was to be burned, but these orders had never reached their destination. More than sixty vessels, frigates, brigs, and other ships, together with the entire naval munitions, fell into the hands of the English, who destroyed or burned whatever they could not carry away. The general feeling in Europe was one of indignant reprobation of this act of savage violence. The English Ministry replied to the vehement attacks, which were made on it on this occasion in Parliament, by declaring that the revelations of secret commitments entered upon at Tilsitt by the two Emperors, had made it necessary to order the Copenhagen expedition, but it was unable to furnish any proof of the truth of these allegations. Suspicions have attached in this matter to M. de Talleyrand's friends. Although these suspicions were never proved to be well-founded, I must say that the Emperor had occasion to find out that breaches of confidence had been committed before that time under M. de Talleyrand's Ministry, and that important documents taken from the Foreign Office had been communicated to foreign powers. An act of treachery of this kind was the reason of the dismissal and banishment of a former head of the secretary's office in this ministry, whom Napoleon did not allow to return to France until long after.

The triumphs of Napoleon and of our armies were counterbalanced by a misfortune which came upon the imperial family in May, 1807. The death of the Crown Prince of Holland overthrew the hopes and the projects which were staked on this child's head, and the realization of which, if he had lived, might perhaps have prevented the Emperor's second marriage with a foreign princess. Napoleon was much attached to this nephew, the son of his adopted daughter. In the summer months which the Emperor was able to spend at St. Cloud, this child used sometimes to be brought under the windows of his cabinet, which opened out on the parterre. When Napoleon saw him he used to go and kiss him. I used sometimes to see him carrying the child in his arms as he came in to resume some work in which he had been interrupted. Napoleon-Charles—such was the child's name—was not yet five years old, when he was suddenly snatched from his mother's arms—leaving her, for some time, demented with sorrow. Napoleon, greatly grieved by this loss, sent his sister Caroline to comfort the unhappy parents, who had retired to the Palace of Loo, in Holland. Queen Hortense left the kingdom on this occasion and went to the springs in the Pyrenees. King Louis accompanied her, wishing to try the effect of these waters on his health, which time and the damp climate of Holland had considerably affected. He spent the months of June and July there. Croup, of which the young prince died, was at that time little known. Napoleon offered a prize of twelve thousand francs to the author of the best essay on the means to prevent and cure this cruel disease, so sudden in its attacks, and so rapid in its progress. It has been noticed that it was on the same date, May 6, fourteen years later, that the Emperor was by death reunited to the young nephew whom he had thought of appointing his heir.

The deposition of Selim, and this monarch's tragic death, which shortly followed, were another misfortune. If this prince, who was worthy of a better fate, had lived, the Treaty of Bucharest, which was so fatal to us in 1812, would doubtless never have been concluded.

On July 9, 1807, after an exchange of the ratifications of the treaties which had been signed the day before, Napoleon, wearing the grand cordon of the Russian Order of Saint Andrew, proceeded to the Emperor of Russia, who received him at the head of his guard, wearing the grand cordon of the Legion of Honor. Napoleon had the soldier of the Russian imperial guard who had most distinguished himself, presented to him, and handed him the golden eagle of the Legion of Honor as a proof of his esteem for the Russian guardsman. He also presented his portrait to General Platov, hetman of the Cossacks.

After three hours' conversation Napoleon accompanied Alexander to the bank of the Niemen, where the Czar embarked. The two sovereigns separated after the most affectionate leave-taking. The King of Prussia, after an exchange of purely formal visits, took leave of the Emperor Napoleon and proceeded to Memel. Napoleon on his side set out at once for Koenigsberg.

The Emperors of Russia and France had spent twenty days at Tilsitt. Their residences in this city were quite close to each other, and in the same street. During all this time Napoleon and Alexander showed the greatest friendship for each other. Who would not have seen in their intimacy a solid guarantee for the peace of Europe? It is necessary to believe that Alexander's professions of friendship were sincere at the time.

Napoleon halted one day in Koenigsberg and settled the dates on which the Prussian provinces still occupied by the French troops, should be evacuated, assigning to each army corps the place which it should occupy.

The Emperor sent General Savary direct to St. Petersburg from Koeingsberg. The mission of this general—who had received instructions both concise and broad, but which had no official character—had for its object the keeping of the Emperor Alexander in the frame of mind which had dictated the Treaty of Tilsitt, and the hurrying on of the execution of the various stipulations of the treaties; he was also to superintend the choice and speedy departure of a Russian ambassador to Paris, and finally to reside in St. Petersburg until further orders.

Napoleon then proceeded to Dresden, where he spent three days. He received sincere proofs of gratitude and attachment from the worthy King of Saxony. He settled with Labouillerie, general paymaster to the Great Army, whom he appointed treasurer of the extraordinary domain, all matters connected with the levies on Prussia and the conquered provinces which amounted altogether to more than six hundred millions of francs.

Napoleon returned to St. Cloud with all speed, and without stopping on the way. He arrived there on July 27, at five o'clock in the morning. He dined with his family, the Archchancellor Cambacérès being present. In the evening he saw the ministers and on the morrow he received the congratulations of the great corporations of state.

The Emperor's return, after an absence of ten months, the longest he had ever made, was hailed with universal satisfaction. The prosperity enjoyed by all classes evoked a feeling of gratitude and warm sympathy for the man who had just crowned the most unheard-of successes with the most glorious peace. The hope that this peace would be durable filled every heart with gladness. Paris was delighted, and a general illumination was spontaneously improvised on the very evening of the Emperor's arrival.

Napoleon's first care was to develop the prosperity of the country at home and to do everything necessary to strengthen its security, a security which had not been in the least disturbed during his long absence from home. He then turned his attention to foreign affairs, and sought the best means for inducing the European powers, including Austria, to declare against England—the realization, in short, of the advantages which he had looked for from the Treaty of Tilsitt.

Napoleon proceeded also with the organization of the kingdom of Westphalia, which had been created by this treaty in favor of Jérôme Bonaparte. This kingdom had been put together out of the Electorate of Hesse-Cassel, joined to the Duchy of Brunswick and other provinces in Germany which had been ceded by Prussia. Hanover also became an integral part of the kingdom of Westphalia in 1810, Marshal Mortier had been commissioned to take possession of these various States.

There was, amongst other rich artistic collections at Cassel, a fine picture gallery; and some of the finest pictures were sent to Paris. Two of these, of the greatest value—the best works of Paul Potter—-were offered to the Empress Josephine, who had them placed in her gallery at La Malmaison. One was "The Farm at Amsterdam," which is more generally known by a vulgar name, and the other was "Men Chased by Animals." I remember seeing these pictures there. They were admired by all connoisseurs, and used to be covered over with green curtains to protect them. When the Emperor looked at them, he seemed to regret that the Empress had accepted them. He used to say that it was robbing the Museum. He would have taken more pleasure in them at the Museum, because the greatest pleasure that he could afford himself was to enrich France with all the masterpieces which he gained by his victories.

Napoleon gave to the new Kingdom of Westphalia a constitution the provisions of which are an answer to the reproach that has been cast upon him of being the defender of privileges and the restorer of absolute power. This constitution, like that of the Grand duchy of Warsaw, and like the constitution of Bayonne, which were drawn up later, consecrated the abolition of Serfdom, the equality of all men before the law, the publicity of trials and the eligibility of all citizens without distinction to fill public offices. Already, as First Consul, he had given a proof of his vigilance for the rights of the people, by causing a special clause to be inserted into the deed by which Louisiana was ceded to the United States, guaranteeing that the inhabitants of this colony should be protected in their liberties, their possessions, and religion. Napoleon sent French commissioners to the new Kingdom of Westphalia, charged with the organization of the various government departments, and to form a regency council pending the king's arrival. The marriage of Jérôme, Napoleon's brother, with the daughter of the King of Würtemberg, was the consequence of the foundation of this new throne.

The interview between the future spouses took place at the castle of Raincy, near Paris. Prince Jérôme, bright, witty, and fond of pleasure, was not yet twenty-three years of age. Princess Catherine was one year older. This union, formed by cold political calculations, was soon strengthened by the mutual affection which sprung up between husband and wife. Catherine of Würtemburg, whose destiny it was to give an example of conjugal fidelity and constancy under adversity, during a period when so many reputations, till then considered above reproach, went to the wall, was a beautiful and interesting princess. From the first moment she won the sympathies of her new family, and the Emperor embraced her affectionately directly he saw her. The civil marriage was performed with great pomp in the Diana gallery, at the Tuileries Palace, and the Prince-Primate gave the nuptial blessing to the young couple in the chapel of the same palace on the following day. There was a reception at court that day, but the bad weather spoiled the illuminations and prevented the firework display.

The King and Queen of Westphalia spent three months in Paris, while the regency council composed of the three councilors of state—Siméon Beugnot and Jollivet and General Lagrange—was organizing the government of the kingdom in the sovereign's name and establishing his authority. Initiated to the science of government by the Emperor, King Jérôme had frequent conversations with his brother, and was in constant correspondence with the regency council. A week after the departure of the Emperor for Italy, the King and Queen of Westphalia left Paris to enter upon their States. They were received all along their route with the enthusiastic welcome which was everywhere accorded to the name which they bore. They spent a week at Stuttgart, where the King of Würtemberg did all in his power to treat his daughter and her husband with respect and honor. The week passed in unending banquets and fêtes. What a change seven years later! The old king seemed then to want to make up for the marks of respect which, in 1807, he had shown, through his guests, to the generous sovereign to whom he owed his royal crown; but Napoleon, in 1814, was no longer anything more in his eyes than a vanquished enemy, whom he had no longer any need to treat with consideration. The change of times can alone explain such changes of conduct and these things are amongst the contemptible features of human nature.

After Napoleon's return from Tilsitt, an important change was made in the Ministry. Prince de Bénévent, who, dissatisfied with the post of Grand Chamberlain, coveted a salary equal to that of the two ex-consuls, was given the choice between the dignity of Vice-Grand Elector and of Secretary of Foreign Affairs. M. de Talleyrand preferred to resign his portfolio, but he considered, and not without reason, that his leaving the Ministry was the beginning of his disgrace. The Emperor, without having material proofs of his minister's infidelity, felt that he could not continue to trust him. Napoleon accordingly thought that it would be more advisable to keep Prince de Bénévent at hand, and only to take advantage of his services as occasion might warrant. M. de Champigny, whom the Emperor had employed in certain negotiations, whose honesty he appreciated, and who seemed to him endowed with the special capacities that were wanted, seemed to him the right man to manage the Foreign Office, under his own direction. It is to be regretted that Napoleon did not remove Talleyrand from public affairs altogether, at the time when he removed the portfolio of the Foreign Office from his hands; for the relations which this minister had formed with certain foreign statesmen, and the way in which he had managed to ingratiate himself with certain sovereigns, gave him powerful resources of influence which he was able to use in a fatal manner against the Emperor.

M. de Champigny gave up the Ministry of the Interior to M. Cretet, who was governor of the Bank of France and who was replaced by Jaubert, the councilor of state. General Clarke replaced Marshal Berthier at the War Office—the Marshal being raised to the dignity of Vice-Constable, while retaining his post as major-general of the Great Army.

M. Portalis, one of the principal writers of the civil code, was succeeded after his death, which occurred in this same month, at the Ministry of Public Worship, by M. Bigot Préameneu, a learned lawyer, who like his predecessor, had worked on the civil code.

The tribunate was suppressed by a senatus consultum of August, 1807. This institution had not fulfilled its object, even at the time when it was created. It was a wheel in the governmental machine, which experience had proved to be useless and even disadvantageous. The tribunate was composed, for the most part, of very capable men, whom a new government could not ignore. The danger lay in the fact that these men, loving to shine by eloquence, and being steeped in the ideas which they had advocated during the Republic, possessed a public tribune from which to preach and maintain the same doctrines. These men brought into their debates, in spite of the fact that nine-tenths of them could not be suspected of ill will or of hostility against the authorities, a spirit of opposition and an instinct of distrust, which prompted them to reject measures of generally acknowledged public utility—amongst others the so anxiously expected provisions of the civil code. The modifications which the Tribune had undergone, a creation incompatible with the idea of stability, did not remedy the fatal objection to the institution as an institution. Its suppression was necessary, and incontestably simplified the elaboration and making of laws. The nation, tired of chatterings and Utopian ideas, had one wish alone—to rest from its agitations in the institutions which it expected from the man in whom its trust had been placed. It saw with displeasure the opposition which was raised against him, and applauded this change in the constitution. Speculative minds have asserted that Napoleon only suppressed the tribunate, because he wished to rid himself of an inconvenient censor, and because he hated any publicity of discussion. Others, more impartial, have found that, on the contrary, by this measure the legislative body was restored to the full exercise of its powers, and that the new method of discussion which was adopted guaranteed better legislation, by doing away with those parliamentary quarrels which kept alive an agitation which was fatal to the steady progress of the government. The examination of the projected laws was as a matter of fact delegated to committees chosen from the legislative body, and including its most experienced members. The Council of State drew up the draft bills and discussed them with the committees. In case of disagreement the sections of the Council of State, and the committees of the legislative body used to meet under the presidence of the Archchancellor or of the Archtreasurer, to come to an understanding. The Speaker for the Council of State expounded the reasons of the law to the legislative body. The president of the Parliamentary committee was next heard. When the matter had been sufficiently discussed a vote was taken. If the committee of the Legislature did not consider the proposed law acceptable, each of the members of the committee was free to explain his objections before the chamber. The Legislature was accordingly vested with the necessary authority, and independence, and the examination of the bills remained entrusted to the pick of its members.

An act which is worthy of mention is the reorganization of the Audit Office. This important measure, which followed closely upon the suppression of the tribunate, has been praised as an act of wise government, the budget committee having been admitted to be insufficient. But even the best things are open to criticism, and fault has been found with the fact that the annual balance sheet submitted to the Sovereign was not made public, and that only the budgets of communes possessing an income of over ten thousand francs a year were audited. The first point was rectified by a subsequent order, by the terms of which the report of the Audit Office had to be annexed to the accounts laid before the Legislature each year. It was in the government's interest to develop this system of public bookkeeping as much as possible, and the reasons for finding fault with the institution of the Audit Office were bound to disappear. Experience, and the Restoration of peace, would have brought with them reforms in turn, as well as the improvement of many other services, for which time was lacking. As Napoleon himself used often to say: "Time is the great master of all things."

M. Barbé-Marbois, from whom the Emperor had been forced to withdraw the portfolio of the Public Treasury, in 1806, received by his nomination to the presidency of the Audit Office, a fresh proof of Napoleon's appreciation of his past services, very different conduct from that of people who, in the day of adversity, have forgotten the injuries they committed against the man who had put a stop to their exile or their proscription, only to remember the disgrace, too often fully merited, which had befallen them later.

One of the principal reasons which had induced Napoleon to sign the peace of Tilsitt was the necessity of securing fresh means for excluding England from the Continent. With this object in view he exerted all the forces of his intelligence, and began by weighing with all his influence on Spain to obtain from this degenerate power an increase of effort against the common enemy. He exacted in consequence the co-operation of the Spanish government in forcing Portugal to accept and carry out the continental system. The Emperor on his side had summoned the Lisbon cabinet to close the ports of Portugal against the English, to seize upon English subjects and merchandise, and to declare war against England. The Portuguese government had not heeded these behests. A secret understanding, which the English government did not conceal in Parliament, existed between England and Portugal, and tended to the evasion by the latter of the decrees of Berlin. Napoleon decided in consequence to fight this country. He assembled an army of twenty-five thousand French soldiers, under the command of General Junot near Bayonne, and ordered them to invade Portugal. The Emperor occupied himself in conjunction with the Minister of Marine (Decrés), in preparing small maritime expeditions, with the object of ruining British trade and shipping in the waters of the island of France, of the Antilles, and on the coasts of Africa. He applied his indefatigable activity to increasing the number of naval constructions, to the creation of new maritime establishments, and, in one word, to every development of the resources of the French navy. His attention was at the same time directed to the best means for providing for the needs of the Treasury by admitting the finances of the state to share in the profits of the war indemnities. This same zeal for the public good extended itself likewise to public works, to the protection required by commerce and industry, to the reform of the magistracy, to the improvement of the positions of parish priests, to the advancement of science, art, and literature. The feast of Saint Napoleon was celebrated with general enthusiasm. The peace of Tilsitt, and the hope that it would be followed by peace at sea, opened every heart to confidence. On the morrow, August 16, Napoleon opened the session of the legislative body with pomp, which was further increased by the presence of an immense concourse of people. In a speech, delivered in a firm and sonorous voice, which thrilled the Assembly, Napoleon related what he had done for the greatness and happiness of France, and described the plans which he was meditating for the perfecting of our institutions. This solemn session was terminated by a statement of the magnificent situation of the French Empire.

The senatus consultum, announced one year previously, which created hereditary nobility, issued from this general state of prosperity. The creation of hereditary titles was the natural sequence of the foundation of the Empire, and the creation of the principalities which had been conferred in 1806. On March 1, 1807, there had been registered at the senate two statutes, one providing for the creation of titles of princes, dukes, counts, barons, and knights; the other establishing the regulation of the institution and composition of settled estates. The nobility founded by Napoleon was no more in opposition to the principles of equality than the institution of the Legion of Honor. That is what distinguished it from the old nobility, which had been a privileged and feudal aristocracy. The new nobility was injured by what was remembered of the old. The imperial nobility would have needed, before being judged, to have undergone the developments which time would have brought with it. It was the fruit of an idea of organization, which, as Napoleon used to say, would have characterized the century. The old aristocracy formed an association outside the people which, separated from it by almost insurmountable barriers, was naturally hostile towards it. In creating a new nobility, open to merit of every kind, Napoleon counterpoised our old close aristocracy and prepared its transformation. In the Emperor's mind the imperial nobility restored the equality which had been proscribed by the old nobility. Napoleon wished to realize three important objects: The amalgamation of old France with the new France; the reconciliation of France with Europe; and the effacement in Europe of the vestiges of feudality, by attaching the idea of nobility to services rendered to the state. The superiority which the old nobility arrogated to itself would have been effaced by its fusion with the new. The Princess de Beauvau, whose merits and attachment the Emperor highly esteemed, hearing that her eldest son had been created a baron, could only bring herself by force to recognize a favor in this gift of a title. She ignored that her son would have recovered, in time, the title to which he had a right. The members of the ancient nobility, bearing names recommended by ancient services, or remarkably illustrious, would have resumed the titles they had formerly borne, after the peace and under conditions which would have made of the two nobilities, one historical nobility.

The Emperor had distributed, on June 30 and September 23, sums of from two hundred thousand to one million francs to each of nine marshals, sums of one hundred thousand francs to each of thirty-four generals—in one word, revenues exceeding a total of fifteen hundred thousand francs. These cash sums did not cost the treasury one halfpenny, for they were taken from the war indemnities levied on the enemy, and paid into a special army treasury. The endowments consisted in domains which Napoleon had reserved to himself in Poland, Hanover, Westphalia, Holland, and Italy. The Arch-chancellor and the Arch-treasurer, several ministers and other civil functionaries, had a share, in a given proportion, in these liberalities. I am only speaking of those who had a first share in these gifts, before and after the Emperor's fête. For, in proportion as victory put these riches into Napoleon's hands, new sums of money and new endowments were used as rewards for old and new services, both military and civil. Nor were the foreigners who had assisted in our victories forgotten. The total resources supplied by conquest composed the extraordinary domain, and this domain was exclusively used for rewarding services rendered to France, and Napoleon always abstained from applying any part of it to his personal use.

The Emperor always wanted me to get married. He was constantly speaking to me on this subject. He was constantly saying: "Well, when are we going to get married?" I had had time to think the matter over. But I was so jealous of my independence that I did not want the Emperor or the Empress to interfere in my marriage. It was only later that I determined to face this great problem, which was solved to my entire satisfaction. I selected my wife from an honorable family and in making my choice was not influenced by anybody else. I did not regret what I had done, for the future which opened before us was sufficiently bright to satisfy all our ambitions. The Emperor, when freedom from worry gave the reins to his benevolence, had more than once said to me: "You have had the fortune to rise with me; I must make your fortune. Peace will at last come to enable me to settle my accounts. You will lose nothing by waiting." I quote these words, which penetrated into my heart too deeply for me to forget them. He put that and other matters off till the period which he so earnestly hoped for. After his second abdication, in 1815, the Emperor expressed his regret to me at not having been able to keep his promises.

Napoleon spent the last days of September, the whole of October, and half the month of November at Fontainebleau. He had given orders, two years previously, for great improvements in this sumptuous residence, and he had considerably added to the splendid furniture of the palace. He received many foreigners and German princes there. Diplomatic introductions took place here, and the Court at Fontainebleau was a very brilliant one. Hunting, theatrical performances of the masterpieces of the French stage, in which Talma and our principal actors took part, were a diversion from the serious business with which the Emperor was taken up.

England's answer to the proposals of France and Russia, and to Russia's offer of acting as mediator, had been the bombardment of Copenhagen. Portugal, who was bound to England by her sympathies and interests, had evaded all cooperation in the efficacious measures adopted by the naval powers against the excesses of English tyranny. The Lisbon cabinet, enslaved by the London cabinet, maintained an attitude of hidden hostility in face of our claims. The Emperor decided to punish this perfidy and to strike a new blow against England by occupying Portugal. A convention was signed on October 27, at Fontainebleau, between General Duroc and M. Izquierdo, a Spanish gentleman who was engaged in the study of natural history in Paris, and who was the devoted agent of the Prince de la Paix. The object of this convention was to settle the basis of the occupation of Portugal by an army of twenty-five thousand men, to which was to be joined a Spanish army of the same force. General Junot, commanding the observation corps which was assembled at Bayonne, received orders to cross the frontier, and to march upon Lisbon by the military route agreed upon with the Spanish government. The Emperor, at the same time gave orders for the formation of a second army, and entrusted its command to General Dupont, whose military talents he had had reason to appreciate during the 1805 campaign. This second army had the same destination as the first, and was to enter Spain to assist it, in case the English joined the Portuguese.

The same plenipotentiaries signed a treaty which divided Portugal into three parts, the first of which was given to the King of Etruria in exchange for Tuscany. The second was to form a principality in favor of the Prince de la Paix, who was pleased at the prospect of having an assured independence in case events forced him to cease his rule in Spain. As to the third part, it was kept in reserve for the purposes of future exchange, or to be bestowed in way of recompense. The reversion of these territories was reserved, in default of legitimate heirs, to the King of Spain, whom the Emperor undertook to have acknowledged as the Emperor of the Two Americas, as soon as the general peace should have been effected.

Two days later a treaty was signed with the envoy from Denmark, also at Fontainebleau. The Crown Prince of Denmark, profoundly incensed by the odious conduct of the English Ministry, and by the barbarous aggression of which his people had been the victims, had rejected all the proposals of England, answering them with a declaration of war, after having denounced the Copenhagen outrage to the whole of Europe. This prince had taken just reprisals by arresting all English subjects, by confiscating their property, by ordering all money due to them to be sequestrated, and by forbidding all communication with England under pain of death. He made common cause with France, on whose support he could rely, and with Russia, whose alliance offered less guarantee of sincerity. Napoleon took into his service the Danish sailors who had been thrown out of work by the capture or destruction of the ships on which they had been engaged.

It was during the last fortnight of his stay at Fontainebleau that the Emperor received a letter dated from the Escurial—October 29, 1807, in which King Charles IV informed him of the discovery of a conspiracy against his throne and the Queen's life—a conspiracy at the head of which was the Prince of the Asturias, the eldest son of the Spanish monarch. The Emperor, without placing faith in this serious accusation, saw in the circumstance another proof of the deep misunderstanding which separated the sovereigns' favorite and the heir to the Spanish crown. On the other hand, Napoleon had received a letter, transmitted by M. de Beauharnais, our ambassador in Madrid, some days before the King of Spain's letter. This letter came from the Prince of the Asturias, who wrote to the Emperor, without his father's knowledge, to implore his protection against the enemies who had decided upon his ruin, and to ask him for the hand of one of the princesses of his family. These letters brought back before Napoleon's mind the thoughts concerning Spain which he had long been meditating. He had long and frequent conversations on this subject with the Prince de Bénévent, who, seeking to penetrate the Emperor's secret thoughts, had skillfully seized upon this opportunity of rendering himself useful. Talleyrand, as a matter of fact, did obtain the favor of being allowed to replace Prince Eugène as Archchancellor of state, during his absence. This title conferred upon Prince Eugène a dignity without diplomatic functions. M. de Talleyrand expected to derive more serious advantages from his honorary title. In the course of confidential conversations with Napoleon, conversations in which he chiefly played the part of listener, he hinted the advice, with all the semblances of a studied reserve, that the Emperor should take advantage of the misunderstandings which divided the Court of Spain, to change the dynasty which would never be a useful ally against England, and which, under circumstances which could not fail to arise, would on the contrary favor this power to our disadvantage. As an alternative to this extreme measure, he proposed that a surrender of territory should be obtained from Spain, to the extent of making her dependent upon us. I was present at several of these conversations, which used frequently to be held in the Emperor's workroom. Napoleon took his time to reflect on this serious matter, before being able to come to any decision himself. Events had to be allowed to ripen with time. He did not answer the letter of the Prince of the Asturias, considering it as an attack on the authority of the head of the royal family. He had a declaration made to Prince de Masserano, at that time Spanish ambassador to France, that it did not suit him to interfere in the domestic affairs of the Spanish sovereign. He answered King Charles, advising him to exercise indulgence and moderation, and made his preparations for his journey to Italy, without having expressed himself in any pronounced way, and leaving the whole matter in suspense. During his stay at Fontainebleau, the Emperor had granted an audience to Madame de Bonchamp, the widow of the Vendéen general of that name, who, dragged into the revolutionary war by a feeling of honor, used to say that he aimed after no human glory, because civil wars can never confer it. His generous conduct won him the esteem of men of all parties. With his dying breath he had saved the lives of six thousand patriots, whose death was being clamored for by the Vendéens. Napoleon, anxious to honor the memory of this distinguished warrior, received his widow with kindness, and promised to endow her daughter, a child of twelve or thirteen, whom she presented to him. He had rather a long conversation with Madame de Bonchamp, and heard with interest that she herself had been saved from a death-sentence by a *conventionnel,* a man called Lofficial, whose name Napoleon heard then for the first time. Lofficial, after having the sentence which condemned Madame de Bonchamp as the widow of a Vendéen general to death, respited, had obtained an amnesty in which her name was included by his care. Napoleon did not limit his interest towards Madame de Bonchamp to sterile expressions of favor, and granted her a pension of six thousand francs.

Towards the same period, the Emperor had appointed General Ordener to the post of first equerry to the Empress. He was a loyal soldier, and an honorable man, but was little accustomed to the ways of the court. This post was equivalent to that of knight of honor, which at that time did not exist. Napoleon had noticed that the ladies and gentlemen in attendance on the Empress put on somewhat forced airs of aristocracy. He had been informed that on a reception day, when several persons belonging to the noble faubourg had been presented to the Empress, her lady-in-waiting had said: "We have received good company today." In appointing General Ordener, the Emperor wished to reward and honor the services of a brave officer, and at the same time to give the Empress's household a lesson. He allowed their vexation at his choice to play itself out in certain sarcastic remarks without appearing to notice them.

When the marriage of Napoleon to the Archduchess Marie Louise was decided upon, General Ordener was replaced as first equerry by Prince Aldobrandi Borghèse. The General was given the governorship of the palace of Compiègne for his retired service. Count Claude Beauharnais, father of the Grand duchess of Baden, became knight of honor to the new empress.

On November 15, the Emperor left Fontainebleau for a tour in Italy. A fully justified distrust of Austria's political feelings towards him, a desire to visit the Venetians and other inhabitants of Italy, and to bind them more closely to his political system, and to confer with his brothers Joseph and Lucien—such were the chief reasons of his journey. While crossing Mount Cenis, Napoleon was overtaken, when on foot, by a storm which put his life in danger. He was fortunate enough to reach a cave in which he took refuge. This cave appeared to him, as he afterwards related, "a palace of diamonds."

Brilliant fêtes were held in Milan and in Venice in honor of the Emperor, and the Court of Bavaria was present. During his stay in Milan the Emperor created Prince Eugène Prince of Venice, and conferred upon him the succession to the throne of Italy in default of male issue to himself. He informed himself on the exact signification of the title of heir presumptive, and himself looked up the exact meaning of this word in the Academy Dictionary. The eldest daughter of Prince Eugène was created Princess of Bologna, with a rich endowment. During the sitting of the three corporations, the Possidenti, the Dotti, and the Commercianti, at which the adoption of Prince Eugène was declared, Napoleon was seen to inform the Viceroy that the applause that burst forth on this occasion was addressed to him, telling him to acknowledge it with a bow. Melzi d'Eril, chancellor of the Kingdom of Italy, was created Duke of Lodi, and richly endowed. During Napoleon's journey at this time, the Queen of Etruria came to Milan to present her son, whose guardian she was, to the Emperor. She left Tuscany, which had just been united to the Empire, after the death of the king her husband.

New edicts from the British government having given an indefinite extension to the maritime blockade, and having subjected all ships belonging to neutral powers to the obligation to put into port in England and to pay duty on their cargoes under pain of confiscation, the Emperor retorted on this piratical legislation with a decree issued at Milan, which declared that any ship which allowed herself to be visited by an English vessel, or which should submit to a voyage to England, or paid any duty whatever to the English should be considered denationalized. After a short stay at Milan, Napoleon went to visit Venice. The population received him with enthusiasm, and splendid fêtes were given in his honor, in which regattas and gondola races naturally played the principal part. The grand canal was covered with boats decorated with the greatest taste, transformed into constructions representing the houses, temples, kiosks, and cottages of different countries, and manned with gondoliers dressed in appropriate costumes. There was not a Venetian noble who did not spend at least a year's income on these fêtes.

Joseph, King of Naples, came to see the Emperor at Venice, and spent six days with him. He accompanied Napoleon when he went to visit the port, the batteries, and the various defense works. The Emperor, in the midst of these fêtes, occupied himself actively with the various improvements which could be introduced into different parts of the government, and with the best means for raising up the Venetians again to the state of prosperity which they had formerly enjoyed. In consequence he increased or improved the civil, military, and maritime establishments of the ancient city of the doges.

Napoleon left Venice to visit the fortified places of the old Venetian state, and stopped at Mantua. King Joseph, who had taken leave of the Emperor, on his way back to his States, received a letter from his brother Lucien, to inform him of his presence in Modena. Two days later, when the Emperor was at Mantua, I received the two following letters:

"MONSIEUR MÉNEVAL—In the annexed letter I inform the Emperor of Lucien's arrival. Be good enough to give this letter with your own hands to the Emperor, and to ask him to authorize you to inform Lucien when he can receive him.

"Your well-disposed,

"(Signed) JOSEPH"

"Mantua, December 11, 1807"

This letter contained another letter, couched in the following terms:

"I beg you, Sir, to hand the enclosed to His Majesty. I am staying at the big inn under the name of secretary to the King of Naples. I beg His Majesty the Emperor to allow you to come and fetch me. The particular feelings of esteem which I have for you will make your selection for this purpose a pleasure to me.

"Your well-disposed,"
(Signed) LUCIEN BONAPARTE"

"Mantua, December 13, 1807"

After having taken the Emperor's orders I went to fetch Lucien Bonaparte at his inn, towards nine in the evening. I brought him into Napoleon's cabinet, bringing him through a secret entry, as he had said that he did not wish to be seen by anybody. The interview between the two brothers lasted till midnight. On leaving the Emperor, Lucien was deeply affected, and his face was streaming with tears. I conducted him back to his inn, and there I heard that the Emperor had pressed him most strongly to return to France, or to accept a foreign throne, but that the conditions which he imposed wounded him in his domestic affections and political independence. He bade me carry his farewell to the Emperor. "It may be forever," he added. Napoleon, finding it impossible to shake his brother's resolution, had given him, nevertheless, full time to consider his proposals. He charged his brothers and his ministers, Talleyrand and Fouché, to renew his remonstrances to Lucien, but was unable to effect any result. Napoleon regretted to be deprived of the cooperation of a man for whose character and rare talents he had the highest respect, but he was unwilling to yield an inch in the matter of what he demanded of him. The promptness with which Lucien rushed to his brother's side when misfortunes came upon Napoleon, prompted only by his brotherly love, is his best eulogy.

It had been agreed, during this interview between Napoleon and his brother, that Lucien should send his daughter Charlotte, who was thirteen or fourteen years old, to Paris. She was the elder of the two daughters which Lucien had by Catherine Boyer, his first wife. It was proposed that this child should become the wife of the Crown Prince of Spain, in the event of Napoleon's deciding to grant the request which Ferdinand himself had proffered in this connection. Lucien's daughter was placed in the house of the Lady Mother, who treated her with kindness, but whose tastes were not sufficiently in sympathy with those of the young girl to captivate her entirely. Educated by a step-mother who had disposed her in no friendly manner towards her father's family, Lucien's daughter did not respond to her grandmother's affections, her letters to her parents were full of bitter complaints about her grandmother's avarice, and of sarcastic remarks against her uncles and aunts. These letters were handed to the Emperor, who amused himself with reading them one Sunday in presence of his family, assembled after a family dinner in the drawing room at St. Cloud. Each member of the family had been made the target of a more or less well-directed satire. After Napoleon had amused himself for a moment with the sight of the vexation caused by the jests of the imprudent young girl on those present, he assumed a graver air, complained about his niece's ingratitude, and decided that she should be immediately sent back to her parents. On the morrow he sent her away from Paris under the care of a person in whom he had confidence, who escorted her back to Italy and placed her in her father's hands. Thus Napoleon's plan of marrying this daughter of his brother Lucien to the Crown Prince of Spain, fell to the ground and was abandoned.

The Emperor returned from Mantua to Milan and spent a week there before returning to Paris. While passing through Alexandria he visited the immense fortification works which he had ordered, and which had transformed this town into the strongest fortified place in Europe. The Austrian and Sardinian governments destroyed these fortifications after the fall of the Empire, and no trace of them remains at the time at which I am writing.

The Emperor was back in Paris from his tour in Italy on January 1, 1808. During his stay in that country, and before his journey to Bayonne, there was published the result of the assembly of Israelites which preceded and followed the convocation of the great Sanhédrin. At the time of the 1805 campaign, Napoleon had been struck by the invasions of the Jewish race. He had given attention to the best means of remedying the damage caused in certain provinces, and notably in Alsatia, by the system of usury, which threatened to cast the finest estates in certain districts into the hands of a vile and degraded race. He wished also at the same time to lead the Jews on to the practice of mechanic and liberal professions, and to engage in industries of which honesty approved. To effect these useful reforms, an assembly of the principal Jews of France and Italy had been convoked in Paris, and there were appointed as commissioners of the government at this meeting, MM. Molé, Portalis and Pasquier. The result of this first meeting was the convocation of a great Sanhédrin, an extraordinary superior council, at which formerly state and church matters were decided upon in Jerusalem, and which had never been called together since the days before Jesus Christ. This council *sui generis,* which was held in Paris, in 1807, while Napoleon was fighting the Russians in Eastern Prussia, was composed in conformity with historical traditions. It was to formulate doctrinally the proposals discussed at the first meeting. M. Molé, the reporter, in his account of the motives which had decided the imperial government to call the Sanhédrin together, gave a magnificent eulogy of Napoleon. The novelty of such a spectacle, this resurrection of an authority and of customs dating from the darkest ages, excited very strong curiosity and interest at the time. Although the sittings were held in camera, a number of people managed to be present and the result was awaited with curiosity by the outside world. To the decisions rendered on political, civil and religious questions, which decisions were sanctioned by a decree, the Emperor added special clauses tending to encourage the Jews to engage in agriculture, and to render all illegal trafficking and practices of usury impossible amongst them. The exceptions from the rights common to other citizens which had necessarily to be imposed on the Jews, were limited to a period of ten years. The Emperor's anxiety to settle all these questions won him the gratitude of the enlightened members of the Jewish world. At the same time, the legislation which was the result of this extraordinary assembly did not sufficiently satisfy all the hopes that had been staked upon it, but it was a useful precedent, and time might also bring with it efficacious reforms amongst the Jews, as well as a cessation of their hostilities against the Christians.

A decree, dated March 1802, had required the Institut to lay before the government, in the Council of State, a general table of the progress and condition of science, literature, and art, from the year 1789 onwards. This report was to have been ready in the month of September, 1803. Extraordinary circumstances, such as the rupture of the Peace of Amiens, the assembling and arming of the Boulogne flotilla, and the wars with Austria and Prussia had prevented the presentation of this important document to the Emperor. It was only in the months February and March, 1808, that, before his departure for Bayonne, the Emperor was able to listen to this report. The deputation from the class of physical and mathematical sciences was admitted first into his presence, and the Academicians Delambre and Cuvier acted as spokesmen. The Emperor was struck with the eloquence and clear-headedness of M. Cuvier, who spoke for several hours. Making an exception to his rule not to remove savants from their studies, Napoleon appointed M. Cuvier *maître des requêtes* to the Council of State, and entrusted him with an important post in the imperial University. On February 19, the class of ancient history and literature presented its report, through M. Dacier. A week later it was the turn of the class of literature and belles lettres, for whom Chénier spoke. This report, in which Chénier displayed both taste and tact, and in which he criticized the powers of contemporary celebrities, who are so easily wounded, with as much impartiality as talent, is a model of the style which has become classical. On March 5 following, the class of Fine Arts completed the table of human knowledge with a report which was presented by M. Lebreton, the secretary to this class. This general review of literature, science, and art which had been brought into existence by Napoleon, showed that human intelligence, far from going back, did not halt in its constant march onward towards progress. Napoleon answered each deputation from the Institute in particular, expressing to the reporters the satisfaction he felt at the results obtained by their researches and labors.

The Spanish correspondence and some fresh letters which the Emperor had received from King Charles IV during his journey in Italy had made him acquainted with the fresh occurrences of which Madrid had been the scene. The Prince de la Paix, having been informed that conferences were taking place between the councilors of the Prince of the Asturias, Escoïquitz, the Duke of l'Infantado, San Carlos and other personages of the court—with the object of deposing him—had had the papers of the Crown Prince seized. Various documents had been found, including a cipher for secret correspondence, and a draft nomination of the Duke of l'Infantado to the command of New Castile, on which the date had been left blank. It was a matter of no difficulty for the favorite to transform these discoveries into proofs of a premeditated plan of attack against the sovereignty and the person of the king. There was also found amongst the Prince's papers the draft of a letter which he had written to the Emperor Napoleon, in which he had asked for the hand of one of the princesses of Napoleon's family. This application had been through the secret agency of the French ambassador, M. de Beauharnais, the eldest brother of the first husband of the Empress Josephine. This envoy whose well-known straightforwardness and fidelity were such as to keep him at a distance from the favorite Godoy, had all the more willingly consented to transmit this request, that he knew that it would not displease the Emperor, and because he had reasons to hope that, in case the Prince's offer was accepted, the choice of Napoleon might fall on one of his nieces, who were also Josephine's nieces. As a matter of fact Napoleon replied to his ambassador that he should listen to all that was being said, should show himself friendly disposed, should bind himself by no commitment, but should learn everything that was going on, and keep Paris constantly informed of what he had learned. These were the only recommendations that could be made to our representative at Madrid, on a question in which no definite instructions could be given, seeing that the government had come to no definite decision, and that the solution of this question had perforce to depend on altogether unforeseen events. It was not diplomacy, but the sword, which was going to play the first and only part in this matter.

The discovery of the ill-considered actions of the Crown Prince and his councilors brought about their arrest. But the council of Castile, to which the matter was submitted, refused to condemn the heir to the throne. The prince was exonerated, and his councilors were exiled.

An apparent calm had followed upon these storms. The Prince de la Paix and the Queen, however much a marriage of the Crown Prince, which would place him under an all-powerful protection, might be distasteful to them, thought it good policy to take advantage of Ferdinand's application to the Emperor. It was on this account that they urged the king himself to ask for a wife for his son, from the French imperial family. The Prince of the Asturias, without dignity and without courage, had denounced his friends, and had expressed his repentance for his fault to the Queen and the favorite, humbling himself before them with all the tokens of the most abject submission. Nevertheless, and in spite of this cowardice, which should have disgusted the pride of the Spanish character, Ferdinand remained the nation's idol, so intense was the hatred against the Prince de la Paix.

This unhappy family, so little worthy of notice, put itself at the mercy of a powerful neighbor, who could accord it neither trust nor esteem. It laid bare before his eyes all its turpitudes, its impotence, and an incapacity which rendered its government worthless, and even a source of danger to France. Spain had indeed fallen, under the reign of Charles IV, to the lowest depths of abasement. Her fleet was nil, reduced to less than thirty seaworthy vessels or frigates, manned by crews short in numbers, whose pay was, for the most part, two years in arrears. The arsenals and the storehouses were empty, the colonies were left to themselves, exhausted, poor, and ready to separate from the metropolis by which they had been deserted. The army numbered about fifty thousand men under arms, badly clothed, badly fed, and badly paid. A staff, out of proportion to the numbers of the land and sea forces, battened on the feeble war supply. Taxation was badly levied and badly collected. The treasury was in debt; industry and commerce had practically ceased to exist; agriculture was neglected—abandoned to old routine and ruined by the annual migrations of innumerable flocks of sheep, which their proprietors had the privilege to drive from the North of Spain to the South, and which devastated the immense districts on which they were allowed to pasture. The monarchy was governed by an incapable and weak-minded king, who abandoned the reins of government to the hands of a vain and unprincipled favorite, who was detested by the nation, and who was the lover of a dissolute queen. The heir presumptive to the crown was a prince lacking in qualities of heart as well as of intelligence, false, profoundly hypocritical, and the blind enemy of France.

Such was the state of Spain, a country on our frontiers, whose neighborhood is of such importance to our safety. Her government and her dynasty crawling at Napoleon's feet when they feared his power or his resentment, had wished to join our enemies in 1807, at the time of the rupture of the negotiations which had been opened between France, Russia, and England; at the time of the declaration of war by Prussia. The Prince de la Paix, thinking that Napoleon would be unable to resist this new coalition, which would increase in size at the first reverse he should suffer, had, by a proclamation dated October 3, called the Spaniards to arms against an enemy whom he did not name, but who was sufficiently clearly indicated to prevent the possibility of any misunderstanding. The victory of Jena had opened the Prince's eyes. He sought, on the one hand, to disavow his proclamation, and on the other, to try and make it believed that it referred to a threatened invasion of the Moors in Andulasia and a landing of the English. In one word he did all that could be done to secure pardon for his imprudent act of bravado. But the Emperor's confidence was destroyed forever. Napoleon made up his mind from that day to take his precautions against a perfidious ally, who would rise to crush him if ever an opportunity of doing so with impunity should present itself. He demanded that the Spanish government should send an army of fifteen thousand men to the island of Elba, to serve as auxiliaries to the French army, and, in case of necessity, to serve as hostages.

The events which had since occurred in Spain had found Napoleon in this state of mind. He did not know what line of action to adopt. Should he ally himself to the Spanish royal house by marriage? Should he seize upon the Spanish provinces on this side of the Ebro, or should he change the Spanish dynasty? In his heart of hearts he inclined towards the last alternative. Without having any fixed plan, the Emperor sent into Southern Spain divisions of French troops assembled under the names of the Gironde and Ocean corps, and divisions of the Eastern and Western Pyrenees. He placed all these corps under the orders of the Grand Duke of Berg, and gave him instructions to advance to Burgos and there to await fresh instructions for his subsequent movements.

The Spaniards at first received the French troops as friends who had come to deliver them from the odious yoke of Godoy and his creatures. Events crowding on, the Grand Duke of Berg had thrown off the mask, and with the corps which, on their entry into Spain, had followed the direction of Lisbon and of Gibraltar, marched upon Madrid. The Spaniards reflected that such a number of troops was not necessary to drive out the Prince de la Paix; the capture by surprise of the fortresses of Barcelona, Pamplona, and Saint Sebastian, only increased their amazement and their suspicions. Napoleon's silence on his plans, his refusal to publish the Fontainebleau convention, which related to the division of Portugal, began also to fill the Spanish court, which had retired to Aranjuez, with anxiety. Secret preparations for a flight to America were made, the pretext of these preparations being that they were in view of a journey to Andalusia. The populations of Madrid and Aranjuez began to grow excited at what was happening. The Court, to reassure the public mind, denied any intention of leaving Spain, and published this denial in a proclamation, but all in vain. In the night of March 18, a revolution broke out in Aranjuez. The maddened mob threw itself upon the house of the Prince de la Paix, broke down the doors of the palace, destroyed the costly furniture in the apartments, and flung the *débris* out of the windows, hunting for the favorite in every recess for the purpose of murdering him. He, escaping the fury of the mob, came forth from the retreat in which he had been able to hide himself from search, after thirty-six hours agony. Recognized by a sentinel, who denounced him, he was handed over to the bodyguards. Protected by them he succeeded in reaching their barracks, pursued by a furious crowd, and wounded by the blows which he received on his way. The Prince of the Asturias, on the prayer of his distracted parents, consented to intercede in favor of his enemy. He desired the pleasure of enjoying Godoy's humiliation, and of casting up in his face, with perfidious joy, the grace which he accorded to the favorite of his family, in return for all the wrong which he had done him.

The King and Queen, terrified by the disaster which had befallen their well-beloved Godoy, feared for a moment for their own safety. Charles IV declared that he wished to abdicate. By a deed written in haste he resigned to his son a crown which he had long worn without glory, and the people of Aranjuez went to hail with their acclamations their new king, in the midst of general transports of delight.

Napoleon, hearing of these events in Paris, at once sent M. de Tournon off to Madrid. M. de Tournon was one of his chamberlains and orderlies, and had recently returned from Spain, where he had been charged with a mission. General Savary, whose skill and devotion were appreciated by the Emperor, whenever there was anything difficult to be done was sent off on the morrow with the same destination.

Here arises a difficulty which till now has remained without solution, as often happens in history. A letter addressed by the Emperor to the Grand Duke of Berg, under date of Paris, March 29, 1808, supposed to have been entrusted to chamberlain Tournon to carry to its destination, has been quoted by numerous writers who have written about the Spanish war and revolution, as though it had reached its destination, although the Grand Duke of Berg never received it. This letter was inserted literally into the Memorial of St. Helena, but cannot have been communicated by the Emperor, who was not in possession of his papers. The dispatch of which I am speaking is in contradiction to all the orders and dispatches which either preceded or followed it. No trace of it has been found either in the archives of the war-office or of the Foreign Office, or in the private archives at the Louvre. No allusion was made to it in any of the letters which followed it. It may be added that it contains several material irregularities. It is dated from Paris, whereas the Emperor was at St. Cloud, where he stayed from March 22, till April 2, 1808—the day of his departure for Bayonne—and he always used to date his letters from St. Cloud when he happened to be there. The form of address which he used in his letters to Murat was not "Sir, the Grand Duke of Berg," but "My cousin." The Emperor did not use the expression "My Minister of Foreign Affairs"—an expression which only dates from the Restoration—but used to say "My Minister of Exterior Relations"—which was the only appellation in use at that time. In spite of these slight anomalies, which may have arisen from unavoidable oversights in the numerous transcriptions of this letter, it has a most authentic character, and can but have been Napoleon's work. He alone knew how to write on such matters. His style might be imitated, his thoughts might be rendered; but there are details and allusions in this letter which nobody but himself could have known without having been initiated to the ensemble of his vast conception and his most secret thoughts.

How did this letter come to be published? What was the filiation? From whose hands does it proceed? Was the draft taken from the archives of the Louvre in 1814, together with the papers referring to the Duke d'Enghien, and the occurrences in Spain, in which Prince de Bénévent was implicated, and at the time when he got possession of all these documents? Was this dispatch neglected by him as of no importance to the object he had in view? or was it saved by chance from the auto-da-fé to which Talleyrand consigned all the papers brought back from the Archives? as was, in so strange a fashion, the First Consul's letter relating to the seizure of the Duke d'Enghien. The most probable hypothesis is that this letter to Murat only existed in the form of a draft, that it was only one of the hundred plans with which Napoleon's mind was taken up during the laborious elaboration of this most difficult enterprise. The Emperor may have been brought to the ideas which predominate in this letter by the reports which he received from M. de Tournon, who had just traveled through Spain, and had pushed on as far as Andalusia; not that Napoleon would have allowed himself to be influenced by the opinions of his chamberlain, but because M. de Tournon quoted actual facts which he had witnessed, and because anything that so candid and truthful an officer might relate could not be listened to otherwise than with great attention.

All the suppositions that one may indulge in will not, as a matter of fact, supply the key to this enigma of history, and the Emperor's letter to his brother-in-law Murat, in spite of all investigation, remains surrounded with a mystery which the author of the "Memorial of St. Helena" did nothing to dispel. The clearness, the precision of the terms of this letter, the allusion to the attitude to be observed towards General Solano amongst others, disposes, in my opinion, of the suggestion of those who have believed that this document was manufactured after the event. Although I have abstained from reproducing in this work historical pieces which are known to the public, I cannot refrain from publishing here, word for word, this most curious letter, so that the reader may have the leading features of the question under his eyes:

"Paris, March 20, 1808

"SIR, THE GRAND DUKE OF BERG—I fear lest you be deceiving me on the situation in Spain, and lest you be deceiving yourself. Events have been singularly complicated by the affair of March 19. I remain in a state of great perplexity. Do not imagine that you are attacking a disarmed nation, and that you have only to show your troops in order to reduce Spain to submission. The revolution of March 18 shows that the Spaniards have energy. You have to deal with a young people. It has all the courage, and will have all the enthusiasm, which are to be found in men who have not been worn out by political passions.

"The aristocracy and the clergy are the masters of Spain. Should they fear for their privileges, and for their existence, they will raise levies in mass against us, which may continue the war for all eternity. I have partisans in Spain, but if I present myself there as a conqueror I shall have no more.

"The Prince de la Paix is hated because he is accused of having surrendered Spain to France. That is the grievance which served Ferdinand's usurpation. The popular party is the weakest.

"The Prince of the Asturias has none of the qualities which are indispensable in the head of a nation, but that does not prevent his being set up as a hero to oppose us. I do not wish any violence to be offered to the persons of this family. It is never a good thing to render oneself odious or to inflame hatred.

"Spain has more than one hundred thousand men under arms, and that is more than is necessary to carry on a war in the interior with success. Divided over several points each division may form the nucleus of a general rising of the monarchy.

"I am placing before you the ensemble of such obstacles as are inevitable. There are others which you yourself will see.

"England will not let this opportunity of increasing our difficulties escape. Each day she is sending *avisos* to the forces which she keeps on the coasts of Portugal and in the Mediterranean, and she is enlisting Sicilians and Portuguese.

"The royal family not having left Spain to go and settle in the Indies, nothing but a revolution can change , the state of affairs in this country. It is perhaps the country in Europe which is least prepared for a revolution. Those who see the monstrous vices of this government, and the state of anarchy which has replaced legal authority, are in the minority; it is the majority who profit by these vices and this state of anarchy.

"In the interests of my empire I can do much good to Spain. What are the best measures to be taken? Shall I go to Madrid? Shall I play the part of grand protector and decide between the father and the son? It seems to me difficult to allow Charles IV to reign. His government and his favorite are so unpopular that they could not survive three months.

"Ferdinand is the enemy of France, and that is why he is being made king. To place him on the throne would be to play into the hands of the parties who for the last twenty-five years have desired the annihilation of France. A family alliance would be a feeble tie. Queen Elizabeth and other French princesses perished miserably when it was possible to immolate them as the victims of hideous vengeance. I am of the opinion that nothing must be hurried on, that it will be a good thing to be guided by the events that will follow. The army corps in position on the Portuguese frontiers should be strengthened, and we should wait. . . .

"I do not approve of Your Highness's plan of seizing on Madrid with such precipitation. The army should be kept at a distance of ten leagues from the capital. You had no reason to be assured that the people and the magistracy would acknowledge Ferdinand without opposition. The Prince de la Paix must have partisans in the public offices. The old king moreover is attached to him by force of habit, and this attachment may produce results. Your entry into Madrid, in frightening the Spanish, has served Ferdinand in a powerful manner. I have ordered Savary to go and see what is going on around the old king. He will confer with Your Imperial Highness. I shall decide later on what must be done, in the meanwhile these are the instructions which I think right to give you. You will not engage me to any interview with Ferdinand unless you deem the position of affairs to be such that I must acknowledge him as King of Spain. You will behave with courtesy and consideration towards the King, the Queen, and Prince Godoy. You will insist that the same honors are paid them as formerly, and you will pay them these honors yourself. You will act in such a way that the Spaniards will not be able to suspect what line of action I intend to adopt, and this will be a matter of no difficulty, seeing that I myself am in ignorance on this point.

"You will give the nobility and the clergy to understand that should France interfere in Spain's affairs their privileges and immunities will be respected. You will tell them that the Emperor desires that the political institutions of Spain should be perfected with the object of harmonizing them with European civilization, and to save the country from the rule of favorites . . . You will tell the magistrates and townspeople, the people of education, that the political machinery of Spain needs recasting, that she is in want of laws which shall guarantee her citizens against arbitrary rule and the usurpations of the feudal families—of institutions which shall revive industry, agriculture, and the arts. You will depict to them the state of ease and repose which is enjoyed by France, in spite of the wars in which she has been engaged, the splendor of the religion which owes its reestablishment to the Concordat which I signed with the pope. You will point out to them the advantages which they would derive from a political regeneration—order and peace at home, respect and power abroad. Such should be the spirit of your writings and of your speeches. Do nothing hastily. I can wait at Bayonne. I can cross the Pyrenees and strengthening myself towards the Portuguese frontier, carry the war in this direction.

"I will attend to your private interests; do not you attend to them yourself . . . Portugal will remain at my disposal . . . Let no personal plan occupy your attention nor direct your conduct; that would injure me, and injure you still more. You go too fast in your instructions of the 14th. The march which you ordered of General Dupont is too rapid, because of what happened on March 19, and there must be changes made. You will give orders for new arrangements; you will receive instructions from my Minister of Foreign Affairs. I command that discipline be most rigorously maintained; no pardon for small faults. The inhabitants must be treated with the greatest consideration. The churches and the convents must especially be respected. The army must avoid any encounter either with the Spanish army or with its detachments. Not a percussion cap must be fired on either side. Let Solano get beyond Badajoz; have him watched; give, in person, orders for the marching of my army, so that it may always be at a distance of some leagues from the Spanish troops. All would be lost if war were to break out.

"The destinies of Spain will have to be decided by politics and negotiations; I advise you to avoid any conversation with Solano, or other Spanish generals and governors. You will send me two couriers each day. Should anything serious happen send me orderly officers. You will at once send the chamberlain Tournon, who carries this dispatch, back to me, and you will hand him a detailed report. And hereupon I pray God, etc.,

"(Signed) NAPOLEON"

In the meanwhile the old sovereigns, who had remained at Aranjuez, were the prey of mortal terrors. Hearing that the Grand Duke of Berg was approaching Madrid they secretly sent their daughter the Queen of Etruria to implore him to protect them. Prince Murat sent them an officer of his staff, M. Bailly de Monthion, to reassure them, and to suggest to them that they should protest against the violence which had been offered to them, a proposal to which they lent a willing ear. On March 21, two days after his abdication, Charles IV signed this protestation, and sent it to the Grand Duke of Berg.

Murat sent it on to the Emperor, who approved of what he had done. Several orders, coming one after the other, had enjoined on Murat to push forward with all speed to Madrid. Napoleon's brother-in-law, in consequence, made his entry into the Spanish capital on the 24th, at the head of a part of his army.

On the following day Prince Ferdinand, who had left Aranjuez in a hurry, made haste to make a solemn entry into Madrid as though to take possession of the rights conferred upon him by his adoption by the popular party. He was on horseback, surrounded by his officers, and was enthusiastically received. The diplomatic corps came to present their respects to the new King. The ambassador of France stayed away, Murat having declared to Ferdinand that he could not acknowledge him as King, as he had received no instructions concerning him from the Emperor.

As soon as Napoleon was apprised of these facts he decided that the time for action had come. In various conferences which he had with MM. de Talleyrand and

Champigny, the Spanish question, once more brought under discussion, came up. Various opinions were pronounced in the course of these conversations on the alternatives of changing the Spanish dynasty, or of maintaining it in power after taking guarantees for the future. At the last conference, which was held on the eve of his departure, Napoleon did not express his own opinion on the matter because his mind was not yet made up as to what line of action he should adopt, and because he wished to see with his own eyes. He appeared, in the course of these conversations to be in quest of either strong objections, or of good reasons for strengthening him in the resolution to which he himself inclined. At the same time nothing was decided upon at this meeting, and the Emperor left Paris without having expressed any fixed determination.

Before leaving Paris the Emperor had written to his brother, the King of Holland, to the effect that in case he should decide to change the Spanish dynasty, he had thought of him for the throne of Spain, that this was only a project, but that it was possible, circumstances aiding, that all would be ready in a fortnight, and asked him for a straightforward answer to this question: "If I should create you King of Spain would you accept the throne?" He added that he expected an answer of "Yes," or "No"; that nobody could be taken into his confidence, as a thing ought to be done before it had been thought over, etc. Louis had refused, and Napoleon answered him that in consequence the matter could no longer be considered.

The Emperor arrived at Bayonne on April 14, after having spent a week at Bordeaux, where his stay was not without profit to the commercial interests of this city. He spent two days at Bayonne, waiting that the Château de Marrac, distant about a league from Bayonne, which he had purchased, should be in a state to receive him and the Empress Josephine, who was to meet him there.

The mission of General Savary, in whom Napoleon had every confidence, was to see the French ambassador to find out all that had happened at Madrid and Aranjuez, to assure himself of the real state of affairs, to see whether King Charles's abdication was genuine, and to ascertain what sort of a man the Prince of the Asturias was, and what degree of confidence he merited. Napoleon made it clear to General Savary that if neither the father nor the son could be trusted, he should make up his mind to dethrone the reigning family.

On his arrival at Madrid, General Savary saw Prince Ferdinand and his private councilors. He found them disposed to go to Bayonne to meet the Emperor, with the idea that so marked an action would render the powerful sovereign who held the fate of Spain in his hand, favorable towards the new king. This journey was accordingly decided upon, and General Savary accompanied the prince.

On arriving at Vittoria, Ferdinand, who had expected to meet the Emperor there, refused to proceed any further, and declared that he would wait for news of Napoleon in that city. Savary, having in vain essayed to get the better of the Spanish prince's obstinacy, proceeded to Bayonne where he arrived some hours before the Emperor. To the searching questions put to him by Napoleon on the character and disposition of Ferdinand, the General answered by expressing his mistrust of the sincerity of the assurances which had been made to him, and declared that in his opinion the prince would be governed by ministers hostile to France.

The Emperor sent General Savary back on the morrow carrying a letter in which he invited H.R.H. the Prince of the Asturias to come to Bayonne, but in which he made no promises, and in no way pledged himself towards him. During Savary's absence, several Spanish persons of importance, amongst others Urquijo, the former minister, had been to see the prince, and had pointed out to him that it would be a want of dignity and of prudence on his part to cross the frontier, especially considering that the Emperor Napoleon had not acknowledged him. Ferdinand and his counselors paid no attention to this advice, and the Emperor's letter having dispelled their hesitations, they decided to leave for Bayonne on the morrow.

Just as Ferdinand was about to enter his carriage a mob of armed peasants, who had joined in with the people who filled the prince's house, wanted to prevent his departure. The traces of the carriages were cut, and the mules were led back to the stables. The Duke of l'lnfantado, throwing himself into the midst of the crowd, succeeded in calming the rioters, so that the mules could be put to again, and the carriages were allowed to drive off without further hindrance. On approaching Bayonne, the prince, who was beginning to be surprised at seeing nothing of the Emperor, met General Duroc, who had been sent to meet him, and to compliment him on his arrival. Napoleon, on his side, hearing of Ferdinand's arrival at Bayonne, jumped on horseback, and rode off to pay him a first visit. He embraced him, but only addressed him as Royal Highness. On his return to Marrac the Emperor sent a chamberlain to invite the Prince and his suite to dinner at the castle.

The conversations which Napoleon had with Ferdinand, and the persons who had accompanied him, very soon showed him the emptiness and vulgar cunning of this prince's character, the mediocrity of his advisers, and their inability to direct their master. These first discoveries were not of a nature to modify the Emperor's way of thinking. His opinion, accordingly, that the regeneration of Spain under such rulers was an impossibility, was confirmed. He was disappointed to find that there was not amongst the Prince's suite a single man with whom he could speak on his political views with regard to Spain. It was to Canon Escoïquitz, the most intelligent amongst them, and the adviser who was most in the Prince's confidence, that Napoleon thought fit to open his mind. He accordingly told this priest that the assistance of Spain was indispensable to him to force England to peace, that the deplorable state of the Spanish monarchy was as disastrous to France as to Spain herself, that the scandal of the scenes at the Escurial and at Aranjuez had shown to what a degree the dynasty was degenerated and degraded, and that it was quite unable to drag the monarchy up out of the slough into which it had fallen. This too plain speaking astounded the canon and brought him down from his castles in the air. In answer to his plea in favor of his pupil, Napoleon made even more positive statements.

Ferdinand, to whom Escoïquitz reported this conversation, protested, alleged the inalienable rights of his family, maintained that he was the legitimate king by his father's abdication, and that if Charles IV wished to withdraw his abdication it was to him alone that he would surrender the crown.

The presence of the old sovereigns being alone likely to put an end to this resistance, the Emperor hurried on their arrival as well as that of the Prince de la Paix in Bayonne. The Prince de la Paix had been treated with extreme severity. Murat was obliged to use force to tear him from the hands of those who detained him, and who were firmly resolved that he should die on the scaffold. Napoleon saw Godoy on his arrival, and disguising the disgust with which this person inspired him, had a long conversation with him, which only gave him fresh cause for persevering in his determination to deprive Ferdinand of his crown. He undertook to assure incomes in proportion to their rank to the old King, the Queen, and the Prince de la Paix.

The Spanish sovereigns arrived at last on April 30. They were received with the etiquette paid to kings. The Emperor went to receive them on their entry into Bayonne. The Empress, who had arrived at Marrac a few days previously, went to comfort the old queen. There was hand-kissing, according to the Spanish custom. Prince Ferdinand came to bow to his father, but Charles indignantly repelled him, and forbade him to follow him into his apartment. There, their dear friend Godoy was awaiting them, and they had the pleasure of embracing him. He told them about Napoleon's plans, and they had no objections to make.

They came to dinner at Marrac on the following day. The old king, weighted by his infirmities, leant on the Emperor's arm as he was mounting the steps of the castle. Napoleon had said to him: "Lean on me, I have strength enough for both of us."

King Charles's protestation against his abdication had been published in Madrid and was addressed to the junta formed by Ferdinand, before his departure from this city, a junta presided over by his uncle Don Antonio. By the terms of this document Charles addressed a severe letter to his son, reproaching him with his guilty conduct, and summoning him to surrender the crown. Ferdinand answered that although he had received the crown by his father's voluntary abdication, he was ready to resign it on condition that the King should reign in person and that the restitution should take place openly at Madrid before the assembled Cortés. But King Charles, retracting his forced abdication, declared himself sole legitimate king of Spain, and added that in view of his absence from his kingdom, he appointed the Grand Duke of Berg his lieutenant general, and invested him with all his powers. At the same time orders were given that the Infant Don Antonio, the King's brother, president of the junta, the Infant Don Francis de Paule, and the Queen of Etruria, who had remained in Madrid, should be sent on to Bayonne.

The Spaniards already excited by the scenes which had taken place, were greatly aroused by the departure of the members of the royal family, one after the other. Ferdinand, by means of letters and couriers, who were dispatched in disguise from Bayonne, inflamed the excitement of the public and kept it aglow. These couriers were watched and arrested, and the papers found upon them were conveyed to the Emperor's cabinet. These letters were filled with invectives and curses against the French and Napoleon. They contained false news, were calculated to excite the anger of the people, and represented the Prince of the Asturias as the victim of the most odious treatment. These lying stories, spread broadcast by means of bulletins and manuscript notes, were read with eagerness everywhere. So greatly did they arouse the popular mind that a general insurrection broke out in Madrid on May 2. Wounded French soldiers in the hospitals, and soldiers and officers, found alone in the streets, were massacred without pity by a furious and savage mob.

The Emperor heard of this sad occurrence as he was returning to Marrac on horseback. The news was brought by one of the Grand Duke's staff-officers, M. d'Haneucourt, who later on became Master of the Hunt. In a violent passion, the Emperor turned his horse round without a moment's delay, and galloped off to find King Charles, to whom he showed these dispatches. The King sent for the Infants, and both he and the Queen spoke to Ferdinand with the extremest severity. The King brandished his stick as though about to strike his son. The Queen was in such a rage that she forgot herself to the point of walking up to her son and making a gesture as though to box his ears. The prince, standing motionless, and with downcast eyes, did not answer a single word. The Emperor put an end to this painful scene by informing the Prince of the Asturias that he was bound only to his father, that he acknowledged Charles alone as King, and that unless Ferdinand surrendered the crown which he had usurped, with all speed, he would be treated as a rebel. Charles IV cried out that he did not want a crown which was tarnished, and that he renounced a country in which an ungrateful son had roused every passion against its sovereign. Ferdinand, covered with confusion and vexation, left the room, followed by the small group of courtiers who had waited for him in the outer drawing room.

After having spent a moment with the old sovereigns, Napoleon left them and returned to Marrac lost in thought, and only emerging from this state of abstraction to utter bitter reflections on the state of degradation into which this family had fallen.

On the same day documents were drawn up which settled the position of the Prince of the Asturias, at the same time as that of the Infants, who were not to return to Spain. The castle of Navarre was given to Prince Ferdinand in fee simple, with an income of one million francs. A pension of four hundred thousand francs was allotted to each of the Infants. The Prince signed, in his own name and that of his family, a renunciation of the crown of Spain and all the rights of succession.

King Charles refusing to accept the crown, whose sole proprietor he was acknowledged to be, he surrendered it to the Emperor to dispose of as he might think fit. He received in compensation the palace and forest of Compiègne, for life, and the castle of Chambord in fee simple, with an income of thirty million reals—seven million five hundred thousand francs—to be paid him from the public Treasury of France.

Such is a plain statement of the facts which brought about this great catastrophe, freed from particulars which certain historians have added in induction to the principal fact, and which they have explained, not always with justice. I have only related what in the sphere of my duties I saw and learned. It does not behoove me to set myself up as the judge of Napoleon's conduct in an enterprise the object of which—as must perforce be admitted—was eminently a national one. If the legality of the means employed did not correspond to the grandeur of the scheme, it remains proved that, in the Bayonne transaction, Napoleon was impelled by the interests of France far more than by any other motive, and that the change of dynasty was only the consequence of, and an accessory to, the system which he wished to establish in Spain.

The forcible act essayed in the peninsula has been explained as caused by a fixed determination on the part of Napoleon to remove the Bourbons from every throne in Europe; but that was only a secondary idea with him; it was rather the state of Spain that awoke his solicitude. Spain, whose prosperity was as important to France as to the country itself, which was the continuation of our soil, was in a state of decay which would inevitably have led to her falling an easy prey to England. The future was not in Napoleon's hands. However much the Spanish government might at that time be subjected to his wishes, this government had none the less desired to join the coalition on the eve of the battle of Jena. As long as Napoleon should feign, this government would not dare to betray him, but would it be the same with the Emperor's successors?

The servile submission of this royal family showed the master of France how foolhardy and dangerous it would be to rely on such princes. The Spanish government placed its ships, troops, and feeble resources at Napoleon's disposal at this moment and without hesitation. In spite of certain secret Communications with England, suspected by the Emperor, but which had remained without any immediate result, France had not a sufficiently strong motive to declare war with Spain, and to expel the Bourbons by force. This line of action, had it been justifiable by apparent causes, would have been worthier of Napoleon, but he could not adopt it in the absence of any plausible motive, without exciting public reprobation. Louis XIV, acting in a dynastic interest, had been admirably served by Charles II's testament. Napoleon, prompted by a national interest, failed; he had no choice of means. He remains exposed to the blame of posterity, which would have absolved him if his work, the defects of which show themselves owing to its want of success, had been able to last and to bring with it the many benefits which would have resulted for France and Spain. This enterprise would have succeeded, as did the War of Succession, if the coalition had not deprived Napoleon of the time and the possibility of applying his strength and his attention to it, by constantly drawing him on to new struggles which removed him from the object in view. The national resistance and antipathy even, would have been overcome in the end; the influence of men enlightened as to the real interests of their country would have prevailed, and the masses would have followed them. The advantages of the constitution of Bayonne, the prosperity which its application would have conferred on the people, the protection which the French alliance would have assured to our neighbors by the interest we had to render them prosperous and powerful—all these causes together Would in time have Subjugated the Spaniards. Napoleon can be blamed in this matter neither for precipitation nor for caprice. His plan had been matured and carried out with the necessary slowness and prudence. He had in his favor his omnipotence, the prosperous state of France, Europe at that time pacified, and a close alliance with Russia. The moment seemed favorable; it was neither too late nor too early. Napoleon himself has said that he was forced to seize the opportunity offered to him by fortune to regenerate Spain, to remove her from the clutches of England, and to unite her closely to our system. In doing so, he was, in his opinion, laying one of the fundamental bases of the repose and security of Europe.

The illegality, however, of the means employed was the frequent subject of Napoleon's reflections, and maintained him in a continual state of perplexity. His mind revolted against perfidious conduct, for he had an instinctive loathing for crooked and tortuous ways. He hesitated for a long time between various lines of action. He had thought of a family alliance; but nothing is more precarious than a political marriage. Another plan was to take, in guise of pledges, the Spanish provinces on this side of the Ebro, but that would have deeply offended the inhabitants of these provinces, and would have kept them continually ready to revolt. He was forced to go back to the plan of dethroning the reigning family; the events that crowded on disposed of the Emperor's irresolutions; an outraged father, supplanted by his son, abandoned by his people, urged on by a fear for his own safety, by the necessity of having recourse to the protection of his ally, and by the fear with which the violence of the factions inspired him—a guilty son, vile and nerveless, dominated by evil passions—both came to throw themselves into Napoleon's arms. This combination of extraordinary circumstances, the news of the Madrid insurrection, which had been encouraged by Ferdinand, an insurrection in the course of which Frenchmen had been massacred in the hospitals and in the streets, all these things together urged the Emperor on. When he saw the Spanish princes at his feet, and had gauged their worthlessness and weakness, Napoleon considered himself "an instrument of Providence." The scandalous scenes which he witnessed amongst the members of this family deprived him of all confidence in the stability of an alliance with these princes. The old king refused to return to Spain. Could Napoleon, even if he had been so disposed, force this prince to resume his crown? King Charles's antecedents, his impotence, the aversion which he had provoked through his favorite, made the Emperor see only too clearly that such a Restoration was not practicable. Should Ferdinand then have been sent back to Madrid? But that would have meant handing Spain over to England, and to the parties which were hostile to France. Napoleon confirmed his resolution, in consequence, to confide the destinies of the neighboring kingdom to the hands of a Frenchman. The generous wish to rescue so interesting a nation from the state of decay to which it had been reduced by the government of a degenerate race of kings had as much to do in forming Napoleon's resolutions as the necessity of putting an end to a line of policy, vacillating in the present, and certain to be hostile in the future.

The Emperor sent a pressing invitation, by courier, to King Joseph, to come to Bayonne. In the interview which he had with his brother at Venice, in 1807, Napoleon had spoken to him of the various chances which might be brought about by the dissensions by which the Spanish reigning house was divided; but without expressing any definite idea on the subject at the time. Napoleon went to meet the King of Naples on his arrival at Bayonne, informed him of the views he entertained concerning him, and urged him to agree to them. He had hoped that Lucien would have accepted the conditions which he wished to impose on him at Mantua. If Lucien had been more docile under his demands, Napoleon would at this time have placed him on the throne of Naples, which was given to Murat, the Grand Duke of Berg. While awaiting the arrival of his brother Joseph, Napoleon occupied himself with providing that the Spanish colonies should remain faithful to their allegiance, With this object in view he had sent out from the various ports of Spain, Portugal, and France a number of light ships freighted with arms and munitions, and carrying proclamations, to the ports of Southern America. The Emperor also ordered reports on the state of the Spanish finances, army, and navy, to be laid before him, and gave orders that a subsidy of twenty-five millions, taken from the funds of the extraordinary domain, should be advanced to the Spanish treasury to meet the most pressing needs of the country. And finally, he ordered the dispersion of the Spanish troops in the peninsula, and the distribution of the French soldiers over various parts of the territory, at the points where they were most needed, to be in readiness to check the first attempts at insurrection.

Napoleon had understood that a change of dynasty could not be effected without the intervention, in some form, of the Spanish nation, and that is the reason why he desired to convoke to Bayonne an assembly of leading men in the various classes of the state. He introduced his brother Joseph to the most influential men, who all offered him their services, and hailed him as the regenerator of their country. The result of this assembly of Spanish notables was a constitution which contained all the elements of the regeneration of Spain. If the fanaticism of the monks, who had a representative in each family; if the influence exercised by the greatness and too generous exaltation of the national feeling of self-respect had not annulled the benefits of this constitution, Spain would today have been far advanced on the road of prosperity, which the constitution drawn up at Bayonne opened out before her feet.

While the deliberations of the junta were proceeding, Charles IV, the Queen, and the Prince de la Paix left for Fontainebleau. The Infants, followed by the Duke of San Carlos and Canon Escoïquitz, were sent to the Castle of Valançay, which had been selected by the Emperor as the residence of these princes. Taken by surprise, and dragged on by the rapidity with which events had crowded on, Napoleon had only just the time to send word to Prince de Bénévent, to whom this estate belonged, and who had remained in Paris, to proceed to Valançay and to receive the Infants.

King Joseph passed from the throne of Naples to the throne of Spain and the Grand Duke of Berg went to take his place in Naples. The Grand Duchy of Berg, left vacant by Murat, was united to the French Empire, and was given, in 1810, to the eldest son of Prince Louis, after the latter had abdicated and renounced the crown of Holland.

This business having been disposed of, the Emperor, accompanied by the Empress, left Marrac to return to Paris. He spent a day at Pau and at Tarbes. At Pau he occupied the castle where Henri IV was born. This castle, situated at a distance of a thousand yards from the town had since been restored, and has become an imperial residence. At Tarbes the Emperor slept at the prefect's mansion, where he noticed, in one of the drawing rooms, a fine portrait of Lays, the celebrated Opera singer, one of the glories of the department.

Napoleon only spent twelve hours at Auch. Hearing that General Dessoles, who had refused to fill the functions of chief of the staff to General Lannes at Boulogne, was living in the neighborhood, retired in a country house, he charged Prince de Neufchâtel to offer him a post. General Dessoles had disapproved of the condemnation of Moreau, and without expressing his discontent, had found some pretext for retiring from the service. He had been chief of the staff to this celebrated general. He had filled the same post in the army in Hanover, when this army was under the command of the Prince de Ponte-Corvo, and had even commanded it during the Marshal's absence. General Dessoles had grown to hate the Emperor with a hidden hatred during these two campaigns, a hatred which he had not dared to make public, but which burst out with violence in 1814. Napoleon, who admired this general officer's talents, had no hesitation in making the first advances. He entrusted him with the command of a division in Spain. General Dessoles asked to be recalled after some time. This inconstancy of humor, or rather this hidden ill will, did not exhaust the Emperor's patience, and at the time of the expedition to Russia he appointed the general chief of the staff to Prince Eugène. After the taking of Smolensk, Dessoles once more asked to be allowed to leave the army on the pretext of bad health. He was present in Paris, in 1814, at the time of the entry of the allies. It is known how he behaved.

The stay of the Emperor and the Empress, for two days, at Toulouse, their journey to Montauban and Agen were marked by the wild enthusiasm which Napoleon's presence excited everywhere. His apparition was always followed by measures calculated to increase the prosperity of the towns and provinces which he visited. Madame de Balbi, an old friend of the Count de Provence, who afterwards became Louis XVIII, happened to be at Montauban at the time. I had occasion to see her in Paris, after the Restoration, and to hear her boast before me of having been an honorable exception to the general joy which was manifested at Montauban at the time of Napoleon's visit.

While the Emperor was pursuing his way through the departments of the South, the insurrection in Spain had become general. The news of the double abdication of Charles IV and of Ferdinand, and King Joseph's proclamation had brought about an explosion of the feelings of hatred which only wanted an opportunity to burst out. In the space of a week, towards the end of May, the East, North, and West of Spain were on fire. The Spaniards had risen as one man. The arsenals had been ransacked, and the people had armed. Juntas had been formed and a mass levy was being organized on every side. The mob took the initiative everywhere, and imposed its umbrageous and savage authority. In the chiefs who were in authority it saw none but traitors. Most of the captains-general were murdered, because they refused blind obedience to the riotous passions of the mob. The least hesitation was punished with a cruel death. Enlightened men, both military and civil, who feared reprisals from France, and who, satisfied with the fall of a shameful government, looked for the reform of abuses and the benefits of a government which was anxious to cause its usurpation to be forgotten, essayed to calm the fury of the mob. They fell victims to their own wisdom and patriotism; the furious mob pursued them into refuges most worthy of respect, murdering them in the arms of their own soldiers, or of their families. Their bodies were dragged through the mud; their heads were carried at the end of pikes. The remnant of the French fleet which had escaped the disaster of Trafalgar had taken refuge in the port of Cadiz. When this insurrection broke out, this feeble squadron, having lost all hope of being rescued by General Dupont's corps, hemmed in by the English and the Spaniards, was obliged to surrender at discretion to the latter, to escape destruction without revenge.

The fury of the Spanish mob kept increasing, and excited the rioters to treat our unhappy prisoners with the refinements of unheard-of ferocity. They crucified some of these wretched soldiers to trees, others were hung up and fires were lighted beneath their feet. Others were buried alive; some were sawn asunder between two planks. The pen refuses to record the acts of horrible and inhuman barbarism which these cannibals indulged in towards their unfortunate victims. Women and children were treated with the most abominable cruelty. It was while at Bordeaux that the Emperor heard the sad news of the capitulation of Baïlen. The dishonorable conditions of this capitulation, the unworthy conduct of the Spanish generals, who, not satisfied with insulting them, had refused bread and water to our soldiers, who were dying of hunger, and who were choking under the burning and implacable sun—all this desolating news filled Napoleon with indignation and grief. These feelings reached their highest pitch when he heard how horribly the ferocious mob had treated those of our soldiers whom it could not kill, pursuing them all along the roads with stones and knives. Able-bodied, invalid, or wounded soldiers, not one had been able to escape the most revolting and most ignominious treatment. To crown these horrible excesses of mob fury, the junta of Seville refused to recognize the capitulation, declared the French prisoners of war, and had them conducted to Cadiz, which they only reached after having faced a thousand dangers—pillaged, robbed, insulted, and running the risk of being murdered every minute of the day.

This disastrous day of Baïlen, during which twenty thousand French soldiers had marched past and laid down their arms before enemies who had always fled before them in the open field, was a reverse without example in the military history of the new France. It put a stain on our arms and dishonored the glory which till then they had enjoyed. It struck a most serious blow against our prestige in Spain. This unexpected success, indeed, electrified the Spaniards, and dragged into the revolution those who were still hesitating. Napoleon was thunderstruck by this unexpected blow. A brave army had been struck by fate, and a spirit of dizziness had disabled its leaders. How, indeed, can so fatal an error be explained on the part of a general—General Dupont—whose military career had been most honorable and often brilliant, and for whom the Emperor destined in the future a Marshal's baton; on the part of another general officer of the highest merit—General Marescot—who till then had been esteemed and appreciated by Napoleon, and finally on the part of General Vedel, who had distinguished himself by brilliant feats of arms before Ulm, and at Friedland, but whose misfortune it was to be too loyal to military discipline? To crown all, one of the Emperor's equerries was one of the staff-officers of this army, and had been sent there on his request to enter the military service. His capacity as an officer of the imperial household had given him, in this deplorable occurrence, a rôle of confidence and a kind of ill-considered authority which had been fatal.

General Marescot, chief inspector of engineers, happened by chance to be at the headquarters of the Dupont corps. Charged to reconnoiter the fort of Cadiz, he had been forced to follow the movements of this corps in consequence of the insurrection of the province of Seville. He was present at the affair at Baïlen, and yielding to pressing instances, he had consented to undertake to negotiate for a capitulation. He had proceeded at once to the Castagno's camp, dressed, it is said, in the Spanish uniform, for what reason is unknown, and had signed at the bottom of this shameful agreement, a name which till then had been without reproach. The necessity of making an example forced the Emperor to punish this general. He was dismissed from all his commissions. His wife shared his disgrace, and lost her place as lady-in-waiting to the Empress Josephine. Although Napoleon felt very sorry to have to act with such severity towards a lady whom he esteemed, Madame Marescot was forced to understand that it was impossible for her to remain at the palace any longer.

The persons who had signed the capitulation of Baïlen were kept in prison for longer or shorter periods. A draft of a decree was presented to the Council of State to decide upon the manner of their being sent to trial, but no effect was given to this measure. The Emperor has been rightly blamed for not having sent the culprits before a court-martial, which would have published their judgment. The interruption of these proceedings has been attributed to an arbitrary will. Napoleon's first impulse was to deal out severe justice, but reflection restrained him. It may be that he thought that publicity would put forward beyond recall these shameful circumstances, and thus add fresh ignominy to the insult which stained our flag. To this consideration may be added another which will be equally blamed by the partisans of national justice. An irrevocable condemnation, such as a sentence of death, would have been the probable result of this trial, besides the scandal. These condemnations would have deprived Napoleon forever of the help of officers whose conduct had been irreproachable until the day of a fatal error which did not in his eyes utterly efface the value of their past services. Extraordinary circumstances might arise, which would give them the opportunity of making up in a brilliant manner for what they had done, as happened in 1813, for the brave General Vedel, amongst others, whom Napoleon only blamed for having shown a too passive obedience to the orders of the commander in chief, Dupont, at Baïlen.

On leaving Bordeaux, Napoleon had proceeded towards the Vendée department, passing by Saintes and Rochefort. He was received as a benefactor. Men and women, old and young, left their farms to rush in crowds to the road on which the Emperor and the Empress were to pass, and to hail them with acclamations of joy, which certainly were not given to order. The traces of the civil war which had devastated these beautiful provinces had disappeared. Large, fine roads in every direction increased the means of communication. From the desert that it had been, this district had become peopled and flourishing. The principal town in the district, Ville-Napoleon, was already supplied with its chief public establishments, others were in course of construction. Numerous private houses, recently built, were all tenanted. In the audiences which the Emperor gave to the mayors and to the priests, who had come together more than two hundred strong, to the soldiery and to the guards of honor, he questioned each on the needs of his department and accorded new favors. The gratitude which the Vendéens displayed towards the hand which had restored their prosperity was the best guarantee of the resistance which, in case of need, they would oppose to any fomenters of fresh discords.

From Napoleon-Ville the Emperor went to spend three days at Nantes, where he was not idle. He visited Angers, Tours, and Blois and arrived at St. Cloud on August 14, 1808.

Chapter VIII

The Emperor's return took place on the eve of his fête, which was celebrated with the customary solemnities. The same day the senate gave a very beautiful fête in the Luxembourg gardens—Free performances were given at all the theatres—The staff officers of the imperial guard celebrated Saint Napoleon with a banquet of three hundred covers in the rooms of the Palais-Royal. The City of Paris offered a banquet, followed by a ball to the Emperor, who was present with the Empress and the whole of the Court.

At the audience on the following Sunday the Russian ambassador presented gifts consisting of jasper vases, and malachite tables, columns, and cups of extraordinary size.

On the same day Napoleon's statue, which was intended for the Place Vendôme, and which had just been cast most successfully, was conveyed to this square. This statue, executed by Chaudet, had been cast out of the metal of the cannons taken from the enemy.

The Emperor spent the five weeks which followed on his return from Bayonne at St. Cloud, He received there the new Persian ambassador at a solemn audience given on this occasion. The ambassador's name was Asker-Khan. He had been sent to him to continue the friendly relations which had been established at Finckenstein by Mirza-Rizza. The ambassador spoke in the name of the hereditary Prince of Persia. He was commissioned to offer the swords of Tamerlane and Thamas-Koulikan to the Emperor. Amongst the presents which he offered were some fine Cashmere shawls, some of which were given to the Empress and the ladies of her court, in the Emperor's name.

Napoleon went to Paris several times, to be present at the fête at the Hotel de Ville, to visit constructions of public utility, to see the panoramas, and for the receptions of the diplomatic corps which took place at the Tuileries. During one of his short stays in Paris he went to view the great picture of the coronation in David's studio. He was accompanied on this occasion by the Empress and her court. Napoleon had pardoned David's errors, on condition that he would devote himself exclusively to the art in which he excelled, and had appointed him his first painter. The Emperor's visit to David's studio was an encouragement given to the arts.

The news of the capitulation of Baïlen, by which twenty thousand French soldiers had laid down arms, in the open field, an event more deplorable for French arms than the surrender of Ulm had been to Austria, had produced the worst possible impression in Madrid. A general defection declared itself, not only amongst the Spanish grandees who after having taken the oath of allegiance to Joseph Bonaparte had accompanied him to Madrid, but even amongst the persons in his service. The wildest and most absurd reports were spread abroad by the monks and all the enemies of France to excite the mob, blind in its anger, to the most extreme excesses. The fiery and savage character of the idle and excitable populations of the towns and country exaggerated these reports still more. The most sensitive fibres of the people were worked upon, its national pride, its religion, its attachment to its princes. A new divine scourge had come upon them to destroy their nationality, to tear them from their homes and to send them to perish in icy climates and in distant wars, victims of an all-devouring ambition. Shackles for chaining them two by two had, it was said, been brought with the French troops. From these impressions greedily accepted by the Spanish mob, there had resulted a hatred of the French, profound, implacable, and exalted to the pitch of ferocity. The occupation of Madrid had become impossible. King Joseph decided to evacuate it. He left in broad daylight on July 31, passing through the town in the midst of the extreme agitation which had been caused by the announcement of his departure. He was followed by some of his ministers and retired to Vittoria with a portion of the first French army which had entered into Spain. The general rising which followed, the animosity which began to characterize the war in this country, the resolution which the Emperor had taken to go there in person, made Napoleon feel the necessity of assuring himself that Russia's disposition was the same, and of conferring on this subject with the Emperor Alexander. An interview was accordingly proposed to the Czar.

The time and place of this interview having been settled, the Emperor left Paris on September 22 to proceed to Erfurth, where the interview was to take place.

On the same day the first column of the Great Army arrived in Paris. It was received at the Pantin gate by the municipal body, and was offered the gold crown which had been voted to the Great Army after the battle of Austerlitz. This column was followed by several others, which passed through Paris one after the other on their way to Spain. All were received with the same solemnity by the municipal authorities, and the City gave banquets and fêtes in their honor on this occasion.

Marshal Lannes had been sent to receive the Emperor of Russia on the frontier of the district occupied by the French army. Napoleon arriving at Erfurth first, went to meet Alexander at a league and a half from the town, which the two sovereigns entered to the sound of bells and the firing of cannon. They had exchanged the insignia of their orders. During the stay of the emperors at Erfurth Napoleon always placed the Emperor Alexander on his right hand to show that it was he who was doing the honors and was in his own place. The houses which they occupied had been furnished by the *garde-meuble* of the French crown and the cost had been paid by the French civil list. The Kings of Saxony, Bavaria, Würtemberg, the Prince Primate, the Grand Duke and Grand duchess of Baden, the Dukes of Saxony and most of the Princes of the Confederation of the Rhine came to Erfurth. The Emperor Napoleon received the Emperor Alexander, the Grand Duke Constantine, his brother, and the sovereigns to dinner every day. At one of these dinners Napoleon noticing that Alexander had forgotten his sword, presented him with his own,

The leading actors of the Théâtre-Français gave numerous performances of our best tragedies. On the first day the emperors occupied a box situated in the center of the theatre. This distance from the stage prevented Alexander from hearing the actors' voices distinctly, he being rather deaf. Napoleon then gave orders that a dais should be raised in the orchestra, and two armchairs for the emperors and chairs for the kings were placed upon it. It was during one of these performances that Alexander, bending over to Napoleon, quoted to him this line of the *Oedipus*, to which Voltaire's great reputation could not give the celebrity, which it acquired after this occurrence: "The friendship of a great man is a gift of the gods."

Alexander's conduct was altogether in harmony with the feeling, feigned rather than sincere, which had prompted him to make this quotation. The two sovereigns spent three weeks at Erfurth, on terms of the most intimate familiarity, riding out together and reviewing the French troops. Hunting-parties, banquets, balls, and theatrical performances were given at Weimar to the whole Court of Erfurth by the Duke of Saxe-Weimar. The battlefield of Jena was visited by the two Emperors.

Goethe and Wieland were presented to Napoleon who was very anxious to make their acquaintance. These two illustrious poets were received by him with the highest distinction and justified in his eyes the opinion he had formed of their merits. Napoleon carried away with him, from the long conversations which he had with them, a high esteem for their talents and for their character. He gave them a proof of this by decorating them with his own hands with the order of the Legion of Honor.

On his return to Erfurth the Emperor gave an audience to Baron Vincent, the Austrian *envoyé*. The suspicious conduct of the Vienna cabinet aroused too much distrust in Napoleon's mind to make him wish to invite the Emperor Francis or his prime minister to the Erfurth meeting. M. de Vincent came to bring to Napoleon the protestations of friendship of which the Austrian cabinet was so lavish; he also came to see what was going on. I will mention later what support this *envoyé* hoped to find at Erfurth for the success of his mission.

On the same day a convention was signed between the two Emperors. Its object was to renew the Tilsitt alliance, to make an application in common to the London cabinet, and finally to acknowledge the new acquisitions of Russia and the new state of things in Spain. After this business had been settled the sovereigns took leave of each other and presents were exchanged. The Emperor Alexander, who professed to treat me with great kindness presented me, as a mark of his favor, with a box ornamented with his cipher in diamonds, worth about ten thousand francs. I first heard of it from the Emperor Napoleon, who authorized me to accept it. Alexander came to take leave of Napoleon, who accompanied him on horseback to the place where his carriages were waiting for him. During this long ride the two sovereigns conversed together alone. Alexander embraced Napoleon, on leaving him, with all the appearances of great cordiality. They were to meet again, sword in hand. The vivacity of these demonstrations was the last expression of a friendship which had no other motive than Alexander's ambition. It had been agreed at Tilsitt that they should meet again later on to come to an understanding, as the Czar hoped, on the Turkish question. Napoleon's refusal to agree to Alexander's demands, or for the time being to permit anything further than the annexation of Wallachia and Moldavia to Russia, began to cool this prince towards an alliance which appeared to him sterile, seeing that it did not carry all the fruits that he had hoped to win from it.

It may not be useless to point out that about two months after Alexander's return from Erfurth to St. Petersburg the King and Queen of Prussia entered the Russian capital. Their Prussian Majesties had arrived the evening before—January 6, 1809—at Strelna, an imperial pleasure house, situated at a distance of two stages from St. Petersburg. Alexander hastened to see them and had a long conference with them. He returned to Strelna on the following morning, before the solemn entry into St. Petersburg and remained closeted for two hours with the King and Queen.

The Emperor Alexander was accompanied to Erfurth by Count Romanzov, whom I mention because Napoleon paid special attention to him. This minister enjoyed his master's entire confidence and showed himself the outspoken partisan of the French alliance. M. de Romanzov urged on the realization of Peter and Catherine's projects on the Orient Empire. When the friendly relations which he had so carefully maintained between Russia and France, broke off, he sent in his resignation from all his posts, either because he saw in this change of policy an abandonment of the scheme of a division of Turkey, or because he did not wish to cooperate in the system of an alliance with England against which he always declared himself. He carried with him, into his retirement, the respect of all and retained his sovereign's esteem, which was frequently expressed in the most honoring terms. He devoted his leisure to letters and science. An enlightened protector of Russian commerce and industry, he employed the largest part of his immense fortune in founding philanthropical establishments, in maritime expeditions, in the publication of articles and ancient documents on the history of Russia. He gave encouragement to Russian and foreign savants and opened his vast and wealthy library to them.

In the memoirs left by M. de Talleyrand, memoirs of which some passages have been made public, which his secretaries copied and in the writing of which some of them even cooperated, there is to be found a curious chapter of which I give the substance further oil. It refers to the conferences which took place between the two sovereigns of France and Russia at Erfurth, in 1808, previous to the campaign which Napoleon made in person in Spain. After the Restoration M. de Talleyrand spoke with complacency of his conduct at that time. The revelations which follow are accordingly no betrayal of a secret. Moreover if I anticipate the time fixed by himself at which the public is to be initiated into his confidence, I shall be pardoned his want of discretion. Already and from now on, this important person belongs to history as a public man. He has fallen into the domain of the chronicler.

When the Erfurth interview had been agreed upon between the two sovereigns, the Emperor Napoleon, although the Prince de Bénévent was no longer a minister and had been replaced by M. de Champigny, took both of them with him to Erfurth. Long accustomed to the Prince's services he could not dispense with him altogether under certain circumstances. He considered that this minister's skill in diplomatic conferences and his knowledge of his political views, might be useful to him. If this imprudence towards a man who had acted badly to him and whom he had not allowed—and rightly so—to add the Ministry of Exterior Relations to the dignity of Vice-Grand-Elector and the post of Grand Chamberlain—was often harmful to Napoleon, it may be said that the fault he committed in allowing Talleyrand to come to Erfurth was fatal to the Emperor. At Erfurth Napoleon specially employed Prince de Bénévent in his confidential communications with the Emperor Alexander. I do not know whether the Emperor was well informed of the nature of the nocturnal conversations which Talleyrand used to have with the Czar at the house of the Princess of Thurn and Taxis, after the theatre, which the sovereigns visited almost every evening. What were these conversations? Prince de Bénévent undertook to answer that question not only in his Memoirs, but in his private conversations.

M. de Talleyrand used to come to the levee every morning at Erfurth. When everybody had left, Napoleon detained him. He spoke to him of his plans, of his views on the Ottoman Empire, of Spanish affairs, of the attitude which he wished to maintain towards the Emperor Alexander, of the advantages which he hoped to derive from his alliance with him, and of the gradual concessions, which he proposed to make him. Prince Talleyrand admits that he had no scruples in betraying these confidences to the Czar in their conversations in the evening. He thus prepared this prince for the communications which were to be made to him by Napoleon warning him of the hidden purpose of the insinuations which would be made to him. Alexander used to speak at Erfurth of his ardent desire to visit Paris, of how pleased he should be to be present at the meetings of the Council of State presided over by Napoleon, and to be able to initiate himself under such a master to the science of government, I do not know how far this wish was sincere. I heard the Czar speak about it with apparent earnestness, but Talleyrand's revelations must have considerably modified the Czar's wish to increase his intimacy with Napoleon. Admitting that this ex-minister did not envenom his master's confidences, it will easily be understood that this kind of confidences always touches on delicate matters, which, when they are approached without mission and without being treated with the necessary opportuneness and circumspection, are liable to be wrongly interpreted and to produce deplorable effects.

Prince de Bénévent did not content himself with abusing Napoleon's confidence, as regards Russia. He rendered Austria—another service. M. de Metternich having been unable to procure an invitation to his sovereign to come to Erfurth, had remained in Paris, where he was kept by his functions as ambassador. The Austrian cabinet could not dispense with the presence of a representative at Erfurth. The Emperor Francis accordingly dispatched an *envoyé* there, bearing a letter of which the apparent purpose was to congratulate Napoleon on the occasion of his presence in Germany and to reassure him on the justly suspected disposition of the Austrian cabinet: the real object of this mission being to find out what was going on at Erfurth and to try and gather what was being planned against Austria. The Baron de Vincent, whom the Prince de Bénévent had already presented to the Emperor at Warsaw, under almost analogous circumstances was, as we have seen, selected for this mission. He received orders to see M. de Talleyrand and to listen to what he would tell him. The Prince de Bénévent used to explain his secret relations with the Emperor of Russia and with the Austrian minister in a manner which is related below. It is difficult, however, to believe that they were totally disinterested on his part, although I have no proof of the price which Austria paid for such precious advice. As concerns the reward given by the Emperor Alexander, we may quote the following fact, amongst other proofs of the Czar's gratitude.

In the course of one of the audiences which Napoleon accorded to the Prince de Bénévent, and of which the latter made the use which has been seen, the Emperor told him that in his private conversations with Alexander the latter had come to speak of the eventuality of a divorce on Napoleon's part and the necessity of his remarrying and at the same time had indirectly offered him the hand of one of the Grand duchesses of Russia.

M. de Talleyrand at once saw the advantage to himself that he could derive from this confidence. He congratulated the Emperor Alexander on the subject and then skillfully seizing his opportunity, said to him: "Sire, since your Majesty is in so happy a matrimonial disposition, you will allow me to ask a favor. I have had the misfortune to lose my eldest nephew, a young man full of promise. There remains one whom I wish to marry with advantage, but there is no prospect of doing so in France. The Emperor keeps all his rich heiresses for his aides-de-camp. Your Majesty has amongst your subjects a family with which it is my greatest desire to ally myself. The hand of the Princess Dorothea of Courland would crown the wishes of my nephew Edmund." The Emperor Alexander, who had often declared his wish to be agreeable to Prince de Bénévent, at once promised him his assistance in the matter and told him that it was his intention on returning to St. Petersburg to stop at the house of the Duchess of Courland, that he would take Edmund de Périgord with him, who being at that time attached to the French embassy in Russia had accompanied the Duke of Vicence to Erfurth, that he would undertake that the Duchess would accept him and that the matter might be considered settled.

After the stories which M. de Talleyrand has told himself, with all particulars, of what passed between him and the Emperor of Russia and the Austrian *envoyé* at Erfurth, one would like to know what pretext he puts forward to justify his conduct. This is the pretext. Frightened by the dangerous progress in power of Napoleon, Prince de Bénévent had the *patriotic* inspiration to endeavor to check the impetuosity of his upward flight and to put obstacles in the way of the execution of his adventurous projects, to bring him back to moderation. He pretended to believe that in arousing the vigilance of Russia and Austria in this matter, he would be rendering a signal service first of all to Napoleon and then to France and Europe. Such an apology reminds one of the excuses made by the unfaithful regimental treasurers, who having been punished by the imperial government, posed before the government of the Restoration as victims of the Empire, alleging in their justification that they had desired to starve the usurper and to reduce him to impotence by depriving him of the sinews of war. It was only much later that the Emperor heard what had been the nature of M. de Talleyrand's night-conversations with the Emperor Alexander at the house of the Princess of Thurn and Taxis.

It was during his stay at Erfurth that the Emperor heard of the Convention of Cintra by the terms of which the French army secured its return to France with arms and baggage, conveyed on English vessels. The capitulation was an honorable one. However much Napoleon was grieved by this issue to the expedition in Portugal he showed no resentment to the Duke d'Abrantès, who was a brave and loyal soldier, of rare courage and entirely devoted to him. The French army landed shortly afterwards at Rochefort. M. de Bourmont, whom General Junot had found in Portugal was amongst them. The commander in chief, in acknowledgement of the services which Bourmont had rendered in Lisbon, had asked the Emperor for a post for him, which Napoleon had refused and it was against his orders that the old Vendéen leader had followed the army.

After the return of General Junot, complaints had been made to the Emperor about the too great extension which the Duke d'Abrantès had given to the right of conquest in Portugal, amongst other things the seizure of the famous Bible at the convent of Belem.

To understand the value attached to this manuscript by the Portuguese government, it is necessary to give a brief outline of its history. At the time of the discovery of the route to East India by the Cape of Good Hope, Vasco da Gama sent the King of Portugal, Dom Manuel, the first fruits of the riches of these countries, consisting in gold, pearls, and diamonds. According to the ideas current at that time Dom Manuel thought it his duty to offer these first fruits to the holy See. Julius II, who at that time occupied the pontifical chair, sent back in return a manuscript to the King of Portugal. This manuscript was remarkable for the perfection of its writing, the beauty of the vignettes, picked out with gold, for the magnificence of its binding and of its clasps which were enriched with precious stones. This manuscript was a Bible with a commentary by Dom Thomas de Lira, in seven big quarto volumes. Dom Manuel had just founded a convent of Hieronymites at Belem with all the magnificence which at that time was the lot of religious foundations. He had the work deposited there and placed it under the prior's care. This book was only shown, even in quite recent times, with the greatest circumspection. The monks were not allowed to part with it without an authorization not only signed but entirely written by the King. General Junot having heard this marvel spoken about, and using the right of conquest, had it brought to him, promising to return it in three days, a promise which he forgot to keep. Events brought on the battle of Vimiero and the Convention of Cintra, which stipulated for the evacuation of Portugal by the French troops. The prior of the Hieronymites made the English general interfere to regain possession of the Bible and an officer was dispatched to General Junot to ask for its restitution. Junot alleged that the manuscript had been sent to France by the *aviso* which had informed the Emperor of the Convention of Cintra and expressed his regret at not being able to restore it. This Bible accordingly remained in Paris in the General's library. At his death his furniture, pictures, and books were sold. The Bible was not included in the catalogue and was reserved for sale by private treaty. A Frenchman who had lived twelve years in Portugal and who had returned to France was charged to write to the Emperor, who was in Dresden at the time, to inform him of the matters related and to solicit his interference for the restitution of this Bible. The Emperor wrote to the Duke of Rovigo, Minister of Police, on the subject who took the steps prescribed by Napoleon. The wretched Duke d'Abrantès had died in consequence of a deplorable mental aberration. Out of interest for Madame d'Abrantès, left a widow and without fortune, and considering perhaps that time had, so to speak, legitimized the possession of a booty taken in war, the Emperor did not insist on the order of restitution which he had given. He was, moreover, much too busy to pay any serious attention to this matter and it remained as it stood. The Restoration came. Marquis de Palmella, Portuguese ambassador to Paris, and Count de Funchal, Portuguese ambassador to Rome, took steps for the restitution of the precious manuscript. Count Funchal asked for an audience with King Louis XVIII. and obtained an order from him, which obliged the Duchess d'Abrantès to restore the Bible. But, in view of Madame d'Abrantès's precarious position, the King insisted that a sum of eighty thousand francs, the sum at which the Bible had been estimated, should be paid to the Duchess. Thanks to this arrangement, the Bible, with the commentary of Dom Thomas de Lira, found its way back to the Hieronymite convent, where it is to this day. The poor prior of the monastery had been exiled for three years for having allowed himself to be deprived of this manuscript, in spite of the fact that he had been quite powerless to oppose it.

On his return to Erfurth, the Emperor only spent ten days at St. Cloud. He heard there of the landing in Spain of the army of the Marquis de Romana, the evasion of which from the Danish islands where it had been in cantonment, had been announced to him in the preceding month of August. This event was calculated to increase the excitement of the inhabitants of the Peninsula and to fortify the spirit of resistance which animated them. The preceding Spanish government, directed by the Prince de la Paix—had on the demand of the Emperor added a corps of fifteen thousand men to the French army in atonement for his hostile proclamation of October 3, 1806, about which we spoke in its place. This corps, the command of which had been confided to the Marquis de la Romana, was intended for the North of Germany. Placed under the orders of the Prince of Ponte-Corvo—Bernadotte—it was charged with the defense of the island of Fionia. The Spanish general, hearing of what had happened at Bayonne, conceived the design of leading his troops back to Spain and depriving the French army of their assistance, to add them as auxiliaries to the insurrection. With this purpose in view he entered into communication with the English Admiral Keates, who was in command in the Baltic, by the intermediary of a Spanish priest of Scotch origin whose name was Robertson. He then set to work to collect his scattered troops, by means of schemes plotted with great dissimulation, on the points on the coast where the boats of the English transport were ready to receive them. La Romana had been able to inspire Bernadotte with such confidence that Spanish companies formed part of the bodyguard of the commander in chief. Thanks to orders supposed to emanate from the staff, he had been able to have marches executed by his troops, on the longest days in the year, which should have aroused suspicion. Detachments dispersed in the island of Fionia and in Jutland were in this way able to reach the island of Langeland which had been fixed upon as a general meeting place, without attracting attention. The Spanish troops who were nearest to Copenhagen, and who had committed certain acts of violence were disarmed by the Danes. All the others were assembled within three days and embarked. During their passage these troops put into port in England where the English government armed and equipped them at the public cost. After a long sea-voyage, General La Romana landed in the first days of October, at Santander, with nine thousand men who went to swell General Blake's army in Biscay.

The Emperor left on October 29 to put himself at the head of the armies in Spain, to which several corps coming from Germany had been added. He only passed the night at Marrac and rode thence to Vittoria where King Joseph was staying. He spent five days in this town to give the soldiers time to come up, and devoted his attention to ensuring his communications and ordering military arrangements in Biscay, Navarre, and Aragon. I left Bayonne on the morrow and rode at full speed to Vittoria with M. Yvan, the Emperor's surgeon in ordinary, leaving my carriage behind me. We were surprised to find at Vittoria the old foot grenadiers of the guard, who had left Bayonne the day before and who had marched nearly twenty-five leagues in two days, laden like Roman soldiers. At Oyarsun the postmaster and his wife did us the excellent turn of keeping us back till daybreak, because armed peasants had been seen on the roads. At a distance of a mile from Oyarsun, as it happened, we found a French officer, who had been murdered, lying by the wayside. Mondragon, through which we passed had a festive air which quite reassured us. However, at different points along our route we came across young conscripts, placed on solitary sentry duty, who were in a very nervous state of mind. At last we succeeded in reaching Vittoria safely. I had had some small pistols sent on to me from Paris and carried them on me. When the Emperor heard of this excess of prudence, he told me that I had acted wrongly as it would make people think that he was in personal danger. But when I had told him about our journey, he did not blame my precaution any longer. It was, however, only necessary in the case of isolated individuals, for the safety of the Emperor and of his household was never for a moment in danger.

On November 11 the Emperor was at Burgos, after having fought an engagement on the outskirts of this town at which flags were captured which Napoleon sent to the Legislative body. The public establishments, the churches of this unhappy town were all given up to pillage. The bivouac fire, established in the bishop's palace, where the Emperor lived, was stoked with broken bits of furniture. The officers warmed themselves at this, sitting round it on gilded armchairs. The abbey, which contained the tombs of the Cid and of Chimenes, received numerous visitors. It was situated outside Burgos. M. Denon with whom I went there brought back with him one of Chimenes's teeth which he placed in a reliquary in which he had collected together fragments of the mortal remains of many celebrated persons.

The Emperor spent ten or twelve days at Burgos. He proceeded thence in the direction of Madrid by the Aranda route. The beautiful Castle of Lerma, which was on our way, contained an enormous quantity of excellent wine in its cellars. This wine was given up to the soldiers. They used it for making cakes which they baked under the warm ashes of their bivouac-fires. Without any exaggeration, the air was scented with the smell of this wine poured about with that careless prodigality which is so characteristic of the soldier.

The defile of Somo-Sierra fortified by the Spaniards who deluded themselves with the hope of holding the French army in check and closing the road to Madrid, a defile defended by ten thousand men and fifteen pieces of cannon, was taken by storm by a brave charge of the Polish light cavalry of the guard, under the command of General Montbrun. Philippe de Ségur was dangerously wounded in this engagement. No further obstacle impeding the marching of the army, it advanced rapidly on Madrid. The Emperor presented himself before the walls of this city on December 2, the fourth anniversary of his coronation and the third of the battle of Austerlitz. King had joined him the evening before at headquarters.

Madrid was in the hands of a fanatical mob. A staff-officer who had been sent in to parley, was attacked in the interior of the town by a gang of murderers and narrowly escaped being killed. The Emperor could have taken this capital by storm, as it was not fortified, but he wished to spare the inhabitants the horrors of an attack. He parleyed for two days with the furies who were encouraged by his humanity. Some Spanish prisoners were brought to the bivouac at which I was, amongst whom were some young monks dressed in long frockcoats buttoned up to the chin, and wearing swordbelts without any sword. They wanted to pass themselves off as officers and affected a military air. Then they were ordered to go through their drill and tried to do so, but did it like men who had never handled any weapons. They were thereupon asked to what regiments they belonged. At last when we had sufficiently enjoyed their embarrassment, their hats were taken off and the fresh shaven tonsures were exposed, which to their great confusion betrayed the disguise which they had assumed.

The occupation of Buen Retiro, a royal castle situated on a height, at one of the gates of Madrid, where certain defense works had been executed, put it in Napoleon's power to annihilate the city. He, however, decided to try the effects of a fresh summons. The junta of the defense answered by sending Captain General Thomas de Morla, one of the generals who had treated the soldiers who had capitulated at Baïlen with such inhumanity. He came to ask that the French troops might be withdrawn so as to give the junta time to calm the popular effervescence. But the Emperor received him with a severity which frightened him. Napoleon addressed him with such crushing and just reproaches that he withdrew in terror without effecting his mission. The ultimatum had been signified to him that unless the city were surrendered within twelve hours, he and his garrison would be shot.

The Emperor gave orders for a general disarming. The authorities of the town came to make their submission and to acknowledge King Joseph, who refused to receive the Spanish grandees who had remained in Madrid. Those who were most compromised had followed the Spanish troops who had left the capital by gates which were not yet occupied by us. Others were arrested and sent to France, Madrid was occupied in a military fashion and the King did not inhabit the palace. He went and established himself at the Prado, a royal castle situated at about one league from the capital. The Emperor also refused to live in Madrid and took up his quarters at Chamartin, a country house situated at about a league's distance from Madrid, the property of the Duke of l'Infantado. Chamartin is a small castle without dependencies, used as a country-box during the fine weather. The cold was rather severe when the Emperor came to live here, and there were no fireplaces in any of the rooms. The only heating-apparatus was some *braseros,* which were great copper basins filled with live coals which were placed in the center of the rooms. Temporary fireplaces were fitted up in his bedroom and study, thanks to which the house was inhabitable during the fortnight he remained there. I may say, in passing, that as a rule he did not feel the cold, though he suffered from the heat. In spite of this he never broke his custom, even in the hottest weather, of wearing his uniform buttoned right up to his neck.

During his stay at Chamartin, Napoleon occupied himself with making arrangements for the complete subjection of Spain. He issued several laws endowing the country with the institutions which it lacked. Each day moreover he reviewed his troops under the walls of Madrid.

Some curious letters from Queen Caroline of Naples to her daughter, the Princess of the Asturias, were found at Chamartin. These letters had been left behind, by forgetfulness, in a drawer.

Some were written in secret ink, and dated in January, 1806. It was at the time that the French were about to enter into Naples. The bitterness with which the unhappy Queen spoke of her allies, the English, whom she accused of perfidy and cowardice—such were her expressions—prompted Napoleon to publish these letters. This correspondence, moreover, did not establish that any great union existed between the royal houses of Spain and Naples, though naturally enough it revealed the existence of strong hatred against the French. There was also found a small almanac of the Court of Naples for the year 1802, which was the year of the marriage of the Prince of the Asturias with the Princess of Naples, a marriage which had been celebrated at Barcelona with great magnificence. This almanac, which was probably a souvenir of the aforesaid royal marriage was ornamented with twelve pretty watercolor paintings representing the town of Naples, the palace, and various royal residences in the Two Sicilies, one painting to each month.

The Emperor's stay at Chamartin was marked by an act of severity and by an act of clemency. An order of the day had commanded that the strictest discipline should be observed—till then it had been too much neglected—and threatened the delinquents with all the rigors of military law. Two light infantry soldiers of the imperial guard, found guilty of pillage, theft, and odious violences committed on the persons of inhabitants of Madrid, were condemned to be shot in sight of the city. The Emperor judging their execution necessary for the maintenance of military discipline, refused to pardon these soldiers although their previous good conduct was urged in their favor. I cannot refrain in connection with this act of severe justice to rebut the accusation brought against Napoleon of having tolerated disorder in his armies, by a kind of tacit understanding between, himself and his soldiers, who, resembling in this the undisciplined hordes of the middle ages, were said to serve their chief only because of his tolerance of their excesses. Those who have followed the imperial armies know with what care Napoleon checked all pillage. If he heard that marauders were behaving in a disorderly manner behind his rearguard, he used to order columns to be formed to pursue them, and rendered the commanding officers in the forts and at the points of defense of his communications, responsible for their crimes. His orders of the day enjoined the greatest respect for property and scathed those who tolerated disorder. Vienna, Berlin, Madrid and other cities witnessed the condemnation and execution of soldiers belonging as well to the imperial guard as to other army corps, when these soldiers had been found guilty of pillage.

The Marquis of St. Simon, a Frenchman in Spanish service, had been taken sword in hand, in command of a troop of rebels and had been sentenced to death by court-martial. Napoleon pardoned him. The daughter of this *emigré,* protected by some officers of the imperial household, who had been touched by her filial piety, and especially by Captain Duchand, orderly on service, was placed on the Emperor's passage and threw herself at his feet imploring her father's pardon. Napoleon could not refuse it at the sight of Mile, de St. Simon's tears. He, moreover, considered that the lesson was a sufficient one.

The Emperor had been a fortnight at Chamartin, awaiting news of the English army with great impatience when he at last heard that it had entered Spain from Portugal, by Salamanca, and that it was marching on Valladolid. Napoleon went off to meet it. He crossed the Guadarrama, which is a mountain situated to the northeast of Madrid. We were overtaken while crossing this mountain by a snowstorm which threatened to swallow us up, and by icy cold which destroyed some of our soldiers. In this crossing our army had a foretaste of the sufferings which we were to undergo, later, at the time of the terrible retreat from Moscow. It was impossible to remain on horseback. The Emperor was obliged to alight and order his light cavalry guards to march on foot, he in the midst of them, thus tracking out the road for the infantry which was coming on behind. On arriving at the bottom of the mountain he halted to assemble all his troops. Impatient as the Emperor was to get up with the English army, which kept retreating before him, he was forced to spend two days at Tordesillas, awaiting the arrival of his regiments. He took up his quarters in a building attached to the Convent of St. Claire, which was reserved for the bishop's lodging, when coming on a pastoral visit.

What follows about Napoleon's stay in this convent, was told me by M. d'Hédouville, who was acting as orderly to the Emperor in Spain and as interpreter.

While at dinner Napoleon ordered this officer to bring the Lady Superior of the convent to him. At first she refused to follow M. d'Hédouville, saying that she was not allowed to go out of bounds and could not pass beyond the gates of the cloister. She gave way when it was pointed out to her that the commands of a sovereign were a dispensation. Hesitatingly she took her conductor's arm. On reaching the wicket, she trembled so that she could not advance and M. d'Hédouville had to hold her up. She told him that it was more than sixty years since she had entered this convent, being at that time six years of age, and that since then she had never been outside its gates. On being introduced into the Emperor's presence, her first impulse was to kneel down before him. On a sign from him M. d'Hédouville held her back. The plate and decorations of the Emperor's orders were what most struck this poor and simple nun and she could not refrain from stretching out her hand to touch them. M. d'Hédouville checked her and pointed out to her how indiscreet was such curiosity. The Emperor asked her several questions. He first of all asked her if she were the abbess of the convent. She said that she only held the second place, and added: "Luckily for me." Napoleon asked her why she said that and she answered that she preferred to obey than to command, that it was more meritorious, and that her conscience was more at ease. The Emperor could not repress a smile at the ingenuousness of this answer. He then asked her if Jane the Mad, mother of Charles V, who had died at Tordesillas, was buried in the convent. She reflected for a moment and in the end answered that there were princes and queens buried in the vaults, but that she did not know their names. Asked whether she knew anything about the history of Spain, she said that she knew nothing but her prayer books and the passages of the Bible which her confessor allowed her to read. The Emperor who found that in spite of her age, her eyes were bright, asked her if she had been pretty. She answered naïvely, that she thought so, but that she had never had a looking-glass and that nobody had ever told her so. The conversation continued in this way for some time and the nun's answers betokened a natural wit. Napoleon, pleased with her innocence and her ingenuousness, told her that he wished to grant her a favor and that she might ask him for anything she chose. Before answering the nun asked if anything that she asked for would be granted to her. On being told that the Emperor did not promise in vain, she asked for the pardon of the director of the convent, who had been taken at the head of an armed gang with his crucifix in his hand. Napoleon granted it, as he had promised, but added that this monk should be careful not to commit such a mistake again as it would be out of his power to pardon him a second time. The nun promised that she would see that he should not leave the convent and answered for him. The Emperor then said that he had granted a favor, on her account, to somebody who was not connected with her family, but that it was for her personally that he wished to do something. As she hesitated about answering, he had her asked if she had any relations. She answered that she had a brother in Holy Orders. "Would she like me to make a bishop of him?" said Napoleon. She knelt down to thank him for this unexpected favor, which, however, as it happened, could not be carried out, the monk in question being shut up in Saragossa. Before the prioress returned to the convent, the Emperor had her served with some coffee. She did not like it, had never tasted coffee and was accustomed to chocolate alone. The poor nun, after having thanked the Emperor again for the kindness with which he had received her and having kissed his hand, was reconducted by M. d'Hédouville to her cloister, touched and grateful.

Before the Emperor left Tordesillas, M. d'Hédouville came to me in his name to ask me for a hundred napoleons to give to the lady superior of the convent. He was received with curiosity and kindness by the sisters to whom the Lady Superior had described her visit. They all ran up to see him, touched his hand and examined him with all the curiosity of islanders seeing Europeans for the first time. When M. d'Hédouville hand the prioress the hundred napoleons, she refused them, saying that if she were to take them, the convent would lose the small merit of its hospitality. On being told, as she frequently had been told before during her visit, that she was not free to refuse a sovereign's gift, she consented to accept it, and gave orders that this sum should be placed in the treasury of the chapter and only be used on extraordinary occasions, so that the proof of the Emperor's goodwill might be preserved as long as possible.

The nun having asked whether these pieces of gold were stamped with the Emperor's likeness, M. d'Hédouville broke open the paper roll and took out some of the coins to show to her. She seized them hastily and examined them with interest, assuring her companions who were watching her eagerly that she found the Emperor's portrait very like him.

On returning to Napoleon, M. d'Hédouville related what had passed. The Emperor had taken a real interest in the nun's visit. He found her full of tact. He regretted that instead of cultivating her natural talents, she had been subjected at so early an age to the education of the convent, the effect of which had been to choke these natural tendencies. And, nevertheless, in spite of the state of ignorance in which she had vegetated, in spite of the horror of the world with which this simple and credulous mind had been inspired, in spite of her minute religious practices, which left no freedom of exercise to the judgment, the gentleness and sweetness of her temper had not been changed and her good natural disposition had resisted these lethargic influences. "After all," he added, "this good soul is happy in her present situation. If convents have often their victims, they have also consoled many." Napoleon spoke of the relative utility of convents and dwelt at length on the subject. It could be seen that he had frequently thought over these refuges of meditation and prayer. He said that there were circumstances where convent life might have its advantages, that the cloisters must often be very well suited to tender minds, resigned and weary of the world, that these retreats might be opened with advantage, for example, to the widows of colonels and general officers, who losing by the death of their husbands the income which they had enjoyed during their lifetime, might combine their pensions and other resources together so as to be able to procure a carriage and other comforts, which singly they would not be able to afford; that in his opinion perpetual vows should be forbidden, and that in any case nobody should be admitted under the age of forty, and so on.

Thus the first impulse of his ardent and dreamy soul bore him towards benevolent ideas, which were matured and modified by time and by reflection, or abandoned when experience showed that they would be dangerous in practice.

During his march on Benavent, while close upon the heels of the English army and almost within reach of it, Napoleon received a courier bearing the portfolio in which the director of the Post office used to place the letters addressed to the Emperor. As I had the key of this portfolio and was at that time a league behind, Napoleon was too impatient to await me. He tore the portfolio open and took out his dispatches. There were amongst them letters from Champigny, the Minister of Exterior Relations, and one from the King of Bavaria to the Prince Neufchâtel (Berthier). These letters announced that Austria was arming her landwehr, that the Bavarian States were threatened with an invasion, that the Austrian troops were maneuvering to cross the Inn and were calling the peoples of Germany to insurrection. This news did not surprise the Emperor. His eye had followed Austria's plots and he was expecting an early outbreak of hostilities, but he was prepared to meet them.

Nor did he ignore the intrigues which were in progress in Paris, as will be seen presently from the violent reproaches which he addressed to Prince de Bénévent. He decided accordingly to hasten his return to France. He pushed on as far as Astorga, and there reviewed his troops as they came up. He then dictated his instructions for Marshal Soult whom he charged with the pursuit of the English army on retreat. Napoleon then returned to Benavent, which he left hastily for Valladolid. In this city he received a deputation of the principal authorities and the most important inhabitants of Madrid. This deputation came to implore him, with the strongest protestations of loyalty to the new king, to put no obstacle in the way of the return of King Joseph into the capital. The Emperor, having spoken to them with severe frankness and having called upon their loyalty, promised to write to the king to advise him to act in accordance with their wishes. He spent a week in Valladolid, awaiting the news of his brother's return to Madrid and attending to the dispatch of the most urgent orders.

Marshal Lannes, recovering from a long illness, had come to meet the Emperor in Spain and had followed the headquarters for some days. As he was still unable to mount on horseback, the Emperor had placed his own carriage, which he did not use, at the Marshal's disposal. I accompanied the Marshal in this carriage. Before Napoleon left Valladolid, Marshal Lannes, who felt himself able to undertake more active service, was sent by the Emperor, who wanted to spare his strength, to take the superior command of the siege of Saragossa.

During our stay at Valladolid, I had the curiosity to pay a visit to the Dominican monastery which the Emperor had ordered to be suppressed because a French officer had been murdered there. In this refuge, consecrated to the patron of the Inquisition, I came across what I had scarcely expected to find there. Amongst the portraits of Saints which covered the walls of the cloister, I saw a picture, representing St. Napoleon, the head crowned with an aureole and wearing the costume of a Roman knight. In one corner of the picture was a brief description in Spanish.

The Emperor during this short campaign of two months and a half, had reoccupied Madrid and the neighboring provinces, and had dispersed like dust the Spanish troops which had opposed his passage. These bands, after being defeated only went off to reassemble again thirty leagues away. At the same time these successes would have effaced the disastrous impression produced on the Spaniards by the catastrophe at Baïlen, if we had been able to follow them up. But their fruit was lost by Napoleon being forced to abandon Spain in great haste, to march against the Austrians who were invading Bavaria, without being able to return.

The Emperor left Valladolid for Burgos and rode this distance at full speed in some hours, by means of relays of horses which had been prepared in advance. He only stopped two hours at Burgos and rode on to Bayonne at such speed that his household could not follow him. He traversed the road from Bayonne to Paris with the same speed and on January 23 was at the Tuileries.

On arriving at Paris, Napoleon without losing a moment, applied himself to making the necessary arrangements to be in readiness to meet the attack with which he was menaced. He gave orders that his corps and the contingents from the Confederation of the Rhine should hold themselves in readiness to begin the campaign. He sent Marshal Berthier off, to assemble the confederate troops on the Danube and to assume the command of the army for the time being.

A privy council was summoned a few days after his return to Paris. The Emperor who had well-founded reasons for displeasure with Prince de Bénévent restrained his resentment as long as the council lasted. At last the dam burst. Napoleon who grew hotter and hotter as he spoke, under the influence of his indignation, lost control of his anger which was only awaiting the opportunity to break forth. He spoke to Prince de Bénévent with the greatest harshness. Thanks to his various sources of information the Emperor had heard things about M. de Talleyrand which perhaps justified the violent scene which was witnessed by certain members of the privy council. In the conversations which Prince de Bénévent had had, on various occasions, with Napoleon, concerning Spanish affairs, I had heard him quote the example of the Jesuits Malagrida and Alexander, and after having insisted on the necessity of the Emperor's presence in Spain, speak of the precautions which he would have to take to defend himself against the poison or the dagger of some fanatical monk. Napoleon felt quite sure that Prince de Bénévent, foreseeing the possibility either of such an event or of his death by means of the bullet of a *guerrillo,* which might strike him down on his triumphant march, had thought of the formation of a government council, the organization of which, in case of need, was quite ready to be carried out. The members of the future government had already been named. Nobody knew the reconciliation, which, with some object or other in view, had taken place between Fouché and Talleyrand. Napoleon, however, showed no resentment towards the former. The confidences and the remarks of M. de Talleyrand on the events in Spain, on the trial of the Duke d'Enghien, his disapproval of these acts and his denial of having taken any part in them were well known to the Emperor. The immobility of the patient, the impassiveness of his features had provoked Napoleon's anger to the point that he forgot his imperial dignity and threatened Talleyrand with his fist. "And you dare," he cried, "you dare to deny the part you took in the condemnation of the Duke d'Enghien. And you dare to say and publish broadcast that you had nothing to do with the affairs in Spain," and so on and so on. The paroxysm of this indignation having reached its climax fell by its own excess and Napoleon, tired of dashing himself against the impassive face, gave up. Prince de Bénévent knew the Emperor well and knew that it was in his nature, the more he had allowed himself to be carried away by his resentment the more to try and have it forgotten. Talleyrand had no real feeling of dignity and he deemed it a good thing to pretend to have forgotten this scene. There was a drawing room at Court on the morrow, which happened to be a Sunday. One of the ministers, the Duke of Gaete—Gaudin—who had been charged by the Emperor with some work that was wanted at once, had devoted this Sunday to finishing it. Remembering that Napoleon liked his ministers to attend the Court regularly, he decided that he. might sacrifice an hour in the accomplishment of this duty. The Minister of Finances, accordingly, went to the Tuileries early, with the intention of placing himself near the door by which the Emperor would enter, so as to be free to withdraw after having saluted him and to return to his work. The minister arrived at the palace before anybody else and while the rooms were being lighted. He wanted to cross the Throne room and place himself where it would be easiest for him to make his escape as he had intended. What was his surprise to see Prince de Bénévent standing alone by the fireplace. A feeling of shame for the man who had so quickly forgotten the humiliation which he had undergone the day before, and his embarrassment at finding himself alone with him after the scene which he had witnessed, prompted the Duke of Gaete to go back into the adjoining drawing room where he spent his time, waiting for the Throne room to fill up, so that he might cross it without coming face to face with Prince de Bénévent, in walking up and down. From the position where he had placed himself, he was the first to salute the Emperor and was free to retire. His curiosity, however, detained him. Napoleon, according to his custom walked round the room, holding his snuffbox, from which he frequently helped himself, standing in the front rank. On reaching the person who was standing on the left of Prince de Bénévent, who had remained rooted to the spot which he had occupied from the beginning, near the fireplace, the Emperor addressed some words to him, passed by Talleyrand with averted head and stopped before the person on the latter's right hand. On the following Sunday, without being in the least disconcerted, Talleyrand placed himself again in the Emperor's way and seeing his neighbor hesitate at a question put to him by Napoleon, answered for him, forcing the Emperor's attention. The ice having been broken in this way, Talleyrand took every opportunity of attracting Napoleon's attention, who in spite of the characteristic attributed to his countrymen, was unable to bear a grudge, because the feeling of his own power and the superiority of his mind over petty passions rendered him naturally indulgent. Prince de Bénévent continued to frequent the *entrées* and was as assiduous as in the days of his favor. The Emperor, who on certain occasions was as severe in public as on the other hand he was indulgent and patient in his private relations, disarmed by so much patience or shaken in his conviction by so much assurance, never thought of forbidding access to his court to a man against whom he had not sufficient proofs to send him to trial, but who in Napoleon's eyes was sufficiently guilty to be removed for ever from all direction of affairs.

This anecdote, of which I heard the first part from members of the privy council, who were present at the scene which Prince de Bénévent had to undergo, was afterwards told me in detail by the man who of all men was most worthy of confidence, My lord Duke of Gaete, Minister of Finances under the Empire. May I be allowed since I have mentioned his name to add that the Emperor had no more devoted nor more skilful minister than he, that no administrator was purer, more honest and more firm, that no man in his private capacity combined more solid and more amiable qualities, that he was good and affectionate, modest with dignity, enlightened without display, and a faithful preserver of those traditions of urbanity and politeness which unfortunately are becoming rarer and rarer every day.

In consequence of this scene Prince de Bénévent lost the post of Grand Chamberlain which was given to M. de Montesquiou. This was the time, indeed, of intrigues of every kind. The faubourg St. Germain had to submit to the exile of Madame de Chevreuse and of several other people whom the Emperor recalled later on, excepting from this amnesty four or five of the most influential persons or those who most strongly persevered in active opposition. Some of these persons had excited Napoleon's anger rather by their sarcasms or spiteful remarks than by their acts. He might have disdained these impotent clamorings. He was strong enough to be able to do so. He used to revenge himself more nobly by granting daily restitutions and favors to members of the old aristocracy. Some members of the former reigning family even received pensions from him. The Duchess of Orléans, the Duchess of Bourbon and the Prince of Conti were living in retirement at Figuiéres in Spain, enjoying a moderate pension which had been granted to them by the Directoire, this pension being subjected to all the formalities exacted in the case of life annuitants. Napoleon on the request of General Canclaux, the warm and persevering friend of the Prince of Conti, increased the pension of each of these members of the royal family to sixty thousand francs which were paid to them at the residence which these princes had chosen, through the agency of a banker who was in account with the Treasury. These pensions were freed from all personal formalities. And consequently the princes whose names we have mentioned, never failed, as each year came round to send the Emperor their wishes for his prosperity.

The Emperor doubled these pensions during the Hundred Days and authorized the Duchesses of Orléans and of Bourbon to continue residing in Paris at the same time. They thanked Napoleon and Queen Hortense, who had interceded for these princesses with the Head of the state, by letter.

A Madame Poitrine, nurse of Madame the Duchess of Angouléme and the nurse of the last Dauphin, whose name I forget, received pensions from the imperial munificence.

In removing to a distance from Paris the malcontents whose opposition became troublesome or harmful, Napoleon was not, as has been said, blindly dominated by a spirit of despotism which could brook no contradiction. Amongst the persons whose exile was proposed to him was the Duchess of Gesvres. When the Emperor heard that this lady was an octogenarian, pity silenced all desire for severity in his heart, and when he had further discovered that this duchess was a descendant of Duguesclin's, this name stirred within him the French fibre. Not only did Napoleon forbid that Madame de Gesvres should be interfered with in any way, but he had inquiries made as to the needs of her old age. To supplement her small fortune the Emperor insisted on granting to the descendant of Duguesclin a pension, the amount of which would allow her to keep a carriage.

Shortly after his return to Paris Napoleon went to live at the Elysée, a beautiful house which he had bought from Prince Murat when the latter, as the soldiers used to say, "had been promoted King of Naples." Murat received in exchange certain estates situated in the Kingdom of Naples which the Emperor had reserved for himself after the conquest of this country. The situation of the Elysée afforded Napoleon a pleasant and commodious residence. Here he was able to walk about in the vast garden attached to this residence, without being importuned, and could go out without being noticed. He found himself delivered here from the pompous imprisonment which he had to undergo at the Tuileries, and only went to the latter palace on Sundays to hear the mass or for ceremonious receptions.

The Emperor had just settled down in the Elysée when he heard the news of the surrender of Saragossa. The remnants of the Spanish army which had been defeated at the battle of Tudela and various scattered corps, composing an army of about fifty thousand men, had shut themselves up in Saragossa, where protected by the walls and energetically seconded by the armed population, they defended themselves with a fanaticism which was kept alive by their leaders and by the monks. The city was not fortified, but was surrounded with a thick brick and granite wall which had been strengthened and covered with parapets. In the interior of the city the entrance to each street was barricaded and in a state of defense. The garrison was provided with numerous storehouses and armed with two hundred pieces of artillery. The commander-in-chief was General Palafox, who being shut up in Saragossa, was elected captain-general. This man dear to the population, whose exaltation he shared, was moreover under the influence of skilful and fanatical monks. He had taken an oath to bury himself beneath the ruins of the city rather than to surrender it to the French. Gallows-trees, permanently standing, threatened the life of anybody who would dare to speak of capitulation. Marshal Lannes had come to take over the superior command of the siege on January 20, three weeks after the trenches had been opened. One of the Emperor's aides-de-camp, General Lacoste, seconded by Colonel Rogniat and Major Haxo, two officers who became famous, commanded the engineering works. General Lacoste met with a glorious death before Saragossa and was deeply regretted by Napoleon. Six days after his arrival Marshal Lannes stormed the city at the head of his troops. All the outer works fell into our hands, and the result should have been the surrender of the place, but the fanaticism of some of the most excited of the inhabitants inspired terror and froze the word, capitulation, on every mouth. Then began a war in the streets and houses, in the defense of which the women and the monks distinguished themselves by their resistance. The ground was fought for inch by inch, each house had to be carried by sap and by mine. Our soldiers, exposed to privations and dangers of every kind, were disgusted with this hideous warfare. The wretched inhabitants of Saragossa were decimated by hunger, disease, and by the losses which resulted from each encounter. Palafox himself was dying, but the monks and the clergy governed in his name. The taking of an important suburb, the destruction of the convents and principal buildings, which were used as places of assembly for the besieged soldiers rendered any continuation of resistance at last impossible. The council of defense, with the mad object of continuing the struggle, had asked for the free pass of officers commissioned to see whether the city could not be relieved. Marshal Lannes refused all conditions and demanded that the city should surrender at mercy. The French army occupied its ruins on February 21 after a siege, which has only been paralleled twice or thrice in history and which had devoured more than half the population. The Marshal moved to pity, treated what remained of the town with the greatest humanity. He protected the inhabitants, their property, and the exercise of their religion. The garrison laid down arms and was made prisoner of war. Travelers' narratives make mention of the inestimable riches of the cathedral of Our Lady del Pilar. On the entry of the French into Saragossa there were found none of the gifts in gold, silver, and precious stones which were said to have been sent there by Catholic sovereigns. These treasures had no doubt been used for the expenses of the siege or for expenses outside, or else had been removed before the invasion of the French. I remember having seen a little box brought to the Tuileries, containing specimens of fragments of ornaments, clumsily carved in open-work, in silver, silver gilt or copper gilt, set with some stones of small value. These *débris* came from the famous chapel of Our Lady del Pilar.

It was at the picture exhibition of this same year, 1809, that the Emperor wished to be represented in full length in his cabinet and gave orders that I should appear in the picture, writing from his dictation. The painter Gamier received the order to execute this portrait. I did not happen to be in Paris while the painter was working at it, for I had accompanied the Emperor on one of his journeys. The painter Isabey was good enough to make up for this drawback by helping Gamier with his memory and on my return to Paris Gamier asked me to sit to him so that he might give the last touches to his work. I do not know in what way it came to the Emperor's ears that the execution of this picture left a good deal to be desired, but he ordered General Duroc to write on the subject to M. Denon, director-general of museums, who took the painter's defense. At last the picture was accepted and was placed in one of the galleries at the Tuileries. In 1814 it was relegated to the lumber room with all those which had for subject the history of "the usurper," or else it was given back to the author as were other pictures of the same kind which were restored to their painters. Found in 1839 at a picture-dealer's, by the son of one of my old friends, Count Lemarrois, he bought it, from attachment to the Emperor's memory and in remembrance of the friendship which bound me to his father.

At the beginning of the year 1809 the Emperor at last decided to fill the two places of secretary to the cabinet which had been created in 1804. One of the new secretaries was charged, amongst other functions with translating the foreign newspapers and periodicals and entered, though rarely, Napoleon's cabinet. This was Baron Mounier, auditor to the Council of State, who had been employed at the time of the war of 1806–1807 in the government of the province of Silesia. M. Mounier was the son of the deputy of the Constituent Assembly, whom Napoleon had recalled from exile and whose capacity and merit he had rewarded by appointing him, on his return to France, Prefect of Rennes, and afterwards by calling him to a post at the Council of State. The Emperor's esteem for the father descended upon the son, who was an intelligent and well-informed young man, of much promise which, later, he fully realized.

The second secretary of the cabinet, who was specially charged with all concerning artillery and engineering, was Baron de Ponthon, at that time colonel of engineers. He had taken part in the memorable campaign in Egypt and enjoyed a well-deserved reputation in his branch of the service. This officer afterwards became lieutenant general and member of the committee of engineers.

The Emperor completed his cabinet later on by placing at the head of his topographical office, Colonel Bacler d'Albe, who afterwards became general. He was the author of the military map of Italy, was endowed with a most happy facility for the arts, and was animated with what Napoleon used to call the sacred fire. D'Albe was assisted by two geographical engineers of merit, MM. Lameau and Duvivier.

In forcing the Emperor to return at full speed from Spain, the coalition effected the objects it had in view, namely of preventing the pacification of this country and of dividing our forces. The Emperor heard, by telegraph, on April 12, that Archduke Charles had entered Bavaria and that his troops had passed the Inn without any previous declaration of war. This declaration was only notified to the outposts on the morrow of the day on which the invasion had taken place. Napoleon left the Elysée on the 13th of April at four in the morning. He passed on with unheard-of speed and reached headquarters at Donawerth on the fifth day, after having stopped at Louisburg and Dillingen to see the Kings of Würtemberg and Bavaria.

The Emperor found Marshal Berthier at Donawerth. He learned here that through a misunderstanding of his orders the communication between the corps of Bavarians commanded by Marshal Lefebvre and Marshal Davout's corps was cut off. New activity was given to his genius by the necessity of repairing this fault. The battles of Thann and of Abensberg, won with the troops of the Confederation of the Rhine and the victory of Ecmuehl, which earned for Marshal Davout the title of Prince of Ecmuehl, bestowed later, were the results of these clever maneuvers. So rapid had been the movements that Napoleon's household had not been able to follow him, and that he had to live like a soldier, only riding borrowed horses.

I have often heard the Emperor complain of how inferior we were to the Romans. Yet, according to the best military writers, he had no reason to envy any one of the heroes of antiquity either for the rapidity of the marches or for the preciseness of the maneuvers which characterized the commencement of this campaign.

Two occurrences marked this victorious march. The first might have deprived the army of its leader. Napoleon was seated on a spot from which he could see the attack on the town of Ratisbon. He was beating the ground with his riding-whip when a bullet, supposed to have been fired from a Tyrolean carbine struck him on the big toe. The news of his wound spread rapidly from file to file and he was forced to mount on horse-back to show himself to the troops. Although his boot had not been cut, the wound was a very painful one. Napoleon, however, put a good face on the matter, but nature would not forego her rights. On returning from this short excursion to a small house which was at a distance of some gun-ranges from the spot where he had been wounded, his courage being exhausted he fainted right away. This wound had fortunately no evil consequences.

A feat of arms of unparalleled bravery, the taking by storm of the Ebensberg position, which was reputed inexpugnable, also marked this campaign. A wooden bridge of more than six hundred feet in length, protected by a stronghold and precipitous heights which were crowned by superior forces and a hundred pieces of artillery, was carried by General Coëhorn. The gates of the city were broken down and a most violent encounter ensued. The houses in which a number of wounded soldiers and combatants had been driven back, without being able to escape, caught fire and were burned down to the ground with every man inside them. The sight presented by this unhappy city, with its streets strewn with corpses half-consumed by fire and spreading a fearful stench, was one of the most horrible that can be imagined. The Emperor was painfully impressed by it. He could not refrain from praising General Coëhorn for his rare courage, but he deplored the losses which would have been avoided if Marshal Masséna had given orders to turn this position.

The Emperor saw for a second time the city of Vienna whose sovereign had sworn to him in 1805, at the memorable interview at the bivouac at Sar-Uschitz, that he would war on him no more. This time Vienna tried to defend herself. Marshal Lannes had sent Captain Marbot, with a flag of truce, carrying a summons. The young aide-de-camp was attacked by a gang of ruffians, ill-treated and even wounded. Archduke Maximilian approved of the conduct of these wretches by allowing it to pass unreproved and kept the captain prisoner. After this violation of international law and the refusal of the Archduke to open the gates of the city a bombardment was decided upon. It has been stated, in error, that Archduchess Marie Louise, being ill, had remained behind in the imperial palace. It has been added that on hearing this the Emperor gave orders that the cannon should not be fired in that direction. The human mind hankers too much after the belief that great men have a mysterious foresight of their destinies. Archduke Maximilian, frightened perhaps at the responsibility which he had assumed left Vienna hastily and crossed the bridges without leaving any orders. On May 12 a French army occupied Vienna after that city had capitulated, at the request of a deputation which was presented to the Emperor at Schönbrunn where he had taken up his quarters. Napoleon assured the delegates of his protection and promised them that the city of Vienna should be treated with the same consideration as at the time of the first occupation in 1805.

The Emperor remained a week at Schönbrunn. In the meanwhile the Island of Lobau, which is situated at a distance of two leagues from Vienna and which divides the Danube into several branches, was occupied by the French army with a view of establishing a point at which our troops could cross the river. Three bridges were thrown across it, thanks to which our army was able to commence to cross on May 20, to attack the enemy on the left bank. But hardly had Marshal Masséna got into touch with the Austrian army when a part of the little bridges was broken. The Austrians, masters of the upper reaches of the Danube set loose large barges filled with stones and cannonballs, which borne along by the rapidity of the current, which had been increased by a sudden rising of the river, dashed against the bridges breaking them down in several places. The inferiority of strength of our fourth corps was compensated for by the heroic tenacity of Masséna and the impetuous courage of Lannes. The latter, separated from his corps by the breaking-down of the bridges, but impatient to take part in the action, marched at the head of the Boudet division, which he directed with the greatest courage. The two armies faced each other during the night. On the morrow the second corps, the guards and the cuirassiers were able to cross the bridges which had been repaired during the night. Marshal Davout's corps was to follow, as also the other corps as they came up. The battle of Essling which had been suspended the day before began again, and victory, the price of the most vigorous efforts, was just about to declare itself for us when the sinister report that the big bridge had broken down was suddenly spread. Anything beyond keeping our ground until the end of the day and returning at nightfall to the Island of Essling, became out of the question. This critical position was to be aggravated by the cruel loss which the Emperor and the army experienced in the person of Marshal Lannes. A spent cannonball shattered both legs of this valiant soldier. When the Emperor saw the litter on which the Marshal was being carried, his face overdrawn with the pallor of death, he ordered it to be carried to one side and walking quickly up to it threw himself upon the hero who was dying, and embraced him with choking sobs. The impression produced by this heartrending scene cannot be described. The Emperor's grief was so great that two days later, the remembrance of it still filled his eyes with tears in spite of all his efforts to conceal them. The Marshal transported to the village of Ebersdorf, died there a week later from the consequence of his terrible wounds.

In Marshal Lannes the Emperor had had a loss for which he could not console himself. He never wearied in his praises of the merits of one of his oldest comrades-in-arms. He used to express his astonishment at the way in which each year the Marshal developed his talents, his prudence, and his knowledge of the military art. Considered apart from his capacity as a soldier, the Duke of Montebello had an extremely original mind. A book could be made of the piquant, energetic and always expressive sayings which escaped him. It was he who said to M. de Talleyrand after the battle of Austerlitz, that victory had sharpened the points of the pens of diplomacy with cuts of the saber.

He used to say of Talleyrand's impassiveness that if he were to receive a kick in his seat of honor his face would not betray the event, and summed him up in this saying which is perhaps strictly true, if expressed in somewhat too military language: "It's a lot of . . . mud in a silk stocking."

By way of an anecdote, I will speak of an accident which will appear the merest trifle compared to the misfortune which had just robbed the army of a glorious captain. I happened to be on foot, on the left bank of the Danube, in front of the bridge which communicated with the Island of Lobau, when I saw the Emperor come up and climb up on to the top of a mill-house to see what was going on. I was looking at him when I felt myself struck with a blow—it was a horse's kick—which stretched me full-length on the ground. Napoleon saw me fall just as he was coming down from his point of observation, thought that I was dangerously wounded, and gave orders at once that I should be picked up and transported to the island. I had only been rendered rather dizzy by the blow so he reassured himself and said: "Get away as fast as you can. You gave me a great fright." I felt no consequences from this accident.

General Espagne, commanding the cuirassiers, was killed by a cannonball, and General St. Hilaire was seriously wounded. It was feared at first that we had to deplore the deaths of Generals Durosnel and Fouler but we had the satisfaction of learning that the first of these officers had not been wounded at all and the second only slightly. They had fallen into the hands of the enemy who sent them back to French headquarters after the battle of Wagram.

The troops who were shut up in the Island of Lobau, and especially the wounded, suffered great privations during the first days. Soon, however, stores of provisions and ambulances were established there. Instead of evacuating the island, the Emperor had works worthy of the Romans carried out there under the direction of General Bertrand. Napoleon spent twelve days at Ebersdorf, a village situated opposite the Island of Lobau, occupied with caring for the wounded and providing for the needs of the soldiers who remained on the island. The works were commenced under his eyes and he distributed the rest of the army into cantonments, after which he returned to Schönbrunn.

The indignation felt by the Emperor at the conduct of the Austrian general Chasteler in Tyrol, where seven hundred French conscripts and eighteen hundred Bavarians had been massacred in his presence by the rebels, had prompted an order of the day providing that this general, in case he should be made prisoner, should be tried by court-martial and put to the edge of the sword. The Emperor of Austria having heard of his order, had declared that the Generals Durosnel and Fouler would be kept as hostages to answer for the way in which General Chasteler was treated. When this declaration was notified to Napoleon, he gave the necessary orders that the persons of the Princes Colloredo and Metternich as well as Counts Pergen and Hardeck who had remained in Vienna should be seized, and that, by way of reprisal, these persons should be conducted to France after their arrest. The Emperor at the same time authorized a deputation from the city of Vienna to go to the Austrian sovereign to enlighten him on the particulars of the massacre of French prisoners in Tyrol. Emperor Francis, better informed, retracted his order concerning the two French generals.

During the months of April and May the intrigues of the agents of England and of the coalition had been directed towards raising to insurrection the provinces in the North of Germany which had belonged to Prussia, or which had been dependent on this power. These provinces were filled with former soldiers, prisoners of war who had returned home or who had escaped from the last defeats. Katt, a Prussian officer, had assembled a large number of these persons, had seized on the public treasuries, and had cut off the communications, seeking to stir up the country to revolt. Pursued by the Westphalian troops he had succeeded in reaching Bohemia, where with the remnants of his gang, he had joined the Duke of Brunswick-Oels, who was organizing a corps of volunteers for Austria. This prince, son of the last Duke of Brunswick—who had lost his life at the battle of Jena—wishing to avenge the death of his father and the ruin of his house, had made himself the leader of secret societies and of insurrections in Germany. He had given his corps a black uniform with the emblems of death.

Towards the end of April an aide-de-camp of the King of Westphalia, colonel of the light infantrymen of his guard, a certain Doernberg, at the head of a troop of smugglers and employees, partly military, partly civilian, which was increased by armed peasants recruited in Westphalia and in Hanover, had raised the standard of revolt and had marched on Cassel, hoping to surprise this city in a defenseless state and had then thrown himself back on Magdeburg. The activity and vigor which the young King of Westphalia, seconded by the leaders of his army, had displayed in dealing with this attempt at an insurrection had ended by getting the best of it. But Doernberg who had been reduced to flight in company with some officers had succeeded in joining the Duke of Brunswick, who was the soul of all these revolutionary movements.

Shortly afterwards, the Prussian major, Schill, former partisan in the war in 1806, marched out of Berlin at the head of five hundred hussars of his regiment on the pretext, as it appears, of maneuvers. He was joined by a battalion of infantry which had formed part of his corps of partisans. After fruitless attempts against the fortresses in the North of Germany he had drawn back on Westphalia to give a hand to the remainder of Doernberg's insurgents. Schill having assembled the forces which he considered sufficient, tried a *coup de main* on Magdeburg and having failed marched on the lower Elbe. In the meanwhile the Duke of Brunswick was tardily entering Saxony to join the Prussian partisan. But the latter was approaching the Baltic to put himself in communication with the English fleet and to receive from it the arms and ammunition, which he lacked. Schill invaded Mecklenberg and, followed by five or six thousand men—Prussian and Austrian deserters—of Mecklenbergers whom he had enrolled, and a multitude of vagrants, had entered the city of Stralsund which he had fortified. General Gratien—I am not quite sure about the name of this general—with a Dutch division, backed up by a column of Danish soldiers, marched on Stralsund and carried its retrenchments by storm. Schill, to cover his retreat had wished to set fire to the city in which a stubborn street-by-street fight was fought. The whole band was taken or killed and Schill himself lost his life.

The Duke of Brunswick, on his side, had broken into Westphalia where he hoped that the people of his ancient duchy would flock under his banner, but he only succeeded in raising a few villagers. Neglected by Austria who was sufficiently taken up with her own reverses, forced to flee by the troops which tracked him on every side, the Duke had to gain the seaside with all speed, where together with the rest of his supporters he was received by the English fleet.

These attempts at insurrection necessarily found support in the anti-French spirit of the provinces whose situations and interests had been changed by our conquests. They were the preludes of a general insurrection in Germany, which was only realized much later, but which the coalition always hoped for. If the ill-arranged enterprises of Doernberg, Schill, and the Duke of Brunswick had taken place simultaneously, French domination in the North of Germany would have been seriously embarrassed at this time.

The French army in Italy, commanded by the viceroy, aided and stimulated by the splendid successes of the Great Army, had taken grand revenge for the reverse which it had experienced at the beginning of the campaign, a reverse which had forced it to retreat as far as the Adige. The battle of Pavia and several encounters in which the Austrian army, under the command of Archduke John lost half of its force, gloriously avenged the army of Italy for this defeat. The Archduke, pursued at the point of the sword, got no breathing-time until he had crossed the frontier which separates Upper Italy from the Austrian hereditary States. The viceroy still on the heels of his adversary reached Bruck on May 26, where he joined in with the Great Army. The appearance of the runners of the army of Italy on the Simmering was quite an event. The Emperor, who expected it, had sent Lauriston, his aide-de-camp to meet it. A chasseur of the 9th regiment of the army of Italy met with a chasseur of the 20th, sent to reconnoiter by General Lauriston. The two soldiers after having watched each other some time saw that each was French and fell into each other's arms. Prince Eugène arrived in Ebersdorf two days later where he received the Emperor's compliments which he had so fully deserved.

Archduke John had joined the army of the Archduke Palatine, his brother. Prince Eugène marched to meet them and came up with them near Raab, a fortified town in Hungary. On June 14, he attacked this combined army which exceeded the French forces by fifteen thousand men. The enemy was completely routed and lost six thousand men, killed and wounded, cannons and flags. Napoleon expressed his satisfaction to the viceroy for a victory which, won on June 14, was honored by him with the name of "Granddaughter of the battle of Marengo," which had been won on the same date, on this spot, eight years previously. On the 24th, our troops entered the fortified place of Raab, the garrison of which, two thousand five hundred men strong, became prisoners of war.

The Island of Lobau had become a large entrenched camp guarded by Marshal Masséna's corps, or rather I should say a fortified place defended by one hundred and twenty cannon of big caliber, by mortars and howitzers in batteries. Three large bridges had been built there of a solidity able to resist anything, which were protected by bridge-heads covering a space of more than sixteen hundred fathoms, composed of palisaded redoubts and surrounded with ditches full of water. During the month which the Emperor spent at Schönbrunn he had made frequent excursions to Ebersdorf and had occupied himself with his usual activity in the reconstruction of the bridges as well as in giving orders for assembling round Vienna sufficient forces to be ready for an emergency. Napoleon's solicitude had been applied to the state of the hospitals which he had made his aides-de-camp visit. They had orders to put sums amounting to sixty francs for a soldier and twelve hundred francs for an officer on the beds of the wounded soldiers and officers.

After the army had rested, the artillery had been reorganized and ammunition of all kinds had been got together, the Emperor left Schönbrunn and transported his headquarters to Ebersdorf. On July 4, the whole army was assembled in the Island of Lobau. On the night of the same day it marched out in perfect order which was not troubled by a fearful storm accompanied by a deluge of rain, crossing six bridges which had been prepared in advance, under the protection of strong stockades, and which had been thrown over the river in a space of two hours with admirable precision.

During this time I was shut up with M. de Champigny, Minister of Exterior Relations, in a room in the Emperor's lodgings at Ebersdorf where we awaited the result of the crossing of the river with keen anxiety. We listened in mute dismay to the peals of thunder which shook the ground and to the torrents of rain which threatened to drown us all, not knowing whether this riot of elements would favor or impede the army's crossing. We heard at last, towards daybreak, of the entire success of this brave operation. A fine day had followed on this terrible night. The enemy deceived by false demonstrations on the other side of the river was astonished to see deploying in the plain of Enzersdorf, the imposing masses of one hundred and fifty thousand men, backed by four hundred pieces of artillery which had appeared as though by magic very far from the spot at which they were expected. On the evening of the same day began the attack on an important position, a combat which was the prelude to the great battle of Wagram which was fought on the morrow, the 6th. I spent this day in the neighborhood of the field of battle, riding about on horseback in company of the Colonels Czernitchev and Gorgoli, aides-de-camp to the Czar, who had been sent to the Emperor and who found themselves at his headquarters. These two officers were rather dissatisfied at not being called to form part of the Emperor's staff during the action. One of them said with a certain amount of vexation that it was no doubt on account of their white crests that they had been excluded.

On the evening of the battle I joined the Emperor's bivouac. Hardly had Napoleon reached it when a cry of *"sauve qui peut"* spread a panic, which fortunately was not of very long duration. A stray band of the enemy had come upon our outposts and had caused this affray.

The battle of Wagram was a murderous one. The Austrians lost twenty-five thousand men, and three of their generals were killed. Our losses were less important, but we also lost three generals including General Lasalle, one of the best general officers in our army. By a sinister presentiment of his approaching end General Lasalle had the evening before recommended his children to the Emperor's care in a touching letter.

Napoleon rode over the field of battle to have the wounded removed and attended to, which was a duty which he entrusted to nobody but himself. From time to time he would halt and order silence so that he might hear the groans of the wounded. He would ride in the direction of these groans, when he was not detained by having to attend to soldiers on the spot where he happened to be, or else he would send people with help. With this object in view he used to spread the men of his escort out in different directions.

Oudet, colonel of the 9th infantry regiment, who died in consequence of the wounds which he received in this battle, has been a great deal talked about. Lying rumors collected by the historian of the secret societies of the army and of the military conspiracies, have represented this colonel as the leader of these imaginary associations and describe him as having fallen a victim to a murder carried out by Napoleon's orders. The falseness of this calumny has already been easily proved, but its very absurdity should have sufficed for its refutation.

On the morrow of the battle of Wagram, the Emperor while visiting the corps and distributing the rewards which each had merited, met General Macdonald and stretched out his hand to him in sign of reconciliation. Macdonald, a friend of Moreau, had been for a long time in disgrace and kept away from the army. On his asking to be allowed to resume his service, Napoleon who esteemed his talents had entrusted him, during this campaign, with the command of the right wing of the army of Italy under Prince Eugène. He created him Marshal of France as well as Generals Oudinot and Marmont.

The victory of the French at Wagram had not destroyed the Austrian army, which in spite of the losses which it had experienced retreated in good order. It was on the 11th of August only that Prince John von Lichtenstein presented himself at Znaim with powers to conclude an armistice and even to treat for peace. The armistice had been proposed by Archduke Charles in virtue of his unlimited powers. The Emperor of Austria, who had retired to Baden, refused to ratify this armistice and removed the Archduke from the command of his army. Napoleon sent him the decoration of a simple Knight of the Legion of Honor. The Emperor Francis, better advised, accepted the armistice five days later, with the mental reservation that it would give him the time to reject it during the period fixed for its duration. The Emperor Napoleon after having distributed his troops over the districts designated by the treaty of armistice proceeded to Schönbrunn. Conferences were opened at Altenburg between M. de Champigny and M. de Metternich. The negotiation dragging, because the Austrian plenipotentiary, counting no doubt on the diversion which the English expedition in the island of Walcheren would cause, wanted to gain time, the Emperor summoned his Minister of Exterior Relations to Vienna. After long tergiversations to which Napoleon's firmness put a stop, peace was signed in his presence, on October 14, by M. de Champigny and Prince von Lichtenstein who had taken Metternich's place.

It is very probable that the signing of the peace was hurried on by an event which produced a strong impression on Napoleon, though he tried not to let this be seen. One day in October, at Schönbrunn, while the troops were marching before him at noonday parade a young man tried to approach the Emperor. This person held a paper in his hands which was thought to be a petition. He was told to hand it to the aide-de-camp in attendance, who was General Rapp, but he answered that he wished to speak to Napoleon. As often rebutted so often he returned. This manner of insisting appeared suspicious, his decided though calm appearance, the expression of his eyes, his right hand which he held in his bosom, struck General Rapp's attention. The General ordered him to be arrested and to be taken to the castle. All this was done without being noticed. It was soon known that a large kitchen-knife had been found on this young man, who was a student of the University of Erfurth, named Staaps. Asked as to what he intended to do with this knife he had no hesitation in declaring that he wanted to kill Napoleon. Informed of this fact, the Emperor on his return to the castle, ordered that the young man should be brought into the drawing room where the Prince of Neufchâtel, Bernadotte and the Generals Duroc and Savary were present. Staaps approached the Emperor with a respectful but determined air. He admitted to Napoleon that he had come with the intention of killing him, although the French sovereign had done him, personally, no harm. He declared that he had the conviction that in killing the Emperor he should render a great service to his country and to Europe, and added that he was neither ill nor mad and that he had spoken of his plan to nobody. Napoleon had Doctor Corvisart, who was then at Schönbrunn, sent for, and asked him if he could not find any traces of madness in this young man. The doctor felt his pulse and declared that he could not find any symptoms of mental alienation in him. Napoleon struck by this fanaticism, and touched with pity for this precocious murderer, offered to pardon him if he would express his regret for the odious act which he had wished to commit. Staaps rejected any idea of pardon, and said that he regretted bitterly that he had not been able to carry out his plan. "But," said Napoleon, "you have a family whose ruin you will cause. You will fill the heart of the young girl who loves you with despair. If I grant you your life will you be grateful to me for it?" "I will kill you none the less." The Emperor gave order that he should be removed, hoping that this young madman would express his repentance and make some revelations. Staaps remained three days without eating and as impassive as ever. He walked on foot to the place of the execution crying: "Long live Germany. Death to the tyrant." Napoleon heard of his execution while on his way from Vienna to Munich.

By the public and secret clauses of the treaty concluded with Austria, this power ceded territories containing a population of three and a half millions of inhabitants, which for the most part fell to the lot of the kings and princes who were allied to France. Austria undertook by the secret clauses to reduce its army to one hundred and fifty thousand men during the war between France and England; to dismiss from the Austrian service all military, civil, and political employees who had been born in French provinces; and finally to pay a war-indemnity of eighty-five millions of francs.

An article of the treaty added a population of fifteen hundred thousand inhabitants to the Grand duchy of Warsaw. To induce Russia to agree to this fresh step towards the reestablishment of Poland, a territory of four hundred thousand inhabitants which rounded off its frontier on the Ukraine was ceded to this power which took part in the treaty. Russia took it over as cheerfully as she had done with the district of Białystock, at Tilsitt, when this province was taken from Prussia, her ally. One might have thought that the Russian government, sharing in the spoils wrested from its allies, kept them back to be restored to them when circumstances should allow it, but the events of 1814 and 1815 occurred without Russia's ever dreaming of restoring her acquisitions.

The conduct of the Russian government during this campaign seemed to justify the extension which was given to the Grand duchy of Warsaw. Alexander had undertaken at Warsaw to declare against Austria in case she should again make war on France. Although Napoleon had no reason to expect that the Russian cabinet would make any great efforts to free the provinces, which formerly had been Polish, and the successive emancipations of which might appear menacing in the eyes of Russia, which had taken a large part in the division, he still was authorized in considering himself discharged of all obligations towards the Emperor Alexander who had not kept the promises which he had made at Erfurth. Napoleon who had counted upon the effective cooperation of Russia, about equal to that which she had formerly tendered to her allies in the wars of the coalition, had just been completely disappointed on this point. The Russian contingent consisted of a body of fifteen thousand men, commanded by Prince Galitzin, who refused to concert with the French army in any way. The cooperation of this corps consisted in re-establishing Austrian authorities everywhere where they had been replaced by Polish authorities, and in seizing upon Cracow by surprise, to establish themselves before the Poles, to whom the Russians refused entrance. On Prince Poniatowski threatening to force his way in, the Russians agreed to occupy the town in common with the Poles. This attitude showed Napoleon how little he could rely on the Russian alliance, but he hid his resentment. What would he have thought if he had known at the time the truth about Prince Schwarzenberg's mission to St. Petersburg? This *envoyé,* who afterwards became ambassador to Paris and negotiator for Napoleon's marriage with Princess Marie Louise and later on commander in chief of the united armies in 1814, had been charged to urge Russia to join Austria in the campaign which had just finished. Alexander, indeed, had refused these proposals, but not for the motive which he alleged to our ambassador at St. Petersburg; when the Czar spoke to the latter of his firm resolution to persevere in the Tilsitt alliance, and to cooperate by his efforts to repel Austria's unjust aggression upon his ally. Emperor Alexander's true motive was to gain time to prepare himself for the struggle which was inevitable in the future, but which at that time he was unable to support against us, owing to the remoteness of his armies, occupied the one in Sweden and the other in Turkey. It was this last motive, the only genuine one, which dictated Alexander's replies to the overtures of the Vienna cabinet. This reply was not a defection on Russia's part towards Austria, for its sincerity could be tested in the Russian declarations which were expressed after Napoleon's fall. It cannot be doubted that if Russia had really wished to prevent Austria from making war against us in 1809, a simple declaration on her part to the Vienna cabinet would have sufficed. Such was unfortunately the sincerity of Emperor Alexander's sentiments. The Mussulman does not consider himself bound by his promises to the unfaithful, and the united armies treated us, it may be said, as the Turks might have done.

The discontent on one side and on the other was strong, and the circumstance of Napoleon's marriage, about which I shall speak in its place, envenomed the already strained relations between France and Russia. The divergence of interests of these two powers, the moral obligation under which France seemed to consider herself to reestablish the kingdom of Poland, Russia's evident hostility towards such a project, all combined to conduct the Paris and St. Petersburg Cabinets, through a series of alternating squabblings and patchings-up, to an irreparable and open rupture.

A deputation of Hungarians had presented itself to the Emperor at Schönbrunn to beg him to take Hungary under his protection and to back up her efforts to separate herself from Austria. Napoleon had at the time conceived the project of placing the Grand Duke of Würtzburg on the imperial throne, but made no fixed determination on the subject. The Hungarian revolution and the change of the Austrian succession were two enterprises which might have led him further than he wished to go, and he did not allow himself to be drawn on. These reasons and the fact that his absence had already been too greatly prolonged under doubtful circumstances, prompted him to sign the peace of Vienna which he did with but little confidence in his mind. Napoleon often afterwards blamed himself for his fault in leaving Austria too strong for future safety, and for not having taken full advantage of his success at Austerlitz when he might have taken or have annihilated the entire Russian and Austrian armies. He had not forgotten that the Austrians had asked for peace twelve years earlier, when the French were at Leoben, that while he was in Egypt Austria had taken up arms again, that she only signed the Treaty of Lunéville after having lost the battle of Hohenlinden, that she had begun war again as soon as she had seen us seriously engaged in making preparations for the expedition to England, that she had only signed the peace of Vienna after the battle of Austerlitz, that Emperor Francis had promised at the interview at Sar-Uschitz not to make war on France again, that this time Austria had once more hoped to surprise Napoleon taken up with the pursuit of the English army in the remotest parts of Spain, and that it was only after Vienna had been occupied a second time that the Austrian government resigned itself to signing peace.

The English, on their side, seeing the Emperor seriously engaged in Germany and encouraged by the hope that the consequences of the battle of Essling would cause him serious embarrassments, attempted an expedition into the island of Walcheren, not indeed to serve their ally's cause but with the very English object in view of seizing upon the fleet at Antwerp and of setting fire to it, and of destroying the dockyards. Napoleon's foresight had assured the defense of this immense dockyard of our navy. At the first report of the invasion of the island of Walcheren, every class of citizen in the neighboring provinces was aroused. Without awaiting orders from the Minister of War, men, horses, carriages, provisions, and fodder were offered to the functionaries of state, who had no difficulty in making a regular use of the same; the national guards hurried up. Marshal Bernadotte had been deprived of the command of the 9th corps of which he was the leader in Germany. The Emperor had sent him back to France on the pretence of taking a cure at the waters. As a matter of fact the Emperor had been seriously displeased with him, because of his insubordinate and violent character, his boasting, and the order of the day by which he arrogated to himself the right of attributing the victory of the battle of Wagram to the Saxons who were a part of his corps, while in his letters he used to complain about their want of vigor and inactivity. This Marshal, well knowing that Napoleon would not have selected him to face the English, greedily seized upon the opportunity to impose and render himself indispensable, in spite of the Emperor, on this occasion. Helped by his friend Fouché, who said that Napoleon must be shown that the territory could be defended and the enemy driven out, without his help, Bernadotte succeeded in getting himself sent to Antwerp by the Minister of War. The English expedition had already failed in its object at the time of his arrival, but King Louis of Holland, who had undertaken the command of the operations out of zeal, seeing Bernadotte arrive, without having received any notice that he was being sent to take over the command in chief, returned to Amsterdam in a very dissatisfied state of mind. Bernadotte made a great deal of noise, but as a matter of fact did nothing more than Marshals Kellermann, Moncey, and Bessières who were very little talked about. The zeal of the officers of all branches of the service, the bravery of the troops and above all the devotion of the national guard and of the inhabitants, the vigorous measures ordered from Schönbrunn by the Emperor, and finally the utter incapacity of the English commander caused the total failure of this gigantic enterprise. The English expedition forced to retire pitifully lost about a third of its men and its material. The unlucky issue of this important attempt brought with it the fall of the English Ministry. Each minister tried to discharge himself of the responsibility, and to shift it on to another of his colleagues, a dénouement which reminds one of Racine's epigram on the subject of the tragedy of *Iphigenia*, the authorship of which two writers, Leclerc and Coras, claimed,

> "But as soon as the piece had appeared,
> "Neither one nor the other wished to have had
> anything to do with it."

I will allude, in connection with this campaign, to the solicitude with which the Emperor insisted that his regiments should be commanded by brave and well-educated officers. The proposals for advancement were submitted to him by the Minister of War. Napoleon charged one of his aides-de-camp, the one whom he considered best suited for work of this kind, to submit the results of this classification for his signature, and weighed each candidate's merits. As he was personally acquainted with each officer, his selections were carried out with discernment. While with the army or when the various corps were passing through Paris, the Emperor used to hold frequent reviews, which were not mere empty parades. He used to cross-examine officers whom he did not know and would invite them to command and carry out maneuvers under his eyes. The maneuvers which were not in the usual routine used sometimes to trouble the officers who had made a special study of their profession. Napoleon obliged the officers with whom he was not altogether satisfied to study these maneuvers, placing them under the supervision of the colonels and generals in command. He missed no opportunity to assure himself that they had profited by this completion of their military education.

Often while reviewing a *corps d'armée* or even on the field of battle the Emperor would pull up in front of a regiment and calling the officers around him would address each by his name. He would ask them to mention whom amongst them they considered most worthy of promotion or of a decoration, and then passed on to the soldiers. Such testimony delivered by the peers bound the various regiments together with the bonds of confidence and esteem, and these promotions, granted by the soldiers themselves, had all the more value in their eyes. In the course of one of these distributions of military rewards, which were like family scenes, an under-officer was designated to the Emperor as the bravest and the best. The colonel while agreeing that he possessed all the qualities necessary to make a good officer added that in rendering him this justice, he regretted that on account of a serious drawback he was unable to recommend him for promotion. "What is it?" asked Napoleon quickly. "Sire, he can neither read nor write." "I appoint him officer, Colonel, you will have him admitted as such."

During these reviews Napoleon used to inform himself of the wants of the soldiers, of the state of their accoutrements and equipments, of the quality of the rations and finally of the way in which the military regulations were carried out. Each soldier was authorized to leave the ranks and to address himself directly to the Emperor, presenting arms, to submit a demand or to make a complaint. No request was ever neglected but was immediately answered. If the petitioner was worthy of interest his request was usually granted, unless it was of a nature to render an inquiry necessary. There is perhaps no example that indiscreet or unfounded complaints were ever addressed to the Emperor in this way.

In the course of one of the reviews which he held at Vienna Napoleon heard that certain regiments had received defective articles of clothing or of equipment, and that embezzlement had taken place in the supply of provisions and fodder. As information had been laid with him on this subject, he ordered that an inquiry should be held. The report having established that these complaints were well-founded Napoleon sent the papers to a court-martial before whom the culprits were brought for trial. They were condemned to death. The Emperor rejected all pleas for pardon, for he wished to make an example. This act of severity acted as a warning to other delinquents. I remember in this connection that one day the Emperor entered his workroom in an excited state:

"Just imagine," he said to me, "that I have just put my hand upon a man who robbed the army in Italy in a disgraceful manner. He had protectors under the Directoire, who assured him of impunity. Thanks to God I have found him again, and I mean to make a severe example of him." The said F—:—had been a contractor for provisions during the first campaigns in Italy at the time when General Bonaparte was commanding the army. His conduct had given rise to the most serious complaints and he had been denounced to the Directoire as guilty of malversations and infidelities in the supply of provisions. This contractor had escaped all prosecution, and since that time Napoleon had heard nothing more about him. I do not know in what way he was put on the scent of his reappearance. He dictated me an order for his examination and confinement. But be it that this individual found the means of evading the vigilance of the authorities, or that Napoleon recoiled before the scandal of a trial in which people whom he did not want to ruin might be compromised, F—— once more escaped all punishment. My object is to show that Napoleon really objected to capital sentences, and that his personal inclinations prompted him to clemency, a virtue which in his case often resembled arbitrariness.

An event of the highest importance which occurred during the Austrian campaign was the forcible removal of the pope from Rome. Apart from the questions which concerned the discipline of the Church, other discussions, which were to be brought to exploding point by the clash of temporal and political interests, had placed fresh storm clouds between the Emperor and the pope. Since the Holy Father's return to Rome the enemies of France had worked upon Pius' vexation at not having brought back with him from France certain concessions to which he considered his condescension had entitled him. However it might be, Rome had become a hotbed of intrigues against the empire. The influence of our enemies, and notably of England, predominated there. Summoned by Napoleon to close his ports upon the English vessels which were cruising in the Adriatic, the pope had replied with a formal refusal, alleging that as the common father of all the faithful he could not and should not enter into any league against any one of his children. This answer gave rise to interminable correspondence, which first of all tended towards a reconciliation, then became menacing on the Emperor's part, while on the part of the pope it remained obstinate, invariably negative, and bearing the imprint of the ideas of the Gregories and Bonifaces, written in a language which was not that of the century. This language irritated the Emperor's patience, who saw each of his requests rejected by the pope from whom he was able to obtain nothing. The discontent of the Roman Court against Napoleon blinded this government to the inequality of the struggle and increased in proportion to the impotent resistance which it opposed to this redoubtable adversary. One might have said that the Court of Rome wished to carry matters to extremes and to defy the Emperor. Napoleon then gave orders that Rome should be occupied, without any interference in the affairs of the pontifical government and with the greatest consideration for the Holy Father and his Court. This violent measure provoked the irritation of the pope's counselors to its extreme limits. The Papal Nuncio, immediately recalled to Rome from Paris, received orders to leave without taking *congé*. Rome raised its temporal and spiritual arms against France. The French General, in command in Rome, received orders in his turn to seize upon the government without interfering with the pope in spiritual matters and to take measures for preserving the tranquility of the country. The state of hostility became bitter. The pope, having issued the bull of excommunication which he held in reserve, shut himself up in his palace, round which barricades protected by armed men were placed. The agitation amongst the Roman population increased when lying reports had spread the rumor of the critical position in which, as it was said, the French army, found itself placed in consequence of the battle of Essling. The open opposition of the partisans of the Holy See became dangerous for the French occupation of Rome. A collision was to be feared which might place the person of Pius VII in danger. The Pontiff, obstinately persisting in his voluntary captivity, deaf to the demands of the governor-general, remained unable to calm the effervescence of the public mind. This functionary accordingly took it upon himself to remove the pope from Rome, and in the night of July 6–7 the pope was kidnapped in his palace. While this extreme measure was being carried into effect the Emperor was on the plains of Wagram. The ever-increasing obstinacy of the pope in refusing what the Emperor asked of him, must have made Napoleon foresee that circumstances might arise which would make such an act of violence necessary. Napoleon, however, denied ever having given any order for kidnapping the pope. He would have wished the pope not to leave Italy so brusquely. But the Grand duchess of Tuscany and the governor-general of Piedmont, who had received no instructions in this matter refused to receive the Holy Father either at Florence or Turin. The Emperor did not wish to disavow the governor of Rome and could not and did not wish to send the pope back to the capital. He accordingly gave orders that the pope should be conducted to Savona, since he had passed Florence and Turin when this order reached its destination. The pope, who was lodged in Savona in the bishop's palace, was treated with the necessary respect and dignity.

A general distribution of promotions and rewards took place after the battle of Wagram, on the Emperor's feast-day, which was celebrated at Vienna in all the army corps. The three principalities of Wagram, Essling, and Eckmuehl were created in favor of Marshals Berthier, Masséna, and Davout. The dignity of Marshal, as we have related was, moreover conferred on Generals Macdonald, Oudinot, and Marmont and the duchies of Gaete, Cadore, Otranto, Massa, Bassano and Feltra were given to Ministers Gaudin, Champigny, Fouché, Regnier, Maret, and Clarke.

At the same time the Emperor issued a decree creating an Order of the Three Golden Fleeces. Napoleon, while increasing his means for rewarding his brave soldiers, wished to eclipse the rival orders of the Golden Fleece which existed simultaneously in Spain and Austria and to resuscitate the order as it had originally been founded by Philip the Good, Duke of Burgundy. He hoped by means of this competition with the Spanish and Austrian orders to annihilate the latter in course of time. All French subjects would be forbidden to accept the orders of these two powers. The reunion of the conditions necessary for admission into the order of the Three Fleeces would have given the French order preeminence over the order of the Legion of Honor. In spite of the publication of the decree of institution concerning this creation, nobody was appointed to the new order. Whatever may have been Napoleon's reasons for abandoning his first idea on this subject, the fact remains that he never spoke of it again. Another decree ordered the erection of an obelisk in Cherbourg granite on the *terre-plein* of the Pont-Neuf, in Paris, bearing the inscription: "Napoleon to the French People." The principal feats of arms of the two campaigns of Jena and Poland were to be represented in bas-reliefs on the pedestal.

The Emperor made a mistake one day which might have had consequences untimely rather than dangerous. It was at Schönbrunn, if I remember rightly, after the signing of the peace with Austria, Napoleon had written to the Emperor of Russia and to the Emperor of Austria at the same time. He wanted, as a pastime, to place their letters in their envelopes, which were ready addressed for the purpose, with his own hands. After having sealed up one he carried it to the Austrian general who was waiting for the letter addressed to his sovereign. Before sealing up the other I took the precaution of looking at the envelope and noticed that it was addressed to the Emperor of Austria, the letter addressed to this prince had been placed in the envelope to the Emperor of Russia. A messenger was immediately sent off at full speed after the Austrian officer, who was carrying off the letter intended for the Czar. This *quid pro quo,* might, had it been repeated, have occurred under circumstances which might have had evil consequences. The Emperor saw this and become so circumspect that whenever he was tempted to close up some letter on which he put his beautiful seals with his own hands, he used to throw it away saying that he had been near placing me under some heavy responsibility.

One day at Schönbrunn, a lady in mourning, accompanied by two young children came to ask for a pardon which the Emperor was forced to refuse. This is what had caused this person's visit. A Mrs. Dombray or Combray—of Caen—had associated herself with certain people of good family, who were committing acts of brigandage of which the whole country complained, but who had the pretension of continuing the Vendee by robbing travelers and stagecoaches. This lady shared the spoils which were carried to the country house which she lived in on the side of the road, with the thieves. Napoleon had given the strictest orders for the repression of these criminal attempts against public safety which were filling the department with consternation. Madame de Combray, arrested, had been found guilty and was condemned. A respite was granted her because the idea had been suggested to her to declare herself enceinte. In spite of the fact that this plea was known to be false, this lady took advantage of the respite to have her pardon prayed for. The Emperor, taken by surprise, having received no report on the appeal for mercy, nor any document which might help him to form an opinion, complained bitterly that the Ministers of Police should grant passports which enabled people to come and take him by surprise at four hundred leagues from Paris leaving to him all the odium of refusing a pardon which he was not in a position to grant. An example moreover was necessary. He expressed to the relation of the sentenced woman, all his regret that she should have had to undertake so hard a journey in vain. He told her that his minister had supplied him with no information, adding that the nature of the crime in question did not, unfortunately, put it in his power to use his right of pardon. He concluded with a few words which showed the compulsion he was putting upon himself, and gave orders that his petitioner should be well treated. I quote this anecdote because people have tried to use it as a pretext for accusing Napoleon of inhumanity. The reader must decide on the point himself.

During Napoleon's stay in Vienna, the inhabitants were the victims of a famine which was caused by the action of the Austrian authorities in forbidding any provisions to be sent into the town, because the French soldiers would have made use of them. A deputation, which the Emperor had authorized to visit the Emperor of Austria to obtain the recall of his order, had returned without obtaining any immediate satisfaction. Napoleon, touched by the distress of the Viennese, paid a visit to the suburbs and, together with the Intendant General of the army, took measures for diminishing the sufferings of the inhabitants. The winter coming on, he authorized the poor of Vienna to help themselves to wood in the imperial forests. We saw files of people passing loaded with stacks of wood which they had cut in these forests, for several days. Napoleon tried to preserve people, as far as lay in his power, from the evils of war.

In 1809, the Emperor had again fallen in with at Vienna, the celebrated singer Crescentini, who had been the delight of the Italian theatres. He remembered with pleasure, that formerly at Milan Crescentini had sung cantatas intended to glorify the triumphs of the French army. Although this clever singer was no longer a young man, Napoleon attached him to the imperial orchestra and sent him to Paris with a salary of thirty thousand francs. From this time on, Crescentini gave up singing on the stage. When age and infirmities had weakened his voice, the Emperor appointed him professor to the Bologna conservatory, where he was ordered to write a book on the laws of his art. At the same time Napoleon created him a knight of the Order of the Iron Crown. It was not only with a view of rewarding his musical merit that the Emperor accorded him this distinction to which his title of professor gave him a claim. In decorating Crescentini, Napoleon had another purpose and was trying an experiment, for he wished to decorate Talma with the Legion of Honor. A foreign distinction awarded to a professor of singing in Italy, the classical home of music, a favor justified by superior merit, was likely to excite less opposition there than in France. At the same time this nomination was generally criticized in Italy and the Emperor was forced to admit that great as was his power, it had its limits. Napoleon saw himself forced to draw back before this manifestation of public opinion, but he regretted that this scruple, praiseworthy in its principle, prevented him from honoring a great artist like Talma, who was endowed with unrivalled talents and whom he held in high esteem.

Corvisart, first doctor to the Emperor, came to Paris during the 1809 campaign. His presence at headquarters gave rise to the belief that Napoleon was dangerously ill, a circumstance which specially attracted the attention of the English government. Corvisart's journey had not been caused alone by a slight indisposition on the Emperor's part, caused by the fatigues of the campaign, but which neither prevented him from riding on horseback nor from holding reviews. The doctor, impelled by curiosity and the interests of science had asked permission on his side to come to Vienna. He wished to visit the medical establishments of this capital and to make the acquaintance of the celebrated Doctor Franck who was first doctor to the Emperor of Austria. Numerous cases of dysentery having declared themselves in the army which it was feared might degenerate into an epidemic, Corvisart's advice became very desirable. I remember that the Emperor jested the doctor on a danger to which the latter had exposed himself while visiting the battlefield of Wagram, where, it is said, he approached a shell which, though the battle had taken place several days before, had not yet been extinguished.

Immediately after signing peace Napoleon left Schönbrunn to return to France. Before leaving he gave orders that the fortifications of Vienna should be destroyed. He remembered how he had been twice stopped before the walls of this capital and, preoccupied with the idea that he might have to come there a third time, thought of the serious embarrassment which an energetic defense of the city might cause him. Such threatening leave-taking struck dismay into the hearts of the Viennese, who considered themselves humiliated by a precaution, which, ordered after peace had been signed, appeared to them to be dictated by a spirit of revenge and rancor.

Napoleon went to await the Emperor of Austria's ratification of the peace at Nymphenburg, where he spent two days, and took leave of the King of Bavaria after having received this ratification. He stopped one day at Stuttgart, passed through Strasburg without stopping and spent some hours at Jeand'heures, near Bar, under Marshal Oudinot's roof. On October 29 the Emperor arrived at Fontainebleau at nine in the morning, without having been announced. Empress Josephine, not having been told in time, was not there to receive him, Napoleon made this a pretext for showing some bad temper. He seemed to wish to prelude the painful declaration which it was in his mind to make by some subject for discontent. As a matter of fact his mind was fully made up on his divorce from Josephine. He prepared himself exclusively for it while at Fontainebleau where for three weeks he held a large and brilliant court.

On his return to Paris, on November 16, Napoleon heard that the ex-Queen of Etruria, who had retired to Nice, with her son, a young child, on the pretext of ill-health, was giving herself up to intrigues of all kinds. She used to write to the English Prince Regent to offer to employ her influence with the Spanish prisoners in cantonment in the depots in the South of France. She wrote to this Prince of the embarrassment which her presence in Spain would cause to the French. The ex-Queen was mistaking matters. There was danger for her alone. The Emperor, not wishing to leave an element of disturbance which might add fresh complications to the state of affairs in Spain, in the hands of the English, gave orders that she should be conducted to Rome. She was placed in a convent of which a Princess of Parma, her relation, was the abbess. Napoleon informed King Charles IV, at that time in residence at Marseilles, of what had happened, and pointed out to him what steps had been, as a measure of prudence, rendered necessary by his daughter's ill-considered conduct.

Before approaching the great event of the Emperor's marriage and divorce, it may be well to pass in rapid survey the state of our affairs in the Spanish peninsula. Austria's declaration of war, in forcing Napoleon to leave Spain, had served the coalition better than the untimely rising of the Spaniards. Napoleon's absence was sadly felt in the Peninsula, where our military operations were characterized by a want of *ensemble* and harmony. Brilliant successes had been achieved but had not been followed by any decisive results. A want of unity in the command and the dissensions of the Marshals amongst themselves prevented the fruits of these victories from being gathered in. To remedy this bad state of affairs, Napoleon replaced Marshal Jourdan in the functions of major general to King Joseph, by Marshal Soult, who was younger and had more experience in making war in the Emperor's own fashion. As to Portugal, she had been abandoned. Military operations were being carried on with more success on the East. General Suchet, appointed commander of the army of Aragon, had restored discipline, abundance, and victory. The taking of the fortified places of Aragon and Catalonia and the occupation of Valentia won this general the *bâton* of Marshal and the title of Duke of Albuféra. It is sad to have to add that Ferdinand, on hearing of the victories which had been gained over his countrymen, who formerly had been his subjects, addressed to the Emperor, in his and his brother's names, the most obsequious congratulations, couched in the most humble expressions and protested his sincere respect for and blind submission to the imperial will.

Chapter IX

Since 1792 Europe had been making war on France—a war of extermination—and France had come forth victorious. The bitterness of her enemies, far from crushing her, had rendered her great and powerful. The Emperor thought that a marriage with a foreign Princess would calm the anxiety of the powers; which would then no longer have reason to fear revolutionary propaganda; that this tie would enforce the acknowledgement of his glory; would diminish the dangers of the retrocessions which France would be obliged to make when universal peace was established, and in one word, would become the means of a lasting peace. He foresaw also that the want of a natural heir would after his death hand the empire over to rival ministers, as had formerly happened to the Empire left by Alexander the Great. Nevertheless, Napoleon hesitated for a long time before breaking the union which was endeared to him by long standing and true attachment. Politics, the future peace of the world, imperiously commanded the accomplishment of his design. Thus age forbade him from longer hesitation. Some have said that he was prompted by the vain desire to mix his blood with that of the royal houses; but it may be asked what reasons he had to envy them, either in greatness or in genius, or in power. If vanity there was in his action, if in this matter Napoleon showed himself open to human weaknesses, it had very little voice in determining his resolution. The assiduity with which the ruling families in Europe sought after an alliance with him by marriage did not raise the merit and value of such an alliance in his eyes, though it was a further guarantee of the advantages which he looked for from it.

Some time previously Fouché had taken the opportunity, without being authorized to do so, to approach Empress Josephine on the necessity of a divorce, and to spread the report that a divorce was imminent. Napoleon had severely reprimanded him, not only because he had come to no definite decision on the subject himself, but because he was anxious to spare the unhappy Princess premature grief, and did not wish to leave her under the continual menace of a separation which was painful for both.

When, on his return from Fontainebleau, at the end of 1809, Napoleon had made up his mind to open this serious question, he allowed the Empress to suspect the separation which he was planning, only a few weeks before the time when this very painful sacrifice had to be accomplished, not in an outspoken manner, but rather by dropping hints which gave her cause for reflection. This man, whom many people have long considered as pitiless, dreaded the sight of tears and of affliction, against which as a matter of fact he was always defenseless. I have often seen him—after certain scenes of jealousy caused by Josephine's suspicious affection—so troubled that he would remain for hours in his workroom given up to silent emotion, and unable to resume his work. Napoleon had retained from his early education, family feelings, and simple ways of life, which in his case were united with the highest political capacities.

Since the interview of Erfurth, time had matured Napoleon's project of a divorce. The cordiality which seemed to reign between the Czar and himself familiarized him with the idea that a family alliance would strengthen between them the intimacy which held out the prospect of great advantages. M. de Talleyrand asserts that he was commissioned by Napoleon to sound the Emperor Alexander on the subject. However this may be it is certain that in the course of one of the familiar conversations between the two Emperors at Erfurth, Alexander offered Napoleon the hand of the Grand duchess Anna. Napoleon bound himself by no commitment, but he had felt pleased and nattered by this offer, which remained a secret between the two sovereigns.

When, towards the end of 1809, on his return from the Wagram campaign, Napoleon made public his decision to seek for children in a new matrimonial alliance, since he could expect no posterity from his marriage with Josephine, his first thoughts were for an alliance with the princess of the Russian Imperial House. While commissioning his representative in St. Petersburg to approach Emperor Alexander in a confidential manner in this matter, two other princesses—one, the only daughter of the King of Saxony, the other, the eldest daughter of the Emperor of Austria—were in his mind. Although his desire to have children as soon as possible threw weight into the scale on the side of the Princess Augusta; or Archduchess Marie Louise, who suited him better, on account of her age, Napoleon still hesitated. The agreement of his political views, with his personal inclination for Emperor Alexander, and the remembrance of the offer made by this Prince at Erfurth, decided him to take up again the proposal, to which he had given no definite answer, and to prefer a marriage with a Russian Princess. It was about a week after the Minister of Foreign Affairs had written in a confidential manner to the Duke of Vicence, our minister at St. Petersburg, charging him to open the subject of the marriage in a categorical manner to Emperor Alexander, when Napoleon made up his mind to break his silence towards Empress Josephine. The minister's letter had been ciphered by himself, and was to be deciphered by the Duke of Vicence alone. Since the insinuations made two years before by Fouché to the Empress, and although this mischievous marplot had been publicly disavowed, Josephine could not help seeing that, sooner or later, she would have to pay for the misfortune of not having given an heir to Napoleon with the loss of her rank. It was the general topic of her conversation, either with me, from whom she hoped to gather some information, or with those with whom she could speak in confidence. But after the Emperor's arrival at Fontainebleau—where, as we have read, he returned after the Wagram campaign—new signs confirmed her suspicions, and made her foresee that the storm might break at any moment. An unaccustomed coldness, the closing of the doors which communicated between their two apartments, the shortness of the rare moments which the Emperor devoted to his wife, certain passing outbursts provoked by the most trifling causes, which troubled this family, usually so peaceful, the arrival in turn of the allied sovereigns whose presence she was not able to understand, inspired the Empress Josephine with the keenest anxiety. So cruelly was she troubled that she was constantly applying to me. I could only answer her in an evasive way, my part became an embarrassing one, and in order to escape from the unhappy Princess's questions, I was obliged to avoid her. But my perseverance in escaping from what I may call her importunities appeared to her more significant than words, and her anxiety reached its highest pitch. When by hazard she was able to keep the Emperor with her for a moment she did not dare to touch on this question for fear that the fatal sentence should fall from his lips. Such a state of things could not be greatly prolonged. Its result had been to strain the relations between the two spouses to a point which was downright torture for both. The Emperor was at last unable to bear it any longer, and one evening, after the most silent and sorrowful of meals, he broke the ice. It may be imagined what was the grief and despair of the Empress Josephine at the moment when her last hope was taken away. Napoleon freed from an insupportable load was deeply touched by the grief which he was causing, and from that moment never ceased to surround her with every care, and to lavish upon her words of comfort, which Josephine in her despair at first listened to with indifference, but which touched her in the end. Napoleon sent for her children Hortense and Eugène, and committed their mother to their care, assuring them of the continuance of his paternal affection and protection. After having calmed the first transports of her grief, Josephine bore her sacrifice with a force of character of which one might not have thought her capable, and resigned herself to this misfortune for which there was no remedy. From that day she was seen no more at court. She, however, came out of her voluntary retirement on two subsequent occasions, once to be present in a pew at Notre Dame at the *Te Deum* which was sung for the Peace of Vienna, and once to accompany the Emperor to the Mansion House to the fête which the City of Paris gave on that occasion. With the exception of these two circumstances she spent, hiding in her apartment, the fortnight which passed between the moment when this cruel revelation was made to her, and the day when the divorce was pronounced. However painful this fortnight must have been for both, it seemed a terribly short time to Josephine, who could not accustom herself to the idea of the loss of her rank, and above all of being separated from Napoleon, whom she dearly loved. The Emperor soothed the last hours of their married life by acts of the kindest consideration and respect, caring for the future of the wife whom he was leaving, advising her, and meeting her every wish.

Josephine had an irresistible attraction. She was not a woman of regular beauty (she had that grace which is more beautiful than beauty's self, as our good La Fontaine used to say); she had the soft *abandon,* the supple and elegant movements, the graceful negligence of Creole women. Her temper was always even. Good, and kind, she was affable and indulgent to everybody without exception of persons. She was not a woman of a superior intellect, but her exquisite politeness, her great familiarity with society and court life and their innocent artifices, always taught her at a moment's notice what to say and do.

The Emperor had loved her much, and retained for her a feeling of affection which had been strengthened by custom and her own affectionate qualities. One would have said that she was born for the part which her elevation in rank at Napoleon's side forced her to play. The partner of his fortune, she had admirably seconded him with the ascendancy of her grace, her gentleness and her goodness. She was the wife of his glory as much as the wife of his person, for she had wedded his glory as much as she had wedded his person. Although she was a total stranger to politics and affairs of government she had, as far as lay in her power, won over to Napoleon the favor of the various political parties. She was fond of luxury, and extravagant perhaps more than her spirit of charity should have warranted; for her extravagance often made it impossible for her to satisfy her charitable tastes. I may add, however, that on frequent occasions Napoleon very generously made up to her the deficiencies caused by her habit of spending money too readily. There was a charm and a delicacy about her way of obliging people, or of thanking them for a service, which won all hearts. In her misfortune she showed a resignation which never failed her; what rendered her sorrow almost too heavy for her to bear was the inflexible necessity of having to separate from the Emperor. He never neglected her.

Prince Eugène and Queen Hortense showed a nobility of sentiment and a dignity under these circumstances which are greatly to their honor—their devotion was admirable. They helped their mother to keep up courage, and yet, while lavishing their tenderness upon her, did not forget their duty to their adopted father. Queen Hortense had been summoned to the Tuileries, and arrived there at the moment when the Emperor was returning from having conducted, or rather having helped to carry, Josephine to her rooms. Accompanying her to the door of her mother's apartments the Emperor said to her, "Go, daughter: keep up courage." "Oh, Sire! I have courage," she answered, barely able to utter the words for her tears and sobs.

Prince Eugène told me at Vienna that in the first interview which he had with his mother in Napoleon's presence after the divorce had been decided upon Empress Josephine had asked for the Crown of Italy for her son, that he (Eugène) did not wish to receive anything except from the Emperor's kindness, fearing that this favor might be considered as the price of his mother's divorce, and had begged her not to insist on this request, that the Emperor, touched by his reserve, had assured him that he did very well to trust himself to his tenderness.

The marriage of Napoleon with Empress Josephine had been declared null by the Senatus Consultum, and after some time the officiality of Paris severed the religious ties. The deed of the civil marriage contained clauses of nullity which would have been enough to justify a divorce. As it was revolting to the Emperor to make use of this means, he would not allow these points to be put forward. The two witnesses had been M. Calmalet, the friend of the Beauharnais family, and Captain Lemarrois, General Bonaparte's aide-de-camp. The latter was not of age for, born in 1776, he was barely twenty years old in 1796, at the time of the marriage. The age of the two spouses had not been correctly stated. The whole proceedings had been marked with the irregularity which was the natural consequence of the time at which the marriage took place. The birth certificates of neither had been asked for, or at any rate had only been casually examined. In the register General Bonaparte was described as having been born on February 5, 1768; as a matter of fact he was really born on August 15, 1769. This made some people suppose that Napoleon was born before Corsica was ceded to France. Was the reason that this date was so given the carelessness of General Bonaparte's solicitor, or did the General himself wish, by adding eighteen months to his age, to make it more on a level with that of Madame de Beauharnais, who, on her side, reduced her age for the same purpose? None of Napoleon's brothers was born on the 5th of February.

After the sorrowful and imposing ceremony, which unloosened the bonds of a union, which, had Josephine been fruitful, would have lasted as long as their lives, she who till then had been Empress went down to her apartment The Emperor reentered his study, sad and silent, and let himself fall on the sofa where he usually sat, in a state of complete depression. He remained there some moments, his head leaning on his hand, and when he rose his face was distorted. Orders for the departure to Trianon had been given in advance. When it was announced that the carriages were ready, Napoleon took his hat and said, "Méneval, come with me!" I followed him up the little winding staircase which communicated between his study and the Empress's apartment. Josephine was alone, and appeared wrapped in the most painful reflection. The noise we made in entering attracted her attention, and springing up she threw herself on the Emperor's neck sobbing and crying. He pressed her to his bosom, kissing her over and over again, but in the excess of her emotion she had fainted. I ran to the bell and summoned help. The Emperor, wishing to avoid the sight of a grief which he was unable to assuage, placed the Empress in my arms as soon as he saw she was coming back to consciousness, ordered me not to leave her, and withdrew rapidly by the drawing rooms of the ground floor, at the door of which his carriage was waiting for him. After the Emperor's disappearance, women who entered laid her on a couch and did what was necessary for her recovery. In her confusion she took my hands and earnestly prayed me to tell the Emperor not to forget her, and to assure him of an affection which would survive any and every event. She made me promise to send her news of him on my arrival at Trianon and to see that he wrote to her. It seemed to be difficult for her to allow me to depart, as if my departure would break the last tie by which she was connected with Napoleon. I left her, grieved at so deep a sorrow and so sincere an affection. I felt very miserable all along my route, and I could not help deploring that the rigorous exactions of politics should violently break the bonds of an affection which had stood the test of time, to impose another union full of uncertainty.

On my arrival at Trianon I informed the Emperor of what had happened after his departure, and gave him the messages with which I had been entrusted. Napoleon, who was still under the impression of the scenes of the day, spoke at great length of Josephine's good qualities, and of the sincerity of her affection for him. He considered her as a devoted friend, and always retained an affectionate remembrance of her. The same evening he wrote her a letter to comfort her in her solitude. Hearing from those who saw her at La Malmaison that she frequently cried, he again wrote to her, complaining tenderly of her want of courage, and telling her how much he suffered by the separation. It was at Trianon that began the official negotiations of Napoleon's marriage, which of course could not be commenced without it being certain that Napoleon's offer would be accepted. The marriage with the House of Saxony, which presented no difficulties, was dropped after careful examination, and in consideration of the dependent position of this state, which could be of no use, and would be rather an embarrassment in case of war. There remained then the Russian marriage, and the Archduchess of Austria. The latter was reserved in Napoleon's secret thoughts. The Emperor spent a week at Trianon in unusual idleness, trying to amuse himself with shooting and hunting. He went to visit at La Malmaison the lady who a few days before had been his wife. On the eve of his return to Paris he wished to receive her at dinner at Trianon with her daughter the Queen Hortense, and having noticed that this palace was not sufficiently protected against the cold authorized Empress Josephine to go to the Elysée, there to wait the conclusion of the necessary arrangements for her definite establishment there. Josephine was obliged shortly afterwards to leave for the Château de Navarre in consequence of the imminent arrival of the new Empress.

Recalled to Paris by public affairs, Napoleon was surprised at the solitude of his palace, no longer animated by Empress Josephine's presence. He felt the want of the domestic life to which he was accustomed, and this void was not always filled by the cares of government which, by reason of his growing activity and foresight, which overlooked nothing, were constantly multiplying. In the meanwhile the answer from St. Petersburg was delayed, and Napoleon began to suspect that this delay covered a hidden refusal. The pretexts given were the question of a difference of creeds, and the necessity of consulting the Dowager-Empress and of overcoming her objections.

In the course of January M. de Metternich had dropped a hint in the course of a conversation which General Narbonne, who having no instructions to answer him on this point, had allowed the insinuation to pass unnoticed. It became necessary to ascertain whether the Court of Austria was disposed as in the past. The first steps with this object in view were made to the Austrian ambassador by MM. Delaborde and Sémonville, in the course of a conversation in the drawing room with the Secretary of the Austrian ambassador, whose name was Floret. These gentlemen spoke as if on their own initiative, so that the Emperor, not being in any way bound by what they said, should be at perfect liberty, in case of need, to refuse any responsibility for their statements. This suggestion which was eagerly seized upon by M. Floret, seemed to confirm what was already known of the friendly state of mind of Austria.

On the other hand, and almost at the same time, letters came from Russia which did not satisfy the Emperor who was not in the least blind to the real reason of the delays of the Russian cabinet. Other considerations which made Napoleon hesitate were the age of Princess Anne, who was not yet of an age to marry; and, supposing the difference of religions to be a genuine objection, the fact that he would be forced to admit Russian priests, and all the intrigues they would bring with them into the interior of the Tuileries Palace. Did the Emperor's feeling of his dignity allow him to renounce the friendly disposition of Austria, to wait until it might suit the Czar and the Dowager-Empress to make up their minds? Such an attitude would have exposed him to the laughter of Europe. Napoleon made up his mind at the right moment, and showed on this occasion, as on a hundred others, that no one better than he knew how to make use of his time. He saw that the Duke of Vicence obtained nothing from Emperor Alexander but evasive answers. In order to avoid being reproached with frivolity and inconstancy and to ascertain exactly how matters stood, Napoleon wrote directly to the Russian sovereign. In this letter he told the Czar that after a series of delays which without any plausible motive were prolonging his state of uncertainty, he could no longer delay from obtaining a clear answer, which would put an end to this equivocal state of affairs. Alexander's answer arrived at last. It was full of flattering protestations; he expressed his desire to multiply the bonds which attached him to the Emperor Napoleon, but left matters exactly where they were after the first overture. Napoleon judging that his own dignity and that of the nation would be compromised by waiting any longer took upon himself the initiative of refusing the marriage. He had taken care before doing so to assure himself of the entire cooperation of Prince Schwarzenberg, Austrian ambassador to Paris, who vouchsafed the disposition of the Court of Austria. From this moment Napoleon's choice was made in favor of the Archduchess. He called together a Privy Council to examine to which of the three marriages, that is to say, the Russian, Austrian, and Saxon alliances, preference should be given. The three questions were freely discussed at the Council, the Emperor listening with the greatest attention to the various opinions for and against these different plans, but did not express his private feelings on the matter. It was only on the evening of the same day that Napoleon signified his decision to the Minister of Foreign Affairs. Prince Eugène was charged with the mission to carry the formal announcement to Prince Schwarzenberg, Austrian ambassador, with whom an appointment was made on the morrow for the purpose of offering the Archduchess's hand. The marriage contract was signed in the evening. The Duke of Cadore's first dispatch to the Duke of Vicence, referring to the proposal of marriage, was sent off from Paris on November 24, 1809. It is true that at the time it reached its destination Emperor Alexander was away from St. Petersburg. On January 10, 1810, the Duke of Vicence asked for a definite answer within a period of ten days. The answer had not yet been given on the 6th of February. Emperor Napoleon—who has generally been represented as a man who would brook no delays, who would have any plan carried into execution as soon as it had been made—had nevertheless been waiting for two months and a half for the solution of a question of capital importance, and the immediate solution of which was of the highest importance to himself.

The Princess whom the Emperor had chosen was the eldest daughter of the Emperor Francis who, until 1805, had been Francis II, the Emperor of Germany. After the creation of the Federation of the Rhine which changed the organization of the German States, this Prince had taken the title of Francis I, Emperor of Austria, a title which since then he has retained. This sovereign was married four times. His first wife, a Princess of Würtemberg, whom he married at the age of twenty, died two years after marriage. His second marriage was with Maria Theresa, daughter of Ferdinand the Fourth, King of the two Sicilies, with whom he lived in a union which the harmony of their tastes rendered a very close one. There may be seen in the Imperial Palace in Austria, and notably in the, Park of Laxenburg small farms, where the illustrious couple delighted in forgetting their rank and giving themselves up to the pleasures and occupations of a country life. It was from this second marriage alone that the Emperor Francis had any children.

The first was Marie Louise, formerly Empress of the French, succeeded, in the following order, by the late Arch-duchess Leopoldine, who was Empress of Brazil; Archduke Ferdinand, who became Emperor; Archduchess Maria Clementina, wife of Prince Leopold of Salerno; late Archduchess Caroline, who married Prince Frederick of Saxony; Archduke Francis Charles, who married the daughter of the late King Maximilian of Bavaria; and finally by the Archduchess Marianne, whose eccentricities have kept her away from the court and which probably stood in the way of any marriage.

The Emperor Francis's third wife, whom Napoleon knew, was the Princess Marie Louise Beatrice d'Este, who was her husband's cousin. She was fond of literature, her favorite author being Augustus La Fontaine, a German author of French origin, who is looked on in Germany as the founder of his school. The new Empress exercised great influence over her husband from the beginning of their married life, an influence which was somewhat to the dissatisfaction of the Emperor's brothers. She hated the French with a hatred which she had inherited from her father. Her life was cut short by her bad health; the Imperial Palace used frequently to resound with the cries torn from her by violent attacks of a nervous disease. She died in 1816, barely twenty-six years of age, leaving the Emperor Francis a widower for the third time. Some surprise was expressed when he married for a fourth time in the same year with the second daughter of the first marriage of King Maximilian of Bavaria. This princess had been married before to the crown Prince of Würtemberg, who, in his turn, had become King. Having been divorced from her husband, she had retired to the house of her eldest sister, the wife of Prince Eugène Beauharnais. She lived there in great retirement, apparently forgotten by the world, and certainly not foreseeing the destiny reserved for her: an Imperial Crown in compensation for the Crown which she had lost.

The history of Empress Marie Louise's first years is the history of all the Austrian Archduchesses, whose education is almost invariably the same. Brought up under their parents' eyes until the day of their marriage, these princesses live in absolute retirement from the court with their women and servants whom, as a rule, they treat with familiar kindness, and whom they even allow to share in their games. Their education is conducted by governesses who are present at the lessons given to them by professors. The grand mistress of the Archduchess Marie Louise was Countess Colloredo, and her governess was Countess Lazanski, a woman of merit, greatly devoted to her pupil, who on her side was extremely attached to her. Marie Louise's education had been a very careful one indeed. She knew several languages—even Latin, which is currently spoken by the Hungarians. Already at an early age she had made great progress in music and drawing. She painted in oil colors, and on her arrival in France took lessons from Prudhon, one of our best painters; but she was forced to give up painting because the smell of the oil and of the colors affected her disagreeably.

The most minute precautions were taken to preserve the young Archduchesses from any impressions which might have soiled their innocence; a praiseworthy object no doubt, but the means employed to secure it were not always very judiciously selected. A spirit of bigotry, and exaggerated scruples were harmful rather than useful. Instead of preventing the Princesses from reading books which contained passages likely to pervert their minds—mutilated books, in which pages, lines, and even single words had been cut out with the scissors, were placed in their hands. A censorship so clumsily exercised could have no other result than one opposite to that which was hoped for. These passages which would be passed unnoticed had they been allowed to remain, were interpreted in a thousand ways by the young minds, all the more ready to suppose all kinds of things because their curiosity had been excited. The harm which it was intended to prevent was thus brought to their notice, and even increased. On the other hand it happened that the Royal pupils had nothing but indifference for their books, which after the mutilations which they had undergone had become in their eyes soulless bodies, totally lacking in interest. The Archduchess Marie Louise, after she became Empress, used to confess that the absence of these passages in her books had aroused the greatest curiosity in her, and the first thing that she did when she became free to read what she chose, was to look up the passages which had been cut out of her schoolbooks so as to see what her parents had wished to hide from her. Shall I add that domestic animals of the male sex were never allowed to enter their apartments, that the only pets they were allowed to have were females, because these were less likely to offend the sense of decency?

This system of education, which was still in practice during Marie Louise's childhood, has probably since then been modified. My remarks apply moreover only to the childhood of the Archduchesses who in their youth received developed education, and had for their masters, professors chosen from amongst the most distinguished writers and savants.

The Archduchess Marie Louise, at the first overtures made to her on the projected marriage, with the Emperor Napoleon, considered herself almost as a victim who was to be sacrificed to the Minotaur. She has frequently told me that she grew up, if not in hatred, at least with very hostile feelings against the man who, on more than one occasion, had put the house of Hapsburg on the brink of ruin; who had forced her family to flee from their capital, and to wander from town to town in the midst of the confusion and consternation which are inseparable from a hasty retreat.

The favorite games of her brothers and sisters consisted in setting up in a row a troop of little wooden or waxen figures, which represented the French army, at the head of which they put the blackest and ugliest figure. They used to stab it through and through with pins, and heap insults on its head, thus revenging themselves on this inoffensive leader for the treatment occasioned to their family by the redoubted chief against whom the efforts of the Austrian armies, and the thunderbolts of the cabinet of Vienna dashed in vain. Brought up to passive obedience Marie Louise was forced to resign herself to the fate which was to be hers. Accustomed to look upon the Princesses of her family as instruments of the greatness of their house, and as destined to avert the storms which threatened it, she did not consider herself the victim of a sacrifice, but contemplated the part which she was called to play not without pride. From that moment she sought to know the man about whom, until then, she had avoided thinking except with hostility. Her former prejudice against him was dispelled by what she heard of his private qualities, of the happiness which he had given to Josephine, and of the love which was borne to him by the French. She left Vienna with the wish to please Napoleon; her subjugation was completed when she had got to know his character. At the time when she spoke to me, in 1813, she felt a real affection for the Emperor, and was sincerely attached to his destinies. It was her dream to be able to go one day with him on a visit to her family, and see once more the delightful surroundings of Vienna, dear to her from the memories of her childhood.

The Emperor had spent about three months in Paris, during which period he had awaited the issue of the negotiations entered upon in St. Petersburg. Then, pledging himself to Prince Schwarzenberg, he gave orders that the deed of betrothal for the marriage of the Archduchess Marie Louise be drawn up. The Duke of Cadore and the ambassador of Austria affixed their signatures. Napoleon appointed by decree, at the same time, the gentlemen and ladies who were to compose the household of the new Empress, and at the same time he dispatched to Vienna, on extraordinary embassy, Prince de Neufchâtel, to wed the Archduchess in his name. During this period of waiting Napoleon, unable to remain quiet in one place, paid visits to La Malmaison, went to spend two days at Grignon, at the house of the widow of Marshal Bessières, and then went on to Rambouillet. On his return home he sent Queen Caroline, his sister, with an escort of honor to the frontier to receive the illustrious bride.

The sovereigns allied to the French Empire, the Kings of Bavaria, Saxony, Würtemberg, Holland, Naples, and the Viceroy of Italy had been summoned to Paris.

King Joseph, detained in Spain by the most serious troubles, could not come to join the royal procession. He did not come to France until the next year, on the occasion of the christening of the King of Rome. The King of Holland had consulted his council on the question whether it would be right to sanction by his presence in Paris his submission to the onerous measures imposed by France on the Dutch Kingdom. The ministers and the grand officers of the crown pronounced themselves in favor of the journey to Paris, and advanced as their reason that marked opposition might be the danger of Holland. The King yielded to this wise advice, which was contrary to his private inclination. He was taken up with the idea that he would be detained in Paris, that use would be made of his name to authorize orders which he would be unable to disavow afterwards, and that advantage would be taken of his absence to occupy Holland. He agreed with his ministers that any writing which did not end up with a word which was agreed upon, and was to be written in Dutch, would be considered as of no value by them. After having left general instructions to the council of ministers as to the government of his country during his absence, King Louis left for Paris. Before his departure he had given written orders to the commanders of the fortress in Brabant that no foreign troops should be admitted into the interior of the fortress without a written order, signed by himself.

Amongst the number of home affairs which at this time were taking up the attention of the Emperor must be mentioned the establishment of the state prisons. Discussed in the council of state, the decree which instituted these prisons is dated March 5, 1810. Although this measure was surrounded with precautions and guarantees, which were intended to soften down its arbitrary nature, and although as a matter of fact, in practice these prisons were only used in a spirit of moderation, I will undertake not to defend, but simply to explain the system. At the time when the measure, of which we are speaking, was adopted and regulated it was one of the vexatious but inevitable consequences of the Imperial dictatorship, at a time when the earthquake caused by our civil trouble was still making itself felt. Without entering into particulars of the arrangements and regime of these state prisons I will say that they were only used for men whom the government could not bring to trial before the ordinary tribunals, and who could certainly not be left unpunished—such as the *Chouans,* battening on civil war, plotters of the murder of the Head of the state, or agents in conspiracy for upsetting the throne; or fanatical or immoral priests. I will add that nobody could be imprisoned in these state prisons without a decision emanating from a privy council, which was composed of the First President and Procurator General of the Court of Cassation, as well as of men who occupied a high position in the administration; and no persons could be detained for more than a year without a fresh decision from the privy council; that the prisons were visited by two Councilors of the state each year, who thereupon presented a report to the council in assembly; that one fourth of the votes was sufficient to set a prisoner at liberty; and that, what is more, the Imperial Procurators had equally a right to visit the prisoners and assure themselves that they had been arrested and were being detained in virtue of a decision of the privy council.

It was in one of these state prisons—Vincennes—that a young Saxon named Lasahla, had to be locked up. Lasahla was arrested in Paris in the month of February, 1811, while watching his opportunity to murder the Emperor. He carried several loaded pistols, and declared that such was his guilty intention, and that were liberty to be offered him on the condition of abandoning his plan it would be impossible to him not to try and find a means for carrying out his object. On the Minister of Police presenting a report, the Emperor dictated the following words, which were written on the margin: "This man's age is his excuse"—he was eighteen years old—"no man is criminal at so young an age, unless born in crime. In some years he will have changed his ways of thinking, and we should be sorry to have inflicted on an estimable family the bereavement which will always be more or less of a disgrace. He must be sent to Vincennes, and receive such medical attention as the state of his brain would seem to necessitate. Books must be given to him, and his family must be written to, and then let time do its work." This young man stayed at Vincennes until 1814, when he was freed by his countrymen. It appears that neither time nor captivity had ripened his intelligence, for he was again arrested during the Hundred Days at the doors of the Legislative chamber on the very day when the Emperor was opening the session. Detected by the explosion of a packet of fulminating powder, which went off in his pocket, Lasahla was arrested, but almost immediately released. Napoleon would not allow any inquiry to be made as to what was Lasahla's object in providing himself with this chemical, the effect of which was more menacing than murderous. Lasahla remained in Paris until the month of August, 1815, when he went to the Charité Hospital, suffering from a slow nervous fever which led him to commit suicide very shortly after leaving the hospital.

Preparations for his marriage did not divert the Emperor from political affairs. During the pope's stay in Savona, Napoleon had offered to conduct him back to Rome if the Holy Father would undertake to recognize the new state of things established in this capital, and would consent to occupy himself with none but spiritual affairs. His Holiness refused. Remaining in his position as a prisoner and as a persecuted man, the pope counted on inspiring that interest which is always attached to the oppressed. The Emperor, on the other hand, could not fail to expose himself to all the odium which attaches to that rôle of oppressor which he had not hesitated to assume in the eyes of Europe. But Napoleon, too accustomed to break down all resistances, supported with impatience the bonds which the Court of Rome imposed upon him. Cardinal di Pietro, to whom Pius VII had left powers in case of need, was sending apostolic vicars into the vacant dioceses, and was corresponding with the members of the different chapters. The pope, by means of his bulls, was seconding his representative in this campaign. Napoleon tired of the troubles which the eternal opposition of the superior clergy caused him, seeing the pope absent from Rome determined to free himself by one stroke of all his difficulties with the Pontifical court. He made up his mind to bring down, at no matter what cost, a resistance to such invincible obstinacy that its determination could not be foreseen. He cut the Gordian knot which he had been unable to untie, and like Charlemagne, whose successor he considered himself, he caused to be issued in the month of February, in the year 1810, a senatus consultum by which the annexation of the Pontifical states to the French Empire was pronounced, and the temporal powers of the pope regulated. A palace was assigned in Paris and in Rome, or in any other part of the Empire which it should please him to reside in, with an annual revenue of two million francs, thus ending this regrettable religious struggle with a Pope who was gentle, a man of good intentions and for whom the Emperor personally had a liking.

About the same time Napoleon ordered the publication, in the *Moniteur,* of a remarkable reply to the King of England's opening speech in Parliament, which was followed by numerous documents relating to Spanish affairs in which the correspondence of the Spanish Bourbon Princes was largely drawn upon.

While occupied in these various matters, the Emperor received one day from some smugglers a packet of English newspapers which were sent to him by the Minister of Police. Before sending them to the translation bureau, he ordered me to look them over, and pointed out to me the Paris correspondence. What was his surprise and mine, on reading that Bonaparte, being seated one evening in his cabinet, had summoned a young secretary, called Méneval—in whom, it was added, he had all confidence—and told him to hold the light while he read a passage; that this secretary had put the light which he held in his hand so close to Napoleon's head that it had caught fire, and that, imagining that an attack was being made on his life Bonaparte had seized a pistol—which he always carried about him—and had discharged it point-blank at his secretary, who had been killed on the spot. It was further reported, amongst other pleasant things of the same kind, that Napoleon had flown into a passion on some slight pretext with Maret, state Secretary, had rushed upon him, knocked him down, and, seizing him by the hair, dragged him on the floor; that shortly afterwards, ashamed at his passion, he had ordered him to sit down and had dictated to him a decree by which he bestowed upon him a gift of a large forest estate. At the time of the planned invasion of England there had been published all along the English coast, a description of Bonaparte, physically, as well as morally, as a man of hideous appearance and character. This description had been printed in large letters by all the English newspapers; such were the shameful means by which the English public was being duped.

The echoes of the English press and the drawing rooms of the Faubourg St. Germain, repeated these absurd stories about Napoleon's brutal manners, not only towards the persons who approached him, but also towards honorable foreigners, and towards the sacred person of the sovereign Pontiff himself. Time, which does justice to errors, and bad faith, has reduced these contemptible inventions to nothing. Even when most displeased Napoleon never gave way to ridiculous passion. Great as was his dignity, and greatly as he commanded respect in public audience and under solemn circumstances, so greatly was he easy, familiar, frank, and gay in private life. An active benevolence which sprang from his heart, as much when he was vexed, as when he was pleased, was felt by his own people, by his ministers and by his officers, and his servants. In short, very often his graciousness and favor went out to seek first some and then others at times when they least expected it.

The Emperor having provided for current affairs on all business which demanded his special attention, prescribed the necessary arrangements for the arrival of the new Empress at Compiègne. Although it is a rule that all letters exchanged between sovereigns must be autograph, the fact that the Emperor could not write legibly had led to the tacit understanding that his letters should be written by a secretary. However, under the extraordinary circumstances of his marriage, Napoleon wanted to write to his future father-in-law, Emperor Francis, in his own writing. But it was a terrible business for him! At last, having taken a lot of pains, he succeeded in writing a letter which was fairly legible. He told me to rectify the badly written letters in such a way that my corrections should not be too noticeable—such as the forming of the letter e, and the dotting of the i's. I did my work as best I could, and sent off, addressed to "His Majesty, Sir, my Brother, The Emperor of Austria"—a letter which this sovereign must have been able to read with ease, and which may possibly have made him think that his son-in-law did not write very badly when he chose. Of course he never knew what trouble it had caused the writer. I remember the King and Queen of Bavaria having come in one day to the Emperor, asking to see the apartment which was intended for the new Empress, Napoleon treated them with a familiarity which altogether pleased the King. He wished to spare them the trouble of leaving the drawing room in which he had received them, and of going down the grand staircase to the ground floor, on which was the Empress's apartment. He accordingly conducted the foreign sovereigns across his workroom, and led them down a small winding staircase which communicated with this apartment. This staircase was no longer lighted, because the apartment was no longer inhabited. It was, moreover, so narrow that the King of Bavaria, who was a very fat man, had the greatest difficulty in walking downstairs, and had to turn sideways. Both the King and the Queen were rather surprised at finding themselves in the dark, and when the bottom of the stairs was reached, to make matters worse, the door was found to be locked. Great was our embarrassment. I was walking in front of their Majesties, the Emperor was following me, then came the Queen, and last of all the King. It looked as if the Emperor had drawn them into an ambuscade, and had this occurred in the Middle Ages what sinister thoughts would have filled the King and Queen! The King of Bavaria cried out that if it were known in what a position Napoleon had placed his guests, people would be very much surprised. However, we got out of it by turning right-about-face and going upstairs again in the reverse order, and the visit to the Empress's apartment was put off until another day. The King remembered this trifling occurrence and did me the honor of speaking about it a long time afterwards, saying that whenever he thought of it, he felt inclined to laugh. A draft of the marriage contract had been sent to the French ambassador at Vienna, together with full powers for signing the diplomatic convention. The minister was Count Otto who had negotiated the preliminaries of the Peace of Amiens, and who had been French ambassador at Munich during the war of 1805; and in the accomplishment of these various missions his zeal had been rewarded by praises which Napoleon by no means lavished. It was thanks to his care that certain difficulties raised by the scruples of the Emperor of Austria and the Archbishop of Vienna on the validity of Napoleon's divorce, were smoothed over. The Emperor of Austria signed the marriage contract on February 16, and, on the 27th, M. Otto exchanged ratifications of this contract with Count Metternich. The Emperor himself had made the arrangements for his marriage. He sent to M. Otto the list of presents which were to be made at the moment when the Archduchess was handed over to the French mission sent to receive her at Braunau. These presents were similar to those which Louis XV had made on the reception of the Dauphiness at Strasburg.

Napoleon wanted everything to be done with magnificence. He expressed the desire that if it were thought necessary to choose one of the Archduchess's brothers to marry the Princess in his name, it should be the Prince Imperial; that if the minority of the Emperor's son be an obstacle it should be Archduke Charles; he added, however, that he would content himself with the Emperor's choice. At the same time Napoleon sent the description of the new Empress's household, and indicated the route which was to be followed. He finally sent Count Anatole de Montesquiou, one of the orderly officers, to Vienna, to carry his portrait to the Archduchess, to be present at the marriage, and to report to him the first news that all these things had been concluded.

The Prince de Neufchâtel and Wagram had been sent on to Vienna as an extraordinary ambassador, and met Prince Paul Esterhazy on the frontier. He conducted him to the Imperial palace, where an apartment had been prepared for him in one of the wings. Marshal Berthier, Prince of Neufchâtel, entered into Vienna, and crossed the bridge thrown over the ruins of the ramparts which the French army had blown up after the last war before evacuating the capital. Such a leave-taking shows how much confidence Napoleon had in the feelings of Austria towards him, and from whom he was constantly expecting fresh perfidy. The ambassador who was conducted on the day of his arrival into the presence of the Emperor to make his solemn demand for the hand of the Archduchess, was treated by the court with unusual distinction. The following day was taken up with the ceremony of handing to the Archduke Paul the powers bestowed by the Emperor Napoleon to wed the Archduchess in his name. On the following day, March 9, the Archduchess, according to the usage, solemnly renounced succession to the Imperial throne, and took the oath. On the evening of the same day the marriage contract was signed with solemn ceremony in the grand apartments of the Palace and the amount of the dowry—five hundred thousand francs—was presented to the ambassador in rolls of gold ducats enclosed in a box.

The religious ceremony of the marriage was performed on the 11th of March, in the Church of the Augustines. The gala banquet given at the court followed this ceremony and the extraordinary ambassador was present. Exception was made in this instance to the ceremonial of the court of Vienna of only admitting Ambassadors to the Emperor's table on very rare occasions, and these, moreover, were obliged to leave the table at dessert, and remain afterwards amongst the crowds of gentlemen who were admitted to the banqueting hall. People did not fail to remember on this occasion, as on the marriage of the French Dauphin with Archduchess Marie Antoinette, that the Marquis Durfort had not been invited to the banquet, so as to avoid any discussion with the Duke Albert of Saxe Teschen, who was present. The same Duke Albert of Saxony, to whom was reserved in his old age the spectacle so extraordinary in his eyes of a new throne being raised in France on the ruins of the old one; and on which another Archduchess went to sit, did not present himself at the banquet which was given in honor of Napoleon's marriage with Marie Louise. The absence of this Prince was explained by the desire of the Court of Vienna to give a particular mark of distinction to the ambassador of the Emperor of the French.

On the morrow after the conclusion of the marriage, Marshal Prince Berthier received the Archduke Palatine and the Archduke Anthony, the Emperor's brothers, who came to take leave of the ambassador, and to present the last adieux to the Imperial family, which was another exception made to etiquette. I could multiply the examples of these concessions made by a court which was scrupulously attached to forms, and which shows to what a degree the Viennese Court, on this occasion, desired to make itself agreeable to Napoleon. They are, moreover, the proof of the care with which Napoleon maintained in his person the dignity of the nation of which he was the head. In order to make certain that everything which his ambassador had a right to demand had been accorded to him the Emperor charged the Masters of Ceremonies to lay before him a report by which he could judge if any slight had been inflicted upon Prince Neufchâtel in the capacity in which he was placed in Vienna. Napoleon had every reason to be satisfied with the report which was laid before him. As a matter of fact, never had an extraordinary envoy been received with such attention, by so brilliant an assembly or had received, as well as his suite, more handsome presents. On the day of the signing of the marriage contract Berthier had received the portrait of the Emperor of Austria, surrounded with diamonds, and attached to the collar of the Order of the Golden Fleece. These outward and visible signs of distinction were not wanting on the part of the Viennese Court, which knew well how to hide the great discontent which it felt. If anybody in these circumstances acted with good faith it was probably Emperor Francis alone. On the 14th of March, the Archduke Charles conducted the new Empress to her carriage. After she had received the farewells of her family she took leave of the people of Vienna, whose blessings mingled with the sound of the bells and the cannon. For the first time tricolor flags were displayed at the windows, and the Austrian Imperial band played French martial airs. When the procession had passed the Burg, the discharge of artillery on the ramparts announced the fact to the town of Vienna. The Emperor Francis had preceded Marie Louise to Saint-Polten, where he hoped to see his darling daughter once more. I will pass over the details of the reception at Branau and the stay of Marie Louise at Munich, at Stuttgart, and at Carlsruhe, where the sovereigns of the different countries, through which they had passed, received her with unusual honors.

In spite of the proofs of deference and the apparent cordiality of the Austrian Imperial family; in spite of the frequent communications which took place between the Burg and the Tuileries after the Empress's arrival in France the reconciliation was not sincere on the part of the Austrian Court and aristocracy; and manifest symptoms were to be seen after the departure of Marie Louise. The population of Vienna, incited by the Russian and English agents, crowded together in the public places and in the streets. Loud complaints were made on the sacrifice which had been imposed upon the Emperor, and on the fate of his daughter, handed over to a man who would crush her with bad treatment. Another complaint was based on the certain humiliation to which Austria would be subjected. The authorities were obliged to take measures against these meetings. M. de Metternich took the occasion of these manifestations to warn the French government that they should be considered in the light of a hint not to carry its exactions too far. In this he made allusion to certain conditions of the last treaty, which had not yet been carried out, adding that the Emperor Francis would prefer to renounce the benefits of peace rather than expose himself to lose the popularity which had helped him to keep up courage in his adversity. This disguised menace could not but irritate a conqueror to whose moderation the sovereign of Austria owed the preservation of his crown. In consequence, Napoleon complained of the confidence reposed in councilors, who made a profession of being his enemies, and demanded their dismissal, but on this point he could obtain no satisfaction.

In reprisal Napoleon maintained the decree which he had issued at the commencement of the campaign, and which ordered that very strict measures should be taken against all persons born in the new or old provinces of France who might be in the service of Austria, and who should not return to French territory before a fixed date. All these circumstances together were not of a nature to calm the reciprocal irritation which kept growing on every side. The Emperor felt it, and not wishing to increase this irritation, for the time being granted an amnesty to the individuals who were menaced by the decree, on condition that those who wished to take advantage of this amnesty should reenter France before July 1, 1811. The convention in consequence of which sequestration had been put upon the estates of those born in the provinces of the Federation of the Rhine, and notably on the estates of Prince Schwarzenberg and of Count Metternich, was removed. Later on the Emperor granted certain individual authorizations to serve in Austria, but did not recall his decrees, which were kept in reserve and ready to receive their application if hostile manifestations forced the French government to bring them into action again.

It will be seen that the peace of Vienna, and even the marriage, had far from reestablished a good understanding between the Cabinets of Paris and Vienna. Austria was humiliated, but was not crushed. She bent her head, but was waiting with the same feelings of ill will and rancor for the opportunity to take her revenge. In signing peace, or in uniting in an alliance by marriage, the two parties kept themselves ready to recommence the war. Napoleon had left Vienna two days after the signing of the treaty with some doubts as to its ratification. He went on to await it first at Passau, then at Munich, as we have seen, and fully made up his mind not to go any further away from Vienna, until he had heard that the ratification of this peace had been consummated. The Emperor had given orders that flags should be used to inform him of the positive or negative result of the negotiations. If the ratifications had been exchanged a white flag was to be hoisted; in case of discussion, a red flag was to be floated as long as the discussion lasted.

Count Stadion, one of the most passionate chiefs of the war party, had been replaced by Count Metternich. The retirement of the former seemed to be a sacrifice made to the desire to maintain peace; but if the minister was changed, the political system was not. An all-powerful oligarchy governed the Viennese cabinet at this time. This oligarchy held in its hands all the departments of the government; conservator of the political traditions of the monarchy—traditions which survive all events—its influence is constantly exercised, in a more or less degree, according to the sovereign's character. The House of Austria, founded by a simple nobleman had raised itself only by marriages and with the assistance of the nobility, which owned two thirds of the territory; it had always been kept the ward of this oligarchy. Of the three hundred families which composed it, a very large majority in quest of Court favors had devoted themselves to the first minister. Amongst the most important may be named the Lichtenstein, the Stadion, the Schwarzenberg, the Esterhazy, and the Lobkowitz families. The tendency of the public mind towards emancipation is each day weakening the influence of these families, which would be destroyed altogether by a strong king. Matrimonial unions which should be a guarantee of reconciliation, were one of the tricks used by Austria to abate the storm, to cover its designs, and to lull its enemies to sleep. Austria had already practiced this tortuous policy before the war of 1809, protesting its pacific intentions, denying its war preparations, but in reality preparing to take advantage of the first favorable opportunity to recommence hostilities. One of the chiefs of the oligarchy—Prince Schwarzenberg—has drawn himself a faithful picture of this situation, when, in 1813, he said: "Politics made this marriage; and politics can undo it."

The ruin of the empire, which was the constant object of the efforts of the coalition, was effected. The admissions of the Cabinets, the narratives of historians, and time, has already raised many curtains; and one can form an opinion upon the open as well as the secret part which each power played in this work. One can, moreover, with thorough knowledge of the matter, cast a retrospective glance on the circumstances which presided over the drawing of the sword in Austria, in 1809. In this war the coalition had extended its combinations. Far from being discouraged, it had learnt lessons from its mistakes, and had taken advantage of the long-suffering of the conqueror who on many occasions had had the opportunity in his hands to dethrone two of his most powerful adversaries, but who nevertheless had left them their crowns. Since 1792 this same coalition had come forward in each struggle with France separately. Since 1808 Austria, who had still been left powerful, had repaired her losses and had secretly organized herself. Secret communications drew together the Courts of Berlin and St. Petersburg. Prussia was greatly abased, but her military system enabled her to treble her standing army with great rapidity. The secret object of the visit of the King and Queen of Prussia to Emperor Alexander on his return from Erfurth was to discuss present and future means for injuring the *common enemy*. It was a renewal of the oath which had been taken in 1805 on the tomb of the great Frederick. The conduct of Russia in the war of 1809 and the proofs of her inaction are sufficiently well known. The admissions of Colonel Bourtourlin have finally placed her attitude in its true light. The bands organized by the Duke of Brunswick-Oels, by Schill, Katt, Doernberg, and others, as also secret societies, were formed or extended. Proclamation of war against *one man alone* was renewed amongst them with the unavowed resentment of the monarchs, and lying pamphlets once more provoked to insurrection or revolt the peoples subjected to the hegemony of France. Agents charged with the work of creating enemies to the French Emperor, and of inciting public opinion against the head of our country, went through Germany, Spain, Portugal, and Italy, flattering the Italians with the prospect of an Italian fatherland which should be independent of the foreigner. In France these agents addressed themselves to men of all parties, to the Royalists as to the Republicans, took advantage of the intriguing spirit of one individual—a busybody who has gained a sad notoriety while another person (let his name be guessed) simply participated in these intrigues, and worked with a purpose no less hostile towards his master, to win favor abroad. These emissaries found their way into the great corporations of the state, and even insinuated themselves into the armies, where they tried to awaken discouragement, and a lassitude for war. Stores of arms and ammunition were collected together in the English possessions, islands, or points under British influence in the vicinity of the continent. A great gathering composed of forty thousand men assembled in various English ports, and held itself in readiness to act; but its destination remained unknown; for what was expected from all these combinations was a general war, the signal for which was to be given by Austria. The slightest success obtained by this power would have sufficed to let loose against France an eighth coalition in which our secret enemies would at last have been able to show themselves unmasked. If in the year 1809, our active enemies were the English, Austrians, Spaniards, and the Portuguese, the Prussians and the Russians were our passive enemies, secretly preparing to take advantage of events. To these may be added the Princes of the Federation of the Rhine, who would have followed the general movement if the Austrian Army had succeeded in making a stand on their territories.

This hasty picture of the secret plan of the coalition is incomplete rather than exaggerated. The observing mind of General Pelet has collected its principal features with ample developments and proofs of what he advances in his excellent *History of the War of 1809*.

Some of these plans at least were known to the Emperor. He had no means of preventing the bad faith of his enemies, and as to the plans which had been decided upon and the means of execution which had been prepared, these were hidden under the greatest mystery, and disguised under false demonstrations.

Count Pozzo de Borgo said to me in 1815, in the boasting way which Italians have: "Napoleon only wanted one man to have become the master of the world. I am that man. I could have revealed to him the secret of the Cabinets, and I could have informed him of what was being planned against him; but there was no possibility of our ever coming together. If he had got me into his hands he would have had me hanged as soon as he had found out who I was." There was a great deal of truth in what Pozzo said.

As a matter of fact Austria's future defection, which took place in 1813, had been decided *in petto,* on the day on which this power signed the Peace of Vienna, which in reality was only a truce, as were all the treaties of peace signed by the Coalition. The result of the marriage was only to suspend the effect of these hostile feelings. The House of Austria, which owes its aggrandizement to matrimonial alliances, hoped to recover possession of the provinces which it had lost by this means. Its hopes not having been realized by the sacrifice of one of its Archduchesses, Napoleon could no longer rely on it. Victory had consecrated the adoption of the master of France into the society of kings, but the kings had protested against his admission amongst royal dynasties. They hoped to be able to cast him out from amongst them sooner or later; with them it was only a question of time. There is where the danger lay for Napoleon. He thought himself sufficiently strong to defy this danger; which meant that he condemned himself to the performance of constant prodigies. He never could believe that the sovereigns of Europe would overthrow him, for he considered that his ruin would be contrary to their interests as best understood. They had no longer reason to fear that he would let loose public passions. England's hatred, England's gold, and England's intrigues aroused their dynastic pride, and kept alive amongst the kings by their ministers and by their aristocracy, blinded them to their true interests. More than one amongst them regretted it after the fall of the Emperor. Some say that they wished to prevent it. It is difficult to believe in the sincerity of these assertions, for their organs have revealed what they did towards this alleged purpose. The league then was general. It would have unmasked itself as early as in 1809, if Austria had been able to surprise us, as she hoped to do. The Emperor, by striking those rapid and decisive blows which upset the plans of the coalition, only postponed for four years what it accomplished in 1814.

I have spoken of Pozzo de Borgo, and I will take advantage to give some details about a person who was one of Napoleon's most active enemies. I hold them in part from Count Pozzo de Borgo himself.

Attached as much by friendship as by conformity of opinions to Joseph and Napoleon Bonaparte, Pozzo was in 1790, a member of the Directorate of the department of Corsica, with Joseph. Pozzo's abandonment of the French party separated them. When the English occupied the island where Lord Elliot, commanded in the capacity of Viceroy, Pozzo accepted employment at their hands and rendered them services. The Corsicans having shaken off the British yoke, Pozzo, who had drawn upon himself the hatred of his countrymen, finding it no longer safe to remain in the island after the departure of his protectors, followed them in their retreat and took refuge in England. Lord Elliot having been sent shortly afterwards to St. Petersburg, Pozzo accompanied him. The English minister entrusted him with several missions to the Emperor of Russia, who appreciated his spirit of intrigue and his talents. The English do not like foreigners, the Russians on the other hand give employment to all who offer themselves. Lord Elliot finding in the Emperor Alexander's good will for Pozzo a means of rewarding him for the services he had rendered to England, and of getting rid of this foreigner in an honorable manner, offered him to the Czar, who admitted him later to his cabinet, and gave him the rank of General-Major. This turncoat, this protégé of the English, having by his past conduct rendered all return to the fatherland impossible, what reasons had he not to persevere in the way on which chance had placed him! He became one of the most active enemies of the French Imperial government. Sent to the various European cabinets he created enemies to France, and signed treaties with them with this object in view. Pozzo de Borgo found himself in 1809 in Austria, charged with a secret mission. At the time of the occupation of Vienna he followed the Court to Buda. The Austrian ministers, feeling that his presence might injure their negotiations with Napoleon, and having learnt that, far from claiming this agent, the Russians disavowed him, then told Pozzo that he could be no longer protected by Austria. Pozzo, fearing to fall into the hands of the French fled to Constantinople, and arrived there after a thousand dangers, crossing over Hungary and the mountain ranges in the greatest state of destitution. I will add to the details which I have given of Count de Borgo, what was said about him to Count d'Orsay, from whom I heard it, by the late Marquis Wellesley, the eldest brother of Lord Wellington, who was at that time head of the English cabinet. Pozzo de Borgo having escaped from Austria, repudiated by the Russian cabinet, retired from Constantinople to Odessa, where he wrote a pamphlet on the politics of the time. The Marquis Wellesley having read this pamphlet was surprised and delighted to find that the ideas expressed in it were absolutely in harmony with his own. He made inquiries as to what had become of the author; if he were any longer in receipt of the pension which the English government had granted him, and gave orders that the arrears should be paid to him, and at the same he brought Pozzo de Borgo to England. Struck by the interest of his conversation and the originality of his views the Marquis would not allow so valuable an agent to remain without employment. In consequence, he sent him off to Russia with very warm letters of recommendation. Pozzo decided that he could do nothing better than take up his cross once more, and forget his grievances. He became more than ever the *âme damnée* of the Russian government, and of the coalition. He resumed his diplomatic missions with renewed ardor, and was especially employed in the last campaign. It was he who contributed in pushing on the Russians to Paris in 1814. He had promised them that it was in his power to open its gates for them. The secret understanding on which he had counted, having failed him, his perplexity was extreme, and he passed the most critical night of his life before Paris. His head was at stake if his promises could not be realized. On the morrow he triumphed as he joined in the procession of the sovereigns on their entrance by the Pantin gate. Grand Duke Constantine came up to him and said: "Pozzo, it is a happy day for you. If we were not here, you would be hanging!."

The Empress had arrived on French territory, and her journey from Strasburg to Compiègne was one continual ovation. Almost at every place where she stopped she found an officer, or page of the imperial household, with letters to her from the Emperor. At Strasburg she saw Count Metternich who was on his way to Paris, and at Vitry she received Prince Schwarzenberg and Countess Metternich, who started back to Paris whence they had come, after having been presented to her. The Emperor had given orders that during the journey, news of the Princess should be sent to her father every day.

Napoleon remained alone at Compiègne for a week. He had the apartment intended for the future Empress fitted up, and presided in person over the arrangements which he thought would please her best. He approved or modified what was being done, hurrying on the preparations for the reception which he intended to give her, and writing to her with his own hand every day. When Marie Louise had set foot on French territory Napoleon sent bouquets of the most beautiful flowers with his letters, and sometimes game which he had shot. He was delighted with the answers which he received from her, many of which were very long. These answers were written in good French, and expressed sentiments marked by delicacy and measure. It may be that the Queen of Naples assisted in their composition. Napoleon's sister used also to write letters to her brother, full of details which interested him greatly.

The Emperor, being pressed by his other sister, Princess Pauline, who was a well-known authority on matters of elegance and good taste, had consented to have a fancy dress ornamented with embroidery, made by Léger, who was then the most fashionable tailor. Napoleon tried it on but did not feel at ease in it. The cut of the coat and the white cravat which was worn with it, did not suit his taste, and deprived him of his usual ease of manner. The uniform which he always wore, and a black cravat were the only things which suited him, perhaps because one was accustomed to see him always dressed in military uniform. However it may be, the Emperor only once wore the costume which Princess Pauline had advised him to have made. He went back to the blue uniform turned up with white, which he used to wear on Sundays and feast days, reserving the green coat of the light cavalry of the guard for ordinary days.

Tents had been put up two leagues from Soissons, and access to these was gained by two inclined planes, one on the Soissons and one on the Compiègne side. According to the ceremonial which had been decided upon, the Emperor was to leave Compiègne with the Princes and Princesses of his family, the Grand Officers, and the officers of the household, preceded and followed by detachments of his guard. He was to pass through the first tent on the Compiègne side, while the Empress was to pass through the tent on the Soissons side. The two spouses were to stop in the middle tent before an ottoman footstool, on which the Empress was to bend down, to be immediately raised by the Emperor, who would embrace her. After this, both would enter a carriage with six places, together with the Princesses. The two processions would then unite and form themselves into one. This ceremonial was not observed, the Emperor having received a letter from the Empress, in which he was informed of her departure from Soissons. He decided to go and meet her at once. He ordered an open carriage, on which no armorial bearings were painted, to be got ready, entered it with the King of Naples, and, preceded by one solitary outrider, started *incognito* from Compiègne. He sent for me, and when I arrived I found him already seated in his carriage with the King of Naples by his side. He ordered me to open all dispatches which might come for him, and to keep them. He told me that he was going to meet the Empress, that he would be back in the evening, and ordered me to keep the object of his journey secret. He returned to Compiègne, as he had said, at ten o'clock in the evening, in fearful weather. He had fallen in with the Empress's procession some leagues beyond Soissons. Napoleon had approached her carriage without being recognized, when the equerry named him, and put an end to his *incognito.* He then entered the Empress's carriage, where the Queen of Naples was sitting, and ordered that instead of staying at Soissons, the carriages should continue to Compiègne. There the rumor had got abroad that the Empress was to arrive that same evening. Illuminations were prepared in haste, the triumphal arches were adorned, and the whole population in crowds went, in spite of the bad weather, to meet Their Majesties. The courts and the galleries of the palace, which were open to the public, were filled with the curious. At ten o'clock the cannon announced the arrival of the procession, which crossed the avenue rapidly by torchlight. The Princes and Princesses who were waiting where the carriages stopped were presented to the Empress by the Emperor. The authorities of the town were assembled in the gallery, and a group of young girls presented to Marie Louise an address and flowers. Prince Schwarzenberg, the Austrian ambassador, was present. After this short ceremonial, the Empress immediately withdrew to her apartment, conducted by the Emperor, who supped with her and with the Queen of Naples.

Marie Louise, then in all the splendor of her youth, had a bust of perfect regularity. The bodice of her dress was longer than used to be worn at the time, which added to her natural dignity, and contrasted very well with the ugly, short bodices of our ladies. Her face was flushed with the journey and by her nervousness. Pale chestnut hair, silky and abundant, framed a fresh full face, over which eyes, full of sweetness, spread a charming expression. Her lips, which were rather thick, recalled the type of the Austrian ruling family, just as a slight convexity of the nose is the characteristic of the Princes of the House of Bourbon. Candor and innocence were breathed from all her person, and a plumpness, which left her after her confinement, bespoke a good state of health.

Napoleon imitated Henri IV towards Marie de Médicis, under similar circumstances. An apartment had been prepared for the Emperor at the chancellor's house, but his impatience preventing him from submitting to this part of the ceremony, he did not leave the palace, which left a free field for conjecture. The first introduction of the new Empress into the interior of the palace took place the next day in the Emperor's cabinet. Did he mean to show her by this that he initiated her into his entire confidence, or did he consider that his workroom was the most important room in his house? It was thus that I was amongst the first who had the honor of presenting my respects to the Empress Marie Louise. At one o'clock took place the introduction of the ladies and gentlemen of the household, who had not taken part in the journey from Braunau, and these took the oath of allegiance. Then came the generals of the guard, the ministers who were at Compiègne, the chief officers, and the ladies and gentlemen in waiting who had been appointed to be in attendance during the journey from Compiègne.

On the following day the court left for St. Cloud, where it spent two days. The civil marriage was celebrated there on April 1, and the religious marriage took place the next day in Paris in the great gallery of the Louvre Museum. The cardinals, who had been present at the civil marriage, with two exceptions, refused to be present at the religious marriage, alleging in justification that the only reason of their absence was that the pope had refused to grant a dissolution of the first marriage. The Emperor would not admit this excuse, refused to receive their protestations of obedience, and exiled them into various departments, forbidding them to wear red, which is the exterior mark of their dignity. This gave them the name of "The Black Cardinals."

On the morning of the day of the celebration of the religious marriage the Emperor was present at the Empress's toilette. The ladies-in-waiting—two French, and one Italian—and the Mistress of the Robes, placed the crown on the Empress's head in his presence. A decision had been made by the Emperor concerning this crown in the following words:

"On the day of the marriage the Empress will wear the coronation crown, which is not handsome, but which has a particular characteristic, and which I wish to attach to my dynasty. This crown will only be worn at the very greatest ceremonies. In ordinary ceremonies the Empress will wear the closed diamond crown, which has no characteristic, and which I am having made for her with the crown diamonds. On the day after the marriage she will wear the closed diamond crown at her reception.

"NAPOLEON.

"Given at Compiègne, 25 March, 1810."

Public rejoicings took place in the park of St. Cloud after the civil ceremony. There was a general illumination, the fountains played under torchlight, and there were repeated salvos of artillery fired at the Invalides in Paris. Immense crowds took part in these rejoicings in spite of the rain.

The solemn entry of the Emperor and Empress into Paris on April 2 was magnificent. The triumphal arch at the Étoile Barrier, under which the sovereigns passed, had been figured by a decoration which showed it as it would be when it was finished. The weather which had been rainy the day before had become fine, and a bright sun shed its rays on the procession, the troops, and the crowd of spectators, composed of almost the entire population of Paris. Their Majesties were received at the Étoile Barrier by the Prefect of the Seine department, and by the municipal body. The procession arrived at the Tuileries Palace by crossing the Champs Élysées, and the garden, at the entrance to which a triumphal arch had been raised. After having rested in the drawing rooms of the palace, and in the Diana Gallery, the procession proceeded towards the great Apollo drawing room of the museum, where a chapel had been installed. The Queens of Spain, of Holland, and of Westphalia, Princesses Elisa and Pauline, carried the train of the Empress's mantle. Cardinal Fesch, the Grand Almoner, pronounced the nuptial benediction over the spouses. After the ceremony the ladies who had placed the crown on the Empress's head, removed it and the imperial mantle, which were carried back to Notre Dame by the First Chamberlain, Master of the Wardrobe. This officer had been to fetch them in the morning with a ceremonial, which was also observed on the return of these insignia to the Cathedral treasury, where they were to remain. Leaving the Apollo drawing room the Emperor, taking the Empress's hand, placed himself with her on the balcony of the *Pavilion de l'Horloge,* where they were present at the march past of the various bodies of the imperial guard. A banquet was given in the theatre, and Their Majesties listened to a concert which was executed under the windows of the palace. This concert was followed by a display of fireworks which reached right down to the whole length of the big avenue of the Champs Élysées.

A description of all the fêtes given on the occasion of Napoleon's marriage with Marie Louise would give but a too feeble and imperfect picture of their magnificence, and the enthusiasm of the Paris population; but they will be remembered for a very long time.

The city of Paris wished the richness and beauty of its presents to correspond to the splendor of such a marriage. It offered a toilette table, with all its fittings, in silver gilt, to the Empress, the armchair and swing-glass being also in silver gilt. This set had been carried out from designs of the best artists and under their personal supervision. So perfect was this masterpiece that when M. Ballouhey, steward of the Empress's purse, demanded it in her name, in 1814, together with the cradle of the King of Rome, Count Beugnot, who was at that time Commissary of the Police Department, refused to hand them over. He alleged, in refusing their restitution, that it would be quite impossible to replace them, considering that the combination of circumstances which had given birth to these masterpieces could not present itself again, and that consequently the artists, in spite of all their talents, would be unable to produce work of equal beauty. This toilette table and accessories were melted down in 1832, and the money was used for relieving families who had suffered by the cholera, but the King of Rome's cradle was spared. Marie Louise had it sent to her son, who had it placed in the Imperial treasury at Vienna, where it still is. The present to Napoleon by the city of Paris consisted of a magnificent table service in silver gilt. By order of the Emperor the two hundred thousand florins given by Austria as the dowry of Marie Louise, were paid into the public treasury.

After the conclusion of the fêtes and ceremonies the court returned to Compiègne where a grand diplomatic reception took place, and distinguished foreigners were presented. While there Napoleon received many letters of congratulation from almost all the foreign courts. The castle of Compiègne had been decorated and furnished with an elegance and taste worthy of its destination. Amongst other rooms in Marie Louise's occupation was a boudoir hung with a profusion of cashmeres of inestimable value. The Princess had these cashmeres taken down later on, but as a matter of fact they had only been placed there as a present to her, and to be used as she thought fit.

The Empress Josephine had enjoyed great liberty at home. She had many acquaintances. Her desire to serve the Emperor, and to increase his popularity, prompted her to cultivate relations which she had preserved, and to extend them. The Emperor's marriage with a foreign Princess, who was not yet very experienced, and was unknown to Parisian society, made it of course necessary to modify this manner of life, and the household of the new Empress had to be organized in a less independent manner. The precautions with which she was surrounded were taken in order to keep her away from all attempts at intrigue and coterie, but the isolation produced by these precautions brought with it grave disadvantages which only became manifest later on. Napoleon appointed the Duchess of Montebello, widow of Marshal Lannes, who had been killed at the battle of Essling, lady of honor to the Empress Marie Louise. He had hesitated some time between her and the Princess de Beauvau. Napoleon abandoned the idea of selecting Madame de Beauvau because he thought that it would not be wise to introduce into his court influences opposed to national ideas, influences to which a German Princess, in whom the prejudice of caste and of birth might be supposed to exist, would have been subjected. Accordingly he decided on the duchess, thinking that he owed this mark of distinction to the memory of one of his oldest and bravest comrades in arms. His choice met with general approval. Madame de Montebello was ten years older than the Empress, a very beautiful woman, cold, calm, and of irreproachable conduct, and in appointing her the Emperor had said: "I am giving the Empress a real lady of honor." The Countess de Luçay, a gentle, inoffensive lady of great morality and excellent manners, became the Mistress of the Robes. The interior service, which at the time of the Empress Josephine had consisted of four *dames d'annonce* was augmented by two more ladies whose attributions were of a more austere nature. They were chosen from amongst the residents of the Ecouen Royal and Imperial House, preference being, given to widows or daughters of officers. One of them, Madame Durand, was the widow of a general. They served the Empress in the same way as the aides-de-camp served the Emperor, except that they did not accompany her out of doors. They were consequently near the sovereign's person during the day, and during the night one of them slept in a room adjoining Marie Louise's apartment. They allowed no man to enter her private apartment; such were their orders. They were present at her drawing and music lessons, they wrote notes at her dictation, or at her order, and presided over the whole interior service.

The Empress's private allowance was £2000 per month. Ten thousand francs were distributed each month to the poor, this distribution taking place with prudence, and after full inquiries had been made. The balance was used for toilette expenses. Marie Louise was economical, and took care never to exceed her allowance. She gave many presents, and always kept in reserve in her writing-table a purse of £1000, which she never touched.

The poets all vied with each other in celebrating the great event of the marriage. Fouché had given them a hint on this subject, but the Emperor had blamed him, because he did not wish to appear to have ordered these praises. Napoleon wished the authors to be left to their own inspirations, which moreover had no need of being stimulated. Later on he made use of a sum of 100,000 francs, which was taken from his privy purse, and distributed it as a proof of his satisfaction.

While the French muses, interpreting the public feeling, were paying their tribute of homage to the spouses, less sincere demonstrations were taking place at the castle of Valençay. Rivalry of adulation established itself there amongst the dethroned Spanish Princes. A *Te Deum* was chanted in their chapel. They presided at a banquet given by themselves in honor of the Emperor and Empress, at which the most flattering toasts, accompanied by the most obsequious compliments were drunk to the health of the royal couple, added to the often repeated acclamations and cheers of Prince Ferdinand. The *Moniteur,* which gave an account of this feast, related that the Prince proposed the health of Their Majesties in the following words: "To the health of *our* august sovereigns, the great Napoleon, and Marie Louise his august wife." A display of fireworks brought to a close a fête the magnificence of which could deceive nobody. To crown it in a worthy manner Prince Ferdinand begged the Emperor to adopt him as his son, and to grant him the honor of allowing him to figure at his Court. Such an entire want of dignity created a painful feeling everywhere.

Another scene, in which Fouché's police played the principal part, took place at the same time at the Château of Valençay. A certain Baron de Kolli, furnished with instructions, powers, and money by the Marquis of Wellesley, had been charged with the mission to help Ferdinand and the other Spanish Princes to escape, and to conduct them to Admiral Cockburn, who, with a small fleet was awaiting the success of this attempt near the coast. The mission of the agent of the English government having become known, he was arrested. His credentials were put into the hands of a police agent, who went and played the part of Baron de Kolli to Ferdinand. But whether the Prince of the

Asturias had been secretly warned of the substitution, whether he suspected a trap, or did not dare to risk the adventure, he received Fouché's agent very badly, and reported him to the governor of the castle. The genuine Baron de Kolli remained in prison in Vincennes until the return of the Bourbons, who restored him to liberty.

After the success of the campaign in Spain, King Joseph had returned to Madrid, and had been able to devote himself to the interior government of the country, in which he had effected some useful reforms. Almost all the powers had acknowledged the new King, and had addressed him letters of congratulation. Ferdinand had not failed to send his congratulations, and had asked him to intercede for him with the Emperor, to induce him to grant him the hand of one of his nieces. The first military events which had happened in Spain had been favorable to our army. Saragossa had surrendered, and important victories had been gained over the enemy. Suddenly a new English army, under Sir Arthur Wellesley, who afterwards became the Duke of Wellington, had joined the Portuguese troops, and restored the confidence of the Spaniards. Our enemies assembled their forces to march upon Madrid which they hoped to surprise in a defenseless state. The King marched out of Madrid with his reserve troops to meet them, and to join the corps commanded by Marshals Soult, Ney, and Mortier. There were alternating successes and reverses. A disagreement which arose amongst the marshals was calculated to help the plans of the English general, their adversary. King Joseph, distinguished by other qualities, was not accustomed to war, and so precarious was the authority which he exercised over the leaders of the French army, that he was unable to remedy the unfortunate effects of their disagreement. This campaign, which might have had decisive consequences, resulted nevertheless in checking the movements of the enemy, and in throwing the Anglo-Portuguese army back into Portugal. Marshal Jourdan returned to France, and Marshal Soult, in whom the Emperor had greater confidence, replaced him as Major-General to the King. The King had returned to Madrid, where his spirit of conciliation seemed to rally partisans around him, even amongst the Spaniards, whose opposition until then had been most marked.

Military operations were being carried out with success on the east of the peninsula. Various successes secured in Aragon, and the taking of Girona, a fortress in Catalonia, which was defended by the Spaniards with as much obstinacy as Saragossa, brought this campaign to a successful close.

After the fêtes occasioned by his marriage, Napoleon, whose attention had been drawn to the Belgian provinces, determined to visit them, together with that part of Holland which had recently been ceded to France. He had another object, besides giving the Empress a change, and showing her to the people of Belgium, and his new provinces. The Emperor's principal object was to see what was going on with his own eyes, to judge of the effect which had been produced by the failure of the English expedition of Walcheren, to see to what an extent the continental system was being violated there. He also wanted to find out what it was possible to do to remedy the damage caused to Dutch trade by the interruption of communications with England, and to conciliate as far as it was possible, the interests of the Netherlands, with the rigor of his prohibitive laws.

To understand the reasons which decided Napoleon to undertake this journey it is necessary to speak of the causes which brought about the annexation to the Empire of the districts situated on the right bank of the Escaut, and, in the end, that of Holland.

The Emperor had seen how feebly the Dutch had cooperated in the defense of the island of Walcheren, against the English invasion under the command of Lord Chatham. He also saw that the authorities of this country did not check the circulation of English goods, with which smugglers, and the English themselves during their temporary occupation of the island of Walcheren, had flooded the Kingdom, not excepting the capital and the King's Court. It has been seen that the King of Holland sympathized but little with the Emperor in the direction which the latter wished to give to the government of his states. The decree, issued in Berlin on November 21, 1806, which put England in a state of blockade, added to their disagreement. Such a measure seemed revolutionary to King Louis, and calculated to ruin Dutch trade. He would not admit that this decree was a necessary and inevitable reprisal on the edicts of the King of England's council. His entire attention was devoted towards attenuating the injury which the blockade system caused to Holland, and to evade carrying it into effect as much as he could, without appearing to violate it openly. To the complaints made to him about the facilities granted to English trade in the ports of Holland, he answered by saying that he could not prevent skin from perspiring. The effect of this opposition was that the Emperor was seriously displeased.

When Napoleon saw himself forced by the decrees of the British council to take recourse to the system of a continental blockade, it was evident that Holland could only preserve her independence by faithfully carrying out this system, or by a maritime peace. The King's answer to the pressing requests of the Emperor that he should close his ports to English trade, was that this system of continental blockade would cause the ruin, of Holland, and that it would be better for her to unite to and incorporate herself with France, which would at least give her free communications with forty millions of men. The King was asked to draw the attention of England to this state of things himself, and to ask her to conclude peace so as to retain the advantages which she derived from the independence of the Dutch Kingdom. With this in view France's conditions were communicated to the English cabinet. These conditions were moderate ones. With Napoleon's consent M. Labouchère, sent by the King of Holland, left for London in February, 1810. Fouché, who was ever on the lookout for the means of rendering himself indispensable, heard of the application which was being made to the London cabinet, and—of his own accord, and without any other authority but his own—began a second negotiation with Lord Wellesley without the knowledge of either King Louis or Napoleon. He charged M. Ouvrard with this mission, but did not satisfy himself with one intermediary alone, and gave orders to another agent whom he had in London, to enter into communications with the English minister. So many overtures aroused the suspicions of a minister who was but little disposed for peace, and he made haste to put an end to the negotiations by giving a negative answer to M. Labouchère.

The Emperor then saw that in consideration of the safety of our frontiers, and the strict carrying out of the continental system, he could no longer postpone the military occupation of the Dutch frontier. Communications between this country and England had not been interrupted, and British trade continued to find markets in the Dutch ports. Negotiations were entered into without further delay, and during the time when King Louis was at Paris, where he had been called at the same time as the other sovereigns allied to France. This prince, who was one of the most honorable men in his kingdom, but who had been embittered by vexations, domestic troubles, and infirmities—placed between the duty which he owed to his brother, and the rigidity of his principles—could not make up his mind to do violence to his feelings in these decisive circumstances. Neither prayers, nor advice, nor remonstrances, nor the promise to indemnify the Dutch for the sacrifice exacted from them, after peace should have been restored, could vanquish the King's scruples, or induce him to give orders for the total exclusion of English trade. King Louis considered his duty, his honor, and even his religion interested in not allowing any sacrifice, from which Holland might suffer, to be imposed upon him; or to admit any composition, or pay any attention to the advantages which an unreserved cooperation in Napoleon's plans promised him. Some very sharp explanations took place between the Emperor and his brother, and it was then that the former first threatened to occupy Holland by force. The King wrote to Holland to order that the French troops should be resisted by all means, even by an inundation of the country. He forbade that any obedience should be paid to his orders if these orders were contrary to those mentioned, and commanded them to hold out until his return.

These orders soon became known. The King, challenged to yield, and having reflected on the responsibility which he was thus assuming in the ruin of his country resigned himself at last to sign a treaty which was forced upon him. This treaty, which is dated March 16, 1810, stipulated the cession to the Empire of the Dutch provinces situated on the right bank of the Escaut, and the interdiction of all trade with England, until such time as the English cabinet should have revoked its decrees in council. During these discussions, which had been so violent that an unpleasant issue could be expected, Marshal Oudinot had received orders to occupy the fortresses of Berg-op-Zoom and Breda.

Amongst other documents relative to the struggle carried on by the King of Holland against the Emperor in Paris, we will quote the following letter, in spite of its length, because it is remarkable for the greatness of national sentiment which predominates in it, and because it epitomizes Napoleon's grievances at the attitude adopted by his brother:

"SIR MY BROTHER—I have received Your Majesty's letter. You desire me to make known to you what are my intentions with regard to Holland. I will do so frankly. When Your Majesty ascended the throne of Holland, part of the Dutch nation desired its annexation to France. The esteem with which the history of this brave nation had inspired me prompted me to desire that it should keep its name and its independence. I wrote its constitution myself, and this was to be the basis of the throne of Your Majesty, and I placed you on it. I hoped that, having been educated with me, you would have had for France that attachment which the nation has the right to expect from its children, and all the more from its Princes. I hoped that brought up in my politics you would have felt that Holland, which had been conquered by my people, owed her independence only to the generosity of France; that Holland, being weak without alliances, without an army, could and must be conquered on the day on which she should put herself into direct opposition with France; that, she had no right to separate her policy from mine; and that, finally, Holland was bound to me by treaties. I hoped accordingly that in placing on the throne of Holland a Prince of my blood, I had found the mean term which would conciliate the interests of the two states and unite them in a common interest and in a common hatred of England, and I was quite proud of having given to Holland what she needed, as by my act of mediation I had found what was needed by Switzerland. But I have not been long in finding out that I had been entertaining a vain illusion; my hopes have been deceived. Your Majesty, in ascending the throne of Holland, forgot that you are French, and even strained all the springs of your reasoning, and twisted the delicacy of your conscience, to persuade yourself that you are Dutch. Those Dutchmen who are friendly disposed towards France have been neglected and persecuted; those who have served England have been put forward. The French, from the officer to the soldier, have been turned out, treated with disrespect, and I have had the pain of seeing the French name exposed to shame in Holland, under a Prince of my own blood. However, the respect for, and honor of the French name cannot with impunity be attacked, either by Holland or by anybody whosoever. This honor, and this respect, lie next to my heart, and I have known how to bear it aloft on the bayonets of my soldiers.

"How badly Your Majesty is disposed is shown in your speeches. In these one meets with nothing but disagreeable allusions to France. Instead of giving the example of forgetting the past, they consequently recall it, and by those means flatter the secret feelings and the passions of the enemies of France, and, after all, about what do the Dutch complain? Were they not conquered by my arms? Do they not owe their independence to the generosity of my people? Should they not rather bless the generosity of France which has constantly left open her canals, and her customhouses to their commerce, which has made no other use of her conquests than to perfect them, and who until the present has employed her power only for the consolidation of their independence. Who, then, can have justified Your Majesty's conduct, which is an insult to the nation, and an offence to me. You must understand that I do not separate myself from my predecessors, and that from Clovis down to the Committee of Public Safety I hold myself responsible for all; and whatever of evil is said light-heartedly against the governments which have preceded me, I hold to be said with the intention of offending me. I know it has become the fashion amongst certain people to praise me, and to cry France down, but those who do not love France do not love me; and those who speak ill of my people, I hold them for my bitterest enemies. Had I only this one cause for discontent, namely, of seeing into what contempt the French name has fallen in Holland, the rights of my crown would have authorized me to declare war on a neighboring sovereign in whose states people allowed themselves to insult my nation. I did nothing of the kind.

"But Your Majesty has been deceived as to my character. You have formed a false estimate of my goodness, and my feelings towards you. You have violated every treaty which you have made with me; you have disarmed your fleets; you have discharged your sailors; you have disorganized your armies; so that Holland finds herself without either army or a fleet, as though storehouses filled with goods, and regiments of tradesmen and clerks could consolidate a power. Such things make a rich association; but there can be no King without finances, without assured means of recruiting, and without a fleet.

"Your Majesty has done more than this. You took advantage of the moment when I had troubles on the continent to allow the relations between Holland and England to be renewed, to violate the laws of the blockade which is the only means of efficaciously injuring this power. I gave you a proof of my disapproval of this conduct in forbidding you France, and I made you feel that, without the assistance of my arms, by closing the Rhine, the Weser, the Escaut, and the Meuse to Holland, I put your country in a more critical condition than if I had declared war upon you, that I isolated it in a way which meant its annihilation.

"This blow reechoed in Holland. Your Majesty implored my generosity and appealed to my fraternal feelings, promising me a change of conduct. And I thought that this warning would suffice. I raised the customs prohibition, when you very soon returned to your first system. It is true that at the time I was in Vienna burdened with a heavy war, Your Majesty received every American ship which presented itself in the ports of Holland, though they were driven out of the ports of France. I was forced to close my customhouses to Dutch trade for a second time. Surely it would have been difficult to have made a more authentic declaration of war. In this state of things we could consider ourselves as really at war. In my speech to the legislative body I hinted at my displeasure, and I will not hide from you that it is my intention to annex Holland to France, both to add to my territory, to strike the most terrible blow in my power against England, and to deliver myself from the continual insults which the ringleaders of your cabinet never cease to direct against me. As a matter of fact the mouth of the Rhine and the Meuse must belong to me. The principle in France that the valley of the Rhine is our frontier is a fundamental principle. Your Majesty writes to me in your letter of the 17th that you are sure of being able to prevent all trade between Holland and England; that you have finances, fleets, and armies; that you will reestablish the principles of the constitution by giving no privileges to the nobility; by abolishing the rank of marshal—a rank which is only a caricature, and quite incompatible with a power of the second order; that you will have the storehouses of colonial goods, and whatever may have been brought on American boats, and ought not to have entered your ports, seized upon. My opinion is that you are undertaking what you will not be able to carry out, and that the annexation of Holland to France is only being postponed. I will admit that I have no more interest in annexing to France the countries on the right bank of the Rhine, than I have of annexing the Grand Duchy of Berg and the Hanseatic cities. I can accordingly leave the right bank of the Rhine to Holland, and I will countermand the prohibition which I had ordered at my customhouses, at all such times as the existing treaties, which will be renewed, shall be carried out. These are my demands:

(1) Prohibition of all trade and all communication with England.
(2) A fleet of fifteen line vessels, seven frigates, and seven brigs or corvettes, armed and equipped.
(3) A land army of twenty-five thousand men.
(4) Suppression of the rank of Marshal.
(5) Abolition of all the privileges of the nobility, which are contrary to the constitution which I gave, and which I guaranteed.

"Your Majesty can negotiate through your ambassador on this basis, with the Duke of Cadore, but you must rest assured that on the admission of the first packet, the first vessel into Holland, I shall reestablish prohibition at my customhouses; that at the first insult which shall be made to my flag I will have the officer who allows himself to insult my flag seized by force and hanged at the mainmast. Your Majesty will find a brother in me, if I find a Frenchman in you. If you forget the feelings which attach you to our common country you will not think it wrong that I should forget the ties which nature has placed between us.

"To sum up: the annexation of Holland to France is what would be most useful to

France, to Holland, and to the continent, because it is what would be most harmful to England. This annexation could be carried out by consent or by force. I have sufficient grievance against Holland to declare war; at the same time I am quite ready to agree to an arrangement which would yield to me the Rhine as a frontier, and by which Holland would engage to fulfill the conditions stipulated above.

"Your affectionate Brother,

"NAPOLEON.

"Given at Trianon, Sept. 21, 1809."

The Emperor and the Empress left Compiègne at the end of April and stopped at St. Quentin, where Napoleon occupied himself with his usual activity with details of government and the needs and resources of industry. His questions, which were always remarkable for their precision and exactness, showed how much he had these interests at heart. Their Majesties visited the canal, and crossed the first part, which was not yet finished, in their carriage. The sovereigns then rowed through the canal in the part into which the water had already been let in, for a distance of about a league and a half. Five days were spent at Antwerp, which were employed by the Emperor, who was on horseback from daybreak, in visiting the harbor works, the arsenal in all its details, and the fortifications; finally in reviewing the soldiers and inspecting the fleet. A ship of several decks, the largest of which had been constructed in this harbor, was launched. The authorities were presented to the Emperor and Empress. Napoleon conversed at length with them all, examining what reforms were possible. The Empress showed herself affable, simple, and unpretentious towards everybody. The remembrance of Josephine's graces, and her ardent desire to please, perhaps injured Marie Louise. Her reserve might have been attributed to the German Schwarzenberg, accompanied the Imperial couple on this journey.

Their Majesties returned to St. Cloud on June 1. This month was consecrated to splendid fêtes which the city of Paris, the Imperial Guard, and other corporations gave to the sovereigns. The people took part in the public rejoicings, and in the interval the Emperor went with the Empress to visit several public establishments, amongst others the National Library, and the Zoological Gardens, and showed himself with her at the principal theatres. On July 1, Prince Schwarzenberg offered a fête to Their Majesties at the Austrian embassy. This fête became sadly notorious by the catastrophe which brought it to a close. A fire broke out in the principal ballroom. The Imperial family, which was the object of the ambassador's first care, was soon placed in safety. Napoleon put the Empress in the carriage and entered it himself to reassure her, but on arriving at the Champs Élysées, left her to continue to St. Cloud, and returned to the embassy mansion to contribute by his presence in rescuing some victims from the flames. The particulars of this catastrophe are well known, and were a sad diversion from the rejoicings which till then had been troubled by no accident. The remembrance of the calamity which saddened the marriage fêtes of Louis XVI. with Marie Antoinette was present in all minds, and the sad presentiments aroused anxiety, the passing impression of which was soon effaced by the prestige of Napoleon's fortune. The Emperor's first care on the morrow was to send to ask for news of the persons who had suffered by this terrible accident.

In the meanwhile the Empress Josephine, after having passed the month of April at Navarre, had returned to La Malmaison, given up to profound melancholy. It was with difficulty that she could accustom herself to her new state. After her divorce she retained the title and rank of Empress-Queen, and the enjoyment of a revenue of three million francs; and held a court at La Malmaison where the same etiquette was observed as at the Tuileries. The Emperor desired that she should continue to receive the persons of the court, the grand dignitaries, the ministers and the principal authorities—to frequent La Malmaison was to please him.

To divert Josephine from this melancholy Napoleon advised her to go to the waters at the end of July; so she left for Aix, in Savoy. After the season of the waters she was anxious to visit Switzerland, which she did not know, but on arriving at Geneva, official advice from Paris caused her to fear that the Emperor was seeking to remove her from France. She commissioned her daughter, Queen Hortense, to speak about the matter with him in a confidential manner. The Emperor, who had not had the least idea of this, and had only wished to give Josephine a change, hastened to write to reassure her. He advised her to go and see the Viceroy at Milan, but gave her the choice between this journey and her return to Navarre, as he wished her to do what would best suit her. Josephine, under the impression of the fear with which she had been inspired, gave up her journey to Switzerland, and made haste to return to Navarre, where she spent the rest of 1810, and the larger part of 1811. It was only in 1812 that she went to Milan to be present at the confinement of her daughter-in-law.

In the course of the month of July of this same year—1810—Lucien wrote to the Emperor to express his desire to retire to America. Since the Mantua interview, of which we have spoken, all attempts to bring about a reconciliation between the two brothers had failed. Napoleon, after having made a last and useless appeal to Lucien, consented to his expatriation, Lucien, however, did not succeed in reaching the United States, for an English frigate arrested him in the waters of Cagliari, and conducted him as a prisoner to England, where he remained until 1814, beguiling his captivity by the cultivation of letters, and by putting the finishing strokes to his poems, "Charlemagne" and "La Cirnéide."

Canova, who had come to Paris in the month of November, 1802, to make the First Consul's bust, returned to our capital in October, 1810, summoned there by the Emperor, who wished to entrust him with the execution of a statue of the Empress Marie Louise. Canova represented this Princess in the character of *Concord,* and this statue is today at Parma. During the course of the sittings which the Empress accorded to the celebrated sculptor, he spoke to the Emperor of the state of distress of the St. Luke Academy in Rome, which had neither revenues nor schools, and the necessity of applying some money to indispensable repairs connected with the Florence Cathedral, as well as for the conservation and maintenance of the numerous monuments and artistic objects with which this city and its churches are filled. Canova, whose acquaintance I had made at the time of his journey in 1802, wrote to me in the first days of November, 1810, to beg me to remind the Emperor of the good intentions in which he had left him, and of the promises which he had received from him. Being about to return to Italy, the great artist desired strongly to hear the news of the fulfillment of the promises. On November 7 I was in a position to answer him that the Emperor had ordered (1) that the part of the German college called *La Fabrica Vecchia* should be accorded to the St. Luke

Academy as a place of meeting for its schools; (2) that an income of one hundred thousand francs should be assigned in fee simple to this Academy, of which sum twenty-five thousand francs should be applied to the Academy, and seventy-five thousand francs to the preservation of ancient monuments; (3) that a sum of three hundred thousand francs should be placed at the disposal of the President of the Academy of Florence: to wit, two hundred thousand francs for digging up antiquities, and one hundred thousand francs for encouragements to be given to artists; (4) that funds should also be granted for necessary repairs. Canova thanked me with effusion for the good news which I had communicated to him, and left Paris highly delighted at being the bearer thereof.

The arrival of Lady Bathurst at Morlaix in the month of September 1810, called attention once more to an extraordinary occurrence which still remains enveloped in mystery. The various recitals which have been made of this event all agree in the matter of detail. I will briefly relate this extraordinary adventure, which is really worth being recorded.

After the Peace of Vienna, in 1809, Mr. Benjamin Bathurst, who, though a very young man, was English ambassador to Vienna, suddenly disappeared on the frontier of Mecklenburg, at the very moment when he was about to embark for England at a port on the Baltic. He was traveling under a fictitious name with a courier of the English cabinet. Mr. Bathurst had set down at the stage house at Perleberg, which is situated outside the town. When he left it he walked towards his carriage in which the courier was already seated, but while putting his hand on the handle of the carriage door the English diplomat seemed suddenly to remember something, turned round, and walked behind the wall of the house. As he did not return they went to look for him, but could not find, him, and not the slightest trace of him could be found. He never appeared again from that hour, and was never again seen; until a fortnight after his disappearance there was found near the stage-house, where he had dined, on the wayside, his trousers, in the pocket of which was the commencement of a letter to his wife. Although it had been raining hard for a fortnight neither paper nor writing had been in the least affected. It could never be found out who had brought the trousers to where they were found.

Mr. Bathurst, during his journey, had been a prey to extreme agitation. He expressed his fear of falling into the hands of enemies. He had walked on foot to the house of the governor of the town, and had expressed great anxiety on this point; then on his return to the stage-house he had burnt his papers. All these matters gave rise to the suspicion that he was mentally affected. The English embassies and the Bathurst family caused all kinds of researches and inquiries to be made, but without any result. Even today complete ignorance exists as to what became of this unhappy man.

It was in order to make in person such inquiries as might lead her to trace her husband that Lady Bathurst came to the continent with her brother. The Emperor in a letter dated June 26, 1810, ordered the Minister of Foreign Affairs and the police to furnish her with passports, and to receive her with favor. He allowed her to remain in France as long as might seem fit to her. She returned to England by way of Germany without having discovered anything concerning Mr. Bathurst's disappearance. It would be superfluous to allude to the thousand conjectures to which this event gave rise. I will, however, say that no suspicion whatever attached itself to the French government in this matter; and that Lord Bathurst, colonial minister, the man who persecuted Napoleon most bitterly at St. Helena, was a near relation of Mr. Benjamin Bathurst. The implacable hatred with which he persecuted the great victim of English perfidy, and the abominable outrages with which he treated him, were the way in which he requited the man who was most kind towards his own kinswoman in 1810. This was not the only occasion, moreover, on which Napoleon gave marks of favor to English subjects in spite of the bitter war which the English government was waging upon him. A certain Mr. Palmer, in whom Mr. Canning took an interest, was sent back to England at the minister's request, and the Emperor informed Mr. Canning at the same time that he was delighted to have had the opportunity of making himself agreeable to him. To finish with the Bathurst family, I will add that another bereavement was in store for Mrs. Benjamin Bathurst. Her daughter, who was endowed with all the gifts of youth and beauty, perished in the Tiber at Rome, in 1828.

Some months after Napoleon's marriage, M. de Talleyrand, tormented by a thirst for intrigue and power, thought a favorable time had come to regain favor, and in consequence made up his mind to write to the Emperor to offer his services. Napoleon replied to this letter on the 29th of August with a formal refusal, written in such terms that Talleyrand gave up all hope. In a very few words the Emperor stated that his letter had given him pain, that he begged him to abstain from writing to him again on the subject, as his letters would recall to him painful memories which he desired to forget.

After the exchange of the ratifications of the treaty of March 16, and having been present at the marriage festivities, King Louis left Paris, where he had been detained till then, on April 8, 1810, to return to Holland. The Queen left for Amsterdam with the Crown Prince at the same time, but went another way. Napoleon and his brother had had a final interview, which, in appearance at least, was a friendly one. The Emperor was holding in his hand a knife, very elaborately worked, representing his statue, and fitted with blades and accessories which made it a masterpiece of the cutler's art. He handed it to King Louis, who hesitated about taking it, saying that that cut friendship. "Bah," said the Emperor, "that only cuts bread!"

The good understanding which appeared to be reestablished between the two brothers was not to be of long duration. The execution of the treaty of March 16, brought with it fresh difficulties. The exigencies of the continental system, the reciprocal broils which envenomed its application, and finally an insult paid to the French ambassador's livery at the gates of the palace, ended in a rupture. One morning while at Rambouillet, the Emperor heard the news of his brother's abdication and flight, no previous warning, no understanding between them being there to cover or to attenuate the bad effect which such an escapade must necessarily cause in Europe. After reading these dispatches, the perusal of which was interrupted by frequent exclamations of surprise and indignation, Napoleon rose and throwing the papers on my table, deplored what he styled his brother's ingratitude, in the strongest terms. Grief and vexation drew tears to his eyes:

"Could I expect," he cried, "such an outrage from a man to whom I acted as a father? I brought him up with the feeble resources of my pay as artillery lieutenant. I shared my bread and the mattress of my bed with him. Where does he go to? To strangers, so as to make people believe that he is no longer in safety in France, or in the States which are subjected to my influence."

During King Louis's stay in Paris, in the first months of the year, the Emperor had threatened to pursue into Amsterdam itself all persons favoring English trade. The King had replied to this threat by giving secret orders that his capital should be defended, even by means of inundation. The Emperor, becoming more and more indignant at the ever-increasing resistance which his continental system, the only means in his eyes for forcing the English to peace, met with, had pushed his custom-house line up to the very gates of Amsterdam, and had even ordered that this city, the seat of the English trade, should be occupied. King Louis, in his extremity, had withdrawn to Haarlem with his young eldest son, who had been brought to him by the Queen in the preceding month of April, determined to submerge Amsterdam rather than to allow it to be occupied by the French troops. He notified this determination to the ministers, but the council unanimously expressed itself opposed to such extreme measures. The King having next proposed the alternative of defending or of abdicating, the ministers advised the latter step. In consequence King Louis addressed a royal message to the Legislature announcing his renunciation of the throne of Holland in favor of his son, and sent with this message a formal deed of abdication. He left Haarlem on the same day to proceed to the waters of Toeplitz in Bohemia, accompanied by two officers of his household, from whom he separated on arriving on the foreign soil. He went by the name of Count de Saint-Leu, which was the name of an estate which he possessed some leagues from Paris. The Emperor sent to his brother, at Toeplitz, M. Decazes, who had been secretary of the cabinet, and who combined the posts of secretary to the commands of the Lady I Mother and of councilor to the imperial court of Paris. M. Decazes was charged to invite King Louis to leave Austrian territory, and to come and inhabit a country governed by a member of the imperial family. At the same time Napoleon wrote to M. Otto, his ambassador to Vienna, who sent off a secretary of his legation to the King, with the purpose of inducing him to act in accordance with the Emperor's wishes. Neither pressing requests nor advice could triumph over Louis's determination, nor make him abandon his resolution not to live under the influence of a government subjected to his brother's power. He even considered his voluntary exile from France as a protestation against the annexation of Holland to the Empire. Napoleon having exhausted all means of persuasion, and being touched by the bad state of his brother's health, did not insist any further, and ended by yielding to his scruples, scruples which were respect-worthy no doubt, inasmuch as they sprang from an upright and sincere mind, but which under the circumstances were eminently regrettable. Louis accordingly was free to choose his own place of retirement, and decided upon the town of Gratz in Styria, situated in the most southern part of Austria. Having heard of the senatus consultum which assigned a jointure to Queen Hortense and her children, he forbade his wife to accept anything, bidding her content herself with the private property which still belonged to both of them, an injunction which Queen Hortense saw herself forced to disobey.

The situation of Holland was such at that time that its best means of safety lay in its annexation to the Empire. In the new state of things in Europe it was impossible to leave this little state to itself. Its incorporation into a great and powerful Empire at least allowed the Dutch to participate in the advantages of more direct protection, thanks to which it was possible for the commercial prosperity of this people to be once more called into life. Sensible people accordingly, and there are perhaps more sensible people in Holland than anywhere else, desired the annexation of their country to the Empire, and this annexation was pronounced. The Emperor ordered the young Crown Prince, who had been left in Haarlem by his father, in care of Madame de Boubers, his governess, and in charge of General Brune, the Grand Equerry, to be brought to France. Napoleon sent Archtreasurer Le Brun to Amsterdam in the capacity of governor-general. There was a resemblance between the character and manners of Prince Le Brun and the tastes and habits of the Dutch, and they agreed very well indeed in consequence.

Napoleon received his nephew, young Prince Napoleon, who was brought to St. Cloud, and who at the time was six years old, in an affectionate manner. He told this child that he would be his father, and that when he became a man he would pay his father's debt and his own. He never missed an opportunity of impressing on those whom he had created kings what he expected from them in the high rank in which he had placed them. "Never forget," he said to his nephew, "that in whatever position my policy and the interests of my Empire may place you, your first duties are towards me, your second duty is towards France, and all other duties, even those towards the peoples whom I may entrust to you, only come after these."

Chapter X

Bernadotte's election as Crown Prince of Sweden was so important an event that it seems to me necessary to speak of it with the most circumstantial details. After the deposition of Gustavus IV, the Duke of Sudermanie, this king's uncle, was called to the throne. As the Duke had no children, the Diet, on his proposal, elected Prince Christian of Schleswig Augustenburg, Crown Prince of Sweden, and he became the idol of the Swedish nation. Unfortunately he died suddenly of a stroke of apoplexy in the month of January, 1810, while engaged in reviewing a regiment. The people, embittered by this death, which they refused to believe was a natural death, broke out into a violent revolt, in which Count Fersen, Marshal of the Court, lost his life. The death of the Duke of Augustenburg was a misfortune profoundly to be regretted. If this prince had lived, a good understanding would have been maintained between France and Sweden. He had asked the Emperor for one of the princesses of his family to wife.

The Swedes, feeling that they needed a soldier, cast their eyes on a French general, and thought that such a choice would be agreeable to Napoleon, whose friendly disposition they were anxious to cultivate.

I am taking part of my story, the exactness of which I can guarantee because its various phases happened under my very eyes, from General Philippe Ségur's work, *The Russian Campaign in 1812, Critically Examined.*

In 1807, at the time of the evacuation of Pomerania by the Swedes, two brothers of the name of Moerner, officers in the regiment of the same name, were brought to Marshal Bernadotte who gave them his house as their prison, and about a month later sent them back to Sweden. In June 1810, one of these officers, who had become colonel, sent in his name to Bernadotte, at his house in the Rue d'Anjou, in Paris, and spoke to him of the desire of the Swedes to put him in the place of their deceased Crown Prince. Bernadotte listened to this offer with amusement, and without attaching any real importance to it at first, determining not to speak of the matter to the Emperor until the proposal should have been made in an official form. Some days later an extraordinary envoy of Sweden, Baron Wrède, came to see the Marshal, and, confirming what Colonel Moerner had said to him, asked for a reply. That was on a Saturday. Next day Bernadotte went to St. Cloud before mass and communicated this news to the Emperor, who said to him: "I know all about it, and I leave you free to accept or refuse. I will act in this matter as you choose. I had charged Alquier to propose a regency, and to await events. The son of the last King might have been recalled later on, but in Sweden they do not want to have anything more to do with this family. I would rather see you there than anybody else. I will support you with my consent; take what steps are necessary."

Bernadotte sent a young man who was a relation of Signeul's, the Swedish consul in Paris, to Stockholm to arrange with his partisans, authorizing him to promise all the money that was necessary. I will add that Bernadotte's agents acted skillfully, using the name of the Emperor Napoleon to bring over those who were hesitating to their side. About two million francs, advanced by Napoleon or lent by General, afterwards Marshal Gérard, was all the money which the future King of Sweden could dispose of to pay into the bank. Bernadotte's election depended entirely on Napoleon's goodwill, and, before appointing him, the Swedes took care to assure themselves of the Emperor's consent.

If the choice of this marshal of the Empire had displeased the French sovereign he would only have needed to express it to prevent his election. The Swedes had only cast their eyes on Bernadotte because he was related to Napoleon by marriage, Madame Bernadotte being King Joseph's sister-in-law, and wishing in this way to conciliate the Emperor's goodwill. Napoleon, however, was prompted to desire that the throne of Sweden should be occupied by a man more loyal to France, and this, through an instinctive distrust of the marshal's feelings, a mistrust which events only too fully justified. Under the influence of this prejudice Napoleon commissioned General Duroc to go one morning to the Elysée where Prince Eugène was living, during the marriage festivities, and to propose to him the future crown of Sweden. Prince Eugène asked for one day in which to consider the proposal. Duroc having come to fetch an answer on the morrow, Eugène replied that after having carefully considered the matter with the vice-queen, and having meditated on the advantages and disadvantages of this new establishment, they had come to the conclusion that they must content themselves with their present situation in Italy. He added that moreover the obligation to abjure the Catholic faith was exceedingly distasteful to his wife, the Princess. Napoleon told Prince Eugène the same day that he had perhaps done right to refuse, although he would have been much pleased if he could have accepted the proposal.

When one considers the lofty fortune to which Bernadotte was raised, one is prompted by the desire to cast a retrospective glance on the career which was followed by this factious soldier, who from a common soldier's dormitory passes through revolutionary clubs to reach a foreign throne, to which the protection of a great man raises him at one stroke without transition, without any apprenticeship to government, and in the capacity of the gratuitous heir of an ancient royal race. Having entered the Royal army as a simple soldier at the age of sixteen, he follows his regiment to Corsica, the cradle of the future Emperor whose arm he uses to raise himself. He works with his hands on the St. Florent road, and is employed in keeping the lists in the office of the Registrar of the superior Council of Corsica. He takes ten years to become a sergeant. The Revolution finds him in this rank which would have been, without it, the highest rank of his military career. At the beginning of the Revolutionary period, when all discipline and subordination was upset, Bernadotte finds himself in his element. He is to be seen in the barracks of Marseilles, perched on a bench, powdered, gaitered, and in elegant military costume haranguing his comrades, and using his Gascony eloquence to persuade them to turn out their former officers and to take their place. His activity and his smartness raise him rapidly to the post of general of division in 1794. After various alternations of success and failure he passes over to the army of Italy under the command of General Bonaparte. Here he displays zeal and adroitness. At the time of the 18th Fructidor, the events on which day were partly brought about because some Royalist letters seized by Bernadotte on the person of Count d'Antraigue, agent of the French Princes, had been sent to the Directoire, the future King of Sweden gets himself sent to Paris bearing petitions from the army which demand the punishment of the traitors. His revolutionary exaltation is noticed and he refuses to take part in the army to England, which had been sent to Egypt, hoping to succeed to the command of the army in Italy.

Appointed ambassador to Vienna he hoists the flag of the Republic over the door of his embassy in a critical moment of popular effervescence: an untimely and unseasonable demonstration which was calculated to provoke some outrage likely to compromise the reestablishment of peace with Austria. This imprudent act obliges the Directoire to retain the army for Egypt in France until fresh orders, in the fear that war might break out again on the Continent. Bernadotte, disavowed by the Directoire, returns to Paris and attaches himself to Joseph Bonaparte, whose sister-in-law he marries—a marriage which was to be the foundation of his fortune. Appointed to the Ministry of War by his brother-in-law's influence he is later on removed by Sieyès, who finds him too ardent. Having returned to private life he shows himself hostile to the revolution of Brumaire 18th, but has not the courage to oppose it openly. He then accepts the advantages of this revolution, having been convinced by the success of the event, and represses the jealous instinct which urges him to paralyze the arm, which, however, he will make use of to raise himself to the highest summit of honors. At the time of the publication of the Concordat of 1802, Bernadotte unites himself to other generals to renew his opposition. Sent back to the army in the west, which he had left to go to Paris on this occasion, he continues the same intrigues and the same plotting. Surprised while conspiring against the First Consul, his brother-in-law, Joseph, intercedes for him, and Bernadotte escapes punishment. But clemency irritates ungrateful hearts, and he finds the weight of gratitude heavy to bear. The demagogue allows himself to be appointed marshal of the empire and Prince of Ponte-Corvo. Vested with the command of an army corps during the Jena campaign, Bernadotte refuses to assist Marshal Davout at Auerstadt, thus compromising for the sake of a detestable feeling of rivalry the safety of the entire army. He only escapes a court-martial sentence for this conduct out of consideration for his alliance with the Emperor's brother, who protects him for a second time. After the battle of Wagram the Prince of Ponte-Corvo addresses a lying order of the day to the Saxons, who formed part of his army corps, an order which was calculated to diminish the credit due to the French troops, and which was contrary to the rules of military discipline. This jealous boasting forces the Emperor to remove him from his command, and to send him back to Paris, covering his disgrace however with indulgent pretexts about the Marshal's health.

In spite of the numerous reasons for displeasure which Napoleon had against Bernadotte, he called him to a high fortune and literally loaded him with gifts and honors.

The sovereign of Sweden comes to be dethroned. His successor, who had no children, adopts a prince of the Danish reigning family. The prince dies as though for the very purpose of leaving Bernadotte free access to the throne of Sweden. Then some Swedish officers, grateful for the treatment they had received at his hands when they were his prisoners, and tempted as much by the hope of the Emperor's protection as by the Marshal's military reputation, proposes his election as hereditary prince. In spite of this reputation, Bernadotte was never a great soldier. There were generals in the French army, having held chief commands, who were worth as much as he was, and some were even superior to him. But in the eyes of the Swedes, Bernadotte was related to Napoleon, and Napoleon had always cast the veil of indulgence over his faults. The Prince de Ponte-Corvo did not hesitate to abjure his religion in order to become king, and declared that Stockholm was well worth a Protestant sermon.

Napoleon's indulgence towards such persons as Bernadotte, Talleyrand, and Fouché cannot be explained in a way likely to satisfy what it is conventional to call public opinion. Napoleon's clemency encouraged such characters to do fresh wrongs, which the Emperor forgot, only remembering the services which they had rendered him. Even after blind Fortune had firmly established Bernadotte on a throne to which a total absence of merit gave him so little claim—after he had gathered in the fruits of his past treacheries and his recent perfidy, when the satisfaction of his ambitious desires should have rendered him well-disposed and inclined to look into his heart—he could not refrain from spreading abroad bitter and dishonoring statements about Napoleon, the first author of his fortune.

The terrible disaster which terminated the reign of that august and most unhappy man, the Emperor, the remembrance of Napoleon's kindness, and an indulgence the effects of which Bernadotte had so often felt, did not suffice to touch a heart ungrateful by nature, and rendered implacable by jealousy and ambition.

The following details will furnish fresh traits of Bernadotte's character. His avarice and the cunning of the means which he employed to avoid paying his debts, or to get the best of his foreign creditors, won him the name of the "Crowned Harpagon," and enabled him at his death to leave behind him a treasure exceeding thirty millions of francs.

The allied powers, while refusing to acknowledge the foreign endowments bestowed by the Emperor Napoleon, nevertheless allotted to the holders of these endowments the arrears which had not been paid up to the day on which the definitive treaty of peace was signed. Bernadotte alone refused to carry this measure into execution, and refused to pay over the arrears due to the titularies. All the efforts of the French ambassador to Stockholm to enforce the claims of those entitled to these arrears, and to establish a principle which was not contested by any other power, remained without effect. This caused it to be said with full justice that "these recipients were, however, his fellow-countrymen, men who had shared the same dangers and the same rewards. They had a right to look upon him, Bernadotte, as their supporter and their protector in this common cause, if by any chance their rights happened to be ignored."

In 1815 there fell to Sweden a sum of twenty-five millions of francs, which was the price of the retrocession of Guadeloupe to France, a colony which the English had given to Sweden during the war, besides twelve millions as an indemnity for the surrender of Pomerania to Prussia. Bernadotte devised the scheme of making Parliament hand over these thirty-seven millions of francs to him, this sum equaling, on a balance sheet which he laid before the States, and which they accepted, the total of the debts of Sweden previous to 1815, and undertook to pay off these debts himself. Having secured the consent of the States General he began by considering himself as a privileged creditor. He kept back, for himself, the amount which he considered due to him in compensation for the loss of the principality of Ponte-Corvo, and of his private fortune, spent for his establishment in Sweden—two claims which he consented to reduce to a total of twelve millions of francs. Bernadotte next devoted his attention to profiting by the remaining twenty-five millions by means of various transactions in which he was seen to display all the subtleness of a procurator combined with the power which he exercised as king. It would take too long a time to relate in all their details the tricks, worthy of Moliere's master, which Bernadotte employed to reduce the total of the debts which the States had charged him to pay off in the lump. We will, however, mention some examples.

Denmark had a claim, for supplies furnished to the Swedish army, to a sum which had already been fixed after discussion at eighty thousand Hamburg crowns. The Danish creditors were so discouraged by the delays and postponements to which they were subjected, that, wearied out, they resigned themselves to the receipt of only thirty-seven thousand six hundred crowns. An American debt which was Duke from the sale of cargoes of cotton seized at Stralsund, in 1812, by the French, but afterwards sold by Sweden, which was to hand over the price realized to the American merchants, was reduced, after ten years' haggling, by two-fifths. The debts contracted with the formal sanction of the States towards the family of Gustavus IV, by way of indemnity for the private property which it possessed in Sweden, were in their turn reduced by twenty-five percent. A Genoese debt of twelve millions, after chicaneries of all kinds, prompted mainly by the intention of realizing profits on the coin-currencies and the exchange, was finally discharged—although it had been declared absolutely lawful—with a draft on London for ninety-nine thousand pounds sterling. The King of Sweden further deducted a sum of four thousand crowns from this sum, pretending that the philanthropy of the Genoese would not refuse this subsidy to one of the philanthropic establishments of Stockholm. And lastly Bernadotte, desiring to liquidate the Saxon loan, offered the bondholders seventy percent, of their claims. The majority resigned themselves and accepted this offer. As to the others, all kinds of maneuvers were brought into play against them to force them to agree. All the preceding details have been taken from official documents.

When, after the death of the Emperor Alexander, Bernadotte's powerful protector, Prince Gustavus Wasa entered the service of Russia, this event caused the royal intruder to fear that the interest taken by the Russian government in the son of the exiled monarch might develop in a perilous manner. A doubt as to the stability of his dynasty arose in the mind of the former Marshal of the Empire, and he expressed himself in the following very characteristic manner: "My son will very probably have a kingdom. He is sure to have thirty millions."

I have to speak of Fouché's disgrace, which is important on account of its cause. The double negotiation opened by this minister in London, without the Emperor's knowledge, concurrently with the overtures for peace which the King of Holland was making there through the agency of M. Labouchère, was the cause of this disgrace. Napoleon had closed his eyes to the agreement which had been made between Fouché and the Prince de Bénévent after the battle of Essling and the landing of the English expedition in the island of Walcheren. Until then an open antipathy had separated these two ministers. Their intimacy manifesting itself under such circumstances was bound to inspire the Emperor with well-founded suspicions. The audacity of Fouché in dealing with a hostile government without Napoleon's participation, could not remain unpunished. It would take up too much space to enter into the details of this culpable intrigue, and these are besides matters of public knowledge. Ouvrard, the agent in this underhand negotiation, had, it is true, written to the Emperor to ask his authorization to act in the matter, but Napoleon, knowing this person's presumption, looked upon his desire to interfere in diplomatic affairs as a ridiculous one, and—never dreaming that he would dare to give effect to these plans without his consent—did not condescend to answer his letter.

The regrets expressed by the Faubourg St. Germain at the news of the dismissal of Minister Fouché, the former bloody terrorist, are worthy of notice. He had known how to persuade this last stronghold of the opposition that it was he who was its protector with Napoleon, and that if any member of this opposition fell into disgrace it was because it had been out of his power to prevent it, but that he might be relied upon to destroy, or at least to attenuate, the effects of this severity. It might have been said that Fouché held Napoleon under the effects of a charm, for with the best reasons for dismissing him, the Emperor still hesitated. One day, at St. Cloud, having, according to a very usual custom of his, come and seated himself on a corner of my writing-table, Napoleon said to me, after some words of no importance, and with a brusque change of subject: "Méneval, I have a mind to dismiss Fouché." This remark seemed to be the expression of a yet undecided state of mind, Napoleon trying to come to some definite determination. I could not prevent myself from exclaiming: "Sire, I expected this, and I am only surprised at one thing, and that is that you haven't sent him away before." He rose slowly without answering me, took one or two turns in the study with his hands behind his back, and then occupied himself with some other matter. This hesitation on the Emperor's part showed to what an extent Fouché possessed the art of rendering himself necessary, or rather what difficulty Napoleon felt in separating himself from persons to whom he had been long accustomed, even when his confidence in them had been greatly shaken.

Fouché, after his disgrace, retired to his château at Pontcarré, but first took care to carry off with him, or to destroy, the most important papers at his ministry. The Emperor not wishing to leave his letters in the hands of a man whom he considered capable of making a bad use of them, sent Prince de Neufchâtel and his friend the councilor of state, Réal, to ask for these papers; but Fouché persisted in denying that he had carried off any papers. Although the Emperor was extremely irritated by Fouché's disguised refusal, he did not wish to take steps against him. Reflection having inspired the ex-minister with the fear of the consequences of the Emperor's resentment, he ended by making up his mind to hand over Napoleon's letters. Napoleon being unwilling to leave the restless mind of this dangerous intriguer without food, and especially wishing to remove him from France, appointed him governor-general of the Illyrian provinces. He had later on reason to repent not having put it out of the power of this unhallowed individual to do harm.

More than one ambition was aroused by the vacancy at the Ministry of Police. The Emperor had reserved this portfolio *in petto* for General Savary, who afterwards became

Duke of Rovigo, and who at that time was one of his aides-de-camp. He was anxious in rewarding the services of this general officer to employ his talents and his devotion to his person in a useful manner. Duke of Bassano had proposed Senator Sémonville, which, without speaking unjustly, was a mistake on his part. Napoleon had not replied negatively. Accordingly, when one day he told M. de Bassano that he would declare his choice on the morrow, the Duke thought the chances in favor of his protégé and advised him in a confidential manner to go to St. Cloud. M. de Sémonville arrived provided with a parcel which contained his senator's coat and sword, and the hat with the white feathers, and waited with anxiety at Madame de Bassano's house. On leaving mass, the Emperor ordered M. de Bassano and General Savary to be brought to his cabinet. The latter, who had no idea of the favor in store for him, was just preparing to return to Paris, his week's service being terminated. The general was on a call to Madame de Bassano, when he saw an outrider from the imperial stables ride up, leading a horse, who told him that the Emperor wished to see him at once. Savary, who could not mount on horseback in shoes and stockings, asked for the loan of a pair of the Duke's riding-boots. Bassano had immense calves, so that Savary had all the room he wanted in his boots. Savary put his shoes in his pockets, so as to have them in readiness to put on again before entering into the Emperor's presence, jumped on the horse which had been brought for him, and rode off on a gallop to the palace. The Emperor, who was tired of waiting, was just going out when the general arrived. Great was the latter's surprise, and no less the surprise of the Duke of Bassano, who was in the Emperor's cabinet, when Napoleon addressing the latter and pointing to General Savary said: "Here is my Minister of Police." It was a *coup de théâtre,* which was repeated at Madame de Bassano's house in front of M. de Sémonville, when the Duke, bringing Savary back told them both: "Here is the Minister of Police."

In the meantime General Foy arrived in Paris. He had been sent by Marshal Masséna to explain to the Emperor the critical position in which the French army found itself before Lisbon, at the end of 1810. Napoleon wishing to reoccupy Portugal, which General Junot had been forced to abandon after the convention of Cintra, had charged Marshal Masséna with this important operation. Prince d'Essling had prefaced the invasion of Portugal with the taking of the towns of Ciudad-Rodrigo and Almeida. After the defeat at the battle of Bussaco, he had arrived in front of the lines of Torres-Vedras, an immense entrenchment covering over fifteen leagues, at which the English general had been working for the past six months, and which was defended by an Anglo-Portuguese army, which was three times greater than ours. Not being able to attack these formidable lines face to face, the Marshal was forced to blockade it while waiting for reinforcements. He then decided to send General Foy to the Emperor to acquaint him with the state of affairs, to ask him for instructions, and especially for funds. General Foy, who in this campaign had displayed courage and talent, was only known to Napoleon by the opposition which he had always manifested against the imperial government. A friend of General Moreau and of General Lecourbe, he had shown himself very partial towards the former at the time of his trial. When Napoleon became Emperor, General Foy refused him his vote, and would not add his name to the congratulations which his comrades addressed to the new Caesar. Foy was colonel of artillery at the time. This inflexibility of principle had not put a stop to his career, for he had been appointed general of brigade on his arrival in Portugal. General Foy's antecedents were not, however, calculated to dispose the Emperor in his favor. But when Napoleon had listened to him he showed himself extremely satisfied with the clear way in which the general had answered his numerous questions as to the position of the French army, its operations, and its resources. The Emperor was much pleased with this officer. Hearing that he had lost his carriages, and had run great dangers on his journey, Napoleon ordered a sum of twenty thousand francs to be paid to him, and appointed him at the same time general of division. He had conceived so high an opinion of General Foy's character and talents that he designed him *in petto* for the dignity of marshal, a distinction which he also reserved for General Gérard and Generals Clausel and Lamarque.

Up till 1814 General Foy continued to show the same bravery and the same talents in war. Having returned at that time to private life, he devoted his leisure to study. Elected by the electors of his department to represent them at the chamber of deputies, this eminent general became one of the most eloquent of orators. He figured in the ranks of the opposition and showed himself the most indefatigable and the most skilled champion of the guarantees stipulated for in the Charter, the most resolute adversary of the unpopular laws proposed by the government of the Restoration. He often used to combine with his magnificent speeches in patriotic defense of public liberties, attacks against the fallen government, which were not always fair or just. He used at times to tell his friends, who blamed him for it, that he did this to be consistent. General Foy, animated, without any possible doubt, by sincere patriotism, charged Napoleon with the commonplace crime of having immolated liberty, so as to strike a simultaneous and indirect blow at the illiberal methods of the royal government, by warning it of the danger of governing in an arbitrary manner, and by accusing it of favoring in this way the underhand growth of the counterrevolution. Mistaking, with this object in view, the spirit of the acts of the preceding government, the general did not take sufficiently into consideration the abnormal and extraordinary circumstances in which the holder of the sovereign power had found himself placed.

After General Foy's death there was published a work on the war in the Peninsula, which this soldier had written during the leisure of peace and of his legislative career. The injustice and the mistakes which disfigure this work, which otherwise is a very remarkable one, are to be attributed, it is said, as much to the author, as to the publisher of this book, who in various places has exhibited his ignorance of military matters in the story of the conduct of this war, and a superficial acquaintance with the events which during this period occurred in Spain and Portugal. General Foy had not had the time to finish this work, and only left behind him unfinished notes, on which the *History of the War in the Peninsula* was written.

In the month of November 1810, the negotiations, opened eight months previously, with the English government for an exchange of prisoners came to an end without any result. These negotiations were being pursued on behalf of France by M. de Moustier, who had been employed with me at the Congress of Lunéville, and on behalf of England by Mr. Mackenzie. The French government had previously proposed various systems of exchange, stimulated by the desire to rescue thousands of French prisoners from hideous captivity on the English pontoons. The system of exchange which England seemed to prefer was the exchange of all the prisoners, both native and allied, *en masse.* When it became a question of drawing up the clauses referring to the arrangement which had to be come to in this matter, difficulties arose. The English plenipotentiary, adopting, in appearance, the bases agreed upon, wished to insert ambiguous clauses, the result of which would have been that the English government would first of all have withdrawn all the prisoners of English nationality, exchanging them for an equal number of French prisoners. Now, from the proportion of French and English prisoners, twenty thousand prisoners would have remained in England to be exchanged for Spanish prisoners. The liberation of these Spanish prisoners was subordinated to the impractical condition of having to open and follow up preliminary negotiations with the Spanish juntas, which were all independent of each other, and which did not compose a regular government. Our wretched countrymen would accordingly have been prisoners for an indefinite time on the English pontoons, for England attached little importance to the lives of the allies who fought for her and who were in her pay. All the efforts of the French government to effect the admission, in an agreement, of equitable and reciprocal conditions remained without result from the British Ministry, and the English negotiator broke off the conferences, and pressed for the return of his credentials. This new attempt in favor of the unhappy victims of war failed before the cold and selfish policy of England.

The events which I have described in a summary manner are not the only occurrences which marked the year 1810, which was more fruitful in important events than any other year of the Empire. 1810 witnessed also the surrender of Hanover to the King of Westphalia; the creation of the Grand duchy of Frankfort, the succession to which became the appanage of the viceroy of Italy; the commencement of the revolution in America, the signal for which was given by Caracas in separating from the metropolis; and the incorporation of Valais, of the Hanseatic cities, and of Oldenburg into the Empire.

The annexation of Valais to the Empire followed that of Holland, and Valais became a new department under the name of the Simplon department.

The immense development which English commerce had taken in the German Ocean, and in the Baltic, where England had important markets, in Heligoland and elsewhere, the evident favor which was accorded to her by the States on this seaboard, rendered the system of a continental blockade an illusory one. The uselessness of the efforts made by France to oppose collusion and smuggling, and to remedy the inactivity of several governments, made Napoleon determine to occupy the German countries situated between these two seas. The edicts of the British council, in tearing up the charters of European international law, authorized the use of even the most violent measures for combating the odious maritime tyranny of England. It was indispensable for the success of the system which had been adopted for the enfranchisement of the seas that the mouths of the Escaut, the Meuse, the Rhine, the Ems, the Weser, and the Elbe should be hermetically closed against the English. The only way of becoming absolutely master of these positions was to place them under French administration. It was for this reason that the French government declared in a senatus consultum, dated December 14, 1810, that the Hanseatic cities, Oldenburg, Mecklenburg, and the districts situated at the mouths of the rivers mentioned, formed integral parts of the French Empire. These acquisitions of territory formed ten new departments.

To these great events, which are of public notoriety, I must add the recital of certain facts of less general interest, which happened about the same time.

A singular occurrence added a fresh grievance to all those which the Emperor already had against M. de Talleyrand and increased the latter's rancor. Talleyrand had a nephew, Augustus de Talleyrand, who had sought in marriage a rich heiress of Orléans. This lady's guardian insisted that the suitor should prove himself possessed of a fortune of three hundred thousand francs before granting his ward's hand. M. Augustus de Talleyrand applied to his uncle, who consented to advance him this sum, his nephew hoping to be able to refund the advance in time. The promissory note which he signed remained in the hands of his uncle, who promised not to let it pass out of his possession. Later on, however, M. de Talleyrand being himself short of money, passed the note on to a third person, who came and asked Augustus de Talleyrand to pay it. He was at that time ambassador to Switzerland. Surprised by this sudden demand, his first impulse was to accuse his uncle of having broken faith. Madame Augustus de Talleyrand, greatly upset by this occurrence, started off at once for Paris from Berne. She presented herself at the Emperor's levee, her husband being one of the Emperor's chamberlains, and told him of the difficulties in which M. de Talleyrand had cast his own nephew. Napoleon, informed of all the circumstances, summoned his Archchancellor, and ordered him to express his displeasure to M. de Talleyrand for the disgrace which his way of behaving had brought upon a man who was representing France abroad, and finally insisted that the note should be called in without delay. M. de Talleyrand was forced to comply, but this direct interference of the Emperor in his family affairs seemed to him a gratuitous provocation, and awoke in him a resentment which poured a fresh dose of gall into his heart.

In these days of extraordinary fortunes, two Frenchwomen who had started from lowly origins acquired an influence in the East which, on more than one occasion, they placed at the service of their countrymen.

One of these modern Roxelanas was the wife of an infantry sergeant, and had been sutler to the regiment in which her husband had served during the French expedition to Egypt. The chances of war threw her into the power of the Pasha of Jerusalem. Claimed by order of General Kléber, at that time in command of the French army in Egypt, this woman, satisfied with her new position, and being in the Pasha's good graces, refused to give up these advantages to return to the precarious position which she had formerly occupied. She remained after that time at the Pasha's court in Jerusalem, but never forgot in the midst of her splendor that she was a Frenchwoman and a Christian. She used the influence which she owed to the Pasha's favor, accordingly, in protecting the Christian establishments in Syria. Napoleon, having heard of this, gave orders to our consuls to put themselves into communication with her, and to profit by her influence. She rendered them certain services for which she was rewarded.

Another Frenchwoman, a Corsican from Balagna, had been taken prisoner by the Barbary pirates, who sold her to the Sultan of Morocco. He made her his favorite. She had a brother in France whom she thought it her right to recommend to the Emperor. Napoleon, yielding to the influence of this woman's strange destiny, was anxious to respond to the confidence which his countrywoman had placed in him. He accordingly gave orders that this brother should be found, and was disposed to do something for him, but was obliged to abandon this project on hearing that the man could neither read nor write, and was totally unfitted for anything.

The story of Roustan, Napoleon's famous mameluke, in some way resembles these extraordinary destinies. I will accordingly take this opportunity of recording it. Roustan received one day a letter from his mother, who was a slave, I believe, in Turkey. She wrote to her son, of whose good position in France she had heard, to give him her news. Roustan was transported with joy on hearing that his mother was still alive. Napoleon ordered me to answer the letter, and to ask Roustan's mother what he could do for her; but my letter for what reason I do not know, was never answered. Roustan was born in Georgia, and his father, who had become doctor to the Pasha, had sent for his wife to join him with their two children. Pirates kidnapped the three during their journey, and divided the prisoners amongst themselves. Roustan, sold in Egypt, was brought up in the house of Koraim, Bey of Alexandria, in the mameluke novitiate. After the death of the Bey, sentenced by court-martial as guilty of having communicated with the English fleet, Napoleon took Roustan into his service, and brought him back to France. Roustan was still in ignorance of what had become of his mother and his sister. He accompanied Napoleon on all his journeys, acting as his outrider and, occasionally, as his valet. He had become inseparable from Napoleon, and no picture of Napoleon was ever painted without the silhouette of his mameluke being placed behind the Emperor's portrait. Roustan adapted himself entirely to French customs. He married a daughter of one of the Empress's ushers, and had several children by her At the time of the abdication, in 1814, Roustan could not stand the test of adversity. He disappeared from Fontainebleau, on the eve of the day on which Napoleon was to leave France for the island of Elba, carrying off a sum of money which had been given him to compensate his wife for the prejudice which his absence might cause her. His weariness of the agitated life which he had been forced to lead for so long a time, the uncertainty of the future, and the pleasures of the domestic hearth, weighed more in his eyes than the fidelity which he owed to Napoleon, and blinded him to the ingratitude of which he was guilty in abandoning a master who had loaded him with acts of kindness.

In 1810 the Emperor ordered the notes concerning several people in the Faubourg St. Germain, whose removal Fouché had demanded, which were in the offices of the Ministry of Police, to be laid before him. He was surprised at the trifling nature of the complaints made against them, and ordered that these persons should be recalled from exile. Four or five of them alone were excepted from his amnesty, amongst others Mesdames de Chevreuse and Staël, whom Napoleon knew personally, and whose malicious way of talking displeased him. One of them was in constant conspiracy against his authority, the other was of an irremediably hostile disposition. The Emperor, deeming them incorrigible, as well as Madame Récamier, one of Madame de Staël's henchwomen, forbade them to live in Paris in the strictest terms, without assigning limits of time to this ostracism.

On the same occasion Napoleon wished to inform himself what was the real state of affairs in the Faubourg St. Germain which certain persons, from prejudice or by interest, tried to make him look upon as a bogey. He ordered information, accordingly, to be supplied of influential families who were known for their active opposition or for their harmless sulking against the new order of things. I drew up a kind of dictionary, with this purpose in view, by help of the contradictory notes supplied by MM. de Talleyrand, Sémonville, Duroc and the Minister of Police; but I do not think that the Emperor ever consulted it, and it has since remained in my hands.

I have related above with what hesitation Napoleon separated himself from Fouché, in spite of the fact that there were reasons for complaint against him, which were only too well-founded, and this in consideration of the useful services which he had rendered him, especially at the time of his accession to power. Bourrienne was another example of that feeling of instinctive benevolence which attached Napoleon to anybody who could invoke "old times" before him. This benevolence, this remembrance of services rendered in an elevated sphere, extended to the most modest posts in his household. No old servant was ever dismissed until the Emperor had approved of the report addressed to him on this subject, and it was only on the second or third relapse that he agreed to a dismissal. A poor devil of a coachman, whose constant state of intoxication rendered him incapable of doing his work, escaped being dismissed for a long time, because he had driven a wagon at the battle of Marengo.

The first usher of the Emperor's cabinet—a man called Landoire—whom the Emperor liked, and whose old and faithful services he appreciated—having lost his wife, desired, on account of family affairs, to remarry with his wife's sister. Such marriages were forbidden by the civil code. The Emperor, to whom Landoire applied, told him that it was impossible for him to grant him this request; but, vanquished by the pressing demands of the man, Napoleon charged the Grand Judge to make a report to him of the matter. The conclusions of the minister's report were to the effect that although the person whom Landoire wished to marry was only his wife's half-sister, the prohibition was so formal that the Emperor could not authorize the marriage without committing a flagrant violation of the law. Napoleon sympathized with his servant's grief and had it suggested to him to go and marry in some neighboring state which was outside the jurisdiction of the civil code. Landoire could only get married in 1814, when marriages of this kind ceased to be absolutely forbidden.

If the examples of Napoleon's goodness were limited to those which I have just quoted, they would not be conclusive in favor of the natural kindness of his disposition. There is no tyrant, however savage he may be deemed to be, who has not his good moments. What I wanted to say was that this kindness was the usual state of his mind, and that it was practiced on every opportunity. Even when Napoleon had thought it his duty to reprimand severely, his real disposition got the upper hand and sooner or later made amends for any injustice in what he had said. I do not want to digress too far, nor to mention the numerous examples of Napoleon's disposition to remember past services. These examples are generally well known, and I will content myself with mentioning the following, which are less so. In 1809, General Carnot found himself in debt. Since Napoleon's accession to the Empire he had constantly maintained an attitude of pronounced hostility towards the new regime. As this general's conduct was the result of his convictions, and not of personal feeling, he presumed on the sovereign's generosity to the extent of asking his support in a critical moment and accordingly sent me, through the agency of M. Collignon, his kinsman, with whom I had been in relations, a letter in which he asked me to ask the Emperor for the loan of a sufficient sum to settle his difficulties. The Emperor being touched by Carnot's confidence in him hastened to assist him. By a delicate feeling he did not ask to be informed of the state of the general's affairs, nor did he ask him to lay his accounts before him. Napoleon simply asked the Minister of War at what time Carnot had ceased to receive his pay as a general, and ordered the arrears with accessories to be paid over to him, which realized more than Carnot needed for his debts. At the same time he granted him a pension of ten thousand francs as a former minister. Carnot, out of gratitude for the Emperor's generosity towards him, offered him his services. An exchange of courtesies then took place between them which honors them both alike. Napoleon, out of consideration for Carnot's political convictions, did not wish to assign him to a post the duties of which might clash with his opinions. He asked him purely and simply to write a book on the defense of fortified places, inviting him to give the authority of his name to the principle of defense carried to its extremest limits. Recent examples had shown the necessity of reestablishing this principle. Carnot lost no time in carrying out the Emperor's wishes, and a few months later sent him the work, together with the following letter:

"SIRE,

"Not having been able to offer your Majesty the first copy of my work on the defense of fortified places, with my own hands, I have begged H. E. the Minister of War to present it to you in my name. My best endeavors have been used in this book to point out to young soldiers intended for this branch of the service, the true path of duty, and to inspire them with «the feelings of honor and of devotion to your person with which they should be animated. I personally have been guided in the course of my work by my feeling of profound gratitude towards you. May this feeling supplement the talent which I should have needed to carry out your wishes in a worthy manner. "I am, Sire, Your Majesty's very humble and very obedient servant, and faithful subject,

"(Signed) CARNOT."

Later on, in 1814, when misfortune fell upon France, and the importance of our fortified places was increased by the invasion of the territory, Carnot offered Napoleon the assistance of his sword and of his experience, in a touching letter. His offer having been accepted he was sent to Antwerp, where he added example to the precept which he had so wisely and so eloquently expounded.

Chénier, having become the adversary of the Emperor, whom he even attacked in his writings, applied none the less to him for a post which he needed. As I had known him formerly it was through me that his letter reached its destination. After Chénier left the tribunate, the First Consul had offered him the place of administrator of the Post office. It was a kind of sinecure which would have enabled Chénier to give himself up to his literary work. Such occupations were better suited for him, and would without doubt have replaced in a profitable and advantageous manner the systematic opposition which had won for him in the tribunate the empty shadow of the influence which he had formerly exercised in the heart of the Convention and of the popular assemblies. Chénier refused this lucrative post, although he was fond of spending money, and combined republican ideas with a little aristocratic display. He proudly wished to earn the salary of the place given to him. He asked for the place of University Inspector, a place which was more suited to his tastes and aptitude, and in spite of the wretched state of his health courageously undertook a long tour on the inspection of schools. His vanity as a poet, which could brook no contradiction, often made him forget that the spirit of conciliation was necessary in the functions which he fulfilled. A spirit of opposition, the recollection of his former political passions led him on to indiscreet attacks against the power of the Head of the state. On a report from Fouché, who until then had been his protector, the place of University Inspector was withdrawn from him. Financial embarrassment, indeed, a state of real distress, to which he was reduced by the loss of his occupation, got the better of his pride. Palissot, who liked him very much, persuaded him after a long resistance to appeal to the Emperor's generosity, and assured him that I would willingly undertake to place his letter before the sovereign's eyes. On reading his letter Napoleon was touched by the sad position into which a man whose talents he respected had fallen, and he made haste to hand over to the poet a sum of money which he needed to pay his debts. At the same time he commissioned him to continue the History of France, and entrusted him with other literary work, rewarding him with a handsome salary. Chénier did not enjoy this new favor for any great length of time, for death overtook him in the prime of life and at the moment when his talents had reached their greatest height.

Charles Pougens, an estimable literary man, and a Member of the Institut, had had the misfortune to lose his sight. This state of blindness had not, however, interrupted him in his literary work. Deprived of all resources by the events of the Revolution, he had succeeded in establishing a printing office, to which he had added a bookseller's shop. He had been known to General Bonaparte, whose library he had formed at the time of his departure for Egypt. A series of bankruptcies ruined Pougens in 1803. In his distress it occurred to him to apply to the First Consul, who at that time happened to be at the camp at Boulogne. The courier who had carried M. Pougens' letter returned with an order that 40,000 francs were to be advanced to him. This loan was to be paid back in a period of four years. Ten years later half this sum was still owing, but touched by the energy of his debtor's efforts, and by his honesty, Napoleon discharged him of the 20,000 francs which remained owing, in a decision issued April 10, 1813. It was stated in this decision that this favor was granted to M. Pougens in compensation for the suppression of his printing office, and as a reward for the labors which he was carrying out for the achievement of his great work *Le Trésor des Origines,* the complete publication of which was prevented by the author's death. Pougens was only able to print one specimen in folio, which shows immense erudition and research, really surprising when one considers that the author had lost his sight.

It would be easy to quote other examples and numerous proofs of Napoleon's liberality as well as of the delicacy which he employed in his way of obliging. Without referring again to his munificence towards his generals I am in a position to say that his ministers, senators, and many other civil functionaries enjoyed the benefits of a generosity to which those who were worthy of it never appealed in vain.

I had asked the Emperor for a pension on the Empire Press Fund in favor of my old friend Palissot. I haggled with him for a long time as to the amount of this pension. He did not want it to exceed 3000 francs, although he had quite recently awarded a pension of 6000 francs to the poet Lebrun (Écouchard). We had a kind of discussion, in which Napoleon consented to engage with me, on the respective merits of the two poets. He authorized me to prepare for him a draft decree granting Palissot a pension, but only one of 3000 francs. As he very readily put up with being contradicted on questions which only interested him slightly, and indeed very often gave way on these points I told him that since he consented to give my protégé a pension, I could not make this amount less than 6000 francs in the decree which I should prepare for him for his signature. He answered nothing; but when I laid the decree before him Napoleon cried out. Turning round towards me he caught hold of my ear, which was a familiar gesture of his, and reproached, me, laughing, at having wanted to get his signature by surprise. Then laying down his pen he repeated his objections on the inferiority of Palissot's merit as compared with Lebrun. At last, after jesting with me in a kindly manner on my tenacity, he was good enough to compound with me, and to award a pension of 4000 francs to my worthy friend, who enjoyed it until his death, which took place just at the time when the Restoration was about to deprive him of his pension.

Napoleon is supposed to have been incapable of friendship. Hatred, which has worked with such assiduity to disfigure this great character, could not fail to seek to strip him of the most precious attribute of true greatness. Napoleon had sincere friends whose friendship he often requited: Desaix, Lannes, Duroc, Bessières, Muiron, and others whose names are not before my memory just now. Misfortune is a crucible in which friendship is refined, and often dissolved, but the friends whom I have named were profoundly attached to Napoleon, and would have remained faithful to him as he on his side was to their memory.

The interest which Napoleon took in those whom he loved proves that he was capable of attachment. A general officer whom he had adopted from the moment of his entering the military profession, whom he had supported and guided with particular interest, and to whom he had given the most favorable opportunity of distinguishing himself in war, had just been raised to the highest dignity in the army. The Duke of Raguse, after having received his nomination as Marshal, presented himself in the Emperor's tent to thank him. Napoleon said:

"I have given you your nomination, and I had great pleasure in giving you this new proof of my affection; but I am afraid I may have incurred the reproach of having listened rather to my affection than to your rights to this eminent distinction. You have plenty of intelligence, but there are needed for war qualities in which you are still lacking, and which you must work to acquire. Be it said amongst ourselves that you have not yet done enough to entirely justify my choice; at the same time I am confident that I shall have reason to congratulate myself on having nominated you, and that you will justify me in the eyes of the army."

The man to whom these words were addressed, touched by such paternal feeling, agreed as to what he owed to the Emperor's goodness, and protested that it was his intention to render himself altogether worthy of it, and to give him fresh proofs of his devotion.

I did not mention Berthier's name amongst the Emperor's friends because of his defection in 1814, and I was wrong. If a moment of error separated this marshal from the Emperor at that time, Berthier had preserved too deeply-rooted a remembrance of his old master not to survive adversity. I very nearly met the Prince of Wagram at Waldsee, a town in Würtemberg, in 1815, when, like a plant which turns its face towards the orb from the rays of which it derives its existence, Berthier was on his way to join the person whom he called his brother-in-arms, his faithful companion in war, his wife. The Emperor on his side could not forget him. He used to say, laughingly, that when Berthier returned—and Napoleon never doubted that Berthier would return—he would take no other revenge upon him than to oblige him to come to the Tuileries in the uniform of Louis XVIII's guards. We may be quite sure that the Emperor would not have insisted on this.

Adversity, moreover, drew close to Napoleon at St. Helena men whose devotion he would never have had full opportunity of judging in the days of his prosperity, and amongst these it is right with others to mention the name of M. de Las Cases, in whose sympathy and fidelity the illustrious captive found consolation in his exile. Napoleon's feelings towards this courtier under misfortune are shown in a letter which is a monument of true friendship, which the Emperor wrote to his faithful servant when England forced him to leave Longwood. M. de Las Cases responded to these feelings by publishing a book, which in spite of its faults became and will remain popular.

The "Memorial of St. Helena" was the first and most powerful protest against an odious system of calumny and libel, inspired by hatred and an abuse of victory. The "Memorial" caused a publication which on its appearance excited general curiosity in Europe, to be forgotten. I refer to the "Manuscript which came from St. Helena in a Manner Unknown." At the time when this book was published the mysterious way in which it reached England and had been addressed to the most celebrated bookseller in London, the strong desire to obtain revelations from Napoleon about himself, the disgust with the diatribes published against him, and finally the interest which was inspired by the greatness of his misfortune, prepared a greedy reception for this alleged St. Helena manuscript. On the other hand, the anachronisms, the improbabilities and the vulgar mistakes interspersed in pages full of lofty ideas and picturesque and characteristic expressions, held the public mind in suspense. The anachronisms were explained by the statement that it had been necessary in order to rescue the sheets of the manuscript from the inquisition of the jailer of St. Helena, to separate them, and to send them to Europe by roundabout ways, so that the confusion which had resulted therefrom had prevented their being put in their right order. Indeed a proof of the authenticity of the book was seen in these very anachronisms because it was pointed out that no spurious author would have committed them. The mistakes about facts were attributed to the loss of several sheets of the manuscript, which had to be rewritten by somebody else's pen. These explanations, good or bad, having been admitted, the book was generally considered to be the work of Napoleon himself, amongst persons whose functions had formerly put them into direct communication with him. Reflection however, and a more careful examination of the manuscript, very soon increased the doubts as to its authenticity. There were mentioned as having been its authors, first of all Madame de Staël, then Benjamin Constant. The Emperor himself attributed it to a councilor of state whom he did not name, who, according to his statement, had been on ordinary service under the Consulate. Public opinion finally settled upon a relation of Count Siméon's, who occupied a place in the financial department in the South of France. Count Siméon, being approached on the subject, admitted that his relation was responsible for the book. The secret which the true author of the book had kept was at last confided to his family. The "Manuscript of St. Helena," which appeared fated to remain enveloped in the mystery which enshrouds to this day the *Letters of Junius,* and other historical writings and deeds, whose authors, or those who took part in them, will probably remain unknown forever, was from the pen of M. Frédéric Lullin de Châteauvieux, a Genevese, already known to the scientific world. This writer has admitted, after keeping silent for twenty-five years, that he wrote this book, in 1816; that he carried it himself to London, and posted it to Murray the publisher. The draft of this little work, entirely written by its author's hand, and covered with his corrections, was found amongst his papers after his death, and M. Siméon's cousin readily renounced a paternity which people persisted in attributing to him.

Napoleon had an inclination for various people who made their mark in the history of this century, and amongst others for M. de Talleyrand. The latter had foreseen the future elevation of General Bonaparte at the time when the Directoire had raised the former Bishop of Autun to the Ministry of Foreign Affairs. The First Consul and Emperor remembered this fact, and there perhaps lies the reason of the sympathy which Napoleon so long retained for Talleyrand. Even when guilty collusions, financial matters, and warnings given by foreign sovereigns obliged the Emperor to remove this minister's portfolio, and to dismiss him from his councils, an instinctive liking drew him back towards him. In 1803, the Emperor had asked the pope to secularize the former prelate, a feeling of propriety making him desire to see the latter in a position better suited to the worldly career which he had embraced; but it was not the same when M. Talleyrand expressed to the Head of the state his wish to marry. The Empress Josephine, Mrs. Grant's friend, helped her with all her influence on the Emperor's mind; but Napoleon remained deaf to all her entreaties. Sometimes Josephine used to go up by the little staircase which communicated between her apartment and the Emperor's cabinet, and would come and knock at the door. One day, being alone, I opened the door. She had come to tell "Bonaparte" that Madame Grant was there, and to beg him to listen to her for a moment. Napoleon at last allowed himself to be influenced and went downstairs to his wife's rooms, where he found Madame Grant in a suppliant attitude, imploring him with clasped hands not to put an obstacle in the way of her marriage. Napoleon could not resist a woman's tears and entreaties, and promised to remain neutral, which was all he could do. The marriage took place, but was not destined to be a happy one.

In 1810, when Talleyrand had lost between fourteen and fifteen hundred thousand francs in banker Simon's bankruptcy, the Emperor, in spite of the fact that he had real grievances against his former minister, came to his assistance. He purchased the Monaco mansion, which M. Talleyrand wanted to sell, for two million and some hundred thousand francs. Now in purchasing this house Napoleon was acting against a rule which he had made of never buying houses or estates which were expensive to keep up, for he had no need of such, seeing that the imperial domains and castles amply sufficed him.

Napoleon also truly loved the Emperor Alexander, whom he found superior to the sovereigns of the day. The Czar's wit, his grace, and his affability had charmed the Emperor. In spite of the most caressing demonstrations, it must be acknowledged today that the Russian monarch's affection for Napoleon was never sincere. As to the latter, he succumbed to the charm of the cunning Alexander, in spite of all the strong reasons which he had to abandon his illusions. Napoleon had retained such feelings for this prince that he used to say that an hour's conversation would have sufficed to efface all traces of resentment between them. I witnessed, at Tilsitt and Erfurth, the charming familiarity which existed between Napoleon and Alexander, and the affectionate intimacy which manifested itself in their private and almost daily correspondence. I like to believe that amongst the causes of the profound melancholy which embittered the Czar's last days were mingled some remembrances of the moments spent at Tilsitt and at Erfurth, and the picture of the agony of St. Helena. Napoleon, without putting aside the requirements of his general policy was filled with condescension towards Alexander. The following incident will serve as an example, albeit it touches Napoleon's military glory as well as his politics. Having noticed that Alexander had retained a bitter remembrance of his defeat at Austerlitz, the victor ordered his cipher to be secretly removed from the bas-reliefs on the column in the Place Vendôme, where it figured on the helmets and the breastplates of the Russian soldiers. The Czar, on entering into Paris, had he paid attention to the matter, might have seen in the absence of this cipher a proof of the delicate generosity of his former ally.

The excommunication fulminated in 1809 by the pope, which had passed almost unnoticed at the time, had not prevented the Emperor's marriage, nor checked the discussion of the religious questions which were being dealt with in an ecclesiastical commission to which the examination of all litigious matters had been submitted.

Towards the end of 1810 the Emperor heard that this excommunication, as well as the Papal bulls directed against the nomination of Cardinal Maury to the archbishopric of Paris, and against the nominations of two other bishops, were in secret circulation. The bull of excommunication had even been clandestinely posted up during the night on the doors of Notre Dame. Abbé d'Astros, grand vicar to the chapter of Paris, was suspected of having had a hand in this matter. The examination of this abbé's papers, and his own confessions, dispelled all doubts on this subject. But what irritated the Emperor in the highest degree was to hear that Portalis, the councilor of state, son of the former Minister of Public Worship, to whom had been extended the same kindness which the Emperor had shown towards his father, had also received communication of these bulls in secret. At the first sitting of the Council of State at which Napoleon presided—January 5, 1811—he addressed Count Portalis in very severe terms, and after a sharp reprimand ordered him to leave the room, and banished him from Paris. At St. Helena Napoleon blamed himself, and perhaps not without reason, for having humbled M. Portalis too deeply in ordering him to leave the room. He said that he should have contented himself with severely blaming him before the whole Council of State assembled. Placed between the severe necessity of denouncing his religion, and his duties toward his sovereign, who had a right to demand unreserved fidelity from him, M. Portalis's position was a difficult one. It is not my place to decide what he ought to have done to conciliate all.

I was much exercised by M. Portalis's disgrace. I had been employed with him at the Congress of Lunéville, and at the Congress of Amiens, and our relations, begun under these circumstances, had been continued. I have even in my possession letters which he wrote to me from Berlin, where he was secretary of legation, letters in which his assurances of friendship towards me are mingled with his expressions of devotion towards the Emperor. When he was recalled in 1813, and appointed first president to the imperial court at Angers, I made haste to go and congratulate him.

The arrest of several prelates and canons, compromised by the papers which had been seized at the house of d'Astros, the grand vicar, followed on the discovery of this religious conspiracy. On the day after the scene at the Council of State, on January 6, 1811, the metropolitan chapter of Paris thought right to present the Emperor with an address exposing its profession of faith in favor of the liberties of the Gallican Church and Bossuet's four propositions. The majority of the archbishops, bishops, and chapters of Italy adhered to the declaration of the Paris chapter.

Napoleon, full of his great designs on Italy, and with a view to opposing an obstacle to the abuse of the Papal authority, convened a national council in Paris, whose apparent object it was to deliberate on the best means of providing for the canonical institution of nominated bishops, when the pope refused to do this. This council, composed of more than one hundred bishops of the churches of France and Italy, assembled on June 17 under the presidence of Cardinal Fesch. The Emperor had reason to complain of the bad direction taken by this assembly. The council did not respond to his views, declared itself incompetent to decide the question of the institution of bishops, and proposed that a deputation should be sent to the pope to come to an understanding with His Holiness on how the precarious state of the Churches of France and Italy could best be remedied. Many French bishops, the Archbishop of Bordeaux amongst others, manifested ultramontane dispositions, contrary to the large majority of Italian bishops, who showed themselves more independent of the Court of Rome.

When the Emperor was informed that the Council had determined to declare itself incompetent, he ordered it to be dissolved. The majority of the bishops reassembled some days later, and this time, admitting the competence of the council, discussed the principal point submitted to them for discussion, and fixed at six months the period accorded to the pope to confer canonical investiture on bishops after which time this investiture was to be carried out by the Metropolitan or, in his absence, by the oldest bishop in the province, *without the pope's interference.*

In the preceding month of January the Emperor had appointed an ecclesiastical commission, composed of nine French cardinals, archbishops, and bishops, for the purpose of settling these questions. This commission, after studying past history, and basing its decision on precedents, expressed the opinion that the investiture of bishops who had been nominated to sees should be entrusted to the Metropolitan, or to his suffragan, in all cases where the pope refused to act. This deliberation was carried to the Holy Father by the ecclesiastical commission, to whom the Emperor had added Abbé Eymeri, the superior of the seminary of St. Sulpice, whom he much esteemed. After long hesitation the pope finally adhered to this proposal. The national council, in consequence, issued a decree in conformity therewith, and charged a large deputation to carry the text of this decree to the pope for his ratification. The pope sanctioned the resolution adopted by the council, but he imposed on the archbishops and bishops who were authorized to give the investiture the formal obligation of declaring that they were only acting in the pope's name. Although the Emperor's object of giving preponderance to the power and right of the national council over the papal authority, and of opposing the former to the Court of Rome, was not altogether fulfilled, since the pope, passing over the council's decision in silence, appeared as the final authority, this first essay appeared nevertheless sufficient to Napoleon for the time being. The convocation of a second council, in 1813, which would have completed the work of the first, was in the Emperor's intention; but events occurred which prevented the realization of this plan. Napoleon at the same time treated three French bishops, two of whom were his almoners, with rigor. They were arrested on the charge of having taken part in intrigues, of having corresponded illegally with the black cardinals, and with Cardinal di Pietro, the clandestine agent of the Papacy in France, and of having fomented rebellion amongst the clergy in underhand ways. These bishops were the Bishops of Tournay, Ghent, and Troyes. The first of these prelates was not to be commended for the austerity of his morality. Napoleon had also to fight against the resistance of his uncle, Cardinal Fesch, who could not be charged with systematic opposition against his nephew, but who disapproved of his open struggle with the Holy See. The Emperor's essay, accordingly, was only partially successful in this first council, and the majority of the upper clergy took advantage of it to preach opposition to the government. The advice of Barral—

Archbishop of Tours—and especially of Duvoisin, Bishop of Nantes, in whom Napoleon had entire confidence, prevented the Emperor's anger from breaking out on those who had opposed him. The Bishop of Nantes, Napoleon used to say, was for him, in theological matters, a torch of which he did not wish to lose sight. The Emperor allowed himself to be guided by this prelate's advice, and checked himself whenever the Bishop of Nantes warned him that he was about to injure the faith, or damage the interests of the Church of France. Napoleon has been blamed for not having allowed any writing or publication either for or against the negotiations of ecclesiastical affairs to appear in the *Moniteur*. Such a polemic was, as a matter of fact, opposed to his views. He was not vexed that public opinion should be lulled to sleep, or even should go astray, convinced as he was that it would come back to his side when the time came for carrying out the plan which he was meditating. Napoleon has stated in his Memoirs that he never wished to publish anything connected with his discussions with Rome. Things were not in a sufficiently advanced state for him to allow anything official to be published. He endured discussions which he looked upon in the light of skirmishing preliminary to the decisive battle that was to be fought, but he did not want these to be made public, because he feared to reveal his private opinions and thus to compromise the success which he hoped to obtain. The Emperor used to say that in depriving the pope of his temporal domain, his object was to fortify and honor his spiritual power. The pope seemed so necessary to Napoleon that he used to say that if he did not exist he would have to be created. But he wished to have him in his hands, and to establish him in Paris, so as to make this capital the metropolis of the Catholic world. In placing the Holy See in the capital of the Empire Napoleon would have surrounded it with magnificence and honors, but at the same time he would always have kept the pope under his eyes. This vast ambition was a permissible one, and he would perhaps have had the power and the genius necessary for realizing it. The establishment of the sovereign pontiff in Paris would have been fruitful in great political results, and the influence exercised by the head of the Church over the whole Catholic world would have become the inheritance of France. That was the time of mighty conceptions; and the generations which shall follow us, in reading over the history of Napoleon, will believe themselves transposed to the heroic ages.

To sum up, Napoleon loved his religion and wished to honor it and render it prosperous. This is proved by the Concordat. But at the same time he wished to employ it as a social force with which to repress anarchy, to consolidate his preponderance in Europe, and finally to increase the glory of France and the influence of the French capital. The Emperor used to say to the Bishop of Nantes, who pointed out to him how useful and how important for the unity of the faith was the visible head of the Church: "Master Bishop, be without anxiety. The policy of my States is closely bound up with the preservation and maintenance of the pope's spiritual power. It is necessary to me that he should be more powerful than ever. He will never have as much power as my policy prompts me to desire for him."

The strict order which Napoleon had introduced into the management of the finances of the state, and of the civil list, had enabled him to amass a treasure, the fruit of his economy, not unproductive indeed, as has been thought, and moreover to have at his disposal private resources, such as the revenues of the extraordinary domain, which placed it in his power to assist banking and commercial houses with loans or advances.

These resources also enabled him to assist families in which he took an interest, and who were obliged by fortuitous circumstances, to appeal to his generosity. The lottery prizes which were not claimed by the holders of the winning tickets, the funds which were derived from farming out the right of working public gaming tables placed at his disposal further resources which he used with prudence and discernment.

He encouraged manufacturers, artists, and workmen with orders, and spent millions of francs in this way. Napoleon had conceived various plans with the object of encouraging merchants and manufacturers. He had thought of establishing in the large manufacturing centers branch offices of the bank, to discount merchants' paper at four percent. He had also a scheme for creating pawnshops where money should be advanced on goods. These plans were abandoned on the advice of the Minister of the Treasury and the directors of the bank, and he limited himself to making advances to merchants of well-known solvency. I am not sufficiently acquainted with financial matters to speak pertinently on Napoleon's financial system. I leave it to his skilful ministers to expound its mechanism, and to point out what were its advantages and disadvantages. I will limit myself to say that without seeking to appreciate the difference between the times and situations that Napoleon had the same views on borrowing as Colbert; but also, there was no deficit. The ordinary taxes and the war indemnities sufficed for all needs. Napoleon was very well acquainted with the resources which could be derived from public credit, but it seemed to him that the time had not yet come for France to found her financial system on borrowing. "What would be my position," he used to say, "towards the whole of Europe, with a government which I built in the midst of ruins, whose foundations are not yet well-established, and the forms of which I am constantly obliged to adapt to new circumstances which proceed from the variations of foreign politics, if I were to subject some of these combinations to absolute methods which do not admit of modification, and which are efficacious only because they are absolute?"

At the same time the Emperor would have lacked neither credit nor lenders if necessity had forced him to have recourse to loans. But he feared the abuse which might be made of this kind of resource and the abyss which he might thereby dig beneath his feet. He did not wish to open new fields to stock-jobbing, nor did he wish to expose himself to have to submit to ruinous usurious conditions. It seemed to him that the institution of a sinking fund would become a delusion if, while reducing the debt with one hand he were to borrow with the other; and finally he did not approve that posterity should be burdened for an indefinite time for the benefit of the present generation. Instead of being tempted by the example of England, the enormous increase of the British national debt scared him. Napoleon had other ideas on the effects of public credit than those which prevail today.

What proves that on the whole the financial system of the Emperor was not altogether defective, and what spirit of order and economy presided over the administration of finance, is that in spite of the wars which were being continually carried on, fed it is true by the indemnities levied on the enemy; in spite of efforts which seemed beyond our strength; in spite of unheard-of disasters and losses, Napoleon was able to do such great things, and in spite of all to leave the finances of France, which he had found in a state of complete ruin, in a more prosperous position than the finances of the other European States.

The question of finances leads me to speak of the manner in which the state budget was regulated under the Emperor. Each year Napoleon, in a financial council, to which all the ministers were summoned, used to fix the amount of the credit assigned to each of them according to his wants, and at the same time decided how much was to be spent in each government Department. Each month the Emperor used to assign to each minister the sums which were to be spent, and which the public treasury would supply to this minister. During the month these sums were entered on a little square of paper ruled in columns, the model of which I had prepared from his design. I add from M. Bresson's *History of Finance* the following details, which are very exact:

"Thus twelve times a year, in one hour's work, the Head of the government passed all the expenses in review, fixed the sum which each should use during the following month, and maintained, as far as it was possible to do so, a balance between expenditure and receipts; slackening or urging on payments, increasing or diminishing the funds of the departmental treasuries according to the amount of sums received, to the urgency of their needs and the changes which current events might bring with them. The Minister of the Treasury, moreover, was not allowed to pay the ministers' drafts unless the minister who signed the order for payment had conformed himself absolutely to the year's budget, and to the monthly sum with which he was credited."

I will add that Napoleon had made the Minister of the Treasury, Comptroller General of Expenditure and kept him acquainted with the movements of the army and other orders involving expenditure which he had given, and he did this with the object of placing the minister in a position to exercise this control in an efficacious manner.

"Never had the tax-collecting department been seen in so well-regulated a state, nor had such absolutely precise book keeping ever been the rule in the French Financial department as under the Empire. True it is that there were some functionaries of the state who made great fortunes, but that was at the expense of foreign kings, and with the Emperor's gifts. It had become almost impossible to rob the state. The accounts were in such perfect order and so greatly simplified that Napoleon could see by the lists he always had in his possession the exact condition of receipts and expenditure, of arrears, and of ordinary and extraordinary resources."

The Emperor did not lose sight of the prosperity of French manufactures, and was constantly thinking about means to enfranchise our industries from the tribute which it paid to the foreigner. The war with England having destroyed our maritime trade, Napoleon applied himself to giving a new impulse to native trade, and to our commercial relations with the allied nations. He sought out in the resources of our country such things as we could no longer import from England, and the wherewithal to replace the produce of our colonies which English supremacy at sea prevented from being landed in our ports, and an equivalent for which had to be found. With this purpose in view, Napoleon created a general council of manufactures and industries, and encouraged the sciences and arts of manufacture, with honorary and pecuniary rewards. He stimulated industries to find the best means of substituting native sugar and coffee for colonial sugar and coffee. He also paid a good deal of attention to the discovery of an article which could be used as a substitute for indigo; and finally the Emperor offered a prize of one million francs as a reward for the inventor of the best machine for spinning flax, the advantage of which would have been to diminish the price of linen, which could then be used as a substitute for cotton. This prize of one million was to be awarded by the terms of the decree which was issued on May 12, 1810, to the inventor of the said machine, no matter what his nationality might be. This decree was translated into all languages, and was sent to our ambassadors and consuls at the various posts which they occupied, to be made public by them. Napoleon forbade the use of cotton or of foreign wood for the furniture of the Imperial Palaces; he desired that the people who were invited to the drawing rooms at court should dress only in silk, so as to encourage the Lyons manufactories. He declared war on Indian cashmeres, but his power was impotent against the tyranny of fashion, and against routine. The Emperor threatened the Empress in vain that he would throw her cashmere shawls into the fire. The Empress used to answer him that as soon as they could give her stuffs as light and as warm as the cashmere woolens she would be very glad to wear them. The Emperor encouraged the manufacturers of French shawls, and commissioned Isabey to make the designs of a magnificent woolen stuff like cashmere, on a white ground, with which a shawl and a dress were made. Marie Louise wore them with some reluctance; these stuffs had not the softness which they have since acquired. The Empress used to complain with reason that her dress "griped" whenever she went near the fire.

The rest of the year 1810 was spent alternately at St. Cloud, Rambouillet, Trianon, Paris, and Fontainebleau. The Court was most brilliant at Rambouillet. There were great hunts, theatrical performances, concerts and frequent drawing rooms. The Empress's pregnancy was declared, and announced to the senate by a message towards the end of November. This event, which crowned the Emperor's desires and the nation's hopes, excited universal interest. The bishops ordained prayers and called down the blessings of Heaven on this happy promise of maternity. M. de Mesgrigny, one of the Emperor's equerries, proceeded to Vienna with a letter for the Emperor of Austria, in which the news of his daughter's pregnancy, then five months advanced, was announced to him. M. de Mesgrigny returned on November 13 with the replies of the Emperor and Empress of Austria, full of their congratulations. On the occasion of the announcement of the Empress's pregnancy there was a theatrical performance at the Court, and a drawing room was held in the grand apartments.

On December 2, the anniversary of the coronation and of the battle of Austerlitz, the Emperor gave an audience to the senate, which came to thank him for the communication of the news of the Empress's pregnancy, and to offer its congratulations on the happy event. There were theatrical performances, illuminations, mass, and a *Te Deum* in the Tuileries chapel. Twelve young women, dowered by the Empress, were led to the altar by the mayors in the metropolitan church, large sums of money were distributed in charity, and, in one word, the greatest solemnity accompanied the announcement of an event which was of national importance.

One circumstance, of little importance in itself, but which nevertheless attracted attention at the time, was the admission of Madame de Mailly, the widow of the marshal of that name, to enjoy the rank and the privileges of the wives of the great officers of the crown, and the authorization which she received to resume her title of *Maréchale.* In consequence, a note of invitation was addressed to Madame de Mailly, on the occasion of the solemnity of January 1 following, and she came to take possession of the rank awarded to her. About the same time the Minister of the Interior introduced a deputation from the Lyons traders to the Empress. The deputation presented her with a magnificent dress of Lyons manufacture, which the Empress wore on New Year's Day.

As soon as the Empress's pregnancy had been made public the Emperor created a society of maternal charity, the purpose of which was to assist poor women in childbirth, and to provide for their needs and the rearing of their children. Napoleon named the Empress patroness of this society, the vice presidents being Madame de Ségur, the wife of the grand master of ceremonies, and Madame Pastoret. This society was composed of one thousand ladies designated by the Empress, of fifteen lady dignitaries, of a grand council which had its seat in Paris, and of councils of administration in the departments, and finally of a secretary-general who was the grand almoner, and of a treasurer-general. Besides the motives of charity which prompted the Emperor to found this association he was anxious to put the Empress forward, and to win public sympathy to her side. The fund of the society was an income of five hundred thousand francs, invested in government stock, drawn from the extraordinary domain, and from voluntary subscriptions, the number of which exceeded that fixed upon.

The Emperor appointed a governess to the children of France and selected the Countess de Montesquiou, the wife of the Grand Chamberlain; a choice which was unanimously approved of. Born in a lofty rank, Madame de Montesquiou enjoyed a reputation which she had worthily won. She was forty-six years old, and a woman of untarnished reputation. Pious, her devotion was free from bigotry. She had great simplicity of manners, a firm character, and solid principles. She united all the qualities which were desirable for the proper fulfillment of the important duties which the Emperor, acting on his own inspiration, had confided to her.

The Empress's pregnancy advanced favorably. Her condition was betrayed by frequent temporary indispositions, which delighted Napoleon. He surrounded Marie Louise with tokens of his solicitude, held her up in his arms, and encouraged her with the kindest attentions. I was often present at these family scenes, in which Napoleon's loving nature showed itself. Only those who did not know him can have accused him of want of feeling. When the weather was fine, the Empress used to walk on the Tuileries terrace, which skirts the river. This terrace had been shut off with breast-high railings, and it was reached by means of a staircase ascending from the ground floor of the palace. Later on a pretty cottage was built at the end of this terrace, where the King of Rome used to spend the fine spring days when the Court was in residence at the Tuileries.

At last arrived the moment when the Empress was to be delivered, a moment waited for with such keen impatience by Napoleon, impatience shared, it may be said in all truth, by the whole of France. One hundred and one cannon shots announced, on the morning of March 20, that the King of Rome was born. The birth of a prince was to be saluted with one hundred and one cannon shots, only twenty-one were to be fired if the child were a princess. One can hardly imagine with what anxiety the first cannon-shots were counted. Deep silence prevailed until the twenty-first. But when the twenty-second boomed forth an explosion of applause and of cheering burst out which was reechoed simultaneously from every corner of Paris. The public enthusiasm was general, and no contemporary will deny this. The bearing of the child, however, on whom such great hopes were fixed, was to be a very laborious one.

Tanta molis erat Romanam condere gentem![*]

The first pains had been felt on the evening before—March 19, 1811. They were endurable until daybreak, when they ceased altogether, and Marie Louise was able to get to sleep. Napoleon had spent the first part of the night by her bedside; then, seeing that she had gone to sleep, he went up to his rooms and took a bath. The members of the Imperial family, the grand dignitaries, the principal officers and ladies of the Court had been summoned to the palace as soon as the first pains had been felt. But, towards five o'clock in the morning, the accoucheur, M. Dubois, being of opinion that the birth could not take place for another twenty-four hours, everybody had been sent away by the Emperor. Mesdames de Montebello, Montesquiou and Luçay had remained alone with the doctor, the nurse, the *dames d'annonce,* and the chambermaids. An hour after Napoleon had returned to his apartments, the Empress woke up in such pain that a speedy delivery was expected. Doctor Dubois, however, saw that the birth would be a very difficult one, and that this was one of the least frequent and most dangerous cases. The Emperor was in a state of perfect serenity, when M. Dubois suddenly opened the door and, in a great state of dismay, announced that the first stages of the accouchement were giving him the greatest anxiety. Without waiting to listen to the explanations which the doctor began to give, Napoleon cried out, from the bottom of his heart: "Above all save the mother." Then springing from his bath he hastily wrapped himself in a dressing gown and ran downstairs to the Empress's room, followed by Dubois. He approached the bed and hiding his anxiety embraced her tenderly, and encouraged her with words of comfort. The presence of the Emperor, the calm which in appearance reigned upon his face, though in his heart he was a prey to mortal anxiety, gave courage to Dubois. The latter had asked that some leading physicians should be called in for a consultation. The Emperor had refused, telling the doctor that he had chosen him because he trusted him, and that the Empress was to be treated just as if she were the wife of any ordinary man. Dubois commenced the painful operation with the skill and the sang-froid which he happily possessed. The labor did not proceed, the child presented itself legs foremost. The pains of the Empress increased in intensity. She was struck with terror, and cried out that they meant to sacrifice her. Dubois saw himself forced to use the forceps to free the child's head. Napoleon, a prey to silent agitation, watched this painful scene, encouraging all present by his brave attitude. At last, after many efforts, and in the midst of so much anguish, the so-impatiently-desired child came to light. It was a son, pale, motionless, and to all appearances lifeless. In spite of all the measures taken in such cases, the child remained seven minutes without giving any signs of life. The Emperor standing in front of him was following in silence and with an air of profound attention, every movement of the accoucheur, when at last he saw the child's breast rise, the mouth open and a breath exhaled. He feared lest it might be the first and last, but a cry escaping from the child's lungs tells him that his son has taken possession of life. All anxiety then ceases. In the effusion of his joy Napoleon bent over the child, seized it in his arms, with a spontaneous movement, carried it to the door of the drawing room in which all the grandees of his Empire were assembled and presenting it to them said: "Here is the King of Rome." He then returned, and placed the child back in M. Dubois's hands saying: "I give you back your child." Archchancellor Cambacérès and Berthier, Prince of Neufchâtel,

[*] Such a great task it was to found the Roman race!

were present in the Empress's bedroom, as witnesses of the accouchement. The Emperor, after he had received the congratulations of those present, insisted on going in person to announce the news of the birth of his son to the whole household. He was still under the influence of the painful sight of the Empress's delivery, and said that he would have preferred being present at a battle. The news of this happy event had spread over Paris as by magic. When the big bell of Notre Dame, and the cannon made it public, a large crowd had already assembled in the garden under the windows of the palace. To restrain the crowd, and to prevent it from disturbing the repose of the august patient, a cord had been stretched along the whole length of this terrace (which since then has been turned into a parterre by King Louis Philippe) from the railing at the Pont Royal to the Pavilion de l'Horloge. This feeble barrier impressed the crowd more than a wall would have done. The spectators, whose number increased every minute, even kept themselves at a respectful distance from the cord. General silence, a proof of popular sympathy and interest, was observed. From the interior of his apartments, Napoleon contemplated with visible emotion, this sight, so pleasant for him.

The officers of the imperial household, pages, and couriers were dispatched with letters and messages for the great corporations of the state, for the "good cities" and for the French and foreign ambassadors and ministers. The pages, sent to the municipal corporations received great marks of favor at their hands. The Paris and Turin municipal councils voted pensions to the bearers of the happy news. The good Empress Josephine was not forgotten. Napoleon sent a page to her in Navarre, and he answered the letter which this page brought back to him, with his usual brevity but with the affectionate cordiality which he always preserved for his first wife.

On the same evening the new-born child was baptized in the Tuileries chapel by the Cardinal Grand Almoner, with all the ceremonies in use at the old court of France.

On the morrow the Emperor, seated on the throne, received the congratulations of the court, the senate, the legislative body and other corporations of the state, the leading authorities and the diplomatic corps. On leaving this solemn audience a visit was paid to the King of Rome who was lying in the magnificent silver-gilt cradle which, on the previous 5th of March, had been presented to the Emperor in the name of the city of Paris, by Count Frochot, Prefect of the Seine, accompanied by the municipal council.

The Grand Chancellor of the Legion of Honor, and the Grand Chancellor of the order of the Iron Crown, laid the grand cordons of their orders on the cradle. Some days later, Prince Schwarzenberg, the Austrian ambassador, presented the decoration of the order of St. Stephen.

The forms used on this occasion, borrowed as they were from the ancient customs of the monarchy, have appeared to some severe critics as servile and frivolous acts. They were, however, only the consequence of the establishment of the Empire. The sage, no doubt, in the independence of his solitude, the speculative philosopher, the austere republican, will look with an eye of pity on this empty ceremonial, and will see in it nothing but the practices of flattery; but it is not with abstract ideas that the exigencies of a crown must be considered. There are usages and conventions consecrated by time, which, although puerile in the eyes of those who ordain them, are nevertheless, in a monarchy, enjoined by the hierarchy of functions, by the necessity of enforcing habits of respect and deference towards those who hold the power, and finally of avoiding that familiarity which is inherent to the national character, but which is infinitely harmful to the prestige which should be preserved by the sovereign power. It would, moreover, have been unwise to isolate oneself from the other European monarchies, and, by exhibiting contempt for their customs, to keep alive a state of distrust which was already in existence, and which it behooved the French government to calm.

I have spoken of the disadvantages of too great familiarity. Military customs indeed, republican manners, and the confusion of ranks, inspired by a spirit of equality, had everywhere authorized an independence of bearing and language which people did not seem able to moderate, even towards those who occupied the highest posts in the state. The dignity of the rank occupied by Napoleon from the time of his accession to the Consulate, and the respect due to his authority, did not allow him to tolerate this excess of familiarity. I was still present at the games of base and of Blind Man's Bluff, at La Malmaison, in which the First Consul used to take part. He had to give them up because these games gave rise to inadvertencies which could be excused by the kind of *camaraderie* which they established, but the abuse of which might degenerate into license and cast ridicule on the person of the Head of the state. The following anecdote, which will support this theory, can do no harm to the respect due to the memory of the illustrious Lannes. One day the First Consul had ordered some Arab horses, which had been given him, to be brought into the courtyard of the castle at La Malmaison. Lannes proposed to the First Consul to play him a match at billiards for one of these horses. Napoleon consented. He wanted to lose, and had to lose, and his adversary won the match with great ease. "I have beaten thee," he said to the First Consul whom he was in the habit of addressing in the second person singular, "and so I have the right to choose." And without waiting for the permission which he did not ask, he runs up and examines the horses one after the other, and choosing the handsomest, has it saddled, and jumping into the saddle says: "Goodbye, Bonaparte. I shan't dine here. I'm off, because if I stayed thou wouldst be capable of taking thy horse back again." The First Consul had no time to answer. Lannes was already out of sight. To prevent a repetition of such scenes, Napoleon thought it right to remove Lannes for some time, but to show him that his friendship for him was still the same, he appointed him to an honorable post, namely that of French ambassador to Lisbon.

General Dutaillis, while still a simple officer, used to address Berthier, who afterwards became Prince of Wagram and of Neufchâtel, in the second person singular. The First Consul put a stop to this familiarity, at least in public.

If Napoleon, recognizing the disadvantages of familiarity, had been obliged to forbid it, he was none the less good and indulgent in his usual intercourse. He was chary of praise, from principle, but his satisfaction manifested itself in more affectionate ways, and by rewards which had sometimes to be waited for, but which always came at the right moment. There are few persons who, by reason of their offices, or through particular circumstances, approached his person who have not some instance of his kindness to relate. It would take too long to quote all the stories that might be cited in support of this statement. Another anecdote, however, which I will relate will prove that Napoleon always endeavored to make amends for the pain he might have caused by the sharpness of his reproaches. During one of the last campaigns made by the Emperor in person, Gudin, a son of the regretted general who was killed at Valoutina, in Russia, was with him as page in attendance. This page, seeing the Emperor getting on horseback in the absence of the equerry on service, wanted to help him. In his eagerness, the young man did it in such a manner that the Emperor hurt himself as he fell into the saddle and cried out involuntarily. Epithets of "clumsy fellow," "lout," and so on, poured forth on the poor page, who slunk off in consternation at his clumsiness. The Emperor, having recovered from his accident, set off at a gallop, followed by his escort. Having reached the place where he wanted to stop, and having spent some minutes in examining the country, he looked round and saw the doleful face of the page. Napoleon motioned to him to approach. The Emperor told young Gudin that he was obliged to him for his attention, and his assistance. "But," he added, "you should set about it differently. When you want to help a man on to horseback, you shouldn't offer him your left arm, but should support him with your right arm until he is in the saddle. Go, my lad, and remember that." So saying Napoleon gave him a little pat on his cheek which was a sign of goodwill on his part, and sent the page away comforted and grateful.

I also wish to relate another occurrence, which chronologically is not in its place, but which can be told here in illustration of what I have said. I cannot omit it, because it merits being told just as it occurred, seeing that either with a bad intention, or perhaps without any such intention, it has been misstated. One day, while Napoleon was crossing the blue drawing room at Saint Cloud, he found a woman there who was remarkably stout, and who waddled up to him as fast as her obesity would allow of, muttering some words, which, owing to the emotion she was experiencing at seeing the Emperor, were totally unintelligible. Napoleon, having asked her for her name, learned that she was Mademoiselle Despaux, a milliner, who, in spite of her marriage with Monsieur Hix, had kept the name by which she was known in business. The Emperor was very angry that, in spite of his formal and often repeated orders that no tradesmen, coming to work upon the Empress Josephine's easygoing nature, were to be admitted into the palace, a milliner should have dared to enter the apartments of the palace and present herself before him. He accordingly at once sent for the officer of the guard, and sharply ordered him to put her out. This officer transmits the order to two gendarmes who were on duty and these led the woman on foot to the bottom of the slope which leads from the bridge of St. Cloud to the palace. Poor Madame Despaux, who was so fat that she could hardly walk, on arriving at the bottom of the slope asked to be allowed to get into her carriage, which was waiting for her, because she was tired out; but this was refused. On arriving on the road to Paris she asked where she was being taken to. The answer was: "A la Force." The officer, seeing the Emperor's excitement, had imagined that this was the severe order which had been given. Napoleon had ordered that Madame Despaux should be put to the door. The officer thought he had said to La Force. At the idea of prison Madame Despaux fell into a violent fit of hysterics. Her husband, who accompanied her, was in a state of great distress about his wife's position, when a savior appeared in the form of a man who ran up and told the gendarmes to set her free. General Duroc hearing with what severity Madame Despaux had been treated, had told it to the Emperor, who, indignant that his orders should have been misunderstood, charged the marshal to have the woman set free at once, and expressed his regret at the mistake, or the excess of zeal, which had been committed in his name. One can now judge how mistaken are those who said that Napoleon had had this woman locked up at Bicètre, where, according to the story, she expiated with a week's imprisonment the crime she had committed in presenting herself at the palace, and in disobeying the order which the sovereign had imposed.

The stage and the poets vied with each other in assiduity in celebrating the birth of the King of Rome. The publishers started a competition on this occasion—a competition of homages, in which the most famous poets took part. It would take too long a time to give all their names, but I will simply mention two young poets who gave a foretaste of their talents on this occasion, and showed signs of the celebrity which their works have since then acquired. Casimir Delavigne, who had only just left school, composed a dithyrambic poem in honor of the birth of the Emperor's heir. This ode, which was full of merit of the first order, awakened hopes for the young author which were fully realized in the future. The poem was brought to me by the good and obliging Guillard, author of *Œdipe à Colone,* a tragedy which has not been surpassed in our days in its class. This author, who formerly had received my first clumsy attempts at poetry with perfect and indulgent good grace, had remained one of my friends. I laid Casimir Delavigne's ode before the Emperor whose penetration excelled in distinguishing true merit in all its varieties. Napoleon judged this piece very much more favorably and rightly than the arbitrators in the competition had done, in which this ode only gained one of the last prizes. The Emperor admired the young author's talent, and gave orders that a special present should be given to him by way of encouragement.

Peter Lebrun, who has become a peer of France, and a director of the Royal Printing House, also paid on this occasion a tribute of homage and gratitude to Napoleon. The Emperor had noticed this young man during one of the visits which he was fond of making to the principal public schools. When Lebrun's ode on the Battle of Jena was presented to him, Napoleon was so pleased that he awarded the author a pension of 1200 francs a year, which the latter retained. The poet's gratitude inspired him, in 1822, with a touching lyrical poem on the Emperor's death.

The feelings of devotion which Madame de Genlis affected for Napoleon and his family prevented her from being silent in the face of the great event of the birth of the heir to the Empire, an event which gave her an opportunity of showing the variety of talents with which she was gifted. She accordingly sent the Emperor a child's song, the music and words of which she had composed. The notes of this lullaby were represented by little roses, which had been delicately drawn and illuminated by her hand. This little composition altogether was carried out with the neatness and elegance which Madame de Genlis displayed in her manual work.

The portraits and presentments of the young King were multiplied by painting, sculpture, modelling, engraving, and medal carving. Gérard made a charming half-length portrait of him, surrounded by the attributes of babyhood. Prudhon painted the imperial child asleep in a shrubbery, in the midst of a group of flowers, amongst which the "Imperial" raised itself, hanging softly over his forehead. The harmony of the composition, the delicacy of the forms, the graceful abandonment of posture, the lifelike sleep, render this picture a delicious one.

Public rejoicings of every kind, a general illumination, fêtes improvised by the corporations, were the manifestations of public happiness. The archbishops and bishops published pastoral letters; all the Courts of Europe, with which we were at peace, sent their congratulations and extraordinary ambassadors to the Emperor. Amongst the number of ambassadors was Prince Poniatowski, who was sent by the King of Saxony, as Grand Duke of Warsaw, to be present at the ceremony of baptism. Napoleon, who was very fond indeed of this sovereign, and of his representative, received Poniatowski with distinction, and made him a present of £12,000 and of an estate in Poland. The Kings of Spain, Naples, and Westphalia had come to Paris in person.

Doctor Dubois, who had delivered the Empress, was magnificently rewarded. He received 100,000 francs, and the title of Baron. This *accouchement,* which had necessitated the use of surgical instruments, had been of so serious a character that the doctor had considered it his duty to tell the Emperor that a second confinement would inevitably put the Empress's life in danger. This revelation made an impression on Napoleon's mind, and had consequences which could not be foreseen at the time. The birth of other children would without doubt have exercised a salutary influence on the Empress's feelings, and, in multiplying, the bonds which united the two spouses, would perhaps have rendered their separation more difficult. M. Dubois, obeying his conviction, had acted as an honest man; but nature, whose power is greater than that of science, has hidden resources of which science has no knowledge and in this case undertook to refute the clever practitioner eight years later.

A month after her confinement the Empress was churched in the Tuileries chapel. The ceremony was performed with a certain amount of solemnity, and on this occasion Marie Louise received the homage of her whole court. The birth of an heir to a lofty position, which had been created by so many efforts, appeared destined to be a guarantee of longevity for the new dynasty. The joy which was manifested by all classes of society was principally caused by the hope, everywhere entertained, of seeing this child become the genius of peace, and close at last the gates of the temple of Janus. The Emperor had no such illusions. England was not yet discouraged. Her intrigues and her gold continued to exercise their influence over the continental powers, and the future, in Napoleon's eyes, was full of storms.

With the return of the fine weather the Emperor and Empress went to spend a week at Rambouillet, to take exercise in hunting. Napoleon was, so to speak, *en famille* in this residence, which was simpler and lest vast than the other imperial mansions; but he was not able to prolong his stay there, because he was too cramped.

Joseph, King of Spain, came to see the Emperor here. Napoleon had sent him General Defrance, one of his equerries, to announce to him the birth of his son, and to inform him that he was to be one of the child's godfathers. Joseph took this opportunity to have an interview, which he deemed indispensable, with his brother, to regulate Spain's present interests, and to come to an understanding on the difficult position which the inevitable presence of an auxiliary army, the leaders of which treated Spain almost like a conquered country, caused him.

Napoleon, weary with the enormous sacrifice of blood and treasure which the occupation of the Peninsula caused to France, had instituted military governments in the country, at the head of which French generals had been placed. King Joseph had sent MM. d'Azanza and Hervas to Paris to complain about this measure. M. Hervas had even brought with him a letter, in which the King offered the Emperor to resign the crown, and asked him for his authorization to withdraw from the country where he was able neither to do good nor to prevent evil. The King stated that the establishment of these military governments was looked upon by the Spaniards—even those who were most attached to his person—as an attack against the integrity of the Kingdom, that this negation of his sovereignty seemed to them to foretoken the future abolition of their nationality, and lastly that this dictatorship, unless it was to be a temporary one, destroyed what little good his efforts had been able to produce.

King Joseph, as a matter of fact, had just reduced Andalusia, as much by persuasion as by force, to a state of submission. He had declared to the Spaniards in this province his firm resolution not to consent to any dismemberment of the monarchy, nor to any sacrifice which was likely to injure the national independence. He had promised that if the English would evacuate Spanish territory, the French troops would also withdraw, and the king with them, if the nation should not adopt him. These assurances had calmed the excitement of the inhabitants of this province, and Joseph had been received in the principal towns of Andalusia with a favor which was calculated to deceive him. The Emperor persuaded his brother to return to Spain by promising him that the institution of military governments, a temporary measure, which had only been demanded by circumstances, should cease as soon as they were no longer necessary. He confirmed his intention of withdrawing the French troops if the English government, to which negotiations were to be proposed, was willing, as he had reason to hope, to evacuate Portugal, and to recognize Joseph, King of Spain, as soon as the Spanish nation should have consented to this; and if, on his side, he replaced the Braganza family on the throne. Napoleon had agreed to place the military governments under the orders of the King, and advised him to call the Cortes together as soon as possible. King Joseph returned to Madrid in the month of July with the hope that the negotiations with England would be successful, and at the same time with a promise that the integrity and independence of the Spanish monarchy should be guaranteed. On his return to Spain he was received with favor, as the bearer of good news which unfortunately was not be destined to be realized.

Chapter XI

About two months after the birth of his son, the Empress having recovered her health, the Emperor wished to go and visit the works at the harbor of Cherbourg, so as, by his presence, to stimulate this important undertaking. The importance of this harbor, situated opposite to England, had attracted all Napoleon's attention, and in consequence, from the time of his accession to power, he had continued the works there which Louis XVI had commenced. The abandonment in which this gigantic undertaking had been left during the crisis of the Revolution had entailed its almost total ruin. During the stay of the Court at Rambouillet, Marie Louise used to be present at the hunts in her open carriage and sometimes on horseback; the sovereigns then left Rambouillet for Caen, where they stayed three days. Napoleon rode over the surroundings of this town, accompanied by the Minister of Marine and the general inspectors of roads and bridges. The journey was continued from Caen to Cherbourg, where, on the day of his arrival, the Emperor, according to his custom, began inspecting from daybreak the fortifications and the heights which commanded the city. He visited the harbor, the dockyards, the roads, and the fleet. He lunched with the Empress on the dyke, and from where they sat at table they could see the English ships cruising in the distance. Napoleon ordered the fleet to perform their evolutions, and took the Empress on board the Admiral's ship, which she examined in all its details—a new spectacle for her. The Emperor, after having inspected the fleet, went down into the vast basin, which for many years past was being cut out of the granite. This gigantic work—a masterpiece of patience—was approaching completion. The basin, which is forty feet deep, accommodates fifty line vessels. It was worked at with picks, which only removed a flake of stone at each stroke. It resembled an immense trough, cut out of one single stone, containing many millions of cubic feet of water.

Having left Cherbourg, the Emperor stopped at Saint Lo, at Alençon, and at Chartres, and was back again at St. Cloud on June 4. This little journey, which lasted three weeks, was the rehearsal of a longer journey which Napoleon proposed to take in Holland, and for which he was preparing the Empress. The health of this princess had been shaken by a most painful confinement but she was now completely restored.

Useful measures and acts of benevolence—by which the cities, which their Majesties passed through profited—as well as almsgiving, marked their passage everywhere. Apart from the grants of assistance, and the pensions which the Emperor awarded on the funds of the Civil List, I was charged to keep a cash-box, to which the treasurer of the crown paid the sum of 10,000 francs each month. This fund was used in connection with the presents or charities which Napoleon distributed, and which I paid over on a verbal order transmitted to me by the aide-de-camp or the equerry in attendance. These expenses were entered into an account book, which the Emperor checked at the end of each month.

The Emperor and the Empress were everywhere received with enthusiasm. The birth of an heir to the name and glory of Napoleon had increased his popularity to the highest degree. The mother of the King of Rome shared in these manifestations of affection, and knew how to respond to them by the amenity of the reception which she accorded to the authorities and inhabitants of the departments.

Her Majesty's return to Paris was hastened by the approach of the fêtes which were being prepared for them at Paris, at St. Cloud, and at Trianon, during the journey to Cherbourg. These festivities, which accompanied the ceremony of the King of Rome's christening, were in point of magnificence in no way inferior to that of the marriage. During the three months and a half which followed on the return from Cherbourg, the Court resided in succession at St. Cloud, in Paris, Trianon and Compiègne.

The young prince was christened at Notre Dame, in the presence of the three great Corporations of state (the senate, the Council of State, and the legislative body), the magistrates and law officers, the Municipal councils, and the deputations from the fifty "good cities," and of the diplomatic corps. The fine bearing of the troops, who made a line from the Tuileries to Notre Dame, and the magnificence of the imperial procession were an imposing spectacle; but what increased the magnificence of this triumphal march was the immense crowd of Parisian and foreign spectators, which was so great that one might have said that the inhabitants of every house had come down into the streets and public squares. All along the route followed by the procession the houses were draped with hangings, and flags floated at every window. At the sight of the carriage in which the imperial child was lying on the knees of his governess and which preceded the carriage of Their Majesties the air reechoed with general acclamations, and cries for his prosperity. Unusual pomp presided over the religious service. The godfather who was the Emperor of Austria, was represented by the Grand Duke of Würzburg. The second godfather was King Joseph. The godmother was the Lady Mother (Napoleon's mother). The second godmother was the Queen of Naples, represented by Queen Hortense. Silence and reserve were maintained during the ceremony; but, when Napoleon, taking his son into his arms, showed him to those who were present, cheers and applause, which had been restrained by the sanctity of the act and by the solemnity of the place, broke out on every side, awakening the echoes of the ancient cathedral.

On leaving the cathedral Their Majesties proceeded to the Hôtel de Ville where the Prefect, followed by the municipal body, received them and offered them a banquet and concert in the name of the city. After the concert the sovereigns walked through the drawing rooms in which had assembled the persons who had been invited, and with whom they conversed. Towards midnight the Emperor and Empress returned to the Tuileries by the light of illuminations which lighted them all the way home. More or less ingenious allegories and emblems interpreted the expression of a genuine feeling. The weather on this fine day was serene and calm. Public rejoicings, consisting of theatrical performances, dances, distribution of provisions, illuminations, and balloon ascents, were offered to the people in the Champs Élysées and other places. Public rejoicings took place in all the provincial departments.

A deputation from the municipal council of Toulouse presented the Emperor with a most costly manuscript on vellum, a masterpiece of calligraphy, enriched with miniatures picked out with gold, and with each page framed in a vignette, the design of which varied on each page. This manuscript, which was of priceless value, forming a quarto volume, bound in *nacarat* velvet, was Charlemagne's book of hours; it had cost the artists who had taken part in its production seven years' labor. This prince had presented it to the abbey of Saint Sernin near Toulouse—destroyed today—in memory of the christening of his son Pepin. The municipal council had considered that this monument of the arts of the ninth century, which had been preserved with religious care, would be properly disposed of if Napoleon became its proprietor. Since Providence had allowed an identical occurrence to renew itself one thousand years later, the presentation of this manuscript to Charlemagne's successor, on the occasion of the birth of his heir, seemed very fitting and appropriate. A deputation of the members of the council proceeded, in consequence, to Paris, to offer the precious manuscript to the new Charlemagne. The Emperor accepted the present and placed the manuscript in his library. This book of hours is at present in the Louvre library.

Some days after the banquet at the Hôtel de Ville a fête took place in the private park of St. Cloud which reminded the Empress of her native country. Orchestras, dispersed in the shrubberies, played dances and waltzes which were performed by the dancers of the Opera dressed in the costumes of German shepherds and peasants. An interlude: *La Fête du Village,* composed by Etienne, and set to music by Nicolo, was performed on an open air stage. A lady aeronaut of the day, Madame Blanchard—made an ascent in a balloon, and remained floating for some time on a level with the tops of the trees.

At a given signal the balloon rose majestically into the air. Then a large firework star exploded, and for the space of some minutes filled the sky with dazzling light. Unfortunately a heavy fall of rain spoiled the end of the evening, and produced some disorder.

The amusements of the Court followed one upon the other almost without interruption. August 15 brought with it the Emperor's fête and the fête of the King of Rome, which were celebrated at St. Cloud with a display of fireworks which was carried out by the artillery of the Imperial Guard, and in which the initials of the two spouses and their son figured. Anthems appropriate for the occasion were sung. Ten days later—August 25—was the Empress's fête, and this was celebrated at Trianon. The weather had become splendid, and the delicious gardens of the Petit Trianon, the buildings, lakes, islands, of this magic resort lent themselves to scenes and combinations of which the organizers of the fête were able to make the best possible use. A piece composed by M. Alissan de Chazet, entitled "*Le Jardinier de Schönbrunn,*" was performed in the theatre at Trianon. This performance was accompanied by a ballet, which was executed by the principal opera dancers. The Emperor, with the Empress on his arm, and followed by almost the entire Court, walked about in the little park for some time. Cantatas, which had been set to music by Paer, were sung in their honor, and the fête terminated with a splendid supper.

This fête, which was the most agreeable of all, ended the series of public rejoicings given to celebrate the marriage of the Emperor and the birth of the King of Rome. The grace and dignity displayed by Marie Louise on this occasion attracted general attention. Napoleon seemed happy. He was affable at home, and affectionate towards the Empress. When he found her grave, he amused her by good-humored remarks, or disconcerted her reserve by embracing her in a cordial and hearty manner. In public he treated her with great respect, and with a dignity which did not exclude a sort of noble familiarity. His manners to her in general expressed an affection full of confidence. At the same time, wishing to preserve in its primitive purity the innocence which had so much charm for him, and to remove from her the suspicions which French lightness usually admits, Napoleon had established in the Empress's household an order of service by which she was so fenced in that one might have thought him jealous. Marie Louise's timidity, her love of family life, her mistrust of herself, and the prejudices with which she had been inspired against most of the persons at Court, and against the spirit of mockery which is so characteristic of the French, kept this princess away from *liaisons* which might have displeased the Emperor, and which, moreover, had no attraction in her eyes. The habits of favoritism in which she had been brought up, and which in her isolation she needed, were bestowed on the lady who, by the advice of her husband, was admitted to her intimacy. The attachment which she conceived for the Duchess of Montebello, her lady in waiting, filled this void. Marie Louise never chatted familiarly with the persons attached to her service, but, however, always treated them with indulgence and kindness.

The Emperor wished her to take horse exercise, and Marie Louise received her first lessons in riding in the riding school of St. Cloud. Napoleon used to walk by her side, holding her hand, while the equerry held the horse's bridle. He calmed her fears, and encouraged her. She took advantage of her lessons, grew courageous, and ended by being able to keep her seat very well. When, to her master's credit, she had become a horsewoman, the lessons were sometimes continued in the avenue of the private park which led out from the family drawing room, so called because it was adorned with portraits of all the members of the imperial family. Napoleon, when he had a few minutes to spare, after lunch, would send for his horse, get on horseback, dressed in silk stockings and buckled shoes, and would ride by the Empress's side. He would excite her horse, and set off at a gallop, laughing heartily when she cried out for fear of falling. It is true that this danger did not exist, for grooms were standing all along the avenue ready to stop the horse, and to prevent a fall.

After the fêtes at Trianon the court returned to Compiègne, where it remained three weeks. This palace, where the Emperor had received Marie Louise on her arrival in France, was at that time the object of his special preference. He had ordered works to be carried out on the estate which were under the direction of Berthault, the architect, and were being executed with a rapidity which was nothing less than marvelous. New gardens had been created by this architect and an entirely new appearance had been given to the residence. So great were the embellishments that had been effected that the park seemed totally transformed. It was now one of the most beautiful and most elegant of the Emperor's pleasure houses. Their Majesties' arrival at Compiègne was saddened by the death of General Ordener, Governor of the Palace, who was struck down on the following day by apoplexy, and who died under the eyes of Doctor Lerminier. The general had come the day before to Compiègne to receive the Emperor and Empress, and Napoleon had complimented him on his good health. He regarded him as one of the bravest and best of his officers. General Ordener had a long time commanded, with distinction to himself, the mounted grenadiers of the guard. His rough plain-spokenness sometimes amused the ladies of the court, but he was one of those men who are endowed with an iron constitution—both moral and physical, rather uncultivated, perhaps; but, in any case, of a loyalty without flaw, of rigid principles, trained in the laws of severe discipline, and incapable of compounding with his duties.

In the meanwhile the King of Rome was growing in strength and beauty, under the vigilant care of Madame Montesquiou, who loved him as a son, and who had for him the most minute solicitude. He was carried every morning to his mother, who kept him with her during the hour of her toilette. In the daytime, in the intervals between her music and drawing lessons, Marie Louise used to go to the young prince's apartment, and work at his side at some piece of needlework. Often, followed by the nurse who carried the child, she would take him to his father while he was at work. When he was announced Napoleon would rise to go and receive him, nobody being allowed to enter his cabinet; the nurse was forced to remain outside, and Marie Louise would be asked to bring her son in herself. The Empress had so little trust in herself in taking the child from the arms of the nurse that Napoleon would hasten to go and meet her, and would take his son into his arms, and carry him away, covering him with kisses. This workroom, which was the scene of the birth of so many skilful maneuvers intended to repel the attacks of our eternal enemies, and so many vast and generous schemes of government, was very often also the silent witness of Napoleon's paternal tenderness. How often have I watched the Emperor there, keeping his son at his side as though he were impatient to initiate him in the art of government. Either seated on his favorite settee near the mantelpiece, which was decorated with two magnificent bronze busts of Scipio and of Hannibal, occupied in reading some important report; or going to his writing table, which was cut out in the center, and the sides of which spread out like wings—covered with his numerous papers—to sign a dispatch, each word of which had to be weighed; his son, seated on his knees or pressed against his bosom, never left him. Endowed with a marvelous power of concentration, Napoleon was able at one and the same time to attend to serious matters, and to lend himself to a child's fancies. Sometimes putting aside all his preoccupations he would lie down on the floor at the side of his darling son and play with him as a child himself, looking out for what would amuse him or spare him vexation.

Napoleon had some little maneuver pieces made. These were little bits of mahogany of different colors and lengths. The tops were fretted, and these pieces represented battalions, regiments, and divisions. When the Emperor wanted to try some new combination of troops, some new military evolution, he made use of these pieces of wood, which he set up on the carpet of the floor so as to give himself a larger field for maneuver. Sometimes his son would surprise him seriously occupied with the positions of these pieces, preparing himself in this way for one of those clever maneuvers which assured him victory in his battles. The child, lying on the floor at his side, pleased with the color and the form of these maneuver pieces—which reminded him of his toys—would at each instant touch them with his hand and disturb the order of battle at a decisive moment just when the enemy was about to be beaten. But so great was Napoleon's presence of mind, and his affection for his son, that he did not allow himself to be disturbed by the disorder into which the child had thrown his strategical combinations, and contented himself, without manifesting any impatience, with putting the pieces back into their right order. His patience and kindness for his child were inexhaustible. At such times it was not only the heir of his name and glory that he loved in this son of his. When he held him in his arms and intoxicated himself with his caresses, it was not pride or ambition which predominated in his mind.

The Emperor used to lunch alone. Madame de Montesquiou used to carry the King of Rome to his father at lunch every day. Napoleon would take him on his knees, amuse himself in petting him and putting his glass to the boy's lips, and would laugh heartily, chiding the child at the grimaces that it used to make when a drop of wine stung its tongue. One day when the child was putting its mouth out to take a piece of some food which his father offered it, Napoleon drew his hand back, and repeated this little practical joke twice. The third time, however, the young prince turned his head away, and obstinately refused to take the tit-bit. The Emperor expressing his surprise at this conduct, Madame de Montesquiou said that the child did not like people to try to deceive it, and added "he is proud and sensitive!" "He is proud and sensitive?" repeated the Emperor. "It is a very good thing. It is because he is like that that I love him!" Delighted to find these two qualities in his son, the Emperor embraced him with tenderness. He used to forget his cares and public business in these short moments, and the very few persons whom he used to admit to his intimacy during this meal hour were assured of being always received by him in the most gracious manner.

The Empress Josephine had asked as a favor to be allowed to have the King of Rome taken to her. Napoleon promised, but feared for her sake the emotion which the sight of this child must necessarily cause her. He, however, gave way before her pressing requests, and Madame de Montesquiou conducted the young prince to Bagatelle, a small pleasure house in the Bois de Boulogne. This took place without the knowledge of the Empress Marie Louise who was animated with a feeling of jealousy, which was based on the fear of the ascendancy which a woman who had been so loved by her husband might still retain over him. The excellent Princess could not restrain her tears at the sight of a child who recalled such painful memories and the privation of a happiness which Heaven had refused to her. She embraced him with transports. She seemed to take pleasure in the illusion produced by the thought that she was lavishing her caresses on her own child. She never wearied of admiring his strength and beauty, and could not detach herself from him. The moments during which she held him in her arms seemed to her very short.

Napoleon, who was the best of fathers, could not be otherwise than a good son, and had for his mother a constant and respectful affection. His tenderness for her in public was mingled with respect and gravity. He had given her a proof of this, a proof which this venerable woman appreciated above all others, when he had appointed her Patroness General of Charitable Institutions. Napoleon's mother was a Roman matron, both in appearance and by the loftiness of her character. Prosperity had no more dazzled her than bad fortune had cast her down. Her parsimony has been jested about, but her children always found her ready to help them with her private fortune. When the Emperor was at St. Helena his mother sent him a full account of her fortune, and begged him to dispose of whatever belonged to her, an offer which Napoleon did not accept. When somebody pointed out to her, at the time when she thus offered her property to her son, that she was reducing herself to indigence in this way: "What does it matter?" she answered; "when I shall have nothing more, I will take my stick, and I will go about begging alms for Napoleon's mother."

A pearl, which was celebrated for its size and the purity of its color, known by the name of the Peregrine pearl, had disappeared from the Spanish crown treasury during the troubles brought on in this country by the change of dynasty. Great search was made for this jewel. I do not know what result it had, but I think, though I cannot affirm it, that these investigations led to a discovery of another kind, namely of several letters addressed to Paris by Joachim, King of Naples. To judge from the terms of this correspondence it appeared certain that Murat's friends had thought that something might happen which would render the imperial throne vacant. Fouché, Talleyrand, and others had already thought of taking their precautions in view of such an event. The Emperor, having neither children nor any fixed successor at that time, King Murat might consider himself authorized to prepare himself to establish the claims he had to this succession. This ambition was perhaps excusable at a time when every head was excited by the splendid instances of prodigious fortunes. Napoleon seemed to think so, for he manifested no resentment against his brother-in-law. Fouché had said one day that if the throne ever became vacant, which with God's help should never be, he would take measures to get as much power into his hands as possible. The Emperor answered this remark with some words which were remembered: "You would do well. It would be your right."

Napoleon, however, thought it right to have the person in whose possession these letters were found—he was a chamberlain to King Joachim—arrested; and he was confined for three months in the prison at Vincennes. On leaving prison this officer was given the choice of returning to Naples or of staying in France, but not in Paris. He retired to an estate which he owned in Poitou, and the famous letters were deposited in the Imperial Archives.

These circumstances, and other reasons for discontent, irritated the King of Naples. His bad temper broke out when he was ordered to send a contingent of Neapolitan troops to join the French army. From the month of August of this year, 1811, the signs of a misunderstanding with Russia, and the hidden preparations for war which were beginning to be made by this power, obliged the Emperor to increase the garrison at Danzig, and to put the French army on a larger footing.

King Murat wished the Emperor rather to recall the French soldiers who had remained in the Kingdom of Naples. Napoleon had refused to do this, and then Joachim wanted to exact that the French who had remained in his service should naturalize themselves Neapolitan subjects. All the French asked for their leave, with the exception of one general, who occupied a high position in the King's household. General Exelmans, and generals and civil officers who were strongly attached to the king, and who had been presented with important offices at court, preferred to give up all these advantages rather than to lose their French nationality. Napoleon received with indignation the news of the pretensions set up by the King, his brother-in-law. A severely-worded decree reminded Murat of the fact that his kingdom was an integral part of the French Empire, and that the sovereign seated on the throne of Naples owed his crown to French valor. This decree proclaimed with cold disdain that every French citizen was *de jure* a citizen of the kingdom of Naples, and that any measure to the contrary, emanating from King Joachim, might in no case be applicable to French subjects. The King of Naples could not endure with calm the humiliation thus inflicted on him. The struggle of the opposite feelings of wounded pride and passionate affection for the Emperor, which raged within him, very nearly drove him mad. I have heard the Queen, his wife, say that she kept her husband isolated from everybody for two whole days, for fear that anybody should see the state of aberration into which he had fallen. In his rage King Joachim had even wished to exile the Queen to Castellamare, because she disapproved of the conditions of naturalization imposed on the French. Returning to a better state of mind Murat sent his wife to Paris to make peace with Napoleon. Napoleon really liked Joachim Murat. He spoke severely at first about his brother-in-law, but soon all traces of dissent disappeared on both sides. The King of Naples returned, as in the good times of the past, to bring to our ranks during the war with Russia, which broke out in the following year, the assistance of his heroic valor and the enthusiasm with which he knew how to inspire his troops, and especially the cavalry.

In the spring of 1811 there was a change in the Ministry, a circumstance which till then had only happened very rarely. As a matter of fact during Napoleon's reign, the ministers were, so to speak, irremovable. The Ministry of Foreign Affairs alone did not participate in this immutability. The vicissitudes undergone in consequence of the troubled state of our relations with Europe necessitated an occasional change in the direction of foreign affairs. In consequence, Count Daru entered the Ministry, where he took the place of the Duke of Bassano, who himself had replaced the Duke of Cadore. Count Daru brought to his new post that indefatigable ardor for work, which had attracted the Emperor's attention, those capacities, that rigidity of morals, and that uprightness which have always characterized the administrative career of this minister. Napoleon had in M. Daru a confidence which was absolute because it was founded on esteem. During the Emperor's stay in Moscow, M. Daru gave him an account of a private letter which he had just received from General Moreau's wife. This lady asked M. Daru to support a request which she was making to be allowed to land in France, where her presence was rendered necessary by certain family affairs. Napoleon, suspecting the real motive of Madame Moreau's request, a motive which was clearly exposed by subsequent events, refused this permission, but bore M. Daru no grudge for his action in this matter. When Moreau's presence at the headquarters of the allied troops, in 1813, was made known, the Emperor contented himself with reminding M. Daru of the communication which he had made to him at the Kremlin. If on the one hand Napoleon had a great respect for Count Daru, it cannot, on the other hand be said that he had any sympathy for him personally. He appreciated his work, and always found him useful, but he never showed him any expansive confidence. M. Daru's attitude towards the Emperor, on his side, was marked by a singular reserve. I am unable to say whether there was any reason for this minister's embarrassment in the presence of his sovereign, and whether the remembrance of his former relations with General Moreau, or some other reason, influenced his feelings towards Napoleon. Whatever may be the conjectures formed on this matter, the truth is that M. Daru served the Emperor with zeal and fidelity, but that the latter did not like him. M. Daru was convinced—I am sure that I do not know for what reason—that Napoleon did not trust him. In the last year of his life this minister did me the honor of telling me that each time that he went to see the Emperor he took the key of his writing-table with him in his pocket—ready, at the slightest expression of discontent on Napoleon's part, to hand him over this key, begging him to send for his family papers. "He would have seen," added M. Daru, "by comparing the inventory of my possessions when I entered his service, with the existing state of my affairs, that I had not increased my fortune in any illegitimate way."

Before speaking of the journey which the Emperor took, in 1811, with Marie Louise, I wish to say a word about a dispatch which was sent to him towards the end of May by Marshal Davout, who was commanding the troops stationed in the Hanseatic provinces. At the time of the first occupation of these provinces serious malversations of public money had been committed. The general who was at that time in command in this district and in Hanover, who since had reached a lofty destiny, was said to have tolerated this disorder. The magistrates of the States occupied by our armies had lent themselves to the sacrifices which were suggested to them as likely to be profitable to the interests of their towns. Prince d'Eckmuehl, who came to Hamburg long after, who was as inaccessible to corruption as he was a strict disciplinarian, insisted on a speedy payment of the taxes. The towns replied that it was only fair that the sums which they had already paid, and which amounted to about four millions, should be taken into account. As these sums had not been paid either into the army treasury or into the treasury of the extraordinary domain, the Marshal replied by demanding the local authorities to produce the proofs of payment of the war indemnities. After long hesitation the senate of Hamburg finally consented to hand in a list of people who had received either money or presents, together with a full account of the sums paid in cash or kind to each person named.

The names of persons of all classes, of officers of every rank, from the Marshal down to the commissary of wars, were to be found on this list; but in still greater number were the names of civil functionaries of every rank, from the ambassador down to his diplomatic agents and simple employees. Some had received sums of money, others presents for their wives or for themselves. The Emperor repeatedly insisting on seeing this list, received it at last from the Prince d'Eckmuehl. Napoleon placed it in the hands of the Minister of the Public Treasury, with orders to sue for the recovery of these sums which had thus been extorted or illegally received. The soldiers, for whom there was more excuse under the circumstances, were less roughly treated than the civilians who could justify themselves by no motive. The latter were accordingly more severely treated, but it was thought advisable to treat certain persons in high positions with tolerance. Some of the fraudulent bailees paid back what they had received. The fall of the Empire saved the most guilty. The resentment retained by the persons compromised in this affair can be imagined. There lies the reason of many desertions and outbreaks of hostility, which manifested themselves against the Emperor when he was no longer to be feared. The Duke of Cadore received orders to inform one of the diplomatic agents whose name was mentioned on the list supplied by the Hamburg senate, who had been plenipotentiary minister to the Hanseatic cities, that he had to count with him as a clerk with his master, and to pay over to the treasury of the Ministry of Foreign Affairs, seventy-five percent of the sums which he had received, this money to be applied to finishing a mansion which had been commenced on the Quai d'Orsay. and which was intended for the Ministry offices and residence. The reason of the order signified to Bourrienne by the Duke of Cadore is more in accordance with truth than the somewhat cynical answer of which the latter boasts in his Memoirs.

Since I have related an occurrence which shows that Napoleon, in spite of his vigilance, was unable to prevent all disorder, I will quote another of the same kind which took place later on, and which was not known, at least officially, by the Emperor, for what reason will be seen. During the 1807 campaign a war indemnity of three hundred thousand francs was imposed on the province of Erfurth. deputies from this province came to headquarters to ask for a reduction. Count Daru, to whom they addressed themselves, received them very badly, but they repeated their application so often that the minister told them that they did wrong to complain, seeing that the sum of three hundred thousand francs which had been demanded of them was not more than the resources of their provinces could afford. "If we only owe three hundred thousand francs," they answered, "we have paid." "Have you receipts in order?" In answer to this question they produced a receipt from the assigner of payments. Count Daru wrote to the latter who admitted to him that the Marshal in command of the army corps which was stationed at that time in the province, and who since was raised to a rank which put him above the reach of all jurisdiction, had allotted two hundred thousand francs out of the money received to himself, and had allowed him to keep one hundred thousand francs. Count Daru informed this functionary that unless the entire sum was paid into the army treasury within an assigned period, the Emperor would be informed of the matter. In consequence of this the assigner of payments made haste to pay over the three hundred thousand francs. He, however, declared that he had paid the whole sum out of his pocket, as the Marshal had refused to restore the two hundred thousand francs which he had appropriated. M. Daru never informed the Emperor of this affair, and it was only twenty years later that he revealed it in private conversation.

On September 19, 1811, Napoleon left Compiègne for his proposed journey in Holland. His object was to visit this peculiar country, the originality of which attracted his attention. He proposed to see the works which had either been finished or were in course of execution, necessary for binding his third capital to the metropolitan seat of the Empire, and intended to render communications between Amsterdam and Paris most rapid. The Emperor accordingly preceded the Empress, giving her rendezvous in Antwerp, as he wished to spare her the fatigues of a military journey, in which, moreover, she would have been forced to dispense with the pomp attaching to her rank. Marie Louise, after leaving Compiègne, proceeded to the castle of Laeken. Napoleon was not displeased at the idea of her appearing in provinces which formerly had been governed by the House of Austria. The Empress made several excursions to Brussels, where she was received as she had a right to expect. She showed herself at the theatre, and visited certain manufactories, where she ordered lace for a considerable amount. The Emperor wished to surround her journey to Holland with considerable splendor, and expressed his wish that the Empress should show herself everywhere surrounded by a brilliant court. As for himself, accompanied by only a small suite, he proceeded to Boulogne, where he spent three days, visiting the little coast harbors, inspecting the flotilla, and engaging it with some English cruisers over whom he secured a victory. From Boulogne Napoleon went towards Ostend and Breskens, a port situated opposite Flushing, where he had ordered certain works to be carried out. The weather was detestable, which did not prevent the Emperor from riding part of the way on horseback. He explored the island of Cadzand, and examined its forts in detail. His plan was to visit one by one the thirty vessels of the fleet at Antwerp, a review which would have benefited the fleet in particular and the navy in general. With this purpose in view Napoleon embarked on the *Charlemagne,* the admiral's vessel, on which Commander Missiessy had hoisted his standard. He was accompanied by his Minister of Marine. The weather was fairly fine, but it changed during the night, and from daybreak a violent storm raged, which lasted three days without diminishing in intensity. The equinoctial winds were so strong that no boat could be put to sea. The Emperor was accordingly forced to remain on board the *Charlemagne* in idleness, without being able to communicate with the land. He took advantage of this enforced stay to examine a report of the state of the fleet, in distributing rewards amongst the sailors, and, armed with his field-glasses, in contemplating the spectacle of the furious waters, whenever he was able to keep his legs on the bridge or on the deck. Napoleon's papers, and almost all his clothes were on board some boats and a yacht, which were dispersed by the wind into various ports along the coast. The pages and people of his household, who were in charge of these boats, were driven about at the mercy of the winds for four or five days, without being able to reach either the Emperor's ship, or to get back to land, menaced with destruction at every moment. Many thought of writing their wills without knowing whether these documents would survive them.

The tempest having calmed at last, and the sea having somewhat quieted, the Emperor took advantage of this circumstance to make his way to Flushing. He spent a day there which he employed in inspecting the immense works which were being carried out by his order, given after the withdrawal of the English expedition. The object of these works was to enable the armed fleet of the Escaut to enter into port, so as to be protected against hostile attack. Napoleon next embarked for Antwerp, sailing up the river and inspecting in turn the various forts which lie on either bank. He arrived at Antwerp in the night, and was joined there by the Empress next day. During a stay of four days in this city, where fêtes of every kind succeeded each other, the Emperor did not remain inactive for a single minute. His attention was entirely taken up with the city, and the military, maritime, and commercial establishments which his genius for organization had created in so short a space of time. In four years he had transformed Antwerp into a new city, a fortified town of the first order, and the most important port in his Empire. Quays, piers, canals, harbor-basins, docks with thirty vessels in process of construction, unbroken roads from Flushing to Antwerp, protected by lines of forts, where one hundred vessels could find shelter in case of danger, all these things had come from hands which seemed to be gifted with the power of a magician's wand.

Napoleon left Antwerp on October 4 at three o'clock in the morning, stopped at Wilhelmstadt and at Helvoetsluis, slept in his yacht, which was at anchor near the island of Gorée, and arrived on the following day at Gorcum, where he found Marie Louise. The Archtreasurer, governor-general of Holland, and Marshal Oudinot, commanding the troops, who had both come to meet him, were there also. The Emperor continued his journey accompanied by the Empress along a road fringed with country houses, each more elegant and better kept than the last. He stopped at Utrecht. Their Majesties were received there by the authorities, and by an immense crowd of people, whom neither the bad weather nor the darkness could prevent from thronging the quays and streets. Before entering the house prepared for his reception, Napoleon got on horseback, and went to review the troops, in spite of the pouring rain. This circumstance reminds me that, during a review which was being held on a rainy day, Napoleon saw some generals who drew aside to wrap themselves up carefully in their mantles. Without appearing to notice care which they were taking of their persons, Napoleon at once made his way to a waterspout and took his stand close to it, thus giving his generals a lesson in discipline and self-denial.

On returning to his house the Emperor, in pursuance of his system of practical education, insisted—without taking the time to change his clothes—on receiving the authorities of the town who had come to await him there. Amongst the corporations admitted to the audience were noticed some Jansenist clericals whose rupture with the Court of Rome had recently been accomplished.

The solemn entry of the imperial couple into Amsterdam was effected on October 9. The Empress was in a state-carriage, gilded and fitted with eight windows. A guard of honor composed of young men belonging to the best families in the town, had come to meet Their Majesties. The Emperor made his entry into the town on horseback surrounded by a brilliant staff. On that day the Dutch seemed to have forgotten their natural stolidity altogether.

Their Majesties spent a fortnight in Amsterdam. The Emperor broke his stay in this city by excursions to the Helder, which was one of his creations, to Texel, and to the famous dykes at Medemblik. Some very lofty dykes had been raised on this point which protected the country against the waters of the Zuyder Zee. The land lies lower than the sea, the waves of which sometimes reach as high as the top of the dyke. The dykes are then covered over with sails to break the force of the waves and to prevent them from overthrowing the ramparts which the industry of the inhabitants had raised. During one of the Emperor's absences, which lasted three days, the Empress made several excursions in the surroundings of Amsterdam. She stopped, notably, at the village of Broeck, which is famed as being the best model of the mincing luxuriousness and excessive cleanliness of the Dutch. No carriages pass through the streets, which are paved with tiles imitating flowers; but an exception was made to this rule in favor of the Empress's carriage. The house which she had come to visit was the mayor's. She saw the state rooms there, which are only opened on days of marriages, christenings, and funerals. Except on these three solemn occasions, the apartment is kept carefully closed up, and even the three steps which lead up to the door are removed. The frontages of some houses are covered with white sand on which patterns are marked out in colored sand. The inside of these houses is as clean and polished as the outside. Curtains of beautiful Chinese silk garnished the windows, large cupboards were filled with rich Japanese porcelain. No traces of any inhabitants were to be seen, nor could one notice any marks of usage on the furniture. These houses appeared to have been placed there like an opera stage scene for the mere pleasure of the eyes. There are in this village, or rather in this symmetrical assemblage of pleasure-houses, of which Nuremberg toys are the miniature, neither barns, nor lofts, nor stables, nor cow-houses, nor kitchens. Whatever of animals or even intellectual life there may be is placed outside the limits of the village. The people sleep and eat no doubt hidden from all eyes for one cannot admit that these houses are only used as the dwelling-places of spirits.

The Mayor or Burgomaster thought he was giving the Empress no mean mark of his respect in breaking for her the rules which he obeyed himself. The entry into one of these houses had even been, on one occasion, refused to Hortense, Queen of Holland, and the King had approved of this because she had not announced her visit in advance. The owners were all millionaires, and had always been carefully treated because they were the pillars of Dutch commerce. Even during the revolution no troops were billeted upon them, nor were they forced to do any personal service. These Republicans, in consequence, are very proud, and make no exceptions of persons nor of ranks.

Another township of celebrated name is Saardam, where the Czar, Peter the Great, passed several months to study the art of ship-building. This township, although this name is no more applicable to Saardam than to Broeck, consists of a succession of houses where modern luxury is combined with the most rare antiquities, and that refined cleanliness which is the mania of the Dutch. These houses cover a space of nearly three quarters of a league. Saardam, like Broek, is inhabited by merchants who have grown rich in the Indian and China trade; but what especially attracts the attention of the curious there is a poor hut of two rooms, made of planks, lacking the comforts of life, without either courtyard or loft, and altogether much resembling a barn. The camp bedstead, on which Peter the Great slept, is kept there. The bare walls are covered with inscriptions in honor of this monarch, who was great even in his eccentricities. There are in a cupboard, in which he put his clothes and provisions, two large volumes, pages of which are covered with the names of strangers who have come to visit this abode, and who remained struck with the contrast between the power of the great prince who inhabited it and the humble condition which he assumed. Napoleon, in honor of Peter the Great, raised Saardam to the rank of a town.

The journey in Holland was very brilliant. The Emperor was followed by his orders by a large court, and by many of his ministers. Talma, Damas, Mademoiselle Bourgoin, and part of the Théâtre Français had been sent for to give performances. The dramatic poet Chazet, during this journey, gave a performance of a piece, *The Saardam Workshop,* which he had written.

The Dutch were much pleased with the Empress Marie Louise. Her simple and affable manners appealed to the Dutch good nature. I do not know whether the love of novelty, or rather the prestige of Napoleon's great name influenced the Dutch. The reception which they everywhere awarded to the Emperor and Empress was such as to make one think that the annexation of their country to France was approved of by them all.

The Emperor allowed no day to pass without going out with no other escort than the guard of honor of the town, either to make excursions to the military and naval stations in the surroundings of Amsterdam, or to visit the manufactories, docks, harbor, arsenal, vessels, flotilla, or to hold reviews. He received all the authorities in audience, conversed with each man on his special subject, asking questions about the various localities, the rules of government, the state of mind of the inhabitants, the material and moral condition of the country, its customs, and so on. From these conversations, from his own observation, Napoleon with that prompt and subtle penetration which has never been equaled, acquired exact notions of everything which attracted his attention. He settled the question of public instruction in Holland by a decree. Imperial Universities were established in the cities of Leyden and Groningen; public schools were established in both these cities and in Utrecht; secondary schools were granted to every town in Holland. It was at Amsterdam that the Emperor created the order of La Réunion. This order, like that of the Legion of Honor, was intended to recompense civil and military services, and remained more especially affected to the cities annexed by the Empire. Napoleon argued with the governor-general and with the indefatigable M. Daru, minister secretary of state, in what way he could remedy the evil results of the suspension of maritime trade which were being felt by the Dutch. He manifested the greatest benevolence towards them, was present at all the fêtes given in his honor, speaking to each man on the subjects which most concerned him, remembering everybody with the amenity and good grace which he knew how to display, and in which it must be said that he was marvelously seconded by the Empress.

The Emperor left Amsterdam very well pleased with the reception which had been awarded to him in this great city, the hopes of which had been revived by his solicitude, his kind nature, and his assurances so full of future promise. He had come to Holland with but little sympathy for its inhabitants, perhaps because he had been told that they were hostile toward him. His feelings about them were changed as soon as he had come into contact with them. He even got a decided liking for their character, to the extent of almost excusing his brother, Louis, for the partiality which the latter had shown them. Generally speaking the morality and the orderly spirit of the Dutch pleased Napoleon, who sincerely desired their prosperity, and who took an interest in the memories of their glorious past. He stayed some hours at Haarlem, which is a half gothic, half Chinese city formerly celebrated for the romantic passion of its inhabitants for tulips and flowers. In passing he visited Cattvick lock and went to sleep at the Hague. Napoleon did not linger in this ancient residence of the Stadtholders, where there was nothing in particular to attract his attention. Rotterdam interested him more. He spent two days there receiving the authorities and the people and in long and frequent conversations with the local functionaries on the best means of alleviating the distress in trade; in visiting the arsenals and the harbor, which is the finest and most convenient in Holland; and applied to the interests of this important city the resources and benefits of his fruitful activity. Napoleon left Rotterdam rather earlier than he had intended to do in making out the plans of his journey, being anxious to hasten his return to Paris. The rain which announced the early approach of the bad weather, rendered the journey, in a country which is cut up by canals and marshes, a laborious one. The weather, indeed, became horrible, and gave this country the saddest of aspects. Napoleon also feared the influence of the damp air on the Empress's health. He accordingly left Rotterdam on October 27, for the Palace of Loo, passing through Utrecht. Marie Louise remained at Loo during the Emperor's excursion to Zwoll, an important fortified place, which is rendered very strong by its advantageous position on the Aa and the Issel, the waters of which fill a double moat. Placed on a height, which commands the surrounding country, this city takes pride in having given birth to the author to whom it attributes the book the *Imitation of Christ*—namely, Thomas à Kempis, whose memory is as much venerated as the name of Erasmus is respected in Rotterdam where a bronze statute has been raised to this *savant* in the market place.

The Emperor returned to the Palace of Loo and left it on the following day with the Empress for Nimeguen. He was anxious to visit the Grand duchy of Berg, which he had bestowed on the eldest son of his brother King Louis, but before proceeding to Düsseldorf, the capital of the Grand duchy, he went to Wesel, where he stayed one day. The Empress left Nimeguen at the same time as the Emperor, and went to pass the night at the castle of Ottenberg, near Xanten, and arrived at Düsseldorf on November 1. Napoleon had joined her there on the following day. After a stay of two days, which were taken up with the cares of government, and the receptions and fêtes which the cities offered to Their Majesties, they returned to France via Cologne, and made their way by Liege, Givet, Mézières, and Compiègne. On November 11 Napoleon and Marie Louise were back again at St. Cloud, after an absence of three months, the longest absence which the Emperor had made in the provinces of old or new France. Wherever he halted during his journey, Napoleon applied his vigilant attention to the most minute details of government, public works, public debts, trade, manufactures, finances, and to the country's means of defense; repelling abuses, dealing out impartial justice to all, rewarding services and talents, occupying himself in procuring for the inhabitants all the prosperity which the difficulty of the circumstances in which they were placed allowed of, and straining all the tendons of his genius to assure and increase their prosperity in the future.

In considering the annexations by force to the Empire on which has been based the accusation of unbridled ambition made against Napoleon—an accusation which the coalition took so much pains to accredit—a reflection, rendered all the more striking by the journey in Holland, presents itself, however, to the mind. It is suggested by the way in which Napoleon acted towards these people.

The necessity of drawing in the circle in which he is bound to enclose England leads him to incorporate into the Empire, for the most part only temporarily, countries which serve as places of refuge or of protection to commerce, and which are either unable or unwilling to protect themselves. At the same time he does not use these countries exclusively for the greatness and domination of France. On the contrary, his best endeavors are applied, with indefatigable peal, towards finding the best ways of relieving them, and each step he takes is marked by some measure of benefit to their interests. In combining their resources with those of the Empire for the kind of war which he is waging upon England, the only means of securing lasting peace, he allows them to participate in the advantages of the French protectorate. He attends to the repression of abuses and to the care of their interests with as much solicitude as for France. He summons to his councils, to the national representation, to various posts in the law-courts and in the government, the most distinguished men, to glide him with their lights and to be to him the advocates and the patrons of their country. And finally Napoleon only makes his appearance in the districts annexed to France to bestow upon them the advantages of his codes, of a skilful government, and a more developed industry, as though to plant in the breast of the people the seeds of a prosperity which the future will take care to develop.

I have not yet spoken of the various people who used to write to Napoleon during the Consulate and the Empire. M. Fiévée was one of Napoleon's oldest and most important correspondents. He had been introduced to Napoleon, at that time First Consul, by M. Roederer. This writer was already known by certain literary successes and by his political acts and writings. Napoleon had charged him with a mission to England in 1802. I will not speak of the reports which M. Fiévée addressed to Napoleon, as M. Fiévée has taken the public into his confidence in this matter himself. His correspondence with Napoleon, both as First Consul and as Emperor, was printed in 1837. If the spirit or the letter of these notes, published thirty years after they were written, and at a time so different, has been modified in some way, these modifications have been so slight that they can neither be recognized nor pointed out. I am inclined to believe that as a whole the reproduction may be considered a faithful one.

M. Desrenaudes, former grand vicar to the bishop of Autun, when M. de Talleyrand held that see, a friend of this minister and long employed in his cabinet, was amongst the persons who were allowed to write to Napoleon on questions of internal government;

excursions into the domain of politics being forbidden. M. Desrenaudes was successively member of the tribunate, archivist to the Council of State, councilor of the University, and censor.

A man who had made an abominable use of his talents, and who never wearied of offering his services to the imperial government, attracted Napoleon's attention: this was Barrère. This man, born, it is said, with a gentle disposition, and even with private virtues, but whom fear had transformed into a man of blood, had been authorized to return to France by favor of a law of the year VIII which allowed the recall of the exiles. Barrère had tried to render himself agreeable to the new power, and to succeed had considered no means, even the act of informer, repugnant. This person, although justly held in bad repute, had been presented by his departments, at the time of the establishment of the Empire, as a candidate to the Legislative body, but the senate had unanimously rejected this candidature. In such a case Napoleon could not act on the maxim which he had adopted of calling to his service everybody likely to be of use to him, and give employment to a man whose notoriety was such as to exclude him from public functions. The Emperor, being unable to reply favorably to the importunities of this discredited former member of the Convention, contented himself with authorizing him to send periodical reports to the Tuileries on the state of public opinion, on administrative matters, and on his old companions in exile. Napoleon found nothing in these reports but the hollow phraseology of the members of the committee of Public Safety at the Convention. Barrère's despatches, which began in 1803, lasted three years after Napoleon's accession to the throne. But the Emperor, tired of finding neither useful expressions of opinion, nor revelations of any value in these reports, which were only filled with words of flattery and vulgar denunciations, put a stop to this insipid correspondence. Then, opining that Barrère's talents as a writer, might be profitably employed in the editorship of some newspaper, he had the idea of placing him at the head of a paper which took the significant name of *The Anti-British Memorial,* and in favor of which I was ordered to pay Barrère five hundred francs a month. This publication was not successful. Napoleon was dissatisfied with his articles, finding in them nothing but empty tirades, arguments without any solidity, and often, as he used to say, stupidities covered over with sonorous phrases. He ceased to take an interest in a man for whom, moreover, he could not have had any kind of esteem. I believe that Barrère afterwards wrote on the staff of *The Argus,* a paper written in the same spirit as *The Anti-British Memorial,* and which derived its inspiration from the offices of the Ministry of Foreign Affairs. M. Andre d'Arbelles, the historiographer of this ministry and M. Lesur, author of the *Annual of Universal History,* a collection of very serious interest to history, presided over the editorial department of this newspaper.

Napoleon's short intercourse with Barrère put me into correspondence with the latter. I had no opportunity of making his personal acquaintance, and only communicated with him by letter. He thought fit to offer me his academical eulogy of Louis XII, a panegyric in which he preached "the advantages of a monarchical government and the fidelity of the people to its kings, the distinctive characteristic of the French people," sentiments which the author, for his part, had so cruelly repudiated.

Nobody will be surprised when I add that Barrère found in 1814, 1815, and 1830, successive occasions for apostasy.

Goldsmith, an English Jew, translator of the articles of *The Argus,* which had been written by MM. Lesur, André d'Arbelles, and others, had also his share in Napoleon's liberalities. He also worked on *The Anti-British Memorial,* but there was no solidarity between him and Barrère. This libeler, who had fled from England to the Continent, had come to offer his pen to the French government. After having lost all credit with this government, and after the Treaty of Amiens had rendered the existence of papers hostile to England no longer necessary, Goldsmith lost his means of existence. He then tried to return home, and was allowed to return to London. Pretending to know the secrets of the French government, this fellow was bought over by Pitt. The price of Goldsmith's return to favor was the publication of the *Secret History of the Cabinet of St. Cloud*, a tissue of lies and calumnies, which, however, the government of the Restoration ordered to be translated and published with additions. Goldsmith also became editor of two newspapers in England, *The Anti-Gallican* and *The Anti-Corsican Chronicles,* which were the counterpart of *The Anti-British Memorial.* This latter newspaper attacked the policy of the British government, while Goldsmith's papers openly preached the murder of Napoleon Bonaparte. In this respect they were unfortunately the organ of certain princes of the House of Bourbon and of the principal members of the French exile party. The publication of the *History of the Cabinet of St. Cloud*, of *The Anti-Gallican* and *The Anti-Corsican Chronicles,* opposed to his collaboration on *The Argus* and *The Anti-British Memorial* have given a sad and but little enviable celebrity to the memory of Goldsmith, that double-faced pamphleteer.

M. M. J. Rocques de Montgaillard, of whom I have spoken elsewhere, also lent the assistance of his pen to the founder of the imperial regime, but that in no very disinterested manner.

Madame de Genlis used also to address periodical reports to the Emperor. This lady, on her return from exile, had found herself like many other honorable exiles, in a state of destitution. The Minister of the Interior, M. Chaptal, gave her an apartment in the buildings of the Arsenal library. Madame de Genlis lived there on the income produced by her numerous books, and some assistance which she received from the funds reserved for literary people. When Napoleon became Emperor he ordered Lavalette to pay her five hundred francs a month, and, in order to spare her feelings, had her told that he wished her to write to him every fortnight on matters of literature and morality. The help which Madame de Genlis received from Napoleon's generosity, the help which was afterwards extended to her by Queen Julia of Naples, and the resources produced from the sale of her works, did not prevent her from being invariably in embarrassed circumstances. She used to apply to me when she wanted some advance on the income allowed her by the Emperor, and at such times would beg M. Sabatier de Castres, whom I used to meet at the house of a mutual friend, to mention the matter to me. This woman of letters, who was prodigiously vain, has published "Memoirs," in which very good measure, in point of quantity, has been dealt out to the subscribers to this work, in which she relates the adventures of her long career. In this book she shows herself faithful to her antipathies as to her sympathies, but the goodwill and the preciseness of her recollections are unfortunately too often in direct proportion to the good or bad fortune of the persons she writes about. A circumstance relating to the imperial family—amongst other examples which I might quote—prompts me to make this remark, and to point out to what an extent, at times, the authoress's memory used to fail her. M. Sabatier, whose name I have just mentioned, had introduced Madame de Genlis to the virtuous Julia

Bonaparte, at that time Queen of Naples, and had advised his friend at the same time to ask to be allowed to take charge of the education of the Queen's daughters. Madame de Genlis, who thought herself born with the vocation for teaching and guiding her neighbor by inculcating her opinions and principles, had jumped at this idea. She wrote in consequence to the Emperor to obtain his consent in the matter. This application was contained in her fortnightly paper, and was accompanied by protestations of gratitude and the expression of her wish to show her gratitude for the kindness of the august head of the family, by assiduous attention in carrying out the duties which such a post would impose. But this letter was not answered, and Napoleon, on the contrary, told his sister-in-law that such a choice would displease him. The Queen on her side had far too much tact to wish to put her neck into such a yoke. She also knew that King Joseph would be very reluctant to give his consent. This consideration would have sufficed to hold the Queen back, even if she could have made up her mind to entrust the education of her daughters to a woman of admitted talents, no doubt, but who was totally unfitted for such a post by associations and prejudices which were incompatible with the new imperial government. To console Madame de Genlis for the Emperor's refusal, Queen Julia, with that feeling of goodness and generosity which characterized her, accorded her a pension of three thousand francs from her private purse. No allusion, as far as I know, to this act of kindness, is contained in the memoirs of the woman who benefited by it.

Let us return to the Emperor's other correspondents, who have been forgotten during this digression.

Doctor Corvisart had proposed M. Lemaire, Professor of Latin Poetry at the Paris Academy, to Napoleon, as correspondent, and he had been accepted. This professor had drawn attention to himself during his lectures, by an ingenious application of certain passages in Virgil's poems to the eulogy of the Head of the government. Napoleon, having noticed in some of the notes sent in by M. Lemaire personalities mixed up with general observations on literature and literary people, ordered him to cease writing to him. The Emperor, as a general rule, forbade his correspondents to speak of persons, wishing them to speak of matters alone.

M. de Montlosier, formerly deputy at the national assembly, where he sat on the right, who did not take pains to soften down the rigidity of his monarchical principles by conciliatory expressions, was also allowed to expound to the Emperor in a series of notes his political, administrative, and even religious plans. He afterwards received an order to write a book on the French Monarchy. I saw the manuscript of this book a long time in Napoleon's study. The multiplicity of the Emperor's occupations had prevented him from reading it, and at last he charged a commission to read it. The opinion of this commission, although it was favorable to the work on the whole, thought that its publication would be untimely. The author has published it since the Restoration with explanatory notes.

These correspondents were more or less remunerated. On the average the pay given for this kind of work was £20 a month.

M. de Dampmartin, a retired Major-General, and a member of the Legislature, author of several historical and literary works, became one of the non-remunerated correspondents of the Emperor by my intermediary, during the years 1813 and 1814.

Another correspondent who was totally disinterested, continued writing to Napoleon from 1800 to 1814, His letters, written with independence and measure, were not particularly brilliant, and dealt with the various acts of his government. I will not betray—as he has not done so himself—the incognito of the author of these letters, who was referendary to the Audit Office, and who hid himself under the pseudonym of "Héléodore." This anonymous writer published his correspondence in 1833 under the title of *Letters of Héléodore Addressed to Napoleon Bonaparte, from March 1, 1800, to March 17, 1814*.

In speaking of the persons who addressed letters or reports to the Emperor I have made use of the word "correspondent," because I could not find a better expression, but as a matter of fact Napoleon never answered these communications.

I had been created Baron of the Empire in 1809, and provided with an endowment in the ancient province of Brabant. In 1811, I was appointed *Maître des Requêtes* of the Council of State, and had received an increase of endowment. I had been successively nominated "Knight," and then "Officer" of the "Legion of Honor," and finally "Knight of the Iron Crown," at the time when this Order was created. The sovereigns who followed each other on the throne of Naples were kind enough to wish to decorate me with their Orders; but although one was a brother and the other the brother-in-law of the Emperor, I respectfully refused, with the Emperor's approval, all the distinctions which they had been good enough to wish to confer upon me. I did violence to the feelings which made me attach great value to the proof of esteem which these sovereigns, for whom I had as much affection as respect, wished to award to me; but I thought that in my capacity as secretary to the Emperor I must be absolutely independent of everybody but himself; and that though I was not the wife of Caesar I must be above all suspicion. The Emperor approving these scruples, thought that I could only wear the two Orders of which he was the head: the decoration of the Legion of Honor, and that of the Crown of Iron, with which he had deigned to honor me.

When the birth of an heir seemed to have seated Napoleon's power on unshakable foundations, at a time when a free and glorious career opened itself out to his creative genius—a genius as wonderful in the works of peace as in the maneuvers of war—while under the shelter of a prosperity, the splendor of which shed its rays on the extremest points of the Empire, he was preparing the success of able measures which were to deal a death-blow to England, and to assure the peace of the world, the coalition—that Hydra with its hundred heads—which ever grew again, was not remaining inactive, and was conspiring against her conqueror. She kept stirring up the ever restless ambition of Alexander, she excited the high aristocracy of St. Petersburg against France, and, in one word, was sowing between the two allies the seeds of a misunderstanding which, though they had not yet germinated, were gradually growing in the secrecy of diplomatic negotiations. These intrigues and these underground conspiracies were soon to cause war to break out.

Napoleon, faithful to the system of the alliance which had been contracted at Tilsitt, was pursuing his great design of forcing England to peace. Amongst the means which it was necessary for him to use to attain his object some, it is true, clashed with Russian interests; but what maritime power in Europe did not suffer by them? Napoleon could not abandon the continental system, the effects of which were beginning to be cruelly felt in England where the distress of manufacturing classes had become extreme. The closing up of the last markets which were opened to English produce, which heaped itself up in the English warehouses, reduced the working classes to misery and to revolt, and this distress reacted on the public fortune of England. Napoleon was studying the best ways of diminishing the damage caused to Russia by the execution of the blockade system; he was seeking to smooth over the difficulties and to reassure the Emperor Alexander. The Emperor's marriage with Marie Louise must have made the Czar imagine that the policy of France had taken another turn. Napoleon's mental reservation, of reestablishing the Kingdom of Poland, was in Alexander's eyes a specter always full of menace.

Counting for little the great advantages which he had gained at Tilsitt, and not hoping for any more, the Czar had once more become accessible to the seductions of England. Alexander willfully exaggerated his reasons for discontent, and rejected all Napoleon's proposals for an arrangement, and all offers of compensation. Russia was secretly preparing for war, and her sovereign denied this when he was asked to explain what the arming meant. He nevertheless kept on assembling troops and accumulating stores, adopted measures which were prejudicial to French commerce, and finally let loose his bad temper on the French ambassador at St. Petersburg. The Duke of Vicence, who had long been the object of the Emperor Alexander's kindest attentions, suddenly saw coolness and repugnance succeed to confidence and the charm of the most intimate intercourse.

The Duke of Vicence, accustomed to the goodwill of a prince who, affecting all the outward signs of friendship, forgot his rank in his presence, could not support the great change which had taken place in his personal position. Persuaded that it was no longer in his power to maintain the friendly relations which till then had existed between the Russian sovereign and himself, he asked to be recalled. Napoleon agreed, giving the Emperor Alexander a proof of his respect in leaving to him the choice of the envoy to replace General Caulaincourt, who would be most agreeable to him, and mentioning the names of MM. de La Rochefoucauld, Narbonne, and Lauriston. Napoleon ordered the Duke of Vicence to declare once more, before leaving St. Petersburg, that his policy had not changed, that he persisted in the alliance, and that he offered any and every indemnity which should be really equivalent to the Duchy of Oldenburg, which he had been absolutely forced to occupy in their common interest, and with the success of his struggle against England in view. The Emperor Alexander answered these new assurances with a protest addressed to every European court against the annexation of the state of Oldenburg to the French Empire.

General Lauriston, aide-de-camp of the Emperor, went to take the Duke of Vicence's place in Russia. During the first audience with the Czar accorded to the new ambassador he checked him at the first word uttered on the subject of the arming which was going on in Russia, and proposed that a French officer should be sent off together with a Russian officer, and simultaneously, with the view of assuring themselves *de visu* of the falseness of the reports which had been addressed to the Emperor Napoleon on this subject. And yet these armaments were only too genuine!

Amongst the causes which contributed to disturb the good understanding between France and Russia, the Polish question holds the first place. Napoleon, resigned to leave the reestablishment of Poland to the future, had done his best to reassure the Emperor Alexander on this point. At his request he had abstained from making use of the word Poland in his home and foreign communications; he had opposed the reestablishment of the Order of the White Eagle, and had insisted that those who were decorated with this

Order should cease wearing it. He had given instruction to the French newspapers that the use of the words "Poles" and "Poland" should be avoided in writing about the Duchy of Warsaw and its inhabitants. And finally, Napoleon had authorized his ambassador in St. Petersburg to negotiate and even to conclude a convention by which France would undertake to refuse all assistance in the Restoration of this ancient monarchy. This convention had been negotiated and signed by the Duke of Vicence on January 5, 1810. It contained the following principal stipulations:

"(1) The Kingdom of Poland shall never be reestablished.

"(2) The words 'Poland' and 'Pole,' shall never figure henceforward in any public deed.

"(3) Any annexation to the Grand duchy of Warsaw of any territory having formerly belonged to the ancient monarchy of Poland, is forbidden."

This convention had been immediately ratified by the Emperor Alexander, and was transmitted to Paris to receive the ratification of the Emperor Napoleon. How much the imperative terms of this document and its unusual form shocked him may be imagined. Napoleon invoked the dignity of France, which was offended by the absolute and exclusive expressions used in this document. He complained of its form, of the violation of accepted customs, and of the anticipated ratifications which the Czar had placed upon it.

He declared that he could not accept the convention without examination, because he had neither approved nor even known the terms in which it was drawn up, before it had been ratified by the Czar. The Russian cabinet, in exacting that no part of the territory which had belonged to ancient Poland should be added to the Grand duchy of Warsaw, refused to declare in a reciprocal manner that Poland should not be annexed to Russia. This exclusion of all reciprocity tended to make France odious to peoples who were attached to her by so many bonds, and even to arm them against her. At the same time it was only in its form that Napoleon disavowed the convention. He wished therefore to consider the act which his representative had signed as a draft to which the future might give the necessary sanction. "He was not," he said, "Destiny, that he should declare Poland would never be reestablished." Might not that take place without his cooperation, and even in spite of himself? Who could foresee the future? Napoleon accordingly substituted for the primitive project a project which was calculated to realize Russia's object. This modified project contained a commitment on the part of France not to favor any undertaking tending to a reestablishment of the Kingdom of Poland, and rendering common to Russia as to the Duchy of Warsaw, the interdiction of any extension of territory by districts taken from the ancient Polish provinces. The Emperor of Russia refused to listen to any modification. The only one that he proposed was that he would join with the Emperor Napoleon in undertaking to prevent any reestablishment of the Kingdom of Poland.

This clinging, on his part, to the terms of a convention which he himself had dictated was not a proof of a friendly disposition, but rather proved a design to transform Napoleon's refusal to ratify the projected convention, into one of those grievances the pretext of which one was certain to arise in a man so jealous of the nation's honor as was the Emperor. It was, then, one grievance the more that the coalition was keeping in reserve to make use of against us when the hour which it was expecting should strike. These hostile mental reservations, about which it would have been difficult to become edified had the idea of them remained hidden in the minds of the princes and the ministers of the coalition, cannot be denied today, when accomplished facts have established their prearrangement and when writers, the agents of this coalition, have even boasted of the skilful way in which they were combined.

Without entering into an examination of the plans of our enemies we will content ourselves with mentioning the facts which took place before 1811, the date of which opposes itself to any admission of the statement that they were only just reprisals provoked by the French government. First of all there is the insignificant cooperation of the Russian contingent in the 1809 campaign, when a Russian force less in numbers than one-fifth of what had been agreed upon, acted with the French army; and then only as an observation corps, rather than as an active auxiliary. This attitude on the part of Russia showed that the St. Petersburg cabinet had not frankly broken off with the coalition—of which, that year, Austria was the vanguard. The confessions of Colonel Bourtourlin, moreover, remove all doubts on this point.

In the second place, the refusal of Princess Anna's hand disguised under the pretext of its being necessary to obtain the consent of the Empress Mother, a consent which was not obtained after a delay of two months, was not any the more a proof than the Emperor Alexander was anxious to tighten his alliance with France. And finally the invincible obstinacy with which this prince persisted in the unacceptable terms which he had imperiously imposed in drawing up the convention concerning Poland, and the preliminary ratification which he wrote at the bottom of this convention, would be inexplicable had they not been calculated.

To these signs of a growing deviation from the Tilsitt alliance must be added: the secret orders given by the Russian government for the execution of works of fortification on the frontier of the Grand duchy of Warsaw, the creation of new regiments, and the extraordinary levy of four men out of every five hundred in all the provinces of the Muscovite Empire, the movements of the troops withdrawn from Siberia, or from the army in Finland, thanks to a secret understanding come to with Bernadotte, the recall of several army divisions from Moldavia and Wallachia, and their assembly on the frontiers of Poland at a time when, apart from the French garrisons left in the forts of Prussia until the payment of the war-indemnities, France had only the corps of Marshal Davout in cantonment in the Hanseatic provinces, in Germany, the immense storehouses of provisions and munitions which were created at Wilna, Minsk, and other fortified places in Podolia and Wolhynia; and, finally, the negotiations which were entered upon at the beginning of 1811, of which I shall speak later on, between the Russian and Prussian Cabinets.

To these preparations, which in spite of their palpability were always denied by the Emperor Alexander, must be added the ukase, which is said to have been issued on December 31, 1810, so that this edict may appear to have been issued by way of reprisal on the senatus consultum of the 13th of the same month, which sanctioned the annexation of the Hanseatic cities to the French Empire; but the Russian decree had been long in preparation in the offices of St. Petersburg before being published. In the form of a custom house regulation, the ukase enforced not only the prohibition, but even the destruction of all French goods. At the same time English goods were allowed to enter all Russian ports, provided the ship was flying a neutral flag, a flag which English commerce never failed to use when it was to its interests to do so. This series of hostilities put forward by Russia was completed by the formation of a corps of 90,000 armed employees, under the command of superior officers of the line, a corps destined to assure the execution of the destructive measures which had been ordered against the produce of French trade. This new corps received the appellation of guardians of the frontier. It would indeed be difficult not to see in the acts which we have just enumerated, a fixed determination on the part of the Russian government to renounce the continental system, and once more to make common cause with England.

Napoleon had been informed that since the spring of 1811, overtures had been made to Prussia to induce her to join with Russia in the attack which she was meditating on France. The dangerous situation in which Prussia would have found herself placed, and the just prudence of the King, kept the Prussian cabinet to its line of duty. The Emperor Alexander, better advised, renounced taking the offensive this time, and postponed carrying into effect the hostile projects which he fostered against us. He wished to leave the apparent wrong of aggressiveness to Napoleon. A new plan of campaign was accordingly concerted, which consisted, as we saw later on, in drawing the French army into the provinces of the Russian Empire, where a desert would be made all round the invaders, who, it was hoped, would perish by starvation, privations of every kind, and the inclemency of an icy climate. Meanwhile the Emperor Alexander, accordingly, remained on the defensive, while secretly continuing his preparations for war.

Although these preparations were enshrouded in deep mystery and publicity only revealed them at the supreme moment, they could not escape Napoleon's farseeing eye. The Emperor on his side was getting ready, and was sending troops quietly on to Danzig to reinforce the garrison. This brought forth autograph letters from the Czar Alexander, who complained of the threatening attitude which France was assuming towards him. These complaints were followed by fresh arming on the part of Russia. Napoleon tried to hold Alexander on the precipitous slope down which he saw him rushing. He assured him of his desire to live in peace and implored him not to listen to perfidious inspirations, the effect of which must end in bringing about an inevitable shock between the two empires. But the Russian sovereign turned a deaf ear to these protestations and to this advice; a feeling of distrust increased by foreign promptings had taken deep root in his mind. The importunities of every kind of the English agents, the obstacles which the ambitious policy of Russia encountered in the power of France, the feeling of spiteful rivalry which had resulted therefrom, envenomed a state of misunderstanding, which, as Napoleon thought, could have been put an end to by a private conversation between the two sovereigns, if Alexander could have been brought to it.

Apart from the grievances which divided the two cabinets on the subject of Poland, their respective recriminations bore upon other very serious points. Russia could not pardon our government the annexation of the Hanseatic cities, and especially the annexation of Oldenburg to the French Empire. The Emperor Alexander's susceptibility had, and not unreasonably, been wounded by the dispossession of the Duke of Oldenburg, the husband of Grand duchess Catherine, the Czar's well-beloved sister. On France's side it was the infraction of the continental system, a system which Russia's attitude struck to the heart, which most irritated the Emperor. Napoleon took pains to demonstrate on his side that the annexation of countries on the northern seaboard of Germany had been caused by the imperative necessity of closing upon English trade the useful markets which she found there for the sale of her merchandise on the continent. We have seen that he also offered the sovereign of Oldenburg, an indemnity fully equivalent to the loss of his duchy, and that he sought to calm, by means of reasonable proposals, the anxieties which were preserved by Russia as to the possibility of a resurrection of the ancient monarchy of Poland. Napoleon's inclinations and interest led him to avoid war; Russia on the contrary, seeing her adversary's reluctance, was trying to throw him into it. Encouraged by our attitude, the Russian cabinet made every effort, both secretly and openly, with a bellicose object in view.

The annexation of the Hanseatic cities, of Oldenburg, and of Pomerania to France, which had taken place after repeated warnings, and when a conviction had been come to as to the real or pretended impotence of these countries to forbid the access of their ports to English trade, could not be looked upon as a violation of the Treaty of Tilsitt, since this annexation, on the contrary, tended to ensure the full and entire carrying into effect of the commitments which had been taken. The connivance of the authorities in these various countries with England was moreover very well known. The voluntary non-observation of the continental blockade rendered many points on this seaboard vulnerable, and forced Napoleon, whose clear-sightedness never failed him, to seize upon it. People have never tired of repeating that the districts situated on the mouths of the Elbe, the Ems, and the Weser had been annexed to the French Empire to be indefinitely incorporated therewith. This erroneous assertion was formulated to give greater weight to the reproaches of provocation which were made against us by Russia, in spite of the fact that the greater part of the hostile measures which this power took against France preceded these alleged provocations. The Emperor wished to keep these different States in his hands as long as the maritime war should last. So penetrating a mind as Napoleon's could not dream of retaining indefinitely, for incorporation in a new empire, these remote regions, which it was his intention to surrender at the time of general peace. He was very well aware that, unless certain restitutions were made, all hope of a European pacification would be a chimerical one. However, in all his messages, the Emperor kept repeating the declaration which he had never ceased to make, that as long as the British cabinet should persist in its attitude, so long would he also persist in the use of measures which this attitude had forced him to adopt.

The thought of rescuing France and the States of the continent from the humiliating supremacy of England was a generous and a lofty one. The Emperor's ardent and exclusive wish was to force peace upon the English government. All attempts to bring this about by negotiations had failed, his plan of invading England had failed, one means alone remained efficacious, that, namely, of closing all access to the continent to the commerce of our enemies. The decrees of the British cabinet, under date of May 16, 1806, which declared the coasts of France and Holland, from the Elbe to Brest, in a state of blockade, had decided the continental system. Napoleon replied to the blockade of the continent with the blockade of the British Isles. The extraordinary measures decreed to bring this great enterprise to a successful issue were its natural consequence. The first clause of the treaties of peace with Russia, Sweden, and Prussia, had been the adhesion of these powers to the continental system. This condition was also imposed on the other states on the continent. In this way England was placed under the taboo of the continent. Once engaged in this mighty struggle Napoleon could draw back before no obstacle in the realization of a plan which promised such useful and such splendid results. There was the price of the efforts of the continental states. One or two years more and the object was gained. Those who have looked upon this conception as a mad and impracticable scheme have not considered that Napoleon's enterprise was easier of execution than was the realization of the threats of the English government, and that the power of the man who had conceived it equaled his genius. Its success would have, as a matter of fact, been infallible. It needed the unheard-of disasters to which France fell a victim to save England, and to bring back to her the states which would have profited by her ruin.

If one passes to considerations of a less general nature it will be found that France was too great and too powerful for England to consent to live in peace with her. Had our country not been sustained by an energetic hand, it would only have been by keeping itself in a state of dependence, and submitting to the laws of its rival, that it would have succeeded in enjoying a delusive calm. As long as England found means to arouse the continent, by exciting the passions of the European cabinets and aristocracy, she employed all her energies for the ruin of France and the imperial dynasty. It was to her the "To be, or not to be" of Shakespeare's Hamlet. The French Empire had either to put its neck under the yoke of this irreconcilable enemy, and submit to the consequences of its implacable hatred, by giving up the only means of bringing her to equitable conditions, or to persist in the rigorous system of blockade which had been conceived by Napoleon. The latter had not always a choice of means, and the calumnies spread abroad against the character of the greatest man of modern times will pass away, together with the many commonplace accusations of despotism and hatred of liberty with which it has become conventional to charge his memory. Impartial posterity will appreciate what he did for France, and what the circumstances in which he was placed prevented him from accomplishing.

The incompatibility of the new France, both under the Republic and under the Empire, with old Europe could only cease by the triumph of the former. The liberal reaction for which the nations were not ripe at the time, and which was progressing secretly, but not without Napoleon's knowledge, would have been inevitably accomplished if peace had crowned our victories. Does one wish to know what was Napoleon's secret, and the reason of a part of his success? It was that he constantly studied the dispositions and the needs of the people, that he could decide what was the general tendency of men's minds, and knew how to seize upon it. Napoleon was ambitious, but always and above all with a patriotic purpose in view. He only undertook what he was able to accomplish, and the unceasing motive of his ambition was an ardent love for his country, on which all his thoughts and all his actions were based. If he committed faults, they always had this noble sentiment for cause and for excuse, and to what a height did not these very faults raise the French name!

The Emperor of Russia had appeared at Tilsitt to share Napoleon's feelings towards England. Alexander's first words on the raft on the Niemen: "Like you, I am England's enemy," had flattered Napoleon's heart, and were destined to smooth away all obstacles which might still separate victor and vanquished. Later on, when the two sovereigns met at Erfurth, the Emperor Alexander pretended to persevere in the same feelings. With a view of assuring himself of the cooperation of a powerful ally against the common enemy Napoleon made up his mind to sacrifices which he afterwards had reason to regret. At Tilsitt he had prevented the Turks from reoccupying Moldavia and Wallachia, at Erfurth he consented to the surrender of these provinces to Russia. The Emperor at Tilsitt had lent his hand to the weakening of Sweden, at that time, it is true, England's most persevering ally, by abandoning Finland to Russia, a concession of inestimable value to that power. He complained later on with reason, in one of his letters to the Emperor Alexander, that he had only contributed to the aggrandizement of Russia to see French trade excluded by the Russians from Moldavia up to Finland, and yet the league formed by the Emperor against England had a future object which would have been profitable not only to France but to Russia herself, as well as to all the maritime powers of the North.

The year 1811, and the first months of 1812, were taken up with an exchange of diplomatic notes between the Russian and French Cabinets, and a correspondence between the two sovereigns, the substance of which, on Napoleon's side, was: "You are preparing for war. It can only be against me; but I am defending our common interests against England, and I have accordingly no wish to attack you. You are obliging me to imitate you; war may be the result, although I do not wish for it, and you perhaps do not desire it yourself. Is there no means of coming to an understanding?" In the meanwhile Russia was secretly preparing to commence the war. Colonel Bourtourlin, whom we have already quoted, relates on page 58 of the first volume of his *Military History of the Campaign of 1812*, "that Russia wished to commence the attack in the spring of 1811, but recognized that she was not ready to do so at that time."

At last in the month of February, 1812, when the formidable display of troops in Russia, ceasing to menace her natural enemies, had been spread out along the frontiers of the Grand Duchy of Warsaw, the Emperor sent for Colonel Czernitchev, Alexander's aide-de-camp, who, since 1808, had been constantly living close to his person in the capacity of confidential intermediary. Napoleon unburdened himself towards him on the causes of the misunderstanding which existed between France and Russia, and charged him with conciliatory proposals for his master. Czernitchev went off, but did not return. He carried away with him reports on the state of the French army which he had succeeded in getting from an employee at the War Office, a man called Michel, who paid with his head for the treachery which he had committed in favor of the Czar's aide-de-camp.

The Emperor applied himself with all his might to minimize the rigorous effect of the prohibitive measures which he had been forced to adopt. He proposed equivalents, the system of licenses, by means of which England was prevented from drawing money from the continent in exchange for the produce of her trade. The licenses allowed merchant vessels to import a certain quantity of colonial produce on condition of exporting the equivalent value in French merchandise. Every ship bearing a license, freighted with a cargo of native productions, was allowed to go and exchange its cargo in England for colonial produce and raw materials alone, but not for manufactured goods. In this way England received no money, and goods of English manufacture could not penetrate on to the continent. The speculators who obtained these licenses very often paid no attention to the condition of exporting French goods, the entrance of which into England was subjected to very heavy duties. They used to load their ships with goods which had the least sale in France and would often throw these cargoes overboard when out at sea, instead of seeking to introduce them into England. Colonial produce and raw materials consequently cost a much higher price, but this sacrifice was largely compensated for by the profits which these speculators derived from such valuable produce as sugar, coffee, and spices, which nobody on the continent was willing to entirely forego. This was an attenuation of the continental system, and although it was no doubt imperfect, it was difficult to go further, seeing what were the exceptional circumstances in which one was placed at the time. Russia could make use of the same means of procuring colonial produce necessary for her consumption or raw material useful for her industries, in exchange for her tars, leathers, and timber. However, the more conciliating and the more desirous of avoiding a rupture did Napoleon show himself, the more did Alexander imagine that the French government was not ready to fight him, and was afraid of him. The Czar, moreover, was free no longer, and had been entirely circumvented by England. There was no kind of intrigue, no perfidious proceeding which our eternal enemy neglected to use, at St. Petersburg and elsewhere, to excite people against the Emperor Napoleon—substitutions of documents, forgery of writings and of signatures, all was good. Towards the end of 1811, a cabal, of which the principal agent was a certain Baron d'Armfeldt—who had been long in the pay of England—trumped up the proofs of an act of subornation of which Napoleon was alleged to be the principal instigator, and Speranski, the secretary of the Russian cabinet, the object and the accomplice. Speranski corresponded with the general secretary of the French Council of State on matters of internal government, a correspondence to which Alexander had appeared to attach importance and which had been authorized by the French government. Although these communications had absolutely nothing to do with politics, the informers did not lose the opportunity of seizing on this pretext and of transforming this exchange of letters into a conspiracy. Speranski saw himself in consequence dismissed suddenly, and banished, without even having been heard. These odious and perfidious machinations still further increased Alexander's mistrust of Napoleon, and contributed towards changing the good relations which had existed so long between them. The Emperor of Russia only discovered the innocence of the privy councilor, Speranski, two years later. He awarded this faithful servant a poor compensation for his undeserved disgrace by appointing him governor of the province of Siberia to which he had been at first banished. Count Nesselrode and Prince Gagarin took Speranski's place as secretaries to the Czar's cabinet. It was by similar lying artifices that England acted upon the suspicious mind of the Emperor Alexander, and succeeded in binding this prince by means of a treaty which it was agreed to keep secret till the day when an open rupture between France and Russia should break out and hostilities begin.

As a matter of fact Napoleon could only lose by the war which was being prepared. The continental system, so disastrous to England, was by this fact postponed, hindered, and subjected to uncertain hazards. The cries of distress and of weariness which were being heard in London, Liverpool, Bristol, and elsewhere, already announced the early and complete success of the system. On the other hand affairs in Spain imperatively demanded all France's efforts. The Emperor was aware of the situation, if one may judge from various notes which he dictated on different occasions. He "worked out his proposition in different ways," and always found, at the end of his calculations that he could not make war upon Russia without incurring risks which it was to his interest to avoid. He would have wished to be able to postpone this war for three years. The object of the continental system would then have been attained, and Spain would have been pacified. He had all to hope for from time, and the consolidation which two or three years more would have given to his power. The coalition understood this perfectly, and put enough occupation in his way to prevent him from returning to Spain. It knew how to work the strings of the most refined intrigue. It influenced the Emperor Alexander with all that was likely to have an effect on his mind, offering baits to his ambition which did not find sufficient satisfaction in Napoleon's condescensions. It constantly put before the Czar's eyes the phantom of the reestablishment of Poland and persuaded him that he was France's dupe, in spite of the genuine advantages which he had derived from the French alliance. It represented the occupation of Oldenburg as a proof of the want of consideration of which the French government rendered itself guilty. It made a skilful use of a suspicious and jealous character and threatened him, needs be, with his father's tragic fate. These maneuvers, skillfully directed, led Alexander on, at first insensibly, and then by a rapid slope to a rupture of the alliance, and to a savage war, fatal to humanity. The pressing need of ending the war in Spain explains Napoleon's reluctance to enter the arena with Russia. He would have preferred to postpone the war, and hoped for some time to be able to avoid it. He spared nothing to obtain this result, apart from the sacrifice of a system the effects of which were about to become decisive. When all hopes of preserving good relations with Russia had been dispelled, the Emperor wished to dispose of all his forces to strike a great blow in the East and to return promptly to Spain. Unheard-of disasters deceived the most clever and most prudent calculations. A happy issue of the affairs in Spain was about to render Napoleon master of the Peninsula and to make him free of action. The English government saw this and could not hesitate. It was accordingly urgently necessary for England to involve her powerful adversary in a new struggle with all the embarrassments inherent to his position.

Napoleon accordingly found himself involved, against his will, in a gigantic expedition, which he would have preferred to postpone, because later on it could have been carried out with better chances of success if any longer necessary. He could not overlook the fact that the immutable tendency of the Russians since Peter the Great, had been to exchange their icy climate for warmer skies, and their arid steppes for the rich and fertile provinces of central Europe. To drive back the Russians into ancient Muscovy, and to raise up the throne to Poland to serve as a frontier to the States of Germany, and to act as the Empire's bulwark against their invasions, such was Napoleon's secret object, a result the realization of which was to be the corollary to and the completion of the success of the continental system. It was to assure the success of this colossal enterprise that Napoleon succeeded in uniting under the French flag the whole of Southern Europe. Unfortunately the danger for him lay in so many precarious alliances, and it was in relying on these that his ruin was consummated. He blamed himself for this fault, which he himself called a clumsy one. It was indeed necessary for him to be absolute victor everywhere and always, and the day of a reverse must necessarily transform the allies whom victory alone kept under his flag, into bitterest enemies.

Matters had grown worse in Spain. The conquest of Andalusia by the French armies had forced the Seville junta to flee to Cadiz. The time it seemed had come to push the war vigorously on at this point, and to profit by the dissensions which divided the councils of the Spanish rebels. A provisional regency, composed of five members, replaced the Seville junta and organized means of defense before which the efforts of the French troops failed. No better success awaited King Joseph's conciliatory measures, so that that important war port Cadiz, key to all the provinces of the South of Spain, became the center of the resistance of the Peninsula.

In Portugal, Marshal Masséna, detained during a month before the lines of Torres-

Vedras, was forced by famine, disease, and daily encounters, which decimated his army by reducing it to the saddest extremities, to approach his victualing centers, to beat a retreat, and finally to evacuate Portugal. He was followed by the English general, who recaptured Ciudad-Rodrigo and Badajoz. Partial insurrections increased in number, and guerillas covered the whole Spanish territory. The recall of the imperial guard and of several regiments, the rumors of an imminent rupture between France and Russia had raised the courage of the Spanish rebels. Famine was reigning in Madrid and in the provinces, owing to the difficulty of communication. The Emperor before leaving to undertake his campaign in Russia, had handed over the command of the French troops in Spain to King Joseph. Napoleon had restored Marshal Jourdan to his brother, with whom the King agreed better than with Marshal Soult. This combination of occurrences shows how greatly the Emperor must have felt the necessity of finishing the war in Spain. A last but feeble hope remained to him. Since 1809 Austria had been keeping an agent, Baron de Wessemberg, in London, with whom it was possible to communicate by Calais. The proposal which Napoleon transmitted to London through this agent had for its principal object the evacuation of the Spanish territory by the French and English armies, and the independence of this country, under the "present dynasty." The negotiation was a very short one, for Lord Castlereagh answered that if the exclusion of Ferdinand VII and his heirs was maintained the commitment undertaken by the British government did not allow him to accede to the proposal of the French government. This very plain spoken declaration broke off the negotiation at its commencement. Napoleon unfortunately thought himself sufficiently strong to carry on two such gigantic enterprises at the same time.

Alliances with Austria and Prussia became necessary to France before entering on the campaign and sending her armies into Russia. Prussia, hemmed in between two giants ready to dash against each other, had made fruitless remonstrances to the St. Petersburg cabinet to avert war. Despairing of preventing a conflict in which, either by remaining neutral or by acting in a hostile manner towards France, the Prussian monarchy ran the risk of definitely disappearing, the Prussian government made up its mind to solicit from the French cabinet an alliance which it had declined at a time when it would have been very useful. But this time the royal government used all its power to bring it about. Although Napoleon could have no real trust in a cabinet which only asked for an alliance with France because it was out of its power to wage war upon us, a purely defensive treaty of alliance was signed with Prussia on February 24, 1812. The King undertook to supply the French army with a contingent of 20,000 men. One of the secret clauses of the treaty revealed the mistrust which, on the part of France, was so justified by the conduct of Prussia in 1806. This power, by a clause in the treaty, deprived itself of the power of making any levy of men, or of ordering any movement of troops, without having previously concerted with France.

Offering easier terms to Austria the Emperor concluded a treaty with her on March 14 of the same year. The contingent of the Austrian monarchy was fixed at 30,000 men. One of the secret clauses stipulated that if, as a consequence of the war, the Kingdom of Poland should be reestablished, Austria would agree to cede a part of Galicia to be added to this kingdom in exchange for the Illyrian provinces, which France then and there agreed to abandon to her by way of compensation. In the case of a happy issue of the war France also promised to procure to Austria indemnities and increase of territory which would not only compensate her for the cooperation in this war, but which would also be "a monument of the intimate and lasting union which existed between the two sovereigns."

Negotiations were at the same time carried on with Sweden, who by her geographical position, in threatening Russia with a formidable diversion, covered the left of our army. But these negotiations were entirely lacking in good faith on the part of the Stockholm cabinet. And to give the proof of this at once, I will mention that while the Crown Prince was haggling with us over his help against Russia—May 29, 1812—he had signed a treaty of alliance with that power two months previously, namely, on March 24. The Swedish cabinet had been frequently warned that if Pomerania continued to serve as a market for English trade, and as the receptacle of the libelous publications directed against France, the French government would be obliged to occupy this province. No satisfactory answer having been received on this subject, Prince of Eckmuehl, commanding the French troops in the Hanseatic provinces, had had possession taken of Stralsund, on January 30, by a premature interpretation of instructions which had been given him against British commerce. Marshal Davout was authorized to take this step by the continual traffic which was going on between Stralsund and Heligoland, a rock near the coast, which had become a rich storehouse of English ammunition, goods, and libelous publications, and the hotbed of active intrigues. The occupation of Pomerania, foreseen at Stockholm, was considered inevitable; a great deal of noise, however, was made about it there. The Crown Prince, who at that time was already engaged in very advanced *pourparlers* with Russia, offered to break them off on a condition which he knew to be unacceptable. He asked that France should guarantee him the acquisition of Norway, by despoiling Denmark, our most faithful ally, whose possessions we had guaranteed. The Emperor Alexander, in order to attach Sweden to the coalition, had promised the Crown Prince to hand Norway over to him in compensation for the annexation of Finland to Russia. England, constant to her hatred for Denmark, on account of the fidelity of this state to the French alliance, not content with ratifying this promise, had further undertaken to help Sweden in the conquest of Norway

The perseverance of the Crown Prince in his pretensions on this country, did not stop Napoleon in his negotiations with the Stockholm cabinet. He employed every means to reach Bernadotte's heart, and to recall him to a sense of duty and of his true interests. The Emperor even caused the Princess Royal, who was at that time in Paris, to act upon her husband with this purpose in view. Napoleon has been reproached for having left the letters which the Crown Prince addressed him unanswered for several weeks. The Emperor's communications with the Swedish cabinet had, perhaps, to be waited for at first, but they were always calm, dignified, and marked by a spirit of conciliation, which gives a denial to the charge of haughtiness and bitterness which has been directed against them. The proof of this will be found in the notes which were exchanged between the two governments, notes which were published after 1815.

Napoleon undertook not to conclude peace until the restitution of Finland to Sweden had been obtained. If the Crown Prince, having other objects in view, could not accept this proposal, nothing in any case prevented him from remaining neutral. Honor, the constancy of France's goodwill towards Sweden, the gratitude due from Bernadotte to his first country—a gratitude which nothing rendered incompatible with his new duties—all his past, in one word, imposed neutrality at least, but his feeling of hatred got the upper hand. Bernadotte did not content himself with declaring against France, he did more, he sent into the wilds of America for an accomplice in his desertion, General Moreau, and obtained not only the cession of Norway, but also of Guadeloupe, the restitution of which France only obtained in 1814.

I speak here for the last time of the relations of the Empire with the Crown Prince of Sweden, in spite of the fact that these perfidious negotiations—for they merit this appellation—continued till the month of June, 1814. Napoleon's cutting saying about Bernadotte is known: "One is not obliged to deny one's mother, in taking a wife, and still less to wish to stab her to the heart."

The defection of Turkey was caused by the belief with which the Divan had been inspired that France was abandoning her alliance for an alliance with Russia, and by the absence at this decisive moment of our ambassador to the Sublime Porte. Since the month of January, 1812, a man eminently French, who from his mission to Turkey had kept up relations from which he obtained valuable and reliable information, the Chevalier Amédée Jaubert—alarmed at the warnings which his private letters from Constantinople gave him of the ever-growing influence exercised on the Divan by the Russians—took it upon himself to acquaint the Minister of Foreign Affairs with the matter. This minister, struck by a state of things the gravity of which had not been revealed to him by his agents, consulted the Emperor on the subject. Napoleon's keen-sightedness, which rarely was at fault, impressed him with the necessity of having at Constantinople an ambassador, whose word would have greater weight than that of a simple chargé d'affaires. He accordingly immediately appointed General Andréossy ambassador to Turkey. This envoy left for Laybach, where he stopped, waiting to receive the usual presents which he was to take with him, and without which he did not wish to present himself before the Turkish authorities. In the meanwhile the, skilful Russian diplomacy had not remained idle; intrigues and corruption had gained ground and made progress, which the authority of a French ambassador would probably have checked. The Emperor, since the month of June, had not ceased insisting that Constantinople should be apprised by every means of his march against Russia, so as to prop up the wavering faith of the Divan. I will not pronounce on the question to what cause the prolonged stay of Andréossy at Laybach must be attributed. The ambassador left it at last and hastened on with all diligence, but though he accomplished a part of the way at full speed, he only managed to reach Therapia on July 25. A fictitious letter from Napoleon to the Emperor Alexander proposing as the first clause of a treaty of peace, the division of Turkey, was put under the eyes of the Grand Vizir. Joseph Fonton, a dragoman in the pay of England, consulted by Ghalib Effendi, attested the authenticity of this document. The fact of General Narbonne's presence at Vilna helped to finally make up the mind of the Ottoman minister, and of the Sultan, who till then had refused to ratify the treaty the preliminaries of which, signed by the plenipotentiaries of the Porte and of Russia, at Bucharest, May 25, had arrived in Constantinople on June 6. It was only on the following 14th of July that the Sultan decided to ratify the treaty which was to become so fatal to us. The error, or the treachery, of the Grand Vizir, which had been so prejudicial to us was punished, though not repaid, by the loss of his head, and the execution of the perfidious agents who had advised him. The ambassador Andréossy only arrived in Constantinople ten days later.

In the course of March, 1812, the Emperor, surmounting the feeling of repulsion with which M. de Talleyrand's spirit of intrigue had filled him had the idea of sending him to Warsaw. He approached him confidentially on the subject, recommending him not to mention it. Shortly afterwards Napoleon learned that ducats were being bought at Vienna on account of his minister, and that the secret of his mission had become known. The Emperor, displeased at seeing his plan exposed, and considering this domestic arrangement as a proof of collusion and a kind of stock-jobbing speculation on the Viennese public funds, abandoned the choice he had made, and appointed Abbé Pradt, who had followed him to Dresden, in Prince de Bénévent's place.

The Emperor strongly desired that the contingent supplied by Austria should be placed under the command of Prince Schwarzenberg who had been ambassador to Paris since 1809; and asked that the rank of field-marshal might be given him with this purpose in view. As the prince was one of the youngest generals of cavalry in active service, this request was evaded, and some private correspondence ensued between the two emperors. The Emperor of Austria, having alleged the rigor of military regulations, consented to be agreeable to Napoleon, while taking care to make it known that the nomination of Prince Charles Schwarzenberg was only due to his respect for the recommendation of his nephew the Emperor of the French.

The answer to the message of reconciliation—with which the Emperor had charged Colonel Czernitchev, at the time of that officer's departure from Paris for St. Petersburg—only arrived six weeks later at the Tuileries. It was Russia's ultimatum. The following were the conditions thereof: The Emperor Alexander imposed on the Emperor Napoleon, as an obligation which must precede all negotiations, the evacuation by the French troops of all Prussian states and of Swedish Pomerania, that is to say, the throwing open of the forts of the Oder and of Danzig to the Russian invasion. These conditions having been fulfilled, Russia would consent to treat on a basis which should put no obstacle in the way of the admission of neutrals into Russian harbors, promising not to aggravate the prohibitive measures which the Russian government had thought fit to decree for the advantage of its commerce; the St. Petersburg cabinet declared itself ready to conclude an arrangement in favor of Sweden, and finally to accept, in exchange for the surrender of the Duchy of Oldenburg, some equivalent compensation. This notification, offensive in its form rather than in its contents, seemed so strange to Napoleon that he suspected that it must be the result of some intrigue, like the one which had just resulted in the banishment of Speranski, the privy councilor. The injunction to evacuate Germany, without any treaty having previously stipulated the terms of this evacuation, deeply wounded the Emperor's pride. It was with no sincere desire for peace that the character and dignity of such a sovereign as Napoleon were put to such a test. In 1806, the King of Prussia had forgotten himself to the point of notifying a similar summons to him. Never had Napoleon in the course of his brilliant victories dreamed of making such insulting demands on his adversaries. A note, drawn up in the sense of the proposals which we have mentioned, was handed in Paris by Prince Kurakin, the Russian ambassador, to Duke Bassano, Minister of Foreign Affairs, who evaded all discussion on this basis. Prince Kurakin asked for an audience with the Emperor, a request which could not be refused. The Emperor hid his resentment. He attributed, he said, the communications made by the ambassador solely to a misunderstanding, which he was anxious to clear up before entering upon any explanations, and added that he reserved to himself to write on the subject to the Emperor of Russia. Napoleon, with this object in view, sent Count Narbonne off to St. Petersburg at once, charged with the mission of endeavoring to find out the secret of the Czar's action, and to discover whether there remained no means of coming to an understanding with Russia. In Paris Prince Kurakin pressed for the acceptance of his proposals and demanded his passports in case of refusal, but only received evasive answers from M. de Bassano.

While matters were in this state the Emperor left for Dresden, whither he was followed some days later by M. de Bassano. As to Prince Kurakin he withdrew to the country to await his passports. These were not sent to him, so as not to break off all relations with Russia.

There remained to Napoleon nothing but to confide the destiny of this great undertaking to the most splendid army which he had ever put into the field. Wishing to dispose of all his forces, to strike a great blow, and to return promptly to Spain (where during two years he kept a detachment of his household with the chamberlain Brigode, equerries, brigades of horses, and pack-mules, and an entire campaign outfit) he awaited the moment for beginning the war, to which he had been forced, with confidence in his strength and in his right. He did not, however, lose all hopes of avoiding it, and up to the crossing of the Niemen, tried to flatter himself that some arrangement was still possible. The Emperor took advantage of every opportunity to reach Alexander's heart. He had a real affection for this prince, and a confidence in his private character which was not justified by events. He was convinced that an hour's conversation with him in private would end in a complete understanding. Later on, when hostilities were at their height, and while the chances of war were not yet unfavorable to him, Napoleon ordered Alexander to be written to. He even wrote to him personally by every way, either on the occasion of the passage of the flags of truce, which the exchange of some Russian generals who had been taken prisoners brought to his headquarters, or under other circumstances, when for example he was trying to minimize the evils caused by the barbarity with which the Russians acted in this most murderous war.

The atmosphere of the Court, the habit which Marie Louise had of living familiarly with the Emperor, who paid her a great deal of attention, treated her with simple and affectionate manners, and often amused her with a gaiety which was often animated, had caused this princess to forget the stiffness and reserve which she owed to her natural timidity at the time of her arrival in France. Her bearing became easy; she had become somewhat less stout, and her figure, which was of perfect symmetry, had very much improved. Fine eyes, full of sweetness, and a beautifully fresh complexion gave to her face an agreeable expression, and rendered the *ensemble* of her person both noble and graceful.

Weighed down by duties and cares on the eve of a rupture with Russia, the Emperor's time was taken up with the multifarious occupations of his cabinets, with reviews, and with the work of his ministers. It was only with his wife and his son that he found agreeable relief from so much fatigue. The little leisure which his affairs left him in the daytime was spent with his son, whose tottering steps it pleased him to guide with quite a womanly care. The frequent falls of this cherished child when they had not been prevented were greeted with caresses and loud shouts of laughter by his father. The Empress, who used to be present at these family scenes, did not take so active a part in them as the Emperor. These three persons, whose simplicity might have led one to forget their greatness, offered the spectacle of a middle-class family attached to each other by the fondest affection. Who could then have thought of the fate which was reserved to them?

This great man, whom so many prejudiced or mistaken minds have been pleased to represent as being inaccessible to any tender sentiment, was both a good husband and an excellent father; never did the Empress find in him the censor of her innocent whims. The following anecdote, which Marie Louise used to be fond of calling to mind, shows the good nature of Napoleon in this respect. The remembrance of a taste, which she had acquired in the very homely sort of life she had led when quite a girl, inspired one day the Empress with a desire to make an omelet herself, and she had had all the necessary ingredients brought into her apartment. While completely taken up with her very important culinary operation, the Emperor entered without having been announced, either by chance, or because he had heard from some officious person what was going on, and wanted to have the pleasure of surprising Marie Louise. The latter, somewhat upset by this unexpected visit, endeavored to prevent Napoleon from seeing what she was preparing. "What is going on here?" asked the Emperor. "There is a singular smell, as if something was being fried!" Then, stepping behind the Empress, he discovered the spirit lamp, the silver frying pan in which the butter was beginning to melt, the salad-bowl, and the eggs. "What!" cries Napoleon, "so you are making an omelet! Bah! you don't know how to do it at all. I will show you how it is to be done." He then set to work, the Empress acting as his assistant, but he was trying to teach an assistant who knew more about it than he did, and whose education had been obtained in a very lofty school. The Empress's parents were passionately fond of rustic occupations, loving to withdraw into some rustic home built in the center of great imperial parks, and there, disguised as farmers, to attend to household duties with their children.

The omelet, then, having been finished, somehow or other, there remained the important operation of tossing it. Napoleon wanted to do this himself; but he had thought himself cleverer than he was, and just as he was trying to toss the omelet there happened to him what happened to the great Condé, who according to Gourville wished to make an omelet at an inn, where he had stopped, and pitched it into the fire when trying to turn it. Napoleon did not succeed any better, and let the omelet fall on the ground. He was then obliged to confess his want of experience, and left the Empress to go on with her cooking alone.

In the spring of 1812 the Emperor was enabled by the return of the fine weather to add to his family amusements excursions on horseback, and hunts, in which the Empress followed him, either at St. Cloud or at Rambouillet—residences of which he was fond because he was surrounded by fewer people, and was more at liberty. Sometimes at break of day he would wake the Empress up to go out riding with her. Together with Marie Louise he would ride through the beautiful woods which surround St. Cloud. Some of these rides had a fixed and useful object, either in the direction of Paris or in the surroundings. On some occasions the sovereigns went to pay a visit to the works of embellishment or improvement which had been commanded by Napoleon. The guardians of these works were sometimes taken by surprise, fast asleep, by these sudden visits, and would look at these new inspectors with amazement, believing themselves in the presence of a vision. As these excursions were never announced in advance the aide-de-camp and equerry in attendance, together with two or three outriders, formed the whole party. The Empress was never accompanied by any of her ladies. Some of these used to meet her on her return, or wait for her in her apartment. Marie Louise used to get into the carriage, which followed them, when she felt tired, but this happened but rarely. The Emperor always came back from these excursions, whether he went out alone or with Marie Louise, with some idea for improving or perfecting the works in his mind. If he found on his road some piece of work to which his attention had been directed, he would examine in person to what an extent the carrying out of such a work would be useful. At the first glance Napoleon would take a survey of the site, and of the works which had been begun, forming a just idea of the best way in which they could be directed, of their duration, and of the expense which they would occasion. On his return he would commission his ministers to call together their heads of departments, the engineers, and scientific men, and unite them in a council over which he used to preside. On hearing the reading of their reports he would apply to them the first notions which he had gathered on the spot itself, having determined in his head in what way the works might be perfected. In spite of the rapidity of his examination he had generally made himself as fully acquainted thereby with all the details of the work as the specialists, who had made it the object of their constant studies, could have done. Nature had lavished upon Napoleon the faculties which she reserves to privileged beings created to command, to conduct, and to enlighten mankind. She had endowed him with a vivid and ardent imagination, united with a cold reasoning power; she had endowed him with genius fortified by study, which the most prolonged and arid labor could not wear out, and which, on the contrary, drew fresh stores of vigor from the diversity of his occupations; she had endowed him with a vast mind, which embraced the *ensemble* of the widest questions, and which descended to the most minute details; she had endowed him with a really extraordinary conception to which sudden flashes revealed the deepest depths of human knowledge; she had endowed him with a prodigious memory. To these gifts of intelligence there was added in Napoleon a lofty and sensitive mind, but a mind which was strongly tempered, and which rose superior to the blows as to the favors of fortune. His *sang-froid* was unalterable in the midst of danger as though he had felt himself invulnerable. A persevering and inflexible will, an instinct of power and superiority which broke down all obstacles, made him smile at the word "impossible," or deny its existence. The study of the human heart had taught him the art of attaching men to him, and of subjugating them. His presence and his language excited enthusiasm, his eloquence was vivacious and rapid, his words were energetic, profound, and often sublime. His simple exterior—simple, but heightened with an air of grandeur and by the habit of command, the fascination of his look—his look, whose sweet or severe expression penetrated to the bottom of all hearts, inspired respect mingled with fear and affection. Never was there a more popular leader in history, and yet he would never consent to lower himself to acquire such popularity. His vigilance was constantly on the alert to reform abuses of every kind, to discover means of raising France to the eminence where his genius dreamt of placing her; at the same time the indefatigable activity of his body and mind induced him to practice the principle that one should not let others do what one could do oneself. The main feeling of what is just and what is unjust dominated within him. So far above other men, he was, whatever may have been said, superior to men's passions, he knew how to pity the weakness and the misery of the human heart. Although as a general rule he was indulgent toward faults and errors, he had thought it sometimes necessary to rebuke severely in public those who had committed them, less to punish those to whom his reproaches were addressed than for an example, and to impress the minds of those who witnessed these scenes. His severity usually limited itself to this.

Often clement towards his adversaries he was reluctant to act against them, and ended by becoming their victim. Those who have represented his government as the type of a military domination have not noticed what a little part in the power Napoleon, who was adored by the army, gave to his lieutenants, and with what care he maintained his soldiers in a state of submission to civil authority. Endowed in the supremest degree with military genius, the reputation of the most illustrious captains pales before his, and yet it is not only to the glory of his army that he owed his reputation and his empire. He was an administrator, a politician, a legislator, a writer, even a savant, and indeed everything that he wished to be—as well as a great soldier. The constant object of his labors, of his conquests, an object which time did not allow him to attain, can be summed up in one phrase: to assure to all men the full exercise and the entire enjoyment of all their faculties. It was Napoleon himself who attributed to himself this lofty ambition, nor will posterity deny him the merit of it. His thoughts, his actions, his very ambition converged towards this lofty object: to regenerate the nations, to scatter broadcast amongst them opinions of progress together with enlightenment, to bestow everywhere and on all classes the inalienable privileges of civil and political liberty.

Preoccupied with his lofty ambition and with the duty of protecting the future of France against the hatreds of the old-world Europe, Napoleon was necessarily forced in the development of his measures for enforcing his conceptions to clash with many prejudices, and to wound many and various susceptibilities. In putting aside the obstacles which impeded his onward march, he could not help injuring many interests of all kinds. Having fallen in the midst of his glorious and laborious career, the elevation of his ideas and the object of his plans have escaped the eye of the vulgar, who only judge by success. Those whom fortune has abandoned are generally judged with but little indulgence. Napoleon has remained after his fall a prey to attacks which are often unjust and undeserved. Even at the time at which I am writing he has not yet been judged with sufficient impartiality, and yet the hatred of him is dying out, passion is losing its force, prejudices are becoming dissipated, and the minds of men enlightened.

The path traced out by his genius, the object towards which he marched, will appear one day freed from the clouds which so long had shrouded them in darkness. This is what in my opinion, will happen for Napoleon, whose glory the future can only increase.

In his private relations Napoleon was simple, natural, an observer of forms towards himself as well as towards others. Of easy manners in his family life, generous, and benevolent, he had orderly morals, religious sentiments, and great tolerance. He was a good father, a good husband, a good son, and a good brother.

Napoleon applied to the acts of his public life the qualities which he had in his private life and which were inherent to his nature. This respect for morality he exacted from his ministers, and from the functionaries of state. Not only did he seek—in those whom he associated with his labors—for talents appropriated to the lofty posts which were entrusted to them, but also a scrupulous probity, a spirit of equity and justice, and honorable morals. Those whom the nature of their functions put into direct relations with him distinguished themselves by these qualities, with one or two exceptions in the case of men who were necessary to him, and who by reasons of prudence or superior political motives could not be definitely removed from his councils. Those who by reason of the secondary importance of their functions did not approach his person were none the less the objects of his attention. Abuses, acts contrary to the respect with which he wished his agents to be surrounded, were immediately repressed by severe reprimands, or punished by dismissal. It must be added that never was sovereign so well served, or inspired so much devotion, never under any reign were services of any and every kind less exposed to hazards, more independent of caprice, or less liable to be forgotten. Those who served Napoleon well were always largely recompensed.

On the 18th Brumaire the future Emperor had found France the prey to the most fatal dissensions, and the care of uniting the French in a common interest of national prosperity and greatness became his constant preoccupation. Everybody of any value in France, both under the Consulate and the Empire was summoned by the Head of the government, without distinction of caste or of opinion, to help him in the task of reorganizing the state, of founding French unity and nationality, and laying the basis of that vigorous administration which Napoleon bequeathed to his successors. All citizens, both in civil and military life, seconded Napoleon with zeal and fidelity, for the spirit and will of the nation were personified in him.

In brief, there were united in the same man all the great qualities which I have only given in outline, crowned with an ardent love for his country.

After the signing of the treaties with Austria and Prussia at the beginning of 1812, of which I have already spoken, the Emperor decided to pay a visit to Dresden before proceeding to the army. He proposed to assemble his allies there. He had not yet given up all hope of avoiding the great struggle which was preparing. Napoleon spoke to the Empress of his intention of inviting the Emperor of Austria to meet him in the capital of the King of Saxony. The Empress Marie Louise received this proposal with great pleasure, for it was her warmest wish to see her father and her family, with whom she kept up a regular correspondence, once more.

In consequence Count Otto, our ambassador in Vienna, was commissioned to invite the Emperor Francis to come to Dresden with the Empress and the Archdukes and Archduchesses, brothers and sisters of Marie Louise, who looked forward with pleasure to spending some days with them.

The necessity of coping with the serious difficulties caused by the lack of wheat, with which France was threatened, delayed the Emperor's departure to Dresden for a month. Since 1811 the scarcity of wheat had been felt, and this scarcity had developed towards the beginning of 1812 in a manner to cause anxiety. Extraordinary measures, and an allotment of 25,000,000 francs for the purpose of reducing the price of bread, ample daily distributions of cheap soups, and above all the promise of a good harvest, dispelled this danger. The Emperor displayed under these circumstances the activity which he knew how to apply to all things. Every two days he presided over councils of maintenance, to which he summoned competent men, and his solicitude and foresight extended to the minutest details of the question.

At the time of engaging in a distant and hazardous expedition, the Emperor feared that during an absence which might be prolonged, the English, whose ships were cruising before Genoa, might attempt to forcibly remove the pope from Savona, in order to make of the Head of the Catholic Church a docile instrument in their hands, in spite of the fact that their hands were the hands of heretics. With a view of providing against this eventuality he ordered that the Holy Father should be invited to go to Fontainebleau, in order to remove him out of the sphere of English intrigues. At the same time Napoleon summoned the Archbishop of Edessa to Fontainebleau, thinking that the society of this prelate, who was much liked by the pope, would be both agreeable and useful to His Holiness.

The Emperor had sent M. de Montholon, who was the son-in-law of Senator Sémonville, to Würtzburg as plenipotentiary minister, because, as he thought, the court of the Grand Duke would be to the French envoy a mirror in which he could see the reflection of all that was going on in Vienna. Prince Ferdinand of Austria, formerly Grand Duke of Tuscany, who had been dispossessed of his States by the Treaty of Lunéville, had obtained in exchange for the Duchy of Salzburg, the Grand Duchy of Würtzburg, in virtue of a clause of the Treaty of 1809. He had come to Paris as a member of the Confederation of the Rhine to be present at the marriage of his niece Marie Louise. He stayed rather a long time in Paris, and lived in the intimacy of the imperial family and court. The object for which M. de Montholon was sent was to a certain extent realized, for the new ambassador gave useful information on the internal state of things in Austria and Germany.

Count Montholon had passed through a brilliant military career. His services previous to the day of Brumaire 18th, and his cooperation on that same day, had been recompensed with the gift of the sword of honor. He was obliged to renounce his military career temporarily, in consequence of wounds and bad health. He then became chamberlain to the Emperor, and was entrusted with various missions, in which he knew how to display his skill. His diplomatic career was however suddenly interrupted by a marriage which displeased Napoleon. General Montholon, as a matter of fact, during his visit to Würtzburg, and without the knowledge of his family, married a woman who had been twice divorced, and whose two husbands were still living. The Emperor had refused his consent to this marriage; but, during his stay in Dresden, he granted M. Montholon permission to marry the niece of President Séguier, because he had forgotten that the lady in question was the identical person whose marriage he had refused to authorize. Napoleon, however, was soon made acquainted with the true state of things, and refused to allow the divorced woman to be presented at the Court of Würtzburg, and this out of consideration for the susceptibility of the small German courts, which in this case at least was very excusable. General Montholon, in consequence, was ordered to retire immediately from his place, and to return to Paris forthwith. The Emperor's resentment, however, was not long-lived. Count Montholon very soon reentered the service and was entrusted with the command of a department. On Napoleon's return from the Island of Elba, this faithful servant made haste to go and meet him, attached himself entirely to his person, and in the end, together with his wife and children, followed him to St. Helena, where, until the very end, he gave the Emperor touching proofs of the most absolute devotion.

Before leaving Paris the Emperor, according to his custom, had dispatched all matters which were behindhand, or which were awaiting his decision. He had established an order of service in virtue of which the government was confided during his absence to the Council of Ministers, presided over by the Arch-Chancellor Cambacérès. An auditor charged with the minister's portfolio was sent each week to the minister secretary of state, who always accompanied the Emperor. The Minister of Police himself wrote every day. Napoleon also used to receive confidential letters or notes from persons who were not employed in the government but who were authorized or permitted to write to him, as the readers have seen, on matters of home politics, on the state of the public opinion, and even on literary subjects. Although distant 800 or 900 leagues from Paris, Napoleon governed the Empire as though he were present. The Empress was at that time only charged with the representative part of the functions. She used to go to mass every Sunday, and all persons who had been presented at Court were allowed to be present on these occasions. After mass she used to walk round the gallery which led into the chapel and converse with everybody present. She used also to receive on certain grand occasions. At such times her timidity was noticeable and the efforts which she made to surmount this timidity gave her an embarrassed bearing. The persons of both sexes whose names were registered on the lists of *entrées* were admitted every evening to her receptions.

It was the Emperor who had drawn up this list, and he had taken care to select persons who were agreeable to the Empress. The consequence was, that at these drawing rooms she was perfectly at her ease, and did the honors with much grace and natural manners. She used to play at billiards with persons whom she selected. Whist tables were set up for form in her drawing room, and the evenings terminated with a concert or theatrical performance.

On May 9, 1812, the Emperor and Empress left St. Cloud, and arrived at Mayence on the 14th, where they stayed. Their Majesties saw the Grand Duke and Grand duchess of Hesse-Darmstadt. The journey from Mayence to Dresden was one unbroken triumphal procession, and the princes of the Confederation of the Rhine, whose States were passed through by the French sovereigns, received them as their Suzerains, and showed them the hospitality of grand-vassals. Many even came to wait for them on the road, amongst others the King of Würtemberg, and the Grand Duke of Baden. It would be a mistake to fancy that the Emperor expected his hosts to pay for his entertainment and that of his suite. Napoleon did not wish his visits to give trouble to anybody. He was preceded and followed by his household, together with all that was necessary for a life of great display. Some leagues from Dresden he met the King of Saxony, who had come to meet him, accompanied by his Queen. The Emperor and Empress made their entrance into Dresden, with Their Saxon Majesties, by torchlight. On the morrow the Emperor and Empress of Austria, and the Archdukes also arrived at Dresden, and were followed in turn by the Queen of Westphalia (the King had already gone to join the army), the Grand Duke of Würtzburg, the King and Crown Prince of Prussia, and many of the princes of the Confederation, the principal ministers, and amongst others MM. de Hardenberg and Metternich.

The Emperor Francis embraced Napoleon with visible emotion. The Empress of Austria and the Archdukes received Marie Louise with an ardor which was mingled with respect. The King of Prussia presented the Crown Prince to the Emperor, and begged him to allow him to follow him as aide-de-camp, and at the same time begged the Emperor's aides-de-camp to bestow their friendship on his son.

The period of Napoleon's stay in Dresden, in 1812, marks the apogee of his power. Words are wanting to describe the effect which his presence produced there. Never perhaps has human greatness reached so high a point. It has been said that Napoleon at Dresden was the Agamemnon, king of kings: it was to his intellectual superiority almost as much as to his power that at that time these spontaneous manifestations of respect and consideration were addressed. An emperor, kings, and sovereign princes, stood at his side as courtiers rather than as peers. The Emperor of Austria was forgotten in

Napoleon's presence, and the latter had to efface himself to draw attention to a Prince whose illustrious son-in-law centered all attention on himself. It must not be judged from their attitude that the Emperor of Austria and the King of Prussia were sincere in their demonstrations towards the man who had conquered them. If these princes had been able for the moment to forget their secret grudges they had near their persons clever ministers who would have taken it upon themselves to remind them of their grievances. The Empress of Austria, a well-read and intelligent woman, came to Dresden armed with her dignity as a beautiful woman and as an Empress, full of prejudices against the man to whom the Austrian monarchy owed its greatest humiliation. Marie Louise's young step-mother came determined to resist the general enthusiasm, and to hold herself in a reserve which should fringe on contempt. In a very short time she had yielded to the influence which Napoleon exercised on all. I had frequent opportunities of observing the aspect of these august assemblies, and I have contemplated the royal assembly, of which Napoleon was the head, in the vast apartment of the Palace at Dresden. The Empress of Austria was in such poor health that she was unable to support the fatigue of walking a long distance in the apartment. The Emperor used to go to meet her, holding his hat in one hand, the other hand resting on the door of the Sedan chair, in which the Empress was being carried, talking to her in a cheerful manner. The Empress seemed to take an interest in his conversation and showed her interest by the attention with which she listened to, and answered him. All those who were present at these moments agree in saying that Napoleon exercised an irresistible ascendency over his noble hosts, as much by the agreeableness of his wit, as by the seduction of his manners. One might have said that this extraordinary man had, since his youth, carried the weight of a great empire on his shoulders, so well did he know how to support the dignity of his rank by his tone and by his manners. Penetrating and profound as was his intelligence, nothing escaped his observing eye. Perfect tact, and a delicate instinct of what was Duke to all, were wedded in this exceptional mind to maturity and education, and this assembly of superior qualities rendered him the most amiable and charming of men *when he chose to show himself as such.*

The first idea of the journey to Dresden had arisen from Marie Louise's desire to see her family again and be once more in the midst of her people. The presence of the Emperor of Austria at Dresden necessarily entailed also the presence of the King of Prussia, who was equally the ally of France in the war which was being prepared. Napoleon's principal reason in assembling the kings and the princes of the Confederation of the Rhine had been to show Russia how strong were the bonds which united these different princes to the system of the French Empire. The Emperor had not despaired of impressing Russia and of leading this power to less bellicose feelings by means of this display of a close alliance with the sovereigns of the whole of Germany, together with a display of considerable forces. As a matter of fact, and I cannot repeat this too often, Napoleon was entering upon this war with extreme reluctance, and until the very last moment in his heart of hearts he hoped to be able to avoid it. Before leaving Paris the Emperor had sent General Narbonne, his aide-de-camp, to St. Petersburg. Having no news of General Narbonne at Dresden, and hearing that the Emperor Alexander had arrived at Vilna, he sent word to Count Lauriston, his ambassador, to proceed to this city and to address himself to the Czar directly. Napoleon accordingly, it cannot be denied, fostered a feeble hope that the difficulties might yet be overcome. He loved to think that reflection having enlightened Alexander the latter would be inclined to withdraw the strong summons addressed by the Russian cabinet to the French government, ordering us to evacuate the territory occupied by our armies before any negotiations or *pourparlers* had taken place. General Lauriston was not even able to obtain authorization to go to Vilna, and as to Count Narbonne he returned to Dresden on May 24, only five days before the Emperor's departure. He had been received by the Russian sovereign, but he had not found him at all inclined to make any alteration in his views. The cold and inflexible attitude of this prince, his reserve, his perseverance in unacceptable demands, convinced Napoleon that the Czar had made up his mind, and that he had engaged himself towards England too far to be able to draw back any more. Unable any longer to deceive himself as to the uselessness of his attempts at reconciliation, the Emperor sent orders to Paris that Prince Kurakin's passport should be returned to him. The Duke of Bassano's letter, which was sent with these passports, was so worded that the ambassador of Russia could not but see that the insistence with which he had asked for them could no longer be considered in any other light than as a declaration of war.

In the midst of imposing fêtes, drawing rooms, and balls, in Dresden, had it not been known that there were stationed around us 500,000 men ready to enter the arena, one would have thought neither of war nor of the great events which were preparing—events in which each one of the actors took a particular and very different interest.

Amongst the persons in the suite of the Emperor of Austria was a man vested with the title of chamberlain, who made himself known in military commands, in diplomatic missions, but who passed unnoticed in the royal and princely crowd. This man was General Count Neipperg. The Empress Marie Louise saw him there for the first time, without attaching the slightest importance to his presence. However, as she was going to the theatre room with the Emperor, she addressed some words to this general because he happened to be standing in her way. How impenetrable are the designs of God! These three persons, whom the festivities of Dresden had drawn together, in such different ranks, were far from suspecting at that time the part which the most humble amongst them was destined to play in the future.

On May 29 the Empress Marie Louise was the only one of the guests who remained in Dresden. The Emperor Napoleon had left her on that day to join the army. The Emperor and Empress of Austria had set out for Prague the same day themselves, to hurry on the preparations for the reception of their daughter and stepdaughter. On the evening before, the King of Prussia and the Crown Prince had left to return to Berlin. Marie Louise remained in Dresden alone for some days, and left on June 4 for Prague. Her journey was an uninterrupted triumph, she was complimented on the Austrian frontier; she was received under triumphal arches, and escorted by numerous squadrons of cavalry in full uniform. The Emperor and Empress came to meet her, and conducted her to Prague, which she entered to the sound of cannon, and church bells. The civil and religious authorities, the court, and the leading nobility of the provinces were presented to her. The Emperor and Empress of Austria gave precedence to Marie Louise both at table and in the carriages, and everywhere she was received with the honors which were reserved for the Austrian sovereigns on gala days. This stay at Prague lasted more than three weeks, and every day was taken up with banquets, balls, excursions, illuminations, or theatrical performances. Alternate receptions were held at the palace of the Emperor of Austria, and at the palace of the Empress Marie Louise. Nothing was wanting in the honors lavished on Napoleon's wife on Austrian territory. It might have been said that the family of Hapsburg, in harmony with fortune, was saluting with a final and splendid homage the man whose star was so soon to wane, and at last to go out—to be altogether extinguished.

In the midst of these enjoyments Marie Louise never for a moment forgot the Emperor, and used to write to him every day. On June 25 she wrote the following letter to Napoleon's mother:

"Prague, June 25, 1812.

"The Emperor is wonderfully well. He is still in the neighborhood of Königsberg, always busy, always on horseback, and all the better for it. The only comfort which I have during his absence is to think that the fatigue which he endures gives me no reason to fear for his health. He writes to me very often, and each day that I receive a letter from him is a day of happiness for me. . . . Nothing can console me for the Emperor's absence, not even the presence of all my family."

On July 1, the Empress Marie Louise left Prague with her father, who accompanied her as far as Carlsbad, and on the 18th she was back again at St. Cloud.

In the meantime Napoleon visited Glogau, Posen, Thorn, Danzig, and Königsberg, in turn. During his stay in the latter city the Emperor held a great review in the plain of Friedland, which reminded him of one of his most splendid triumphs. He inspected the various army corps, and conducted them to the Niemen which was crossed on June 24. On the 22nd of the same month a proclamation, dated from Wilkovicki, had announced the declaration of war on Russia. On the 25th of May previously, this power had endeavored to sign the Treaty of Bucharest with the Porte, and on the 29th of the same month, had declared all its ports open to ships of all nations, which meant to say that they were open to English trade.

On the morrow of the day on which the proclamation of Wilkovicki had been entered on the order of the day, Napoleon went to reconnoiter in person which point on the Niemen was most favorable to crossing. He put a hood over his coat, and placed on his head the forage cap of one of the Polish Light Cavalry of the Guard. Three bridges were thrown over the river, near Kovno, by his orders, and it was by these bridges that the army crossed the river in the night of the June 23, and during the whole following day. After the Niemen had been crossed, and during the march from Kovno to Vilna, no Russian soldiers were met with, except some light troops near the latter town, which was entered by the French without any fighting. The weather had changed suddenly after the crossing of the Niemen, and the rain, which fell in torrents, inundated the roads, and this disorganized all the army transport service. The Emperor entered Vilna on June 28, and he was received there like a liberator, and as the restorer of Polish independence. I will now speak of an incident which happened to a Polish squadron, and which occurred while crossing a small river. I do so because the losses which it is alleged were suffered by these squadrons have been stated with a great deal of exaggeration. The bridge having broken down, the Poles bravely swam across the river—which was much swollen by the rain—in the way practiced by the Tartars. Their loss amounted to one light cavalryman, who was carried away by the current, separated from his comrades, and drowned.

The Emperor Alexander had left Vilna three days previously to join his headquarters at Sventziani.

The narrative of the military events of the Russian campaign is not within the scope of this work. Conscientious historians have already fulfilled this task with impartiality. Memoirs which are still unpublished will relate all the occurrences which took place, and make all the conduct of this fatal war better known. The majority of writers who have undertaken to relate them have not justified their mission with sufficient impartiality. One animated with hostile sentiments against the fallen Imperial government has in his narrative shown all the ardor of his hatred and all the injustice of his prejudices. Another devoted to the Bourbon government has tried to offer them a sacrifice of the great victim. A third, seeing in the events of this war the subject of a somber epic, which tempted his literary ambition, has strained his dreamy imagination to compose a drama, which by the manner of its exposure, its action, and its *dénouement,* should realize the object which he had proposed to himself to attain. Although the causes and the combinations of this memorable expedition were in part unknown to him, the author has known how to suit them to the object he had in view *(aegri somnia).* His melancholy genius took pleasure in painting, in the blackest colors, misfortunes which were cruel enough to need no exaggeration and to excite the minds of men, already struck with this immense catastrophe, those deep emotions of which the human heart is so greedy.

The mission of the Russian general, Balakov, at Vilna, the object of which is hardly known, was a preliminary of this fatal war, and was perhaps its most certain precursor. The Emperor of Russia had received Count Narbonne at Vilna, in a manner which dispelled all hopes for the preservation of peace. He had moreover refused to see Count Lauriston, our ambassador, and even to allow his prime minister to confer with him. War had already begun, Napoleon was already in the center of Lithuania, all communications seemed broken off between the two States, when the arrival of a Russian officer at the Imperial headquarters excited general surprise, and brought back a ray of hope. This general officer, Minister of Police, whose mission no doubt was purely one of observation, bore an autograph letter from the Emperor of Russia to Napoleon. In this letter Alexander complained of the violation of his frontiers, declaring that "Prince Kurakin had not been authorized to ask for the return of his credentials, that if this was the reason why the Emperor had considered himself at war with him it was a great misunderstanding, that if Napoleon was content to withdraw his troops from Russian territory, he was prepared to shut his eyes to what had happened, and that an arrangement was still possible." The Emperor, comparing this step taken by Russia with the insistence with which Prince Kurakin had demanded his passports in Paris, with Alexander's refusal to listen to our ambassador, and the cold reception which he had awarded to Count Narbonne at Vilna, was greatly surprised at this so tardy a communication. He, however, asked the Russian envoy if he had powers, and offered to treat for peace then and there. General Balakov had neither instructions nor powers. His mission was limited to renewing the injunction which had been made in Paris by Prince Kurakin, and to demand the evacuation of the territories. The Emperor, concealing the resentment which he felt on the receipt of a notification which he was unable to define, received the bearer thereof very well, spoke to him of his master in a friendly way and with interest, but, could not but consider Alexander's message as a message intended to humiliate him, the effect of which had been well calculated by those who had advised it.

Chapter XII

Another incident which marked Napoleon's stay at Vilna was the reception of a deputation from the Diet of Warsaw, which came to ask him to declare himself in favor of a reestablishment of Poland. The address in which this wish was expressed, which had been written by Abbé de Pradt, who had not found the address written by the deputation sufficiently academical, was of a kind to embarrass the Emperor. If he did not pronounce the decision which the Poles asked for, namely: "The Kingdom of Poland is reestablished," it was because he could not and would not guarantee anything at the beginning of a war the chances of which could not be foreseen. Nor was he prepared to bind himself to the promise that he would not lay down arms until after the accomplishment of a commitment on this head. He wished, indeed, in case of a want of success, to be able to conclude peace and not to prolong a struggle which, while exhausting the forces and the resources of France, would bring with it no decisive result for Poland. A fortunate war, followed by peace, could alone allow him to enfranchise this nation and to proclaim its independence. All therefore had to depend on the issue of this war and on the way in which the Poles should conduct themselves during its course: such was the Emperor's way of thinking.

It has been seen that in the alliance which was concluded with Austria before the campaign was entered upon, the cession of a part of Galicia had been stipulated for in case Poland should come to be reestablished as a consequence of the war, that is to say after the conclusion of peace. When in 1806, Prussian Poland was created the Grand Duchy of Warsaw, Napoleon had acted with the same circumspection and had refused to pronounce himself until after victory was his.

The reasons which dictated the Emperor's answer to the Poles were just and sincere. A prudent reserve dictated the language in which he spoke to them, although his mind was fully made up to make the reestablishment of the Polish monarchy one of the conditions of peace if victory once more remained faithful to the French flag. However, this declaration produced a bad effect on the Poles and even in France. Napoleon has been blamed for having been too prudent in this matter. On reading over his declaration attentively, it will however be found that he promised his support to the Polish nation in no ambiguous terms. If he did not add to the number of Russo-Polish provinces which he advised to revolt the provinces which belonged to Austria, it was because the war being exclusively directed against Russia, it was to the Russo-Polish provinces alone that his call to arms had exclusively to be addressed. Napoleon had moreover no wish to reveal the secret of his plans nor to alienate Austria to whom he was bound by a treaty, by a want of consideration at the very outset of the campaign. What moral force would have remained to him if, in the course of a solemn audience, he had offended, by the use of indiscreet expressions, a power whose troops with the Prussian contingent formed the wings of his army? If the war had been crowned with success, the Austro-Polish provinces would necessarily have been returned to the reconstituted monarchy of Poland, Austria being compensated by means of an indemnity which would have been equivalent and even superior.

To appreciate Napoleon's interest in the reestablishment of Poland it is necessary to make known the instructions which he had given to his ambassador at Warsaw, and above all it is necessary to know why he had chosen him. With a view of assuring to his representative preponderant authority, for it was his to exercise a veritable vice-royalty in Poland, the Emperor had chosen him from amongst the high dignitaries of the Church. The rank of archbishop gave to the French envoy a political character which gave him an exceptional position, an advantage which neither a general nor a civil functionary would have enjoyed in presence of the Polish generals and ministers. Only his choice of the man was a most unfortunate one. It is one of the few reproaches of the kind which can be addressed to Napoleon, who, as a rule, was so well able to find men fitted for the functions with which he intended to entrust them.

The résumé of the instructions given to M. de Pradt, was to see all, to know all, to direct all, to animate all, but he was not to let his hand be seen. What the Emperor could not or did not wish to say was to be done by the country through the ambassador's influence. The latter was ordered to obtain from the Polish nation the revival of the great confederations, a pronouncement of its wishes, a vigorous display of all its forces, and a general revolt against Russia. The ambassador did exactly the contrary. He made it his task to calm all agitation, to annihilate all manifestation, to cool all enthusiasm. He was ordered to keep the Diet constantly assembled, to inspire it, to keep up the warmth of its patriotic feelings and the excitement with which its members were animated, and finally to keep it permanently in session, so that there should always be a tribune from which the voices of those authorized to speak could address the country, inflame the minds of men and keep the holy flame aglow. M. de Pradt dismissed this assembly after a three days' sitting; he sent the deputies back to their homes and retained alone a committee which he only assembled on rare occasions and which he prevented from acting in any way. A manifesto, comprising addresses by Polish ministers of approved talent and patriotism, whose voices were known to the Polish people, had been written. The ambassador rewrote these according to his own way of thinking, considering that they were written in savage style, and thus stripped these of their national character. In this same way he disfigured the very pronouncement of the confederation.

The Emperor hearing, at Vilna, of conduct so opposed to the orders he had given and so utterly inconsistent, regretted his choice and thought of recalling M. de Pradt; but fearing that such a recall, under existing circumstances, might produce a bad effect, contented himself with sending him a severe reprimand and renewing his instructions in a positive and peremptory manner. The delirium of pride however blinded the archbishop.

He woke up one day with the idea that the duchy was threatened by sixty thousand Russians, and at once thought of flight. He is urged to take advantage of the anxiety caused by this rumor to excite the Poles, to urge them on to levy troops, to organize guerillas and to increase the numbers of agents of the insurrection. On the morrow, this imaginary danger having passed away, M. de Pradt considers these measures useless and falls back again into a state of apathy.

There can be no doubt that the cooperation of the Poles would have been unanimous if the Emperor's instructions could have been faithfully carried out, but the man who represented France at Warsaw seemed to make it his duty to paralyze their efforts.

When one considers how M. de Pradt behaved in his embassy, as proved by his own dispatches, by the Emperor's instructions and the correspondence of the Ministry of Exterior Relations, one is tempted to accuse this fatal person of treachery, but the frivolity and the inconsistence of his character exclude such an idea. One cannot admit the suspicion that he had conceived two years in advance the plan of working in an underhand way towards the overthrow of the Empire. All the evil he occasioned in the course of the mission to Warsaw with which Napoleon had entrusted him, was inspired to him by his overweening arrogance and his foolish and ridiculous vanity.

It remained only for the man who had basely flattered Napoleon in the days of his power, who had caused him such serious damage by his incapable conduct in Poland, to hurl calumny and insult in the face of the august and unhappy man; nor did he fail to do so, acting like a faithless servant, as soon as, having nothing more to expect from his ancient benefactor and master, he had, at the same time, no more reason to fear him. The *History of the Embassy to Warsaw* is a monument of ingratitude and cowardice, to which History ought to do justice had it ever occasion to deal with its author.

A provisional government was established at Vilna. It was composed of seven members belonging to the most important families in Lithuania. Here are their names: Count Soltan, Prince Alexander Sapieha, Count Potocki, Count Sierakowski, Count Prozor, Count Tysenhaus, and the President of the University of Vilna, M. Sniadecki. A guard of honor under the command of Count Oginski was placed at the Emperor's service, followed him to Moscow, and accompanied him on his retreat as far as Vilna. This guard of honor, which was small in number, but whose zeal never slackened for an instant, formed the nucleus of the second regiment of light Polish cavalry of the Guard. Many leading Poles, prompted by patriotic feelings, and animated by the hope of contributing in a more efficacious manner to the reestablishment of the Polish nation, followed the Imperial headquarters as volunteers, sharing the vicissitudes and the dangers of the French army.

The Emperor appointed the Duke of Bassano governor of Lithuania, but established him at Vilna with a mission to act as the center of correspondence and organization. M. de Bassano was charged with publishing the news concerning the operations of the French army, with corresponding with Austria, Prussia, and especially with Turkey, whom it was a matter of great importance to watch over, and if needs be to excite against Russia. This last part of Napoleon's instructions could not always be carried out with the required promptitude. Various causes contributed to this, especially the slowness and difficulties of communication, which increased as the army moved further and further away from Vilna. The Duke of Bassano was also ordered to correspond with the Warsaw government, and sometimes to transmit orders to the corps which were ranged on the rear of the army; and finally to provide for stores, war ammunition, and provisions. The couriers, officers, and auditors, who came from France, called in at Vilna on their way, and were sent on from thence by M. de Bassano to the Emperor's headquarters.

It was near Vilna that Napoleon met the Crown Prince of Würtemberg at the head of his contingent. He blamed this Prince severely for the insubordination of the Würtembergs, who committed such disorders that complaints were being made on every side against these ruthless pillagers, both from the French and Polish authorities, and from the inhabitants. The Emperor pointed out to the Crown Prince in a very violent manner, how urgent it was that these disorders should be checked. He listened to the remonstrances with coldness, and did not answer. The Crown Prince considered himself humiliated, and bore a grudge in consequence.

We think that the following extract from General Gourgaud's work, entitled *A Critical Examination of the Count de Ségur's Work* will be read with interest. It gives some particulars of the way in which Napoleon usually spent his time when he was on campaign:

"The active life which he (the Emperor) led was subordinated to the military operations. As a rule he used to ride along with the army when in pursuit of or near the enemy. When the army was engaged in grand maneuvers and the operations took place at great distances he waited until the corps which were to march by approached the positions which he had ordered them to take up, and would then remain at headquarters. There he used to receive the reports which were addressed to him either directly or through the Major-General by the officers in command of the various corps. In the meantime he used to give his attention to the home government of France, answer the reports which were sent to him from Paris by the ministers, who were in the habit of writing to him every day, and the reports of the ministers in council which were carried to him every week by an auditor of the Council of State, who was put at the disposal of the Intendant General of the army to be used in different missions. In this way he governed his Empire, at the same time that he directed his army. Economical with his time he calculated the moment of his departure so as to find himself at the head of his troops at the moment when his presence there became necessary. He would then proceed thither in his carriage with full speed. But even during this journey he did not remain idle, but busied himself in reading his dispatches, and very often received reports from his generals, and answered them forthwith. Estafettes brought his dispatches from Paris enclosed in a portfolio which was locked, and these dispatches were sometimes given to him at the same time. By means of a lamp which was placed at the back of his carriage, and which lighted up the carriage during the night, he was able to work as though he had been in his workroom. The Major-General usually accompanied him in these journeys. His aides-de-camp and orderlies marched by the door of the carriage, and a brigade of his saddle horses followed with the escort.

"Such was the privileged constitution of this extraordinary man that he could sleep an hour, be awakened to give an order, go to sleep again, be awakened anew, without suffering for it in his health or in his rest. Six hours of sleep were sufficient for him whether taken consecutively or whether spread over intervals in the twenty-four hours.

"On the days which preceded the battle he was constantly on horseback, reconnoitering the enemy's forces, deciding upon the battlefield, and riding round the bivouacs of his army corps. Even in the night he used to visit the lines to assure himself once more of the enemy's forces by the number of its fires, and would tire out several horses in the space of a few hours. On the day of the battle he would place himself at some central point, whence he could see all that was going on. He had his aides-de-camp and orderly officers by him, and used to send them to carry his orders in every direction. At some distance behind the Emperor were four squadrons of the guard, one belonging to each branch of the service, but when he left this position he only took a platoon with him as escort. He used usually to inform his marshals of the place which he had chosen, so as to be easily found by the officers whom they might send to him. As soon as his presence became necessary he would ride off there at a gallop."

I, on my side, can add to these details that everywhere where the Emperor halted, whether at a castle, a cottage, or a hovel, his first care was for his workroom. As soon as Napoleon had taken possession of his temporary lodging, the portfolio containing his papers, his maps, and two or three mahogany boxes divided into compartments which contained his traveling library, were set out on tables, when tables were to be found, or on planks, or doors laid upon trestles. When there was only one room, his little iron bed and his toilet-bag were also placed there. There he would dictate the numerous orders which it was necessary for him to send off. The Major-General who always lived within call used to lay the reports which he had received before him, and carry back the answers forthwith.

When the operations of the war obliged Napoleon to remain for any length of time in one of his winter quarters, or in one of the capitals which he had conquered, his time was for the greater part taken up with the occupations of his cabinet. He attended to the needs of the army without neglecting the affairs or the details of the government of the Empire. He used to summon to him the minister secretary of state, who brought him the work which had been dispatched by the council of ministers and received instructions, orders, and decisions, which he was charged to forward to Paris. The Emperor dispatched numerous orders providing for the repose of the troops, to assign the places which they were to occupy, to reorganize them, to prepare them to be in a better position to resume hostilities. He watched over the carrying out of his orders with the greatest care, and in order to better obtain this result he would frequently repeat them. He used to go out every day, no matter what the weather might be, to hold reviews. Sometimes he would undertake short excursions to visit the corps of his army or strategical positions. In the train of each corps he had a brigade of saddle horses composed of six or seven horses, two of which were for his personal use, the others for his officers, a field bedstead, and a portmanteau containing changes of clothes. Napoleon used to lunch and dine every day with the Major-General, and with some marshals or general officers. He was fond of playing at whist after dinner, and sometimes at vingt-et-un, a game which he preferred because everybody present could take part in it. Over these games of cards he would forget the labors and the cares of the day. As a general rule he would never occupy himself with two things at the same time, his entire attention being given to the pleasures as to the duties of the moment. Moderate stakes only were played for, none the less Napoleon took a great interest in the game. He would sometimes associate one of the officers present in his game as a half partner, and if fortune favored the Emperor, would hand over all his winnings to him.

Familiar with the soldiers, benevolent towards the officers, Napoleon was accessible to all in the army. In the camp all etiquette was banished in the entirely military relations between the sovereign and his comrades-in-arms. The private was authorized to leave the ranks, on presenting arms, and to lay any request he might have to make before the Emperor, either verbally or in writing. Such requests, whether they were granted or refused, were immediately attended to by the Emperor. When it happened that the petition could not be granted the soldier was always told the reason of such refusal, which was explained to him with kindness. Very often the refusal was compensated for by the grant of some other favor. If any officer had a confession to make to Napoleon, the Emperor was always ready to hear him, and would listen to him in a paternal manner.

Before continuing the account of the Russian campaign, I must rectify a certain error which has been repeated by some of Napoleon's historians. It is a fact that the Prince of Wagram has been accused of having on various occasions transformed or even suppressed orders which the Emperor had given him, or of having delayed to forward them. To make such a statement is to show one's ignorance of the way in which the Major-General used to work with Napoleon. The Major-General, who was always lodged within call of the Emperor, was, so to speak, endowed with the faculty of sleeping with one eye open, and he needed very little sleep. He was always found awake by the officer who bore the dispatch which was sent to him. He would then proceed to the Emperor, followed by the officers, so that Napoleon, in case of need, could examine the latter. If the Emperor were in bed he would get up at once, put on a white swanskin or *pique* dressing-gown and dictate an answer to the Major-General. The latter would send it as it was written to the marshals or generals, having at the same time copied into his book of orders the name of the officer who was charged with carrying it to the address, and the mention of the hour on which this officer had been dispatched. Before giving another order the Emperor used to have the book of orders laid before him, and would re-read the preceding orders. The marshals and the generals never failed to add with the date of their letters the mention of the hour on which they wrote them.

Anybody who knew Prince de Wagram is well aware that this marshal was incapable of committing such an abuse of confidence, both by the loyalty of his character, as by the feeling of his responsibility. Nature moreover had given him neither the spirit of intrigue nor the audacity requisite to defy the consequences of forgetting his duties in such a manner.

I have heard it said that Prince de Wagram was a model of chief staff-officers, that his absence during the 1815 campaign was fatal to the Emperor. I am far from wishing to contest the talents of General Berthier, displaying in the campaigns of Italy, Egypt, the Consulate, and during the first campaigns under the Empire. He was young at that time, as Napoleon used to say of himself, and his comrades-in-arms, and he had his fortune to make; but I should not be telling the truth if I did not add that in proportion as honors and riches came to General Berthier the solid and real qualities which had distinguished him diminished. In this connection I will simply relate what I witnessed during the 1812 campaign. The Emperor would often blame him for his carelessness in my presence. "Berthier," he used to say to him, "I would give an arm to have you at Grosbois. Not only are you no good, but you are actually in my way." After these little quarrels Berthier would sulk, and refuse to come to dinner (he was Napoleon's habitual table-fellow). The Emperor would then send for him, and would not sit down to dinner until he had come;

he would put his arms round his neck, tell him that they were inseparable, etc., would chaff him about Madame Visconti, and in the end would seat him at the table opposite him.

On arriving in the evening at any place where he was to pass the night, the Emperor would often think it his duty to provide at once for the establishment of his guard, and the troops who had followed him, unless he had some pressing orders to give.

He would remain on horseback and visit the bivouacs round his house to see if the soldiers had food, if communications between them were easy and, in one word, would fulfill the functions of a simple staff-officer. While Napoleon was absent himself in this way the Major-General, leaving him to the occupation, would hurry off to his house, and settle himself in it.

It happened that I was sent one day by the Emperor to the Major-General—I do not remember what for—and I found him alone in his bedroom, with his head on his hands, and his elbows on the table. He raised his eyes up to me glistening with tears. When I asked him what was grieving him he broke out into bitter complaint of the wretchedness of his position. "What is the good," he said, "of having given me an income of £60,000 a year, a magnificent mansion in Paris, a splendid estate, in order to inflict the tortures of Tantalus upon me. I shall die here with all this work. The simplest private is happier than I am." Then wiping his eyes with his hand: "Well! What is up now? Must send for Salamon, Leduc." These were his secretaries. Of course I took very good care not to repeat these remarks to the Emperor, who by the way, was only too well aware of the state of things. Napoleon was attached to Berthier, in spite of all his imperfections, by a bond which was a very strong one with him, the tie of custom. Later on, he regretted the absence of his old comrade-in-arms, not on account of the qualities which the Major-General no longer possessed, but because, having been long accustomed to his services, the Emperor remained in the illusions of the past. A more capable chief of the staff would perhaps have rendered Napoleon better services, but nobody, in his eyes, could replace Berthier, who had begun with him, and who had never left him. Born in prosperous times, this superstitious confidence inspired the Emperor with a feeling of security, more apparent than real, in the collaboration of this old comrade-in-arms. I have heard Napoleon say that he had taken Berthier as a "gosling," and had transformed him into an eagle; and it must be admitted that he knew the man whom he had created Prince de Wagram. In 1814, indeed at Fontainebleau, when Berthier asked his leave to go and spend two days in Paris, to put his affairs in order, the Emperor, having seen him depart, could not refrain from exclaiming: "There's one who won't come back."

The false position in which Major-General Berthier placed the French army at the beginning of the 1809 campaign, has been censured from a technical point of view, and his military capacities have been disputed; but this is a point on which I cannot dwell, because, in the first place, I am no judge of such matters and secondly because I do not wish to expose myself to the accusation of having vilified him. Why, indeed, speak of the military talents of Prince de Wagram, who never was in chief command.... If he was in the secret of the most skilful combinations, of the most marvelous plans of campaign, genius cannot be acquired, nor did the Major-General do more than order the details of their execution. He can console himself for having occasionally drawn the Emperor's reproaches upon himself; for there is nothing humiliating in certain criticisms, when they proceed from so superior a man as Napoleon. There are however, some people who are not convinced of the prodigious genius which is personified in the name of Napoleon.... Now Berthier, Talleyrand, and so many others *never gave an order, and never wrote a dispatch which had not been dictated by Napoleon.* Napoleon had not alone the initiative of the conceptions, but further reserved to himself the details of all these matters. I do not say that he was altogether in the right in wishing thus to do all himself; but the superhuman activity of his genius carried him away, and he felt that he had the means and the time to suffice for all. His part was to organize, to create, and he filled this part in all its details; writing dispatches, no matter of what nature; giving instructions for missions of every kind, military, administrative, financial, literary; drawing up notes to be presented by his ambassadors to the Courts to which they were accredited, and so on, all was written by him, as though at play, and without any apparent mental strain. In this way Napoleon glorified the men whom he employed, since everything appeared to have been conceived and drawn up by them, whereas in truth it was all done by him.

These digressions have made me lose sight of my subject. I hope the reader will pardon me. I am carried away, in spite of myself, by the tyranny of old remembrances.

Having left Vilna on July 18, the Emperor marched to Glubokoï where he established the army magazines, and thence to Becken-Kovitski, where, for a moment, he hoped to come up with the Russian army; and spent a day at the country house of the Polish Count Kreptovich. This beautiful residence, the abode of the arts, decorated with very fine pictures and with flowers everywhere, which contrasted strangely with the horrors of war, was in perfect order when we entered it. This house had been so suddenly abandoned that every trace of its recent occupation still remained. There was still to be seen a cradle in which was the soft impress of the body of the child which had lain in it. The marriage of the master and mistress of this house had been accompanied by a tragical circumstance, which was told to me on the scene of the drama. Mademoiselle de Renn, a Russian by birth, was loved by an officer named Arseniew, who was in the Russian Emperor's guards. This officer hearing of the projected marriage between Count Kreptovich and Mademoiselle de Renn, went to his rival and threatened to kill him if he persisted in his design. Kreptovich answered that this threat only decided him to hurry on the marriage; a Duel followed in which M. Arseniew lost his life. A taste for the arts, for music and painting was stronger in Count Kreptovich than his love for his wife whom he had won at the point of his sword. He left his home for the hazards of a wandering life, went round the world, explored Asia and Africa, always bearing with him two inseparable vade-mecums, his violin, and a picture which he could not live without.

After having lost at the battle of Ostrovno, in which it was at first thought that the entire Russian army would take part, the hope of inducing Barclai de Tolli, the Russian general, to engage in a great battle, Napoleon made his way to Vitepsk. He was tired of uselessly pursuing an army whose chief—and this is nothing but the truth—could not make up his mind to fight him. One day the Russian general seemed full of fire, determined to retreat no further without engaging in a decisive encounter The next day the phantom of Napoleon's presence once more impressed itself on his mind and all his resolutions of the day before vanished.

The fact that Napoleon spent a fortnight at Vitepsk, and that during that time he gave orders for the construction of certain defenses and the establishment of a large bake-house, gave rise to the idea that he wished to camp round this city and select this point for his line of defense. But it was impossible for him to terminate the campaign in the month of July without even having been able to come into contact with the enemy's army. The object of this halt was to rest the army, which stood in need of repose, and to watch the movements of the Russians. Hearing that they were leaving the vicinity of Smolensk to come and attack him the Emperor made haste to march to meet them, proceeding rapidly along the left bank of the Dnieper and ascending the course of this stream to reach Smolensk, before they had had time to return there. This movement, hiding the march of the French army from the enemy placed it on their flank and rear. The audacity and skill of this maneuver have been admired by the Russians themselves and it has been considered the finest of the campaign. But Napoleon's star was already waning. The eight corps commanded by General Junot went astray on the road, and Marshal Ney's attack on the citadel of Smolensk was unfortunately unsuccessful. General Barclai, tardily apprised of the movements of the French army, hastened to return to Smolensk which was successfully defended during a whole day by two Russian divisions who were shut up in this fortified place, time being thus given to the two Russian armies to come to the rescue. Napoleon had hoped that Barclai would not let this city, the key of old Russia, fall into our hands without a decisive battle, but he only resisted long enough to cover his retreat and operate his junction with Bagration, whose army had got past the French corps which had been ordered to cut off his retreat.

The question as to whether a halt should be made at Smolensk was again discussed between Napoleon and his lieutenants. The reasons which had prompted the Emperor at Vitepsk to continue his march forward remained the same at Smolensk. The French army could only have ceased its movements and have taken up its quarters in these two cities if one of those splendid victories to which the French were accustomed had come to give hopes for peace. The Russians on the contrary had fought no battle to defend this bulwark of Russia and did not show themselves on the other hand at all disposed to open negotiations. It was then the month of August and it was quite out of the question for the French army to spend the rest of the summer at Smolensk. There was at that time no reason for retreating or for taking up a position behind rivers, which, frozen hard in the winter, would no longer be a protection against the enemy. Were we to wait in a continued attitude of defense, a kind of war which is antipathetic to the French character, at a distance of five hundred leagues from our frontiers....to give our adversaries time to look round and to employ for our destruction the resources of every kind which they so easily derived from their native soil? Napoleon did not think so. The Russians would at last be forced to stand to battle to defend Moscow. There then lay peace. That is what the Emperor thought. One great victory and this great object was attained. The Emperor Alexander would be forced to treat. This peace, added Napoleon, would have limited our war expeditions. It was the crown of our efforts, the commencement of security.

During the march of the French army on Smolensk, the encounter with a Russian division gave rise to the combat of Krasnoi. It was during one of the brilliant cavalry charges which were carried out during this combat that young Marbeuf was mortally wounded. The loss of this officer gave great grief to the Emperor. This young man had been presented to him by his mother, widow of Count Marbeuf, the former governor of the Island of Corsica, whom she had married, when a widower. When Madame de Marbeuf presented her son to the Emperor in 1805, he was twenty years old. Napoleon admitted him amongst his orderly officers. The following letter, which we think right to reproduce, will show what remembrance Napoleon had retained of the interest formerly shown to the Bonaparte family by M. de Marbeuf.

"Paris, 18 Ventôse, Year XIII (March 9, 1805)

"M. DE MARBEUF—officer in the 25th regiment of dragoons—I have granted you for life a pension of six thousand francs on the crown treasure, and I have given orders to M. de Fleurieu, my intendant, to send you the warrant for the same. I am giving orders that there shall be paid to you out of my privy purse, a sum of twelve thousand francs for your outfit. It is my wish to give you, under all circumstances, a proof of the interest I take in you on account of the good recollection I have of the services rendered to me by your father, whose memory is dear to me. I rely in the hope that you will follow in his footsteps. And hereupon I pray God to have you in His holy keeping.

"NAPOLEON"

The Emperor, so to speak, adopted this young man whom he intended to raise to a high degree of fortune. He had entailed a fine house at No. 11, Rue de Montblanc, upon him. This house had been bought from the Receiver-General Pierlot and, after M. de Marbeuf's death, the Emperor bestowed it on the Duke of Padua.

Napoleon always used to treat young Marbeuf's mother with great respect. It had been related that at the time of the establishment of the imperial households the Lady Mother suggested to Napoleon that he should appoint Madame de Marbeuf one of her ladies-in-waiting and that Napoleon refused from a feeling of delicacy. He is said to have answered: "After what M. Marbeuf was for us, it would not be right for his widow to be in our service."

Madame de Marbeuf, inconsolable for her son's death, separated herself from her daughter, who had married Count Louis d'Ambrugeac, who owed the favor in which he stood with the Emperor to this marriage, and who was a colonel in 1813. She retired into the convent of the Sacred Heart and died there in 1839, at the age of seventy-six, the same age at which her husband, whom she survived fifty-three years, had died.

After having set fire to Smolensk before leaving it, the enemy continued its retrograde movement. One half of the Russian army was attacked on the heights of Valoutinia-Gora by Marshal Ney's corps, supported by the Gudin division. These corps performed prodigies of valor in this encounter. The inconceivable action of General Junot, in command of the Westphalian troops, in refusing to march to the rear of the Russians and to cut off their retreat, saved the enemy's forces once more. Brave General Gudin had both his legs shot off by a cannonball in this engagement. As to Junot, he had disobeyed not only the repeated orders of the Emperor to march to Ney's assistance, but also the pressing request of the King of Naples, who had gone to him to convince him of what he ought to do. The Emperor heard what was going on, at Smolensk where he had remained, not foreseeing that this encounter might develop into a battle. When he arrived the struggle had nearly finished and the Russian army was continuing its retreat. Napoleon addressed the severest reproaches to General Junot but this unfortunate general was then already experiencing the first attacks of the mental malady which broke out with such violence a year later. The Emperor had chosen Rapp, who spoke German, and who had all his wits about him, to take his place. The refusal of Rapp, who interceded for his brother-in-arms, and a feeling of benevolence, which Napoleon could not help feeling for the oldest of his aides-de-camp, maintained the Duke d'Abrantès at the head of his army corps. General Gudin was transported to Smolensk but all the Emperor's care was unable to preserve his life. He died regretted by his sovereign and the whole army, who appreciated his eminent qualities. Gudin was buried in the citadel of Smolensk.

Certain advantages gained by the right wing of the army, under the command of Prince Schwarzenberg, and an important success achieved on the left wing by General Gouvion Saint-Cyr, who had replaced Marshal Oudinot, who had been seriously wounded, in command, a success which won a Marshal's *bâton* for the General, consoled the Emperor in some measure for all these mishaps. The army followed the Russians on their retreat without respite. After having set fire to the cities of Gjatz and Viazma and their rich bazaars, the enemy's forces halted at last at Mojaisk. There it was learned that Marshal Kutosov had replaced General Barclai de Tolli in the command-in-chief of the Russian army.

On the eve of the memorable battle of Moskova, in the midst of the serious anxieties occasioned by the murderous fight in which he was about to engage, the Emperor received the portrait of his son. The Empress had commissioned M. de Bausset, who was proceeding to headquarters, to carry the young prince's portrait to his father. In his impatience the Emperor ordered the box containing the picture to be opened at once, under his eyes. The royal infant was represented sitting in its cradle playing with a cup and ball. The ball might have been taken for the globe of the world and the cup-stick for a scepter. Napoleon contemplated his son's picture with an emotion which was increased by the recollection of the distance which separated him from France as well as by the preparations for a battle which he had long wished for, but the approach of which filled him with anxiety. He ordered one of his valets to carry the picture outside his tent and to hold it up high enough that the sentry of the guards might see it. This sight brought all the officers and soldiers who were in the neighborhood running up. To satisfy the curiosity of the military crowd, which kept increasing, the Emperor ordered the portrait of the King of Rome to be placed on one of the folding-chairs in his tent and left it standing all day in sight of the army. The sympathy and the sentiments of all these good soldiers ended by breaking out into a manifestation which deeply touched the Emperor.

Marshal Kutosov awaited the French army, near the Borodino, in a fortified position defended in the middle by means of a great bastioned redoubt, flanked with other defense works. These redoubts, stubbornly fought for, taken by the French and retaken by the Russians in turn, finally remained in our hands. General Montbrun and after him General Caulaincourt, brother of the Grand Equerry, met with a glorious death there. Three hundred thousand men fought on this murderous day of September 7 with an unexampled implacability. Eight hundred cannon vomited forth death into the ranks of the two armies. This battle to which the Russians have given the name of Borodino and which the French call the battle of La Moskova is one of the most murderous battles which were ever fought. It may rightly be styled a battle of giants. The Russians admit having lost fifty thousand men, killed, wounded, or taken prisoners. This enormous loss must be attributed to the passive courage which they opposed to the attacks on the redoubts, allowing themselves to be killed rather than to surrender them. The losses of the French army may be estimated at thirty thousand men put *hors de combat*. Thirty Russian generals and fifteen French generals were killed, wounded, or made prisoners. The two armies, sated with bloodshed, stayed their hands towards the end of the day, the French army remaining master of all the positions and the Russian army preparing for a retreat.

The Emperor Napoleon has been blamed for not having completed the routing of the enemy by ordering out the imperial guard which took no part in the action. He answered the remonstrances which were made on this subject with the following words: "If there's a second battle to-morrow, with what shall I fight it?" As a matter of fact Kutosov thought of fighting a second battle on the morrow. If the respective states of the two armies be considered, one will be seen with its back to its capital, from which it is able to draw reinforcements and resources, an army fighting for its home and animated with religious and patriotic fanaticism; the other more than eight hundred leagues distant from France, without any means of receiving immediate reinforcements, and obliged finally to return home sooner or later. So great a captain as was Napoleon could not commit the imprudence of remaining disarmed before the possible return on the offensive of an adversary who did not consider himself defeated. A reserve force of twenty thousand fresh men, as bold as were the imperial guards, could decide a victory in case a second battle became necessary. Was it not, indeed, the guard which later on protected our retreat? The Emperor allowed the young guard to occupy the field of battle, giving orders for its support in case the enemy, receiving reinforcements, should attempt a fresh attack during the night.

After the bitterly contested day of La Moskova, Napoleon halted at a little country house, situated at no great distance from the field of battle. The nights which he had passed in four consecutive bivouacs, where he had constantly been on his legs, and the great fatigues which he had had to undergo, gave him a cold which very soon degenerated into an extinction of the voice, which greatly annoyed him. He, whose hand could not suffice to write down the thoughts which flooded his volcanic brain, was seen reduced to the necessity of scribbling roughly the multifarious orders which had to be given in every direction, on little squares of paper. On the morrow he had already got rid of this passing ailment.

After an encounter which was fought outside Moscow, an encounter which at first induced the belief that the Russians really intended to defend the city, the front-guard of the French army arrived in front of this old capital of the Russian Empire, and the sight of Moscow, which was to be seen from the heights, filled it with a joy which rapidly communicated itself to the rest of the army. It was hoped that repose and especially abundance would be found there. A curious and impressive sight was this sudden appearance of this great city, Asiatic rather than European, spreading out at the end of a desert and naked plain, topped with its twelve hundred spires and sky-blue cupolas, strewn with golden stars, and linked one to the other with gilded chains. This conquest had been dearly paid for, but Napoleon at that time lulled himself in the hope that he would be able to dictate peace there. The King of Naples, who entered it first, sent word to the Emperor that the city appeared to be deserted and that no civil or military functionary, nor nobleman, nor priest had presented himself. The Russian army had taken away the majority of the inhabitants of Moscow in its train. Some Russian and foreign dealers, who had managed to escape this order, came to see the Emperor and implored him to protect them against the pillaging with which they thought themselves menaced.

There had remained in the city only a few thousand people belonging to the lowest classes of society, who had nothing to lose by awaiting the course of events.

Napoleon passed this night of September 14 in the Dorogomilov faubourg, and only entered Moscow on the morrow. This entry was not accompanied by that tumult which marks the taking possession of a great city. No noise disturbed the solitude of the city streets, save only the rumbling of the cannon and of the artillery caissons. Moscow seemed asleep in deep sleep, like one of those enchanted cities of which we read in Arabian tales. The streets through which we passed were lined with houses of fine appearance for the most part, with closed windows and doors. Palaces with colonnades, churches and beautiful buildings glittering with the luxury of Europe and of Asia raised themselves side by side with very modest habitations. All bespoke the ease and wealth of a great city enriched by trade and inhabited by a wealthy and numerous aristocracy. Some of the principal houses which we were able to enter were well appointed and well furnished, many even magnificently so, and their inhabitants did not appear to have abandoned them forever.

The Emperor proceeded directly to the Kremlin, a large citadel placed in the center of the town, on the top of a hill, surrounded with an embattled wall and flanked at intervals with towers armed with cannon. The Kremlin is a second city. It contains the imperial palace, the arsenal, the senate palace, the archives, the principal public establishments, a large number of churches, temples filled with historical curiosities, objects serving for the coronation of the sovereigns, and lastly trophies and flags taken from the Turks. It is in one of the principal temples that are the tombs of the Czars. In this imposing fane reigns a magnificence which is half barbaric and of a primitive character. The walls are covered with thick plates of gold and silver on which are figured in relief the principal incidents of the Sacred History. Enormous silver lamps of Byzantine shape hang from the arches of the building, large many-branched chandeliers of the same metal stand on pedestals on the floor. There is also to be seen in this sanctuary a portrait of the Holy Virgin attributed to St. Luke, the frame of this picture is enriched with pearls and precious stones. A great bell-tower, known as the Ivan tower was surmounted by a gigantic cross in the center of which was enchased a cross of pure gold containing a fragment of the true cross. This cross and a number of curious objects which could be removed were to be sent to Paris from the Kremlin.

Hardly had the Emperor entered the Kremlin than fire broke out in the Kitaigorod, or Chinese city, an immense bazaar, surrounded by porticoes, in which were heaped up, in large shops or in cellars, the entrances to which were placed in the middle of the streets, precious goods of every kind, such as shawls, furs, Indian and Chinese tissues. Fruitless efforts were made to extinguish the flames, and the burning of the bazaar became the signal for a general conflagration in the city. This conflagration, spreading rapidly, devoured three-quarters of Moscow in three days. Each moment one saw smoke followed by flames breaking out of houses which had remained intact and in the end the fire broke out in every house in the city. The town was one mighty furnace from which sheaves of fire burst heavenwards lighting up the horizon with the glaring flames and spreading a burning heat. These masses of flame, mingling together, were rapidly caught up by a strong wind which spread them in every direction. They were accompanied by a succession of whistling noises and explosions caused by the falling walls and the explosion of inflammable materials which were stored in the shops and houses. To these roaring noises, to these sinister outbreaks added themselves the cries and yells of the wretched people who were caught by the flames in the houses which they had entered to pillage and which many escaped only to perish in the streets which formed a blazing labyrinth from which all escape was impossible. Motionless and in the silence of stupor we looked on at this horrible and magnificent spectacle, with the feeling of our absolute helplessness to render any assistance.

Rapid and frequent gunshots announced that prompt justice was being meted out to the incendiaries who were taken in the act, still holding their sulphur fuses in their hands, and flying from the houses to which they had just set fire. The Emperor had given orders that a house which he could inhabit during his stay in Moscow should be found for him. The Sloboda palace, built and decorated with great luxury by the Empress Catherine, had been selected for this purpose. The Major-General and M. de Narbonne, one of the Emperor's aides-de-camp, went by his order to inspect this palace and found it perfectly suited for the purpose. The chandeliers were still filled with candles. This royal abode seemed to be deserted and entrance had to be made through a window. When General Narbonne returned to take possession of it, after having informed Napoleon of the result of his visit, the fire had already broken out in it in several places simultaneously, and on the morrow this palace was completely destroyed.

Count Rostopchin, governor of Moscow, after having employed every means of acting upon the stupid minds of a credulous population, had had sufficient audacity to take upon himself the responsibility of destroying the second capital of the Empire. Did he take so cruel a resolution alone, or was he authorized by Alexander's secret consent to carry out this fearful auto-da-fé? Did the incitations of the old Russian party weigh with all the weight of their fanaticism on the governor's savage decision? One and all reject the responsibility of this terrible catastrophe. To accomplish his detestable project, Rostopchin set a number of galley-slaves at liberty, distributed them over different quarters of the town, where they hid themselves in the principal buildings and in houses which had been abandoned. Under the pretext of constructing an enormous balloon which was to pour down inflammable material on the French troops Rostopchin ordered the manufacture of fireworks for setting fire to the houses and of fuses to be thrown on the roofs of the houses. On leaving Moscow the governor had sent the inhabitants of every class on before him, who carried off their most valuable belongings. He had even had the infernal inspiration of removing the fire-engines with him. Certain writers have had the courage to admire such a resolution. What advantage had Russia to gain from this fearful sacrifice? The examples of moderation given by the French army, during our soldiers' occupation of nearly every capital in Europe, did they not guarantee the victor's protection to the city of Moscow? If the author of this destruction, after really being cruelly inspired thereto, had shared the dangers which resulted there from and had buried himself under the ruins of the city which he had doomed to the flames, one might in an extremity excuse the excess of his fanaticism. But since then Paris has seen this same man, protected by our hospitality, seeking after the most refined pleasures of our civilization, applauding the jokes of our mountebanks, and manifesting the most profound indifference for a disaster for the horror of which his heart should ever have bled, even in the consciousness of having accomplished an act of lofty patriotism.

The flames which were consuming Moscow reached the Kremlin and threatened the safety of its walls. The wind blew sparks and blazing fragments with violence, which falling into the courtyard of the arsenal, set fire to the tow with which the ground was covered. There was danger of the artillery caissons exploding. This danger, which was fortunately avoided, did not shake Napoleon's resolution, for his soul never knew the feeling of fear. He did not think it necessary as yet to leave the Kremlin, the danger which he ran there, deciding him, on the contrary, to remain. Prince Eugène and the Marshals of his guard in vain implored him to withdraw and in the meanwhile the conflagration, drawing closer, increased in intensity. The panes in the windows of the apartment occupied by the Emperor became red-hot and flames shooting out everywhere, threatened to surround the Kremlin and to utterly destroy it. Napoleon, however, still hesitated. He was loth to flee from danger and to abandon a conquest which he had bought at such a price. He only yielded when it was pointed out to him that if he did not leave he might be separated from the corps which were stationed outside Moscow, with which all communications would be cut off, in case of an attack by the enemy. Napoleon then at last decided to leave the city and withdrew to Petrovskoi, an imperial residence situated at a distance of about one league from Moscow, whence the Czars used to depart to make their solemn entry into their ancient capital where the ceremony of coronation used to take place. The Emperor left the Kremlin, by one of its big gates, on foot, followed by his officers, and without any accident. On arriving at the Moskova quay he mounted on horseback and safely accomplished the ride from Moscow to Petrovskoi, passing through the quarters of the town in which the houses were entirely consumed and avoiding the streets where the fire was still in full activity. Napoleon thus avoided the danger of being crushed beneath the falling varnished iron plates, with which most of the buildings were covered, as the houses in the quarters through which he passed were already reduced to smoldering ashes. As a matter of fact, however, even in the quarters where the flames were at their height, the fall of these iron plates was menacing rather than dangerous and it was easy to avoid them. My colleague Mounier and myself drove through these quarters in a carriage and met with no accidents. Napoleon spent two days at Petrovskoi and then returned to the Kremlin.

On his return to Moscow, the Emperor did not limit himself to providing for the needs of the army alone, but gave the reins to his usual prodigious activity. He threw open to the wretched inhabitants who had remained in the town and who had been reduced by the fire to a state of utter destitution, refuges and shelters and at the same time ordered provisions and money to be distributed among them. He extended his solicitude to the wounded Russians and to the various establishments in Moscow. Amongst other establishments he protected the Foundling Hospital whither he betook himself, desired to see General Tutolmine, the director of this establishment and asked him to acquaint him with the situation of his institution. Napoleon also visited the hospitals, which he found wanting in necessaries. He gave orders that all available medical assistance should be brought together, and established a kind of medical agency for diseases of all kinds which he placed under the direction of the surgeon-in-chief of the army, the respected Doctor Larrey. The Emperor allotted convenient houses for the reception of the sick and wounded and ordered frequent reports on the situation to be laid before him. In one word Napoleon did everything in his power to assist this unhappy city which had been given over to anarchy, and to save for his army the resources which had escaped destruction. The arrival of M. de Lesseps, French Consul General to Russia, who had come from St. Petersburg to join the Emperor in Moscow, gave

Napoleon the opportunity to organize a municipal organization and local committees composed of natives of the place, at the head of which this agent was placed. Vested with these difficult functions, M. de Lesseps took all the advantage that could be hoped for from intelligent zeal and sustained activity, of these feeble means of keeping order.

When the fire had ceased, provisions of wines, brandies, meal, biscuits, potatoes, salted meats, sugar, coffee, and tea were found in the cellars, to which the flames had not penetrated. These provided ample resources. The houses were provisioned for several months and the inhabitants had left whatever could not be easily carried away. The starving Russian population rushed on all the places where they knew that some prey, easy to be devoured, was to be found and pointed out hiding-places to our soldiers to share the spoils with them. The Emperor was even forced to place sentries in all the shops and other provision storehouses to preserve them from being pillaged by this mob whose greediness was insatiable.

After having in this way provided for the material wants of the army and of the inhabitants the Emperor devoted his attention to the soldiers' minds. He knew that theatrical performances were an excellent means for diverting the human mind from sorrowful thoughts and for recreating it. A troop of French comedians who had remained in Moscow under the management of Madame Aurore Barsay gave a number of performances which were enthusiastically attended by our soldiers. A clever Italian singer, who had come to Russia to give singing lessons, organized some concerts which were given before Napoleon at the Kremlin. And lastly the famous Moscow decree on the *Comédie Française* dates from this period.

The director of the Foundling Hospital having asked Napoleon for permission to write to the Dowager Empress, to inform her of the preservation of the establishment confided to his care, this princess being the patroness of the hospital, was asked to add pacific overtures to his letter. Two days later Napoleon wrote to the Emperor Alexander and commissioned the brother of the Russian ambassador to Stuttgart, who was at Moscow at the time, to carry this letter. Almost at the same time the Emperor sent General Lauriston to Kutosov, the commander-in-chief, under the pretext of proposing an armistice, and carrying a second letter to the Czar. Kutosov, pretending that he was obliged to ask for instructions, contented himself with sending the document which had been brought by Lauriston, by Prince Volkonski, the aide-de-camp, but would not allow the French general to go to St. Petersburg. The commander-in-chief, moreover, an old Scythian, supple and cunning like half-civilized barbarians and like many other Russian generals, professed the friendliest disposition, while as a matter of fact the burning of Moscow which was attributed to the French, was already bearing its fruits. The authors of the destruction of the great capital, the sacred city of the Empire, had wished, by exciting the hatred of the nation to the highest degree against the invader, to render all reconciliation between the combatants impossible. And as a matter of fact, all attempts made to snatch Alexander away from British influence remained fruitless and without result.

Napoleon did not yet despair of receiving some answer to his proposals but he spent all his time while waiting in Moscow in reorganizing and reinforcing his army, in completing the artillery teams with the horses of the great pontoon-train, which we were forced to leave behind in the Kremlin, and with the horses of persons in the army who had more than was authorized by the regulations. The value of these horses was paid to their owners. By the Emperor's orders the ammunition of our army was increased by means of the stores of powder which had been found in the buildings outside Moscow, which Rostopchin had forgotten to destroy, and by cannonballs picked up on the field of battle. In one word nothing that might be of service to the French troops amongst the things found in this city after the conflagration was discarded. While organizing assistance for our numerous sick and wounded Napoleon did not lose sight of the necessity of providing sufficient means of transport to remove them to Smolensk. He gave orders at the same time for the formation of stores of provisions, equipments and ammunition on our rear, and for the concentration at Smolensk of the artillery caissons and carriages which had been abandoned on the road over which the army had marched. Napoleon wished to make a great depot of this city, a center and point of support for his present and future operations of war. He also had given orders and detailed instructions for the marches and destination of the 2nd and 9th corps commanded by Marshals Dukes de Bellune and de Reggio, who had been summoned to Lithuania to support and reinforce the army.

The disasters which fell upon the French army have prompted many well-thinking men to blame Napoleon for having stayed a month in Moscow. This halt, however, far from being a waste of time, was on the contrary barely long enough to enable the Emperor to put his army in a position to commence the retreat. The complete burning of the ancient capital of Russia was an occurrence which could not in the least be foreseen and which by disconcerting all Napoleon's plans was the chief reason of all the cruel misfortunes from which our brave army suffered afterwards. Did Count Rostopchin foresee this when he gave orders that Moscow was to be burned? One may be allowed to doubt it. This individual's palace was one of the few houses which were spared by the flames. A memorandum was found there which he had laid before the Emperor Paul when he was at the Ministry of Foreign Affairs. In this memorandum he submitted to the prince the line of policy which he advised in the relations of Russia with France. This memorandum had been drawn up after a conversation with the Czar at the time when the latter reconciled himself with the First Consul, in 1801, after the seven thousand Russian soldiers who were prisoners in France, had been sent back to St. Petersburg. The policy developed in this memorandum consisted in leaguing Russia with the head of the French government, while secretly fomenting all causes of misunderstanding between England and France, exciting the spirit of natural rivalry which existed between these two countries, so as finally to drive them to war, and so to succeed, by means of their common enfeeblement, in raising Russian influence on the ruins of their preponderance.

The news which we received from St. Petersburg apprised us that this city was greatly disturbed by the fear of seeing the French come there, after the taking of Moscow. As by an audacious maneuver on Napoleon's part, this new capital of the Empire might fall into his power, the archives and precious objects had already been removed, and the Court as well as the, leading families were already preparing to depart. The burning of Moscow seemed to show that Russia was decided to resist our armies to the death. In spite of this, so great was Napoleon's partiality for Alexander that the Emperor still flattered himself with the hope of removing the Czar out of the reach of the importunities and threats of the enemies of France, by enlightening him on his real interests. Alexander would soon recognize, he thought, the selfishness of the warlike counsels of Great Britain, in whose interests the coalition had each time stupidly gone to war. This hope was again deceived. Nearly a month had passed and no answer had come from St. Petersburg. The hopes which had been conceived and awakened both by the King of Naples and General Lauriston, were in no wise realized. Napoleon was forced to admit how completely he had deceived himself in hoping that Alexander would approach him with the purpose of peace.

In the meanwhile Kutosov was preparing an attack on the vanguard commanded by the King of Naples—by favor of a verbal promise which he had given to Murat that both armies should remain in their respective positions until the return of Prince Volkonski, who had gone to St. Petersburg to deliver Napoleon's letter. A sudden attack of nearly the whole Russian army on our outposts decided the Emperor to begin his movement of evacuation and to approach himself to his reinforcements and storehouses. He had done all that duty and conscience prescribed to obtain peace. This object of the campaign and of so many efforts not having been obtained, Napoleon's plan was to retreat to Smolensk, to take up his winter quarters in Lithuania, and to prepare himself to commence the war again in the spring. The terrible severity of this exceptional and premature winter, which disorganized our fine army and caused it such cruel sufferings, opposed an insurmountable obstacle to the realization of these plans. The terrible cold which assailed our unhappy soldiers during the retreat, and killed them by thousands, was the cause of the disastrous issue of this memorable expedition.

Already on October 6, the Emperor had ordered arrangements to be made for the evacuation of such of the wounded as could be removed. A convoy, in which was General Nansouty, who was wounded himself, left some days later under command of General Claparède. Trophies which consisted of the valuable historical relics taken from the Kremlin were sent off from Moscow at the same time.

Napoleon left the Russian capital on October 19, a very fine day. He only left seven or eight thousand men behind him who were to follow him under Marshal Mortier after they had blown up the fortifications of the Kremlin. In the rear of the army, marched in numerous lines of extraordinary length a huge number of carriages filled with sick and wounded; chariots, *berlines,* open carriages, wagons laden with provisions, clothes and booty of every description.

The army took the road to Mojaïsk by which it had come, but in order to hide his march from General Kutosov, the Emperor feigned a march on Kaluga. Napoleon was two leagues beyond Borovsk and twenty leagues from Moscow when he heard that Prince Eugène's corps had been attacked at Malojaroslavetz by superior forces. He marched there forthwith and was able to reach it with sufficient speed to give his orders in good time. In this bloody encounter sixteen thousand French and Italian soldiers triumphed over sixty thousand Russians. This victory, dearly paid for, was marked by the death of the intrepid General Delzons and of his young brother who, covering the general with his body, as a rampart against the enemy, fell struck by a ball near his brother's corpse, the victim of his touching devotion. This attack by the Russians at Malojaroslavetz had generally given rise to the idea that they were anxious to engage a decisive action, and this decided Napoleon to halt in a little village called Gorodnia, in the vicinity. But having scoured the plain, it appeared to him that the enemy was preparing to retreat. Napoleon in consequence returned to the place from which he had come, strengthened in his resolution to follow the direction which he had ordered for the retreat.

On his return at nightfall to the poor weaver's cottage which he occupied at the Gorodnia bivouac, the Emperor narrowly escaped being carried off in a sudden dash made by some Cossacks. He was escorted only by three platoons of chasseurs and Polish lancers belonging to his guard, besides whom were the aides-de-camp and orderly officers who accompanied him. One of these officers, named Lecoulteux, was struck, in the course of the medley, by a chasseur of the Emperor's escort who ran him through the body. This chasseur had mistaken the officer for a Cossack, because he wore a green coat over his uniform and was holding a lance which he had wrested from a Cossack in his hand. By an extraordinary piece of good fortune, this terrible wound did not kill M. Lecoulteux, who only died in 1845.

The army saw the field of battle of La Moskova again, with emotion. The great abbey of Kolotskoi which had been used as a hospital, was still occupied by Russian and French wounded soldiers whose lives had been preserved by the devotion of some of our surgeons. Napoleon ordered all the sick and wounded French soldiers who could be moved to be placed on the carriages which followed the army.

We passed through Gjatz and Viazma, once so prosperous, but where now, since the passage of the Russian troops who had set fire to them and driven the wretched inhabitants out before them, solitude and death reigned. At Viazma the enemy tried to bar our way, but was dispersed by the corps under the command of Prince Eugène and Marshal Davout.

Till then the weather had been fairly mild with a bright sun, but on November 6, when the army was about two days' march from Smolensk, the first snow fell. In one night the thermometer went down to twelve degrees below zero and two days later to eighteen degrees. From that time forward the cold grew worse and worse. We hoped to find provisions, clothes, and fodder at Smolensk, for Napoleon had frequently repeated his orders that stores of all kinds were to be collected in abundant quantities in this town. But this expectation was doomed to disappointment, owing to an incomplete execution of his orders and the perfidy of various agents in the supply department, and the army was forced to continue its march in the same state of destitution. Before arriving at Smolensk the Emperor had heard of the Mallet conspiracy of which I shall speak later.

An act of neglect on the part of General Baraguay d'Hilliers who was in command at Smolensk and the capture of one of his brigades who capitulated and laid down arms, greatly angered the Emperor against this general, whom he deprived of his command and sent off to Berlin. It was a complications of misfortunes.

Napoleon remained several days in Smolensk to rally the laggards and to give some rest to the remnants of his army which was literally melting away under the influence of the cold and the privations. It became, however, necessary to leave the town. From that time forward the most hideous calamities never ceased to assail the French army. Each night at the bivouacs we lost thousands of horses whose flesh served to stay the hunger of the soldiers. Our cavalry found itself on foot, our artillery was without teams. Napoleon's great fame however influenced the enemy, and no serious action was attempted. At Krasnoi, wishing to instill prudence into the enemy, and to prove that our disasters had not abashed the courage of our army, the Emperor ordered General Roguet who was commanding a division of the young guard, to make a night attack on a Russian corps which was stationed near this town and which threatened the left of our road. This brave attack was fully successful although the hands of our soldiers were so numbed by the excessive cold that they could hardly hold their rifles.

A young auditor to the Council of State perished in this encounter, victim to his devotion. M. de Villeblanche had been sent to headquarters with the portfolio containing the work of the ministers. The Empress Josephine had charged me in a pressing letter to recommend him in her name to the Emperor as the son of one of her best friends. This interesting young man had been left at Smolensk in the capacity of intendant. He would certainly have experienced the effects of Napoleon's goodwill later on, had he not been reserved for a tragic end. As the army was leaving Smolensk, the auditor followed it on its retreat. Falling in during an encounter with one of the viceroy's officers, who was wounded and could hardly drag himself along, he ran up to him and supported him in his arms to help him along, when a cannonball came and finished off the wounded man, at the same time killing his generous supporter.

On leaving Smolensk the Emperor had ordered Marshal Ney to act as his rear-guard and not to leave the town until he had destroyed its fortifications. Ney, who was to be supported by Marshal Davout, set out on November 17. But in the night of the same day, the enemy maneuvered so as to separate Marshal Ney's corps from Davout's corps. The latter was one march ahead of Ney. The Emperor on hearing at Krasnoi of the movement which had been effected by the Russian troops, thought only of the best means of freeing the corps of his two marshals, whom he considered in common danger, by drawing the enemy upon himself. Free to continue his retreat or forced to fight so as not to abandon these two corps, Napoleon's choice was never doubtful. He returned in consequence to attack the enemy on the morrow. Having left Krasnoi at daybreak with a handful of men he attacks the Russian army, protected by powerful artillery, marches upon the enemy at the head of his guards, disconcerts it by this audacious aggression, forces it to leave its position on the road and give free passage to Marshal Davout's corps. In the meanwhile however Marshal Ney's corps does not appear. Indeed no news can be heard of it, and the rear guard left by the Emperor at Krasnoi is on the point of being carried, and the army's retreat is in danger of being cut off by Orcha. Napoleon makes up his mind to return to Krasnoi, grievously anxious in his mind by the uncertainty which overhangs Marshal Ney's fate, and to continue his retreat. The Emperor considers Marshal Ney lost.

Napoleon's generous resolution in this circumstance, where he exposed himself to being surrounded by the Russians in order to rescue his two marshals did him great honor even in the eyes of the enemy. It also shows the vigor of mind which he knew how to preserve in the midst of the greatest disasters.

The episode of Marshal Ney's separation from the army after his departure from Smolensk, has excited so much interest that I cannot resist the temptation to relate the principal phases of this adventure, although the story has already been told.

The corps of Marshals Ney and Davout, had been left at Smolensk, as I have already related, to protect the retreat and to blow up the fortifications of this town before abandoning it. Marshal Davout left Smolensk on November 16 to reach Krasnoi. Marshal Ney's corps which was under orders to form the extreme rear guard, only left it on the morrow to follow the same direction. It consisted of about six thousand soldiers with twelve cannon. It was followed by a large quantity of baggage which had remained behind and by a multitude of laggards from the other corps whom the fear alone of the Russian cannon determined to place themselves under the Marshal's protection. But during the night and before it was dislodged, as has been seen, by Napoleon, the enemy had occupied a strong position on the road from Smolensk to Krasnoi, and Ney—in spite of unheard-of but fruitless efforts to force his way through—remains with his single corps, separated from the whole of the French army. In this critical situation, reduced to his own scanty forces, surrounded by enemies ten times superior in numbers, in an icy and unknown land, the Marshal never wavers and buoys up his comrades in misfortune. He marches on with his troops in good order harassed by the Russian army, forced to restrain an undisciplined gang which at each cannon-shot rushes into the ranks of his soldiers. Marshal Kutosov sends him a summons by an officer to surrender, pointing out to him that no chance of escape remains to the little French troop. Ney replies to this summons, which it may be added was accompanied with the flattering expressions and courtesies which were thought the due of so great a warrior, by detaining the officer who brought it as prisoner of war. Eighty thousand Russians, occupying the heights, batter down his feeble troops. Instead of weakening, the Marshal's courage rises to the pitch of heroism. He reassures his soldiers and fills them with his intrepid valor. They follow their chief blindly in a furious attack against these masses and break down their first line. This courage of despair impresses the enemy, which contents itself with following them, without essaying to attack them. Ney's soldiers close round their Marshal in whom alone they personify safety, drawing indomitable resolution from his eyes. In searching a village they find a peasant who conducts them to the banks of the Dnieper. This great river has to be crossed, but they have no pontoon-train and the ice is floating down the river, except at one point where owing to some obstacles the ice-floes have stuck fast. The Marshal might have taken advantage of the rest of the day to try and cross, but half his men are still in the rear. He will halt to rally them, and while awaiting their arrival, this valiant man of war, who carried in a robust body a soul which was inaccessible to fear, wraps himself up in his cloak and goes to sleep on the snow. His troops having come up, they begin to cross the river at midnight. The first battalions succeed in reaching the other side. Those who come last and the artillery break in through the ice floes. The Marshal strains every muscle, present everywhere, he stretches out his hand to the one, encourages the other. This difficult crossing takes place in spite of a thousand dangers, but a part of the small army, which there is no means of getting across, remains on the left bank with the laggards, the baggage and the artillery train.

In the meanwhile the Marshal and his decimated troops set out on the weary march, and arrive at a big village where each and all hope to get some rest after so many terrible fatigues, but thousands of Cossacks, commanded by Hetman Platov, pour down upon our soldiers on every side. Ney's heroic attitude, however, restrains these savages. The Marshal wishes to take advantage of the night to decamp without noise, but scarcely has he taken his first steps than he is received with a rolling fire of artillery. He marches thus, during three days, followed by six thousand Cossacks, before whom he retires slowly, with no cannon, ho cavalry, even as a lion pressed by the hunters, advancing from wood to wood, taking advantage of all the cover afforded by the ground, keeping the enemy at a respectful distance, turning upon them when this enemy pressed him too close and putting them to flight with a handful of men, weak or wounded, all exhausted with cold, fatigue, and hunger. Each step taken by this valorous cohort is marked by a fierce encounter. At last after so much misery and so many cruel adventures, in which it is seen what the energy of a single man can accomplish for the safety of all, Ney and his soldiers arrive in sight of Orcha, with the fear lest this town be in the hands of the enemy. The Marshal detaches some Poles to reconnoiter. On seeing them Prince assembles some thousand men and at once marches to Ney's rescue, falling into his arms when he meets him, with tears of joy and emotion. No words could describe the astonishment, the emotion, the curiosity with which the two corps received each other, mingled and embraced, so greatly do men's minds unite and exalt them in the presence of a common adversity. The Emperor who had been filled with grief and anxiety by Ney's disappearance, hears of this veritable resurrection from his orderly officer, Gourgaud. He doubted the truth of the news of this unhoped-for return, then transported with joy, he cried out: "I would have given the treasure in my vaults in the Tuileries palace rather than have lost so brave a man." Marshal Ney fully justified that idea expressed by Napoleon in the hyperbolical language which he was accustomed to use: "Better an army of deer commanded by a lion, than an army of lions commanded by a deer."

I saw that the Emperor was troubled with grievous anxiety during all the time that he was without news of Marshal Ney. Napoleon could have found some comfort for the death of this illustrious warrior on some glorious battlefield, but he would have suffered bitter regret at the obscure immolation of a whole army corps and its valorous chief.

Napoleon's remark about Ney, in which he alludes to his treasure, gives me the opportunity of remarking that it was not three hundred nor two hundred millions which the Emperor had in his vaults in the Tuileries. This treasure, which was the result of savings during ten years out of the civil list—and only a part of which was in specie—never exceeded one hundred and forty millions. Almost this entire sum was used in days of adversity, in reorganizing the army, or in providing for the needs of the different public services during a time of crisis. The rest, about twelve millions, was confiscated in 1814, by the provisional government, under a notoriously lying pretext.

Such of the wounded as could be moved had been placed in all the carriages without exception, in the Emperor's carriages as well as in the carriages of the army. Napoleon's own horses had been used for this purpose. His solicitude for the honorable victims of this war and his indefatigable activity displayed themselves on this occasion as they had done during all his campaigns in Italy, Egypt, Germany and Spain. The following letter addressed to Marshal Mortier who remained the last in Moscow, is a proof which may be quoted amongst others. The Emperor writes:

"I cannot too strongly commend all the wounded that are left to you. Place them on the carriages of the young guard, on those of the cavalry on foot, in short on every carriage that you can find.—The Romans used to give crowns to those who saved the lives of citizens, how many crowns will you not deserve in my eyes for all those whom you shall save? Put them on our own horses, on everybody's horses; it is what I did at Acre. Begin with the officers, take the under-officers next, and give the preference to the French. Assemble the generals and the officers who are under your command and impress upon them what humanity expects of them under these circumstances."

The two sons of Prince Mark of Beauvau, who had made a very brilliant commencement in this campaign, were now following the retreat. The elder, a lieutenant of carabineers, was seriously wounded, having had his thigh broken with a lance-wound in the affair at Winkovo. He owed his life to the Emperor, for Napoleon had him placed in one of his carriages, recommending him specially to the Grand Equerry, and frequently asked with interest for news of him during the retreat. The Emperor held the parents of the young Beauvaus in high esteem and these on their side never forgot the kindnesses which they had received from him. Prince de Beauvau was one of the chamberlains who had been most in attendance. On Napoleon's return from the island of Elba, M. de Beauvau resumed the functions of his post and sat in the imperial chamber of peers. Princess de Beauvau was a lady-in-waiting in the Empress's palace. The Emperor had a particular regard for this lady and had thought to give her a striking proof of this regard—as I mentioned in its place—at the time of the formation of the Empress Marie Louise's household.

Chapter XIII

The Emperor's firmness and resolution grew in proportion with the dangers of the critical position in which he found himself placed. At Doubrovna a singular alarm spread round the bivouac. Dawn was beginning to break, when the camp was thrown into a state of tumult. At the first sounds thereof I made haste to dress and hurried to the house where the Emperor had passed the night, near which I was lodged. I met Count Daru under way, also going there and fully as anxious as I was. We found Napoleon, half-dressed, on the threshold, giving orders that the Cossacks who no doubt had caused this scrimmage should be driven off. But it was not an attack by the enemy which had caused all this confusion. It was the loud cries of calling somebody whose name was Ozanne. This name, repeated from bivouac to bivouac, had given rise to the belief that a call "*aux armes*" was being made. Such an alarm might any day entail serious dangers in the state of disorder inseparable from the disorganization of the army corps and in view of the fact that the camp was very carelessly guarded. Napoleon rode through the camp, ordering the guards and the troops to redouble in vigilance and to charge themselves with the care of seeing that a supervision and a discipline which had become more than ever necessary were maintained.

This circumstance, the remembrance of the alert at Gorodina and similar dangers to which he saw himself exposed, the anxiety which he felt at the time as to what had become of Marshal Ney, of whom we had no news, filled the Emperor with grave and sad reflections. In 1805, after Austerlitz, the respect of a Marshal of France for a king's word of honor, given with but little scruple, had preserved Alexander from the misfortune of falling into the hands of a detachment of French troops—but Napoleon had seen that this prince had retained no friendly recollection of the tacit approval which he had given to Marshal Davout's conduct on this occasion. The Emperor knew that the Czar was today dominated by the more than hostile influence of his enemies, from whose fury he might expect anything. Napoleon could not bear the idea of having to serve, in case of misfortune, to adorn the triumph of these implacable adversaries. He asked his ordinary medical adviser, Doctor Yvan, in consequence, to give him a dose of poison, which was contained in a sachet which he could carry round his neck, and which was to spare him the humiliation of falling alive into the hands of the Cossacks and of being exposed to the insults of these savages.

The army found some stores, forty cannon, and two pontoon trains at Orcha. The two heavy pontoon trains were sacrificed (a sacrifice which later on was to be very fatal to the issue of our retreat) because they would have stuck in the broken-down roads, and in order to employ the few horses that remained for the artillery trains. To leave as little as possible to serve as trophies to the enemy, Napoleon ordered almost all his carriages, his luggage, and the secret papers contained in the portfolio which was in my hands to be burned. It was from this portfolio that I derived the title of "Secretary to the Portfolio" with which the Emperor had invested me.

The cavalry being entirely on foot, there was spontaneously formed a squadron of from five to six hundred men, composed of officers who still had a horse each, to watch over Napoleon's person. The officers formed the privates of this squadron, the non-commissioned officers were colonels and the officers, generals. This squadron later on took the name of "the cursed battalion" because those who composed it lost their horses one after the other. It was commanded by General Grouchy under the orders of the King of Naples.

The Emperor having fully informed himself which was the best road to take, decided to march rapidly from Orcha to Boristov hoping to reach the Bérésina before the enemy who were maneuvering to close the road of Vilna against us. Admiral Tchitchakow, commanding the army of Moldavia, who by a treaty of neutrality concluded with the Russians by the Austrian general, Prince Schwarzenberg, enjoyed full liberty of action, had marched to this river. He had crossed it at first, but having been driven back by Marshal Oudinot, had recrossed it and had destroyed the bridge. Napoleon and the French troops then found themselves in a more dangerous position. The Emperor had with him less than forty thousand men, including the corps of Bellune and Reggio, surrounded by more than one hundred thousand Russians supplied with everything, fighting on their own native ground, while half our soldiers, were exhausted by the cold and by horrible fatigues, being moreover mentally depressed by so many reverses and the great distance which separated them from their fatherland. The imminence of the danger, far from weakening Napoleon's energy, tempered all the valor of his vigorous mind and indefatigable genius. Having succeeded in duping the enemy by feigned maneuvers, he succeeded in crossing the Bérésina beyond Boristov. The change to mild weather which, under all other circumstances would have been a blessing to our soldiers, brought on the contrary fresh misfortunes upon us; for the solid ice would have served us as a bridge, whereas the thaw having broken up the ice, the Bérésina drifted innumerable ice-floes. In order to construct trestle-bridges, our brave sappers and pontoniers, under command of General Eblé, were frequently forced to plunge into the icy water up to their shoulders, hampered in their movements and often wounded by the ice-floes which were dragged along by the current. In spite of so much suffering and so many obstacles, these brave fellows constructed several bridges, rapidly and with admirable devotion, over which the remnants of our unhappy army crossed the river in turn in an order which had been commanded by the Emperor who superintended the operation in person. The bridges broke down several times, a circumstance which aggravated the fatigues of our brave pontoniers, who were forced to repair the damage and begin their work over again. In spite of Napoleon's exhortations and repeated commands sent over the water that the opposite bank should be evacuated, there remained behind some thousands of laggards and non-combatants who could not make up their minds to abandon their innumerable carriages of every kind and their baggage. They only could make up their minds to do so when the enemy's cannon began to scatter dismay and death in the midst of this frantic mob. The confusion then became inexpressibly horrible, and the breaking-down of the bridges which gave way beneath the weight of these unhappy men, left all those who had not been able to cross the river in the power of the Russians. It would be a task beyond my power to describe the misfortunes of this day so deplorable under one aspect and yet at the same time so full of glory for the bravery of our army. It is in the midst of great dangers that the character of the French soldier reveals itself. Never did he show himself so great as in this catastrophe, emulating his chiefs in heroism. Napoleon's presence of mind and indefatigable activity, as he multiplied himself, taking every measure, keeping his eye on everything, is the best answer that can be made to those who have insinuated that on this memorable occasion he was afflicted with absolute mental and physical prostration. Never on the contrary did he display greater strength of mind nor exercise more genius than in these terrible moments. So also will he be found in the midst of the grave events of the campaigns of Saxony and of France.

All justice must also be rendered to Marshal Ney for his bravery and admirable firmness. This Marshal was the hero of the retreat. What devotion and presence of mind in the midst of danger, what familiarity with war and courage can produce of miracles, was realized by this intrepid warrior, who turn by turn was general and common soldier. How was it that the remembrance of his heroic conduct, of the thousand civic crowns and laurel-wreaths which adorned his brows, did not preserve him from the thunderbolt that struck him down?

It was no longer possible to preserve even the shadow of discipline, and each man left to himself tried to reach Vilna as best he could. At last, having reached Molodetchno, the Emperor found there a great quantity of dispatches which had been brought by estafettes who had not been able to reach him till then. These letters contained particulars of the Mallet attempt, the news of which he had first heard of on the evening before his arrival at Smolensk. Public security had not till then been troubled in Paris by the announcement of any disaster, but the distance by which the chief and the army were remote, the savagery of the Russians' means of defense and the burning of Moscow created a vague feeling of anxiety in France. Suddenly the foolhardy enterprise of Mallet broke out, the audacity of which stupefied Paris and the authorities. The desultory nature of the measures which were taken to oppose it show a state of uncertainty which might have proved fatal if the agents of the conspiracy had been on a better understanding. The Empress was living very quietly with her son at St. Cloud, when she was suddenly alarmed as to her son's safety and her own by the appearance of a detachment of guards sent on by the Minister of War, which galloped into the palace courtyard in great precipitation. She at once ran out in a dressing gown, with her hair flying out behind, on to a balcony which overlooked the courtyard and it was there she received the first news of an attempt which she had little expected. Her consternation did not, however, last a long time. But what produced a profound impression in France and in Europe, was the audacity with Which an obscure man, without money or credit, alone and without accomplices had escaped from prison to try a *coup de main* which had very nearly succeeded. Other reasons for amazement were the facility with which he had succeeded in persuading the troops that the Emperor was dead and that consequently the Empire was at an end, the passive submission of the municipal authorities to his behests, and finally the way in which the King of Rome and his mother had been forgotten.

The project of profiting by Napoleon's absence, when engaged in some distant expedition, with a view of overthrowing the Empire, was a fixed idea which had long been growing in the head of Mallet, that monomaniac of conspiracy. In 1806, after the battle of Eylau, and in 1809, after the battle of Essling, Mallet counting on the serious embarrassments which would keep Napoleon away from France, had tried to make use of the same means for provoking an upheaval. The first indications accused him of participation in these revolutionary intrigues, but convicting documents being wanting for the definite establishment of his complicity, Mallet was not sent for trial; a decree ordered his detention only in one of the state prisons. In 1809 the police were informed that Mallet had organized a plan of insurrection in the Force prison, which was to break out on a Sunday, on the day fixed for the chanting of a *Te Deum* at Notre Dame in honor of the entry of the French troops into Vienna. The indulgence with which he was treated having encouraged him, Mallet thought that the misfortunes of the retreat from Moscow at last offered him an opportunity of realizing the design, the execution of which he was pursuing with such constant obstinacy.

Seeing the necessity of his presence in Paris, the Emperor who had not wished to separate himself from the army as long as it was being menaced by imminent dangers, at last made up his mind to start for France. Dressed in a fur-lined pelisse, a present from the Emperor Alexander in happier days, and wearing an Astrachan cap on his head, Napoleon during the retreat had most often walked on foot, with a stick in his hand, taking the arm of the King of Naples or of one of his Marshals, in the midst of his troops and escorted by the sacred—or cursed—battalion. He only very rarely got into his carriage or mounted on horseback.

On December 5, on the day of his arrival at Smorgoni, the Emperor assembled the leaders of his army, and informed them of his departure, provided for all things with detailed instructions and left the supreme command to his brother-in-law Murat with Prince de Neufchâtel as his major-general. On December 2 he had sent Colonel Anatole de Montesquiou on to Paris charged with the mission of publishing good news all along the way, in towns as well as in simple villages, so as to reassure Poland, Germany and France, who must have been rendered anxious by the absence of all reports from the army. Napoleon sent the 29th bulletin on ahead of him, and in this bulletin he concealed none of our disasters. He left on December 5 with the Duke of Vicence in a sledge, with no other escort than his mameluke Roustan and one groom. Count Vonsovich who was seated on the box of the sledge, acted as interpreter. Napoleon made his way to Warsaw where he found fresh reasons for displeasure with Abbé Pradt and thence proceeded to Dresden, where were his ambassador Serra and the King of Saxony. He continued his way by Erfurth and Mayence, halting at Erfurth to send letters to his envoys at the courts of the princes of the Confederation of the Rhine, and orders to the generals in command of our military forces in Germany. He then proceeded from Mayence to Paris without stopping on the way. The Emperor arrived very late in the evening of December 18 at the Tuileries. The Empress who was sad and unwell had just gone to bed, for Napoleon had given her no notice of his approaching arrival. Frightened by the noises which she heard in the drawing room which opened out of her bedroom, Marie Louise was rising to find out what was going on when she saw the Emperor enter, rush up to her and clasp her in his arms. The noise outside which had rather frightened the Empress was caused by a discussion between two men hooded and wrapped up in fur cloaks, with the lady-in-waiting who slept in the room adjoining the Empress's bed-room. This lady, as was her bounden duty, was defending the entrance to the bedroom, when one of these men throwing open his mantle disclosed the Emperor to her stupefied gaze.

Napoleon saw the soil of his country again, as great, greater perhaps, than when he had left it. More than once had his audacious and skilful maneuvers, and the ascendancy of his genius saved the remains of the French army from a destruction which appeared inevitable. Adversity had found him strong and even immovable. Adversity had awakened in him that vigor of mind and those qualities which that hard school develops in chosen natures. Fortune, then, in betraying, had not diminished him, but she had weakened his prestige of invincibility. The army had lost none of its glorious reputation. It had displayed in these evil days an intrepidity, a constancy and warlike virtues which have amazed the world. It was only beaten by the elements, and if the bodies of the soldiers succumbed their hearts had never failed. The leaders of this valiant army had shown themselves worthy of it. Attacked by every kind of disaster, reduced to a handful of soldiers with barely enough strength to carry their arms, the army had still imposed respect on the enemy. No doubt that among so many brave soldiers there were numerous exceptions, as must necessarily be the case in any large agglomeration of men exposed to the direct calamities, for all characters are not tempered alike. But why make mention of such exceptions when the bulk showed such endurance and such courage? Those whose names might be mentioned as having been exceptions to the rule were for the most part men who had no need of the test of adversity to show their imperfections, their weaknesses, or their vices.

The 29th bulletin which had preceded the Emperor to Paris, where it was delivered thirty-six hours before his arrival, had explained the long silence of the Great Army and had thrown a sad light on the disasters of the retreat. The minds of men were struck with these sinister pictures, and comparisons were instituted between the expedition of Cambyses to Egypt and the retreat from Moscow. Some thick-headed people applied to Napoleon a passage, sufficiently striking it is true, out of the "Considerations on the Causes of the Greatness and Decline of the Romans"—chapter XVII—where Montesquieu, after having spoken of the invasions of the barbarians into Europe, emboldened as they were by the enfeeblement of Charlemagne's empire, adds: "If a prince were to create such ravages in Europe today, the nations driven back in the North to the limits of the Universe would keep their stand there until the moment when they would inundate Europe for the third time."

Victories dearly purchased and fruitless, unheard-of disasters, the destruction of the finest army which France ever possessed, such were the results of this fatal expedition to Russia. How wide a field was thrown open to accusations, to complaints, and to the expressions of regret of even the best-disposed party in the nation and of our allies the Poles! Many people have been pleased to describe Napoleon's confidences delivered at St. Helena, as ingenious and tempting fictions, intended to deceive his contemporaries and posterity. May I be allowed to oppose to these severe judgments, the following extract from Napoleon's Memoirs; it is a *résumé* of his plans and of his conduct at this most important epoch in his reign, which, in my opinion, is as sincere as it is free from boasting?

"The history of the Russian campaign will never be well known, because the Russians either do not write or write with no regard for truth, and because the French have been seized with a fine frenzy for dishonoring and discrediting their own glory.—The war with Russia became the necessary consequence of the continental system on the day on which the Emperor Alexander violated the conventions of Tilsitt and of Erfurth, but a consideration of far greater import influenced Napoleon and decided him. The French Empire, which he had created with so many victories, would inevitably be dismembered at his death, and the scepter of Europe would pass into the hands of a Czar, did he not throw the Russians back on to the farther side of the Borysthenes, and reestablish the throne of Poland, the Empire's natural barrier. In 1812, Austria, Prussia, Germany, Switzerland, and Italy marched under the eagles of France. Was Napoleon not obliged to think that the moment had come for consolidating the immense edifice which he had erected, but on the summit of which Russia would weigh with all the weight of her power, as long as she was able at pleasure to march her numerous armies to the Oder. Alexander was young and full of strength like his empire; it was to be presumed that he would survive Napoleon. All the secret of the war is there. No personal feeling weighed in the matter as certain writers have alleged. The Russian campaign is the most glorious, the most difficult and the one fullest of honor for the Gauls of which either ancient or modern history makes mention.

"This war should have been one of the most popular of modern times; it was a war of common sense and of true interests; it was a war for the repose and security of all; it was Conservative, European, and Continental. Its success was to consecrate combinations which would have caused the dangers of the times to disappear, yielding a quiet future in their place, and ambition had no place in my views. Could one believe that it was there that I was to fail and to meet with ruin? Never had I acted better, never had I better deserved. But as if opinion also were subject to epidemics, lo! in one moment, there was but one outcry, one feeling against me. I was proclaimed the tyrant of the kings, I, who had given them a fresh lease of life! I was no longer anything more than the destroyer of rights of the nations, I, who had done all and was about to undertake all for them! And the peoples and the kings, these irreconcilable enemies, allied themselves, concerted in conspiracy against me! No account was taken of all the acts of my life. I knew very well that the opinion of the people would come back to my side with victory, but I failed to secure victory and found myself crushed. Such are men and such is my history. But the people and the kings, and perhaps both together, will regret me; and my memory will be sufficiently avenged for the injustice which has been done to my person."

After having described the great advantages of Russia's position with regard to Europe, Napoleon adds:

"One cannot refrain from shuddering at the thought of such a mass of men, which one can attack neither on the flank nor on the rear, pouring out with impunity upon you, flooding all if it triumph—or retreating into the midst of its icy regions, into the bosom of devastation and death, which are its reserves, if defeated, ready to reappear again if needs be. Have we not here the hydra's head, the Antaeus of the fable, which cannot be vanquished except by seizing it body to body, and smothering it in one's arms? . . . . But where to find the Hercules? It appertained to us alone to dare to assume that part ....

"Was it, however, the efforts only of the Russians which annihilated me? No, it was a capital burned down in spite of the inhabitants, and by means of foreign intrigues; it was a winter, a frost, whose sudden appearance and excessive rigor were phenomenal; it was the false maneuvers, the countermarches of the Austrian corps, false reports, low intrigues, treachery, stupidity, and many other things, in one word, which will be known one day perhaps and which will be able to extenuate the one clumsy fault in diplomacy and in war which can be justly laid to my charge, namely, having undertaken such an enterprise in leaving on my flanks, which soon became my rear, two Cabinets of which I was not the master, and two allied armies which the slightest reverse would transform into enemies: and in conclusion on this point and indeed to cancel all that I have said by one word, this famous war, this audacious enterprise, were never desired by me; I had no wish to fight. Alexander had no wish to fight either, but once face to face, circumstances drove us one against the other and fatality did the rest."

Napoleon was right in saying that he did not wish to make war on Russia in 1812 and that he did all he could to avoid it; his first need was to finish the war in Spain. The conferences, the explanations, which the Emperor had with his ministers and with persons who were best acquainted with the Russian empire are sufficient proofs of his anxiety. When the indispensable necessity of taking steps was made clear to him, and when his mind was firmly made up and he had assumed its entire responsibility, he considered it superfluous to enter upon any controversy on this point. When on the contrary he had reasons for hesitation, he would sound the opinions of competent persons either directly or indirectly; he would put forward paradoxical proposals in his conversations, and would provoke arguments destined either to enlighten him and confirm him in the resolution which in his eyes seemed the best, or to modify it or even to abandon its execution. He would then weigh the pros and cons in his heart of hearts and never took any serious resolutions without having thought them over for a long time and with the deepest attention.

In the midst of his meditations I often heard Napoleon characterize his position with this expression to which he gave vent in the silence of his cabinet: "The bow is overstretched." Who had created this situation? Did it depend on him alone to slacken this bow? I am aware of all that might be said on this great question; but I cannot discuss it here. It was opined that Napoleon's dictatorship had lasted too long a time does not the exclamation which I have referred to above prove that Napoleon, more than anybody else, understood the danger this situation implied?

The situation in which the gravity of circumstances placed France at that time did not diminish the Emperor's courage, but brought out all the vigor of his mind, giving new food to his energetic activity. His first care was to inform himself on what had happened in Paris at the time of Mallet's audacious conspiracy. Napoleon feared the misfortunes of every kind for which his death might give the signal. He blamed the hastiness of the judgment which had been pronounced on the authors of the conspiracy, and especially on those who had only been implicated in it; but feeling how imperatively necessary it was to recall the civil magistrates to a rigorous observance of their duties Napoleon pronounced, although with regret, the dismissal of the Prefect of the Seine, for yielding with too great ease to Mallet's declarations and injunctions.

The Emperor received the principal corporations of the state in solemn audience. The senate, encouraged in the expression of a wish to which Napoleon had not answered in an explicit manner, spoke of the advisability of proceeding to the coronation of the King of Rome. Arrangements were even projected for the eventuality of a coronation of the Empress and of her son; but there were things of greater urgency to be performed, and for the time being the project in question was not carried into effect.

The former King Louis of Holland, who was living in absolute retirement in Gratz, on hearing the news of the disasters which had befallen the French army in the Russian campaign, and the return of the Emperor to France, wrote to him to ask to be allowed to return to Holland. King Louis thought the moment a favorable one for reestablishing the French dynasty in the Low Country, and considered that Napoleon ought not to hesitate to replace him on the throne which was about to become a prey to the allied forces. Napoleon answered his brother's letter by asking him to come to Paris, where he said he would find, not an offended brother, but a father who had brought him up. He further declared to him that Holland had become French, and that Louis, having of his free will abdicated his crown could not think of taking it back again. The Ex-King of Holland made another fruitless application with the same object in view to the Congress of Prague, at a later period. He left the Austrian states at that time, and withdrew to Switzerland so as to be in a more favorable position for following the course of events.

The Emperor's first care was the reorganization of the army, and he worked without respite to repair its losses. He met with a goodwill and an ardor in the country which powerfully seconded his efforts in the accomplishment of this great task. Old and new France and Italy seemed to have renewed their strength in the terrible days of the calamities of the last campaign, just as after the battle of Cannas, the Roman senate went to meet Varro to thank him for not having despaired of the safety of the republic. The city of Paris, all the provinces of the Empire made haste to sacrifices of all kinds, convinced as they were that Napoleon was more than ever necessary to France and that they had lost nothing since he remained to them, armed with all his energy. The speeches which were addressed to him, the letters which were written to him, the addresses which were presented to him were proofs of the sincere and spontaneous expression of the feelings of the country. The artillery, both in men and material, as well as all other military branches were reorganized and completed, and very soon, in one word, the French army was once more in a position to present itself afresh on the field of battle, as numerous as it was before its disaster. Three months had sufficed to obtain these prodigious results. The young soldiers who for the most part had been employed to reinforce the army, were as brave and as formidable in the face of the enemy as our veterans, after a day's fighting. Unfortunately they were not inured to fatigue like the latter, nor as accustomed to forced marches as were their seniors: it will be remembered that Napoleon used to say that it was chiefly with his soldiers' legs that he waged war.

Wishing to attach to the fate of the Empire the young gentlemen belonging to old families, whom laziness and discontent had cast into the ranks of the adversaries of the Imperial regime, Napoleon created regiments of guards of honor in which the privates had the prospect of becoming officers with one year's service. His object was to avoid leaving behind him any elements of disturbance, and at the same time to increase his cavalry. The creation of the regiments of the guards of honor was as successful as had been desired by the Emperor, and this new corps supplied the army with 10,000 excellent horsemen whose education was either complete, or easily to be completed. The *esprit de corps* and the natural taste of the French for the profession of arms very soon aroused in these young gentlemen the love of the Fatherland and of the flag. At the beginning, however, a spirit of resistance and insubordination natural enough manifested itself amongst these forced recruits, especially in the first regiment, which was assembled at Tours, under the command of General Philippe de Ségur. There had been formed in this regiment, which was made up of young gentlemen from Brittany and Vendée, a kind of association, the object of which was to kidnap the Emperor. To obtain this result the association counted on the hazards which might arise to approach the regiment to the sovereign's person. Louis de la Rochejaquelein, with this purpose in view, had placed himself in communication with the principal members of the association, notably with a certain Charette, who was a relation of the Vendéen general of that name. The police, informed of this intrigue, arrested and transported to Paris some of the ringleaders. The regiment was excited by their long absence, and a deputation came to ask the Colonel what had been done with their comrades, and imperiously demanded that they should be set free. On the firm refusal of the Colonel one of the guards of honor, whose name was Des Nétumières, shot at him point-blank with a pistol, which merely grazed his face, the bullet entering the collar of his coat without wounding him. This outbreak had no other consequences. The authorities satisfied themselves with the arrest of Nétumières and some other young fellows who were implicated in the matter, and imprisoned them at Saint Pélagie They were treated with indulgence, the Restoration found them in prison in 1814, and set them at liberty.

The Emperor had received the most disastrous news from the army in Russia. After his departure from Smorgoni the army had continued its march to Vilna under the command of the King of Naples. The absence of Napoleon, whose presence inspired all with courage, left it exposed to new disasters. The intensity of the cold, which increased to thirty degrees below zero, completed their disorganization and the road from Smorgoni to Vilna was strewn with corpses; With Napoleon's forethought they collected at Vilna immense stores of every kind, besides provisions which had been brought from Koenigsberg, and towns in Lithuania; but it was impossible to distribute these provisions with any order. Famished gangs of men rushed on the storehouses and pillaged them, so that all these immense resources, which would have revictualled and provisioned an army of 300,000 men, were wasted and lost. Vilna was in the midst of horrible confusion. At a league from this city a hill which was one mere ice-block opposed an insurmountable obstacle to the horses and carriages, and these had to be abandoned at the foot of the hill. The army treasure was distributed amongst the soldiers, who faithfully brought back the sums which had been entrusted to them. At last the remnants of this noble and heroic army arrived at Kovno, after six weeks of disasters and misfortunes without a parallel. They recrossed the Niemen which six months earlier a splendid, large, and brilliant army had crossed. Reduced to one quarter of its numbers, this army retreated, after having suffered all kinds of misfortunes; but although vanquished by the atrocious severity of the elements, the

Queen Marie Louise, Napoleon's second wife, for whom he divorced Josephine, leaving Paris with her son, the young King of Rome. "Don't go to Rambouillet," he cried out to his mother. His sentiments of honor and of loyalty had remained unshaken. Marshal Ney, the hero of this retreat, at the head of a handful of men of the rearguard, carrying a rifle like a private forced himself over the bridge of Kovno and was the last to leave this inhospitable land.

It is a poor consolation to think that this campaign had been no less disastrous to the Russians than to us. Their army had been decimated during our retreat by disasters and the rigors of the weather, from which the Russian troops had suffered as much as the French army. According to Sir Robert Wilson, English commissioner with the Russian army, more than 200,000 regulars perished there. The second capital of the Russian Empire had been totally consumed together with immense riches, and many provinces had been devastated by the Russians themselves, to make a desert around us. While so many sad events were taking place, a Prussian auxiliary force, commanded by General York, separated itself from Macdonald's army corps and treated with the enemy. Disavowed at first by the King of Prussia, York was recompensed two months later by the same Prince, on signing a treaty of alliance with Russia at Breslau. Prince Schwarzenberg, who commanded the Austrian corps, after having left an open field to the Russian troops who came to cut our way across the Bérésina, evacuated the Russian territory and returned to Galicia in virtue of a convention which he had signed with the Emperor Alexander's generals.

The *Moniteur* of June 27, 1813, reported the King of Naples' departure to his states in the following terms: "The King of Naples, being unwell, has left the command of the army which he has handed over to the viceroy. This latter is more accustomed to great administrations: he enjoys the Emperor's confidence."

Matters were no better in Spain. King Joseph had made proposals to the Cortes assembled in the town of Leon, where deputies were occupied in laying down the basis of their constitution. The successes of the French army in Aragon and Catalonia had given some weight to the proposal made by the King to recognize the fundamental clauses of this constitution. But in the meanwhile the loss of the battle of Salamanca, which had been fought by Marshal Marmont without awaiting the re-enforcements which the King was bringing to him, and the occupation of Madrid by the English General, which was the result of this serious reverse, once more modified the more conciliatory disposition of the Spaniards. The evacuation of Galicia and Andalusia, to which Marshal Soult resigned himself after repeated orders, brought him back to Madrid, which the English General made haste to leave to avoid being surrounded. After having besieged Burgos, which was valiantly defended by General Dubreton for thirty-five days, without any result, the English army withdrew to Salamanca pursued by the army from Portugal, which inflicted serious losses upon it. The reunion of the French armies on the Tormés, the command of which the King handed over to Marshal Soult, gave him the hope of avenging the defeat of Salamanca, but floods of rain, which rendered the roads impassable, delayed the movements of our troops and gave the English General time to decamp. The King had entered Madrid, where he hoped to be able to maintain himself. In spite of the numerous detachments which Napoleon had withdrawn from the French armies in Spain, these armies still numbered ninety thousand men in the center and west of the Peninsula, and forty thousand men in Aragon and Catalonia with Marshal Suchet at their head.

One of the Emperor's first cares was to endeavor to put an end to his dispute with the Pontifical Court. On January 19, 1813, he escorted the Empress to Grosbois, where Prince de Wagram gave a grand hunt in Their Majesties' honor. But instead of returning to Paris, Napoleon went to pass the night at Fontainebleau, where he was not expected: the Empress joined him there on the morrow. Several Italian and French cardinals, archbishops, and bishops, assembled around the pope in this residence, were busy in negotiating the arrangements which should put an end to the disputes which had taken place for several years between the Holy See and Tuileries Court. Napoleon, growing impatient at the slowness of these negotiations, and relying on the influence which he knew himself to possess over Pius VII, wished to take advantage of this to deal directly with the Holy Father without any intermediary. In consequence the Emperor had several private conferences with his Holiness, the result of which was that a new Concordat was signed in the Empress's apartments in the presence of their councilors and of the court. The Empress Marie Louise had taken a great part in bringing this reconciliation about. She had been to call upon the sovereign pontiff at the time of his arrival at Fontainebleau; she returned there of her own accord after the signing of this Concordat, to offer the Holy Father her congratulations. The pope, who was a very apostle, full of sweetness and charity, loved Napoleon in spite of all; and Napoleon on his side had for him esteem and even affection. It is almost certain that they would have come to an understanding if the pope's Roman councilors had not unceasingly held up before his eyes to check him the menace of the anathema with which he would be struck in case he were to abandon the rights of the church, or sacrifice the smallest fragment thereof. The Fontainebleau Concordat was destined to dry up at their very fountain head all these religious quarrels. It provided for the solution of all the most important questions. First, the establishment of the pope at Avignon, which was to become the See of Christendom; secondly the fixing of a delay of six months in which the briefs of canonical investiture were to be delivered to the Bishops by the Metropolitan in case there had not received, during the period stated, the bull of investiture from the Pontifical Court. The Concordat of 1801 had passed this matter over in silence, and the Pontifical Court had taken advantage of these circumstances, on more than one occasion, to leave churches in France, Italy, and Germany unprovided with priests. No sooner had the pope been left alone than he once more fell under the influence of his former counselors, who had been recalled from exile by Napoleon, and who were in the pay of the enemies of France and initiated in their secret designs. They worked upon the conscience of the gentle and venerable Pontiff to bring him to refuse the concessions which he had freely made in a spirit of concord and pacification. The pope, obedient to their suggestions, addressed the Emperor two months after the signing of the new Concordat, a letter, in which he explained his scruples and the reason which induced him not to carry the conditions of this covenant into effect. The Emperor's only answer was a decree in which he commanded the archbishops, bishops, and chapters to see that these conditions were rigorously carried out.

Affairs in Germany, and especially the precarious state of our alliance with Austria, demanded Napoleon's serious attention. Austria professed the friendliest feeling and was not chary of protestations, but the always equivocal conduct of the Vienna cabinet kept alive the Emperor's distrust which was certainly thoroughly justified. Every report he received from Vienna informed him that in political circles the dissolution of the Confederation of the Rhine and of the Grand duchy of Warsaw was being talked of. These pretensions, it is true, were attributed to the allied forces, but the language in which these rumors were hawked about revealed a desire to see these things realized. To enlighten doubts which were still existent in his mind Napoleon thought it better to replace M.

Otto, our ambassador in Vienna, by Count de Narbonne, his aide-de-camp, whose old-standing relations with the Viennese aristocracy, during the exile, might render him better able to sound the private intentions of the Vienna cabinet. The new ambassador was not long in obtaining the revelation of the intention of this cabinet to propose an armed mediation, thanks to which it should become the arbitrator of peace. The new rôle which Austria was trying to assume changed our situation, for it was evident that France was about to lose the best guarantee she possessed against Austria's bad faith. In declaring herself mediator, the contingent supplied to our army by this power would be no longer forthcoming; and from that time forward the alliance would rest on the most fragile foundations imaginable, and on assurances of friendship of which the Vienna cabinet was never chary, but whose sincerity Napoleon had reasons to mistrust.

While awaiting the turn which these events were about to take Napoleon devoted himself to details of home government. Without neglecting the achievement of works which had already been begun, he reduced the sums of money allotted to each. He paid visits to the public establishments and showed himself in the faubourgs, where his simple and homely manners aroused the enthusiasm of the people. These walks in Paris were constantly inspiring the Emperor with ideas for improvements, embellishments and useful reforms. He notably gave orders for municipal works for the distribution of water in the various quarters of the town, and the increase in the number of fountains; for the achievement or construction of market-houses, slaughterhouses, sewers, bridges; for the erection of large buildings intended to receive the archives of the Empire, the University and its dependencies, a school of Fine Arts, with studios and exhibition rooms; and finally for the establishment of four large cemeteries at the four cardinal points of Paris. This useful employment of the few moments which the constant anxiety of war left free to Napoleon is an example of the advantages of every kind which the departments would have derived from the journeys which he proposed to make, as soon as lasting peace should give him leisure to do so.

Napoleon also went with the Empress to the Invalides, reviewed the old soldiers there, inquired as to their wants, tasted the food provided for them, and made the Empress do the same. The sovereigns walked through the gallery in which were exhibited the raised plans of the fortified towns and harbors. The Emperor remarked amongst others the plan of the harbor of Brest, which had just been finished and which he praised highly.

In the beginning of this year, 1813, the Emperor had opened the session of the Legislative body in person, with a speech in which he had spoken of his losses, of his hopes, and of his desire for peace, with the greatest frankness. This speech had been followed by a speech by the Minister of the Interior, in which he read out a statement of the situation of the Empire during the two preceding years.

Napoleon had also busied himself in constituting the Regency, the exercise of which he had decided to confide to the Empress. It had been proposed to him to give a special household to this princess, at the head of which a *"surintendant"* should be placed. However much the Emperor objected to the creation of any fresh charges at court, this proposal had seemed to find favor in his eyes. He had then cast his glance on M. de Narbonne, whose distinguished intelligence and courteous manners had always pleased him, as a fit man to fill this post. But he soon abandoned this project and took this officer as his aide-de-camp, until the time when he sent him to Vienna. M. de Narbonne justified the favor shown him by Napoleon, and served him with constant fidelity until his death, which occurred at Torgau, where he had been appointed governor of the town, in 1813.

The liking attributed to Napoleon for the representatives of the ancient nobility was part of his system of fusion and proceeded from the resolution he had taken to render himself at one with all that was distinguished in France. This consideration outweighed what attraction he may have felt for those polished manners, those delicate flatteries, that fine and often ornate wit, those traditions of good taste and of urbanity, which especially formerly, distinguished the pick of the nobility at court. The ensemble of these reasons had prompted Napoleon from the moment of his accession to power to make advances to the representatives of these families, making use of M. de Talleyrand in this work of amalgamation and reconciliation which he had undertaken. It was thus that he had placed the Dukes of Choiseul-Praslin and de Luynes in the senate at the time of its formation.

Various persons had been proposed to fill the post of secretary to the commands of the Empress-Regent, amongst others M. Ferrand, a former councilor to the Parliament of Paris, the same gentleman who became Louis XVIII's minister under the first Restoration and who intrepidly assumed the responsibility of laws best calculated to exasperate public opinion; then M. Duchesne de Gillevoisin, another parliamentarian. These selections not having been approved of, the post of secretary to the commands of the Empress-Regent remained vacant. When the Emperor decided to constitute the Empress's Regency I was seriously ill, for I had returned exhausted with the fatigues of the retreat from Moscow. Napoleon, whom I was consequently unable to attend, ordered Duroc, the Grand Marshal of the palace to write to me, that the need I had of repose, and his wish not to remove me from his person, had prompted him to register me as "in convalescence," to use his expression, near the Empress's person, and that in consequence he had appointed me secretary of the commands of this princess. Some days later he conferred the title and powers of Regent on the Empress by letters patent, and she took the oath in this capacity in a cabinet council which was convened for the purpose at the Elysée. King Joseph was acknowledged lieutenant-general of the Emperor, and the Prince Archchancellor first councilor to the Regency, and charged with giving his visa to all documents emanating there from. A Minister of State, the Duc de Cadore, was appointed secretary to the Regency and filled the post of secretary of state during Count Daru's absence, when the latter accompanied the Emperor beyond our frontiers. At the same time Marshal Duke of Conegliano was designed to fill the functions of colonel-general of the guard and General Caffarelli, the Emperor's aide-de-camp, was charged with the command of the detachments of the said guard which remained in Paris.

In my new capacity as secretary to the commands of the Empress, I received through the agency of Count Daru, minister secretary of state, the Emperor's instructions with a copy of the letters patent which bestowed the title of Regent on the Empress Marie Louise, a copy of the senatus consultum constituting the Regency, and of the senatus consultum fixing the Empress's jointure.

This is Count Daru's letter:

"MONSIEUR LE BARON.—The Emperor having appointed you secretary of the commands to the Empress-Regent has commanded me to communicate to you the documents of interest to H.M. which it is necessary for you, for this reason, to be acquainted with. In consequence I have the honor to send you herewith copies of the organic senatus consultum on the Regency, and of the senatus consultum which fixes the Empress's jointure.

"It is right that you should hold these documents at the Empress's disposal and that you be able to lay them before H.M. whenever She desires to see them. The Emperor also wishes you to prepare the protocol of the Empress's cabinet and that you should present it to the Minister of Exterior Relations who will submit it to H. M. The original of this protocol will remain in your hands. It is also necessary that you should withdraw all letters and communications which may have been addressed to the Empress from the Ministry of Exterior Relations, and that in future you should write the answers to such communications.

"It is essential, M. le Baron, that you should procure everything concerning the statutes of the imperial family and the constitutional acts of the state, to place them at the disposal of H.M. the Empress whenever She may need to see them.

"Such, Monsieur le Baron, are the Emperor's desires, which H. M. has charged me to acquaint you with.

"I have the honor to offer you the assurance of my high esteem.

"(Signed) DARU."

When I was appointed secretary of the commands of the Regent, and as this appointment was only a temporary one, I did not draw the salary attached to this post. The Emperor provided the funds for this salary with an allotment of four thousand francs a month and furnished a very fine house at St. Cloud, for my use, requesting me to live there with my family, whenever the Empress should be in residence in the palace there. At the same time he gave my wife and myself our daily *entrées* to the Empress's evening drawing rooms. And lastly he ordered me to write to him every day, which I never failed to do and without a single interruption.

I took possession of my functions in the Empress's service some days before she was declared Regent. I had had frequent opportunities of appreciating the gentleness and the kindness of this princess; my frequent relations with her taught me to know these winning qualities still better. She took pains to render the exercise of my functions as easy and as pleasant as possible, so that they were a real sinecure. The order established in the dispatch of affairs was so well arranged that the intervention of the Regent was hardly noticed. She was in reserve for extraordinary circumstances, which fortunately did not occur (the death of the Emperor for example). My chief employment was my correspondence with the Emperor when he was away, and my work at the Council of State where I was on ordinary duty.

After having provided for all matters which claimed his foresight, matters which we have just enumerated in part, Napoleon at once prepared himself to join his army. Almost on the eve of his departure Prince Schwarzenberg, announced long previously as a bearer of good news, at last arrived in Paris. The Emperor contented himself with putting him into communication with the Duke of Bassano, so anxious was he to find himself on the scene of the military operations. The Russians had crossed the Elbe and were occupying Dresden, which the King of Saxony had left in going to Prague. Prussia had concluded a treaty of alliance with Russia, at Kalitch, on February 27. The Emperor left St. Cloud for Mayence on April 15, at four o'clock in the morning.

In the morning of the same day I received the following note from the Empress:

"You are sure to know that the Emperor has gone. I like to think that you also are a good deal grieved at this. I beg you, if M. Fain has not yet left, to tell him that I want him very much to give me news of the Emperor. I did not find time to tell him so myself. I beg you also to send me the list of entrées, the Emperor wishing them to be sent to me in the course of the day. I beg you to believe in the assurance of the sentiments with which I am your much attached

"LOUISE."

"Saint Cloud, April 15, 1813."

The first essay in her new rôle which the Empress made was a reception of the diplomatic corps, which took place on the following Sunday. She sustained the character of Empress-Regent with nobility and affableness.

The first success of the campaign of 1813, gained six days after the Emperor's arrival at the army, a success which was violently contested, was the battle of Lutzen, which opened the gates of Dresden to the French army. The King of Saxony made haste, immediately afterwards, to return to his capital.

In the meanwhile conferences were taking place in Paris between Prince Schwarzenberg and the Duke of Bassano. They were limited on the part of the Austrian envoy to an abundance of friendly protestations which lost in value on account of the manner in which they were lavished. In one of these conferences, however, the prince let slip a very significant statement. Apropos of obligations which seemed to be a natural consequence of a family alliance, Prince Schwarzenberg said: "Politics made the marriage, politics can unmake it." Although M. de Bassano did not acquaint the Emperor with this remark, the reserve of the Austrian ambassador who formulated no declaration aroused the suspicion that he had a mental reservation and that he was trying to gain time. In the end however came the proposal of an armed mediation, accompanied by a renewal of friendly protestations, and the assurance that if Austria presented herself under arms it was in order to force the allies to make peace. Napoleon then decided to send Prince Eugène off to Italy, where he considered his presence would be more useful, in case of a rupture. At the same time he recalled Marshal Soult, whom he wished to employ in the Great Army, from Spain.

While the Emperor was in Dresden, the Austrian general, Bubna, was sent to him. It was always the same language that was held, but after a great deal of reticence it was hinted that Austria's fidelity to the French alliance merited as a compensation, on the part of France, a renunciation of the protectorate of the Confederation of the Rhine, the dislocation of the Grand Duchy of Warsaw, and the restitution of Illyria to Austria, the said restitution not being the subject of any contestation. M. de Bubna at the same time proposed that a general congress should be opened, declaring "that Russia and Prussia admit Austria's mediation, but that he cannot explain what will be the nature of this mediation."

Napoleon losing all trust in the friendly dispositions affected towards him by Austria, but still dissembling, decided to send the Duke of Vicence to Russian headquarters to come to an understanding with the Czar on the basis of general pacification, preferring to deal with an open enemy rather than with a perfidious ally. The Emperor Alexander who was already engaged to Austria refused to receive the Duke of Vicence.

In the meanwhile the victories of Bautzen and Wurtschen determined the allies to propose an armistice during which, they added, the mediating power would expose the basis of peace, the armed mediation having accordingly been denounced as disposed of. Napoleon once more agreed to this armistice, and had reason to regret doing so thereafter. But he hoped, to make use of his expression, "to get a better insight of the pieces on his chessboard," to find means, thanks to this truce, of approaching the Emperor Alexander and of making Austria pay the price of her bad faith.

While I was fulfilling my functions in the Empress's service as secretary of her commands, this princess received one day the following letter from the Emperor:

"MADAME AND DEAR FRIEND—I send you an open letter for the Duke of Otranto; you will send for the duke and you will hand him this letter yourself. If he needs a passport you will order one to be given to him, my desire being that this mission should remain secret. You may however speak of it to the Archchancellor, my desire being that nothing be ever kept secret from him. But you will arrange that, while the Archchancellor is with you, the Duke of Otranto shall have been already sent for and be present.

"(Signed) NAPOLEON."

"Dresden, May 11, 1813."

In conformity with the request contained in this letter which was handed to him, Fouché left for Dresden. Napoleon thought it prudent not to leave this individual in Paris under the grave circumstances in which France and the Empire were placed. The object of this letter was to remove Fouché from Paris and to send him to Illyria to replace General Bertrand, whose presence was more useful with the army.

By a letter on the same day the Emperor commissioned the Empress to send the Duke of Bassano to Dresden also, but these two letters had been written with very different purposes.

Since I have begun quoting letters written from Napoleon to Marie Louise, I will copy two more, the first of which will show both the Empress's ingenuousness and the Emperor's extreme delicacy in all matters concerning the proprieties, and to what a pitch he carried his scruples in these matters:

"MADAME AND DEAR FRIEND—I have received the letter in which you inform me that you received the Archchancellor while you were in bed. My pleasure is that, under no circumstances whatsoever, and on no pretext, you receive anybody while you are in bed, no matter who he may be. That is only permissible after thirty years of age.

"(Signed) NAPOLEON."

"At Haynau, June 7, 1813"

Another letter from the Emperor:

"MADAME AND DEAR FRIEND—I receive your letter of May 30. I think that it is useless for you to go to Notre Dame for the *Te Deum* for the battle of Wurtschen. It will be sufficient for you to go to the Tuileries, and that the *Te Deum* be chanted with pomp in the chapel there at the ordinary hour of the court, and that you hold a grand drawing room in the evening. I am writing this in the supposition that it has not been officially announced that you will go to Notre Dame, for, of course, if the programme has appeared, it must not be countermanded, and there would be more inconvenience in not going than in going. (Signed) NAPOLEON."

"Liegnitz, June 9, 1813."

In another of his letters to Marie Louise, Napoleon reverts to the same subject: he tells the Empress that she did well to go to the *Te Deum* which was chanted for the battle of Lutzen, but that such ceremonies should not be too frequent, and that it is because they are rare that they are imposing. "As a general rule," he adds, "it is suitable that the *Te Deum* should be chanted on the Sunday following: it is a mistake to delay it. I do not see why Pentecost should prevent the singing of a Te *Deum.* When an event has passed by, other events happen, and that may give rise to all sorts of inconveniences. Have a grand theatrical performance and a large Court at St. Cloud on that day."

These letters arrived at the time when the programme of the ceremony was published in the *Moniteur;* the Empress accordingly proceeded with great pomp to Notre Dame, to conform with the orders which she had received.

In the course of these glorious commencements of the 1813 campaign the Emperor and the army had experienced two notable losses. In a reconnoitering expedition, effected on the eve of the battle of Lutzen the Duke d'Istrie—Bessières—was struck by a bullet in the head and killed. Colonel of Napoleon's guides in the army of Italy, and afterwards commander of the imperial guards, Bessières had followed the Emperor in all his campaigns. His bravery, his great experience in the cavalry branch, as much as his devotion to Napoleon's person, had raised him to the rank of Marshal.

The grief occasioned to the Emperor by Marshal Bessière's death was raised to the highest pitch by the death of the Duke of Frioul—Duroc—who, less fortunate than the former, survived for twelve hours a terrible wound which he received on the evening of the battle of Wurtschen. The enemy's last cannonball sought him out far from the firing, in the midst of a group where he was conversing with General Kirgener and Marshal Mortier. This ball opened the Grand Marshal's stomach, killed General Kirgener, and only grazed the Duke of Trevise. Napoleon was present at Duroc's last moments. He went to see him after the sentries had been placed, at the house to which he had been transported, and found him fully conscious. This interview was a most poignant one. Napoleon exchanged some words with the most regretted of his officers, in which Duroc expressed sentiments of the purest devotion and the Emperor his bitter regrets and the hope that they might meet again in another world. Napoleon, a prey to the most terrible emotion, remained more than a quarter of an hour grasping Duroc's right hand with his head resting upon it. The deep silence which reigned during this painful scene was broken by Duroc, who begged the Emperor to go away from so sad a sight. And Napoleon, unable to speak, could say nothing to him but: "Farewell, then, my friend." He thereupon withdrew, leaning on Marshal Soult and the Grand Equerry, and went to shut himself up in his tent where he spent the night alone weeping for his friend and reflecting on the painful warnings which the genius which presided over his destinies seemed to be giving him.

After his return from Mayence, where he went to spend some days with the

Empress, Napoleon halted in the course of one of his marches before the house in the village where the Grand Marshal had died. He sent for the pastor and commissioned him to have a small monument raised in the interior of this modest abode, in remembrance of the loss which he had experienced there. Napoleon wished the tenant of the house to become its owner, with the charge of preserving the monument in it, and ordered the amount of the purchase money as well as the sum of the mausoleum to be paid over at once.

One might have said that Napoleon who had been so long favored by fortune brought evil fortune to all his people; on the morrow of Duroc's death, Colonel Bernard, one of the Emperor's aides-de-camp, broke his leg while escorting Napoleon's carriage.

After the conclusion of an armistice, signed by the French, Russian, and Prussian commissioners, M. de Metternich arrived in Dresden. On the 28th of June he had that famous interview with Napoleon in which, casting off the mask, he demanded, as the price of Austria's fidelity to the French alliance, the cession of Illyria, and half of Italy, the renunciation of the Protectorate of the Confederation of the Rhine, the abandonment of Holland and of Spain, of the Swiss mediation and that of the Duchy of Warsaw. The answer which the Emperor made, in an outburst of just indignation which he could not control in face of so arrogant an expression of wishes, is well known: "Ah! Metternich. How much has England paid you to make me such proposals?" The explanation of this language was indeed soon arrived at by the news of the convention, which M. de Stadion, the Austrian minister, had signed on June 27, the day before Metternich's audience with Napoleon—a covenant by virtue of which the allies accepted the offer of the mediation of the cabinet of Vienna, and settled the conditions which should be imposed on France. These conditions were still more implicitly determined by the Treaty of Trachemberg, dated the 9th of July following, which laid down the plan of the military operations of the campaign, and the distribution of the subsidies supplied by England to the coalition. Austria and Sweden were the contracting parties in this treaty, and united their contingents to the Russian and Prussian forces.

After the preceding explanations it would be of little interest to investigate at what period the Austrian cabinet commenced negotiations with the allied Cabinets. Various indications would suggest that this took place as far back as the time when Prince Schwarzenberg was sent to Paris bearing professions of friendship and fidelity to the French alliance. It was, as the reader has seen, just at the time of Napoleon's departure for the army. Bad faith could not be carried any further!

While awaiting the opening of the congress which was to be held at Prague, and the end of the negotiations with the object of prolonging a truce, Napoleon, who could no longer have any doubt about the understanding come to by Austria and the alliance, left for Mayence. He wanted to spend some days there to give orders for various arrangements which he considered necessary for the truest interests of the Empire, in case of a resumption of hostilities.

He had asked the Empress to come and meet him there, in a letter in which he mentioned the names of the persons who were to accompany her. I was mentioned by name. At the same time as he wrote to the Empress he addressed a letter to the Archchancellor on the same subject. He even took the precaution to send an article which was to be published in the *Moniteur* to announce this journey.

The Empress left St. Cloud on July 23, at six o'clock in the morning. She slept at

Chalons and Metz, received the principal authorities there, and arrived at Mayence on the 25th at three o'clock in the morning, in very bad weather. She was afraid that the Emperor might have got there before her, but he only arrived at six o'clock in the evening of the same day. Napoleon was in good health, his complexion was heightened and bronzed by the air of the camps. It was with real pleasure that I saw the Emperor again, and he received me very kindly. I once more attended him as secretary until the arrival of his cabinet, and was entrusted with numerous commissions by him. It pleased me to find myself once more living in this familiar and confidential manner with him, and I witnessed Napoleon's departure with sorrow. My heart was oppressed as I took leave of him, for I was worried with Austria's suspicious conduct, and the doubtful issue of the congress of Prague.

During his stay in Mayence the Emperor lived in a very retired manner, very busy in his cabinet with military and diplomatic correspondence, working with his ministers in turn, but especially with the Minister of Finance, on matters of inner administration, and also in view of the uncertain duration of the struggle which was about to begin. The princes adjoining the Confederation of the Rhine, amongst others the Grand Duke and Grand Duchess of Baden, the Prince Primate, the Prince of Nassau, the Grand Duke of Hesse-Darmstadt, took advantage of the Emperor's stay at Mayence to come and pay him court. The beauty of the weather which had become quite serene again enabled the Empress to drive out every day in an open carriage; her court had been increased by the arrival of the Princess de Wagram who had come with her children to Mayence to see her husband. The Countess de Lobau was impatiently expected there by her husband, who was very much upset by the delay in her arrival. When she at last arrived it was on the day before that fixed for Napoleon's departure. During his stay at Mayence the Empress, who wished to give the Emperor a present on his name day, which was approaching, commissioned Isabey, who was taking the waters at Vichy, to paint the portrait of herself and her son in a group on a snuff box.

Napoleon left Mayence on August 1 at six in the evening to return to Dresden, and arrived there at nine o'clock in the morning of the 4th. It was from this city that was issued a decree which has been styled an act of excessive arbitrariness. At the time of Napoleon's journey to Holland in the Autumn of 1812, he had heard at Antwerp, that the mayor and the directors of customs were charged with fraud, having caused a loss of over two millions to the city, this sum having been divided amongst the embezzlers. The Emperor had issued a decree at Flushing, which sent the individuals who were accused of having embezzled this money, to be tried at the Court of Sessions to be held at Brussels. A very long trial ensued which ended in the accused being acquitted, on the dishonest verdict of a jury, which had probably been won over to the side of the embezzlers in advance. As was to be expected this verdict produced a great scandal. Napoleon, who had the reports of his Inspectors of Finance, knew that the receiver of customs, directed by the mayor, and by the head of the department at the prefecture, had double sets of books for registering the receipts from the customs, and would not allow such a swindle to remain unpunished, and of his own authority suspended the verdict which acquitted the cheats. At the same time he commissioned the Court of Cassation to designate another tribunal before which the trial should be commenced. This decision was without any doubt a blow to the independence of the jury, but corruption triumphing, morality was on the other hand outraged and the conscience of the sovereign in whose name justice was rendered was charged with an obviously iniquitous judgment. In this state of things was the embezzlement of public money to be encouraged with immunity, or was the insufficiency of the law to be remedied by an act of vigor? Napoleon could not be expected to accept the responsibility of a decision which was calculated to injure public morality, and this proves his vigilance for the interests of the citizens even in the midst of the cares of war.

At the same time the harbor basin of Cherbourg was finished, and the letting in of the sea into this basin, was an important event. The Emperor expressed his wish to the Empress that she should be present at this inauguration, in order to add to its solemnity. It was in consequence decided that Marie Louise should proceed to Cherbourg on her return to Paris. I give below the letter which Napoleon wrote on this subject to the Arch-chancellor, when he had returned to Dresden. The letters which I gave above, and the following one, will suffice to show the reach of the Emperor's foresight, and to what minute details he could descend:

"MY COUSIN—I shall be pleased that the Empress should go to Cherbourg, first of all to enjoy the beautiful sight of the sea being let into the basin, and secondly, to invest this operation with solemnity. The Minister of Marine can precede the Empress to Cherbourg to prepare her reception, and the best means of amusing her during her stay. The Empress will leave on the 17th or the 18th, and the operation can take place on her name day. The principal authorities of the department will be present, and so interesting a spectacle will not fail to attract an immense crowd of sightseers. Insert all the particulars of the Empress's journey and return to Mayence in the papers. And hereupon I pray God, etc.

(Signed) NAPOLEON."

"Dresden, 7th Aug. 1813."

Leaving Mayence, the Empress returned to Paris by way of Aix-la-Chapelle, following the banks of the Rhine. She left on August 2 on board a yacht which the Prince of Nassau had placed at her service, the honors on board being done by an officer of the house of Nassau. Her suite was composed of the Duchess of Montebello, Count de Beauharnais, Knight of Honor, who had followed her to Mayence; Mesdames de Talhouet, and Lauriston, General Caffarelli, the chamberlains Vaulgrenand and Cornélissen, Cussy, the Prefect of the Palace, and myself. On arriving at Saint Goar the Empress's first care was to write to the Emperor. She continued her journey on the Rhine on the morrow, stopping at Coblentz and at Cologne. She left her yacht at the latter place, and took to her carriage. She arrived at Aix-le-Chapelle on Aug. 5, visited the cathedral, and returned to St. Cloud by way of Liége, Namur, Soissons, and Compiègne. She was received in the cities in which she stopped by the principal authorities and never failed to give them an audience before her departure. On our arrival at Coblentz I found to my great surprise the wife of my colleague in a waiting-room in the house which was intended for the Empress's residence. Her husband who had remained at Dresden during the Emperor's journey to Mayence had taken advantage of his absence to pay his wife a visit at Coblentz. Madame Mounier came with the wish to be presented to the Empress and I was delighted to be able to render her this slight service. Madame de Montesquiou was waiting where the Empress's carriage stopped to place her son in her arms. He was then a very fine child, with every appearance of strength and health, and his intelligence was developing in a remarkable manner. The Queen of Naples presented him with a little open carriage in which he used to drive about the castle gardens in great glee. This carriage was drawn by a team of sheep which had been trained by the clever equerry.

The inauguration of the Cherbourg harbor, which at first was to have taken place on the 15th of August, the Emperor's name day, in order to give the Empress time to rest from the fatigues of the journey from Mayence. She was kind enough to dispense me from following her to Cherbourg. She arrived there: "half dead with fatigue, and quite broken up by the bad roads which she had met with after passing Carentan, suffocated with the dust, and with a very bad cold on the chest," as she herself expressed it in letters dated August 25 and 26. In another letter which the Empress was good enough to write to me she further told me in speaking of this inauguration: "the basin was opened yesterday, but the fine moment at which the water burst in with a rush and a roar happened just at the time when everybody was at dinner, and nobody saw it, and, as a misfortune never comes alone, I also missed seeing the fireworks."

The congress had been opened at Prague to treat for peace. The disposition of the allies was by no means pacific, but they were obliged to dissemble the fact. Austria had need of time to furnish her preparations for war. As a matter of fact the Prague Congress was only a lure. Exchange of credentials even could not take place. The plenipotentiaries did not even see each other. Austria who had set the price of the abandonment of Illyria, half of Italy, the abandonment of Holland and Spain, on her alliance with France when Napoleon had 300,000 men in the center of Germany and as yet had not succeeded in her object, dominated in the congress as mediator. Forgetting her part and the necessity of holding the scales with an equal hand, she looked after her own interests while pleading the cause of the coalition. The congress which was to have opened on July 5 did not begin until the 29th. The allies attributed the delay in the opening of the negotiations to the late arrival of the French plenipotentiaries, who did not assemble at Prague until the 27th. One was the Duke of Vicence, the other the Count de Narbonne. The latter was at Prague at the same time as the Russian and Prussian plenipotentiaries. The Duke of Vicence, commissioned to treat for the prolongation of the truce was detained at Neumarkt by the real or alleged non-arrival of the papers of the allied commissioners, which delayed the signing of this convention until the 27th. Another motive which made the Emperor haste to send the Duke of Vicence immediately to Prague was the insulting choice, so Napoleon considered it, made by the Russian government in the person of M. d'Anstett, a born Frenchman who was serving against France, to represent Russia. He had been rejected by an Imperial decree as a Frenchman intervening in the name of a foreign power, in a treaty in which French interests were being discussed. The maintenance of the choice of this person was a sign that the allies, who were sure of the cooperation of Austria, considered it unnecessary to treat us with ordinary courtesy. A general plan of campaign had been definitely decided upon in the conference at Trachemberg, in which Austria and Sweden had equally taken part. The Russian and Prussian envoys were sure in their minds, and knew perfectly what to think of the real intentions of these two powers. The strong suspicions, amounting almost to certitude, which Napoleon had conceived of what was being plotted against him for several months past, forced him to circumspection, and made it necessary for him to find out what were the traps which were being laid for him, as well as the end and the imminence of the dangers to which he was exposed. The armistice was to expire on August 10. Could 12 days, a part of which was passed in discussion of the forms or of the traditions of usages observed in similar congresses, suffice to resolve the question, complicated by the conflict of so many different interests which had to be reconciled, and to effect the general pacification of Europe? These pressing and various interests were moreover complicated by the pretentions, both patent and dissimulated, of the mediating power. Other incidents provoked by the Russian and Prussian commissioners, who were backed up by the mediator, helped towards the utter waste of precious time. All three of them were at a loss what to imagine to shorten the duration of this ephemeral congress. The mediator hid her perfidious designs under a show of goodwill towards the French negotiators, but her flagrant perfidy and her whole conduct showed that Austria had only intervened in the congress at Prague with the object of forcing our hands. At last, three days before the expiration of the truce, an ultimatum was notified to the French plenipotentiary. No ultimatum, even when it is expected, can be accepted without final examination. Time, which is materially necessary to grasp the nature of sacrifices against which there can be no appeal, is requisite. One must be able to yield with honor and without a loss of dignity.

On the second day following, August 9, Napoleon made known what concessions he consented to. They were those which had been asked for by the allies, except the reserve of the harbor of Trieste, the possession of which interested the mediating power alone. France simply insisted on obtaining a guarantee of the integrity of Denmark, this last restriction in favor of a faithful ally was an act of loyalty. On the following day, the 10th, at midnight the allied plenipotentiaries, encouraged by the news of the reverses which our arms had suffered in Spain, and especially by our defeat at Vittoria, which put an end to French domination in that country, without answering the last proposals of our envoys contented themselves in declaring through the Austrian plenipotentiary that their powers had expired. The Austrian plenipotentiary in communicating this declaration added that his mission was also terminated. Even in admitting that Austria's mediation had come to an end all negotiations with this power should not have been refused to us. The Austrian cabinet, it is true, had prostituted the part of mediator by uniting itself to our enemies in spite of or rather thanks to this title, but we were not nominally at least at war with the Emperor Francis. Austria had to justify the attitude which she was about to take towards us: neutrality, alliance, or declaration of war. She preferred roughly to tear off the transparent mask, with which she had so long covered her face, and to declare war on France without any previous explanation. She was ready; all her arrangements with the coalition had been decided upon—her act of treachery was accomplished. Napoleon was expecting an answer to his proposals when General Narbonne came to inform him of the dissolution of the congress; a last hope still kept the Duke of Vicence back at Prague. On hearing this news, however, Napoleon gave his consent to all that had been asked of him, and sent General Bubna off at full speed to carry it to the Emperor of Austria. The answer was that it was too late (some hours too late!) and that he must address himself to the Emperor Alexander. This prince who had arrived on the 16th at Brandeitz, where the Emperor of Austria was staying, rejected all proposals and urged the Austrian monarch to run the risk of war; at the same time Austria's manifesto appeared. M. de Bassano in a final note addressed to M. de Metternich, after having pointed out to him the perfidy of this conduct, proposed to him the reunion of a congress at which all powers, both great and small should be represented, where all the questions should be solemnly laid down, and where it would not be expected that they should be decided upon either in a week, or a month; where it would be their task to consult all interests, to compensate sacrifices which had been made, and to render peace advantageous and honorable for all. The Austrian minister answered in an evasive manner to this note, and the resumption of hostilities was fixed for August 16. If a peace, concluded at Prague, should have become a reality, it would without doubt have been a good thing, especially compared with the rigorous conditions which were afterwards imposed upon France. But we have been able to form an opinion upon the insincerity of the intentions of our enemies as well as of the mediating power. In the audience which Napoleon had awarded to the Minister Metternich at Dresden in the previous month of June, he had reproached him with having allowed himself to be won over by England. The reproach was an imprudent one, but it was not this reproach which brought about Austria's desertion. The sole and real motive for this desertion was that the cabinet of Vienna and the other cabinets of the coalition whose common interest it was to take advantage of our misfortunes in order to crush us out, were too closely bound up together. Austria had long since made the calculation that it would be better for her to unite herself to friends, strong in numbers, than to expose herself to the danger of remaining the benevolent auxiliary of an isolated ally. If instead of taking recourse to treachery and bad faith, the Austrian cabinet had frankly and without ambiguity expounded wishes, which were quite natural in the position in which it was placed, Napoleon, convinced of its sincerity, would certainly have consented to sacrifices loyally asked for, feeling as he did that concessions on the part of France had become necessary. When one remembers the treaty which had been concluded one year previously between Austria and France—a treaty by which the two forces mutually guaranteed the integrity of each other's territory—one will understand all the fragility of political alliances. The indemnities and the increase of territory asked for by Austria, which we had promised to grant her, were not only a compensation for the charges of her cooperation in the Russian expedition, but further—do not let us forget it—"a monument of the intimate and lasting union which existed between the two sovereigns."

The unfortunate issue of the war of 1812, having made it impossible for France to keep her promises, Austria thought it safer to forget her commitments and to crush us. Already in the month of February, she had changed her feelings, without however having as yet modified her language. The Vienna cabinet has itself admitted that the allies and Austria were already agreed in principle, before this union was consecrated by treaties. Why then such a profusion of lying protestations? Because Austria needed the time to complete her armaments and to prepare her desertion. It is admitted that this crafty derogation on the part of the Vienna cabinet from the spirit which had dictated the terms of Austria's alliance with France in 1812, and this violation of plighted faith, can be excused as very skilful political calculations. However this may be, the Austrian government, according to our opinion, was called to play another part, the effects of which would have been more profitable to Austria in the future and above all would have been more honorable to the character of the Austrian minister. The cabinet of Vienna ought to have remained faithful to the policy which had led to the sacrifice of one of the Austrian archduchesses, to have united itself closely to France from that day forward, and thus have forced Napoleon to take this attitude of Austria, both wise and loyal at the same time, into account. Instead of following this line of action, the Austrian government, without at first conceiving the idea of overthrowing Napoleon, thought only of profiting by his despoilment, by entering into the general European coalition. It has frequently been said that if we had thrown gold into the scale, the balance would have been in our favor. That is still the opinion of a number of people who think corruption an important element of success. That was also Fouché's doctrine. During the Prague congress, the Emperor showed him a very handsome snuffbox enriched with diamonds, which he intended for M. de Metternich. "Do you know," said Napoleon, "that this is a present of thirty thousand francs?" "And it is with that," cried Fouché, interrupting him, "that you expect to win over the Austrian minister! It's not thirty thousand francs that you ought to give him, but millions." The Emperor answered with a gesture of disgust to the cynicism of this remark, addressed to the man who had the greatest horror of corruption. A fact which appears to be above doubt, and which will be entirely revealed in time, is that a secret council, presided over by the Emperor of Austria, and composed of a very small number of his most intimate councilors, was held at Vienna before the departure of Minister Metternich to Dresden. The names of the persons who composed this council are mentioned, and it is stated that at this council the reasons which should engage the Austrian cabinet to remain true to the French alliance, or to abandon and make common cause with the allies, were vigorously discussed. A former minister, Count Baldani, known for the energy of his opposition to France, was summoned to this council. Set aside at the moment of Marie Louise's marriage, the enmity with which the French press treated this minister had caused the Emperor of Austria, whose confidence in him was increased by this circumstance, to recall him. One can easily imagine what opinions were expressed by this person during the discussion of this serious question. Suffice it to say that the majority of the council expressed the opinion that the alliance with France had not produced the favorable results which had been hoped for, that fidelity to this alliance would be sterile, and that Austria on the other hand would derive real and decisive advantages by placing herself on the side of the allies. The Austrian government accordingly made up its mind to come to an understanding with the allies and to prepare for a rupture with France. Furnished with instructions in this spirit, M. de Metternich left for Dresden. The result of this minister's mission and his conversation with Napoleon—a conversation in which Metternich, so to say, laid at one stroke the foundations of the monument, brilliant rather than solid, which he proposed to raise in reestablishing the greatness of the Austrian empire—these things are well known. Metternich, moreover, in putting on the maintenance of his master's alliance the price of the abandonment of Illyria, of one half of Italy, of the protectorate of the Confederation of the Rhine, of Holland and Spain, was sure of revolting Napoleon's legitimate pride and of bringing him to break the feeble bonds, between the two empires, which he still hesitated to destroy.

These cunning negotiations bring me to speak of the reproach made against the Duke of Bassano of having dissuaded the Emperor from signing the peace at Prague, and under other decisive circumstances. I do not know on what foundations such an accusation has been based. It shows but a poor knowledge of Napoleon's character to imagine that he was accessible to the insinuations and influence of those about him, when capital resolutions, of which he considered himself the sole judge, had to be taken, no matter how great his confidence might be in the lights of his councilors. This reflection moreover cannot be applied to the Duke of Bassano, who was in favor of peace. This minister will hold an honorable place amongst the faithful men who placed their faculties and their devotion at the Emperor's service, who helped him in his noble task of working for the good and for the greatness of his country, and whose zeal was neither servile nor blind. His will always be the merit of having served France, in the person of his chief, with fidelity and discernment, of never having deserved ill of his confidence, and of having remained true to him in adversity.

The Emperor had once more to fight against the allied armies, increased by the entire force of Austria, while but for the intervention of this power peace would have been concluded. Austria's partiality at the congress of Prague which would be better described by the name of treachery, the refusal to admit the free discussion of concessions which were certainly worthy of debate, the cold and insulting rupture of the negotiations, which le ft no door open to pacification, convinced Napoleon that he had no other alternative than to conquer or to die, or to abdicate if the nation abandoned him. Later on, Napoleon abdicated under circumstances where the welfare of France seemed to render such a step necessary, but that was not the case at that time and the Emperor did not consider himself at liberty to surrender to foreigners provinces which composed the integrity of the territory which had been confided by the French nation to his keeping. With what applause would not his contemporaries and many of his traducers themselves have hailed him, what blessings would have been reserved for his memory, had he only been successful.

The fatal news of Austria's desertion deeply affected the Empress Marie Louise. She feared that it might result in a diminution of the Emperor's affection for her, but he did not cease to give her proofs of his confidence. She on her side tried to inspire her husband with the trust she had in her father's probity and offered, prompted by a feeling which may be styled French, to act as peacemaker between them. Marie Louise had indeed at that time so entirely assumed French habits that in her letters to her father which were written in German, she was often forced to make use of French expressions, having forgotten the German equivalents.

It is known that up to August 30, 1813, the French army won victories which revived hopes which had been weakened by Austria's desertion. The Empress shared in the general satisfaction created in our country by this good news. She did me the honor of writing to me from Cherbourg, on August 31, on the occasion of the victory at Dresden on the 27th. This is her letter:

"My health would be good enough, but for a bad cold on the chest which tires me greatly. I shall, however, do nothing to cure it until I get back to Paris. Besides the good news which I have received today will do me much more good than all the drugs imaginable. I hope that this great victory will soon bring back the Emperor and peace with him."

Another letter, dated from Rouen, September 2, Marie Louise having stopped in that town on her way back to Paris, ran as follows:

"You must be very pleased with all the particulars of the splendid victory which the Emperor has just won. What pleases me most is to know that he did not expose himself.

God grant that it may bring us peace. I want it badly, as do all persons who are devoted to the Emperor."

The desertion of Austria, which had added to the forces of the allies 200,000 men, seemed to forebode that fresh enemies would rise up against us, and Napoleon had been obliged to prepare himself to meet this new situation. Already on the 16th of August, he had set out from Dresden, after having confided to the corps of Marshal Saint-Cyr the defense of this central point. Having traveled into Silesia in order to reconnoiter the Prussian army, which he defeated in several engagements, the Emperor then returned against the great Austrian army which had just entered Saxony. Deceived by the departure of Napoleon whom they believed to be in Silesia the Austrians wished to profit by his absence to take possession of Dresden, and crush the corps of Marshal Saint-Cyr. But Napoleon, wishing above all to save Dresden, returned rapidly to the capital of Saxony which was menaced by the great army of the allies. He arrived there on the 26th of August in the morning, followed by the corps of Marshal Ney. The town was already surrounded by immense forces before which the feeble corps of Marshal Saint-Cyr was bound to succumb. The unlooked-for arrival of Napoleon restored confidence already in several German corps, allied to the French, and reassured the king and his family who were preparing for flight. The people hailed him as a liberator. The Emperor's plans were quickly made. In the night of the 26th to the 27th of August the Austro-Russian army which was commanded by Prince Schwarzenberg gave the signal for the attack, and a general and terrible battle ensued. Napoleon had some officers killed and wounded at his side, the strife only ceasing at nine o'clock at night. The allies lost thirty thousand men killed, wounded, or prisoners, a part of their artillery, and an enormous quantity of equipages, stragglers, and convoys of wounded. The French general, Moreau, returned from America at the instigation of Bernadotte to aid the Emperor of Russia in his councils, assisted at this battle. Injured by a mortal wound which necessitated the amputation of both legs, he expired the following day. Such was the sad end of a Frenchman, crowned with a splendid military aureole, whom death seized upon in the midst of the enemies' ranks while committing a flagrant crime against his country.

The Emperor of Russia had the body of General Moreau buried in the catholic church of Saint Petersburg. He addressed a letter of condolence to his widow, presented her with 500,000 roubles, and conferred upon her a pension of thirty thousand roubles. The Emperor had assuredly the right to render these honors to the memory of Moreau and to accord these favors to the family of that general which was quite willing to accept them. But what is to be said of the King of France—Louis XVIII—who after his Restoration conferred on Madame Moreau the Marshal's staff which he had intended for the husband of this lady, and further conferred on her the honors and prerogatives which the wives and widows of Marshals enjoyed?—what is to be said of the proposition made on the 26th of April, 1814, to the senate by one of its members and supported by several of his colleagues, a proposition which had for its object to declare that General Moreau had merited public esteem and the gratitude of his country?—of the religious service ordered on the 23rd of June of the same year in the church of Saint Paul at Paris, with the approbation and at the expense of the king, for Pichegru, Georges, and Moreau, and for the eleven assassins who had perished with Georges?—of the royal decree of the 27th of February, 1815, which decreed the erection of statues to Moreau and to

Pichegru? Public opinion revolted against such an interpretation of national honor, it would not allow the crimes committed against the country to the profit of a single family to be glorified. The ennoblement of the family of Georges Cadoudal was tolerated, but public honors rendered to these turncoats, who carried arms against France, were the fruit of an unhallowed policy, insulting and humiliating to the great mass of the nation.

After the letter which informed the Empress of the result of the great battle of Dresden this Princess remained eight days without any news of the Emperor. She was good enough to send me the following letter very early in the morning of September 11 at St. Cloud:

"I send you a letter from the Emperor which I received very late yesterday" (just a minute after I had left the Empress). "I think you will be glad to read it because you share my anxiety. As soon as you have read it be so good as to send it back."

The glorious victory of Dresden was dearly paid for by the succession of reverses which followed, by the defeat which Oudinot, Duke of Reggio, met with at Grossbeeren, by the disaster which the Duke of Tarente, Macdonald, met with at Katzbach, and by the loss of the battle of Dennewitz where Marshal Ney was commanding. At Grossbeeren and at Dennewitz, Bemadotte had the questionable honor of defeating French soldiers commanded by two of his oldest comrades-in-arms. The reverse which proved most fatal to us was the defeat at Culm where General Vandamme, who had remained behind with a corps of 30,000 men in consequence of some misunderstanding which has never been explained, lost half his troops, 60 pieces of cannon, and fell into the hands of the enemy with General Haxo. Shamefully treated by an ungenerous enemy, the French general was made the butt of the insults of the Russian and Prussian people and soldiers. General Corbineau was fortunate enough to force his way with a corps of cavalry which he commanded and with 12,000 infantry soldiers who were following him, and to be able to come up with the army. General Vandamme's false maneuver on which the success of the campaign was to depend had a powerful influence on the unhappy issue of events. Unfortunately Napoleon had not the gift of ubiquity and fortune was withdrawing little by little from him, whom she had so often favored. The sudden illness with which Napoleon was stricken after the victory of Dresden may also be looked upon as the effect of fatality. Just as he was about to enter Pirna in pursuit of the enemy, a passing but violent indisposition, which had probably been caused by the quantity of rain to which he had been exposed, seized suddenly upon Napoleon, whose frequent vomiting gave rise to the fear that he might have been poisoned. This great soul, an emanation from a divine source, yielded to this moment of enfeeblement of his mortal coil, and the Emperor had to be brought back at full speed to Dresden in a state of absolute mental and physical prostration. The allied army was at that time in such a state of confusion that it has been admitted by the enemies themselves that had it been vigorously pursued it would infallibly have been destroyed. This fatal incident saved it, and all hope of winning peace disappeared. The series of our misfortunes dates from this day—misfortunes which were hurried on by the disaster of the days at Leipzig which brought about the successive desertion of Bavaria, Würtemberg, and of the Confederate States of the Rhine. Another desertion, if I may use such an expression, which must greatly have affected the Emperor was the spirit of hidden opposition which was to be noticed in several generals of the French army. This inclination to rebel which was but poorly dissimulated dated back from the time of our disasters during the Russian campaign. It developed into more definite resistance when Napoleon announced his bold plan of leaving the road of the Rhine open to the allied troops, maneuvering on their rear, threatening Potsdam and Berlin, which the enemies were leaving unprotected, and of raising the siege of the various fortresses in which we had left garrisons. A maneuver of the same kind which had been successfully carried out by the great Frederick in the Seven Years' War, promised a good result. Seeing that he would be badly seconded, Napoleon hesitated; moreover, news of the various adhesions to the coalition obliged him to abandon this plan. The positive assurance of the fidelity to the French alliance which had only shortly before been given by the King of Bavaria and his minister to the Emperor had made him hope that this desertion would only take place later on. I have heard Napoleon complain bitterly of this conduct at a sitting of the Council of State. The King of Bavaria, who was a well-intentioned but easy Prince had been dragged away by the rapidity of the events and by the persuasions of a faction which had at its head the ambitious General Wrède, who had been loaded with kindnesses by the Emperor. On September 27 Napoleon addressed the following letter to the Empress-Regent:

"MADAME AND DEAR FRIEND—You will go and preside at the senate and will make the following speech. The Minister of War will make a report and the orators of the council of state will present a senatus consultum for the levy of the conscription. You will go in a gala carriage with all suitable pomp, as is the custom when I go to the legislative body.

"(Signed) NAPOLEON"

"Dresden, Sept. 27, 1813"

"P.S. As the speech had to be written in cipher Duke of Bassano will have it translated, and will send it to the Archchancellor who will hand it to you."

The speech referred to is the one which was published in the *Moniteur* of October 8. The senatus consultum ordered the levy of 280,000 conscripts, 120,000 of which were to be taken from the soldiers whose service was to begin in 1814 and earlier, and 160,000 of the year 1815. This anticipation of the conscription of two years, which was not a reassuring sign, filled the Empress with sad thoughts. She was anxious about the future. The part which she was to play at the senate also frightened her by its novelty. However her youth, ability, and the modesty of her attitude produced an impression upon the senators. M. de Talleyrand said in the evening as he was going to the theatrical performance at the court that she had been neither bold, nor timid, and that she had shown dignity, combined with much tact and propriety.

The reverses which followed on the victory of Dresden, and Bavaria's desertion having put it out of the Emperor's power to maneuver at ease between the Elbe and the Oder, he decided to precede the enemy to Leipzig, where Prince Schwarzenberg's army was also marching. On October 7, Napoleon left Dresden, which till then had been the center of his operations, leaving Marshal Saint-Cyr with an army of twenty-five thousand men in this city, and garrisons in the forts of Magdeburg, Wittenburg and Torgau. The Emperor arrived at Leipzig on October 15, where he was joined by the King and Queen of Saxony.

On the morrow of his arrival, the allied armies attacked the French army at Wachau. They were defeated and lost twenty thousand men. Poniatowski won his marshal's bâton there. But what was such a loss, however great it may appear, to an enemy which was constantly replacing its tired and defeated soldiers with fresh troops? The Austrian general Meerfeldt, who was taken prisoner in this battle, was sent by Napoleon to the Emperor of Austria, with pacific proposals which were coldly received by the allies.

The enemies renewed the attack on the morrow. In spite of their extreme inferiority in point of numbers, the French troops sustained the fight, thanks to their heroic efforts, with advantage, but the impossibility of turning or breaking into an impenetrable line, formed of an accumulation of three hundred thousand hostile troops protected by more than one thousand cannon, the desertion of the Saxons and the Würtembergers, made the scale in which the destinies of France and Europe were being weighed in the balance, turn in favor of the allies.

All military writers have recorded the disasters which marked this bloody day and morrow. I cannot, however, refrain from speaking, after them, of the shameful incident which marked the day of mourning—*nigro notanda lapillo*—; the desertion to the enemy of an allied army corps, which took place on the field of battle itself, in the heat of the fight, an occurrence unheard of in the history of modern war. In one of those critical moments when everybody rushes to the spot where there is the greatest danger, the Saxons, feigning to follow the general movement, advanced upon the enemy....but to join it. It was seen with stupor that the ranks of a foreign army, commanded by a Frenchman—Bernadotte—opened to receive our faithless allies, marching under a flag stained with the vilest treachery. Need it be added, alas, that this Frenchman threatened the general commanding the Saxons with branding, because, with some last traces of decency, the latter hesitated to turn against our troops the cannon which a moment before had been fired in their defense.

The exhaustion of the army and the want of ammunition rendering a fresh battle impossible, the Emperor decided to retreat. He returned to Leipzig to take leave of the King and Queen of Saxony, who begged him to withdraw, lest to so many disasters should be added his capture by the enemy, adjuring him to leave them to their sorrowful fate. Napoleon, moved to tears, and kept back by his gratitude for such great devotion, hesitated about separating from them, In the meanwhile the danger of being surrounded by the enemy becoming imminent, the Emperor yielded to the pressing entreaties of his faithful and venerable allies. He bade them farewell and embraced them, assuring them that one day France would discharge her debt towards them, whatever might be the fate to which Providence destined him personally.

The calamities which accompanied the retreat of the army after the battle at Leipzig, the untimely breaking-down of the Elster bridge, which resulted in the capture of several divisions, and the death of the brave Poniatowski in this river, are well-known matters. The allies, having entered the city of Leipzig, seized upon the King of Saxony and sent him under escort to Berlin, to expiate the crime of his inviolable fidelity to France.

Napoleon fell back on Erfurth with the remnants of his army. The King of Naples took leave of the Emperor there, not without emotion on both sides, for each felt that it was their last farewell. The insinuations which the Austrians had made to King Joachim, at his outposts, had it must be said been listened to with more attention by him than by the venerable King of Saxony. Our army's retreat was effected with fairly good fortune in spite of the numerous partisans who harassed our troops during their march. However, near Hanau, sixty thousand Bavarians and Austrians undertook to bar the way to the French army. General Wrède commanded them. In the ardor of his zeal for the new cause which he had embraced the day before, this general—formerly so proud, as he used to say, of the esteem of the first hero of the century—and of the endowment of thirty thousand francs a year which he had received from him—thought to have little difficulty in disposing of a vanquished and retreating army. Success did not justify these ungrateful and culpable hopes. The lion, although sorely wounded, was not yet dead. The victory of the battle of Hanau opened the road back to its frontiers to the French army. The Austro-Bavarians lost more than ten thousand men in this murderous encounter. General Wrède was dangerously wounded there and his son-in-law, Prince d'Oettingen, lost his life.

The Emperor wrote on this occasion to the Empress, the following letter which was intended for publication in the *Moniteur:*

"MADAME AND VERY DEAR WIFE,

"I send you twenty flags taken by our armies at the battles of Wachau, Leipzig and Hanau; it is a homage which I am pleased to render you. I wish you to consider it as a proof of my great satisfaction with your conduct during the regency which I entrusted to you. This letter having no other purpose, I pray God that He may have you in His holy and worthy keeping.

(Signed) NAPOLEON."

"*Given at* Frankfort, November 1, 1813."

These trophies were a very poor compensation for the losses experienced by our armies in this disastrous campaign; but they threw a last luster on our arms, which Fortune, if not Glory, was preparing to abandon.

The Emperor followed the letter which I have just quoted very closely. He arrived at Mayence on the morrow and the remnants of the army crossed the Rhine here. He only remained the time necessary to make the first arrangements for the defense of our frontiers, which were menaced by the coalition and by the entire forces of Germany, which only shortly before had been assembled under the French flag. After having given the most urgent orders for the reorganization of the army, Napoleon left for St. Cloud, and arrived there on November 9.

Chapter XIV

The pleasure of seeing his wife and son again was balm upon Napoleon's wounds, and it was only a momentary diversion from all the cares with which he was besieged. Every moment of his time was taken up by the necessity of providing for the defense of the territory. Councils of administration presided over by the Emperor were held every hour in the day. Extraordinary efforts were made to recruit the army, to remount the artillery, manufacture arms, and so on. The treasure which had been amassed during ten years in the cellars in the Tuileries was employed to meet this extraordinary expense. This treasure was the product of the fourteen million francs annual savings realized on the funds of the Civil list, a circumstance which had not prevented the Imperial court from being the most splendid in Europe. Such was the result of a well-regulated administration free from abuses.

On his return to Paris the Emperor heard of the capitulation of Marshal Saint-Cyr's corps which he had left in Dresden. By the terms of this capitulation these troops were to reenter France, with the commitment taken in their name not to serve against the allies during a period which was fixed. The General in Chief, Schwarzenberg, refused to ratify this clause, making Marshal Saint-Cyr the ridiculous offer to return to Dresden where the French army placed as it was at the moment of the capitulation would be at liberty to recommence the struggle. In consequence the Marshal, remained a prisoner of war with his army corps. This sad example of a violation of plighted faith given by the Austrian General in Chief was followed by the allied sovereigns with regard to the Danzig garrison. The allied forces refused to ratify the capitulation, which granted the return to France of General Rapp and the French garrison. These honorable victims of the bad faith of our enemies were shut up in the prison at Kiev. The allies also violated the commitments which had been stipulated by them, with regard to our garrisons, at the time of the capitulation of Wittemberg and Torgau. The other forts which were still occupied in Germany fell one after the other into the hands of the enemy. The French garrisons which we had left there would have sufficed to compose a large army.

News from Spain was no better. The Spaniards who had placed the command of their forces in the hands of Lord Wellington, were now no longer fighting for their freedom; they were threatening the territory of France. The Emperor had resigned himself to conclude a treaty with Ferdinand, who had remained a prisoner at Valençay, dated Dec. 11, 1813—a treaty which sent back to the Spaniards a master who was to avenge the French conqueror. By this treaty Napoleon acknowledged Ferdinand as King of Spain and of the Indies, and undertook to withdraw the French troops from the Spanish territory. The King on his side promised to make the English troops evacuate Spain; prisoners on both sides were to be exchanged. Amongst other stipulations the King of Spain undertook to pay his father King Charles IV and the Queen, an annual pension of 30,000,000 of reals—7,500,000 francs. I must not omit to relate, because it is another trait of Ferdinand's character, that while this prince was signing the treaty which he had no intention of carrying out, he renewed his request to obtain one of the Emperor's nieces in marriage, the lady whom he asked for being one of King Joseph's daughters.

Marshal Suchet was commissioned to receive King Joseph and the princes of his family on their return from Spain. He had maintained himself in the provinces in the East with brilliant success for a long time. This Marshal was in occupation of Valençay when he received the news of the defeat of Vittoria, and the order to approach the frontiers without abandoning the principal forts, which he left in a good state of defense and provided with garrisons whose total amounted to about 20,000 men. The retreat of the French had begun on July 5; Marshal Suchet, who had become Duke of Albuféra as a reward for his splendid services, set up his cantonments in the neighborhood of Barcelona, after having rallied the army in Aragon. He handed over the forts in Aragon and Catalonia to Ferdinand, who undertook by a written covenant to return the French garrisons who might still be there at the earliest possible opportunity; but he did not keep this promise. The violation of his promises and the non-execution of the clause of the Valençay treaty, left Marshal Suchet no other alternative than to recross the Pyrenees.

King Joseph, whom we left reestablished in his capital, not having been able to maintain himself there was forced to think of leaving Madrid. The French army in the Peninsula had further been weakened by the loss of 12,000 men who had received orders to return to France. The disasters which our soldiers had encountered in Russia, published in the fatal twenty-ninth bulletin, hastened on the evacuation of Madrid which this time became definite. Joseph proceeded to Valladolid and Burgos, where he remained for some days on the defensive with an army of about 30,000 men, escorting long columns of equipages of every kind, and the baggage of more than two thousand Spanish families who were following the fortunes of Napoleon's brother. The operations of the enemy's general obliged King Joseph to fall back upon Vittoria; a part of the convoy was sent in the direction of Tolosa. Attacked on June 21 before Vittoria by hostile forces, three times superior in numbers, coming from the left and from the right, King Joseph's army was completely routed, without General Clausel's corps being able to rejoin him. This disastrous day settled the fate of Spain, when however the loss in men was not as great as was to be feared from the obstruction which hampered the movement of the French army; this loss consisted of about 5,000 men killed, wounded or prisoners. The enemy lost about as many, but all our war material fell into their hands. The French left a garrison of four thousand men in Pamplona, and the remnants of our army withdrew to Bayonne. Joseph cast off his empty title of King and went to seek in his fatherland rest, if not oblivion, after a life so alien to the gentleness of his manners and character.

It became necessary to bestow on the army in Spain a leader able to unite its debris, and check the progress of the enemy. The Emperor sent off Marshal Soult, invested with the chief command, at full speed. The Anglo-Spanish armies could not be checked in their march from the Pyrenees, and Marshal Soult, after having disputed the ground inch by inch was forced to draw back to Bayonne, where the victorious army of the enemy followed him. The battle of Toulouse was violently contested and both armies experienced heavy losses. It remained without any useful result, and was the last act of this great drama.

Thus ended the important expedition to Spain, where, as in the memorable Russian campaign the bravest soldiers in the world commanded by generals educated in a great school, and guided by the most illustrious captain of ancient and modern times, ended in immortal struggles a career of twenty years of glory. These struggles will not be sterile, these bands of veterans nobly fulfilled their task. Marching victoriously through Egypt and the capitals of the continent, from the icy regions of the north, down to the Pillars of Hercules, they scattered broadcast on their way the seeds of civilization, of generous and valiant ideas, which will surely bear their fruits. They displayed a heroism and military virtues which will serve as an example and as a lesson to those who shall come after us.

The Emperor's brothers were assembled in Paris, with the exception of Lucien, who remained in Rome, and who did not return to Napoleon until 1815. King Joseph after the Anglo-Spanish armies had crossed the Pyrenees had returned to the fatherland, which he had only quitted to act in conformity with the desires and views of his powerful brother. The King of Westphalia, forced by the insurrection in Germany and by our enemies to abandon his kingdom, had sought refuge in France with Queen Catherine. The violation of Swiss territory by the allies did not allow the former King Louis of Holland to prolong his stay there. He arrived in Paris on January 1, 1814, and was coldly received by the Emperor, but he found assistance and protection in France. Still anxious to recover the throne of Holland he had made a fresh application with this in view to the Emperor in the month of March, 1813, and towards the end of September to the authorities in Amsterdam; but Holland was waiting for the allies to lay down the law. The reestablishment of the House of Nassau having destroyed all King Louis's hopes, he resigned himself to forget them, and thought of nothing more than to live in retirement. He was in a deplorable state of health, nearly crippled in all his members, no remedy having been able to check the progress of his disease. King Louis came to Paris with a hope of being able to go and live on his estate at St. Leu, but followed the Empress on her departure from Paris to Blois. When the Bourbons had returned to Paris he took leave of the Empress and of her son and returned to Switzerland whence he afterwards proceeded to Rome. King Joseph also took refuge in Switzerland, and lived there very quietly until the Emperor's return from the Island of Elba. The King of Westphalia returned with his Queen to the States of the King of Würtemberg, his father-in-law, who treated him like a proscript. He was at Trieste and preparing to make his way to Rome, when the events of March, 1815, recalled him to Paris.

The state of religious affairs and the absence of the sovereign Pontiff from Rome caused an irritation which was to be removed by the return of the pope to Rome. *Pourparlers* with this object in view were held at Fontainebleau. This negotiation was entrusted to Countess Brignole, lady in waiting to the Empress and mother of the ambassador of Sardinia to Paris under the Restoration. She is the only woman ever employed by the Emperor in diplomatic negotiations. It is necessary to add that the friendship which bound this lady to Cardinal Consalvi and her relations in Rome, where one of her sons was a prelate, decided the Emperor in his choice, as much as her personal qualities.

In short every effort calculated to remedy our evils or to increase our resources was tried. In the meanwhile however the allied powers were intoxicated with the successes they had gained. They worked Napoleon's pride and misfortunes to their advantage and seemed to sport with his agony. They stirred up the hotbeds of Jacobinism, of national prejudices, of fanaticism, to inflame with their sparks the passions of the peoples of Germany against the man who had extinguished the hatreds and furies of the French Revolution. They blindly hurried on the destruction of the sovereign who had saved the royal houses from the effects of the revolutionary propaganda and who reassured the thrones by the establishment in France of a political state which resembled the forms of European governments. Napoleon might have appealed against them by calling out a mass levy of the nation; if the great corporations of the state, joining their voices to that of the Emperor in one patriotic thought, had sanctioned this appeal to the nation, France might still have been saved. But to reduce himself to play the part of an adventurer, to put his glory into the lists with evil passions, to resuscitate, by illegal and disturbing measures, the factions and the anarchy which he had destroyed, to organize, it might be, a civil war, these things Napoleon was not willing to do. He sacrificed to the fear of such great calamities, his crown and the future of his son and of his family; he did not wish to appear in the eyes of posterity as a mere vulgar ambitious man; and the French people, rejecting the vulgar accusation which has been made against Napoleon by the Utopians, of having been the enemy of public liberties, has done him justice.

Lying words of peace, dictated by a false semblance of moderation, were transmitted from Frankfort by M. de Saint-Aignan, who had been detained prisoner at Weimar, where he occupied the post of French ambassador. While the ambassadors of Austria, Russia, and England, with whom M. de Saint-Aignan had been put into communication, were appearing desirous of opening out negotiations, the enemy's generals were deciding on the plan of an invasion of France. It suited the allies to show themselves under a pacific exterior, so as better to dupe the French nation and to isolate Napoleon, by pointing him out as a man whose personal ambition was the only obstacle to complete pacification. The Emperor had however caused M. de Saint-Aignan's proposals to be answered to the effect that he consented to the proposed conditions: France to be limited to her natural frontiers, the Rhine, the Alps and the Pyrenees; Spain to be restored to her former dynasty; Italy, Germany, and Holland to be reestablished in their independence. Napoleon proposed the meeting of a congress at Mannheim to treat on this basis. The Austrian ambassador answered that the two Emperors and the King of Prussia had been pleased with his consent to their proposals, that they transmitted them to the co-allies, and that they accepted the selection of the town of Mannheim. And while the allies allowed the Austrian ambassador to dupe Napoleon with the hope of a pacification which was very far from their intentions, they published the declaration of Frankfort, of December 1, in which they made it public that they were not making war on France, but on the Emperor alone and the preponderance which he had too long exercised beyond the limits of his empire. They protested the most liberal intentions towards France, which they desired to see remain "great, strong and happy," assurances which were as sincere as were their overtures of peace. This was to be seen very soon, when our enemies had accomplished the resolution—about which they had hesitated—

of crossing our frontiers. In spite of M. de Metternich's fine promises the Duke of Vicence, who was waiting at the outposts for them to be carried into effect, could not succeed to be admitted to negotiate for peace, and hostilities which had not been interrupted, were pushed on with new vigor.

On his return to France the Duke of Vicence was appointed Minister of Exterior Relations, replacing the Duke of Bassano, who was, unjustly, supposed to have been sacrificed to the intrigues of the peace party. The real reason of the selection of the Duke of Vicence was the hope that the favor which this minister had enjoyed with the Emperor Alexander, during his mission to St. Petersburg, would place him in a position to render useful services, and fitted him more than anybody else to bring affairs to a happy termination.

M. de Bassano returned to the Ministry of State Secretaryship. Count Daru passed to the Ministry of War Administration, which had been left vacant by the retirement of Count Lacuée de Cessac. The Emperor, in appointing a successor to this honest and rigid administrator, endowed with the same qualities, considered Monsieur Daru more accustomed to the prompt dispatch of business and the details of so vast an administration.

The Duke of Massa—Régnier—who needed rest on account of his bad state of health, ceded the Ministry of Justice definitely to Count Molé, who had been directing it in his place since the preceding month of June. His name, one of the most illustrious in the magistracy, and his familiarity with hard work, which was proved by a book of real value which M. Molé had published at the age of twenty-five, had attracted the Emperor's attention. The young author of the *"Essai de Morale et de Politique,"* was included in the first list of auditors, created in 1806, and was rapidly promoted to the posts of prefect, councilor of state, and director-general of the department of bridges and highways. Napoleon liked M. Molé very much and treated him with a kindness which the latter returned with a great devotion. On his return from the Island of Elba, the Emperor proposed the Ministry of Exterior Relations and then the Ministry of the Interior to M. Molé, which the former Grand Judge refused to accept, believing himself, it is said, bound by the oath which he had taken to the reestablished monarchy. Although personally I must regret that M. Molé refused the Emperor the assistance of his talents under such grave circumstances, his scruples in any case are worthy of praise rather than of blame. What cannot be denied to Count Molé is a loyal heart and a distinguished intelligence. He showed great wisdom and no ordinary capacity in the administration of business. His honorable character won for him general esteem and respect.

The Emperor opened the legislative session on December 19, 1813; his words to the representatives of the nation were noble and touching. The deputies appointed a committee to draw up the address. The answer of the Legislative body was bound to have great weight not only on public opinion but also on the intentions of the allies. Napoleon, trusting to the patriotic feelings of the majority of this assembly, wished the committee to be composed of men not dependent on the government. And, as a matter of fact, men who were strangers to public functions were chosen, men devoted to the study of literature and laws, but who thought less of serving the interests of the country than of parading their independence; the royalists' way of thinking even found echoes amongst them. The deputies who composed this committee were MM. Lainé, barrister at Bordeaux; Raynouard, author of the tragedy *Les Templiers*; Gallois, a former tribune;

Flaugergues, a barrister at Toulouse, and Maine de Biran, a former *"garde-du-corps,"* a man who was generally respected, but who did not understand the situation in which France and the Emperor were placed at that time. M. Gallois drew up a report. Napoleon had accused M. Lainé of having been in secret intelligence with the English government with a view of restoring the Bourbons. I know that he had very strong suspicions in the matter. M. Lainé himself undertook to justify the accusation brought against him. M. Raynouard attracted attention to himself by his violence. His tragedy called *Les États du Blois* which had been performed in 1810 at the theatre at St. Cloud, and also his tragedy *Les Templiers,* had been severely judged by the Emperor. The poet's self-esteem is very touchy. Might not one think that M. Raynouard was influenced in this matter by his recollection of the way in which Napoleon had criticized his plays? Instead of calling upon the nation to unite itself closely to its Chief the commission, while agreeing that an energetic defense was necessary to obtain peace, complained about the oppression of the people, asked for guarantees against arbitrary power, and demanded the execution of laws favorable to liberty and to the free exercise of political rights. These remonstrances which would have been admissible at any other time but which were most untimely then constituted a bill of indictment against a man in whose power alone it lay to save the state; they discredited him in the eyes of Europe and of the nation, the nation which had to be called to arms to defend an invaded territory. In the same way the Greeks were busy with religious squabbles, when the battering-ram of Mahomet II was already dashing against the doors of Constantinople. The legislative body adopted the report of the committee by a large majority. A proof of this report having been carried to the Emperor he summoned a Privy Council at the instance of which the violent measure of dissolving the legislative body was adopted. Since there was no means of coming to an understanding this measure imposed itself. The legislative body instead of being a lever became a club in the hands of the intriguing ringleaders. In my audiences in the evening with the Emperor, rendered deeply anxious by the spirit of opposition which took advantage of his adversity to crush him at the very time when he stood in need of help, he used to ask me what the Empress thought of this struggle so new for this princess, and the measure which had been its consequence. I must mention that I used to see the Emperor with the same intimacy as in the past. I found him careworn although he did his best to master his anxiety. But in public his face was calm and reassured. In our conversations he used to complain of feeling tired of war and of not being able to endure horse-exercise any more. He reproached me in jest with having fine times, while he painfully dragged his plough—such was his expression; in one word, he felt that he was no longer happy. One could not help looking at him with melancholy interest, and seeing Napoleon unhappy my veneration for him increased.

The enemy crossed the Rhine on the last day of 1813. The allied armies had hesitated a long while; the prestige of glory still covered our frontiers, besides, a divergence of the political interests of the various powers divided them on the great question of an invasion of France. The promptings and the encouragements of conspirators in the interior of the country made them waver without deciding them. What at last put a stop to their hesitations was an offer which was made to them of a passage through Switzerland. The oligarchical party in Berne, which before the act of mediation had asked for Austria's intervention in the interior affairs of Switzerland, was raising its head again. This party encouraged by Baron Senft de Pilsach who was a turncoat from the Saxon military service, proposed to Prince Schwarzenberg who had become commander-in-chief of the allied armies to surrender him the way through the valleys. Switzerland, heedless of her independence and forgetting the benefits which she had derived from the act of mediation, allowed her neutrality to be violated, a neutrality the inviolability of which the Diet had only just solemnly proclaimed. She thus opened the way to the allied forces, who were in this way able to cross our frontiers without hindrance, for France reposing too great confidence in the good faith of Switzerland had neglected to fortify them on that side.

Five days after the adjournment of the legislative council, January 4, 1814, the Emperor sent the Duke of Vicence to the headquarters of the allies with instructions, which have been made public, and which show Napoleon's desire for peace. It was said in these instructions that if fortune betrayed him his mind was made up, that he did not care for the throne, and that he would leave it rather than submit to shameful conditions. The Duke of Vicence who was detained a fortnight at Lunéville at last obtained an invitation to proceed to Châtillon, where Lord Castlereagh had just arrived. A sham congress was to be assembled there at the same time that the armies of the enemy were pursuing their march onward in the French provinces. The Empress Marie Louise kept up a vigorous correspondence with her father. She used to receive from him nothing but assurances of interest and repeated promises that he would never sacrifice, whatever might happen, the cause either of his daughter or of his grandson. Such however was not the intention of the coalition. As a general rule the sovereigns personally were not at all hostile towards the Emperor, they were influenced and even dominated by the ascendancy which England and the high aristocracy of Europe exercised on their cabinets and on the leaders of their armies. Napoleon used to say at St. Helena that democracy was violent, but that one could come to an understanding with it, that the aristocracy, on the other hand, was cold and implacable and never surrendered.

Napoleon having realized in six weeks all that will, energy of character, and superhuman activity could create in the way of resources, he could no longer put off his departure for the army. On January 23, two days before his departure, the Emperor assembled the officers of the legions of the National Guard in the Tuileries Palace, and presenting the Empress and the King of Rome to them he said: "I am going to fight the enemy. I entrust to you what I have dearest—the Empress, my wife, and the King of Rome, my son." He confirmed the Empress's Regency with fresh letters patent and left on the 24th, after having embraced his wife and his son whom he was never to see again. Before leaving this palace which he quitted full of care and at the same time full of hope, Napoleon had the sorrow of hearing that Joachim Murat the King of Naples, his brother-in-law, had declared himself in favor of the allies in treaties signed with Austria and England, and was marching with a Neapolitan army against the French troops under the command of Prince Eugène. I will not speak at any length on the sad consequences which this fatal error had for Napoleon's political and military arrangements, although the war between Eugène and Murat was limited to an exchange of proclamations. My respect for the memory of the valiant and unfortunate King of Naples, and the bitterness of my regrets, invite me to keep silence. I know that King Joachim had a terrible struggle with himself before coming to so fatal a decision. He flattered himself that having taken this extreme step he would be able to reserve himself the means of serving the Emperor in the future. He was very far from thinking that this enterprise would lead him very shortly afterwards to the loss of his throne and of his life.

On the morrow of Napoleon's departure to the army, a deputation of the National Guard with Marshal Moncey, assistant-Major-General, who was commanding it in the Emperor's absence, at its head, was presented to the Empress Regent by Cambacérès, the Archchancellor. Marshal Moncey read out an address in answer to the words which the Emperor had addressed to the officers of the National Guard, which we have quoted higher up. Very late on the same day I had received the following letter from the Empress:

"I want you to come to me rather earlier tomorrow. There is nothing less to do than to write an answer to the speech of the National Guard. I hope that your advice will help me to make a fine speech as I am totally lacking in ideas for the time being. I beg you to believe in all the sentiments with which I am your very affectionate

"LOUISE."

I went to the Empress very early on the morrow, and, under her eyes, wrote the following answer to the deputation of the National Guard:

"GENTLEMEN, OFFICERS OF THE GUARD, I am deeply touched by the sentiments which you have just expressed, and am happy to have to transmit them to the Emperor. In the midst of the anxieties and cares of every kind with which he is surrounded his heart will be nattered with the new assurance of fidelity and devotion of which the National Guard of Paris has so often given him proofs. The Emperor, in placing me and my son in your midst fulfilled a wish which was dear to me. My confidence in the good inhabitants of Paris is entire. The proofs of affection which I have received from them are pledges of what I may expect. Present circumstances would be very fitting to tighten the bonds which attach me to them, had not our sentiments and our interests been made one long ago, were not my cause inseparable from those of all the French."

Marie Louise, who felt the necessity of winning the confidence and interest of the people of Paris in provision of events which might bring the enemies to the gates of the capital, adopted this answer, but she was obliged to submit it to the approval of the Archchancellor, who was the first councilor of the Regency. The Archchancellor did not find it sufficiently dignified. It also seemed to him too personal. He contented himself with making the Empress say that she had shared the sentiments expressed by the Emperor in his speech to the National Guard, that like him she had entire confidence in the courage, the devotion, and the fidelity of the officers of this guard, and that she would give orders that their address should be transmitted without delay to the Emperor. The Empress told him that she feared this answer might be found rather cold; the national guard was full of such a spirit of patriotism that it never failed in its duty in the moment of danger. I have quoted this fact because it is a proof of the goodwill and the praiseworthy sentiments which at this time animated the Empress Marie Louise.

The territory was invaded, the Emperor had marked the commencement of his immortal campaign in France with the glorious battle of Brienne, but attacked afterwards by forces three times superior in numbers, he had just lost the battle of La Rothière. It was feared in Paris that the enemy would be seen before our walls; and so great was the alarm that for a moment the question was discussed whether or not the great city should be evacuated. The Emperor himself was troubled by the prospect of this danger, and of the critical circumstances in which the Empress-Regent's government and the cabinet of the Empire might find themselves involved. Several letters were addressed by him from the army to his brother Joseph. As these letters are well known today, and have appeared in various publications, we will only quote here those which seem to us of most interest. On Feb. 8th the Emperor wrote the following letter from Nogent to his brother:

"Nogent sur Seine, Feb. 8, 1814

"MY BROTHER,

"Hand this letter into the Empress Josephine's own hands. I write to her that she should write to Eugène. Tell her to send you the letter she writes, and send it off at once by estafette.

"Your affectionate Brother

"NAPOLEON."

King Joseph answered the Emperor on Feb. 10, and informed him that the Empress Josephine's letter to Eugène had been sent off by estafette, and that this letter had been as pressing as it could be. This letter referred to the order given to Prince Eugène to march with his army to Geneva to join Marshal Augereau. If subsequent events, notably what was going on in Naples, had not obliged the Emperor to renounce this movement, the consequences might have been most important. The entrance of Prince Eugène and his troops on French territory would indeed have given fresh and fruitful activity to the military operations which were so feebly directed by Augereau on this side. The imminence of the danger which was menacing Italy, in consequence of the desertion of the King of Naples, caused the Emperor intense anxiety and he wrote the following letter to King Joseph:

"Troyes, Feb. 26, 1814

"MY BROTHER,

"It appears that the allies have not yet ratified the King of Naples' treaty. I wish you to send one of your people to proceed with all haste to the King, that you should write to him in a very plainspoken manner on the iniquity of his conduct, offering to be his intermediary to bring him back again, and that this is the only thing that remains for him to do or else his ruin is certain, either at the hands of France or of the allies. I need not remind you here all that you can say to him. The English themselves do not acknowledge him as king. It is not too late to save Italy and replace the viceroy on the Adige. Write also to the Queen of her ingratitude, which nothing can justify and which disgusts even the allies....write that as no battle has yet taken place between the French and Neapolitan troops all can yet be arranged, but that there is not a moment to be lost. Senator Fouché is still in these cantons. You might write to him to deal with these matters with the person whom you will send.

"(Signed) NAPOLEON."

This episode which relates to King Joachim, must not delay me any longer in the chronological recital of the events of this sad year, 1814. In these times of trouble and anguish King Joseph's prudence and firmness were not wanting to Napoleon, as is proved by the following letter, full of energetic sentiments and a noble resignation.

Letter from Joseph to Napoleon:

"Paris, February 9, at 11 o'clock in the morning.

'SIRE,

"I receive a letter from the Minister of War, and send your Majesty the original copy. You will see that our resources in rifles are reduced to six thousand and that it is consequently impossible to hope for a reserve army of from thirty to forty thousand men in Paris. Events are stronger than men, Sire, and when that is established it appears to me that it is true glory to preserve what one can obtain. It is not glorious to expose a precious life to a too evident danger, since it is not advantageous for a great number of men who have attached their existences to yours. . . Nobody here has anything to do, either directly or indirectly, with what I am writing to your Majesty, with entire freedom of speech, just as it strikes my mind.

"You must submit to fate with courage, whether fate allows you to hope to be able to cause the happiness of a great number of men, or that it forces you to commit yourself, giving you no choice except between death and dishonor, and I see no dishonor for Your Majesty, as things stand, except in abandoning the throne, because such an abandonment would cause the misfortune of a large number of people who have staked their all on you. If then you can make peace, make it at any price. If you cannot, you must perish like the last Emperor of Constantinople; there is a splendid end for you!—In this case your Majesty can be assured, that in all and for all, I will obey your behests, and that I shall never do anything unworthy either of You or of myself. JOSEPH."

While the military operations were following their course, the congress opened at Châtillon-sur-Seine. On February 7 the allies, full of pride at the success which they had gained at La Rothière, disavowed the bases which they themselves had proposed at Frankfort, which the Emperor had accepted and which assigned her natural frontiers to France. They demanded that she should return to the limits which had bounded her before 1792, that she should renounce all sovereignty or protectorate in Italy, Germany and Switzerland. The Duke of Vicence, already on February 5 had full powers for signing peace. Napoleon in vesting him with unlimited powers, was not aware of the new pretensions of the allies. The Duke of Vicence did not think that he could take upon himself to make use of his full powers. He informed the Emperor of the communication which had been made to him. Napoleon declared that he was unable to leave France smaller than he had received her in 1800; that he would not purchase the conservation of his crown with a degrading treaty, and that he would abdicate if the nation did not support him. The Duke of Bassano and the Prince de Wagram implored the Emperor to yield to necessity. Napoleon consented to close his eyes, but refused to dictate himself the conditions of his humiliation, or to consecrate, by an order signed with his own hand, the degradation of France. He did not however revoke the unlimited powers which he had given to the Duke of Vicence. The latter fulfilled the painful part with which he was charged at the congress, with courage and devotion. He resigned himself in consequence to the hard condition of the former boundaries, but demanded that hostilities should cease at once. For all answer the ambassadors of the allies, satisfied at having obtained this concession, brusquely suspended the conferences. They alleged that they needed fresh instructions. They feared that perhaps they had not exacted enough. Considering no doubt that France had not fallen low enough, they thought to inflict a still crueler degradation upon her.

Napoleon hoping for nothing more from such enemies, far from allowing himself to be cast down by their exactions, found in the resources of his genius one of those heroic maneuvers which were familiar to him, with the result that he won the battles of Champaubert, Montmirail and Vauxchamps, besides several combats which filled the allied forces with terror. Their plenipotentiaries made haste to have recourse to their usual tactics. They renewed the fallacious proposal of an armistice. This is the letter which Napoleon wrote to his brother Joseph on this subject:

"Nangis, February 18, 1804

"MY BROTHER,

"Prince Schwarzenberg has at last given signs of life. He has just sent a flag of truce to ask for a suspension of hostilities.

"It is difficult to be cowardly to this degree. He had constantly refused, and in the most insulting terms, any kind of suspension of arms or armistice, and even to receive my flags of truce, after the capitulation of Danzig and of Dresden, a horrible thing of which but few examples can be found in history. At the first shock these wretches fall down on their knees. Fortunately Prince Schwarzenberg's aide-de-camp was not allowed to enter; I only received his letter, which I shall answer at leisure. I shall grant no truce till they have quitted our territory. According to the news in my possession all has changed amongst the allies. The Emperor of Russia, who a few days ago had broken off negotiations, because he wished to inflict worse conditions on France than that of the former frontiers, is anxious to resume them; and I hope very shortly to conclude peace on the Frankfort basis, which is the minimum of peace with honor that I can conclude. Before commencing my operations, I have offered them to sign for peace on the condition of the former limits, provided they should immediately cease fighting. This demand was made by the Duke of Vicence on the 8th. They answered negatively, saying that the signature of the preliminaries would not put a stop to hostilities, and that this could only take place when all the clauses of the treaty of peace had been signed. This inconceivable answer was published and yesterday, the 17th, they asked me for an armistice. You can imagine that seeing myself on the eve of a battle in which I was decided to conquer or to die, and in which if I yielded, my capital would have been lost, I would have consented to anything to avoid so great a risk. I owed this sacrifice of my self-respect, to my people and to my family. But, since they refused, since the hazard of the battle was played and that all has returned to the chances of an ordinary war, where the result of a single battle can no longer menace my capital, when all possible chances are in my favor, I owe it to the interests of the Empire and to my glory to negotiate for a real peace. If I had signed peace on the condition of the former limits, I should have rushed to arms two years later; and I should have told the nation that it was not peace but a capitulation that I had signed. I could not say so, under the new state of things, since, fortune having returned to my side, I am master of my conditions. The enemy is in a very different position from the one in which it was placed when the Frankfort treaty was proposed and pretty well assured that it will bring few of its soldiers back over our frontiers. Its cavalry is nearly worn-out; its infantry is exhausted by all these marches and countermarches. In one word it is completely discouraged. I accordingly hope to be able to conclude a peace, such as should satisfy any reasonable man, and my wishes do not extend beyond the proposals made at Frankfort.

"(Signed) NAPOLEON."

The mission of Prince Schwarzenberg's aide-de-camp, sent with a flag of truce, prompted Napoleon to write directly to the Emperor of Austria to express the desire that negotiations might take a more conciliatory turn and might lead to a speedy signing of the peace. The victories of Nangis and Montereau gave Napoleon fresh hopes.

In the meanwhile, the conference had recommenced on February 17, at Châtillon. On the same day the Emperor had revoked the unlimited powers which he had granted to the Duke of Vicence, the victory of the French armies having apparently modified the respective positions of the enemies. But Lord Castlereagh had just arrived and was present at the congress. The object of the first *pourparlers* was the resumption of negotiations on the basis of a restitution by France of all the territory which she had acquired since 1792, a restitution in which the surrender of Antwerp, England's *sine quâ non,* was formulated. At the same time the allies demanded that certain fortified towns in the interior of France should be surrendered to them; they founded their pretensions on the concession made by the French plenipotentiary, at the time of the suspension of the congress, on February 9.

On the 23rd, Prince Wenzel-Lichtenstein brought back the Emperor of Austria's answer to Napoleon's letter. The terms of this answer were conciliatory. Prince Lichtenstein protested that the allies had no evil intentions either against the dynasty or against the Emperor's person. Even had this not been the case the Emperor of Austria's envoy declared that Austria would never lend herself to such maneuvers, that all she sincerely desired was peace. This power had, as a matter of fact, very much less interest in a continuation of the war than the others. The principal object of her ambition was fulfilled, since she recovered Italy and her influence in Germany. Prince Lichtenstein renewed the proposal of an armistice which, in his ardent desire for peace, Napoleon decided to accept.

The allies, discouraged by a series of defeats, had decided upon a retreat which almost became a disaster, in proportion as the accumulation of their masses of troops in the outlets gave rise to greater encumbrance and disorder. A terrible panic seemed to have struck Prince Schwarzenberg's great army, the columns of which, dragged on by the fugitives and by streams of equipages, retrograded with all speed towards the Rhine.

Napoleon, having returned to Troyes, made his arrangements for maneuvering on the rear of the army command by Blücher, who tempted by the numerical inferiority of the corps of the Marshals Mortier and Marmont was advancing in a foolhardy way upon Meaux, while Schwarzenberg was continuing his retrograde movement.

Napoleon's letter to his brother Joseph:

" Troyes, February 24, 1814, 7 a. m.

"MY BROTHER,

"I have entered Troyes. The army of the enemy are besieging me with flags of truce to ask me for a suspension of arms. A truce will perhaps be negotiated this morning; but that can only be on the condition that the Châtillon negotiations are pursued on the basis of the Frankfort proposals.

"The Minister of the Interior is a 'funk,' he has a very wild idea about men: neither he, nor the Minister of Police have any more notion about France than I have about China.

N."

Letter from King Joseph to the Emperor:

"Paris, February 25, 9 p. m.

'SIRE,

"I have had occasion to see the ministers today in the council which was held by the Empress. I spoke to them of Your Majesty's successes and of your hopes. The Minister of the Interior is working hard on the lines marked out by you. A council will be held tomorrow.

"M. de Montalivet is very zealous in your Majesty's service. J."

The Emperor flattered himself or pretended to flatter himself that the resumption of negotiations would have a successful issue. He wrote from Troyes, on February 26, at six in the evening:

"In the meanwhile the congress is in our hands; which proves that all the enemy's calculations have been upset. Lord Castlereagh has asked if his person will be in safety, in view of the fact that he has no official position as ambassador. That of course cannot be questioned. Anybody touching the congress, either directly or indirectly, is under the protection of international law.

" N."

The demand for an armistice had been made at a time when the Emperor's rapid movements and his unexpected successes had filled the allies with discouragement. Having got over this first impression, and the Russian and English plenipotentiaries predominating at the congress, they broke off the conferences at Lusigny under the pretext that Napoleon was mixing up with the military question points of discussion which were without the scope of the Châtillon congress. These conferences had not lasted more than four days.

In the meanwhile the only retreat open to the Silesian army, under the command of Blücher, was by Soissons. The French army occupied the roads by which the Prussian general was forced to pass. If Blücher did not succeed in forcing his way through Soissons, his position, driven as he was into a corner against the Aisne river, would become extremely critical. Soissons had been put into a good state of defense and was provided with a garrison of 1500 men, but the incapacity of the general in command threw it into the hands of the enemy. Not understanding the importance of the fortress which he was charged to defend, he capitulated on the morrow of the day on which the enemy presented itself before Soissons, satisfied with obtaining that his garrison should not be taken prisoners of war. It was in this wise that Blücher in the night of March 3, was able to cross the river with the whole of his army, and join forces which brought the total number of the soldiers with whom we had to fight to one hundred thousand.

The unexpected surrender of Soissons upset the Emperor's plans and had a fatal influence on the issue of the campaign. This success raised the courage of the allies, who reassured by their immense numerical superiority passed from a state of depression to one of exceeding confidence. Their shame at flight, the dangers to which numerous armies marching with their sovereigns at their head, across a country in a state of insurrection and ready to bar the way of their return to the Rhine, without stores and without ammunition, and finally the encouragement which they received from Paris, determined them to cease their retrograde movement. They had succeeded in duping their adversary with sham negotiations and in winning time.

The allies far from reducing their pretensions, had accordingly come to the opinion that they would have every advantage in persisting in their claims. They saw that the successes obtained by Napoleon which were owing to the heroism of a handful of heroes who were not supported, cost the victor dearly, and that these successes themselves served but to weaken him. The four great powers signed a treaty at Chaumont on March 1, by which they allied themselves still closer. They engaged in consequence to act on the offensive and not to retreat separately. They invited the other powers to join them and exerted extraordinary efforts to realize their object, which was to overthrow the Emperor. England furnished fresh subsidies.

On March 2, King Joseph received the following letter from the Emperor:

"Jouarre, March 2, 1814

"MY BROTHER,

"I desire you on receiving this letter to assemble under the presidency of the Regent, the great dignitaries, my ministers and the presidents of the Council of State, and to read to them, the note containing the proposals of the allies, my letter to the Emperor of Austria, Prince Schwarzenberg's dispatch to the major-general, and the draft of the note which I have just dictated to be handed by the Duke of Vicence to the Congress: in one word, all the papers which explain the state of affairs. The Duke of Cadore will record what each one says. I do not want formal opinions, but I shall be glad to know each person's way of thinking."

King Joseph answered this letter as follows:

"Paris, March 4, 1814

"SIRE,

"The Empress held the extraordinary council, which Your Majesty commanded, today. I ordered the papers which had been sent to me to be read. All the members of this council seem to share the same opinion. They found the enemies' proposals very unjust, and they showed absolute confidence in whatever Your Majesty might order to your plenipotentiaries, so that France might enter into immediate enjoyment of the immense sacrifices which are demanded of you, and which we well know will only be granted by Your Majesty in the last extremity. You, better than anybody else are judge of that. But, with fairly general unanimity, we are united in thinking the necessity of seeing France reduced to the territory which she possessed in 1792 should be accepted rather than to allow the capital to be threatened. The occupation of the capital is looked upon as the end of the present order, and the commencement of great misfortunes. Europe, entirely united, wishes to reduce France to what she was in 1792. Let this be the basis of a treaty which is imposed upon us by circumstances, but let the territory be immediately evacuated. In one word, prompt peace, no matter what it may be, is indispensable. It will be a truce for two or three years; but good or bad, peace must be made. The Emperor will make it as little unfavorable as possible. In the present state of things it will always be an advantage, since it will allow the Emperor to occupy himself exclusively with home affairs, and that by good management he will be in a state to take back what has been unjustly demanded of him and which he has wisely accorded. The natural frontiers would be a real benefit for France and for Europe; they would give the hope of long peace, but nobody is forced to do what is impossible. Peace is indispensable today, this peace could cease on the day when France would be in a position to demand her rights. Conclude then a truce *in petto* since the injustice of our enemies will not allow you to conclude a just peace, and when the state of things and of public opinion does not allow you to hope from France efforts proportionate to the object which has to be attained. The Emperor of Austria's letter was found full of nobility and good sense. You will remain to France and France will remain to you as she was in the days when she filled Europe with amazement, and you who saved her once will do so a second time by signing peace today, and by saving yourself with her. Be acknowledged by England, deliver France from the Cossacks and the Prussians, and France will render to you one day in blessings that which superficial minds might think you have lost in glory. I notice that I am indulging in too much verbiage. Whether Your Majesty has gained a victory or not you must have peace. This sums up what everybody here thinks and says.

"J."

The Privy Council indeed was unanimously of opinion that peace was the first need of France. The condition however of having to give up, by the occupation of Besançon and our principal fortresses, the key of our frontiers caused some to hesitate. Amongst those who were consulted I may mention M. de Cessac and General Dejean, first inspector of engineers, as having shown the most firmness on this solemn occasion. General Dejean was a noble character, and it is known with what generous indignation he combated in 1815 resolutions tending to submit to laws imposed by the foreigners. Napoleon had had occasion in 1810 to give this general publicly a high proof of his esteem.

On March 9, King Joseph congratulated the Emperor on the victory of Craonne, and pressed him in a most eloquent manner to take advantage of this success and to conclude peace. But the victory of Craonne was balanced by the issue of the battle of Laon, in which the Emperor had to fight against an army which was five times stronger than his own. Napoleon was forced to retreat, to avoid being surrounded by forces so vastly superior. He wrote as follows to King Joseph:

"Chavignon, March 11, 1814

'MY BROTHER,

"I have examined the enemies' position. It was too strong to be attacked without incurring great loss. I have accordingly made up my mind to return to Soissons. It was probable that the enemy would have evacuated Loan, for fear of being attacked there, but for the skirmish of the Duke of Raguse, who behaved like a sub-lieutenant. The enemy experienced enormous losses when attacking the village of Clacy, five times yesterday, and was always repulsed. The young guard melts away like snow, the old guard keeps firm. My mounted guards are also greatly diminished. It is indispensable that General Ornano should take every means to remount all the dragoons and chasseurs, beginning with the veterans. Orders must be given for redoubts to be constructed at Montmartre.

"N."

Another letter from Napoleon:

"Soissons, March 13, 1814.

"MY BROTHER,

"Before beginning the works for the fortifications of Paris the plan of these works must be known. The one which was presented to me seems very complicated. What one wants is something very simple. On every side of me I receive complaints of the people against the mayors and leading citizens, who prevent them from defending themselves. I see the same state of things in Paris. The people have energy and honor. I very much fear there are certain leaders who don't want to fight, and who will be very much dazed after the event at what they have brought upon themselves." J."

Another letter from Napoleon:

"Rheims, March 14, 1814

"My BROTHER,

"I arrived yesterday at Rheims which was occupied by the General in Chief, St. Priest, with three Russian divisions and a new Prussian division which came from the blockade of Stettin. I defeated him, recaptured the city, 20 pieces of cannon, a quantity of baggage, and caissons, and made 5,000 prisoners. General St. Priest was mortally wounded and has been amputated at the thigh. The thing to be noticed is that St. Priest was wounded by the same gunner who killed General Moreau. One may exclaim: 'O Providence!'

"N."

Another extract from a letter from the Emperor, dated at:

"Epernay, March 17, 1814

"I am expecting great results in my movement which will throw great disorder and great confusion on the rear of my enemy, and its headquarters if it be still at Troyes. The couriers must be sent to me by Ferte-sous-Jourre, and thence to Arcis-sur-Aube by way of Epernay and Montmirail. You must tell the ministers of war and of police not to say anything which is not necessary, and to write anything of importance in cipher until my communications by way of Nogent have been established. Send officers to Soissons, to Compiègne, to Rheims, and to Epernay. I have given orders for a division of 12,000 men whom I am bringing from Metz to proceed to Chalons. I do not know whether this order will reach its destination. It would be a great piece of good fortune.

"N."

Another letter from Napoleon:

"Epernay, March 18, 1814

"MY BROTHER,

"The whole army is in movement, to pass the night beyond Fère-Champenoise and thence to proceed in the direction of Arcis-sur-Aube, and the enemies' bridges. I am in communication with our garrisons of Verdun and Metz. I am expecting a division of 12,000 men whom I am withdrawing from these forts. It appears that the enemy has left Noyon which clears the ground round Compiègne. The conduct of this commune was perfect."

"N."

The success over General Saint-Priest, the occupation of Rheims, Napoleon's presence in this city and in Epernay had surprised the allies in the midst of their movement, and had thrown them back into a state of indecision which was revealed by a general retreat of their troops. The army of the enemy fell back upon Troyes preceded by its baggage. Paris seemed threatened no longer. The Emperor Alexander sent word, it is stated, to Prince Schwarzenberg in the middle of the night, that he wished a courier to be sent off immediately to Châtillon, with orders to sign peace on the conditions asked for by the French negotiator. The Emperor of Austria had fled in the direction of Dijon, with a single officer and a valet-de-chambre, to place himself in safety. M. de Metternich succeeded in joining him there with some secretaries. They remained there without communications from the outside for a period of thirty hours.

On the eve of evacuating Troyes to continue his retreat, the Emperor Alexander, recovering from his panic, convoked a council of war. At this council he declared with emphasis that he was tired of fleeing before a handful of men, with such formidable armies as were under his command, and that the only means of dictating peace was to march with all the forces, of the coalition on Paris. Having countermanded the retreat, the concentration of the two great allied armies was decided upon, and a meeting fixed in the plains of Châlons. The allied forces looked for safety not only in the inertia of a part of the nation, which was being worked upon with magnificent promises with the object of detaching it from Napoleon, but further in the prayers and encouragements of the Royalist committees in Paris, whose communications with the congress of Châtillon had remained permanent. Prince de Bénévent, bound by secret relations with influential persons in the foreign cabinets and courts, was in correspondence with the ministers present at the congress; making ready to profit by events whatever they might be, and redoubling the activity of his intrigues both in Paris and abroad.

Duke Dalberg, whom the Emperor had naturalized a Frenchman but whose heart he had been unable to change, whom he had loaded with kindness, whom he had created a duke and endowed with two hundred thousand francs a year, the relation and friend of Nesselrode and Stadion, the ministers, seconded Prince de Bénévent, with all the zeal which his deep ingratitude could inspire him with. Every day at the Council of State, where he had been placed in the section of home affairs to which I belonged, as there was no section of exterior relations, he used to bring us desperate tidings; his language was that of a man who was initiated in the plans of the allied forces. Thus when an immense array of hostile forces, seconded by the perfidy of foreign diplomacy, was rendering the glorious efforts of Napoleon and of his army of no avail, treachery at home was noiselessly consummated within the ruin of the imperial edifice.

Simultaneously with their decision of uniting their forces and of marching in one body upon Paris the allies abandoned their empty show of negotiations. They declared that the congress of Châtillon was closed, taking as a pretext that the French plenipotentiaries based themselves on certain apparent successes of the French army to go back on arrangements which they themselves had proposed. The representatives of the allied powers alleged that there was no possibility of coming to an understanding and imputed the rupture of the negotiations to France. In vain did the Duke of Vicence ask for twenty-four hours grace in which to receive the instructions which he was expecting, instructions which were to authorize him to make what concessions were deemed possible and to discuss further concessions; the ministers of the coalition persisted in considering the negotiations as at an end. They withdrew declaring the congress dissolved, on their own authority, in spite of all the protestations of the French plenipotentiaries. At Châtillon, as at Prague, every way was blocked to freedom of discussion, and that in despite of diplomatic usages and the consideration with which civilized states treat each other. The courier who carried the dispatches from the Emperor to his envoy to the congress, met the Duke of Vicence on the road, on his way back to headquarters. The latter stopped to write to Metternich that he regretted the brusque breaking-off of the negotiations all the more because he had received certain dispatches which put him in a position to smooth over many difficulties: a final and useless step, which only proved more clearly how great was our distress and how implacable the ill will of our enemies.

Joseph Bonaparte had thought of the means of detaching the Prince Royal of Sweden (Bernadotte) from the coalition before the Emperor had told him to attempt to do so. Joseph, Bernadotte's brother-in-law, as is known, retained the feeble hope, that after having betrayed his country and having handed it over to the vengeance of the enemy, this erring son, might, as he set foot upon his native soil, feel some remorse. He thought that the remembrance of their family alliance might contribute to arouse some generous feelings in the heart of an old French soldier who had risen to become a French marshal. King Joseph accordingly sent off Doctor Franzenberg, to his brother-in-law, by the agency of Chiappe, a former *conventionnel,* a mutual friend of the two families, and he succeeded in reaching the Swedish headquarters. This step remained without result, Bernadotte alleging that it was too late. He had engaged himself still further with the coalition, and had rendered them fresh services for which he expected his reward. It appears certain that he had been duped with the hope of succeeding the Emperor Napoleon on the throne of France. M. de Langeron, an *émigré* in the command of a Russian army corps, declared that he transmitted to the Emperor of Russia intercepted letters which inspired the allies with the fear of seeing Bernadotte lend his ear to overtures coming from Paris, a discovery which had induced the Emperor Alexander to lavish fresh promises and fresh flatteries upon Bernadotte. From that time forward the fatal ambition of the ex-marshal of the Empire knew no limits; rendering him deaf to the promptings of honor and of duty. The Emperor had written to King Joseph from Troyes, on February 25, as follows:

"It is said that the Prince Royal of Sweden is at Cologne. Could you not, on your own initiative, send somebody to him to make him feel the folly of his conduct and induce him to change it? Try it, but without involving me in any way.

"N."

The following is the letter in which King Joseph informed the Emperor of the steps that had been taken, in conformity with the wishes which his brother had expressed to him:

"Paris, March 13, 1814

"SIRE,

"The person whom I sent to the Prince of Sweden returned today. He left the prince at Liége on the 10th instant. If Your Majesty wishes to examine him, you have but to give orders to the Prince of Neufchâtel for whom I will give him a letter. If Your Majesty should not desire to see him, he could give military information of some importance on the districts which he had just traveled through.

"The Prince of Sweden speaks frequently and quite openly of the return of the Bourbons. He is temporizing to give you time, as he says, to conclude peace, which he desires, as he wishes to return home. "J."

Letter from the Emperor to King Joseph:

"Rheims, March 17, 1814, noon

'My BROTHER, I have seen the officer attached to the Queen, whom you sent me. Amongst good things he tells me many which are false. If you can trust him, I think it would be important to send him a second time, and to send other messages; would that not give us the advantage of learning what is going on in these provinces?

"Duke of Bassano has written to Count d'Hauterive to hand you a copy of the declaration which was made by the allies at Châtillon, who wanted, being four, to treat for all the other powers. You may communicate this document in a confidential manner to the Prince Royal, pressing him to make efforts to have a minister at the congress. For after all Sweden can have no interest in allowing a *quatrumvirate* to put hands on the whole of Europe. It is for her, as has always been the case, to look after her affairs herself. Before sending this person, be sure that he is no traitor.

"N."

The Emperor had many reasons for being suspicious. But King Joseph's envoy was a loyal man, a good Frenchman who had fulfilled his mission with zeal and fidelity. These communications had no further result and remained fruitless.

The Emperor excited the spirit of resistance in the hearts of the French against these hordes of barbarians which the allies vomited forth on to the center of civilization, and who committed atrocities surpassing all that can be imagined. He endeavored to keep men's courage alive by the display of trophies wrested from the enemy. On February 27 the Minister of the Interior had presented the Empress with ten Russian, Prussian, and Austrian flags taken at the battles of Montmirail and Vauxchamps, and at the encounter at Montereau. These flags, carried by officers of the imperial guard and the national guard, had been brought to Paris by Baron, today Duke, de Mortemart, the Emperor's orderly officer.—The papers were filled with reports made by the auditors who had been commissioned to establish and put on record the cruelties and vexations committed by the allies at every place which they had occupied, in spite of the presence of their sovereigns. The Paris municipal council received deputations from the towns in Champagne and Burgundy, who related the misfortunes which these provinces had had to suffer by the foreign occupation. But so great was the weariness with war that these reports did not produce the indignation which might have been expected. At the same time Dupaty's rondos, with the choruses of "Let us guard her well" and "He has gone" were being sung in all the theatres.

In spite of all Paris was filled with alarm. The two letters following from the Empress describe the feelings which agitated the population of Paris sufficiently clearly. On February 12 Marie Louise wrote to me:

"Good news. The Emperor has destroyed York's corps and has taken his material: the rest has got stuck in the crossroads. The Emperor was to sleep at la Ferté-sous-Jouarre and was in good health. This is what M. Anatole reports to the Archchancellor at half-past three. I hasten to acquaint you of it and beg you to believe in the sentiments of esteem of your very well-affected.

"LOUISE."

On March 27, she wrote to me:

"I send you back the letter which you lent me this morning, and add to it two petitions which I beg you to send to the ministers, adding that I interest myself in them. It appears that our affairs are going so badly on the Duke of Raguse's side that we may very easily receive visitors here very shortly. What a terrible prospect!

"LOUISE."

The Emperor in maneuvering on the flank of the enemy fell in with Schwarzenberg's army, which was operating a new movement on this side, at Arcis-sur-Aube. After having fought all day against overwhelming masses, after having personally incurred the greatest dangers, and having obstinately sought after death which refused to take him, Napoleon recrossed the Aube in the night. He arrived at Saint-Dizier on the 23rd, where he found the Duke of Vicence, who had returned from Châtillon which he had left on March 20 after the rupture of the congress.

In the critical situation in which he found himself, Napoleon thought of putting into execution the project of which he had spoken to his brother, in his letters of March 2 and 4: namely of stopping the enemies' march upon Paris by maneuvering on their rear, a movement which was to allow him to rally the garrisons of the fortresses in Alsace and Lorraine, to organize a formidable insurrection and thus to cut off the communications of the allied armies. Before taking this resolution, which presented some chances of success, and which might if carried out effectually save France, the Emperor wished to procure certain information on the real movement effected by the enemies. With this object in view he sent out strong reconnoitering parties to the lines of operations, and established himself at Doulevent where he spent the 25th awaiting the result of these reconnoitrings. There Napoleon was able to convince himself how well his apprehensions had been founded; Schwarzenberg and Blücher's immense forces had effected a junction. The Emperor learned that new and pressing advices from the royalists had emboldened the allies, and dissipated their hesitations; and that their armies, taking once more to the road to Paris which they had abandoned, were now in full march upon the capital.

Having heard this news, Napoleon returned to Saint-Dizier where he spent the night in thinking over the advantages of his plan and the disadvantage of exposing Paris, which it was his so anxious desire not to leave to the enemy. The discouragement of the leaders of his army, which had reached the point of disorganization, the fear of not being seconded or of being badly seconded, the importunities of those who surrounded him, importunities which under different circumstances he would not have tolerated, the news he had of the audacity of the counterrevolutionaries and the lukewarm state of public opinion in Paris, the responsibility of the disasters with which the capital was threatened, so many considerations taken together troubled this mind, generally so firm. A secret advice, transmitted by a sure and loyal man, Count Lavalette, informing the Emperor of the secret intrigues of the royalists and of their communications with the enemy, confirmed Napoleon in his resolution to return at full speed to the rescue of Paris.

Before leaving Saint-Dizier, the Emperor charged M. de Wessemberg, the Austrian envoy in London, with a confidential letter to the Emperor of Austria. M. de Wessemberg had been arrested in company with several civil and military officers belonging to the enemy by some peasants and had been brought to the imperial headquarters. M. de Vitrolles, charged with a secret mission by the royalists in Paris, happened to be amongst them in disguise but was not recognized. The mission confided to M. de Wessemberg remained without result. The envoy alleged that he had been prevented from reaching the Emperor of Austria, who was sequestrated at Chanceaux, near Dijon.

A vexatious occurrence had aggravated our anxieties at the Tuileries. The Emperor had written to the Empress of his maneuver in the direction of Saint-Dizier, a maneuver the object of which was to check the enemy's march upon Paris and to force it to a retrograde movement. Unfortunately this letter fell into the hands of the Prussians. It informed the enemy of the Emperor's plans, and after reading it the Prussians sent it on to the Empress with every mark of respect. The Empress thought it right to keep this disturbing communication secret, but considered it full of dire forebodings.

The vague rumors of the disgust with war which reigned in the French camp and which was said to have reached the pitch of insubordination, which came to our ears about the same time, were another cause of alarm.

While the women of the royalist party, in the hope of a return of the ancient dynasty, were busying themselves in the most private rooms in their houses in making white cockades, the Empress Marie Louise and the ladies of her court, like the queens and ladies of the Middle Ages, assembled in a large drawing room in the palace, prepared lint for the wounded.

A hidden fermentation reigned amongst the corporations of state. Indirect insinuations, which were soon followed by more transparent actions, produced themselves with the object of removing Napoleon from power, and of inducing him to abdicate in favor of his son. A member of the senate went so far as to sound several of his colleagues, amongst others Count Ségur, who consented to keep the matter secret, on the advisability of inducing a belief in the Emperor's insanity with a view to his suspension. Other intrigues had as a purpose to make use of the foreigners with a view to restoring the Bourbons. The ungrateful Duke Dalberg did not disguise this guilty hope in the very Council of State, where, as I have recorded, he had been placed in extraordinary service.

M. de Talleyrand concealed under the mask of his customary indolence, and under a language which was full of feigned patriotism, the activity of his communications with the enemies at home and abroad. But he took good care, as he always did, not to show himself in anything and to write nothing which might compromise him. Napoleon was not in ignorance of the fact that his enemies at home and abroad were planning to make use of the senate to proclaim Napoleon II, and that the allies hoped to excite civil war in France by separating the Emperor from his son and family; events justify this supposition. Without thinking that the Bourbons had much chance of success, Napoleon knew that the ringleaders, except those of the Mortfontaine committee, who possessed but little influence, had no other object than to force him to surrender his crown to his son. King Joseph had been sounded on this point by some senators; the general-lieutenantship of the empire under the Emperor's minority, had been offered to him. The loyalty of Napoleon's brother revolted at the thought. Disturbed by this inner danger he desired that peace should be concluded at no matter what cost. At the end of some work which had been done at the Empress's, King Joseph and the Archchancellor suggested to me that I should express this wish to the Emperor. Before taking this step, I asked to be allowed to inform him of it, for I had a presentiment that it would be very badly received by him. As a matter of fact, I received a letter from Soissons, *written in Napoleon's own hand,* dated March 12, at two o'clock in the afternoon, which began with the words:

"I have received your letter; you answered rightly. I shall consider the first address presented to me to ask me for peace as an act of rebellion.

"NAPOLEON."

Napoleon saw very well that if peace were still possible, nothing would be more likely to delay it than a manifestation in its favor on the part of the corporations of state, a manifestation by which the foreigners would not fail to profit to create the belief that there was a misunderstanding between the Emperor and the nation. King Joseph had never thought of making the communication which he had entrusted to the public. His choice of me proved moreover that it was to be quite confidential. At the same time the Emperor had gladly taken advantage of this circumstance to prevent any official application to him in this direction, in case anybody might have thought of attempting it.

The presence of the scouts of the allied army outside the gates of Paris had driven the inhabitants of the surrounding country into the metropolis, and their furniture, provisions and live stock, encumbered the various entrances. Rich families were fleeing in the direction of the Loire. A part of the population of Paris, impelled by a vague anxiety, wandered about the streets, on the squares and boulevards, or hastened to the termini of the country roads or to the heights around the city.

During the last days which preceded the entry of the allies into Paris, pressed with the anxiety by which the minds of all were preyed upon, I used to go very frequently to the office of the general director of the post office to learn what news there was of the enemy's approach; the news received from French headquarters was rare and not calculated to calm the anxiety. Couriers and persons of every condition, fleeing from the scene of the war, used to come to the general post office to relate what they had undergone and to seek for the means of communicating with the relations and friends who had remained behind in the towns and country districts which they had just left. I frequently met M. de Bourrienne there, who used to come with a purpose less innocent than mine, but who disguised it under exaggerated demonstrations of zeal for the imperial government. He had every reason to go away with satisfaction for the news was far from being reassuring. The enemy did not slacken in its onward march.

The orders which the Emperor had given for the defense of Paris had been for the most part carried out. The committee of defense had provided for matters of detail. The necessity, however, of conferring with the Emperor, and various obstacles over which his presence and energetic will alone could have triumphed, prevented the necessary extension and perfection from being given to the various works which had been projected.

Nobody ignored the fact that Napoleon, endowed with devouring activity, with a mind rich in resources and an ever sustained power of attention, embraced in his vast genius all the details of the war at the same time as all the branches of his government; that even in the midst of the most active military operations, he found time to occupy himself with home affairs; that his orders always reached his ministers in good time; that he kept himself informed on everything, that everything was under his control and that he thought for everybody. The result was that those who acted for him, whose prudence increased in proportion to the responsibility which weighed upon them, did not dare take any steps on their own authority and awaited his orders instead of acting. Thus the Emperor's absence in these troubled times, paralyzed the zeal which his presence on the contrary would have stimulated in the highest degree.

On March 27, King Joseph reviewed the national guards, who were incompletely equipped and dressed, and the feeble corps of the Paris garrison made up of depots of the imperial guard. So scarce were arms that part of the national guard had to be armed with lances, which they only used with repugnance. These troops marched past the Empress who was with the King of Rome. They were filled with the best feelings and full of ardor to defend the capital as well as to protect Marie Louise and the young prince.

The following letter addressed by the Emperor to King Joseph determined the latter, some days later, to hurry on the departure of the Empress and of her son:

"Rheims, March 16, 1814

"In conformity with the verbal instructions which I have given you and the spirit of all my letters you must not allow the Empress and the King of Rome to fall into the hands of the enemy, in any case whatever. I am about to maneuver in such a manner that it may be some days before you receive any news of me. If the enemy advance upon Paris with such forces that all resistance is out of the question, send the Empress-Regent, my son, the great dignitaries, the ministers, the grand officers of the crown, Baron de la Bouillerie and the treasure off in the direction of the Loire. Do not leave my son, and remember that I would rather know him at the bottom of the Seine than in the hands of the enemies of France. The fate of Astyanax, prisoner to the Greeks, always seemed to me the saddest fate that history records.

"Your affectionate brother,
"NAPOLEON."

When the corps of Marshal Marmont and Marshal Mortier, reduced to very small numbers, had been driven back on Paris by imposing forces of the enemy and the capital was menaced, when this danger had been still further aggravated by the Emperor's letter to the Empress falling into the hands of the enemy, King Joseph considered that the case provided for by the Emperor's verbal and written communications in such precise and positive terms, had come into existence; and he accordingly showed the letter which he had received to the Empress and to Cambacérès. A privy council, composed of the great dignitaries, of the ministers and the president of the senate, assembled on the evening of March 28. The Emperor's letter was not at first communicated to the council, to form the text of its deliberations; the question whether the Empress should remain in Paris with her son, or leave it, was alone mooted. The majority of the members of the council, Count Boulay de la Meurthe amongst others, were of opinion that the Empress ought not to leave, that her presence would reassure the capital, and would impose respect upon the invaders. M. Boulay expressed this opinion and argued with much energy in support thereof. He even proposed that the Empress should go to the town hall and show herself to the people of Paris, holding her son in her arms like another Maria Theresa. But the resolution of remaining in Paris was contrary to the wishes expressed by the Emperor, and the responsibility of the council risked being seriously involved if the majority of its members pronounced themselves in favor of an opposite decision. The government of the Regency then produced the Emperor's letter of March 16. It put an end to all discussion and determined the departure, only Joseph explained that it was necessary to be informed of the real strength of the enemy's army, which was following the troops of Marshals Marmont and Mortier, and offered to remain behind in Paris with the Ministers of War, of the War Administration and of Marine. It was agreed that the decision of the council should be published, that the enemy's forces should be reconnoitered, and that in case they were so great that all resistance was out of the question, King Joseph and the three ministers should follow the government to the Loire. A proclamation which was posted on the walls, appeared after the departure of the Empress and of her son to temper the discouragement of the inhabitants. The Minister of War, questioned during the council on the number of guns which he could dispose of in case of need, had answered that only very few were in a state of repair, because the guns which were fit for use were distributed daily amongst the conscripts on their way to the army.

At the end of the sitting of the council, which lasted past midnight, King Joseph and the Archchancellor followed the Empress to her rooms; I was present also. After having exchanged some words on the disastrous consequences which might result from abandoning Paris, King Joseph and the Archchancellor ventured to tell the Empress that she alone was in a position to decide what steps should be taken in such a grave state of affairs. The Empress answered them that they were both her forced councilors, and that she could not take it upon herself to give an order contrary to the Emperor's, confirmed by the deliberations of the privy council, without first having obtained their formal advice in a signed document. Both refused to assume this responsibility.

Now that the past can be examined in cold blood, has one the right blame this conduct? If honor and loyalty be not empty words, were Joseph and Cambacérès allowed to sacrifice the man who had given them his confidence and to treat with his enemy in his absence? If they had consented to sanction Napoleon's deposition, for to disobey his orders was to provoke it, they could no doubt obtain for the Empress the acknowledgement of her son, King Joseph the general-lieutenantship of the empire, and the Archchancellor the preservation of his dignities....but at what a price!

The conversation was brought to a close by a declaration on the part of the Empress that were she to fall into the Seine with her son, as the Emperor had said, she would not hesitate one moment about leaving. A wish so formally expressed as that of her husband was a sacred command to her.

Napoleon has since complained that his order was too strictly interpreted; he had said that the execution of this order was subordinated to circumstances, which had changed since the day on which he had given it. There can be no doubt that the Empress's presence in Paris might have checkmated guilty maneuvers and have given Napoleon time to arrive to the rescue of his capital by preceding the enemy there. The privy council had felt this; the Empress and her councilors understood it, but who would have dared to disobey the formal instructions which we have recorded? Moreover the subsequent letters of the Emperor, during the fortnight which had elapsed between the time when they were given and the day on which they were carried out, had neither cancelled nor modified these orders.

The treasure and the most valuable things were loaded upon vans which were to follow the Empress's escort. I sent for the archivist attached to the Emperor's cabinet and named to him, according to instructions which I had received, the most important papers which Napoleon had not taken away with him, so that they might be burned. This order was only partially carried out, and the government of the Restoration found a sufficiently large number of papers which ought to have been destroyed. I carried away with me family papers and letters to preserve them until they were in danger of being taken, in which case I was to destroy them. I then withdrew to my dwelling, where I made my arrangements for following the Empress with my family on the following day. It had been agreed that King Joseph should proceed to the outposts to acquaint himself personally with the situation of the Marshals Marmont and Mortier, and that the Empress should await his return before taking her departure.

The departure had been fixed for the morrow, March 29, at eight o'clock in the morning. The carriages with the horses put to were waiting in the Carrousel courtyard. The Empress, dressed and ready to go, had been in her apartments with her son and the ladies in waiting, since seven in the morning. Distracted and with her mind full of sorrowful presentiments, she evaded the questions of her son, whose happy carelessness was disturbed by this unusual movement. Already at break of day the drawing-rooms had filled with the people who had been appointed to follow the sovereign. A painful silence had succeeded the noisy conversations which had at first been exchanged on the subject of what was the object of general solicitude, but the anxiety was none the less great. A sudden noise, the opening of a door, was sufficient to agitate everybody present. We were expecting to see King Joseph, who had proceeded to the gates of Paris before daybreak, or at least somebody sent by him. Suddenly the officers of the national guard on service at the Tuileries, together with other officers entered precipitously, and gaining access to the Empress implored her not to leave Paris, and promised to defend her. Marie Louise, touched to tears by their devotion, told them of the Emperor's orders. She however delayed her departure, hour by hour, and sought to gain time, feeling that her departure would be a public disaster; she hoped without daring to admit it that some fortuitous occurrence would prevent it. Clarke, the Minister of War, who the previous evening had insisted on the necessity of the Empress's departure, had sent an officer in the morning to point out to the Empress how urgent it was that she should start. Pressed by some to hasten away, and by others on the contrary to remain, Marie Louise was a prey to extreme agitation. She once reentered her bedroom, threw her hat on the bed in a temper, and sat down on an easy-chair. There, resting her head on her hands, she began to cry. In the midst of her complaints broken with tears, she was heard to repeat with impatience: "My God, let them make up their minds and put an end to this agony." At last towards ten o'clock, the Minister of War sent word to her that there was not a moment to lose, and that if she tarried any longer she would expose herself to falling into the hands of the Cossacks.

The Empress, receiving no message from King Joseph, then decided to leave. When the time had come to enter the carriages, the young King of Rome refused to leave his apartment. The poor child seemed to guess what the future reserved for him. "Don't go to Rambouillet," he cried out to his mother, "it's a nasty palace; let us stop here!" He struggled in the arms of M. de Canisy, the equerry who was carrying him, saying: "I don't want to leave my house"—such was the expression that he kept repeating—"I don't want to go away, since papa is absent it is I who am the master." He clung to the doors and to the balustrade on the staircase. This obstinacy on his part excited a painful astonishment in the minds of all who witnessed this sorrowful scene, and awoke I know not what sad and gloomy presentiments.

The carriages drove out slowly, and as though a counter-order was hoped for, by the Pont-Royal gate. Ten heavy green berlines, with the imperial arms painted on the panels of the doors, a crowd of carriages, baggages and vans formed a line which stretched right across the courtyard. Sixty or eighty sightseers contemplated this sorrowful procession in gloomy silence, as though they had been looking at a funeral procession; they were indeed present at the funeral of the Empire. Their feelings were manifested in no way; not a voice raised itself to salute with an expression of regret the bitterness of this cruel separation. If somebody had had the inspiration to cut the traces of the carriages, the Empress would not have left, she passed out through the gateway of the Tuileries courtyard, with tears in her eyes and death in her soul. On arriving at the Champs Élysées, she saluted the Imperial city which she was leaving behind for a last time and bade it farewell forever.

The danger which threatened the capital had aroused great agitation in Paris. The general alarm had been beaten all night, the national guard was assembling at full speed. Some battalions of volunteers, with some artillery served by the brave scholars of the Polytechnic School, who paid their debt to the country before their time, marched out to support the corps of Marshals Dukes de Raguse and de Trévise. Others collected at the barriers of Paris to defend the entrance to the city. All emulated in zeal, and harmed the enemy sufficiently to oblige it to call up its reserve forces. The population of the faubourg was filled with ardor and clamored for arms, but arms and ammunition were alike wanting. The news of the transfer of the government of the Regency to the provinces took Paris by surprise in the midst of this agitation. The hatred of the foreigners and the imminence of the danger to which the city was exposed prevented the disorders which the absence of the government and of all force able to repress them would have occasioned.

On March 29, at daybreak, a regiment of the Prussian vanguard, the scouts of Europe under arms, appeared under the walls of the capital of France, which a handful of its brave children attempted though in vain to defend against too numerous enemies. The Emperor and the bulk of his army were far away; no news had been received of them since nine days. The city of Paris would have needed on such a day a Camillus or the heroism of a senate, like the senate whose majesty Brennus, long ago, was able to contemplate in the Capitol.

In the meanwhile King Joseph was with the Ministers of War, of the Administration of War and of Marine, outside the barriers; it was there that they learned from the engineer of the Paris fire-brigade who had been made a prisoner in the morning, that almost the entire allied forces were under the walls of Paris. This officer, after having been conducted before the Emperor of Russia, the King of Prussia and Prince Schwarzenberg had been sent back to the outposts; he had reported what he had seen to Marshal Marmont, who had sent him on to King Joseph.

It was not long moreover before the Duke of Raguse warned the prince of the danger of his position, which would not allow him to resist more than a few hours; he asked to be allowed to conclude an arrangement with the enemy, the French troops not being in a position to prevent the occupation by force, an occupation with which Paris was perhaps menaced during the night. King Joseph and the ministers recognized that resistance was impossible and that Paris was exposed to be carried, so to speak, by storm. General Hulin was sent to Marshal Marmont with authority to treat, for the urgency of the matter began to be felt. Indeed the columns of the enemy were already appearing in the plain and began to overwhelm the feeble forces of the two marshals; they were maneuvering in the direction of St. Denis, approaching the bridges of which they took possession, only a few minutes after King Joseph and the ministers had crossed them. The latter had nothing left for them to do than to follow the Empress and the Regency council in conformity with their instructions.

King Joseph had promised the citizens of Paris to remain with them. He had kept his promise. His place was not within the city walls, but at the gates where the danger lay. While there was the faintest hope of defending Paris he did not give up the struggle. When after a heroic resistance Marshals Mortier and Marmont declared that they could hold out no longer it became the King's duty to save the capital from the horrors of an occupation by force; he authorized the Marshals to treat. His presence in Paris could be of no use whatever after the departure of the Empress and the King of Rome. He had done to prevent this departure what his conscience and his honor allowed him to do; he had shown himself a good citizen as well as the Emperor's devoted brother. If King Joseph had remained any longer in Paris what just reproaches would he not have merited from his contemporaries and from history! He would have remained there, but to become in the hands of the allied powers, the instrument of his brother's dethronement, an odious rôle which he could not have escaped, and which would have been imposed upon him by his desire to defend the interests of his nephew.

In one word, as long as Joseph Bonaparte preserved the hope of being of any use, he remained; when this hope vanished, he departed, but he departed the last of all.

Chapter XV

The Empress Marie Louise, who had left the Tuileries on March 29, towards midday, was sadly making her way towards Rambouillet. We had a vague idea that we might stop at this palace, although this hope was not authorized by any plausible motive. The suite of the fugitive sovereign was composed of the Duchess of Montebello, lady of honor, Countess de Luçay, mistress of the wardrobe, Mesdames de Castiglione, Brignole arid Montalivet, ladies of the palace, Count Beauharnais, knight of honor, MM. de Gontaut and d'Haussonville, chamberlains, Prince Aldobrandini, first equerry, MM. d'Héricy and Lambertye, equerries, de Cussy and Bausset, prefects of the palace, de Seyssel, master of ceremonies, de Guerchy, quartermaster of the palace, and finally MM. Corvisart, Bourdier, Lacourner and Royer who formed the medical staff in attendance. The King of Rome was accompanied by Countess de Montesquiou, his governess, Mesdames de Bourbers and Mesgrigny, under-governesses, M. de Canisy, equerry, and by M. Auvity, doctor. The Prince Archchancellor and the great officers of the crown who happened to be in Paris followed the Empress. An escort of about twelve hundred men, composed of grenadiers, chasseurs, dragoons and lancers of the Imperial guard and picked gendarmes, accompanied the carriages.

The Empress arrived at Rambouillet on the same day—March 29—and left it on the morrow to sleep at Chartres, without having received any news from Paris. The prefect was absent. Marie Louise passed the night at the prefect's house; she was very impatient to receive news of the Emperor. Kings Joseph and Jérôme with their Queens, the Ministers of War, of the Administration of War and of Marine arrived in Chartres during the night, they had all left Paris at five o'clock in the evening. There was no direct news from Napoleon except that it was heard that General Dejean, one of his aides-de-camp, had arrived, sent by him, to announce his march on Paris. We also heard of the proposals which had been made to the Emperor of Austria—proposals which seemed of a nature to remove every obstacle towards the conclusion of peace. To conform himself to the instructions notified by General Dejean to Marshal Mortier, this marshal had sent to Prince Schwarzenberg to ask for a truce, basing himself on the fact that negotiations had been commenced with the Emperor of Austria, but the Austrian commander-in-chief had answered that he had no knowledge of this fact and had refused the suspension of arms, having already concluded with Marshal Marmont a covenant for the surrender of Paris. We also heard that the Prefect of the Seine and the Prefect of Police had alone remained in the capital. Prince de Bénévent, desirous of being prepared for any event, had asked the Minister of Police for authorization to remain in Paris, on the pretext that he might be useful there. Although it could easily be seen what part he was playing, the authorities were no longer powerful enough to force him to follow the government to Blois. He was accordingly told that there were no orders to be given him. This opinion not shielding him sufficiently to his way of thinking, M. de Talleyrand wishing to make everything straight, left his hotel with a certain amount of display and pretended to be on his way to join the Empress, but took care to get himself arrested at the gates of Paris. Having thus put appearances on his side, Prince de Bénévent returned home to await events. Queen Hortense had returned to Navarre with the Empress Josephine.

Such was the news we received at Chartres. Our original intention was to travel to Tours, but in Vendôme the Empress received a letter from the Emperor which was forwarded by King Joseph. In this letter Napoleon announced his arrival at Cour-de-France, on March 30, where he had heard the news of the capitulation of Paris. This letter contained the order that the Empress was to go to Blois. At the same time we heard in Vendôme that the allied troops with the Emperor of Russia and the King of Prussia at their head had just entered Paris, and that Prince de Bénévent was presiding at the senate. The Empress arrived in the evening of April 2 at Blois, and was received by the Prefect, Baron Christiani. She established herself at the Prefecture mansion. It was there that the ministers and various councilors of state, who had already proceeded to Tours, joined the Empress. This Princess stayed at Blois until April 8, and it was here that we learnt the succession of events which had happened in Paris since the departure of the Regency government.

Marshal Marmont taking advantage of the authorization which had been awarded him by King Joseph, had sent one of his officers to Prince Schwarzenberg to treat on the capitulation with the allies, and it was in virtue of this capitulation that the allied sovereigns, except the Emperor of Austria, had entered Paris on March 31, preceded by the Russian and Prussian corps. The Emperor Alexander personally had not much liking for the Bourbons. The King of Prussia had identified himself both in his language and attitude with the Emperor of Russia. Prince Schwarzenberg, in the absence of the Emperor of Austria and his principal minister, remained undecided. The Emperor Alexander had established himself at the Talleyrand Mansion in the Rue St. Florentine where he had been preceded by his minister Nesselrode. The Russian sovereign was there surrounded by people who persuaded him that the French nation entirely rejected Napoleon. The principal object of the discussions which were entered upon bore on the troubled question of knowing whether the Emperor should be retained, whether a regency should be declared, or whether the Bourbons should be recalled. Talleyrand, now already deeply compromised, seeing that the Emperor's cause was lost had thrown off the mask. Presenting Duke Dalberg, Abbés Louis and Pradt, General Dessoles, and some others as organs of public opinion he had decided the two Emperors to declare that the allies would no longer treat with Napoleon. Prince Schwarzenberg maintained a silence which caused some anxiety to Talleyrand and his accomplices. At last, not wishing to take upon himself the responsibility of a refusal, the Austrian commander-in-chief yielded and took the same commitment in the name of his sovereign. The renegade faction encouraged by this adhesion added to the declaration by which the allies forbade themselves to treat with the Emperor Napoleon the words: "Nor with any member of his family." If one could doubt that the Restoration was the work of the foreigners it would suffice to remember that the allied sovereigns would only permit the publication of the document which recalled Louis XVIII to the throne of France, when they found themselves free from all fear, and able to dispense with considerations of every kind by the desertion of the commander of the third corps.

Thus, as it has already been very justly pointed out, it was not the national wish nor the authority of the rights of legitimacy, nor the title of a family to the crown which reestablished the throne in the elder branch of the Bourbons, but it was the mere good will and pleasure of two foreign monarchs assisted by an Austrian general who without the nation's knowledge opened the doors of France to King Louis XVIII and set him on the throne. The declaration of the allies which Michaud, the printer, had waited for in an adjoining drawing room, had been printed and posted in Paris without loss of time. It remained to be decided what government should replace the government which these intrigues and this juggling had overthrown. A certain number of Royalists who had surrounded the Emperor Alexander from the moment of his arrival at Prince de Bénévent's house, implored him to give them back their old masters. The municipal council of Paris through the mouthpiece of its president, Bellart, had expressed a wish that the Bourbons might be recalled; the Emperor of Russia had not yet expressed his opinion. The Emperor Napoleon possessed in the person of the Duke of Vicence an advocate whose zeal and devotion no difficulty could cool. As to Prince de Bénévent, he had burnt his ships behind him. Unwilling and unable to remain behind he had convoked the senate. The result of the deliberations of this assembly had been the appointment of a government commission charged with the administration, and the drawing-up of a draft of the constitution. This Provisional government had Prince de Bénévent at its head as President, and as members General Beurnonville, Duke Dalberg, Senator Jaucourt, and Abbé Montesquiou. The General of Division, Beurnonville, surnamed the French Ajax in Dumouriez's army, and who was known by the exaggeration of one of his reports in which he related that the enemy had lost 10,000 men, and that the loss of the French consisted in the little finger of a chasseur, had been loaded with dignity and favors both in the army and in diplomacy by the Imperial government. General Beurnonville had left M. Lavalette very late in the evening of March 31. They had been deploring together the fatal events which had just occurred and had agreed to meet again on the morrow morning. On arriving at Beurnonville's house Lavalette heard that the general had been sent for during the night to Prince de Bénévent's, for what reason was explained to him by the list of members of the Provisional government. Talleyrand needed a general in the Provisional government, and had chosen his man well; General Beurnonville displayed the greatest zeal.

Duke Dalberg, of whom we have already had occasion to speak, nephew of the Prince Primate, at first ambassador of Baden in Paris, afterwards naturalized by the grace of Napoleon, created a Duke, Councilor of state, and married to Mlle. Brignole with an endowment of four million francs, was also reaping the reward of his perfidy towards the sovereign who had so generously adopted him. M. de Jaucourt had drawn attention to himself at the constitutional assembly and later on at the senate by the liberalism of his principles and by his honorable character. Taken up and protected by King Joseph, he had been drawn away by old remembrances, and by twenty-five years' relationship with M. de Talleyrand—a relationship which had never been interrupted even during the exile. The fifth member of the provisional government was Abbé, afterwards Duke, de Montesquiou, formerly agent general of the clergy and member of the national assembly where he defended the privileges of his order with apparent moderation and with energy. He had served the interests of the Bourbons under the Consulate and under the Empire with zeal, he had been the agent in 1800 in the application made by the Count de Lille to the First Consul. Exiled at first he obtained without difficulty and in spite of his suspicious conduct permission to return to Paris where he lived in obscurity until the occurrences of 1814. He was on good terms with the family of Count de Montesquiou, the Grand Chamberlain, who protected him with the Imperial government. Abbé de Montesquiou used sometimes to go and see the King of Rome's governess. During one of these visits he had begged his cousin to show him the Emperor without being seen. To oblige him Madame de Montesquiou placed him where he could see Napoleon crossing a gallery. The Abbé having looked at him with attention could not help murmuring between his teeth, yet loud enough for his cousin to hear him, "Will no one deliver us from this little man?" Madame de Montesquiou, rather disturbed by the perseverance of this hatred hidden under gentle and inoffensive appearances, treated her relation with the circumspection and prudence in the future.

Prince de Bénévent, whose greatest skill always consisted in turning events to his profit, and giving the last blow to the different governments who employed him, when fortune abandoned them, made use of a corporation which bore the title of conservative, to consummate the Emperor's ruin.

This corporation, to which Napoleon in his order of the day of April 4, addressed to the army, made such just and such killing reproaches, disposed of the government of France without having the authority to do so, and was careful not to forget in its draft of a constitution, to stipulate for the permanent enjoyment of its salaries, and the privileges which it had received from the Emperor himself. The legislative body adhered to all the acts of the senate. A nucleus of deputies was got together to represent this assembly some way or other; it was completed later on. Whatever it may have done it was anticipated and excelled in servility by the senate. A torrent of insults, libels, and calumnies of all sorts suddenly took the place of the demonstrations of respect, and the protestations of devotion towards the Emperor who only the day before had been incensed to the extent of adulation. Every feeling of decency and respect was from that time cast aside by the majority of the corporations of the state. To many intelligent and impartial minds Napoleon was at that time our only chance of safety. Those who not understanding this separated from him, had the right to abandon him when by patriotism he abandoned himself, but to lose all dignity in this common misfortune, to throw themselves at the feet of foreigners, to give a display of total want of decency in desertion, to insult the genius who had been smitten by adversity, these are things which we regret to have seen, and which will long live amongst us in sorrowful remembrance. The national character will not be stained by these things because it can be rightly said that this deplorable error was the error only of some individuals, and that unlike them the nation did not insult nor repudiate the master when the day of misfortune came upon him.

In considering with greater coolness the desertions which took place at this painful time one sees there a new example of the inevitable effect of reactions which is to raise up around a man who has held great power and who has fallen, traducers of every kind. It is not from contemporaries who are always actuated by more or less vivacious passions that one can expect an impartial judgment. In their eyes the greatness of the genius and of the character of the man who has presided over important events which they witnessed has always a contestable greatness; and even those who have taken no part in these events are infinitely more prone than others to severity and to criticism. Most of the persons to whom I am alluding yoked themselves to the chariot of a new master, trampling beneath their feet the idol whom they had so long incensed, in order to preserve the estates, the honors, and the advantages with which the Imperial government had loaded them. For these turncoats of honor, Napoleon's unpardonable crime was to have lost together with his power all means of exercising his generosity in their favor. There are some people who do not forgive a reproach which they have merited, or who think they have not been sufficiently recompensed for their services. Certain generals, certain administrators, in whom the old jealousies of the army of the Rhine fermented, or who regretted the favors of those who had formerly been in power; certain others who were imbued with republican or indeed Royalist opinions gave vent at the sight of the fallen Colossus to hostile sentiments which till then they had very carefully kept down in the remotest recesses of their hearts. Napoleon would not admit that any obstacles were insurmountable; he would not accept the excuses of those who pleaded such obstacles in justification of their failure. This incredulity on his part was only feigned, but he considered it useful and even necessary to keep alive what he used to call the sacred fire amongst those whom he used for objects which audacity alone could attain. Those only saw in his conduct a gratuitous injustice, forgetting that in face of the resistances which crossed his plans Napoleon would have wished to have effaced the word "impossible" from the French dictionary. At the same time if he placed his confidence in those whose assertions he distinctly contradicted, this proved to them that they had not deserved ill in his eyes and that he on his side did not cease to appreciate their talents and their fidelity. The Emperor indeed took into account as occasion might be all the good will which had been displayed in his service, but the reward of the moment, the tacit reparation accorded by Napoleon did not efface in the eyes of some the injustice of the reproaches to which they had formerly been exposed. There may still be met today men who have kept up these old grudges, probably finding in these childish sufferings of their vanity a plausible excuse for their desertion.

A certain number of persons bore Napoleon a grudge for not having appreciated the wisdom of their advice, and for having opposed their calculations, and crossed their views for the future in the accomplishment of his designs. Others no doubt with more susceptible but not more equitable feeling remembered that their demonstrations of devotion had not always been received with the show of sympathy proportionate to the outward signs of their assiduity. Those however ought to recognize the fact—they suffered no harm thereby—that the mind unconsciously possesses mysterious instincts which attract or repel, but which in no way bring about any alteration in point of esteem and confidence. Do not their tardy complaints on this head tend to prove that their devotion was not really very sincere?

The Emperor's disapproval of certain alliances which had been contracted by people whom he liked, with families who were rich but not respected, excited the resentment of those who had contracted these marriages. But he was prompted by the fear lest the respectability of the corporations to which they belonged might in some way be attained.

If promotion for certain people was not as rapid as they might have hoped, instead of attributing this to want of opportunities they blamed the Emperor for having treated them unjustly. It would however be difficult to mention genuine examples of real services or of acknowledged talents which were neglected by Napoleon, even in the case of men whom he had authorized to consider his enemies. No considerations of a man's opinions, nor of wrongs he might have committed against him, ever made him deviate from his rule of leaving no kind of merit without employment, that is to say, without reward.

A longer enumeration of the causes which raised up enemies for Napoleon amongst those who served him, would be superfluous. When in order to rescue France from the tyrannical pretensions of England, and to replace her in the rank whence the successive aggrandizements of her neighbors tended to bring her down, Napoleon charged himself with labors, with privations, with dangers of every kind; when he renounced all the pleasures of life and disdained that material comfort, which even the loftiest minds sometimes need; when he exposed himself to temporary unpopularity in order to assure the success of plans fertile in great future results, the secrets thereof being alone known to him—he had a right to exact the same sacrifices from those whom he employed. If he was exacting he was more so towards himself than towards others.

I have pointed out the wrongs committed by such of Napoleon's antagonists as I may call his domestic enemies. I will not undertake to define the numerous varieties of adversaries to whose passions and feelings the fall of the Imperial government gave a free field. The principal head of indictment in which they unite against the Emperor is that after the splendid victories which he gained over the coalition he did not relax the springs of his dictatorial government. They will not recognize the understanding which existed amongst our enemies, nor the persevering system of hostilities of that coalition whose immense resources enabled it to repair its losses and unceasingly recommence the struggle. It was not while in the face of numerous active enemies constantly springing up afresh that Napoleon could indulge in such experiments as the extension of political liberties. These reproaches springing from bad faith, from ignorance, or from want of sense, we have seen them serving the hatred and the implacable rancor of the foreign powers, associating themselves with the interested passions of the princes and courtiers following in their train.

And this concert of complaints and recriminations which are but little justifiable has created a current of opinion hostile to the Emperor, in accrediting calumnies with which for a long time the present generation has been duped in France as well as abroad. The contagion of these feelings of opposition to the unhappy Emperor had not spared the majority of the leaders of the army. Instead of answering Napoleon's vibrating appeal, they forced him to abdicate. The Emperor had consented to this sacrifice in order to protect the rights of his son. The Duke of Vicence to whom the Emperor added the Duke of Raguse and the Prince de la Moskova, and in the absence of the former, Duke of Tarente, were charged by Napoleon to carry this document to the allied sovereigns. But Marmont, on whose attachment he thought he could rely in days of adversity, urged on by the fatality which seemed to weigh upon his name, abandoned the French eagles at this moment. M. Laffitte, pressed by the firm of Lassabathie of Bordeaux to make the Duke of Raguse's family act upon him had persuaded the Marshal's brother-in-law a few days before to go to him so that he might point out to him the uselessness of any further resistance. This seed of insubordination fell on a soil which was not prepared at that time to receive it, but it later on bore fruits.

Marshal Marmont's desertion was a mortal blow to the Imperial cause. It decided the Emperor Alexander, who till then had appeared to hesitate on the question of a regency, to exact in the name of the allied powers the unconditional abdication of the Emperor. This notification was handed to the French Imperial plenipotentiaries in the night of April 4. On the 6th a document, by which Louis XVIII was recalled to the throne of France, was published in Paris.

The unexpected return of the Bourbons to France after an exile of twenty-five years, naturally makes one think of the vicissitudes which this prince experienced during that long period. Louis XVIII who was at that time known by the name of Count de Lille had at first gone to Mittau in the month of March, 1798, on the invitation which had been made to him by Czar Paul I, out of hatred for the French revolution. But his sentiments for Louis XVIII changing completely, he very roughly sent him a command to leave Russian territory. The Emperor Alexander having broken off with France reestablished only four years after this expulsion the pension of 200,000 roubles which his father had granted to Count de Lille, and invited this Prince to return to Mittau. At the time of the conclusion of the Tilsitt peace, Count de Lille left Mittau suddenly; the variations of Russian politics were during ten years the thermometer of the favor or the disfavor in which the head of the house of Bourbon was held. Count de Lille had left Mittau without having been asked to do so by Alexander, but the Czar in transmitting to the Emperor Napoleon the news of the Prince's departure, informed him at the same time that he did not know what had prompted it. Napoleon sent word to Alexander that he attached very little importance to the Pretender's movements, and that he would very gladly give him Versailles to live in if Count de Lille cared to come to France. The future King of France afterwards went and established himself in England, but did not receive the authorization to reside in London. He afterwards went to settle himself at Hartwell, where he hired the mansion and remained there until 1814 at the time when he returned to France.

Count d'Artois, who afterwards became Charles X, had left French territory in 1789. He resided in turn in Turin and in Mantua, where he had an interview with the Emperor Leopold. After numerous peregrinations in Germany, to London, and to Edinburgh, this prince traveled to St. Petersburg, where the Empress presented him with a useless sword. On his return from Russia, Count d'Artois showed himself on the coasts of Brittany and even landed in the Ile Dieu. In 1813, he was in Germany and in 1814, in Bâle, whence he returned to France by way of the Franche-Comté, with the title of lieutenant-general of the kingdom.

Apart from their intelligences with the foreign powers, Louis XVI's brothers never ceased, from the time of their exile, to keep agents in Paris and to make overtures, through these agents, to members of the Convention or the Directoire, to high civil functionaries or to generals.

The immense popularity which Pichegru had enjoyed in France, after the conquest of Holland, drew the attention of the royalists upon him. Since 1795, relations had been established between this general, the Prince de Condé, and other Bourbon agents. The reward of services at first clandestine, intended afterwards to become public, which had been or were to be rendered by Pichegru to the royalist cause was to be the governorship of Alsace, a million in money, two hundred thousand francs a year, the Arbois estate, which was to bear the name of Pichegru, twelve cannon, the grand cordon of the orders of the Holy Ghost and of Saint Louis, and finally the dignity of Marshal of France. The importance of the price was proportioned to the greatness of the treason.

The part intended for Barras was less magnificent. In the month of April, 1799, the Marquis de Maisonfort proposed the assistance of this Director to the Count de Lille. In the month of July following, Barras received letters patent signed by the King and countersigned by M. de Saint-Priest, sealed with the Great Seal, which after assuring him of amnesty, awarded him twelve million francs for himself and two million francs for his collaborators. This was four months before Brumaire the 18th. This secret covenant was not known to Napoleon who heard of it from Consul Le Brun to whom Abbé Montesquiou had revealed it.

On June 9, 1796, the Count de Lille had authorized Pichegru to approach certain influential generals in the army in Italy. M. Rocques de Montgaillard was also charged, shortly before Fructidor 18th, to offer General Bonaparte the vice-royalty of Corsica, the post of Marshal of France and the blue cordon; but this agent was unable to fulfill his mission and could not reach General Bonaparte.

The silence which General Moreau observed during six months on the seizure of General Kinglin's vans, in which Moreau had found the correspondence of Pichegru with the Prince of Condé, this silence, we say, has seemed to some a proof of Moreau's interested complicity in the royalist conspiracy. However, half a century has passed since that event took place, and as no fresh revelations have been made on the subject, it remains established that Moreau was not mixed up in Pichegru's machinations.

With regard to the Pretender's alleged relations with the revolutionary party, history may perhaps disclose these someday; but up to the present time it has been impossible to obtain other than obscure and incomplete information on this point.

Apart from the letters which the Count de Lille wrote to the First Consul and the applications made in his name by Vendéen and other chiefs, the Count d'Artois, faithful to his habits of gallantry, had entrusted the beautiful Duchess of Guiche with a mission of seduction at the court of the First Consul. Believing Josephine to have an inclination towards royalist ideas and an influence over Napoleon which she did not possess, the future King Charles X had caused the most magnificent assurances of the gratitude of the Bourbons to be made to her through Madame de Guiche if the First Consul should consent to favor their reestablishment. Josephine had received the duchess with affability, and had even asked her to lunch; but she also very politely refused her offers. The answer which the First Consul made to the proposal that there should be erected on the Place du Carrousel, a column surmounted with his statue crowning the Bourbons, is well known. "My tomb," he said, "will serve as pedestal to this statue."

The emissaries of the two brothers often arrived with contradictory instructions. The Count de Lille feigned to lend himself to ideas of constitutional monarchy, of amnesty and of amicable arrangement with the persons who had bought national property. Count d'Artois spoke of nothing but absolute monarchy and revenge. These princes were assisted by Russia and by England.

A fact worthy of mention is that the princes of the House of Orléans figured in no intrigue against their country, took no part in any league with foreigners, and placed themselves in the pay of no European powers. The only exception to this line of conduct which can be quoted is the relations between the head of the Orléans family and the Cadiz Regency in the month of May, 1810.

The abdication of the Emperor brought with it the proscription of the national colors which he had covered with glory and rendered the object of the respect of all the world. This great event was carried through with an ease which astonished the foreigners. One of the first acts of the new government, in its contempt for the national glory, had been to invite the Paris national guard to assume the white cockade. The leaders of the twelve legions had at first not seemed disposed to obey, but a week later, on a second order, the tricolor disappeared. This apparent resignation emboldened the provisional government to order that the white cockade and the white flag should in future be the cockade and flag of France. The army and the navy submitted to this humiliating necessity with a shudder, and bitter resentment was pressed down to the bottom of the hearts of our officers and even of the private soldiers.

The allies were alarmed by the bombast and the pretensions of the royalists. They begged the new king to make use of the elements of the Revolution in governing and to give France a constitution. Nevertheless they looked upon the proscription of the national colors as a reason for security. These colors reminded them of things which they preferred to forget, and moreover they feared that unless the white flag were hoisted the whole country might rise to arms against their soldiers. Other foreigners, endowed with more foresight, feared on the contrary lest the proscribed colors might become a formidable rallying sign for the partisans of the fallen Emperor. The white cockade, which was forced upon France during fifteen years, the last symbol of the counter-revolution, could not survive the government which was overthrown by the Revolution of 1830. A national government reestablished on that day in France the tricolor, which had been adopted by the French nation, which will know no others after all the remembrances of triumphs and greatness of which the blue, white, and red flag had become the emblem.

After signing the abdication at Fontainebleau after his abandonment by his comrades-in-arms who were impatient to enjoy in peace the honors and riches which he had loaded them, Napoleon kept up an active correspondence with Marie Louise. Not a day passed without his sending her an officer, in spite of the fact that the road to Blois was intercepted by the enemy. Marie Louise sometimes expressed her regret at having left Paris and spoke of her wish to rejoin the Emperor. The obstacles which opposed themselves to the realization of this desire, the conflict of contradictory opinions expressed on the subject by those who surrounded her, made her postpone endeavoring to bring this meeting about, much as it was in her thoughts. Her anxiety had reached its highest pitch; the violent emotions which she had undergone, the tears which she was constantly shedding, her painful sleeplessness had cast her into a state of nervousness which nearly approached a convulsive state. She could not imagine what passions were agitating France. The assurances which she had received from her father constantly reverted to her mind; she could not persuade herself that the Emperor of Austria would sacrifice her husband and her son. At the same time the events which hastened on in Paris left her with few illusions; she was confounded; but like a drowning woman she clung to the paternal affection which seemed to her her only means of safety. Hearing that the Emperor of Austria was not in Paris, she hoped that he would not consent to what had been done in his absence and that her voice would be listened to; she sent him the Duke of Cadore with a pressing letter. The Duke of Cadore, former ambassador of France to Vienna, had been treated with the greatest kindness by the Emperor Francis who had deigned to be the godfather of one of his children. He left Blois on April 6, and was replaced by M. de Montalivet in the post of secretary of state to the Regency. On the morrow, Count Regnault de Saint-Jean d'Angély was sent on the same mission; on the 8th, MM. de St. Aulaire and Bausset left charged with fresh letters from the Empress to the Emperor of Austria. The Empress's stay in Blois alternated between fears and hopes, in the expectation of what Napoleon should decide to do, and especially in the expectation of the turn of events; it was not marked by any important act of government. The Empress presided at Regency councils every day, the object of which was rather to communicate the news that had been received and to exchange opinions than to attend to business; he who put all things in motion was there no more. As nobody could foresee what any day might bring forth, the ministers used to come to the Empress's house in their traveling suits. The only act which emanated from the government in its retreat in Blois was a proclamation to the French, which, so to speak, attracted no attention whatever.

The Emperor's brothers Joseph and Jérôme, as well as the Archchancellor made an application to the Empress on the morning of April 8, which has given rise to erroneous interpretations. The Regent's counselors had fears, for which there was good foundation, for the safety of Napoleon's wife and child; and it was with this in their minds that they came to point out to the Empress that it was necessary for her to leave Blois to proceed with the young prince over the Loire and to transport the seat of the government thither. Marie Louise, tired of the hazards of a wandering life, remained immovable in the resolution of not going further away; in spite of the vivacity with which Jérôme explained the reasons why he insisted on the matter, the princess would not yield. The officers of her suite, General Caffarelli at the head of them, thinking wrongly that violence was being done to Napoleon's wife, interfered in her favor in a somewhat tumultuous manner. Three hours later a Russian commissioner arrived to secure the persons of the Empress and of her son.

Count Schouvalov arrived in Blois at two o'clock in the afternoon. This commissioner of the allied powers, aide-de-camp of the Emperor of Russia, was accompanied by Baron de Saint-Aignan, equerry of the Emperor Napoleon and brother-in-law of the Duke of Vicence; he communicated the object of his mission, which was to conduct the Empress and her son to Orléans. General Schouvalov's arrival gave the signal for the departure of the principal persons who had accompanied the Empress. Each went to fetch his passports at the mairie to have them viséed by the Russian officer, whose lodgings were filled with people all day long. The majority of the ministers and councilors of state left for Paris. I saw the Minister of War the Duke of Feltre—Clarke—who with the smile which he always wore told me that he had come to take farewell of his old colleague—he had been secretary to the cabinet—and to hand him a letter which he had written to the Emperor to take leave of him. He added that when one left people it ought to be done politely; that he had to give an account of the state of the war-archives, the depot of maps and so on; that he did not want to be considered a thief.

From that moment forward it was put out of the Empress's power to join the Emperor. Whatever illusion she may have wished to retain on this point, the separation of the two spouses was decided. If the assurances since given by the Austrian ministers, and by the Emperor Francis himself, that she would be left to inhabit the Island of Elba or her new States, or to divide her residence between Parma and the Island of Elba, were sincere, it was no longer in their power to keep their promises as had to be admitted later on.

On April 9, very early in the morning, I went to the Empress's house. I found her up and rather nervous as to how the journey would pass off. She sent for the crown jewels, which she did not very well know what to do with. Knowing that she would have to pass through posts of Cossacks and be escorted by foreign troops, she feared lest her carriages might be looted; she thought of carrying the various parures into which these jewels had been made, upon her person, never doubting that her person would be respected. There remained the imperial sword on the hilt of which the Regent diamond had been mounted, and the blade of which was in the way. Unable to take anybody into my confidence, I was reduced to separate this blade from its handle by myself. As I had no tool at my disposal fit for such work, I had the idea of placing the blade under one of the firedogs in the fireplace of the Empress's apartment, and to my great satisfaction, I discovered that it was made of brass; so that I had little trouble in breaking it. I hid the hilt under my clothes, and I proceeded to my carriage through the hindrances occasioned by the block of horses and carriages, not without trembling for the safety of my precious burthen. I had preserved the family papers and other valuable documents which the Emperor had ordered me to carry away from the Tuileries, at the moment of our departure, to destroy them if they ran any risk of being seized or lost, till then; I now thought that the latter circumstance had arrived and threw them into the fire.

I think it necessary to say that amongst these papers there were not the letters addressed by foreign sovereigns to Napoleon; had they formed part of this collection, we should know definitely what became of these curious documents, over the fate of which there has till now reigned an impenetrable obscurity.

All the searches which were carried out by the Emperor's orders, for these papers, by King Joseph, the Duke of Bassano, and myself remained without, result.

After having been stolen from the Count de Survilliers—the name which King Joseph had taken—in the portmanteaux sent from Paris to Point Breeze near New York, they are said to have fallen, according to the statement of Doctor O'Meara, into the hands of Murray, an English publisher in London. M. de Liéven, the Russian ambassador to England, it is said, bought back his sovereign's letters for the sum of ten thousand pounds.

As far as I can remember, the letters of this important collection which possessed the greatest interest, had been written by the Emperor Alexander. Those written by the Spanish, Bavarian and Würtemberg princes and some of those written by Prussia were also of a nature to excite curiosity, inasmuch as they were historical documents. The rest of the collection, so far as my memory serves me, was not of the same interest; however, as copies had been taken of them by the Emperor's orders, it is possible that this correspondence will appear one day.

At ten o'clock in the morning after having received Count Schouvalov, the Empress, accompanied by her son and the princes and princesses of the imperial family, left Blois on her way to Orléans. At Beaugency the Cossacks stopped the last carriages of her suite and looted them, but at General Schouvalov's command everything that had been taken was restored. Maris Louise arrived in Orléans at six in the evening and was received on her entry into the city by the civil and military authorities. The national guard and the garrison formed in line along her way up to the bishop's palace, where she alighted. These troops hailed her arrival with cries of "Long live the Emperor" and "Long live the Empress."

During the night which followed on our arrival at Orléans I received a ciphered letter, which had been dictated by the Emperor on April 8. This letter had been after me to Blois and had been forwarded on to Orléans; it filled me with grief and consternation. It had been written in a moment of discouragement and bore the impress of deep sorrow. The substance of this letter was: that it had been agreed with the Emperor of Austria that the crown should pass to the King of Rome under the Regency of the Empress; that M. de Metternich was charged to formulate this covenant; that in this state of affairs it was necessary that the Empress should always be acquainted with the whereabouts of the Emperor of Austria, to have recourse to his protection, and that everything was to be looked for, *even the Emperor's death.* I was ordered to burn this letter after having read it and to make what use of its contents I should think fit. I burned the letter in conformity with a behest which I was tempted to consider as the expression of a dying will. I was so disturbed by this fatal confidence that I thought it right to inform the Duchess of Montebello, who enjoyed the Empress's greatest confidence, and who by reason of her position was best able to keep up her courage and to comfort her if the misfortune which I feared were to come upon her; I then waited for news from Fontainebleau in terrible anxiety. The Empress had anticipated the wish expressed by the Emperor that she should keep herself in communication with her father in sending the Duke of Cadore, and MM. Regnault de Saint-Jean d'Angély, de Bausset, and de Saint-Aulaire, one after the other to the Emperor of Austria.

Since the withdrawal of the ministers and the great officers of the crown the Emperor had no intermediary between the Empress and himself; I was the only person remaining with the Empress whom he was accustomed to confide in. An exchange of letters was then established between the Emperor and myself, through the agency of my colleague, Baron Fain, until the moment of his departure from Fontainebleau, and after his departure through the agency of General Bertrand. M. Fain took care to inform me that every letter that he wrote to me had been dictated to him from the first word to the last. I received one letter and sometimes two, sent off at different hours, every day. I will not transcribe these letters textually; I will only copy the passages which can throw a light on events and reveal the thoughts which occupied the Emperor's mind and his solicitude for the Empress.

To the letter of April 9 was annexed the armistice concluded with Prince Schwarzenberg by the commissioners invested with full powers by the Emperor, the Marshals, Prince de la Moskova, the Duke of Tarente and the Duke of Vicence. In virtue of this armistice of forty-eight hours, preliminary of the negotiations, a line of demarcation was drawn, starting from the sea and following the limits which separated the departments of the Somme, the Oise, Seine-et-Oise, Seine-et-Marne, the Yonne, the Côte d'Or, Saône-et-Loire, Rhône, Seine-Inférieure, Eure, Eure-et-Loire, Loiret, Nièvre, Allier, and Loire. Thence this line followed the frontier of the Isère department up to Mont-Cenis. In the department of Seine-et-Marne the line of demarcation followed the bed of the Seine, the right banks of which were occupied by the allied troops and the left banks by the French.

Since the opening of the negotiations which had been entered upon by Napoleon's three plenipotentiaries with the allies, Prince Schwarzenberg, in spite of the friendly disposition which the Emperor of Austria had manifested towards his daughter, opposed that Tuscany, which had been asked for Marie Louise by Napoleon, should be granted to her. A certain latitude was left to the Emperor to select his personal residence, but he preferred the Island of Elba to any other arrangement.

Another letter of the 9th, addressed to me, informed me that Napoleon

"was expecting news from Paris before deciding about his journey; that he wished to join the Empress near Gien; that he supposed that *Madame* (his mother) and his brothers were already on their way to Provence ....

"He wished to know whether the Empress was traveling by stagecoach or with her own horses."

Passing on to subjects personal to me,

"he supposed that it was my intention to follow the Empress wherever she might go; he said that he considered that warm climates were favorable to my health; that my wife and children could follow me there; that in taking a step which was in conformity with my sentiments, I could also be useful to the Emperor; that his greatest sorrow was to think of the troubles which the Empress was undergoing and the harm that they must do to her health."

A letter written on the evening of the 10th, stated that, according to letters received by the Emperor, the Empress seemed disposed to go and see her father:

"But," he added, "does she know where her father is? It was reported yesterday that he must be at Brie-Comte-Robert, and would arrive in Paris today; all these reports are very vague. If you have any more positive information, acquaint us with it. The Emperor expects the Duke of Vicence this evening, who will bring him some definite decision on his affairs. The Emperor wishes you to find out what are the Empress's real intentions and to know whether she prefers to follow the Emperor in all the hazards of this evil fortune or to retire, either into a state which will be given to her, or to her father's palace with her son. The Emperor would also like you to inform yourself what each of the Empress's or King of Rome's 'red' ladies wishes to do . . . Try and find out also what each of the Emperor's three brothers wishes to do; of course this communication will be in confidence."

I answered that I feared that the Empress was no longer at liberty to join the Emperor; that I thought that personally she wished to do so but that she still trusted in her father's affection who, as she used to say, would not allow her to be separated from her husband and from her son; that she authorized herself by the wish expressed by the Emperor to await the effect of the applications which she had made to the Emperor of Austria. I added that the fear of being arrested on her way might keep her back, and that the idea of flight was repugnant to her.

In a later letter of the same day the Emperor asks me to send him news as to the

Empress's health. He would like to have Doctor Corvisart's opinion on this subject.

In a letter dated the 11th, at four o'clock in the morning, Napoleon sent me word:

"that M. de Metternich has arrived in Paris but does not seem better disposed than M. de Schwarzenberg; that the Empress's plan of going to see her father still seems advisable; that however it is not yet known in Paris where the Emperor of Austria may be, that if the Empress knows it, he would like her to tell him before setting out on her journey."

In a letter sent off at noon the same day the Emperor informs me of what follows:

"It appears that arrangements were signed this night between the Duke of Vicence and the ambassadors of Russia, Austria, and England; that the island of Elba is given to the Emperor; Piacenza, Parma and Guastalla to the Empress and the King of Rome. It would be well however for the Empress to continue pressing her father for Tuscany, and if that be impossible at least to obtain in addition to Parma and Piacenza the territories of Lucca, Piombino, Massa di Carrara, and the Pontremoli enclosures; by this means the Empress would be in communication with the island of Elba . . .

"The Emperor's plan would be to proceed to Briare, as soon as his affairs are settled, the Empress to join him there, so as to continue their journey by Nevers, Moulins and Mont-Cenis as far as Parma. The Empress and the King of Rome might rest at Parma, while the Emperor would go on to the island of Elba to prepare everything necessary for the Empress's arrival. It is stipulated in the treaty that every Frenchman who shall follow him shall preserve his rights as a Frenchman and his estates, and will be at liberty to return to France . . . ."

He also spoke in this letter of replacing Madame de Montesquiou as governess to his son, for he had heard that the Countess did not wish to leave Paris, though I do not know who told him so. The Emperor also strongly insisted in the same letter on the indispensable restitution of the crown jewels.

I communicated the substance of this letter to the Empress. She said that she would acquaint her father of the arrangements which were proposed in it. I sent word to the Emperor that the sword in the hilt of which the Regent diamond had been set, and all the diamonds of the crown, had been handed over to M. de Bouillerie, in conformity with his orders.

As regards Madame de Montesquiou and her alleged intention, I informed Napoleon that his son's governess had never expressed any intention of returning to Paris, and that on the contrary she charged me to inform him that whatever might happen, she was decided not to separate herself from her royal pupil, unless he was torn from her arms by force.

The Emperor had expressed the desire of seeing the Queen of Westphalia, born Princess of Würtemberg, remain in Paris in spite of what had happened, but nothing could determine this very model of conjugal devotion to live away from her husband.

Napoleon had hopes in King Jérôme, and it was just at the time when the maturity of his judgment was developing his natural qualities that fortune came to overthrow the edifice of which he was called to be one of the strongest supports. Jerôme seconded the Emperor with the ardor of absolute devotion in his days of adversity. He gave him the last proofs of this devotion during the short campaign of Waterloo, where he was the last to leave the field of battle after having accomplished prodigies of valor.

On the day of her arrival at Orléans (it was Easter Day) the Empress received the Duke of Cadore after mass, on his return from his mission to the Emperor of Austria whom he had only been able to join at Chanceaux, near Dijon. This prince had been dragged away with the fugitives in consequence of Napoleon's movement upon Saint-Dizier. He found himself there, separated from his army and from his minister.

The Empress was under the empire of the reflections which were suggested to her by Napoleon's advice to put herself in communication with her father. She was alarmed by precautionary measures which seemed to warn her that the protection under which she had been always sheltered was no longer as efficacious as in the past. The Emperor of Austria's letter, which was handed to her by the Duke of Cadore, in which this prince protesting his goodwill, expressed his fear that his allies might not share in his zeal for her interests, increased the Empress's anxieties. She had received so many sterile protestations that she had ceased to place any reliance upon them. Her reunion with the Emperor Napoleon depicted itself in her mind, troubled by so many emotions, as an imperative duty, and she reproached herself for having so long delayed in carrying it out.

Fleeing from counsels which were not in harmony with the thought which preoccupied her mind, she rushed one day out of her dressing-room, and half-dressed, crossed the terrace which separated her apartment from that of her son, and threw herself into the arms of Madame de Montesquiou whom she held in great esteem. Intrigues had always been busy at work to separate the Empress from this lady, whose rigid character and well-known inflexibility in the accomplishment of every virtue prompted her to remind Marie Louise of the duties which some people had at times endeavored to induce her to forget. The recollection of good advice given under important circumstances and an absolute confidence in her wisdom and the purity of her principles attracted her irresistibly towards Madame de Montesquiou. This lady had never any other thought than to remain faithful in adversity. The Empress strengthened herself under her influence in her resolution to go and join the Emperor at Fontainebleau. She then made serious preparations for her departure which was to take place as soon as she had received an answer to her letters to the Emperor of Austria, which had been carried by MM. de Bausset and Saint-Aulaire; she awaited the return of these gentlemen with great anxiety. They had been obliged to go as far as Paris, where they hoped the Emperor of Austria might at last have arrived.

During the day of April 11 a great part of the Empress's household, chamberlains, ladies in waiting, and equerries, came to take leave of the dethroned sovereign; this leave-taking could not but be very painful to her.

M. de Metternich, who had left the Emperor of Austria at Troyes only arrived in Paris on the morning of April 11. Lord Castlereagh had gone to meet him, and entering his stagecoach had informed the Emperor Francis's minister of what had been done during his absence and pressed him to agree to these things in the name of his master. Metternich's arrival was awaited by high persons and by all who were compromised in any degree in having contributed to the overthrow of the Imperial government. M. de Nesselrode, who happened to be in M. de Talleyrand's drawing room, which was the meeting-place of the deserters from the vanquished party and the admirers of the rising sun, left precipitously on hearing of the arrival from the Austrian minister, and returned two hours afterwards to Talleyrand's mansion. The high priest of this temple of perfidy, after having spoken for a moment with the Russian minister turned round to his friends, and with an expression of joy on his face, which was usually so impassive, said to them: "Gentlemen, the Emperor of Austria approves of what we have done."

In the meanwhile the Emperor Napoleon accompanied by some faithful servants and followed by 600 braves who attached themselves to his bad fortune was preparing to leave France with a sum of 3,400,000 francs. It is with these feeble resources that the man who had been master of Europe, who had disposed of the finances of the Empire and of the treasures which victory had poured into his hands, was about to gain the humble retreat which his enemies had not dared to refuse to the mighty vanquished. No idea of preparing a comfortable position for himself in case of adversity had ever entered Napoleon's mind; he had so completely identified himself with his country that on the day when he separated from France he deemed that he had no longer need of anything.

While Marie Louise was still in Orléans, M. Dudon, formerly *maître des requêtes* to the council of state, who thanks to the protection of the Archchancellor had been rapidly promoted, arrived there charged with a special mission. He had incurred Napoleon's disfavor for having abandoned his post in Spain. The Provisional government who considered the malcontents of the Imperial regime as excellent agents, commissioned M. Dudon to go and lay hands on the Emperor's treasure. At the same time in order to justify this iniquitous robbery the Provisional government pretended to have been informed that considerable sums of money had been removed from Paris before the occupation of this city by the allies—sums of money augmented by the pillage of the public municipal treasuries, the funds of the pawn-broking establishments, and even of the hospitals. The decree issued with this in view commanded all persons detaining these funds to immediately declare and pay them over to the municipal and general receivers of taxes, under penalty of being declared despoilers and as such being prosecuted according to the law both criminally and civilly. This decree, which was dated April 9, was signed by the five members of the Provisional government, Talleyrand, Dalberg, Francois de Jaucourt, Beurnonville, and Abbé de Montesquiou.

On arriving at Orléans where he knew that he would find the Imperial treasure, which was the object of the Provisional government's decree, M. Dudon betook himself to the house of Baron de la Bouillerie, Treasurer General of the Crown, who had nothing to do with any public funds; informed him of his quality as government commissioner, and had the books of the treasurer laid before him. He thence proceeded to the house of General Caffarelli, and notified to him the decree which confiscated the Emperor's treasures as being the product of a spoliation of the public funds. In spite of the protestations of this general and of the Duke of Cadore, who persisted in denying that the decree which was exhibited by M. Dudon was applicable to the Imperial treasure, which was purely the Emperor's private property, and the product of savings on his civil list, as was clearly established, M. Dudon, assisted by the officer of picked *gendarmes* who were entrusted with the guard of the treasure, removed the vans which contained it in the course of the evening. These vans were standing in the square and contained about 10,000,000 francs in gold and silver coins; 3,000,000 francs in silver and gilt plate; and about 400,000 francs worth of snuff-boxes and rings enriched with diamonds which were intended to be given as presents; the Imperial clothes, and ornaments which were covered with gold embroidery; and even the Emperor's pocket-handkerchiefs which were marked with an N, and the Imperial crown. The Russian General Schouvalov, who was appealed to to interfere, in no way opposed the execution of so revolting a deed.

On the morrow—April 13—General Cambronne arrived in Orléans with two battalions of the guard. The Emperor hearing that one of the reasons which might prevent Marie Louise from coming to Fontainebleau was the fear of being arrested on the way by the enemy, doubtless sent her this escort to protect her. I am however not acquainted with what were General Cambronne's instructions, though we received no notice of his expedition. He did not find the Empress in Orléans, for she had left the day before for Rambouillet. The general's mission was limited to protect the transport to Fontainebleau of the remains of the treasure which had been in the keeping of M. Peyruses, whose zeal and fidelity, which at one time had been misunderstood by the Emperor, had never once failed him.

The vans containing Napoleon's private treasure which had been seized in Orléans by M. Dudon were transported to Paris. I heard from M. de la Bouillerie, who having been Treasurer of the Imperial Civil List passed to the same functions under Louis XVIII, that the remains of this treasure were conveyed to the Tuileries, that one of the barrels of gold was broken open, and the contents distributed amongst such of the *émigrés* as were besieging the court of Count d'Artois, who was at that time lieutenant-general to the King; and that this Prince had not opposed this distribution in any way. Baron Louis, who had him appointed to the Ministry of Finance, having been informed of this pillage, made haste to come up and rescue the rest of the money. But when M. de la Bouillerie had asked for the two millions requisite to discharge a commitment taken by Napoleon in favor of the officers and servants of his household, a commitment guaranteed by Article nine of the Treaty of Fontainebleau, "Monsieur" had ordered on the unanimous advice of Baron Louis and M. de Talleyrand that the remnants of the Imperial treasure, eight or ten millions, should be purely and simply paid into the public exchequer, at first as a loan, and afterwards definitely.

Such was the fate of this treasure, the fruit of the savings which Napoleon had made out of the revenues of the civil list during ten years. Of the 120,000,000 of which it was composed at first, 100,000,000 had been employed in the noblest manner, since it had been used in reorganizing the army, and in meeting the wants of the public exchequer. The rest became as I have just related the prey of violence and of bad faith.

On the same day on which this crime was committed against the poor remnants of his material resources the Emperor had signed his abdication at Fontainebleau.

On the moment of his embarkment at Fréjus Napoleon sent me through General Bertrand a note, which will be found lower down. I handed it by his orders to the Empress, informing her that the Emperor wished her to transmit it to the Emperor, her father, a commission which was faithfully discharged by the Empress Marie Louise. The following is the note in question:

"According to Article 11 of the treaty the proceeds of the Civil list belong to the Emperor—the Duke of Cadore has the balance sheet of all which belongs to the Civil list, and of the savings which have been accumulated during 14 years.

"A treasure of from ten to twelve millions has been unjustly seized in Orléans and is today in sequestration in Paris.

"The Duke of Cadore and M. de la Bouillerie, the Treasurer of the Crown have in their keeping all scrip belonging to the crown, such as bank paper and investments in various establishments.

"It is evident that as the French government is acting with ill grace in all matters, and contrary to every idea of justice, it is no use to hope for the two millions invested in government stock, and intended for the maintenance of the Island of Elba, unless some foreigner interferes in the matter.

"There are four or five hundred thousand francs worth of presents, with portraits of the Emperor which had been bought out of the funds of the Civil list, and which were seized in Orléans together with all his plate and silver. The Emperor has also been deprived of his library, and of everything in daily use by the Emperor and the Empress."

In spite of the Empress Marie Louise's pressing applications to her father, not only were none of the stipulations of the Treaty of Fontainebleau in the Emperor Napoleon's favor, respected, but even his furniture and real estate, the property of which had been guaranteed to him or the members of his family by the same treaty, were put under sequestration. This is proved by the following document addressed to King Louis XVIII, and bearing his approval:

"Paris, Dec. 18, 1814

"SIRE,

"Your Majesty's ministers think that it is necessary to put a stop to any further disposal of the furniture and real estate belonging to the Bonaparte family, and to preserve them, by putting them under sequestration, until such times as Your Majesty may have otherwise ordained; they beg the King to authorize them to take this measure.

"(Signed:) DAMBRAY, Chancellor of France; ABBÉ MONTESQUIOU, FERRAND, LOUIS, Count BEUGNOT, Marshal Duc de DALMATIE, BLACAS D'AULPS, FRANCOIS DE JAUCOURT.

"(Approved, and signed) LOUIS."

On April 12, which was the last day spent by Marie Louise in Orléans, M. de Bausset had arrived very early in the morning, bearing a letter from Napoleon which he had taken as he passed through Fontainebleau, and a letter from Prince Metternich. M. Regnault de Saint-Jean d'Angély had not been able to reach his destination. MM. de Saint-Aulaire and Bausset, having proceeded to Paris had not found the Emperor Francis there. They handed their letters to Prince Metternich who had just arrived in Paris and had alighted at the house of Prince Schwarzenberg where these gentlemen had gone to await him.

M. de Metternich answered the Empress from Paris, on April 11, as follows:

"That MM. de Saint-Aulaire and de Bausset had handed him the letters which she had written to her august father, the Emperor; that having arrived in Paris during the course of the day he had made haste to forward them to their lofty destination; that he should have the honor of furnishing her on the morrow with fresh proofs of the Emperor's solicitude for herself and for the King of Rome; that he had preceded H.I.M. so as not to be foreign to the arrangements which were being negotiated with H.M. the

Emperor Napoleon; that, as soon as this arrangement was signed, he should have the honor of sending her somebody; that he was, however, able to assure her in advance of an independent existence to which her august son would succeed; that it would be superfluous to assure her that the Emperor took the greatest interest in her, and of the satisfaction with which he would receive her at his palace; that the most suitable arrangement would be that she should betake herself for the time being to Austria with her child, while awaiting the time when she should have the choice between the place where the Emperor Napoleon might be and her own residence; that in this wise the Emperor would have the satisfaction of drying the tears which she had only too much reason to shed; that she would be at peace for the time being and free to act as she pleased in the future; that she would take with her the persons in whom she reposed the greatest confidence; that the Emperor would be here in two or three days."

M. de Metternich adds:

"That what he tells her concerning her journey to Austria must be considered as entirely in conformity with the paternal desires of her august father; that he cannot beg her sufficiently to be entirely at her ease as regards the actual safety of all touching her; that she has often deigned to give him her confidence, and that she should not do less in the crisis of the moment, and that he gives her an assurance which is based on an entire knowledge of the state of things."

When Prince Metternich arrived in Paris, all had been decided and even carried out between the allied sovereigns and Prince Schwarzenberg; the latter was as anxious to break the family ties and the marriage bond as he had been assiduous in the work of forming them. M. de Metternich had contented himself with ratifying all that had been done, and Lord Castlereagh had taken upon himself to dispel all his scruples.

The wish expressed in the Austrian minister's letter that the Empress should proceed to Vienna was the only sincere one in the letter. The assurance of the reversion of the state which should be given to her and to her son, and the promise that she would be free to choose between the place where the Emperor Napoleon was living and her own residence, are two statements which need not be commented upon.

Only a few hours after the reception of this letter, Prince Paul Esterhazy and Prince Wenzel-Lichtenstein arrived in Orléans bringing with them another letter from Prince Metternich, which informed the Empress of the conclusion of the arrangements which in conformity with his letter of the nth was to give her the proof of the Emperor's solicitude for her and for her son, that is to say the cession of the duchies of Parma and Piacenza. This letter had the further object of inviting Marie Louise to come to the castle of Rambouillet to meet the Emperor of Austria who, on his side, was to come there from Paris.

The Austrian envoys urged on the Empress's departure with her son for Rambouillet, and decided her to set out on the evening of the same day—April 12.

She only had time to write to her husband the Emperor, to inform him of the fresh delay in their meeting, and to acquaint him with the order which she had received to start at once for Rambouillet where she was to have an interview with her father.

At the same time as the Empress announced her departure for Rambouillet to the Emperor, this prince sent me the following letter dated April 12, at 10 a.m.:

"How greatly must the Empress have been afflicted with the harshness with which she is being treated. The Emperor sends you a copy of a letter written yesterday by M. de Metternich to M. de Caulaincourt. H.M. supposes that M. de Saint-Aulaire came straight to you from Orléans with tidings. Rambouillet seems rather far off to the Emperor, and he further does not see the necessity of going to an imperial residence which can but awaken sad recollections in the Empress's mind; it is however for the Empress to see what it is best for her to do. M. le Duke of Vicence has not yet arrived with the arrangement; we expect him in the course of the day. I will send you a courier at once. What seems most suitable is that the Empress, the King of Rome, and the Emperor Napoleon should travel all together . . ."

Copy of a letter which the Duke of Vicence had just received from M. de Metternich, annexed to the preceding letter:

"I am sending MM. the Princes Esterhazy and Lichtenstein to H.M. the Empress Marie Louise, to invite H.M. to a meeting with her august father. Rambouillet seeming to us the most suitable place for this meeting, I beg your Excellency to use your best endeavors so that H.M. the Emperor Napoleon may also agree to it. Care will be taken to neutralize Rambouillet and a suitable space round it. My master, the Emperor, would doubtless see with great pleasure that it be you, My lord Duke, who should accompany the Empress.

"Receive, My lord Duke, the assurance of my high consideration.

"METTERNICH."

This letter written from Paris was dated, April 11, 1814.

Although M. de Metternich seemed to desire to have the Emperor Napoleon's consent to the choice of Rambouillet as a place for the meeting between the Empress and her father, the departure of this princess was so hurried on that she left Orléans at the very moment when M. de Metternich's dispatch to the Duke of Vicence reached the Emperor. Besides, though Napoleon disapproved of the selection of Rambouillet, his disapproval would in any case have arrived too late. The apparent consideration of the Austrian cabinet was mere mockery, since it took care to arrange matters so as to render all its promises vain words.

I had received, previous to the letter which I have quoted, another letter, dated the same day, at four o'clock in the morning; it will be found further on.

I cannot help saying in this connection that I refuse to believe in Napoleon's alleged sentiments of confidence—sentiments openly professed by himself—in the perfidious enemies who were about to separate him from his wife and child. It may be that he hoped by this attitude to disarm their ill will against him.

In any case the Emperor when at the summit of his power, displayed more generous sentiments, and did not seek to separate husbands from wives and children from their fathers. I don't want any better proof of this than the following anecdote:

In 1806, or 1807 I saw a young man arrive at St. Cloud. He was a man of elegant figure, of an interesting and noble face, and he wore a hussar's uniform with a chamois-colored dolman. It was the Hereditary Prince of Würtemberg who came to thank the Emperor for the kindness with which he had been treated by him and the good offices which he had received from him. This young prince, forced to leave his father's court to escape his tyrannical domination, had taken refuge in Paris. He frequented with much assiduity the house of M. Abel, the resident of the Hanseatic cities in Paris, and the charms of the daughter of this ambassador had produced so strong an impression on the mind of the prince that he thought of marrying her. A reciprocated affection as much as the state of discouragement into which the severity of the sovereign of Würtemberg had thrown him, had prompted the heir to the throne to take this resolution. Napoleon, having been informed of the position in which the Prince of Würtemberg found himself in Paris, had invited him to come and see him. He received him with kindness, gave him paternal advice, and even charged his treasurer to supply him with the funds of which he might stand in need. At the same time the Emperor opened a correspondence with the King of Würtemberg with a view to recalling this prince to more tender feelings towards his son. He succeeded in inducing the king to reconcile himself with his son and to restore him to his good graces. The Prince Royal, protected by the ascendancy which the Emperor naturally exercised over the princes who owed their elevation to him, returned to Stuttgart, where the King agreed to forget what had happened. He afterwards lived with his father on fairly good terms and succeeded to his throne in 1816.

I continue my narrative with the quotation of another letter:

"Fontainebleau, this 12th of April, 1814,
at 4 o'clock in the morning."

"The courier bearing your letter of yesterday, referring to the Duke of Cadore's mission, has just arrived. I immediately forward you the answer dictated by the Emperor.

"It appears that the Emperor of Austria has arrived in Paris. He will be very badly received by the people who are indignant at his treatment of the Empress; he will propose to see his daughter at Rambouillet. The Empress would accordingly be obliged to travel twenty-five leagues. It is for her to decide what to do; but after such harsh treatment it seems that she will gain nothing by this interview. If the Emperor of Austria really wishes to see her, she might send him word to come to within eight or ten leagues of Orléans, her health barely allowing her to go so far. Besides, Caulaincourt has not yet arrived, we only expect him in the course of the day and the Emperor will then write again. You are now aware that Parma has been given to the Empress.

"The Emperor still thinks that it would be best for the Empress to travel with him by short stages. She might stay at Parma or at Piacenza or at some mineral water station in Italy. The Emperor thinks that nothing could be better for the Empress's health than to be with the Emperor, and he thinks that Corvisart will share this opinion."

Doctor Corvisart obstinately insisted upon the waters of Aix in Savoy, and maintained that no others would be suitable, but that, on the contrary, they would injure the Empress's health.

These letters and the letter of the same day sent off at ten in the evening and containing the copy of the treaty signed on April 11, reached me at Orléans. I made haste to communicate the treaty to the Empress and to forward to King Joseph the articles concerning the members of the Imperial family. These left for Switzerland directly afterwards. *Madame* (the Emperor's mother), King Louis, and Cardinal Fesch had left Orléans the day before to proceed to Italy. Queen Julia, Joseph's wife, returned to Paris with her children. These princes and princesses had taken leave of the Empress on the day before their departure.

Marie Louise leaving Orléans at eight o'clock in the evening reached Rambouillet the next day at twelve, exhausted with fatigue. At Angerville she fell in with the Russian troops. It was here that the Imperial guard, which was escorting the Empress, was dismissed and proceeded thence to join the Emperor at Fontainebleau. General Schouvalov, who accompanied the Empress on this journey, took an escort of twenty-five Cossacks who accompanied us to Rambouillet. The avenue and the interior of this castle were guarded by Russian soldiers.

The Empress entered by the park; but she could not help seeing the foreign uniforms. Russian sentinels were posted at all the gates. On arriving there she had reason to regret the haste with which she had been forced to leave Orléans; she learned that the Emperor of Austria was only to arrive in Paris on the 14th, and that he would be unable to come to Rambouillet before the 16th; but the allies were no doubt aware of General Cambronne's march with the two battalions of the Imperial guard, with which he arrived at Orléans on the day after the Empress's departure.

This princess spent two days in Rambouillet, guarded by the Russians, and anxiously awaiting her father's arrival. He arrived on the 16th, accompanied by Prince de Metternich. In the morning of the day she was in a continual state of excitement, and the future appeared to her eyes only in the gloomiest colors. Informed of the approach of the Emperor she went to receive him at the door of her palace, followed by her son who was conducted by Madame de Montesquiou, and certain officers and ladies of her household. The Empress, deeply touched, snatched up her son and threw him, weeping, into the arms of her father, to whom in a grievous tone she said some words in German. The Emperor embraced his grandson; but the young prince seemed very indifferent to this sign of tenderness; he looked at his grandfather's long grave face with astonishment. When they were taking him to see his grandfather, he had said: "I am going to see the Emperor of Austria!" When he returned to his apartment, he said: "I have just seen the Emperor of Austria. He is not good-looking." The precocious intelligence of the poor fatherless child revenged itself in a very gentle manner, by this innocent epigram, for the harm which his grandfather's weakness had caused him. He had grasped the fact that this important person, whose name and whose presence created so much stir, was one of the principal authors of his mother's anguish and tears and the cause of all the fuss that had been made round about him since he had left the Tuileries; he used to say that Blücher was his greatest enemy; that Louis XVIII had taken his papa's place and was keeping back all his toys, but that he would "jolly well" have to give him back both his papa and his toys. Madame de Montesquiou's prudence removed from the child's mind whatever might have excited a dangerous irritation in him; but a word overheard as it passed, in the midst of his sports, without his appearing to understand it, fixed itself in his young imagination.

The Empress was anxious to find herself alone with her father; she accordingly barely took the time to introduce the various persons of her household who were with her, to him, and passed rapidly into her apartment with the Emperor Francis.—In the effusion of their common emotion, the father and the daughter embraced each other several times, shedding tears. The little prince was sent for. The Emperor never wearied of admiring him, and said that it was truly his blood that flowed in his veins. He told his daughter that he would take his grandson under his protection and would be a father to him. He also told her amongst other things that everything that had been done in Paris had been done without his consent, because fatality had willed it that he should be detained at Chanceaux, near Dijon, by the movements of the French army, without being able to communicate with Prince Schwarzenberg. One must after all give the Austrian sovereign and his minister the credit of having acted with a feeling of propriety in not sanctioning by their presence the dethronement of the mother and the son.

From this day forward the Empress and her son became the wards of Austria. Two battalions of infantry and two squadrons of Austrian cuirassiers replaced the Russian guards. The Russian sentinels were relieved by Austrian grenadiers, two cuirassiers being posted at the principal entrance to the palace.

Since the fatal letter of April 8, which had caused me such keen anxiety about Napoleon's person, the terrible impression which I had felt had gradually been effaced from my mind. I had received, as had been seen, several letters from Fontainebleau which showed me that the Emperor was occupying himself with his affairs with his usual clearheadedness. The Grand Equerry, Duke of Vicence, and Colonel Montesquiou came in turn to Rambouillet and told me the first news I had had till then of the sad event which I had only suspected and feared. Marie Louise, on her side, was, I believe, a long time in ignorance of the Emperor's attempt against his own life; in any case she never spoke to me of it.

In the night of April 11, Napoleon, whose mind was so strongly tempered, had yielded to an access of discouragement and had tried to accomplish the sinister project which it seemed evident to me had preoccupied him since the 8th. The overthrow of all his hopes and of the illusions to which he in vain essayed to cling, the ruin of the magnificent edifice which he had built up with so much trouble, but above all the consciousness of the implacable hatred of his enemies, who as long as he should live would be an insurmountable obstacle in the way of his son, excited to the highest degree the bitterness of his cruel sorrows. He bent beneath the terrible blow which struck him down.

But Providence would not yet permit the sacrifice of his life, to which he was inclined. She reserved him for other trials and for an end which was to add to his past glories. This end was to be that of a great man in the hands of adversity, mastering it with supreme dignity and calm.

This is what is certain about this painful attempt at suicide. I have related that during the retreat from Moscow, on November 18, 1812, the army passing the night at Doubrovna an alert which was thought to have been caused by the Cossacks took place in the morning. I added that wishing to prevent the misfortune of falling into an ambuscade, Napoleon had asked Yvan, his doctor in ordinary, to give him a sachet of poison of which he could make use to preserve himself by death from an odious captivity. The Emperor was fortunately not obliged to take recourse to this extreme measure at that time. On his return to Paris he removed the black taffeta sachet, in which the poison had been placed, from his neck, and deposited it in one of the boxes in his traveling-bag where it remained until 1814. At the time of his great paroxysm of discouragement Napoleon remembered this sachet. One day, after having consulted Yvan on the various means of putting an end to one's life, he drew out the sachet in question before the doctor's eyes and opened it. Yvan, terrified by this action, seized part of its contents and threw it into the fire. It appears that on the morrow, a prey to the blackest thoughts, despair seized upon the Emperor's mind. Napoleon rose, without summoning anybody, diluted the rest of the poison in a goblet, and swallowed it; what remained of this lethal substance was no doubt insufficient in quantity or had been too much diluted to cause death. On April 11, 1814, towards eleven in the evening the silence of the palace of Fontainebleau was suddenly disturbed by the sound of groans and the noise of comings and goings. The Duke of Bassano and de Vicence, and General Bertrand rushed to the Emperor's side, while Yvan himself was sent for. Napoleon was stretched out on a sofa in his bedroom, with his head leaning on his hands. He addressed himself to Doctor Yvan: "Death will have nothing to do with me. You know what I have taken." Yvan, dumbfounded, troubled, stammered, saying that he does not know what H. M. means, that he gave him nothing; at last he loses his head altogether and rushes out of the room to throw himself into an armchair in the adjoining room, where he has a violent fit of hysterics.

Napoleon passed a fairly quiet night. On the morrow Doctor Yvan, M. de Turenne and others presented themselves at the Emperor's levee and found him almost recovered from this violent moral and physical shock. He was calm, deeply sad, and deplored the unhappy state in which he was leaving France. As to Doctor Yvan, still troubled by the scene of the previous night, and under the impression of the terror with which it had filled him, his mind was made up to remain no longer in the palace. And so, on leaving the levee, he rushed down into the courtyard, and finding a horse tied to one of the gates, jumped on its back and galloped away.

The Emperor of Austria spent the night at Rambouillet and left on the morrow at nine o'clock in the morning for Paris, after having taken leave of the Empress Marie Louise. What happened during this interview? With what object did Metternich accompany his sovereign? What revelations were made to Marie Louise? What secret reasons were given to her to decide her to go to Vienna and to remain there till she could go to Italy, instead of awaiting this moment in the Island of Elba? Did they think fit to reveal to her the resolution which they had taken of separating her from her husband? These are questions, the answers to which may be conjectured but which can with difficulty be solved. The Empress's respect for her father, who expressed his keen desire to have her for some time in Vienna, naturally influenced this princess, as well as the prospect of being sent at an early date to take possession of the States which were promised to her, and where she would enjoy complete liberty. She thought that she would then be free to divide her time between her new residence and the Island of Elba. However this may be the emotions to which events so extraordinary, which had followed on each other with such rapidity, had subjected this princess, had sensibly injured her health and plunged her into the deepest melancholy. The happiness of having seen her father again under the sad circumstances in which she found herself had not diminished her affliction. She used frequently to withdraw to her chamber and there, with her elbows on her knees and her head in her hands, she would give way to all the bitterness of her thoughts, and shed bitter and abundant tears.

Already on the morrow Count Trautmansdorff, the Grand Equerry of the Court of Austria, came to Rambouillet to settle the details of the journey to Vienna. The Russian General Schouvalov left Rambouillet to betake himself to Fontainebleau, having been appointed to accompany the Emperor on his journey to Elba. He was replaced by the Austrian General Wroleck. The Duke of Vicence, the Count de Flahaut, and several ladies, amongst others Mesdames de Luçay and de Plaisance, came to take leave of the Empress.

On the 19th the Emperor of Russia arrived at Rambouillet and lunched with the Empress. This visit seems to have been forced upon her by the Emperor of Austria, this princess at least complained bitterly of having been obliged to submit to it. Nothing could cause her greater pain than to be forced to receive the Emperor Alexander at that time—with whatever care she had dried her tears and had composed her features. The King of Prussia's visit followed on that of the Emperor of Russia, two days later. These princes could not help knowing that Marie Louise was well aware of the part they had taken in the overthrow of the empire. It must have been a poor satisfaction for them to see the abasement of a woman whom they had involved in the ruin of her husband and of her son. It is said that the object of this step was to mask the true feelings of this victim of an odious policy and to arouse the belief that she had renounced of her own free will to make common cause with the Emperor, and that she separated herself from him to throw herself into the arms of his enemies. If such were not the motives of the visits of the King of Prussia and of the Emperor of Russia it must be admitted that their visits to Marie Louise, under such circumstances, gave a great appearance of truth to this opinion, especially on the part of the Emperor of Russia. It contrasted strongly with that magnanimity and that delicate appreciation of the proprieties which people have been pleased to attribute to him.

This prince made very ardent offers of service to the Empress and begged her to apply to none but to him. He asked to see the King of Rome whom she had had no intention of showing to him. The Czar went to the young prince alone, and saw him in the company of Madame de Montesquiou. The sight only inspired him with cold compliments. The King of Prussia arrived at Rambouillet in the afternoon of the 22nd, and only spent a few minutes there. He also expressed a wish to see the King of Rome. This interesting child was considerably bothered by these visits; he saw very well, in spite of his tender years, that these visits were not prompted by any feeling of interest in him and that he was only the object of an indiscreet curiosity.

I received, with regard to these visits, a letter from Fontainebleau, dated April 18 at five in the morning. Here are some extracts from it:

"It is inconceivable that the Emperor of Austria should not have seen the indecency of bringing the King of Prussia and the Emperor of Russia to Rambouillet, especially at a time when the Empress was ill.

"The Empress must try to go to the waters at once since this is the season.

"The Emperor is pleased to hear that you will accompany the Empress. H.M. wishes you to take every opportunity of sending him information of her."

I communicated this letter to the Empress. She disapproved of the visits of the foreign sovereigns as much as the Emperor, but it was then no longer in her power to undo them.

Napoleon left Fontainebleau for the Island of Elba on April 20, at noon, accompanied by the Russian General, Schouvalov, the Austrian General, Koehler, Count Truchsess-Waldbourg, a Prussian officer, and the English Colonel, Campbell, after a memorable and touching scene, in which he took leave of his eagles and of the brave officers and soldiers of his old guard.

Chapter XVI

On April 22, after the King of Prussia's short visit, Major-General Kinski, accompanied by his adjutant, Count Desselbrune, Count Eugene Wrbna, son of the Grand Chamberlain, Taffe, chamberlain, and Karaczaï, staff officer, appointed to accompany the Empress Marie Louise, arrived at Rambouillet, and provided for the arrangements of the journey. At the same time care was taken to verify the amount of the sums which had been placed in the Empress's carriages on her departure from Orléans. The amount was found to agree with the Treasurer's balance sheet. I had the chests fastened up, and in conformity with injunctions contained in the Emperor's letter I took the keys of these chests and handed them to the Empress together with the audited balance sheet. This princess recognized the good effects of the foresight which had induced me to insist upon these resources being put at her disposal, and she was good enough to express her satisfaction. She then assembled for form's sake Generals Caffarelli and Fouler, MM. de Saint-Aignan, Bausset, and myself to discuss the ways of regulating the administration of her household. We separated without having regulated anything. MM. Caffarelli, Fouler, and Saint-Aignan were to return to France after having conducted the Princess to Vienna. They refused to assume any responsibility. I urged M. de Bausset in his capacity of Prefect of the Palace to charge himself with the registration of all the larder and other expenses. The Empress, who seemed to wish to abdicate all authority in this matter, approved of this arrangement. I for my part wished to have nothing to do with the handling of monies, and I had every reason to applaud myself for having taken this resolution.

Rambouillet was the last Imperial residence which Marie Louise inhabited. She left it never to return to France again, making her way to Vienna. She stayed one day at Grosbois where the Emperor of Austria was expecting her. This prince received her as she was alighting from her carriage. Prince de Wagram, in order to place his principal house at the disposal of Marie Louise and her father, had retired with his wife and children to Marolles, a small château adjoining Grosbois. M. de Montesquiou, the Grand Chamberlain, was there with them. Prince de Wagram came to Grosbois to present to the Emperor of Austria some officers and ladies in waiting of the household of the Emperor Napoleon and of the Empress. Marie Louise received these people, who had come from Paris to take leave of her at Grosbois. When the last of them had withdrawn, the fallen sovereign felt herself in a state of isolation which warned her that the last bond which attached her to France had been severed.

During the Empress Marie Louise's stay in Rambouillet and Grosbois I traveled to Paris several times to carry out various orders which this princess had given me. In the course of one of these excursions I had the curiosity to go and see Prince de Bénévent. He charged me to express to the Empress his regret for what had happened as concerned herself and her son. He said that all combinations had had to fail before the fact of Napoleon's existence; that if the Emperor had died all would have been easy; but that as long as he lived his abdication would have been mere sham; that if the regency had been adopted and the son of the Emperor had been acknowledged, his father would have come back and would have put himself back in its place. After this scantily disguised confession of his conduct and of a perfidy which did not seem to trouble him in the least, M. de Talleyrand spoke to me of my personal position. He tried to dissuade me from following the Empress. He said that I had nothing to gain in leaving the country, that I should have no reason to regret staying in France, and accepting an order of things which was irrevocably established. As I persisted in silence M. de Talleyrand changed his attitude and appearing to disavow these indirect efforts, told me amongst other things that he had but little part in the distribution of offices, that till then he had not yet been able to get appointments for capable persons whom he wished to serve. He mentioned to me M. de Rémusat whom he had not yet been able to appoint to a prefecture. He added that when the Bourbons had no other money they distributed written promises of posts amongst their partisans. These promissory notes were to be met on their Restoration. When this unhoped-for time arrived he for his part was assailed with demands from people who presented him letters which promised them posts in his department. It seemed to me as far as it was possible to read this impenetrable man's mind that he would have preferred the Regency to the Restoration, if Napoleon's death had allowed him to take the direction of affairs into his own hands. Some years later I had occasion to meet M. de Talleyrand at the Salon, or annual exhibition of pictures. He came up to me, although I tried to avoid him, and said to me in an ironical tone: "You have seen finer salons than this. Have you not?"

Before commencing the account of the Empress Marie Louise's journey to Vienna I must revert to the state of things in Italy. In consequence of the desertion of the King of Naples the Viceroy of Italy had concentrated his forces on the Mincio, and had established his headquarters at Mantua. The Vice-queen had joined him there, and gave birth on April 13, to her fifth child. When the Vice-queen left Milan a coterie was already secretly agitating against French domination. General Pino, who had been Minister of War, abandoned the French cause at the same time. The Austrian General, Neipperg, who three months previously had signed the treaty against France with the Neapolitan Minister of Foreign Affairs, presented himself at Prince Eugène's headquarters accompanied by the Count de Wartemberg, aide-de-camp to the King of Bavaria. This officer carried a letter from the king inviting his son-in-law to abandon so desperate a cause, and follow his own example. General Neipperg also acquainted the Viceroy of the occupation of Paris by the allied troops and of the dethronement of the Emperor. Prince Eugène answered these communications with these noble words: "I understand nothing about politics, but simple good sense in default of every other feeling shows that the only thing to be done under these circumstances is to unite the French and Austrian forces and to march upon Paris, there to protect the rights of Marie Louise, and of her son." Such were certainly not the intentions of General Niepperg.

On the morrow, the 17th, Prince Eugène concluded a convention with Marshal Bellegarde for the return of the French troops to their country. While these things were going on news of the Treaty of Fontainebleau arrived, a treaty by which Napoleon abandoned all his claims to Italy. This was followed by the news of his abdication. These two pieces of news excited terrible fermentation in the Peninsula. On April 20 an insurrection broke out in Milan in the course of which Prina, Minister of Finance, was killed with umbrella blows. Prince Eugène's position in Italy was not long tenable. On April 25 he left Mantua with the Vice-queen, who had hardly recovered from her confinement, and proceeded by way of Verona to Munich. There he found letters from his mother which called him away, and having left his wife in Munich he proceeded immediately to Paris.

On April 25 the Empress Marie Louise, who had been styled Duchess of Parma, but who continued to wear her first title, received the farewell of her father who was returning to Paris to dine at the house of the Count d'Artois, and then proceeded on her journey which was not to be interrupted any more. Marie Louise was accompanied by Mesdames de Montebello and Brignole, by General Caffarelli, by Barons de Saint Aignan, Bausset, and myself. The Prince of Parma who had lost the title of King of Rome was accompanied by his noble and faithful governess Madame de Montesquiou, who had refused to separate herself from him, and by Madame Soufflot. We traveled under the guard of the Austrian General, Count Kinski, and his staff. On the way from Grosbois to Provins we passed Austrian and Cossack camps. The country presented a desolate aspect. Swarms of horses let loose in the fields were destroying all hopes of a harvest. The Empress wrote to the Emperor from Provins. I posted her letter and mine at Provins to the care of General Bertrand. These letters reached their destination and were received at Porto-Ferraio on May 25 following. We saw the same spectacle of devastation on the way from Paris to Troyes, which had saddened our departure from Grosbois; the country ravaged, villages burned, and the little village of Nogent nothing but a heap of ruins. There were not two houses standing intact. Brick chimneys alone were standing. The Empress lodged at Troyes at the house of M. de Mesgrigny, father of the Emperor's equerry, and father-in-law of the under-governess of the King of Rome. We arrived at Dijon on the evening of the 28th, after having slept at Châtillon, the city of sinister memories.

General Giulay, military governor of the district, General Fresnel, and several other Austrian generals and superior officers received their master's daughter. All the Austrian troops were under arms and lined the streets of Dijon. General Giulay had given orders that the cannon should be fired and the city be illuminated. Fortunately the Empress, informed in time, was able to escape this surfeit of untimely homages.

The Austrians affected to pay great honor to their sovereign's daughter: it was to the Archduchess and not to the Empress that these manifestations of deference and respect were addressed. Marie Louise arrived in Bâle, escorted by a detachment of Swiss cavalry which received her at the frontier, and she entered into this city between rows of Austrian and Bavarian troops. The house which she occupied had been inhabited by the Emperor of Austria; care had been taken to prepare her lodgings, all the way, in the same houses where her father had lived. Fearing lest the journey might tire her son, and anxious to escape the importunate marks of respect with which she was pursued, Marie Louise decided to rest a day in Bâle.

The courier whom the Empress had dispatched from Rambouillet to Fountainebleau, brought her back a letter from Napoleon dated from Fréjus on April 28. The Emperor had embarked for the Island of Elba the same day, at Saint-Raphael. I received by the same courier two letters from General Bertrand, also dated the 28th. These letters aroused in Marie Louise's heart regret for not having joined the Emperor in Fontainebleau; it was a secret sorrow, a kind of remorse which often manifested itself, in spite of the efforts which she made to hide her feelings. The view of the picturesque sites and the various sights afforded to the eyes by a journey through Switzerland were not sufficient to divert her from this preoccupation. At Schaffhausen the Empress saw the Falls of the Rhine under their various aspects; in Zurich she rowed out on the lake. M. de Lebzeltern, the Austrian Chargé d'Affaires at the Diet during the absence of the ambassador, asked to be presented to her with the representatives of Russia, Bavaria and others members of the diplomatic corps; but Marie Louise refused to receive them, alleging her incognito as the reason of this refusal. She stayed twenty-four hours at Constance, made an excursion on the lake, and paid a visit to the island of Meinau. At Waldsee, she lodged at the château of the prince, who presented his wife, who was about to be confined of her seventeenth child, and his daughter, canoness of a chapter in Salzburg, to the Empress. Marie Louise's melancholy had increased during her sad journey through our desolated provinces and the Austrian States. Her nights were disturbed by painful fits of sleeplessness, and her face was often steeped in tears. After one of these sleepless nights, one day in the Tyrol, she said to me with tears in her eyes that she had lacked in resolution in Blois and that no reason ought to have delayed her departure for Fontainebleau. A praiseworthy but useless regret, which time perhaps has not altogether effaced. The guides which the Emperor Francis's solicitude had given to his daughter, faithful to their instructions, neglected nothing to awaken in Marie Louise's mind the remembrance of her German fatherland. In France and as far as the Swiss frontier, they had surrounded her, as we have related, with homage and honors, but when this princess entered Tyrol, the demonstrations of popular enthusiasm knew no limits. At Fuessen, at Reitti, at Innsbruck and as far as Salzburg, the delirium was universal.

The inhabitants of the villages rushed in crowds to see the daughter of their well-beloved sovereign go by. Songs were heard all along the road, echoed by troops of singers placed for the purpose some distance away. The Tyroleans excel in open air concerts performed without instruments. At Fuessen, mortars were fired; at Reitti, no sooner had the Empress's carriage been seen from afar, than twenty Tyroleans, carrying ropes, rushed to meet it, unyoked the horses and dragged it to her house. During dinner, a troop of men and women sang verses in her praise outside her windows. On the morrow at seven o'clock, a Capuchin monk, followed by two or three young people, entered the passage which led to the princess's apartment and sang a number of songs with his companions before the door of her chamber.

Snow had been falling all the morning but this did not slacken the ardor of the Tyroleans. All the way from Reitti to Innsbruck, the inhabitants of all the villages were under arms, singing national anthems in chorus, saluting with flags and firing off mortars as soon as they saw the carriages. They saw in the Empress an Austrian princess only. Perhaps not one of these men who indulged in such noisy joy knew that she had reigned over France as the wife of the Emperor Napoleon. At Innsbruck, where she arrived at eight in the evening, she found the city illuminated; she was received there with the same transports and her carriage was dragged, or rather carried to the château, where she alighted.

The crowd was so great that two men and a child were crushed to death at the gate of the town. The Bavarian functionaries were awaiting the Empress at the foot of the grand staircase of the château and seemed to place themselves under her protection. The poor Bavarians who held public offices in Tyrol were dying to get away, considering that their lives were not safe in the midst of this popular excitement. Their authority, however, was exercised in a moderate and liberal manner. The vivacity of the attachment of the Tyroleans for the house of Austria, which had been still further excited by the pretence of showing them a princess of this house, was a warning, given to Bavaria, not to think of keeping the provinces in which this affection and a hatred for foreigners had such deep roots. Tyrol was accordingly given back to Austria one month later.

From Innsbruck where she stayed two days, Marie Louise proceeded to Salzburg. The Marshal of the Court of the Prince Royal of Bavaria awaited her at the door of the château where she alighted. She was visited there by the Princess Royal, a very handsome woman, at that time about twenty years old, and she returned this visit on the following day at the Château de Mirabelle, where this princess lived. All these royal or princely residences were large and spacious.

The young prince, entrusted to the care of Madame de Montesquiou, only saw his mother at the places where she stopped. He had forgotten the grief with which he had left the Tuileries; the novelty of what he saw amused him and he enjoyed it all in the happy carelessness of childhood.

Having rested a day at Salzburg, the Empress continued her journey to Vienna by way of Moelck. Prince Trautmansdorff, Grand Equerry, came to receive her there and to ask in the name of the Empress of Austria, who was coming to meet her, by what road she proposed to travel.

She met the Empress of Austria between Saint-Polten and Siegartskirchen, at a distance of four leagues from Vienna. The Empress of Austria gave up her carriage to Madame de Montebello and Countess Lazanski, former Grand Mistress of the Archduchess Marie Louise, and entered the latter's carriage. The same evening the Empress arrived in Schönbrunn, the destination of her journey. The princes of her family, uncles and brothers, had come there from Vienna to receive her. Her sisters were awaiting her at the door of the apartment to which she was conducted by the Empress of Austria. The young Archduchesses threw themselves on her neck as though she had just escaped from some danger and they were glad to see her safe and sound.

Marie Louise had returned to Vienna in about the same position as when she had left it four or five years previously, with bitter remembrances to boot, fallen from the lofty rank which the policy of the Austrian cabinet had temporarily bestowed upon her, and decoyed with the enjoyment of a principality which she was to purchase with the most painful sacrifices. When she had been destined to become Napoleon's wife, her father, the Emperor, had said, in taking leave of her: "Be a good wife, a good mother, and render yourself agreeable in everything to your husband." Austrian politics had mentally added: "as long as he is powerful, happy, and useful to our house." Marie Louise, on the throne on which Napoleon's choice and the eager consent of her father had placed her, had docilely obeyed her father's orders. There had never been anything to blame in her conduct as a wife. If it had been the destiny of the Empire to survive its disasters, she would have left behind an honored memory, after having given the example of private virtues, equal to those of the wife of Louis XIV or the wife of Louis XV. As Empress, either from self-love or from a sense of duty she had seemed to take pride in the prosperities of the Empire. She had not shown herself indifferent to our misfortunes. She tolerated no machinations against the safety and the repose of France. In the days which preceded its agony, she was the zealous and straightforward intermediary between the Emperor and her husband, but she had never identified herself with her adopted country. Passive, a stranger to politics, contemplating with terror the sight so new to her of party struggles—not having resided in France long enough to contract ties of any strength there, she did not take in our misfortunes that active and passionate part which induced Anne of Austria and Marie Antoinette to make the cause of the country in times of trouble and danger, their personal causes. She had renounced her new country without much opposition, to take refuge in her family as a harbor where she would be sheltered from new storms. Imbued with the impression which she had received in early youth, with the idea that the interest of the house of Austria cannot be weighed in the balance with any other interest, when her father said to her, in Schönbrunn, after her return: "As my daughter all that I have is yours, even my blood and my life; as a sovereign, I do not know you," she could but bow her head and confirm the irresistible force of such an argument by her silence. This saying of the Emperor Francis would justify the popular prejudice which attributes to the Austrian princesses, a fatal influence on the destinies of France.

Marie Louise's family received her with all the outward signs of cordiality. The Empress of Austria and the other Archduchesses had come to reside in the palace of Schönbrunn to receive her and to live with her. During the first days, numerous visits were exchanged amongst these princes and princesses and interminable conversations were indulged in. The Empress divided the rest of her time between her son, whose apartment adjoined her own, and the French persons who had accompanied her during her journey but who were to leave her after a short stay. Count de Lobau, who had been kept a prisoner in spite of the capitulation of Dresden, came to Schönbrunn and spent two days there before continuing his journey to Paris. He left on June 29; the 30th was the day fixed for the departure of the Duchess of Montebello. This separation, which was extremely painful to the Empress, was tempered only by the hope of seeing the Duchess again at the springs of Aix. MM. de Saint-Aignan and Corvisart, who left with the Duchess of Montebello, also took leave. On the morrow General Caffarelli, in his turn, left for France. These successive departures revived the pain which the Empress felt in losing persons whose fidelity and devotion she had been able to appreciate. She handed the noble and loyal Caffarelli a small morocco pocketbook, which she had used, and wrote some friendly words on the first page.

On the day after Marie Louise's arrival at Schönbrunn, she settled the order of service of her household; but no particular regulations were laid down. She even wanted to banish all etiquette and realize her pet dream of a private life. She refused to live in common with her family and preserved her domestic independence. She used to lunch and dine at her usual hours, at eleven in the morning and seven in the evening, with Countess Brignole, M. de Bausset and myself who alone remained with her.

She used to invite, in turn, a small number of persons of her family, ministers and their wives, gentlemen and ladies of the Emperor of Austria's household, and certain persons holding high rank or dignities in the state. The reception accorded to us in this court differed for each of us, but we were not treated as friends. Generally speaking we had reason neither to complain of, nor to praise the reception which was given us.

The Empress stayed about six weeks in Vienna, awaiting the return of the Emperor of Austria, who was to bring her the authorization to go to Parma and to the island of Elba. One of the consolations which she enjoyed during this first stay in Schönbrunn was the society of the Queen of Sicily, her grandmother, whose sincere attachment and vigorously expressed opinions, though they rather frightened her, helped to comfort her. This princess, the last daughter of Maria Theresa and sister of Marie Antoinette had arrived in Vienna at about the same time as Marie Louise. Unable any longer to support the authority which the English had arrogated to themselves in Sicily, she had escaped from their yoke, secretly making her way from Palermo and braving the dangers of a dangerous sea-voyage, had come to interest her son-in-law the Emperor in the restitution of the Kingdom of Naples. She had made up her mind to see each sovereign in private and not to slacken her assiduities until she had obtained King Joachim's expulsion. Her enterprising character and her tenacity gave some trouble to the Austrian government, which on her side she accused of egotism. This queen, who in the days of Napoleon's prosperity had been his declared enemy, and whose opinion in consequence could not be accused of partiality, professed the highest esteem for his great qualities. Hearing that I had been attached to him as secretary she sought me out to speak of him. She said that formerly she had reasons to complain of him, that he had persecuted her and hurt her feelings "for I was fifteen years younger at the time"; but that today that he was unhappy she forgot all. She could not check her indignation at the sight of all the maneuvers which were being made to sever the bonds which were the glory of her granddaughter and to deprive the Emperor of the sweetest consolation which could be his after the immense and cruel sacrifices which had been wrested from his pride. She added that if they were prevented from meeting, Marie Louise ought to tie her bedsheets to her window and escape under disguise. "That's what I should do in her place," she said, "because when a woman's married, it's for life." Such an act of boldness, which pleased the enterprising spirit of the old queen, was not in the scope of Marie Louise's character and contrary to her ideas of the proprieties. She was moreover lulling herself in the hope of being soon placed in possession of Parma, where she would be her own mistress and able to go where she pleased. Marie Louise used frequently to visit her grandmother; the old queen resided in the small château of Hetzendorf which was reached by one of the avenues of the Schönbrunn park. She gave her granddaughter advice, which was too energetic to please the Empress of Austria and the Austrian cabinet. The Queen of Sicily, having found a portrait of Napoleon enriched with diamonds, while looking over the contents of Marie Louise's jewel-case, urged her granddaughter to wear it. More ardent than Marie Louise in the expression of her feelings, she said one day to her lady-in-waiting that it did not suffice to wear this portrait on the breast, that it must also be worn in the heart. And finally the excellent princess showed a great liking for Napoleon's son and loaded him with caresses.

The kindnesses which were bestowed on Marie Louise by her step-mother and the Court of Vienna, masked a design to get possession of her mind, to confine her in the midst of her family, and to seek to guide her conduct and all her actions. They began to express doubts on the possibility of the journey to Aix, although she had obtained the Emperor's consent to this plan. They spoke of a château in Hungary where she could pass the summer very agreeably, and which she could inhabit during the time that the allied sovereigns were in Vienna, where they had fixed a meeting for the middle of July. It was thought that it might be disagreeable to her to be too near a city in which the congress was being held and that the sight of it would but cause her pain. If she absolutely needed a cure, why go to Aix? The Carlsbad waters or other springs in Germany might suit her state of health. Besides there would be the advantage of her not being too far away from her family. She was even made to fear that something might arise which would prevent her establishment in Parma. These hints troubled the Empress; but she clung to the idea of going to Aix, because her father had promised her that after the season at the springs she would be at liberty to proceed to Parma directly. Another reason was that she had appointed to meet Madame de Montebello, whose absence she much regretted, at Aix. Her recollections of France and the Emperor had an attraction for her at the time.

The Empress seemed to see, as in a glass, darkly, through the worrying to which she was subjected, the secret intention to separate her from Napoleon. She blamed herself then for having too much believed in the impossibility of joining him, and for having placed too much confidence in the promises which had been made to her. It must be added that the Emperor in his letters, kept speaking of plans for their coming together.

These vexations in some degree disturbed the calm of the peaceful life which Marie Louise was leading in Schönbrunn. She devoted her mornings to her son; she drew, played, and studied Italian, a knowledge of which would be necessary to her in her new States. Madame de Montesquiou used to bring in the young Prince of Parma at the end of luncheon. The young prince's treat was what he used to call "the nice dish"; it was generally one of the hundred kinds of cakes which are to be seen on every table in Austria.

In the afternoon Marie Louise used to mount on horseback or walked out in the beautiful gardens of Schönbrunn, every building in which she saw again with pleasure.

In the first days of her arrival Napoleon's wife was the object of the curiosity and interest of the people of Vienna. During her drives in the city, her carriage was followed by a silent crowd anxious to catch a glimpse of her. On the first Sundays, the gardens of Schönbrunn were the general meeting-place of the inhabitants of Vienna, who in their respectful whisperings seemed to congratulate Marie Louise on her return amongst them and admired the beauty of her son's face.

On June 15 the Empress left Schönbrunn early in the morning to go and meet the Emperor of Austria. She stopped at Siegartskirchen, two stages from Vienna where the Empress of Austria and the Emperor's children had preceded her. She received her father in the same room in the stage-house in which, in 1805, Napoleon had received the deputation which presented him with the keys of Vienna.

The remembrance of the scene which I had witnessed nine years previously, retraced itself in my mind with curious vividness. I saw once more the glorious victor, before whom Count Zinzendorf and the magistrates of Vienna bent down low, presenting him on a silver tray the keys of the haughty capital of Austria. I saw once more the faces and the attitudes of the deputies recommending their city and its inhabitants to

Napoleon's generosity. So strongly had this hallucination seized upon me that involuntarily I closed my eyes. How different the sight that met my eyes today. In the place of the victorious soldier, whose proud attitude was tempered by a feeling of natural generosity, I beheld a princess, almost on her knees, with wet eyes, bending before a sovereign who raised her up with a gesture half of pride and half of tenderness. This princess was the wife of Napoleon, and the sovereign who today proscribed her husband was the same who formerly at the bivouac of Sar-Uchitz had implored the clemency of the French Caesar.

Marie Louise accompanied the Emperor Francis, alone, in his carriage to the last stage. On arriving there, she left him, as she was anxious to get to Schönbrunn a quarter of an hour before him, so to be able to present his grandson to him on his arrival. An extraordinary crowd of people from Vienna and the surrounding districts filled the road, the avenues of the park, and had even invaded the outer rooms of the palace.

The Austrian monarch left Schönbrunn on the morrow to make his solemn entry into the Austrian capital. He was on horseback, accompanied by the Archdukes, his brothers, preceded and followed by his guard at the head of which marched Prince Lambesc, who was styled Prince of Lorraine in Vienna, captain of the first guard of archers, Prince de Ligne, captain of halberd-bearers, and Prince Esterhazy, captain of the Hungarian guard of nobles. The uniform of the latter as well as the harness of his horse was covered with pearls and diamonds of considerable value. According to the custom, there was perhaps not one street through which the Emperor and his procession did not pass to the acclamations of an immense crowd. This march through the city lasted five hours and terminated at the Metropolitan church of St. Stephen, at the door of which the Archbishop of Vienna harangued the Emperor Francis, who was afterwards present at the *Te Deum.* The Emperor of Austria had been advised to make his entry into Vienna on an Arab horse which had been used by Napoleon, and which had been brought to Paris with the Empress's equipages, but he had the good sense to refuse this kind of triumph.

The Austrian sovereigns returned to Schönbrunn on the morrow and remained there until the departure of the Empress Marie Louise to the waters of Aix. While granting her permission to undertake this journey, it was impressed upon her that it was necessary that in the future there should be at her side a person destined to act as her adviser and as a go-between between her and the Austrian cabinet. The Emperor had selected Prince Nicolas Esterhazy. This person's rank, age, and prudence justified this selection, but the Vienna cabinet caused Prince Esterhazy to be replaced by General Count Neipperg, who was commanding a division of Austrian troops in Pavia and who was ordered to proceed to Aix.

The Austrian General, Count Nugent, having taken possession of the Duchy of Parma in the name of the sovereign, Marie Louise had sent an agent to obtain first information as to the state of affairs in the country and its situation. This agent no doubt did not meet with the favor of the Austrian authorities who treated the Italian provinces like conquered territories. Badly treated, badly received, and even locked up in jail, the Duchess of Parma's envoy only secured his liberation by means of the pressing appeals made by this princess to her father, the Emperor of Austria.

When Marie Louise had been of opinion that she would be free to proceed directly to Parma, she wished to take with her two celebrated artists from whom she was receiving lessons. They themselves had asked to go. One was M. Paer. Born in Parma he was pleased with the prospect of going to end his days in his native country; a feeling of gratitude engaged him to follow the fortunes of his royal pupil, and to go and establish himself in her new States. He had been loaded with kindnesses by the Emperor who after the victory of Jena, had brought him to Paris with his wife to attach both of them to the palace musical service, with large salaries. He had been appointed director of the court theatrical performances and master of singing to the Empress. He had succeeded Spontini in 1812 in the management of the Italian Theatre. Hardly had the negotiations for his establishment in Parma been begun than he was appointed director of the concerts to Louis XVIII, to which post he afterwards added that of director and composer of music to the Duchess of Berri. The other was M. Isabey. The Empress was accustomed to the drawing lessons of this skilful and witty artist. She liked him very much and was much pleased with his good-natured humor. He was moreover the friend of Corvisart, and was protected by the Duchess of Montebello, in whom Marie Louise had great confidence. Isabey, in going to settle in Parma, wished to find there compensations for the advantages which he lost in leaving Paris. His pretensions appeared too great to the Empress who was no longer rich enough nor great enough a sovereign to satisfy them as she would have wished to have done. "And besides," she did me the honor of writing to me, "even were he to come for nothing, I should never allow myself to take him without first having obtained the Emperor's consent. You know how he objected to him and I must respect his prejudices, for though I am separated from him I am none the less responsible for my conduct to my husband."

The Emperor of Austria had deigned to receive Madame de Brignole, M. de Bausset and myself. He received us with kindness and prolonged a conversation in which no political questions were raised, for some time. The Emperor above all spoke with satisfaction of the paternal forms of his government and of the intimate, almost family, relations which existed between the different provinces and the hereditary States. He told us amongst other things that it had sometimes happened that the harvests in various parts of his hereditary states having been insufficient, cities wanted grain, that he then sent them corn from his private estates carried on his own carts and that these cities paid him it back after the harvest of the following year. It seemed to me that I was listening to a patriarch of primeval days speaking of his patronage and protection of his tribe, and not to the chief of a great empire, discoursing on the forms of government of his vast states.

A circumstance connected with this introduction struck me. The room in which the Emperor Francis received us was the same which had been used as Napoleon's cabinet in 1805 and 1806. This cabinet, filled with souvenirs of a great queen—Maria Theresa, decorated with her statue and portraits of her descendants, had reechoed with the severe words of Napoleon against the persons of the court whose influence tended to alienate the heart of his subjects from their sovereign. The picture which the Emperor of Austria drew of the good harmony which existed between his peoples and himself, and his solicitude for their needs seemed to be in protest against the reproaches which the Emperor Napoleon had addressed to him.

During the five weeks which the Empress spent in Vienna at the time of this first journey she received several letters from the Emperor Napoleon, one through General Koehler on his return from the island of Elba whither he had accompanied the Emperor in the capacity of Austrian commissioner; the others enclosed in letters from General Bertrand to myself. Marie Louise answered them punctually. She even took advantage of the departure of a former courier, called Sandrini, to whom Countess Brignole had given a letter of recommendation, to the island of Elba, to write to Napoleon.

These are General Bertrand's letters written to me by order of the Emperor or dictated by the latter:

"His Majesty has received your letter and read the particulars it contained with interest. He desires the Empress to make the state of her pecuniary affairs known, as otherwise the Emperor, her father, may think that she has large resources, whereas as a matter of fact she has nothing. You will find annexed a note which the commissioners have consented to take; the Empress might speak in conformity therewith." (This note refers to the seizure of the Emperor's treasure and personal belongings at Orléans.)

. . . .

"I had written you a line this morning fearing that the Emperor might not write to Her Majesty, because we have to start early, but the departure has been put off on account of the wind having failed us. The Emperor has vomited a little bile; you know that this indisposition only lasts a few hours. At the time of writing the Emperor is in wonderful health. He has just written to the Empress.

"Please receive, etc., etc.

"(Signed) BERTRAND"

"Fréjus, April 26, 1814, 6 o'clock in the evening."

"I receive your letter at the moment of starting for the island of Elba. The weather is fine; and we hope to arrive there in less than two days. We had a very sad journey, as you may imagine, fairly good throughout almost the whole of France; but in Provence, we were exposed to insults which fortunately had no consequences . . . . You can imagine that we are very anxious that the Empress should come and divide her time between Parma and the island of Elba. It would make an enormous difference to the Emperor and to all of us; we should be happy to see her now and again: she was so kind to my wife and to myself that nobody desires it more than I do. Lay my homage at her feet, my respect, and my devotion. The Emperor has always been in very good health in spite of the cruel position he has been in during the last month. He handed his answer to the Empress to General Schouvalov's aide-de-camp who is proceeding to the Emperor of Austria. As this letter will not be carried there directly, the Empress may perhaps be anxious at receiving no answer. I hand my letter to the courier, so that you may be informed of the early arrival of the Emperor's answer. You will hardly be able to read my writing; but I am in a great haste and my heart is so full that I hardly know what I am writing. My sentiments are none the less for you what, as you know, they have been for a long time.

"(Signed) BERTRAND"

"Fréjus, this 29th April, 1814, at 7 a. m."

"General Koehler is leaving the island of Elba and will probably go to the Empress. He will thus be able to give you particulars about our island, which is prettier than we thought. It is in a good state of cultivation; the heat is not excessive. The Emperor will be fairly well lodged. His health is excellent. Please present my respects to the Empress.

"(Signed) BERTRAND"

"Porto-Ferraio, this 9th May, 1814"

"I have received your letter from Provins of April 26. The newspapers have informed us of H.M.'s visit to Schaffhausen. She must have arrived in Vienna on the 16th. I have delivered the letter which was enclosed in yours. The Emperor wished to answer the Empress through the under-officers Schopff and Hertlieb who are returning to join General Koehler; but the Emperor is out riding and the ship is under sail, so that they are obliged to go off without the Emperor's letter. I regret it very much.

"The Emperor is very happy here and seems to have forgotten that only a very short time ago he was in such a different position. He is very busy getting his house into order, furnishing it, and looking out for the site of a pretty country house.

"We often speak of our excellent Empress. The officer of the guard whose wife is in H.M.'s service, and who had the honor of presenting his respects to her at Dijon has just arrived, and gave us your news.

"I repeat, etc., etc.

"(Signed) BERTRAND"

"Porto-Ferraio, this 27th May, 1814"

"We have heard no news of you since the letter which you wrote to me from Provins on leaving Paris. We learned by the newspapers that the Empress had arrived in Vienna on May 18.

"The Emperor continues in good health. We ride and drive and boat a great deal. The Emperor's house has already been greatly improved. We are busy arranging different residences for him in various parts of the island.

"We are anxious to receive news as early as possible of the health of the Empress and her son. The heat is beginning to make itself felt. Please lay my respects at the feet of the Empress.

"(Signed) BERTRAND"

"Porto-Ferraio, June 28, 1814"

"I received your letter of June 4, a few days ago and yesterday your letter of June 21.

"Since the letter you wrote me from Provins I had had no news of you. Your letter of the 4th contained two letters from the Empress to the Emperor, numbered 5 and 6. The preceding ones have not been received. Your letter of the 21st contained another for the Emperor; his answer is being sent off today. Communications not being yet reestablished H.M. wrote but little. I imagine that you will soon receive one or two letters which I have written to you. I know that there is a letter from you which I shall no doubt receive very soon, under way.

"If the Empress awaited the answer to her letter in Vienna, the Emperor wishes her not to go to Aix, and if she has already gone there, not to pass the season there but to return to Tuscany as quickly as possible, the waters there being the same as in Aix. These springs are nearer to us."

. . . .

"We have learned from the newspapers that M. Marescalchi was commissioner to Parma for the Emperor of Austria. If you see General Koehler remember us to him. He is an excellent man and we have nothing but praise for his conduct towards us. You are thanked for the details which you give us about the King of Rome, they interested us greatly.

"May the Empress's health soon be reestablished. We often speak about all concerning her. I need not tell you with what interest we read all that you send concerning her occupations and her way of living. I am asking General Rospigliosi to send you this letter by a courier. Receive, etc., etc.

"(Signed) BERTRAND"

"Porto-Ferraio, July 3, 1814"

"I have received your letter of June 6, in which you inform us of your departure from Schönbrunn. We read of your journey through Switzerland in the papers; we are surprised to receive no news of you. The Emperor expects the Empress for the end of August and wants her to bring his son with her. H.M. has certainly written much more frequently to the Emperor; but her letters are probably intercepted by some secondary agent's orders, or perhaps by her father's command. At the same time nobody has any rights over the Empress and her son."

"*Madame* has arrived in good health. She has already taken up her abode in her house; although the house is not a handsome one, she has plenty of room and certain comforts . . . . The Emperor is wonderfully well. Our amusements are always the same; certain occupations during the day; in the evening excursions on horseback, in our carriages, or in a boat. The heat has been felt for some days past but the mornings and evenings are cool. I presume that you have received the letter that I wrote you by return of the Grand Duke's courier in which I informed you that my letter of the 9th was the one that I entrusted to General Koehler, which was handed to you. My wife who has arrived safely saw M. Marescalchi in Genoa. Madame Brignole's family were all well.

"(Signed) BERTRAND."

"Porto-Ferraio, this 9th August, 1814"

"P.S. The officer who was to take this letter to you has left without coming to my house. I take advantage of M. Hurault's departure to send it to you. He is very anxious to see his wife again. We hope to see you in the month of September when H.M. has finished taking the waters."

"This 20th August."

The day on which the Empress was to leave for Aix was approaching. As the young prince was not to accompany his mother on this journey she sent for Doctor Frank, the Emperor of Austria's doctor, and charged him with the care of her son's health during the child's stay in Vienna. She wrote to the doctor on this matter officially.

Napoleon's son, left under the vigilant maternal care of Madame de Montesquiou, remained accordingly with her in Schönbrunn. This young prince, whose birth had been hailed with so many blessings in our country, and who seemed destined for so lofty a future, was not to leave Austria where he had found a prison for a refuge, while awaiting the tomb which was to open so prematurely for him.

Two days before the Empress's departure, the Emperor Francis went to the Baden baths with his family. These baths are situated at a distance of four leagues from Vienna in a pretty valley called Saint Helena. Marie Louise went to take leave of him, and on her return received almost the entire court which came to take leave of her. An indisposition of Madame de Brignole's, which had at first given us some anxiety, but which fortunately had no consequences, delayed our departure twenty-four hours. The Empress of Austria came to Schönbrunn after dinner to say good-bye to her stepdaughter and only left her after having put her into her carriage.

The Empress Marie Louise assumed the name of Duchess of Colorno for this journey, Colorno being one of the pleasure-houses of the Duchy of Parma. She traveled without stopping till we reached Morsburg where we found M. de Bausset, who had preceded us, ill with the gout. She stayed one day in this town. The road which she was following obliged her to pass through Munich. She found the viceroy and the vice-queen of Italy waiting for her at the stage-house and they took her to sup with them. Madame de Brignole and myself, untidy as we were in our traveling costumes, followed her. We supped at the viceroy's palace with the Princess Royal of Würtemberg, sister of the vice-queen. This princess, after her separation from the husband whom Napoleon's politics had bestowed upon her, had come to seek comfort with her sister. Providence held a splendid reparation in store for her, by placing her a year later on the Imperial throne of Austria.

Having continued her journey by way of Berne, Payerne and Chamonix, Marie Louise reached Aix on July 17. She was received at Carrouge by General Neipperg who came to meet her on horseback, saluted her at the door of her carriage and accompanied her to Aix. This was the second time that she saw him. The sight of him created a disagreeable impression on the Empress, which she did not dissimulate.

Count Neipperg was not, it must be said, particularly well favored. A black bandage covered the deep cicatrice of a wound by which he had lost an eye, but this disadvantage disappeared when one looked at him attentively. This wound rather suited the *ensemble* of his face, which had a martial character. His hair was of a light blonde color, scanty and curly. His glance was bright and penetrating. His features were neither vulgar nor distinguished; taken altogether they betokened a clever and subtle man. His complexion, full-colored on the whole, lacked in freshness, it was marked with the impress of the fatigues of war and his numerous wounds. He was of the middle height, and well-built, and the elegance of his figure was heightened by the loose cut of the Hungarian uniform. General Neipperg was at that time about forty-two years old.

This man played so important a part in Marie Louise's life and exercised so great an influence on her destiny that I must try and explain what were the qualities with which he won her confidence. His general appearance was an amiable one, mingled with alacrity and gravity. His manners were polite, insinuating and flattering. He possessed agreeable talents, and was a good musician. Active, clever, possessed of little scruple, he knew how to conceal his acuteness under an exterior of simplicity. He expressed himself and wrote with grace. He added to much tact a spirit of observation and he knew how to listen, listening with studied attention to what was said to him. His face would now assume a caressing expression, and now his glance would seek to fathom the secret thoughts. He was as clever in reading the designs of others as he was prudent in the conduct of his own. Adding to the outward signs of modesty an immense vanity and ambition, he never spoke of himself. He was brave in war and his many wounds show that he had not spared himself.

M. Armandi, colonel of artillery in the Italian army, who acted as Minister of War during the troubles in Romagna in 18— has assured me that General Neipperg was in Milan, in 1814, at the house of a lady whose lover he was, when he received notice that he had been selected to reside with the new Duchess of Parma, together with his instructions. His mistress tried in vain to keep him back, ambition was stronger in him than love. This Italian mistress having asked him what he would do with Marie Louise and whether this new position would at least bring him more forward, Neipperg is said to have answered:

"I hope to be on the most intimate terms with her before six months are out, and soon to be her husband."

To complete these data on Neipperg, I must further mention a curious peculiarity of this strange destiny. The Austrian general was the son of a Frenchman. While Count Neipperg, the putative father of the general, was filling a diplomatic mission in Paris, he made the acquaintance of a French officer belonging to a distinguished family. He received him with familiarity at his house and Countess Neipperg did not remain insensible to the merits of Count d'H— who repaid her with assiduous attention. An intimacy arose accordingly between the countess and the young officer and General Neipperg was the fruit of it. The proof of this fact lies in a letter from Countess Neipperg which was found in the papers left by Count H— after his death. This concatenation of circumstances will afford a fresh subject of reflection to those who admit that fatality always plays some part in human events.

Marie Louise alighted in Aix at a house situated outside the town, belonging to a M. Chevalley. It had been prepared for her reception by care of M. Ballouhey, the intendant of the Empress's household, and was the same which Queen Hortense had already occupied. The Empress during my stay in Aix only received General Neipperg in official audiences. This princess had not yet had time to become German again and the presence of a few French people who had remained faithful to her cause still attached her by some ties to France. The Empress found MM. Corvisart and Isabey awaiting her at Aix. The Duchess of Montebello did not arrive before the beginning of August. I left Marie Louise, on the second day after her arrival at Aix to go and spend the time of a double season at the springs with my family.

The Empress did not neglect means of corresponding with the Emperor, but opportunities became more and more scarce and difficult. She had commissioned M. de Bausset with a letter thinking that he would find facilities in Parma, where she was sending him, to forward it to Elba.

I extract from the long and numerous letters, written to me entirely by the princess herself during the seven weeks that I spent in Paris, the passages which depict the state of her mind as well as her sentiments towards the Emperor. I hope that she will pardon me for having published this correspondence during her lifetime. However it may be, I am certain that I have not committed any abuse with this publication of my communications with Parma, and the silence that Marie Louise has observed towards me since the revolution of 1830 prevented me from obtaining the consent from her which I should have been glad to be in a position to ask for.

First Letter.

"August 4, 1814

"I am still expecting an answer from my father to know the date of my departure for Parma. I will let you know at once. Though I should be very pleased if you would soon return to me, still I feel how much you must wish to remain a little longer with Madame de Méneval. I am sure it is very unselfish on my part to allow you to do so.

"Your very affectionate

"(Signed) LOUISE"

Second Letter.

"August 9, 1814

"I thank you very much for all the trouble you have taken about my boxes. What you write me concerning the remarks of M. de Bombelles on this subject does not seem to portend much good. I am still in the most painful uncertainty as to my future fate. I sent a letter by M. de Karaczaï to my father in which I asked him for permission to establish myself at Parma on Sept. 10 at the latest. Will this be granted to me? I fear not. If my presentiment is wrong I will let you know at once so that you can send for Madame de Méneval and her children. I know that will please you. It will be very hard for you to have to pass the winter without having seen them, and I should be very sorry for you. If the answer is a negative one I shall never consent to return to Vienna, before the departure of the sovereigns, and I shall try to have my son back. I shall establish myself in Geneva or in Parma while awaiting the congress; but it is impossible for me to remain here after the season is over. I cannot tell you with what impatience I am waiting an answer. I want you to help me with your advice in my determination. Do not be afraid to tell me the truth if my determination appears inconsistent to you. I want your advice as from a friend, and I hope you will give me your opinion quite frankly. I have just received a letter from the Emperor from the Island of Elba, dated July 4. He begs me not to go to Aix, but to go to Tuscany to take the waters. I shall write about this to my father. You know how anxious I am to do what the Emperor wishes. In this case ought I to do it if it is not in harmony with my father's intentions? I send you a letter from Porto-Ferraio. I was very much tempted to open it. It would have given me some particulars. If it contains any particulars please let me know them. I thank you very much for those you gave me, I wanted them badly, for it was a long time that I had been without news. Generally speaking I am in a very critical and in a very unhappy condition. My conduct has to be full of prudence. There are some moments when my head is so troubled that I think the best I could do would be to die.... My health is fairly good. This is my tenth bath. They would do me good if my mind were easier. I shall not be happy until I have got out of this fatal state of uncertainty. I am very pleased to think that you will soon be here, to reason with me, and calm my poor head. I need it badly. M. de Bausset left some days ago, taking with him all the papers which I wanted to see, so that I have not been able to examine all this month's accounts as I had a wish to do. I am awaiting the couriers which he sent from Parma with impatience. I did not carry out all the extravagances which I had planned for the 28th. I had Madame de Brignole to *Goûter,* but when the moment came for carrying out my plans I was afraid that they might not be very successful and so I gave them up. I am sure you will laugh at my cowardice. The account of my journey which I am writing has only got as far as my visit to the Bossons Glaciers. The other day at the ball we were speaking about it and about my plan of having it printed, and Madame Hurault added: "Yes, with M. de Méneval's little printing press." Somebody whom she did not know said behind her: "M. de Méneval has got a printing press! That is worth knowing." M. Hurault informed me of this remark, and begged me to let you know of it; so that you can get rid of your press as soon as possible, or send it to Parma with my carriage. I am told that a very heavy penalty is inflicted on private individuals who are detected with printing presses. Imagine what it would be in your case who have been working so long in the Emperor's cabinet. It worries me; I can assure you that I shall not be at ease until I hear you have got rid of it.

"Your affectionate

"MARIE LOUISE"

"P.S. My son is wonderfully well and gets sweeter every day, according to what they write me. I am very anxious to see the poor child again."

Third Letter.

"This Aug. 15, 1814

"I have had no answer yet from my father to the letter which I spoke to you about in my last. This uncertainty seems to me very cruel and very long. I am awaiting for the answer with a great deal of impatience and I will let you know about it at once. I have a black presentiment that it will be nothing pleasant to hear, but I am in one of my sad moods today, so maybe I am mistaken. How can I be happy on the 15th when I am obliged to pass this feast-day, so solemn to me, far from the two persons who are dearest to me. I beg your pardon for thus speaking to you of my sad thoughts, but the friendship and the interest which you have always shown me embolden me, provided you will let me know when I bore you. I beg you to believe in my sincere friendship.

"Your affectionate

"LOUISE."

"P.S. I have just received a letter from Parma which informs me that M. de Marescalchi has been replaced by M. de Magawly, who has just upset the entire Provisional government. M. de Marescalchi is now nothing but Austrian ambassador at my court. My father has also appointed M. de San Vitale as my grand chamberlain, and that without consulting me. This grieves and vexes me. M. Magawly said in Parma that my father had sent M. de San Vitale to go to Vienna to fulfill his functions in my service, and that I should be invited to go to Vienna during the whole period of the Congress. What a sad prospect! I have half a mind to ask him to allow me to spend the winter in Florence, promising him to write to the Emperor only through the Grand Duke. It seems almost certain that he will refuse. But about one thing my mind is made up. I will not go to Vienna while the sovereigns are there. Advise me, I beg of you. I assure you I am much to be pitied."

Fourth Letter.

"This 15th August in the evening'

"I have just received your letter of August 9. I am really much distressed at the time that letters take to come, one gets such old news. I send you a copy of a letter from Prince Metternich which will acquaint you with the news which M. de Karaczaï brought me. I am very unhappy indeed at the idea of being forced to return to Vienna, all the more so that no good reason for it is given to me. I do not think I shall go to Vienna before the end of September or the beginning of October. I shall leave here on Sept. 3 or 4th and shall go to Geneva, and thence to Berne where I shall spend a fortnight, besides a week in Geneva, and after that I shall go on to Vienna. I am very vexed about this on Madame de Méneval's account. If you can bring her to Geneva she can follow you after her confinement. If you come and share my exile I know how tedious it will be for you, at the same time I am too selfish not to desire it. I want your advice, I need your conversation. You know all the confidence which I have in you. One of the pleasantest thoughts which I can have just now is the thought of keeping you by me.

• • • • • • •

"I also send you a letter which came here for M. Amelin. Be good enough to send it to him. As regards the paymaster I can promise nothing: less now than ever, for you see I am consulted about nothing. I do not think it at all right, they ought at least to treat the unfortunate with a little delicacy of feeling. The Duchess will tell you a lot of things by word of mouth which I cannot write for I am very sad, although resigned. The hardest blow will be struck tomorrow when I have to say good-bye to the Duchess, but I do not complain. I ought to be accustomed to every possible misfortune. But what comforts me is the thought that there are still some good people who have pity for me, and I have pleasure in thinking that you are one of these. Begging you to believe in all my esteem and confidence.

"Your affectionate

"LOUISE."

Fifth Letter.

"This 20th of August in the evening.

"I received your letter of the 12th of this month yesterday, and I see with pleasure that you received some of my letters, but surely you must have received one in which I spoke of the wretched answer which my father gave me. I am very much touched by your offer to follow me under any circumstances whatsoever, and I stand in great need of good advice. It is more necessary to me now than ever, and so I hope I shall soon have the pleasure of seeing you again. I wish you to arrange it so that you will be deprived of Madame de Méneval's society as short a time as possible. I quite see how sad that would be, and I am afraid she will get to have a grudge against me. I have answered my father as well as Prince Metternich, and used fine phrases in writing to the latter about all the confidence I had in him, and I especially insisted on the satisfaction I felt in the promise which was given me that I could go to Parma. It appears that M. Magawly has made some very good changes and reformed many of the abuses of the Provisional government. I have received long letters from M. de Bausset which I will communicate to you when I return. I want to bother you with all my affairs. I have received news of the Emperor on August 6. He speaks very well of you and begs me not to believe all that may be said against him. He was in good health, happy, and quiet, and was thinking greatly about my son and myself.

"Write to me I pray you with great punctuality, and believe in all my friendship from

"Your very affectionate

"MARIE LOUISE"

I do not want to reproduce too large a number of the letters which I had the honor to receive from the Empress Marie Louise. The literal extracts which I have just given, suffice for the purpose which I had before me in quoting them. One month after the Empress's arrival in Aix, the Duchess of Montebello, MM. Corvisart and Isabey, left this city one after the other, the first two to return to Paris. M. Isabey went off to Vienna where he was to paint the portraits of the sovereigns assembled in the congress. After their departure the Empress remained another fortnight in Aix, anxiously awaiting the effect of the promises which had been renewed to her when she left Vienna.

The letter from Prince Metternich which was alluded to in one of the letters from Marie Louise, which I have reproduced, destroyed some of the Empress's illusions. This letter informed her that the possession of the sovereignty which had devolved upon her by the treaty was no longer certain and invited her in the Emperor's name to return to Vienna, and to put her interests into his hands. A letter from the Emperor of Austria contained the same invitation. The Empress, abandoned to sad presentiments, losing a hope which she had entertained till then of being free to enjoy the independence of which she had dreamt, gave way to a new influence which shook the constancy of her attachment to the Emperor and persuaded her that she stood in need of other protection. She grew to think that by submission she might be able to remove the obstacles which stood in the way of her possession of Parma, and she resigned herself to obey orders which it was no longer in her power to avoid. General Neipperg, placed exclusively in her confidence, and who was to be united to her by much closer bonds later on, was commissioned to conduct her to Vienna.

Before continuing this narrative I desire to tarry over the first period of the life (still innocent, as I judged it) of a princess born with qualities which would have commended her to the respect of France, if Nature in endowing her with these qualities had added a greater firmness of character. Extraordinary circumstances had united her destiny to that of a great man. These bonds had been violently severed by the selfish and cold policy which had formed them, on the day when Napoleon was no longer to be feared. The faults into which Marie Louise fell must above all be imputed to those in whose hands she was the instrument of hatred and revenge. Our compatriots, under the influence of recent impressions, or of recollections the bitterness of which no revelations have come to temper, have blamed Marie Louise with almost unanimous reprobation. This anathema, I can assert, would grieve the Emperor Napoleon were he still living. The woman whom he honored with his alliance, to whom he owed some happy days, the mother of his much beloved son, the woman of whom he never ceased to speak with generous kindness, who was passive but not aggressive towards him, whose difficult situation he appreciated, whose long struggles he took into consideration, has a right to some indulgence on our part also. Let us reserve our indignation for those who have caused and hurried on her downfall.

I left Paris on September 6, but in spite of the haste with which I traveled I could not reach Geneva before the morning of the 9th. I proceeded without waste of time to Secherons where the Empress was living since she had left Aix, and I was received by her in an extremely friendly manner. She was just about to leave for Berne, and then to undertake an excursion in the Oberland. Her plan was to visit several parts of Switzerland and to prolong her stay so as to arrive as late as possible in Vienna. She was good enough to ask me to accompany her on her excursions, and appointed a meeting at Berne. I had occasion to congratulate her on the happy state of mind in which she seemed to be. Countess de Brignole, several persons of her household, and General Neipperg, who had attached himself to her footsteps in order to carry out the mission which he had received, were with her at Secherons. I saw her a short time at Secherons and she put off, until her arrival in Berne, the opportunity of speaking to me about a number of things which she wished to discuss minutely with me. On leaving her I heard that an officer, who is a General today, the husband of one of her *dames d'annonce,* who had arrived some days previously from the Island of Elba, had brought her a letter from the Emperor. This officer was commissioned to conduct her to the Island of Elba, where she was expected, but he left for Paris on the day before my return without having been able to fulfill his mission.

After having rested a day at Secherons I went to spend a day at Prangins, an estate situated a distance of four leagues from Geneva, on the shores of the lake, where the excellent Queen Julia, wife of Joseph Bonaparte, had recently arrived with her children. I was very anxious to see this noble and virtuous family once more. They had received me in my youth with very much kindness, and with them I had spent many happy days at Mortfontaine. I had not seen the Prince or the Princess since I had taken leave of them at Orléans. I found King Joseph just as he had always been, amiable and unpretentious, returned like Cincinnatus to his plough, much more taken up with the details of his rustic life and his brother's future fate, than with the remembrance of the brilliant and stormy career, which he himself had just brought to a close. Joseph Bonaparte loved Napoleon as much as he had admired him. There existed between the two brothers a sympathy which the difference in their characters, apart from the bond of fraternity, no doubt contributed to strengthen. Napoleon, a mighty mind carried on to splendid actions by the sublimity of his genius, can be compared to nobody. The glory of brilliant enterprises which would not have been above his faculties did not tempt Joseph Bonaparte's ambition; but he knew how to display in business, when once he was engaged in it, the activity and energy which it demanded. To the negotiations which occupied the first period of his political career he had brought the lights of a keen and profound mind, clear and easy eloquence of discussion, and a straightforwardness which was proof against anything. He displayed the same talents and the same qualities in his administration of the two countries which he was called upon to govern. A gentle philosophy, the qualities of a gentleman, a straightforward heart, a noble character would have drawn attention to him in any condition of life, and as the Emperor used to say, would have made him the ornament of society.

The difference in the characters of the two brothers is characterized by a remark which was sometimes addressed to me by Napoleon as First Consul, before Joseph Bonaparte had consented to take an active part in this system. "Why is Joseph with all his talents so lazy?" Napoleon applied the term laziness to the moderation which kept his brother away from the pompous cares and brilliant chains of a rank which is the object of the envy of almost all mankind.

King Joseph's wife was a type of goodness. In the most fragile frame she hid a strong mind, and a lofty reason. Her life was one continued exercise of kindnesses. The time she spent on the two thrones (of which she said with very rare philosophy, that the woman who comes down from a throne is perhaps happier than she who ascends one) was particularly distinguished by the fact that the sphere of her benevolence extended itself more widely.

This digression has taken me away from my subject. I allowed myself to be carried away by the pleasure of speaking of my host at Prangins, and of seeing friends, whom one is glad to find again, after the tempest is over. The time which I spent at their house passed rapidly, and I only arrived at Berne after the Empress. She had left word for me to follow her together with the itinerary of her journey up to the 21st. As at the same time she had been good enough to give me the choice of remaining in Berne, I preferred to do the latter. The Empress was followed in this journey by Count Neipperg, and by one of this General's officers. Countess de Brignole, and one of the *dames d'annonce* were the only French people who accompanied her on this journey.

On my way from Prangins to Berne I stopped at Payerne. Just as I was leaving I was told that a traveler who had passed the night in the hotel wished to speak to me. I followed the host, who conducted me to a room, where I was as surprised as I was pleased to find King Louis, who was traveling in Switzerland under the name of Count St. Leu. I had not seen him since the marriage festivities, not even at Blois, where I had not been acquainted with his presence until the moment when he had left the town. He was in bed, and was suffering greatly from the disease, which had only grown worse as years went on. I spent an hour by his bedside. He spoke to me of recent events with bitter regret, and of his brother with sentiments of true affection. He was still under the sad impression of the Emperor's attempt on his life at Fontainebleau, and judged the immensity of his unhappiness by this desperate action. He said that Heaven, which had prevented so great a disaster, doubtless reserved him for fresh glories, but also for fresh trials. "If Louis XVIII had killed himself," he added, "he would not be today in the palace of the Tuileries." Count St. Leu was that day a prophet without knowing it. He charged me with a letter for the Empress, and I left him very pleased with the unexpected hazard of this meeting.

While awaiting the Empress's return I made some excursions, having nothing else to do, in the pretty country round Berne. On the 21st, which was the day on which Marie Louise was to return from the glaciers, in my impatience to see her again I went to meet her at Thun. I found her well pleased with her journey which according to those who accompanied her had been a fatiguing one, but she had not suffered much thereby. She was kind enough to come and see me at Madame de Brignole's house where I had alighted. I followed her into her apartment and she said the kindest things to me about my return and the mark of affection which I had given her in leaving my family to follow her. She spoke to me at length of the difficulties which were put in the way of her establishment in Parma, and of the bitter regret which she felt at being obliged to return to Vienna, where her position during the congress would be most equivocal. I spoke to her of the Emperor; she said she had received no news of him since the arrival of Colonel Hurault, and that she had been unable to comply with Napoleon's request that she should join him on the Island of Elba without having consulted her father, whose intentions must have been known to him since reading the letter from Prince Metternich, which she had sent him. It was Count Neipperg, as one may well think, who had pointed out this objection to her. Marie Louise had heard, during her journey, of the death of the Queen of Sicily, her grandmother, who succumbed to a night attack of apoplexy. This princess had tried in vain to reach the bell-pull, and when she was found in the morning, it was seen that her hand was stretched out to grasp it, but had not been able to reach it. So as not to sadden the pleasures of the congress with a spectacle of mourning, it was decided in a lofty place, that the official notification of the death of the Emperor Francis's mother-in-law should not be made till its close. Thanks to this fiction, which left the dead queen still living, the festivities were not interrupted.

The Empress spent two days in Berne. She received the Princess of Wales, who had stayed there to see her on her way to Rome where she intended to spend the winter, and invited her to dinner. The princess seemed to be about forty-five years old at that time. She was short and very fat, she had large pronounced features, and eyes which rightly or wrongly, betrayed some of the adventures which were generally attributed to her. Her suite was composed of a lady-in-waiting and four officers. I admit that I was very curious indeed to see this princess who became historical by the scandal with which the English filled Europe, concerning her and the Prince Regent. The evening was of the gayest. We had some music with General Neipperg at the piano. The Empress asked the Princess to sing, and she consented to do so, on condition that Marie Louise should sing with her. The Empress said that she was so timid that she was unable to bring forth a sound, when anybody was listening to her. The Princess encouraged her, saying that as far as she was concerned she was never frightened except for her friends. As a matter of fact, and to tell the truth, she sang with a voice of which I will say nothing, except that it really showed this princess's courage. One of her plans was to go and visit the Emperor at Elba. She was traveling with a child about twelve years old which had a very pretty face. She had not brought him to the Empress's house. This was the famous "Austin" who was so much spoken about in the memoirs published under her name, memoirs which she publicly disavowed as a libelous pamphlet. She said that she did not know who was this child's father, but she loved it just as much as she loved her daughter.

She was dressed in an ample white muslin dress trimmed with lace; her head was adorned with a large veil, rather like those worn by the priestesses of Greek tragedies, which covered her waist, her shoulders and both sides of her bosom. This veil was fastened with a diadem of diamonds. She also wore a magnificent necklace of several rows of pearls and traveled in this array. Apart from this, in spite of her figure and dress, which frankly might be styled curious, the Princess of Wales had the appearance of an excellent woman, simple, straightforward and putting everybody at his ease. Her lady-in-waiting's figure was not less singular than her mistress's. The officers were of very good appearance; one of them was the son of a celebrated Englishwoman, Lady Craven, who married the Margrave of Anspach; the other two were young officers of the Prince of Wales's regiment; the fourth was Doctor Holland, who was said to be a very good doctor.

We left Berne to return to Vienna, traveling through the small cantons. The Empress was accompanied by General Neipperg and his adjutant Hrabowski, Countess de Brignole, Madame Héreau and her husband, etc., etc. M. de Cussy had returned to Paris; M. de Bausset and Madame Hurault de Sorbée, one of the two *dames d'annonce* who had followed the Empress on her departure from Paris, had preceded her to Lindau where they were awaiting her with the carriages.

Marie Louise desired also to visit the ruins of the castle of Rudolph de Hapsburg. General Neipperg, charged to recall her to the seductions of her native land, could not dispense her from a visit to the cradle of the founder of the house of Austria. He even declared that a piece of iron which he found there was a fragment of Rudolph's lance. The Empress lent herself complacently to this fiction. Little pieces of this iron cut up were used for the settings of some rings which she had made in Vienna and which she gave to General Neipperg, M. de Bausset and myself as the insignia of a new order of knighthood and to Madame de Brignole as a souvenir of this journey. The Empress took so much pleasure in all her excursions that I had reason to expect that her journey would be prolonged. I understood only too well how disagreeable her position would have been in Vienna to be surprised at this, but I was impatient to get there. The necessity of getting the letters which were waiting for me in this city, and my interest in their contents, made it imperative for me to return; I was moreover of no utility whatever to the Empress. After having urged me to continue, she was good enough to yield to my arguments, and grant me permission to go. I left her at Schweitz; but to my great surprise she arrived at Schönbrunn three days after me, on the feast day of the Emperor Francis, to whom she had given me a letter.

She had made her way to Vienna from Schweitz, by Saint-Gall, Constance, Munich, and Braunau. She had passed the night in the last town, her memory taking her back four years, when she had been received there as Empress of the French, and when she left it to go and take triumphant possession of a throne the glory of which she came to share. What feelings must have agitated her on finding herself back in this town in so different a position!

She had the pleasure of embracing her son, who had remained at Schönbrunn with Madame de Montesquiou. The young prince was tender and caressing towards her; he was in a flourishing state of health and had not suffered from the slightest indisposition during his mother's absence. The Emperor Francis came to see his daughter as soon as he had heard of her arrival. The Empress of Austria, who was somewhat indisposed by the fatigues of the various ceremonies in which she had been forced to appear, had remained in Vienna. The way in which Count Neipperg had fulfilled his mission was approved of by Their Majesties, for he was at once appointed to act as chamberlain to the Duchess of Parma during the Congress.

Marie Louise found all the sovereigns assembled in Vienna. The kings of Denmark, Bavaria, Würtemberg and other princes had preceded the Emperor of Russia and the King of Prussia there. These sovereigns had made their solemn entry into Vienna, on September 25, 1814, accompanied by the Emperor of Austria who had gone to meet them and followed by the whole of his court. The imperial family of Austria had received all these sovereigns in a magnificent manner. The Emperors and the Kings lodged in the imperial palace where they were entertained with the most sumptuous hospitality. The expense which the assembly of these various princes occasioned to the court was enormous. Fifteen hundred servants and twelve hundred horses were added to the imperial household. Carriages with horses constantly put to and saddle horses were at the service of each sovereign and the officers of his household. Each had a private table sumptuously served at the Emperor's expense. Dinner was served at two in the afternoon, and supper at ten in the evening. Splendid fêtes diverted these noble guests from their political labors, for the Congress had not yet been opened at the time of which I am speaking. It was only to last a few weeks, to settle the interests of the secondary German states, the Treaty of Paris having vested the great powers with the territories which they had adjudged themselves and put them in possession of the same.

The Empress Marie Louise, confined with her son in the château of Schönbrunn, lived there in absolute retirement, a stranger to all the amusements and display which surrounded the sovereigns in Vienna. She awaited the day when justice should be done to her, relying on the faith of a treaty and on her father's feelings. Five days after her return to this château, a fête was given there at which all the sovereigns were present. There were drives in open carriages in the gardens, a theatrical performance, and supper in the orange-house. The Empress remained shut up in her apartments all day long, not daring to go out for fear of meeting faces whose triumphant expression would have contrasted too strongly with the obscurity of the position which had been forced upon her. Although the sight of the amusements which celebrated events which had been so disastrous for her could not but afflict her, she had nevertheless curiosity enough to enjoy the sight of the court ball incognito, watching it through a window let into the attic of the grand hall of the palace of Vienna. Four years ago she had been the queen of a brilliant fête given in this same hall on the occasion of her marriage. The reflections which the contrast of her past greatness with her present situation awoke in her should have sufficed to make her turn her back for ever on such sights. At the same time her want of occupation and the need of emotions caused by souvenirs, although these were importunate, sometimes attracted her back to them.

Marie Louise was presented to the Empress of Russia by the Empress of Austria, and the same time returned the visit of the Grand duchesses of Russia, who had called on her at Schönbrunn first, two days after her arrival. The sovereigns were waiting for somebody to break the ice before going to call upon her. The King of Bavaria had said that if the Emperor of Russia would set the example they would all follow it. Alexander's gallantry, or rather his vanity, had no need of any such stimulus. He came to Schönbrunn with the Austrian general, Count Hardegg; the kings and princes followed.

The Empress received the kings and queens, the princesses and princes whom the Congress had assembled in Vienna, one after the other. She also admitted to pay their court the same persons whom she had seen before her departure for Aix. Prince de Ligne was one of the most attentive. He was an old man of eighty, whom time seemed to have forgotten. His straight figure, above the middle height, his noble gait, even his Field marshal's uniform and the grace with which he used a stick, which he did not seem to want for the purpose of support, gave an air of distinction to his person. His head was crowned with a forest of grey hair, the parasite denizens of which used sometimes to stray out on to the chairs on which he sat. He had a fine face, but his sodden eyes did not betoken the keen wit and power of vivacious repartee which won for him a European reputation. I remember one of his good sayings about the Emperor, whom he described as afflicted with a satyriasis for glory; the saying was in conformity with the style of wit in vogue at the Congress. Prince Lambesc, whose name is inseparable from the first events of the Revolution of 1789, used also to come rather often to present his homage to the Empress Marie Louise. He used to wear long riding-boots, covered with a varnish which he asserted that he prepared himself, but the smell of which did not say much in favor of his olfactory nerves.

On her return to Schönbrunn she resumed the mode of life which she had followed during her first stay. We took our meals, so to speak *en famille,* in dress coats and top-boots. Walks, some visits, billiards, music were the chief amusements of this familiar country house life. Tuesdays and Saturdays were devoted to some invitations, as the Empress wished to be free during the rest of the week. She used to leave Schönbrunn almost every day at one o'clock to go and see her father; sometimes she would take her son with her. This young prince was only taken to the Empress of Austria on solemn occasions, on feast or birthdays. The youngest of the Emperor's sons, Archduke Francis, whose age most nearly approached his nephew's, used to come rather often to Schönbrunn to spend a few days with him. Marie Louise met with real kindness towards herself and her child only from her father and her sisters. The rest of the imperial family did not take the interest in the child which was due to his age and his position. The Empress and her brothers-in-law spoke of nothing less than making a bishop of him; the Emperor was sometimes obliged to force them to keep silence. These hostile sentiments against Napoleon and his son were shared by a crowd of subaltern agents and writers whom the sharing of the spoils of the French Empire had attracted to Vienna, and found an echo in a certain class of Viennese. During one of the Empress's visits to one of the foreign princesses, a crowd of sightseers, who had gathered round her carriage, expressed their opinion that it was very bad taste on her part to have retained the Imperial French arms on the panels of her carriages and on the buttons of her servants' liveries. These remarks obliged Marie Louise to change them.

Her uncles rarely came to see her. The youngest, Archduke Rudolph, who under the appearance of health, hid a complication of diseases, took advantage of the moments when these diseases left him at peace to visit his niece. He was very amiable and very gentle, his constant sufferings had given an expression of melancholy of his features. He was a great musician and painted agreeably. Sometimes he would improvise at the piano and while doing so would often be attacked by a nervous attack, the violence of which used to make him faint.

The Emperor of Austria, accompanied by the Emperor of Russia and the King of Prussia left at the end of October for Hungary. The Emperor Alexander showed himself at the Emperor Francis's side, on his entry into Buda, dressed in a Hungarian uniform. The Austrian monarch's confidence taken in connection with the secret designs attributed to the Czar on some of the provinces of Hungaria, seemed imprudent to the Hungarians attached to the house of Austria.

We had reached the last days of October and the Congress had not yet set to work, which justified Prince de Ligne's well-known saying: "The Congress dances but does not go." At the same time, in the midst of the tumult of balls, banquets, and amusements of every kind which each day brought with it, the most serious questions were being debated; but they were so complicated, and so divergent were the interests at stake, that it was difficult to establish the bases on which to found the drafting of the various definite treaties. The Empress's interests were subjected to the same oscillations. On her return to Vienna there began for her a series of vicissitudes, the object of which was to gain time, and to complicate the question of the possession of the duchies of Parma. The Vienna cabinet pretended to decline, from a feeling of delicacy, to listen to any proposal in favor of Marie Louise. The Emperor Alexander protested his intention of maintaining the stipulation of the Fontainebleau treaty of April 11, which assured the sovereignty of Parma to the Empress; the politics of Russia were not interested in this question. Prussia and England only attached but slight importance to it. The government of Louis XVIII and Spain on the other hand manifested the most violent opposition. Marie Louise once so lofty had fallen so low that she and her son could be disposed of without consulting her. The interest which she could hope for was purely gratuitous; it could only become efficacious by a docility on her part which would suffice to dissipate the mistrust which as the wife of Napoleon she inspired. The only prince who seemed to defend her cause, then, was Alexander, who never lost an opportunity of parading chivalrous sentiments. The lady who had been Empress of the French played in Vienna the rôle of a suitor who has no access to her judges, whose family, though strong enough to defend her, observes a despairing neutrality, and who has no support but the interested zeal of a friend and the protection of a powerful man, anxious rather to do himself credit by his good offices than to render her real services.

Her declared, adversaries were the Spanish plenipotentiaries. The former Queen of Etruria, charged with the guardianship of her son, not having been able to obtain for him the restitution of Tuscany, ceded in 1801 to the Infant of Parma, her husband, had thrown herself back on the duchies of Parma, the paternal inheritance of this son. This princess's claims were supported by the Spanish legation with an obstinacy, to which the most hostile feelings against the Emperor Napoleon gave fresh force; the French plenipotentiaries favored this pretention. The Austrian cabinet, whose policy tended to the invasion of the Italian peninsula, strongly desired, though without letting it be seen, to see an Austrian Archduchess in possession of the duchies of Parma, amongst which Piacenza moreover afforded a strong military position. The Emperor Francis, however, to whom his cabinet wished to give the merit of disinterestedness or whose scruples it apparently wished to respect, offered to leave the decision as to his daughter's interests in the hands of the allies, as well as the settlement of the indemnity to which she was entitled. He carried his abnegation to the point of consenting to the proposal made by France that this indemnity should be taken out in fiefs in Bohemia, known by the name of the Bavarian Palatinates, belonging to the Grand Duke of Tuscany, with reversion to the Emperor Francis's domain. These fiefs were later on assigned to Napoleon's son, in compensation for the succession to the States of Parma which was refused to him. These estates consisted of lands situated in the Buntzlau, Czaslau, Klattau, Leumeritz, and Raconitz districts.

The estimated value of these estates and the revenues derived therefrom valued in currency, Vienna rate, represented a capital of thirteen millions, three or four hundred thousand francs and a revenue of about six hundred thousand francs, French currency. This concession on the part of Austria was never made in earnest. The cession to the son of the Queen of Etruria of the duchy of Lucca, with the enjoyment of an annual income of five hundred thousand francs charged on these estates the fee-simple of which was not alienated, definitely assured to the Empress Marie Louise the integral life possession of the States of Parma.

The pretensions raised by the Court of Spain did not displease the allied sovereigns who were not reassured by the prospect of the establishment of the wife of Napoleon in Italy. They provided the text of new arguments which were employed with success to obtain from her that she should at least appear indifferent to the Emperor's prospects. It was pointed out to her that any suspicion of complicity with him would deprive her forever of the advantages which the friendly feeling of Austria reserved for her, the loss of which would not only have been injurious to her but also to the Austrian Empire. These considerations skillfully placed before her, the fear inspired into the Empress of injuring her father, her respect for whom increased in proportion to the affection, sterile as it was in appearance, that he manifested towards her, the impossibility demonstrated to her of ever being reunited with the Emperor, the Austrian public opinion which influenced her, so to say, on every side, found her without defense. Later on it was tried to push her docility to its extreme limits and to induce her to make a public manifestation against the Emperor, but this she refused to do. This was a concession to old memories, weak it is true, but not yet effaced.

At the same time, General Neipperg, whose functions as chamberlain, Grand Equerry, and Chargé d'Affaires attached him to the inner service of the Empress, was busying himself to assure her the free possession of the sovereignty which the treaties had granted to her. He made use of his influence with the prime minister, wrote memoranda, and pleaded her cause with ardor. The Emperor arranged for interviews between his daughter and his all-powerful minister, so that she might speak to him of her affairs. Each day there was a fresh story: today Parma was assured to her, on the morrow it had been given to somebody else. These alternatives of fear and hope kept her anxiety alive and had the effect of disposing her for the sacrifices which were demanded of her and of increasing her desire to have her fate decided upon. They seemed calculated to aggravate the sad effects of the change which this dependent and undignified position had brought about in her ideas about France.

General Neipperg came almost every day, in the evening, to dine and play music at Schönbrunn; he afterwards returned to Vienna. His every nerve was strained towards one single object, to succeed in the mission with which he had been charged to make the Empress forget France and in consequence the Emperor. The progress which he succeeded in making in the Princess's confidence recommended him to the gratitude of the Austrian cabinet. As a natural consequence the French, especially those whose attachment to the Emperor Napoleon was well known, were badly looked upon. The suspicion which they aroused had caused them to be excluded from any public post in Parma; if the Empress went there, no Frenchman was to follow her. She would only go under the guardianship of an Austrian minister, with an Austrian governor, who alone would be admitted to her confidence and to the directions of public business. The bishop of Piacenza, M. Fallot de Beaumont, made useless endeavors to preserve the episcopal see to which he had been appointed by Napoleon. Count San Vitale was introduced to Marie Louise as Grand Chamberlain of the Duchy of Parma, in the course of November, and this revived her hopes. This seemed to her the effect of General Neipperg's energetic measures, and a foretoken of her speedy occupation of the throne of Parma. By this general's advice she addressed letters to the Emperor of Russia and the King of Prussia to commend her interests to their attention. These letters which were approved of by her father were carried by Neipperg. The General at the same time was commissioned to make a verbal communication on the subject to Lord Castlereagh who showed himself well disposed. Without admitting Count Neipperg to their presence the two princes answered the letters of the Empress. Alexander's answer was in harmony with the character which he assumed in public. It contained promises expressed in kindly terms. The King of Prussia's letter contained nothing but vague and general assurances. Lord Castlereagh, who had answered General Neipperg by word of mouth, did not think it necessary to write; but a week later presented himself at Schönbrunn, with his brother Lord Stewart, in ordinary riding costume, top boots, and a whip in his hand. Not having been received they asked to write down their names and being told that that was not the custom they withdrew. The English minister made a large use of the protectorate, in harmony with the way of thinking of the British cabinet, and thought no doubt than an archduchess who had become the wife of the Emperor Napoleon had on that account lost her rights to any kind of respect. The assurances of the Agamemnon of the coalition and England's toleration gave the Empress some kind of security. Parma seemed likely to be assured to her in the future. There remained the question—a capital question in her eyes—to know whether she would be allowed to reside there.

Chapter XVII

The congress which had progressed so slowly was beginning to give signs of life, but nothing had been practically concluded, except the surrender of Genoa to Sardinia, which made Countess de Brignole say that it was little to the honor of her country that all the sovereigns of Europe should have assembled in Vienna to decide about its fate, and that that was the only reason for which they had come. Indeed that was all that the congress could boast about at that time, besides the death of the poor Prince de Ligne who had been finished off by the festivities. A much more grievous act—an act really iniquitous—was in preparation, namely the expulsion of the King of Saxony from his States. This good and unoffending prince, the most loyal and the most friendly of kings, in whom they were pitilessly persecuting the faithful and constant friend of Napoleon, protested against so revolting an abuse of force. The alleged decision of the congress which was notified to him, handed over the government of the kingdom of Saxony to Prussian commissioners. The declaration made public by the king proclaimed his opposition. At the same time he made it public that he would never consent to surrender the states which he had inherited from his ancestors, nor would he accept any compensation or equivalent which might be offered to him. Generosity was this time in harmony with the politics of the French cabinet. The French plenipotentiaries pleaded the King of Saxony's cause with force. The protection of France to which that of Austria was added, a noble and generous protest from the princes of Ducal Saxony, who declared that they would not accept any portion of territory taken away from the king of Saxony, a declaration made by the small German states against any kind of parceling out of the German states, recalled the great powers to moderation. They contented themselves with depriving the King of Saxony of half his kingdom, the whole of which was swallowed up by Prussia. England who laid claim to the rôle of being alone the Savior of Europe prided herself on asking nothing for herself. The war and the Treaty of Paris had realized her ambitious views. She had acquired Malta and the Ionian Islands in Europe, and had laid hands on almost all the French colonies. She had seized upon offensive and defensive points in all the seas which favored her commerce and gave her the means of injuring the trade of other nations. She wished to establish her supremacy, and render her rôle as a continental power more important by peremptorily declaring that she raised her Electorate in Hanover to a kingdom, and that she increased this territory by such of the neighboring lordships as might best suit her. Venice had asked for her independence. Austria answered this demand by imposing her rule on this republic.

On Dec. 12, the anniversary of the Empress's birthday, the foreign princesses sent her their compliments, according to the German custom. She had gone away to spend this day in Baden so as to escape the bother of visits and compliments. Two days previously the Empress of Austria had gone to Schönbrunn accompanied by the Archdukes and Archduchesses, Marie Louise's brothers and sisters, to celebrate the occasion *en famille*. The Emperor Francis who had announced his intention of being present had been detained in Vienna by unforeseen business and had been unable to come.

About this time Fouché wrote letters from Paris to Prince Metternich. Napoleon's former minister, bored at having nothing to do, wished to take part in all and to set his mark on everything. He wrote to the Austrian minister that there could never be a more favorable opportunity for establishing the Empress Regent in France; that the new government had so offended public opinion that if the Emperor's son riding on a donkey and led by a peasant were to make his appearance in Strasburg, the first regiment to which he would be presented would lead him to Paris without any obstacles being put in his way. I heard of these letters from Count Aldini to whom they had been shown by Prince Metternich. Count Aldini had been minister secretary of state to the King of Italy in Paris. The Austrian cabinet who had feared his influence had summoned him to Vienna under the pretext of consulting him about Italian affairs. He had frequent opportunity of seeing the prime minister, but rather to show himself than to work with him.

Since the letter which the Empress had written from Aix to the Emperor and which M. de Bausset had sent from Parma in the preceding month of August, all communications between her and the Island of Elba appeared to have been forbidden. I wished to know what reasons she had for not writing. Shortly after her return to Schönbrunn, whence I used to send news of the Empress and her son to the Emperor, I asked Marie Louise for a letter to enclose in mine. I then heard to my sorrow that Prince Metternich in the course of a long interview which she had had with this minister had made her promise not to carry on any correspondence with the Emperor without her father's consent, and to hand him the letters which she might receive. The Empress added that she had consented very much against her will to this cruel necessity, despairing of being able to do otherwise. One day, on her return from one of the daily visits which she paid to the Imperial palace in Vienna, she brought back a letter from the Emperor Napoleon dated November 30 which her father had handed her. The Emperor complained of the Empress's silence and begged her to write to him to give him news of herself and of his son. This letter had been four days in the hands of the Emperor of Austria. One of the Grand Duke of Tuscany's couriers had brought it. It had no doubt been shown to the sovereigns, for it was for this purpose and in order to prove his good faith to his allies that the Emperor Francis had exacted from his daughter that all letters which her husband should write to her should be handed to him. The Empress did not answer because the permission to do so had not been granted to her. I made up for her silence by writing myself. The Emperor as soon as he had been informed that the privacy of his letters was no longer respected, and that the Empress had been forbidden to write to him, ceased writing. In spite of the minute supervision to which I was subjected, Napoleon had not remained without news of his wife and son. I used to write to him by every possible means. I found facilities amongst the Viennese merchants which I took advantage of to fulfill my duty. Some worthy merchants whose heart had not been hardened by politics, and who had lost nothing in business during the stay of the French at the time of the occupation in 1805 and 1809—can say this without in any way diminishing the merit of their kind behavior—lent themselves in a very friendly manner to forwarding the letters which I addressed to General Bertrand by way of Leghorn or Florence.

The Empress who since her departure from France had neglected her drawing took advantage of the presence of Isabey of Vienna to recommence her lessons. I have said that this clever artist had come to paint the portraits of the sovereigns, and he was, as a matter of fact, working at his picture of the assembly of the congress. This picture is as remarkable from the good likenesses of the people as from the clever way in which Isabey grouped them. His brush must often have fallen from his hand for he was engaged on a piece of work which must have been painful to a Frenchman. He used to sacrifice some hours of each week to go to the Empress and repeat the lessons by which she had so much profited.

The want of occupation, the influence of her recollections, favored by the atmosphere in which she was jiving, prompted her also to seek relaxation in the childish amusements which had been familiar to her youth; she gave herself up to these frivolous and innocent pleasures when the bad weather interrupted her usual walks or her daily visits to the Imperial palace. Sometimes she would master her dislike for business and attend to the reports which were sent or read to her by General Neipperg, or by the minister who was governing the Duchy of Parma, and who had come to Vienna for this purpose. The former read her one day a very serious memorandum, which she appeared to listen to with interest. It was a series of political and military considerations about Italy, in which the author had inspired himself rather with the political maxims of Themistocles, than with Aristides' principles of virtue. This project of one of the men who used to accuse Napoleon the loudest of iniquitous ambition, was *very useful* to Austria but at the same time very unjust. Count Neipperg's memorandum recommended the adoption in Italy of a confederative system, which in course of time would deliver up the whole Peninsula to Austrian rule, and cause all the little sovereignties which were not held by princes of the House of Austria to disappear imperceptibly. This memorandum might perhaps be found even now in the deed boxes of the Vienna Chancery. The annexation of the state of Genoa to the kingdom of Sardinia was the first step in the direction of the establishment of a confederation intended to unite the small Italian states against France to the advantage of Austria. This enlargement of the territory of a prince who had always been our adversary and the ally of our enemies, was destined in the opinion of the great powers to increase his means of action and to render him master of France's outlets in Italy. The purpose of the allies was in one word to turn against us the immense fortifications of Alessandria and protect Lower Italy from a French invasion by the sea.

My greatest pleasure was to pass a few hours in the young prince's apartment. His prettiness, his gentleness, the vivacity of his repartee were full of charm; he was about four years old at the time, strong, well-built, and in excellent health. Fair, abundant curly hair framed his fresh face, the regular features of which were animated by fine blue eyes. His intelligence was precocious and he was better educated than many children older than he was. Madame de Montesquiou, who never left him and who cared for him with a mother's solicitude, used to rise every morning at seven o'clock and begin his daily lessons immediately after prayers. Not only did the young prince read quite fluently, but he also knew a little history and geography and was acquainted with the first elements of knowledge. A certain Abbé Lanti, almoner to the French legation, used to come and talk Italian with him; a valet used to speak to him in German only. The child could already make himself understood in these two languages, but he greatly disliked speaking German which he found hard and unpleasant to pronounce.

New Year's day of 1815 revived remembrances of France in the Empress's heart, remembrances which had so roughly been repelled. In France New Year's day is a solemn feast day; in Vienna it is little more than an ordinary day, for it is during the week that precedes it that people make presents to each other and that the compliments of the season are exchanged. The streets of Vienna are then filled with carriages and foot-passengers in Sunday clothes. The Viennese seem rather to bury the old year with honor than to celebrate the new. This return to the customs of our country made us think for a moment that France had not been altogether forgotten in Schönbrunn. The Empress received all the persons of her household after mass. She was so kind as to give me some charming articles of Viennese manufacture for my New Year's presents, adding one of those little colored picture-cards which it is the custom to give in Germany, at certain periods in the year, and which conveyed the wish for a future better than the present and which might in some way resemble the past. Even General Neipperg showed himself attentive and affectionate.

On Twelfth-night the sovereigns assembled at a great banquet at the court. I forget which of them got the bean and was king of the feast. At Schönbrunn, the Empress gave a *goûter* to her son, her young brother Archduke Francis, and his sisters. The ephemeral royalty fell to her son; it was unfortunately the emblem of the royalty which had been bestowed on him at his birth.

On the 12th the Empress went to return calls on the Empress of Russia and the Grand Duchesses, on the occasion of New Year's day according to the Russian calendar which corresponds to January 13 of the Gregorian calendar.

About the same time Baron d'Erbeck, tutor of the Prince Imperial, who is Emperor today, had a violent attack of epilepsy in the midst of a drawing room at court, as a result of which he fell into a state of furious madness, which caused his death shortly afterwards. This event produced a very strong impression on his august pupil; the matter was variously spoken about, various also were the comments made on the strange things which the tutor had said while in delirium, and which were only the utterances of a diseased mind. As far as I can remember he spoke about menaces of death or of an attempt that was to be made against the exercise of the Prince Imperial's intellectual faculties.

Abbé Werner, a great preacher, who was considered one of the first poets in Germany, was the author of tragedies which had a success of "runs." Being in Vienna, Count Neipperg thought it would give the Empress pleasure to hear this poet. The impression created by beautiful verses recited in an inspired manner, would tend to reconcile the princess to the German language. Several Archdukes, her uncles, and her two former Grand Mistresses, Mesdames de Colloredo and Lazanski, were invited to these readings; my ignorance of the German language dispensed me from attending them. Abbé Werner read his tragedy, *Cunégonde*. He was a man of exalted imagination, whose austere face gave him the appearance of a fanatic. At first a Lutheran, he had turned

Roman Catholic; and had gone to Rome ostentatiously to abjure his faith in the pope's presence.

We were awaiting the issue of the congress with impatience. It was expected to end each day, but the lofty persons who presided over it appeared to be too much taken up with ceremonies and festivities to pay much attention to business. On January 21, the minister of France had the anniversary of the death of Louis XVI celebrated in the cathedral of St. Stephen. The Archbishop of Vienna officiated with great pomp. All the sovereigns, in mourning garb, and the princesses wearing mantles of crape over their black dresses, were present at this ceremony in a pew of the choir. To divert the spectators of this lugubrious solemnity, the sovereigns gave the spectacle of a sledge-race conducted by themselves at Schönbrunn. Prince Eugène was invited to it. The château was crowded with people. Madame de Montesquiou and Madame de Brignole were forced to allow the sovereigns to go through their rooms on their way to the theatre. The Empress's apartment was alone respected. The great questions of the possession of Saxony and Poland disturbed the harmony which appeared to exist amongst the principal powers represented at the congress. By the treaties which the allies had concluded amongst themselves since Austria's desertion, when fortune favored their arms, it had been secretly agreed that the States of the great powers should be reconstituted as they had been before the wars, at the expense of the French Empire and even of the secondary states whose possessions might be to their liking. As long as the common adversary of the allies had remained standing they had been faithful to the motto "Union gives strength," but if the needs of conquest had united them, the sharing of the spoils was to divide them. The powers separated into several camps; it was whispered that secret treaties had been concluded between England and Austria, who later on admitted France thereto, against Russia and Prussia. France, in spite of or perhaps by reason of the skill of her representatives, was the disinterested spectator of these redistributions of states. In spite of her benevolent rôle she did not obtain the concession of the slightest advantage; she did all in her power, on the contrary, to destroy the only French power that remained in Italy and to assure the rule of Austria. When it has been said that the French plenipotentiary had a personal interest in the preservation of the principality of Bénévent, which he owed to Napoleon's munificence, or in the large indemnity which he was to receive from the gratitude of the Bourbons of Naples, one has enunciated a fact so entirely in harmony with the well-known conduct and character of this minister that it is not possible to consider such an imputation as entirely libelous. M. de Talleyrand allied himself with the Spanish envoys to deprive the wife of his former master of the States of Parma, thrown to her in guise of alms; his zeal in favor of the House of Bourbon and legitimacy *devoured* him. The interests of the royal family of Naples outweighed the interests of France, just as the interests of the people were sacrificed to the interests of the dynasties at the Congress; but all the efforts of France could not prevent the virtuous King of Saxony from losing half his States.

One of the greatest cares of the powers assembled at the Congress was the fear with which the vicinity of the Island of Elba inspired them. Intrigues were set on foot in mysterious conferences, to act by violence or ruse against the redoubtable sovereign of this imperceptible speck in the Mediterranean. The French legation associated itself in the secret measures proposed against him and urged his transportation. Whatever may have been the resolutions taken concerning him, whatever may have been the reasons why all the troops of the coalition were kept under arms, certain it is that instead of being disarmed the foreign armies were, from the end of December, increased in number and put on a war footing.

The great Russian army remained under arms. It was recruited and fully completed. A Polish army was organized, before the annexation of Poland to Russia, and a Russian corps marched on Posen; still larger corps received orders to advance on Hanover. Prussia drew up the troops which were stationed in the North of France and transferred the general headquarters to Brussels. At the same time her garrisons in Luxembourg, Coblentz, and Treves were increased. The King of Bavaria increased the corps which he had on the two banks of the Rhine by one third, and put the fortifications of Cleves and Juliers into a state of defense. The Dutch army was increased by several new battalions. Austria exerted the greatest activity in her armaments, and great energy was displayed in the staffs of her army. By order of the aulic council of the Empire all the regiments of the Austrian Empire were put on a war footing and fully completed. The purchase of several thousands of horses was ordered in the country to complete the parks of artillery and the military equipages. General Frimont's corps received orders to cross back to the left bank of the Rhine. And finally there was formed in Italy a reserve army of forty thousand men. The Austrian military lists placed the total effective forces of the Empire at four hundred and fifty thousand men. The official Gazette of Vienna published in part an account of the military measures and preparations which had been adopted. An imperial decree: "that as passing from a state of war to a state of peace presented difficulties, it had appeared necessary to preserve a great army under the flags, and that in order to provide for the expenses caused by its maintenance, a tax of 50% was placed on the various branches of manufacture." Other clauses made public the fact that no soldiers would be discharged until the political situation had cleared up. One of the King of Bavaria's orders announced: "that affairs abroad having rendered it impossible to recall the troops who were outside the frontiers of the kingdom back to their garrisons, to put the army on a peace footing and to discharge the corps of volunteers, an extraordinary tax intended to meet the expenses of these troops would be levied."

The Vienna Gazette announced, in the month of December, that the sittings of the congress would be closed towards the end of January; then, towards the end of January the same paper stated that the sovereigns would not be able to leave Vienna until the end of February. It was again stated in this paper that it was impossible to say how long the stay of the sovereigns in the Austrian capital would last.

All these military movements and arrangements, which had been commanded from the middle of December, continued during the months of January and February. The reason for some of these arrangements might have been the taking possession of the various parcels of territory which had fallen to each of the allied powers, but no satisfactory explanation can be given for the rest. A curious book might be written on the secret history of the Vienna congress, a work of varied interest, well calculated to tempt the pen of some talented writer. Passions, abuses of power, jealousies, grudges, fear covered themselves with the brilliant varnish of the festivities. Balls and routs blinded the idlers to the real reasons of the apparent stagnation of business. The Austrian court must have found that the stay of the allies, from a financial point of view, was prolonging itself beyond measure. The expenses in which it was involved became as ruinous as a war would have been. This court would really have had a right to ask for some indemnity; it is true that it found sufficient compensation for its pecuniary sacrifices in the restitution of the provinces which it had lost.

The plenipotentiaries of Spain and France in most urgent notes demanded the expulsion of King Joachim. Already in the month of December the following proposal had been made, in a confidential way, to Lord Castlereagh by M. de Talleyrand, and had been eagerly approved of: "Europe assembled in congress acknowledges King Ferdinand as King of Naples; all the powers mutually engage themselves one towards the other not to support, either directly or indirectly, any claim opposed to his right to assume this title."

At the same time the hostile steps taken against King Joachim by the two courts which were allied to the old reigning house of Naples, were personally only aimed against Austria, whose interest and whose views on this question—far from being definitely pronounced—remained, on the contrary, equivocal. The other great powers, who had influence at the congress, took very much less interest in a change of dynasty in Naples. What injured King Joachim the most in the mind of the allies was the suspicion that he remained secretly attached to the Emperor.

Lord Castlereagh laid copies of letters from Napoleon to King Joachim and the Queen, his wife, before the English Parliament, on May 2, 1815. The minister wanted to prove by means of these letters that King Joachim in signing the treaty by which he had engaged to make common cause with the allies, had had no intention of fulfilling the obligations which he had contracted. It has been proved that these letters, handed by the French cabinet to Lord Castlereagh, bore a date which was not the date of the time when they had really been written—that they referred to older occurrences, and that the text of some of them had even been forged. Copies of the Emperor's letters, taken in 1814 or in 1815, from drafts which remained in the archives of the Imperial cabinet and which were left by Minister Blacas when Louis XVIII had left the Tuileries on March 19, 1815, were found on the return from the Island of Elba. These copies were written on paper doubled lengthwise—one half being left blank, and the alterations which had been made in the text were marked with red ink. I saw them in June, 1815, and everybody else could have seen them as I did, as they were shown to anybody who wanted to convince himself of the fact. It was only when King Joachim had strong reasons to suspect the designs of the allies and of the government of the Restoration against his crown that he thought of putting himself in a state of defense, by approaching Napoleon on the Island of Elba. When he could no longer doubt Austria's intentions of dethroning him Murat determined to act on the offensive.

The Emperor Alexander, accompanied by Prince Eugène with whom he used to walk out alone every day, used sometimes to come to Schönbrunn at the luncheon hour. He used to come without being announced, and would sit down to table next to the Empress in a familiar manner. He remembered having seen me at Tilsitt and Erfurth, showed himself very well disposed towards me, and gave me marks of his interest. He even made me the offer through Prince Eugène that I should go to Russia, assuring me that I should find all the advantages that I had lost in France there. There was every conceivable reason for my not accepting this offer, but none the less I was very grateful to him for it. I do not know whether I have already mentioned what the Czar was good enough to tell me about the continental system, and the infallible ruin which would have resulted therefrom to England if this system could have lasted another year. Alexander had come to this conviction after the visits which he had paid to the leading manufacturing establishments in that country and his conversations with the principal manufacturers.

He was thinking no doubt at the same time of the advantages of the impetus given to the industries of the various States of the continent and to Russian industry in particular, a result which alone would suffice to justify this great conception. There was a little bitterness in his tones when he spoke about England. He was not charmed with London society. He was specially shocked by the custom, which was then still in use, for the men to remain at the dinner table to drink after having sent the ladies off to the drawing-room. He sought after popularity in Vienna. In his walks abroad he used to salute all the officers he met and went up to them, sometimes shaking hands with them and saying nattering things. Always either in a dress or frock coat he used to go out and come in without allowing military honors to be paid to him. If a guard who did not know of this wish of his saw him coming, and recognizing him were about to present arms to him, he would motion to them to return into their guardhouse and not to pay any attention to him.

The circle of Marie Louise's little court had greatly shrunken; it was almost entirely composed of General Neipperg and myself. Countess de Montesquiou used sometimes to come and join us, but not very often; in her scrupulous attachment to the duties of her place she did not wish to leave her pupil. From the beginning of the year Countess de Brignole had become very ill; she was forced to keep her room almost without interruption and often had to take to her bed.

M. de Bausset, on his side, was bedridden with a stubborn attack of gout which did not give him a moment's respite. Owing to the absence of these two persons, the Tuesday and Saturday receptions had been interrupted.

Towards the middle of February, when no doubt ought to have subsisted concerning the possession of the duchies of Parma, definitely acquired, General Neipperg took me aside and spoke to me with apparent emotion of the disquieting turn which the Empress's affairs were taking. On my expressing my surprise to him, at this sudden alarm, he told me that he had just had an hour's conversation with Prince Metternich on this subject and that the minister had made him understand, amongst other reasons which called the Empress's rights into question again, that it would be impossible for them to allow her son to go to Italy for the time being. He did not appear to doubt that the friends of the princess would entreat her to leave her son in Vienna, if his presence in Italy might injure her interests, reserving to herself the right to go and see him every year. This hint was calculated to give rise to the thought that the determination to deprive the young prince of the succession to the States of Parma had either been taken or was just about to be taken. On the morrow Count Neipperg, apparently thinking that he must convert me to his opinion, spoke to me of the matter again in the presence of M. de Bausset; at the same time he asked me to listen to his memorandum on the vicissitudes which the duchies had undergone, and on the inalienable rights of the House of Austria over these states. This memorandum and the one written by Baron de Wessemberg on the same subject were handed to the Italian committee.

The Emperor Alexander, constant in his affection for Prince Eugène, pleaded his cause at the congress. He had at first thought of securing the Ionian Islands for him. It is a fact worthy of remark that in the dismemberment of a great Empire, when each of the sharing powers was urgently occupied in appropriating the fragments of it which best suited it, the Ionian Islands should have remained untouched for some time—left, so to speak, at the disposal of the first comer. The annexation of these Islands by England opened their eyes to the forgetfulness which had made them neglect this rich prey, or to their want of sufficient boldness to take possession of them. The Emperor of Russia afterwards laid a note before the congress, the purport of which was that a territory with 300,000 inhabitants, on the left bank of the Rhine, should be accorded to Prince è. The choice of a district in the neighborhood of France for the territory in which the Emperor Alexander wished to establish Napoleon's adopted son did not show any great solicitude on his part for the interests of the French princes, who had been recently recalled, and as a matter of fact his language did not bespeak much interest on their behalf. I have sometimes heard him speak quite bitterly about them. He said that he had known Louis XVIII since Mittau; and in his eyes they were nothing but *parvenus* in all the Royal Houses of Europe. "They are back again on the throne now," he added, "let them keep there. If they fall off it is not I who will help them up again."

The hint which Prince Metternich had given to General Neipperg induced the Empress to obtain an interview with the prime minister. She saw him in the Emperor of Austria's palace and received the assurance that her right to the duchy of Parma would be vigorously defended, and that her docility was being taken into consideration. General Neipperg asked Lord Castlereagh for an audience, and he appointed it at eleven o'clock in the evening; he received assurances of interest from this minister and from Lord Wellington. The Empress wrote on February 16 to the Emperor of Russia. Her letter contained, together with new assurances of her confidence in the support he was giving her, a declaration to the effect that she would accept nothing from France, that she would renounce the reversion of, the revenue of a million francs which was assured to her by Article III of the treaty of April 11, and all claims to the fiefs in Bohemia. General Czernitchev brought back the Emperor Alexander's answer. It renewed his promises to remain of the same way of thinking *in the manner desired by the Empress.* He asked her for a meeting on the morrow. He arrived just at the moment when the Empress, who did not know whether he was coming to luncheon, was sitting down to table, and renewed the assurances which he had made in his letter. Since the concession which had been obtained from the Empress that she would not take her son with her to Italy the most comforting assurances reached her from every side. General Neipperg returning one day from Vienna assured her of the Austrian cabinet's firm resolution to maintain her rights, and even not to allow any discussion on this point, which was considered as definitely settled by the treaty, and by the fact of the occupation, the taking possession of and government of the duchy in her name ten months ago. The French legation was far from sharing these views. The Spanish plenipotentiaries joined with it in manifesting a violent opposition. Duc Dalberg asserted at the house of the Countess de Brignole, his mother-in-law, that the Empress would not have Parma, and that the allies would not allow the Bonaparte family to own an independent principality. Count Anatole de Montesquiou arrived about that time to spend a few weeks with his mother, and I was exceeding glad to see him, for friends of the Emperor had become very rare at Schönbrunn. I also received a letter from General Bertrand from Porto-Ferraio, dated January 28, and a letter from Cardinal Fesch which had been written from Rome on Feb. 4. The Emperor was in good health, and had received no news of the Empress and his son for more than a month, a matter which was causing him great anxiety. I showed these letters to the

Empress. On the morrow at lunch she told me that if I had not yet answered the letters of which I had spoken to her the day before I was not to answer them; that she would tell me why later on, that the reason referred personally to me rather than to her. Whatever respect I might have for this wish of the Empress which was prompted by nothing less than her natural kindness, I did not consider myself able to dispense with answering these letters, and I have no doubt that if I was not disturbed in my correspondence with the Island of Elba it was owing to her protection. A powerless but not indifferent spectator to all that was going on around me I could not but be painfully affected to see the Empress placed between her duty as wife and mother, and her desire to go and reign in Parma (which she could only obtain by means of a double sacrifice), so easily choosing between these vexatious alternatives which till then had caused her so much anxiety. Passing storms had changed neither her gentleness nor her kindness, but to her anxiety there had succeeded a security which it was difficult to disturb. I ought perhaps to have sought for the reason of this serenity of hers in the confidence with which she was inspired by the powerful protection of her father, who absolved her of all, and in the sacrifice of her French sentiments to which she had fully made up her mind.

When I used to go and spend a few hours at the bedside of poor Countess de Brignole, who was very ill indeed, I found food for other reflections. The habit of intrigue—even innocent intrigue—which had become a real want in this remarkable woman, accustomed to the respect which distinguished men of every class had always had for her, found but little food in the society of a princess who took nothing seriously to heart. Countess de Brignole enjoyed all the influence to which she could reasonably lay claim on the Empress's mind; but she was forced to exert more suppleness and intellectual resources, put up with more vexations, anxieties, and cares, involuntarily aroused, than when she was governing the Republic of Genoa by her influence on the statesmen of this country, or when she was negotiating with the pope at Fontainebleau. This violent state of affairs in which this woman, of so fine and delicate an organization, who needed rest and quietness of mind, was placed was to end in killing her. I often advised her to go to seek for rest in Italy, but all her past there had been overthrown, and besides, how could she make up her mind to renounce even the shadow of an influence?

When I used to go from Madame de Brignole's to M. de Bausset's I found him, on the rare occasions when he was not in bed, almost swooning in his armchair, wrapped up in an old cashmere shawl and a largely flowered counterpane, *sweating in this harness,* and casting glances now supplicating, now furious, towards the ceiling. This other patient was entirely given up to his sufferings, and remained sometimes for three weeks without interruption fastened down to his bed of pain, which he watered with his perspiration and his tears, for he literally used to cry like a child when his nerves were tortured by the gouty humor.

To pass on to less sorrowful scenes I will speak of a wager which the Emperor Alexander made with a Viennese lady. The wager was to see which of them would change clothes the quicker. The scene took place in a drawing room which had been divided into two by a screen behind which each was to undress and dress again. The witnesses handed each article of clothing, so that there could be no doubt that the undressing and dressing had been completely carried out. The lady must have exerted great haste, or the Czar must have allowed her to get ahead of him, for she won the bet. It is true that she shortened the operation, which in a woman's toilette takes the most time, by putting a cap on her head. Thus no difficulty was made in the choice of amusements, for anything in the way of diversion was welcomed. The same day there took place at the court a ballet-pantomime representing Olympus. They had been unable to find any Venus, or rather no lady had claimed to represent this Goddess. A certain Princess Bagration had more courage, but before the curtain went up she withdrew the offer which she had only made to get the performers out of their difficulty. The ingenious Isabey, to conciliate matters had the idea of showing a back view of Venus, draped with all the grace and elegance of which this clever artist possessed the secret.

The French and Spanish plenipotentiaries persevered in their applications for the dethronement of King Joachim. The latter had given Austria no pretext for declaring against him, but the Congress wanted nothing better than to have its hand forced. To effect this purpose the French government manifested its intention of resorting to the force of arms. The Austrian cabinet was only awaiting this hostile demonstration to declare that it intended to observe a neutral attitude, and that it would repel by force any French or Neapolitan troops which should set foot on its territory in Italy. To assure this neutrality in appearance, a neutrality behind which it could prepare itself to act, it assembled an army of one hundred and fifty thousand men in Italy under the command of General Frimont. Count Saurau was sent to Milan, at the same time, in the capacity of governor of Lombardy, and General Goertz was sent to Venice. This declaration was notified to the Courts of Paris and Naples. The French government then appeared to occupy itself in organizing an expeditionary army to embark at Toulon, land in Sicily, and joining the Sicilian troops, to attempt a landing on the Neapolitan coast. The Minister of War sent General Ricard at the same time to Vienna to come to an understanding with the French ambassador on the subject of this expedition, which however never got beyond the mere proposal.

General Neipperg being at the Court Theatre met M. de Metternich and was told to prepare to leave for Turin; his adjutant, Colonel Hrabowski received orders at the same time to proceed to Milan to be employed in General Frimont's staff. General Neipperg rushed off at once to inform the Empress Marie Louise of the decision which had been taken with reference to him. On the morrow this Princess left early for Vienna where she begged the Emperor to postpone the general's departure until her affairs had been finally settled; the Emperor Francis refused to make any promises. Count Neipperg wrote from Vienna to Marie Louise urging her to carry out the intention which she had expressed of asking for an interview with Prince Metternich; she at once sent off a letter, which had been prepared in advance, to the minister. At two o'clock Marie Louise drove to Vienna with her son, whom she sent back in the carriage to Schönbrunn. She had to wait a long time for Count de Metternich at the house of the Archduchess Leopoldine, her sister, where she had appointed to meet him. The minister arrived at last and the Empress obtained a promise from him that General Neipperg should not go away before the decision of the congress on the Parma question; his opinion was that all would be finished from the 8th to the 10th of March.

In the meanwhile King Joachim was not in ignorance of the danger which threatened him, nor of the agreement come to between France and several other powers with the object of dethroning him; the crafty conduct of Austria, and the assembling of a formidable Austrian army which was six times greater than a simple observation corps needed to be, caused him anxiety. Considering, and rightly so, that this army was simply directed against himself, he determined to get the start of his enemies. During the Emperor's stay in the Island of Elba, communications had been established between Napoleon and the King of Naples. At the time when the Emperor decided to leave the Island of Elba it was agreed by word of mouth that the King of Naples should remain with his army on the frontiers of Lombardy, thus threatening Austria without attacking her. A convention to this effect was carried to Naples by one of the Lady Mother's chamberlains. The hurrying on of events prevented this treaty from being signed. A council was held at Ancona, at which three ministers, one French and the other two Neapolitan were present. At this council the question was discussed whether advantage should be taken of the King of Naples' favorable situation, to profit by this situation and to get the start of Austria. The two ministers who were born Neapolitans expressed the opinion that apparent neutrality should be observed, basing themselves on the danger to which the King would expose his crown if by a premature attack he justified Austria's secret designs. The King answered them by saying that since Austria had made up her mind to overthrow him, he must get the start of her by assuming an offensive attitude without waiting any longer. One of the Neapolitan ministers, Zurlo, who was for a long time thought to be the creature and secret agent of the Queen of Sicily, which was not the case, insisted with much loyalty and talent on the various considerations which should keep the King on the defensive. These views were strongly supported by the third minister, who was a very honorable man, animated with French sentiments and devoted to King Joachim. He especially insisted on the faithful execution of the arrangements which had been come to with the Emperor Napoleon. The King, whose bellicose and impatient character urged him to war, and who was indignant with Austria's ill will towards him, inclined to act on the offensive. A letter from one of the Emperor's brothers, the contents of which are not known, which was handed to him at a ball which was given to him by the city of Ancona, it may be, referred to some secret plans, and decided him. He threw down the glove and crossed the Rubicon.

Some of the sovereigns had left Vienna, others were preparing to depart, or had fixed the date of their departure at an earlier or later period, in one word, the Congress appeared to be drawing to a close, when the Duke of Wellington arrived in Vienna to take the place of Lord Castlereagh who was being called back to London by the impending opening of Parliament. Whatever may have been the real reason why so important a person was sent to the Congress at the time when the most important business had, been settled, the arrival of the hero of the coalition gave a fresh impetus to the amusements which, for the last five months, had not been able to weary the august guests of the Emperor of Austria. It was in the midst of a renewal of festivities and enjoyments, that the unexpected news was thundered forth: *the Emperor has left the Island of Elba.* It is impossible to describe the sensation which was produced by this news. It was brought to Schönbrunn on March 7 at two o'clock in the afternoon by a certain Abbé Zegelius, priest of the parish of St. Anne in Vienna, who came to see Madame de Montesquiou.

The coachman who had driven this abbé had heard the news at the Chancery of state, whither it had been brought by a courier. The Empress was absent at the time. She had gone out riding accompanied by General Neipperg. On his return the General found a note from his adjutant Lieutenant-Colonel Hrabowski, which informed him that he had been ordered to go to Milan as a courier, and that he was starting at once. Marquis

Brignole, who arrived in the course of the evening, informed Marie Louise that couriers coming from various parts of Italy since noon had brought the news that the Emperor had indeed left the Island of Elba. Till then doubt had been permissible. Extreme was the agitation amongst the sovereigns and their ministers. On the evening of the day an extraordinary spectacle was given at the court. The news was the object of the most animated conversations. The French plenipotentiaries, and some other foreign ministers who were present, maintained that the Emperor had made his way to Naples; which was to them a fresh grievance against King Joachim. Those who thought that he had made his way to France were in a great minority and could find nobody to believe them; but all were unanimous in the resolution to take energetic measures against Napoleon. The King of Bavaria pushed his way through the crowd to come and tell Prince Talleyrand that he would *make one of them.* His son the Prince Royal said that the Emperor Napoleon and King Joachim, would be taken together and both sent to trial. It would be difficult to describe the various impressions of stupor, fear, hope, in one word, of the genuine or feigned feelings which were expressed by the lofty persons present at this assembly.

The Empress no doubt heard the news on her return from her ride. At least there is nothing more probable, but she appeared to ignore it. There was dinner, billiards, and music as usual. On the morrow the news spread rapidly in the little French colony of Schönbrunn, and gave rise to such remarks and expressions of opinion that an officious individual thought fit to suggest that an order of the day forbidding the people of the household to make any reflections on the subject be issued. The Empress no longer sought to dissemble the emotion which this *coup de main,* as it was called, caused her. She spoke a great deal about it on the next day; she was alarmed at the dangers to which the Emperor had exposed himself, being persuaded that he would not succeed. She afterwards expressed a fear lest the effects of such an enterprise might be to spoil her affairs in Parma, and compromise her son's future. She went to Vienna to take leave of the Empress of Russia, who was leaving for Munich. On her return she said that the Emperor of Austria had expressed his great displeasure at what the Emperor Napoleon had done and had manifested his intention of sending powerful forces into Italy to oppose anything that he might endeavor to do there. Orders indeed were given to put the Italian navy in movement and to march an army of 180,000 men to Italy under the command of Prince Schwarzenberg. As usually happens in occurrences the importance of which exceeds all others, everybody tried to find a reason for this evasion, and tried to fix the responsibility of it on somebody else. The Emperor of Austria reproached the Emperor of Russia and the King of Prussia for having rejected the proposal of sending a foreign garrison to the Island of Elba, and of forbidding French soldiers to live there. All festivities ceased in Vienna from this time and gave way to silent activity; the sitting of the Congress was involved in impenetrable mystery; the Vienna Gazette (the *Beobachter,* a newspaper which was written under the inspiration of the prime minister) remained silent, the simplest news of the city came there through the newspapers of the other states of Germany. All communication with France was rigorously forbidden. The supervision became insupportably wearisome. The police, like so many wasps, assailed one as one went by, followed one everywhere, and invaded one's privacy on a thousand pretexts. The German servants were thrown into a state of desperation by the Vienna police who exacted with menaces revelations which they were unable to make, as most often they had nothing whatever to disclose. The uncertainty of the events which might be brought about by Napoleon's audacious attempt did not stay the allies in their plans of despoiling the unhappy King of Saxony. This very uncertainty made them hasten it on. This prince had retired to Presburg, determined to consent to no dismemberment of his states. Lord Wellington, Prince Metternich, and Prince de Bénévent went there on the morrow of the day on which the news of Napoleon's departure from the Island of Elba had become public, to endeavor to persuade the King to consent to the arrangement which deprived him of the half of his kingdom. They found him immovable. This unhappy sovereign was, however, obliged later on to yield to force.

It was not only the lofty persons assembled at the Congress who were anxious as to what might be the nature of Napoleon's plans, the event was in everybody's mind. Two days elapsed before it was known that the Emperor had landed in France. The Emperor Francis, reassured as to Italy, then told his daughter that if Napoleon, against all likelihood, was to succeed, he would not allow her to return to France until experience had taught him that he could trust in his son-in-law's pacific intentions and prudence. The first impulses of this monarch were always good, but his good sense and natural loyalty always yielded to the exigencies of politics.

Already on March 8 all the sovereigns who were still present in Vienna had come to an agreement to put the armies of the coalition once more in march. Lord Wellington—accused of having opposed the plan which had been discussed before his arrival in Vienna, of removing the Emperor from the Island of Elba and of transporting him to some island in the Ocean—said that a campaign against the Emperor Napoleon was about to be entered upon; that he would be taken prisoner and conducted to England, where he would enjoy the consideration and the respect due to the part which he had played in the world.

During the three weeks which had elapsed since the news of the Emperor's departure from the Island of Elba had become known in Vienna, the most contradictory rumors followed upon each other. Now, Napoleon, having failed before Antibes, where he had presented himself, had re-embarked; according to other versions he had been received there by General Vandamme. Now, he had marched upon Lyons, but had been attacked on his march and had lost three pieces of artillery. The provinces through which he passed, so went the report, placed themselves once more under the rule of the Bourbons, after he had left them behind him. Now, he was at the head of six thousand men, and Marshal Soult had joined him; now, Count d'Artois, at the head of a corps commanded by Gouvion Saint-Cyr, had fallen in with the Emperor on this side of Dijon and had inflicted a defeat upon him! now Louis XVIII was prisoner at Compiègne; now Marshal Ney had defeated the Emperor; now he had joined him with his army. According to others he had joined the Emperor alone, because his troops had abandoned him, etc., etc. These rumors did not spring from the lower classes; they were the *résumé* of the letters received by the two Emperors and the King of Prussia. The Empress of Austria took care to forward the news which she received, more often false than true, to her stepdaughter. French newspapers were forbidden and were carefully hidden by the Austrian ministers and the ministers of the allied powers who received them. French news was published in the German newspapers alone.

King Joseph, at that time in retirement in Switzerland, did not leave me without news of the Emperor's march. He sent me emissaries to acquaint me with the real state of affairs and to put me in a position to counteract the effect produced by the calamitous reports which Fauche Borel scattered broadcast amongst the members of the congress and in the city of Vienna, which was the only source whence they reached the Empress's ears.

The Empress was so agitated by the rapid succession of events, by the continual alternations of the Emperor's success and failure, that she lost her peace of mind altogether. Careful as I was to inform her of the truth, as I was not always able to reveal to her the source of my information, she was inclined rather to believe the news which reached her from the Court in Vienna than to trust in mine; any piece of news, no matter what it might be, agitated her in the same manner. One day she would say that she would not return to France, because she could see no chance of repose for this country; the next day she would say that if the Emperor would give up his plans of conquest, and would consent to reign peacefully, she had reason to believe that no obstacle would be put in the way of her return to France, and that she would have no objection to appear there again, as she had always had a liking for the French.

The resolution which had been taken, of separating the young prince from his worthy governess, began to manifest itself in complaints which were made against Madame de Montesquiou. It was said that she was guilty of having spoken to the young prince of the future which would be the result to him of his father's enterprise. M. de Bausset was in consequence commissioned to see Colonel Montesquiou and to point out to him how very necessary it was that his mother should be careful about what she said, so great was the supervision to which she was subjected; a very superfluous recommendation, seeing that Madame de Montesquiou was prudence itself. She had no difficulty in convincing the Empress that she was not inconsiderate enough to disturb a young child's mind with untimely revelations the gravity of which he could not appreciate, and to say things to him which were calculated to excite him in a manner likely to injure him physically as well as mentally.

The state of the Countess de Brignole's health continued a cause for serious anxiety. On March 11 she had several severe fainting-fits, in consequence of which Madame de Montesquiou induced her to receive the last sacraments. At three o'clock the Empress followed by Madame de Colloredo, M. and Madame Antoine Brignole and persons of the household proceeded to the chapel, according to the custom observed in the imperial households. There both she and her suite received lighted tapers, and we followed the priest who carried the Holy Sacrament to the sick woman's room in processional form. We all were present at the prayers and the extreme unction, on our knees. Countess de Brignole edified us all with her piety and her resignation. She asked forgiveness for any injuries that she might have done in a firm and loud voice, without either boasting or baseness. After the conclusion of the ceremony, we reconducted the priest back to the chapel in the same procession and in the same order. This scene, touching and imposing at the same time, supported by the sick lady with all her presence of mind seemed to restore her to her strength. On the morrow she was well enough to receive the Empress and even to converse with each of us, with a serenity and clear-headedness that deceived us as to the danger which menaced her.

In the midst of this visit Marie Louise whispered to Count Neipperg proposing that they should go and finish a letter the object of which we did not know till the morrow. The purport of this letter was to declare to M. de Metternich that she had nothing whatever to do with the Emperor Napoleon's plans, and that she placed herself under the protection of the allies. This declaration, which was immediately communicated to the sovereigns and their plenipotentiaries assembled at the congress, seemed to have been what they had been waiting for to decide upon the terms of the manifesto directed against the Emperor. This manifesto was the famous declaration of March 13, 1815, an incitement to murder, worthy of the days of barbarism. Why need it be added that the terms of this *factum,* which had been elaborated at the French legation, were found too violent by the allies themselves, who changed its wording. The treaty of March 25 following, was the application and completion of this manifesto, a veritable document of proscription dictated by fear, by pride, and by all hateful passions exaggerated to their extremist degree. The French plenipotentiary no doubt did not foresee that in stirring up the hatred of the foreigners against France, and in provoking the renewal of the Chaumont treaty, he was preparing the disastrous and humiliating Treaty of Paris of November 20, 1815, to which too late he recognized that it was impossible for him to affix his signature.

The Empress appeared sad and afflicted. Her mind was secretly agitated by a fluctuation of painful feelings and reflections; she had not enough confidence in Madame de Montesquiou or in me to unbosom herself to us without reserve. She had even made a remark—so I was assured at the time—which I did not think it right to pass over in silence. She is said to have said: "If I were sure that I have not been blamed for not going to the Island of Elba . . . ." then, without giving full expression to her thought, to have added: "But I am surrounded by people here who, to be sure, have not missed the opportunity of accusing me." No misunderstanding of these words was possible to me. I accordingly took the first opportunity that presented itself to complain of the bad opinion which she had of me, if she deemed me capable of abusing the honorable hospitality which she was according me, to play the part of informer. I told her that nobody better than myself knew the desire which she had always had to join the Emperor, and that events alone, the severe watch which was held over her person, and the precautions with which she was surrounded, had not left her free to obey what she had considered as a duty. What motive, I added, could I have had to lack in the respect which I owed to her? When she had spoken of the Emperor was it not always with the remembrance of the consideration and affection which she admitted to have always found in him? I took advantage of the opportunity to express to her my regret for the declaration which she had made some days before and which had been turned to so bad a use by the Congress. I exhorted her in the most pressing manner to sign nothing which might engage her either to the allies or against the Emperor; it seemed to me the only attitude which she could assume in the vexatious position in which she found herself. She listened to my advice without impatience and told me that she saw its prudence; that if I was alluding to the declaration of March 13 she regretted it as much as I did; that it was a declaration of unparalleled violence, and that the allies in the future would regret having allowed themselves to give way to it; but she added that she was no longer mistress of her actions, that she had promised her father to place herself entirely in his hands and to conduct herself only in accordance with his advice; that she could not, without breaking her word, or failing in her duty towards her father, thenceforward her son's only guardian, to whom he showed constant affection, oppose anything that he might wish to do, not only in her personal but in their common interest; that the Austrian princesses were mere instruments in the hands of the head of their house; that she had been brought up in the principle of absolute submission to this authority; that she was no longer an independent sovereign; that she was without protection and incapable of resistance; that she could but yield under the yoke which would be put upon her, or openly rebel against her father and her family; that I could imagine what would be the consequences of such rebellion on her son's future; that she had been born under a fatal star; and that she was doomed never to be happy.

The thought that Napoleon's son was in the hands of people who were devoted to his father filled the masters of Europe with anxiety. The Emperor of Austria declared to his daughter that the sovereigns desired that, under existing circumstances, the young prince should reside in Vienna. On March 18, the Empress on her return from Vienna, whither she had taken her son to see the Emperor Francis, sent word to Madame de Montesquiou to prepare to take the young Prince back to reside in the palace of Vienna, and occupy the apartment of the hereditary prince. In consequence of this order, arrangements were made for going to Vienna on the second day following, the sad anniversary of a great day. When this dear object of the wishes and hopes of a great and powerful nation had come to the light of day, who could have foreseen that four years later, he would be in Vienna, a new Astyanax, a prisoner to the coalition, and that he would suffer the fate from which his father had tried to preserve him. On the 19th the Empress, returning from Vienna, went to her son's apartment and informed Madame de Montesquiou of the wish expressed by the Emperor of Austria, inviting her to get ready to start at eight in the evening, without mentioning the reasons which rendered this sudden departure necessary. At the hour mentioned she entered the carriage with Madame de Montesquiou and her son, and accompanied them to the imperial palace, where she left them.

On her return to Schönbrunn, the Empress informed me that she had been forced to write to her father to place herself and her son under his protection; that the necessity of this step had been imperiously pointed out to her; that the Emperor Francis was determined to assure the succession to the States of Parma to his grandson, and would ask the King of France for his consent to this arrangement, as the price of the efforts made to maintain him on his throne. In the meanwhile the Austrian cabinet availed itself of the step taken by Marie Louise to order the administration of the duchies in her name, but on behalf of Austria, on the pretext that the Emperor Napoleon might send a governor into these states to take possession of them in the Empress's name.

The Prince de Bénévent was an object of so much suspicion in Vienna that all his actions were supposed to be dictated by double and contradictory motives. On the one hand it was said that, informed of the progress which Napoleon was making in France, and knowing that a decree issued from Lyons excepted him from the amnesty, he had had the idea of making his way to London where his niece would have followed him with her children and the Duchess of Courland, but that his favorite principle of awaiting events had prevented him from carrying this plan into execution. On the other hand, known as he was as a man most inconsistent in his fidelity, it was supposed that he had come to a secret understanding with Napoleon. It was added that it had been proposed in Congress to put his papers under seal. On March 27, after having received a special messenger who had been sent to him from Paris, M. de Talleyrand announced that he was closing his house and that his mission was terminated. Of the four French plenipotentiaries, M. de la Tour du Pin left Vienna; Prince de Bénévent, Duke Dalberg, and

Count Alexis de Noailles remained there until further orders. M. de Talleyrand duly left a few days after the various deeds of the Congress had been signed. M. de la Besnardière had separated himself from M. de Talleyrand towards the end of April; he had returned in the beginning of May to Paris and everything that he said there seemed calculated to create discouragement. In order to hide the real motive which had brought him back to Paris he pretended to blame M. de Talleyrand. His real motive was to keep the latter acquainted by letter with what was going on. I had had frequent opportunities of seeing this person in Vienna. I had found him exceedingly badly disposed towards the Emperor and towards the army, and in general very hostile to the acts of the Imperial government. He seemed unable to speak on this subject without giving way to the most violent tirades. On his arrival in Paris M. de le Besnardière put himself at Fouché's disposal and became his tool. Fouché chose him as one of the commissioners who were charged to negotiate for the armistice with the generals of the enemy after the battle of Waterloo. In this capacity he was sent with Generals Valence and Andréossy, and MM. Boissy d'Anglas and Flaugergues. Although M. de la Besnardiére's exaggerated opinions were well known, and although only a fortnight previously he had been attached to the Royal Legation at the Vienna Congress, Fouché insisted on his choice. He answered any objections which were made on this score with the remark that the commissioners would want a man who was acquainted with diplomatic forms. The mention of this fact dispenses with any considerations. I have neglected to say in what capacity M. de la Besnardière was in Vienna. Before the Restoration he had been head of the northern division at the Ministry of Exterior Relations, at the time when political direction was divided into two divisions, a northern and a southern. Appointed Councilor of state he had been attached to Prince de Bénévent's mission. On his return from Vienna M. de la Besnardière attained in September 1815, in recompense for his "loyal services" to the Bourbons a very large pension and retired to an estate which he possessed in Touraine, where he died leaving a fortune of one million. His retirement was on the pretext of his health, for which he took the most extraordinary care. This imaginary invalid never traveled without being accompanied by his doctor, his sister, and his dog.

On March 20, the day on which the Emperor retook possession of the Tuileries palace, which King Louis had abandoned during the night, the Grand Chamberlain Count Wrbna called upon Madame de Montesquiou, and told her that he had been the day before to Schönbrunn charged with a disagreeable mission which he had not had the courage to fulfill, and informed her with all possible consideration that the Emperor had given orders that she should be separated from his grandson the Prince, and leave for France. The well-known opinions of the worthy countess, and the tender affection which she considered it her duty to foster in her pupil's heart for the Emperor his father, had rendered her an object of suspicion to the Court of Vienna. In spite of her prayers, her entreaties, and her protests, she was forced to obey this cruel order. She was forced to abandon the child which she had received in her arms, which she had not left for a single moment since its birth, and which had been the object of her constant care. She refused, however, to relinquish this precious charge except on a written order from the Emperor of Austria, protesting against the violence which tore her from functions which she could only resign into the hands of him who had entrusted her with them. She demanded in addition to a written order from the Emperor that a doctor's certificate should be given to her to prove that she had left the young prince in a perfect state of health. In reply she received a letter from the Emperor of Austria in which she was informed that new circumstances having arisen which rendered it necessary to make a change in the Prince's household, he could not allow Madame de Montesquiou to go away without assuring her of his gratitude for the care which she had bestowed on his grandson since his birth. To this expression of esteem, which he could not refuse to conduct so noble, the Emperor Francis added the gift of a set of sapphires. The same day we learned the reason which had hastened on the young Prince's departure for the Imperial palace. Madame de Colloredo who had come to lunch with the Empress told us that Count Anatole de Montesquiou had wanted to kidnap the Prince, that the proof of this was contained in reports which had reached the Emperor during the night, and that relays of horses had been prepared for this purpose as far as Bâle. This story about an imaginary conspiracy with the object of kidnapping the Emperor's son and restoring him to his father has been accredited in memoirs published about this period; but the reports spread with reference to this matter, have no real foundation. On the morrow, March 21, the Empress went and spent several hours in Vienna with her son and then returned to Schönbrunn. In the evening Madame de Montesquiou arrived with Count Anatole, in a court carriage which had been sent her by the Grand Chamberlain. She had only left the Prince after he was asleep and after having received a visit from Count Sickingen, the Emperor of Austria's chamberlain and friend.

M. de Sickingen's name reminds me that the Emperor Napoleon out of respect for a request made by the Emperor Francis, had accorded a revenue of 50,000 francs to this chamberlain, the capital of which was taken from the funds of the extraordinary domain. This revenue had been given as a special favor to Count Sickingen as a compensation for the loss of estates which he possessed on the left bank of the Rhine.

As Madame de Montesquiou was to return on the morrow to France with her son, the Empress wrote her an affectionate letter in which she enclosed her a lock of her hair. Difficulties which they experienced in obtaining passports delayed the mother and the son in Vienna until the evening and they were waiting with a certain impatience, when Count Wrbna called again and informed Madame de Montesquiou that in consequence of the events which were taking place in France the Emperor of Austria had made up his mind to cancel the authorization which he had given her to depart, and that an apartment would be prepared for her and her son in the palace of Schönbrunn. Madame de Montesquiou refused it, saying that the "persecuted would be too near the persecutor." She asked one of three things, either to be free to return to France, to resume her service with the young prince, or to withdraw to the Convent of the Visitation until the time when she would be allowed to depart. The reason why she wished to go and live in this convent was, that having been brought up in a house of this order she had acquired there those sentiments of religion and honor which had been the rule and the consolation of her life, sentiments which had also made her considered worthy of the charge that the Emperor Napoleon had entrusted to her. Count Wrbna promised her an answer for next morning. This answer arrived at noon. The Emperor Francis gave Madame de Montesquieu leave to go and live in the Convent of the Visitation. M. de Wrbna answered that he had just been there, only that there was no apartment vacant in this convent, and that he had chosen an apartment of three rooms in Vienna at the house of M. d'Enzenberg, Arch-Duke Louis's chamberlain, where she could live. Madame de Montesquiou accepted, resigning herself to go and live in the apartment which had been prepared for her. So painful a separation was bitterly felt by the poor little prince, who had become accustomed to the care lavished upon him by his affectionate governess. He was constantly asking for *Mamma Quiou,* and the regrets which he expressed at no longer seeing her by his side were the only consolation which she could receive under these painful circumstances.

In a letter which the Emperor addressed from Lyons to Marie Louise, under date of March 12, he informed her that summoned by the French people he yielded to their wishes, that he was received with acclamation everywhere, that he should be in Paris in a few days, and that he expected her and his son at the end of the month. This letter had been handed to the Empress on the same day on which the young prince had been taken to Vienna. It had been sent on by the Austrian General Bubna together with a very similar letter addressed to the Emperor. These two letters had been laid before the Congress. I do not know to what extent they influenced the decision which was taken in Vienna for detaining Madame de Montesquiou and her son. The latter received permission some days later to return to France, but on arriving at Lambach, the frontier of the Austrian states, he was arrested on some pretext or other, brought back to Vienna, and detained in secret confinement for four days. M. de Montesquiou only regained his liberty, partly thanks to M. de Talleyrand's interference on his behalf, and on a promise which he was forced to make that he would not leave Vienna without permission. These gratuitous severities exercised against an officer full of honor, whose social position and well-known loyalty should have protected him from such vexations, were carried out by the most servile and most brutal police in Europe. This police was moreover stimulated by the mistrust which was inspired by the few French people who had remained in Vienna in the Empress's service—a mistrust which the presence of one of the Emperor's aides-de-camp, whose mother was the governess of Napoleon's son, was bound to still further increase. Countess de Montesquiou, greatly hurt by the accusations which had been made against her son, demanded in vain that the official Gazette of Vienna should publish a denial of the alleged conspiracy for kidnapping the young prince; no attention whatever was paid to this request.

During Passion Week the Empress Marie Louise attended mass with great assiduity, leaving Schönbrunn at nine o'clock in the morning to be present at the religious ceremonies. On the Thursday before Easter the Emperor and Empress of Austria washed the feet of twenty-four old men and women whose total ages amounted to nearly two thousand years. Marie Louise continued her devotional exercises in Vienna up to Easter Day. She attended mass on that day in the chapel of the château of Schönbrunn, but went to Vienna to be present at the benediction in the Cathedral Church. At that time she sought relief from her sad thoughts in pious exercises, and consolation which she said she could no longer find anywhere else than in religion.

Reports of every kind provoked by the escape from Elba continued to circulate, supplying food to the curiosity of the idle, to the anxieties and hopes of those who were interested in the result of this extraordinary enterprise.

All eyes were turned to Napoleon at this time. It was said that King Joachim had assembled his council and the principal persons in his state, that he had made a speech to them, that his son, Achilles, had been carried in triumph, that the King had set out to put himself at the head of his army and to proclaim the independence of Italy. In order to increase the effect of this dramatic recital, which was so favorable to the views of the

Austrian government, it was falsely added that the Princess of Wales, having fallen in love with King Joachim, had refused to embark on board a frigate which had been sent to convey her back to England, and that she had followed the King with the army.

On Easter Monday the Empress was present at a family banquet given in Vienna on the occasion of the renewal of the Emperor's oath-taking to protect and support the Catholic religion, in the presence of the Archbishop of Vienna. The Emperor and Empress of Austria proceeded with this purpose to St. Stephen's church in great state with a procession of carriages of gothic shape and covered with gold, with all the corps under arms, and the pages in grand livery, escorting the Imperial carriage on foot. At the same time when the young prince was removed from Madame de Montesquiou's maternal care, orders were given that members of the French Imperial family should be arrested and detained in Austria. Prince Schwarzenberg sent two officers to the château of Prangins in the canton of Vaud, to seize the person of King Joseph and conduct him to Brunn in Moravia, but the prince had left Prangins when they arrived. Princess Elisa, Grand duchess of Tuscany, had been arrested in Bologna and conducted to Brunn. She had only been allowed two hours to prepare for her departure, in the presence of several officers and non-commissioned officers who crowded her apartment. She left her son at Bologna, her daughter accompanying her to Brunn. She had asked to be allowed to go and live in the country near Vienna, or at Baden, because the climate of Brunn was injurious to her health. This permission was not granted.

The childhood of Napoleon's son needed gentler and more attentive cares than could be given him by the men to whom he had been handed over since Madame de Montesquiou's forced retirement. A certain Madame de Mitrowsky, widow of an Austrian general, was provisionally appointed the young prince's governess, and was presented in this capacity to the Empress. This lady appeared to be thirty or thirty-two years old. She was not pretty, but had a refined appearance, and seemed amiable and anxious to please. Her daughter who was then about ten years old was. with her. Her re-marriage with a M. Scarampi had been decided upon. This M. Scarampi was a superior officer in the Austrian Lusignan regiment and he was leaving the army to enter the civil service. He was to have been attached to Baron de Vincent's legation in Ghent, but on his marriage with Madame de Mitrowsky, the Duchess of Parma gave him a post in her household, in order that he might be near his wife. This lady after her presentation to the Empress, and at the death of Madame de Brignole, was appointed lady-in-waiting, by a decision emanating from the Emperor of Austria's cabinet. She fulfilled these double duties during the first year.

The Empress of Austria who protected Madame de Mitrowsky gave orders in person that on her return to the château of Schönbrunn, Madame de Mitrowsky's apartment should be got ready for her with all speed.

The turn for the better in Madame de Brignole's health was not of long duration. She had grown weaker each day and was devoured by an ardent fever. I used to spend most of the day at her bedside speaking to her, chatting to her, or reading passages which she would sometimes interrupt with judicious and remarkable reflections. Her language was full of eloquence, and impressed with a loftiness of thought which was almost sublime. In her calmer moments she would return to her memories of the past or occupy herself with her last arrangements. One day she charged me with various private commissions which she begged me to keep secret. She also dictated me a note containing certain arrangements referring to charities, and presents which she wished to be distributed, and provided that all her papers should be sent to her business man in Genoa.

I made haste to send this note to her son directly after her death. It was not possible for me to be present with her during her last few moments, for I myself was ill and unable to leave my room. The state of excitement in which she found herself during the last days which preceded her death prevented me from speaking to her of what was going on in France. The fear of provoking an emotion which might have been injurious to her obliged us to observe prudent discretion on events so important. I heard from Madame de Montesquiou that she had told her all these things on the day before her death. Countess de Brignole at least carried into her grave with her the hope which it needed but two months to destroy for those who survived. After she had breathed her last Count Dalberg, her son-in-law, hastened to come and see me, being very anxious to know whether his mother-in-law had made any arrangements in his favor with which I might be charged to acquaint him. I bitterly regretted the premature death of this lady who was as distinguished by her mental gifts, as by her qualities of heart; she was not yet fifty years old. She died during the night in her doctor's arms, assisted only in this supreme moment by two faithful servants. She was deprived of the comfort of taking farewell of her son who was the Genoese minister at the Congress. The state in which he had left his mother on the previous evening had not made him think that the end was so near. When he arrived it was to find that she was dead. While he was accomplishing this painful journey his daughter, a child of five years, who had been suffering from croup for several days past also breathed her last. Thus in a few moments he lost the dearest objects of his affection; death seemed to have awaited his absence to remove them both. Few misfortunes could be compared to the misfortune which thus fell upon the unhappy Marquis de Brignole.

On the second day following Madame de Brignole's death, after the doctors had carried out the post-mortem examination, her body was buried in the cemetery at Hitzing, which is a village near Schönbrunn, where some Frenchmen who died in exile—amongst others Cléry, Louis XVI's old valet-de-chambre—were buried. Marie Louise was present at the funeral service in the church in the company of Madame de Mitrowsky, who had just been appointed her lady-in-waiting.

The treaty of March 25 had been signed. The operations of the Congress had been followed by military movements. The Emperor Alexander seemed to have assumed the rôle of quarter-master to the Austrian troops. Every day, dressed in Austrian uniform, he used to go either to the Burg Square, or to the Prater, to review the regiments on their way through the city of Vienna; he used to take the Prince Imperial of Austria with him. The good citizens of Vienna had a change in their sight-seeing: instead of tournaments, carriage and sledge races, there were military parades, the rolling of drums, the rumbling of cannon and artillery caissons. The majority of the princes of the secondary States had left Paris. The Emperor of Austria dragged in the train of the Emperor of Russia, was to follow the latter to Prague to review the Russian troops there. Prince Schwarzenberg was leaving to take over the command-in-chief of the Austrian troops. Archduke Charles had accepted the government of Mayence.

The Emperor of Russia was in a state of violent excitement. Prince Eugène, whose intimacy he had sought after, had become an object of suspicion in his eyes. A groom attached to the latter's service, returning from France where he had been to visit his family, and who had left Paris on March 22, had brought back letters from Queen Hortense, Count Lavalette, and M. Soulange Bodin, the prince's intendant, which spoke of the enthusiasm with which the Emperor's return had been met, of the hopes which had been conceived as to the speedy return of the Empress and her son, and of Queen Hortense's intention of going to receive them at Strasburg. Certain expressions which had offended the Emperor Alexander had crept into the Queen's letter. This courier was arrested at Stuttgart and sent to Vienna, and the letters which he carried were read out to the Congress. It was concluded from this that Prince Eugène was an accomplice in Napoleon's return to France. General Czernitchev came to inform the prince in his master's name that the Emperor Alexander was obliged to break off all communication with him and, in spite of all his efforts, Prince Eugène was unable to entirely justify himself. To clear himself of all suspicion of being in connivance with the Emperor Napoleon, he was obliged to promise not to leave Germany. If it was important to the allies that Prince Eugène should not return to France, where his help might have been useful to the Emperor, Austria feared his presence in Italy still more. No sooner had she reentered into possession of the provinces of which the hazard of war had stripped her, than she neglected nothing to assure herself of their quiet possession to extend her influence. Her first care had been to remove the generals and principal officers of the Italian army, sending them to serve in Hungary and replacing them by Austrian officers. I was constantly seeing, at Prince Eugène's house, Italian generals passing through Vienna on their way to their new destination. The measure taken with them seemed to affect them very disagreeably. They were deprived of the order of the Crown of Iron, for which another order bearing the Emperor Francis's effigy, accompanied by emblems recording the events by which Italy had again been placed under the rule of Austria, was substituted. Archduke John was sent to these provinces, with the title of viceroy, provided with extraordinary powers for assuring the Emperor's authority in this country. Count Aldini tired of his useless sojourn in Vienna had asked to be allowed to return home, but this had been refused.

I had occasion to see M. de Talleyrand at the time, having various communications to make to him. Till then I had avoided meeting him, although he had made me offers of service. I took advantage of this opportunity to thank him for the interest which he had shown in my favor—although, it is true, it had been without result—in seconding the wish expressed by the Emperor Alexander that some compensation should be awarded to me for the loss of my endowments in the former Escaut department. He asked me what I proposed to do. I told him that I intended to return to Paris as soon as I was free to do so. His question emboldened me, in my turn, to ask him what were his intentions. "Mon Dieu!" he cried. "Who can make any plans at such a time? You ask me what I mean to do. I don't know at all. I shall wait." This complete and unexpected frankness on the part of the most subtle of diplomats would give a great appearance of truth to what General Langenau, quartermaster of Prince Schwarzenberg's army, told me when some time later I had to apply to the Austrian commander-in-chief for my passports. This general officer assured me that Prince de Bénévent and M. de la Besnardière had wished to return to France; that Prince Metternich had made no objections to their being supplied with passports, but that Prince Schwarzenberg had held a different opinion on the subject. According to the General's story the Austrian commander-in-chief had pointed out how very disadvantageous M. de Talleyrand's return to Paris would be, in view of the fact that he was in the secret of all the affairs that had been discussed at the Congress. M. de Metternich, convinced by his representations, had refused to grant the passports. I, for my part, have every reason to place faith in the revelation which precedes, and I may add that it is only another proof of the little confidence which the allies reposed in M. de Talleyrand. According to their statements, this ambassador had not been sufficiently carefully watched, even while at Ghent, for them to feel quite at their ease about him.

M. de Talleyrand spoke to me of the two heavy losses which he had experienced within the last month, in the persons of Countess de Brionne and of Countess de Brignole. Madame de Brionne was the mother of Princess Lambesc, and of a Princess Charlotte, who was formerly notorious for her relations with Abbé de Perigord, who was none other than M. de Talleyrand. Countess de Brionne had come to die at Presburg where her daughter's former lover had been to take a last farewell of her. He told me that the Empress had lost in Madame de Brignole a person who was able to give her "strong advice." He insisted on this word, but I did not ask him what he meant by it. I found that I had been indiscreet enough already in asking him what his plans were.

I cannot speak of M. de Talleyrand without expressing my surprise at the way in which his friends and those who have echoed them attributed to him a large part in the direction of Napoleon's politics. His greatest skill lay in his *savoir faire,* in the science of intrigue, and in his way of hiding his secret dislikes. He always sheltered himself behind some great capacity, so as to ride in its shade and found his reputation. First of all, behind Mirabeau, and then behind Napoleon. It is not thanks to luminous conceptions matured in the work of the study, nor to a talent for developing them in searching debates, nor to his eloquence as an orator that this statesman raised himself to the rank where public opinion has placed him. The secret of the superiority attributed to him by his contemporaries dwells, above all, in the prestige of the great diplomatic transactions of the Consulate and the Empire, in which he was the keen and intelligent agent, in the long career of public honors in which he knew how to maintain himself, and finally in the art of resuming in witty or sententious sayings the gravest and most important questions. How often have I been present at the ordinary weekly work which this minister had with the First Consul or Emperor, when he was at the head of the department of Exterior Relations! Napoleon used to read the dispatches which his minister handed him and would speak in detail about the matters contained therein. M. de Talleyrand appeared to listen to him with attention, but I rarely heard him express his own opinions, and as a general rule he only used to answer in monosyllables. Was this circumspection on his part, or was it a wish to clearly understand the Emperor's views before expressing himself on the subject? When the conversation was drawing to a close, it would sometimes happen that Napoleon would be summoned to an audience which he had to give. He would then leave M. de Talleyrand, saying: "You have quite understood, make a summary of what I have said on the paper. I shall come back." And as a matter of fact he would return an hour or two later, but M. de Talleyrand had written nothing. Then Napoleon without appearing surprised and without making any complaint, would collect the papers on the table and dictate at great length what had to be written in answer. He would then charge his minister to take away what he had written from dictation and make a fair copy of it. It would be sometimes myself who wrote from his dictation. M. de Talleyrand on his return home would summon his heads of department and set them to work. It has sometimes happened that I found him in the morning lying in a little room in which two or three of his writers, standing up before a Tronchin writing-table, were giving the last touches to a report which M. de Talleyrand was to carry to Napoleon, and which he would afterwards patiently copy out in his own writing. Although this minister was incurably lazy, he spared no pains to prevent any loss of his reputation for skill and discretion. There is reason to believe that even the letters which were written from Vienna to Louis XVIII by Prince de Talleyrand, were written by M. de la Besnardière and afterwards copied by the chief. Volumes of these letters exist in the archives of the Foreign Office, the drafts of which, written in M. de la Besnardière's writing, have been found.

But what made M. de Talleyrand's co-operation especially precious to the Emperor was that this minister was unequaled in diplomatic conversations. In comparing him to another of his ministers Napoleon used to say of him: "One speaks with so much ease, that yielding to the pleasure of talking he lets his secret escape him and comes away without having found out the secrets of the Others, while Talleyrand on the other, hand allows nobody to fathom him and extracts all that it is of interest for me to know, out of the person to whom he is speaking." In this respect Talleyrand was a useful and skilful coadjutor to the Emperor. It has been so often repeated that success abandoned Napoleon's operations from the day on which M. de Talleyrand was no longer in a position to enforce his political ideas, that I fear lest those who hear me speak in this way of this celebrated person, may accuse me of resembling that Athenian peasant who recorded his vote of ostracism against Aristides, whom he did not know, because he was tired of always hearing this great citizen styled The Just.

In our opinion, M. de Talleyrand owes the best part of his reputation to his circumspection and the prudent silence which he was careful to observe. He never allowed himself to be carried into a discussion with anybody; his principle was to let people talk and not to answer. I have heard General Lamarque relate the following anecdote on this point: The general had formerly had a dispute with a certain General Canuel, an ardent republican who afterwards became a royalist. General Lamarque defended himself vigorously against Canuel's attacks by means of letters to the papers. One day when he had published a letter in the *Constitutionnel,* with which he was very well satisfied, he found himself at dinner, placed next to Prince Talleyrand. The Prince nudged him with his elbow and said: "General Lamarque, I thought you were an intelligent man." On the general's expressing surprise at this remark, the Prince continued: "I say that because I read a letter of yours in a paper this morning. How can you be simple enough to enter the arena with people who attack you? You cannot imagine how you please them by so doing. Trust me, let them talk, and do you keep quiet. Do as I do; I have never answered anybody and you see that I have had no reason to complain of the result."

General Neipperg had left for Italy on April 1, leaving a long letter full of recommendations and advice for Marie Louise who could no longer do without them. During the general's absence an active correspondence established itself between the princess and himself. Count Neipperg's letters were real memoirs; some of them were not less than eight or ten pages in length.

M. de Montrond arrived in Vienna some days after Count Neipperg's departure. He handed me a letter from the Emperor for the Empress and letters addressed by the Duc de Vicence to Madame de Montesquiou and myself. M. de Montrond, according to what he told me, had only been able to enter into Austria thanks to the passport of Abbé Altieri, who had been sent by the pope to withdraw the archives of the Vatican which had been transported from Rome to Paris after Napoleon's victories. He informed me that the Emperor had in vain endeavored to send couriers and several officers, amongst others, M. de Flahaut and M. de Stassart, to Vienna and that all the passages were hermetically closed.

Count de Flahaut, aide-de-camp to the Emperor, and Baron de Stassart, who had been auditor and prefect under the Empire and who was at that time chamberlain to the Emperor of Austria, had not been able to get beyond Lintz which they had reached after surmounting many obstacles. M. de Stassart went to Munich there to await the answer to a letter which he had written to the Emperor of Austria, in forwarding to him the dispatches with which he had been entrusted, a letter in which he renewed the offer made by Napoleon to maintain the Treaty of Paris; it was then the beginning of May. He had been some days in Munich when he was sent for by Prince Eugène who had been there for about a month past. This Prince informed M. de Stassart that M. de Metternich invited him through Prince Wrède, who had arrived the day before from Vienna, to inform him that if the Emperor Napoleon would consent to abdicate immediately in favor of his son, not only would Austria consent to acknowledge the imperial dynasty, but would even in case of need make common cause with France. It was demanded at the same time that Napoleon should surrender into the hands of his father-in-law and, while waiting for the sovereignty, which was intended for him, to be assigned to him, should go and live in one of the cities of the hereditary Austrian states. Napoleon, to whom M. de Stassart made haste to communicate this offer which had been passed on from hand to hand in the way described, may have hesitated over some of the proposals which were made to him, but his want of confidence in the loyalty of the Vienna cabinet and in the dispositions of the allies definitely prevented him from accepting it.

At the same time M. de Metternich caused an overture of an almost similar nature, but addressed to the Duke of Otranto to be made through M. Werner, whom the Austrian minister sent to Bâle with this object in view. A month earlier M. Bresson had also been sent from Vienna with an analogous secret mission. These were the last attempts at an arrangement which can be mentioned on the part of Napoleon's irreconcilable enemies who were preparing themselves, at the same time, to give him his death-blow.

M. de Montrond had told me, laughing, that he had a free hand to kidnap Marie Louise, disguising her, if need be, in man's clothing and "without having to pay any attention to her prudery, etc."

Various indications and his customary tone of witty jesting proved to me, as I already had reason to suspect, that this plan of removing the Empress, was only a joke on his part and not the object of his mission to Austria. He expressed his surprise at the sudden confidence which the Imperial government in Paris had placed in him, who till then had been exiled and prosecuted. My surprise was even greater, for I thought that he had come to Vienna rather to help M. de Talleyrand's affairs than to serve Napoleon's interests. And as a matter of fact M. de Montrond was charged with a private mission from Fouché to King Louis XVIII's former plenipotentiary at the Congress. He had alighted at the mansion of the French embassy. We used to meet each other by appointment at Vienna or in the gardens of Schönbrunn where he passed himself off as an amateur of horticulture and hothouse forcing, so as to deceive the numerous spies who followed us.

The Duke of Vicence in informing me that M. de Montrond was to bring back answers to the letters which he had to hand me, stated that the Emperor was without news of the Empress and his son, and that it was of extreme importance to him to know what he was to think about what interested him in Vienna. I made haste to answer M. de Caulaincourt. It was impossible to write in a letter all that I wanted to tell the Emperor. Nor could I foresee what questions I should have had to answer could I have seen Napoleon and have spoken with him. At the same time my letter dealt with the principal points on which I thought that he required enlightenment. The letter which I wrote to the Duke of Vicence, and the draft of which I have found, contained particulars which must naturally find their place here. Although this letter was written in great haste and without any order, it has the merit—for want of a better—of offering a summary of the principal facts relating to the Emperor and the Empress, of retracing local impressions, and of presenting a character of actuality, if I may make use of an expression which is in great favor today.

This letter, the text of which follows, was deposited by chance in the archives of the Paris Foreign Office, where it still remains.

Copy of my Letter to the Duke of Vicence

"Vienna, April 7, 1815

"MY LORD DUKE,

"Your note of March 26 was handed to me this morning. The French newspapers are carefully hidden by the Austrian ministry and by those of the allied princes who receive them. It is the German newspapers which give us any news of France. All the negotiations of the Congress have been suspended: everybody remains *in statu quo,* awaiting fortunate hazards. The troops are in movement in every direction. The Emperor of Austria is to follow the Emperor of Russia to Prague at the end of the month, to see the Russian troops. The Emperor of Russia is madly excited against our Emperor and supports and stimulates all the allies against him.

"It is said that he has sworn on the Gospel not to lay down arms as long as the Emperor is master of France. A treaty, with this purpose in view, was signed by the allied ministers on March 25; we are expecting its publication. The Emperor Alexander reviews the Austrian regiments as they leave Vienna or pass through it; he is accompanied by the hereditary prince alone. As long as he keeps the princes assembled either at Frankfort, whither he is proceeding, or anywhere else, he will animate them and keep their ardor against Napoleon alive, but it may be that they will grow tired of his fury, especially in consideration of the fact that their finances are exhausted and that their troops have stayed so long a time in Germany. There is reason to believe from what has transpired of the opinions of these princes, and from various speeches that have been made, that they will not be the first to enter into France.

"Paper stands today at 450, that is to say that 450 paper florins are only worth 100 silver florins. This depreciation, the end of which cannot be foreseen, is already making the Viennese grumble.

"The government here has just issued a loan of fifty million florins in paper, promising to pay the interest of two and a half percent, in silver. This loan has accelerated the fall in paper.

"M. Bresson has left for Paris, charged with a mission, the object of which you are no doubt acquainted with.

"Two days ago, by a general order, the decoration of the Iron Crown was taken away from the Italian generals, with the promise that it would be replaced by a new decoration, which has not yet been decided upon.

"M. de Talleyrand is today an object of suspicion to the allies and everybody else. Any form of French government, democratic, monarchical, aristocratic, anything except Napoleon's government would suit the Emperor of Russia. If anybody can get anything from this prince, there is no doubt that it is you.

"I do not know when the Empress will go to France. I have no means of foreseeing such an event. The cabinet here is far from being disposed to it at present. The Empress's mind has been so worked upon that she can think of a return to France only with terror. During the last six months all possible means have been used to turn her away from the Emperor. So that she should not be compromised by the confidence which she might have bestowed on the *Emperor's man,* I have not been allowed, for the last six months, to receive any orders from her. When by any chance I have been able to say a word to her, I have implored her to remain neutral and to sign nothing. But on several occasions she has been pressed to declare herself alien to the Emperor's plans, to place herself under the protection of her father and the allies, and to ask for the crown of Parma. General Neipperg, who is accredited to her by the Austrian Ministry and who has acquired great influence over her, has left for Italy. He has placed a certain Madame de Mitrowsky in her service, who is destined to be the young prince's governess, but who for the time being replaces Madame de Brignole of whose death you will have heard.

"On Sunday last happening to be alone at dinner with the Empress, H.M. told me after dinner that an act of the Congress which had just been signed assured her the possession of Parma; that for the time being the government of this duchy would be left to Austria who would pay her one hundred thousand francs a month; that she had been unable to obtain the reversion of these duchies for her son; that the son of the Queen of Etruria would be her heir, but that she would obtain the fiefs of the Archduke Ferdinand of Tuscany in Bohemia for her son, the total revenue of which amounted to about six hundred thousand francs; and that she had made an irrevocable resolution, namely, that she would never join the Emperor again. Pressed for the reason of so strange a resolution, after advancing several reasons which I undertook to destroy, she confessed that not having shared his disgrace she cannot share a prosperity which she had done nothing to bring about. She added that she had written nothing on this subject; that she reserved it to herself to settle this matter with the Emperor as soon as she was able to write to him; that she is well aware that she will not be able to establish her son in Parma; that terrible as this sacrifice is she will submit to it; and that she has consulted only two persons, the Archduke Charles and a lawyer, who consider that nothing can stand in the way of this arrangement. You will recognize the influence of the Empress's uncles in this matter. However this may be, that is her dream today. I beg you to make such use of this information as your prudence may suggest to you. I am afraid of the effect that it will produce on the Emperor.

"On Easter Sunday the annexed note from King Joseph was brought me at six o'clock in the morning by a Swiss."

[This note informed me of the unhoped-for success of the Emperor's march through France and of his very speedy arrival in Paris, of his wish to reestablish pacific relations with Austria and the other powers, and of his hope that his wife and child would be restored to him. I was charged to communicate this information in a confidential manner to the Empress.]

"I was able to carry out this mission the same day, without showing the Princess the note, naming anybody, nor compromising the Emperor's name, because she had told me that she had sworn to her father that she would hand over to him everything that came to her from the Emperor. She therefore mentioned my name to her father as having been charged to beg her to give this assurance. The Emperor of Austria sent me his thanks through her, so she told me, no doubt to encourage me to name my correspondents and to tell her all I might learn in the future. This partial neutrality on the part of the Empress prevents me from unbosoming myself to her. I spoke to her today of M. de Vincent in a roundabout manner. She assured me that she had not seen him, and had received nothing from him. She added that she had heard that he had not seen the Emperor but that he had seen you as well as M. Flahaut, that you wanted to give him some letters which he refused to take, that nevertheless she thinks that she remembers that her father spoke to her of a letter written to her which was brought by M. de Vincent's secretary who left Paris on the day after the ambassador's departure, but that her father would not give it to her as he did not wish her to communicate with the Emperor, any more than he himself wished to communicate with him. While awaiting for all this tangle to unravel itself and for the Empress to return to a better way of thinking, I speak to her of the happiness which the Emperor's return to France has brought to his country, of the impatience with which she is expected there, of the Emperor's desire to see her again, etc., etc., but I do it quietly because it is a topic which embarrasses her. All must be looked for from time and from the Emperor's moderation. However great my circumspection I am the victim of the lowest kind of espionage; a swarm of ignoble spies crawl around me and study my gestures, my steps, and my face. I fear that I may be kept here a long time; I want to breathe another air. I want to see you all again. My health is breaking up. It is only the Empress and her son who enjoy splendid health. The Empress has grown much stouter; the Prince Imperial is an angel of beauty, strength, and sweetness. Madame de Montesquiou weeps for him every day. This poor lady is treated with great severity, she is shut up in a small apartment of two rooms in a private house in Vienna. Her son who had obtained his passports for France was arrested at Lambach six days ago. He was brought back to Vienna and was kept in solitary confinement for four days. He was only restored to his mother, whose sole comfort he is, yesterday. He has given his word of honor not to leave Vienna without permission. It is to M. de Talleyrand's frequent applications on his behalf that he owes this alleviation of his captivity. The particulars of the circumstances and causes which separated the young prince from his mother would take too long a time in describing, and besides I know that she is going to write to you.

"Prince Eugène left this morning at three o'clock in the suite of the King of Bavaria.

He had come to Vienna to take the necessary steps for obtaining the establishment which was promised to him by the treaty of April 11. He was received with suspicion and mistrust. At last, for the last three months he appeared to have won the Emperor Alexander's affection and used to walk out with him every day for two hours. Since the letters which were sent to him from Paris on March 22 last were seized the Emperor Alexander has stopped seeing him. So that the Congress might not separate without having done something for him, the principality of Ponte-Corvo was proposed to him, some days ago. A condition imposed was that he should not reside there until fresh circumstances had arisen but should go and live at Bayreuth with his family. On his refusal the Congress admitted that an establishment was due to him and that until it could be given to him, he should be placed in the enjoyment of his estates and revenues in Italy; but till today, April 7, no orders have been given.

"Last night at half-past twelve, Prince Eugène had not received his passports. Since April 3 they have been deliberating as to whether they ought to be given to him. They wanted him to give his word of honor that he would not leave Bavaria but he refused to do so as he is not a prisoner of war. He intends to stay one or two weeks in Munich to take the princess and his children, and to accompany them to Bayreuth.

"During the last six months I have written several letters to General Bertrand and have sent him two pamphlets. I do not know whether he has received them."

(PS.—this 8th April.)

"I wrote to you yesterday in great haste and without any order. I have a thousand other things to tell you which it would take ages to write. What I venture to commend to your prudence is what relates to the Empress's person; this princess is good at heart, but for the time being she is under foreign influences."

In the preceding letter I have spoken of Prince Eugène, but I neither said how nor why Napoleon's stepson found himself in Vienna. We related that after the fall of the Empire, the Viceroy of Italy had been forced to take refuge in Munich and that then he had been sent for to Paris by his mother the Empress Josephine. Prince Eugène was well received there by the Bourbons and the allied sovereigns, and particularly by the Emperor of Russia who pressed him to come to Vienna during the Congress. Alexander appointed a meeting with him in the Austrian capital, promising him to support his claims for the establishment which had been stipulated for him by Article VIII of the Treaty of Frankfort. In Vienna the preponderating influence exercised by the Emperor Alexander had won the favor of the Austrian government, and of the other sovereigns assembled in congress, for Prince Eugène. He was treated like a royal prince and invited to all the fêtes. Napoleon's return from the island of Elba, to which the Emperor of Russia suspected Prince Eugène of having contributed, put an end to the friendly relations which had existed between them till then. The Emperor Alexander bore a grudge against Prince Eugène as long as he remained in Vienna. It was only at the time of his visit to Munich, whither the prince had retired, that the Czar restored him to his friendship. So lavishly had the territories been distributed that there remained nothing available to be given to Prince Eugène, in execution of the Treaty of Fontainebleau which assured him an establishment outside France. A decision taken under the Emperor Alexander's influence converted this stipulation of the treaty of April 11—concerning the Empress Josephine's son—into an indemnity, the amount of which was to be taken out of the

Kingdom of Naples and which should be the equivalent of a principality of fifty thousand inhabitants. Prince Eugène estimated the total value at twelve million francs, but the Neapolitan government reduced this indemnity to five millions. The estates which the prince derived from the Kingdom of Italy, and the endowments which the Emperor had bestowed upon him in Rome and Lombardy, were left in his possession. Two million seven hundred thousand francs which he had left on his departure in the Italian treasury were restored to him. And finally the King of Bavaria, his father-in-law, vested him with the principality of Eichstadt taken from the Bavarian States. Prince Eugène was at the same time created premier peer of the Kingdom of Bavaria (taking precedence after the princes of the royal family) and Duke of Leuchtenberg. A regiment of Bavarian chasseurs was further given to him.

Count Las Cases, on his return from St. Helena, had a communication to make to Prince Eugène, which the latter received after having been authorized to do so by his father-in-law the King of Bavaria. In 1814, the Emperor had deposited with Count Lavalette, a sum of sixteen hundred thousand francs, which he hid under the flooring of one of the rooms in the château of La Verrière, an estate in the neighborhood of Rambouillet which belonged to him. The château was occupied by the allied troops who, fortunately did not discover the treasure. After their departure, Count de Lavalette, alarmed for the safety of the trust confided to his keeping, begged Prince Eugène to take upon himself to keep one half of the amount. The Prince made various payments, and held at Napoleon's disposal during the last two or three years of the Emperor's life, twenty thousand francs a month, which he took from the fund in his keeping. When this fund was on the point of being exhausted, Eugène asked the members of the imperial family to contribute their share of expenses the object of which might be considered sacred. Napoleon's death happening in the meantime put an end to the negotiations which had been entered upon for this purpose.

Prince Eugène died in February, 1824, less than a year after the marriage of his eldest daughter to Prince Oscar, son of the King of Sweden—Bernadotte. Thus, unless anything happens to prevent it, the throne of Sweden, which Napoleon wanted to give to Prince Eugène in 1810 will descend to his daughter.

The two main points in my letter to the Duke of Vicence were the obligation enforced upon the Empress Marie Louise to consent to her son's forfeiture of the right of succession to the States of Parma, and her determination never to reunite herself to the Emperor. On considering what had been going on around me during the preceding six months, I had understood that some unfortunate *dénouement* of the critical situation in which so many events had placed the Empress must be expected. This princess, deprived of all protection, surrounded by pitfalls, led astray by perfidious advice, had become the too docile instrument of unscrupulous politicians. In spite of my previsions, which had never been very optimistic, I was painfully affected to see that Marie Louise abandoned the only line of conduct which any care for her own glory ought to have kept steadfastly before her. Amongst the reasons which decided the Empress to leave her son in Vienna and to go and establish herself in Parma without him, she gave the following, to which no allusion is made in my letter: that she was forced to make this sacrifice, painful as it was, because it was in her son's interest. She added that, if she did not obtain the sovereignty of some state of some importance, she would be able to do nothing for him; whereas, once established in Parma, it would be possible for her to save five hundred thousand francs a year, which, added to the revenues of the fiefs in Bohemia, would assure an independent position to her son after her death. I permitted myself to answer the Empress, that pecuniary considerations had very little weight in the position in which her son found himself placed; that if his name and quality as Napoleon's son did not make him great enough and recommend him sufficiently to the sympathy of the world, a million francs a year would not compensate him for the loss of the rank from which he had been cast down; that she could not resign herself thus to the disinheriting of her son, who, already deprived of his paternal inheritance was also being stripped of his maternal inheritance by an unjust decision on the part of the Congress, and who in consequence would live outside the pale of the law, without fatherland, without a title, and, so to say, without a name—for nobody would know how to call him. With regard to the idea which she had expressed of separating herself from the Emperor I did not fail to remind Marie Louise of the affection of which Napoleon had so often given her proof, and of the grief which he had felt at the obstacles which were placed in the way of their meeting, obstacles the responsibility of which he was very far from attributing to her. I spoke finally of the pain which her husband would feel at a separation the whole blame of which would fall upon her. I told her that she would be received in France like an angel of peace, and that the boon of her return would win her the eternal gratitude of the French nation; that I hoped that she would change her mind and give up the violent resolution, in forming which she could have consulted neither her heart nor her interests. I assured her that if she would make a statement in exactly the contrary sense expressing herself forcibly, this manifestation of her will would have very great weight. All that I could say on this matter made very little impression on Marie Louise. She repeated that she had not been able to consult her own feelings nor to rely on her own judgment in a question where such grave interests were involved; that the advice of her uncle Charles and a lawyer had dispelled her uncertainty; that moreover she had signed nothing and would sign nothing before she had come to an understanding with the Emperor Napoleon; that she had fully made up her mind not to consent to any divorce from him, but that she personally would come to a friendly agreement for their separation with him as soon as she had liberty to write to him. I gave my letters to M. de Montrond begging him not to deliver them to anybody but the Duke of Vicence. He promised me to do so, and faithfully carried out his mission. I learnt later, on my return to France, that this minister had immediately taken the letters to the Emperor. Napoleon, in his anxiety to receive news from Vienna, wanted to read the original copy, and therefore the precaution which I had wanted to take when I asked the minister to make prudent use of my communication was of no avail. I asked M. de Montrond before his departure if he had been charged with any messages from M. de Talleyrand. M. de Montrond gave me to understand that this minister could for the time being be of no service whatever to the Emperor's cause. As a matter of fact the hostilities of the allies against Napoleon, and the array of force which they were marshalling against him, were so great that any wish to serve the Napoleonic cause would have been considered a crime in the eyes of the allied powers. It certainly could not be M. de Talleyrand who would defy the resentment which an attitude, so little in conformity with his character, and so audacious, would have excited against him in the coalition.

Chapter XVIII

I have related how the King of Naples had made up his mind to act on the offensive. The Austrian manifesto had been published in the official Gazette of Vienna, and war had broken out between the two States. Each day different reports were current as to the march of the Neapolitan troops, as well as to the advantages which had not yet been obtained by the Austrian army; these reports kept all minds in suspense.

The events of this campaign excited the greatest interest, especially at Schönbrunn. Archduke Rainier came to see the Empress one day and informed her that General Neipperg had marched 5000 men against a corps of Neapolitan troops near Medina, that he had defeated them, and had taken 800 prisoners; that he had taken the fort of Carpi by surprise and captured it with his cavalry alone, this ranking with General Lasalle's feat of arms at the taking of Stettin during the Jena campaign. Finally, it was said, that after several fruitless attacks on Occhiobello to force a crossing over the Po, King Joachim had been obliged to retreat. Such were the reports which were circulating in Vienna during the whole month of April.

Before relating the sad issue of the struggle which the King of Naples had entered upon with Austria, I must throw a retrospective glance on the causes which decided the unhappy Murat to take so desperate a resolution. After having left the French army in Posen on January 16, 1813, the King immediately returned to Naples. He felt that his crown would be in danger by the consequence of the failure of the war against Russia. He lent his ear to the insinuating proposals made to him by Austria—Austria maintains that Joachim took the initiative. *Pourparlers* took place with the English General, William Bentinck. The King offered, without the Emperor's sanction to do so, to mediate between France and hostile powers. However, the remembrance of the glory which he had won under the French flag, the feeling of what he owed to the country where he had been born and raised to a high rank, his gratitude to and attachment for Napoleon brought him back into the midst of his brothers-in-arms during the 1813 campaign. The fatal project which he had been turning over in his mind so long a time past, and to which a new impetus was given by the battle of Leipzig, recalled him a second time to Italy. At Erfurth he took what was to be a last farewell of the Emperor, and then returned to Naples. He was more than ever convinced that Napoleon's power was shaken to its foundation, and that it would not be long before he would succumb, without any possibility of saving him. The Neapolitans, who had King Joachim's confidence, maintained him in this way of thinking by false or true reports which contributed to lead him astray. Fouché's advice finally persuaded him that the time had at last come when he must separate his fortunes from Napoleon. This calculation was based on a principle which proceeded from a feeling of generosity which calls for indulgence, and diminishes the culpability of his desertion; he had said to himself that if he, the King of Naples, the only ally remaining to Napoleon, were to be dragged down with Napoleon in a common fall, all hope would be forever lost, but that if on the contrary he remained standing on the ruins of the Empire he would have a chance of being useful to his benefactor and of being able to hold out his hand to him. The splendor of such a rôle dazzled him. It must be admitted also that a less chivalrous motive had great influence on his determination. He had learnt as a fact, and supposed friends had assured him of it, that it was Napoleon's intention to incorporate the state of Naples into the Kingdom of Italy. According to these rumors it was proposed to offer the dethroned monarch an indemnity, which, no matter how great it might be, could not be an equivalent of the crown of Naples—a crown which he hoped to transmit to his children. Murat had accordingly come to the conclusion that his throne would not be in safety so long as Napoleon's rule remained preponderant in Italy. It was thus that he was brought to reenter upon negotiations, which he now approached without the same advantages on his side as formerly. On January 11, 1814, after a violent struggle between his good and evil genius, Murat signed an offensive and defensive alliance with Austria, who went surety for her allies. By this treaty Joachim engaged to pursue the war against France, assisted by the united efforts of the allied powers, in the reestablishment of a fair balance of power; and to assure peace to Europe and particularly to Italy, where the two contracting states mutually guaranteed each other's possessions. The avowed object of this treaty was to limit Napoleon's Empire to the Alps, the Rhine, and the Pyrenees. But Joachim, trusting in the apparent force of the bonds which attached the Austrian Emperor to Napoleon's family, could not imagine that the war against France would be transformed into a personal war against the daughter of the said Emperor of Austria, against his son-in-law, and his grandson. General Neipperg, Prince Metternich's great agent in seduction, was sent to Naples to conclude this treaty. Lord W. Bentinck arrived in Naples at the same time and signed a convention with the Neapolitan government, which was simply entitled an armistice but which proclaimed the state of Naples as at peace with England. Free communication was reestablished between the two States, and the ports of both countries were reciprocally opened to trade, while the Neapolitan flag was acknowledged and protected by England.

The covenant concluded with General Bentinck was considered as being virtually of the same strength as a treaty, and was reserved for signature on a future occasion, it having been recognized as necessary not to lose any time in deciding on the plan of the campaign which the Austrian, English, and Neapolitan troops were to take part. Lord Aberdeen was to receive the full necessary powers for the conclusion of a definite treaty at a subsequent period. The convention was the preliminary of this treaty. One of the articles of this convention stipulated that in case any unforeseen event stood in the way of its ratification, the two parties undertook not to recommence hostilities before having given each other due preliminary notification. We shall see lower down with what object this clause was inserted. The promise of a definite treaty was never concluded, the English government, whose good faith was with good reason open to suspicion, having alleged that if it put off concluding this treaty, it was by motives of delicacy and honor which did not allow it to impose on a prince allied to England (the King of Sicily) a sacrifice of his hereditary states before an indemnity had been paid to him. Letters from Lord Castlereagh containing the commitment to carry out this covenant faithfully were communicated to the King. Thus the English government had only bound itself towards the King of Naples by a military convention, a convention which the occurrences of war might modify entirely.

In the meanwhile King Joachim, full of confidence, immediately opened the campaign, and marched upon Bologna without having the ratification of the treaty with Austria. A variety of circumstances inspired him for a short time with doubts as to the sincerity of his allies. The delay of the Emperor of Austria's ratification showed that there was some hesitation on the part of this prince. The equivocal attitude of Lord Bentinck, who was placed at the head of the Sicilian troops, manifested to the former sovereign of the Two Sicilies that these troops were intended to conquer back again the throne which had been usurped at Naples, the summonses addressed to the generals and the officers of King Joachim's army to induce them to pronounce themselves against the reigning dynasty, all these threatening communications troubled King Murat as well they might. On another side the declaration of Sir Robert Wilson, English commissioner with the Austrian army in Italy, charged by Lord Bentinck as well as by Marshal Bellegarde, to dissipate all misunderstanding, tended to reassure the reigning sovereign of Naples. General Wilson declared to him that he considered Lord Castlereagh's letters containing promises of a formal treaty, as documents of a value equal to a treaty itself, and that neither the British parliament nor any executive authority would hesitate to recognize the validity of such an commitment. In his personal opinion, the English commissioner said, this promise was more binding than a regular treaty because it constituted at the same time an appeal to honor, and an obligation of good faith. Lord Bentinck himself hastened to King Joachim's headquarters and declared anew that his government fully adhered to the treaty concluded on January 11 between the Emperor of Austria and the King of Naples. He also confirmed England's consent to the advantages stipulated in Murat's favor, that is to say, the cession of the Marches of Ancona, on condition that the Neapolitan army should give its immediate and active cooperation to the allies. The non-payment of the indemnity due to the King of Sicily still remained the only alleged cause of delay in the conclusion of a formal and definite treaty. Murat contented himself with these explanations and no longer hesitated. While the King of Naples was relying on the good faith of the allies, with whom he was making common cause, the ambassador of France at the Congress of Vienna was making every effort to obtain from the Austrian government that they should break off this alliance with Napoleon's brother-in-law. Talleyrand was seconded in his task by the English ambassadors who, hiding their double game, pressed Austria to undertake what they called the Holy War of Legitimacy, against a sovereign with whom this power was bound by a treaty and to whom she had guaranteed the integrity of his states. The Austrian government, while listening to these proposals, adjourned its final acquiescence, alleging as an excuse that its finances were exhausted. The English minister offered to dispose of this difficulty by paying the cost of this expedition and even consented to assist the Austrians in their movements with an

English fleet. When King Joachim was informed of these treacherous negotiations, he was either in ignorance of the part which the English ministers had taken in it, or else he closed his eyes against proof. When it became impossible to doubt any longer that he would sooner or later be attacked by Austria he decided to prepare himself thoroughly to repel any aggression. He entered into communications with the Island of Elba and obtained from Napoleon that he would forget what had passed, and once more made common cause with him in secret.

While this redoubtable adversary of the allies, leaving the obscure retreat from the depths of which he still made them tremble, went off to reconquer his Empire with one battalion of his faithful guard, the King of Naples attacked the Austrians, and drove them back from position to position to the banks of the Po. Fickle fortune who had so long protected her two favorites, luring them on with her last favors, was soon to swallow them up in the abyss. Murat advanced rapidly upon Reggio, having directed his right flank on Occhiobello and his left on Florence. Pushing his outposts as far as Pistoia he marched in the direction of Milan, where he was expected, believing that he had only to deal with the Austrians. Flattering himself with the thought that the English would not interfere in his quarrel with Austria, he gave satisfaction to the request which was addressed to him by Lord Bentinck, not to violate the territory of the King of Sardinia, who was England's ally. This condescension on his part was to become fatal to him. Crossing a corner of the Piedmontese territory Murat could easily have crossed the Po at Piacenza which was then in a very weak state of defense. He directed his principal efforts against Occhiobello, which he was unable to carry by storm. His respect for the Sardinian frontier did not preserve him from the discomfiture which a treacherous enemy inflicted upon him in notifying to him that a union of the English forces to the Austrian army had been effected, on the pretext that the King of Naples had violated the convention between him and England, a convention, one of the stipulations of which provided that he should not attack them without having given three months' notice of his intention of doing so.

Joachim then repented that he had not remained on the defensive in conformity with his agreement with the Emperor Napoleon, and of having yielded to the repeated and pressing requests which his ambassadors in Vienna and in London had addressed to him, to urge him to act on the offensive. Not allowing himself to be cast down, however, by a blow which had not altogether taken him by surprise, Joachim undertook to reestablish his forces by means of a decisive act. He assembled his army, which was still of a strength of more than 30,000 men, in a retrenched camp between Ancona and Rimini. Two days later he gave a great battle with the Austrians which lasted two days in the plain of Tolentina. The Neapolitan army, weakened and demoralized by previous defeats, succumbed to the force of an enemy numerically superior, in spite of the prodigies of valor of its chief. Disbanded, and the greater part cut off by the Austrian troops, some fell into their power. The rest fled towards Naples and dispersed in every direction. This retreat would have been perhaps less disastrous had not General Pignatelli-Strongoli, who commanded the left wing of the Neapolitan army, prematurely quitted Florence, leaving the road open to Rome to the Austrian General Nugent. Some attribute this disastrous negligence on the Neapolitan general's part to want of order, others to treachery. This fatal incident, the false reports of Murat's death and of the landing of the English in Naples, the open treachery of certain officers who propagated discouragement and desertion by their speeches and by their example; all these causes together caused a panic in the Neapolitan army. Joachim, abandoned by his people, had nothing left to do but to return to Naples. He arrived there followed by some horsemen. He entered his capital accompanied by Colonel Bonafous, his nephew, and your lancers. He went straight to the palace where he appeared before the Queen, pale and emaciated, in his lancer's uniform, covered with dust. He embraced his wife tenderly and said to her: "All is lost except my life, and I was not fortunate enough to find death." In taking leave of the Queen and his children, King Joachim cut his hair, which fell in long ringlets on his shoulders, and putting off his decorations dressed himself in clothes which did not attract attention. He walked along the coast until he was opposite the Island of Nisida, and there got into a boat which landed him on the Island of Ischia, where he passed three days without being recognized. On the fourth day, as he was walking along the beach accompanied by his faithful nephew, and was deliberating with him on the best means for escaping to France, he noticed a little sailing ship on the east which was approaching them. The King hailed the vessel and flinging himself into a fishing smack, ordered its owner to go and meet it. What were his surprise and joy when he recognized on board the Duke of Rocca-Romana, his Grand Equerry, and Marquis Giulani, his aide-de-camp, who had succeeded in escaping from Naples, and who were looking for their unfortunate sovereign. The King before his final departure from Naples had divided a considerable sum in gold between these two officers, and had told them of his plan of going to Ischia with his nephew and of embarking there for France. Their meeting, which had been delayed by obstacles as one can easily understand, having thus fortunately been effected, the King landed in Cannes with his faithful companions towards the end of May, 1815, after a crossing which had been disturbed by no incident.

During the Odyssey which we have just related Queen Caroline had opened negotiations with Lord Exmouth, who was commander of the English fleet before Naples, offering him two Neapolitan ships of war on condition that she should be transported to Toulon with her children, whom she had already placed in safety at Gaëta; but Admiral Exmouth, who knew that the ships would be his in any case, refused to receive the Queen except to conduct her to Trieste, and to place her in the hands of the Austrian authorities. Forced to submit to these humiliating conditions, and having fortunately escaped the effects of a riot which she quelled by her courage and calmness, Caroline Murat embarked on the English frigate, and making sail for Gaëta where Napoleon's sister took in her young family, she was conducted to Trieste. King Joachim immediately on landing in Cannes, wrote to Fouché charging him to speak for him to the Emperor and to ask the latter to allow him to go to Paris. Napoleon's only answer was to ask his brother-in-law what treaty of peace had been concluded between France and Naples since 1814. Fouché in consequence advised Murat to remain where he was, adding that it was still possible for him to render service to his native country by exciting the inhabitants and the troops to vigorous resistance to the enemies within and without—a kind of service which Murat was never to render, for he had no weight whatever with the French, who did not forget his desertion in 1814. Murat then retired into a little country house in the neighborhood of Toulon.

In the meanwhile took place the battle of Waterloo, in consequence of which Napoleon definitely abdicated in favor of his son and a provisional government commission entered into functions. After Louis XVIII returned to Paris, Joachim who until then had been protected by the Imperial authorities found himself placed in a most critical position. He was forced to quit the retreat where he had passed six weeks without being interfered with. Exposed to danger by murderers, who were seeking for him to kill him, he dared not go out to change his refuge except in the night, fearing if he were taken to have to submit to the fate of the unfortunate Marshal Brune. Murat had spread the report that he had escaped to Tunis, but his persecutors did not long remain the dupes of this strategy. The Marquis de Rivière, the same who had been condemned to death for his cooperation in Georges's conspiracy, and whose pardon Murat had obtained, wrote to him and advised him to surrender into his hands. M. de Rivière exhorted Joachim to trust to the humanity and good faith of the King of France, as well as to the word of Lord Exmouth who associated himself in this application. The letter which I have just spoken of was handed to King Joachim by a M. Joliclerc, general commissary of police, who knew Murat's hiding-place, and who refused to reveal it. His refusal to become an instrument of treachery procured this honorable man's dismissal from his post. Joachim, having declined Marquis de Rivière's offer, as he might be expected to do, would not have any more confidence in Admiral Exmouth, who had previously refused him an asylum on board his fleet while awaiting the decision of the allied powers about him, unable to find any safety in France made up his mind to go to Havre and to proceed thence to Corsica. With this purpose in view Duke of Rocca-Romana freighted a vessel and embarked for this port with Colonel Bonafous and two of the King's servants, and they were charged with his money and his clothes. As soon as they were on board they were to send a boat to a distant point in the bay of Toulon where the King would hold himself in readiness to embark. Unfortunately the boat went out of its way, and after having searched for the King in vain returned to the ship without having found him. The murderers, who had heard of this plan of escape and who thought that Joachim had gone in the boat, boarded the vessel and, unable to find the man whom they were looking for, obliged the captain to hoist sail forthwith. The King left his hiding-place after nightfall and tried to find the boat, but as he was in ignorance of the mistake which had occurred, passed the night in the most anxious waiting. As soon as the day broke he ran along the shore climbing up every eminence to try to discover the vessel which meant freedom for him. He at last saw it under sail, but was unable to find any means of drawing attention to himself. Each moment removed the ship further and further away from his eyes, until at last he lost sight of it altogether. Heartbroken with this new misfortune Murat did not know what was to become of him. Fortunately, however, in the midst of his misfortunes he did not return to the asylum which he had left, and it was well he did not do so for he would have fallen into the hands of his persecutors, who not having found him on board the vessel hoped to lay hands upon him in this retreat. The wretched man walked as chance guided his steps, avoiding the neighborhood of the ports and big buildings, and wandered thus for several days and nights through the woods and the vineyards. Finding barely enough to eat, worn out by fatigue, urged on by hunger, the unhappy proscript ventured to enter a farm. He only found an old woman there, and introducing himself to her as an officer of the Toulon garrison who had lost his way asked her to give him something to eat. The good woman receiving him with cordiality told him that in the absence of her master who had gone out for a walk she would make him an omelet. While she was busying herself in preparing it the master of the house returned. Seeing a stranger sitting at his table he asked for another omelet and sat down by the side of his guest to share this modest repast with him. The resemblance between the stranger and the portrait of the King of Naples which he had seen in the Imperial Hall at the Tuileries Palace struck the newcomer. He told the King so, and Murat confessed who he was. This excellent man then rose with tears in his eyes, begging the King to forgive him for the liberty with which he had acted towards him, and placed himself and everything he possessed at his entire disposal. The good wife troubled by this sudden recognition, hearing what her master said, was seized with a fit of nervous trembling and dropped the omelet which she held in her hand.

The King remained hidden in this house for several days while its owner, who was a naval officer, busied himself in conjunction with some friends whom he had taken into the secret with the best ways of providing for the subsistence and wants of his illustrious guest. In the meanwhile the King's enemies, excited by the hope of getting hold of the gold and diamonds which they believed he carried with him, had been hunting for him with renewed activity. The old woman who was charged to guard King Joachim discharged this duty with indefatigable perseverance. She watched all night while he was asleep, sitting at the window of the house, which was situated on an eminence, from which she could see all that was going on around. During the night of August 13, a gang of about sixty men came up the path which led to the house where Murat was hiding, but the vigilant old woman saw them by the light of a lantern which they were carrying. Suspecting their evil purpose she hastened to waken the King and told him of the danger which he was running. Joachim was sleeping in his clothes, his dagger and two pairs of pistols beside him. He covered himself with all speed with a great frock coat under which he hid his arms, and then this intrepid Paladin, this fearless knight, who so many a time had confronted death at the wars, was forced to hide himself under the foliage of a vine which was situated less than thirty paces from his refuge. Barely had he got out of the house when it was surrounded. The old woman had shut the door to get rid of the mattress on which the King had been sleeping and put everything in order in his room. She kept the brigands waiting outside the door, pretending that she had to dress herself. As soon as she had opened the door they rushed into the house, searching everywhere, while some of them explored the garden and the vineyards, passing and repassing many times near the spot where the King was hidden, vomiting forth imprecations against him, expressing their hopes of finding him, of taking him alive or of killing him, and of sharing his spoils. Joachim's mind was fully made up in case he were discovered, to rush upon his murderers and sell his life dearly; and, rather than fall into their hands, to blow his brains out with his own hands. Having escaped from this danger he returned to the house because he thought that as it had been searched through and through he would be safer there than anywhere else. His faithful host had given it up to him and had gone to sleep in the city, so as to divert attention from it. The unfortunate Joachim had addressed himself to the authorities of the department to ask for their protection, assuring them of his firm resolution not to trouble public repose either by words or by acts. At the same time he wrote to Louis XVIII appealing to his generosity and magnanimity, but he received no answer to his letter. Tired at last with uselessly awaiting a message from the allies, under whose protection he pressingly demanded to place himself, he began to despair of ever receiving it. It was impossible for him to remain in hiding any longer. A price had been placed on his person, or rather on his head; 24,000 francs reward was offered to the man who should give him up. That meant the sale of his life, because it was very well known that he would not be taken alive. In this terrible position he did not know what would become of him. There was no chance of safety for him in a journey by land and it was too late to go and join the Duke of Rocca-Romana and his nephew at Havre.

Corsica was the only country which could offer him an asylum. The adventurous character of the inhabitants of this island, with their mountains, and the thick jungles in their woods, offered him a safe retreat until the day when the intentions of the allies with reference to his person would be known to him. It was accordingly decided upon that the King and his host should make an attempt to reach Corsica in an open boat. The King's host offered himself to conduct this expedition with the assistance of his friends. On August 22 Joachim wrote to Fouché to inform him of his plan, and on the evening of the same day he embarked at Toulon with his three friends. On the 24th a violent storm broke out. The fragile boat kept filling with water, which they were forced to bail out with their hats. In the afternoon, seeing a ship sailing in an opposite direction they approached it and asked to be taken on board, offering the captain a sum of money to take them to Bastia. The captain of this ship, which was freighted with wines for Toulon, alarmed at being thus accosted by four men who were heavily armed, and whom he suspected of having evil designs, not only refused their offer but did his best to sink their boat, and probably would have succeeded in doing so, but for the coolness and skill of the King and his companions, who thanks to their presence of mind were enabled to escape this danger. Under the first impulses of their indignation they wanted to board the ship and revenge themselves on the ill-conditioned crew, but on reflection, however, they abandoned this plan. A few minutes later the King and his friends were fortunate enough to fall in with the packet which plied regularly between Toulon and Bastia.

It was in the nick of time, for it would have been no longer possible for them to keep afloat. Their boat had been seriously damaged by the storm and in the course of the encounter which they had engaged in against the trading vessel. The King met several eminent people on board the packet-boat to whom he was known, and who were leaving the South of France from motives of prudence. Murat spent a day at Bastia, and on the morrow proceeded with his three comrades to Vescovato, which is a big village fifteen miles to the south of Bastia. He went straight up to the biggest house, which belonged to M. de Colonna-Ceccaldi, mayor of this village, who was a warm partisan of the Bourbons for whose cause he had endured many years of exile. M. Ceccaldi enjoyed a well-merited reputation for uprightness and generosity in the country. The King disclosed himself to him, informing him of the reasons which obliged him to seek refuge in Corsica, and begged him to grant him his hospitality until it would be possible for him to know the decision of the allied sovereigns with reference to him. M. Colonna-Ceccaldi received King Joachim with respect, and assured him that the laws of hospitality were sacred to the Corsicans: he added that no order emanating from the government obliged the subjects of the King of France to treat a Frenchman who had been sovereign of Naples as an enemy. The King had the greatest satisfaction in meeting one of his aides-de-camp in this house, an officer named Franceschetti, who had retired there quite recently with his wife, M. de Ceccaldi's daughter.

In the meanwhile the commander of the town of Bastia having heard of King Joachim's presence in Corsica sent him orders to consider himself a prisoner until the King of France's decision concerning him should be made known. Murat refused to obey the orders of an officer in whom he recognized no authority whatever over his person. The military commander of Bastia then declared Joachim the enemy of Louis XVIII, and a perturbator of the public peace. He sent some hundred soldiers to Vescovato to capture him, but in the meanwhile M. Ceccaldi's friends and relations had united to repel this attempt at violence, for they considered it their bounden duty and a point of honor to assist in defending their host's glorious guest, who had placed himself under the protection of their hospitality. To this force which in the course of a few days had reached the number of over six hundred men who had hastened from every point in the island, two hundred more men, veterans and for the most part officers who had formerly served under the King's orders, and who had come back home after the fall of the Empire, added themselves.

The soldiers who had been sent from Bastia might consider themselves very lucky to be able to return without injury. The men who had helped King Joachim urged him to seize upon Bastia and even the whole of the island, promising him the assistance of the troops and of the greater part of the inhabitants. Murat thanked these good people for their zeal, but had no hesitation in saying that he considered himself a fugitive who had come to Corsica in search of hospitality alone, and had no right to make any attempt against the sovereignty of King Louis XVIII. Three weeks having passed by without his having received any answer whatever to his letters from the allies, which made him suppose that he was abandoned and proscribed by the European powers, and persuaded that there was no other resource for him than to listen, to the promptings of his despair, he took the resolution to endeavor to win back his crown by conquest, even were he to find death in the adventure. To avoid coming to blows with the superior commander of Bastia, Murat left Vescovato. He accepted the services of four hundred men selected amongst the braves who had offered him their help, and proceeded with them to Ajaccio. On his approach the authorities of the town retired with the exception of the mayor, who remained behind to protect public peace. The inhabitants received King Joachim with respect and his troops behaved with absolute discipline. The King refused the hospitality which was offered to him in private houses, so as to compromise nobody, and went to live in an inn. It was there that he arranged for the purchase of five ships, and collected the arms and ammunition necessary for his expedition. These preparations lasted several days.

While the adventures of which we have spoken were taking place, one of King Joachim's aides-de-camp of British origin, Captain Macirone, who happened to be in Paris for reasons which have nothing to do with this story, and from whose book I have already taken a great part of these particulars, and who was busying himself to be useful to King Murat, knowing Fouché's former relations with his dethroned king, had approached this minister, who had made use of his services with the Duke of Wellington at a time when the Duke of Otranto was secretly treating with the English general. Macirone taking advantage of his relations with Lord Wellington had implored the latter's aid to obtain from M. de Metternich the promise of a refuge in Austria for King Joachim, and he had succeeded in his application as will be seen by reading the following document:

"M. Macirone is authorized by these presents to inform King Joachim that his Majesty the Emperor of Austria will grant him an asylum in his States under the following conditions:

"1. The King will take the name of a private person. The Queen having assumed the name of Lipona it is proposed that the King should do so also.

"2. The King will be at liberty to select a town in Bohemia, Moravia, or in Upper Austria, and to take up his abode there. Should he wish to settle in the country there would be no objection to his doing so in the same provinces.

"3. The King will give his word of honor to his Imperial and Royal Majesty not to leave the Austrian States without the express sanction of His said Majesty, that he will live as a distinguished private person who is subject to the laws in force in the Austrian States, in favor of which and in order that suitable use may be made of it the undersigned has received the Imperial orders to sign the present declaration.

"Given in PARIS on Sept. 1, 1815.

"(Signed) METTERNICH."

Provided with this declaration and with passports, Macirone proceeded to Toulon, where he heard that King Murat had left for Corsica. Thereupon Captain Macirone, being anxious to carry out his mission successfully, embarked for Bastia. In this port he had an interview with the English Captain Bastard, who was in command of the *"Meander,"* a frigate of the British navy. This officer having informed him of King Joachim's preparations, and of the expedition which he was preparing, did not conceal from Macirone that there was great excitement at Naples, but that necessary arrangements were being made to repel this audacious attack. The commander of the English vessel declared at the same time that he had received orders to oppose Murat's adventurous enterprise by force, and that he should make his arrangements so as to capture the king's flotilla after he had left port, and was at some distance from the coast. Before leaving Bastia himself Macirone received a visit from two Corsicans there who had come from Leghorn on the *"Meander."* One of them was a captain in the Royal Corsican Regiment in British service. The other was a civil servant in the new government of the new King of Naples. These emissaries carried orders from the Neapolitan minister, who enjoined upon them to resist King Joachim's expedition by every means in their power. Like Captain Bastard they thought that having seen M. Macirone, Murat would accept the refuge offered him by the Emperor of Austria. Macirone arrived in Ajaccio on September 28, bringing two servants who had been in the service, with money, linen, and clothes. In spite of the affectionate cordiality with which the king received Macirone he refused to listen to his advice. The captain in vain urged him in the most pressing way to make up his mind to accept the offers of hospitality of the Austrian government. He had given orders that Joachim should be received at Trieste whither he would be transported by an English vessel. The King answered that it was too late, that the die was cast; that he had already waited for the decision of the allied powers for a space of three months, during which time his life had been constantly menaced; that finally, persecuted as he was by the sovereigns of Europe, he had made up his mind to risk all and to endeavor to recover the throne which he had lost. King Murat further added that in spite of all the confidence in his success, with which he was animated, he cared very little for the result of his expedition. If he failed in his enterprise he would at least have the comfort of losing his life, after having so often confronted death on so many fields of battle. He also said that the failure of his campaign against Austria could not deprive him of his right as a king which had been acknowledged by the whole of Europe, and that he had signed no abdication. The final reason which urged him to persevere in his determination to vindicate his rights to the crown was that in acting otherwise he would have gratuitously compromised three hundred brave officers and soldiers, who had wished to follow him, and whom it was impossible to abandon to the revenge of the French Royal government. Captain Macirone despairing of turning King Joachim away from his foolhardy enterprise begged him at least for a written answer to the proposal which he had been commissioned to lay before him. The King, who did not wish to make his plans public yet, informed Captain Macirone in a letter that he "accepted the passport which had been sent him, that he intended to make use of it to proceed to the destination which was mentioned upon it." But subsequently, on the night which preceded his departure, King Murat addressed another letter to Macirone in which he admitted that his first communication had been dictated to him by the necessity imposed upon him of hiding his true designs, and that he *owed it to truth, to his own dignity, and to the noble frankness and good faith of the captain, to acquaint him at last with his real intentions.* This very long letter, in which King Joachim bitterly complained of the way in which the allied forces had treated him, terminated with the declaration that he was leaving to go and reconquer his kingdom, and that he would already be some distance on his way at the time when Captain Macirone should receive his letter.

Macirone thought it his duty to inform the commander of the English vessel of King Joachim's departure, but took care not to do so until the King's little fleet had got forty-eight hours start. Murat's intention was to land at Salerno, which is a port situated about thirty miles from Naples, where a considerable number of the old Neapolitan troops were being reorganized; but, a storm having separated him from his flotilla, he made up his mind, instead of returning to Salerno, to rally the rest of his forces, and to land immediately in the neighborhood of Pizzo. The felucca, on board which King Joachim found himself, carried about thirty old officers of his, amongst whom was General Franceschetti. This little troop, at the head of which Murat placed himself in a general's uniform, was pacifically received by some coastguards who happened to be on the beach, and who recognized King Joachim. They marched without loss of time to the town of Pizzo and entered the marketplace. Murat addressed the inhabitants who surrounded him, and some saluted him as their King, offering him horses which served to mount his troops, but the majority displayed timidity and hesitation. Joachim continued his march on Monteleone without respite. The agent of the Duke of l'Infantado, who enjoyed great influence with the inhabitants on account of this duke's immense possessions at Pizzo and elsewhere, addressed them after Murat's departure and threatened them with the vengeance of Ferdinand's government if they did not oppose the usurper's march. He even succeeded in making a troop take arms, and placed himself at their head. On this march on Monteleone King Joachim fell in with a colonel of gendarmerie named Trentacapelli, who was on his way from Monteleone to Pizzo. Murat invited him to join them, but this officer who had little confidence in resources so feeble for so great an enterprise respectfully declined the offer. The colonel said, pointing to Monteleone, that he could only recognize as King the man whose flag should float on those towers. Trentacapelli, whom the King had very imprudently allowed to continue his way to Pizzo, met the Duke of l'Infantado's agent there urging the people to take up arms for King Ferdinand. The colonel added his efforts and the influence of his authority to the agent's exhortation; then placing himself at the head of a large troop he marched rapidly in pursuit of King Joachim and came up with him very soon about half way to Monteleone. King Joachim and his friends seeing Trentacapelli's troops coming along at great speed in the distance imagined that they were coming to join them. Actuated by this idea the King interrupted his march, thinking that it would be a good thing to await reinforcements before entering Monteleone. On the approach of this imaginary reinforcement Murat walked a few paces towards this troop, when some of his followers shouted out: "Long live King Joachim." To their great surprise this was answered with a discharge of musketry. A fierce encounter ensued and the party of King Murat, who defended himself with the courage of despair, lost some men killed, and many wounded. Having to deal with an enemy numerically much superior, and unable to advance on Monteleone with his enemies behind him, the King made up his mind to return to his ship, and followed by General Franceschetti and a dozen others he cut his way through the thick of his enemies wounding several with his own hand and discharging his pistol point-blank at Colonel Trentacapelli, whom he missed. The vigor of his attack disconcerted the enemy and filled their ranks with confusion, of which the King took advantage to run to the place in the bay where he had left his ship. He had received no injuries although all his comrades had been wounded.

In the meanwhile the commander of the expeditionary fleet, Barbara, a Piedmontese officer, now in the King's service, having heard firing and considering his personal safety only, or perhaps bought over by Ferdinand's agent, had left the coast, abandoning King Joachim to his fate. In this desperate situation the King jumped into the water to reach a fishing boat which was within reach, followed by Franceschetti and the remainder of his followers. Fate would have it that this boat had unfortunately settled in the sand, and the united efforts of the fugitives to run it out into the sea were in vain. They then ran up to a smaller boat which was within twenty paces, and meanwhile the coast was covered with the King's enemies who watched them with astonishment, without firing or without approaching them. To make matters worse, this little boat in which the King could have escaped with his followers was chained to the shore, and all efforts to break the chain were fruitless. The fisherman to whom the boat belonged, and who was perhaps afraid of losing his boat, pulled at the chain, while another fisherman who had run up seized on the King, who with one blow on his head butted him into the sea. The example given by these two fishermen was followed by other assailants, and the boat was soon completely surrounded. No violence was committed upon the King, who stood up in the midst of his assailants, adjuring them to let him go, and as a last hope showing them his passport for Trieste. Finding them deaf to his appeals Joachim was obliged to give himself up into the hands of his enemies. News of this important capture having been telegraphed to the Neapolitan Ministry an order was sent back by telegraph that a court-martial should be called together to try, and to sentence, King Joachim. It is known how very expeditious was this trial. Murat listened to his sentence with a smile of contempt. He had written the following letter to his wife, enclosing a lock of his hair:

"MY DEAR CAROLINE,

"My last hour has come. In a few moments I shall have ceased to live, in a few moments you will have no husband. Never forget me, do not curse my memory. I die innocent. Farewell my Achilles, farewell my Laetitia, farewell my Lucien, farewell my Louise—show yourself worthy of me to the world. I leave you without a kingdom, without wealth, in the midst of my enemies. Remain constantly united, show yourselves superior to misfortune. Think of what you are and what you have been. God will bless you. Know that my greatest grief in the last moments of my life is to die far from my children. Receive my paternal blessings; receive my kisses and my tears, and ever hold in your memory your unhappy father.

"Pizzo, Oct. 13, 1815.

"(Signed) JOACHIM."

King Murat declared that he died in the Roman Catholic religion and begged the assistance of a priest, who comforted his last moments. He placed a portrait of his wife and his children on his bosom, and then refusing to sit down on the bench which was offered him or to allow his eyes to be bandaged, he himself gave the word of command to fire, and not a single muscle of his face betrayed that he felt the slightest emotion. Thus perished by an obscure death a man to whom fortune, having taken him from a very lowly position, had reserved the loftiest destiny. An intrepid soldier, frank, loyal, generous, throughout his whole career and on the throne which he had admirably occupied he had carried all these brilliant qualities to excess. Animated by too much confidence he made peace with his enemies when he should have continued to make war, and recommenced war when he should have maintained an expectant attitude, which is what brought about his ruin.

Chapter XIX

Various letters which I had received recalled me to France. I myself felt that the lack of information which was experienced there rendered my early departure necessary, and I accordingly made up my mind to ask for the necessary authorization for going there. On April 9 I begged the Empress to ask the Emperor of Austria to grant me a passport, which could only be delivered with the special permission of this prince. After some very affectionate attempts to dissuade me from going, Marie Louise was good enough to promise to speak to her father on the subject. I awaited the result of this promise for some days, at the end of which the Empress told me that she had had great difficulty in getting the Emperor of Austria to allow me to go; and that before ordering a passport to be given to me he wanted me to see Prince Metternich, and that I should be sent for at any moment by this minister. I resigned myself without reluctance to this delay. Half-confidences, the variations in the language of the influential people with whom I was brought into contact, comparisons which I was enabled to draw, thanks to the rôle of observer to which I was reduced, the indefinite adjournment of the Emperor of Austria's departure for Prague, a whole concatenation of circumstances and indications had given birth to certain hopes in my heart, which were unfortunately never to be realized.

I had no doubt that some event or other was being waited for, it may be one of those lightning-strokes to which the Emperor Napoleon was so accustomed, which might encourage the tendencies of the Austrian cabinet and induce it to charge me with some message for him. M. de Talleyrand had told somebody that he worked a great deal with the prime minister, and that he had noticed that he often varied. In telling the reader of these deductions of mine I only give them as conjectures on my part, seeing that I was never called to the audience to which I expected to be summoned.

Life at Schönbrunn and in Vienna had become intolerable for French people: the police behaved brutally towards them. Count Anatole de Montesquiou was coming one day from Vienna to Schönbrunn when he was detained at the Mariahilf barrier by an agent who informed him that he was not allowed to cross the lines. M. de Montesquiou went to the police-office and not finding any explanation of this order went home to his mother to wait for it there. A quarter of an hour later a messenger came from M. de Hager, director of police, with apologies for the misunderstanding which had interrupted his excursion and the assurance that such a thing would never occur again. In spite of this assurance we were frequently exposed to similar unpleasantness.

Since General Neipperg's departure for Italy, Baron de Wessemberg, the Austrian minister, one of the negotiators at the Congress, acted as intermediary between the Empress and Prince Metternich whom she used to see at her son's apartment every time that she went to Vienna. He was often charged with letters from General Neipperg. Archduke Charles appeared also to enjoy the Empress's confidence.

On April 13, a religious service was celebrated in Vienna in commemoration of the anniversary of the death of Maria Theresa, Marie Louise's mother, and she was present with her family. On her return to Schönbrunn she did me the honor of telling me that a letter which had been brought by M. de Flahaut had arrived in Vienna, and that she had been told its contents verbally. They persisted in not handing her the Emperor's letters, so as to cut short all communications between her and her husband. M. de Flahaut had been arrested at Stuttgart just as M. de Stassart had been arrested at Lintz, and had been forced to turn back after having handed over to the Austrian authorities the dispatches with which he had been charged.

On the same day the Vienna Gazette published the Emperor of Austria's edict, relating to the institution of the "Lombardo-Venetian kingdom," under date of April 7. Ambitious motives prompted the sovereigns of the great powers to erect into monarchies the spoils of the colossal power from which they were inheriting. Thus the Emperor of Russia took the title of King of Poland, the King of England that of King of Hanover; Holland, with Belgium added, also definitely became a kingdom.

The Empress returned one day to Schönbrunn, much upset by a remark which had reached her ears as she was coming out of the imperial palace in Vienna. Two men, who spoke in French, had said loud enough for her to hear: "This lady does very wrongly to act as a spy here on her father; she would do very much better to return to France and to live with her husband there." This reproach wounded her deeply, but as moderation was the basis of her character she refused to have the people who had made this remark looked for, contrary to what she had been advised to do. Count Aldini had just brought a letter from the Princess Elisa, Napoleon's sister, to Schönbrunn, in which she begged Marie Louise to use her influence with the Emperor of Austria to enable her to return to France. In spite of the goodwill of the Empress who went specially to Vienna to ask for this permission for her sister-in-law her application remained without any result and no answer was vouchsafed by the Austrian cabinet.

On April 16 there began in the Austrian capital a series of prayers and processions for the success of the war against France and against Napoleon. These processions composed of schools of young girls and boys, together with people of the working-classes, lasted a fortnight. Preceded by banners and flags of every color they marched through the streets and suburbs of Vienna, and went to pray in the cathedral of Saint Stephen and the principal churches. The court did not fail to be present at these prayers. The Empress of Austria formally asked her stepdaughter to be present with the rest of her family, but was unable to induce her to do so. So pressing were her requests that the case was submitted to the Emperor of Austria and to two of his brothers, and their opinion was opposed to such an action. The sentiments manifested by the Empress were in harmony with her position; but I am sorry to say that she appeared only to make this concession so as to be able to persist in her determination not to return to France. I had just received a letter from the Emperor, another from King Joseph, and another from the Queen, his wife, addressed to the Empress, by special messenger, and I handed them to her telling her that I was discharging a duty which had been laid upon me. She reminded me that she could only take them to hand them over to her father, and that if I thought right to keep them she would act as if she had heard nothing about them. As these letters were intended for her and it was better that they should be read, I begged her to take them and to do what she thought right with them. Some words were afterwards exchanged between us on the very painful subject of her refusal to join the Emperor. She answered with some vivacity, but, however, with her usual gentleness, that her resolution on this head was irrevocable. When I objected that there was no such thing as an irrevocable commitment, and that circumstances might arise which would render her return to France obligatory, she made haste to answer that even her father's rights did not extend as far as that. I could not help remarking, in my turn, that the sentiments which she was manifesting were unjust and quite out of harmony with her character; that if the French nation were to hear of her repugnance, it would be much hurt, for nothing could be more painful to the French than to see their affection despised; and that then they would reject her, after having ardently desired her as a pledge of peace. This conversation was the last I ever had with her on the subject. She seemed to have made up her mind with so much obstinacy that it appeared to me quite useless to refer to the subject again. Time and events, moreover, were our only masters.

Prince Anthony of Saxony, the King's brother, was living in retirement and in bad health at Schönbrunn. The Empress Marie Louise frequently went to see him. This family was under a ban, on account of the affection which its head had shown for Napoleon. Poor Prince Anthony—although he was the Emperor of Austria's brother-in-law—had an army of bailiffs in his palace in Dresden, and was forced to pay for their keep. The King, who was even worse treated, was entirely without resources and lived on the proceeds of the sale of some diamonds which did not always suffice for paying all his household expenses, limited as his household was to a very small number of faithful servants, whose keep cost him about sixteen thousand francs a month. The Prussians seemed to have formed the plan of reducing this Prince by means of starvation, and they were pitilessly pursuing the invasion of one half of his States. The King had for a long time refused to agree to this dismemberment of his territory, but he was at last obliged to resign himself to the painful sacrifices which were imposed upon him by brutal force. This expression will not appear too strong when it is compared with the odious principles enunciated in a letter from Lord Castlereagh to Prince Hardenberg, which was produced at the debates in the English Parliament. This letter strikes the keynote of the abuse of prepotency which marked the majority of the acts of the Congress. The King of Saxony was not only despoiled of the Duchy of Warsaw, but of one half of his hereditary States, with which Prussia, in her moderation, was good enough to content herself. He had left Presburg to come and reside in the château of Laxemburg, where he was near the tribunal which was to pronounce without appeal on the fate of Saxony. He wanted to return to Dresden. In spite of his resignation permission to live in his capital during the war was for a long time refused him, nor was it hidden from him that there were good reasons why he should be treated with distrust. He was forced to send two of his nephews, sons of Prince Maximilian, to serve in the Austrian army, as hostages who would be a guarantee of his fidelity. He came incognito to see his brother at Schönbrunn, and these two Pariahs of royal blood wept in unison over the disasters of their house.

The cessation of festivities and the absence of Prince Eugène appeared to have disturbed the Emperor Alexander's habits. He used to go and kill some of his time every day at the house of Prince Schwarzenberg. I was constantly hearing of the complaints made by the Field marshal at the way in which he was bothered. When he had arranged to spend a day with his family and had selected one of his châteaux, so as to be more at his ease, he would see Alexander come and insist on forming one of the party. Prince Schwarzenberg, who was a man of independent character, did not always dissemble his irritation at these constant assiduities on the part of the Czar. His departure for the army at last delivered him from them. He had announced that he would come and take leave of the Empress, but no doubt a feeling of decency prevented him from keeping this promise.

A piece of news which at that time passed unnoticed, except at Schönbrunn where it created great excitement, was the death of Countess Neipperg. This lady who had remained in Würtemberg, which was General Neipperg's birthplace—while he came to employ his talents in Vienna—died in the month of April, after an illness of two days, leaving four boys behind her. She was said to have been very pretty but only moderately intelligent. Count Neipperg had run away with her from her first husband, who was still living a few months before his wife's death. The way in which Marie Louise announced this death, one day at table, showed that she did not regret it very much.

The Empress of Austria had taken care to keep her stepdaughter informed of what was going on in Italy. The last news which she sent her was altogether unfavorable to the Neapolitans, and this was confirmed by letters from General Neipperg. This general informed the Duchess of Parma that the regiment of her bodyguards, having refused to march against the Neapolitans and having shouted "Long Live the Emperor," had been disbanded. The Empress Marie Louise blazed up on reading this. She did not speak of punishing the authors of what she at least had no right to consider a rebellion, because by her character she had a dislike for severity, but she reserved to herself to reward those who had remained faithful. The Emperor of Austria anticipated her, informing her that he was going to reorganize her regiment and reduce it to three thousand men instead of the five or six thousand who had formerly composed it. This was a favor which looked very much like an increase of charges.

It was to be noticed that since the news of the military events which forejudged the issue of the Neapolitan question and ensured the pacification of Italy, the animosity of the high personages at the Congress had increased in intensity, and that the violence of the German newspapers had increased. The Congress busied itself with nothing but deliberations against the common enemy. The offensive treaties were renewed, and the sovereigns were pledged by transactions about which no time was given them to reflect. Austria, Russia, and Prussia signed new conventions for subsidies with England. The whole of Europe was set on foot as one man. Three great Russian armies were set to march through Hungary and Silesia.

Austria was assembling an army in Piedmont, and another on the Rhine. Prussia was making extraordinary efforts. She was organizing two armies in the Netherlands and on the Rhine. All the princes of Germany were sending their contingents in soldiers of the line and *landwehr;* England was landing troops in Holland; Spain was assembling troops;

more than a million soldiers were marching against Napoleon. At last, on May 12, all the powers confirmed their declaration of March 13, and declared war upon France if she recognized Napoleon as her sovereign. The Emperor Alexander had been the most animated. This prince who had been Napoleon's guest, whom he had loaded with apparent expressions of friendship, declared with the greatest vehemence and under an oath, that he would let his last soldier be killed and would spend his last rouble, to prevent Napoleon from ascending the throne of France once more and remaining there.

The decisive successes of the Austrians in Italy against King Joachim had dissipated the doubts which the Empress had had till then as to the fate of her States of Parma. No obstacle seemed, in her eyes, to stand in the way of her taking speedy possession of these territories. From that time on, all thought of returning to France was effaced from her mind and all her thoughts turned towards Parma. She occupied herself with unusual attention, in studying the principal branches of the administration of the country, but above all the resources which it offered for private life.

She informed herself with all details on the most comfortable way of establishing herself there, of the internal arrangements of the Palace of Parma, of the new disposal of rooms which would have to be carried out, of the summer country houses, and finally of the various improvements which could be carried out in the various residences. She gave orders for the organization of the ducal household, and for the nominations to all the functions at court. These occupations, which I am far from speaking of in a spirit of blame, took up all her time during several days. She attached to her establishment in Parma, the interest which is felt by a new landowner, who never having had the free disposal of the estates which he has inhabited, finds himself at last master of a domain where he is able to exercise an undivided authority. She planned out excursions to Florence, Genoa, Rome, Naples, where King Joachim would no longer be reigning; to England, etc., and annual visits to Vienna to see her son. This was the unvarying subject of her conversations.

The Official Journal had published an edict on April 14, ignored till then, by which the Duchess of Parma, begged her father to administer the duchies provisionally in her name, until circumstances would allow her to proceed there in person. This edict, dated March 3, bore the Emperor of Austria's acceptance.

Before leaving for the army, the Archduke John, Viceroy of Italy, came to take leave of Marie Louise. This visit having given her the opportunity of speaking of a remark which had been made by this prince on hearing the first news of the Emperor's departure from the island of Elba: "My poor Louise, I am sorry for you; what I hope for you and for us all is that he may break his neck," I could not help remarking to the Empress, that without any doubt she disapproved of such words. She admitted that these words were to be blamed, but she found that the feeling which had dictated them was excusable on the part of princes for whom the Emperor's return to France was a great calamity. On the same day she was called on by the Grand Duke of Baden who was to leave on the morrow; but who, according to his statement, was detained in Vienna to give certain explanations on a note which he had addressed to the Congress—a note the object of which was certain claims relating to the supremacy of the Federative Diet established by the same Congress, according to which all German affairs were to be decided by Austria's influence, and under the presidence of an Austrian minister.

It seems to me that it will not be entirely without interest to relate here the last act of the Empress Marie Louise, which I witnessed before my departure from Vienna, although it only interested this princess's conscience. If I allude to it at all, it is because it is an indication of her religious feelings. She discharged her devotional duties, in the chapel of Schönbrunn, at seven o'clock in the morning in her father's presence. On that day Count San Vitale, who had been appointed her grand-chamberlain, fulfilled the functions of his post for the first time.

More than three weeks had passed by since I had been ordered to await an audience with Prince Metternich before returning to France. Counting no longer on this audience with the prime minister, I regretted to see my departure delayed in pure waste of time. If it entered into the secret views of the Austrian cabinet to resign itself to a reconciliation with the Emperor Napoleon, it seemed evident to me that events still uncertain, and perhaps remote, would alone be able to force it to such a step. There was accordingly no further reason for my presence in Vienna, nor were there any motives for prolonging it. I renewed my request for a passport, but the Emperor Francis was at that time suffering from an indisposition which prevented him from attending to business of any sort. Later on another objection was made against the realization of my plan, connected with the visa, which was described as indispensable. This visa had to be given to my passport by Prince Schwarzenberg. An order having forbidden all communication with the left bank of the Rhine, the signature of the commander-in-chief of the Austrian army had become necessary for crossing the river. Now M. de Schwarzenberg had already left for his general headquarters, and this absence complicated the difficulties. After much opposition I was given to hope that I should be able to leave if I took a place in the carriage of an Austrian officer, a proposal to which I eagerly agreed. At last I received a passport from the state chancery, but another week was lost in the formalities of the visa and complications of every kind. It was only after a quantity of applications and negotiations with Generals Stipsicz and Langenau that I definitely obtained permission to start, on accepting the escort of an Austrian officer. I could have no politer nor more attentive traveling companion than Captain Karaczaï, a young Hungarian officer who had already accompanied the Empress Marie Louise, when she was leaving France after the events of 1814, and later on also during this princess's journey to Aix in Savoy.

Before leaving, I went to take leave of the young prince at the imperial palace of Vienna. It grieved me to notice his serious and even melancholy air. He had lost that childish cheerfulness and loquacity which had so much charm in him. He did not come to meet me as he was accustomed to do, and saw me enter without giving any sign that he knew me. One might have said that misfortune was already beginning its work on this young head, which a great lesson of Providence seemed to have adorned with a crown on his entrance into life, so as to give a fresh example of the vanity of human greatness. He was like one of those victims destined for sacrifice who are adorned with flowers. Although he had already spent six weeks with the persons to whom he had been confided, with whom I found him, he had not yet got accustomed to them and seemed to look upon their faces, still strange to him, with distrust. I asked him in their presence if he had a message which I could take for him to his father. He looked at me in a sad and significant way, then gently freeing his hand from my grasp he withdrew silently into the embrasure of a window some distance off. After having exchanged some words with the persons who were in the drawing-room, I approached the spot to which he had withdrawn and where he was standing looking on with an attentive air. As I bent down to him to say farewell, struck with my emotion, he drew me towards the window and looking at me with a touching expression he whispered to me: "M. Méva, you will tell him that I am still very fond of him!" The poor orphan already felt that he was no longer free and that he was no longer with his father's friends. He had had great difficulty in forgetting his "Mamma Quiou," as he used to call her. He kept asking for her of Madame Marchand who had been left with him and who was very fond of him. This excellent woman, who had received him in her arms at his birth and who had identified herself with him, returned to France a year later. Her departure was a fresh source of sorrow for the young prince. When they ceased calling him by the name of Napoleon, he was greatly displeased, for he found the name of Francis, which had been forced on him, both trivial and ugly. I admit that such impressions are the impressions of children of his age whose habits have been brusquely broken in upon, that they are only temporary and soon give way before the happy mobility of their character. One might have said that the gravity of the circumstances in which the young prince found himself placed had been revealed to his intelligence and had hastened on his maturity.

I left him in a state of flourishing good health. His constitution was robust and promised a long life, free from infirmities. He was handsome, good, and full of amiable qualities which later on won for him his grandfather's affection.

When he was deprived of the succession to the States of Parma and his name had been taken away from him, it became necessary to provide for his present and future position. By an edict issued in July 1818, he received the title of Duke of Reichstadt, which was the name of one of the estates in Bohemia which were to form his appanage. The same edict settled his armorial bearings and gave him precedence immediately after the princes of the Austrian imperial family: another deed had six months previously conferred upon him the property of the Bavaro-Palatinate fiefs in Bohemia with reversion to the crown of Austria in default of male issue. He was only to enjoy the revenues of these estates on reaching his majority or on his mother's death; this princess being obliged to provide for her son's maintenance as long as the duchies of Parma, Piacenza, and Guastalla remained in her possession. The poor child never came to the enjoyment of his estate, for death awaited him at his majority. Thus the Emperor of Austria, although he was very fond of his grandson, gave him nothing. Marie Louise provided largely for her son's expenses and the cost of his education. Count Dietrichstein was with the Emperor Francis's consent appointed his tutor. His masters were learned and distinguished men who gave to his precocious intelligence the development to which it was prone. Count Dietrichstein, who came to Nice for the sake of his health, during the winter of the years 1831–1832, frequently conversed with General Bertrand's daughter about Napoleon's son. The gist of his remarks was that the young prince was tall and well-made, that he resembled both his father and his mother, that he had not the simplicity and the good-nature which are the basis of the character of the Austrian Archdukes, but that he had a great distinction and dignity in his manners, that a touch of melancholy and a habit of meditation had left their impress on his features, that he was well-informed and had a taste for serious studies and for the military state, that he had retained a recollection of France, although he had left it in his early childhood, and that he took pleasure in seeing French people, which revealed itself by the animated attention with which he looked at them and tried to recognize them. "It does not befit me," added Count Dietrichstein, "to boast of a young man whose education I directed, but I may say that my efforts were seconded by the very best natural dispositions and that the Duke of Reichstadt is a man." Six months later this young prince was no more.

It was on May 6, at ten o'clock in the evening, that I took my last farewell of the Empress. She was much touched on this occasion. She was good enough to express her regret at my departure and said that she felt that in future all relations between her and France would cease, but that she would always remember this land of her adoption. She charged me to assure the Emperor of all the good she wished him, and told me that she hoped he would understand the unhappiness of her position. She repeated that she would never consent to a divorce, that she flattered herself with the belief that he would agree to a friendly separation, that this separation had become inevitable, and that no change had occurred in the feelings of esteem and gratitude which she felt for him. She presented me with a snuffbox ornamented with her cipher in diamonds, as a souvenir, and left me to hide the emotion which was mastering her. I myself left her with a heavy heart and in a state of veritable affliction.

I left on the morrow at six in the morning, with my traveling companion. I met Baron de Vincent at Enns, on his way to resume his functions as ambassador at Ghent, with Louis XVIII. On the way from Vienna to Munich, I met with conveyances full of recruits, with the cavalry corps on march, together with artillery regiments and parks. The headquarters of Prince de Hohenzollern, commanding the first corps were at Stockach.

Prince Eugène was at Munich when I passed through. He was there in so equivocal a situation that I avoided seeing him for fear of exposing him to some unpleasantness. He had, besides, warned me, begging me in secret not to visit him on account of the supervision to which I was subjected.

The postmaster at Waldsee told me that Prince de Neufchâtel had passed the day before, in company of his princess and an officer, on his way to Bâle, but had returned a few hours later, having been forced to go back at Stockach and that he had made his way to Bamberg, from whence he had come.

I arrived at Bâle on May 11, at six in the morning. I separated myself from my traveling companion there. I had nothing but praise for the way in which he had treated me during the journey. He had exercised a mission of protection over me rather than of supervision. On the frontiers, at the forts, and in the various stations of the allied troops through which we had passed he had preserved me from the annoyance of visits to and appearances before the civil and military authorities. I found the people of Bâle much disturbed by the battery which had been constructed at Huningue, which menaced the bridge and town of Bâle. I saw M. Harel, extraordinary commissioner of police, at Bourglibre or St. Louis and found him very distrustful of their feelings towards us. From that city to Paris I met with an enthusiasm for the Emperor and an ardor for the war which I cannot describe, not only amongst the soldiers and the fresh recruits but also amongst the majority of the people. At Belfort I was called upon by the chief of the staff of General Lecourbe who had his headquarters there. He came to us in Lecourbe's name, to ask with great anxiety, whether I brought the news of the speedy arrival of the Empress and her son and if there was reason to hope that the war would not take place. I met the loyal M. de Marmier, the Emperor's aide-de-camp, on my way. He had raised a free company at his own expense, and he asked me the same questions with the keenest interest.

I was expected with impatience by the Emperor. I went at noon to the Élysée where he had established himself. I was introduced into his room, immediately after my arrival, and I found Napoleon there seated on a settee with his head leaning on his hand, wrapped in profound meditation. He rose to receive me and took my hand, which he grasped with great cordiality; then, opening a glazed door, he preceded me into the garden where he kept me till six in the evening, overwhelming me with questions of every kind. He told me to return on the morrow at his levee. I arrived just as he had finished dressing and followed him again into the garden where his questions recommenced. These conversations lasted several days. The levee usually took place at nine o'clock, but it was often eleven o'clock before the Emperor thought of leaving me to attend it. When I fancied that I had exhausted all the subjects which seemed to me likely to interest him, or to satisfy his curiosity, he found means to extract fresh details from me by searching in the innermost recesses of my memory. I will not endeavor to transcribe these conversations in the form of a dialogue. They were an exchange of questions and answers of infinite variety and detail and turned on most of the things of which I have spoken higher up. Generally speaking the subjects of the Emperor's conversation on these occasions were serious, and seemed to affect him painfully He rarely dropped a grave way of speaking. One day, however, after having listened to certain particulars on the Empress's domestic life, he asked me, in a jesting tone, whether one of her uncles had not paid her attentions. Napoleon spoke to me of his son with great tenderness and listened with marked emotion to the most insignificant particulars about this darling child. All that he said about the Empress was full of respect and consideration for her. He pitied her for the trials to which she had been exposed, anticipated whatever I had to say in her favor, and expressed no doubt that her feelings for France and for himself had been forced. He ordered me to write to her, so that the weak thread which still connected Marie Louise with France might not be severed.

I informed the Emperor of the order given me by the Emperor of Austria to delay my departure until I had been summoned by Prince Metternich. I told him of the strong reasons which I had for thinking that the object of this audience, although I had not been told so, but which I could suspect from certain half-confidences, was a pacific one, if subsequent events should bring the Austrian cabinet to make an overture to the French government. I told the Emperor that having waited for this audience for a month, without its being brought about by any occurrence, and seeing precious time go by, I had feared lest it might be indefinitely postponed. The cabinet of Vienna, if its dispositions grew more favorable, could easily find an intermediary and charge him to carry its offers to Paris. I had therefore thought that my place was at the Emperor's side, and that my return to France would be more profitable to his interests than a prolongation of my stay in Vienna, were it only to carry the news of this incident to his ears. Napoleon approved of my conduct. He considered that the delay which had occurred in the delivery of my passport had been occasioned by the confidential negotiations which had been established about that time in Bâle between Metternich and Fouché. It was one of Napoleon's secretaries who received these communications from Vienna instead of the emissary of Fouché, who wanted in this matter to act without the Emperor's knowledge.

Speaking of the princes who had been brought back by the Restoration, the most remarkable thing that the Emperor told me was "that in returning from the Island of Elba, it was not Louis XVIII—for this prince could not have kept himself on the throne of France for another six months—whom he had dethroned, but the Duke of Orléans, that he was sorry for this, because this prince was the only Frenchman in his family, the most capable, and so on, and so on." Napoleon was touched by the patriotic sentiments which had been displayed by the Duke of Orléans, two months earlier, when he had gone to take command of the army in the North, placed under the orders of Marshal Mortier, with the letter which he had written to this Marshal on returning into retirement, but above all with the words which had been reported to him by Captain Athalin, one of his aides-de-camp, whom the Duke of Orléans had authorized to resume his post as orderly officer to the Emperor. This prince had told him that a new invasion of France by foreign troops must be prevented above all, esteeming him happy to find once more the colors which he himself had only left with regret. The Emperor judged the policy of the sovereigns with a great abnegation of his own interest. He considered it violent, but such as he was bound to expect; that it might have been more generous, for he had given them the example; that the princes given over to the inspirations of their ministers were naturally led to make a bad use of prosperity. He told me that all that was happening could not in consequence surprise him; and that it was in the nature of things, that in making his attempt, he had understood that he could appeal only to the courage and patriotism of the nation, and to his sword. "And for the rest," he added with a melancholy smile, "God is great and merciful." All his words were stamped with a calm sadness and a resignation which produced a great impression upon me. I no longer found him animated with that certainty of success which had formerly rendered him confident and invincible. It seemed as if his faith in his fortune, which had induced him to attempt the very hardy enterprise of his return from the island of Elba, and which had supported him during his miraculous march through France, had abandoned him on his entry into Paris. He felt that he was no longer seconded with the ardent and devoted zeal to which he was accustomed, and that, hampered as he was with the shackles which he had allowed to be placed upon him, he was no longer as free as formerly.

The Emperor, after his first curiosity had been satisfied, prompted by his natural kindness, could not fail to attend to my personal affairs. He was the first to speak to me of the kind of occupation which would suit me best, and encouraged me to express my wishes on this head to him. One of Napoleon's ministers, remembering the example of M. Augeard, secretary of commands to Marie Antoinette, who had been at the same time treasurer of the city of Paris, thought that this latter function—the holder of which had provoked the animadversion of the government by his exaggerated royalist fervor—should become the appanage of the secretary to the commands of the Empress. This lucrative post was occupied at that time by the son-in-law of Count de Ségur, Grand Master of Ceremonies, and as this circumstance prevented me from desiring it, I did not entertain the proposal. In the course of one of his audiences, the Emperor told me that this arrangement had been mentioned to him but that he did not think that a financial post would suit me and that he intended to entrust me with the Postmaster-General's place as soon as he found some other employment for M. de Lavalette. He added that the general guardianship of the state archives would be the post in the administration in which my services would be most useful to him, that I could occupy it temporarily and that he would add the title of Councilor of state to this post. On his departure for the army he charged King Joseph to have a report and the draft of a decree with this purpose in view prepared. The events of the campaign of 1815 and the catastrophe which terminated them prevented any realization of Napoleon's kindly intentions concerning me.

I learned in Paris that M. de Talleyrand, on April 2, 1814, in the midst of the cares which were caused to him by the enterprise of which he was the pivot and which ended in the Emperor's overthrow, and in spite of the multifarious obligations imposed upon him by the necessity of ensuring the success of all his intrigues had thought of removing from the state archives all papers which were of a nature to compromise him. On the day after the Emperor Alexander's arrival at the mansion in the rue Saint Florentin, M. de Talleyrand had charged two persons on whom he relied to go and explore the archives at the Louvre, and on some pretext or other to examine the cases or boxes containing letters, notes, or reports emanating from himself or addressed to him, concerning the trial of the Duke d'Enghien and affairs in Spain, as well as documents which might cast a light on the abuses of confidence, or money questions in which he might find himself implicated. As soon as the report concerning these investigations had been handed to him, M. de Talleyrand, who had become head of the provisional government, made use of his power to appoint a M. Devillers as chief to the imperial archivist. This temporary conservator naturally withdrew from the archives all the papers which were mentioned to him by the exalted person whose creature he was. When the former Minister of Exterior Relations under the Empire saw himself in possession of these documents he burned them so as to destroy the proofs which sooner or later might have been used against him. As soon as M. Devillers had accomplished his mission his provisional functions ceased.

The desire to know whether the return of the Empress and her son could be hoped for was general. So great was the anxiety on this point that all the persons with whom I came into contact overwhelmed me with questions. Fouché in his capacity as a policeman was the most inquisitorial. He wanted to know what had happened in Vienna during the last year. He urged me to come and see him. I had no inclination to do so, because this minister had always inspired me with an invincible dislike. I told the Emperor of the way in which he had pressed me to come and he advised me to see him, but to listen to him rather than to tell him anything. I went to his house and, after his first questions, he said of the Emperor—speaking with his usual assurance: "Well, there he is. It was not he who was wanted, but he can't be removed as you remove a pawn from the chessboard. We will see what we can do to keep him." These are the exact words which he used. I reported them to the Emperor who knew no doubt what to expect from him, for he contented himself with shrugging his shoulders in sign of his contempt. Fouché's hardy words agreed with what had been told me on my return to Paris of his mysterious understanding with Prince Metternich since the Emperor's return from the island of Elba. Communications had been exchanged through a secret agent with a view to concerting the Emperor's dethronement in favor of his son. I was surprised that Napoleon, after the discovery of treachery so flagrant, should have kept Fouché at the Ministry of Police. I learned in my conversations with the Emperor that he had been informed by the Duke of Vicence of this new intrigue on Fouché's part, and that he was acquainted with his previous intrigues as well as with the mission which he had given to M. de Montrond, behind his back, at the time when the latter was sent to Vienna with dispatches from the Duke of Vicence. It was only later that I learned, and M. de Stassart himself confirmed this, that a communication of the same nature had been addressed to the Emperor by his intermediary, simultaneously with the dispatch of M. Werner to Bâle.

A fortnight after my return to Paris I was present as a simple spectator at the ceremony of the Champ de Mai, during which the acceptance of the Additional Act to the Constitution of the Empire was proclaimed. On this occasion Napoleon presented the Paris national guard and the imperial guard with eagles. The deputations of the army received their eagles three days later, in the great gallery of the Louvre. The Additional Act was greatly criticized, and yet this act contained more liberal dispositions than the Charter which was granted by Louis XVIII. I for my part regretted this isolated act which opened the door to all kinds of polemics and passionate discussions, at a time when it was the first need of France and of the Emperor to face the enemy. It would have been, we consider, better to have postponed to quieter times the elaboration of a new constitution, for the situation in which the French nation found itself in the spring of 1815 lent itself more than ever to a continuation of the dictatorship, and the danger which was menacing the country at this time made everybody feel its necessity. These reflections concerning the Additional Act give me the opportunity of mentioning in what terms Madame de Staël expressed her approval of it. These are the very words which Napoleon's persevering enemy wrote to King Joseph from Coppet: "The additional clauses are all that France needs, nothing but what she needs, and not more than she needs. Your brother's return is prodigious and surpasses anything that one could have imagined. I commend my son to you."

The Emperor on his return to France had found the army reduced to less than one hundred thousand men; in two months he had increased its force five times. A zealous and active administration had seconded Napoleon's efforts, and the nation by its sympathy and by means of spontaneous gifts, by levies of free troops had proved its ardor for the defense of the soil of the fatherland. The Emperor hesitated some time before deciding whether to remain on the defensive and to draw the enemy on either to Lyons or Paris, or whether on the contrary to take the offensive. He ended by deciding on the latter. After having armed and provisioned all the fortresses on our frontiers, having settled on a system of fortifications for the defense of Paris and Lyons, and having established supplementary gun-factories and collected considerable quantities of ammunition of every kind, Napoleon left Paris on June 12. At Avesnes he decided the first operations of the army by an order of the day which he wished to keep secret. On the 14th General Bourmont, commanding a division of the 4th corps, Clouet, colonel of engineers, and Major Villoutreys, staff-officer, and formerly equerry to the Emperor, followed by some officers, to the disgrace of French honor passed over to the enemy and betrayed the order of the day of June 13 to them.

In spite of this unqualifiable treachery, the campaign had opened under the happiest auspices for French arms. Napoleon had been able to hide his first movements from the eyes of the enemy and had succeeded in taking the Prussian and English armies by surprise. His skilful maneuvers which had separated these two armies and brought about the victory of Ligny gave one reason to hope that these successes would be followed by decisive victories. There was no doubt of this in Paris, and news from the army was being awaited with confident security, when the report of a great disaster came to trouble every mind. Soon the defeat of Waterloo was a mystery to nobody. This fatal news spread consternation in our capital, and this consternation was raised to its highest pitch by the desolating reports which kept coming in. In spite of the faults committed during this short campaign, and notably on this fatal day; in spite of the slowness and want of decision with which orders, for the execution of which the greatest speed was necessary, had been carried out; in spite of the fact that Marshal Mortier's retreat had left the command-in-chief of the imperial guard vacant; the battle of Waterloo, which was won in the middle of the day, would have been a complete and decisive victory but for the arrival on the field of battle of Bulow's Prussian corps and Blücher's army, in turn, and finally without the absence of Marshal Grouchy's corps. A caprice of fortune upset the best-laid plans, and snatched from Napoleon's hands the triumph which was within his grasp. Wellington had even said to General Hill, who came to take his orders, at the most critical moment of the battle: "I have no orders to give you. There is nothing left for us but to die here. Our retreat is even cut off behind us." Chance came to transform the vanquished into victors and success into defeat.

It can be said that Napoleon and his soldiers fell gloriously. On no encounter of such importance did the French army display more heroism and more resolution than at the battle of Waterloo. The young generals, the young colonels, the officers of the various corps were animated with the same ardor and the same enthusiasm. On the other hand certain of the principal leaders of the army, demoralized by the recollection of the events of 1814, had lost that energy and confidence which often forces the hand of success. Treachery and desertion helped to transform our defeat finally into a rout. The French army, whose attitude and warlike qualities had been worthy of admiration up to the time of this catastrophe, retreated in fearful confusion.

The Emperor arrived at Charleroi and stopped there some hours. He sent out orders for rallying the army, and made arrangements for checking the enemy's march. He then proceeded to Laon where he established Marshal Soult in general headquarters, and designed this place as the point where the various corps were to meet. After having received more satisfactory news from his brother Jerôme whom he had charged to rally the remnants of the army and to reduce this confusion to order, Napoleon hesitated some time as to whether he should remain in the midst of his troops or return to Paris. He decided that his presence would not be necessary to the army until his columns had been rallied, and that it was more important to return to Paris, from which, besides, he was not more than thirty leagues distant. The Emperor accordingly returned to his capital, arriving there at eight o'clock in the morning of June 21. As soon as I heard of his return I hastened to the Élysée. I found Napoleon there, overwhelmed with fatigue and care, and yet mastering the grief with which he was devoured. He was in a bath into which he had plunged himself on his arrival, to promptly restore his exhausted strength. He had left the army, in spite of pressing entreaties to the contrary, but he was not only a general, he was also Head of the Empire. Napoleon had come to ask the Chambers for their help, with which he did not want to dispense, to check the onward march of the enemy, who were once more advancing upon Paris. But mad divisions, the conflict between republican and royalist passions, the ambitions of certain influential persons, a spirit of vertigo, in one word, were troubling every head in Paris; and there was soon nothing left for Napoleon but to abdicate for a second time. During the two hours which preceded and followed the Emperor's second abdication, I saw him absorbed in cruel reflections and hesitations. His foresight of the fate which was reserved to France if he abdicated, or if he remained in power, deprived of the assistance of the Chambers and reduced to a factious rôle, inspired him with a thousand conflicting resolutions and the most painful anxiety. An apparent want of feeling rendered him indifferent to the devotion of his brothers and to the remonstrances of certain faithful servants who urged him to adopt energetic resolutions. But the trial to which he had just submitted had opened Napoleon's eyes. He did not wish to add the horrors of a civil war to the evils resulting from a foreign invasion, by provoking a redoubtable conflict between the Chambers and himself. He felt that his mission had come to an end and that he could no longer recommence a career of prodigies; the times, the elements, the tendencies of men's minds were no longer the same. A close union of the great corporations of the state with himself could alone save France for a second time. This harmony of tendencies and will not existing in the circumstances in which the country found itself, Napoleon deemed that success was impossible. He might, no doubt, have appealed to the nation and to the army whose feelings were not to be doubted, but he feared to raise internal dissensions amongst the French.

The Emperor accordingly preferred to resign his crown, after having in vain endeavored to draw the Chambers out of their state of blindness; and not without having pointed out to them in the most vivid colors all the misfortunes which his abdication would entail. He addressed himself, as the continuation of my story will show, to ears that would not hear, for rest, at no matter what price, had become the first need of one and all.

The intentions of a great part of the chamber of Representatives may have been pure and patriotic, and yet the majority of its members only knew how to work with passion in breaking the sword and shield of France. It is painful to have to say that never was the nation represented by a political assembly more ignorant of its true interests, more below its mission, in presence of circumstances of such extraordinary gravity. While numerous hostile armies were pressing in upon us on every side, this majority gave voice to none but vain tirades and untimely discussion on abstract constitutional theories. It was unable either to inspire the hearts of Frenchmen with a hatred for foreign domination and to proclaim the danger which was menacing the fatherland, or to rally itself to Napoleon's dictatorship; the only means which remained to triumph, perhaps, over a formidable league. After having provoked and obtained the abdication of the Emperor, whom it feared more than the enemy, it at last understood the imminence of the danger and felt the necessity of seconding the ardor which animated the national guard, the federates as well as the army. This assembly, invariably inconsistent, not knowing what use to make of the power which it had snatched from Napoleon's hands with violence and not daring to assume the weight of it itself, entrusted it to a government commission which was unable or unwilling to make use of it. This commission undertook to cool the national enthusiasm against our invaders. It decided upon the timid resolution to send five plenipotentiaries, chosen amongst the members of the two Chambers, to demand the fulfillment of illusory promises, which had been made by the allies under circumstances which imposed a certain amount of prudence upon them. Anxious as to the issue of the struggle in which they had engaged, the allies, at the commencement of the 1815 campaign, had declared their intention of respecting the independence of France and of preserving the integrity of her territory. It was easy to foresee what would be the value of our demands upon them, the day when these demands were no longer backed by arms, And so we had the grief of seeing the deputies of a great people, which so often had triumphed over these same enemies, present themselves as supplicants in the cabinets of the ministers and the camps of the generals of the coalition, and expose themselves to the humiliations and disdain of a victor intoxicated with his successes.

I saw Fouché myself at the time and he charged me to tell Napoleon that the plenipotentiaries had been instructed to demand that Napoleon II should be recognized and, in one word, to accept anything except a return of the Bourbons.

While these plenipotentiaries, furnished with illusory instructions, were making their way towards the headquarters of the allied sovereigns, Fouché was sending confidants to Lord Wellington and to Prince Metternich to negotiate for the return of the Bourbons. It is here that we meet again with Macirone, who was one of the secret agents employed by the Duke of Otranto. This former aide-de-camp to King Murat has given curious particulars about the missions with which Fouché charged him to Lord Wellington. Captain Macirone, who had witnessed, in 1815, the exaltation of the French soldiers, whose ranks he had passed through, and who had narrowly escaped being killed because they took him for a spy, was astonished at the facility with which Napoleon had abdicated when there remained to him, round Paris alone, a reorganized army of more than 80,000 men filled with fanatical enthusiasm for his person, shaking with indignation at the yoke which it was wished to lay upon them, and burning with an ardor which was proof against anything; and that at the very time when Macirone had just seen that the Prussians and the English, on the contrary, were divided on the question of the reestablishment of Louis XVIII. We ourselves saw the Prussian cannon pointed against the Tuileries palace. M. Martial Daru, the military intendant, has assured me that overtures had been made by General Gneisenau to General Maison, at that time governor of Paris, to induce him to join with Field Marshal Blücher for the purpose of driving the Bourbons out and of proclaiming a Prussian prince King of France. General Maison, while asking for time to consider his answer, had come to the conclusion that it was better to keep Louis XVIII than to accept the Prussian yoke.

The judicious reflections made by Joseph Bonaparte on the conduct of the French Chambers during the last years of the Empire will not, we think, be read without interest. One might say that these reflections had been written by Napoleon himself. They are as follows:

"One must not cast on the nation the blame which is deserved by the members of the chamber of deputies, who, in 1813, joined themselves to M. Lainé, whose opinions at the time may be judged by those which he has since professed for the Bourbons; nor by the opinions and conduct of the chamber of 1815, presided over by Lanjuinais, an honest but short-sighted man, a bourgeois Cato and the eternal dupe of intriguers of every color and every party. The French nation is no more in a coterie of peers, than the Italian spirit is in the sacred college and amongst the Neapolitan barons. The French nation is in the day laborer's workshop, in the middle-class family interior, in the workroom of the busy man, in the peasant's field, in the minds of all who palpitate at the remembrance of our national glory, in these old remains of so many heroes. The French nation is the nation which received Napoleon on his return from the Island of Elba, which is conscious of what is right and what is wrong, which does not accuse the man whom she admires and whose widow she will long consider herself. This nation is not frivolous, capricious, changing, as people would have one believe. It feels today what it felt on the morrow of Austerlitz. But Europe has been pressing her down for the last fifteen years; and though it has crushed its will, it has not yet killed it.

"In all nations there are weak individuals who have been lifted by chance to eminent places. These individuals, in decisive circumstances often decide the fate of nations, by little personal passions by which, without suspecting it themselves, they are dominated. Unfortunately there were many such individuals in the Chambers of 1813 and 1815, and when they saw the precipice which they had opened beneath their feet they could do nothing but groan and lament themselves.

"For France's misfortune it was fated that men like Sieyès, Merlin, Carnot, Roederer, Boulay de la Meurthe, etc., etc., were not in the majority in the chamber. The leaders of the majority were either men of bad faith or lacking in foresight of the future, guided by petty vanity, wishing to play the Romans of the time of Brennus or the Mirabeaus of the Jeu de Paume at a time when they should have rallied themselves to the dictatorship of Camillus to expel the Bourbons, that is to say the foreigners.

"I remember in this connection to the eternal honor of Sieyès that when he heard of the loss of the battle of Waterloo he came to see me. Finding me in conversation with Lanjuinais, president of the chamber of deputies, he said to me: 'If you want to persuade them with speeches, your work is cut out for you. Allow me to speak. Lanjuinais,' he said, 'Napoleon has at last lost a battle. He stands in need of us. He is coming. Let us go to his assistance, so that he may drive the barbarians out. He alone can succeed in doing this with our help. After that, if he wants to become a despot, once the danger is passed we will unite to hang him if that is considered indispensable. But today let us march with him, that is the only hope we have of safety. Let us save him that he may save us. The nation will be grateful to us for this, for he is today the man of the nation.'

"France is full of people who think so. It would be unjust to judge the nation otherwise than by them or by itself, by the force of its resistance and the example it has given in so many important circumstances.

"Napoleon without any doubt desired France and Italy to enjoy all the happiness, all the liberty of which they were capable. 'Time,' he used to say, 'will do the rest. *Il tempo è un galantuomo*. Suffice it for me to pacify them at home and to put them on the right road.'

"The Concordat, the Empire, the imperial nobility, his marriage, all these things were maneuvers to attain an object ignored by the incorrigible, with their assistance, by making everybody take part in bringing them to a successful issue. 'Mr. Colonel of the 4th,' he would sometimes say to me in jest, 'wheel to the right to march to the left.' Napoleon wished to attain peace with England, the conquest of all the rights which the Revolution had proclaimed and which the Terror had exaggerated in 1793. To succeed in this it was necessary to unite all parties, to make them all work towards a common object, which would have been the happiness of France, of Italy, of Europe, and at the same time an immense glory for himself. England successfully opposed this object and Napoleon perished in the midst of his plan, at a time when his real system and his real object were yet neither known nor unmasked."

Napoleon had signed his abdication in spite of certain generous opposition. General Drouot groaned over the misfortune of two abdications in the same year; Carnot saw in it France's death warrant. While this illustrious citizen—who had opposed Napoleon's elevation in 1804—dominated by the gravity of the situation in 1815 and foreseeing the sad consequences which would be entailed by the loss of a man whose military genius might still save the country, did all in his power to prevent his abdication, La Fayette urged it on with all his might.

A comparison between the conduct of two men, known for their patriotic sentiments, who played an important part at this time and whose political opinions were opposed to the Emperor, may, in our opinion, teach a useful lesson. Carnot was a sincere, straightforward man eminently patriotic. Easy to deceive as are all upright and guileless men he was Fouché's dupe. If his politics were not always clear-sighted, he understood, in 1815, all the harm that the politicians who dominated in the chamber were about to bring on France. I can still see him taking leave of the Emperor who was leaving the Élysée to go to La Malmaison. He halted on the top of the stairs which led down into the garden and there this austere citizen, yielding to the excess of his emotion, threw himself on Napoleon's neck and leant his head on his shoulder to hide the tears which were streaming from his eyes. La Fayette, a republican of good faith, moved by a sincere love for his country, but unenlightened by experience, dreamed only of the means of realizing an impossible Utopia; the state of France in 1815 seemed to him a favorable opportunity to enforce his theories. More ardent than ever he raised a voice which was all the more powerful because it had not been heard for many years and recalled remembrances dear to the nation. He made use of a popularity which admired without investigating it the strange phenomenon of a man who had persevered in the same principles for twenty-five years, to break his tutelary sword in Napoleon's hand.

The same regrets followed the so different conduct of these two citizens. Carnot died in exile deploring the blindness which had destroyed the only instrument of our safety. La Fayette was not long in recognizing the effects of the unfortunate influence which he had exercised on our destinies. I have in my hands a letter which is the proof of this. It was forwarded to me by M. de La Fayette himself, together with the following note, written in his own handwriting:

"La Grange, November 5, 1825.

"I have the honor of saluting M. le Baron de Méneval and I make haste to send him a letter which I ought to have received at Washington but which reaches me here through American hands. He will greatly oblige me by informing me that he has received it. I beg him to accept the assurance of the pleasure which I take in discharging this commission towards him.

"(Signed) LA FAYETTE"

The letter which M. de La Fayette sent me, dated September 8, 1825, from Breezy Point, near New York, contained these words which allude to the occurrences of 1815:

"MY DEAR MÉNEVAL,

"M. de La Fayette will hand you this letter. He came to see me twice and spoke to me at length on the source of the mortal error which has been so fatal to us. He deplores the situation of France and appears to me to be animated with the best intentions ….

"(Signed) JOSEPH, COUNT DE SURVILLIERS."

(JOSEPH BONAPARTE)

I have extracted the passage referring to M. de La Fayette from King Joseph's letter; the rest only contains general reflections on the advantages of the American government and on the satisfaction which is derived from a straightforward and honorable conduct. In the midst of the ovations with which the guest of the Americans, the friend and comrade-in-arms of Washington was everywhere received, the remembrances of 1815 pursued him. M. de LaFayette during a journey in America and a short stay in this country may have heard the words addressed by the venerable John Adams, former president of the United States, to a French general, and a member of the provisional government of 1815, Baron Quinette, who had both taken refuge in America: "Gentlemen, you did not understand the Emperor Napoleon."

The abdication by which the Emperor proclaimed his son, under the title of Napoleon II, could not satisfy Fouché who wanted a free field for the Bourbons. The Chambers appointed a provisional government commission and Fouché, although he was distrusted by all parties, had a great influence in the selection of the five persons who composed it. These five commissioners were, Fouché, Carnot, General Grenier, of the chamber of deputies; Quinette, and Caulaincourt, members of the chamber of Peers. Fouché naturally was elected president of this commission. He spoke to each and all in the language which best suited his listeners, but he, above all, endeavored to impress on everybody below his breath that Napoleon was an insurmountable obstacle in the way of peace. He found people of good faith in both Chambers, who were disposed to propagate his opinions openly, to listen to his insidious advice and without knowing it to second his secret designs. In adopting the order of the day proposed by Manuel, based on the fact that by his father's abdication alone, Napoleon II was emperor, the Chambers had settled the question of the acknowledgment of Napoleon's son. The government commission, dominated by Fouché, did not think itself bound by this equivocal consecration of the usages of the old monarchy. It placed at the head of its acts: "In the name of the French people," and Napoleon's name was omitted. Some isolated voices protested in vain against this omission, they found no echo.

Amongst the members of the provisional government figured, as has been seen, Caulaincourt, Duke of Vicence, whose devotion to the Emperor none could doubt. This faithful servant of Napoleon was fated to be called to play a last part in the denouement of the great imperial drama, after having raised himself with the Emperor and having served him faithfully in good as in evil days. The Emperor always had sympathy and esteem for Caulaincourt. This officer, the son of the Marquis de Caulaincourt and nephew of General d'Harville, both old friends of the Empress Josephine, was colonel of the 2nd regiment of carbineers, when the First Consul attached him to his person in the capacity of aide-de-camp and afterwards employed him in various diplomatic missions. The very secondary part which Napoleon's orders and the passive obedience to which soldiers were subjected had given to Caulaincourt in the arrest of the Duke d'Enghien, this indirect participation, as we have already related, contributed to his fortune. Napoleon wished to compensate by all the means in his power, his aide-de-camp Caulaincourt for the attacks, as unjust as they were passionate, of which on this occasion he had been the victim on the part of the royalists. Accordingly, at the time of the formation of the imperial household, he was appointed Grand Equerry and afterwards Duke of Vicence. As Grand Equerry he established, in the services which depended from his post, an order and a discipline which greatly pleased Napoleon. The Emperor allowed his

Grand Equerry sometimes to give orders contrary to his own injunctions, whenever he recognized that the reason of these orders was in the interest of his service. The Emperor liked to travel with extreme haste and would always have ridden his horses at a gallop. The Grand Equerry on the other hand wanted to spare them, and he was besides frightened of accidents which might occur by riding at too great a speed. Napoleon in his impatience often used to order that the speed of his carriages should be increased. Then one might see the Grand Equerry, whose carriage followed the Sovereign's, leaning out of the window ordering the equerries and postilions at the top of his voice to slacken the speed of their horses. Napoleon, who heard him countermanding his orders, did not seem dissatisfied with him and perhaps in his heart of hearts thought that he was perfectly in the right.

During the negotiations which occupied the last period of the Empire the Duke of Vicence acquitted himself with a zeal which never failed him of the thankless mission with which Napoleon had charged him. Imbued with the principles of a purely military education he was a strict observer of discipline. Hard upon himself, during the retreat from Moscow, when there were twenty-five degrees of cold, he neglected to protect himself by wearing either a cap or a mantle. He only wore a spencer lined with fur, on which were embroidered the insignia of his rank and which blended itself with his uniform. Vivacious and even rather brusque, with a habitually calm and serious expression, his manners were polite and often affectionate. His sentiments were chivalrous. He justified the opinion which Napoleon expressed about him when he said that he was an upright man and a man of heart.

After the fall of the Empire, the Duc de Vicence married Madame de Canisy, who had been married for the first time at the age of fifteen to her cousin M. de Canisy. This lady's father, who would not admit that there was any family superior to the Canisys, had insisted upon this marriage. Mademoiselle de Canisy was still of an age when discernment and experience are wanting to make a choice, and her father had not taken into consideration the harmony of tastes and tempers which renders marriages happy. This marriage accordingly did not present the conditions necessary for happiness. And so the two spouses were not long in separating. The husband was one of the Emperor's equerries of the household; the wife was one of the Empress Josephine's ladies and afterwards lady-in-waiting to the Empress Marie Louise.

The Duke of Vicence, won over by the graces of Madame de Canisy, whose wit equaled her beauty and who was one of the ornaments of the imperial court, had asked the Emperor to consent to Madame de Canisy's divorce so that he might marry her. Napoleon, who had considered divorce necessary to society, had an instinctive repugnance to authorize it amongst the persons by whom he was surrounded and in whom he took a real interest. The quality of a divorced woman seemed a blot to him. Madame de Canisy, one of the Empress's ladies-in-waiting, enjoyed a well-deserved respect in his eyes; the Duchess of Vicence in spite of all his friendship for the Duke could not have retained her place as lady-in-waiting. Napoleon accordingly used his influence over General Caulaincourt to dissuade him from this marriage. It was only after the second Restoration, and before divorce was abolished that this marriage could be effected.

Having accomplished his last painful sacrifice, the Emperor, who was as great in his misfortune as at the time when he wore or distributed crowns, left the Élysée for La Malmaison, escaping the acclamations of an immense crowd which pressed itself every day in the Avenue de Marigny in the hopes of seeing him, and saluting with his hand the *fédérés* who with loud shouts offered to follow his fortunes and to defend him.

I continued to see Napoleon at La Malmaison, on that estate where the dawn of his greatness had shone, and which reminded him at one and the same time of things so sweet and so bitter. It was not without emotion that my eyes once more rested on this château where step by step I had been able to follow the progress of his astonishing fortune. I had found him there invested with a power temporary at first, but already crowned with the halo of great personal glory, spending the summer in this charming retreat with his seductive wife, the most amiable, the best of women, and the personification of female graces, as he himself used to say. I had seen him there, surrounded by his family and some faithful friends and servants, sharing in their games, seeking some relaxation from his labors in the cool shade of the gardens, sowing the treasures of his fruitful imagination in conversations now serious now humorous but always full of original and profound remarks. I myself, at that time, humblest of guests, had sat down at his table. Soon the people's gratitude had raised him higher, and the procession which follows on greatness had grown larger behind him. He had been forced first of all to have a private table, next a court, but never had the exigencies of etiquette changed the kindness of his nature. When the venerable Head of the Catholic Church had come to France to crown and consecrate the Emperor, he had been received at La Malmaison with the filial deference which was due to him. Kings had come to this residence to pay homage to the great man as much as to the powerful sovereign.

The rupture of a union formed by mutual affection, and dissolved by the exigencies of politics, had caused Napoleon to leave this place which became the witness and the confidant of the regrets of a forsaken wife, as also the scene of a little court, the pomp of which often veiled the bitterest regrets. A premature death had snatched away the princess who adorned this abode, as though Josephine, to whom sovereign greatness had formerly been predicted, had accomplished her destiny and had no further part to play on this earth after she had lost her crown. Napoleon returned hither fallen from his high estate to take a last farewell of the tomb of his first wife; he was received here in his adversity by his adopted daughter, Queen Hortense, whose generous care and filial piety comforted him in his evil days. I saw there the noble courtiers of adversity, ready to run all the risks of their illustrious chief's bad fortune; the Duke of Rovigo so energetic and so devoted, whose presence at Napoleon's side would have been so useful to him; General Bertrand and his wife, whose persevering loyalty only increased under adversity; M. and Madame de Montholon, who were to give him, in hard captivity, the care of devoted children; Gourgaud, whose devotion bore the stamp of a chivalrous mind and an ardent imagination; the virtuous Las Cases and his young son, whose adolescence formed in a great school was to bring forth excellent fruits; Marchand, whose noble master was to reward his touching services by calling him his friend.

Walking one day with the Emperor in the private garden which adjoined his cabinet, he told me that he counted on me to follow him. I had no other intention. As I needed a little time to put my affairs in order, I asked him where I was to meet him. He told me that his first intention had been to go to America, but as there were some obstacles in the way of the realization of this plan, he intended to go and live in England, and added that he meant to insist on the rights which were enjoyed by every English citizen. As I expressed some surprise at this resolution, he exclaimed: "Without that condition I shall put myself at the head of affairs again." My surprise increased on hearing this sudden revelation and I could not help saying: "But, Sire, if such is your thought, do not wait until the time has passed: at some paces from here devoted generals and a faithful army call for you; you are not a prisoner here, I suppose." "I have here," he answered, "a battalion of my guard who would arrest Becker, if I said one word, and would act as my escort. Young man," he added, after a moment's silence, and with the gesture of pulling my ear, "such resolutions are not improvised." I then saw that the threat of placing himself at the head of affairs had only been torn from him by a flash of natural pride, and that it had never really been in his thoughts. This scene has remained engraved on my memory. At the end of this conversation he told me that he wanted me to remain at La Malmaison, and bade me ask Queen Hortense to give me a room. I accordingly stayed to dinner and I spent the evening with the Queen, preoccupied with the thought that I was expected in Paris.

At nine o'clock I heard that the Emperor had retired to his apartments. One of my friends who had dined at La Malmaison and who had no carriage told me that he counted upon me to take him back to Paris. I told him what the Emperor had said to me and he replied that I had no reason to fear that he would send for me before the morning. This should not have been sufficient reason for my going away, because I knew that Napoleon often used to get up in the night. I very much wanted to return to Paris when I thought how anxious my wife and children would be at not seeing me come back to them. Absorbed as I was by these preoccupations, I did not reflect, a very simple reflection, after all, that I could lend my carriage and send a letter to my people. I compounded with my irresistible desire to go home and waited another hour until I heard that the Emperor had gone to bed. I then yielded to the promise which was made to me by my friend that he would come and fetch me very early next morning to take me back to La Malmaison. On leaving I begged the Duke of Rovigo, who was remaining, to tell the Emperor that I should be back before the hour of his levee and I set out for Paris. On the morrow I waited for my companion of the previous night until six o'clock. Having no news of him, I sent to inquire as to the reason of this delay and heard that he had started at five in the morning. I immediately set out for La Malmaison, but the barriers of Paris had just been closed when I presented myself and I was told that nobody was allowed to go out. I returned at full speed to get this order countermanded as regarded myself. After a great deal of running about, I was just about to start off again for La Malmaison when I heard the news that Napoleon had just entered his carriage to go to Rochefort. Nothing had occurred the night before to make me suppose that his departure would be so sudden. I was painfully affected by this unexpected news, and my first apprehension was lest the Emperor had gone away with the idea that I also was abandoning him and that I had repented of having promised to follow him wherever he might go. This thought tortured me for a long time, until Madame de Montholon, on her return to France in 1819 or 1820, and later on the Emperor's faithful companions in exile, freed me from my apprehension by assuring me that Napoleon had never once alluded to the circumstance which I have related, that he had never ceased to speak of me with kindness, and that he had praised my fidelity; assurances the confirmation of which I found in the souvenir which the Emperor deigned to bequeath to me in his will. However this may be I have always blamed myself for my want of presence of mind in this circumstance, and for my unpardonable weakness. I had separated myself from

Napoleon, never to see him again here below. All my attempts to obtain an authorization to go and share his exile remained of no avail. I took recourse to the obliging intervention of General Wilson, who was the principal author of Count Lavalette's evasion, to reach the English Secretary of state for the Colonial Department. All that could be accorded to me—such was the answer vouchsafed—was permission to go to the Cape. Once there I should have been forced to write to the governor of St. Helena to ask for permission to come to this island, Sir Hudson Lowe being entirely master to grant or refuse this permission. It was impossible for me to obtain any other answer than this disguised refusal.

I heard afterwards that Napoleon during the night which preceded his departure from La Malmaison had thought of rendering a final service to the fatherland. In the rapidity of their march upon Paris the Prussian and English armies, intoxicated with their successes and full of imprudent confidence, had separated at the gates of the capital. The Prussians had crossed the Seine, and it would have been possible to crush them before the English army was in a position to assist them. Napoleon was of opinion that so unfavorable a position gave France a real chance to fight the enemies one by one, to drive them off, or at least to obtain, by inflicting defeat upon them, more favorable conditions of peace. He had accordingly proposed to the provisional government that he should assume the temporary command of the army, undertaking to resign after the victory. Fouché's perfidy and the mistrust of some members of the Commission caused Napoleon's offer to be rejected. Not one of them dared assume this responsibility towards a chamber which feared Napoleon more than it feared the enemies. This proposal especially crossed Fouché's plans, for he had come to a secret understanding with the allies. He was afraid lest Napoleon should win back an authority and a prestige which should restore the nation to energy. The understandings which the allies had with Paris, thanks to Fouché's connivance, gave them a feeling of security which might have been fatal to them if the offers of the great captain had been accepted. In allowing for the unforeseen chances of the events of war, it was in any case a remedy *in extremis,* and in this desperate situation nothing stood in the way of an attempt in this direction. While brazenly betraying the Emperor and the national cause, Fouché hurried on Napoleon's departure, under the pretext of caring for his personal safety—and really so as to rid himself of the vicinity of the great victim whom he still feared. The Emperor in speaking of the Duke of Otranto, had said of him the evening before at La Malmaison "I ought to have had him hanged. I leave that for the Bourbons to do." The Bourbons were to make a minister of this regicide. Thanks to Fouché's patriotism, the Prussians certain of not being disturbed in their movements had come up to the walls of Paris. Napoleon by prolonging his stay at La Malmaison ran the risk of being captured by them. The Emperor's departure, which was urged on by the provisional government, took place on June 29. On that day Napoleon left his retreat at La Malmaison, never to return there again, accompanied by some faithful servants who followed him into exile.

Such was the end of the most splendid, perhaps the most glorious reign of all those which history will have to register. It will be meet, we consider, to interrupt this narrative for a moment, to cast a glance at the various causes which prevented the consolidation of the great Empire and entailed its fall; these causes are many. Amongst them must be placed in the front rank, the hatred for the French Revolution implanted in the heart of the old European dynasties; and next England's successful resistance of Napoleon's efforts to enfranchise the sea. Above these two primary causes floated the fear inspired in the foreign sovereigns by the superiority of the powerful, innovating, and regenerating genius, devoted to the triumph of principles which were incompatible with the spirit of the old-world monarchies.

As auxiliaries to these implacable enmities were:

1. The condemnation of the Duke d'Enghien, a painful event, a fatal episode in Napoleon's reign, of which the enemies of our country in their bad faith and their animosity did not fail to take advantage in their campaign against France and her chief.

2. The war in Spain, a disastrous enterprise, which divided our forces and perhaps prevented Napoleon's definite triumph over the sovereigns of the coalition.

3. The 1812 expedition against Russia which was doomed to failure in consequence of the severity of an exceptional winter, and whose deplorable issue had such fatal results.

And finally, a fourth factor, a dissolvent to which reference must be made and the force of which must be admitted, was treachery at home, treachery, timid and underground at first, but hardy in the end, and stalking abroad with uplifted head.

Two men, or rather, two evil genii, had attached themselves to Napoleon's fortunes; everybody will know that I am referring to Fouché and Talleyrand.

Talleyrand, the last representative of the *grands seigneurs* of former times, supple, insinuating, prudent to excess, always master of himself, without any conscience, grown grey in political perfidies, and selling his influence to the enemy, surrounded his hidden intrigues with mystery.

Fouché, the former fiery demagogue who had exchanged the red cap for a ducal coronet, a foolhardy marplot, who needed intrigue as he needed air to breathe, falling into his own pitfalls, was less secret in his maneuvers. Napoleon despised him because of his political immorality, but made use of him, because he was convinced, I do not know for what reason, that he was necessary to him. The Emperor believed that the apostasy of the one and the regicide of the other guaranteed their fidelity. In dismissing the first from his councils he was unable to deprive 'him of the power for evil which Talleyrand's influence abroad conferred upon him; in retaining the other he was nurturing a serpent in his bosom. These two men were equally harmful to Napoleon, one by his retirement, the other by his constant presence in the councils of the crown. They were not men of transcendent intelligence, but they had vices and capacities which stood them in stead with Napoleon. They might have been considered sufficiently guilty to have incurred a judicial sentence, but Napoleon, trusting in his force, thought the noise and scandal of a trial useless and even harmful.

His pride would, moreover, have suffered by the public confession that ministers vested with his confidence had been bold enough to conceive the plan of turning against him the power which he had delegated to them, and besides they had risen with him, and he could not forget their first services. The man who used to say that the statesman's heart should be in his head always felt his own heart in its right place, in spite of what he might say. It is especially against these two men that Napoleon pronounced an anathema when, on taking his last farewell of France, as the shores which he was never to see again faded from his sight, he cried out: "Farewell thou land of heroes....farewell thou dear France; a few traitors the less and thou wouldst still be the great nation, the mistress of the world."

The Emperor had left La Malmaison and had gone to pass a night at Rambouillet, On July 3 he was at Rochefort, where his brother Joseph followed him. During the twelve days which Napoleon spent either in Rochefort or in the Island of Aix, he was undecided what to do. Should he go to America or to England? He received proposals from various French and foreign naval officers and from several generals who sent him messages. The blockade of the English cruisers and the declarations made by the captains in command of the vessels in this fleet barred the way to America. Of the various measures which were proposed to give the English cruisers the slip some were declared impracticable, others were considered inadmissible. Napoleon was loath to be the direct cause of the loss of the ships and the crews who should sacrifice themselves entirely for him. He preferred to wait for the safe-conducts which were to be sent from England. These safe-conducts did not arrive, and on the other hand assurances which he could consider official were given him that he would be received in England with the respect to which he had a right. As he was assured that in any case he would have every facility in this country for proceeding to America he decided to go on board the *Bellerophon,* the principal vessel of the English naval station. He sent on before him an autograph letter addressed to the Prince Regent of England and charged General Gourgaud to hand it to him in person. After having accomplished this act the Emperor Napoleon surrendered, with all the confidence of a mighty foe, to British hospitality. The *Bellerophon* set sail for England the same day and dropped anchor at Plymouth. The moment for landing was being awaited on board this boat, when on July 30 two English commissioners came to notify the decision of the British Ministry to Napoleon, by which he was to be transported to the Island of St. Helena. I will not relate a matter of common knowledge, how the Emperor protested, nor the various incidents which marked this most painful epoch in his life, nor will I dwell on the manifestations of respect which he received from the English sailors and soldiers, nor on the curiosity which was excited by his presence near the English coast. I will content myself with putting on record the sentiments of universal sympathy of which Napoleon became the object in the midst of a crowd ever growing larger, packed in innumerable boats, which had come to contemplate him.

The *Bellerophon* not being in a state to undertake a long voyage the Emperor, and a small number of his faithful servants who were allowed to follow him, embarked on board the *Northumberland,* which set sail without delay to the place of exile which has been immortalized by the greatness of soul with which Napoleon supported his adversity there, and by his death. The Emperor spent two days of his captivity in the house of an honest Englishman where he was compensated for the insufficiency and discomfort of this poof abode by the care and the respect which were lavished upon him by this excellent family. Two months later Napoleon went to live in the house at Longwood where began for him that long agony which was to last six years and to end in the tomb.

The Triumvirate of allied sovereigns left Vienna at the end of May; the generals in command of their armies had already preceded them on their road to France. A fortnight after the departure of the two Emperors and of the King of Prussia all the plenipotentiaries who had remained in Vienna, with the exception of the representatives of Spain, signed the Acts of Congress. The refusal of Spain was prompted by the objections raised by the former Queen of Etruria against the cession, to the former Empress of France, of the Duchies of Parma and Piacenza, the paternal inheritance of the Infant,

Don Carlos, this Queen's son. A subsequent convention, which settled the reversion of these states in favor of the Infant on the death of Marie Louise, ended this dispute. Amongst the illegalities and the arbitrary spoliations which were consecrated by the Acts of the Vienna Congress, figure the arrangements which deprived the son of the Duchess of Parma of his mother's inheritance. This famous Congress of Vienna which should have been an honest senate assembled to found a new public law intended to assure the peace of Europe and to protect her from fresh commotions was in reality nothing but an arena opened to spoliations and oppressive ambitions. Four great powers made use of the forces which the peoples had placed in the hands of these sovereigns, to ignore the social interests of these peoples and the promise which they had given to ameliorate the condition of these masses. Sovereigns and their ministers had been interested only in enforcing dynastic prerogatives and in enlarging their territories at the expense of their weaker neighbors, and in the sole interest of ambition bringing about antipathetic fusions, dismemberments, barterings, traffickings, without either consulting public interest or decency, and with a total indifference to vested rights. The consequence has been that these arbitrary decisions scattered the seed of discontent, the ferments of discord, and future wars broadcast over Europe. Finally, having shown so much indifference for the rights of morality and justice, these powers, on the instigation of the Emperor Alexander, did their best to hide under the mantle of religion their selfish and greedy policies. The sovereigns signed a mystic treaty called the Treaty of the Holy Alliance, without the intermediary of their ministers, by which adopting Jesus Christ as their model and their master, they undertook to take as the rule of their conduct the principles of justice, charity, and peace which had been taught by the Savior, to allow themselves to be guided under all circumstances by principles which they had most certainly repudiated only too often in their acts.

General Neipperg covered with the laurels which he had gathered in his last campaign in Italy had returned with fresh claims on the gratitude of the Austrian government, to resume his rôle as supreme director of Marie Louise's sentiments and will. This Princess remained another year in Austria before she went to take possession of her new states. Although she was preceded there by an edict of the Austrian government which imposed a war contribution of three millions to the benefit of Austria, these peoples, happy to be delivered from the scourge of a military occupation which had lasted more than two years, received Marie Louise like a second providence. She seemed to have been sent to put an end to their evils and to bring an era of prosperity back amongst them. The most powerful reason of the flattering reception which was accorded to Marie Louise by her new subjects was, it must be said, the fact that she had been Napoleon's wife. In the solemn entry which she made into Parma there appeared by her side, and in the front rank Count Neipperg, who was then her *chevalier d'honneur,* and the guardian of her authority.

The task which I undertook has reached its end.

Index